T0181501

# IFIP Advances in Information and Communication Technology

592

## Editor-in-Chief

# IFIP – The International Federation for Information Processing

IFIP was founded in 1960 under the auspices of UNESCO, following the first World Computer Congress held in Paris the previous year. A federation for societies working in information processing, IFIP's aim is two-fold: to support information processing in the countries of its members and to encourage technology transfer to developing nations. As its mission statement clearly states:

*IFIP is the global non-profit federation of societies of ICT professionals that aims at achieving a worldwide professional and socially responsible development and application of information and communication technologies.*

IFIP is a non-profit-making organization, run almost solely by 2500 volunteers. It operates through a number of technical committees and working groups, which organize events and publications. IFIP's events range from large international open conferences to working conferences and local seminars.

The flagship event is the IFIP World Computer Congress, at which both invited and contributed papers are presented. Contributed papers are rigorously refereed and the rejection rate is high.

As with the Congress, participation in the open conferences is open to all and papers may be invited or submitted. Again, submitted papers are stringently refereed.

The working conferences are structured differently. They are usually run by a working group and attendance is generally smaller and occasionally by invitation only. Their purpose is to create an atmosphere conducive to innovation and development. Refereeing is also rigorous and papers are subjected to extensive group discussion.

Publications arising from IFIP events vary. The papers presented at the IFIP World Computer Congress and at open conferences are published as conference proceedings, while the results of the working conferences are often published as collections of selected and edited papers.

IFIP distinguishes three types of institutional membership: Country Representative Members, Members at Large, and Associate Members. The type of organization that can apply for membership is a wide variety and includes national or international societies of individual computer scientists/ICT professionals, associations or federations of such societies, government institutions/government related organizations, national or international research institutes or consortia, universities, academies of sciences, companies, national or international associations or federations of companies.

More information about this series at http://www.springer.com/series/6102

Bojan Lalic · Vidosav Majstorovic ·
Ugljesa Marjanovic · Gregor von Cieminski ·
David Romero (Eds.)

# Advances in Production Management Systems

## Towards Smart and Digital Manufacturing

IFIP WG 5.7 International Conference, APMS 2020
Novi Sad, Serbia, August 30 – September 3, 2020
Proceedings, Part II

*Editors*
Bojan Lalic (iD)
University of Novi Sad
Novi Sad, Serbia

Ugljesa Marjanovic (iD)
University of Novi Sad
Novi Sad, Serbia

David Romero (iD)
Tecnológico de Monterrey
Mexico City, Mexico

Vidosav Majstorovic (iD)
University of Belgrade
Belgrade, Serbia

Gregor von Cieminski (iD)
ZF Hungária Kft.
Eger, Hungary

ISSN 1868-4238          ISSN 1868-422X (electronic)
IFIP Advances in Information and Communication Technology
ISBN 978-3-030-57999-9          ISBN 978-3-030-57997-5 (eBook)
https://doi.org/10.1007/978-3-030-57997-5

This Springer imprint is published by the registered company Springer Nature Switzerland AG
The registered company address is: Gewerbestrasse 11, 6330 Cham, Switzerland

# Preface

We live in a time where just one factor (i.e., COVID-19) could change the game plan for the global manufacturing economy. Digital transformation has been going on in the last decade, and it seems that not all the countries and companies are utilizing all the opportunities that it could provide to build new digital capabilities such as 'digital resilience.' A digital transformation path towards Industry 4.0 in manufacturing is more important than ever. Yet, how to approach the development and scaling of digital technology is a question that keeps executives awake at night and academics in a constant quest. The current digital transformation of manufacturing has so far mostly been studied from the perspective of the cyber-physical production system as drivers of change. However, there are several other enablers, including artificial intelligence; additive and hybrid manufacturing; 5G-enabled manufacturing; digital assistance systems based on augmented, virtual, and mixed reality; industrial, collaborative, mobile, and software robots; advanced simulations; cloud and edge technologies; and data-driven product-service systems. These are the key components of a digital transformation and the main research thrusts in the production management systems research community. Thus, the question of how to find the path to the digital transformation and innovation of production management systems is of eminent importance.

The International Conference on Advances in Production Management Systems (APMS 2020) in Novi Sad, Serbia, brought together leading international experts from academia, industry, and government in the area of digital transformation and innovation to discuss globally pressing issues in smart manufacturing, operations management, and supply chain management in the Industry 4.0 era. Under influence of COVID-19, the event was also digitally transformed: For the first time in its history the APMS conference was organized in a 'hybrid mode,' meaning face-to-face as well as online conference sessions. A large international panel of experts reviewed all the papers and selected the best ones to be included in these international conference proceedings. The topics of interest in APMS 2020 included Digital Supply Networks, Data-Driven Production Management, Sustainable Production Management, Cloud and Collaborative Technologies, Smart Manufacturing and Industry 4.0, Data-Driven Services, Digital Lean Manufacturing, and Digital Transformation Approaches in Production Management.

The proceedings are organized into two parts:

- The Path to Digital Transformation and Innovation of Production Management Systems (Volume 1)
- Towards Smart and Digital Manufacturing (Volume 2)

The conference was supported by the International Federation of Information Processing (IFIP) and was organized by the IFIP Working Group 5.7 on Advances in Production Management Systems and University of Novi Sad, Faculty of Technical Sciences, Department of Industrial Engineering and Management. We would like to thank all contributors for their high-quality work and for their willingness to share their innovative ideas and findings. We are also indebted to the members of the IFIP Working Group 5.7, the Program Committee members, and the Scientific Committee members for their support in the review process of the papers. Finally, we appreciate the generous support from both the Ministry of Education, Science and Technological Development and Provincial Secretariat for Higher Education and Scientific Research of the Republic of Serbia.

August 2020

Bojan Lalic
Vidosav Majstorovic
Ugljesa Marjanovic
Gregor von Cieminski
David Romero

# Organization

## Conference Chair

Bojan Lalic          University of Novi Sad, Serbia

## Conference Co-chair

Gregor Von Cieminski      ZF Hungária Kft., Hungary

## Program Chair

Vidosav Majstorovic      University of Belgrade, Serbia

## Program Co-chair

David Romero      Tecnológico de Monterrey, Mexico

## Program Committee

Thorsten Wuest      West Virginia University, USA
Paolo Gaiardelli      University of Bergamo, Italy
Ilkyeong Moon      Seoul National University, South Korea

## Organizing Committee Chair

Ugljesa Marjanovic      University of Novi Sad, Serbia

## Doctoral Workshop Chair

Milan Delic      University of Novi Sad, Serbia

## International Advisory Committee

Farhad Ameri      Texas State University, USA
Ilkyeong Moon      Seoul National University, South Korea
Hermann Lödding      TUHH, Germany

## Organizing Committee

Danijela Gračanin      University of Novi Sad, Serbia
Nemanja Tasić      University of Novi Sad, Serbia
Nenad Medić      University of Novi Sad, Serbia

| Tanja Todorović | University of Novi Sad, Serbia |
|---|---|
| Slavko Rakić | University of Novi Sad, Serbia |
| Marko Pavlović | University of Novi Sad, Serbia |
| Jelena Ćurčić | University of Novi Sad, Serbia |
| Dragana Gojić | University of Novi Sad, Serbia |
| Nemanja Majstorović | University of Belgrade, Serbia |

## Scientific Committee

| Erry Yulian Triblas Adesta | International Islamic University Malaysia, Malaysia |
|---|---|
| Erlend Alfnes | Norwegian University of Science and Technology, Norway |
| Thecle Alix | IUT Bordeaux Montesquieu France |
| Susanne Altendorfer-Kaiser | Montanuniversitaet Leoben, Austria |
| Farhad Ameri | Texas State University, USA |
| Bjørn Andersen | Norwegian University of Science and Technology, Norway |
| Eiji Arai | Osaka University, Japan |
| Frédérique Biennier | INSA Lyon, France |
| Umit S. Bititci | Heriot Watt University, UK |
| Magali Bosch-Mauchand | Université de Technologie de Compiègne, France |
| Abdelaziz Bouras | Qatar University, Qatar |
| Jim Browne | University College Dublin, Ireland |
| Luis Camarinha-Matos | Universidade Nova de Lisboa, Portugal |
| Sergio Cavalieri | University of Bergamo, Italy |
| Stephen Childe | Plymouth University, UK |
| Hyunbo Cho | Pohang University of Science and Technology, South Korea |
| Gregor von Cieminski | ZF Friedrichshafen AG, Hungary |
| Adolfo Crespo Marquez | University of Seville, Spain |
| Catherine Da Cunha | École Centrale de Nantes, France |
| Frédéric Demoly | Université de Technologie de Belfort-Montbéliard, France |
| Shengchun Deng | Harbin Institute of Technology, China |
| Melanie Despeisse | Chalmers University of Technology, Sweden |
| Alexandre Dolgui | IMT Atlantique, France |
| Slavko Dolinšek | University of Ljubljana, Slovenia |
| Sang Do Noh | Sungkyunkwan University, South Korea |
| Heidi Carin Dreyer | Norwegian University of Science and Technology, Norway |
| Eero Eloranta | Helsinki University of Technology, Finland |
| Soumaya El Kadiri | Texelia AG, Switzerland |
| Christos Emmanouilidis | Cranfield University, UK |
| Åsa Fasth-Berglund | Chalmers University of Technology, Sweden |

| | |
|---|---|
| Manuel Fradinho Duarte de Oliveira | SINTEF, Norway |
| Jan Frick | University of Stavanger, Norway |
| Paolo Gaiardelli | University of Bergamo, Italy |
| Adriana Giret Boggino | Universidad Politécnica de Valencia, Spain |
| Samuel Gomes | Belfort-Montbéliard University of Technology, France |
| Bernard Grabot | INP-ENIT (National Engineering School of Tarbes), France |
| Gerhard Gudergan | FIR Research Institute for Operations Management at RWTH Aachen University, Germany |
| Thomas R. Gulledge Jr. | George Mason University, USA |
| Hironori Hibino | Tokyo University of Science, Japan |
| Hans-Henrik Hvolby | Aalborg University, Denmark |
| Dmitry Ivanov | Berlin School of Economics and Law, Germany |
| Harinder Jagdev | National University of Ireland at Galway, Ireland |
| John Johansen | Aalborg University, Denmark |
| Hong-Bae Jun | Hongik University, South Korea |
| Toshiya Kaihara | Kobe University, Japan |
| Duck-Young Kim | Ulsan National Institute of Science and Technology (UNIST), South Korea |
| Dimitris Kiritsis | École Polytechnique Fédérale de Lausanne, Switzerland |
| Tomasz Koch | Wroclaw University of Science and Technology, Poland |
| Pisut Koomsap | Asian Institute of Technology, Thailand |
| Gül Kremer | Iowa State University, USA |
| Boonserm Kulvatunyou | National Institute of Standards and Technology, USA |
| Thomas R. Kurfess | Georgia Institute of Technology, USA |
| Andrew Kusiak | University of Iowa, USA |
| Lenka Landryova | Technical University of Ostrava, Czech Republic |
| Jan-Peter Lechner | First Global Liaison, Germany |
| Gyu M. Lee | Pusan National University, South Korea |
| Ming K. Lim | Chongqing University, China |
| Hermann Lödding | Hamburg University of Technology, Germany |
| Marco Macchi | Politecnico di Milano, Italy |
| Gökan May | École Polytechnique Fédérale de Lausanne, Switzerland |
| Jörn Mehnen | University of Strathclyde, UK |
| Joao Gilberto Mendes dos Reis | UNIP Paulista University, Brazil |
| Vidosav D. Majstorovich | University of Belgrade, Serbia |
| Hajime Mizuyama | Aoyama Gakuin University, Japan |
| Ilkyeong Moon | Seoul National University, South Korea |
| Dimitris Mourtzis | University of Patras, Greece |
| Irenilza de Alencar Naas | UNIP Paulista University, Brazil |
| Masaru Nakano | Keio University, Japan |

# Contents – Part II

**Digital Transformation for more Sustainable Supply Chains**

## Data-Driven Applications in Smart Manufacturing and Logistics Systems

## Operations Management in Engineer-to-Order Manufacturing

**Gastronomic Service System Design**

**Product and Asset Life Cycle Management in the Circular Economy**

## Production Ramp-Up Strategies for Product

# Contents – Part I

**Digital and Virtual Quality Management Systems**

**Novel Production Planning and Control Approaches**

**Machine Learning and Artificial Intelligence**

**Connected, Smart Factories of the Future**

**Manufacturing Systems Engineering: Agile, Flexible, Reconfigurable**

## Circular Products Design and Engineering

## Circular, Green, Sustainable Manufacturing

## Environmental and Social Lifecycle Assessments

## Socio-Cultural Aspects in Production Systems

## Data-Driven Manufacturing and Services Operations Management

## Product-Service Systems in DSN

## Collaborative Design and Engineering

# The Operator 4.0: New Physical and Cognitive Evolutionary Paths

# Facilitating Operator Participation in Continuous Improvement: An Investigation of Organizational Factors

Eirin Lodgaard(✉), Silje Helene Aschehoug, and Daryl Powell

SINTEF Manufacturing, Enggata 40, 2830 Raufoss, Norway
eirin.lodgaard@sintef.no

**Abstract.** Continuous improvement (CI) is a fundamental part of lean thinking and practice and will remain critical for the success of manufacturing firms during the fourth industrial revolution. The realization of CI is based on the active participation and involvement of the firm's entire workforce – with everybody making incremental improvements, every day. This of course includes shop floor operators. In this paper, we explore various aspects that influence the successful involvement of shop floor operators in CI activities, by adopting a case study approach. The case company has achieved only partial success with CI on the shop floor, despite repeated efforts. As a result of the study, several organizational factors emerge as critical success factors for securing involvement and engagement of operators in CI, with positive results. Raising awareness of these critical factors may help manufacturing firms adopt an alternative approach to CI which promises to increase the level of operator participation in CI.

**Keywords:** Continuous improvement · Operator · Shop floor · Case study

## 1 Introduction

The increasing challenges faced by manufacturing firms in the global marketplace are currently forcing companies to think in new directions. To remain competitive, the continuous improvement of manufacturing processes is necessary. As a result, manufacturing companies have introduced lean as a management approach, with the aim of improving competitiveness by creating and delivering value to customers, while continuously eliminating waste in the organization [1]. Lean thinking and practice, which is primarily inspired by the successes of Toyota Production System (TPS), has to some extent been introduced by the most significant actors and is known as a crucial strategic weapon [1, 2].

Despite an abundance of research within the field of lean production, there is no clear consensus among the research community on a common definition or approach to lean. However, one of the most commonly used approaches is based on a framework developed in [1]. This framework presents five principles with the aim of helping organizations to realize lean production as a coherent system:

© IFIP International Federation for Information Processing 2020
Published by Springer Nature Switzerland AG 2020
B. Lalic et al. (Eds.): APMS 2020, IFIP AICT 592, pp. 3–10, 2020.
https://doi.org/10.1007/978-3-030-57997-5_1

- Identify customer value
- Identify and manage the value stream(s)
- Create flow
- Achieve pull
- Strive for perfection

The core objective of applying these principles is to provide customer value and to increase the ratio of value-added activities in the value stream. In practice, this includes identifying all types of waste and continuously looking for improvements to eliminate them. Hence, integrating a culture of sustained improvement is of highest importance, targeting the elimination of waste in all systems and processes of an organization [3]. In organizations, this means implementing continuous improvement (CI) by involving everyone to make incremental improvements through ongoing efforts.

Much research has been conducted on CI success factors and enablers [4]. However, there has been little focus on how to succeed with ensuring the active participation and involvement of shop floor operators in CI activities, given that operators are essential in the day-to-day success of CI. Against this background, this paper aims to answer the following research question: *how can an organization successfully involve shop floor operators in the process of CI, targeting the elimination of waste in the value stream?*

The article is structured as follows: First, we provide an outline of the theory of CI including a review of select literature regarding how to organize for CI. Secondly, we present a case study from a company specializing in the development and manufacturing of products for the automotive industry. The results of CI initiatives at the case firm are mixed, with only partial involvement of shop floor operators. Thus, we identify opportunities for successfully engaging operators in the process of eliminating waste and improving the CI process itself. Finally, we present conclusions and implications for both researchers and practitioners.

## 2 Continuous Improvement

CI is a core principle regardless of which kind of management system the organization has chosen [5]. There exist several definitions of CI, for example: *"A continuous stream of high-involvement, incremental changes in products and processes for enhanced business performance"* [6], and *"A company-wide process of focused and continuous incremental innovation"* [7]. Both definitions emphasize the involvement of everyone in making improvements, including shop floor operators. This is in accordance with the following definition of lean manufacturing: *"...the systematic removal of waste by all members of the organization from all areas of the value stream"* [8]. Waste is defined as unnecessary activities that do not add value for the customer.

CI may occur through incremental improvements or through radical change [3]. Incremental improvements refer to small and gradual improvements, while radical change refers to improvement based on new, innovative ideas or new technologies that may require investments. Moreover, an extended period with several incremental improvements may result in major improvements or a radical change. Consequently, CI is a change process in which superior performance is achieved [9].

# 3 Organizing for Continuous Improvement

The organization of CI activities transpires over at least three levels: management level, team level and the individual level. Firstly, CI at management level involves the organization's strategy. Secondly, CI at team level involves all kinds of tasks, broadly defined. Finally, CI also deals with improvements in day-to-day tasks at individual level [10]. [3] suggests that it is management's responsibility to address CI at each of these levels. In a manufacturing organization, shop floor operators may be involved both at team level and at the individual level. More specifically, a shop floor team will be responsible for improving day-to-day operational activities, in addition to their own practices aiming to improve overall equipment efficiency (OEE) [11].

Designing, executing and achieving CI represents a variety of challenges [12]. Fortunately, there are several known factors that influence successful implementation of CI. Among these are management commitment and involvement, leadership, cultural issues, a need to measure the progress, motivation of workers, resources and working in cross-functional teams [4].

In the literature, management commitment and involvement are highlighted as the most important success factors in CI [4]. Hence, without visible, committed and active support and engagement from management, CI is unlikely to succeed. Improvement programs will suffer where there is an absence of strong leadership. As such, the existence of a charismatic leader will contribute in a positive way [4, 13]. In addition, it is important to understand that CI leadership must be performed by all managers, not only the top management. Furthermore, good leadership will influence the motivation for shop floor operators in a positive manner [14]. Consequently, when considering implementing CI in an organization, the management team must not underestimate the managerial effort required.

Like any change program, the implementation of CI will require change management. This requires available resources, and at the same time, people in a position of influence. These people must work consciously to develop the ability to implement and to sustain CI in the organization. Another important factor is involvement of operators to ensure that improvements in the CI implementation process influence and reach work practices [4]. For most people, it is easier to accept changes when personally involved in the process. This view is supported by [15] which points out the importance of gathering and involving relevant experts, and consequently ensuring acceptance through participation. Through involvement, employees gain a sense of belonging and satisfaction, and are allowed to put their creativity, knowledge and skills to good use. The intrinsic motivation of individual team members is another factor that influence CI implementation [19].

CI may be achieved through the application of a number of methods and techniques [3]. If the overall goal is to reduce waste, streamline the flow of the manufacturing process and improve product quality, then a systematic approach to problem-solving is required. A systematic approach helps people stay focused on completing the improvement initiative, by carrying out pre-defined steps until goal satisfaction prevails [16]. A study by [17] points out that an effective communication channel between management and employees working with CI is important to ensure sustainability.

At the individual level, improvements are normally driven by a suggestion system. The actual implementation of the improvement ideas can be carried out by shop floor operators or can be left to specialists. [18] points out that shop floor operators are the experts within their work area and are therefore those who can best solve their own problems, though they may require support in the process.

## 4   Research Design

We adopt a case study design, the purpose of which to better understand how to successfully involve shop floor operators in CI work to target the elimination of waste in their value streams. A case study can use an appropriate approach when the area being studied is in progress or has recently been in progress, and where research variables cannot be controlled [19]. The case company had an ongoing CI program which could be studied, and consequently met these requirements.

Operators working in different shop floor teams, but within the same manufacturing department, were interviewed to identify success factors regarding involvement and active participating in their ongoing CI process. Ten semi-structured interviews were carried out across five shop floor teams. They had a range of work experience from 1 to 30 years. Five of the interviewees had a combined shift leader job in addition to their regular work at the production line.

The questions were formulated to cover both how they approach CI activities and to gather their opinions of what could have been done differently. Face to face interviews is a commonly used method to collect information. Well-informed interviewees can provide important insight into facts and opinions [19]. The actual interviews were conducted as semi-structured conversations, in which the informants were asked pre-developed questions. The informants were allowed to answer freely. The aim of the conversations was to create an informal setting in which the interviewees would open up and provide rich data. All interviews were recorded and later transcribed to provide an accurate representation of the conversation [19]. All interviews were conducted at the company's production site. In addition, observations were made during frequent company visits, as well as examination of written documentation (minutes of meetings, procedures, improvement database etc.) to allow for triangulation.

## 5   The Case: The Process of Continuous Improvement

The case company is a large subsidiary of a global corporation located in Norway. It operates as a first-tier supplier to original equipment manufacturers (OEMs) in the automotive industry and has a long term and strategic relationship with customers worldwide. The production is highly automated and has a functional structure with eight different production lines. This case is limited to one of the production lines only. The production line is operated in five shifts with three operators at each the shift. One of the operators at each shift also has the function of shift leader, and consequently has the responsibility for organizing the shift and the work in the production line.

The case company has been working with lean as a management approach for decades. One of the main purposes of their chosen lean approach is to systematically reduce waste in the workplace and to improve the manufacturing processes by working with CI. To address progress, they measure the overall equipment efficiency (OEE) a product of the availability of the equipment, the actual operating speed compared to ideal speed, and the quality of products (measured as right-first-time).

Every morning they have a team meeting, where the shift leader, team leader, process engineer, quality engineer, maintenance workers, logistic planner and production manager participates. The core activity is information exchange regarding production performance for the last 24 h, in addition to planning for the next 24 h. A standardized board is used to follow up on OEE and accompanying activities. Major outputs from these meetings are the identification of problems and areas for improvement.

The team board used in the meetings has a pre-defined area dedicated for improvement suggestions. Suggestions may come from everyone, including operators that do not participate in the daily team meeting. Before the meeting starts, the shift leader has a discussion with the other two operators about issues which are important to address. For example, small improvements at the individual level and more complex suggestions which need to be solved at a team level.

Improvement suggestions from both the team members and from other operators is divided into two levels: individual- and team level. At individual level it is decided in the team meeting the responsible person and due date. All suggestions involving more complex issues are transferred into a system for escalating the improvement. This is taken care of in an additional improvement meeting once in a week with a cross functional team, where the participants are those responsible for issues in addition to the production manager and logistics planner. In addition, other functions are invited where it is necessary to solve the improvement issues.

# 6 Case Analysis and Discussion

Everyone is expected to contribute with suggestions covering all kinds of operational problems and improvements in their daily work. As a rule, both minor and large improvements are implemented every day. Still, the teams experience that the same type of problems and quality issues repeat themselves, often on multiple occasions. This finding indicates that the company may in fact struggle to identify and eliminate the actual root causes, or rather struggles with learning, standardizing and communicating the results of the improvement activities.

## 6.1 Management Support

All informants claimed that many of the improvement initiatives experienced problems. For example, operators explained that their improvement suggestions were at times not followed up in a serious and systematic manner. In some cases, they experienced little or no information about what happened to their suggestions after a decision had been made. In other instances, the implementation period for a solution was considered too long. This is in line with the experience of disappointment and failure with CI reported by shop floor operators who highlight that this derives mainly from limited support and commitment from managers [20].

## 6.2   Involvement of Operators

All ten interviewees highlighted the importance of their individual involvement in CI. In addition, CI was regarded as a useful approach for their desired results. This is in line with recommendations in literature which emphasis CI as useful if the aim is to reduce waste, streamline the flow of the manufacturing process and improve the quality of the product [3]. Nevertheless, the shop floor operators reported that they were only partly involved in systematic CI activities. Shift leaders were currently more involved in dealing with improvement suggestions due to their daily participation in the team meeting.

However, it was apparent that the operators in the case company were motivated to produce high quality parts in an efficient way to meet the customers' requirements and expectations. This is a good starting point for improvement activities. These findings may indicate that the organization has not sufficiently reflected on how to organize for CI at the shop floor level.

## 6.3   Knowledge and Skills

The findings indicate that CI training at this level is inadequate. To improve the situation, the case company may allocate more managerial time at shop floor level to communicate, discuss and listen to operators. Such activities are known to lead to empowerment [14]. Additional training should also be considered to make both shift leaders and shop floor operators aware of how they can work with CI together. In this respect, it is interesting to observe that most of the operators did not see the need for training in the use of improvement tools and practices. Although none of the informants were willing to miss the opportunity to expand their knowledge about CI tools and practices if asked. Existing research shows that an important driving force for successful CI is knowledge of CI techniques, combined with the knowledge and skills to perform necessary activities [20].

## 6.4   Communication Interface

The interviews with the shift leaders and operators revealed that the list of improvement suggestions was not actively used outside the team board meeting, as intended. Consequently, many opportunities for discovering problems early on and working with CI is lost today. Investigating this issue further, it appears that most of the operators and shift leaders did not see the need of a common system to document improvement suggestions.

A common opinion prevailed among the interviewees, concerning that verbal messages to support functions and leaders was considered enough. These functions are responsible to decide whether a suggestion should be put into effect, and who should be the person responsible for this. A plausible interpretation of this insufficient documentation and information handling may be that many operators at shop floor level are still quite unfamiliar with CI as a concept and practice. Consequently, they do not know what to expect.

# 7 Concluding Remarks

Worldwide, CI is regarded as a valuable approach to increase the competitiveness of organizations. However, implementation of CI at the shop floor level with the active participation of all operators is not a trivial task.

This study indicates that identifying and understanding organizational aspects is a critical success factor for involving shop floor operators in CI activities. The case study findings point towards managerial efforts as the most vital organizational aspect to consider. More specifically, facilitating and engaging operators are vital to enhance proactive improvement initiatives on the shop floor. Managers cannot give the full responsibility to the shop -floor operators and expect them to succeed without support and engagement. Standardized work requires capabilities and mindsets for routine processes, while CI activities have a non-routine character and require a greater level of thinking and analysis. Due to the non-routine character of working with all types of incremental improvements, operators will need management support in their CI work until a culture of common and systematic way of thinking and acting have been rooted in the entire organization.

Moreover, the study illuminates the importance of having a digital system to document all improvement suggestions with easy access for the entire shop floor team. More specifically, – a digital communication interface facilitating communication, planning, executions of actions and monitoring the progress of the CI activities

Raising awareness of these organizational factors may help manufacturing organizations to arrive at the correct approach and increase the odds of a successful CI program in a lean perspective. These indicative findings may be used when launching CI activities in a lean context. Notwithstanding, more research is needed to enhance the result and to increase generalizability. The future research should include multiple organization trying to implement and improve their CI process in a lean perspective.

**Acknowledgement.** The research was funded by the Research Council of Norway through the research project *Lean Digital*.

# References

1. Womack, J.P., Jones, D.T.: Lean Thinking. Simon & Schuster, New York (1996)
2. New, S.J.: Celebrating the enigma: the continuing puzzle of the Toyota production system. Int. J. Prod. Res. **45**(16), 3545–3554 (2007)
3. Bhuiyan, N., Baghel, A.: An overview of continuous improvement: From the aast to the present. Manag. Decis. **43**(5), 761–771 (2005)
4. Garcia-Sabater, J.J., Marin-Garcia, J.A.: Can we still talk about continuous improvement? Rethinking enablers and inhibitors for successful implementation. Int. J. Technol. Manag. **55**(1), 28–42 (2011)

5. Dahlgaard-Park, S.M.: The quality movement - where are you hoing? Total Qual. Manag. Bus. Excel. 22(5), 493–513 (2011)
6. Ljungström, M., Klefsjö, B.: Implementation obstacles for a workdevelopment-oriented TQM strategy. Total Qual. Manag. 13(5), 621–634 (2002)
7. Bessant, J., Caffyn, S., Gilbert, J., Harding, R.: Rediscovering Continuous Improvement. Technovation 14(1), 17–29 (1994)
8. Worley, J.M., Doolen, T.L.: The role of communication and management support in a lean manufacturing implementation. Manag. Decis. 44(2), 229–245 (2006)
9. Juran, J.M., Gryna, F.M.: Juran's Quality Handbook. McGraw-Hill, New York (1988)
10. Imai, M.: Kaizen. The Key to Japan's Competitive Success, 1st edn. Random House, New York (1986)
11. de Lange-Ros, E., Boer, H.: Theory and practices of continuous improvment in shop floor teams. Int. J. Technol. Manag. 22(4), 344–358 (2001)
12. Lillrank, P., Shani, A.B.R., Lindberg, P.: Continuous improvement: exploring alternative organizational designs. Total Qual. Manag. 12, 41–55 (2001)
13. Chiarini, A.: Japanese total quality control, TQM, Deming's system of profound knowledge, BPR, lean and six Sigma. Int. J. Lean Six Sigma 2(4), 332–355 (2011)
14. Lodgaard, E., Johannessen, L.P.: Shop floor teams and motivating factors for continuous improvement. In: Wang, K., Wang, Y., Strandhagen, J.O., Yu, T. (eds.) IWAMA 2018. LNEE, vol. 484, pp. 467–474. Springer, Singapore (2019). https://doi.org/10.1007/978-981-13-2375-1_59
15. Jarvinen, J.: PDCA-cycle in implementing design for environment in an R&D unit of Nokia Telecommunications. In: Proceedings of the 1998 IEEE International Symposium on Electrics and Environment (1998)
16. Reid, R.R., Koljonen, E.L.: The Deming cycle provides a framework for managing environmentally responsible process improvements. Qual. Eng. 12, 199–209 (1999)
17. Yan, B., Makinde, O.D.: Impact of continuous improvement on new product development within SMEs in the Western Cape, South Africa. Afr. J. Bus. Manag. 5(6), 2200–2229 (2011)
18. Deniels, R.C.: Performance measurement at sharp and driving continuous improvement on the shop floor. Eng. Manag. J. 5(5), 211–218 (1995)
19. Yin, R.K.: Case Study Research. Design and Methods, 4th edn. Sage Publications, Thousand Oaks (2009)
20. Lodgaard, E., Ingvaldsen, J.A., Aschehoug, S., Gamme, I.: Barriers to continuous improvement: perceptions of top managers, middle managers and workers. In: Proceeding of the 48th CIRP conference on Manufacturing Systems, vol. 41, pp. 1119–1124. Procedia CIRP (2016)

# Improving the Safety of Using Didactic Setups by Applying Augmented Reality

Srdjan Tegeltija(✉) , Vule Reljić , Ivana Šenk , Laslo Tarjan ,
and Branislav Tejić

Faculty of Technical Sciences, University of Novi Sad, 21000 Novi Sad, Serbia
srkit@uns.ac.rs

**Abstract.** The application of didactic setups is one of the commonly used teaching methods at schools and universities nowadays. By using the didactic setups, students are introduced to real components and real processes that take place in the industry. However, the students often need to use the didactic setups outside of regular teaching activities and at times when teaching staff is unavailable. This paper presents a solution for improving the safety of using the didactic setups by applying an augmented reality solution. The presented solution was implemented on a didactic setup for control of a three-phase asynchronous motor. In addition to improving the safety, the proposed solution allows the students to autonomously use the didactic setups beyond regular teaching hours.

**Keywords:** Didactic setup · Remote control · Augmented reality

## 1 Introduction

In order to provide training for the use of various equipment, there are numerous different solutions aiming to provide simple, fast and safe training for people. One of the possible ways is that the trainees learn solely from literature [1, 2]. In such a setting, the users are introduced to the equipment and its use through printed literature (textbooks, books, operating instructions, etc.) or through literature in a digital format (PDF, audio and video, etc.). By following the descriptions and instructions, the users are introduced to the equipment and its operation. The obvious advantage of this type of training is simplicity. However, its main disadvantage is that it is completely theoretical, and lacks hands-on trainings which are essential for real acquisition of knowledge and skills. After such a training, the trainees need some time to become familiar with the real equipment, which might additionally pose a potential safety risk. Another disadvantage of this type of training is that certain instructions may be difficult to read and incomprehensible to the trainees without experimenting with the actual equipment. Also, there may be errors in the text that may lead the users to the wrong conclusions, which also poses a safety risk (for example, electric shock, injuries due to contact with actuators, etc.). Another training possibility is to apply didactic setups [3–5]. The didactic setups serve as system models with actual parts of equipment, which are used to simulate the systems and processes that are executed in real industrial and

B. Lalic et al. (Eds.): APMS 2020, IFIP AICT 592, pp. 11–18, 2020.
https://doi.org/10.1007/978-3-030-57997-5_2

non-industrial systems under controlled and laboratory conditions. The main advantage of this type of training is the hands-on experience of working with real components of the system. The didactic setups are often created by the producers of the equipment to make it easier and faster for the users to familiarize themselves with the equipment, or by companies in order to train new employees as quickly as possible. After such a training, the trainees can apply the acquired knowledge directly in real systems because they have the hands-on experience with working with real components during the training. A disadvantage of this type of training is that there are some, although minimal, safety risks. Even though the didactic setups simulate the operating processes in the controlled laboratory conditions, there is a possibility of electric shock if the trainees would accidentally touch metal parts which could get connected to the power supply, as well as injuries from physical contact with actuators, or burns from handling high temperature fluids (hot water or steam), etc. Consequently, in order to minimize the safety risks, at least one responsible person must be present to supervise the training process (instructor, laboratory assistant, etc.). Thus, the availability of didactic setups for the users depends on the availability of the responsible personnel for supervising the training as well as on the availability of the laboratories in which the didactic setups are located. Further disadvantage of this type of training is that didactic setups cannot be used by a large number of users at the same time, i.e. there is a limit on the number of the trainees per training. In recent years, following the development and popularization of virtual and augmented reality technologies, training systems which utilize these technologies have been developed [6–8]. The advantage of this type of training is that, similarly to hands-on trainings, the users are introduced to a model of the system with real system components, but in a virtual environment, so there is no possibility of physical injury. In addition, a large number of trainees can attend the training at the same time, and there is a possibility of conducting the trainings from remote locations. The disadvantage of this type of training is that the virtual reality systems can cause side effects on the user such as a headache, blurred vision and nausea, so planned breaks are recommended during the training at regular time intervals. Another disadvantage of this type of training is that it employs emerging technologies whose cost is still relatively high, and many organizations may not have the resources to make the initial investment, although the costs are usually justified in the long run. To overcome the disadvantages of the individual training types, the trainings for users who will work in more complex industrial and non-industrial environments often utilize a combination of multiple training methods.

Educational institutions such as schools and universities commonly use dedicated didactic setups as a training method in order to provide hands-on experience to the students. By using the didactic setups, students are introduced to real components as well as to the models of real systems and processes under controlled laboratory conditions. A disadvantage of using such didactic setups at schools and universities is that they are available to pupils and students only during regular teaching activities with the presence of teaching staff (professors, assistants, laboratory assistants). However, the students often need to use the didactic setups outside of regular teaching hours, including times when the teaching staff is not available for them. This paper presents a concept for a solution that increases safety of using the didactic setups as well as enables autonomous use of didactic models by pupils and students beyond regular teaching hours by applying augmented reality technology.

## 2   The Proposed Solution

The proposed solution is based on a combination of using didactic setups and the augmented reality concept. The augmented reality is a concept that expands a user's view of the world with computer-generated text, images and sound. The idea behind the augmented reality concept is not new. The concept was created in the 1960s, and its foundations were laid by Ivan Sutherland through the development of a system with a head mounted display which was used to show a simple wireframe cube overlaid onto the real world [9]. This technology has long been neglected due to the limitations of hardware and software resources (large computers with low performances, cameras and displays with large dimensions but low resolutions, etc.) [4]. With the emergence and widespread use of smartphones with built-in high-speed processors, high-resolution displays and cameras, the augmented reality concept has gained in popularity and became implemented in a number of fields, such as industry, medicine, education, and other areas [10–17]. In the meantime, a variety of glasses that allow augmented reality to be displayed have been developed [18]. All this leads to new possibilities of implementing the augmented reality concept in various areas.

In this paper we propose a solution for using the augmented reality concept in order to enhance the existing didactic setups used for teaching students through hands-on experiences with a model of a system that includes real industrial equipment. The proposed solution is based on using a server application, a smartphone with a dedicated user application providing the augmented reality features and the remotely controlled didactic setup. The concept diagram of the proposed solution is shown in Fig. 1.

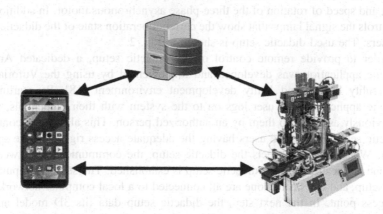

**Fig. 1.** The concept diagram of the proposed solution for improving the safety of using the didactic setups by applying augmented reality: server, smartphone and the didactic setup.

The server application is designed to store the user profiles and the didactic setup data. When creating the user profile, each user is assigned adequate access rights for the didactic setup along with dedicated timeslots when they can access it. The didactic setup data includes the 3D model of the setup as well as the descriptions of its functions required for using the augmented reality options in the smartphone application. The smartphone application allows the user to log on to the system, and based on their defined access rights it grants or denies the user control of the didactic setup. After the user has logged on, a connection between the smartphone application and the didactic setup is established, in order to establish communication and enable sending commands to the didactic setup, as well as downloading data from the didactic setup to display them on the smartphone through augmented reality. Communication between the smartphone application and the didactic setup can be established either via Bluetooth or via Wi-Fi communication, depending on the actual equipment of the didactic setup.

## 3 The Realized Solution

As a proof of concept, an experimental system was developed and realized for use in hands-on teaching activities. This experimental system serves as an upgrade of a didactic setup for control of a three-phase asynchronous motor, previously developed at the Faculty of Technical Sciences in Novi Sad. The didactic setup consists of a pro-grammable logic controller (PLC), type Siemens Simatic S7-1200, frequency converter type Danfoss FC51, a three-phase asynchronous motor, command buttons and switches, signal lamps and auxiliary components (fuses, power supply, etc.) [4]. The command buttons are connected to the PLC, and allow executing basic commands such as starting or stopping the three-phase asynchronous motor, changing the direction of rotation of the motor, or changing (reducing or increasing) its speed. Following the user commands, the PLC sends commands to the frequency converter, which controls the direction and speed of rotation of the three-phase asynchronous motor. In addition, the PLC controls the signal lamps that show the current operation state of the didactic setup to the users. The used didactic setup is shown in Fig. 2.

In order to provide remote control of the didactic setup, a dedicated Android smartphone application was developed and implemented by using the Vuforia aug-mented reality library and Unity development environment [18]. By starting the smartphone application, the user logs on to the system with their credentials, which were previously assigned to them by an authorized person. This allows the control of the didactic setup only to the users having the adequate access rights for the specific time slot. When the user selects the didactic setup, the communication between the smartphone application and the didactic setup is established. The server computer, the didactic setup, and the smartphone are all connected to a local computer network via a WiFi access point. In the next step, the didactic setup data (its 3D model and the descriptions of its functions) become visible to the user. By directing the camera of the smartphone towards the didactic setup, the image processing algorithms implemented in the Vuforia library recognize the didactic setup and, implementing the concept of augmented reality, the information on the didactic setup and commands for its control

**Fig. 2.** The didactic setup for control of a three-phase asynchronous motor

are displayed on the screen of the smartphone. Figure 3 shows the flow diagram for the user side of the developed solution.

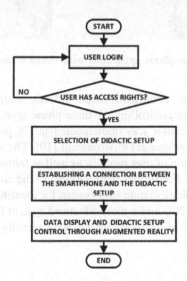

**Fig. 3.** The flow diagram of the developed solution

The control of the didactic setup by using a smartphone and augmented reality was realized through the use of virtual buttons. Figure 4 shows the smartphone application with virtual command buttons "S", "R", "−" and "+". The virtual control button "S" is used to start and stop the three-phase asynchronous motor. The virtual control button

"R" is used to change the direction of rotation of the three-phase asynchronous motor. Virtual command buttons "−" and "+" are used to reduce or increase the speed of the three-phase asynchronous motor. Virtual buttons do not physically exist but are displayed to the user's smartphone screen as augmented reality. By activating the virtual control buttons, the smartphone sends adequate commands to the didactic setup. This way, the control of the didactic setup (starting and stopping the motor rotation, changing the motor rotation direction, changing the motor rotation speed) without physically touching the control buttons on the didactic setup is enabled.

**Fig. 4.** User smartphone application with virtual command buttons.

In order to allow sending commands to the didactic setup, the existing PLC program of the didactic setup for controlling the three-phase asynchronous motor has been modified. The server application was implemented in C# programming language in Microsoft Visual Studio development environment [19]. The server application allows easy creation and modification of user profiles, as well as transferring the data about the didactic setup upon request. For further improvement of the concept as well as increase of general security, the implementation of a system for identification of didactic setups (for example 2D barcodes [20]) and a more advanced system for identification of users (for example access control as a service for software security [21]) is planned.

## 4   Conclusion

This paper presents a solution for improving the safety of using didactic setups by applying the concept of augmented reality. This system enables the control of the didactic setup from a dedicated smartphone application through augmented reality, which enables the control without physical contact of the user and the didactic setup. Such a solution improves safety as during its intended use there is no possibility of injury due to electric shock or contact with actuators. The advantage of the proposed and realized solution is that students can control the didactic setup without supervision of the teaching staff with minimal risks, assuming that they follow the safety regulations for handling the machines in the laboratory. In such a setting, the physical buttons on the didactic setup can be completely disabled, or the access to the buttons or even to the whole didactic setup can be physically disabled (e.g. by locking the control cabinet or putting the safety barrier between the students and the didactic setup), as the solution allows control of the didactic setup by using only the smartphone application and the virtual command buttons. It is important to note that even if full control of the didactic setup is available through the smartphone application, a physical emergency stop button has to be available to the students at all times for unexpected situations. A preliminary assessment and validation of the developed solution was conducted in collaboration with five students. All five students gave a positive assessment of the realized solution regarding the safety aspect, with only a single comment that it is not always easy to simultaneously keep a phone directed at the didactic setup and command virtual buttons. To confirm this preliminary assessment, an extensive user study is planned, which would include a larger number of students, in order to assess the applicability and usability of the presented solution. The study would also extend the developed solution to include additional didactic setups located at the Faculty of Technical Sciences in Novi Sad. As further development of the system it is planned to include the use of augmented reality smartglasses to facilitate the manipulation of the setup by the users and improve usability (instead of holding the smartphone directed toward the didactic setup, the students could control the setup simply by looking through the smartglasses).

**Acknowledgment.** This research has been supported by the Ministry of Education, Science and Technological Development, Government of the Republic of Serbia, through the project: "Innovative scientific and artistic research from the FTN activity domain".

# References

1. Bhutkar, G., Rajhans, N., Konkani, A., Dhore, M.: Usability issues of user manuals provided with medical devices. Br. J. Healthc. Comput. Inf. Manag. (2009)
2. Møller, M.H.: Usability testing of user manuals. Commun. Lang. Work. **2**, 51–59 (2013)
3. Cunha, B.G.P., et al.: DidacTronic: a low-cost and portable didactic lab for electronics: kit for digital and analog electronic circuits. In: 2016 IEEE Global Humanitarian Technology Conference (GHTC), pp. 296–303 (2016)
4. Ostojic, G., Stankovski, S., Tarjan, L., Senk, I., Jovanovic, V.: Development and implementation of didactic sets in mechatronics and industrial engineering courses. Int. J. Eng. Educ. **26**, 2 (2010)
5. Stankovski, S., Tarjan, L., Skrinjar, D., Ostojic, G., Senk, I.: Using a didactic manipulator in mechatronics and industrial engineering courses. IEEE Trans. Educ. **53**, 572–579 (2009)
6. Van Wyk, E., De Villiers, R.: Virtual reality training applications for the mining industry. In: Proceedings of the 6th International Conference on Computer Graphics, Virtual Reality, Visualisation and Interaction in Africa, pp. 53–63 (2009)

7. Gavish, N., et al.: Evaluating virtual reality and augmented reality training for industrial maintenance and assembly tasks. Interact. Learn. Environ. **23**, 778–798 (2015)
8. Hasan, R.B., Aziz, F.B.A., Mutaleb, H.A.A., Umar, Z.: Virtual reality as an industrial training tool: a review. J. Adv. Rev. Sci. Res. **29**, 20–26 (2017)
9. Billinghurst, M., Kato, H., Poupyrev, I., et al.: Tangible augmented reality. ACM SIGGRAPH ASIA **7**, 1–10 (2008)
10. Marescaux, J., Rubino, F., Arenas, M., Mutter, D., Soler, L.: Augmented-reality–assisted laparoscopic adrenalectomy. JAMA **292**, 2211–2215 (2004)
11. Fraga-Lamas, P., Fernández-Caramés, T.M., Blanco-Novoa, Ó., Vilar-Montesinos, M.A.: A review on industrial augmented reality systems for the Industry 4.0 shipyard. IEEE Access **6**, 13358–13375 (2018)
12. Yuen, S.C.-Y., Yaoyuneyong, G., Johnson, E.: Augmented reality: an overview and five directions for AR in education. J. Educ. Technol. Dev. Exch. **4**, 11 (2011)
13. Kounavis, C.D., Kasimati, A.E., Zamani, E.D.: Enhancing the tourism experience through mobile augmented reality: challenges and prospects. Int. J. Eng. Bus. Manag. **4**, 10 (2012)
14. Fischer, J., Neff, M., Freudenstein, D., Bartz, D.: Medical augmented reality based on commercial image guided surgery. In: EGVE, pp. 83–86 (2004)
15. Yovcheva, Z., Buhalis, D., Gatzidis, C.: Smartphone augmented reality applications for tourism. E-Rev. Tour. Res. **10**, 63–66 (2012)
16. Pettersen, T., Pretlove, J., Skourup, C., Engedal, T., Lokstad, T.: Augmented reality for programming industrial robots. In: The Second IEEE and ACM International Symposium on Mixed and Augmented Reality 2003, Proceedings, pp. 319–320 (2003)
17. Peng, F., Al-Sayegh, M.: Personalised virtual fitting for fashion. Int. J. Ind. Eng. Manag. **5**, 233–240 (2014)
18. Cherdo, L.: The 8 best augmented reality smartglasses in 2020. https://www.aniwaa.com/buyers-guide/vr-ar/best-augmented-reality-smartglasses/. Accessed 26 Mar 2020
19. Microsoft: Visual Studio tutorials—C#. https://docs.microsoft.com/en-us/visualstudio/get-started/csharp/?view=vs-2019. Accessed 26 Mar 2020
20. Tarjan, L., Šenk, I., Kovač, R., Horvat, S., Ostojić, G., Stankovski, S.: Automatic identification based on 2D barcodes. Int. J. Ind. Eng. Manag. **2**, 151–157 (2011)
21. Dašić, P., Dašić, J., Crvenković, B.: Applications of access control as a service for software security. Int. J. Ind. Eng. Manag. **7**, 111–116 (2016)

# Production Management as-a-Service: A Softbot Approach

Brunno Abner[1(✉)], Ricardo J. Rabelo[1(✉)], Saulo P. Zambiasi[2(✉)], and David Romero[3(✉)]

[1] UFSC - Federal University of Santa Catarina, Florianopolis, Brazil
brunnoabner@gmail.com, ricardo.rabelo@ufsc.br
[2] UNISUL - University of Southern Santa Catarina, Florianopolis, Brazil
saulopz@gmail.com
[3] Tecnológico de Monterrey, Monterrey, Mexico
david.romero.diaz@gmail.com

**Abstract.** Production management involves many activities. In order to deal with Industry 4.0 requirements, many systems have developed solutions to gather real-time information from the shopfloor for more reliable decision-making. Empirical studies have been showing that this has created a tremendous overload of information to be handled by managers, causing stress, incorrect analyses and sometimes guessing-based decision-making, especially in SMEs. Using data analytics and maturity models concepts, this work shows *Livia*, a softbot with chatting capabilities. Deployed in a cloud and working on companies' shopfloor information got via a MES system, *Livia* helps managers to identify their main problems, suggests corrective actions, and proactively performs many supporting actions. Results are presented and discussed in the end.

**Keywords:** Production management · Softbot · Maturity model · Business analytics · MES · Manufacturing Execution System · Software-as-a-Service · SaaS

## 1 Introduction

*Production management (PM)* comprehends the sort of activities related to the planning, coordination, supervision, control and decision-making upon resources and business processes' outputs [1]. In Industry 4.0, PM should also consider the increasing digitalization and interconnection of smart products, services, manufacturing systems, value chains and business models in the Internet of Things, Services, and People [2].

This brings up new general technical requirements for enterprise information and operational systems and technologies, such as [3, 4]: distributed and decentralized control; decision autonomy; collaboration of cyber-physical systems (CPS); virtualization; adaptation and plug-and-play capabilities; emergent behavior & self-organization; supervision and resilience; data-driven & real-time control and optimization; and symbiotic interaction of CPSs and humans.

B. Lalic et al. (Eds.): APMS 2020, IFIP AICT 592, pp. 19–30, 2020.
https://doi.org/10.1007/978-3-030-57997-5_3

In order to deal with that, some works have been pursuing the development of environments where managers can be provided with easier, quicker, more systematic and more accurate access to information related to companies' shopfloor, to support more agile and confident decision-making with higher man-machine symbiosis (e.g. [5, 6]).

Implementing such environments is however complex. Regarding its basics – the real-time gathering of information from the shopfloor – some works have been proposing Business Intelligence-based as well as integrated and more interoperable approaches, making easier and more reliable the access to company's information as well as some basic support for decision-making via production dashboards (e.g. [7, 8]).

This is crucial, as information is normally spread over many disparate systems that use different technologies, formats and terminologies, which turns the access, understanding and usage of the right information sometimes even challenging for managers.

Despite the benefits brought up by such environments, they can bring additional complexity to managers. The practice has been showing that they are making managers be increasingly exposed to massive amounts of information about their companies, where lots of checking, analyses and supervision actions as well as critical decision-making need to be more often and rapidly performed [9, 10].

Some approaches have been proposed to handle this, being *software robots* (or just *softbot*) one of them. A softbot can be defined as a virtual system, deployed in a given computing environment, that automates and helps humans in the execution of some tasks with variable levels of intelligence, autonomy and proactivity [11].

In two previous works the authors demonstrated in near-real shopfloor scenarios that softbots can help mitigate some of those problems [6, 10]. Nevertheless, empirical evaluations have been demonstrating that, even though, managers keep being required to check and to do many things, repetitive actions, and without much guidance.

This paper presents a contribution to mitigate these issues. This also includes the consideration of SMEs reality and the coping with some observations came from those two previous works as well as from a MES (Manufacturing Execution System) provider: many SME managers are not used to data-driven philosophies, and they do not have enough or up-to-date theoretical background to more properly manage their companies' production. More specifically, managers are limited: (i) to filter which information from the shopfloor is indeed relevant to consider in the many different situations of analyses; (ii) to properly interpret the actual meaning of the many generated performance indicators and KPIs even though displayed in cute dashboards; and (iii) to reason about them to be more confident on which decisions are suitable for each situation.

These issues are addressed applying the foundations of maturity models and business analytics, employing a *softbot* with chatting properties. It has been developed using Action-Research methodology close to *Harbor*[1], one of the leading software providers of MES in Brazil. Using the Platform-as-a-Service (PaaS) *ARISA NEST* framework to derive particular softbots, this development has been gradually integrated into Harbor's MES and initially used by some of their industrial customers.

---

[1] https://www.harbor.com.br/.

# 2 Basic Foundations and Related Work

## 2.1 Basic Foundations

Production Management (PM) refers to planning, coordinating, and controlling the resources required for fabricating specified products by specified methods [1]. It handles activities like selection of products, production processes, and right production capacity; production planning; inventory control; maintenance of machines; production control; and quality and cost control [1]. Last two activities are the main focus of this work.

*Production Control* means ensuring that production is running as planned. If any deviation is found, then corrective actions should be taken. *Quality & Cost Control* means that good quality products should be produced at the lowest possible cost, with minimum possible delay, in a way that the company remains sustainable [1].

*Maturity* is a measurement of the ability of an organization to continuously improve some of its capabilities. Maturity is typically expressed in levels. The higher the maturity the better the company [12]. One referential model is CMMI[2], which allows assessing software companies based on processes and further assigning a given maturity (from 1 to 5) depending on which set of processes have been properly implemented.

*Business Analytics* refers to methods and techniques used to measure an organization's performance exploring its data to gain insight and drive business [13]. In general, there are five types of analytics [13]: Planning analytics: *What is our plan?;* Descriptive analytics: *What happened?;* Diagnostic analytics: *Why did it happen?;* Predictive analytics: *What will happen next?;* Prescriptive analytics: *What should be done about it?*

*Softbots* in an Industry 4.0 scenarios mean 'talking' to operators about their daily workflows, technical problems, and work-related topics [11]. Softbots represent novel human-machine/computer interfaces. In [6] & [14] are listed eleven softbots activities.

## 2.2 Related Works

Few works have been found in the literature combing *softbots* and *Industry 4.0* with a focus on PM. Schwartz et al. [15] proposed softbots to support hybrid teams to increase collaboration between humans, equipment, and software. Kar et al. [16] proposed a cloud-based system architecture for softbots to handle communication between humans and IIoT environments. Kassner et al. [17] proposed a general architecture for softbots to interact with a single machine to illustrate their benefits in smart factories. Dersingh et al. [18] developed a chatbot to monitor and record issues of a production line, notifying workers for appropriate actions. Longo et al. [19] implemented a framework to support the interaction of humans with physical equipment and their digital twins.

---

[2] https://cmmiinstitute.com/.

Chen et al. [20] developed an engine that adapts production plans to the skills and experience of workers aiming at improving factory efficiency as well as human satisfaction.

In previous research [6, 10], the authors implemented a scenario where a *single softbot* helped machine operators in some tasks via a high-level and voice-enacted interaction. In the second stage of this work, they implemented a scenario of *collaborative softbots* on top of a group of CPS to enhance operation excellence in a shopfloor.

Despite the important contributions of these works, no work has been found using softbots for the envisaged PM support, combining smart chatting, real-time information and alarms, maturity analysis upon companies' shopfloor status, and some business analytics to guide managers in their final decision-making against identified problems.

## 3 Production Management as-a-Service

*Production Management as-a-Service (PMaaS)* is a general business term for a system module that works together with a given commercial MES system called as *LiveMES®*.

This module works as a softbot (called *Livia*[3]) with chatting properties that: (i) evaluate companies' shopfloor information, identifying current problems in the production against what was planned (e.g. by the ERP) or what it is expected (e.g. based on operational metrics); (ii) identifies company maturity model so that managers can be aware of its operating excellence level; (iii) helps managers in decision-making thanks to some business analytics; and (iv) can be accessed *as-a-service* from the Internet.

Figure 1 shows the general architecture of the PMaaS environment the developed work – the dashed square – is inserted in. Next sections complement this explanation.

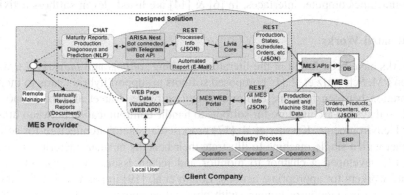

**Fig. 1.** General systems' architecture

---

[3] The name *Livia* comes from the union of *Live*MES with the *i*ntelligent *a*nalysis words.

The architecture follows the ISA-95 five-layer model. "Industry Process" encompasses layers 0-1-2 (machines, local controllers, industrial networks, sensors, IoT, etc.); "MES" represents layer 3; and "ERP" system the layer 4. The PMaaS approach is implemented via *Livia*, which works as a (new) module of LiveMES. The ERP feeds MES with the production plan.

LiveMES is a fully cloud-based system, deployed at *Amazon*, also proving mobile access via a Web app, from anywhere, anytime. Although companies' machines can be equipped with controllers, industrial networks, etc., LiveMES only requires an Internet connection and that given (simple and low cost) IoT-based data collectors are installed in the machines under supervision in the different production processes.

Data collectors grab every change in the (predefined) information about each machine (e.g. production counting and machine status) and keep it in memory. The information is sent to the cloud in batches every ten seconds, where they are properly handled and stored in a database (DB), per company. Some manual data entry is complementarily supported, regarding companies' possibilities and needs.

LiveMES has the sort of functionalities (exposed via an API implemented as *REST/JSON*-based microservices), being their invocation and results (including dashboards and emails) mostly performed via GUIs. There are different permissions, granting access to allowed system's functionalities, information filters and reports.

### 3.1   The ARISA NEST Tool and the *Livia* Softbot

*ARISA NEST*[4] is a PaaS-based-academic tool that allows the derivation of ("instances-of") both single and groups of service-oriented softbots [6], which can be accessed via Web or mobile phones. ARISA (which is deployed in another cloud/server) supports the communication between it and the derived softbots in different ways and protocols.

User communicates with *Livia* via *Telegram* – *Livia* communicates with LiveMES and its DB by invoking their API. It has been specialized via coding the envisaged functionalities (in *Python* language), whereas some functionalities are provided by the own ARISA tool (like chatting via *Telegram*, messages modeling and their processing).

*Livia*, via ARISA, supports three types of softbot's behavior modes in its communication with end-users: (i) *reactive*, when the softbot acts in response to direct users requests via chatting (e.g. to ask about more detailed information from a given machine); (ii) *planned*, when the softbot acts in response to predefined scheduled tasks (of different types and complexities), bringing their results to users after their execution (e.g. to generate consolidated performance reports weekly); and (iii) *pro-active*, when the softbot performs predefined tasks autonomously on behalf of users or of LiveMES, bringing their results to users if needed (e.g. to continuously checking communication problems between data collectors and LiveMES and promptly take measures to solve them, or sending warnings and alarms).

---

[4] ARISA NEST tool for softbots derivation – https://arisa.com.br/ [in Portuguese].

In Arisa, all dialogues between a softbot and users were inspired by AIML[5] concept, where key elements are the contexts. *Contexts* mean domain's subjects (and the related key terms in a dialogue) users are supposed to express when asking things or ordering actions to the softbot. A dialogue is modeled as a flow of inter-related contexts in a tree. Users can write (or say) whatever they want since the expected keywords are provided. New contexts, keywords and communication flows can be added, removed, or modified anytime during the softbot's lifecycle.

### 3.2 The "Real-Time" Maturity Model

In this work, the concept of maturity models has been adapted to the envisaged PMaaS environment. However, instead of checking if given very formal processes are or aren't implemented in the companies, *Livia* checks if some expected actions have been performed. Once this is assessed then the company's maturity level is identified and a set of improvement actions are suggested to its managers (see next section).

Another difference is that *Livia* assesses maturity in "real-time". Given the required time to do that, managers usually do wider analyses once a week based on what happened in the production during this time horizon. With the real-time mode, managers can be permanently aware of the most important problems in the shopfloor.

Applying the descriptive and bottom-up approaches, four maturity levels have been conceived: the "4R". Roughly, level 1, *Resources*, assesses if the shopfloor's supporting instrumentations are properly running and measuring the expected information. Level 2, *Rigor*, assesses if the set of expected assets and production entities are properly registered and communicating with the MES system. Level 3, *Routine*, assesses if the set of predefined management and supervision actions and processes have been executed. The highest level, 4, *Run*, assesses if a high-level set of production data is being used to manage the production. The calculated assessment level is displayed in a *Radar*-like interface. This creates the so-called *RA-RE-RI-RO-RU* measurement cycle of the company's maturity evolution.

Besides identifying the maturity level, *Livia* computes a grade within it. Grades range from 1 to 4, indicating how much of the expected actions, information, processes, etc., have been performed within the given maturity level. This computation basically considers if each action, etc., has been done ("OK"), hasn't been done ("NOK") or it is not supported/non-available ("NA"). For example, a company can be measured as Level 3, but has a grade "2.75", indicating that some aspects need to be improved towards reaching Level 4. Section 4 shows some *Livia* interactions related to this.

### 3.3 The Business Analytics and Decision-Making Support

One of the most relevant goals of the PMaaS approach is helping managers in better, less stressing and more agile decision-making.

---

[5] https://web.archive.org/web/20070715113602/http://www.alicebot.org/press_releases/2001/aiml10.html.

Making use of those three softbot's behaviors (see Sect. 3.1) and via interacting with *Livia*, four types of business analytics are provided: *description, diagnostic, prediction* and *prescription*. They can be triggered either sequentially or independently one from another, depending on the situation in place. For example, when a given problem happens, it is identified (*description*) and its cause(s) named (*diagnostics*). Possibilities to solve it can be generated and evaluated (*prediction*), and straight-forward measure(s) are suggested (*prescription*). However, depending on the problem, the solution is so simple or clearly known that there is no need to generate predictions.

Considering that each maturity model addresses very different production and MES related aspects, that four types of analytics are executed per level, and not globally.

Business analytics can be extremely complex and can use sophisticated software tools, AI-based methods and big data, for example. In this initial version of PMaaS, it is however relatively simple, also considering the envisaged market niche of SMEs. On the other hand, the algorithms of each type of analytics are implemented as loosely-coupled services, following that general sequential logic, meaning that different and more powerful algorithms (or even external tools) can be added in the future replacing current services by the new ones.

That inter-related logic is modeled as a forward rule-based decision-tree, similar to some expert systems. Starting from the set of predefined problems to be detected from the information received by the data collectors, the system is prepared to identify the one(s) that can indeed take place. For each problem there is a direct relation to the prediction method to be used. Finally, predefined management measures to face the identified problems (within the previously identified maturity level) are suggested.

Applying again the descriptive and bottom-up approaches, these suggestions were conceived based on good practices and managerial foundations, combined with the solid empirical knowledge from the MES provider's professionals got along years.

# 4 Experimental Setup and Preliminary Results

This section provides a broader view of the main steps of one example scenario of *Livia* execution[6] under the *reactive* mode, which is based on a real case.

In this example, *Livia* is running in stand-by waiting for some requests from the manager (called *Brunno*). The conversation style tried to let the interaction the most symbiotic/user-friendly as possible. *Brunno* is interested to make the maturity analysis of his company (see Fig. 2a). *Livia* asks *Brunno* if he wants to run the weekly-basis general analysis (which is set up by *default*), or if he wants to apply a different time frame or to focus on some specific shopfloor's work centers[7].

---

[6] All the conversations and figures' texts were translated *ipsis litteris* to English only for the purpose of this paper. All the *liveMES* and *Livia* user interfaces are written in Portuguese.

[7] A work center can embrace one or more machines, depending on local installations.

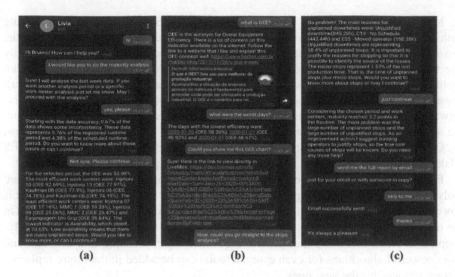

(a)                           (b)                           (c)

Fig. 2. Chatting between *Livia* and the Manager

Following the maturity model, one level of analysis (*Routine*, in this example) refers to data integrity and consistency. For example, due to some reasons, some operators forgot to register some information or did it wrongly; or the data collected is actually an outlier; or the observed production rate of a given work center was higher than its standard rate. All this is informed to *Brunno* by *Livia*. If this analysis is not done, then the quality of other higher-level analyses and further decisions will be impacted by those problems. It is important to also highlight that the softbot does this analysis over hundreds of data, which would be not feasible at all for humans to do.

In the example, the *descriptive* analytics for the Routine level has started, checking lots of related data. It has detected that only 0.67% of all the considered data has some inconsistency. However, it is important to check the data related to production time. Livia detects that 9.76% of the time that work centers are at runtime state and 4.38% of the time that work centers should be at runtime state (i.e. planned production time) have some kind of inconsistency detected. Given that none of these values were greater than the accepted default tolerance (10%), the manager decides to continue the analysis.

The analysis goes on and gets into the *diagnostics* analytics. The machines' OEE (*Overall Equipment Effectiveness*) are shown, and *Livia* also provides references to *Brunno*, indicating the best and the worst cases. She also tells that the main reason for the low mean OEE (a low *availability*, of 70.63% in the case) was the too many unplanned stops in the work centers.

*Brunno* can ask for complementary information about the calculated OEEs, for more detailed information about given work centers, etc. In the case (see Fig. 2b), he is not so sure about what OEE is, for which an answer is provided, including a deeper explanation about it via a suggested Internet URL. Yet, he gets interested to know more about the calculated OEEs and asks about the worst days.

As this information/functionality is casually already provided by LiveMES, *Livia* indicates the URL through which *Brunno* can directly have access to this. Figure 3 shows the OEE analysis for the evaluated period for all the work centers. Several filters can be applied to this afterwards. Many other equivalent graphics are provided by LiveMES, which *Brunno* can just request to *Livia* to have access to.

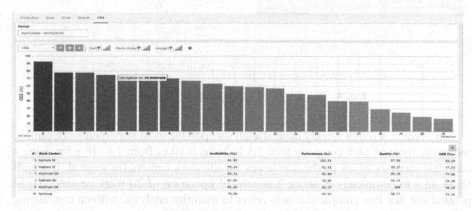

**Fig. 3.** General OEE dashboard

Some *predictive analytics* might be done in the case *Brunno* requested that (e.g., *Livia* could predict the OEE for the next week considering that the issue would be half-solved – *feature in development). *Livia* then goes directly to the *prescriptive* analytics phase (see Fig. 2c), suggesting a good practices-based measure to tackle the cause(s) of the problem. In the case, the real cause may be related to how operators handle stops in the work centers, for which some training activities are initially recommended.

This example showed how the whole analysis can be done in a "step-by-step" basis, with lots of interactions, intermediate analyses, and requests from *Brunno* to *Livia* being made in her *reactive* mode. In the case *Brunno* wants to have a complete executive report about the whole production (within a given period) or some work center(s), he can just request *Livia* to send it via an email (see Fig. 2c).

Likewise the reactive mode, equivalent actions can be carried out in the *planned* or *pro-active* modes. For example, *Livia* can autonomously start conversations with the manager during the execution of scheduled tasks to ask for some confirmations; or when she detects some serious problem during its supervision activities and decides to inform the manager about it; or to ask him to decide out of given possible solutions.

Figure 4 shows the final Radar view of maturity, also helping managers in having wider perspectives of analysis. It is so far manually generated via LiveMES. However, most of this will be automatically done by *Livia* when it gets fully operational.

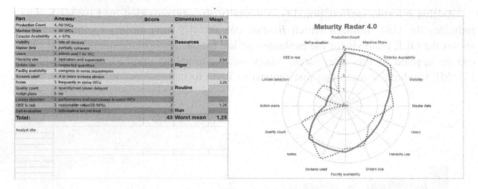

**Fig. 4.** The *RA-RE-RI-RO-RU* maturity assessment

On average, a rough weekly manual analysis upon the most important work centers. (normally four) of each company took 2.5 h. Now, it takes from 7 to 16 s for doing a complete analysis of all production issues for all work centers (in general, it spends about 15 s to completely evaluate 2 months of operation of 20 work centers). To be pointed out that this comparison only refers to maturity analysis, without considering the many actions that now the softbot does automatically and more accurately in the background on behalf of the managers in the *planned* and *proactive* modes.

## 5 Final Considerations

This paper has presented an approach on how softbots can help managers in their daily management of production, called as *Production Management as-a-Service (PMaaS)*.

Differently from larger companies, many SMEs are very limited to permanently check their shopfloors, to reason about hundreds of information and of many KPIs usually displayed in managerial dashboards, and to further take decisions based on that.

*Livia* is a SaaS softbot that has been developed to offer some help and guidance in that, attending companies' managers' requests and performing some actions automatically. It was created to work as a module of a cloud-based MES system (called *LiveMES*), using the real-time data gathered from the shopfloor. To be highlighted a dedicated maturity model, allowing managers to be aware of their data, production and MES issues, and that is the basis for suggesting appropriate decisions.

*Livia* and *LiveMES* provide an integrated environment. Managers can work without having to spend their time looking for relevant information in the companies' different systems, in a more reliable and less stressing "habitat" for better, agile decisions.

Before the utilization of the softbot, the average time for just doing a rough assessment of the main production issues of a single company was about 2.5 h. Now the complete assessment of all the involved issues of a company is automatically done in few seconds. However, deeper and complementary analyses on top of this can take much longer. Training is also essential to properly to interact with *Livia*; to understand the terminologies' meaning; and to correctly implement the suggested actions.

The developed softbot does not intend to replace managers, but to help them instead. If on one hand it could be observed that the softbot aids managers in faster and more comprehensive analyses, on the other hand, the practice has also shown that managers' experience and insights keep being as essential to interpret the provided analyses and the suggested actions to their companies.

Both Harbor's users and the early company adopters have evaluated this beta-like solution very positively, confirming its claimed benefits. It has also made Harbor and companies strengthen their partnerships, better understanding companies' effective production problems and so helping them in more assertive improvement measures.

*Livia* implementation has shown very promising results so far. However, being an initial work, some limitations were identified and represent the main next steps of this work: (i) improvements in the messages modeling and handling for more complex interactions; (ii) more clever algorithms for data analytics are very simple, deterministic, and based on a previously known small set of problems; and (iii) expansion of the problems to be considered in the different maturity levels.

**Acknowledgements.** This work has been partially supported by CAPES Brazilian Agency for Higher Education, project PrInt "Automation 4.0". Authors would like to thank Harbor company and their managers, Mr. Paulo Narciso and Mr. Tulio Duarte, for the deep support to this work.

# References

1. Kaushik, S.: Production and Materials Management. Centrum Press, London (2014)
2. Camarinha-Matos, L.M., Fornasiero, R., Afsarmanesh, H.: Collaborative networks as a core enabler of Industry 4.0. In: Camarinha-Matos, L.M., Afsarmanesh, H., Fornasiero, R. (eds.) PRO-VE 2017. IAICT, vol. 506, pp. 3–17. Springer, Cham (2017). https://doi.org/10.1007/978-3-319-65151-4_1
3. Lee, J., Bagheri, B., Kao, H.A.: Recent advances and trends of cyber-physical systems and big data analytics in industrial informatics. In: Proceedings of IEEE Industrial Informatics (2014)
4. Lamnabhi-Lagarrigue, F., Annaswamy, A., Engell, S.: Systems & control for the future of humanity, research agenda: current and future roles, impact and grand challenges. Ann. Rev. Control **43**, 1–64 (2017)
5. Romero, D., Vernadat, F.: Enterprise information systems state of the art: past, present and future trends. Comput. Ind. **79**, 3–13 (2016)
6. Rabelo, R.J., Romero, D., Zambiasi, S.P.: Softbots supporting the Operator 4.0 at smart factory environments. In: Moon, I., Lee, G.M., Park, J., Kiritsis, D., von Cieminski, G. (eds.) APMS 2018. IAICT, vol. 536, pp. 456–464. Springer, Cham (2018). https://doi.org/10.1007/978-3-319-99707-0_57
7. Vukšić, V.B., Bach, M.P., Popovič, A.: Supporting performance management with business process management and business intelligence: a case analysis of integration and orchestration. Int. J. Inf. Manag. **33**(4), 613–619 (2013)
8. Méndez, J.D., Rabelo, R.J., Baldo, F., Cancian, M.H.: A plug and play integration model for virtual enterprises. In: Camarinha-Matos, L.M., Afsarmanesh, H., Rezgui, Y. (eds.) PRO-VE 2018. IAICT, vol. 534, pp. 312–324. Springer, Cham (2018). https://doi.org/10.1007/978-3-319-99127-6_27

9. McDermott, A.: Information overload is crushing you. Here are 11 secrets that will help. https://www.workzone.com/blog/information-overload/

10. Rabelo, R.J., Zambiasi, S.P., Romero, D.: Collaborative softbots: enhancing operational excellence in systems of cyber-physical systems. In: Camarinha-Matos, L.M., Afsarmanesh, H., Antonelli, D. (eds.) PRO-VE 2019. IAICT, vol. 568, pp. 55–68. Springer, Cham (2019). https://doi.org/10.1007/978-3-030-28464-0_6

11. Kim, J.H.: Ubiquitous robot. In: Reusch, B. (ed.) Computational Intelligence, Theory and Applications. Advances in Soft Computing, vol. 33, pp. 451–459. Springer, Heidelberg (2005). https://doi.org/10.1007/3-540-31182-3_41

12. Mettler, T.: Maturity assessment models: a design science research approach. Int. J. Soc. Syst. Sci. 3(1/2), 213–222 (2011)

13. Pochiraju, B., Seshadri, S.: Essentials of Business Analytics: An Introduction to the Methodology and its Applications. Springer, Heidelberg (2019). https://doi.org/10.1007/978-3-319-68837-4

14. BCG Boston Consulting Group. https://www.bcg.com/en-br/publications/2015/technology-business-transformation-engineered-products-infrastructure-man-machine-industry-4.aspx

15. Schwartz, T., et al.: Hybrid teams: flexible collaboration between humans, robots and virtual agents. In: Klusch, M., Unland, R., Shehory, O., Pokahr, A., Ahrndt, S. (eds.) MATES 2016. LNCS (LNAI), vol. 9872, pp. 131–146. Springer, Cham (2016). https://doi.org/10.1007/978-3-319-45889-2_10

16. Kar, R.: Applying chatbots to the internet of things: opportunities and architectural elements. Int. J. Adv. Comput. Sci. Appl. 7(11), 147–154 (2016)

17. Kassner, L., Hirmer, P., Wieland, M., Steimle, F.: The social factory: connecting people, machines and data in manufacturing for context-aware exception escalation. In: Proceedings 50th Hawaii International Conference on System Sciences (2017)

18. Dersingh, A., Srisakulpinyo, P.: Chatbot and visual management in production process. In: International Conference on Electronics, Information and Communication, pp. 274–277 (2017)

19. Longo, F., Nicoletti, L., Padovano, A.: Smart operators in Industry 4.0: a human-centered approach to enhance operators' capabilities and competencies within the new smart factory context. Comput. Ind. Eng. 113, 144–159 (2017)

20. Chen, X., Bojko, M., Riedel, R., et al.: Human-centred adaptation and task distribution utilizing levels of automation. IFAC PapersOnLine 51(11), 54–59 (2018)

# Knowledge Strategies for Organization 4.0 – A Workforce Centric Approach

Magnus Bjerkne Gerdin[1,2] (ID), Åsa Fast-Berglund[2(✉)] (ID), Dan Li[2] (ID),
and Adam Palmquist[1,3] (ID)

[1] Insert Coin, 411 37 Gothenburg, Sweden
magnus@insertcoin.se, adam.palmquist@his.se
[2] Chalmers University of Technology, 412 96 Gothenburg, Sweden
{asa.fasth,dan.li}@chalmers.se
[3] University of Skövde, 541 28 Skövde, Sweden

**Abstract.** This paper aims at presenting an overview of how the manufacturing industry formulates business transformation and knowledge strategies, to find gaps in Industry 4.0 concepts' impacts on the workforce. The results indicate that the industry is still focusing on the digital transformation era that was adopted at the end of the 20th century, and how to adopt computing technologies to work more efficiently in existing business processes. The approach of this article is to adopt a methodology of three areas; (a) Human resource processes, (b) Industry 4.0 pillars and (c) Process knowledge, where links between these three generate opportunities to address for further research.

**Keywords:** Industry 4.0 · Automation technologies · Collaborative robots · Business transformation · Human resource management · Knowledge strategies · Skills requirements · Employee education

## 1 Introduction

Industry 4.0 has started to make an impact in the industry and many manufacturing companies need to start a business transformation to adopt new technologies with more complex IT infrastructures [1]. Technology advancement requires new management strategies to close the gap between technology and skills, to avoid a drop-in performance and competitiveness. Personalized training, collaboration and knowledge transfer will be needed for operators and managers to handle and adapt to the enabling technologies within industry 4.0. With the technology shift, in all areas especially the growth of cumulative self-improvement AI, algorithms for big data with pattern recognition and advanced robots [2], humans need to develop new strategies to interact with robots. The accelerating technological unemployment raises a question if new jobs will be generated or will the technology increasingly be making skilled workers obsolete. Knowledge management strategies should be aligned with the 4.0 implementation in industrial enterprises and been taken in several phases [3].

The core of Lean is about three essential areas [4]: Learning, Leadership and Long-term perspective. This requires a special form of leadership. Lean innovation is very much built on a scientific method of learning, it is all about quickly train the workforce

B. Lalic et al. (Eds.): APMS 2020, IFIP AICT 592, pp. 31–36, 2020.
https://doi.org/10.1007/978-3-030-57997-5_4

in the new and better standards. Taking from a view of retraining we can assume that employees will be difficult in the first two steps which Human Resource need to consider in the knowledge strategies. The situation has called for more effective methods of retraining in companies. Academic institutions will be needed to create opportunities for lifelong learning with massive open online learning that is personalized to stay relevant [5] in the new industry ecosystem. The paradigm of teaching factory [6] has therefore entered to keep up with the rapid advances in education-related technologies, tools, and techniques. The concept comprises the relevant educational approach for the facilitation of interaction between industry and academia [7]. Research, Education, and Innovation are the pillars in the triangle of the teaching factory, which has been the new way of industrial learning [8]. This paper aims at answering the question; *How does the manufacturing industry formulate business transformation and knowledge strategies connected to workforce transition within industry 4.0?*.

## 2 Methodology

Three industrial studies have been performed in order to get a first indication on how manufacturing industry formulate a strategy for Human Resources and management. The study examined the overall training instead of specific groups of employees. In order to do these two different methods were used (1) direct observations in production and (2) semi-structured interviews with HR managers and training directors at the companies. Interviewees represented the major stakeholders responsible for the overall training strategies for each group. More specific questions were asked to as require ensuring that the data from each case would allow a cross-case comparison [9].

### 2.1 Within-Case and Cross-Case Analysis

**Case 1.** The company has been working with Industry 4.0 several years in a program called "Digital Transformation". The program aims to prepare managers for the future in terms of new technologies and digital maturity. Furthermore, the program has a cross-functional knowledge sharing platform with the purpose to stay on top in the digital transformation process. At the company, leadership is seen as an important skill in digital transformation. A leadership is defined by a person who is influencing others and does not necessarily have a formal responsibility as a manager or group leader.

The "*Learning Organization*" is a toolkit that is integrated into the training strategy where the focus has been to adopt knowledge sharing. The company pinpoints three main areas for knowledge; (i) Vertical integration experience (ii) Cross-company experience and (iii) Behavioral pattern management. The main strategic focus of Human Resource is a business transformation from a people perspective, with focus on how to capitalize on knowledge in areas as; (a) Business, (a) Knowledge and (c) Technology, and how to adopt technologies to work more efficient in process management.

*"The most demanding part of this transformation is to change the view of what people can achieve in technology adoption. It is important that managers rethink the way to creating results. Managers need to get dressed in new capabilities. Even if the organization is hierarchical the decisions need to be decentralized to build a network culture where knowledge is collected cross-functional, to build network clusters with a span from inside to outside the share experiences and share knowledge. The historical way of building teams based on experts is contra-productive. In the era of business transformation, it is more important to know what questions to raise instead of knowing the answers".*

The company have implemented a new talent review process to be able to meet the business transformation, where new demands of skills are established where managers are facing needs of multi-skilled profiles with technology skills added to the core skills. The group started a training program within technology innovation where employees could apply for a project and dedicate one day per week to experiment.

**Case 2.** Industry 4.0 is not yet implemented, even if the company is a manufacturing company. The main perspective is digital transformation, with a focus on modifying existing business processes and customer experiences to meet the new business requirements. The organizational structure is a matrix that facilitates the horizontal flow of skills and information, mainly in the management of product development. The company has moved from a product-centric to a customer-centric approach, where the focus is on; (a) How do we think in processes, (b) how do we engage with customers. The overall purpose is using data to simplify processes to work faster and more efficient when data is instantly accessible. In the context of digitalization, the group has revisited all processes, from internal systems to customer interactions. The company pinpoints three main areas for knowledge; (i) horizontal integration along the value creation chain (ii) vertical integration from the field to control level and (iii) information transfer from planning to maintenance, to ensure consistent engineering.

*"The main challenge in this new technology era is knowledge. Workforce transition is about switching skills from operators/mechanics skills to technical/electricity skills. Operators/Mechanics are in educational programs to manage the transformation. The knowledge strategy is organized in a Competence Development Center to match the vertical and horizontal perspectives. Different programs are established based on needs and opportunities addressed from organizations. The center is organized based on geographical areas to meet the local needs in each market. The center is primarily focusing on hard skills while the Groups University is focusing primarily on soft skills. The group has recently updated their reskilling approach where the learning is integrated into practice. The programs run online with an agile approach where employees can learn daily. The Universities plays an important role for the group when it comes to building a platform of roles with scientific methods, critical thinking and statistic models. Reward programs today are connected to employee's skill-building and community knowledge sharing".*

There is a gap identified today when it comes to soft skills development, either in production or sales & aftermarket. On a yearly base, the company has established a skill mapping program that all HR executives. This to be able to set real-time training programs with the purpose to adopt the changing business models. The group has recently updated their reskilling approach where the learning is integrated into practice.

**Case 3.** Industry 4.0 is not yet implemented, but the digital transformation is making a huge impact, and has started in the product phase of R&D that is years ahead of the production. In workforce transition the group focus on overall purpose and goals. The main strategy in training today is to focus on job training where the group have adopted the agile lifelong learning approach. The group has an academy that is responsible for all training and educates both in soft and hard skills. The company pinpoints two main areas for knowledge; (i) robots and physical automation (ii) Knowledge transfer from automation engineers to maintenance engineers.

*"Industry 4.0 is not a commonly used term internally within the group. Strategies are about speed and scope in digital transformation. The group need to shift complete focus when it comes to business transformation. The workforce transition is more of a strategic level now starting with the managers, and not the operators. The automation impact on operators is highly connected to labor costs depending on low- or high wage countries, where the breakeven for investments differs dramatically. Another important angle of automation is new versus old factories, where it is easier to automate a new greenfield factory project. In a new factory, it is easier and more cost-efficient to plan for automation. Hard skills are easier and have a clear vision and path for learning, while soft skills are much more difficult when it comes to willingness and motivation to adopt new insights. From an operational perspective in the factories, the group work with training academies, as leadership programs, hard skills training related to production and basic training routines. The training strategy is taking from two models; 5 whys root cause analysis and 5 S workplace organization method. The main challenges right now begin already in an earlier stage than the Universities, where younger people are not attracted to technology engineers. The group work close to senior high schools as well as building the groups own senior high schools to be able to meet future demands".*

The company expects the employees to adopt an agile lifelong learning approach where they learn "on the go" by combining the theory into practice. Redundancy as a state occurs based on knowledge strategies. Continuous feedback loops are a critical part. The group has a cultural talent management program, where the real talents appear in different vertical processes. Workforce transitions are addressed from executives, where executive HR translating directions into future. The group has a task-oriented approach and collects knowledge from verticals toward an agile methodology. Universities is an important link to collect knowledge.

## 3   Discussion and Conclusion

The current exploratory study examined how three manufacturing companies reflect on how the transformation of the workplace with new technologies impacts the employment and if there is a gap between skills available and skills needed. Furthermore, the study explores how the industry formulates and implements training strategies for skills retraining and how they invest in training systems.

The results shown a slow adoption of Industry 4.0 and the term is not commonly used within the HR-departments. The focus when it comes to re-skilling within the companies are still focusing on the digital transformation era that was adopted in the 1990s, and how to adopt computing technologies to work more efficient in existing business processes. The analysis shows that a common focus within the companies and a step towards industry 4.0 is the integration of existing data where integration needs to be aligned horizontal along the value chain, vertically from the field of production control and from planning and maintenance. Based on the within-case analysis assumption can be drawn that these companies still are in an early phase of business transformation. Related to a product lifecycle, the transformation has started at the beginning of the process in R&D and Product Design. However, the study has shown that the gap between skills available and skills needed is increasing. The focus is the soft-skills training program for leaders to prepare for the business transformation. Technical-, process- and network agility are important skills sets as well as emotional awareness. The focus is concentrated on overall purpose and goals within the organization, and how to transform this to an organizational structure based on knowledge. The talent management strategies are important workforce strategies, where the support of employees in retraining has decreased. The prioritized talent management programs strengthen this analysis. The redundancies of workforce will take place but are still in an early phase, because it is difficult to find the right skills sets. The case studies also show that the "learn as you go" trend has been adopted where theory and practice are implemented. Universities are an important link to close the early stage gap in Research and Product Design phases as well as in Engineering to be able to balance the higher theory with real-world practice. A higher level of advanced process knowledge is required to meet the increased demands.

In the future, further research should focus on the development of specific training systems, as well as on the integration of individual training methods to support the knowledge within the enabling technologies of industry 4.0. This will enhance the speed and agility of closing competence gaps in the manufacturing processes. Further research is needed within Education 4.0 and Organization 4.0. Managers and Human-resource departments need to build a literacy within digitalization ad automation in order to handle the needed re-skilling in future manufacturing.

**Acknowledgement.** The authors would like to give gratitude to the Swedish government of research, Vinnova for enabling the research.

# References

1. Alcácer, V., Cruz-Machado, V.: Scanning the Industry 4.0: a literature review on technologies for manufacturing systems. Eng. Sci. Technol. Int. J. **22**, 899–919 (2019)
2. Kagermann, H., Wahlster, W., Helbig, J.: Recommendations for implementing the strategic initiative INDUSTRIE 4.0. Final report of the Industrie 4.0 Working Group (2013)
3. MacCarthy, M.: Time to kill the tech job-killing myth (2014). http://thehill.com/blogs/congress-blog/technology/219224-time-to-kill-the-tech-job-killing-myth
4. Rentzos, L., Vourtsis, C., Mavrikios, D., Chryssolouris, G.: Using VR for complex product design. In: Shumaker, R., Lackey, S. (eds.) VAMR 2014. LNCS, vol. 8526, pp. 455–464. Springer, Cham (2014). https://doi.org/10.1007/978-3-319-07464-1_42
5. Richert, A., Shehadeh, M., Plumanns, L., Groß, K., Schuster, K., Jeschke, S.: Educating engineers for Industry 4.0: Virtual worlds and human-robot-teams: empirical studies towards a new educational age. In: 2016 IEEE Global Engineering Education Conference (EDUCON), Abu Dhabi, United Arab Emirates. IEEE (2016)
6. Netland, T.H., Powell, D.J.: The Routledge Companion to Lean Management. Routledge, New York (2017)

36     M. B. Gerdin et al.

7. Chryssolouris, G., Mavrikios, G., Rentzos, L.: On a new educational paradigm for manufacturing: the teaching factory (2014)
8. Selamat, A., Taspir, S.H., Puteh, M., Alias, R.A.: Higher education 4.0: current status and readiness in meeting the fourth industrial revolution challenges, pp. 23–24 (2017)
9. Dillman, D.A.: Mail, and Internet Surveys: The Tailored Design Method. Wiley, New York (2007)

# Challenges for the Operator 3.0 Addressed Through the Enabling Technologies of the Operator 4.0

Malin Tarrar[1]([✉]) [iD], Peter Thorvald[1,2] [iD], Åsa Fast-Berglund[1] [iD],
and David Romero[3] [iD]

[1] Chalmers University of Technology, Gothenburg, Sweden
{malin.tarrar,asa.fasth}@chalmers.se,
peter.thorvald@his.se
[2] University of Skövde, Skövde, Sweden
[3] Tecnológico de Monterrey, Monterrey, Mexico
david.romero.diaz@gmail.com

**Abstract.** Just as human operators are important production enablers in the factories of today, they are expected to stay key enablers also in future manufacturing. In today's factories, operators often meet challenges related to poor information and communication design, which affects their possibilities to perform with higher efficiency levels. Therefore, they need to be provided with better cognitive support tools that are relevant to the challenges to be met. To ensure efficient and effective operator work in the factories of the future, operator support needs to be adequate for the new tasks arising from the evolving operators' roles and work. Within this paper, the results of current operators' work and challenges, based on six case studies, are combined with an outlook of the future of work of operators, based on the Operator 4.0 vision. The challenges categorized in this paper can be used to identify opportunities for improvement in the operators' cognitive support in present factories as well as for researchers and developers of Operator 3.0 support solutions.

**Keywords:** Cognitive ergonomics · Operator support · Operator 4.0 · Tasks

## 1 Introduction

In recent years there has been a massive and broad technological development in society, with opportunities as computing, analysis, information and communication technologies (ICT) as a few examples [1]. The anticipated benefits of applying advanced technology in production companies have led to initiatives such as *Industry 4.0* and *Smart Manufacturing* among others [2], and the appearance of the *Fourth Industrial Revolution* [3].

Even though the operational and informational technologies have evolved, the challenges of the operator of today remain. In current factories, operators face difficulties relating to information and communication, these challenges affect their possibilities to perform with higher efficiency levels. Therefore, operators need to be

© IFIP International Federation for Information Processing 2020
Published by Springer Nature Switzerland AG 2020
B. Lalic et al. (Eds.): APMS 2020, IFIP AICT 592, pp. 37–45, 2020.
https://doi.org/10.1007/978-3-030-57997-5_5

provided with better cognitive support tools, relevant for their tasks and challenges to be met. However, what should this type of cognitive operator assistance support?

Technology focus and usage is often the starting point for discussing "operator support", which is not surprising considering the technology drive of *Industry 4.0*. It could lead to shortages of a holistic perspective on the operators' tasks. Tarrar [4] attempted to identify and describe the challenges met by operators regarding information and communication processes from a holistic perspective, studying issues and improvement potential in the operators' work. This paper builds upon these challenges that are further developed. To ensure efficient and effective operators' work in the factories of the future as well as in the present factories, operators' support needs to be adequate for the new tasks arising from the evolving operators' roles and work.

This paper aims to analyse and connect the challenges from Tarrar [4] with the recent development of *Industry 4.0*, and specifically the *Operator 4.0 vision*. Furthermore, the paper will discuss potential benefits relating to the enabling technology scenarios of the Operator 4.0 in combination with the aforementioned challenges.

## 2 Challenges for the Operator 3.0

The challenges, first published in Tarrar [4], were based on six case studies in four large Swedish companies from the medical equipment, tooling, component, and automotive industries. The companies were considering improvements in information and communication support for their operators. The operators performed: (I) Machine/process supervision and maintenance, disturbance handling, production improvements, planning of work, and to some extent assembly; or (II) Assembly of special features, pre-assembly and planning of work all requiring high product and production knowledge; or (III) Machine/process supervision with testing, with either some assembly or maintenance. The operators in four of the cases (Tasks I & II) had broader responsibilities and conducted more tasks themselves than the common operators in the industry [5]. The connection between the companies, cases and operator tasks are displayed in Table 1.

**Table 1.** Industrial cases serving as the foundation for identifying the Operator 3.0 challenges

| Company | Medical equipment | Medical equipment | Tooling | Automotive | Component | Component |
|---|---|---|---|---|---|---|
| Operator tasks | I | III | I | II | III | I |
| Challenges | 3, 4, 5 | 2, 3, 4, 7 | 1, 2, 3, 5, 7 | 1, 3, 4, 6, 9 | 2, 3, 5, 6, 9 | 1, 3, 4, 8 |

In each case, data was gathered through: semi-structured interviews held with managers and operators; observations; and surveys. Difficulties and opportunities were identified from the gathered data, through content analysis and grounded theory these were combined into ten general operator challenges relating to the information and communication requirements in the operators' work.

Despite the variability of operators' tasks, there could be challenges not included here. The identified challenges can exist in different combinations within companies and departments. From the original challenges, the first three were combined into two and the following were kept. Totally nine challenges are presented below:

1. *Know what task to perform* – For common tasks, knowing what task to perform is often done by memory, i.e. an assembly worker knowing what part to assemble to a workpiece. However, infrequent tasks are easily forgotten and this coupled with poor quality or availability of instructions, may lead to work performance issues.

2. *Know how to perform a task* – The knowledge of how to perform a particular task is often acquired during training. However, updates to the task, disturbances, or contextual changes might require new tasks or ways to perform a task. The memory of how to perform a specific task is also highly affected by the level of variation in work tasks, a high product variation entails a higher cognitive demand as more bits of information needs to be remembered. Furthermore, the challenge can occur for complex and difficult analysis and problem-solving tasks, were experience is acquired slowly. It can also occur in very long tasks or task times. A task which recurs rarely is naturally more difficult to remember.

3. *Knowing and conveying what tasks have been carried out* – Keeping track of task status and the status of the overall objectives is as much a matter of securing relevant information to perform a job as well as a psychological aspect that influences mental workload and operator wellbeing [6]. It could be challenging when several operators share the responsibility; or when assembly times are long. To a large extent, this is aided by properly designed information interfaces, especially made easier through digitalized information systems. And further simplified where connections between the information system and the tools used can help the user keep track of the work status. The challenge also includes communicating task status to others or even to the operator himself at another point in time. David Kirsh discussed the term entry points [7] to describe an "invitation to do something" (p. 311). Other works [8] have identified similar aspects of leaving cues in the environment for oneself where a worker when leaving their work station to take a break or help a colleague, would leave their work gloves or a particular tool on the workpiece to indicate task status once they returned. Essentially creating an entry point for themselves to resume work.

4. *Passing on information and communicating statuses* – such as audio or visual impressions of the product, process, or machine, to others not present. Also, information to oneself in the future to remember some characteristics of a situation. An example could be an operator experiencing a possible miss-sound and wondering if there is a problem or if it is okay, the sound is hard to capture in text and not always possible to transmit through tools and systems available.

5. *Finding and understanding products, machines, or process statuses and information* – is relevant in situations with e.g. alarms or breakdowns. Difficulties are typically caused by difficult interfaces or codes (e.g. error messages/codes, given by the product or a system interface) that are unintuitive and hard to understand; or

when process information and statuses are hard to find. An example is to discover what caused the machine to stop when there are very many error codes following the stop.

6. *Handling different computer systems* – caused by poor usability, overlapping systems or systems with low perceived benefit of using. The issues could result in operators asking someone else to use the system(s) and perform the task, or complete circumvention of the system, for example, calling maintenance personnel instead of reporting in the system. Systems smartly designed with perceived usefulness largely addresses the issues.

7. *Performing task(s) and supervising machines, or processes at the same time* – when reviewing automatic process steps, it may be necessary to carry out other tasks such as tending to other processes, machines or quality controls. This implies that visual or audible contact with the machine or process interface may be lost, which could cause stress or late responses to deviations.

8. *Transmit health and safety information in, case of an emergency* – in case of personal health issues or risks in the environment of the operator. For example, while working in locations difficult to see for others. Or in case something happened, send information so the rescuer can deal with the specific threat.

9. *Locating products, tools, and materials* – when these are not at the desired place, or when one does not know where to go. For example maintenance personnel looking for the exact location of a machine or a specific small detail in a large process.

# 3   The Operator 4.0 and the Future of Work

Perfect forecasts of future manufacturing and operators' work are impossible to make. However, researchers have suggested possible paths of development for the future of work of operators, in this paper the focus is on the Operator 4.0. The *Operator 4.0* was introduced by Romero, et al. [9] as a way to highlight the role of the operator as a smart and skilled worker enhanced through technology within the Industry 4.0 context. Furthermore, it has been predicted that the future of work of operators will include increased problem-solving and analysis [10–12], indicating a need for further information to facilitate decisions [13]. Parts of these decisions could be made through the information systems, however, data availability and quality need to be improved [9, 10, 13].

## 3.1   The Skills Forecast for the Operator4.0

The vision of the *Operator 4.0* is to create trusting and interaction-based relationships between humans and machines and to empower the "smart operators" with new skills and gadgets to fully capitalize on the opportunities being created by the enabling technologies of *Industry 4.0* [9]. Within the enabling technologies [14], seven out of nine can be connected to information and communication processes considering the operator, i.e. IIoT, Big Data, Real-time Optimisation, Cloud Computing, Cyber-Physical Systems, Machine Learning, Augmented Reality (or xR-Technologies). These technologies have a machine and technology focus but to create wellness for the operator a strategy based on the *Operator 4.0 vision* is needed [15]. Within the taxonomy of *Operator 4.0*, skills needed from both the enabling technologies and wellness of the operator are included, however, the collaborative and super-strength operators are not applicable here and are therefore omitted. Different types of Operators 4.0 are discussed:

- *Augmented and Virtual Operator* – uses xR technologies as assisting means in training, maintenance, and complex tasks [16–18].
- *Healthy Operator* – uses smart wearable solutions (i.e. wearable trackers for health-related metrics) including data analytics capabilities together with advanced human-machine and human-automation interfacing/interaction technologies for his/her physical and physiological wellbeing management [19].
- *Smarter Operator* – uses an intelligent personal assistant, or other types of softbots, which have been developed to help an operator in interfacing with machines, computers, databases, and other information systems as well as managing time commitments and performing tasks or services in a human-like interaction [20, 21].
- *Social Operator* – uses social networking services, enabled by real-time mobile communication capabilities, to empower his/her colleague operators by contributing with his/her expertise across the production line and the whole shop-floor. *Social Operators* can accelerate ideas generation for product and processes innovation and can facilitate problems-solving by bringing together the right people with the right information within the enterprise [22].
- *Analytical Operator* – uses (big) data analytics techniques to leverage real-time information for driving the right response to prevent mistakes, quickly identify problems, and call for the right decisions to improve operational efficiency [9].

## 4 Addressing Challenges for the Operator 3.0 Through Enabling Technology Scenarios from the Operator 4.0

Many of the challenges of the *Operator 3.0* can be addressed through the technological enablers of the *Operator 4.0*. In Table 2, the challenges and technologies are mapped together.

The Xs in Table 2 indicate the *Operator 3.0* challenges that can be supported by the *Operator 4.0 vision*, and will be discussed in the following bullet-points:

- *Know what task to perform* (challenge) – can be addressed by (i) the *xR Operator*, which uses xR technologies as visual triggers that quickly prompt the operator's memory on what to do; (ii) the *Smarter Operator* and his/her intelligent personal assistant (e.g. a softbot) that would enable hints to ensure the operator is aware of product/process/machine characteristics affecting a task; and (iii) the *Analytical Operator*, who leverages the data available on the task at hand (e.g. a report) combined with the operator's previous experience/performance to support "remembrance/remembering/acknowledging" what to do and draw attention to differences.

**Table 2.** Challenges of the Operator 3.0 connected to the skills of the Operator 4.0

| Challenges/Skills | xR operator | Healthy operator | Smart operator | Social operator | Analytic operator |
|---|---|---|---|---|---|
| 1. Know what task to perform | X | | X | | X |
| 2. Know how to perform a task | X | | | X | |
| 3. Know and convey what tasks have been carried out | | | X | X | |
| 4. Pass on information and communicate statuses | | | X | X | X |
| 5. Find and understand products, machines, or process statuses and information | | | X | | X |
| 6. Handle different computer systems | | | X | | X |
| 7. Perform task(s) and supervise machines or processes at the same time | X | | X | | X |
| 8. Transmit health and safety information in case of an emergency | | X | | | |
| 9. Locate products, tools, and materials | X | | X | | X |

- *Know how to perform a task* (challenge) – can be addressed by (i) *the xR Operator* enhancing his/her understanding of the task at hand (i.e. the procedure) through a digital-assistance system providing visual instructions overlaid in real-time in the operator's field of view; and (ii) the *Social Operator* that enables real-time interactions with other smart, connected operators and things (e.g. machines, computers, databases, and other information systems) using mobile and social collaborative methods to retrieve advice and know-how on how to perform a task.
- *Knowing and conveying what tasks have been carried out* (challenge) – can be addressed by (i) the *Smarter Operator* through alerts provided by his/her intelligent personal assistant on tasks not performed yet according to a working plan, and (ii) the *Social Operator*, when the reminders could come from his/her "connected" supervisor or a smart, connected machine "calling" for attention (e.g. a digital Andon system) so the task gets performed.
- *Passing on information and communicating statuses* (challenge) – can be addressed by the (i) the *Smarter Operator*, which shares information and sends updates on statuses with the help of his/her intelligent personal assistant that sorts, filters, and delivers the information collected and statuses of machines and processes validated to the right persons and/or systems to get a task performed; (ii) the *Social Operator*, who uses mobile devices and enterprise social networks to share the right information, at the right time, to the right person) and/or systems to get a task performed;

and (iii) the *Analytical Operator* that uses data analytic techniques to automatically transform data into information to support and accelerate a task performance.

- *Finding and understanding products, machines, or process statuses and information* (challenge) – addressed by (i) the *Smarter Operator*, who receives statuses and relevant information previously found, sorted, and filtered by his/her intelligent personal assistant so he/she can react on time to the task at hand; (ii) the *Social Operator*, which is real-time connected with other smart, connected operators and things that he/she can reach out to consult and query to support and accelerate a task performance; and (iii) the *Analytical Operator*, which uses data analytic techniques to obtain insights from (big) datasets that can help to improve a task performance.
- *Handling different computer systems* (challenge) – addressed by (i) the *Smarter Operator*, which receives support from his/her intelligent personal assistant to oversee all computer systems and receive an alert when human intervention is needed; and (ii) *Analytical Operator*, who uses artificial intelligence to automate certain tasks to reduce the handling effort of different computer systems.
- *Performing task(s) and supervising machines or processes at the same time* (challenge) – addressed by (i) the *xR Operator*, who uses digital assistance systems and digital poka-yokes to prevent mistakes and perform all his/her tasks without errors; (ii) the *Smarter Operator* that counts with an intelligent personal assistant to support the performance of his/her tasks; and (iii) the *Analytical Operator*, which uses real-time data analytics techniques (e.g. computer vision systems) to analyse a task as it is being performed, and receive immediate feedback to quickly identify problems and take the corrective actions on time.
- *Transmit health and safety information in case of emergency* (challenge) – addressed by the *Healthy Operator* who uses smart wearable solutions to track his/her health-related metrics to self-manage his/her physical and cognitive workload, and if this information is shared in an anonymized way could help production planners to foster better industrial hygiene by better planning and controlling the workforce workloads as they perform their tasks.
- *Locating products, tools, and materials* (challenge) – addressed by (i) the *xR Operator* which shows directions (ii) the *Smarter Operator*, who uses the support of his/her intelligent personal assistant to locate smart things, which have a smart tag such as a GPS, so his/her task performance doesn't get delayed due to the search; and (iii) the *Analytical Operator*, which uses data analytic techniques to obtain insights on data related to assets location, condition, availability, etc.

## 5  Conclusions and Further Work

Several challenges concerning information and communication processes were identified covering current and future work of operators. The industry of today is still facing a lot of challenges when it comes to information and communication technologies, and foremost support for the operators. Even if the technologies are evolving, the organisations, the smart factories, need to evolve at the same pace to get skilled *Operators 4.0*. To know what tasks and how to perform them together with knowing what steps of the tasks have been carried out, are the most general challenges for the operators with the others being more specific to the operator work/task at hand. The challenges identified in this paper could be used to identify the needs to support the operators at the factories of the future.

Further work is needed to address the severity of the information and communication challenges in correlation to different types of operators' tasks, operator experience and production types. Moreover, the tasks of operators in the factories of the future need more attention to understand/predict possible challenges for future operators.

**Acknowledgement.** The research presented was part of a VINNOVA funded projects, the *Operator of the* Future and *Smart Digitalisation for Operators*. The work has been carried out within the Production Area of Advance at Chalmers. This support is gratefully acknowledged.

# References

1. Lu, Y.: Industry 4.0: a survey on technologies, applications and open research issues. J. Ind. Inf. Integr. **6**, 1–10 (2017)
2. Thoben, K.-D., Wiesner, S., Wuest, T.: Industrie 4.0 and Smart manufacturing: a review of research issues & application examples. Autom. Technol. **11**, 4–16 (2017)
3. Liao, Y., et al.: Past, present and future of Industry 4.0: a systematic literature review and research agenda proposal. Prod. Res. **55**, 3609–3629 (2017)
4. Tarrar, M.: supporting operators with their daily tasks in complex production environments – a perspective on ICT tools. Licentiate, Chalmers University of Technology (2018)
5. Mattsson, S., et al.: Managing production complexity by empowering workers: six cases. In: 47th CIRP Conference on Manufacturing Systems, Canada, pp. 212–217 (2014)
6. Lindblom, J., Thorvald, P.: Manufacturing in the wild-viewing human-based assembly through the lens of distributed cognition. Prod. Manuf. Res. **5**, 57–80 (2017)
7. Kirsh, D.: The Context of Work. Hum.-Comput. Interact. **16**, 305–322 (2001)
8. Andreasson, R., Lindblom, J., Thorvald, P.: Interruptions in the wild: portraying the handling of interruptions in manufacturing from a distributed cognition lens. Cogn. Technol. Work **19**, 85–108 (2017). https://doi.org/10.1007/s10111-016-0399-6
9. Romero, D., Stahre, J., Wuest, T., Noran, O., Bernus, P., Fast-Berglund, Å., et al.: Towards an Operator 4.0 typology: a human-centric perspective on the fourth industrial revolution technologies. In: International Conference on Computers and Industrial Engineering (2016)
10. Berlin, C., et al.: Workshop – a method for identifying and consolidating industrially perceived needs and requirements of future operators. In: Swedish Production Symposium (2012)
11. Gorecky, D., Schmitt, M., Loskyll, M., Zühlke, D.: Human-machine-interaction in the Industry 4.0 era. In: IEEE International Conference on Industrial Informatics, pp. 289–294 (2014)
12. Romero, D., Noran, O., Stahre, J., Bernus, P., Fast-Berglund, Å.: Towards a human-centred reference architecture for next generation balanced automation systems: human-automation symbiosis. In: Umeda, S., Nakano, M., Mizuyama, H., Hibino, H., Kiritsis, D., von Cieminski, G. (eds.) APMS 2015. IAICT, vol. 460, pp. 556–566. Springer, Cham (2015). https://doi.org/10.1007/978-3-319-22759-7_64

13. Segura, A., Diez, H.V., Barandiaran, I., et al.: Visual computing technologies to support the Operator 4.0. Comput. Ind. Eng. **139**, 105550 (2018)
14. Bortolini, M., Ferrari, E., Gamberi, M., et al.: Assembly system design in the Industry 4.0 era: a general framework. IFAC-PapersOnLine **50**, 5700–5705 (2017)
15. Mattsson, S., Fast-Berglund, Å., et al.: Forming a cognitive automation strategy for Operator 4.0 in complex assembly. Comput. Ind. Eng. **139**, 105360 (2020)
16. Fast-Berglund, Å., Gong, L., Li, D.: Testing and validating extended reality (xR) technologies in manufacturing. Procedia Manuf. **25**, 31–38 (2018)
17. Syberfeldt, A., et al.: AR smart glasses in the smart factory: product evaluation guidelines and review of available products. IEEE Access **5**, 9118–9130 (2017)
18. Kim, M., Park, K.-B., Choi, S.H., Lee, J.Y., Kim, D.Y.: AR/VR-based live manual for user-centric smart factory services. In: Moon, I., Lee, G.M., Park, J., Kiritsis, D., von Cieminski, G. (eds.) APMS 2018. IAICT, vol. 536, pp. 417–421. Springer, Cham (2018). https://doi.org/10.1007/978-3-319-99707-0_52
19. Romero, D., Mattsson, S., Fast-Berglund, Å., Wuest, T., Gorecky, D., Stahre, J.: Digitalizing occupational health, safety and productivity for the Operator 4.0. In: Moon, I., Lee, G.M., Park, J., Kiritsis, D., von Cieminski, G. (eds.) APMS 2018. IAICT, vol. 536, pp. 473–481. Springer, Cham (2018). https://doi.org/10.1007/978-3-319-99707-0_59
20. Boesl, D.B.O, Liepert, B.: 4 Robotic revolutions - proposing a holistic phase model describing future disruptions in the evolution of robotics and automation and the rise of a new generation 'R' of robotic natives. In: IEEE/RSJ International Conference on Intelligent Robots and Systems, pp. 1262–1267 (2016)
21. Rabelo, R.J., Romero, D., Zambiasi, S.P.: Softbots supporting the Operator 4.0 at smart factory environments. In: Moon, I., Lee, G.M., Park, J., Kiritsis, D., von Cieminski, G. (eds.) APMS 2018. IAICT, vol. 536, pp. 456–464. Springer, Cham (2018). https://doi.org/10.1007/978-3-319-99707-0_57
22. Romero, D., Wuest, T., Stahre, J., Gorecky, D.: Social factory architecture: social networking services and production scenarios through the social internet of things, services and people for the social Operator 4.0. In: Lödding, H., Riedel, R., Thoben, K.-D., von Cieminski, G., Kiritsis, D. (eds.) APMS 2017. IAICT, vol. 513, pp. 265–273. Springer, Cham (2017). https://doi.org/10.1007/978-3-319-66923-6_31

# Agent- and Skill-Based Process Interoperability for Socio-Technical Production Systems-of-Systems

Åsa Fast-Berglund[1]([⊠])(iD), David Romero[2](iD), Magnus Åkerman[1],
Björn Hodig[3], and Andreas Pichler[4]

[1] Chalmers University of Technology, 412 96 Gothenburg, Sweden
{asa.fasth,magnus.akerman}@chalmers.se
[2] Tecnológico de Monterrey, Monterrey, Mexico
david.romero.diaz@gmail.com
[3] PTC, Gothenburg, Sweden
bhodig@ptc.com
[4] PROFACTOR GmbH, Steyr, Austria
andreas.pichler@profactor.at

**Abstract.** In this research work, we take an interoperability point of view on "production systems-of-systems". Interoperability of production processes requires a stepwise planning of resources. An approach supporting the orchestration and coordination of human and artificial agents (i.e. collaborative robots) is developed. First tasks are assigned to production resources/agents, followed by an interaction and task execution design. Another step taken into account is the technology used as a human-robot interface.

**Keywords:** Production systems · Systems-of-Systems · Processes interoperability · Collaborative robotic systems · Flexible automation · Balanced automation systems · Cooperative agent systems · Operator 4.0

## 1 Introduction

Manufacturing enterprises are facing increasing uncertainty in demand and variety in product types. This implies an increasing need for "flexibility" in the structure and configuration of manufacturing processes [1]. To cope with this situation, *Production Systems-of-Systems (PSoSs)*[1] have to be effective, efficient, yet still flexible. One type of system that addresses the flexibility needs of modern manufacturing processes is "collaborative robotics systems" [2, 3]. In collaborative robotics, human and robots work together to execute a common task. The optimisation and control of processes involving human and artificial agents (i.e. a cobot) is a challenge nowadays faced by "smart manufacturing" enterprises [4]. Hence, *interoperability* and *flexibility* have to be

---

[1] *Production systems-of-systems* are production systems composed by multiple production lines, with multiple manufacturing cells, with multiple workstations in which human-human, human-robot or robot-robot collaborations can take place.

© IFIP International Federation for Information Processing 2020
Published by Springer Nature Switzerland AG 2020
B. Lalic et al. (Eds.): APMS 2020, IFIP AICT 592, pp. 46–54, 2020.
https://doi.org/10.1007/978-3-030-57997-5_6

assured in such novel socio-technical system-of-systems composed by the human system and the collaborative robot (cobot) system [5]. Moreover, future manufacturing jobs in smart production systems will require new technical skills from the operators to work as part of these novel socio-technical systems-of-systems at the production line.

In this research work, we discuss technologies and approaches, supporting process planning for the *Operator 4.0* [6] interacting with a collaborative robotic system as part of a production system. This discussion is an extended version of our work presented at the IEEE International Conference on Intelligent Systems [7]. It has been extended and the overall human-robot collaboration is discussed as a "system-of-systems" within a production system that requires a "human-robot interoperability" approach.

## 2  Theoretical Foundations: Systems-of-Systems Interoperability

The term "system" has been coined in the General System Theory (GST) [8]. GST aims at supporting the identification of general principles that are valid for many different types of systems. In the GST, a system is a structure of connected elements; like in a production system where a production line, a manufacturing cell, or a workstation are a group of interrelated production resources. Each part, and therefore, the overall system shows a behaviour (i.e. producing a part, assembly, or final product). According to [9], a system is separated from the environment by a boundary or interface; a system (e.g. a workstation) fulfils one or more functions providing some outcome concerning its objectives; systems interact with the environment and other systems through interfaces (e.g. a human and a robot interact using a human-robot interface to become a team in a workstation); and the environment and other systems may influence the system's behaviour and structure (e.g. the type of a manufacturing cell or production line). Moreover, the possibility of a system to change its behaviour allows a system to evolve from a given state to another one over time (e.g. a flexible or reconfigurable manufacturing cell or system [1]). A system may influence its environment in turn. The behaviour of a system is determined by the functions that the system executes (e.g. its production capabilities). A system has an objective that it wants to meet, its purpose (e.g. its production objectives).

In a system-of-systems, multiple systems act together, forming a "supra-system" (i.e. a production system can be composed by multiple production lines, with multiple manufacturing cells, with multiple workstations). It is important to understand that the systems forming a system-of-systems, remain independent. The systems still follow their individual purpose. The formation of a system-of-systems does not allow to integrate systems which would lose their own freedom and/or purpose. Systems in a system-of-systems may leave or join a system if it does not fit to their individual purpose. In this view, systems actively manage their own state. In case of high dynamics (e.g. due to frequent changes in behaviour) such system-of-systems may be seen as *Complex Adaptive Systems (CAS)* with many human and artificial agents interacting with each other [8]. Such is the case of flexible/reconfigurable manufacturing cells/systems [1].

A system-of-systems can be analysed from two points of views: (i) the resource point of view, and (ii) the interaction point of view. In this paper, our focus is the interaction point of view, which requires understanding to which degree the systems need to be "interoperable".

An *agent-based system* is a system-of-systems where the agents have their individual goals. Some sort of negotiation needs to take place for cooperation and alignment of the activities of the agents. Often using some money or equivalent mechanism [10].

## 2.1  Interoperability of Interacting Systems

Before being able to choose a mechanism for coordination of systems in a system-of-systems (i.e. a production system-of-systems), the degree of coupling between systems needs to be considered, which is the focus of research of "enterprise interoperability".

Recently, steps towards a formulation of *enterprise interoperability* using the GST as their baseline have been started [9, 11]. Special attention is being put to the gaps and barriers between systems interaction. Figure 1 presents the European Enterprise Interoperability Framework, where several areas of research have been marked in dark grey circles [4]. The semantic alignment in the middle relies on technical interoperability (i.e. syntax of data and transport). On the organisational level, process interoperability is important. Moreover, process interoperability can also be referred to as interoperability on a pragmatic level. The pragmatics relies on a common semantics. On this level also knowledge transfer between systems and actors is important [12].

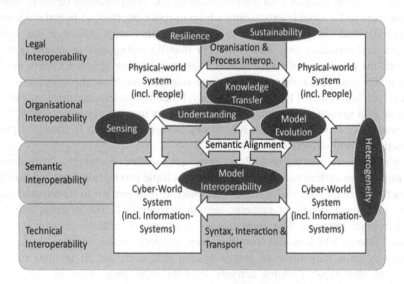

**Fig. 1.** European Enterprise Interoperability Framework (EEIF) [4]

## 2.2    Interoperability Approaches, Timing and Barriers

Interoperability barriers are discussed in the domain of enterprise interoperability along the following dimensions [13]: (i) interoperability approaches (i.e. federated, unified, and tight integrated), (ii) interoperability timing (i.e. a priori/design-time solutions, and a posteriori/run-time solutions), and (iii) interoperability levels/barriers (i.e. legal, organisational (business, processes), semantic-conceptual, and technological). Furthermore, interoperability approaches can be classified according to their degree of coupling: (i) Systems are *tightly integrated* by definition. The elements of the system are dependent on each other. The breakdown of one element will lead to the breakdown of the overall system. (ii) A *unified approach* supports interoperability by establishing a common reference. Different systems can reference the common reference. Through this a layer of abstraction, a common layer for communication is established. This implies an additional indirection in the communication. The systems' internal states and messages need to be translated into the common language. This supports the independence of the individual systems. Any system that is knowledgeable of this reference can participate in a system-of-systems. (iii) The most loosely coupled approach is a *"federation"* where the participating systems negotiate over the interfaces at run-time.

In *integrated approaches* (e.g. integrated manufacturing cells or systems), the interoperability is often established at design-time. This requires to anticipate problems and to overcome barriers before systems are built. *Federated interoperability* approaches establish interoperability at run-time. Such approaches allow reacting to problems after their occurrence in the running system (flexible or reconfigurable manufacturing cells or systems) [1].

The interoperability problems can occur on different levels of the enterprise. The system-of-systems discussed in the following includes human, robots for collaborative applications and artificial agents. Therefore, interoperability at the *process level* and *unified interoperability* are the most relevant.

# 3    Systems-of-Systems: Task and Resource Planning

To be able to plan "interaction" in systems-of-systems, both *task* and *resource planning* needs to be done. The resources are mostly discussed in the physical world in the EEIF framework in terms of organisation and process interoperability. Hence, to achieve self-organisation and self-maintenance systems; data, information and knowledge transfer is vital. One of the important interoperabilities to achieve this is the "semantic interoperability". The complexity is to include both resource allocation and function allocation [14] in the planning system of different resources with different levels of automation (i.e. humans, machines, and robots). A lot of research is addressing the complexity of including skills to automatic systems [15–17].

## 3.1    Task and Resource Allocation in Systems-of-Systems (SoS)

Within the research field of human factors, two well-known approaches have been used for task and resource allocation: (i) HTA (Hierarchical Task Analysis) [18], and (ii) CTA (Cognitive Task Analysis) [19]. When comparing these two approaches, HTA focuses on the goal, while CTA uses a qualitative method mix (i.e. interviews and observation strategies) for capturing the knowledge that experts use for tasks operation [7]. Both methods aim at optimising the task allocation for human resources. In the context of balanced automation systems, where human and robots cooperate, optimisation does not only refer to time and costs dimensions but also to a "cognitive" dimension. Human operators' cognitive load needs to be taken into account to provide a "good" plan. Cognitive overload and cognitive underload (i.e. boring tasks) both have an impact on the performance of the human operator. *Interoperability* in this context refers to the suitability of a process that a human operator has to execute. Allocation of tasks usually happens at "design-time". This implies less flexibility and less resilience. To have an adoptable SoS, the optimisation needs to be executed more frequently than it is today. By using the *semantic interoperability* together with the *organisational interoperability,* data from the system in terms of deviation in cycle time can be used together with the information and knowledge transferring systems in the organisational interoperability. In our approach, the tasks are defined from a CAD model to a Bill-of- Material (BOM). A two-steps approach to optimise task allocation to resources have been identified, illustrated in Fig. 2 [14]: (Step 1) – Global optimisation, containing both tasks and resources and is product depended (i.e. what components will be assembled). A digital product is defined in the PLM system. The HTA is used to determine the Bill-of-Process (BOP) that is later used for instructions and orchestration; (Step 2) – Local optimisation is competence dependent: (Step 2a) Task allocation with resource alternatives – here, alternative resources (i.e. redundancy) are made. For the resource allocation and integration between humans and robots, five different scenarios, working individually or in teams has been identified by [20], which should be considered in (Step 2b) to plan for collaborative applications, as illustrated in the Fig. 2. The complexity (depth of the diagrams) increases a lot when both humans and robots are part of the same operation and task. The "competence" of the production resources can be pre-defined by using the ontology of S-BPM that will be discussed in Sect. 3.2.

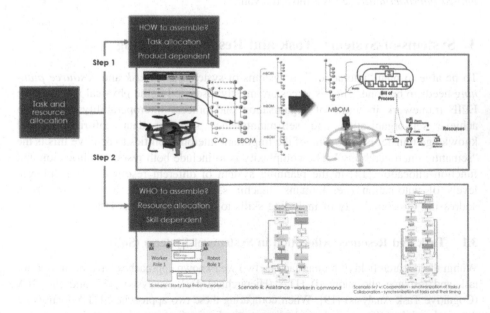

**Fig. 2.** Task and resource allocation

## 3.2    Message-Based Systems Used for Interaction Between Resources

To increase flexibility during task execution and to increase the interaction between the resources, *message-based systems* can be used. S-BPM (Subject-oriented Business Process Management) is an approach that mixes message-based systems with process-based systems [21]. At its heart, it is a communication-oriented approach. Two subjects are modelled that exchange messages, called: "business objects". The subject is similar to a process-oriented role. A subject is responsible for the execution of a part of the process. The S-BPM modelling language separates the two points of view in two diagrams. [7]. Coordination and interoperability of human and robots are through communication. Here, the interaction is driven by messages exchange. These messages trigger a certain behaviour, which then can result in a particular action or another message being sent [22]. Multi-Agent Systems (MAS) [10], and Actor-based Systems (ABS) [22] are a particularly well-known approach where agents are interacting through sending and receiving messages. Taking the term "skill", it is possible to implement different subject-behaviours for different skills. The other subjects in a process are not influenced when the same message-based interaction protocol is executed. However, the human may be guided by the workflow system implementing the S-BPM workflow according to different levels of automation. Skills can be modelled as subjects. In this approach, skills are not static properties of an actor but define the behaviour. Having predefined processes that determine the behaviour support "design-time planning" for a structured process. While this reduces flexibility, it also reduces the complexity. Dynamics is introduced when at "run-time", a different subject-behaviour is executed (e.g. because a different operator with a different skill is collaborating with the robot).

## 3.3    Interaction Between Humans and Robots

After determining the details of the interaction and establishing interoperability on the process level, the technology on the interface between systems needs to be determined. The *Operator 4.0 typology* provides several technologies that support the interaction of humans and robots [6]. Only the relevant ones have been selected. The technology used will be the interface through which the interaction happens. As such, the kind of message exchanged will depend on technology as well. In some cases pressure sensors with trigger events (i.e. simple messages): (i) Operator + Exoskeleton = Super-Strength Operator – The robotic system directly supports the worker in her/his doing. The message exchange happens through sensors. Messages as such are simple. Here the response time is essential; (ii) Operator + Augmented Reality = Augmented Operator – The interaction will be visible on the Augmented Reality (AR) technology. This allows reaching message exchanges in both directions; (iii) Operator + Wearable Tracker = Healthy Operator – Trackers may be used as sensors that trigger events. These events (again) can be used as messages for the interaction protocol between subjects; and (iv) Operator + Collaborative Robot = Collaborative Operator – The robot itself may be equipped with sensors that may be capable of understanding natural language. In this solution, a technology used for the interaction might be needed so that the operator knows the next position and task that the robot shall do and vice versa. For robotic tasks planning it has been extended by a skills/competency matrix to better support human operators in planning [23].

### 3.4   Orchestrating the Planning in Process-Oriented Systems

*Resource planning* is often done for the implicit "happy" path only. Unexpected events (e.g. running out of materials, machine break-down) require ad-hoc replanning and design time solutions have no flexibility, and therefore no resilience. For more robust plans, the number of alternative resources (i.e. humans as well as robots) that need to be included needs to be higher. To increase the predictability of a system-of-systems, process-based systems have been created. Process models and process management supports the orchestration of an integrated system. In our approach, the PTC IIoT platform ThingWorx (TWX) is used for orchestration and cellular management [24] as illustrated in Fig. 3.

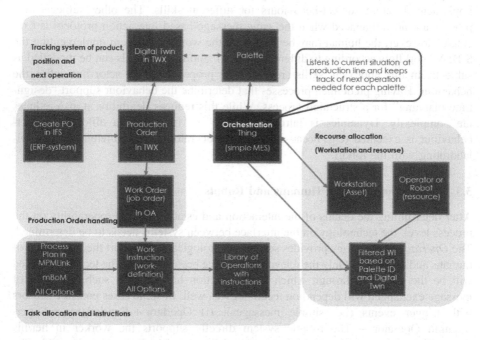

**Fig. 3.** Orchestration and cellular management between resources and systems

The *orchestration* is used as a simple MES (Manufacturing Execution System) that listens to the current situation regarding the product, components, and task allocation. Furthermore, the "thing" also keeps tracks of the assets and the resources. To create an SoS ecosystem, interoperability across platforms must be enabled. Such interoperability will let developers create applications by combining data from multiple platforms [24]. Further research will be to connect the *actor-based system* with the orchestration of the ThingWorx platform to increase the interaction between resources with higher levels of automation, both physical and cognitive by combining different platforms.

# 4 Conclusions

In this work, we focused on process interoperability of socio-technical systems-of-systems. The described approach makes use of the skills and capabilities of human and artificial agents. Multiple instruments have been aligned to support the *Operator 4.0*. First tasks are assigned to resources, for optimisation a priority with respect to the level of automation is determined. The skills also determine the detailed interaction on process level between the participating systems (i.e. human and artificial agents). Finally, we also determine the technologies used on the interface between the human and the robot.

# References

1. Brettel, M., Klein, M., Friederichsen, N.: The relevance of manufacturing flexibility in the context of Industrie 4.0. Procedia CIRP **41**, 105–110 (2016)
2. Bortolini, M., Ferrari, E., Gamberi, M., Pilati, F., Faccio, M.: Assembly system design in the Industry 4.0 era: a general framework. IFAC-PapersOnLine **50**(1), 5700–5705 (2017)
3. Fast-Berglund, Å., Palmkvist, F., Nyqvist, P., Ekered, S., Åkerman, M.: Evaluating cobots for final assembly. Procedia CIRP **44**, 175–180 (2016)
4. Panetto, H., Iung, B., Ivanov, D., Weichhart, G., Wang, X.: Challenges for the cyber-physical manufacturing enterprises of the future. Ann. Rev. Control **47**, 200–213 (2019)
5. Åkerman, M., Fast-Berglund, Å.: Interoperability for human-centered manufacturing. In: Debruyne, C., Panetto, H., Weichhart, G., Bollen, P., Ciuciu, I., Vidal, M.-E., Meersman, R. (eds.) OTM 2017. LNCS, vol. 10697, pp. 76–83. Springer, Cham (2018). https://doi.org/10.1007/978-3-319-73805-5_8
6. Romero, D., et al.: Towards an Operator 4.0 typology: a human-centric perspective on the fourth industrial revolution technologies. In: International Conference on Computers & Industrial Engineering, Tianjin, China, pp. 1–11 (2016)
7. Weichhart, G., Fasth-Berglund, Å., Romero, D., Pichler, A.: An agent- and role-based planning approach for flexible automation of advanced production systems. In: IEEE International Conference on Intelligent Systems (2018)
8. von Bertalanffy, L.: General System Theory. George Braziller, New York (1969)
9. Naudet, Y., Latour, T., Guédria, W., Chen, D.: Towards a Systemic Formalisation of Interoperability. Comput. Ind. **61**, 176–185 (2010)
10. Wooldridge, M.: Introduction to Multi-Agent Systems. 2nd Edn. (2009)
11. Ducq, Y., Chen, D., Doumeingts, G.: A contribution of system theory to sustainable enterprise interoperability science base. Comput. Ind. **63**, 844–857 (2012)
12. Fast-Berglund, Å., Thorvald, P., Billing, E., Palmqvist, A., Romero, D., Weichhart, G.: Conceptualizing embodied automation to increase transfer of tacit knowledge. In: IEEE International Conference on Intelligent Systems (2018)

13. Weichhart, G.: Requirements for supporting enterprise interoperability in dynamic environments. In: Mertins, K., Bénaben, F., Poler, R., Bourrières, J.-P. (eds.) Enterprise Interoperability VI. PIC, vol. 7, pp. 479–488. Springer, Cham (2014). https://doi.org/10.1007/978-3-319-04948-9_40

14. Fasth-Berglund, Å., Provost, J., Stahre, J., et al.: From task allocation towards resource allocation when optimising assembly systems. Procedia CIRP **3**, 400–405 (2012)

15. Epple, U., Mertens, M., Palm, F., Azarmipour, M.: Using properties as a semantic base for interoperability. IEEE Trans. Industr. Inf. **13**(6), 3411–3419 (2017)

16. Perzylo, A., et al.: Capability-based semantic interoperability of manufacturing resources: a BaSys 4.0 perspective. IFAC-PapersOnLine **52**, 1590–1596 (2019)

17. Theorin, A., et al.: An event-driven manufacturing information system architecture for Industry 4.0. Int. J. Prod. Res. **55**, 1297–1311 (2017)

18. Annett, J., Duncan, K.D., Stammers, R.B.: Task Analysis. HMSO, London (1971)

19. Clark, R.E. et al.: Cognitive task analysis. In: Handbook of Research, pp. 577–593 (2008)

20. Weichhart, G.: Representing processes of human-robot collaboration. In: S-BPM-ONE Workshop Proceedings, CEUR Workshop Proceedings (2018)

21. Fleischmann, A., et al.: Subject-Oriented Business Process Management. Springer, Heidelberg (2012). https://doi.org/10.1007/978-3-642-32392-8

22. Hewitt, C.: Viewing control structures as patterns of passing messages. Artif. Intell. **8**, 323–364 (1977)

23. Fasth-Berglund, Å., Stahre, J.: Cognitive automation strategy for reconfigurable and sustainable assembly systems. Assem. Autom. **33**(3), 294–303 (2013)

24. Bröring, A., et al.: Enabling IoT ecosystems through platform interoperability. IEEE Softw. **34**(1), 54–61 (2017)

# Digital Transformation Approaches in Production Management

# Challenges in Data Life Cycle Management for Sustainable Cyber-Physical Production Systems

Mélanie Despeisse$^{(\boxtimes)}$ and Ebru Turanoglu Bekar

Chalmers University of Technology, Gothenburg, Sweden
{melanie.despeisse,ebrut}@chalmers.se

**Abstract.** Rapid technological advances present new opportunities to use industrial Big Data to monitor and improve performance more systematically and more holistically. The on-going fourth industrial revolution, aka Industrie 4.0, holds the promise to support the implementation of sustainability principles in manufacturing. However, much of these opportunities are missed as social and environmental performance are still largely considered as an afterthought or add-on to business as usual. This paper reviews existing data life cycle models and discusses their usefulness for sustainable manufacturing performance management. Finally, we suggest possible directions for further research to promote more sustainable cyber-physical production systems.

**Keywords:** Data life cycle · Industrial big data · Sustainability assessment · Sustainable manufacturing · Sustainability performance

## 1 Introduction

Over the last four decades, sustainable development gained importance and is now a top priority in many organizations' and governments' agenda. While sustainability is widely recognized as an imperative for all human activities conceptually, it still lacks presence in organizations' operations as evidence by the lack of action to tackle global challenges and to respect planetary boundaries [1]. Recent technological progress present new opportunities to address these global challenges. Several studies have looked at the sustainability implications of digital technologies in manufacturing [2, 3]. Most notably, advanced data management systems and cloud computing hold promise to systematically collect and manage the data necessary for a sustainability assessment [2]. In turn, this would allow a more holistic approach to improve the performance of manufacturers and their value chain [3] while avoiding rebound effects.

This study aims to reconcile digital technologies and sustainability in manufacturing by investigating how data life cycle models—note that the expression "life cycle" is used in two manners in this paper: "data life cycle" and "life cycle perspective"—can be combined with and support the implementation of sustainability methodologies. We discuss common challenges encountered along the data life cycle,

© IFIP International Federation for Information Processing 2020
Published by Springer Nature Switzerland AG 2020
B. Lalic et al. (Eds.): APMS 2020, IFIP AICT 592, pp. 57–65, 2020.
https://doi.org/10.1007/978-3-030-57997-5_7

and provide recommendations for sustainability performance management. Finally, we suggest directions for further work to promote more sustainable cyber-physical production systems based on the challenges identified and recommendations listed in this paper.

## 2 Background

### 2.1 Sustainability Methodologies

Numerous methodologies have been developed and demonstrated as effective to support sustainability performance management at different levels [4]. These methodologies can be broadly categorized according to four dominant purposes: *(1) assessment tools* are used to quantify the system's performance or impacts; *(2) improvement tools* are used to identify potential solutions to increase performance or decrease negative impacts; *(3) decision-making tools* help prioritize the solutions to meet predefined targets; finally, *(4) enforcement tools* (e.g. policies and regulations) have a strong influence on decision-making. Many of these tools require high-quality data to generate meaningful and useful results. On-going efforts and collaborations have increased data availability and quality [5], most notably for life cycle-based methodologies [6] such as life cycle assessment (LCA), life cycle costing (LCC), social life cycle assessment (sLCA), and their combination in life cycle sustainability assessment (LCSA) [7]. But these methodologies are still rarely used by organizations.

### 2.2 Data Life Cycle Models

Data life cycle refers to the entire process from generation to use and possibly destruction of the data, sometimes divided into two, three or more stages. In 1993, Levitin and Redman presented two cycles for data acquisition and data usage with the addition of data storage connecting these two cycles [8]. They went on to detail those cycles into a data life cycle model with the enhanced acquisition and usage cycles. To address comprehensively such data quality issues, an extension of Levitin and Redman's data life cycle model [8] was developed by Yoon et al. [9] to include additional phases focusing on metadata before dealing with the data itself. More recently, data life cycle models used by Big Data researcher included the same three main of activities for data management (data generation/collection, storage, processing/utilization), e.g. [10]. Some models detail further some intermediate and end-of-life activities with added emphasis on Big Data and data security [11, 12]. Other models focus on Big Data analytics and machine learning [13–15]. Major differences between models: inclusion of a planning phase before the collection phase, a pre-processing/calibration/refinement phase before the use phase, and an assessment/improvement phase either alongside or integrated in the use phase. These phases are indeed not always included in industrial practices, resulting in poor data quality, suboptimal exploitation, or data misuse/misinterpretation.

## 2.3 Cyber-Physical Production Systems

The technologies comprised under the trend of "digitalization" can be categorized using the smart factory architecture or cyber-physical production systems (CPPS) comprising four layers: *(1) physical resources, (2) network, (3) cloud services,* and *(4) terminal* (edge computing) [16]. In addition, a better understanding of Big Data characteristics and research challenges [17] also helped develop more effective data management systems and data analytics to support process control [18] and decision-making [19]. Finally, the 5-level cyber-physical systems (CPS) architecture [20] and Big Data architecture [19], as well as the maturity model for CPPS [21] provide good foundations to address some of the technical challenges in the digital transformation of manufacturing systems. Much of the work done has potential to align with and support sustainability methodologies (e.g. resource efficiency and collaboration for circular economy). But digitalization can also unlock new levels of productivity and accelerate our linear economy, thereby further transgressing planetary boundaries already exceeded.

## 2.4 Industrial Big Data

Research challenges, opportunities and enabling technologies for Big Data analytics have been discussed from the different perspectives in recent literature studies [22–24]. Big Data challenges can be grouped into three categories [22]: *(1) data challenges* related to data characteristics, e.g. "the seven Vs" [11]; *(2) process challenges* related to data handling, e.g. capture, clean, integrate, transform, store, visualize, etc.; *(3) management challenges*, e.g. security, privacy, information sharing, operational costs, data ownership, governance and ethical concerns. Specific challenges for sustainable smart manufacturing from a product life cycle perspective have been reviewed and categorized into data storage, analysis and processing, and value, also raising concerns about security and ownership [23]. In addition, inadequate technical infrastructures remains one of the biggest challenges of industrial Big Data [24]. Therefore, effective data management using appropriate expertise and secure infrastructure are necessary for Big Data analytics to support smart and sustainable manufacturing [25, 26].

# 3   Challenges in Data Management for Sustainability

In this paper, we have adopted advanced data life cycle model shown in Fig. 1 based on Levitin and Redman [8] and using the terminology from Yoon et al. [9] as we found it adapted to focus on challenges associated with each stage of the data life cycle. We also put a strong emphasis on intermediate activities related to data quality assessment and continuous improvement of the data model from the more experimental and innovative approaches to data management. This is to highlight typically overlooked activities, e.g. assess data quality, repair data if possible, discard faulty data which cannot be repaired, obtain new values, and update metadata when necessary.

This section presents typical challenges and resulting recommendations for industrial data management to support sustainability performance monitoring and

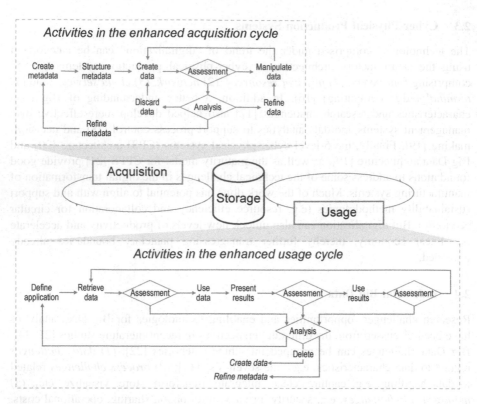

**Fig. 1.** Data life cycle model (adapted from [8, 9]).

improvement. We especially emphasize the importance of planning, quality check-points, data manipulation, and feedback loops which are often overlooked. To structure our discussion, we grouped activities as follows:

- Data model architecture: metadata creation, structure and refinement;
- Data acquisition and storage: data creation, manipulation, storage and refinement;
- Data exploitation: data assessment, representation/visualization and utilization.

## 3.1  Data Model Architecture: Create, Structure and Refine Metadata

We assume a manufacturing organisation is developing a new data management system for their operations, thus starting the data life cycle with goal and scope definition, which in turn informs the metadata creation. This first planning stage is overlooked. With the cost of information and communication technology (ICT) assets rapidly falling, data is easily collected, much of which is of limited usefulness as little consideration was given to the (long-term) applicability and purpose of the data model. Thus, it is critical to reflect on what is to be achieved, and when possible, experiment with small-scale projects to develop organisational capabilities. Lessons learnt from such pilot applications are invaluable in developing a more robust data model before scaling up. This also allows clarification and alignment with organisational sustainability goals.

The data model architecture is then defined and documented accordingly. A typical limitation encountered at this stage is a reductionist view of manufacturing (gate-to-gate), thereby ignoring externalities and indirect impacts outside the manufacturing site. Lack of standards for system boundaries lead to inconsistencies in sustainability indicators and incompatibilities when combining different assessment methods. This issue is exacerbated with the intrinsic complexity and interdependencies between the three dimensions of sustainability.

Another typical weakness in developing data management systems is the lack of feedback loop and maintenance activities resulting in missed opportunities to correct structural flows and other recurring defects in the data model. This problem is particularly present in organization relying on outdated ICT infrastructure and legacy systems. Although such systems still perform satisfactorily, the organization may miss on new value opportunities and lag behind competitors who are making the transition to state-of-the-art practice and technology. However, upgrading ICT assets as well as skills and capabilities are costly and take time. This has been a central question surrounding the changing nature of jobs in manufacturing to leverage new digital technologies.

Recommendations regarding desired data model characteristics:

- **Model relevance & usefulness:** the model addresses organizational sustainability goals and effectively supports sustainability performance management.
- **Model scope & completeness:** the scope is comprehensive enough to capture relevant physical and information flows, and to enable a holistic performance assessment which accounts for externalities and potential rebound effects.
- **Model essentialness & minimally redundant:** the model complexity is minimised by including only data elements fundamentally required to meet the organization's goals, and is implemented using minimal duplication to meet user needs.
- **Model correctness & consistency:** the model is developed and maintained with appropriate standards to maintain uniform data definitions and avoid data misinterpretation, especially given the multidisciplinary nature of sustainability.
- **Data management:** the model is developed and maintained by a central function which applies systematically data quality engineering methods, and data is managed with distributed control and appropriate data representation to meet end-user needs (local exploitation under the coordination from the central function).
- **Accessibility & searchability:** the model is structured so it is possible to access specific data based on end-users' requirements.
- **Data sharing:** the model addresses data sharing requirements within the organisation and among its collaborators based on accepted standards for metadata definitions to support data exchanges; especially critical given the importance of collaborative networks to achieve higher levels of industrial and societal sustainability.
- **Continuous improvement:** the model is regularly assessed and maintained in a flexible, adaptable manner to meet future requirements (including new applications) using user feedback to determine the value provided to end-users and implement corrective measures (updates) based on lessons learnt.

## 3.2    Data Acquisition and Storage: Create, Manipulate, Store and Refine Data

To create data, various means are used, such as measurement, observation, analysis, or copy. A first challenge related to this activity is a lack of purpose in data collection which can lead to an ineffective model as discuss in the previous section. Another challenge in this early stage of data creation is data improperly recorded, especially for raw data acquisition through sensing, measuring and/or manual entry. Due to a lack of quality checkpoints, flawed and potentially useless data are recorded, contributing to the typical problems of data overload, especially considering the sheer volume of data generated by modern ICT systems. It is therefore crucial to ask the questions "why do we need the data?" and "is it the correct data for our purpose?" before collecting data.

Data scarcity and unreliability are common hurdles in system modelling and assessment. Implementing sustainability methodologies is often limited by external data availability, trustworthiness, transparency and other data quality issues leading to incomplete or unreliable assessment results. Estimations, calculations and assumptions are sometimes necessary to fill gaps in data, for instance due to inaccessibility to the process or lack of technical solutions for what needs to be measured, e.g. sensor technology does not exist. Incompleteness can also result from other technical issues, e.g. data collected by smart agents and stored in server, but missing connection thus cannot be transferred.

Other gaps are associated with data not collected due to lack of interest or awareness, e.g. waste, pollution and other non-value adding flows not monitored unless unregulated, or data collected with inadequate granularity and quality to be useful in assessing manufacturing performance/impact and identifying improvements. In manufacturing systems, data granularity and sparsity issues are often due to unavailability of machine-level data. However, progress in sensing technologies are quickly removing these barriers (while creating new ones, such as the aforementioned data overload problem).

Even when the right data is collected and stored, there are a number of common pitfalls organizations need to avoid, such as inconsistent terminology or coding practices, inaccurate or missing contextual information (metadata) leading to misinterpretation and misuse, amongst other issues. Once again, these issues need to be addressed in early planning stages and when creating the data model architecture (Sect. 3.1).

Recommendations regarding desired data acquisition characteristics:

- **Completeness, conciseness & relevance:** all (and only) data values necessary for the agreed purpose are acquired.
- **Correctness, reliability & accuracy:** data values are assessed and (when possible) repaired/corrected to ensure they are free from faults or recording defects.
- **Precision & granularity:** data values match the level of detail (e.g. machine, plant, company levels), the time period, and the precision required by the user.
- **Currency & timeliness:** data values are updated as often as required by the user.

### 3.3 Data Exploitation: Assess, Present and Use Data

After data is created, manipulated and stored, it can be accessed and used for different applications. Here, a typical challenge result from misaligned objectives between the model developers and model users as they are often at different levels in the organization. Most of the challenges related to data model architecture and metadata during the planning stages (Sect. 3.1) will have an impact in the usage cycle, thus need to be addressed early. Other challenges regarding data accessibility, searchability and usability can prevent end-users from engaging with the data management system. A typical cause for this disincentive to use data is the lack of tools and user-friendly interfaces to help access and make sense of the data easily. Recent developments in cloud computing, connectivity as well as mobile devices are helping in this regard. Augmented, virtual and mixed reality tools are also increasing the usability and intuitiveness of the data by using (more) realistic representations and context-sensitive information.

Despite the rapid growth in industrial Big Data, there is still a lack of tools to make use of this data and especially real-time data to perform continuous sustainability assessments. While sustainability assessment may not be necessary for day-to-day management of operations, it should not be considered as a mere reporting exercise, but as a basis for decision-making. We strongly advocate that data should be used more systematically to support sustainability performance management, thus should be integrated in business-as-usual rather than treated as the occasional "sustainability project".

Recommendations regarding desired data exploitation characteristics:

- **Accessibility:** data can be retrieve when needed by the user.
- **Timeliness:** data is presented only when needed.
- **Correctness & consistency:** the data is free from retrieval fault, data is presented unaltered from what was stored and according to established standards.
- **Detail & conciseness:** data is presented at an appropriate level of detail according to the user requirements without data loss.
- **Clarity & intuitiveness:** data is presented in a manner that ensure it is understood and used as intended.
- **Presentation & visualization:** data is presented in a manner that facilitates user comprehension.
- **Flexibility & customizability:** data presentation can be customized between systems, formats, media to match user specific needs.
- **Portability & compatibility:** data can move between applications without data loss.

## 4 Conclusion

With advances in ICT, collecting data is becoming ever easier, resulting in industrial Big Data with large amounts of data from multiple sources using different representation methods and structural characteristics. But many organizations still lack data management strategies and architectures to define key parameters and to ensure data quality. To solve these problems, a systematic and standardized approach is needed. This papers describes some typical challenges in data management for sustainability and outlines recommendations regarding desired characteristics for various stage of the data life cycle. Further research is required to identify critical data and prepare the data adequately to enable advanced analytics, and especially machine learning methods for industrial applications of sustainable production strategies.

# References

1. Rockström, J., et al.: Planetary boundaries: exploring the safe operating space for humanity. Ecol. Soc. 14 (2009)
2. Stock, T., Obenaus, M., Kunz, S., Kohl, H.: Industry 4.0 as enabler for a sustainable development: a qualitative assessment of its ecological and social potential. Process Saf. Environ. Prot. **118**, 254–267 (2018)
3. Li, W., Alvandi, S., Kara, S., Thiede, S., Herrmann, C.: Sustainability Cockpit: an integrated tool for continuous assessment and improvement of sustainability in manufacturing. CIRP Ann. - Manuf. Technol. **65**, 5–8 (2016)
4. Finnveden, G., Moberg, A.: Environmental systems analysis tools - an overview. J. Clean. Prod. **13**, 1165–1173 (2005)
5. Fazio, S., Kusche, O., Zampori, L.: Life Cycle Data Network — Handbook for Data Developers and Providers (2016)
6. Bjørn, A., Margni, M., Roy, P.-O., Bulle, C., Hauschild, M.Z.: A proposal to measure absolute environmental sustainability in life cycle assessment. Ecol. Indic. **63**, 1–13 (2016)
7. Sala, S., Farioli, F., Zamagni, A.: Progress in sustainability science: Part 1. Int. J. Life Cycle Assess. **18**, 1653–1672 (2013)
8. Levitin, A.V., Redman, T.C.: A model of the data (life) cycles with application to quality. Inf. Softw. Technol. **35**, 217–223 (1993)
9. Yoon, V.Y., Aiken, P., Guimaraes, T.: Managing organizational data resources: quality dimensions. Inf. Resour. Manag. J. **13**, 5–13 (2000)
10. Jain, P., Gyanchandani, M., Khare, N.: Big data privacy: a technological perspective and review. J. Big Data 3(1), 1–25 (2016). https://doi.org/10.1186/s40537-016-0059-y
11. Khan, N., et al.: Big data: survey, technologies, opportunities, and challenges. Sci. World J. **2014** (2014)
12. Borgman, C.L., Wallis, J.C., Mayernik, M.S., Pepe, A.: Drowning in data: digital library architecture to support scientific use of embedded sensor networks. In: Proceedings of the ACM International Conference on Digital Libraries, pp. 269–277 (2007)
13. Chi, M., Plaza, A., Benediktsson, J.A., Sun, Z., Shen, J., Zhu, Y.: Big data for remote sensing: challenges and opportunities. Proc. IEEE **104**, 2207–2219 (2016)
14. Monostori, L., Markus, A., Van Brussel, H., Westkämpfer, E.: Machine learning approaches to manufacturing. CIRP Ann. - Manuf. Technol. **45**, 675–712 (1996)
15. Fisher, D., DeLine, R., Czerwinski, M., Drucker, S.: Interactions with big data analytics. Interactions **19**, 50–59 (2012)
16. Chen, B., Wan, J., Shu, L., Li, P., Mukherjee, M., Yin, B.: Smart factory of industry 4.0: key technologies, application case, and challenges. IEEE Access **6**, 6505–6519 (2017)
17. Costa, C., Santos, M.Y.: Big data: state-of-the-art concepts, techniques, technologies, modeling approaches and research challenges. Int. J. Comput. Sci. **44**, 285–301 (2017)

18. Schmidt, M., Moreno, M.V., Schülke, A., Macek, K., Mařík, K., Pastor, A.G.: Optimizing legacy building operation: the evolution into data-driven predictive cyber-physical systems. Energy Build. **148**, 257–279 (2017)
19. Santos, M.Y., et al.: A big data analytics architecture for industry 4.0. In: Rocha, Á., Correia, A.M., Adeli, H., Reis, L.P., Costanzo, S. (eds.) WorldCIST 2017. AISC, vol. 570, pp. 175–184. Springer, Cham (2017). https://doi.org/10.1007/978-3-319-56538-5_19
20. Lee, J., Bagheri, B., Kao, H.-A.: A cyber-physical systems architecture for industry 4.0-based manufacturing systems. Manuf. Lett. **3**, 18–23 (2015)
21. Monostori, L., et al.: Cyber-physical systems in manufacturing. CIRP Ann. - Manuf. Technol. **65**, 621–641 (2016)
22. Sivarajah, U., Kamal, M.M., Irani, Z., Weerakkody, V.: Critical analysis of big data challenges and analytical methods. J. Bus. Res. **70**, 263–286 (2017)
23. Ren, S., Zhang, Y., Liu, Y., Sakao, T., Huisingh, D., Almeida, C.M.V.B.: A comprehensive review of big data analytics throughout product lifecycle to support sustainable smart manufacturing. J. Clean. Prod. **210**, 1343–1365 (2019)
24. Al-Abassi, A., Karimipour, H., HaddadPajouh, H., Dehghantanha, A., Parizi, R.M.: Industrial big data analytics: challenges and opportunities. In: Choo, K.-K.R., Dehghantanha, A. (eds.) Handbook of Big Data Privacy, pp. 37–61. Springer, Cham (2020). https://doi.org/10.1007/978-3-030-38557-6_3
25. Dubey, R., Gunasekaran, A., Childe, S.J., Wamba, S.F., Papadopoulos, T.: The impact of big data on world-class sustainable manufacturing. Int. J. Adv. Manuf. Technol. **84**, 631–645 (2016)
26. Raut, R.D., Mangla, S.K., Narwane, V.S., Gardas, B.B., Priyadarshinee, P., Narkhede, B.E.: Linking big data analytics and operational sustainability practices for sustainable business management. J. Clean. Prod. **224**, 10–24 (2019)

# Explainable AI in Manufacturing: A Predictive Maintenance Case Study

Bahrudin Hrnjica[1] and Selver Softic[2(✉)]

[1] University of Bihać, dr. Irfana Ljubijankića bb, 77000 Bihać, Bosnia and Herzegovina
bahrudin.hrnjica@unbi.ba

[2] IT and Business Informatics, CAMPUS 02 University of Applied Sciences, Körblergasse 126, 8010 Graz, Austria
selver.softic@campus02.at

**Abstract.** This paper describes an example of an explainable AI (Artificial Intelligence) (XAI) in a form of Predictive Maintenance (PdM) scenario for manufacturing. Predictive maintenance has the potential of saving a lot of money by reducing and predicting machine breakdown. In this case study we work with generalized data to show how this scenario could look like with real production data. For this purpose, we created and evaluated a machine learning model based on a highly efficient gradient boosting decision tree in order to predict machine errors or tool failures. Although the case study is strictly experimental, we can conclude that explainable AI in form of focused analytic and reliable prediction model can reasonably contribute to prediction of maintenance tasks.

**Keywords:** Explainable AI · Predictive Maintenance · Production management

## 1 Introduction

Predictive Maintenance (PdM) anticipates maintenance needs to avoid costs associated with unscheduled downtime. By connecting to devices and monitoring the data the devices produce, we can identify patterns that lead to potential problems or failures. Those insights can be used to address issues before they happen. This ability to predict when equipment or assets need maintenance allows us to optimize equipment lifetime and minimize downtime [1].

The fundamental litmus test for explainable AI (XAI) – that is, machine learning algorithms and other Artificial Intelligence systems that produce outcomes that humans can readily understand and track backwards to the origins [2].

In this case study we will consider the field of maintenance in manufacturing. More precisely we will deal with PdM by involving explainable AI outputs as base for our decisions and predictions.

B. Lalic et al. (Eds.): APMS 2020, IFIP AICT 592, pp. 66–73, 2020.
https://doi.org/10.1007/978-3-030-57997-5_8

## 2  Explainable AI - XAI

Recent success of Machine Learning (ML) led to series of application scenarios for Artificial Intelligence (AI) applications. Continued advances promise to produce autonomous systems that will perceive, learn, decide, and act on their own. However, the effectiveness of these systems is limited by the machine's current inability to explain their decisions and actions to human users.

The Explainable AI (XAI) program introduced by DARPA[1] aims to create a suite of ML techniques that:

- Produce more explainable models, while maintaining a high level of learning performance (prediction accuracy); and
- Enable human users to understand, appropriately trust, and effectively manage the emerging generation of artificially intelligent partners.

For decision makers who rely upon Data Analytics and Data Science, explainability is a real issue. If the computational system relies on a simple decision model such as logistic regression, they can understand it and convince executives who have to sign off on a system because it seems reasonable and fair. They can justify the analytical results to shareholders, regulators, and other involved stakeholders. But for "Deep Nets" and ML systems, this is no longer possible.

There is a need to find ways to explain the system to the decision maker so that they know that their decisions are going to be reasonable. The goals of explanation involves reaching a persuasion, but that comes only as a consequence of understanding the how the AI works, the mistakes the system can make, and the safety measures surrounding it.

Meanwhile, AI is increasingly allowed to make and take more autonomous decisions and actions. Justifying these decisions will only become more crucial, and there is little doubt that this field will continue to rise in prominence and produce exciting and much needed work in the future [3].

The importance of explanation, and especially explanation in AI, has been emphasized in numerous popular press outlets over the past decades, with considerable discussion of the explainability of "Deep Nets" and ML systems in both the technical literature and the recent popular press [2, 4–13].

## 3  Predictive Maintenance

PdM extracts insights from the data produced by the equipment on the shop floor and acts on these insights. The idea of PdM goes back to the early 1990's and augments regularly scheduled, preventive maintenance. PdM requires the equipment to provide data from sensors monitoring the equipment as well as other operational data. Humans act based on the analysis. Simply speaking, it is a technique to determine (predict) the failure of the machine component in the near future so that the component can be

---

[1] https://www.darpa.mil/program/explainable-artificial-intelligence.

replaced based on the maintenance plan before it fails and stops the production process. The PdM can improve the production process and increase the productivity. By successfully handling with PdM we are able to achieve the following goals:

- Reduce the operational risk of mission-critical equipment.
- Control cost of maintenance by enabling just-in-time maintenance operations.
- Discover patterns connected to various maintenance problems.
- Provide Key Performance Indicators.

Usually PdM uses descriptive, statistical or probabilistic approach to drive analysis and prediction. There are also several approaches which used Machine Learning (ML) [1, 14]. Through the literature [15] there can be found the following types of PrM in the production: reactive, periodic, proactive and predictive (Fig. 1).

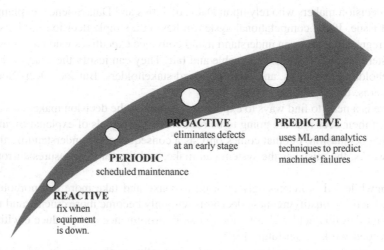

**Fig. 1.** Different types of maintenance in the production

# 4   Case Study

In order to handle and use this technique we need a various data from the machines in production. In this case study we used the freely available data from a data source generated as test data set for PdM containing information about: telemetry, errors, failures and machine properties.

The data can be found at Azure blob storage. The data is maintained by Azure Gallery Article[2]. Once the data is downloaded from the blob storage, local copies will be used for further observations in this contribution.

---

[2] https://gallery.azure.ai/Experiment/Predictive-Maintenance-Implementation-Guide-Data-Sets-1.

## 4.1 Methodology

Usually, every PdM technique should proceed by the following three main steps:

- **Collect Data** – collect all possible descriptions, historical and real-time data, usually by using IoT (Internet of Things) devices, various loggers, technical documentation, etc.
- **Predict Failures** – collected data can be used and transformed into ML ready data sets, and build a ML model to predict the failures of the components in the set of machines in the production.
- **React** – by obtaining the information which components will fail in the near future, we can activate the process of replacement so the component will be replaced before it fails, and the production process will not.

## 4.2 Data Preparation

In order to predict failures in the production process, a set of data transformations, cleaning, feature engineering, and selection must be performed to prepare the data for building a ML model. The data preparation part plays a crucial role in the model building process because quality of the data and its preparation will directly influences the model accuracy and reliability. The data used for this PdM use case can be classified to:

- Telemetry – which collects historical data about machine behavior (voltage, vibration, etc.).
- Errors – the data about warnings and errors in the machines.
- Maint – data about replacement and maintenance for the machines.
- Machines – descriptive information about the machines.
- Failures – data when a certain machine is stopped, due to component failure.

**Errors data** represents the most important information in every PdM system. The errors are non-breaking recorded events while the machine is still operational. In the experimental data set the error date and times are rounded to the closest hour since the telemetry data is collected at an hourly rate. What we get to insight is shown in the left chart of Fig. 2.

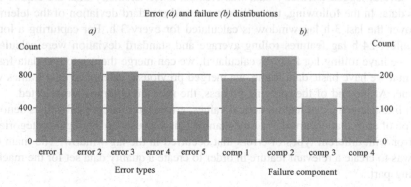

**Fig. 2.** Error and failure distributions across machines

**Failures data** represents the replacements of the components due to the failure of the machines. Once the failure is happened the machine is stopped. This is a crucial difference between errors and failures. Failure distribution produced by certain component across machines is shown in the right chart of Fig. 2.

**Maintenance data** tells us about scheduled and unscheduled maintenance. The data set contains the records which correspond to both, regular inspection of components as well as failures. To add the record into the maintenance table a component must be replaced during the scheduled inspection or replaced due to a breakdown. In case the records are created due to breakdowns are called failures. Maintenance contains the data from 2014 and 2015 years.

**Machine data** includes information about 100 machines which are subject of the PdM analysis. The information includes: model type, and machine age. Distribution of the machine age categorized by the models across production process is shown in the following Fig. 3.

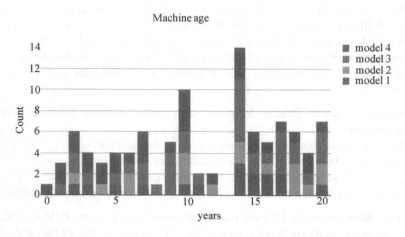

**Fig. 3.** Machines overview grouped by different types of models and age.

### 4.3  Feature Engineering

First, several lagged telemetry data was created, since telemetry data are classic time series data. In the following, the rolling mean and standard deviation of the telemetry data over the last 3-h lag window is calculated for every 3 h. For capturing a longer term effect 24 h lag features rolling average and standard deviation were calculated. Once we have rolling lag features calculated, we can merge them into one data frame. Now that we have basic data frame, we merged previously calculated data frames with this one. At the end of the merging process, the relevant columns are selected.

Unlike telemetry that had numerical values, errors have categorical values denoting the type of error that occurred at a time-stamp. This was used to aggregate categories of the error with different types of errors that occurred in the lag window. The main task here was to create a relevant feature in order to create a quality data set for the machine learning part.

One of the good features that has been chosen was the number of replacements of each component in the last 3 months to incorporate the frequency of replacements. Furthermore, we calculated how long it has been since a component is last replaced as that would be expected to correlate better with component failures since the longer a component is used, the more degradation should be expected. The machine data set contains descriptive information about machines like the type of machines and their ages which is the years in service.

As the last step in feature engineering, we are performing merging all features into one data set. The label in PdM should be the probability that a machine will fail in the near future due to a failure certain component. If we take 24 h to be the period (task) for this problem, the label construction consists of a new column in the feature data set which indicate if certain machine will fail or not in the next 24 h due to failure one of several components.

In this way, we are defining the label as a categorical variable containing: – none – if the machine will not fail in the next 24 h, – comp1 to comp4 if the machine will fail in the next 24 h due to the failure of certain components. Since we can experiment with the label construction by applying different conditions, we can implement methods that take several arguments in order to define the general problem.

## 4.4 Preliminary Results

We analyzed 5 data sets with information about telemetry, data, errors and maintenance as well as failure for 100 machines. The data were transformed and analyzed in order to create the final data set for building a machine learning model for PdM.

Once we created all features from the data sets, as a final step is to create the label column so that it describes if a certain machine will fail in the next 24 h due to failure a comp1, comp2, comp3, comp4 or it will continue to work. In this part, we performed a part of the ML task and start training a ML model for predicting if a certain machine will fail in the next 24 h due to failure, or it will be in functioning normal in that time period.

The model which we built was multi-class classification model since it has 5 values to predict: comp1, comp2, comp3, comp4 or none – means it will continue to work. We used the DART Booster hyper-parameter tuning along with Light- GBM[3] [16] which is a gradient boosting framework that uses tree based learning algorithm. It is especially efficient on small data sets. We evaluated the trained model first with training data set (see Table 1).

As can be seen the model predicts the values from the training data set correctly in most cases. In order to see how the model predicts unknown data entries we used the test data. The result is shown in Table 2. We can see, that the model has overall accuracy 99%, and 95% average per class accuracy which is very promising for experimental case.

---

[3] https://lightgbm.readthedocs.io/en/latest/.

**Table 1.** Results on training data set.

| Predicted truth | none | comp1 | comp2 | comp3 | comp4 | Recall |
|---|---|---|---|---|---|---|
| none | 165371 | 0 | 0 | 0 | 0 | 1,0000 |
| comp1 | 0 | 844 | 26 | 4 | 8 | 0,9588 |
| comp2 | 0 | 22 | 1097 | 8 | 31 | 0,9473 |
| comp3 | 0 | 4 | 8 | 576 | 13 | 0,9548 |
| comp4 | 0 | 16 | 25 | 11 | 772 | 0,9369 |
| Precision | 1,0000 | 0,9546 | 0,949 | 0,9616 | 0,9369 | |

**Table 2.** Results on test data set.

| Predicted truth | none | comp1 | comp2 | comp3 | comp4 | Recall |
|---|---|---|---|---|---|---|
| none | 120313 | 15 | 0 | 0 | 6 | 0,9998 |
| comp1 | 2 | 464 | 24 | 24 | 14 | 0,8788 |
| comp2 | 0 | 22 | 1097 | 8 | 39 | 0,9382 |
| comp3 | 0 | 0 | 0 | 412 | 4 | 0,9904 |
| comp4 | 1 | 10 | 17 | 4 | 552 | 0,0,9452 |
| Precision | 1,0000 | 0.9489 | 0.9532 | 0.9035 | 0.8976 | |

# 5  Conclusions, Limitations and Outlook

In this paper we conducted a case study in the field of Predictive Maintenance (PdM) with sample machine data to demonstrate how explainable AI can be reached in the field of manufacturing. Although the study is strictly experimental, we can conclude that explainable AI in form of reliable prediction model and visualizations can reasonably contribute to avoiding unnecessary costs associated with unscheduled downtime caused through machine errors or tool failures.

The basic limitation of this contribution is that this experiment was conducted with generic data set, however the presented concept shows high maturity with promising results.

The next step in the future would be to engage the trained model with some data collected directly in real world manufacturing settings and involving data from different manufacturer. In this way the reliability of presented results could be approved and through the comparison of results from different data sources and adjustment of the prediction model.

# References

1. Lee, W.J., Wu, H., Yun, H., Kim, H., Jun, M.B., Sutherland, J.W.: Predictive maintenance of machine tool systems using artificial intelligence techniques applied to machine condition data. Procedia CIRP **80**, 506–511 (2019). 26th CIRP Conference on Life Cycle Engineering (LCE) Purdue University, West Lafayette, IN, USA May 7–9, 2019

2. Kim, T.W.: Explainable artificial intelligence (XAI), the goodness criteria and the grasp-ability test. arXiv preprint arXiv:1810.09598 (2018)
3. Biran, O., Cotton, C.V.: Explanation and justification in machine learning: a survey or (2017)
4. Bornstein, A.M.: Is artificial intelligence permanently inscrutable?
5. Clancey, W.J.: Intelligent tutoring systems: a tutorial survey. Technical report, Stanford Univ CA Dept of Computer Science (1986)
6. Core, M.G., Lane, H.C., Van Lent, M., Gomboc, D., Solomon, S., Rosenberg, M.: Building explainable artificial intelligence systems. In: AAAI, pp. 1766–1773 (2006)
7. Hawkins, J.: Special report: can we copy the brain?-what intelligent machines need to learn from the neocortex. IEEE Spectr. **54**(6), 34–71 (2017)
8. Marcus, G.: Deep learning: A critical appraisal. arXiv preprint arXiv:1801.00631 (2018)
9. Monroe, D.: AI, explain yourself. Commun. ACM **61**(11), 11–13 (2018)
10. Sheh, R.K.M.: "Why did you do that?" explainable intelligent robots. In: Workshops at the Thirty-First AAAI Conference on Artificial Intelligence (2017)
11. Voosen, P.: How AI detectives are craking open the black box of deep learning. Science (2017)
12. Wang, D., Yang, Q., Abdul, A., Lim, B.Y.: Designing theory-driven user-centric explainable AI. In: Proceedings of the 2019 CHI Conference on Human Factors in Computing Systems, pp. 1–15 (2019)
13. Weinberger, D.: Our machines now have knowledge we'll never understand. Backchannel (2017).     https://www.wired.com/story/our-machines-now-have-knowledge-well-never-understand
14. Susto, G.A., Schirru, A., Pampuri, S., Mcloone, S., Beghi, A.: Machine learning for predictive maintenance: a multiple classifier approach. IEEE Trans. Ind. Inform. **11**, 812–820 (2015)
15. Selcuk, S.: Predictive maintenance, its implementation and latest trends. Proc. Inst. Mech. Eng. Part B: J. Eng. Manuf. **231**(9), 1670–1679 (2017)
16. Ke, G., et al.: LightGBM: a highly efficient gradient boosting decision tree. In: Guyon, I., et al. (eds.) Advances in Neural Information Processing Systems 30, pp. 3146–3154. Curran Associates, Inc. (2017)

# Retrofit Concept for Textile Production

Felix Franke, Susanne Franke, and Ralph Riedel[(✉)]

Department of Factory Planning and Factory Management,
Chemnitz University of Technology, Chemnitz, Germany
{felix.franke,susanne.franke,
ralph.riedel}@mb.tu-chemnitz.de

**Abstract.** In production, an intelligent analysis of the data provided along the production line bears huge potential for increasing process efficiency and reducing production costs. The (continuous) collection of relevant data is a crucial precondition for every Industry 4.0 or smart technology. While new machines have internal controllers and sensors to meet those requirements, this is usually not the case for machines being already in use. Especially in the textile industry, it is often standard to keep old machines since the manufacturing methods themselves haven't changed significantly over the past decades. Hence, the successful exploitation of digitalization advantages requires these companies to first develop and implement a digitization strategy. In this paper we present a concept which allows to develop modular, scalable, flexible solutions considering the whole digitization process from data acquisition to storage. The concept is complemented by a guideline for its application in industry. Experience from a prototypical application in a textile company is described. The concept enables companies to determine the various conditions and requirements for digitization, to analyze different possibilities and to deduce scenarios that lead to a solution for the effective utilization of Industry 4.0 technologies.

**Keywords:** Industry 4.0 · Textile process chain · Modularization · Digitization · Digitalization

## 1 Introduction

Being one of the most important trends of our time, digitization and digital transformation are the key for production companies to secure their long-term competitiveness. Industry 4.0, a synonym for the digitalization process, provides new opportunities for optimizing the entire value-added chain [11]. A modern IT infrastructure, digital applications as well as intelligent data and networked systems are the decisive factors for the fourth industrial revolution. In this context, the following two aspects have to be considered. First, the available standard digitization solutions do not apply to every sector (in Germany, best practice solutions usually aim at the dominating sectors of automotive and microelectronic industry). Second, the fitting accuracy of existing solutions to small and medium-sized enterprises (SMEs) is generally not considered. However, SMEs are an important economic factor in Germany as they make up more than 99% of all enterprises [15]. Especially in the textile sector, one of the oldest industries in Germany and still of vital importance for manufacturing high-quality

© IFIP International Federation for Information Processing 2020
Published by Springer Nature Switzerland AG 2020
B. Lalic et al. (Eds.): APMS 2020, IFIP AICT 592, pp. 74–82, 2020.
https://doi.org/10.1007/978-3-030-57997-5_9

technical textiles as well as custom products, the majority is SME [12]. We want to close this gap and develop tools that enable the textile production SMEs to be digitized, to adapt to the fast-paced change and to benefit from the advantages.

The paper is structured as follows. Section 2 comprises an investigation of the relevant aspects of the textile industry and an overview of the digitization process we want to implement. In Sect. 3, we deduce the requirements that our solution has to meet in this context, derive the concept and propose a guideline for a proper application in the industrial environment. The paper concludes with the results of a prototypical application of the concept as well as an evaluation of the obtained knowledge.

## 2   Theoretical Background

### 2.1   Preconditions of the Textile Industry

In order to establish a concept for the digitization of textile companies, it is crucial to analyze the prevalent procedures, methods and manufacturing facilities. As relevant fields, filament and textile production and textile finishing were identified. The linked procedures (and, hence, machines and technology) vary strongly, as Table 1 shows.

**Table 1.** Procedures and relevant parameters in textile production

| Field | Product (selection) | Procedures (selection) | Relevant parameters (selection) |
|-------|---------------------|------------------------|---------------------------------|
| Filament production | Natural fibers | Preparation (carding, drawing, combing), spinning process | Air flow, heterogeneity of the fiber |
| | Synthetic fibers | Preparation (liquefying raw material, wet/dry/melting procedure, drawing), spinning process | Type of separation, spinneret pressure |
| Textile production | Tissue | Preparation (spooling, twisting, sizing, warp beam provision), weaving (rapier/air jet/shuttle) | Thread stability |
| | Knitted goods | Thread provision, structure formation | Thread tension, thread velocity |
| Textile finishing | | Preparatory treatment (brushing/tapping/singeing, washing/bleaching), dyeing (padding and exhaustion; for synthetic fibers: within preparation process) | Temperature and chemical composition of the dye, direction of the good |

The process parameters of and even within the three production fields differ in most cases, which means that it is not possible to identify universal parameters as a baseline. As a consequence, the concept has to be very abstract in order to provide a common guideline for the different textile production procedures and heterogeneous machinery.

Since most of the basic operating modes in textile production have been established years ago and still prove to be state-of-the-art, the machines are generally not equipped with control units or sensors for gathering data. Accordingly, the internal IT infrastructure is not fully digitally evolved, implying that data measurement from the viewpoint of digitalization is insufficient (which is characteristic for SMEs [8]). This leads to two main tasks: appropriately equipping the machinery and improving the IT infrastructure. Particularly, retrofitting of the "digital process chain" (collect, transmit, save and make data available) is part of the main goal. The purpose of retrofitting "is to transfer the aspects of the Industry 4.0 visions to machines and processes with the least possible financial and time expenditure" [6].

## 2.2   The Process of Digitization

It is our goal to transform the analog world of the textile companies into a digital one, i.e. to map the relevant data into a digital model, on which then a defined action is performed. According to [7, 14], this process is defined as digitization, which has to be distinguished from digitalization: the latter one corresponds to making use of the data gathered within the digitization process. Digitization builds the basis for digitalization. The gathered data should be stored in a database in order to have access to relevant information for evaluation and to possibly share it via Internet of Things (IoT) systems. Hereby, the focus is set on condition monitoring as the basis for optimizing the production process as it is one of the most important and profitable topics.

The digitization process consists of the three steps collecting data, transferring data as well as storing data [16]. We have to adjust them to our problem, and then a method for a proper implementation has to be formulated.

# 3   Methodology

## 3.1   Requirements

Starting point of developing the concept is the deduction of the requirements it has to meet. Based on the knowledge gained about the textile sector in combination with digitization and our interviews with textile companies, we identified the five main requirements modularity, scalability, open interfaces, data security and technical flexibility. In the following, they are explained and investigated w.r.t. this paper's context, hereby providing a deeper understanding and the fundamentals for the concept.

*Modularity* is described as "a structuring principle which enhances clarity, reduces complexity, provides flexibility and has some organisational advantages" [9] and demands for both separability and functional independence. Separability addresses the possibility to interchange certain components without negatively affecting the system as a whole. The second dimension, functional independence, assigns a uniquely defined and self-contained task to every component. The main advantage of modularity is the high flexibility of the digitization solution w.r.t. extension and substitution.

*Scalability*, "the ability of a system to accommodate an increasing number of elements or objects [...] and/or to be susceptible to enlargement" [1], can be understood in a vertical (i.e. increasing performance by improving/upgrading the system without raising the number of modules) and a horizontal way (in the sense of achieving increased performance by adding components, e.g. gradually digitizing the company).

The next requirement, *open interfaces*, stems from the goal of retrofitting the textile machines. It is defined as the ability to include data from various sources and combines them into a consistent system [4]. For the realization of Industry 4.0 applications, an integration of the machines into the IT infrastructure is mandatory as well. Because of the heterogeneity of the textile machinery, numerous different systems with varying data sources need to be linked.

*Data security*, defined as a set of standards and technologies that protects data from intentional or accidental destruction [3], was identified as one of the main obstacles in the process of the digital transformation of SMEs [17].

The users' claims, varying strongly due to the wide range of the processes and machines, call for *technical flexibility*: the concept has to be capable of including both easy in-house developments and highly advanced, industry-standard solutions.

The five requirements have to be fulfilled throughout the digitization process. In addition, we want to achieve a high abstraction level such that the field of application meets the diversity of the textile production processes.

### 3.2   Derivation of the Concept

First we have to ensure that the three steps collecting data, transferring data and storing data as the basis of the digitization process fulfill the five abovementioned requirements. Data collection combines the different functionalities of acquiring signals as well as converting them into measurable information and, as a consequence, might contain parts of data transfer. This contradicts the required functional independence. Hence, we divide data collection into the two parts acquisition of a physical value and conversion of the signal (both will be connected via data transfer). This is especially necessary in the context of retrofitting, i.e. equipping machines such that a digital signal or an interface for data transfer is supplied. Having a closer look at data transfer and data storage, we conclude that a further separation is not expedient.

Figure 1 depicts the results obtained so far: in order to meet the requirements explained in Scct. 3.1, we derived five functional sections of the digitization process in a logical order. Every section is strictly separate from the adjacent ones, modularity and scalability are fulfilled. The latter three requirements (open interfaces, data security and technical flexibility) will be significant w.r.t. the content of the five sections.

ACQUISITION     TRANSFER     CONVERSION & MEASUREMENT GENERATION     TRANSFER     STORAGE

**Fig. 1.** Five sections of the digitization process

We will now use this fundamental structure to develop and explain the modules that form the sections. Those modules correspond to the means and ways of how to realize the action that has to be performed on the data. For every component to be digitized (e.g. a machine), suitable modules within each section have to be chosen.

Considering the sector acquisition, we identified the relevant modules sensor, control and manual input. The module sensor, a crucial tool for retrofitting, establishes a connection between a physical quantity and, generally, an electric signal. Since we aim at high technical flexibility for the diverse textile machinery, a division of sensors with and without industry standard is reasonable. The module control, comprising control units already integrated in machines to gather data, is important in the context of retrofitting: it has to be distinguished whether the control provides data or not. This allows the user to identify controls that need to be equipped with an extra module to guarantee the desired functionality. The module manual input covers data that is included in the system manually, with the help of a special device or a software.

The sector transfer comprises wired and wireless, which both occur in textile factory halls. To meet the company's demands on the requirement data security, encrypted and non-encrypted transfer is distinguished. Here, encryption refers to a technical solution that protects data classified as critical against unauthorized access.

The tasks of the sector conversion & measurement generation usually are fulfilled by a powerful computer. Depending on the digitization goal, additional controlling beyond the possibilities the machines provide is in need. The relevant modules are micro-PC for easy controlling tasks, programmable logic controller (PLC) to control one special machine, IoT gateway mainly for forwarding data and industrial computer as high-end solution for complex tasks as well as controlling many machines. Considering that retrofitting machinery in the textile industry is our main task, open interfaces (especially w.r.t. the two adjacent sectors data transfer) must be given throughout the whole chain of collecting, processing and storing data.

The sector storage comprises modules that ensure the long-term storing of the acquired data in a secure way. The two prevalent concepts are cloud (private or public) and server (centralized or non-centralized). Note that cloud computing has been identified as one of the key technologies for digitalization initiatives [2], but at the same time the safety standards imposed by the company have to be met (see Sect. 4).

Figure 2 visualizes the obtained results. The concept, following the five identified sectors in a logical order, forms the basis of the development of the digitization solution, which is realized by selecting the proper modules within this chain. The desired high abstraction level is achieved and offers a broad spectrum of application within the textile production industry. We suggest that for a specific application in a company, the abstraction level of the concept is reduced by identifying and selecting the available and relevant technical solutions within each module. This leads to a specification of the modules and provides a more tailored, transparent solution [10].

## 3.3  Guideline for Concept Application

Because of the modularity of the concept, a variety of combinations arises as possible digitization solutions. However, since a company is only interested in one very suitable solution, a multi-stage procedure, depicted in Fig. 3, is applied: First, both the present

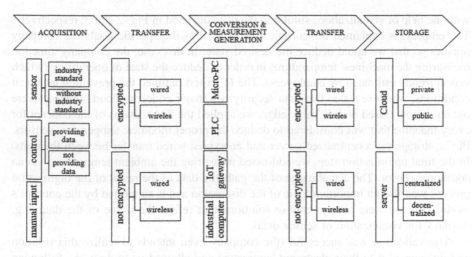

**Fig. 2.** Concept sections and corresponding modules

and the desired state w.r.t. the five requirements have to be determined. Here, the company's specific goals have to be taken into account (for example, enhancing the internal IT infrastructure or implementing a cloud solution). In the next step, the technical conditions of the company (e.g. availability of a network) are identified. Then, the user repeatedly passes through the five sections of the concept, starting with acquisition and ending with storage. With every cycle, a new component of the company (e.g. a machine) is included. This corresponds to the horizontal scalability of the concept. As a last step, an improvement cycle is performed, which helps detecting previously unrecognized optimization potential. This is justified for example by the broad overview over all modules that are included now, or the optimization potential may occur late in the process due to the gradual integration of components which has not yet been revealed. It corresponds to the vertical scalability of the concept.

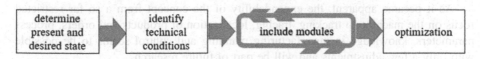

**Fig. 3.** Guideline for the application of the concept

## 4   Experience from Practical Application and Conclusions

In order to validate the applicability of the concept and to detect chances for improvement, we performed a test in a small-sized German textile company. In coordination with the production manager, we selected part of their machinery with no control unit and no sensors, i.e. machines specifically in need of retrofitting. We then tested the concept together with the production manager, the maintenance manager and the company's IT expert. First we introduced the concept and the intended procedure with the help of visualizations similar to the ones depicted in Fig. 2 and 3, respectively. The employees explained the current state as well as the specific goals the company pursues so that we could deduce the desired state. In this case, the company aimed at measuring the machines' temperatures in order to deduce the state of operability (which was currently estimated by employees). The IT expert outlined the prevailing technical conditions, which revealed that data security is a major concern: cloud solutions were not an option. Based on this knowledge, we applied the five sections of the concept for every machine that was considered to deduce the proper modules: temperature sensors, PLCs, storage via a centralized server and encrypted wired transfer between the units. In the final optimization step, we addressed measuring the ambient temperature via an additional sensor. The actual usage of the gathered data as the result of the digitization process was also an important topic of the discussion and is supported by the concept's modularity: we were able to choose solutions that reflect the usage of the data (e.g. displays for visualization of sensor data).

The validation was successful (the company even intends to realize this solution and outsourced it to their electronic contractor) and allowed us to draw the following conclusions. Decoupling the detection of the present state and the technical conditions turned out to be useful: it helped the employees making deductions from the present state and not focusing on current technical restrictions. Including all decision-makers of the different involved departments proved to be important. Internal processes and conditions (e.g. directives from the works council or for data security) are crucial for a valid implementation and have to be considered. Furthermore, we found that even though we aimed at formulating the concept self-explanatory, a dialogue with responsible company members is indispensable for a successful digitization process: the company's process knowledge in combination with our digitization experience and an unbiased view from the outside leads to a solution-oriented exchange. According to a study [13], German companies lack structured strategies to implement Industry 4.0 solutions. This was confirmed during the real-life test. However, the test also revealed the general huge interest of the managers in the company's digital transformation. The concept turned out to be a very helpful enabler for this process: the discussions led to many valuable digitalization ideas that the concept was able to reflect.

As it became apparent, the expendability of the concept from a so far restricted focus on the machine to tracking, tracing, localization of products and orders, process parameters, knowledge in manufacturing planning and control seems to be possible with only a few adjustments and will be part of future research.

From the high abstraction level of the concept (which was necessary due to the diversity of the textile production processes), we can deduce two important aspects. First, the typical fears and wishes of companies – they want to implement solutions that are low-cost and easy to understand [5] – can easily be met due to the modularity, technical flexibility and scalability of the concept: it provides a classification of the modules, whereas the final technical solution is subsequently selected in coordination with the company (this was indicated in Sect. 3.2). Second, the high abstraction level is likely to allow the transfer of the gained knowledge to other fields of the production industry. This will also be part of our future research.

**Acknowledgments.** The authors would like to thank Sächsische Aufbaubank - Förderbank - for funding this work, which is part of the research and development project retroTEX. (Diese Maßnahme wird mitfinanziert mit Steuermitteln auf Grundlage des von den Abgeordneten des Sächsischen Landtags beschlossenen Haushaltes./This measure is co-financed by taxes based on the budget concluded by the parlamentarians of the Saxonian Landtag.)

# References

1. Bondi, A.B.: Characteristics of scalability and their impact on performance. In: Proceedings of the 2nd International Workshop on Software and Performance, Ottawa, Ontario, pp. 195–203 (2000)
2. crisp Research. https://www.crisp-research.com/publication/public-cloud-key-successful-digital-transformation. Accessed 02 Mar 2020
3. Forcepoint. https://www.forcepoint.com/cyber-edu/data-security. Accessed 02 Mar 2020
4. Gharbi, M., Koschel, A., Rausch, A.: Software Architecture Fundamentals, 1st edn. dpunkt. verlag, Heidelberg (2019)
5. Halse, L.L., Jæger, B.: Operationalizing industry 4.0: understanding barriers of industry 4.0 and circular economy. In: Ameri, F., Stecke, K.E., von Cieminski, G., Kiritsis, D. (eds.) APMS 2019. IAICT, vol. 567, pp. 135–142. Springer, Cham (2019). https://doi.org/10.1007/978-3-030-29996-5_16
6. Hamrol, A., Zerbst, S., Bozek, M., Grabowska, M., Weber, M.: Analysis of the conditions for effective use of numerically controlled machine tools. In: Hamrol, A., Ciszak, O., Legutko, S., Jurczyk, M. (eds.) Advances in Manufacturing. LNME, pp. 3–12. Springer, Cham (2018). https://doi.org/10.1007/978-3-319-68619-6_1
7. i-SCOOP. https://www.i-scoop.eu/digital-transformation/digitization-digitalization-digital-transformation-disruption. Accessed 02 Mar 2020
8. Luco, J., Mestre, S., Henry, L., Tamayo, S., Fontane, F.: Industry 4.0 in SMEs: a sectorial analysis. In: Ameri, F., Stecke, K.E., von Cieminski, G., Kiritsis, D. (eds.) APMS 2019. IAICT, vol. 566, pp. 357–365. Springer, Cham (2019). https://doi.org/10.1007/978-3-030-30000-5_45
9. Miller, T.D., Elgård, P.: Defining modules, modularity and modularization. In: Proceedings of the 13th IPS Research Seminar, Fuglsoe, Aalborg University (1998)
10. Napoleone, A., Andersen, A.-L., Pozzetti, A., Macchi, M.: Reconfigurable manufacturing: a classification of elements enabling convertibility and scalability. In: Ameri, F., Stecke, K.E., von Cicminski, G., Kiritsis, D. (eds.) APMS 2019. IAICT, vol. 566, pp. 349–356. Springer, Cham (2019). https://doi.org/10.1007/978-3-030-30000-5_44
11. PriceWaterhouseCoopers: Industry 4.0 - Opportunities and Challenges of the Industrial Internet (2014)
12. Richter, U.: Perspektiven der ostdeutschen Textilindustrie - Grundrisse einer arbeitsorientierten Branchenstrategie. In: Schallmeyer, M., Gerlach, F. (eds.) Otto Brenner Stiftung-Arbeitsheft, vol. 50, pp. 1–32. Frankfurt/Main (2007)
13. Satyro, W.C., et al.: Implementation of industry 4.0 in Germany, Brazil and Portugal: barriers and benefits. In: Ameri, F., Stecke, K.E., von Cieminski, G., Kiritsis, D. (eds.) APMS 2019. IAICT, vol. 567, pp. 323–330. Springer, Cham (2019). https://doi.org/10.1007/978-3-030-29996-5_37
14. Schuh, G., Anderl, R., Gausemeier, J.: Industrie 4.0 maturity index: managing the digital transformation of companies. In: ten Hompel, M., Wahlster, W. (eds.) acatech STUDY, Herbert Utz Verlag, München (2017)

15. Statista.    https://de.statista.com/statistik/daten/studie/731951/umfrage/anteil-des-umsatzes-von-kmu-am-gesamten-umsatz-in-deutschland-nach-wirtschaftszweigen. Accessed 14 Feb 2020
16. Wolf, T., Strohschen, J.-H.: Digitalisierung: Definition und Reife. Informatik-Spektrum **41** (1), 56–64 (2018). https://doi.org/10.1007/s00287-017-1084-8
17. Zimmermann, V.: SMEs and digitalisation: the current position, recent developments and challenges. KfW Research, Focus on Economics, vol. 138. Frankfurt/Main (2016)

# Organizational Enablers for Digitalization in Norwegian Industry

Lars Harald Lied$^{(\boxtimes)}$, Maria Flavia Mogos, and Daryl John Powell

SINTEF Manufacturing AS, S.P. Andersens Vei 3, 7491 Trondheim, Norway
{lars.harald.lied,maria.flavia.mogos,
daryl.powell}@sintef.no

**Abstract.** Norway has a long cultural tradition for organizing its working life. A dialogue-based and cooperation-oriented model constitutes the way work life functions locally in companies as well as at the national level. This article addresses how the basic values of this practice promote processes of industrial digitalization in Norway. The digitalization of industry and society has many faces, but the focus here is on organization, forms of collaboration and management that create the foundation for successful digital implementation in the industry. Within the framework of a working life that requires ever-increasing competence at all levels, this article shows that intra-corporate collaboration between management and employees generates common goal understanding and process commitment. This paper highlights seven organizational enablers for digitalization in a Norwegian industrial context. Our findings from a cross-case analysis of data collected through 33 case studies of successful digitalization processes at Norwegian companies in a diverse set of industries suggest that the digitalization of industry requires cross-functional and inter-organizational collaboration to develop more specialized expertise from all employees, and this serves as a key element for success within industrial digitalization.

**Keywords:** Digitalization · Operations management · Multiple case study

## 1 Introduction

Today's industrial challenge is largely about how to generate increased competitiveness through the strategic implementation of digital technologies. Operators and machines must cooperate with an interaction we have not envisaged before [2]. Technological impact will again alter our ways of organizing and manage industrial production. Access to current information is no longer reserved for managers only [3]. Hierarchical organizations are replaced by flatter structures with autonomous production teams. These teams have access to all the data needed to do a good job. The operator must increasingly communicate with the robot through programming, computing has become cloud-based and information is visually distributed via screens and other digital platforms. This new human – machine interface (HMI) calls for specialized skills among operators and a reconsidered understanding of being a leader. The communication and division of responsibilities between manager and employee are changed in a way that requires a dynamic organization that can cope with change.

Published by Springer Nature Switzerland AG 2020
B. Lalic et al. (Eds.): APMS 2020, IFIP AICT 592, pp. 83–90, 2020.
https://doi.org/10.1007/978-3-030-57997-5_10

Digital solutions create a framework for how to organize processes, workplaces and communication in the future.

## 2 Theoretical Background

### 2.1 The Norwegian Model as an Enabler for Industrial Development

In Norway there is a well rooted tradition based on dialogue and involvement. It is a tripartite co-operation with the Norwegian Confederation of Trade Unions (LO), the Confederation of Norwegian Enterprise (NHO), and the Norwegian government constitute this model. Formal cooperative measures go back to 1935 when board representation for employees was fixed by law [4]. The Norwegian model (NM) for work-life design is a cooperative model based on trust and respect among the parties involved. Trust is the key element for success in this model. Both the employer and the employee side of work-life have agreed upon a series of tools to avoid unnecessary use of energy in search of best performance. The unions, and specifically the employee representatives, have a demanding role in such a model. On one hand, they are the representatives of the employees' interests. On the other hand, they are obliged to co-operate with the employer, and align the company's goals and employees' interests. This challenging role has been described as the balance between "boxing and dancing" [5]. The model is culturally embedded in all levels of Norwegian work life, and it sets a strong guideline for priorities made in work-life. Management and organization mirror this in a direct way. This dialogue based and involving way of organizing generates a true feeling of motivation and a sensation of being both useful and important. The voice of the employees is heard, and they feel ownership to both process and result. This way of organizing work-life has also produced a higher level of trust between leaders, employee representatives and unions in Norway compared with other countries [7].

### 2.2 Industry 4.0

Germany launched its so-called "Industrie 4.0" initiative in 2011 as part of the country's high-tech industrial strategy, introducing the idea of a fully integrated industry [6]. Since then, Industry 4.0 has gained worldwide interest and has opened up a range of new business potential and opportunities [7]. A commonly accepted overview of Industry 4.0 technologies includes: Autonomous robots, simulation, horizontal and vertical integration, industrial internet of things, cybersecurity, cloud computing, additive manufacturing, augmented reality and big data analytics [8]. Together, these technologies are considered to be the pillars of Industry 4.0, presenting manufacturers with opportunities for digitalization and integration of physical and virtual environments building capabilities for better problem-solving and learning in action – leading to increased operational performance and competitiveness. Inspired by Industry 4.0, the Norwegian government announced a strategy for a 'greener, smarter and more innovative' industry in 2017, which has become commonly known simply as "digitalization" [9]. Thus, in recent years, Norwegian industrial companies have been increasingly adopting Industry 4.0 technologies.

## 3 Methodology

Our research design is guided by the following research question: *What are the organizational enablers for digitalization in the Norwegian industry?* Given this what-type question, we selected a multiple case study approach [10], as this enabled the identification of organizational enablers in real digitalization processes and with a relatively full understanding of the nature and complexity of digitalization. This article is built on a multiple case-study conducted among Norwegian industrial companies in 2019. The study was called, *Pioneering Norwegian industrial companies and their experiences from digitalization.* The research foundation SINTEF was given a mandate by the Ministry of Trade, Industry and Fisheries (NFD) to explore how digitalization could strengthen future industrial production in Norway. Over a six-month period, SINTEF conducted a total of 170 interviews distributed across 33 *successful companies*[1] in a diverse set of industries including automotive, defense, food, maritime and process industry. The set of selected companies included all the finalist of *Årets smarteste industribedrift* (Smartest Industrial Company of the Year in Norway). A written report summarized the semi-structured interviews at each company. Trade union representatives, production and top leaders responsible for digitalization and technology developers were interviewed about their experiences with digitalization and their thoughts about its effects on future manufacturing. Responses were triangulated with company documentation and extensive field notes that were collected during company meetings and tours. For an increased accuracy of the empirical findings and increased construct validity [11], the results have been reviewed by a working group that included participants from industry, research/academia, NFD and the SINTEF researchers that conducted the interviews. The study of 33 cases enabled a fruitful cross-case analysis, an easier identification of representative relationships between the informants' experiences during the digitalization processes and their causes, and thereby a higher internal and external validity [12]. An interview guide was used, which focused on four main areas: (i) Curiosity in using new technology, (ii) Integration and utilization of digital tools (technology opportunities) throughout the business, (iii) Changing business models as a result of digital opportunities, and (iv) Reflections on the future. Potential benefits of using the NM of work-life organisation was defined as an overarching focus.

## 4 Discussion

When focusing on organizational enablers for implementing digitalization in the industry, the analysis of the SINTEF study data can be summarized in the following emergent themes:

**Ensuring Company Democracy.** Decisions regarding the implementation of new digital technology includes the employees in a direct way. Job content becomes altered,

---

[1] A *successful company* was defined as a company that can demonstrate successful development and implementation of digital technology.

new skills are required and processes must be reorganized due to new and increasingly complex technology [13, 14]. Within such a framework, it is most important to make sure that the "voice of the employee" is heard. Our study showed that the industrial companies genuinely involved the employees at an early stage in the process. By doing so, the company management gained trust, transparency and support from the union. By establishing this relation early on, several major elements were secured:

- The management secured a higher degree of momentum in the upcoming process of implementing new digital technology
- The union could influence decisions along the process
- The process produced less errors since decisions were considered from different angles during the process. A clean process requires less adjustment afterwards
- Collective goals generated a collective feeling of ownership to the solution. A broad involvement also creates a common vision
- Employees understood that digital technology also includes jobs with more stimulating content, which may replace tedious operations [14]
- Employees felt increasingly comfortable, since they mastered the new technology.

For instance, one of the case companies, a manufacturer of heavy mechanical parts for offshore installations, has managed to streamline their well-rooted internal processes by giving their operators a smartphone with digital work instructions. However, right from the start, they involved relevant operators in the team that was developing the technological solution, alongside technology developers. Moreover, during many days the operators were observed while working and their feedback during and after the workshops that were organized along the project, were recorded and they were the starting point for real improvements. The company regarded this close and early involvement of the operators as decisive for the smooth adoption of the new technology among employees with very different background. This and all the other effects listed above are a product of organizing the process in accordance with the NM.

If one compares the implementation of new digital technology with the introduction of robots in the 70s and 80s, then this study shows a distinct difference in the attitude of the unions. Back then, the unions tried to hold back the implementation of robots due to the fear of losing jobs. The confrontation between trade union and management characterized the international automotive industry to a great extent [15]. The SINTEF study of Norwegian industrial companies show that employee representatives today sees digital technology as a necessity to safeguard future jobs and competitiveness. They genuinely support the measure and most of the companies involve employees in the whole process. It is important for companies to take advantage of this common attitude as they work on digitalization.

**Safeguarding Well-Balanced External Relations.** Digital implementation calls for digital skills. Medium sized and smaller companies do often lack internal IT skill required for identifying and implementing digital technologies [16]. Organizing processes is often left with the option of using external consultants. Such solutions bring both pros and cons, but our study showed that a company easily can become too dependent on a single sub-contractor/supplier. A company's IT solutions require a high degree of trust in the relationship between customer and supplier. On one side, it is important for an IT provider to know the company well. On the other hand, such a customer-supplier relationship can develop into something unhealthy if the relationship leaves the customer in a lock-in position. The customer must use his/her position in an active manner which indicates that the customer - supplier relationship is of a positive nature. For industrial companies, it is important to secure healthy and well-balanced relations to external support when implementing new digital solutions. For instance, another company in the survey developed in-house a dashboard and decision-making system for production management, by help of an off the shelf Microsoft app. Earlier, the company would have contracted consultants for this type of development. However, their experience was that the process took too long and there was insufficient collaboration with their personnel during the process. Thereby the technology adoption was more cumbersome, and the development contributed to a much lesser extent to organizational learning and growth than during the in-house development. Nevertheless, the in-house development required a broad set of competences, that traditionally, many industrial companies did not have. The personnel needed to understand how to extract the necessary data, structure the data, analyze it, and ensure a user friendly and real-time presentation of the results on the dashboard.

**Valuing Internal IT Skills.** The SINTEF study also showed how important internal IT skills can be when digitalizing the industry. Employees with "above average" IT interest can make a huge difference in these processes. By actively searching for new IT solutions in their daily work, they can combine their personal IT interest with IT situations needed to be solved at work. Leaders who understand this potential organize for joining internal opportunities with company needs. Such processes often show the company what choices and opportunities that exist. Employees with IT skill knows company routines, products and internal affairs, and therefore they can also play the role of a bridge builder. For instance, at a tool producer in the survey the operators are allowed to program the machines that they use. To this end, the company created a forum for knowledge sharing and joint learning that included both senior operators and apprentices, and both older and young personnel. By seeing their digital competencies valued, the operators' motivation for their working place and for contributing to digital improvements increased even more. Thus, employees' own commitment and knowledge thirst increases the company's opportunities to capture new technology/opportunities.

**Recognizing Young Talent.** Another key element for a successful digital implementation is how the company organize their internal resources in general. Leaders need to understand what a digital transformation really is about. The SINTEF study showed some examples of processes that were suffering from insufficient digital maturity and understanding at management level. Leaders must enter these digital processes at an early stage and then follow up by taking an active and genuine part. Several companies in the survey stated a distinct awareness to join younger employees with leaders responsible for decision making, rather than sideline young talent – which is often a symptom of "Big Company Disease" [17]. A number of respondents reflected that the younger "digital native" generation often has a greater ease of understanding the opportunities and limitations of key enabling technologies, than the older and more "analog" generation, to which many of their leaders belonged. By actively including young employees in the project teams, companies can improve the outcomes of their digitization endeavor. Moreover, by organizing pre-projects, project groups, pilot projects, etc. companies ensured a higher degree of digital competence in digitalization projects. This shows that different forms of conscious diversity enhance the quality of a digitalization process.

**Building Cross-Functional Autonomous Teams.** Teamwork in the industrial production has been the way to organize production for a long time [18]. Analyzed data from the study show that operators still work in teams, but they work more autonomously due to the implementation of digital technologies. Relevant information has become more visual and accessible [19]. Due to this development, operators have gained the opportunity to see and understand a broader part of the value chain. Some of the companies also stated an awareness to organize teams in a cross-disciplinary manner. By doing so, they also created a unit more capable of thinking in an innovative way. This trait can be helpful since product development and improvement related work often is initiated at the shop floor.

**Promoting Learning in Action.** Operators and engineers work more closely when using digital solutions. They unite in digitized processes with digital tools in their common quest for improved practice. One of the companies located their engineers in the areas of manufacturing in order to safeguard a close relation between engineers and operators. Operators and engineers may have different ways of interpreting a problem, but by joining efforts, they are able to reach a higher level of understanding which again adds value to the product/process. This way of work organization was not common earlier when the work force was organized in traditional silos – a further symptom of "Big Company Disease" [17].

**Organizing for Flexibility.** A common mention for many of the companies in the study was their awareness to organize for change. Flexibility, therefore, stands out as a key feature for a successful digitalization. Quick responses, flexible solutions and an adjustable structure of organizing work has become essential for preventing loss of time and other resources [20]. The ability to continuously adapt to changing circumstances has become a key feature. Systems and processes need to solve contextual changes in order to perform optimally. The companies in the study organized their processes accordingly to safeguard these features.

## 5   Conclusion

There are numerous ways to derive great value from digitalization. Fostering internal collaboration through greater engagement of employees is one of them. This paper has highlighted seven organizational enablers for digitalization in a Norwegian industrial context. The findings are based on a cross-case analysis of data collected through 33 case studies of successful digitalization processes at Norwegian companies in a diverse set of industries. Collaboration between management and employees also emerged as a necessary success criterion for digitalization. Flatter and cooperation-oriented models are well suited to cope with the dynamic and demanding processes of digital transformation. Such an approach can prevent the loss of useful energy on resistance through building a joint taskforce promoting digitalization. The NM holds traits that give Norwegian companies a potential and valuable advantage that can be useful for industrial digitalization. Finding the best way to digitalization will vary from company to company depending on their competence, resources and digital maturity. Thus, our findings suggest that it makes sense to utilize both external and internal organizational possibilities. They may, together with digital technologies, boost the digital transition in search of more efficient industrial production.

In terms of limitations, we recognize that the Norwegian context specifically represents both the major strength and weakness of the study. This is because the NM appears to present us with an advantage for industrial digitalization. However, further work should test the seven enablers in other industrially developed countries.

**Acknowledgements.** The authors would like to thank to the SFI Manufacturing research program and to all 33 companies who took part in this SINTEF study. Their participation made a difference, and we strongly believe that dissemination and sharing of experiences from digital implementation processes generates useful knowledge for further development.

# References

1. Ashrafian, A., et al.: Sketching the landscape for lean digital transformation. In: Ameri, F., Stecke, K.E., von Cieminski, G., Kiritsis, D. (eds.) APMS 2019. IAICT, vol. 566, pp. 29–36. Springer, Cham (2019). https://doi.org/10.1007/978-3-030-30000-5_4
2. Romero, D., et al.: Towards an operator 4.0 typology: a human-centric perspective on the fourth industrial revolution technologies. In: Proceedings of the International Conference on Computers and Industrial Engineering (CIE46), Tianjin, China (2016)
3. Kotter, J.P.: Leading Change. Harvard Business Press, Brighton (1996)
4. Bergh, T.: Avtalt spill. Hovedavtalen 75 år. LO/NHO, Oslo (2010)
5. Huzzard, T., Gregory, D., Scott, R.: Strategic unionism and partnership: boxing or dancing? Book of Abstracts (2004)
6. Brettel, M., et al.: How virtualization, decentralization and network building change the manufacturing landscape: an industry 4.0 perspective. Int. J. Mech. Ind. Sci. Eng. **8**(1), 37–44 (2014)
7. Hofmann, E., Rüsch, M.: Industry 4.0 and the current status as well as future prospects on logistics. Comput. Ind. **89**, 23–34 (2017)
8. Powell, D., Romero, D., Gaiardelli, P., Cimini, C., Cavalieri, S.: Towards digital lean cyber-physical production systems: industry 4.0 technologies as enablers of leaner production. In: Moon, I., Lee, G.M., Park, J., Kiritsis, D., von Cieminski, G. (eds.) APMS 2018. IAICT, vol. 536, pp. 353–362. Springer, Cham (2018). https://doi.org/10.1007/978-3-319-99707-0_44
9. Industrien – grønnere, smartere og mer nyskapende. Det kongelige Nærings og Fiskeridepartementet (2016–2017)
10. Meredith, J.: Building operations management theory through case and field research. J. Oper. Manag. **16**, 441–454 (1998)
11. Karlsson, C.: Researching operations management. In: Researching Operations Management, pp. 20–55. Routledge (2010)
12. Eisenhardt, K.M.: Building theories from case study research. Acad. Manag. Rev. **14**(4), 532–550 (1989)

13. Holm, M.: The future shop-floor operators, demands, requirements and interpretations. J. Manuf. Syst. **47**, 35–42 (2018)
14. SINTEF: Lær av de beste - Hvordan skaffe seg konkurransekraft gjennom digitalisering. SINTEF (2020)
15. Stewart, P., et al.: We sell our time no more: workers' struggles against lean production in the British car industry. Pluto Press (2009)
16. Romero, D., Bernus, P., Noran, O., Stahre, J., Fast-Berglund, Å.: The operator 4.0: human cyber-physical systems & adaptive automation towards human-automation symbiosis work systems. In: Nääs, I., et al. (eds.) APMS 2016. IAICT, vol. 488, pp. 677–686. Springer, Cham (2016). https://doi.org/10.1007/978-3-319-51133-7_80
17. Ballé, M., et al.: The Lean Sensei. Lean Enterprise Institute (2019)
18. Van Dun, D.H., Wilderom, C.P.: Lean-team effectiveness through leader values and members' informing. Int. J. Oper. Prod. Manag. (2016)
19. Romero, D., Gaiardelli, P., Powell, D., Wuest, T., Thürer, M.: Digital lean cyber-physical production systems: the emergence of digital lean manufacturing and the significance of digital waste. In: Moon, I., Lee, G.M., Park, J., Kiritsis, D., von Cieminski, G. (eds.) APMS 2018. IAICT, vol. 535, pp. 11–20. Springer, Cham (2018). https://doi.org/10.1007/978-3-319-99704-9_2
20. Suri, R.: It's About Time: The Competitive Advantage of Quick Response Manufacturing. CRC Press, Boca Raton (2010)

# Concept of PLM Application Integration with VR and AR Techniques

Jan Duda[1(✉)] and Sylwester Oleszek[2]

[1] Politechnika Krakowska, al. Jana Pawła II, 31-866 Kraków, Polska
duda@mech.pk.edu.pl

[2] Transition Technologies PSC sp. z o.o., ul. Piotrkowska 276,
90-361 Łódź, Polska
sylwester.oleszek@gmail.com

**Abstract.** Nowadays, many industrial companies, including small and medium-sized ones, are adopting virtual manufacturing concepts to face global competition and major manufacturing challenges. The aim is to improve quality, shorten delivery time and reduce costs. However, most virtual manufacturing methodologies, tools and software are not integrated well enough to perform the required activities efficiently. Attention is usually focused on local and specific proficiency, thus jeopardising information exchange between departments, parallelism of work and communication along the product lifecycle. In these circumstances, the use of virtual production and digital representation of the production system and its processes becomes even more important to optimise production activities. Manufacturing industries are evolving towards digitisation, networking and globalisation. In the process of rapidly evolving information technology, digital tools and systems are being used in all industries, managing a variety of tasks throughout the product lifecycle with the use of PLM (Product Lifecycle Management) applications. PLM class systems integrate a set of applications supporting product development.

The paper presents the concept of the integration of PLM application with VR (Virtual Reality) and AR (Augmented Reality) techniques based on the example of the proprietary system integrating advanced PLM app with a mobile application in which AR technology has been implemented.

**Keywords:** Augmented reality · Virtual reality · Product lifecycle management

## 1 Introduction

VR is a medium composed of interactive computer simulations that determine the position and actions of the participant and replace or extend the feedback to one or more his senses, giving him a sense of immersion or mental presence in the simulation, that is, in the virtual world [11]. The key elements of the ability to experience virtual reality are: virtual world, immersion, sensory feedback on user actions and interactivity [11]. Virtual reality is also a scientific and technical field that uses IT tools and behavioural interfaces to simulate the behaviour of 3D objects in the virtual world so they can interact with each other in real time in pseudo-natural immersion through sensomotor channels.

B. Lalic et al. (Eds.): APMS 2020, IFIP AICT 592, pp. 91–99, 2020.
https://doi.org/10.1007/978-3-030-57997-5_11

Augmented reality, unlike virtual reality, includes techniques for adding virtual objects to the real world [8]. Augmented reality techniques are therefore defined as those which, in real time and in a three-dimensional environment, make it possible to connect the real world with the virtual one [1, 5]. In other words, the AR system is a system that connects the real world with a computer-generated world.

Virtual Manufacturing (VM) is a concept of planning production activities using virtual models and simulation tools instead of objects and their operations in the real world [6]. The way to implement this concept is a computer system that generates information about the structure, states and behaviour of the manufacturing system as observed in the natural production environment. In other words, the process of virtual production does not involve materials or physical products, but information about them. Virtual manufacturing can therefore be defined as an integrated computer model that represents the physical and logical scheme and behaviour of the actual manufacturing system [10]. Some scholars define virtual manufacturing in relation to virtual reality by describing this technology as a virtual world for manufacturing at the same time presenting virtual reality as a visualisation tool for virtual manufacturing. With this approach in mind, we can define VM as an application of integrated technologies of simulation, modelling and analysis with the use of models and virtual processes in a virtual reality environment. This integration makes it possible to identify potential problems before the actual production takes place. As a result, it is possible to improve the design of the production system, make decisions and control all stages of this process [2]. Thus, the general premise present in most definitions is that "Virtual production is nothing more than production on a computer".

The Virtual Factory (VF) paradigm is the basis for dealing with the problem of implementing methodologies to support the design of production systems, processes, simulation, production control, visualization and other.

The ideal implementation of a virtual factory should therefore include the creation of a comprehensive, integral, upgradeable and scalable representation of the actual factory. It should provide a virtual representation of buildings, resources, processes and products. The entire factory should be simulated as a continuous and coherent digital model that can be used throughout the entire product lifecycle - from the product idea to the final disassembly of production plants and buildings [4].

## 2   Interactive Product Development Cycles

A modern company has to cope with the co-evolution of products, processes and production systems through strategic and operational management, promotion of engineering changes depending on market requirements and the dynamics of legislative changes. The essence of these changes is to manage the implementation of development phases based on a common model of product, process and resource data (Product, Process, Resource). Figure 1.

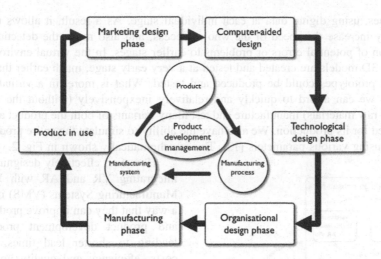

**Fig. 1.** Management of development phases based on a common model of product, process and resource data

One way to implement the idea of a virtual factory is to use PLM class systems. They integrate a set of applications supporting product development which include [3]:

- Product and Portfolio Management (PPM),
- Computer-aided technologies (CAx),
- Manufacturing Process Management (MPM),
- Product Data Management (PDM).

Although these systems provide support for most areas related to the planning and design phases, and effectively support product data management and process virtualization, they do not provide certain functionalities relevant to business needs, especially in the area of interoperability [14–16]. As a result, the whole process of virtual factory realisation cannot be carried out with the use of PLM systems in a continuous and coherent way. This is particularly visible in the lack of integration between technologies and data model used in the product design and the production systems design phases [7].

One of the important features of the product development process is concurrency. The essence of this process is the implementation of product development phases and the possibility of evaluating possible product, process and system variants in the context of the implementation of subsequent development phases. The achievement of this postulate has been made possible by separating the conceptual and detailed design stages in subsequent development stages [3]. The assessment of the obtained design solutions, apart from the application of simulation programs, may be supported by the application of VR and AR virtual manufacturing techniques. Assuming that the product development process consists of subsequent stages, where the quality of each stage depends directly on the quality of data from the previous one, the above mentioned approach allows the performance of interactive design cycles using CAx (Comuter Aided x) systems and then testing using DFx (Design for x) systems, AR and VR techniques, using digital data at each individual stage. As a result, it allows to significantly increase the speed of the whole process, and also move the detection and resolution of potential errors or problems to earlier stages. In the virtual environment process, 3D models are created and tested at a very early stage, much earlier than any physical prototypes could be produced and tested. What is more, in a virtual environment we can afford to quickly and relatively inexpensively (without the use of physical raw materials) manufacture and test many variants of both the product and the tools used for its production. We also have the ability to simulate the entire production process using various parameters [13]. This is schematically shown in Fig. 2.

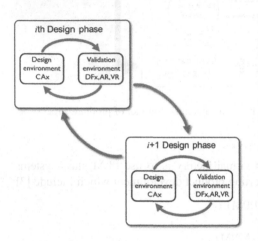

**Fig. 2.** Interactive product development cycles

However, effectively designing and integrating VR and AR with Virtual Manufacturing Systems (VMS) in such a way that they can improve production and product development processes, leading to shorter lead times, lower costs, efficiency and quality improvement along with a clean and eco-friendly process, is a major challenge. One of the biggest difficulties to overcome is the absence of system and data interoperability, i.e. the lack of consistency in data transfer between systems (in case of many software-integrated system platforms) or between system modules performing different tasks (in case of e.g. PLM systems).

## 3    PLM System Architecture Integrated with the Service Performing Tasks Related to VR and AR Technologies

Modern PLM systems operate according to the client-server model, and communication between system clients (the client can be a web browser, another system or system component), and the system is based on HTTP protocol, i.e. in request-response mode. Thus, it is possible to propose a generalised PLM system architecture integrated with modules performing tasks related to VR or AR technologies.

The architectural pattern of WWW application for client-server system in the most general sense assumes organizing the whole system into three layers: database, processing (business) and presentation (client) [12]. At the level of the processing layer, where PLM system services realizing business logic are located, an application performing tasks related to the preparation of data for use in VR or AR environments may be integrated. These tasks may include e.g. conversion of 3D data from native engineering formats (.prt,.CATPart,.sldprt, etc.) to a neutral or lightweight format, which enables easier transfer via HTTP protocol and easier display in mobile multimedia applications. They can also be more complex tasks, i.e. processing and preparing 3D models in such a way that they can be used directly in client applications, e.g. in mobile applications or augmented or virtual reality glasses.

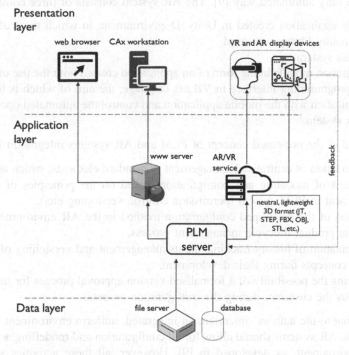

**Fig. 3.** Generalised architecture of the PLM system integrated with the service performing tasks related to VR and AR technologies

Response information from the client application, e.g. in the form of metadata, can be sent directly to the PLM system business layer - for further processing - via communication protocol requests. A proposal of a generalized PLM system architecture integrated with the service performing tasks related to VR and AR technologies is presented in Fig. 3.

## 4 The Proposal of the Procedure for Technical Implementation of PLM System Integration with VR and AR Techniques

This chapter presents the concept of the procedure for the technical implementation of the integration of the PLM commercial system with the proprietary AR system, where the integration of an advanced CAx class system with a mobile application - in which the AR technology has been applied - was accomplished. This solution enables 3D modeling activities (based on techniques adopted from product configurators) directly in AR environment. Simultaneously, in the CAx system, a parametric 3D model is created in a fully automated way [9]. The AR system consists of three components:

1. A mobile application created in Unity3D environment, in which the Vuforia augmented reality library was used,
2. CAx class system,
3. An integration module in the form of an application created with the use of the CAx system programming interface in VB.net language, the aim of which is to provide communication with the mobile application and control the automated operations of the CAx system.

The goal of the presented concept of PLM and AR systems integration is:

- implementation of centralised management of standard elements, which are used in the process of modeling and configuration, based on the principles of standards management in PLM system (permission control, versioning etc.),
- integration of the developed configuration method in the AR environment with a consistent product lifecycle management process,
- implementation of history tracking, status management and versioning of modeled product concepts during their development,
- introducing the possibility of a formalised version approval process for the product created by the customer during the configuration process.

According to the authors' intention, an integrated, uniform environment including the PLM and AR systems should allow for all configuration and modelling activities in the AR environment, as developed in [9]. However, all these activities should be performed within a PLM environment. To enable this, it is necessary to automate operations such as:

- establishing a connection between the AR and the PLM systems,
- loading elements used in the configuration process from the PLM system standard library,
- saving the 3D model developed in the process of configuration to the development container of the PLM system,
- management of the lifecycle state of the 3D model developed in the configuration process,
- end of session and logout from PLM system.

In order to implement the above mentioned actions, the following steps are necessary:

- developing a method of automatic login into the PLM system using credentials (login and password),

- creating a standard library of elements used in the configuration process in the PLM system and modifying the AR system to enable loading these elements directly from the created library,
- developing a method of automatic saving the 3D model developed in the process of configuration directly to the development container of the PLM system,
- developing a method to automatically change the state of the 3D model lifecycle developed during the configuration process (this will also enable version management).

The diagram in the BPMN notation of the product configuration process in the AR system with integrated PLM system is shown in Fig. 4.

## 5  Summary

This paper presents practical definitions of virtual and augmented reality, virtual manufacturing and virtual factory. The authors highlighted that one of the possible, although not perfect, implementations of the virtual factory paradigm is using modern PLM systems. In these systems, AR and VR technologies can be implemented in the presentation layer level. However, this requires the development and integration of additional services with the PLM system, the purpose of which is to carry out tasks related to data conversion and processing in a specific way (depending on the technology and purpose), so that they can be displayed in AR or VR devices.

The paper also proposes a concept of PLM system integration with VR and AR techniques based on generalised PLM system architecture. This concept is based on the assumption that at the level of processing layer integrated with PLM system there is a software service, by means of which tasks related to VR and AR technologies are performed.

The last part of the paper presents the proposal of the procedure of technical realization of integration based on the example of a commercial PLM and a multi-module proprietary AR systems. The aim and benefits of obtaining a uniform PLM and AR environment have been defined and additional functionalities that are possible to achieve (e.g. version control, status management, management of elements used in the configuration process based on the principles of the standards library in the PLM system) have been highlighted. This part of the paper also presents actions that need to be performed in order to create a prototype version of the integration.

The authors intend to continue their work in order to implement the concept mentioned and also to examine the functionality and practical usefulness of such a solution.

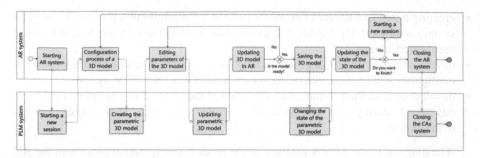

**Fig. 4.** Diagram of the product configuration process in the AR system integrated with the PLM system

# References

1. Barfield, W.: Fundamentals of Wearable Computers and Augmented Reality, 2nd edn. CRC Press, Boca Raton (2015)
2. Bharath, V.G., Rajashekar, P.: Virtual manufacturing: a review. Int. J. Eng. Res. Technol. (IJERT) (2015). NCERAME-2015 Conference Proceedings
3. Duda, J.: Zarządzanie rozwojem wyrobów w ujęciu systemowym. Cracow University of Technology (2016)
4. Ghielmini, G.: Virtual factory manager for semantic data handling. CIRP J. Manuf. Sci. Technol. **6**, 281–291 (2013). https://doi.org/10.1016/j.cirpj.2013.08.001
5. Januszka, M.: Metoda wspomagania procesu projektowania i konstruowania z zastosowaniem poszerzonej rzeczywistości. Ph.D. thesis, Silesian University of Technology, Gliwice (2012)
6. Keyvani, A., Danielsson, F.: A virtual manufacturing approach for integrating fixture design with process planning. In: Huang, G.Q., Mak, K.L., Maropoulos, P.G. (eds.) Proceedings of the 6th CIRP-Sponsored International Conference on Digital Enterprise Technology. Advances in Intelligent and Soft Computing, vol. 66, pp. 483–496. Springer, Berlin (2010). https://doi.org/10.1007/978-3-642-10430-5_37
7. Lafleur, M., Terkaj, W., Belkadi, F., Urgo, M., Bernard, A., Colledani, M.: An Onto-Based Interoperability Framework for the Connection of PLM and Production Capability Tools, pp. 134–145 (2016). https://doi.org/10.1007/978-3-319-54660-5-13
8. Mann, S.: Intelligent image processing. Adaptive and learning systems for signal processing, communications, and control. IEEE, New York (2002)
9. Oleszek, S.: Metoda wspomagania projektowania naczyń szklanych z zastosowaniem konfiguratora w środowisku poszerzonej rzeczywistości. Ph.D. thesis, Silesian University of Technology, Gliwice (2018)
10. Sharma, P.: Concept of virtual manufacturing. GRD J. – Glob. Res. Dev. J. Eng. **2**(6), 285–292 (2017)
11. Sherman, W.R., Craig, A.: Understanding Virtual Reality: Interface, Application, and Design. The Morgan Kaufmann Series in Computer Graphics, San Francisco (2002)
12. Sienkiewicz, J.E., Syty, P.: Architektura warstwowa aplikacji internetowych. Oblicza Internetu. Conference Proceedings, PWSZ, Elbląg (2008)
13. Souza, M., Sacco, M., Porto, V.: Virtual manufacturing as a way for the factory of the future. J. Intell. Manuf. **17**, 725–735 (2006). https://doi.org/10.1007/s10845-006-0041-1

14. Terkaj, W., Pedrielli, G., Sacco, M.: Virtual factory data model. In: CEUR Workshop Proceedings, vol. 886, pp. 29–43 (2012)
15. Tolio, T., et al.: SPECIES - co-evolution of products, processes and production systems. CIRP Ann. – Manuf. Technol. 59(2), 672–693 (2010). https://doi.org/10.1016/j.cirp.2010.05.008
16. Tolio, T., Sacco, M., Terkaj, W., Urgo, M.: Virtual factory: an integrated framework for manufacturing systems design and analysis. In: Forty Sixth CIRP Conference on Manufacturing Systems (2013)

# The Big Potential of Big Data in Manufacturing: Evidence from Emerging Economies

Marko Pavlović[⊠], Uglješa Marjanović, Slavko Rakić,
Nemanja Tasić, and Bojan Lalić

Faculty of Technical Sciences, University of Novi Sad, Novi Sad, Serbia
{m.pavlovic, umarjano, slavkorakic, nemanja.tasic,
blalic}@uns.ac.rs

**Abstract.** In the last years, the manufacturing sector of developed economies is going through extensive changes to adopt Industry 4.0 principles. Prior studies investigated key enabling technologies for Industry 4.0 and their applications focusing on developed economies. However, there is a lack of studies covering emerging economies (e.g., Serbia). This research provides an overview of the use of technologies for automatic storing of operational data and the exchange of operational data between different entities from the manufacturing sector. For this purpose, the Serbian dataset of 240 companies from the European Manufacturing Survey gathered in 2018 is used. The empirical results indicate that 43% of manufacturing companies are utilizing the systems that automatically record operational data, 88.3% of manufacturing companies are creating an immense amount of data through ERP systems, and 78.6% of companies are using a digital exchange with suppliers or customers. The results reveal the big potential for the Big Data in the manufacturing sector in emerging economies.

**Keywords:** Industry 4.0 · Big Data · Manufacturing

## 1 Introduction

The transformation of manufacturing systems characterizes Forth-Industrial Revolution or Industry 4.0 through deeper digitalization [1]. The concept of Industry 4.0 was first declared as a German strategic initiative in 2013 [1]. Industry 4.0 is enabled through the use of technologies like Cyber-Physical Systems (CPS), Internet of Things (IoT), Cloud Computing, Big Data, and Data Science [2]. Prior studies investigated key enabling technologies for Industry 4.0 and their applications focusing on developed economies. However, there is a lack of studies covering emerging economies (e.g., Serbia). In this paper, the analysis will be conducted on how many companies from the manufacturing sector of the Republic of Serbia automatically record data from their production and examine the potential for the use of Big Data in the manufacturing sector of the Republic of Serbia. Moreover, we investigate which systems are used to record data automatically and in which manufacturing sectors. Our analysis used the Serbian dataset from the European Manufacturing Survey (EMS) conducted in 2018.

© IFIP International Federation for Information Processing 2020
Published by Springer Nature Switzerland AG 2020
B. Lalic et al. (Eds.): APMS 2020, IFIP AICT 592, pp. 100–107, 2020.
https://doi.org/10.1007/978-3-030-57997-5_12

The remainder of the paper is structured as follows. A literature review is presented in Sect. 2. Section 3 describes the research questions and method that has been used in this paper, Sect. 4 presents the research results and discussion, and Sect. 5 presents the conclusion of this paper with identified limitations of the study and suggestions for further research.

## 2 Literature Review

One of the turning points of human history is the emergence of the First-Industrial Revolution, which dramatically changed human production. The use of water and steam powers introduced mechanized industry systems in the manufacturing sector. Second-Industrial Revolution introduced the use of electrical energy in manufacturing that paved the path to mass production. Third-Industrial Revolution saw further automation in manufacturing through increased use and development of informational technologies. For the implementation of Industry 4.0 in their operation, companies can use various novel technologies that include CPS, automated robotics, Big Data analytics, and cloud computing, etc. [3]. Developed countries formed government strategies, which included Industry 4.0 as guiding principles. Germany created "High Tech Strategy 2020" and "Industry 4.0" [1], the United States "Advanced Manufacturing Partnership" [4], China "Made in China 2025" [5], and the United Kingdom "The Future of Manufacturing: A New Era of Opportunity and Challenge for the U.K." [6]. Prior studies investigated key enabling technologies for Industry 4.0 and their applications focusing on developed economies [7]. However, there is a lack of studies covering emerging economies (e.g., Serbia). In this paper, we will focus on the connection between CPS, IoT, Big Data, and Data Science regarding Industry 4.0, specifically the manufacturing sector. To respond to constant pressure from the competitors and to improve total production performance, companies in the manufacturing industry are integrating new solutions [8]. CPS presents one of the essential pillars of Industry 4.0 implementation [9]. CPS is defined as processing technologies with the high interconnection between physical assets and computational tools [10]. CPS provides integration of objects from the virtual world with artifacts from the physical world through embedded computing technologies [11]. Regarding manufacturing, every component of CPS will be capable to sense environment, itself and to collect and transmit data and consequently take actions that will be constructed through input from the acquired information [12]. Likewise, one of the critical pillars of industry 4.0 is IoT. IoT will completely change current ways of manufacturing and set-up a path to advanced manufacturing [13], and manufacture will progress from automated to intelligent manufacturing [14]. IoT is defined as a network of interconnected devices, systems, and services through Internet infrastructure. IoT enables mutual communication between connected devices, systems, services and objects and provides deeper integration and joint relations among the virtual and physical world [15]. Implementation of IoT in production will inevitably be followed by the creation of massive amounts of data from manufacturing processes and the stacking of data from various devices will create Big Data [16]. Prediction from Cisco and Ericsson is that by 2020 there will be 50 billion devices connected to the internet and Machine Research predicted that the total number of M2M connections would grow from 5 billion in 2014 to 27 billion in 2024 [17]. There can be found a lot of various predictions about the number of connected devices in the future. Still, all of the projections are united in the conclusion that the number will grow substantially. Big Data is defined as dynamic information that is generated in complex systems that is characterized by three V's, by volume represented in enormous amount of the acquired data, by velocity represented in pace of data processing and by variety represented in data coming from highly diverse sources [18]. Permanent acquiring, storing and exchanging of data from different devices from miscellaneous sources and systems will form Big Data. The manufacturing sector generates and stores a larger amount of data than any other sector [19]. Only one particular device, from production, could generate thousands of records within a second, which would amount to several trillion records in a year. Beside large amount of data that is generated from the companies internally, also horizontal integration through value networks that includes processes and data flows between customers, suppliers and various external partners, will produce enormous quantities of data [1, 20, 21]. Trough processing and analysis of data provided by the implementation and use of IoT in the manufacturing sector, valuable information can be extracted that could provide useful knowledge to companies to face the business challenges and to recognize opportunities and form competitive advantages [22]. Gaining insight from data is achieved through the use of artificial intelligence technologies, like Data Science, Data Mining, and Machine Learning [23]. Using Data Mining or Machine Learning algorithms to analyze and study collected data can significantly improve the efficiency of companies' operations in a very efficient manner [24]. In the manufacturing sector Data Science can facilitate better production rates, supply chain innovations, reduction in malfunction rates, improved decision making, development of new business models, etc. [25, 26].

## 3   Research Questions and Method

Based on the literature review, the following research questions were proposed to increase the available knowledge about the potential for the use of Big Data in the manufacturing sector in developing countries:

- **RQ1:** What is the utilization of the systems that automatically record operational data in the manufacturing sectors of an emerging economy?
- **RQ2:** Which systems for automatic recording of operational data are used and which are the most common?
- **RQ3:** Is it and to what extent Electronic Data Interchange between manufacturers, suppliers, and customers is represented?

Our analysis used the Serbian dataset from the European Manufacturing Survey (EMS) conducted in 2018. EMS investigates technological and non-technological innovation in the European manufacturing sector [27]. The survey is carried out on a triennial basis and targets a random sample of manufacturing companies with more than 20 employees (NACE Rev 2 codes from 10 to 33). The dataset includes 240 companies. Concerning descriptive statistics, the sampled companies report, on average, a company size of 124 employees (SD = 207). In total, 110 companies are small firms (fewer than 50 employees), 103 companies are medium-sized (between 50 and 249 employees), and 27 companies are large enterprises (more than 250 employees).

## 4    Research Results and Discussion

This section presents the results of the research and discusses the results. The presentation of results follows the order of the research questions introduced in the previous section.

### 4.1    Automatically Recording Operating Data

To provide the answer on RQ1 (i.e., What is the utilization of the systems that automatically record operational data in the manufacturing sectors of an emerging economy), we used the data gathered through the following question:

*Do you use machines or systems in your production that automatically store operating data?*

We found that a large number of manufacturing companies (103 or 43%) already in their operations use systems that automatically record operational data.

Table 1 depicts an overview of companies that automatically record operating data by manufacturing industries. Most of the companies are manufacturers of fabricated metal products, except machinery and equipment, manufacturers of rubber and plastic products and manufacturers of food products.

**Table 1.** Companies automatically recoding data by industries

| NACE | Manufacturing industry | Nb. of companies | % of companies |
|------|------------------------|------------------|----------------|
| 25 | Fabricated metal products, except machinery and equipment | 21 | 20.1 |
| 22 | Rubber and plastic products | 15 | 14.6 |
| 10 | Food products | 15 | 14.6 |
| 28 | Machinery and equipment | 7 | 6.8 |

Since the largest number of the all companies that were included in the survey are NACE 10, 22, 25 and 28, it is logical that most companies which already automatically record data are coming from specified manufacturing sectors. No significant deviations have been established by manufacturing sectors.

## 4.2    Technologies Used for Automatic Storage of Operational Data

To provide the answer on RQ2 (i.e., Which systems for automatic recording of operational data are used and which are the most common), we used the data gathered through the following questions:

*Which of the following technologies are currently used in your factory?*

- *Software for production planning and scheduling (e.g., ERP system)*
- *Near real-time production control system (e.g., Systems of centralized operating and machine data acquisition, MES – Manufacturing Execution System)*
- *Systems for automation and management of internal logistics (e.g., Ware-house management systems, RFID)*
- *Product-Lifecycle-Management    Systems    (PLM)    or    Product/Process    Data Management*
- *Which of the specified technologies do you plan to use by 2021?*

The results in Table 2 show that most of the companies use ERP and MES systems. Also, we can see that a certain number of companies plan to implement and use specified systems in their production by the year 2021.

**Table 2.** Technologies used/planned to be used for automatic data storage

|       | Companies using 2018 [%] | Planned use by 2021 |
|-------|--------------------------|---------------------|
| ERP   | 91 [88.3]                | 24                  |
| MES   | 66 [64.0]                | 32                  |
| WMS   | 38 [36.9]                | 33                  |
| PLM   | 29 [28.2]                | 23                  |

Results are in line with the findings from studies covering developed countries, in which most common systems used are ERP and MES [28]. So, there is no deviation regarding systems used for automatic data storage. Thus, already in the manufacturing sector of the Republic of Serbia, we have a lot of operational data recorded and stored through various specified systems. Also, we can conclude that the number of companies that automatically store operational data will rise in the future.

## 4.3    Electronic Data Interchange

To provide the answer on RQ3 (i.e., Is it and to what extent Electronic Data Interchange between manufacturers, suppliers, and customers is represented), we used the data gathered through the following questions:

*Do you use digital exchange of product/process data with suppliers/customers (Electronic Data Interchange – EDI)?*
*Do you plan to use digital exchange of product/process data with suppliers/customers (Electronic Data Interchange – EDI) by the year 2021?*

The results in Table 3 show that 81 companies use EDI, and 21 companies plan to implement EDI by the year 2021.

**Table 3.** Overview of companies using/planning to use EDI

| Technology | Companies using EDI 2018 [%] | Planned use EDI by 2021 |
|---|---|---|
| EDI | 81 [78.6] | 24 |

The substantial number of companies exchange their data with other companies, suppliers, and customers, thus creating additional quantities of different operational data across the manufacturing sector of the Republic of Serbia. These results indicate the existence of a reasonable basis for the use of Data Science, Data Mining, and Machine Learning to extract hidden knowledge from Big Data.

## 5 Conclusion

This paper focuses on determining the potential for the use of Big Data in the manufacturing sector of the Republic of Serbia. The empirical results indicate that 43% of manufacturing companies are utilizing the systems that automatically record operational data. Our results show that 88.3% of manufacturing companies are creating an immense amount of data through ERP systems. Moreover, 78.6% of companies are using a digital exchange of product/process data with suppliers/customers. These findings indicate actionable insights for managers of manufacturing firms to expand their understanding of how to use various systems to collect data and provide a proper application for the use of Big Data analysis. Furthermore, there are significant quantities of operational data that are recorded and stored, which represents an appropriate basis for the use of Big Data in the manufacturing sector in emerging economies.

Through this research, we have shown that companies from emerging economies, to some extent, already use technologies for automatic recording of operational data. We have shown that a certain number of companies, from the manufacturing sectors, exchange operational data with suppliers and customers. Moreover we have determined that part of the companies also plan to implement technologies that automatically record operational data and to exchange data with other entities. Furthermore, this research contributes to the existing literature by showing the potential for the creation of Big Data and the possibilities for further use in emerging economies.

This research is limited to the dataset from the manufacturing sector of the single country. There are other emerging economies and companies from their manufacturing sector that could be included in future research. Also, future research could include the potential for the use of Big Data covered through different manufacturing sectors, company sizes, regions, etc.

# References

1. Kagermann, H., Wahlster, W., Helbig, J.: Securing the future of German manufacturing industry: recommendations for implementing the strategic initiative INDUSTRIE 4.0. Final Report of the Industrie 4.0 Working Group (2013)
2. Hermann, M., Pentek, T., Otto, B.: Design principles for industrie 4.0 scenarios. In: Proceedings of the Annual Hawaii International Conference on System Sciences (2016). https://doi.org/10.1109/hicss.2016.488
3. Fedorov, A., Goloschchapov, E., Ipatov, O., Potekhin, V., Shkodyrev, V., Zobnin, S.: Aspects of smart manufacturing via agent-based approach. Procedia Eng. (2015). https://doi.org/10.1016/j.proeng.2015.01.530
4. Steering Committee of the Advanced Manufacturing Partnership 2.0, "Accelerating U.S. Advanced Manufacturing." Report to President on Accelerating U.S. Advanced Manufacturing (2014). https://doi.org/10.1111/j.0033-0124.1964.033_g.x
5. The State Council, "Made in China 2025' plan issued," People's Republic China (2015). https://doi.org/10.2332/allergolint.r-07-146
6. Department for Trade and Industry, "Future of manufacturing: a new era of opportunity and challenge for the UK - summary report - GOV.UK," [Online] Gov.uk (2013)
7. Oesterreich, T.D., Teuteberg, F.: Understanding the implications of digitisation and automation in the context of Industry 4.0: a triangulation approach and elements of a research agenda for the construction industry. Comput. Ind. (2016). https://doi.org/10.1016/j.compind.2016.09.006
8. Zhao, H., McLoughlin, L., Adzhiev, V., Pasko, A.: "Why do we not buy mass customized products?"- An investigation of consumer purchase intention of mass customized products. Int. J. Ind. Eng. Manag. (2019). https://doi.org/10.24867/IJIEM-2019-2-238
9. Lu, Y.: Industry 4.0: a survey on technologies, applications and open research issues. J. Ind. Inf. Integr. (2017). https://doi.org/10.1016/j.jii.2017.04.005
10. Baheti, R., Gill, H.: Cyber-Physical Systems: From Theory to Practice (2011)
11. Gunes, V., Peter, S., Givargis, T., Vahid, F.: A survey on concepts, applications, and challenges in cyber-physical systems. KSII Trans. Internet Inf. Syst. (2014). https://doi.org/10.3837/tiis.2014.12.001
12. Dassisti, M., et al.: Industry 4.0 paradigm: The viewpoint of the small and medium enterprises. In: International Conference on Information Society and Technology, ICIST 2017 (2017)
13. Trappey, A.J.C., Trappey, C.V., Hareesh Govindarajan, U., Chuang, A.C., Sun, J.J.: A review of essential standards and patent landscapes for the Internet of Things: a key enabler for Industry 4.0. Advanced Engineering Informatics (2017). https://doi.org/10.1016/j.aei.2016.11.007
14. Weber, M., Chatzopoulos, C.G.: Digital customer experience: the risk of ignoring the non-digital experience. Int. J. Ind. Eng. Manag. (2019). https://doi.org/10.24867/IJIEM-2019-3-240
15. Lalic, B., Marjanovic, U., Rakic, S., Pavlovic, M., Todorovic, T., Medic, N.: Big data analysis as a digital service: evidence form manufacturing firms. In: Wang, L., Majstorovic, V.D., Mourtzis, D., Carpanzano, E., Moroni, G., Galantucci, L.M. (eds.) Proceedings of 5th International Conference on the Industry 4.0 Model for Advanced Manufacturing. LNME, pp. 263–269. Springer, Cham (2020). https://doi.org/10.1007/978-3-030-46212-3_19
16. Zhong, R.Y., Xu, X., Klotz, E., Newman, S.T.: Intelligent manufacturing in the context of industry 4.0: a review. Engineering (2017). https://doi.org/10.1016/j.eng.2017.05.015

17. Maple, C.: Security and privacy in the internet of things. J. Cyber Policy (2017). https://doi.org/10.1080/23738871.2017.1366536
18. Laney, D.: 3D Data Management: Controlling Data Volume, Velocity, and Variety. Appl. Deliv. Strateg. (2001). https://doi.org/10.1016/j.infsof.2008.09.005
19. Chen, Y., Chen, H., Gorkhali, A., Lu, Y., Ma, Y., Li, L.: Big data analytics and big data science: a survey. J. Manag. Anal. (2016). https://doi.org/10.1080/23270012.2016.1141332
20. Guido, V.S.R., Mirabelli, G., Palermo, E.: A framework for food traceability: case study – Italian extra-virgin olive oil supply chain. Int. J. Ind. Eng. Manag. 11(1), 50–60 (2020)
21. Medić, N., Anišić, Z., Lalić, B., Marjanović, U., Brezocnik, M.: Hybrid fuzzy multi-attribute decision making model for evaluation of advanced digital technologies in manufacturing: Industry 4.0 perspective. Adv. Prod. Eng. Manag. (2019). https://doi.org/10.14743/apem2019.4.343
22. Chong, D., Shi, H.: Big data analytics: a literature review. J. Manag. Anal. (2015). https://doi.org/10.1080/23270012.2015.1082449
23. Siryani, J., Tanju, B., Eveleigh, T.J.: A machine learning decision-support system improves the internet of things' smart meter operations. IEEE Internet Things J. (2017). https://doi.org/10.1109/JIOT.2017.2722358
24. Wang, X.V., Wang, L., Mohammed, A., Givehchi, M.: Ubiquitous manufacturing system based on cloud: a robotics application. Robot. Comput. Integr. Manuf. (2017). https://doi.org/10.1016/j.rcim.2016.01.007
25. Manyika, J., et al.: Big data: The next frontier for innovation, competition and productivity. McKinsey Global Institute (2011)
26. Da Xu, L., Duan, L.: Big data for cyber physical systems in industry 4.0: a survey. Enterp. Inf. Syst. (2019). https://doi.org/10.1080/17517575.2018.1442934
27. Lalic, B., Rakic, S., Marjanovic, U.: Use of industry 4.0 and organisational innovation concepts in the Serbian textile and apparel industry. Fibres Text. East. Eur. (2019). https://doi.org/10.5604/01.3001.0013.0737
28. Niebel, T., Rasel, F., Viete, S.: BIG data–BIG gains? Understanding the link between big data analytics and innovation. Econ. Innov. New Technol. (2019). https://doi.org/10.1080/10438599.2018.1493075

# A Conceptual Model for Deploying Digitalization in SMEs Through Capability Building

Zuhara Chavez[✉], Jannicke Baalsrud Hauge, and Monica Bellgran

KTH Royal Institute of Technology, Kvarnbergagatan 12,
151 36 Södertälje, Sweden
zuhar@kth.se

**Abstract.** This paper proposes a conceptual implementation model for small and medium enterprises (SMEs) to follow as part of their digitalization implementation. It can later be translated into a practical step by step guide for SMEs to practice during their digital transformation. The model is based on gradually developing industrial capabilities that can influence production processes performance. The model development was based on a critical literature review and a real case industry application. The case data served as direct feedback to the model to assess both the model validity and the actual SMEs needs. The capabilities included in the model are proved to directly influence the performance positively. In comparison with existing models and frameworks, this model envisions the company a full digital shift by proposing an achievable sequence which SMEs in a resource-efficient way could start deploying in compliance with their business needs. SMEs can utilize the capabilities as a foundation for a system that supports continuous improvement in the whole factory.

**Keywords:** Sustainable production · Managerial capabilities · Digital transformation · SME · Manufacturing industry

## 1 Introduction

The Industry 4.0 (I4.0) concept is based on the emergence of new technologies so that business process and engineering process are deeply integrated enabling production to operate in a flexible, efficient, and green way with high quality at low cost [1, 2]. Such technologies should improve the transmission of information throughout the entire system, and thereby enable better control and operations to be adapted in real-time according to varying demand [3]. The concept is being widely spread around the world, given the trust that incorporating emerging technical advancement can improve the industry's ability to deal with global challenges [1]. However, the SME perspective has not sufficiently been taken into account in terms of framing the appropriate I4.0 policies [4] even though they form the backbone of the European Economy.

The terminology and the so-called nine elements i.e. "foundational technology advances" [5] connected to I4.0 are defined conceptually and treated as single elements both in research and in application [6–9]. However, the reality of SMEs positioning in

© IFIP International Federation for Information Processing 2020
Published by Springer Nature Switzerland AG 2020
B. Lalic et al. (Eds.): APMS 2020, IFIP AICT 592, pp. 108–116, 2020.
https://doi.org/10.1007/978-3-030-57997-5_13

such a context is not clearly defined. I4.0 projects in SMEs often remain cost-driven initiatives and there is still no evidence of real business model transformation at this time [3]. The practical cases of deployment found in research are often centered around showing single applications, highlighting the low-cost factor as a main advantage and strength of their application [2, 10–15].

One major challenge faced by the implementation of the I4.0 concept is the robustness and resilience of the manufacturing production system, that is, the ability to absorb manufacturing disruptions without failing or breaking and to adapt to major variations/disturbances and gradually return to its original level of performance [16, 17]. New technologies enable an entirely new set of capabilities, which according to [18] can be grouped into four areas: monitoring, control, optimization, and autonomy. There is a close relation between these capabilities and the technologies or technical resources available in order to achieve the performance targets. Given the defined four capabilities, little is said about how can SMEs develop each one of them to achieve "self-awareness and autonomy" and how they can connect to production performance.

SMEs might struggle to adapt to external market forces and to make the next step in expanding their business due to a lack of expertise and resources [9]. Therefore, it is necessary to embrace a well assessed and affordable path for the adoption of new technologies that allow them to develop the needed managerial capabilities and create the ability to better handle deviations in their production system. In order to contribute to knowledge building within the area, this paper focuses on a main research question: *How can SMEs conduct a digital transformation that supports and aligns with deviation handling for production system performance improvement?* The results will be demonstrated by a model that connects the mentioned elements and depicts the digitalization deployment for SME; which to the best of our knowledge is lacking.

## 2 Theoretical Background

### 2.1 Managerial Capabilities of Production Processes

Acknowledging the technical, managerial and operational aspects of digitalization will make SMEs more aware of their own organizational dimensions like finance, product, process, and people. This awareness will result in informed decision making [19], which leads to more accurate judgments and results in close coordination with production plans, operations and supply chains. New technologies are designed to support processes such as data collection, integration, storage, analysis and visualization [20] and they can be deployable in a variety of industries. However, those technologies can generally not be adopted independently, and they require management involvement and support to succeed. It is also important to understand the circumstances of technologies being adopted, the extend of the technology adoption i.e. incremental or radical [19, 21], as well as the system, process or the activity that needs to be improved by technologies. SMEs, in particular, may not always be aware of the understanding and capabilities required from management to implement such technologies.

In a model [3] connect [18] managerial capabilities with the concept of I4.0 (as means of implementation) their analytical model stated the importance of classifying

I4.0 elements in terms of the desired performance objective and the corresponding managerial capacity that needs in place. It shows a close relationship between the targeted objectives, the levels of managerial capacity pursued and the technical resources required to achieve them.

## 2.2   Disturbance Handling as Part of the Industry 4.0 Paradigm

The ability to absorb manufacturing disruptions and to adapt is a crucial characteristic to achieve with the support of the I4.0 concept and elements implementations. According to [16, 22] robustness and resilience do not necessarily co-exist, but both provide production systems with a sustainable competitive advantage. When trying to connect disturbances and deviations to I4.0, the terms are assessed in works that address resilience and robustness [16, 23, 24], with focus on a) analyzing the variation and its adjustability, b) analyzing variation in terms of disturbances propagation and their effects and that leads to c) concentrating on the characteristics necessary to build resilience.

Research highlights the principle of adjustability as one of the aspects that comply with I4.0 demands when focusing on proactive communication [23]. The deviation is mentioned only as variation in the physical product specification related to quality and design. On their work [16] studies the propagation of disturbances, making a clear distinction between resilience and robust system and highlights the objective of systems for I4.0, which are intended to be robust i.e. have the ability to absorb disruptions without failing or breaking and resilient i.e. have the ability to adapt to major disturbances and gradually return to its original level of performance. According to [24], six characteristics are necessary to achieve resilience in I4.0: flexibility, diversity, connectivity, knowledge, redundancy, and robustness. Resilience is highlighted as a competitive approach, and robustness is mentioned as one of the characteristics for resilience. One common factor presented in the mentioned studies is the variation analysis in the production processes and operations; they all agree that it is necessary to control and stabilize variation to reduce disturbances and deviations. However, the spectrum is closed to product variation, which is far from the aim of full integration with I4.0 or full digital transformation. The characteristics to be resilient may be identified in works like [24], but models and guidelines on how exactly this can be achieved are lacking.

## 3   A Model for Digitalization Deployment in SMEs

The literature review indicates that analytical models for managerial capabilities exist but there is a practical approach missing in terms of sequence and concrete simplified guidance on how to integrate performance objectives. For our theoretical model, we adopted the analytical model proposed by [3] as a building base, due to the elements it comprehends: capabilities, means of implementation and operational performance objectives. The four capabilities defined initially by [18] are to be linked together, each capability builds on the next one, as valuable in its own right and also sets the stage for the next level. In that sense, a company won't be able to control and optimize without first having a monitoring system in place.

Figure 1 represents the elements in three main categories: 1. managerial capabilities, 2. means of implementation and 3. operational performance objectives. They are arranged in a suggested deployment order from left to right.

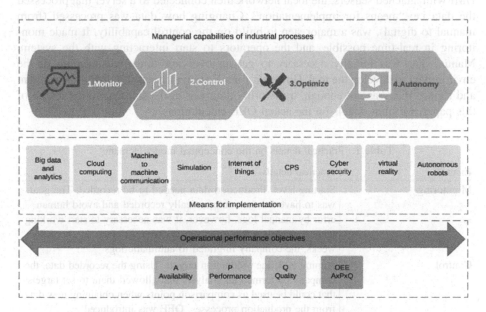

**Fig. 1.** Model for deploying manufacturing digitalization in SMEs based on [3].

SMEs are sometimes lacking formal systems to control and measure their performance. That was the reason why we considered the operational performance to be initially measured by the three elements of the OEE KPI. To our knowledge, most SMEs independent of industry and production strategy, often have an initial understanding of these three elements. The OEE data is not always analyzed, but that data itself is often generated. With the introduction of OEE as an initial step, a gradual connection to production disturbances is expected, as is the propagation and their effects on performance. A reactive approach is often common practice among SMEs, therefore our model's goal is to make the shift to a proactive approach possible, by developing capability three and four.

### 3.1 Practical Application on the Capabilities Building

**Practical Case: A Deployment Process**
The case selected is a Swedish SME with more than 75 years of experience in manufacturing of fasteners and industrial components for the automotive and engineering industries. In 2019, with the objective to improve its disturbance handling and become more autonomous, the company formally started its digital transformation by the

development and implementation of a low cost and tailor-made digital tool. The project was interlinked with a research team (advisors) and a couple of students (developers). Table 1 describes the practical implications of the implemented elements in the case study as illustrated in Fig. 2, which is a visual representation of the elements that the prototype tool covers. A local network was built around a system containing a PLC and HMI with attached sensors, the local network then connected to a server that processed the data i.e. "means for implementation". Changing how data was processed (from manual to digital), was a major step to build on the control capability. It made monitoring in real-time possible, and the operators to start interacting with the system. Manual data was initially necessary to get an overview and understanding of the environment to develop the tool. However, for a system that was required to be resilient and robust, that was not enough, trustworthy data was also vital. Due to the length of this paper, we omit details on the actual OEE calculations.

**Table 1.** Practical details on the conceptual model elements.

| Element | Practical details |
|---|---|
| Monitoring | Starting level. Production data needed to be recorded. The goal was to have the data automatically recorded and avoid human error by manual logs, however, it was necessary to start working with manual data while the sensors were in place. In about 8 weeks, the company migrated to automatic logs |
| Control | Aiming to define production targets. Using the recorded data, the company performed an analysis that allowed them to set targets that could be used as comparison points when obtaining new data from the production processes. OEE was introduced |
| Optimization | On plan - not deployed at the moment. The goal will be to improve by monitoring data, system models, simulation systems, production system, and resources |
| Autonomy | On plan and set as the ultimate goal, when the system can learn from the inputs and its own behavior and can adapt itself. Shift from reactive behavior to proactive response will be enabled |
| Operational performance objectives | OEE in terms of AxPxQ<br>A: Availability %. Data became available digitally from the machines (configurable, initial data was collected manually by the operators, special attention on downtime)<br>P: Performance efficiency %. Data became available digitally from the machines (configurable, initial data was collected manually since the only existing records were in ERP system and not updated, special attention on cycle times)<br>Q: Quality. Data is both available from manual records and digitally, depending on the machine. Some quality measures are digitalized but not part of this calculation |

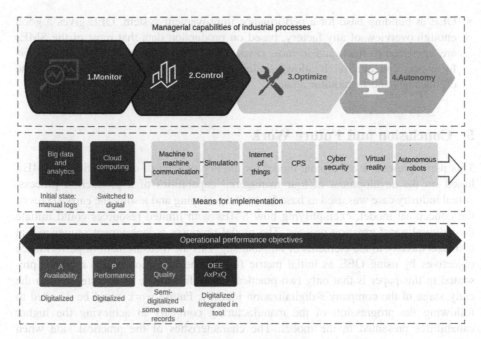

**Fig. 2.** Exemplification of model deployment: industrial case.

## 4   Discussion

Being the topic of digitalization in a novel field, it becomes harder to create a model that fits in a higher set of manufacturing/production environments. Nonetheless, the deployment case allows us to offer some analytical generalization as a result of the lessons learned:

- Means of implementation in higher capabilities. The path for deploying the four managerial capabilities in the proposed conceptual model is set systematically and in a defined order. However, we can infer that the means of implementation may not necessarily follow a strict order of deployment, especially for the last five blocks: internet of things, CPS, cybersecurity, virtual reality, and autonomous robots. The deployment order may highly depend on the company strategy and business needs. For instance, a company may decide to prioritize virtual reality for training purposes without necessarily have a CPS in place.
- Adapting I4.0 elements. Taylor-made digital solutions could be a more reliable way for SMEs to develop managerial capabilities. The key lays in incorporating their needs into a digital system that integrates the generated data for analysis purposes to support decision making.
- Resilience and robustness coexisting in I4.0 for SMEs. Robustness is a priority when discussing disturbance and deviation handling. With the introduction of digital tools, SMEs can little by little develop their production systems to have the desired abilities.

- OEE as building base for a performance improvement system. OEE gives a good enough overview of any factory, based on production data that most of the SMEs are interested to track and in most cases already are generating: availability, performance, and quality. It allows setting realistic thresholds to integrate into the digital tools and to monitor against.

## 5   Conclusion and Future Work

This paper presents a conceptual model for the deployment of digitalization in SMEs, based on the development of four managerial capabilities of a production process. A real industry case was used as base for both developing and testing the early stages of the conceptual model, exemplifying how SMEs with limited resources could initiate their digital transformation process. The model proposes a deployment sequence that connects directly to the elements of I4.0 and suggests the measurement of performance objectives by using OEE as initial metric (KPI). The limitation of the research presented in this paper is that only two practical capabilities have been tested due to the early stage of the company's digitalization journey. Future work could be devoted to following the progression of the manufacturing company in achieving the higher capabilities presented in the model. The characteristics of the practical side when talking about resilience and robustness is furthermore interesting to explore, to build new knowledge ensuring that SMEs build on their digitalization based on a good theoretical foundation.

**Acknowledgements.**  This work is part of the project ASPIRE "Automation solutions for production deviation management", funded by Sweden's Government Agency for Innovation VINNOVA (Programme Produktion 2030). The authors thankfully acknowledge the funding agency, the good collaboration and support from the case company and the feedback from Alvis Sokolovs which helped to improve the manuscript.

## References

1. Wang, S., Wan, J., Li, D., Zhang, C.: Implementing smart factory of industrie 4.0: an outlook. Int. J. Distrib. Sens. Netw. (2016) https://doi.org/10.1155/2016/3159805
2. Mukhopadhyay, A., Murthy, L.R.D., Arora, M., Chakrabarti, A., Mukherjee, I., Biswas, P.: PCB inspection in the context of smart manufacturing. In: Chakrabarti, A. (ed.) Research into Design for a Connected World. SIST, vol. 134, pp. 655–663. Springer, Singapore (2019). https://doi.org/10.1007/978-981-13-5974-3_57
3. Moeuf, A., Pellerin, R., Lamouri, S., Tamayo-Giraldo, S., Barbaray, R.: The industrial management of SMEs in the era of industry 4.0. Int. J. Prod. Res. **56**(3), 1118–1136 (2018). https://doi.org/10.1080/00207543.2017.1372647
4. Mittal, S., Romero, D., Wuest, T.: Towards a smart manufacturing maturity model for SMEs (SM$^3$E). In: Moon, I., Lee, G.M., Park, J., Kiritsis, D., von Cieminski, G. (eds.) APMS 2018. IAICT, vol. 536, pp. 155–163. Springer, Cham (2018). https://doi.org/10.1007/978-3-319-99707-0_20

5. Lasi, H., Fettke, P., Kemper, H.-G., Feld, T., Hoffmann, M.: Industry 4.0. Bus. Inf. Syst. Eng. **6**(4), 239–242 (2014). https://doi.org/10.1007/s12599-014-0334-4

6. Lee, J., Bagheri, B., Kao, H.A.: A cyber-physical systems architecture for industry 4.0-based manufacturing systems. Manuf. Lett. **3**, 18–23 (2015). https://doi.org/10.1016/j.mfglet.2014.12.001

7. Lee, J., Bagheri, B., Jin, C.: Introduction to cyber manufacturing. Manuf. Lett. **8**, 11–15 (2016). https://doi.org/10.1016/j.mfglet.2016.05.002

8. Baheti, R., Gill, H.: Cyber-physical systems. Impact Control Technol. **12**(1), 161–166 (2011)

9. Gomes, R.L., Rigley, M., Bacon, D., Watson, N., Porcu, L., Fisher, O.: Cloud manufacturing as a sustainable process manufacturing route. J. Manuf. Syst. **47**, 53–68 (2018). https://doi.org/10.1016/j.jmsy.2018.03.005

10. Ud Din, F., Henskens, F., Paul, D., Wallis, M.: Agent-Oriented Smart Factory (AOSF): an MAS based framework for SMEs under industry 4.0. In: Jezic, G., Chen-Burger, Y.-H.J., Howlett, R.J., Jain, L.C., Vlacic, L., Šperka, R. (eds.) KES-AMSTA-18 2018. SIST, vol. 96, pp. 44–54. Springer, Cham (2019). https://doi.org/10.1007/978-3-319-92031-3_5

11. Veres, P., Illés, B., Landschützer, C.: Supply chain optimization in automotive industry: a comparative analysis of evolutionary and swarming heuristics. In: Jármai, K., Bolló, B. (eds.) VAE 2018. LNME, pp. 666–676. Springer, Cham (2018). https://doi.org/10.1007/978-3-319-75677-6_57

12. Wieland, M., et al.: Towards a rule-based manufacturing integration assistant. Procedia CIRP **57**, 213–218 (2016). https://doi.org/10.1016/j.procir.2016.11.037

13. Dallasega, P., Rojas, R.A., Rauch, E., Matt, D.T.: Simulation based validation of supply chain effects through ICT enabled real-time-capability in ETO production planning. Procedia Manuf. **11**(June), 846–853 (2017). https://doi.org/10.1016/j.promfg.2017.07.187

14. Bi, Z., et al.: Real-time force monitoring of smart grippers for Internet of Things (IoT) applications. J. Ind. Inf. Integr. **11**(February), 19–28 (2018). https://doi.org/10.1016/j.jii.2018.02.004

15. Wang, Z., Shou, M., Wang, S., Dai, R., Wang, K.: An empirical study on the key factors of intelligent upgrade of small and medium-sized enterprises in China. Sustainability **11**(3) (2019). https://doi.org/10.3390/su11030619

16. Martínez-Olvera, C., Mora-Vargas, J.: A max-plus algebra approach to study time disturbance propagation within a robustness improvement context. Math. Probl. Eng., 1–18 (2018). https://doi.org/10.1155/2018/1932361

17. Spiegler, V.L.M., Naim, M.M., Wikner, J.: A control engineering approach to the assessment of supply chain resilience. Int. J. Prod. Res. **50**(21), 6162–6187 (2012). https://doi.org/10.1080/00207543.2012.710764

18. Porter, M.E., Heppelmann, J.E.: How smart, connected products are transforming competition. Harv. Bus. Rev. **92**, 64–88 (2014)

19. Mittal, S., Khan, M.A., Romero, D., Wuest, T.: Smart manufacturing: characteristics, technologies and enabling factors. **233**(5), 1342–1361 (2019). https://doi.org/10.1177/0954405417736547

20. Tao, F., Qi, Q., Liu, A., Kusiak, A.: Data-driven smart manufacturing. J. Manuf. Syst. **48**, 157–169 (2018). https://doi.org/10.1016/j.jmsy.2018.01.006

21. Stoldt, J., Trapp, T.U., Toussaint, S., Süße, M., Schlegel, A., Putz, M.: Planning for digitalisation in SMEs using tools of the digital factory. Procedia CIRP **72**, 179–184 (2018). https://doi.org/10.1016/j.procir.2018.03.100

22. Kristianto, Y., Gunasekaran, A., Helo, P.: Building the 'Triple R' in global manufacturing. Int. J. Prod. Econ. **183**(December), 607–619 (2017). https://doi.org/10.1016/j.ijpe.2015.12.011

23. Boorla, M.S., Eifler, T., McMahon, C., Howard, T.J.: Product robustness philosophy – A strategy towards zero variation manufacturing (ZVM). Manag. Prod. Eng. Rev. 9(2), 3–12 (2018). https://doi.org/10.24425/119520

24. Morisse, M., Prigge, C.: Design of a Business Resilience Model for Industry 4.0 manufacturers. In: Twenty-third Americas Conference on Information Systems, pp. 1–10 (2017)

# The Potential of Game Development Platforms for Digital Twins and Virtual Labs

## Case Study of an Energy Analytics and Solution Lab

Ali Abdallah$^{(\boxtimes)}$ ⬦, Matthias Primas, Ioan Turcin,
and Udo Traussnigg

CAMPUS 02, University of Applied Sciences, 8010 Graz, Austria
ali.abdallah@campus02.at

**Abstract.** In this paper, we present the first steps towards realizing a digital twin with integrated virtual laboratory possibilities, for a newly established Energy Analytics and Solution lab, using the Unity3D game development platform. The presented example is a case study that shows the possibilities of such development environment for creating a fully connectable digital twin of an energy analytics lab and other more complex industrial environments.

**Keywords:** Virtual reality · Virtual lab · Digital twin · Unity 3D · Energy analytics lab

## 1 Introduction

The digitalization of a physical object or system can be done at various levels; ranging from a simple digital model that has no exchange of data between the model and the real entity, to a digital shadow where there is a one way data transfer and last but not least a digital twin (DT) [1]. A widely accepted definition of a digital twin was introduced by [2], and subsequently by [3]: a DT is defined as an integration of multi-physics and multi-scale simulation of a complex product. These simulations use available physical models and outside sensor data (or other measurements) to mirror a corresponding physical twin.

Big advancements in DTs are enabled by developments in the areas of simulation, communication protocols and very important visualization [1]. Virtual reality (VR), and by extension augmented reality (AR), offers itself as very strong and immersive tool for the visualization of DTs and game development engines such as Unity 3D offer a free access tool for developing VR applications with high levels of integration possibilities. The uses of VR for DT applications in various areas are discussed in works such as [4–6].

In this paper we introduce the first step towards creating a DT for a newly established energy analytics and solution lab (EAS-Lab), where Unity 3D has been used to digitalize the lab and connect various relevant measurements and other elements from the actual lab to the virtual world. The developed virtual lab is also intended for teaching purposes. The use of virtual labs for various teaching purposes is reviewed in [7].

© IFIP International Federation for Information Processing 2020
Published by Springer Nature Switzerland AG 2020
B. Lalic et al. (Eds.): APMS 2020, IFIP AICT 592, pp. 117–121, 2020.
https://doi.org/10.1007/978-3-030-57997-5_14

## 2    Energy Analytics and Solution Lab

The aim of the project Energy Analytics and Solution lab (EAS-Lab) is to be able to analytically describe and develop core areas in the existing and future energy value chain in lab conditions. For this purpose, a digital energy research laboratory, the EAS-Lab, was built both at the University of Applied Sciences JOANNEUM in Kapfenberg and at CAMPUS 02 in Graz. The project, which was concluded in the beginning of 2020, includes the installation of renewable energy generation systems, hybrid energy systems with energy storage hubs, charging stations for electric mobility, and measurement and automation components on both sites. With these components, it will be possible to analyse, develop and improve existing and future questions relating to energy and business models. In addition, the labs will be suitable for investigating innovative charging technologies for electric mobility and their technical implications.

The EAS-Labs consists of a network of highly connected renewable energy generators (mostly photovoltaic cells), energy management, storage and testing loads covering a wide range of typical household and industrial loads including e-mobility. A smart home infrastructure ensures the high level of connectivity and control needed to create an effective testing lab environment. Several software tools for simulation, visualization and energy management, automation and control supplement the hardware components of the EAS-labs. One of the most important tools in use is the XAM-Control software, which is an industrial tool used for visualization, programming and control of automated processes.

All measured values are transferred to a server on which the XAM Control software is installed. All components (measuring devices, energy storage devices, charging stations...) must therefore have a suitable interface for data transmission (e.g. Modbus TCP, Ethernet). The XAM Control takes over the control of all energy flows in the laboratory (energy and load management) (Fig. 1).

## 3    EAS-Lab Case Study: Digital Twin and VR-Lab

In this section we shortly introduce the first steps taken towards the realization of a DT and virtual lab of the above introduced EAS-Lab.

The motivation of the presented work is to create an environment that replicates the EAS-Lab in both presentation and functionality, and going along the definition of a DT, offers communication in both ways, between the virtual and the physical lab. This also allows for the implementation of a connected virtual laboratory, where various energy systems concepts can be presented to students in a safe environment.

Unity 3D, a game development engine, is chosen for the implementation of the EAS-Lab DT. Unity supports C# scripts allowing for great flexibility in the implementation of the communication protocols needed to connect the EAS-Lab to its DT and vice versa. The implementation of serial and Modbus TCP communication was the

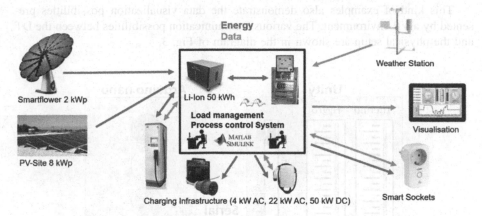

**Fig. 1.** Diagram depicting the core elements of the Energy Analytics and Solution Lab (EAS-Lab). This diagram shows how all the main elements of the lab connect together on both energy and data exchange levels.

first step, and was realized in the scope of a master thesis [8]. These communication protocols were specifically chosen because they are often used in energy management and home/facility automation systems.

In the above-mentioned master thesis, the successful implementation of both communication protocols was demonstrated through the integration of a measurement station in the EAS-Lab DT. The temperature and humidity measurements were made in the lab using a DHT11 sensor and a microcontroller (Arduino) setup. Data communication to the physical EAS-Lab was demonstrated through the control of various LEDs. Figure 2 below shows the digital setup and the corresponding physical prototype.

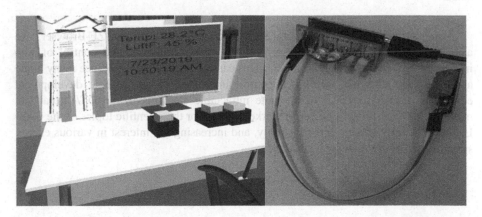

**Fig. 2.** Figure showing the lab measurement station setup introduced in [8] in both its digital form (left) and as a physical prototype (Right).

This kind of examples also demonstrate the data visualization possibilities presented by a VR environment. The various communication possibilities between the DT and the physical setup are shown in the diagram of Fig. 3.

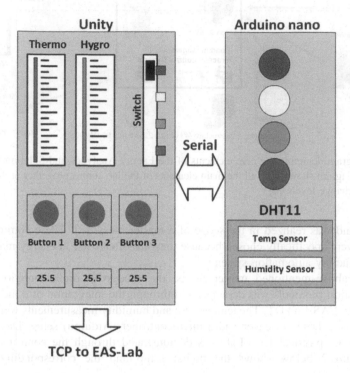

**Fig. 3.** Diagram depicting the various communication and control possibilities between the implement experimental setup in the DT and both the physical lab and the developed Arduino board.

Using software development kits (SDK) available for Unity 3D (ZF-Browser), we also implemented a web based interface, allowing the display and control of web interfaces through the VR-environment. This can be especially useful since many home automation systems use web-based control interfaces. Using a game development engine makes it also easier to integrate intractable elements in the DT/Virtual lab, making the DT also into a powerful marketing tool for the scientific topics of the EAS-Lab, significantly adding to the visibility, and increasing the interest in various energy systems and energy management topics.

# 4   Conclusion

In this work, we have introduced a DT implementation of an energy analytics lab using a game development engine in an interactive VR environment, in addition to introducing the newly established Energy Analytics Solution (EAS)-Labs.

We have shortly shown the integration of a virtual lab module and the implementation of various communication protocols in the virtual presentation of the lab, thus creating the basic building blocks for a scalable DT of the EAS-Lab. This was established by communicating from a Unity 3D environment with a microcontroller in the physical lab through both a serial and a TCP protocol. Successful communication in both direction, i.e. from and to the microcontroller, is a successful first step towards a full DT of the EAS-lab. In addition, the creation of the VR-environment is important for various visualization applications in the newly established labs.

The work shown here holds great potential for the EAS-Lab, opening the door for future scientific work in the areas of VR-based energy systems simulations and visualization and digital twins of renewable energy systems, all while acting as a marketing tool with great reach.

# References

1. Kritzinger, W., et al.: Digital twin in manufacturing: a categorical literature review and classification. IFAC-PapersOnLine **51**(11), 1016–1022 (2018). https://doi.org/10.1016/j.ifacol.2018.08.474. ISSN 2405-8963
2. Glaessgen, E.H., Stargel, D.S.: The digital twin paradigm for future NASA and U.S. air force vehicles. In: 53rd Structural Dynamics and Materials Conference Special Session: Digital Twin, Honolulu, HI, US (2012)
3. Tao, F., Cheng, J., Qi, Q., Zhang, M., Zhang, H., Sui, F.: Digital twin-driven product design, manufacturing and service with big data. Int. J. Adv. Manuf. Technol. **94**(3563), 3576 (2018). https://doi.org/10.1007/s00170-017-0233-1
4. Schroeder, G., et al.: Visualising the digital twin using web services and augmented reality. In: 2016 IEEE 14th International Conference on Industrial Informatics (INDIN), Poitiers, pp. 522–527 (2016)
5. Laaki, H., Miche, Y., Tammi, K.: Prototyping a digital twin for real time remote control over mobile networks: application of remote surgery. IEEE Access 7, 20325–20336 (2019)
6. Andaluz, V.H., et al.: Unity3D-MatLab simulator in real time for robotics applications. In: De Paolis, L.T., Mongelli, A. (eds.) AVR 2016. LNCS, vol. 9768, pp. 246–263. Springer, Cham (2016). https://doi.org/10.1007/978-3-319-40621-3_19
7. Potkonjak, V., et al.: Virtual laboratories for education in science, technology, and engineering: a review. Comput. Educ. **95**, 309–327 (2016). https://doi.org/10.1016/j.compedu.2016.02.002. ISSN 0360-1315
8. Semler, B.: Visualisierung und virtuelle Steuerung eines Messtisches in einem realen Labor

# The Application of ICT Solutions
# in Manufacturing Companies in Serbia

Danijela Ciric$^{(\boxtimes)}$ ⓘ, Teodora Lolic ⓘ, Danijela Gracanin ⓘ,
Darko Stefanovic ⓘ, and Bojan Lalic ⓘ

Faculty of Technical Sciences, University of Novi Sad, 21000 Novi Sad, Serbia
danijela.ciric@uns.ac.rs

**Abstract.** Information and Communications Technology (ICT) integration in
the entire process of manufacturing management is necessary and obliging from
the perspective of efficient resource allocation, time-saving, broadening the
variety of products, reducing waste, and increasing the productivity and economy of production. Delivering competitive advantage needed for being successful in the new digital era is of crucial importance for the Serbian
manufacturing industry. This research, in the first instance, seeks to examine the
empirical link between the ICT software solutions importance and the actual
software application, and in the second instance, to explore the empirical link
between ICT software solutions application and the company's competitive
position, as perceived by the respondents from 74 Serbian manufacturing
companies included in the study. Research results have shown that if the
managers in manufacturing companies believe that the usage of the specific
software solution is vital for their business, the usage of that software will be
empowered and, therefore, will positively impact the company's competitive
position.

**Keywords:** ICT software solution · Manufacturing sector · Industry 4.0 · SEM

## 1 Introduction

The business environment today has been undergoing unprecedented changes, and
constant technological advancement is keeping manufacturing companies in a continuous state of disruption, in order to be competent to handle huge amount of extrinsic
data, and rejoinder to vibrant and dynamic worldwide markets [1]. Many manufacturing companies are seeking new ways to stand out from the competition by transforming their traditional business processes and sustaining their competitive advantage
through the application of ICT software solutions in a wide range and operations areas.
Nowadays, ICT integration in the entire process of manufacturing management is
necessary and obliging from the perspective of efficient resource allocation, time-
saving in production, broadening the variety of products, reducing waste, and
increasing the productivity and economy of production. The application of advanced
digital technologies and software solutions has become the focus of the research related
to Industry 4.0, as they are considered as one of the main enablers of this new paradigm
[2]. Taking into account that manufacturing is destined to play the most significant role

© IFIP International Federation for Information Processing 2020
Published by Springer Nature Switzerland AG 2020
B. Lalic et al. (Eds.): APMS 2020, IFIP AICT 592, pp. 122–129, 2020.
https://doi.org/10.1007/978-3-030-57997-5_15

in the reindustrialization of Serbia [3], delivering competitive advantage needed for being successful in the new digital era is of crucial importance for the Serbian manufacturing industry. This research, in the first instance, seeks to examine the empirical link between the ICT software solutions importance and the actual software application, and in the second instance, to explore the empirical link between ICT software solutions application and the company's competitive position, as perceived by the respondents, from 74 Serbian manufacturing companies, included in the study.

## 2 Theoretical Background

The advent of digitalization and ICT is reshaping the manufacturing sector to highly interconnected but, at the same time, increasingly complex and dynamic [4]. The strategic role of ICT highlights the importance of ICT usage in developing products, services, and capabilities that help a company gain a competitive advantage or meet other strategic objectives [5]. Today's successful companies are deploying ICT to enhance performance and continually renew their ability to manage their interfaces with the environment dynamically [6]. The accelerated development of communication technologies driven by computer hardware and system software solutions has conditioned the overcoming the application of manual systems for production control and enabled the adoption of new processes and operations [7]. This has led to sustainable gains in productivity, quality, and responsiveness [8] today, there is a large number of commercial ICT software solutions that are available for manufacturing management. Software solutions are used to automate a business process, streamline and improve operations, make the supply chain more transparent, or improve the enterprise asset management. The emergence of change in the manufacturing sector to ensure the pathway to Industry 4.0 is evident. For example, enterprise-resource-planning (ERP) systems, as one of the modern ICT solutions are being used in the majority of companies. In the manufacturing sector, ERP system implementation benefits are concentrated in quickly providing high-quality information within a company [9]. Other authors [10] pointed out that the benefits of ERP systems differ by company size, so larger companies emphasize improvements in financial measures. In contrast, smaller companies report better performance in manufacturing and logistics. On the other side, there are social media, as one of the most widely used IT application [12], which contains valuable information collected from the customers. Companies can use data not only for the prediction of customer behavior but also for making decisions on product and process design [11]. Still, there is no evidence in the literature about the connection between social media and its impact on business process performing [12]. One of the major developments in business has been the emergence of the Internet as a channel for commerce [13]. Cyber-physical system (CPS), Internet of Things (IoT), digital twins, and other available ICT solutions should be used for design or redesign of the production landscape, and these technologies are being cultivated around large multinational companies [14]. Currently, in Serbia, there is little interest and very modest results in the development of Industry 4.0. However, orientation to Industry 4.0 could provide a chance for its revitalization. Industry 4.0 is based on rapidly evolving

ICT capacities starting already from the production planning process using ICT solutions for operational planning and manufacturing resource planning [15].

# 3 Research Methodology

## 3.1 Research Instrument

The questionnaire was used as a research instrument. In the first section, respondents gave their background information. In the second section, respondents were asked to rank the importance of different ICT software solutions in their business. In the third section, the actual software application was assessed, and the fourth section was dedicated to the company's competitive position. This research used a self-reporting (subjective) assessment of software importance and usage and the company's competitive position, as perceived by respondents. The importance and actual application of various software solutions in manufacturing were operationalized with 26 questions. The variables were classified into seven groups, representing different software products (office, email, enterprise resource planning, production, marketing, calculation, and simulation software, business processes). To capture respondents' subjective perception of software importance, a continuum of five-point, unipolar, Likert type scale was used (1 = not important at all; 2 = of little importance; 2 = of average importance; 3 = very important; 4 = absolutely essential). To capture respondents' subjective perception of actual software application, a continuum of five-point, unipolar, Likert type scale was used (1 = not using at all; 2 = of little usage; 2 = of average usage; 3 = very important; 4 = absolutely using it). The company's competitive position, as the dependent variable, was operationalized with 11 questions. The variables were classified into five groups (1) quality, (2) delivery, (3) price, (4) flexibility, and (5) innovativeness. To capture respondents' subjective perception of the company's competitive position, a continuum of four-point, unipolar, Likert type scale was used (1 = behind the competitors; 2 = the same as competitors; 3 = better than competitors; 4 = much better than competitors).

**ICT Software Solutions Used in This Research**
In this research, we included those software solutions that are most commonly found in manufacturing companies. The list of software, divided into seven groups, is given in the following section.

1. Office
– Text editing (MS Word, OpenOffice…)
– Spreadsheets (MS Excel, OpenOffice Calc…)
– Communication
2. Email
– Project and team management software (Trello, Slack, Jira…)
– Conference and messaging (Zoom, Skype, Messenger…)

5. Marketing
– Company website
– Social network accounts (Facebook, Instagram…)
– Survey and market research tools (Mailchimp, SurveyMonkey…)
– E-commerce
6. Calculation and simulation software (Matlab, Simul, Solid Works…)

3. Enterprise Resource Planning (ERP)
- ERP Sales and CRM
- ERP Production planning and scheduling
- ERP Logistics & warehouse (WMS)
- ERP Finance and accounting
- ERP Document management (DMS)
- ERP Human resource (HR)
4. Production
- Production lifecycle management (PLM)
- Computer-aided engineering (CAE)
- Computer-aided design (CAD)
- Computer-aided manufacturing (CAM)
- Product data management (PDM)
- Finite element method (FEM)

7. Business processes (Visio, Mind Jet, Org Plus...)
- Business process modeling
- Business intelligence systems
- Internet of things/digital platforms
- Intelligent business process automation suites

## 3.2 Data Collection and Sample Demographics

Respondents from 74 Serbian manufacturing companies were included in the study. The sample consisted of companies across different manufacturing industries and companies sizes. To present the determined fundamental indicators of statistical series, authors have used descriptive statistical analysis. Sample demographics are shown in Table 1.

**Table 1.** The demographic composition

| Characteristic | Mean | St. dev. | Freq. | % |
|---|---|---|---|---|
| **Industry** | 4.46 | 2.882 | | |
| (1) Metal production and machine work | | | 14 | 18.9 |
| (2) Manufacture of computer, electronic and optical products | | | 7 | 9.5 |
| (3) Food and beverage industries | | | 16 | 21.6 |
| (4) Textile industry (clothing, footwear) | | | 7 | 9.5 |
| (5) Wood and furniture industries | | | 3 | 4.1 |
| (6) Chemical, biotechnology and pharmaceutical industries | | | 8 | 10.8 |
| (7) Tobacco, oil and gas, sports | | | 3 | 4.1 |
| (8) Rubber, plastics and packaging ind. | | | 6 | 8.1 |
| (9) Construction + ceramics | | | 6 | 8.1 |
| (10) Automotive | | | 4 | 5.4 |
| **Size** | 3.0 | 0.936 | | |
| (1) From 1 to 9 | | | 7 | 9.5 |
| (2) From 10 to 49 | | | 11 | 14.9 |
| (3) From 50 to 249 | | | 31 | 41.9 |
| (4) More than 250 | | | 25 | 33.8 |

## 3.3    Research Model and Hypotheses

The questionnaire has been structured into three sections forming three factors. Fist independent factor – ICT software usage importance described the importance of different ICT software solutions in respondents' business. Second, the dependant factor – ICT software actual application showed the actual application of different types of software solutions. The third dependant factor addressed the respondents' subjective perception of the company's competitive position compared to competitors. To assess if the perceived importance of ICT software solutions influences the actual software usage, the authors proposed the first hypothesis.

*H1 – ICT Software Usage Importance has a positive influence on the ICT Software Actual Application.*

However, if the company applies a particular software solution, believing it will gain a competitive advantage, it is essential to know if that influence exists. Thus, the second hypothesis is proposed.

*H2 – ICT Software Actual Application has a positive influence on the Company's Competitive Position.*

## 4    Results and Discussion

Based on the collected data, a measurement instrument consisted of 26 indicators was tested. Exploratory factor analyses (EFA) was conducted in an iterative procedure until an adequate model, and factor structure satisfied the criteria [16]: validity of variance higher than 1 (applying the Keizer-Guttman's rules), visual representation of variance value using scree plot, elimination of the variables that have been creating other, not relevant factors, and suitability of the Chi-square index and usage of the suitability index.

## 4.1    Reliability and Validity Assessment

By calculating the Cronbach's alpha coefficient for each factor, the reliability of the measurement instrument has been determined. All factors Cronbach's alpha values are higher than the minimum criteria (0.70 or more), as it is suggested by the authors [18]. The reliability and convergent validity of the factors were estimated, and the results are presented in Table 2. Ultimately, the measurement model had adequate reliability, convergent, and discriminant validity.

**Table 2.** Reliability, convergent validity and construct correlation

| Factor | α | CR | AVE | MSV | ASV | SwApp | SwImp | Comp |
|--------|-----|-----|-----|-----|-----|-------|-------|------|
| SwApp | 0.950 | 0.952 | 0.665 | 0.160 | 0.101 | 0.816[a] | | |
| SwImp | 0.924 | 0.925 | 0.674 | 0.160 | 0.097 | 0.400 | 0.821[a] | |
| Comp | 0.860 | 0.861 | 0.556 | 0.042 | 0.038 | 0.204 | 0.187 | 0.746[a] |

[a] Indicates the square root of AVE construct; SwImp – ICT Software Usage Importance, SwApp – ICT Software Actual Application, Comp – Company's Competitive Position

## 4.2 Structural Model

To test the proposed research hypotheses, the structural model has been created (see Fig. 1). The model had adequate suitability indexes with the values shown in Table 3. Observed indexes' values are in the acceptable range, which presents a proper fitting of models. All obtained values for part coefficients were above-recommended values of 0.20 [19]. Results of the Structural equation modeling (SEM) reveal that both explored hypotheses are confirmed and accepted.

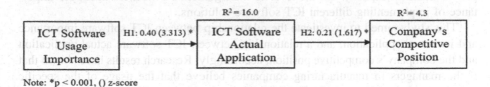

Note: *p < 0.001, () z-score

**Fig. 1.** Structural model

**Table 3.** Suitability indexes for Confirmatory factor analyses (CFA) and SEM

| Model | $\chi^2$/df | NFI | CFI | RMSEA |
|---|---|---|---|---|
| Measurement model | 1.497 | 0.802 | 0.923 | 0.080 |
| Structural model | 1.493 | 0.802 | 0.923 | 0.080 |
| Recommended value | <3 | >0.80 | ~0.95 | 0.05–0.10 |

Relationship between factors ICT software usage importance and ICT software actual application resulted as statistically significant and positive (path coefficient = 0.40; t = 3.313). Therefore we can conclude the following: if the managers from Serbian manufacturing companies believe that the usage of the particular software is vital for their business, chances for the actual application of the software are increasing. Proposed relationship between factors ICT software actual application and company's competitive position has been confirmed and shown as statistically significant and positive (path coefficient = 0.21; t = 1.617), however, on the border of the significance.

Finally, two presumed factors explained 20.3% of the variance in the structural model. According to the respondents' subjective perception, presumed factor ICT software usage Importance has an influence on presumed factor ICT software actual application by 16%. ICT software solutions with the highest importance are ERP systems – Sales and CRM, WMS, Production planning and scheduling, and HR. Previous research in the Serbian manufacturing sector also showed the most significant software solutions for the enterprises are the ones for the production planning and scheduling, near real-time production control systems, as well as the systems for the automation of the logistics [20]. On the other side, factor ICT software actual application shows a significantly lower effect on the assumed factor company's competitive position, with 4.3%. The respondents addressed that ICT software solution application will make the most significant influence on their flexibility and innovativeness – as the key indicators of their competitiveness.

# 5  Conclusion

What is quite certain is that almost all companies in the world use some kind of ICT solutions in their business. The manufacturing companies are not lagging behind either. Still, the question is whether they use narrowly specialized software intended solely for direct use in the production or whether they use a spectrum of various ICT solutions to support their business. The choice of ICT solutions to be applied depends primarily on the activity of the company, then the goals to be achieved, but most of all, the company's financial capacity and the level of management's awareness about the importance of implementing different ICT software solutions.

This study aimed to investigate the relationship between ICT software importance and its actual application, and a relationship between ICT software actual application and the company's competitive position, accordingly. Research results have shown that if the managers in manufacturing companies believe that the usage of the specific software solution is vital for their business, the usage of that software will be empowered and, therefore, will positively impact the company's competitive position. ERP systems are shown to be the most important ones. Moreover, the actual application positively affects companies' competitiveness with the most significant influence on their flexibility and innovativeness. Taking into account that H2 with the competitiveness implication is very tightly on the border of significance, the conclusions drawn in this work can also be observed as partly interpreted assumptions.

It is of massive importance for the companies to carefully choose and invest in new ICT software solutions, which they find as ones potentially improving business processes, having in mind that investment will increase their competitiveness. For Serbian manufacturing companies to embark on this reindustrialization and keep up with current trends, it is necessary to implement at least some or all of the elements of Industry 4.0, including the application of various ICT software solutions.

This study has potential limitations. The first is the respondents' subjective perception of the research constructs. The second limitation concerns the use of unipolar scales to measure the ICT software solutions application level and the company's competitive position. What has undoubtedly not been sufficiently explored is the impact that the application of ICT software solutions has directly on profitability and cost-effectiveness. Also, the insights are focused on Serbia with no comparison to some other referential economies. Future research should overcome these limitations, and also take into consideration the influence of the company's size on ICT software application.

# References

1. Prasad, K., Shankar, C.: A QFD-based decision making model for computer-aided design software selection. Int. J. Ind. Eng. Manag. 7(2), 49–58 (2016)
2. Droege, H., Hildebrand, D., Forcada, M.A.H.: Innovation in services: present findings, and future pathways. J. Serv. Manag. 20(2), 131–155 (2009)

3. Jovanovic, B., Filipovic, J., Bakic, V.: Prioritization of manufacturing sectors in Serbia for energy management improvement – AHP method. Energy Convers. Manag. **98**, 225–235 (2015)
4. Jaewon, K., Abe, M., Valente, F.: Impacts of the digital economy on manufacturing in emerging Asia. Asian J. Innov. Policy **8**(1), 1–20 (2019)
5. Seev, N.: Strategic Information Systems: Competition Through Information Technologies. MacMillan College Publishing Co., New York (1994)
6. Olamade, O.O., Oyebisi, T.O., Olabode, S.O.: Strategic ICT-use intensity of manufacturing companies in Nigeria. J. Asian Bus. Strategy **4**(1), 1–17 (2014)
7. Berić, D., Stefanović, D., Lalić, B., Ćosić, I.: The implementation of ERP and MES systems as a support to industrial management systems. Int. J. Ind. Eng. Manag. **9**(2), 77–86 (2018)
8. Brynjolfsson, E., Hitt, L.M.: Beyond computation informational technology, organizational transformation and business performance. J. Econ. Perspect. **14**(4), 23–48 (2000)
9. Hasan, M., Trinh, N., Chan, H., Chan, K., Chung, S.H.: Implementation of ERP of the Australian manufacturing companies. Ind. Manag. Data Syst. **111**(1), 132–145 (2011)
10. Mabert, V., Soni, A., Venkataramanan, M.: The impact of organization size on Enterprise Resource Planning (ERP) implementations in the US manufacturing sector. Omega **31**(3), 235–246 (2003)
11. Chan, H.K., Lacka, E., Yee, R.W.Y., Lim, M.K.: The role of social media data in operations and production management. Int. J. Prod. Res. **55**(17), 5027–5036 (2017)
12. Annisa, L.H.: Impact of alignment between social media and business processes on SMEs' business process performance: a conceptual model. Procedia Comput. Sci. **161**, 1106–1113 (2019)
13. Weber, M., Christos, C.G.: Digital customer experience: the risk of ignoring the non-digital experience. Int. J. Ind. Eng. Manag. **10**(3), 201–210 (2019)
14. Hansen, G., Malik, D., Ahmad, A., Bilberg, A.: Generic challenges and automation solutions in manufacturing SMEs. In: Proceedings of the 28th DAAAM International Symposium, pp. 1161–1169 (2017)
15. Dakic, D., Sefanovic, D., Lolic, T., Sladojevic, S., Anderla, A.: Production planning business process modelling using UML class diagram. In: Proceedings of 17th International Symposium INFOTEH-JAHORINA, pp. 1–6 (2018)
16. Tabachnick, B.G., Fidell, L.S.: Using Multivariate Statistics. Pearson Education, Inc., Boston (2007)
17. Chin, W.W.: Issues and opinion on structural equation modeling. MIS Q. Soc. Inf. Manag. **22**(1), 1–4 (1998)
18. Hair, J., Black, W., Babin, B., Anderson, R.: Multivariate Data Analysis, 7th edn. Prentice Hall, Upper Saddle River (2009)
19. Lalic, B., Rakic, S., Marjanovic, U.: Use of industry 4.0 and organisational innovation concepts in the Serbian textile and apparel industry. Fibres Text. Eastern Europe **27**(3), 10–18 (2019)

# Achieving Business Model Innovation with the Personalized Product Business Model Radar Template

Egon Lüftenegger[1,2(✉)] (iD)

[1] IT & Business Informatics, Campus 02 University of Applied Sciences, Graz,
Austria
egon.lueftenegger@campus02.at
[2] BusinessModelRadar.com, Salzburg, Austria

**Abstract.** Industry 4.0 is changing companies' business by introducing new manufacturing techniques. Personalization is one key goal of Industry 4.0 that is transforming companies' business models by bringing the customer's preference in the production process. Companies require to adapt their business model to these disrupting manufacturing approach. In this paper, we present a management tool for guiding the business model innovation towards personalized products: The personalized product business model radar template. This template implements a pattern that guides the business model design process by introducing predetermined values that are common in the personalized product business model in Industry 4.0. We apply this management tool in a business case scenario in a workshop setting with professionals from smart manufacturing.

**Keywords:** Business model radar · Service-dominant business model · Digital transformation

## 1 Introduction

Digital transformation and Industry 4.0 (I4.0) are disrupting production management from design and production processes to the underlying business models. The digital transformation is bringing tailored and affordable products to customers by digitalizing the manufacturing process. I4.0, also known as the fourth industrial revolution, drives the digital transformation within the manufacturing context [7].

Academics are researching highly automated processes driven by robots and cyber-physical systems. I4.0 recognizes the transformation towards personalization as a strategic goal [12]. Furthermore, smart manufacturing promise advances in production towards mass-customization and personalization at a competitive cost [7]. However, small and medium enterprises (SMEs) get less attention. Challenges for SMEs include limited financial resources and staff qualifications. Conveying the benefits of I4.0 from vision to practice is difficult because most I4.0 findings are laboratory experiments results. Hence, we notice a knowledge gap in solving current SMEs' challenges regarding personalization with I4.0 for designing cost-effective solutions.

© IFIP International Federation for Information Processing 2020
Published by Springer Nature Switzerland AG 2020
B. Lalic et al. (Eds.): APMS 2020, IFIP AICT 592, pp. 130–137, 2020.
https://doi.org/10.1007/978-3-030-57997-5_16

Most academics are focusing their attention on the shift from products towards services with servitization [8]. However, the inclusion of products to services know as productization has less attention from academics [2]. Through productization, firms try to improve the implementation of the service [21], facilitate the dissemination of the service across the organization through replication [5], improve the efficiency of service operations, and render the service more accessible for customers to perceive and use [4]. Productization is important in I4.0-driven innovation because it enables non-manufacturers to adopt smart production technologies for offering complete new solutions. For instance, additive manufacturing is a smart production technology that is ideal for offering personalized products.

In this paper, we present a pattern for designing personalized product business models in Industry 4.0 by using a networked business model management tool as a foundation. We use the pattern for achieving business model innovation of a service company towards a solution-driven by additive manufacturing.

This paper is structured as follows: In Sect. 2, we present a tool for designing networked business models: The business model radar. In Sect. 3, we present a business model pattern for designing personalized product business models: The personalized product business model radar template. In Sect. 4, we apply the personalized product business model radar pattern in a workshop setting. Finally, we end this paper with conclusions.

## 2  The Business Model Radar

The business model radar (BMR) is a novel business model tool for analyzing and designing business models as ecosystems, also known as value networks [13, 14]. The BMR implements the concept of service-dominant business models [16]: A business model that uses a value network as an organizational structure for the value co-creation between the business network actors. This organizational structure enables the adoption of an actor-to-actor value co-creation perspective instead of the typical firm-to-consumer creation one. The actor-to-actor value cocreation implies a shift from a passive customer role as a value receiver towards an actual value co-creator [10]. This co-creation perspective is derived from a strategic focus on the service-dominant logic [15, 17, 18].

As shown in Fig. 1, each co-creation actor $Ai$ $Ai$ from $A1$ to $An$ is represented as a BMR slice. There is only one Solution (S) in a business model radar: S is represented at the center of the BMR. The central position embodies that the solution is co-created by all the co-creation Actors in the business model. Each co-creation actor $Ai$ can collaborate with the solution with value propositions $AiV$ $Pj$, performing co-creation activities $AiCAk$. Each co-creation actor $Ai$ can incur in costs $AiCl$ and gain benefits $AiBm$ by participating in the networked business model. We describe further the BMR elements as follows [10]:

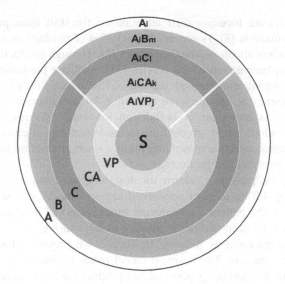

**Fig. 1.** Business Model Radar's multi-actor perspective

**Solution (S).** The solution is the goal of the business model. We can think about the solution as the co-created value between the co-creation actors of the business model.

**Co-Creation Actors (A).** This element represents the entities collaborating in a business model. We denote each co-creation actor as Ai. We can distinguish between the following types: users (U), focal organization (FO), and partners (P). The focal organization is the co-creation actor that is behind the business model. The FO collaborate with partners and users for co-creating a solution.

For each co-creation actor Ai defined above, we can distinguish the following four elements:

**Value Proposition (VP).** This element represents the value proposition of each co-Creation actor into the solution. We can see each actor's value proposition as a contribution to the overall solution. We denote the value proposition of a co-creation actor as AiV Pj.

**Co-Creation Activities (CA).** This element represents the activities that a co-Creation actor performs for delivering a value proposition into the solution. We denote the co-creation activity CAk of a co-creation actor Ai as AiCAk.

**Costs (C).** This element represents the costs that a co-creation actor incurs by performing co-creation activities and by participating in the business model. We denote the cost Cl associated to a co-creation actor Ai as AiCl.

**Benefits (B).** This element represents the benefits that a co-creation actor gain by performing co-creation activities and by participating in the business model. We denote the co-creation activity Bm of a co-creation actor Ai as AiBm.

## 3   Personalized Product Business Model Radar Template: A Pattern for Business Model Innovation

Business model innovation is the capacity to reframe an existing business model in new ways that create new value for the customers. Furthermore, business model innovation can be a path to gain competitive advantage [9]. Business model patterns are a tool for business model innovation [5]. Entrepreneurs and innovators can use these patterns to generate a new business model systematically or adapt an existing one. Patterns are reusing solutions that are documented generally and abstractly to make them accessible and applicable to others [1]. Work on patterns in the context of business models has been done by several authors [3, 12, 22].

In Fig. 2, we present a template for the personalized product business model pattern based on the literature on business models in the industry 4.0 [6]: The customized product BMR template[1]. In the template, we have three predefined co-creation actors: The focal organization, the manufacturer, and the customer. The focal organization is the company behind the business model innovation towards a customized product solution, the manufacturer is a partner from the focal organization that brings personalized manufacturing capabilities for delivering personalized products, and, the customer bring the customer's specification or needs as value propositions.

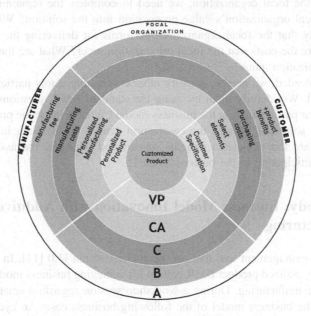

**Fig. 2.** Personalization BMR pattern as a template

---

[1] The template is available at businessmodelradar.com.

The resulting BMR is not limited to three co-creation actors. The quantity of actors depend on the specific business scenarios. The BMR can be used in workshop settings with a printed poster and post-it notes to capture the values within the management tool [10]. For using the personalized product BMR template in workshops sessions, we established a sequence of steps as the usage method. The steps order can vary depending on the interaction between the workshop participants and the workshop facilitators. We describe the usage method as follows:

First, we need to answer the following question: Who plays the role of the focal organization? Then we place the name in the co-creator actor area in the template. Second, we identify the value that want to co-create as the solution by answering the following question: What kind of customized product do we want to produce?

Second, by using the predefined values from the template, we modify the values according to our specific business case by answering the following questions for each predefined co-creation actor: the manufacturer and the customer. For the manufacturer, located at the left side in Fig. 2, we need to answer the following questions: Who is the manufacturer? What is the manufacturer's personalized product? What is the manu- facturing fee? What are the manufacturing costs? For the customer, located at the right- side in Fig. 2, we answer the following questions: Who is the customer? What is the specification provided by the customer? What is the product element selection? What are the purchasing costs for the customer? What are the product benefits for the customer?

Third, for the focal organization, we need to complete the remaining questions: What is the focal organization's value proposition into the solution? What is the co- creation activity that the focal organization performs for delivering the value propo- sition? What are the costs that the focal organization incur? What are the benefits that the focal organization gains?

Finally, if needed, we need to identify other co-creating actors participating in the business model. We identify them by using the standard BMR questions: Who is the co-creating actor participating in the business model? What is the value proposition that brings into the solution? What is the co-creation activity of the actor in the business model? What are the associated benefits gained and what are the associated costs involved by participating in the business model?

# 4    Case Study: Business Model Innovation with Additive Manufacturing

The BMR is a management tool that can be applied within I4.0 [11]. In this case, we can use the personalized product BMR pattern for achieving business model innovation with additive manufacturing. During a workshop session regarding smart production, we innovated the business model of the following business case: An eyeglasses retail company wanted to innovate their business model from selling standard eye-glasses towards customized eyeglasses. By this way the company could differentiate their offer from the massive eyeglasses retail market. The design process consisted in two stages: First, we explained the pattern to the workshop participants. Secondly, we used this pattern as a guide for identifying the values for the manufacturer and the customer in this specific business instance: The Additive manufacturer and the buyers. Then, we proceeded to identify other actors in the business models. In this case, the focal organization behind this business model is an eyeglasses company that does not manufacturer their own glasses. Then the additive manufacturer plays the role as a partner for the eyeglasses company in this specific business case. The resulting customized eyeglasses business model radar is shown in Fig. 3. In the workshop, the smart production professionals identified additive manufacturers' 3-D printing as an innovative approach within the industry 4.0 initiative for producing customized products.

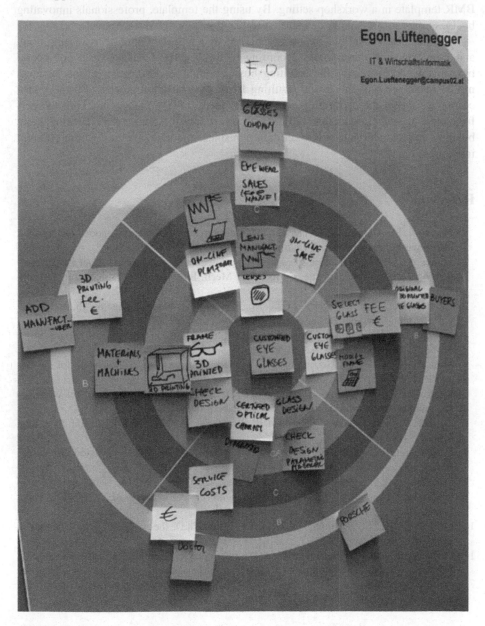

**Fig. 3.** Resulting personalized product business model for an eyeglasses focal organization

## 5 Conclusions

In this paper, we present a pattern for designing personalized business models. The pattern was implemented as a template by using the business model radar: A networked business model tool. The resulting pattern is the personalized business model radar template that serves as a foundation for innovating a business model towards customized products. The template enables a service provider the productization of their business models towards customized products. We tested the personalized product BMR template in a workshop setting. By using the template, professionals innovating business models are able to develop customized product business models.

The business model innovation is achieved by using the template as starting point and then changing these values according to the specific business case. For operationalizing and evaluating the resulting business models designed with the business model radar, we can convert the resulting BMR to a business process. Business processes are useful for performing cost-benefits analysis [19] and for tracking the performance in smart production [20]. As future work, the author will develop more business model radar patters for facilitating business model innovation within different industries.

## References

1. Amshoff, B., Dülme, C., Echterfeld, J., Gausemeier, J.: Business model patterns for disruptive technologies. Int. J. Innov. Manag. 19(03), 1540002 (2015)
2. Baines, T., Lightfoot, H., Evans, S., Neely, A., Greenough, R., Peppard, J., et al.: State-of-the-art in product-service systems. Proc. Inst. Mech. Eng. Part B: J. Eng. Manuf. 221(10), 1543–1552 (2007)
3. Gassmann, O., Frankenberger, K., Csik, M.: The Business Model Navigator: 55 Models that will Revolutionise your Business. Pearson, New York City (2014)
4. Jaakkola, E.: Unraveling the practices of "productization" in professional service firms. Scand. J. Manag. 27(2), 221–230 (2011)
5. Johnson, M., Lafley, A.: Seizing the White Space: Business Model Innovation for Growth and Renewal. Harvard Business Press, Boston (2010)
6. Kaufmann, T.: Geschäftsmodelle in Industrie 4.0 und dem Internet der Dinge: der Weg vom Anspruch in die Wirklichkeit. Springer, Heidelberg (2015)
7. Lasi, H., Fettke, P., Kemper, H.G., Feld, T., Hoffmann, M.: Industry 4.0. Bus. Inf. Syst. Eng. 6(4), 239–242 (2014)
8. Lüftenegger, E., Angelov, S., Grefen, P.: A framework for business innovation di-rections. BETA publicatie: working papers 351 (2011)
9. Lüftenegger, E., Angelov, S., van der Linden, E., Grefen, P.: The state of the art of innovation-driven business models in the financial services industry. BETA Working Paper Series, vol. 310 (2010)
10. Lüftenegger, E.: Service-dominant business design. Ph.D. thesis, Tech-nische Universiteit Eindhoven, Eindhoven (2014)
11. Lüftenegger, E.: Management-tools in smart service engineering für industrie 4.0. In: Intelligente Produktion: intelligente Produktion - Management- und Mitar- beiteraspekte, pp. 208–230. Pearson/Univerza v Mariboru, Ekonomsko-poslovna fakulteta, Harlow/Maribor (2019)

12. Lüftenegger, E.: Servitization und industrie 4.0: Neue geschäftsmodelle in der service-dominant industrie 4.0. In: Intelligente Produktion: intelligente Produktion - Management-und Mitarbeiteraspekte, pp. 255–277. Pearson/Univerza v Mariboru, Ekonomsko-poslovna fakulteta, Harlow/Maribor (2019)
13. Lüftenegger, E.: Using action design research for co-creating service-dominant business artifacts between academia and industry. EMISA Forum (2020, in Press)
14. Lüftenegger, E., Comuzzi, M., Grefen, P.: The service-dominant ecosystem: mapping a service dominant strategy to a product-service ecosystem. In: Camarinha-Matos, L.M., Scherer, R.J. (eds.) PRO-VE 2013. IAICT, vol. 408, pp. 22–30. Springer, Heidelberg (2013). https://doi.org/10.1007/978-3-642-40543-3_3
15. Lüftenegger, E., Comuzzi, M., Grefen, P.: Designing a tool for service-dominant strategies using action design research. Serv. Bus. 11(1), 161–189 (2017)
16. Lüftenegger, E., Comuzzi, M., Grefen, P., Weisleder, C.: The service dominant business model: a service focused conceptualization. BETA Working Paper Series, vol. 402 (2013)
17. Lüftenegger, E., Grefen, P., Weisleder, C.: The service dominant strategy canvas: defining and visualizing a service dominant strategy through the traditional strategic lens. BETA Working Paper Series, vol. 383 (2012)
18. Lüftenegger, E., Grefen, P., Weisleder, C.: The service dominant strategy canvas: towards networked business models. In: Camarinha-Matos, L.M., Xu, L., Afsarmanesh, H. (eds.) PRO-VE 2012. IAICT, vol. 380, pp. 207–215. Springer, Heidelberg (2012). https://doi.org/10.1007/978-3-642-32775-9_21
19. Lüftenegger, E., Softic, S.: Service-dominant business model financial validation: Cost-benefit analysis with business processes and service-dominant business models. In: Proceedings of 30th Central European Conference on Information and Intelligent Systems (CECIIS), Croatia, pp. 161–172 (2019)
20. Lüftenegger, E., Softic, S., Hatzl, S., Pergler, E.: A management tool for business process performance tracking in smart production. Mensch und Computer 2018- Workshopband (2018)
21. Menor, L., Tatikonda, M., Sampson, S.: New service development: areas for exploitation and exploration. J. Oper. Manag. 20(2), 135–157 (2002)
22. Osterwalder, A., Pigneur, Y.: Business Model Generation: A Handbook for Visionaries, Game Changers and Challengers. Wiley, Hoboken (2010)

# Integrating Electronic Components into 3D Printed Parts to Develop a Digital Manufacturing Approach

Ioan Turcin[1,2(✉)], Ali Abdallah[1] ⓘ, Manfred Pauritsch[1],
Cosmin Cosma[2] ⓘ, and Nicolae Balc[2]

[1] CAMPUS 02 University of Applied Sciences, Körblergasse 126, 8010 Graz,
Austria
ioan.turcin@campus02.at
[2] Technical University of Cluj-Napoca, Muncii 103-105, 400641 Cluj-Napoca,
Romania

**Abstract.** Digital manufacturing (DM) processes such as additive manufacturing (AM) technology, allow a high degree of integrability and functionality of printed parts. In this work, we present a proof of the DM concept focused on the integration approach where a product is developed and embedded with sensors. We also take this example one step further and introduce a method that allows 3D printing of heating elements into the specimens. The thermal characteristics of the developed heaters are investigated, and the results detailed. The novelty relates to a heater prototype injected and solidified into a curved 3D printed channel, which can produce a temperature between 23–46 °C on the printed surface of the sample both in a dry and wet environment. This research demonstrates that it is possible to construct parts with embedded electrical structures using the described method.

**Keywords:** Digital manufacturing · Stereolithography · Sensors · Conductive ink

## 1   Introduction

This work uses complex methods, tools, and processes to demonstrate the possibilities of digital manufacturing (DM). The proposed approach combines the design and manufacturing information with the concept of functionalizing additively manufactured parts in various aspects. As a practical case study, we present an anatomical sweat glands module, which was developed with DM instruments, starting from design and conception to the direct fabrication by additive manufacturing (AM). This prototype will be further developed to optimize textile materials and to elaborate specific analysis of this industry.

The sweating glands are all over the human body surface within the first 3 mm of the skin. Their density is between 80 to 100 glands/cm$^2$ and they have 40 µm diameter. These reduced characteristics of sweat glands are not possible to be fabricated with standard AM machines. Due to AM limitations, we concentrated on considering the

© IFIP International Federation for Information Processing 2020
Published by Springer Nature Switzerland AG 2020
B. Lalic et al. (Eds.): APMS 2020, IFIP AICT 592, pp. 138–145, 2020.
https://doi.org/10.1007/978-3-030-57997-5_17

surface and the sweat rate. Thus, an anatomical module was designed that offer the possibility to bring the same amount of liquid to the required surface. The armpit area was selected to develop a complex sweat glands module [1]. Regarding the AM possibilities, various scientific papers shown that 3D printing technologies can produce complex prototypes for different applications under the "layer by layer" principle [2–11]. Comparing with conventional manufacturing methods [12–14], 3D printing provides reduced time to market, lower product development costs, and improved design process [15]. Emerging technologies such as 3D printing and robotics [16] accelerates a sustainable developing of Industry 4.0 with DM. Analyzing the literature recommendations, the actual sweat glands module can be manufactured by stereolithography (SLA) technology. This AM process can produce directly accurate parts with good surface quality. A sweat glands module was designed according to AM requirements. To design the sweat glands module, boolean and CAD operations were developed using Creo Parametric and Meshmixer software. Boolean operations offer a versatile tool for editing or modifying the STL format, adding artificial constructions [17, 18]. With the design freedom afforded by the SLA process, atypically channels networks were developed for liquid flow. The designed and printed part is illustrated in Fig. 1. This module contains more than 600 outlet glands on the anatomical shape of the armpit. All the parts from this study were fabricated using a Form2 SLA system and a standard photo-polymer (Clear Resin-Formlabs).

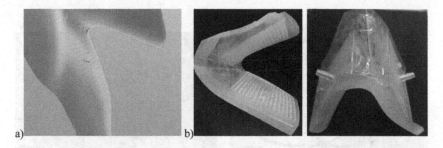

**Fig. 1.** Sweat glands module of armpit: a) virtual model, b) SLA manufactured

To add functional requirements to the actual sweat glands module, the study was focused on embedding electronic components into the 3D printed parts. This work combines additive polymer printing with liquid metal infiltration for use in potential practical applications. The novelty of this study relates to a heater prototype developed by injecting a silver conductive ink into a curved channel, which can produce a temperature between 23–60 °C on the printed surface of the sample.

## 2  Integrating Electronics in SLA Parts

AM technologies offer the possibility to integrate electric components and sensors in complex parts. Various applications of 3D printed sensors were reported for measuring the following: strain, pressure, ultrasounds, gas detection, food quality, biosensor, or even brain activity [19]. This paper describes two practical examples of how electronic components could be integrated into a sweat glands module. The first method is a straightforward one, where traditionally manufactured electronic components and sensors are integrated into pre-designed holes in the printed part. After the part was SLA manufactured, additional sensors were integrated into the pre-designed holes. The concept is presented in Fig. 2, where humidity and a temperature sensor are connected. The humidity sensor is Honeywell HIH-4000-003 and has the following features: near linear voltage output versus relative humidity, laser-trimmed interchangeability, low power design, enhanced accuracy, fast response, and low drift performance and chemical resistant. The temperature sensor is a PTF type produced by TE Connectivity. It combines a resistance temperature detector using a platinum resistor in the thin film as a sensing element. This sensor contains a structured platinum film on a ceramic substrate, passivated by glass coating [20]. The main features of it are the following: resistance tolerance $\pm 0.12\%$, application temperature $\pm 200\ ^\circ C$, and silver wire. As shown in Fig. 2, a specially printed circuit board (PCB) was designed, equipped with an ARM controller (STM32C476), which controls the electronics. This board enables the connection of various sensors and actuators and controls the integration of the components. After setting up the controller via an ST-Link (Nucleo-F103RB), the first data from the sensors (temperature and humidity) were read (Fig. 2b). Furthermore, this sweat glands module, and electronics will be implemented in a mechatronic system, which will allow us to simulate the sweating process in various conditions.

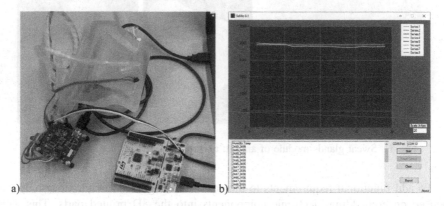

**Fig. 2.** Sweat glands module with integrated sensors: a) setting up the controller b) sensors data

The second example is based on a previous report focused on 3D printed micro-electronics for integrated circuitry and passive wireless sensors [21]. In this method, some channels are left intentionally hollow in the part, and after manufacturing, they are filled with conductive ink. In this manner, interesting components such as micro-electro-mechanical-systems (MEMS) could be developed [22]. Using this technique, we produce integrated paths in the 3D printed sample, which can be used for actuating, in this case, thermal regulation, or even sensing purposes. Several samples were SLA manufactured with "U" channels (Fig. 3b). Each sample has three channels with a

1.00 mm diameter and 26 mm length. The SLA parts were post-cured with 1.25 mW/cm$^2$ of 405 nm LED for 60 min at 60°C. For these conditions, the heat deflection of SLA parts is approx. 58.4 °C for 1.80 MPa load value (according to ASTM D 648-07). Using a normal syringe, all the channels were injected with a conductive liquid (Fig. 3a). The material used is based on silver conductive element and has a volume resistivity of 0.001 Ω cm (product code RS PRO 186-3600). According to the material data sheet, this conductive ink contains 50–75% silver, 10–25% 2-methoxy-1-methyl ethyl acetate, and 10–24% n-butyl acetate. In general, this conductive ink is used to repair circuits on printed circuit boards or to make electrical connections to non-solderable surfaces. Figure 3b shows a sample developed using this procedure, which contains three resistive elements.

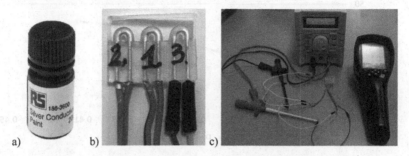

**Fig. 3.** a) Silver conductive ink used, b) 3D printed heater: SLA sample where the "U" channels injected with silver conductive ink, c) instruments used for temperature sensitivity experiment

To investigate the heating behavior of these elements integrated into the SLA part, they were characterized for temperature sensitivity. In this step, we analyzed their suitability as heating elements. To undertake this work, a programmable DC power supply from Instek PSS-3203, and an infrared thermal camera from Flir i7 was used (Fig. 3c). The power was varied from 0 to 300 mW and the surface temperature of SLA parts was recorded. Typical temperature maps at different power values are shown in Fig. 4. Moreover, Fig. 5 shows the temperatures measured in air and with the elements immersed in a liquid with respect to increasing power. The results presented are the mean values recorded on the surface. All the measurements were made until the part was no longer conductive.

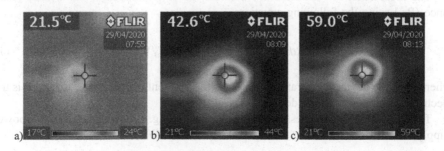

**Fig. 4.** Temperature maps at different values of power: a) 0.002 W, b) 0.107 W, c) 0.226 W

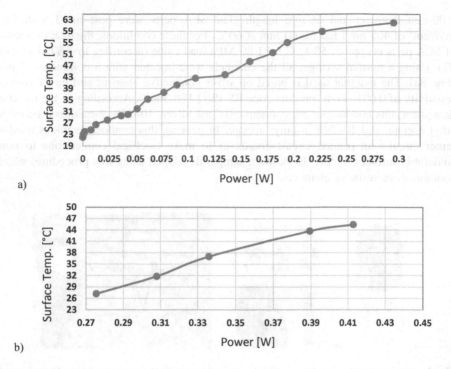

a)

b)

**Fig. 5.** Chart with surface temperature versus power: a) dry environment, b) wet environment

The interruption appears at maximum resistance, where a voltage supply of 1.15 V was applied (power of ~298 mW). The resistance of samples varied between 3.278 and 3.727 Ω. These results show that temperature from 31 °C to 42 °C can be achieved using a power input from 40 to 107 mW in a dry environment (Fig. 5a).

To investigate this system in a sweating environment, other samples were tested in water at room temperature (18 °C). The results are exposed in Fig. 5b. In this case, the power was increased up to 420 mW. In a wet environment, temperature from 32 °C to 44 °C can be archived using an input between 310 and 390 mW.

For better mechanical and electrical properties, the conductive ink could be cured at 121–148 °C for 5 to 10 min. To achieve this, another resin must be used for the printing process (e.g. High Temp Resin from FormLabs).

The measurements conducted above allow the determination of the thermal resistance ($R_{th}$) using the following equation:

$$cRth = \frac{\Delta T}{P} = \frac{(Td - Ta)}{P} [°C/W] \tag{1}$$

where $T_d$ is the device temperature (°C), $T_a$ is the ambient temperature (°C) and P is the electrical power through the device (W).

The results of thermal resistance are shown in Fig. 6. Depending on the power supply, the thermal resistance varies from 34 to 142 °C/W.

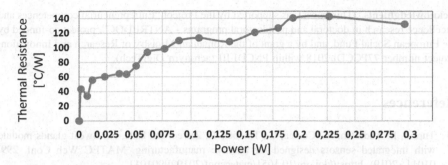

**Fig. 6.** Thermal resistance ($R_{th}$) versus power consumption

The presented results showed that this concept of resistive elements can be used as a heater. Future studies will integrate this heater concept into the anatomical shape of the sweat glands module, allowing us to simulate the sweating process at various temperatures in a dry or wet environment. To create an instrument, which combines both fluidic channels and sensing elements, the actual study shows a possible method to integrate electronic components into a 3D printed part.

The results reported brings a valuable contribution and useful reference for future applications of DM. The work was focused on functional design and the high levels of integration enabled by DM. In this study, the SLA process has been utilized to develop a sweat glands module with integrated electronic components such as temperature and humidity sensors, and a heating component made of silver conductive ink. Combining the 3D printing process and liquid metal paste filling method, a heater prototype was developed. The heating results show that it is possible to obtain a temperature from 36 °C to 46 °C both in a dry or wet environment using this heater. This preliminary study demonstrates that it is possible to develop an embedded heater into the SLA parts. From the manufacturing point of view, these findings suggest that a future heater can be constructed into the anatomical shape of the sweat glands module.

## 3 Conclusion

With the increase in the quantity and quality of computer systems in production facilities, the transition to a DM approach has become popular. DM concept refers to smart, networked methods, techniques, and tools that enable more flexible and customized manufacturing, increasing productivity and strengthening competitiveness [23]. In this study, a practical implementation of DM was developed which explores the benefits of 3D printing. Due to enabling to produce prototypes, tools, and final parts directly from virtual models, DM fosters dramatic reductions in delivery times and production costs while improving overall product quality. From our perspective, the technique described can be used to produce various electrical components with an atypical structure such as resistors, capacitors, inductors, circuits, and wireless sensors.

**Acknowledgments.** This paper was supported by the Project "Entrepreneurial competences and excellence research in doctoral and postdoctoral programs - ANTREDOC", project co-funded by the European Social Fund, and by a grant of the Romanian Ministry of Research and Innovation, project number 77PCCDI/2018 within PNCDI III (acronym DigiTech).

# References

1. Turcin, I., Abdallah, A., Cosma, C., Thiebet, T., Zavec, D., Balc, N.: Sweat glands module with integrated sensors designed for additive manufacturing. MATEC Web Conf. **299**, 01011 (2019). https://doi.org/10.1051/matecconf/201929901011
2. Ispas, A., et al.: Influence of Ti-Ceramic or Ti-composite crown on stress distribution: finite element study and additive manufacturing. J. Optoelectron. Adv. Mater. **18**, 904–912 (2016)
3. Popescu, A., Hancu, L., Sabau, E.: Effect of temperature on the mechanical properties of extrusion glass fibre reinforced polyamide 6.6 composites (GFRPA 6.6). Acta Technica Napocensis Series: Appl. Math. Mech. Eng. **61**, 213–218 (2018)
4. Gowda, R.B.S., Udayagiri, C.S., Narendra, D.D.: Studies on the process parameters of rapid prototyping technique (stereolithography) for the betterment of part quality. Int. J. Manuf. Eng. (2014). https://doi.org/10.1155/2014/804705. Article 804705
5. Pacurar, R., Berce, P.: Research on the durability of injection molding tools made by selective laser sintering technology. Rom. Acad. Ser. A – Math. Phys. Tech. Sci. Inf. Sci. **14**, 234–241 (2013)
6. Kocisko, M., Teliskova, M., Torok, J., Petrus, J.: Postprocess options for home 3D printers. Procedia Eng. **196**, 1065–1071 (2017). https://doi.org/10.1016/j.proeng.2017.08.063
7. Molnar, I., Morovic, L., Delgado Sobrino, D., Lecky, S., Michal, D.: Medical applications of biomaterials: the case of design and manufacture of orthopedic corsets made of polylactic acid by additive manufacturing. Mater. Sci. Forum **952**, 223–232 (2019). https://doi.org/10.4028/www.scientific.net/msf.952.223
8. Monkova, K., Monka, P.: Some aspects influencing production of porous structures with complex shapes of cells. In: Majstorovic, V., Jakovljevic, Z. (eds.) NEWTECH 2017. LNME, pp. 267–276. Springer, Cham (2017). https://doi.org/10.1007/978-3-319-56430-2_19
9. Grobelny, P., Furmanski, L., Legutko, S.: Investigations of surface topography of hot working tool steel manufactured with the use of 3D print. MATEC Web Conf. **137**, 02004 (2017). https://doi.org/10.1051/matecconf/201713702004
10. Miron-Borzan, C.S., Popan, A., Ceclan, V.A., Popescu, A., Berce, P.: Custom implants: manufacturing principles and determination of psychological price. Appl. Mech. Mater. **808**, 169–174 (2015). https://doi.org/10.4028/www.scientific.net/amm.808.169
11. Loginov, Y.N., Stepanov, S.I., Mukanov, G.Z.: Finite element simulation of cellular structure built from orthogonal cylindrical struts. Mater. Sci. Forum **989**, 856–860 (2020). https://doi.org/10.4028/www.scientific.net/MSF.989.856
12. Sobotova, L., Kralikova, R., Badida, M.: The analysis of chosen material properties at thermal drilling. Key Eng. Mater. **635**, 35–40 (2015). https://doi.org/10.4028/www.scientific.net/KEM.635.35
13. Harnicarova, M., Valicek, J., Cep, R., et al.: Comparison of non-traditional technologies for material cutting from the point of view of surface roughness. Int. J. Adv. Manuf. Technol. **69**, 81–91 (2013). https://doi.org/10.1007/s00170-013-4992-z

14. Popan, I.A., Popan, A.I., Carean, A., Fratila, D., Trif, A.: Study on chip fragmentation and hole quality in drilling of aluminium 6061 alloy with high pressure internal cooling. MATEC Web Conf. **299**, 04014 (2019). https://doi.org/10.1051/matecconf/201929904014
15. Chua, C.K., Leong, K.F., Lim, C.S.: Rapid Prototyping: Principles and Applications, 2nd edn. World Scientific Singapore, Singapore (2003)
16. Pisla, D., et al.: Risk management for the reliability of robotic assisted treatment of non-resectable liver tumors. Appl. Sci. **10**(1) (2020). https://doi.org/10.3390/app10010052
17. Guo, K.B., Zhang, L.C., Wang, C.J., Huang, S.H.: Boolean operations of STL models based on loop detection. Int. J. Adv. Manuf. Technol. **33**, 627–633 (2007). https://doi.org/10.1007/s00170-006-0876-9
18. Herle, S., Marcu, C., Benea, H., Miclea, M., Robotin, R.: Simulation-based stress analysis for a 3D modeled humerus-prosthesis assembly. In: Sobh, T., Elleithy, K. (eds.) Innovations in Computing Sciences and Software Engineering, pp. 343–348. Springer, Dordrecht (2010). https://doi.org/10.1007/978-90-481-9112-3_58
19. Xu, Y., et al.: The boom in 3D-printed sensor technology. Sensors **17**, 1166 (2017). https://doi.org/10.3390/s17051166
20. PTF temperature sensor. Data sheet, www.te.com. Accessed 03 Mar 2020
21. Wu, S., Yang, C., Hsu, W., et al.: 3D-printed microelectronics for integrated circuitry and passive wireless sensors. Nat. Microsyst. Nanoeng. **1**, 15013 (2015). https://doi.org/10.1038/micronano.2015.13
22. Birleanu, C., Pustan, M., Voicu, R., Serdean, F., Merie, V.: Humidity influence on the adhesion of SU-8 polymer from MEMS applications. MATEC Web Conf. **137**, 08002 (2017). https://doi.org/10.1051/matecconf/201713708002
23. Digital Manufacturing 4.0. Fraunhofer Institute IAO, www.iao.fraunhofer.de. Accessed 03 Mar 2020

# Digital Transformation and Its Potential Effects on Future Management: Insights from an ETO Context

Antoni Vike Danielsen[(✉)]

Department of Ocean Operations and Civil Engineering, Norwegian University of Science and Technology, Aalesund, Norway
antoni.v.danielsen@ntnu.no

**Abstract.** Digitalization has penetrated and transformed entire business models irrespective of industry belonging. Thus, digital transformation launches both possibilities and challenges for firms and their managers in how to execute (intra) organizational operations and strategies. This paper provides findings derived from an explorative interview study targeting required skillsets for future Engineer-to-Order (ETO) operations within the maritime industry. It has an introspective perspective, focusing on managerial perception of current and future needs to enhance efforts to digitalize ETO work further. Hence, as ETO firms tends to be conservative in their underlying dynamics of work it is important to gain insights on important skills and mindsets for successful leadership of digital transformation. The study heightens the effects of previous and future implications of digital transformation, while accentuating that new required skills are not only restricted to operators and engineers, instead it is equally relevant for managers to embrace such changing needs, as digitalization has resulted in blurred mechanisms for how to conduct management.

**Keywords:** Digitalization · Engineer-to-Order · Leadership change

## 1 Introduction

The Internet boom started 20 years ago and then exaggerated on the promise as a source of fully disruptive technology- turning it into a speculative bubble. However, from the start of the internet boom the technology has eventually materialized into more rational business fundamentals who have become mainstream and in many cases mission and operational critical. Digitalisation, as such has become a *"global mega-trend that is fundamentally changing existing value chains across industries and public sectors"* [1].

Based on these foundations we are today in the early loop of even more disruptive technologies as artificial intelligence, internet of things (IOT), cyber currencies as bitcoin, gamification, visualisation and augmented reality (AR), robotics, driverless cars, autonomous ships, whereas parts of these technologies has already become ubiquitous within selected industries and businesses during the last decade. Embarking and aiming to make the best use of the aforesaid technologies implies that a firm will face a digital transformation process. According to Parvainen et al. [2] *"Digital*

© IFIP International Federation for Information Processing 2020
Published by Springer Nature Switzerland AG 2020
B. Lalic et al. (Eds.): APMS 2020, IFIP AICT 592, pp. 146–153, 2020.
https://doi.org/10.1007/978-3-030-57997-5_18

*transformation is changes in ways of working, roles, and businesses offered caused by adoption of digital technologies in an organization, or in the operation environment of the organization".*

The definition mirrors the traditional research conducted in studies investigating manufacturing environments and systems, while missing (or intentionally disregard) its effect on management. However, this might have its consequences in not having managed to clarify some distinct differences in its dimension. For instance, digitalization and digital transformation are often used interchangeably, which has resulted in a blurred terminology usage, both in academic and professional environments [4, 5].

Hence, a digital transformation implies a larger change than e.g., converting a paper transcript into a digital representation (i.e. digitalization) as well as the process of technologically induced change that e.g., a software program can provide (i.e. digitalization) [3, 4]. As such, digital transformations have greater impact on organizations as they affect both intra and inter organizational aspects and thus, enforce a re-evaluation of future manufacturing strategies. Extant studies on technological advancement in manufacturing has greatly improved the understanding of effectiveness and efficiencies with regards to production processes, tools for information sharing, design, delivery and payment, including operator- and engineer perspectives, however, less has been said about its effects for managerial actions and possibly styles to handle its outcome.

This study picks up this deficit and aims to sharpen the understanding of potential changes to required skillsets for managers during digital transformations in the context of ETO. Based on theoretical and conceptual groundwork, the study delineates potential implications and opportunities regarding future required managerial capabilities. While the analysis is performed by the author, the recommended and reflected skillsets are defined and elaborated by 8 different executives and top managers operating in ETO firms.

The rest of the composition of the paper is as follows: A short presentation of relevant theory targeting ETO characteristics is introduced in Sect. 2, and Sect. 3 describes the methodological choices. Section 4 presents the findings, which also represents the frame of reference for the discussion and the concluding remarks in Sect. 5.

## 2 The Engineer to Order Business

In ETO firms the product produced are often one of a kind, or one of very few. The products in question are often very different from each other. Repeat orders might be made where the manufacturer can use already made and tested design and fabrication processes. There are often very strict customer requirements, and they tend to be very specific, technical and precise, thus ETO products tend to be complex, highly technical and comprise a high level of added value with many levels of assembly [6, 7].

These firms tend to operate as project-based organizations [6, 8], where engineering is the core activity [9]. In addition to its unique characteristics in production methods, design and engineering, the human and organizational factors are built on long traditions, posing hinders for new management approaches [10]. Despite this notion, there is an increasing focus on bringing new functionalities into ETO products, as well as introducing new business models, such as 'power-by-the-hour' and conditional maintenance, moving away from the core paradigm of construction to a level of servitization, where new business models will be pushed forward and introducing new challenges. Also worth mentioning, is that ETO differs from firms working by the Make-to-Order (MTO) principles, which is heavily based on lean methodologies with a high level of standardization and manufacturing planning. Interestingly, MTO firms are already achieving a high level of benefits from an extensive use of digital tools, such a robotics and virtual reality, while ETO firms are more in its infancy in the implementation and the search for how to reap the benefits of extensive digitalisation and digital transformation. These new processes, activities and business models will in turn affect organizations, workers and hence, its management.

This development in combination with the increased competition from developing countries located in Asia, which previously were delivering low cost to an acceptable quality, now moving up the value chain due to learning outcomes derived from foreign direct investments, Joint ventures, offshoring and atomization and robotics, is pushing Western companies to speed up and reap the benefits of what digitalization might provide, in terms of new products and services creating new business models as well as increasing effectivity and quality of their production offerings.

The above development induces not only a focus towards potential benefits in form of digital improvements and efficiency but also in terms of organizational strategy and management skillsets.

## 3   Approach and Methodology

The present research is conducted as a continuation of the former research project "Human Side of Digitalization" [3], which focused on organizational structures, leadership, employee skills and work-life balance in a digital context. As an extension to the results in the first phase, this study provides an additional understanding targeting potential challenges managers might need to reflect and act upon when entering a phase of digital transformation.

Based on a list of 14 identified experts in the Norwegian maritime industry we managed to interview 8 experts from equal number of firms during the period of April–August 2019. The experts were all top managers and senior executives within the firms they were working. They were carefully recruited based on their merits as experts recruited through the researcher's network.

Data collection was performed through semi structured interviews carried out in a maritime ETO environment, lasting on average 60–90 min. The interviews focused on managerial perception and understanding of past, present and future skillset requirements in the context of digital transformation [10].

To improve transparency, the findings and analysis is illustrated with quotes from the interviews.

# 4 Findings and Discussion

Overall, issue addressed by the executives interviewed where aspects they considered as important during a digital transformation, as well as their interpretation of it as a phenomenon in itself.

Almost all interviews started with some sort of reflection to digitization mentioning the use of e-mail as a tool for communication and Cad/Cam as a tool for engineering, which is understandable as both tools have been around for at least two decades. However, they should not be considered as a transformation neither as something new nor innovative. Thus, they all agreed that digital transformation is something more, and something that changes the business and the business offerings made possible. Our research thus takes a wider perspective on digitalization to contribute a better understanding of the challenges facing leaders in their effort for digital transition within their ETO based firms. Next section presents three key areas which according to the experts/executives deserve further attention: i) changes in leadership behaviour, ii) decision making and iii) social and cultural structures.

## 4.1 Top Management

The first sub grouping found in the key area of top management are the conflicting perceptions and actions of becoming more efficient while being explorative and innovative. These conflicting interests are termed ambidexterity. Ambidexterity is the notion of doing things with both hands. In business this means to pursue and balance exploration and exploitation, in terms of innovation and operational efficiency. An ambidextrous organization loosens up the rigidity and strict organizational hierarchies and enforce self organizing [11]. This is in line with Snow et al. [12] perspective that digitalization will alter the ways of working both in terms of exploration and exploitation. All interviewees stressed the importance of acting on the dualism that ambidexterity presents. However, the focus of pursuing and managing this dualism within the organization, by enforcing an explorative perspective introducing new digital products and services seems to fade in the day to day operations, whereas 'the next day' operations are the most important. The findings point in the direction that firms tend to maintain focus on efficiency. Digital transformation is, as such, perceived more as a driver for increased efficiency, where new products and services are perceived more as tools to achieve greater efficiency. As one interviewee stated: *"The driver for [digitalisation] is not to follow the buzzwords and all the issues around internet, and words like artificial intelligence and big data, that is not the driver....[...] ... we have a very practical approach to this, thus making things more efficient and do it right the first time, that is what the driver is".*

The second main grouping found under the key area of top management is the need for an effective strategy. Strategy is about setting a target for the firm and what the firm will become in the future. Our research indicates that the focus for creating and following a digital strategy is made on an ad hoc basis, although there were exemptions. Thus, there is an interest to follow through on working on a digital strategy, but firms seem to lack a strong, dedicated and deliberated strategic focus. A common expression from our interviews is that there is an expressed wish for enhancing digitalisation and to move towards digital transformation of the firms, but in practice the firms fall easily back into day to day operations, where the focus on digital transformation becomes blurred. As one interviewee stated: *"... without any comparison, here we have the entire office, and then outside on the other side of the parking lot there are some barracks where they have put the IT department. Thus, every time, anyone has a problem with a computer, they have to put on outerwear to approach them..."*.

The third grouping found under the umbrella of top management is strategic decisions. Strategic decisions are decisions made by the top management to enhance and push the strategy forward. One component and decision commonly made by ETO firms is the implementation of organizational wide ERP systems. It is acknowledged that implementing ERP systems are difficult. The majority of the experts agreed that the use of digital communication as ERP systems introduce and promote are not well utilised. One argument acknowledging their statement is that the input, output and use of information between the different software systems were difficult and not sufficiently taken care of or managed during the implementation and later the use of the ERP system. The lack of effective implementation leads to suboptimal processes and intra organizational communication outside the system and integrated processes the ERP presents. Further, leading to flow of data outside the dedicated channels and systems. Organization wide system integration is expressed as difficult, and in some cases could lead to operational interference. These integration difficulties are seen as barriers for the further digitalisation processes, and in particularly where developing digital services are the objective. Decisions on the scale of IT and ERP system integration needs to be made in front of, or in parallel of the development of new digital services. As one interviewee stated:

*"...thus, a senior executive need to have interest to know that if we were to be a global organisation working digital, it has to be anchored at executive level and distributed down throughout the organization".*

## 4.2 Organization

Trust is an essential component of organizational life and leadership. The greater the trust the less the control and surveillance mechanisms will be within the organisation. Trust is also a component between the leaders, managers and co-workers, and that each part act in the best interest for all parties and the company as a whole. In our research we found that the experts believed that the co-workers and managers need to have a high level of trust and confidence that the development and implementation of new digital technologies will be beneficial for them, and not seen as tool for reduction in manning and layoffs. As one interviewee stated: *"...and that I think a digital leader also has to understand. He cannot know, and he needs to have trust and confidence in his organization... that they work for the best for the company".*

Organizational culture is another subgroup found and derived from Organization as a key subject. Organizational culture is evolving within the borders of the organization, with an explicit focus on thoughts and opinions among people. Our research shows that the experts perceive that there need to be a strong culture and attitude within the organization to accept new thoughts and ideas. This implies that there has to be a culture and attitude accepting new and innovative tools, processes and technologies within the organization. As one interviewee stated:

*"... I do not believe the curiosity regarding digitalization, is a culture per se, it is more a culture of being curious of new innovations and technical developments...."*.

Motivation and a will to change among the co-workers are important both in terms of implementing new technologies and products within the organization, but also as a mean for providing new product and service offerings. It is acknowledged that there will be opposition to changes made in organizations. It should be reasonable to suspect that, due to the form and type of change that digitalization represents, the older should express greater resistance and be in a stronger opposition to this category of change. However, our experts perceive that resistance and opposition in the context of digitalization is not about age, but more about general interests in digital technology. Their expression was that many youngsters (digital natives), are not necessarily digital savvy. There is a difference in being fluent on social media and superficial use of software, versus being skilled in digital technology and sophisticated use of software. Thus, our findings indicate that the willingness to change and adapt is more about the interests of the individual rather being a digital native or digital immigrant. As one interviewee stated: *"...I have many reports who are positive to those things [digitalization and digital technologies], but the knowledge and understanding for it and how to benefit from it [make effective use of the technology] is scarce... and when the day it comes that they will have to change, then it becomes a challenge."*

### 4.3 Leadership

The ability to understand the business you are in are paramount in being able to exercise effective leadership. This implies that effective leaders need to have the skills and know-how, not just about the business they are in, but also to understand the principles of the technology that render the industry and businesses. During our research we found that the majority of the respondents acknowledged their belief that there is a lack of skills and understanding of new digital technologies among leaders and executives. Our interviewees believe there are many thoughts and wishes of new product and service offerings due to digitalization. The lack of a sufficient skillset renders the leader less likely to understand how to, why doing and what resources and expertise will be needed to explore the opportunities digitalisation may provide. As one interviewee stated: *"A leader, an executive, in a firm cannot know everything about digitalization, but he has to surround himself with people who can give advice, who knows and have competence within that area"*.

Another interviewee stated: *"...you have to express a clear opinion on what you want to achieve. This will challenge leaders in a greater degree, as more technical savvy environments in the organization are very keen to continuously find an try new technology and create intelligent things... but you need to have a business case. You cannot just do it for the sake of technology but do it because you will earn money on it"*.

Following Shipper and Davy [13] leadership skills follow two broad categories a) interactive skills and b) initiating skills. Their model is useful in the context of traditional industries with less extensive rate and pace of environmental and organizational change, as most ETO firms have traditionally operated within. However, such a model falls short in a digital context with high pace and scale of change. Because of digitalization and the increasing complexities of technology and organizational structures, the power will tip more from the vertical to the horizontal organizational axis. This will challenge leaders, as their behaviour will face greater scrutiny and decisions more questioned due to a broader and deeper skillset among peers and reports. Thus, leaders must accept greater transparency of their decisions. As one interviewee stated: *"For some leaders, especially those of age, who are used to withhold and govern through access to information, [...]. That will not work, it will hit them hard. They do not understand that there is so much available information from other sources, which makes people able to verify what has been done. Especially in the aftermath." [...]... that means that those leaders that are used to govern and manage by withholding information, will face a real backfire. It will not work. A leader has to acknowledge that issues has to be transparent"*.

The third grouping under the umbrella of leadership is the skills and expertise in change management. Change management per se is not about operational leadership nor management. It is more about changing the organization to work differently in its environment. With the increasing pace of change due to digitalization, some of our interviewees believe that organizations will be kept in a continuous state of change. Change initiatives and implementation of new technology and processes will not manifest itself throughout the organization. This leave organizations in a state of continuous flux. Leaders will have to manage and lead in a more fluid environment with higher pace and a higher level of uncertainty. As one interviewee stated: *"With digitalization you got the technological development a different way. You got continuously improvements, you needed and wanted more. Also specialised workers. It became necessary to digitalize drawings. Everything. And now we have the possibility to automate our warehouses and automate our logistic operations. It is like a tsunami"*.

# 5   Conclusion

ETO firms can be innovative and explorative in terms of product development and one-time technical solutions, but digitalization proves novel challenges and new forms of innovation, both in terms of developing new products and service offerings as well as novel processes and the utilization of the new technology within the organization. This alteration requires new skills and different mindsets for successful leadership and management of digital transformation. The new technological trajectory may render parts of the traditional management and leadership skillset outdated and in extreme cases obsolete. Through our research we have identified three key areas which according to the experts/executives deserve further attention: i) changes in leadership behaviour, ii) decision making and iii) social and cultural structures.

Our contribution is twofold. For the practitioners we provide insight into key areas a leader should give attention to and address while implementing and developing new leadership- and management skills pursuing digital transformation. For the academic community we provide additional insight into the scarce literature of the possible effect that digitalization might have on management and leadership within ETO firms.

# References

1. Collin, J., Hiekkanen, K., Korhonen, J.J., Halén, M., Itälä, T., Helenius, M.: IT leadership in transition - the impact of digitalization on finnish organizations. In: Science + Technology, Aalto University, vol. 7, p. 121 (2015)
2. Parviainen, P., et al.: Tackling the digitalization challenge: how to benefit from digitalization in practice. Int. J. Inf. Syst. Project Manag. 5(1), 63–77 (2017)
3. Mustafa, G., et al.: Human Side of Digitalization, Aalesund, p. 56 (2019)
4. Bloomberg, J. Digitization, digitalization, and digital transformation: confuse them at your peril (2018). https://www.forbes.com/sites/jasonbloomberg/2018/04/29/digitization-digitalization-and-digital-transformation-confuse-them-at-your-peril/#4a0ea6f22f2c. Accessed 20 Feb 2020
5. Khan, S.: Leadership in the digital age - a study on the effects of digitalization on top management leadership. Stockholm Business School, Stockholm University, p. 54 (2016)
6. Hicks, C., McGovern, T.: Product life cycle management in engineer-to-order industries. Int. J. Technol. Manag. 48(2), 153–167 (2009)
7. Brady, T., Davies, A., Gann, D.M.: Creating value by delivering integrated solutions. Int. J. Project Manag. 23(5), 360–365 (2005)
8. Hobday, M.: The project-based organisation: an ideal form for managing complex products and systems? Res. Policy 29(7–8), 871–893 (2000)
9. Hicks, C., Earl, C.F., McGovern, T.: An analysis of company structure and business processes in the capital goods industry in the UK. IEEE Trans. Eng. Manag. 47(4), 414–423 (2000)
10. Arica, E., Magerøy, K., Lall, M.T.M.: Barriers and success factors for continuous improvement efforts in complex ETO firms. In: Moon, I., Lee, G.M., Park, J., Kiritsis, D., von Cieminski, G. (eds.) APMS 2018. IAICT, vol. 535, pp. 124–130. Springer, Cham (2018). https://doi.org/10.1007/978-3-319-99704-9_16
11. O'Reilly, C.A., Tushman, M.L.: The ambidextrous organization. Harv. Bus. Rev. 82(4), 74–81, 140 (2004)
12. Snow, C.C., Fjeldstad, Ø.D., Langer, A.M.: Designing the digital organization. J. Organ. Des. 6(1), 7 (2017)
13. Shipper, F., Davy, J.: A model and investigation of managerial skills, employees' attitudes, and managerial performance. Leadersh. Q. 13(2), 95–120 (2002)

# Applying Contextualization for Data-Driven Transformation in Manufacturing

Sonika Gogineni[1(✉)], Kai Lindow[1], Jonas Nickel[2],
and Rainer Stark[1,3]

[1] Fraunhofer Institute for Production Systems and Design Technology IPK,
Berlin, Germany
sonika.gogineni@ipk.fraunhofer.de
[2] Rolls-Royce Deutschland, Eschenweg 11, 15827 Blankenfelde-Mahlow,
Germany
[3] Chair Industrial Information Technology, Technische Universität Berlin,
Berlin, Germany

**Abstract.** Manufacturing is highly distributed and involves a multitude of heterogeneous information sources. In addition, Production systems are increasingly interconnected, hence leading to an increase in heterogeneous data sources. At present, data available from these new type of systems are growing faster than the ability to productively integrate them into engineering and production value chains of companies. Known applications such as predictive maintenance and manufacturing equipment management are currently being continuously optimized. While these applications are designed to help companies manage their manufacturing and engineering data, they only use a fraction of the total potential that can be realized by linking manufacturing and engineering data with other enterprise data. In the future, the context in which the data can be set will play an essential role. A meaningful added value in manufacturing can be achieved only with context specific data. Against this background, this paper presents three main areas of application for contextualizing data (semantics, sensitivity and visualization) and explains these applications with the help of a contextualization architecture. The concept is also evaluated using an industrial example. Furthermore, the paper describes the theoretical background of contextualization and its application in industry. The major challenges of the ability of engineers to adapt their activities and the integration of process knowledge for semantic linking are addressed as well.

**Keywords:** Contextualization · Manufacturing planning · Semantics

## 1 Introduction

An increasing number of data sources is leading to larger pools of data being collected in manufacturing for diverse applications (scheduling, quality monitoring, maintenance, new design assumption etc.). The data is then being converted into information that helps users perform their activities. Increasing information implies that users need to find, understand, process and act on additional information. Which leads to increasing efforts and perhaps to frustration, especially for the information discovery

© IFIP International Federation for Information Processing 2020
Published by Springer Nature Switzerland AG 2020
B. Lalic et al. (Eds.): APMS 2020, IFIP AICT 592, pp. 154–161, 2020.
https://doi.org/10.1007/978-3-030-57997-5_19

and usage (e.g. searching relevant information across various tools and databases against the unclear background of responsibilities and rights). At this point, the context of data becomes relevant. Until now, various domains have already largely defined the context [1]. In the information technology (IT) environment context means any kind of information that can be used to characterize the situation of an entity in interaction with other entities. Context can be a single piece of information or a combination of many pieces of information from different sources or at different points in time. For example, a CPS (Cyber-Physical System) interacts with a CPPS (Cyber-Physical Production System). Examples of such contextual information could be location, product identification number, machine identification number, time, energy consumption, etc. From the manufacturing user's point of view, the appropriate situational context must be established (e.g. "I want to know why my bearing is not available at work station three."). From a data processing point of view, the interaction between the entities has to take place (e.g. work station three reports that the bearing is not available and an automated search finds possible solutions based on historical data, the worker has to make a solution respectively "I decide to take the bearing from workstation one, because there is still one available and the station is currently in maintenance mode."). Eventually, a decision can be made on the basis of the respective situation and the data. Hence, contextualization contributes to saving time and efforts involved in carrying out an activity and making decisions. A connection to Industry 4.0 as well as data allocation and contextualization of this data is an ongoing challenge: research gaps are becoming apparent [2]. So far, there are only partial solutions in individual technology domains, but no general industrial approach is apparent [3]. To fill this gap, the research methodology followed is to identify the main aspects of contextualization, develop a suitable architecture to integrate them and evaluate the same with an industrial application. The effective evaluation of the contextualization concept and its future scope are further detailed in this paper.

## 2 Technological Approach

Contextualization consists of three major aspects which have to be combined: context sensitivity, semantics and visualization. These three aspects are described in detail below:

**Context sensitivity** is becoming increasingly important to ensure that systems are situation-dependent. By using a knowledge base and linking it with context data, information can be provided to the right user at the right time. According to [4], context-sensitive systems can be divided into four levels of interactivity: active execution, active configuration, passive execution and passive configuration. Active executing systems make independent decisions based on the current context and execute the necessary measures to implement the decision independently. Active configuring systems get to know the user over time and adapt accordingly. Passive executing systems understand the context and, based on this, develop proposals of action for the user, who then decides on the next steps. Passive configuring systems offer the user configuration options depending on the context, allowing the user to influence the system configuration.

**Semantics:** Production and production planning are highly distributed and involve a multitude of heterogeneous data. Necessary distributed systems and their heterogeneous databases require adequate technical possibilities to present (e.g. production and planning) information in a semantic context, otherwise the interpretation of the information is difficult or impossible. Ontologies have proven to be suitable technologies for modelling these semantic relationships in application and research. In the industrial environment, semantics modelled by ontologies are currently mainly used for semantic searches. Ontologies can be created automatically and manually. Automated ontologies can be created efficiently without human intervention and are thus suitable for large amounts of data, but do not represent the implicit knowledge of engineers. Therefore, the literature recommends creating semi-automated ontologies according to templates such as ISO 15926 "Industrial automation systems and integration—Integration of life cycle data for process plants including oil and gas production facilities". Technically, the trend is towards cloud-based applications based on Semantic Web technologies. Semantic Web offers a good basis for doing this in an enterprise context: [5] for example, presents a concept for the automated creation of an enterprise-wide, semantically linked knowledge base.

**Visualization** of primary abstract data and the interaction with it is important for the development of modern user interfaces. A widely accepted definition of information visualisation is "The use of computer-supported, interactive, visual representations of abstract data in order to amplify cognition" [6]. Information visualization should help to prepare and visualize abstract data accordingly. Therefore, information visualization also supports the cognitive processes of the user, i.e. all processes related to perception and recognition. The aim is to understand semantically analysed and sensitive data more quickly. This forms the basis for human-centred decision making or at least decision support. In the understanding of manufacturing, the development and planning of complex systems requires visualizations that provide an overview of the complex and extensive models. Visual validation can be performed in immersive (virtual) environments where data/information can be experienced [6].

## 2.1   Contextualization Approach

Contextualization of data can be seen as a valuable input for various applications along the lifecycle of products. Figure 1 shows how the data can be exchanged across the different phases of product lifecycle by using a contextualization architecture as a backbone. The contextualization architecture, which consists of semantics interconnection, context sensitivity and visualization elements supports the users with relevant data from various phases. For example, a designer can benefit from contextual information about market research. This helps the designer to design a product closer to the market needs. Another example is contextualization of production information with regards to the machines available and their capabilities, which helps production planners to plan future production better.

To illustrate the above approach, a real case from the production of aero engines is presented here: in terms of manufacturing, the efficiency of execution of processes, such as production, assembly, maintenance or quality assurance, is directly related to the availability of up-to date product data. The product data has to be updated,

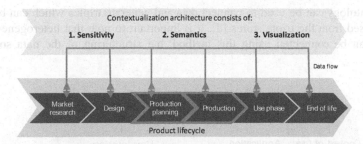

**Fig. 1.** Contextualization across product lifecycle

available, manageable and traceable throughout the lifecycle. Increasing product variance leads to complexities in production. Complexities in turn cause difficulties in flexible production management, as resources have to be rescheduled and managed across various production programs. This increased complexity creates a challenge for employees who have to be informed and qualified to run the different production programs. In order to support the future of flexible production, it is important to provide the production employees with the workplace of the future equipped with contextualized information.

## 3 Development of a Contextualization Architecture

The basis for the development of a contextualization architecture is formed by the three essential components "context of origin", "context of processing" and "context of use" (cp. [7]). The "context of origin" is the information about origin of the data. This is linked to the question of "who organized and performed the actions; what were the objects; which features have been measured; what were the reasons or motives for collecting the data; when and where the data were collected; who were the owners; what were the licences used, etc." [7]. The "context of processing" is on a technological level and describes "formats, encryption keys, used pre-processing tools, predicted performance of algorithms etc" [7]. Eventually, the "context of use" describes the "potential domains, potential or known applications, which may use the data or the knowledge extracted from it, potential customers, etc." [7].

The three components are shown on the left hand side in Fig. 2. Furthermore, Fig. 2 shows the application of the components to a general contextualization architecture. Since the processing component is the technological advanced one, it has to be divided into several sub-components to be made applicable. That way, four layers describe the architecture, namely: data layer, semantic middleware layer, context-algorithm layer and the application layer. The application layers host the user interface with which the user interacts with and has contextual information using suitable visualization techniques. Based on the users tasks or request context algorithms pull or push requests to adjacent layers. The request to pull the relevant data is interfaced with the semantic middleware which can be any form of a semantic network which connects various data sources present in the data layer. For example, an ontology web language

(OWL) ontology can be used to connect data and generate triples which can be stored and accessed from the triple stores [8]. It is important to note that heterogeneous data sources can be connected using this method, but structuring of the data sources is required.

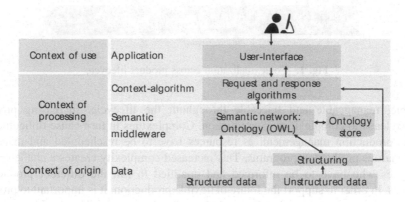

**Fig. 2.** Contextualization architecture

# 4   Evaluation of Contextualization in Manufacturing

The evaluation of contextualization is conducted as part of a project called Cockpit 4.0 (funded by the Berlin Senate, the State of Brandenburg and the European Regional Development Fund – ERDF 1.8/03) in which a consortium of Rolls-Royce Germany, Fraunhofer IPK and the BTU Cottbus are working together to address different challenges in the context of digitalization [9]. The aim of the project is to address industrial challenges by assisting in making process data available and interconnected across various processes such as production, assembly, maintenance or quality assurance. Hence, users can work with contextual information to obtain a big picture of the entire lifecycle, track changes, manage, collaborate and interoperate across processes. This helps in improving efficiency of processes, therefore, leading to time and cost savings.

## 4.1   Goal of the Research

The goal of the project is to develop and study concepts that support the navigation and data analysis in heterogeneous information ecosystems by providing relevant data in context to the current use case activity.

## 4.2   Methodological Approach

The research approach was based on the Design Science Research Methodology (DSRM) for Information Systems Research [10]. Initially the needs or requirements from the company were derived through a series of workshops with various stakeholders. The needs were then converted to user stories and further grouped and detailed to form use cases. The use cases enabled capturing of the features that needed to be developed. One suitable use case was then selected and developed into a demonstrator with a contextualization architecture. The demonstrator and its user interface were then evaluated by the users.

### 4.3 Concept

The concept of the demonstrator that was developed together with Rolls-Royce was an assistance system for the assembly of aero engines. The purpose of this demonstrator was to assist a team, called Voice of the Fitter (VoF), in their daily tasks to solve issues faced by the fitters during assembly processes. Examples for the problems occurring are part shortages, tool related issues, non-conformances identified during the assembly and others. As the team had to often search for causes of the problem and solve the problem by searching through various data sources, the assistance system was equipped with contextualization fields to address this situation. The aim was to provide useful information and suggestions, to help speeding up finding and solving problems which occur on the assembly line.

### 4.4 Implementation

The architecture for the assistance system is based on the contextualization architecture discussed in Sect. 3. It provides context sensitive information to the VoF team from various data sources. The data sources comprise information about the parts of the aero engine, current and historic problems recorded by the team called VoF-cases and reported non-conformances (concessions) associated with a specific engine type. These data sources are generated by different processes along the product lifecycle of the engine. Data from these various sources were connected using an ontology, this represents the connection of data layer with the semantic middleware layer. The ontology is mined for context relevant data through contextualization algorithms. The contextualization algorithms used data fields such as part number and engine type to identify associated information relevant to the user. The algorithms also relied on natural language processing (NLP) to identify datasets with contextually similar and relevant information.

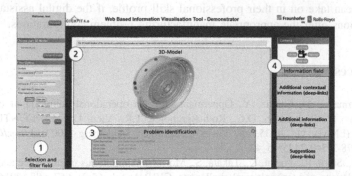

**Fig. 3.** Front end of assistance system [9] (numbers 1 to 4 are explained in the text below)

The assistance system's front end is shown in Fig. 3. This is a part of the application layer where the user interacts with the system. The first field, indicates the selection and filter field which was designed to provide the team with options to obtain relevant problem information on the part having the problem. The part is displayed in the 3D viewer ($2^{nd}$ pane) this helps the team to visualize the part on which they are planning to solve a problem. The problem identification field ($3^{rd}$ pane) provides information about the problem. The fourth field, is an information field which provides additional context sensitive information (including deep links) from various data sources such as non-conformances, historic problems, similar problems and their solutions, hence, saving research time for the team. This helps in avoiding delays which are extremely critical on the assembly line. The assistance system was evaluated twice with a gap of six months. A VoF team member was briefed about the features available and then was interviewed to receive qualitative feedback and suggestions for improvement. The user then filled the questionnaire presented by F.D Davis to measure perceived usefulness, perceived ease of use, and user acceptance [11]. The results indicated that the user acknowledged the advantages of the system to support daily work. However, highlights scope for improvement with respect to the user interface and additional features to integrate it into the work environment.

## 5  Conclusion and Potentials for the Future

Data contextualization becomes a base foundation for the design and operation of manufacturing systems. In this paper, the authors have introduced the foundation for data contextualization in the heterogeneous field of data sources in the product and assembly context. The main potentials of data contextualization can be realized in the processes of decision making, knowledge reuse, knowledge transfer and user (planer, fitter, and maintenance personnel) experience. It became clear throughout the execution of this research that new capabilities in designing, planning and executing manufacturing with respect to the collection, identification, interpretation and digital composition of the right or decisive data sets will form a new discipline in manufacturing. This discipline will need competence in manufacturing/engineering process know-how, data analytics, data contextualization, human-machine interaction and IT knowledge. Data contextualization will be a competence that process planners and manufacturing engineers can take on in their professional skill profile, if the digital assistant system configurations offer the appropriate manufacturing problem configurations.

## References

1. Zimmermann, A., Lorenz, A., Oppermann, R.: An operational definition of context. In: Kokinov, B., Richardson, D.C., Roth-Berghofer, T.R., Vieu, L. (eds.) CONTEXT 2007. LNCS (LNAI), vol. 4635, pp. 558–571. Springer, Heidelberg (2007). https://doi.org/10.1007/978-3-540-74255-5_42
2. Roy, R., Stark, R., Tracht, K., Takata, S., Mori, M.: Continuous maintenance and the future – foundations and technological challenges. CIRP Annals 65(2), 667–688 (2016)

3. Erkoyuncu, J.A., del Amo, I.F., Dalle Mura, M., Roy, R., Dini, G.: Improving efficiency of industrial maintenance with context aware adaptive authoring in augmented reality. CIRP Annals **66**(1), 465–468 (2017)

4. Augusto, J., Kramer, D., Alegre, U., Covaci, A., Santokhee, A.: Co-creation of smart technology with (and for) people with special needs. In: Proceedings of the 7th International Conference on Software Development and Technologies for Enhancing Accessibility and Fighting Info-Exclusion - DSAI 2016, Vila Real, Portugal, pp. 39–46 (2016)

5. Khilwani, N., Harding, J.A.: Managing corporate memory on the semantic web. J. Intell. Manuf. **27**(1), 101–118 (2014). https://doi.org/10.1007/s10845-013-0865-4

6. Card, S.K., Mackinlay, J.D., Shneiderman, B.: Readings in Information Visualization: Using Vision to Think. Morgan Kaufmann, San Francisco (2007)

7. Weichselbraun, A., Gindl, S., Scharl, A.: Enriching semantic knowledge bases for opinion mining in big data applications. Knowl Based Syst. **69**, 78–85 (2014)

8. Mapping to RDF Graphs for OWL. https://www.w3.org/TR/owl-semantics/mapping.html. Accessed 02 Apr 2020

9. Gogineni, S., Exner, K., Stark, R., Nickel, J., Oeler, M., Witte, H.: Semantic assistance system for providing smart services and reasoning in aero-engine manufacturing. In: Garoufallou, E., Fallucchi, F., William De Luca, E. (eds.) MTSR 2019. CCIS, vol. 1057, pp. 90–102. Springer, Cham (2019). https://doi.org/10.1007/978-3-030-36599-8_8

10. Peffers, K., Tuunanen, T., Rothenberger, M.A., Chatterjee, S.: A design science research methodology for information systems research. J. Manag. Inf. Syst. **24**(3), 45–77 (2007)

11. Davis, F.D.: Perceived usefulness, perceived ease of use, and user acceptance of information technology. MIS Q. **13**(3), 319 (1989)

# Digital Transformation for more Sustainable Supply Chains

# Smart Contract-Based Blockchain Solution to Reduce Supply Chain Risks

Fabian Dietrich[1,2(✉)], Ali Turgut[3], Daniel Palm[1,4] ⓘ,
and Louis Louw[2] ⓘ

[1] ESB Business School, Reutlingen University, Alteburgstr. 150,
72762 Reutlingen, Germany
fabian.dietrich@reutlingen-university.de
[2] Department of Industrial Engineering, Stellenbosch University,
145 Banghoek Rd., Stellenbosch 7600, South Africa
[3] Steinbeis Innovation gGmbH, Alteburgstr. 150, 72762 Reutlingen, Germany
[4] Fraunhofer Institute for Manufacturing Engineering and Automation,
Alteburgstr. 150, 72762 Reutlingen, Germany

**Abstract.** Companies are becoming aware of the potential risks arising from sustainability aspects in supply chains. These risks can affect ecological, economic or social aspects. One important element in managing those risks is improved transparency in supply chains by means of digital transformation. Innovative technologies like blockchain technology can be used to enforce transparency. In this paper, we present a smart contract-based Supply Chain Control Solution to reduce risks. Technological capabilities of the solution will be compared to a similar technology approach and evaluated regarding their benefits and challenges within the framework of supply chain models. As a result, the proposed solution is suitable for the dynamic administration of complex supply chains.

**Keywords:** Blockchain · Smart contract · Supply chain risk management · Sustainability · Supply chain control

## 1 Introduction

Companies are becoming increasingly aware of the potential risks arising from supply chains (SCs). Studies reveal that SC risks and associated business interruptions are considered to be one of the most important global business risks [1, 2]. This results in a growing need for proactive risk management in the SC across industries. Companies need to respond to these challenges in order to fully identify and manage risks in their SCs in order to understand and manage the risks and vulnerabilities [3].

Innovative and Industry 4.0 technologies like tracking and tracing with RFID, sensors and IoT-devices can be used to overcome these challenges [4, 5]. One of the current emerging technologies is blockchain technology, a distributed and immutable database that allows transactions to be conducted directly and transparently between parties [6] while at the same time permitting the programming of algorithms and rules

© IFIP International Federation for Information Processing 2020
Published by Springer Nature Switzerland AG 2020
B. Lalic et al. (Eds.): APMS 2020, IFIP AICT 592, pp. 165–173, 2020.
https://doi.org/10.1007/978-3-030-57997-5_20

of so-called 'smart contracts' [7]. Smart contracts are computer protocols which are developed and used to run decentralized applications on the blockchain [8].

Christopher and Peck [9] proposed to dividing risks in a SC context into three main categories: organizational risk sources that are internal to the company, network risk sources that are external to the company but within the supply network, and environmental risk sources that are external to the network. This classification clarifies the relevant dimensions of potential disruptions in a SC environment and thus provides the basis for a comprehensive risk analysis. The three main categories can be further broken down into five different areas of the SC where risks may occur (see Fig. 1).

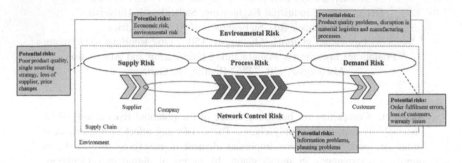

**Fig. 1.** Areas of supply chain risks (own illustration based on [4, 9, 10])

Based on the potential of the blockchain technology, research approaches use the technology as an innovative solution for challenges in the area of Supply Chain Risk Management (SCRM). Layaq et al. [11] for example, examined the potential of the blockchain in the area of supply risks which revealed that the use of blockchain and smart contracts can lead to improvements in material and information flows in order to reduce disturbance risks. This is enabled by increasing visibility (accessing or sharing information with participants of the SC network [12]), transparency (disclosure of information to all stakeholders, including customers [13] and transaction automation along the SC. Due to their structural design, traditional SCRM tend to take action reactively after damage has occurred. With blockchain technology it is possible to design action proactively and preventively as well as manage non-physical risks – such as cyberattacks or miscommunications – more efficiently [14].

This paper focuses on the area of network control risks, since the proposed smart contract-based blockchain solution aims to enhance the transparency and efficiency of information flows. Therefore, the paper briefly presents current problems with conventional token standards in this context. Subsequently, a new extended token-based approach is proposed. Finally, the characteristics of the two solutions are compared.

## 2  Background and Rationale of the Paper

Nowadays, companies have to deal with the growing interests of customers, governments, and non-governmental organizations in having a greater transparency of brands, manufacturers, and producers throughout the SC [15, 16]. As a result, social and environmental sustainability issues have become increasingly important for manufacturers in order to maintain the flawless reputation of their brand [17]. However, as SCs become more global, many suppliers in the network can be located in developing economies where governments have only limited ability and willingness to enforce their own laws [16]. In addition to the risk of being unintentionally involved in social and environmental sustainability issues, a lack of transparency also increases the probability of counterfeit components being introduced into a SC. For example, the counterfeiting of electronic parts causes potential risks including safety and loss of profits to companies, as well as maligning the reputation of manufacturers and distributors [18–20]. It can therefore be summarized that the dispersed nature of today's SCs creates increasing levels of network control risks for multinational businesses, making transparency of SCs both critical and complex [21, 22]. Notably, the problem of incorporating tampered counterfeit parts in assemblies introduces a vulnerability that must be prevented and a gap in present research [18].

In particular, when applying the blockchain technology to SC management, companies have high expectations to solve transparency and auditability issues of complex collaborative SCs [7, 23]. A first approach by Abeyratne et al. proposes that physical assets in combination with their 'unique digital profiles' on the blockchain can solve transparency problems of manufacturing SCs [24]. Based on this approach, Westerkamp et al. developed a solution using special non-fungible tokens in order to represent batches of manufactured products on the blockchain [25]. However, conventional non-fungible token standards such as the ERC-721 [26] are not specifically designed to map SCs. In combination with the immutability of the blockchain technology [25], non-fungible tokens enable a static reconstruction of SCs but show weaknesses when mapping dynamic changes in the composition of products or the structure of the SCs.

## 3  Extended Token-Based Solution

This paper proposes a new solution aiming to create a smart contract with a static address on the network, but still enabling a dynamic mapping of changes in the SC. In conventional token standards, a transaction to change a token's ownership does not send the token itself to a new address; it is an interaction with the token contract assigning a new owner address to the token. This fundamental functionality of tokens is used to create a new approach specifically designed to adopt supply chain characteristics.

From the very beginning, this extended smart contract-based approach includes the identification and mapping of all stakeholders in the supply chain. For this purpose, the SC participants are divided into SC partners (suppliers, producers and service providers), customers and certifiers [25, 27].

Similar to the token standard-based approach [25], the creation of virtual identities on the blockchain is strictly connected to dependencies reflected in their 'recipes'. In this context, a distinction can be made between two types of assets:

- *Assets without dependencies*: can be created without depending on previous actions (e.g. raw materials or certificates).
- *Assets with dependencies*: can only be created when previous actions have been successfully conducted.

In order to map SC processes, the virtual identities of assets must have the same ownership and conversion characteristics as their physical counterparts. They must be able to change their owners when the physical product is transferred in the SC or sold. Furthermore, the virtual identities must be able to be summarized when combining several components into a new product. These events can then be tracked in the blockchain and are accessible for all partners in the SC. All nodes of the network agree on a common time by implementing a consensus algorithm. As a result, the immutability of the network guarantees that a certain event on the network happened at a certain time Fig. 2.

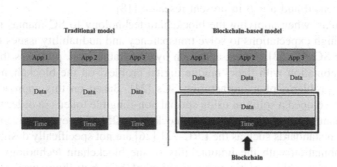

**Fig. 2.** Blockchain technology as verified public timestamps (based on Grossman [28])

To ensure this traceability by using the blockchain technology, a link between the blockchain and the physical product must be established. Accordingly, this approach assumes that all data can refer to an asset itself. For this purpose, the smart contract generates unique identification identities (IDs). A unique ID refers to the virtual identity of an asset. For the uniqueness of these IDs the extended solution proposes hashing the asset's information. Therefore, Hash IDs are a logical result of their input data and provide initial information about the origin, composition, and time of creation. Hash IDs can also be referred to as the smart contract version of conventional primary keys. Within the smart contract, these Hash IDs refer to the virtual identity of their physical counterparts. Similar to other blockchain approaches, these Hash IDs can be attached to the physical parts in the form of barcodes, RFIDs or QR codes [24]. The smart contract logic of a function creating an asset with dependencies is shown in Fig. 3. To map such a logic, it requires the modelling, planning, and definition of further various smart contract functions. Therefore, it is necessary to carefully design all required conditions to create the virtual identity of an asset and its associated Hash ID. The creation of assets is firmly bound to the address of the responsible entity. This means that only a selected authorized entity is able to create the respective virtual identity. The address of the creator is then authorized to send this virtual identity to a new owner. As soon as the transaction has been successfully confirmed by the network, only the new owner has the rights to cause further actions related to the sent virtual identity. In this way, the same functionality in terms of asset 'moving' and asset 'recipes' as with non-fungible token standards can be achieved, except that there is now more scope to link the respective smart contract functions to defined authorities and to execute dynamic adjustments.

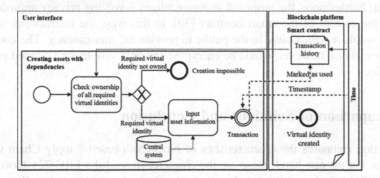

**Fig. 3.** Model to create virtual identities for assets with dependencies

Since the structure of SCs is subject to dynamic influences, the smart contract must also allow dynamic changes of its content. This not only affects the modification of structural elements but also the composition of products. An initial design of such a dynamic smart contract structure is presented in Sect. 3.1.

### 3.1 Holistic Smart Contract Structure

The assigned authorities and the functions for creating virtual identities are embedded into algorithms allowing the mapping of dynamic changes in the SC while the smart contract's address remains static. For these complex algorithms, this paper proposes to include existing approaches to continuously update and generate smart contracts [27, 29]. Figure 4 shows the design of the holistic smart contract structure.

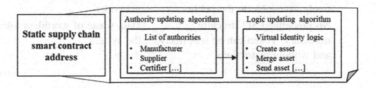

**Fig. 4.** Holistic smart contract structure

Such a structure allows a wide range of possibilities in terms of the allocation of authorities, which is determined in the dynamic updating algorithm related to the list of authorities. It is possible to virtually represent decentralized and open SCs with an even distribution of power, as well as strictly regulated SC structures with only one central authority. As illustrated in Fig. 4, this determines to what extent the authorities can have an impact on changes in the virtual identity logic.

It is important to state, that such smart contract constructs are affected by the immutability of the blockchain technology. Consequently, any eventuality that could affect the SC or product structure must be considered in the program code before its deployment. If, for example, the addition of new suppliers is not taken into account in the code, they cannot be added. A new smart contract with a new address must be deployed. Furthermore, the proposed structure allows involving privacy approaches to encrypt the content of the smart contract [30]. In this way, the interactions with the contract would remain visible to the public to provide SC transparency. The content of these transactions, however, would be encrypted and only visible for a defined group of authorities.

## 4   Comparison of Solutions and Conclusion

This section compares the characteristics of blockchain-based Supply Chain Control Solutions. On the one hand, these are the characteristics of the ERC-721-based smart contracts [26] (non-fungible token-based standard) which was adopted by Westerkamp et al. [25] for manufacturing SCs and on the other hand, the characteristics of the extended token-based solution proposed in this paper (see Table 1).

**Table 1.** Comparison of blockchain-based Supply Chain Control Solutions

|  | Advantages | Disadvantages |
|---|---|---|
| Conventional token-based solution | No central authority necessary, changes in Supply Chain (SC) can be decided decentrally and must be made downstream | End producer can only react to changes in the SC and product changes require new tokens downstream. This leads to high change effort in complex SCs |
|  | Fast technical implementation | Structural changes in the SC difficult to implement (the more complex the SC, the more difficult) |
|  | Standarized tokens (e.g. ERC-721) freely accessible to the public | Privacy is not given in public networks |
|  | No predefined SC-structure necessary. Token can be sent freely and without restrictions | Data waste of worthless tokens in the system |

*(continued)*

**Table 1.** (*continued*)

|  | Advantages | Disadvantages |
|---|---|---|
| Extended token-based solution | Definition of authorities facilitates coordination of SC partners | More elaborate planning necessary since all change contingences must be considered in advance |
|  | Complex SCs can be mapped easier through central control | Not necessarily open to the public; private, semi-private or public smart contract on a public blockchain possible |
|  | Parts of smart contract can be encrypted for the public (only accessible for selected partners) | Possibly no balanced distribution of power in the administration of the smart contract (some authorities may receive additional power over the SCs) |
|  | Enabling product and structure changes by continuously updating the smart contract | The complexity of the technical implementation increase with the degree of individualization of the solution |

An analysis of the two solutions in terms of suitability for SC types (see, for example, Lee [31]) shows that the conventional non-fungible token standard is mainly suitable for simpler SCs following an efficient strategy with a single source approach with a low number of changes over time. This makes it much easier to implement and manage downstream changes in the SC. In responsive scenarios the flexibility also means that the product must be constantly adapted and changed according to the requirements of the customer [31]. Therefore, a responsive strategy is preferably suitable in combination with the proposed smart contract-based solution allowing continuous configurations. This also applies to companies choosing more flexible strategies, such as the risk-hedging strategy and agile strategy. Especially in complex SCs, this solution allows a continuous administration of the SC and the adoption of structural changes. To what extent the changes of such complex SCs can be foreseen when designing the smart contract, should be further investigated. The limitations of the dynamics in the SC in terms of product composition and SC structure also need to be researched. Since the flexibility and the resulting complexity of SCs depicts a challenge [5], the proposed solution represents a promising approach for industry sectors with a high degree of product customization like the automotive industry or sectors following Industry 4.0 concepts. Further research on this topic is currently being conducted. Furthermore, it is necessary to investigate the scalability of such solutions, since the scalability currently represents a limitation of the blockchain technology.

# References

1. Dobie, G., Hubmann, et al.: Allianz Risk Barometer - Results Appendix 2020. Allianz Global Corporate & Specialty (2020)
2. Dobie, G., Milla, et al.: Allianz Risk Barometer. Allianz Global Corporate & Specialty (2019)
3. Palm, D., Kales, P.: Efficiency-oriented risk prioritisation method for supply chains in series production. In: International Conference on Competitive Manufacturing, pp. 417–422 (2016)
4. Kersten, W., Schröder, M., Indorf, M.: Potenziale der Digitalisierung für das Supply Chain Risikomanagement: Eine empirische Analyse. In: Seiter, M., Grünert, L., Berlin, S. (eds.) Betriebswirtschaftliche Aspekte von Industrie 4.0. Z, vol. 71/17, pp. 47–74. Springer, Wiesbaden (2017). https://doi.org/10.1007/978-3-658-18488-9_3
5. Ivanov, D., et al.: The impact of digital technology and Industry 4.0 on the ripple effect and supply chain risk analytics. Int. J. Prod. Res. 57(3), 829–846 (2018)
6. Bosch, R., Penthin, S.: Blockchain als Treiber im modernen Supply Chain Management 4.0. BearingPoint (2018)
7. Iansiti, M., Lakhani, K.R.: The truth about blockchain. Harvard Bus. Rev. 95, 118–127 (2017)
8. Buterin, V.: Ethereum White Paper: A Next Generation Smart Contract & Decentralized Application Platform (2013). https://blockchainlab.com/pdf/Ethereum_white_paper-a_next_generation_smart_contract_and_decentralized_application_platform-vitalik-buterin.pdf. Accessed 20 Mar 2020
9. Christopher, M., Peck, H.: Building the resilient supply chain. Int. J. Logist. Manag. 15(2), 1–14 (2004)
10. Kales, P.: Development of an efficiency-oriented risk prioritisation method for supply chains in series production. Thesis, Reutlingen University (2015)
11. Layaq, W., et al.: Blockchain technology as a risk mitigation tool in supply chain. Int. J. Transp. Eng. Technol. 5(3), 50–59 (2019)
12. Barratt, M., Oke, A.: Antecedents of supply chain visibility in retail supply chains. J. Oper. Manag. 25(6), 1217–1233 (2007)
13. Doorey, D.: The transparent supply chain: from resistance to implementation at Nike and Levi-Strauss. J. Bus. Ethics 103, 587–603 (2011)
14. Min, H.: Blockchain technology for enhancing supply chain resilience. Bus. Horiz. 62(1), 35–45 (2019)
15. New, S.: The Transparent Supply Chain (2010). https://hbr.org/2010/10/the-transparent-supply-chain. Accessed 20 Mar 2020
16. Chen, S., et al.: Impact of supply chain transparency on sustainability under NGO scrutiny. Prod. Oper. Manag. 63(9) (2018)
17. Lemke, F., Petersen, H.L.: Managing reputational risks in supply chains. In: Khojasteh, Y. (ed.) Supply Chain Risk Management, pp. 65–84. Springer, Singapore (2018). https://doi.org/10.1007/978-981-10-4106-8_4
18. Collier, Z.A., et al.: Supply chains. In: Kott, A., Linkov, I. (eds.) Cyber Resilience of Systems and Networks, vol. 2, pp. 447–462. Springer, Cham (2019)
19. Pecht, M.: The counterfeit electronics problem. JSS 01(07), 12–16 (2013)
20. DiMase, D., Collier, Z.A., et al.: Traceability and risk analysis strategies for addressing counterfeit electronics in supply chains for complex systems. Soc. Risk Anal. 36(10), 1834–1843 (2016)
21. Linich, D.: The path to supply chain transparency. Deloitte Uni. Press (2014)

22. Brandon-Jones, E., Squire, B., et al.: A contingent resource-based perspective of supply chain resilience and robustness. J. Supply Chain Manag. **50**, 55–73 (2014)
23. Hackius, N., Petersen, M.: Blockchain in logistics and supply chain: trick or treat? In: Hamburg International Conference of Logistics (HICL), vol. 23, pp. 3–18 (2017)
24. Abeyratne, S.A., Monfared, R.P.: Blockchain ready manufacturing supply chain using distributed ledger. Int. J. Res. Eng. Technol. **05**(09), 1–10 (2016)
25. Westerkamp, M., et al.: Tracing manufacturing processes using blockchain-based token compositions. Digit. Commun. Netw. **6**(2), 167–176 (2019)
26. Entriken, W., Shirley, D., et al.: EIP 721: ERC-721 Non-Fungible Token Standard (2018). https://eips.ethereum.org/EIPS/eip-721. Accessed 31 Mar 2020
27. Bechini, A., et al.: Patterns and technologies for enabling supply chain traceability through collaborative e-business. Inf. Softw. Technol. **50**(4), 342–359 (2008)
28. Grossman, N.: The Blockchain as verified public timestamps (2015). https://www.nickgrossman.is/2015/the-blockchain-as-time/. Accessed 20 Mar 2020
29. Frantz, C., Nowostawski, M.: From institutions to code: towards automated generation of smart contracts. In: International Workshops on Foundations and Applications of Self-Systems, vol. 01, pp. 210–215 (2016)
30. Yuan, R., Xia, Y.-B., et al.: ShadowEth: private smart contract on public blockchain. J. Comput. Sci. Technol. **33**(3), 542–556 (2018)
31. Lee, H.: Aligning supply chain strategies with product uncertainties. Calif. Manag. Rev. **44**(3), 105–119 (2002)

# Towards Sustainability: The Manufacturers' Perspective

Olena Klymenko(ID), Lise Lillebrygfjeld Halse$^{(\boxtimes)}$(ID),
and Bjørn Jæger(ID)

Molde University College, Specialized University in Logistics, Molde, Norway
{olena.klymenko,lise.l.halse,bjorn.jaeger}@himolde.no

**Abstract.** Moving towards more sustainable operations is a challenging goal for industries. The growth of interest in corporate sustainability performance has brought attention to the importance of accounting and transparency across economic, environmental and social dimensions. This paper provides an explorative study addressing sustainability from the perspective of industrial firms. The paper presents case studies on the application of the Triple Layered Business Model Canvas, which allows for relevant insight into how firms account for economic, environmental and social values. The findings show that while accounting for economic values is well taken care of, accounting for environmental values are at an initial stage, and accounting for social values are virtually lacking. Thus, the ability for the industrial firms to conduct a sustainability assessment is limited. The opportunities lie in the adaptation of digital technologies providing cost efficient feedback mechanisms for environmental and social values. This can support environmental and social accounting, giving industrial managers a decision management tool to guide their transition towards more sustainable operations, and aligning company goals with the UN Sustainable Development.

**Keywords:** Sustainability · Manufacturing · Triple layered business model · Digitalization

## 1 Introduction

Sustainability and digitalization are two terms that have gained increased attention since they are representing potential transforming forces of businesses and the society. Sustainability has moved from being a regulative pressure from the surroundings and a corporate buzzword, to becoming a concept that businesses have to relate to and implement in their activities [1, 2]. The growth of interest in corporate sustainability performance has brought attention to the importance of accounting and transparency across economic, environmental and social dimensions [3]. This study focuses on how industrial companies are accounting for economic, environmental and social values. The paper presents case studies on the application of the Triple Layered Business Model Canvas (TLBMC) [2]. TLBMC add an environmental layer based on a lifecycle perspective and a social layer based on a stakeholder management approach, to the traditional business model canvas. Among other tools for sustainability measurement

B. Lalic et al. (Eds.): APMS 2020, IFIP AICT 592, pp. 174–181, 2020.
https://doi.org/10.1007/978-3-030-57997-5_21

(LCA, Social LCA, GRI) that are complex, time-consuming and require detailed data, the TLBMC gives an understanding of how organizations generate impacts and how to evaluate these impacts in terms of the triple bottom line perspective. The TLBMC also integrates the evaluation of impacts throughout supply chain to customer and stakeholders.

Financial accounting has evolved over several centuries giving companies a detailed, high quality, view of its financial operations. Accounting systems for environmental operations and social values are, however, under development [1, 3, 4]. Furthermore, the fourth industrial revolution based on innovations in technologies, smart materials and innovative manufacturing operations is a driving force for using technology for collection and handling data [5, 6]. Digitalization will play a vital role in providing data feeding the economic, environmental and social accounting systems, giving companies powerful business decision analytical tools to move towards making their businesses more efficient and sustainable [7].

In order to transform companies to become sustainable, a new theoretical and practical basis within operation management is called for. This paper explore how and to what extent the manufacturing companies currently are accounting for economic, environmental and social values. In-depth case studies were conducted in two companies, one in the maritime and one in the marine sector in Norway [8]. In these case studies, the Triple Layered Business Model Canvas (TLBMC) [1] was applied to identify how the companies' accounted for operations within the economic, environmental and social domains. Based on this, we discuss how digital technologies may contribute to improve measurement of environmental and social values.

## 2 Sustainability Accounting

Digital technologies provide the means for detailed accounting across the economic, social and environmental domains. Coupling digital technologies with sustainability principles can help companies to acquire information that is more accurate on their operations. Digitalization can be identified as one of the enablers of sustainability in terms of improving resource efficiency, manufacturing performance and as an opportunity to establish accessible data system and obtain flexible and smart use of data through application of information technology [7]. Of particular interest for our study is the ability of using technology to support the triple layered business model. For the economic layer, existing financial accounting systems have long been highly optimized giving companies detailed real-time data on the economic status of the company.

For the environmental layer, it is much harder as the operations are affecting our physical environment. Obtaining detailed real-time data on the environmental status can be done in a cost efficient manner by utilizing emerging digital technologies like internet of things (IoT). This creates intelligent assets that report on environmental factors of interest, including energy consumption, chemical constituents involved, temperature, and other physical conditions. IoT provide us with the means to link the physical world with the virtual world, allowing for detailed information on all aspects having an environmental effect. This enables calculation of the environmental bottom line in the same manner as the financial bottom line in the profit and loss statement.

Such detailed information is valuable input to management for further improvement of the environmental bottom line.

For the social layer, the use of social software emerging from innovations in social media is promising, as it can provide industrial companies with detailed data on social factors allowing the calculation of the social bottom line for a company. However, as identifying what social factors to measure for an industrial firm is an emerging area of research [4]. This study aims at contribution to this research by investigating how the companies currently are approaching triple bottom line accounting.

# 3   The Triple-Layered Business Model Canvas (TLBMC)

The literature suggests a large number of frameworks and methodologies on sustainability. Some scholars propose various business models, for instance business models for sustainability and circular business models [1, 9, 10]. The TLBMC is a tool for developing sustainable business models. A business model (BM) is a conceptual model that integrates coherence of processes and information necessary for value creation of a firm [11]. The TLBMC tool extends the original business model canvas by adding two layers: an environmental layer based on a lifecycle perspective, and a social layer based on a stakeholder perspective. In combination, the three layers of the business model can show how an organization generates economic-, environmental-, and social value [1, 12]. According to Joyce and Paquin [1], there are horizontal and vertical coherences between each layer. The horizontal coherence of TLBMC is assured by examining each of three layers separately, while the vertical coherence combines the value creation of the three canvas layers [13].

The Economic layer encompasses the assessment of nine interdependent components, such as customer value proposition, segments, customer relationship, channels, key resources, key activities, partners, cost and revenues. The Environmental layer is based on a life cycle perspective of the environmental impact. The layer assesses environmental benefits and environmental impacts of the company. As the business model canvas evaluates how revenues outweigh costs, the Environmental layer aims at assessing whether the company's highest environmental impact is within their sustainability goals [1]. Following this approach, organizations might search for environmentally oriented solutions, especially when the environmental impacts are large. The Environmental layer consists of nine components, which together give the bottom line on environmental performance of the company.

The Social layer rests on a stakeholder management approach to explore an organization's social impact [1], seeking to balance the interests of an organization's stakeholders rather than maximizing the gain for the organization itself. Examples of stakeholders are employees, shareholders, customers, suppliers, and governmental bodies.

# 4  Methodological Approach

The sustainability accounting issues addressed in this paper are explorative in their nature, calling for an open and explorative approach. We have carried out in-depth case studies in two Norwegian companies. In order to find what data was available in the three layers in the TLBMC, we interviewed key personnel in the company, and investigating internal company documents. The TLBMC model was governing the questions as well as the document analysis. The findings lay the foundation for discussed how digitalization and Industry 4.0 can contribute to sustainability accounting along the three dimensions.

# 5  The Case Companies

The methodology of the TLBMC was applied on two companies from marine and maritime industries. The companies were selected based on their practices and focus towards sustainability. Company A is a maritime mechanical equipment supplier and is an important actor in the region's maritime industry. The company controls the complete value chain, involving various activities starting from design, manufacturing, marketing and after-sales service for maintenance and repair. The production facilities are located in the region. The firm focuses on providing maintenance, upgrade service for the equipment in order to extend the lifetime of equipment. The product range includes environmentally friendly products with lower energy consumption, low noise and vibration. Company B is a fishing company that provide catching, processing and delivery of fish fillets. It uses eco-friendly factory trawlers with hybrid propulsion and low nitrogen oxide (NOx) emission. The company focuses on sustainable harvesting techniques that minimizes emissions and utilize 100% of the fish and aims to provide a high degree of transparency as all fish caught are traceable. Both companies are categorized as small and medium-sized companies representing two different and important industries in Norway.

# 6  Findings

Most information related to the economic layer in the TLBMC was easy accessible by the companies' managers. The data and information for the environmental layer provided a generalized understanding of the impact of business operations on the environment. The study revealed, however, that there is a lack of data on greenhouse gas (GHG) emission for distribution and energy requirements during the operation. Some components of the social layer were difficult to define and measure, for instance, social value, scale of outreach and social impacts.

Company A emphasizes the differences regarding product types, as this have impact on manufacturing, energy consumption for product use, and finally the environmental impact. The products in Company A were very complex, which led to challenges in applying the TLMBC framework. Nevertheless, Company A makes several kinds of products and some of them were identified as environmentally friendly products. They have lower energy consumption, lower noise and vibration than comparable products. The interviews revealed that Company A does not have a single accounting system for data. Data are distributed according to the organizational structure of the firm and separate pieces of data belong to specific department or to responsible of those employees. Consequently, there is a lack of a systematic approach to information storage with data organized in an accessible and structured way. Sustainability from the perspective of the TLBMC, was directed towards detailed review of all business processes, starting from raw materials delivery by suppliers, along the manufacturing, logistics, warehousing, towards customer use, and finally finishes at the end of use stage. For the environmental and social layers we were not able to map the different elements in the TLBMC due to the lack of available data.

Compared to Company A, Company B has a shorter value chain, which is mainly integrated in one vessel. In this case, fishing is one of the central activities of the company. However, information about fuel consumption and NOx emission were not available. General information about consumption level came from the shipbuilding company in Spain. To apply life cycle approach to the environmental value, it is imperative to take a broader view on the entire life cycle. Trading partners include firms who provide packaging material, processing factory manufacturers, fuel providers, and vessel maintenance companies among others. In this case, the conduction of a more comprehensive sustainability assessment was limited due to the absence of necessary information about suppliers that are part of the product's life cycle and hence are contributors to the emission level of the product. Table 1 shows the data and information collected for the Environmental Layer for both companies.

Exploring the interrelations between digitalization and sustainability measurement, the findings reveal that the data requirements are high, especially regarding the environmental layer of the TLBMC. The case studies show that the information collected partly fulfills the requirements for production phase analysis for both companies A and B. For Company A, data on energy consumption in production facilities for 2012–2017 was received. According to the findings in Company B, the resulting data consisted of information regarding fuel used for catching, processing, freezing on the vessel, and storage/freezing after taken from the vessel per 1 kg of fish. The information for material phase for Company B provides particular insight on packaging materials. The first common issue for those companies is absence of the information from the suppliers, for instance, environmental impact from raw materials supply and logistics. Furthermore, customer use and end of life stages are not at the main scope of these companies. As a result, the responsibility for the product impact often ends when the suppliers' role finishes. At the same time, the information flow on business activities generally is not completely shared between supplier firms across the value chain. Consequently, based on the data and information collected during the interviews and secondary data assessment, the measured environmental impacts and benefits are not addressing total impacts and benefits of the activities of the companies in this study.

The findings show that important data and information related to environmental and social aspects are not available or even not accessible for the companies. For example, the information on products delivered by suppliers such as raw materials and equipment for Company A, and packing materials and processing factory for Company B, is missing. Radio Frequency Identification (RFID) technology can help to identify at what

**Table 1.** Data collected for the environmental layer for company A and B

| Environmental layer | Company A | Company B |
|---|---|---|
| Supplies and outsourcing | *** | *** |
| Production | ** Energy consumption Waste for recycling, hazardous waste | ** Estimated fuel consumption |
| Materials | *** | ** Information about reduction of pollutants from supplier |
| Functional value | One type of mechanical system | 1 kg fresh frozen fish |
| Distribution | *** | *** |
| Use phase | *** | *** |
| End-of-life | *** | ** |
| Environmental impacts | ** Electricity use in production facilities Data on noise and vibration Hazardous waste | ** NOx production Disposal of packing material |
| Environmental benefits | ** ISO 14001 Three environmentally friendly products Waste for recycling and further processing | **Reduction of $NO_x$ (2016–2017) 100% use of fish Modern trawler prevents catching of small fish which secure future stock |

\* - Data available
\*\* - Partly available data
\*\*\* - No data

stage the components or equipment were produced along the supply chain, and the materials it consists of. This can contribute to simplify recycling processes by identifying how and where it can be recycled, or what components can be reused or replaced to extend the life cycle [14]. Furthermore, from the social and ethical perspective, RFID technology can trace the location history of a product and can prove the authenticity of a product, hence customers and firms can make more environmentally and socially informed decisions [14]. Additive manufacturing can offer opportunities to improve and optimize materials and design of a product in order to enhance recycling and remanufacturing of components and decrease waste [15].

Another essential phase for sustainability assessment is the use phase and end of life of a product, which also lacked data. Cyber-physical systems (CPS) that establish connective and communicative solutions can allow sufficient information exchange and control between humans, machines and products. The collection of data and information can be carried out through installed sensors, actuators and communication technologies, which can be used to capture data on emissions of a product during the use phase for Company A. Thus, digitalization and novel emerging technology solutions are crucial for industrial sustainability accountability, directed to redesign for value creation in sustainable production and consumption.

## 7 Discussion and Conclusion

The case study findings of the TLBMC application emphasize that sustainability is a data- and information-demanding area. The study indicates that the case companies are at a stage of development where they are not capturing sufficient data and information along the supply chain in order to conduct overall sustainability assessment across the economic, environmental and social domains of sustainability. This indicates that the companies are not able to manage their processes in an efficient way towards their sustainability goals.

High data requirements for sustainability measurement underline the importance of digitalization of businesses. Digitalization from the perspective of business model for sustainability requires a common system for data and information, its processing and structuring. This will support the effective interpretation of data, which is crucial for business model redesign and sustainability assessment. This study illustrates the importance of data availability for sustainability measurement across each domain of the triple bottom line. Managers should consider the opportunities represented by digitalization, and provide support learning programs for employees to obtain the digitalization skills required [16]. The opportunities lie in adaptation of new technologies, which allow collection of data for the environmental and social layers in a similar manner as the economic layer.

Having said that, we acknowledge that the implementation of technology will not solve all challenges in the path to sustainable manufacturing and supply chains. Technology can contribute to collecting, sharing and analyzing data, but does not solve the trade-offs that have to be made between different and conflicting issues. In particular, there may be conflicting goals between the layers, which call for an interdisciplinary dialogue and approach, which cannot be solved by technology alone.

## References

1. Joyce, A., Paquin, R.L.: The triple layered business model canvas: a tool to design more sustainable business models. J. Clean. Prod. **135**, 1474–1486 (2016)
2. Grin, J., Rotmans, J., Schot, J.: Transitions to Sustainable Development; New Directions in the Study of Long Term Transformative Change. Routledge, New York (2010)
3. Rodriguez, A., Cotran, H., Stewart, L.S.: Evaluating the effectiveness of sustainability disclosure: findings from a recent SASB study. J. Appl. Corp. Finan. **29**(2), 100–108 (2017)
4. Hourneaux Jr., F., da Silva Gabriel, M.L., Gallardo-Vázquez, D.A.: Triple bottom line and sustainable performance measurement in industrial companies. Revista de Gestão **25**(4), 413–429 (2018)
5. Porter, M.E., Heppelmann, J.E.: How smart, connected products are transforming companies. Harvard Bus. Rev. **93**(10), 96–114 (2015)

6. IEC, Factory of the Future, White Paper, Switzerland (2015)
7. EMF, Intelligent Assets: Unlocking the circular economy potential. Ellen-MacArthur-Foundation (2016)
8. Klymenko, O., Nerger, A.J.: Application of the Triple Layered Business Model Canvas-A case study of the maritime and marine industry. Master thesis, NTNU, Ålesund, Norway (2018)
9. Schaltegger, S., Lüdeke-Freund, F., Hansen, E.: Business cases for sustainability: the role of business model innovation for corporate sustainability. Int. J. Innov. Sustain. Dev. 6, 95–119 (2012)
10. Bocken, N.M., de Pauw, L., Bakker, C., van der Grinten, B.: Product design and business model strategies for a circular economy. J. Ind. Prod. Eng. 33(5), 308–320 (2016)
11. Teece, D.J.: Business models, business strategy and innovation. Long Range Plann. 43(2), 172–194 (2010)
12. Osterwalder, A., Pigneur, Y.: Business Model Generation: A Handbook for Visionaries, Game Changers, and Challengers. Wiley, Hoboken (2010)
13. Lozano, R.: Envisioning sustainability three-dimensionally. J. Clean. Prod. 16, 1838–1846 (2008)
14. Denuwara, N., Maijala, J., Hakovirta, M.: Sustainability benefits of RFID technology in the apparel industry. Sustainability 11(22), 6477 (2019)
15. Bonilla, S., Silva, H.R.O., da Silva, M.T., Gonçalves, R.F., Sacomano, J.B.: Industry 4.0 and sustainability implications: a scenario-based analysis of the impacts and challenges. Sustainability 10(10), 3740 (2018)
16. Eller, R., Alford, P., Kallmünzer, A., Peters, M.: Antecedents, consequences, and challenges of small and medium-sized enterprise digitalization. J. Bus. Res. 112, 119–127 (2020)

# Data-Driven Applications in Smart Manufacturing and Logistics Systems

# Smart Factory Competitiveness Based on Real Time Monitoring and Quality Predictive Model Applied to Multi-stages Production Lines

Nicola Gramegna[1(✉)], Fabrizio Greggio[1(✉)], and Franco Bonollo[2(✉)]

1 EnginSoft SpA, Padua, Italy
{n.gramegna, f.greggio}@enginsoft.com
2 Università di Padova – DTG, Padua, Italy
bonollo@gest.unipd.it

**Abstract.** Smart Factories are complex manufacturing ecosystems where the converging of ICT and operational technologies and competences drive the digital transformation. Smart manufacturing operations planning and control program, as defined by NIST, implement advances in measurement science that enable performance, quality, interoperability, wireless and cybersecurity standards for real-time prognostics and health monitoring, control, and optimization of smart manufacturing systems.

The traditional production processes and plants are evolving following this digitalization combining the long experience and the AI-driven methods to improve the production efficiency, to accelerate the fine-tuning and real-time adjustment of the process parameters oriented to the zero defect quality. The digitalization of multi-stages production processes (e.g. foundry) plays a key role in competitiveness introducing new integrated platform to monitor the process through an intelligent sensors network and predict quality and cost of castings in real-time.

The application presented in this paper is the main outcome of EU FP7-MUSIC project giving a new age to the traditional multi-stages production. The actual regional project PreMANI (POR FESR 2014–2020) is a new extended application of AI-driven digital twin in manufacturing process and quality control. This paper demonstrates the applicability of data-driven digital twins to small and medium-sized enterprises (SME) and to complex manufacturing sectors integrating the process monitoring with advance data mining and cognitive approach to predict the quality, the efficiency vs cost and react in real-time with the support of decision support system.

**Keywords:** Industry 4.0 · Digital twin · Overall efficiency · Zero defect manufacturing · Data mining · Predictive modeling · Cost model

**Special Session:** Data-Driven Applications in Smart Manufacturing and Logistics Systems

© IFIP International Federation for Information Processing 2020
Published by Springer Nature Switzerland AG 2020
B. Lalic et al. (Eds.): APMS 2020, IFIP AICT 592, pp. 185–196, 2020.
https://doi.org/10.1007/978-3-030-57997-5_22

# 1  Introduction

Industry 4.0 is the industrial revolution based on Cyber-Physical-Systems (CPS) in the context of Factory of Future. The digital investment grow is estimated of 1,7% in digital economy, +40% of smart factory in the next 5 years, if technology potential is released thanks to an appropriate governance and soft skills and data-driven culture. In the new digital era, a Manufacturing Execution System (MES) is a first form of Digital Twin (DT), the evolution of the Internet of Things (IoT) and Industry 4.0 manufacturing concepts have opened new possibilities regarding how real-time data can be used to better control and optimize production [1]. Recent data-driven Digital Twin is enabling the advanced real-time data mining and the machine learning technologies to support the prediction of failures, defects and the impact on production key performance indicators (KPIs).

Today, however, there are three main categories in which a digital twin can be utilized: product design, process planning and validation, and execution. The product design, is more associated with product lifecycle management (PLM) and is probably the area of application for the digital twin that is most familiar in manufacturing industries; MES helps with planning and testing manufacturing models, including planning processes and resources; the DT in manufacturing execution, which this paper is referring, is the least explored of the three categories and it offers huge potential in helping drive production efficiency, especially in the manufacture of sophisticated technological products.

In this paper the definition of DT is the digital modelling representing of assets and processes to understand, predict and optimize performance of a process, product or service. DT consists of three components: a system model, the data gathering with intelligent monitoring and the real-time data knowledge extraction and response prediction connecting the virtual and real worlds. The system model of Digital Twin, based on reference architecture us RAMI, has to be flexible, with high interoperability, data-centric combining tools of data mining and Artificial Intelligence (AI) to support the decision making process in a collaborative way [2].

In the context of data gathering with intelligent monitoring, the large data management and data quality are ingredients to capture the process stability, to elaborate the KPIs and to improve fast and proper decision making supported by A.I. The data standardization (e.g. defects classification) and the right communication protocol (e.g. OPC_UA) are pre-requisite applied to the multi-stages production to improve the communication [3].

Meta-modeling for manufacturing processes describes a procedure to create reduced numeric surrogates that describe cause-effect relationships between setting parameters and sensors as input and product quality variables as output for manufacturing processes. In-process, such advanced models can be used to determine the operating point and to search for alternative setting parameters in order to optimize the objectives of the manufacturing process, the product quality [4].

In agreement with this definition, the implemented cognitive meta-model, or Artificial Intelligence (AI) model, is defined and customized to the specific set of variables and output in order to assure reliability and maximum accuracy.

The automatic learning process is applied to improve the meta-model by re-training approach including new data from production.

Data-Driven Digital Twin for manufacturing has to be flexible, with high interoperability, data-centric combining tools of data mining, statistic model e cognitive met-model to support the decision making process by Operator (Quality oriented), Production manager (Efficiency oriented - OEE) and Business manager (Cost-oriented).

In the context of multi-stages production processes, metal and polymer manufacturing current trends show an improvement in demand for light products considering the material substitution for complex structural parts, the design and technology innovation as well as the evolution in smart production (e.g. smart foundry). The foundry case study of this paper starts from existing data from machine and some devices, but never used in a predictive quality model or real time efficiency elaboration. Due to the high number of process variables involved and to the non-synchronisation of all process parameters in a unique and integrated process control unit, High Pressure Die Casting (HPDC), as well as Plastic Injection Molding (PIM), is one example of the most "defect-generating" and "energy-consumption" processes in EU industry [5, 6], showing less flexibility to any changes in products and in process evolution. In both, sustainability issue imposes that the production cells are able to efficiently and ecologically support the production with higher quality, faster delivery times, and shorter times between successive generations of products.

The development and integration of a completely new ICT platform, based on innovative Control and Cognitive system linked to real time monitoring, allows an active control of quality, minimizing the presence of defects or over-cost by directly acting on the process machine variables optimisation or equipment boundary conditions [7, 8]. The AI-driven manufacturing approach works at machine-die level to optimise the production line starting from the management of manufacturing information. An Intelligent Sensor Network (ISN) monitors the real-time production acquiring the multi-layers data from different devices and an extended meta-model (the Cognitive model) correlates the input and sensors data with the quality indexes, energy consumption cost function. Data homogenization, centralization and synchronization are the key aspects of control system to collect information in a structured, modular and flexible database. Process simulation, data management and training of the meta-model are key factors to generate an innovative Cognitive system to improve the manufacturing efficiency.

## 2 Multi-source Data Flow in Production Line

The multi-source data flow from heterogeneous devices and controllers in the same production is requiring a new flexible, secure and interoperability platform in agreement with RAMI4.0 architecture [1].

The essential elements that characterize a Digital Twin (DT) are: *Connectivity* based on appropriate ICT architecture (e.g. RAMI) and communication protocol (e.g. OPC_UA); Traceability of data that flows towards a structured and secure repository by storing setup information and sensors together with classified quality values;

*Data Mining* which ensures the reliability of the data and the processing of the stability of real and virtual sensors where the latter can rely on mathematical applications also useful for the management of alerts; *Cognitive* model which has its roots in the programming of the instructive DOE suitable for the construction of predictive models with advanced self-learning and cross-validation algorithms; *Interoperability* offers a collaborative platform for different and multi-site users where the key performance indicators (KPIs) and cost index useful for a decision making process to optimize the process and apply the retrofit in the right and efficient time.

The structured and secure database is the ingredient to acquire all sensor signals by server-client connection. Remote real time visualization of the pure sensor measurements, as well as the preliminary data elaboration (e.g. velocity curve form movement in time and its relevant points), are the key metrics of process stability and alerting.

The reliability of data is evaluated in terms of *Validity, Accuracy, Consistency, Integrity, Timeliness, Completeness*. Data *Accuracy* can be defined as the degree to which data correctly reflects the real world object or an event being described. On fast changing processes like HPDC and PIM, data must be accurately and quickly collected and aggregated to represent the interesting process transactions.

Data *Timeliness* must be grant within the Control & Cognitive platform and can be measured as the time between when data is expected, from the Intelligent sensor Network, and when it is available by the Cognitive System and the user. Data *Completeness* is the extent to which the expected attributes of data are provided. So the Data Completeness means the expected completeness from the user or application requirements, but has strong impact on future elaborations. Data *Consistency* means that data across the system should be in synch with each other. Data is inconsistent, when it is in synch in the narrow domain of a system, but not in synch across the system. On the Factory 4.0 it must be trusted that all data coming from different production plants must be available and aligned each other. Data *Auditability* means that any transaction or statement of the identities represented can be tracked to its original state, that contextualized in the Digital manufacturing process means that all product quality and traceability data must be available for each process state. Data *Integrity* signify that data collected and stored is intact and unchanged, and in the Factory 4.0 this is achieved using correct saving, backup and security technologies and policies.

Standardization in communication and data mining is mandatory for future statistical model and KPI elaborations. Any production line is configured for the specific product and any volume of production, so the database has to be dynamic flexible to be connected with all possible sensors from various equipment as well as to archive the predicted output by Artificial Intelligence (AI) model. OPC and OPC UA (Unified Architecture) are industry standards that enable software to connect devices, machines and systems from different manufacturers using same interface. OPC servers add value for any device, machine or system, as it reduces any integration or application software development costs. Similarly OPC clients and application software utilizing OPC client features can be connected to any OPC server in a standard way without customization. OPC Foundation is dedicated to ensuring interoperability in automation by creating and maintaining open specifications that standardize the communication of acquired process data, alarm and event records, historical data, and batch data to multi-vendor enterprise systems and between production devices [3].

Within this context, the cognitive approach of data-driven digital twin (Fig. 1) predicts the quality, energy and cost in near real-time, covering the 100% of products, and suggests the appropriate re-actions to adjust the process set-up and/or mechanism.

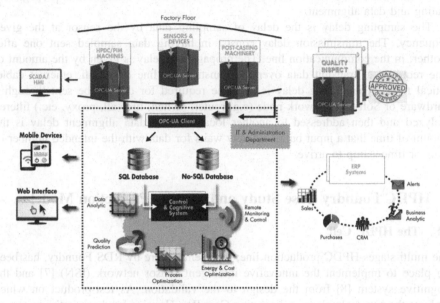

**Fig. 1.** Introducing the *Data-Driven Digital Twin* with the OPC_UA client–server in the production line

The client-server connection works in combination with the real time monitoring system to elaborate instantaneously the production data set with respect to quality/energy/cost prognosis.

The database is collecting all process data, via OPC UA protocol, coming from all existing devices and active sensors in the production line. This communication protocol was chosen since it meets all the requirements needed by the ICT platform.

A fundamental innovative characteristic of digital twin platform, *called Smart Prod ACTIVE,* is the predictive Quality model integrating multi-resolution and multi-variate process data in a collaborative way to support the decision making process by Operator (Quality oriented), Production manager (Efficiency oriented - OEE) and Business manager (Cost-oriented).

The real-time visualization of elaborated data, including warning and safety messages and statistic production diagrams, can be customized for multiple users' interfaces as machine operator, production manager and plant director. The standardization of quality classification and investigation methods [5, 6], as well as the traceability, are fundamental to train the quality model guiding the minimization of relevant indexes affecting the scrap rate. The current version of the *Smart Prod ACTIVE* platform has a smart web application to visualize, share and communicate the significant data and to support the decision making with proper reactions in real-time based on the captured signals from the process.

To achieve this goal, the latency of data is always kept under control and the main delays trusted by the *Smart Prod ACTIVE* system are due to transmission, propagation, routing and data alignment.

The sampling delay is the delay of sampling data by the sensor at the given frequency. The transmission delay consist in having data sampled sent one after another, in the communication line. The propagation delay is given by the amount of time required to transmit data over the transmission line (e.g. wifi, ethernet cable, optical fiber). The routing delay is the time required for data to be sent through a Hardware or Software network node (e.g. router, switch, firewall, proxy, etc.) filtered analyzed and then addressed to another location. The data alignment delay is the amount of time that a input buffer actively waits for data with the intended number of shots or time-stamp to arrive.

# 3   HPDC Foundry Case Study and Quality Prediction Model

## 3.1   The HPDC Cell

The multi-stages HPDC production line, represented here by RDS Foundry, has been the place to implement the innovative intelligent sensor network (ISN) [7] and the Cognitive system [8] from the design to the validation. As test-product on which evaluate the new technology, a diecasting Gear Box Housing has been individuated, as well as the priority list of defects/imperfections to be minimized/avoided: lamination, cold shots, flash, blister and incomplete casting.

In the foundry case study, a new die has been designed and built introducing various advanced sensors and in-line thermo-camera. All process parameters possibly affecting the quality of Gear Box Housing have been taken into account (Fig. 2), and used in the training stage of a meta-model, both virtual and real, correlating input process variables and data from sensors with quality indexes in the areas of interest, based on CEN Standard on defects classification in Aluminium foundry products [6].

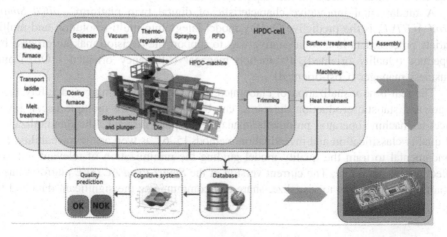

**Fig. 2.** The application of *Data-Driven Digital Twin* in Foundry 4.0

The correlation matrix, based on 185 evaluated designs (Fig. 3), is one method to visualize the dependency of quality indexes from process parameters and virtual sensor measurements (e.g. temperature, pressure, velocity). As expected, defects such as misruns are strongly affected by the plunger position, when switching from first phase velocity to second fast velocity – the quantitative correlation is now available – but there are small opposite effects due to second phase velocity of the plunger and initial temperature of the alloy. Similar comments are possible for shrinkage porosities depending from overpressure and spray time, or blister correlated with second phase velocity.

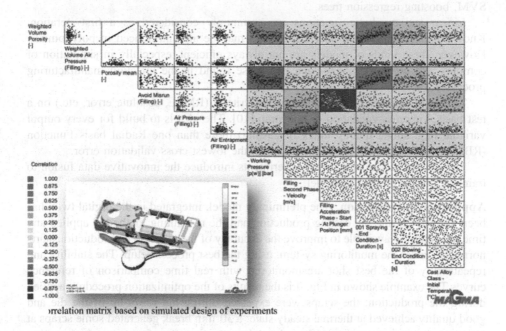

Fig. 3. Correlation matrix based on simulated design of experiments

## 3.2 Quality Prediction Model

The prediction model needs to be trained with reference to a specific product and process, because the quantification of correlations are unique and not generalized. Typically, a meta-model is constructed based on data generated from a complex deterministic simulation of the system in which the random variation that exists in the real system is not represented. Design decisions, then, are based on system analysis and evaluation by approximating the system performance using the constructed meta-model. The primary objectives of metamodeling are to obtain an accurate estimation of the response and to minimize the required computational effort. This includes minimizing the necessary number of sample points and utilizing a computationally efficient modeling method valid for multi-layer and non-linear correlations like those found in the manufacturing processes. In addition, an important item underlying both tasks is the issue of performance evaluation and optimization of the system.

The main quality requirements for an experimental design are: the robustness (ability to analyze different models), the effectiveness (optimization of a criterion), the goodness of points repartition (space filling property) and the low cost for its construction. Several studies have shown the qualities of different types of experimental designs with respect to the prediction capabilities of the meta-model [9]; the choice of the meta-model that can be derived from any linear regression model, nonlinear parametric or non-parametric. The most used meta-models include polynomials splines, generalized linear models, generalized additive models, Kriging, neural networks, SVM, boosting regression trees.

Linear and quadratic functions are commonly considered as a first iteration. Knowledge on some input interaction types may be also introduced in polynomials. However, these kinds of models are not always efficient, especially in simulation of complex and nonlinear phenomena like those found in the injection manufacturing processes.

The usual practice is to estimate global criteria (RMSE, absolute error, etc.) on a test basis, via cross-validation or bootstrap [10]. The idea is to build for every output variable (e.g. single quality index of casting) more than one Radial basis Function (RBF) model and to choose the model with the lowest cross validation error.

The dataset of virtual and real experiments introduce the innovative data fusion to train the quality prediction model.

**Application in Production.** The preliminary model, integrated in the digital twin, has been applied starting the casting production and the re-training method is applied any time new data are available to improve the accuracy of the model. The production starts normally, under the monitoring system, using the best process setup. The stability and repeatability of the best shot are monitored with real time comparison of reference curves The example shown in Fig. 4 is the results of the optimization procedure applied during the production: the scraps were expected during the warm-up of the die and good quality achieved at thermal steady state; a 30 min break generated some scraps at re-start (e.g. casting number 157) and good production after 5 castings (e.g. casting number 162) has been recovered and automatically identified.

**Fig. 4.** LAN network connection and real time prediction of Waste and Good castings shown on tablet

At the end, the introduction of the *Smart ProdACTIVE platform* in the factory floor needs a simple installation of LAN network connecting all devices of the production line, and it has been validated in an industrial production context of Al-alloy gear box housings.

## 4 Cost Model and Decision Making

The Data-Driven Digital Twin includes a cost model, properly developed to consider and manage costs related to the whole multi-stages HPDC production process [11]. This model is characterized by the presence of both real-time measurements, thanks to the positioning of an intelligent sensor network within the production process, which will guarantee a real-time quality and cost management as and a comparison of company's past production data. The structure of the HPDC cost model has been developed based on the main units that are composting the entire process: the melting, the process, the post-processing and the quality. Four cost centers were thus identified for each the cited units. In particular the melting, the process and the post-processing centers reflect the real production process and are considered to be different cells characterized by different equipment. The melting cell is composed of all the activities starting from the arrival of raw materials till the movement of the cast material in the holding furnace; the die-casting cell includes all the activities starting from the holding furnace till the trimming activity that is the last activity realized close to the die-casting machine; the post-processing centre is composed by different cells that include heat treatment, machining and finishing before the final assembly. The fourth cost center is dedicated to the quality control activities to check how quality costs can influence the final product cost. The control of quality in different moments of the production could increase production efficiency thanks to the possibility to avoid waste and reworks within the production and accordingly to these considerations, the quality center aims to monitor all the quality control costs during the melting, the process and the post-processing activities. Specific cost voices are collected in Table 1.

**Table 1.** Cost voices for each cost center.

| Cost center | Cost voices |
|---|---|
| Melting | Labour cost, depreciation cost, cell maintenance cost: scheduled or extraordinary maintenance, resource cost, consumption material cost, liquid/waste disposal cost, setup cost |
| Process | Labour cost, depreciation cost, cell maintenance cost: scheduled or extraordinary maintenance, resource cost, consumption material cost, liquid/waste disposal cost, warm-up cost, permanent mould cost, trim cost |
| Post-processing | Labour cost, depreciation cost, cell maintenance cost: scheduled or extraordinary maintenance, resource cost, consumption material cost, liquid/waste disposal cost, setup cost |
| Quality | Cost for control activities allocated into the melting, the process and the post-processing |

The developed cost model is applicable at preliminary estimation of die-casting cost, but also during the real time monitoring of the production since it is connected in real-time with sensors and the database of the process parameters to estimate the cost impacts. The reduction of scrap is instantaneously translated in cost minimization, as well as the reduction of cycle time or alloy temperature and/or of energy consumption within the thermoregulation channel. As result any variations introduced to optimize the process or to satisfy the customer is tracked and optimized in terms of quality and cost.

With reference to the current production of the HPDC case study, the cost of material is predominant with 52% of the total cost per single piece, the melting process is 18%, the HPDC transformation process accounts for 19% while post-processing impacts for 10%. Quality affects 1% of total cost.

The cost model can provide projections in different scenarios: in case of two cavities per die, the estimation of industrial cost reduction is 19%. The potential reduction of 10 s per cycle impacts of −4.6% industrial cost and 13% reduction of energy.

## 5    The Expected Impacts and Conclusions

The *data-driven digital twin* in production line is a solution to measure, analyze and react oriented to zero defect manufacturing and to the maximization of the OEE improving the sustainability and profit of factory of future.

With reference to the foundry application, the expected benefits are summarized as follow:

- 40% reduction in scrap rate for the involved HPDC foundry,
- −3% in no-quality costs for the involved automotive company,
- up to 40% decrease in the cost of quality control, to be applied only to specifically individuated products,
- 5–10% reduction in energy consumption, due to scrap reduction and increased production efficiency,
- better knowledge and control of the process, resulting in time to market reduction and minimization of trial & error approaches.

The application of *Smart Prod ACTIVE system* has been demonstrated and validated at foundry level. In the frame of HPDC production process, Operator and Process manager take advantage by adopting a centralized remote control system supporting process monitoring and quality prediction in real time. The decision is supported by cause-effect correlations, and proper reactions suggested by a continuously updated meta-model. Re-usability and flexibility of the *Smart Prod ACTIVE system* also allow agile re-start in case of small batches production.

The "zero defect" target is always the first priority of the approach, to minimize the defects with real-time retrofit suggested by the tool. The scrap rate reduction is focused on those defect factors mainly contributing the overall quality requirements of the product. Being the energy consumption connected to the production rate, the cycle time optimization (more pieces per hour) and the improved management of energy-demanding devices (furnace, thermal units, etc.) lead to cost reduction.

The digitalization of manufacturing plays a key role in competitiveness introducing new integrated platform to Control the process and predicting in real-time quality and cost of castings.

The new ICT technologies at manufacturing plant introduces significant potential impacts: (i) strengthened global position of EU manufacturing industry; (ii) larger EU market for advanced technologies such as electronic devices, control systems, new assistive automation and robots; (iii) intelligent management of manufacturing information for customization and environmental friendliness.

The application of data-driven digital twin has the natural extension to further multi-stages and multi-disciplinary production lines (e.g. sheet metal forming, forging, rolling, thermoforming, machining, welding, trimming, or the innovative additive manufacturing) is planned to exploit the same methodology in different industrial contexts.

**Acknowledgments.** The authors would like to thank the kind and professional technical support of RDS Moulding Technology staff involved in the industrial case study. The supports from EU FP7-MUSIC project (multi-stages production) and from PreMANI (POR FESR 2014-2020) project (new extended application of AI-driven digital twin in manufacturing process and quality control) are gratefully acknowledged.

# References

1. Weber, C., Konigsberger, J., Kassnera, L., Mitschanga, B.: A maturity model for data-driven manufacturing. Procedia CIRP **63**, 173–178 (2017)
2. Lu, Y., Liub, C., Kevin, I., Wang, K., Huang, H., Xua, X.: Digital twin-driven smart manufacturing: connotation, reference model, applications and research issues. Robot. Comput. Integr. Manuf. **61**, 101837 (2020)
3. OPC Foundation, OPC Unified Architecture Interoperability for Industrie 4.0 and the Internet of Things, version 10, November 2019
4. Auerbach, T., et al.: Meta-modeling for manufacturing processes. In: Jeschke, S., Liu, H., Schilberg, D. (eds.) ICIRA 2011. LNCS (LNAI), vol. 7102, pp. 199–209. Springer, Heidelberg (2011). https://doi.org/10.1007/978-3-642-25489-5_20
5. Bonollo, F., Gramegna, N., Timelli, G.: High-pressure die-casting: contradictions and challenges. JOM **67**(5), 901–908 (2015)
6. CEN T/R 16749: Aluminium and aluminium alloys — Classification of Defects and Imperfections in High Pressure, Low Pressure and Gravity Die Cast Products, CEN, Brussels (2014)
7. Bonollo, F., Gramegna, N.: The MUSIC guide to the key-parameters in High Pressure Die Casting. Assomet servizi srl, Enginsoft SpA (2014). ISBN 978-8887786-10-1
8. Bonollo, F., Gramegna, N.: Smart Control and Cognitive System applied to the HPDC Foundry 4.0. Assomet servizi srl, Enginsoft SpA (2016). ISBN 978-8887786-11-8
9. Simpson, T.W., Poplinski, J.D., Koch, P.N., Allen, J.K.: Metamodels for computer-based engineering design: survey and recommendations. EWC **17**(2), 129–150 (2001). https://doi.org/10.1007/PL00007198

10. Kleijnen, J.P.C.: Regression metamodels for simulation with common random numbers: comparison of validation tests and confidence intervals. Manag. Sci. **38**(8), 1164–1185 (1992)
11. Macchion, L., Kral, G., Bonollo, F., Gramegna, N.: Application of cost model approach in HPDC contexts. HTDC, Venice (Italy), 22–23 June 2016

# A New Application of Coordination Contracts for Supplier Selection in a Cloud Environment

Reza Tavakkoli-Moghaddam[(⊠)], Mohammad Alipour-Vaezi, and Zahra Mohammad-Nazari

School of Industrial Engineering, College of Engineering, University of Tehran, Tehran, Iran
tavakoli@ut.ac.ir

**Abstract.** Cloud manufacturing (CMfg) is considered to be a facilitator for mass manufacturing resources. It is a paradigm of intelligent systems, which makes the manufacturing procedures easier. In this regard, the most important issues of the manufacturing environment are discussed in the literature. Supplier selection and order allocation have been great concerns for researchers in all manufacturing systems, even in a cyber-physical environment allocating orders to the best supplier is of great importance. Hence, this research highlights one of the most challenging issues in a cloud environment which is related to supplier selection in CMfg. A hybrid multi-criteria decision-making framework (i.e., fuzzy DEMATEL-VIKOR) considering sustainable criteria is proposed to help the decision-makers for better dealing with supplier selection in a cloud environment. Selecting the best supplier is not the only issue discussed in this paper. Coordinating the suppliers is also taken into account because a better partnership supplier and the client need to work in a coordinated structure. In the second stage of this paper, the best coordination contract is proposed based on the client's given score on some predetermined criteria. The results indicate that a revenue-sharing contract is an ideal coordination framework, which will satisfy the client and supplier and help them to work in a coordinated environment.

**Keywords:** Cloud manufacturing · Coordination contract · Supplier and contract selection · Multi-criteria decision-making · Uncertainty

## 1 Introduction and Literature Review

With the existing change in a manufacturing system toward intelligent manufacturing technologies, new manufacturing modes have been presented; global manufacturing, manufacturing grid, cloud manufacturing (CMfg) are great examples in this regard. It is worthy to note that the complexity of manufacturing systems and the importance of resource sharing highlight the importance of distributed intelligent manufacturing. CMfg is a service-oriented manufacturing system that can be considered a distributed intelligent manufacturing system, which seeks to transform today's manufacturing industry toward the collaborative and innovative manufacturing system [1]. In a CMfg environment, manufacturing resources support costumers in a form of service. A service platform is used as a determiner in a CMfg system. A cloud manufacturing

© IFIP International Federation for Information Processing 2020
Published by Springer Nature Switzerland AG 2020
B. Lalic et al. (Eds.): APMS 2020, IFIP AICT 592, pp. 197–205, 2020.
https://doi.org/10.1007/978-3-030-57997-5_23

platform can provide manufacturing services by manufacturing resource access from different suppliers. A service-oriented architecture is of high prominence in the scope of developed technologies in the integration of distributed systems and software [2].

Centralized and decentralized operating modes are two main methods in a cloud environment, in which CMfg can be operated. To the best of our knowledge, in a centralized operating mode, the platform investigates the services to fulfill the clients' requirements. In this case, clients do not choose their providers (suppliers) by themselves. In general, centralized networking has had problems regarding flexibility, efficiency, availability, and security [3]. On the other hand, decentralized operating mode gives the clients the volition to make decisions regarding service and provider selection. Each client can choose the desired services based on his requirements. But, there is a point that can't be neglected in this scope, owing to the selfish behavior of clients the overall productivity of the system can be decreased [4]. A CMfg system is a new manufacturing system that emerged based on Industry 4.0 guidelines. Also, the critical role of contracts for supply chain coordination is not covered for anyone.

Wang et al. [5] asserted as logistics-based industries and information technology developed manufacturing models to get more innovative. Thus, manufacturing enterprises became eager to outsourcing different parts of their manufacturing process to contractors, who were more proficient so the enterprises could reach their goals for their main occupation core. They presented a manufacturing resource selection strategy based on a distributed genetic algorithm (DGA) to optimize the combination of manufacturing resources in CMfg. Raj et al. [6] studied coordination issues of a supply chain that formed due to concurrent consideration of green supply chain (GSC) and corporate responsibility on social issues that are done by supply chain agents. They considered the situation that responsibility of greening is on suppliers or supply agents and so on, in which the vendee is responsible for social responsibility. With this regard, Lu et al. [7] proposed some beneficial approaches to make improvements in this field and proposed a cloud model for optimal green supplier selection considering the fuzziness of evaluation information. In their research, a fuzzy analytic hierarchy process (AHP) was applied to determine the index weight. In the case of CMfg and supplier selection, an online evaluation of the supplier's service capability was proposed by Jain et al. [8].

To the best of our knowledge, online evaluation of the supplier's service capability is the key to efficient service matching. It is worthy to note that we gather the related data for the performance test of the supplier's machine tools, which are taken from the cloud platform [8]. In the second stage, supplier's machine tools are evaluated and then their processing stability is evaluated. Simeone et al. [9] presented a framework, in which CMfg enables the resource sharing. To increase the resource efficiency in a manufacturing network, an intelligent CMfg platform is proposed through dynamic sharing of manufacturing services that can be offered on demands according to a service-oriented paradigm. In the scope of supplier selection, on the other hand, Luthra et al. [10] proposed a framework for evaluating sustainable supplier selection by using AHP and VIKOR methods. They considered three criteria (i.e., economic, environmental, and social). In the scope of coordination contract selection, Zhou et al. [11] investigated three contracts for a monopoly firm, which acts as a transaction platform between clients and providers. The mentioned platform can charge different rates of commissions and select the optimal contract. Zhen et al. [12] developed a model, in which a retailer sells products through offline, online, and third party platform channels, and then the best contract is considered in the proposed platform. Sun et al. [13] proposed a framework for Cloud Service Selection in which they applied a fuzzy measure to measure and aggregate non-linear relations between criteria. They introduced a non-linear constraint optimization model to determine criteria interaction indices.

As investigated in the reviewed articles, researchers in recent years have paid much attention to CMfg systems. This issue has been welcomed by researchers in particular with the advent of the 4th Industrial Revolution (i.e., Industry 4.0). According to the reviewed articles, the following research gaps are identified by:

We found no article in the CMfg field examined the importance of contract selection. However, there are a few articles used a multi-criteria decision-making (MCDM) method in the process of contract selection [14, 15]. Supplier selection is neglected in the research agenda in cyber-physical systems, such as a CMfg system. There are a few real-life cases used CMfg principles, especially in Iran.

In this paper, we propose a new methodology for CMfg systems that considers a variety of coordination contracts from different providers. Then, based on client criteria, it chooses the best provider and after that, the best coordination contract is chosen.

MCDM techniques are applied based on the expert's opinion and the reviewed articles in the proposed framework (as it has been reviewed through articles by [16, 17]. We apply from a fuzzy DEMATEL method to allocate weights to criteria and the VIKOR method for ranking the alternatives. At the end of this stage, the best provider is chosen. Like Stage I, in Stage II, client criteria are defined based on the expert's opinion and the literature review of this field. The first step after the identification of criteria is to determine the proper weight of each coordination contract, so we use the best-worth method (BWM). A TOPSIS method is applied for ranking the options in the second step. For illuminating this concept, it is worth to say that the options are the different coordination contracts of different providers.

The objective of this paper is to help the managers in CMfg systems to choose the best providers and select the best coordination contracts.

## 2 Problem Description and Methodology

This paper examines the application of the supply chain coordination contract advanced by Industry 4.0 principles in the CMfg platform. The proposed methodology considers a data-based agent, whose duty in the proposed cyber-physical system (CPS) of CMfg is to connect the best provider to the client under the best coordination contract. These data-based agents are connected to a variety of different providers and clients, which are acting in the manufacturing of a specific product. When a client ordering on a system, he/she is asked about his/her criteria for selecting a supplier, in which the Likert's program for converting expressions into triangular fuzzy numbers is used. We develop a two-stage method, which in the first stage, the best supplier (i.e., provider) is selected based on the clients' criteria and in the second stage, the selected supplier proposed its coordination contract and the client according to the criteria that identified based on reviewed articles and experts' opinion, select the optimal coordination contract.

Owing to the fact that selecting the best supplier for cloud manufacturing (CMfg) is momentous; by reviewing the articles in this case, the hybrid fuzzy DEMATEL-VIKOR method is found applicable. In the process of data gathering, some questionnaires have been filled with the help of experts, who utilize CMfg to help us identify the criteria that influence on the supplier selection procedure profoundly. These questionnaires have been filled using the 5-point Likert scale. By identifying the criteria and their weights with the help of the above-mentioned questionnaires and fuzzy-DEMATEL, it is worthy to find the best supplier based on the predetermined criteria. In this case, the VIKOR method is of great help, due to the fact that we need to apply a compromising method among MCDM methods. In this case, it is found the most applicable one.

By identifying the best supplier, selecting the coordination contract for suppliers is the next decision problem, in which managers face with. In this step, the best-worst method is applied to determine the criteria, which affect that contract selection. It is worthy to note that the best-worst method is a novel outstanding method introduced in 2015 with so many applications in various decision problems. As a compromising method needed to be implemented for best contract selection, the TOPSIS method is found exemplary. Figure 1 shows the summary of this two-stage methodology.

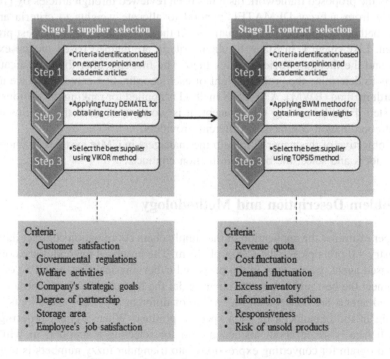

**Fig. 1.** A proposed two-stage methodology

# 3  Case Study and Results

To better understanding, the subject here is one of the projects that took place based on this articles' method in Iran. An "Indamin Saipa" company located in Iran is one of the "Saipa Group" companies that is responsible for manufacturing the shock absorbers for Saipa cars. One of the components designed for shock absorbers production is cylinders' tubes that are made in such a way that there is no seam or in other words, they have to be en bloc. Since these monolith cylinders' tubes had a 3-micrometers surface smoothness in the design process and no machinery is available to produce such a product in Iran, we should replace the product and produce the alternative product with innovative processes (the alternate production) method is out of this paper scope so no further explanation is proposed. Due to internal policies and existing conditions, senior management decided to use CMfg techniques for alternative manufacturing steps. For each step, numbers of providers, candidate, and each of them proposed a variety of coordination contracts.

**Stage I:**
In this section, the information of the providers and the reports of this paper's method for supplier selection and contract selection is provided. In the first step, the criteria for the first stage of supplier selection based on a sustainable triple bottom line are identified. The predetermined criteria in this part and their discerption are shown in Table 1.

In this stage, the obtained weights of each criterion are obtained by using the fuzzy DEMATEL technique. This technique will not provide us with the weights; however, the weights of criteria are found by using this technique. Table 2 shows the obtained weights using the fuzzy DEMATEL technique.

**Table 1.** First stage criteria for supplier selection

| Notation | Criteria | Description |
|---|---|---|
| C1 | Customer satisfaction | In every organization and company, customers play a decisive role |
| C2 | Governmental regulations | Government as another stakeholder in a project supply chain is a key element |
| C3 | Welfare activities | Company must consider its visions to assign expenses to the activities |
| C4 | Company's strategic goals | Branding and the company's competitive advantage |
| C5 | Degree of partnership impact on objectives fulfillment | Supply chain partnership is also an important factor that can enhance the satisfaction of final customers |
| C6 | Storage area | Storage area is the other criterion considered to be a constraint for suppliers |
| C7 | Employee's job satisfaction | Employee's satisfaction is the final criterion, which influences the process of decision making |

**Table 2.** Obtained weights of each criteria using the fuzzy DEMATEL technique

| Criteria | C1 | C2 | C3 | C4 | C5 | C6 | C7 |
|---|---|---|---|---|---|---|---|
| Weights | 0.1470 | 0.1522 | 0.0863 | 0.1653 | 0.1474 | 0.1481 | 0.1532 |

In the following procedure of supplier selection in a CMfg environment, the VIKOR method is applied to help the client choose the ideal supplier. The obtained results of the VIKOR method indicates that among 5 suppliers, which are compared, supplier 2 is superior to suppliers 4 and 5. And supplier 3 has shown a better performance based on the mentioned criteria; however, the superiority of suppliers 2 and 3 over each other is not identified as they have the same performance in most of the criteria.

**Stage II:**
In the second stage by identifying the best supplier with the help of the fuzzy DEMATEL-VIKOR method, the best contract is chosen by using the BWM-TOPSIS method. In the following paragraph, the criteria used for the process of the cloud supplier selection based on coordination contracts are identified. Table 3 asserts the criteria of the contract selection in this methodology.

**Table 3.** Second stage criteria for contract selection

| Notation | Criteria | Description |
|---|---|---|
| A1 | Revenue quota | As supply chains are becoming more global worldwide, in the competitive market of which depends heavily on the application of internet and smart manufacturing, the global supply chains investigate to find the best suppliers based on the gained revenues of their partnership |
| A2 | Cost fluctuation | Because we are living in the world, in which the uncertainty and cost inflation are an undetached part of it, and considering cost fluctuations is momentous |
| A3 | Demand fluctuation | Uncertainty in demand and demand fluctuations is influencing the process of selecting the most appropriate contract |
| A4 | Excess inventory | Suppliers need to vigilant regarding the inventory that they hold, because the excess inventory can impose costs to the suppliers |
| A5 | Information distortion | information distortion is a great concern in the process of exchanging the information |
| A6 | Responsiveness | Responsiveness of the service provider and the predetermined lead time of each supplier must be taken in to account as a factor for contract selection |
| A7 | Risk of unsold products | The last factor, which influences the contract selection, is the risk of unsold inventory because unsold inventory needs to be brought back or to be sold to the client |

By considering the above-mentioned factors and by using the experts' ideas, we find that the revenue quota (A1) is the most important criterion, besides, the information exchange is the worst one. By using the best-worst method (BWM), the weights are obtained as shown in Table 4.

Criterion 1 as the most important one has a higher weight. In Table 5, the ranking of criteria is obtained by using the TOPSIS method, in which the BWM weights are taken into account as inputs for the TOPSIS method.

**Table 4.** Obtained weights for each criterion

| Criteria | A1 | A2 | A3 | A4 | A5 | A6 | A7 |
|---|---|---|---|---|---|---|---|
| Weights | 0.379 | 0.166 | 0.100 | 0.125 | 0.032 | 0.125 | 0.079 |

**Table 5.** Ranking of criterion

| Revenue sharing | 0.701 | Option contract | 0.336 |
|---|---|---|---|
| Buyback | 0.256 | Quality flexibility | 0.372 |

The results of the supplier selection procedure show the significant role of the company's strategic goals in decision making. In this process, the welfare activities are considered a factor because the client cares about the supportive role of his supplier in nonprofit organizations. Governmental rules and regulations and the hindrance that the government causes for the supplier during the production is taken into account for a supplier selection process. Among the mentioned factors for the first stage, the obtained results indicate that the employee's job satisfaction is in the second rank for the decision-maker (i.e., client). In the second stage, the desired contract is selected based on the determined criteria. The obtained results indicate the fact that the revenue sharing contract is the most applicable one. This is mostly because of the importance of the first criterion (i.e., revenue quota). In the other mentioned contracts (e.g., buyback, option contract, and quantity flexibility), the excess inventory and unsold products play a decisive role. In the quantity flexibility contract, the fluctuation in demand is the pivotal factor for the selection procedure of the contract. Since the experts' interviews do not show the superiority of demand fluctuation over gained revenue the quantity flexibility contract is in the last rank.

## 4   Conclusions

This paper proposed a framework for cloud manufacturing (CMfg) supplier selection, in which the last step was the determination of the best contract for the selected supplier. The proposed framework consisted of two stages. In the first stage, the best supplier was identified by using the fuzzy DEMATEL-VIKOR method. The predetermined criteria in this step were based on experts' interviews. In the second stage, as the beginning of the partnership period, the coordination contracts were the alternatives. The best coordination contract was presented by using the BWM-TOPSIS method. By using the BWM method, the criteria's weights were determined and the TOPSIS method helped the decision-makers to rank the contracts. To the best of our knowledge, this study was the first research, which was conducted in the field of supplier selection in CMfg by using MCDM methods. Furthermore, the application of contract selection improved the partnership, which was the main objective in SCM.

# References

1. Wu, Z., Yang, K., Ting, L., Cao, Y., Yang, J., Gan, Y.: Study on the robust tolerance design with multiple resource suppliers on cloud manufacturing platform. Proc. CIRP **75**, 63–68 (2018)
2. Yu, J., Han, Y.: Service Oriented Computing-Principle and Application. Qinghua University Press, Beijing (2006)
3. Li, Z., Barenji, A.V., Huang, G.Q.: Toward a blockchain cloud manufacturing system as a peer to peer distributed network platform. Robot. Comput.-Integr. Manuf. **54**, 133–144 (2018)
4. Chen, J., Huang, G.Q., Wang, J.-O., Yang, C.: A cooperative approach to service booking and scheduling in cloud manufacturing. Eur. J. Oper. Res. **273**, 861–873 (2019)
5. Wang, L., Guo, S., Li, X., Du, B., Xu, W.: Distributed manufacturing resource selection strategy in cloud manufacturing. Int. J. Adv. Manuf. Technol. **94**, 3375–3388 (2016). https://doi.org/10.1007/s00170-016-9866-8
6. Raj, A., Biswas, I., Srivastava, S.K.: Designing supply contracts for the sustainable supply chain using game theory. J. Clean. Prod. **185**, 275–284 (2018)
7. Lu, Z., Sun, X., Wang, Y., Xu, C.: Green supplier selection in straw biomass industry based on cloud model and possibility degree. J. Clean. Prod. **209**, 995–1005 (2019)
8. Jian, W., Jianfeng, L., Tiaojuan, H.: Application and research on online evaluation for service capability of cloud manufacturing supplier. IFAC-PapersOnLine **52**(13), 1555–1559 (2019)
9. Simeone, A., Caggiano, A., Boun, L., Deng, B.: Intelligent cloud manufacturing platform for efficient resource sharing in smart manufacturing networks. Proc. CIRP **79**, 233–238 (2019)
10. Luthra, S., Govindan, K., Kannan, D., Kumar Mangla, S., Prakash Garg, C.: An integrated framework for sustainable supplier selection and evaluation in supply chains. J. Clean. Prod. **140**, 1686–1698 (2017)
11. Zhou, Y.-W., Lin, X., Zhing, Y., Xie, W.: Contract selection for a multi-service sharing platform with self-scheduling capacity. Omega **86**, 198–217 (2019)
12. Zhen, X., Xu, S., Hu, C.: Contract selection of platform selling under spillovers from offline to online sales. In: 2019 16th International Conference on Service Systems and Service Management (ICSSSM). IEEE, Shenzhen, 13–15 July 2019
13. Sun, L., Dong, H., Hussain, O.K., Hussain, F.K., Liu, A.X.: A framework of cloud service selection with criteria interactions. Future Gener. Comput. Syst. **94**, 749–764 (2019)
14. Schnjakin, M., Alnemr, R., Meinel, C.: Contract-based cloud architecture. In: Proceedings of the 2nd International Workshop on Cloud data Management, New York, USA (2010)
15. Clemons, E.K., Chen, Y.: Making the decision to contract for cloud services: managing the risk of an extreme form of IT outsourcing. In: The 44th Hawaii International Conference on System Sciences. IEEE (2011)

16. Önüt, S., Kara, S.S., Işik, E.: Long term supplier selection using a combined fuzzy MCDM approach: a case study for a telecommunication company. Expert Syst. Appl. **36**(2), 3887–3895 (2009)
17. Xu, Z., Qin, J., Martínez-López, L.: Sustainable supplier selection based on AHPSort II in interval type-2 fuzzy environment. Inf. Sci. **483**, 273–293 (2019)

# Workforce Assignment with a Different Skill Level for Automotive Parts Assembly Lines

Hyungjoon Yang[1] , Je-Hun Lee[2] , and Hyun-Jung Kim[1(✉)]

[1] Korea Advanced Institute of Science and Technology (KAIST),
Daejeon 34141, Republic of Korea
hyunjungkim@kaist.ac.kr
[2] Sungkyunkwan University, Suwon 16419, Republic of Korea

**Abstract.** One of the most important operational issues in an assembly line is to allocate workers to tasks (or workstations) so that their workloads can be well-balanced. We address a new workforce assignment problem in an assembly line where workers can perform all tasks but have a different skill level, which affects not only the throughput but also the number of defective products. We derive two mathematical programming models that can be used in various production environments. One is with the objective of the throughput maximization while keeping the defect rate under a given criteria and the other is for the minimization of the total rework time while achieving a given throughput. Several experiments are performed with the proposed two models by changing the number of workers and a proportion of skilled workers. We also compare the two models and provide managerial insights.

**Keywords:** Workforce assignment problem · Different skill level · Defect rate · Rework time

## 1 Introduction

Allocating tasks to assembly lines in order to optimize a certain objective is called an assembly line balancing problem (ALBP), which was introduced in 1955 [1]. The problem has been known to be NP-hard due to its high complexity [2]. A basic problem of ALBP is called a 'simple ALBP', which does not consider the skill difference of workers and only assigns one worker to each workstation [3]. Most previous studies on worker assignment problems have assumed homogeneous worker skills, and less attention has been paid to the quality problem caused from heterogeneous performance levels of workers [4]. There have been a few approaches on assigning workers with different skill levels to tasks, which was known as an assembly line worker assignment and balancing problem (ALWABP) [5, 6]. They typically consider two objectives, which are the minimization of the number of workers while achieving a given cycle time (ALWABP-1) and the minimization of the cycle time with a given number of workers (ALWABP-2) [4, 6]. These studies have assumed that only one worker is assigned to each task, and there have recently been some studies that consider tasks requiring multiple workers [7, 8].

© IFIP International Federation for Information Processing 2020
Published by Springer Nature Switzerland AG 2020
B. Lalic et al. (Eds.): APMS 2020, IFIP AICT 592, pp. 206–212, 2020.
https://doi.org/10.1007/978-3-030-57997-5_24

We address a workforce assignment problem for multiple assembly lines for automotive parts where products are assembled while moving on a paced conveyor belt. The assembly process consists of multiple operations, each of which is composed of several tasks. Workers can perform all the tasks but have a different skill level. Multiple workers, at most $M_{max}$ workers, can be assigned to a task. The number of assigned workers and their skill levels affect the throughput and defect rate of the task. After a product is assembled, its quality is checked, and rework is done if any defect exists. Hence, we need to assign workers to tasks efficiently in order to maximize the throughput or minimize the total rework time.

## 2   Problem Definition

This assignment problem takes place in multiple wiring harness assembly lines. The wiring harnesses are the organized sets of wires, terminals, and connectors that run throughout the entire vehicle. Each assembly line consists of three operations, cable grapping, clipping, and taping, which are performed sequentially, and each operation consists of multiple tasks. The task time and the number of defects in each task depends on the number of assigned workers, their skill levels, and characteristics of vehicles assembled.

Figure 1 shows an example of two assembly lines that have five and four hetero-geneous tasks, respectively. The skill levels are divided into three, A, B, and C, and the number of assigned workers in each level, called a worker set, is represented as well. The workload of these tasks is all different depending on product types assigned to each line. If we assign more highly skilled workers to a task, the task time can be reduced significantly, which increases the throughput, and the defect rate of the task can also be reduced. In this problem, we assume that workers in the same skill level have the same performance. We also assume that the throughput and defect rate of a task are deterministic functions of a worker set, which will be discussed in Sect. 3.1.

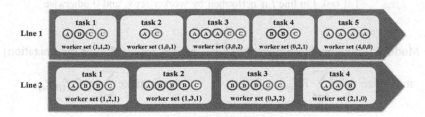

**Fig. 1.** Example of assigning workers to tasks

After a product is assembled in a line, its quality is checked, and the rework is performed if a defect is observed. This procedure is done by some specified workers who are not considered in the problem. Rework of defective products is an inefficient process which lowers the productivity, thus it is reasonable to consider the minimization of the total rework time as the objective in our problem. We also consider the throughput as another objective. The assembly lines we assume have many workers who are often absent without notice and leave the workplace during working hours. Hence, an efficient assignment of workers needs to be made frequently, several times a day, while considering various skill levels of workers and the remaining number of workers.

## 3  Approach

### 3.1  Problem Formulation

Table 1 shows the parameters and decision variables we use.

**Table 1.**  Notations for problem formulation

| Indices & Sets | |
|---|---|
| $i \in I$ | Index of lines |
| $j \in J$ | Index of tasks |
| $k \in K$ | Index of worker sets |
| $l \in L$ | Index of skill levels |
| Parameters | |
| $M_{kl}$ | Number of workers with skill level $l$ in worker set $k$ |
| $N_l$ | Number of workers with skill level $l$ |
| $TH_{ijk}$ | Throughput of task $j$ in line $i$ when performed by worker set $k$ |
| $f_{ijk}$ | Defect rate of task $j$ in line $i$ when performed by worker set $k$ |
| $A$ | Upper limit of the defect rate |
| $r_{ij}$ | Rework time for task $j$ in line $i$ |
| $D_i$ | Daily demand assigned to line $i$ |
| $t$ | Daily operating hour of factory |
| Decision variable | |
| $x_{ijk}$ | 1 if task $j$ in line $i$ is performed by worker set $k$, and 0 otherwise |

Model 1 (throughput maximization)

$$\text{maximize } \min_{i,j}(\sum_k TH_{ijk}x_{ijk})$$

$$\text{s.t. } \sum_k x_{ijk} = 1, \qquad \forall i \in I, j \in J \quad (1)$$

$$\sum_{i,j,k} x_{ijk}M_{kl} = N_l, \quad \forall l \in L \quad (2)$$

$$\sum_k f_{ijk}x_{ijk} \leq \alpha, \quad \forall i \in I, j \in J \quad (3)$$

Model 2 (rework time minimization)

$$\text{minimize } \sum_{i,j,k} r_{ij}D_i f_{ijk}x_{ijk}$$

$$\text{s.t. } \sum_k x_{ijk} = 1, \qquad \forall i \in I, j \in J \quad (4)$$

$$\sum_{i,j,k} x_{ijk}M_{kl} = N_l, \quad \forall l \in L \quad (5)$$

$$\sum_k TH_{ijk}x_{ijk}t \geq D_i, \forall i \in I, j \in J \quad (6)$$

The proposed two models have the following objectives; one is to maximize the minimum throughput of assembly lines and another is to minimize the total daily rework time. Two models share some constraints; Constraints (1) and (4) and Constraints (2) and (5) are the same. Constraint (1) indicates that one worker set must be assigned to each task in a line, and Constraint (2) is used to ensure that the number of workers assigned to each task is equal to the total number of workers we have. Constraint (3) restricts the maximum defect rate that needs to be achieved in Model 1, and Constraint (6) controls the minimum throughput to meet the daily demand.

A worker set indicates the number of workers in each skill level, and one worker set is assigned to a task. For example, a worker set $(2, 0, 1)$ for a task means that 2 workers in level A, 0 worker in level B, and 1 worker in level C are assigned to the task. The workers who are absent or leave the workplace are considered when counting the number of workers and creating worker sets in the models.

## 3.2   Estimation of Throughput and Defect Rate

The throughput and defect rate of each worker set are calculated by considering the fact that as more workers are assigned, the task time is reduced and less mistake is made. We assume that a worker with level A is 15% faster than a level B worker, and 29% faster than a level C worker, based on the data we have and interviews with production managers. We then designed a simple linear model to express the throughput $TH_{ij(n_A,n_B,n_C)}$ of worker set $(n_A, n_B, n_C)$ where $n_A, n_B$, and $n_C$ are the numbers of workers in levels A, B and C, respectively.

$$TH_{ij(n_A,n_B,n_C)} = n_A TH_{ij(1,0,0)} + n_B TH_{ij(0,1,0)} + n_C TH_{ij(0,0,1)}$$
$$= \left( n_A + \frac{1}{1.15} n_B + \frac{1}{1.29} n_C \right) TH_{ij(1,0,0)} \qquad (7)$$

However, the throughput does not increase infinitely and tops out at a certain point in practice. Hence, we use a square root transformation with $\epsilon$ for considering randomness in the model.

$$TH_{ij(n_A,n_B,n_C)} = \sqrt{n_A + \frac{1}{1.15} n_B + \frac{1}{1.29} n_C} \times TH_{ij(1,0,0)} + \epsilon \qquad (8)$$

We can now calculate the throughput of all tasks for each worker set if $TH_{ij(1,0,0)}$ is given. In a similar way, we assume that a defect rate of a level A worker is reduced by 20 and 43% compared to a level B and C worker, respectively. For the defect rate $f_{ij(n_A,n_B,c_C)}$ of a worker set $(n_A, n_B, n_C)$, we have the following.

$$f_{ij(n_A,n_B,c_C)} = \frac{f_{ij(1,0,0)}}{\sqrt{n_A + 0.8n_B + 0.57n_C}} + \epsilon \qquad (9)$$

# 4 Result

The proposed models were solved by using ILOG CPLEX 12.10. We assume that the factory runs 8 h a day, with 8 assembly lines each of which has 9 different tasks. There are 55 possible worker sets when the maximum number of workers ($M_{max}$) is 5.

The defect rate, $\alpha$, is set to 0.04, and the rework time for each task, which is independent from the worker assignment of the assembly line, is randomly generated from $N(80, 16)$ where $N(\mu, \sigma)$ is a normal distribution with the mean of $\mu$ and standard deviation of $\sigma$. The daily demand of each line $D_i$ is 320 for all lines, and $TH_{ij(1,0,0)}$ and $f_{ij(1,0,0)}$ for all $i$ and $j$ are randomly generated from $N(100, 10)$ and $N(5, 0.005)$, respectively.

Since we consider absenteeism of workers, the total number of workers at assembly lines varies every day. There are 72 tasks (8 lines * 9 tasks) where each task may contain up to 5 workers, so at most 360 workers can be hired in the whole assembly line. We denote the ratio of the total number of workers we have to 360 as a worker capacity ratio (WCR). The experiments are performed by changing WCR from 20 to 100%, and the results are shown in Table 2. When WCR is small (i.e., less than 40%), the problem becomes infeasible because the demand and defect rate constraints cannot be satisfied. When WCR is larger than or equal to 80%, the throughput is the same with Model 1 regardless of the worker skill ratios. We can also observe that as the number of level C workers becomes smaller, the throughput and rework time are enhanced.

The ratio of the throughput difference to the rework time difference from the two models, denoted as TH/Rework in Table 2, is computed by (throughput from Model 1 – throughput from Model 2)/(rework time from Model 1 – rework time from Model 2). This value means a tradeoff between objective values of Models 1 and 2, and Model 1 becomes more favorable in a high TH/Rework condition. As WCR is smaller, TH/Rework becomes larger, which means that the rework time reduction from using Model 2 becomes much smaller than the throughput improvement from Model 1 when the number of workers we have is small. Hence, when WCR is large, it is more reasonable to use Model 2, and Model 1 is appropriate when WCR is relatively small.

**Table 2.** Experimental results (TH in unit/hour, Rework in hour)

| WCR | Distribution of worker skill levels (A : B : C) | | | | | | | | | | | | | | |
| | Distribution 1 (4.5 : 1 : 4.5) | | | | | Distribution 2 (3 : 4 : 3) | | | | | Distribution 2 (2 : 6 : 2) | | | | |
| | Model 1 | | Model 2 | | TH/Rework | Model 1 | | Model 2 | | TH/Rework | Model 1 | | Model 2 | | TH/Rework |
| | TH | Rework | TH | Rework | | TH | Rework | TH | Rework | | TH | Rework | TH | Rework | |
|---|---|---|---|---|---|---|---|---|---|---|---|---|---|---|---|
| 100% | 74.25 | 13.68 | 68.36 | 13.18 | 11.83 | 74.25 | 13.51 | 68.06 | 13.15 | 16.96 | 74.25 | 13.44 | 68.84 | 13.13 | 16.93 |
| 95% | 74.25 | 14.06 | 68.36 | 13.52 | 10.93 | 74.25 | 14.00 | 68.36 | 13.49 | 11.44 | 74.25 | 13.82 | 62.96 | 13.46 | 31.40 |
| 90% | 74.25 | 14.48 | 67.26 | 13.90 | 11.88 | 74.25 | 14.36 | 66.36 | 13.86 | 15.73 | 74.25 | 14.26 | 66.51 | 13.83 | 17.93 |
| 85% | 74.25 | 14.75 | 62.08 | 14.30 | 27.25 | 74.25 | 14.70 | 61.67 | 14.26 | 28.35 | 74.25 | 14.65 | 61.67 | 14.23 | 30.17 |
| 80% | 74.25 | 15.17 | 60.64 | 14.74 | 31.50 | 74.25 | 15.17 | 60.64 | 14.70 | 28.92 | 74.25 | 15.13 | 60.64 | 14.67 | 29.26 |
| 75% | 74.25 | 15.68 | 56.23 | 15.22 | 39.39 | 74.25 | 15.61 | 56.23 | 15.18 | 42.06 | 73.81 | 15.54 | 55.87 | 15.15 | 46.08 |
| 70% | 71.89 | 16.22 | 54.90 | 15.76 | 36.86 | 71.78 | 16.16 | 54.52 | 15.71 | 38.56 | 71.44 | 16.08 | 54.52 | 15.68 | 42.87 |
| 65% | 68.78 | 16.82 | 52.70 | 16.35 | 34.39 | 68.78 | 16.73 | 52.70 | 16.30 | 37.68 | 68.56 | 16.68 | 52.70 | 16.27 | 38.68 |
| 60% | 65.60 | 17.46 | 47.74 | 17.02 | 40.64 | 65.60 | 17.38 | 47.74 | 16.97 | 43.65 | 64.78 | 17.32 | 47.74 | 16.94 | 44.57 |
| 55% | 62.02 | 18.16 | 46.16 | 17.78 | 41.27 | 62.02 | 18.13 | 46.16 | 17.73 | 38.86 | 61.67 | 18.06 | 46.16 | 17.69 | 42.52 |
| 50% | 58.07 | 18.95 | 46.96 | 18.65 | 36.42 | 58.07 | 18.93 | 46.96 | 18.59 | 33.25 | 56.75 | 18.85 | 46.94 | 18.56 | 33.60 |
| 45% | 50.93 | 19.90 | 44.98 | 19.66 | 24.98 | 53.05 | 19.84 | 44.98 | 19.60 | 33.31 | 50.97 | 19.79 | 44.52 | 19.56 | 28.42 |
| 40% | inf. | inf. | 43.29 | 20.86 | – | inf. | inf. | 43.29 | 20.79 | – | inf. | inf. | 41.44 | 20.75 | – |
| 35% | inf. | inf. | inf. | inf. | – | inf. | inf. | inf. | inf. | – | inf. | inf. | inf. | inf. | – |
| 30% | inf. | inf. | inf. | inf. | – | inf. | inf. | inf. | inf. | – | inf. | inf. | inf. | inf. | – |
| 25% | inf. | inf. | inf. | inf. | – | inf. | inf. | inf. | inf. | – | inf. | inf. | inf. | inf. | – |
| 20% | inf. | inf. | inf. | inf. | – | inf. | inf. | inf. | inf. | – | inf. | inf. | inf. | inf. | – |

*inf.: infeasible

# 5 Conclusion

In this study, the two optimization models were presented to address the workforce assignment problem. Worker sets are assigned to each task in a line to maximize the throughput or minimize the total rework time. The throughput and defect rate of each worker set have been computed by analyzing product data and used in the formulation. We then compared the two models and provided some managerial insights. In the future, an efficient algorithm needs to be developed to handle a large-sized problem.

**Acknowledgement.** This is a project funded under the SMART EUREKA CLUSTER on Advanced Manufacturing program. This research was supported by the Ministry of Trade, Industry and Energy (MOTIE) in South Korea and the Korea Institute for Advancement of Technology (KIAT) through the International Cooperative R&D program [P0009839, Cyber Physical Assembly and Logistics Systems in Global Supply Chains (C-PALS)].

# References

1. Salveson, M.E.: The assembly line balancing problem. J. Ind. Eng. **6**(3), 18–25 (1955)
2. Gutjahr, A.L.: An algorithm for the line balancing problem. Manage. Sci. **11**(2), 308–315 (1964)
3. Scholl, A.: Balancing and Sequencing of Assembly Lines, 2nd edn. Physica-Vertag, Heidelberg (1999)
4. Baybars, I.: A survey of exact algorithms for the simple assembly line balancing problem. Manage. Sci. **32**(8), 909–932 (1986)
5. Miralles, C.: Advantages of assembly lines in sheltered work centres for disabled. A case study. Int. J. Prod. Econ. **110**(1–2), 187–197 (2007)
6. Mutlu, Ö.: An iterative genetic algorithm for the assembly line worker assignment and balancing problem of type-II. Comput. Oper. Res. **40**(1), 418–426 (2013)
7. Araújo, F.F.B.: Two extensions for the ALWABP: parallel stations and collaborative approach. Int. J. Prod. Econ. **140**(1), 483–495 (2012)
8. Giglio, D.: Multi-manned assembly line balancing problem with skilled workers: a new mathematical formulation. IFAC-PapersOnLine **50**(1), 1211–1216 (2017)

# A Framework of Data-Driven Dynamic Optimisation for Smart Production Logistics

Sichao Liu[1], Lihui Wang[1(✉)], Xi Vincent Wang[1], and Magnus Wiktorsson[2]

[1] Department of Production Engineering, KTH Royal Institute of Technology, 10044 Stockholm, Sweden
lihui.wang@iip.kth.se
[2] Department of Sustainable Production Development, KTH Royal Institute of Technology, 15181 Södertälje, Sweden

**Abstract.** Production logistics systems in the context of manufacturing, especially in automotive sectors today, are challenged by the lack of real-time data of logistics resources, optimal configuration and management strategies of materials, and optimisation approaches of logistics operations. This turns out to be the bottleneck in achieving flexible and adaptive logistics operations. To address these challenges, this paper presents a framework of real-time data-driven dynamic optimisation schemes for production logistics systems using the combined strength of advanced technologies and decision-making algorithms. Within the context, a real-time data sensing model is developed for the timely acquisition, storage, distribution, and utilisation of equipment and process data in which sensing devices are deployed on physical shop floors. The value-added data enable production logistics processes to be digitally visible and are shared among logistics resources. A multi-agent-based optimisation scheme for production logistics systems based on real-time data is developed to obtain the optimal configuration of logistics resources. Finally, a prototype-based simulation within an automotive manufacturing shop floor is used to demonstrate the proposed conceptual framework.

**Keywords:** Production logistics · IoT · Data-driven optimisation · Multi-agent system

## 1 Introduction

Production logistics in the context of smart manufacturing aims for flexible and adaptive production and logistics operations by using integrated information technologies that can combine advanced computing power with networked equipment [1, 2]. Production logistics systems are multidimensional and complex systems that cover material handling, planning, scheduling, and management of logistics resources and control of manufacturing execution systems [3]. Smart production logistics systems depend on the timely acquisition, storage, distribution, and utilisation of equipment and process data [4], as well as advanced analytic tools [5], amplifying the human ability to improve productivity and quality in production logistics. The rapid development of

© IFIP International Federation for Information Processing 2020
Published by Springer Nature Switzerland AG 2020
B. Lalic et al. (Eds.): APMS 2020, IFIP AICT 592, pp. 213–221, 2020.
https://doi.org/10.1007/978-3-030-57997-5_25

manufacturing requires advanced production and logistics strategies in global supply chains. Therefore, there has been an increasing interest in the field of production logistics from both academia and industry. With the advancement of the latest technologies such as the Internet of Things (IoT) and mobile internet [6], production logistics systems used today show the potential of meeting the expectation of Industry 4.0 and smart manufacturing. These technologies will facilitate real-time information sharing, knowledge discovery, and informed decision making [7].

In production logistics, i.e. factory internal logistics, companies are still facing typical challenges that lie in a lack of concrete models used for real-time data acquisition and sharing and digital visualisation of production logistics systems. This has led to the difficulties in monitoring and controlling physical resources on shop floors. Exception events (i.e. failures and breakdown) that may occur on the shop floors cannot be actively sensed and timely handled, which may trigger the rescheduling of logistics resources. Numerous logistics tasks and production demands from upstream and downstream suppliers also call for an efficient resource management system. In addition, the optimal configuration of logistics resources fails induced by the lack of real-time data and optimisation algorithms, which can increase the cost of transportation and material handling. To address such challenges, this paper proposes a framework of data-driven dynamic optimisation for production logistics systems which is for the digital visualisation and optimal configuration of logistics resources. Within this framework, an IoT-enabled real-time data sensing and visualisation model is developed to acquire equipment and process data by deploying sensor networks on the physical shop floor. Digital visualisation of production logistics systems is for the virtual control and management of materials, status monitoring and tracking, and ease-to-use visualisation services on the shop floor. Then, a real-time data-driven dynamic optimisation strategy using multi-agent technologies is developed for the optimal configuration of logistics resources and efficient material handling.

The remainder of this paper is organised as follows: Sect. 2 describes a real-time data sensing and visualisation model. Data-driven optimisation configuration of logistics resources is presented in Sect. 3. In Sect. 4, a prototype-based simulation focused on an automotive shop floor is proposed to demonstrate the proposed framework. Section 5 draws conclusions and highlights future work.

## 2 Real-Time Data Sensing and Visualisation

An IoT-enabled real-time data sensing model for production logistics systems, as shown in Fig. 1, is developed for the timely acquisition, processing, and utilisation of production and logistics data in which smart devices are deployed on the physical shop floors. Through the use of acquired data, digital visualisation of production logistics systems is designed to offer end-users easy-to-use services of production status, logistics planning, and path navigation. In this model, it consists of three modules, i.e. configuration of smart devices, sensing and processing of data, and visualisation.

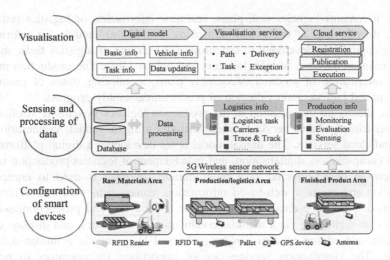

**Fig. 1.** A real-time data sensing and visualisation model for production logistics systems.

Configuration of smart devices is used to deploy smart sensing devices/sensors on the physical shop floors such that a sensing environment can be developed where production equipment/logistics resources can be monitored, tracked, and traced. The physical shop floor is classified as a raw material area, a production/logistics area, and a finished product area. For each area, Radio-frequency identification (RFID) technologies [8] are applied to sense and capture the real-time information of logistics resources, production processes, and WIP (Work-in-Progress) inventories. RFID readers installed with antennas are used to capture the production/logistics items attached with RFID tags. For example, when an item passes through the sensing area embedded with sensor networks, this event can be timely sensed and the information of this event is acquired. Then, the real-time status of this item can be monitored and traced. A real-time location system of transportation carriers on the shop floors is developed where the real-time location information acquired is used for the dynamic optimisation of the production logistics system. For the production/logistics area, external interfaces of some devices allow to get access to machining/assembling progress, and the traceability and monitoring of raw materials and WIPs make the status of buffers between devices transparent and visible.

Using 5G wireless sensor networks, real-time data acquired from the physical shop floor are transmitted to the module for sensing and processing of data and stored in the dataset. These data can match the specified events on the shop floor and they can be defined as a form of events, e.g., basic, complex, and key events. A basic event contains general information of production/logistics items (e.g., event ID and temporal and spatial attributes). The information included in a complex event reflects the status updating of logistics resources and production processes. A key event defined in the production logistics system impacts the overall performance of the system (i.e. production exception and urgent task delivery). The event-based data processing model simplifies the classification and management of primitive data. For the logistics module, it contains logistics task plans, real-time information of logistics tasks and carriers, delivery lists of tasks, and path plans. Within this module, an information updating approach is developed to synchronise the change of logistics tasks and carriers in terms of volume, weight, location, and delivery lists. The production module has the information of production/assembly plans, monitoring status of production equipment and buffers, and evaluation of production/assembly progress.

Then, the digital visualisation of the production logistics systems is to offer endusers user-friendly digital services, which includes a digital model, visualisation services, and cloud services. The digital model is for developing a digital platform used for data encapsulation, digitalisation, and management of logistics/production resources where an object-oriented Java programming language is used to encapsulate information and create a web-based information management platform. Within this digital model, real-time data of logistics tasks and carriers and production/assembly processes are digitalised via a modular combination of interfaces, and display, query, invocation, and editing of data can be performed by users via a human-computer interface. The visualisation services are of importance for operators to perform tasks/operations in which path plans and navigation of carriers, lists of tasks, delivery status, and exception events can be digitalised. These available services can be embedded and displayed in a portable mobile device. A typical example is that a delivery request of logistics tasks can be displayed to instruct operators to perform related operations. In addition, exception events (i.e. errors of task delivery/loading) can trigger a signal alarming to eliminate operator-made mistakes. Cloud services offer opportunities for extendable applications across the whole production logistics network.

# 3 Data-Driven Optimisation Configuration of Logistics Resources

In this section, a data-driven dynamic optimisation strategy using multi-agent technologies is presented for planning, scheduling, and allocation of logistics resources based on the collected data form Sect. 2 as shown in Fig. 2. A logistics resource module is for management of logistics resources and offering data input for a multi-agent-based hierarchical optimisation model with constraints. Then, the output results are sent to and stored in a logistics system module where the status of the shop floor can be monitored and digital logistics services can be built. Updated logistics data (i.e. new tasks and exceptions) from the logistics system module are transmitted to the logistics resource module. Then, a closed-loop dynamic optimisation scheme for logistics resources is developed by integrating the blocks of monitoring, scheduling, optimisation, and digitalisation into the production logistics system.

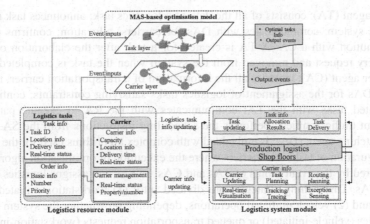

**Fig. 2.** A conceptual framework of data-driven dynamic optimisation for logistics resources.

A production logistics system that focuses on a factory-internal part of logistics is to deliver tasks efficiently and effectively to machines/workstations within a highly dynamic environment where unpredicted events that may occur can be prevented. For this purpose, algorithm-driven negotiation and communication among tasks, carriers, and workstations (or machines) are essential. Agent technology is considered as a promising approach used for dynamic optimisation for production logistics [9] and a network of agents, will create a multi-agent system (MAS) whose members not only are responsible for satisfying their local objectives, but also can interact and cooperate with each other to satisfy a global objective. Using the real-time data sensing model, factory-internal logistics resources that have the main characteristics of an agent [10] can be defined as agents. The factory-internal part of logistics prioritises accurate logistics material delivery to ensure the runtime of production lines while minimising logistics cost and improving the efficiency of production logistics systems. Within this context, a multi-agent-based architecture is presented as shown in Fig. 3(a), and interaction and communication of agents (as shown in Fig. 3(b)) are introduced as follows.

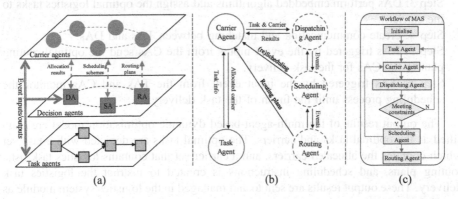

**Fig. 3.** (a) A hierarchical architecture of MAS; (b) Interaction and communication of agents; (c) A workflow of MAS.

- Task agent (TA): consists of all the data of a logistics task; announces task requests in the system; communicates with DAs for carriers' allocation; confirms the task distribution with a CA. A TA is created for a task after the elaboration of a task delivery request and removed from the system when the task is completed.
- Carrier agent (CA): includes all the information of a transportation carrier; interacts with DAs for the assignment of logistics tasks satisfying constraints; confirms the allocated tasks with the TA; communicates with the RA to execute path plans without traffic conflicts; performs the scheduling instructions from the SA.
- Dispatching agent (DA): is embedded with complex algorithms used for the optimal configuration of tasks and carriers where the execution of optimisation algorithms is triggered by the event inputs of TAs and CAs; selects and assigns logistics tasks to the CAs. Dispatching strategies are divided into: (1) workstation-initiated operations and (2) vehicle-initiated operations, depending on whether the system has idle vehicles (vehicle-initiated) or queued transportation requests (workstation-initiated).
- Routing agent (RA): is embedded with dynamic routing algorithms; makes routing decisions based on real-time information; outputs specific paths that each carrier will execute to accomplish its transportation tasks; interacts with the CA to offer path instructions.
- Scheduling agent (SA): is embedded with real-time scheduling algorithms; monitors and manages the entire scheduling process in interaction with other agents; is encapsulated with a reactive mechanism that triggers a rescheduling in case of failure of scheduling plans and handles unexpected events; outputs scheduling instructions.

An event-based communication protocol between agents is adopted for interaction and collaboration according to the definition of event-based data structure in Sect. 2.

When triggered by input events, the agent will start tasks/operations execution by activating the embedded algorithms/behaviours used for task allocation, routing planning, and scheduling planning. Finally, when the task is finished, the agent's event output will send triggering signals to related agents. The procedures of a MAS-based scheme, as shown in Fig. 3(c), are summarised as follows:

Step 1: initialise TAs and CAs by the input events from the logistics resources module.

Step 2: send the output events of TAs and CAs to trigger DAs.

Step 3: DAs perform embedded algorithms and assign the optimal logistics tasks to the carrier.

Step 4: create communication and matching between TAs and DAs.

Step 5: RAs triggered by the event inputs from the CAs send the optimal routing plan to the CAs for the task delivery.

Step 6: SAs triggered by the input event from the TAs and CAs monitor the scheduling process until the finish of the task delivery.

The output results of the multi-agent-based dynamic optimisation model are classified as the optimal tasks and carriers. The optimal tasks are depicted with a task set which contains the allocated carriers, and a carrier set that contains logistics task lists, routing plans, and scheduling instructions is created to instruct the logistics task delivery. These output results are sent to and managed in the logistics system module as shown in Fig. 2. A submodule of task information is for task updating initiated from carrier/workstation sides, managing the allocated task results, and monitoring task delivery, and a submodule of the carrier is for carriers' status updating, managing task plans and routing plans, offering digital visualisation services, and handling task delivery and exception. Then, data of these two submodules are stored in the database used for the historical task tracking.

## 4   A Prototype-Based Simulation

This section introduces a prototype-based simulation within an automotive manufacturing shop floor as shown in Fig. 4. Digital services designed aim for data visualisation of elements and monitoring and managing the production logistics systems on the shop floor, which offers easy-to-use interaction with operators. Function tabs located on the top of the visualisation interface are designed. *Home* tab allows an operator to create/logon an account and external interfaces to be connected for extended functions/services. This enables the traceability of the operations performed by operators. *Task IF* and *Carrier IF* are used to show real-time data of the tasks and carriers registered on the shop floor. *Path plan and navigation* is to show the path results optimised by the embedded algorithms and offer the path navigation services for the carriers. *Shop floor* is to show and monitor the real-time status of the shop floor, i.e. machine and buffer status, machining progress, inventory information, and exception events. *Bulletin* is to show instructions and event information when clicking on the tab including data of tasks and carriers, task demands, and exception events from the shop floor. Rescheduling/re-navigation will be performed followed by the optimisation triggered by exception events.

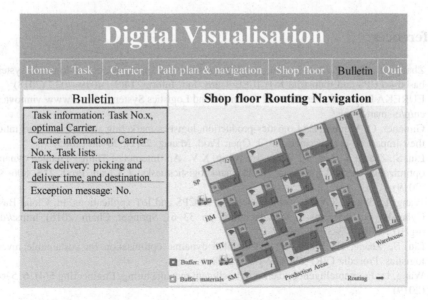

**Fig. 4.** A prototype-based simulation and digital visualisation.

A use case focuses on a factory-internal part of the shop floor in an automotive manufacturing company, which consists of a warehouse, two transportation carriers, and a production area for soft machining (SM), heat treatment (HT), hard machining (HM), and shot peening (SP) as shown in the right side of Fig. 4. Machines and buffers are defined as a numbered workstation cell that can trigger the workstation-initiated dispatching requests. The signals marked on the workstation show the varying priorities of task demands with different colours. Within the sensing and communication network in Sect. 2, the real-time status of elements on the shop floor can be sensed and monitored. Then, the event inputs of tasks and carriers trigger the runtime of the MAS-based optimisation approach, which sends output events. The output results are transmitted to the carriers and displayed through the digital visualisation interface. Finally, the path plan marked by red arrows is used to directly navigate operators to finished the task delivery, which can avoid the time-consuming path search.

# 5   Conclusions

This paper proposes a framework of data-driven dynamic optimisation for production logistics systems, aiming for the optimal solutions of logistics resources configuration. Within this context, a real-time information sensing and visualisation model is developed for timely acquisition, processing, and digital visualisation of production and logistics data. Then, a data-driven optimisation configuration scheme for logistics resources is presented for planning, scheduling, and allocation of logistics resources in which multi-agent technologies are adopted. Finally, an industrial case study focused on an automotive factory-internal part of logistics is carried out to illustrate the proposed framework. Our future work will focus on advanced algorithm development for real-world complex industrial practices.

# References

1. Zhang, Y., Guo, Z., Lv, J., Liu, Y.: A framework for smart production-logistics systems based on CPS and industrial IoT. IEEE Trans. Ind. Inform. **14**(9), 4019–4032 (2018)
2. EUREKA Project: Cyber-Physical Assembly and Logistics System. https://www.vinnova.se/en/p/e-smart-c-pals/
3. Gimenez, C., Ventura, E.: Logistics-production, logistics-marketing and external integration: their impact on performance. Int. J. Oper. Prod. Manag. **25**(1), 20–38 (2005)
4. Liu, S., Zhang, Y., Liu, Y., Wang, L., Wang, X.V.: An 'Internet of Things' enabled dynamic optimization method for smart vehicles and logistics tasks. J. Clean. Prod. **215**, 806–820 (2019)
5. Wang, L., Wang, X.V.: Latest advancement in CPS and IoT applications. In: Cloud-Based Cyber-Physical Systems in Manufacturing, pp. 33–61. Springer, Cham (2018). https://doi.org/10.1007/978-3-319-67693-7_2
6. Liu, S., Zhang, G., Wang, L.: IoT-enabled dynamic optimisation for sustainable reverse logistics. Procedia CIRP **69**, 662–667 (2018)
7. Wang, L.: From intelligence science to intelligent manufacturing. Engineering **5**(4), 615–618 (2019)

8. Zhang, Y., et al.: The 'Internet of Things' enabled real-time scheduling for remanufacturing of automobile engines. J. Clean. Prod. **185**, 562–575 (2018)
9. Shen, W., Wang, L., Hao, Q.: Agent-based distributed manufacturing process planning and scheduling: a state-of-the-art survey. IEEE Trans. Syst. Man Cybern. Part C Appl. Rev. **36** (4), 563–577 (2006)
10. Wang, L., Haghighi, A.: Combined strength of holons, agents and function blocks in cyber-physical systems. J. Manuf. Syst. **40**, 25–34 (2016)

# Decentralized Industrial IoT Data Management Based on Blockchain and IPFS

Xiaochen Zheng[1]([⊠]) [iD], Jinzhi Lu[1] [iD], Shengjing Sun[2] [iD],
and Dimitris Kiritsis[1] [iD]

[1] Institute of Mechanical Engineering, EPFL, 1015 Lausanne, Switzerland
{xiaochen.zheng,jinzhi.lu,dimitris.kiritsis}@epfl.ch
[2] ETSII, Universidad Politécnica de Madrid, 28006 Madrid, Spain
shengjing.sun@alumnos.upm.es

**Abstract.** The wide application of Internet of Things (IoT) has fostered the development of Industry 4.0. In manufacturing domain, Industrial IoT (IIoT) are key components of the Factories of the Future (FoF). The big IIoT data are the foundation of implementing data-driven strategies. In current industrial practice, most of these IIoT data are wasted or fragmented in data silos due to security and privacy concerns. Novel data management approaches are required to replace traditional centralized data management systems. The rapid development of blockchain technologies provides a novel solution for this challenge leveraging its unique characteristics such as decentralization, immutability and traceability. However, blockchain is inefficient for exchanging big data due to transaction throughput limits. The peer-to-peer InterPlanetary File System (IPFS) provides a suitable complement for blockchain. Therefore, this paper aims to propose a decentralized IIoT data management approach based on blockchain and IPFS technology. The architecture and enabling technologies of the proposed system are introduced. A proof-of-concept implementation is realized and relevant experiments are conducted. The results demonstrated the feasibility of the proposed approach.

**Keywords:** Blockchain · IPFS · Data management · Industrial IoT

## 1 Introduction

The advancements of digital technologies, such as Internet of Things (IoT), Artificial Intelligence (AI) and Cyber-Physical Systems (CPS) etc., are reshaping different sectors of the modern society. In industrial domain, the Industry 4.0 paradigm has been proposed empowered by Cyber-Physical Production Systems (CPPS), Industrial Internet of Things (IIoT) and big manufacturing data analytic etc. [1–3]. To realize the vision of Industry 4.0, all these enabling technologies and systems need to be integrated seamlessly. A smart manufacturing system requires connectivity among various

Supported by EU Commission within the research projects QU4LITY (EU H2020 825030) Digital Reality in Zero Defect Manufacturing and FACTLOG (EU H2020 869951) Energy-aware Factory Analytics for Process Industries.

manufacturing units, facilities, machinery, suppliers and retailers as well as other manufacturing supporting industries, to form a valuable smart manufacturing network through the entire manufacturing value chain [4, 5]. This remains a challenging task for manufacturing enterprises due to the concerns about security, trust, traceability, reliability, and agreement automation within the manufacturing value chain [6, 7].

According to the Data-Information-Knowledge-Wisdom (DIKW) model [8], data are the basis of higher levels of intelligence. For the Factories of the Future (FoF), the heterogeneous data produced by the wide deployed IIoT devices are the foundation of all data-driven applications for smart manufacturing. However, in reality the storing and sharing of big IIoT data are still challenging tasks for most manufacturing companies. Overwhelming amount of these data are either discarded due to high storage and processing cost, or remain fragmented in isolated data bases [9].

One of the main obstacles hindering IIoT data sharing is the concerns about data privacy and security issues. Traditional centralized databases and data exchange protocols might be susceptible to various attacks and tampering risks [10]. The cost of data transferring is another limitation preventing IIoT data flow freely. Although, from a technological point of view, data sharing cost is relatively lower than before, in reality it is still expensive for manufacturing companies to transfer large volume of fine and granular IIoT data in real-time due to intermediary fees [11]. To cope with the above mentioned issues, advanced data management systems are required. Distributed Ledger Technologies (DLT), which have been developing rapidly in recent years, provide suitable solutions for this purpose. A distributed ledger is a distributed database, maintained by a consensus protocol run by nodes in a peer-to-peer network without any central administrator [12]. Popular DLT structures include blockchain and Directed Acyclic Graph (DAG) among others [13]. Blockchain was first successfully applied to cryptocurrency field, such as Bitcoin [14] and Ethereum [15], and has gained attention from both academia and industry owing to its unique features, such as decentralized control, high anonymity and distributed consensus mechanisms [16–18].

In recent years, blockchain technology has been widely adopted in manufacturing domain to enable smart manufacturing under the Industry 4.0 context [19]. Many Blockchain-based applications have been developed such as cloud manufacturing [20], manufacturing supply chain management [21], manufacturing processes tracing [22] etc. Some recent studies have investigated the application of blockchain in industrial IoT data exchange [23], knowledge management [24] and trading and energy trading in smart grid [25–27] among others. Despite of the such advantages, blockchain protocols are facing some challenges in terms of throughput limitations, high transaction fees and long approval time.

DAG-based protocols, such as IOTA [28], have been proposed as the new generation of DLT to solve the scalability and transaction cost limitations of blockchain. Theoretically they can reach unlimited throughput without transaction fees, making them suitable to transfer high frequency and large amount of data [29]. However, currently they are still in their early phases with limited throughput. The InterPlanetary File System (IPFS) [30] provides a suitable complement to DLT protocols for big data handling. IPFS is a content-addressing, peer-to-peer network for storing and sharing arbitrary data in a distributed file system. It uses a hash to access a stored file and the hash value changes when any changes are made in the file content. This paper aims to propose a decentralized data management system by combining IPFS and DAG-based DLT to address big IIoT data storing and sharing challenges.

The rest of the paper is organized as follows. The architecture of the proposed data management system and the key components are introduced in Sect. 2. A proof-of-concept prototype implementation and experiments are demonstrated in Sect. 3. The paper is concluded in Sect. 4.

## 2   System Architecture

The architecture of the proposed IIoT data management system is as shown in Fig. 1. It includes four main components: IIoT data providers, IPFS data storage, blockchain-based meta data sharing platform, and IIoT data consumer.

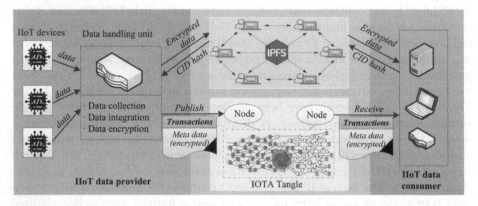

**Fig. 1.** Architecture of the proposed IIoT data management system based on IOTA Tangle and IPFS.

- IIoT data providers refer to the IIoT devices and relevant data handling units in a manufacturing system. The raw data generated by IIoT devices are transferred to a connected handling unit which can be a normal computer or any edge devices with certain computing capabilities like local servers and single-board computers. The handling units collect and integrate the raw data before uploading to IPFS in batches. Depending on the privacy by design, the data can be encrypted before uploading.
- IPFS data storage: Once the data are stored in the IPFS network, a cryptographic hash is generated as the Content Identifier (CID), which can be used to retrieve the uploaded data. After received the CID, the handling unit encode and encrypt the CID together with other meta data to create a transaction, to be transmitted to data sharing platform.

- Blockchain-based meta data sharing platform: The adopted protocol in this study is DAG structured IOTA Tangle, which is considered as the third generation blockchain. Although it is not exactly 'blockchain', we follow the common naming rules [13] to avoid confusing. The main reason of choosing this solution is that it solves the main limitations of previous blockchains, i.e. scalability and transaction fees. The transactions published on the Tangle can be searched or recommended to interested stakeholders. The content of a transaction might have different privacy levels depending on if it is encrypted or not. If encrypted, only receivers with authenticated decryption keys can consume the content.
- IIoT data consumers decode, and decrypt if required, the content of the transaction. Following the CID in the content, they can retrieve the data stored in IPFS. Another decryption might be required depending on the privacy level.

## 3 Proof-of-Concept and Experiments

A prototype of has been developed as proof-of-concept based on the IOTA Tangle API *(iota.lib.js)* and IPFS API *(ipfs Javascript implementation)*. The Javascript source codes with implementation instructions are open access on GitHub (https://github.com/zhengxiaochen/ipfs_iota_data_management.git).

### 3.1 Experiment and Result

Experiments are conducted simulating the process of storing and sharing sensor data in JSON format collected from environment monitoring devices located in a factory. Details about data collection are introduced in a previous study [31]. As shown in Fig. 2, the raw data generated by different sensors were streamed to the data handling unit, where they were integrated into JSON format. Then the JSON data were encrypted according to a certain interval and uploaded to the IPFS network. Once stored successfully, a CID *(e.g. QmbF-PdXRP8EuEHNuZuoqJ3vZeSzyE8TnKy7 djLsrYf9rHE)* was created and return to the data handling unit. The uploaded content can be viewed on the IPFS network *(https://ipfs.io/ipfs/)* using the CID as shown in Fig. 2.

After received the CID, the handling unit created a transaction containing the CID and other meta data describing the shared data, such as data owner, data type, brief description and decryption keys to the IPFS content etc. The transactions can be published in different privacy modes [29]. For example, in Fig. 2 the transaction was published in public mode so that anyone who knows the transaction address can view the content of the transaction. In restricted mode, a extra key will be required to view the content, enabling the data publisher to flexibly control the access to the data.

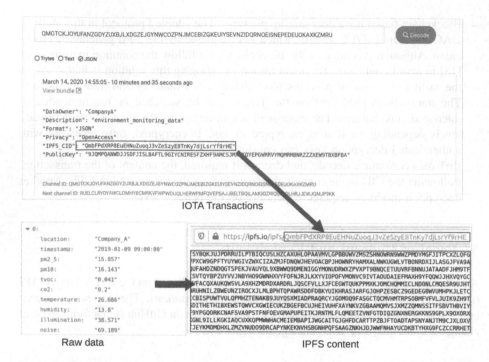

**Fig. 2.** Screenshots of the experiment for storing and sharing JSON sensor data using proposed approach.

Once the transaction is published on IOTA Tangle, interested data consumers can find it by proactive searching or passive subscription and recommendation. As shown in Fig. 2, the consumer followed the IFPS CID to retrieve the raw data from IPFS network. After downloaded the content, they might need to decrypt it with a specific key (the *"PublicKey"* in Fig. 2), which can be included in the transaction or distributed in separately.

### 3.2   Privacy and Security Analysis

The proposed data management system supports different privacy modes as demonstrated in the experiment. It allows nonsensitive data to be shared in public mode making them accessible to as many users as possible. For sensitive data, it provides two layers of encryption to protect the privacy and security. First, the data uploaded to IPFS are encrypted before uploading. It prevents data leakage even the IPFS network is compromised. Second, the transactions published to the Tangle can also be encrypted with the signature of the publisher and an extra key. Moreover, both IOTA protocol and IPFS are designed to be decentralized and distributed. This could eliminate the single-point-failure risks, and increase the tamper-resistance capability of the system. After a transaction is confirmed, it cannot be modified unless the majority of the computing power of entire network is controlled the attacker. Any modification to the original content stored in IPFS will also produce a totally different CID because of the hash function.

# 4 Discussion

With the evolution of the Industry 4.0 and smart manufacturing, the needs of data integration and sharing from different sources is increasing. The proposed approach can be applied as an enabling tool for many aspects of advanced manufacturing. As an example, the proposed approach is been applied in a factory producing construction materials. This factory is facing difficulties in handling the data related to customer orders data from the Enterprise Resource Planning (ERP), Manufacturing Execution System (MES) data, the loading and delivery monitoring data etc. Due to privacy and security concerns, the manufacturer, logistic providers and customers are reluctant to share their data, which is essential for data integration and higher level data analysis. The proposed approach has been adopted in a more complex data management system to support data sharing among different stakeholders. By combining the proposed approach with semantic modelling and machine learning, advanced data handling solutions can be developed thus to empower the development of Industry 4.0.

# 5 Conclusions

This paper proposed a IIoT data storing and sharing approach by integrating advanced blockchain and IPFS technologies. A DAG structured IOTA Tangle was used to empower high scalability, low cost and tamper-resistance data sharing; and IPFS was adopted to handle the large volume data storage challenge. The proof-of-concept implementation and experiment results demonstrate the feasibility of the proposed approach. Such data management systems could accelerate IIoT data exchange among FoF manufacturing systems enabling higher level data-driven strategies for smart manufacturing.

# References

1. Wang, L., Törngren, M., Onori, M.: Current status and advancement of cyber-physical systems in manufacturing. J. Manuf. Syst. **37**, 517–527 (2015)
2. Wang, J., Ma, Y., Zhang, L., Gao, R.X., Wu, D.: Deep learning for smart manufacturing: methods and applications. J. Manuf. Syst. **48**, 144–156 (2018)
3. Ordieres-Meré, J., Villalba-Díez, J., Zheng, X.: Challenges and opportunities for publishing IIoT data in manufacturing as a service business. Procedia Manuf. **39**, 185–193 (2019)
4. Lee, J., Bagheri, B., Kao, H.-A.: A cyber-physical systems architecture for industry 4.0-based manufacturing systems. Manuf. Lett. **3**, 18–23 (2015)
5. Lu, Y.: Industry 4.0: a survey on technologies, applications and open research issues. J. Ind. Inf. Integr. **6**, 1–10 (2017)
6. Mohamed, N., Al-Jaroodi, J.: Applying blockchain in industry 4.0 applications. In: 2019 IEEE 9th Annual Computing and Communication Workshop and Conference (CCWC), pp. 0852–0858. IEEE (2019)
7. Zhou, K., Liu, T., Zhou, L.: Industry 4.0: towards future industrial opportunities and challenges. In: 2015 12th International Conference on Fuzzy Systems and Knowledge Discovery (FSKD), pp. 2147–2152. IEEE (2015)

8. Frické, M.: The knowledge pyramid: a critique of the DIKW hierarchy. J. Inf. Sci. **35**(2), 131–142 (2009)
9. Industrial-Internet-Consortium-(IIC): Smart factory applications in discrete manufacturing, Industrial Internet Consortium White Paper (2017)
10. Callegati, F., Cerroni, W., Ramilli, M.: Man-in-the-middle attack to the https protocol. IEEE Secur. Priv. **7**(1), 78–81 (2009)
11. David, S.: IOTA data marketplace (2017)
12. Brogan, J., Baskaran, I., Ramachandran, N.: Authenticating health activity data using distributed ledger technologies. Comput. Struct. Biotechnol. J. **16**, 257–266 (2018)
13. Xiao, Y., Zhang, N., Lou, W., Hou, Y.T.: A survey of distributed consensus protocols for blockchain networks. IEEE Commun. Surv. Tutorials **22**(2), 1432–1465 (2020)
14. Nakamoto, S.: Bitcoin: a peer-to-peer electronic cash system, Technical report, Manubot (2008)
15. Wood, G., et al.: Ethereum: a secure decentralised generalised transaction ledger. Ethereum Proj. Yellow Pap. **151**(2014), 1–32 (2014)
16. Böhme, R., Christin, N., Edelman, B., Moore, T.: Bitcoin: economics, technology, and governance. J. Econ. Perspect. **29**(2), 213–238 (2015)
17. Harlev, M.A., Sun Yin, H., Langenheldt, K.C., Mukkamala, R., Vatrapu, R.: Breaking bad: de-anonymising entity types on the bitcoin blockchain using supervised machine learning. In: Proceedings of the 51st Hawaii International Conference on System Sciences (2018)
18. Zheng, X., Mukkamala, R.R., Vatrapu, R., Ordieres-Mere, J.: Blockchain-based personal health data sharing system using cloud storage. In: 2018 IEEE 20th International Conference on e-Health Networking, Applications and Services (Health- com), pp. 1–6. IEEE (2018)
19. Lee, J., Azamfar, M., Singh, J.: A blockchain enabled cyber-physical system architecture for industry 4.0 manufacturing systems. Manuf. Lett. **20**, 34–39 (2019)
20. Yu, C., Zhang, L., Zhao, W., Zhang, S.: A blockchain-based service composition architecture in cloud manufacturing. Int. J. Comput. Integr. Manuf. 1–15 (2019). https://doi.org/10.1080/0951192X.2019.1571234
21. Mondragon, A.E.C., Mondragon, C.E.C., Coronado, E.S.: Exploring the applicability of blockchain technology to enhance manufacturing supply chains in the composite materials industry. In: 2018 IEEE International Conference on Applied System Invention (ICASI), pp. 1300–1303. IEEE (2018)
22. Westerkamp, M., Victor, F., Küpper, A.: Tracing manufacturing processes using blockchain-based token compositions. Digital Commun. Netw. **6**(2), 167–176 (2019)
23. Liu, C.H., Lin, Q., Wen, S.: Blockchain-enabled data collection and sharing for industrial IoT with deep reinforcement learning. IEEE Trans. Ind. Inform. **15**(6), 3516–3526 (2018)
24. Lin, X., Li, J., Wu, J., Liang, H., Yang, W.: Making knowledge tradable in edge- AI enabled IoT: a consortium blockchain-based efficient and incentive approach. IEEE Trans. Ind. Inform. **15**(12), 6367–6378 (2019)
25. Li, Z., Kang, J., Yu, R., Ye, D., Deng, Q., Zhang, Y.: Consortium blockchain for secure energy trading in industrial internet of things. IEEE Trans. Ind. Inform. **14**(8), 3690–3700 (2018)
26. Wang, S., Taha, A.F., Wang, J., Kvaternik, K., Hahn, A.: Energy crowdsourcing and peer-to-peer energy trading in blockchain-enabled smart grids. IEEE Trans. Syst. Man Cybern.: Syst. **49**(8), 1612–1623 (2019)
27. Zhou, Z., Wang, B., Dong, M., Ota, K.: Secure and efficient vehicle-to-grid energy trading in cyber physical systems: integration of blockchain and edge computing. IEEE Trans. Syst. Man Cybern.: Syst. **50**(1), 43–57 (2019)
28. Popov, S.: The tangle. White paper, p. 131 (2016)

29. Zheng, X., Sun, S., Mukkamala, R.R., Vatrapu, R., Ordieres-Meré, J.: Accelerating health data sharing: a solution based on the Internet of Things and distributed ledger technologies. J. Med. Internet Res. **21**(6), e13583 (2019)
30. Benet, J.: IPFS-content addressed, versioned, P2P file system (2014)
31. Sun, S., Zheng, X., Villalba-Díez, J., Ordieres-Meré, J.: Indoor air-quality data-monitoring system: long-term monitoring benefits. Sensors **19**(19), 4157 (2019)

# Integrated Platform and Digital Twin Application for Global Automotive Part Suppliers

Jinho Yang[1] ⓘ, Sangho Lee[1], Yong-Shin Kang[1],
Sang Do Noh[1(✉)] ⓘ, Sung Soo Choi[2], Bo Ra Jung[2], Sang Hyun Lee[2],
Jeong Tae Kang[2], Dae Yub Lee[3], and Hyung Sun Kim[3]

[1] Sungkyunkwan University, Suwon 16419, Republic of Korea
sdnoh@skku.edu
[2] Yura, Seongnam 13494, Republic of Korea
[3] DEXTA Inc., Suwon 16419, Republic of Korea

**Abstract.** For global automakers that manufacture products through a globally distributed supply chain, it is essential for this supply chain to be managed efficiently to enhance the efficiency and responsiveness to uncertain changes in the market. These manufacturers face limitations associated with independent applications, such as difficulties in collecting information from distributed sites and the inability to make quick decisions. To solve this problem, researchers have been actively investigating the application of smart manufacturing technology to improve productivity as well as the optimal use of manufacturing resources in dynamic environments. Furthermore, different countries have different cultures, regulations, and policies. Hence, a universal integrated platform is required to address these difficulties. Accordingly, this study proposes an integrated cyber-physical system-based platform that reflects international standards and has versatile applications. This platform can be used to utilize information from various distributed manufacturing sites in real time. In addition, the proposed system was verified through a field application case study.

**Keywords:** Cyber-Physical System (CPS) · CPS-based platform · Digital twin · Global supply chains · Smart manufacturing

## 1 Introduction

Currently, several manufacturers design, engineer, and produce their products through a globally distributed supply chain. In particular, the automotive industry is a typical assembly industry wherein a small number of automakers procure tens of thousands of parts from several suppliers to produce automobiles. These agents form a global supply chain in which suppliers provide parts to automakers. It is estimated that more than 1,000 part suppliers directly or indirectly affect a single automaker [1].

Global automotive supply chains are also expanding geographically, owing to the increasing globalization and the reductions in production costs. As consumer preferences become more individualized, production systems have been recently shifting toward the build-to-order (BTO) model; such changes have been observed in Eastern

© IFIP International Federation for Information Processing 2020
Published by Springer Nature Switzerland AG 2020
B. Lalic et al. (Eds.): APMS 2020, IFIP AICT 592, pp. 230–237, 2020.
https://doi.org/10.1007/978-3-030-57997-5_27

Europe, Southeast Asia, South America, and India [2]. In such an increasingly complex and uncertain automotive manufacturing environment, part suppliers must effectively manage their distributed global supply chains to enhance their efficiency and responsiveness [3]. Firms must manufacture high-quality, reasonably-priced products that satisfy the needs of various customers, while simultaneously meeting delivery times. For this purpose, researchers have been actively investigating the application of smart manufacturing (SM) technology to improve productivity as well as the optimal use of manufacturing resources in dynamic environments [4, 5]. SM is a collection of advanced technologies that facilitate effective and accurate real-time decision-making by combining various information and communication technologies (ICTs) with the existing manufacturing industry [6]. Although SM has not been clearly defined thus far, it can be described as "a fully-integrated and collaborative manufacturing system that responds in real time to meet the changing demands and conditions in the factory, supply network, and customer needs." This enables technologies and systems to respond to internal and external changes in real time, thereby facilitating the construction of lighter and more flexible production systems [7, 8]. However, the production plants of global manufacturing companies are spread across different countries, which have different cultures, systems, regulations, units of measure, and languages. This introduces limitations for independent applications, such as difficulties in collecting information from distributed sites and the inability to make quick decisions [9, 10]. Consequently, studies on the design and application of cyber-physical systems (CPSs) have been conducted to address these limitations [11]. A CPS, which is a core technology of SM, extends beyond static systems and recognizes, adapts, and variably responds to situations, based on the data collected in real time in the field, thereby enhancing the efficiency of the entire production process [12, 13]. A cyber-physical production system (CPPS) is created by applying a CPS for manufacturing using a variety of technologies [6, 14]. A digital twin (DT) is one of the core technologies that constitutes such a system; it is a virtual model that can analyze, evaluate, optimize, and predict current situations by synchronizing and simulating the information and functions of the production site [15].

To address the difficulties faced by global automotive manufacturers who deal with different cultures and systems, this study proposes an integrated CPS-based platform that reflects international standards and has versatile applications. This platform can be employed to utilize site information from various distributed external data and systems in real time. In addition, a system that provides a cloud-based service to add and extend various applications is proposed.

## 2 Research Backgrounds

A CPS is defined as an innovative technology for managing interconnected systems between its physical assets and computational capabilities [16]. Currently, to realize competitive advantages in advanced ICT technology and big data, numerous manufacturers and researchers are investigating methods to implement the CPS structure and methodology in their respective industries [17]. A CPPS consists of autonomous and cooperative elements and subsystems based on the data collected throughout the production and logistics system; it comprises three main characteristics: intelligence (smartness), connectedness, and responsiveness towards internal and external changes [17]. To implement a CPPS, the integration of analyses and simulation-based approaches for big data collected in large quantities is considered more important than other components [17]. In this regard, a DT is a core technology that can more quickly and accurately conduct simulations by synchronizing the information and functions of the production site [15].

Grieve first introduced the concept of DT in 2003. Since then, it has continued to develop [18]. A DT is defined as "an integrated virtual model of information and functional units based on the composition of heterogeneous physical elements." In the manufacturing field, a DT is also defined as a virtual factory that reflects the config-uration information of a physical factory, for synchronizing information and functions related to the design, operation, and production in real time [18–21].

Compared to conventional simulation models, a DT possesses several advanced features. By combining predefined models and functions with ICT, it can quickly generate models that reflect site information as well as enhance processes through optimization and conduct dynamic diagnoses and predictions by calculating repeated simulation results [18, 21–24]. To apply a DT, a data exchange system that can be connected to the site must be constructed; four studies are actively being conducted to create this data exchange system [19, 25, 26].

To utilize CPS and DT for integrating and linking the information in distributed environments and for providing various services, a platform that provides a large-scale service system must be constructed. This is a highly complex problem [26]. Each component of a DT is configured as a heterogeneous system; to utilize these compo-nents for monitoring and predictions, an efficient platform that employs distributed computing-based modeling and simulation must be developed. Moreover, interoper-ability is essential to ensure the exchange of information between these systems [26].

## 3    CPS-Based Integrated Platform and Applications

### 3.1    Platform and Applications

The proposed CPS-based integrated platform supports various design, engineering, manufacturing, and logistics applications and services for SM in global manufacturing companies. This platform integrates real-time information from heterogeneous envi-ronments and incorporates DT technology to construct virtual factories and site applications for smart assembly systems. The smart assembly system largely consists of 1) a smart quality control system comprising a quality impact analysis model between processes and a quality prediction algorithm that considers the characteristics of an operator performing manual assembly processes, and 2) a smart production control system comprising an analysis and control model for factors that impact productivity in the assembly process, such as the number of workers at the production site, skill levels, and task difficulties, and an optimal production control algorithm. The core advanced technology proposed in this paper is an advanced analytics technology based on DT and machine learning; it serves as a basis for service applications applicable to logistics and production processes in the global automotive industry environment. Figure 1 depicts the conceptual architecture of the proposed CPS-based platform, and Table 1 presents an overview of the major technologies and applications that constitute this platform.

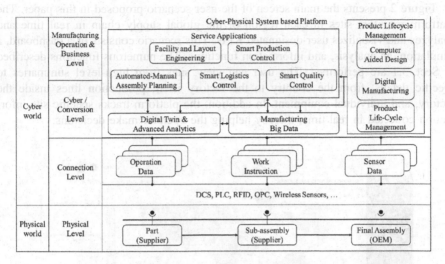

**Fig. 1.** Conceptual architecture of Cyber-Physical System (CPS)-based Integrated Platform

**Table 1.** Summary of CPS-based platform and services

| Name | Sub-technology or service name |
|---|---|
| CPS-based platform and cloud service | Digital-twin |
| | Advanced analytics |
| | Manufacturing big data & repository |
| Cloud based application service | Facility and layout engineering |
| | Smart production control |
| | Smart quality control |
| | Smart logistics control |
| | Automated-manual assembly planning |

## 3.2 User Scenario

Primary users of the proposed platform and services are supervisors, operators, and managers. Operators are the personnel who directly operate equipment in the field, supervisors are those who direct operator activities, and managers are those who manage the overall production process. Each user has different strategic goals depending on his/her purpose of using the platform and services. Appropriate selection and operation of these key performance indicators (KPIs) are critical success factors for an enterprise [27]. Therefore, considering the environment of global manufacturers, this study proposes the use of KPIs based on international standards for the proposed platform [28, 29]. International Standard ISO 22400 presents 34 KPIs for understanding and improving the performance of manufacturing systems. In the proposed platform, the KPI screen can be configured according to the specific purposes of each user.

Figure 2 presents the main screen of the user scenario proposed in this paper. The platform monitors sites in each region of the global supply chain in real time and analyzes and visualizes user-designated KPIs. This scenario consists of a dashboard, a simulation, an analysis, and information functions. The numerous functions described in Sect. 3.1 are performed. The user can view sites from high-level summaries to specific details, from the country to the factory itself, production lines inside the factory, and individual equipment. In addition, the platform tracks specific site information collected in real time, thereby helping the operator make decisions.

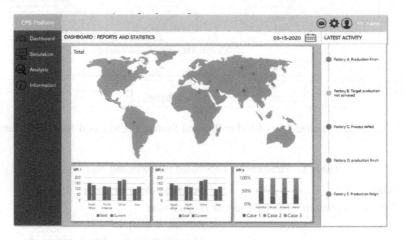

**Fig. 2.** Conceptual scenario main screen of CPS-based platform

## 3.3   Information Model for Digital Twin

This study proposes an information model for creating a virtual factory model that reflects real-time site information. To employ a DT, tuning is required to construct a simulation model from the collected site data. To reflect these requirements, this study used the Core Manufacturing Simulation Data (CMSD) proposed by the National Institute of Standards and Technology (NIST) of the United States. The information model proposed in CMSD was utilized for the configuration and tuning of parts, resources, production operations, and production planning [30]. The information model defined in this study consists of a header, a resource instance, a simulation execution, and results for the DT construction. The header corresponds to the simulation model and the library information in the model; the resource instance represents the instance configuration information of the manufacturing resource for constructing the cyber model.

# 4 Implementation

This study is currently being conducted as part of an international joint research between South Korea and Sweden. It involves the design and implementation of various applications for the CPS-based platform, such as cloud service, DTs, advanced analytics, and site applications. To construct the CPS-based platform, research is being conducted on detailed design, analysis of user requirements and standards, scenario establishment, and platform implementation. Moreover, a library that defines the information model and various data for DT construction is being built. A virtual factory model linked to the data of operators and processes collected in real time at the production site is also being built. Figure 3 presents a DT model for site application and the verification of the CPS-based platform. The model is linked to operator information collected at the site in real time using a short-range wireless communication device; a global automotive wiring harness manufacturer from South Korea is considered as the site. This can be used to construct a system that predicts a variety of problems and evaluates alternatives by linking algorithms for production management and predicting various quality issues. Furthermore, a platform that reflects international standards through a cloud-based service is provided, and it can be used in global environments involving different cultures and systems.

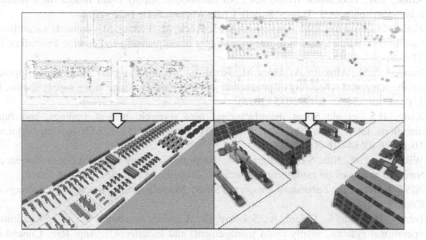

**Fig. 3.** Virtual factory model synchronized with real-time data

# 5 Conclusion

This paper presented a CPS-based integration platform for integrating and efficiently managing information from the distributed sites of global automotive manufacturers. The proposed platform was verified through a case study involving a global automotive wiring harness manufacturer from South Korea. The CPS-based platform and various service applications were designed and implemented in accordance with international standards, and a detailed information model for the DT was defined. However, there are a few limitations associated with collecting various data to implement smart manufacturing, in addition to the problem of identical data requiring different management systems. Future studies must investigate the construction of a data collection system to obtain valuable, high-quality data and support more accurate and rapid decision-making.

**Acknowledgment.** This research was supported by the Ministry of Trade, Industry and Energy (MOTIE) and Korea Institute for Advancement of Technology (KIAT) through the International Cooperative R&D program [P0009839, Cyber Physical Assembly and Logistics Systems in Global Supply Chains (C-PALS)] and this study is part of the Cyber Physical Assembly and Logistics Systems in Global Supply Chains (C-PALS) project funded by Eureka SMART and Vinnova.

# References

1. Jung, J.-S.: Logistics Innovation in the Automotive Industry, Research Report. Korea Institute for Industrial Economics & Trade, Sejong (2001)
2. Lee, C.-B., Lee, J.C.: A classification of logistics outsourcing in the global automotive industry. Korea Logist. Rev. **29**(6), 163–174 (2019)
3. Ambe, I.M., Badenhorst-Weiss, J.A.: An automotive supply chain model for a demand-driven environment. J. Transp. Supply Chain Manag. **5**(1), 1–22 (2011)
4. Pires, M.C., Frazzon, E.M., Danielli, A.M.C., Kück, M., Freitag, M.: Towards a simulation-based optimization approach to integrate supply chain planning and control. Procedia CIRP **72**, 520–525 (2018)
5. Frazzon, E.M., Albrecht, A., Pires, M., Israel, E., Kück, M., Freitag, M.: Hybrid approach for the integrated scheduling of production and transport processes along supply chains. Int. J. Prod. Res. **56**(5), 2019–2035 (2018)
6. Kang, H.S., et al.: Smart manufacturing: past research, present findings, and future directions. Int. J. Precis. Eng. Manuf.-Green Technol. **3**(1), 111–128 (2016). https://doi.org/10.1007/s40684-016-0015-5
7. Wiktorsson, M., Noh, S.D., Bellgran, M., Hanson, L.: Smart factories: South Korean and Swedish examples on manufacturing settings. Procedia Manuf. **25**, 471–478 (2018)
8. NIST Engineering Laboratory Program: Smart Manufacturing Operations Planning and Control (2014)
9. Ivanov, D., Sethi, S., Dolgui, A., Sokolov, B.: A survey on control theory applications to operational systems, supply chain management, and Industry 4.0. Ann. Rev. Control **46**, 134–147 (2018)
10. Ivanov, D., Sokolov, B., Kaeschel, J.: A multi-structural framework for adaptive supply chain planning and operations control with structure dynamics considerations. Eur. J. Oper. Res. **200**(2), 409–420 (2010)
11. Ivanov, D., Dolgui, A., Das, A., Sokolov, B.: Digital supply chain twins: managing the ripple effect, resilience, and disruption risks by data-driven optimization, simulation, and visibility. In: Ivanov, D., Dolgui, A., Sokolov, B. (eds.) Handbook of Ripple Effects in the Supply Chain. ISORMS, vol. 276, pp. 309–332. Springer, Cham (2019). https://doi.org/10.1007/978-3-030-14302-2_15
12. Miclea, L., Sanislav, T.: About dependability in cyber-physical systems. In: 2011 9th East-West Design and Test Symposium (EWDTS), pp. 17–21. IEEE (2011)

13. Ribeiro, L., Björkman, M.: Transitioning from standard automation solutions to cyber-physical production systems: an assessment of critical conceptual and technical challenges. IEEE Syst. J. **12**(4), 3816–3827 (2017)
14. Monostori, L.: Cyber-physical production systems: roots, expectations and R&D challenges. Procedia CIRP **17**, 9–13 (2014)
15. Tao, F., Zhang, M., Nee, A.Y.C.: Digital twin driven smart manufacturing. Academic Press, Cambridge (2019)
16. Rajkumar, R., Lee, I., Sha, L., Stankovic, J.: Cyber-physical systems: the next computing revolution. In: Design Automation Conference, pp. 731–736. IEEE (2010)
17. Monostori, L., et al.: Cyber-physical systems in manufacturing. CIRP Ann. **65**(2), 621–641 (2016)
18. Lee, J., Bagheri, B., Kao, H.A.: A cyber-physical systems architecture for industry 4.0-based manufacturing systems. Manuf. Lett. **3**, 18–23 (2015)
19. Grieves, M.: Digital twin: manufacturing excellence through virtual factory replication, White paper, pp. 1–7 (2014)
20. Cheng, Y., Zhang, Y., Ji, P., Xu, W., Zhou, Z., Tao, F.: Cyber-physical integration for moving digital factories forward towards smart manufacturing: a survey. Int. J. Adv. Manuf. Technol. **97**(1–4), 1209–1221 (2018)
21. Liu, Q., Zhang, H., Leng, J., Chen, X.: Digital twin-driven rapid individualised designing of automated flow-shop manufacturing system. Int. J. Prod. Res. **57**(12), 3903–3919 (2018)
22. Gabor, T., Belzner, L., Kiermeier, M., Beck, M.T., Neitz, A.: A simulation-based architecture for smart cyber-physical systems. In: 2016 IEEE International Conference on Autonomic Computing (ICAC), pp. 374–379. IEEE (2016)
23. Tao, F., Cheng, J., Qi, Q., Zhang, M., Zhang, H., Sui, F.: Digital twin-driven product design, manufacturing and service with big data. Int. J. Adv. Manuf. Technol. **94**(9–12), 3563–3576 (2017). https://doi.org/10.1007/s00170-017-0233-1
24. Uhlemann, T.H.J., Schock, C., Lehmann, C., Freiberger, S., Steinhilper, R.: The digital twin: demonstrating the potential of real time data acquisition in production systems. Procedia Manuf. **9**, 113–120 (2017)
25. International Standard, 008-01-2012: Standard for Core Manufacturing Simulation Data–XML Representation, Simulation Interoperability Standards Organization (2012)
26. Yun, S., Park, J.H., Kim, W.T.: Data-centric middleware based digital twin platform for dependable cyber-physical systems. In: 2017 Ninth International Conference on Ubiquitous and Future Networks (ICUFN), pp. 922–926. IEEE (2017)
27. Kang, N., Zhao, C., Li, J., Horst, J.A.: A hierarchical structure of key performance indicators for operation management and continuous improvement in production systems. Int. J. Prod. Res. **54**(21), 6333–6350 (2016)
28. International Standard, ISO 22400–1: Automation Systems and Integration – Key Performance Indicators (KPIs) for Manufacturing Operations Management - Part 1: Overview, Concepts and Terminology, International Standard Organization (ISO), Geneva (2014)
29. International Standard, ISO 22400–2: Automation Systems and Integration - Key Performance Indicators (KPIs) for Manufacturing Operations Management - Part 2: Definitions and Descriptions, International Standard Organization (ISO), Geneva (2014)
30. Riddick, F.H., Lee Y.T.: Core manufacturing simulation data (CMSD): a standard representation for manufacturing simulation-related information. In: Fall Simulation Interoperability Workshop (Fall SIW) SISO (2010)

# Analyzing the Characteristics of Digital Twin and Discrete Event Simulation in Cyber Physical Systems

Erik Flores-García[1]([✉]) [ID], Goo-Young Kim[2] [ID], Jinho Yang[2] [ID],
Magnus Wiktorsson[1] [ID], and Sang Do Noh[2] [ID]

[1] KTH Royal Institute of Technology, 15136 Södertälje, Sweden
efs0l@kth.se
[2] Sungkyunkwan University, Suwon 16419, South Korea

**Abstract.** Digital Twins (DTs) are described as the next wave in simulation, a critical component of Cyber Physical Systems (CPS), and a key enabler for data-driven decision-making. Yet, the literature presents limited understanding about the characteristics of DTs and their relation to current simulation capabilities. Addressing this problem, the purpose of this study is to analyze the characteristics of DTs and simulation models for CPS in production logistics. This study reviews extant literature on DTs and presents findings from a single case study at a South Korean manufacturing company developing a DT including Discrete Event Simulation (DES). The findings of this study highlight the importance of DES in DTs focusing on increased production logistics performance. The results of this study indicate that the use of DES may promote the development of DTs, but be insufficient in the characterization of DTs for CPS in production logistics.

**Keywords:** Digital Twins · Discrete Event Simulation · Production logistics

## 1 Introduction

Digital Twins (DTs) are proposed as the next wave in simulation and optimization technology, extending simulation along the life cycle of products and production systems [1]. Research posits that DTs are essential for Cyber Physical Systems (CPS) and data-driven decision-making [2, 3]. The benefits of DTs facilitating data-driven decision-making along the value chain include facilitating product customization, flexibility, operation and monitoring leading to increased performance [4]. However, the literature presents limited understanding about the characteristics of DTs and their relation to current simulation capabilities [2]. This situation is problematic because inadequate understanding of the characteristics of DTs and simulation may translate to increased costs when implementing DTs and limited benefits to key stakeholders along the value chain [5]. Addressing this problem, the purpose of this study is to analyze the characteristics of DTs and simulation models for CPS in production logistics. This study presents findings from a case study at a manufacturing company developing a Discrete Event Simulation (DES) model in a context of DTs for

© IFIP International Federation for Information Processing 2020
Published by Springer Nature Switzerland AG 2020
B. Lalic et al. (Eds.): APMS 2020, IFIP AICT 592, pp. 238–244, 2020.
https://doi.org/10.1007/978-3-030-57997-5_28

CPS. These findings of this study contribute to existing understanding by describing the limitations and coincidences between the characteristics of DTs and DES for CPS in production logistics which may be essential for increased performance.

## 2 Frame of Reference

### 2.1 Characterizing Digital Twins in Cyber Physical Systems

The literature describes CPS as the integrations of computation and physical processes [5]. CPS and DTs share common principles including the interconnection and interoperability of a physical shop floor and corresponding cybershop floor [6]. However, CPS and DTs refer to distinct constructs with unique compositions, cyber-physical mapping, control and core elements [3]. For example, data and models are the core elements of DTs, which differ from the core elements of CPS (e.g. sensors and actuators). Data and models in DT play an important role helping interpret and predict the behavior of the physical world based on data. Currently, literature focused on DTs supporting data-driven decision-making for production logistics in CPS follows three lines of inquiry: Firstly, studies providing a general understanding of DTs [7]. Secondly, conceptual studies proposing the models, operating mechanisms, or architectures for DTs [8]. Thirdly, studies exploring the use of DTs in practical applications [9]. The study of DTs is a dynamic field. One of the more recent reviews [10] presents the characteristics of DTs shown in Table 1.

**Table 1.** Characteristics of Digital Twins in Cyber Physical Systems based on [10].

| Characteristic | Description |
|---|---|
| Networking devices | Physical or cloud-based communication devices for data exchange |
| Synchronization | Real-time convergence of physical systems and its digital counterpart |
| Multi-communication environment | Communication processes between production systems, environment, domain experts and DTs for interaction and operation |
| Data storage | Acquiring historic static data of products, processes, production planning and ontologies for data comprehension |
| Data analysis | (De)coding and analyzing data for integrating multiple data sources |
| Information selection | Identifying, extracting and storing useful information |
| Pattern identification | Identifying changes and trends by analyzing data |
| Self-adjustment | Self-adaptation and parametrization capabilities following production system changes during its lifecycle |
| Predictive analytics | Predicting future status and important changes of production systems |
| Prescriptive analytics | Specifying high-value alternatives given objectives, requirements, and constraints |
| Optimization | Achieving best outcomes while addressing data uncertainty |
| Closed loop feedback | Feedback to production systems and to other DTs, using interfaces to access the computed information |
| Simulation | Representing current status and what-if scenarios |

## 2.2    Characterizing Discrete Event Simulation in Production Logistics

DES is one of the most commonly used techniques for understanding the dynamics of production logistics [11]. DES involves the experimentation of a simplified imitation of a production system as it progresses through time, for the purpose of understanding and/or improving that system [12]. Recent publications reviewing DT literature underscore the importance of DES in data-driven decision-making [8]. The literature presents alternative processes for developing DES models, but largely coincide on the activities of structured process [13]. Beginning with a clear problem definition, DES in production logistics frequently focus on operational performance including work in progress, lead-time, throughput, or utilization of resources. In addition, DES involves activities specifying the useful information according to the purpose of a model and acquiring data from multiple sources (e.g. ERP systems and domain experts). Frequently, DES depends on multiple sources of communication, data storage systems, and statistical analysis to synthesize and comprehend the interrelation of variables and outputs. Increasingly, DES research emphasizes the need for identifying a best alternative (optimization), and increasing understanding of results to non-experts (for example through 3D visualization).

## 3    Method

To meet its purpose, this research is based on a single case study. This study adopts case study research because of its appropriateness for investigating novel scientific inquiries with scant theoretical background [13]; namely, the need for empirical insight about DTs for CPS in production logistics [3]. Case selection followed from the correspondence between four DT implementation features [8] and the attributes of DTs at a manufacturing companies. These features included an explicit description of acquired dataset and acquisition protocols, specification of simulation model objectives, cloud usage, and control of the real system from the DT. Data collection occurred between July 2019 and February 2020 including participant observation, company documents, and DES models. Data analysis relied on a comparison between identified characteristics of DTs and DES described in the frame of reference and collected data.

## 4    Empirical Results

The manufacturing company is a global producer of wire harnesses and electronic components for the automotive industry that undertook the development of a DT based on CPS principles. The purpose of the DT involved improving performance in the areas of production logistic, quality, and production control based on data-driven decision-making. The development of the DT focused on the assembly process of wire harness products including sub-assembly, main assembly, inspection, and product buffer areas.

Acquired data sets for the DT included CAD files for factory layout, bills of materials and processes, production cycle times and disturbances, and real time data of resources (machines, assembly stations, forklifts, and buffers). Data was acquired via systems for Enterprise Resource Planning (ERP), Manufacturing Execution (MES), and Real Time Location (RTLS) systems. The DT enabled cloud services such as facilities/configuration engineering service, smart quality prediction service, production control service and production logistics management service.

The DT included quality predictive model, production optimal control model and DES model. The purpose of the quality model was that of identifying and prescribing actions for correcting quality problems. The purpose of the production control model included determining the optimal production process based on production environmental conditions for improving production throughput. DES included a 3D visualization of material flow with the purpose of predicting resource utilization and production throughput. Managers and operators performed control of the real life system based on the visualization of the system behavior and guidelines presented through user interfaces included in the DT. Figure 1 presents the DES model visualization of sub-assembly, main assembly, inspection, and product buffer included in the DT.

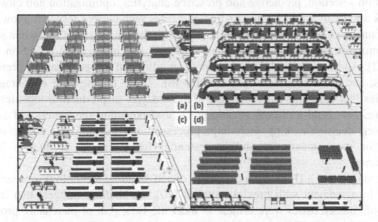

**Fig. 1.** DES model visualization of (a) sub-assembly, (b) main-assembly, (c) inspection, and (d) product buffer included in the DT.

The DES presented a simplified imitation of the production process. Managers identified parameters including utilization rate, idle rate, poor quality rate, production throughput, and buffer levels for calculating production logistics performance. Production staff examined information, selecting or excluding data, required as input data. A multi-communicational environment was essential for DES. For example, historical data stored in ERP and MES systems and the outputs of the production control and quality models provided to and facilitated the verification and validation of the DES model. In addition, the knowledge of domain experts was crucial for modeling the production process. DES produced two types of results. First, DES predicted future status of production logistics performance based on demand and operational prognosis. What-if scenarios including changes in demand or resources enabled this type of predictive analysis. Second, DES utilized optimization algorithms linking various design variables (e.g. buffer size or number of forklifts) to the production logistics performance. Adopting optimization in DES helped identify and prescribe high-value alternatives and their trade-offs including for example minimum buffer sizes and production lead-time and maximum production throughput. Feedback from DES to the performance of the production system depended on the interpretation of production staff and their corrective actions based on quantitative data analysis and 3D visualization.

## 5 Analysis

The purpose of this study is to analyze the characteristics of DTs and simulation models for CPS in production logistics. The findings of this study suggest that the use of DES may promote the development of DTs in CPS for production logistics. This study reveals that eight characteristics of DTs were facilitated by DES in production logistics including: multi-communication environments, data storage, data analysis, information selection, predictive and prescribe analytics, optimization and closed loop feedback shown in Table 2. This finding coincides with current research showing that manufacturing companies benefit from the prescriptive analysis of DES when securing multi-communication, data storage, data analysis, and information selection competences [2]. Additionally, publications report on advanced in optimization, prescriptive analytics, and close loop feedback in DES [8]. These findings are encouraging for companies that currently embrace DES in the analysis of production logistics. These companies may hold a critical advantage for understanding the benefits of DTs and data-driven decision-making including: processes and technologies increasing data quality, or data analytic capabilities essential for increased production logistics performance.

Data shows that a DT is not a collection of self-standing technologies or simulation models. In agreement with previous studies [10], the findings suggest that interconnection of characteristics were critical to meet the DTs goal of increasing production logistics performance. For example, case data revealed that achieving quality prediction and production optimization for smart automated-manual production required fulfilling 14 DT characteristics described in literature and shown in Table 2. This finding suggest that the benefits of DTs, including data-driven decision-making for production logistics, depend on fulfilling individual DT characteristics and establishing a link between these. This finding underscore the importance of identifying the elements, processes and operating mechanisms and their interrelation required for fulfilling the characteristics of DTs in CPS for production logistics [2].

The findings of this study suggest that DES is supportive but not sufficient for developing a DT in production logistics. DTs include a complex human, machine, material, and environment interaction throughout the lifecycle of a production system. Achieving this interaction requires the coordination and linkage between relevant data and models to fulfill the purpose of a DT [3]. Empirical data presented in Table 2 reveal the absence of networking devices, synchronization, pattern identification, and self-adjustment in the DES model. The absence of these four characteristics do not constitute a failure to the success of a DES project, but do limit the characteristics of DTs in CPS aimed at improving production logistics performance [8]. In addition, data suggests that DES may facilitate one, or several, characteristic of DTs, but the use of DES brings no assurance that DT characteristics will be fulfilled. For example, information selection which is both a characteristic of DTs and DES found in case data as shown in Table 2. In DES, information selection is an iterative activity traditionally entrusted to simulation specialists and domain experts [12]. However, DTs require extracting useful information in a manner that reduces cost storage and computational processing but does not compromise the volume of data and dynamic services [6]. This finding is important because it underscores the need for increased understanding of shared characteristics between DTs and DES, and the extent of their fulfillment towards a common goal.

**Table 2.** Case analysis of DTs and DES characteristics for CPS in production logistics

| Observed DT characteristics | Observed DES characteristics |
|---|---|
| Networking devices x | |
| Synchronization x | |
| Multi-communication Environment x | ERP, EMS, simulation models, domain expert knowledge |
| Data storage x | Historical data for DES model inputs |
| Data analysis x | Production logistics resource utilization, quality rate, production throughput, and buffer levels |
| Information selection x | Non-automatic identification of useful information |
| Pattern identification x | |
| Self-adjustment | |
| Predictive analytics x | What-if scenarios with changing production demand and resources |
| Prescriptive analytics x | Identifying high-value alternatives including minimum buffer size and resource quantity and maximum production throughput |
| Optimization x | Linking design variables to production logistics performance |
| Closed loop feedback x | Staff-dependent, based on DES output and 3D visualization |

# 6   Conclusions

This study analyzed the characteristics of DTs and simulation models for CPS in production logistics. This study indicated that the use of DES may promote the development of DTs, but may be insufficient towards their characterization. Future research could verify the findings of this study with additional cases, and understand the precedence of DT characteristics and their alignment to current DES capabilities at manufacturing companies.

**Acknowledgement.** This research was supported by the Ministry of Trade, Industry and Energy (MOTIE) in South Korean and the Korea Institute for Advancement of Technology (KIAT) through the International Cooperative R&D program [P0009839] and the Fostering Global Talents for Innovative Growth Program [P0008746]. In addition, this study is part of the Cyber Physical Assembly and Logistics Systems in Global Supply Chains (C-PALS) project funded by Eureka SMART and Vinnova.

# References

1. Park, K.T., Lee, J., Kim, H.-J., Noh, S.D.: Digital twin-based cyber physical production system architectural framework for personalized production. Int. J. Adv. Manuf. Technol. **106**(5), 1787–1810 (2019). https://doi.org/10.1007/s00170-019-04653-7

2. Tao, F., Zhang, H., Liu, A., Nee, A.Y.C.: Digital twin in industry: state-of-the-art. IEEE Trans. Ind. Inform. **15**(4), 2405–2415 (2019)

3. Tao, F., Qi, Q., Wang, L., Nee, A.Y.C.: Digital twins and cyber–physical systems toward smart manufacturing and industry 4.0: correlation and comparison. Engineering **5**(4), 653–661 (2019)

4. Schleich, B., Anwer, N., Mathieu, L., Wartzack, S.: Shaping the digital twin for design and production engineering. CIRP Ann. **66**(1), 141–144 (2017)

5. Monostori, L., Kádár, B., Bauernhansl, T., et al.: Cyber-physical systems in manufacturing. CIRP Ann. **65**(2), 621–641 (2016)

6. Ding, K., Chan, F.T.S., Zhang, X., Zhou, G., Zhang, F.: Defining a digital twin-based cyber-physical production system for autonomous manufacturing in smart shop floors. Int. J. Prod. Res. **57**(20), 6315–6334 (2019)

7. Negri, E., Fumagalli, L., Macchi, M.: A review of the roles of digital twin in CPS-based production systems. Procedia Manuf. **11**, 939–948 (2017)

8. Cimino, C., Negri, E., Fumagalli, L.: Review of digital twin applications in manufacturing. Comput. Ind. **113**, 103130 (2019)

9. Lu, Y., Liu, C., Wang, K., Huang, H., Xu, X.: Digital twin-driven smart manufacturing: connotation, reference model, applications and research issues. Robot. Comput.-Integr. Manuf. **61**, 101837 (2020)

10. Barricelli, B.R., Casiraghi, E., Fogli, D.: A survey on digital twin: definitions, characteristics, applications, and design implications. IEEE Access **7**, 167653–167671 (2019)

11. Flores-Garcia, E., Wiktorsson, M., Bruch, J., Jackson, M.: Revisiting challenges in using discrete event simulation in early stages of production system design. In: Moon, I., Lee, Gyu M., Park, J., Kiritsis, D., von Cieminski, G. (eds.) APMS 2018. IAICT, vol. 535, pp. 534–540. Springer, Cham (2018). https://doi.org/10.1007/978-3-319-99704-9_65

12. Robinson, S.: Simulation: The practice of model development and use, 1st edn. Wiley, Chichester (2008)

13. Yin, R.K.: Case study research: Design and methods, 5th edn. Sage, Thousand Oaks (2013)

# Streaming Analytics in Edge-Cloud Environment for Logistics Processes

Moritz von Stietencron[1], Marco Lewandowski[1], Katerina Lepenioti[2],
Alexandros Bousdekis[2(✉)], Karl Hribernik[1], Dimitris Apostolou[2,3],
and Gregoris Mentzas[2]

[1] BIBA - Bremer Institut für Produktion und Logistik GmbH at the University of
Bremen, Bremen, Germany
{sti,lew,hri}@biba.uni-bremen.de

[2] Information Management Unit (IMU), Institute of Communication and
Computer Systems (ICCS), National Technical University of Athens (NTUA),
Athens, Greece
{klepenioti,albous,gmentzas}@mail.ntua.gr,
dapost@unipi.gr

[3] Department of Informatics, University of Piraeus, Piraeus, Greece

**Abstract.** The recent advancements in Internet of Things (IoT) technology and
the increasing amount of sensing devices that collect and/or generate massive
sensor data streams enhances the use of streaming analytics for providing timely
and meaningful insights. The current paper proposes a framework for supporting
streaming analytics in edge-cloud computational environment for logistics
operations in order to maximize the potential value of IoT technology. The
proposed framework is demonstrated in a real-life scenario of a large transportation asset in the aviation sector.

**Keywords:** Data analytics · Machine learning · Predictive maintenance ·
Aviation

## 1 Introduction

Having an expected economic impact of $2.7 to $6.2 trillion in 2025 [1], Internet of
Things (IoT) has already started to have a crucial role in every aspect of production,
logistics and transportation operations [2, 3]. Among others, a promising application
deals with logistics operations, which usually consist of low value-added activities
combined with a high degree of manual work. High information visibility achieved by
real-time data processing has the potential to allow improved decision making and thus,
increased efficiency and responsiveness [3]. The use of technologies for real-time
condition monitoring and streaming data analytics for fleet maintenance can lead to
optimization of maintenance costs, vehicle availability, operational efficiency, and
lifetime [4]. Although the use of IoT technologies in public transportation is a well-
studied area, the transportation means of manufacturing or product assets to maintenance providers are subject to different processes within the supply chain. Such
operations pose significant challenges to the scheduling and planning decisions of the

© IFIP International Federation for Information Processing 2020
Published by Springer Nature Switzerland AG 2020
B. Lalic et al. (Eds.): APMS 2020, IFIP AICT 592, pp. 245–253, 2020.
https://doi.org/10.1007/978-3-030-57997-5_29

maintenance service providers. The current paper proposes a framework for supporting streaming analytics in edge-cloud computational environment for logistics operations in order to maximize the potential value of IoT technology. It consists of three main components: SENSE for data acquisition and edge analytics, DETECT & PREDICT for cloud analytics, and DECIDE for actions planning. The rest of the paper is organized as follows: Sect. 2 briefly presents the key enabling technologies of the proposed framework. Section 3 described the proposed framework, while Sect. 4 demonstrates a case study from the aviation sector. Section 5 concludes the paper and presents our plans for future work.

## 2  Key Enabling Technologies

### 2.1  Streaming Analytics

The fast development of IoT promotes an enormous amount of sensing devices that collect and/or generate massive sensor data streams over time for a wide range of fields and applications [5]. Data streams, i.e. sequences of unbounded tuples generated continuously in time, open new perspectives for extracting meaningful and timely insights from data-in-motion through streaming analytics (e.g. detect anomalies, predict future insights, make decisions) [1, 5]. By bringing streaming data analytics closer to the source of data (i.e. IoT devices or edge devices) the need for data parallelism and incremental processing is less sensible as the size of the data in the source allows it to be processed rapidly. However, bringing fast analytics on IoT devices introduces its own challenges such as limitation of computing, storage, and power resources at the source of data [1].

### 2.2  Edge and Cloud Computing

Cloud computing enables ubiquitous, convenient, on-demand network access to a shared pool of configurable computing resources that can be rapidly provisioned and released with minimal management effort or service provider interaction [6]. With the growing volume of data generated at the logical extremes of the network, and the fact that network bandwidth is not scaling at the same speed as with computing power, data mitigation is becoming a bottleneck constraining the cloud computing paradigm for delay-sensitive IoT services [7]. Consequently, data must be processed at the edge of the network for shorter response times, more efficient processing and significantly less network pressure [8]. Edge computing refers to the computation at the logical extremes of the network, enabling the conversion of raw signals to contextually relevant information in proximity of the data source [7].

# 3  The Proposed Framework for Streaming Analytics in Edge-Cloud Environment

The proposed framework aims at supporting streaming analytics in edge-cloud computational environment for logistics operations in order to maximize the potential value of IoT technology. It consists of three main components, described in the following sections: SENSE for data acquisition and edge analytics, DETECT & PREDICT for cloud analytics, and DECIDE for actions planning.

## 3.1  SENSE for Data Acquisition and Edge Analytics

SENSE performs data acquisition and edge analytics. It has two main levels denoted "SENSEcore" and "SENSEnode", as shown in Fig. 1. Table 1 provides a summary of the hardware specifications.

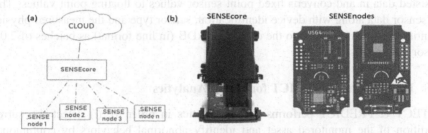

**Fig. 1.** (a) SENSE connections; (b) SENSE subcomponents.

**Table 1.** SENSEcore technical specifications.

| Product specification | Technical information |
| --- | --- |
| Processor/architecture | i.MX 6Quad/ARM Cortex-A9 |
| Clock frequency | 4 × 1 GHz |
| Memory | 1 GB DDR3 RAM 64 Bit, 1 GB NAND Flash, 16 MB NOR, 4 kB EEPROM |
| Hardware interfaces | • Ethernet: 1 × 10/100/1000 Mbits/s<br>• USB<br>• Serial: 1 × RS232<br>• CAN Bus<br>• I2C, 2 × SPI, UART, JTAG, SATA |
| Power supply | 12–24 V |
| Wireless connectivity | 802.11 WLAN (WiFi)/Bluetooth |
| Operating system | Linux 4.1.36 |

The *SENSEcore* is one unit per monitored asset and consolidates all data from this asset. It also adds metadata for the integration of the asset data with the context model. It allows for performing edge data analysis and state detection and forwards the information set to the cloud.

The *SENSEnode* firmware acquires data from motion sensors (e.g. accelerometer, gyroscope, magnetometer), environment sensors (e.g. barometric pressure, humidity, light intensity, air temperature), etc. at a fixed sampling rate. The acquired raw data is processed on the sensor controller of the SENSEnode to derive measurable physical quantities - e.g. raw value from accelerometer is processed to get acceleration in G's. These processed values are then converted from floating point to fixed point format in order to reduce the data bytes required to be persisted. The data is then mapped to a timestamp and persisted on a SD card. Each node captures and pre-processes specific sensor data from the asset and forwards this dataset to the SENSEcore unit.

Once data acquisition from the SENSEnodes is complete, the forwarding of the data to the cloud is facilitated by a data parsing script. The data parser reads the persisted data in and converts fixed point sensor values to floating point values. Then the sensor data along with device identification, sensor type and the measured physical quantity are batch uploaded to the cloud InfluxDB (in line format) as batches of 2,000 sensor data points.

## 3.2    DETECT and PREDICT for Cloud Analytics

DETECT & PREDICT performs cloud analytics in order to: (i) detect the current condition of the monitored asset and identify abnormal behaviors by continuously processing sensor data streams; and, (ii) estimate remaining useful life and predict future states. It has been developed using the OpenJDK 10 and it is deployed with an application server like Tomcat as the underlying server structure.

At design time, the user (data scientist) uses the following functionalities: (i) *Connection to sensor data streams and definition of queries*: The component has access to a time-series DB (based on InfluxDB) including discrete measurement points and additional meta-information describing the sensor stream, such as "location", "installation point", "reference to a technical equipment", "type", etc. Based on this connection, it provides the capability to define queries on the data streams using detection and prediction algorithms from various libraries. The query may provide a list of applicable sensor streams for a later analysis based on the provided meta-data, and a subset of the data within each previously selected sensor stream, e.g. based on a time range; (ii) *Engineering, instantiation and deployment of calculation flows*: The component provides a web-based interface in which the algorithms of the toolbox are orchestrated through the use of calculation flows, which can be considered similar to flowchart-based workflows, in order to be linked to continuous data streams and process them to more aggregated information. The component gives the opportunity to establish rules which define time- or event-based triggers for the later deployment.

At runtime, the component performs *deployment, monitoring and persistent storage of calculation flows* in order to collect the latest required data by executing the queries, execute the algorithms defined by the calculation flow and monitor the calculation flows. The outputs are communicated through an event message broker (Apache Kafka) for further processing.

### 3.3 DECIDE for Actions Planning

DECIDE implements a prescriptive analytics approach [9] in order to provide proactive recommendations and plans about optimal actions by receiving streams of predictions about future states (e.g. failures) through the event message broker.

At design time, the user (domain expert) inserts proactive decision rules, i.e. rules that correlate sets of predicted failure modes with sets of (alternative) proactive actions along with their parameters, in order to create the *knowledge base* (implemented with Drools Rule Engine). At runtime, the real-time predictions are received through subscription to prediction message topics and feed into the *inference engine* which retrieves and fires the related rules from the working memory associated with the knowledge base. On this basis, the *proactive decision making* functionality, implemented as a Kafka Topology and incorporating the Brown-UMBC Reinforcement Learning and Planning (BURLAP) library, embeds reinforcement learning algorithms in order to jointly minimize the maintenance costs and maximize the positive human feedback over the generated recommended actions.

The recommendations are accompanied with explainable graphs that visualize the decision model and the resulting policy. The recommended actions are either approved or rejected by the operator according to their knowledge, experience and preference. This *human feedback* is taken into account in two ways: (a) The approved actions formulate the actions plan to be followed once the vehicle arrives for maintenance; (b) It is taken into account in order to perform policy shaping and adapt the decision models for building optimized human-machine collaborations.

## 4   Case Study in Maintenance Service Logistics of Aviation

The proposed framework was validated in FFT Produktionssysteme GmbH & Co. KG, a company with core business, among others, the design, realization and maintenance of production systems in aerospace industry. Typical maintenance projects include both fixed (stationary production equipment, test rigs) and mobile assets (jigs and tools, transportation jigs). The case under consideration deals with the maintenance of mobile assets, which are subjected to a wide range of external influences affecting their condition, while they are maintained on geographically dispersed locations. Specifically, the type of mobile asset is a large transportation jig for major aircraft wing shells (Wing Upper Cover Transportation Jig - WUCTJ) (Fig. 2). It consists of a steel structure (the main jig) and an associated light-weight roof component (Top Weather Protection) made from aluminum profiles. It is 40 m long with an empty weight of around 2,350 kg and is designed to transport wing covers of a commercial aircraft between plants of a transnational manufacturer in Germany and the United Kingdom. During its journey, the asset is moved by different means of transportation on land, water, and air (by Airbus Beluga).

**Fig. 2.** The transportation jig during loading at the Airbus Beluga.

All these environments impose different kinds of stress on the asset. For example, since the cargo hold of the Beluga transport aircraft is not pressurized or air-conditioned, the transportation jig is subjected to extreme temperatures (−60 to +50 ° C) additionally to a multitude of loads, shocks and weather influences. There are many situations where damages can occur (e.g. mishandling of the asset during the loading and unloading between different transportation modes). However, FFT, as the manufacturer and maintenance provider of the transportation asset, will see such damages only at the end of a transportation cycle and then, urgent repair activities will need to be applied. Due to the fact that both production and logistics schedules can be significantly affected by the availability and plannability for transportation jig deployment, there is high benefit of having comprehensive condition information and proactive meaningful insights for maintenance operations of the jig.

The SENSE component of the proposed framework acquires and pre-processes sensor data related to GPS location, temperature, humidity, gyroscope, acceleration, magnitude and light. To do this, ten SENSEnodes have been applied to the jig. Figure 3 shows example graphs of the condition monitoring, as well as the map showing the drive and the current location of the jig. Then, the DETECT & PREDICT component implements an outlier detection algorithm in order to identify abnormal frequencies and amplitudes that lead to predictions about failure modes. Figure 4 depicts an example of a pattern that, according to the stored predictive analytics models, leads to a prediction of the failure mode "Crack of the light-weight frame". Based on this trigger, the DECIDE component generates the recommendation "Re-welding of light-weight frame" along with the explainable visualization of the decision model shown in Fig. 5a. Upon user approval, the action is inserted to the maintenance plan (Fig. 5b), and the decision model is updated accordingly.

In order to perform a preliminary evaluation of the proposed framework on the process improvements, we performed simulations involving a typical WUCTJ transport cycle based upon the methodology described in [10]. Specifically, discrete event simulations were performed and compared under an "as-is" and a "to-be" scenario, using ARENA simulation software. The results showed, among others, that the "to-be" scenario has about half the Non-Value Added Cost (49,052 instead of 107,523 Euro), while its "efficiency gain" is more than double comparing to the "as-is". This translates to less risk of production blocking events and the possibility to increase capacity

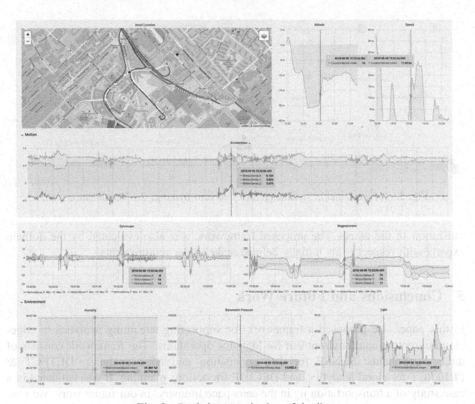

**Fig. 3.** Real-time monitoring of the jig.

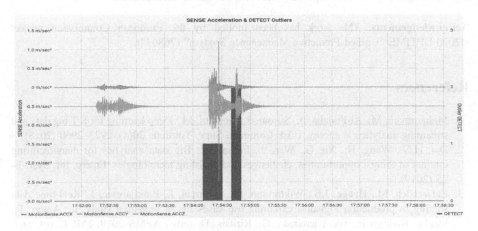

**Fig. 4.** Outlier detection of the jig health status.

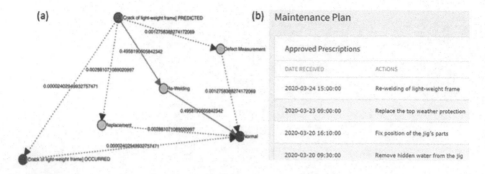

**Fig. 5.** (a) Explainable visualization of decision making; (b) Maintenance plan.

utilization of the assets. The proposed framework was also evaluated by the domain experts with respect to its initially defined stakeholder requirements.

## 5   Conclusions and Future Work

In this paper, we proposed a framework for supporting streaming analytics in edge-cloud computational environment for logistics operations. The framework consists of three components: SENSE for data acquisition and edge analytics, DETECT & PREDICT for cloud analytics, and DECIDE for actions planning. It was validated in a case study of a transportation jig in the aerospace industry. In our future work, we plan to further validate our approach in additional use cases, as well as to take advantage of legacy data analytics that represent different levels of information.

**Acknowledgements.** This work has been funded by the European Commission project H2020 UPTIME "Unified Predictive Maintenance System" (768634).

## References

1. Mohammadi, M., Al-Fuqaha, A., Sorour, S., Guizani, M.: Deep learning for IoT big data and streaming analytics: a survey. IEEE Commun. Surv. Tutorials **20**(4), 2923–2960 (2018)
2. Dai, H.N., Wang, H., Xu, G., Wan, J., Imran, M.: Big data analytics for manufacturing internet of things: opportunities, challenges and enabling technologies. Enterp. Inf. Syst. 1–25 (2019)
3. Zafarzadeh, M., Hauge, J.B., Wiktorsson, M., Hedman, I., Bahtijarevic, J.: Real-time data sharing in production logistics: exploring use cases by an industrial study. In: Ameri, F., Stecke, Kathryn E., von Cieminski, G., Kiritsis, D. (eds.) APMS 2019. IAICT, vol. 567, pp. 285–293. Springer, Cham (2019). https://doi.org/10.1007/978-3-030-29996-5_33
4. Killeen, P., Ding, B., Kiringa, I., Yeap, T.: IoT-based predictive maintenance for fleet management. Procedia Comput. Sci. **151**, 607–613 (2019)
5. Isah, H., Abughofa, T., Mahfuz, S., Ajerla, D., Zulkernine, F., Khan, S.: A survey of distributed data stream processing frameworks. IEEE Access **7**, 154300–154316 (2019)

6. Miyachi, C.: What is "Cloud"? It is time to update the NIST definition? IEEE Cloud Comput. **3**, 6–11 (2018)
7. Shi, W., Dustdar, S.: The promise of edge computing. Computer **49**(5), 78–81 (2016)
8. Cao, H., Wachowicz, M.: An edge-fog-cloud architecture of streaming analytics for Internet of Things applications. Sensors **19**(16), 3594 (2019)
9. Lepenioti, K., Bousdekis, A., Apostolou, D., Mentzas, G.: Prescriptive analytics: literature review and research challenges. Int. J. Inf. Manag. **50**, 57–70 (2020)
10. Nikhil, B.H.: Modelling and simulation of an industry 4.0 based predictive maintenance system in an aerospace value chain, Vellore Institute of Technology, School of Mechanical Engineering, Vellore (2019)

# An Improvement in Master Surgical Scheduling Using Artificial Neural Network and Fuzzy Programming Approach

Ahmad Ghasemkhani, Reza Tavakkoli-Moghaddam, Mahdi Hamid,
and Mehdi Mahmoodjanloo[⊠]

School of Industrial Engineering, College of Engineering, University of Tehran,
Tehran, Iran
mehdi.janloo@ut.ac.ir

**Abstract.** In this study, a new mathematical model is presented for the master surgical scheduling (MSS) problem at the tactical level. The capacity of the operating room for each specialty is determined in the previous level and used as an input for the tactical level. In MSS, elective surgeries are often performed in a cycle for a cycle. However, this problem considers both elective and emergency patients. The model of this problem is specifically designed to achieve this tactical plan to provide emergency care, as it provides the possibility of reserving some capacity for emergency patients. The current study, forecast emergency patients by applying an artificial neural network, and reserve capacity for them are based on the demand. Fuzzy chance-constraint programming is employed to handle the uncertainty in the model. The data of a private hospital in Iran is used to solve the problem using GAMS software. The results show that the performance of the proposed method against the solution in the hospital performed better.

**Keywords:** Master surgical scheduling · Fuzzy mathematical programming · Prediction · Neural network

## 1 Introduction

Due to an increase in society's ages and medical progress, the demand for health services worldwide is increasing [1, 2]. Besides, lower costs and a lack of human resources lead to increased pressure on hospital resources. Therefore, the importance of optimizing the use of scarce resources in hospitals is quite evident. The most valuable resource in most hospitals are in operating rooms (ORs). ORs are strongly linked to downstream resources, such as the post-anesthesia care unit (PACU), the intensive care unit (ICU), and the patients' general ward [3]. One of the major activities at a hospital is providing surgery to patients. Freeman et al. [4] stated that 60 to 70 percent of all hospitalized patients require surgery, and Hans [5] stated surgery costs account for approximately 40% of total hospital costs and operations generate about 67% of hospital revenues. Appropriate surgical planning methods are essential for the proper utilization of scarce hospital resources and the need to treat most patients.

© IFIP International Federation for Information Processing 2020
Published by Springer Nature Switzerland AG 2020
B. Lalic et al. (Eds.): APMS 2020, IFIP AICT 592, pp. 254–262, 2020.
https://doi.org/10.1007/978-3-030-57997-5_30

Patients are usually divided into two groups: elective and emergency patients. Elective patients are not on medical emergencies, and their surgery can be pre-planned, depending on the availability of the surgeon and the patient. On the other hand, emergency patients may need surgery within a few hours or up to a few days. Surgery planning may be divided into three decision stages [6]. At the strategic level, the number of blocks assigned to the specialties. A master surgery schedule (MSS) is developed at the tactical level to schedule different specialties to the ORs through the week. Finally, at the operational level, the patients are scheduled to the ORs.

The primary purpose of this paper is to provide a tactical decision for the departments that provide surgery to both elective and emergency patients. More specifically, we consider both elective and emergency patients in the master surgery scheduling problem (MSSP). The schedule is typically made for one cyclic week, and this weekly schedule is generally applied for a period of six to twelve months [7]. The rest of this paper is organized as follows: Sects. 2 and 3 present literature review and the problem; the artificial neural network and fuzzy methods are explained in Sects. 4 and 5, respectively. In Sects. 6, a case study and the numerical results are discussed, respectively. Finally, Sect. 7 concludes the research and provides suggestions for future research.

## 2   Literature Review

The master surgical scheduling problem has been the object of several studies. Most authors considered only elective patients, arguing that the emergencies are taken care of by dedicated resources [8]. On the other hand, Adan et al. [9] considered the emergencies by estimating their arrivals based on simulation and Poisson process and reserve capacity for the patients based on this.

In addition to including the surgical specialties and the operating rooms, some authors include other resources, such as wards and intensive care units, as they may impose bottlenecks for efficient patient flow [10]. In contrast, others neglected wards in their model because they believed that access to beds does not impose a bottleneck on the efficient flow of patients [11]. Several authors include aspects of uncertainty when handling the MSSP. Ma and Demeulemeester [12] included probability distributions to account for uncertainty in the patient's length of stay (LOS) following surgery. Van Oostrum [13] dealt with the uncertainty of surgery duration by providing probability distributions. They calculate the distribution of patients resting in both the wards and the ICU resulting from a cyclical MSS. Most papers have used stochastic programming to deal with uncertainty in the MSS level [14]. Many predictive methods have been used in the literature to predict hospital demand. Batal et al. [15] estimated the demand for an emergency department by using a stepwise linear regression model. Jones et al. [16] used regression models, including climate variables, to estimate patient demand. Boutsioli [17] investigated the unpredictable hospital demand variations by using two types of forecast errors. The autoregressive integrated moving average (ARIMA), exponential smoothing (ES), and multiple linear regression (MLR) were found to be the most widely used techniques [18]. In this paper, we use a neural network to predict the emergency department admissions to achieve an efficient optimization model.

Our main contribution to the present literature is the inclusion of emergency patients and the development of a mathematical model to simultaneously handle the uncertain demand of elective patients and emergency patients. Moreover, we provide an artificial neural network and a fuzzy method to cope with unknown parameters in the model.

## 3  Problem Definition

In this paper, the overall goal is to construct a cyclic schedule (MSS table) where each subspecialty is scheduled for surgery slots in one or several of the ORs to perform surgeries efficiently. By efficiently, we mean scheduling many elective patients for surgery and handling a fluctuating demand of emergency patients without having to cancel the elective surgeries. In developing MSS, the capacity for the non-elective operations shall be reserved. To avoid elective patients' cancellations in periods of high emergency demand for surgery, we want to devote surgery slots for emergency patients in the elective ORs. The resources considered in this problem are the ORs, the wards, the surgeons.

Determining the optimal mix of patients is referred to as the case-mix planning problem (CMPP). The target of case-mix planning is used to feed downstream issues such as MSS. We assume that the target throughput of elective patients to be scheduled within each patient category for the cycle is known, and we aim to schedule as many of these patients as possible. Also, we need to forecast the number of emergency patients entering the department each week and devote additional capacity for them. In this study, a mathematical model is developed to construct the MSS for elective surgeries while using the results obtained from solving CMPP as input. Moreover, based on the hospital requirements, a part of the OR's capacity is reserved for emergency surgeries.

Following is the new mathematical model presented in this paper.

| Sets: | |
|---|---|
| $S$ | Surgical specialties |
| $R$ | ORs |
| $L$ | Block types |
| $D$ | Working days (five days a week) |
| $K$ | Surgery time for each specialty (1: short, 2: medium, 3: Long) |
| Parameters: | |
| $CL_{lrd}$ | Block time for elective patients for OR $r$ in day $d$ in block l |
| $AP_{sr}$ | 1 if OR $r$ is suitable for specialty $s$ |
| $DE_s$ | Demand of elective patients for surgery $s$ |
| $DM_{ks}$ | Demand of emergency patients for surgery $s$ and index $k$ |
| $d\tilde{u}r_{ks}$ | Fuzzy surgery duration $k$ for specialty $s$ |
| $T$ | Length of cycle |
| Variables: | |
| $X_{slrd}$ | 1 if surgical specialty $s$ is assigned to OR $r$ in block l on day $d$; 0, otherwise |
| $E_s$ | Total idle time of OR assigned to specialty $s$ |

$$\text{Min } E_s \tag{1}$$

s.t.

$$\sum_s X_{slrd} \leq 1 \quad \forall l, r, d \tag{2}$$

$$X_{slrd} \leq AP_{sr} \quad \forall s, l, r, d \tag{3}$$

$$\sum_{s,r,l,d} X_{slrd} \times CL_{lrd} \leq T - \sum_{k=1}^{3} \sum_s d\bar{u}r_{ks} DM_{ks} \tag{4}$$

$$\sum_{r,l,d} X_{slrd} \times CL_{lrd} \leq DE_s \times d\bar{u}r_{ks} + E_s \quad \forall s \tag{5}$$

$$X_{slrd} \in \{0,1\} \quad \forall s, l, r, d \tag{6}$$

$$E_s \geq 0 \quad \forall s \tag{7}$$

The objective function minimizes the underutilization of the operating room. Constraints (2) and (3) ensures the assignment of OR blocks to specialties. Constraint (4) determines that OR block time of elective patients assigned to each specialty should not exceed the total time of elective patients. Constraint (5) describes the amount of underutilization of the idle time related to specialties. Constraints (6) and (7) are the domain of the variables.

# 4  Forecasting Emergency Demand

Among various intelligent methods, artificial neural networks (ANNs) are suitable instruments to solve complicated problems. In this study, 24 months of data were used, and the data were extracted from a private hospital in Tehran. The data were divided into two: the training and test sets.

## 4.1  Data and Variable Selection

The daily number of patients visiting the ED was employed as a dependent variable, whereas information including the month, day of the week, a quarter of the year, holidays, seasons, weather, rate of insurance and number of accidents per area were employed as independent variables [19–21].

## 4.2    Artificial Neural Network

The most conventional ANN model is the multilayer perceptron (MLP). It has one or several layers between the input layer and the output layer. In this research, we predict the demand for emergency patients, then, we determine the capacity of ORs for emergency patients. To implement the ANN depending on the purpose, different types of neural networks can be used. In this study, MLP is used. Every MLP neural network has three parts, including the input layer, the hidden layer(s), and the output layer. Mean arctangent absolute percentage error (MAAPE) is an indicator to assess a neural network structure. The equation of this criteria is given below. In this equation, $N$ indicates the number of samples, $F_t$ shows the predicted value of the model for sample $t$, and $A_t$ represents the real demand for sample $t$.

$$MAAPE = \frac{100}{N} \sum_{t=1}^{N} \arctan\left(\left|\frac{A_t - F_t}{A_t}\right|\right)$$

Based on a trial and error method, several neural network structures are evaluated to find an appropriate configuration for MLP (see Table 1). According to column MAAPE, the best configuration is MLP 9 that is highlighted. The output of the designed model is the number of emergency patients refer to the hospital that is 374 in the mentioned hospital.

Table 1. Parameters of the neural network

| Structure code | MLP | | First hidden layer | | Second hidden layer | | Transfer function in output layer | MAAPE |
|---|---|---|---|---|---|---|---|---|
| | Learning function | Number of hidden layers | Transfer function | Number of neurons | Transfer function | Number of neurons | | |
| MLP 1 | GDX | 2 | Tansig | 6 | – | – | Purelin | 4 |
| MLP 2 | BFG | 2 | Logsig | 11 | Tansig | 13 | Purelin | 5 |
| MLP 3 | GDX | 1 | Tansig | 10 | Logsig | 15 | Purelin | 5 |
| MLP 4 | LM | 2 | Tansig | 4 | – | – | Purelin | 3 |
| MLP 5 | GDA | 1 | Logsig | 9 | Tansig | 10 | Purelin | 3 |
| MLP 6 | OSS | 2 | Tansig | 18 | – | – | Purelin | 4 |
| MLP 7 | LM | 2 | Logsig | 7 | – | – | Purelin | 5 |
| MLP 8 | BFG | 1 | Logsig | 15 | Tansig | 23 | Purelin | 3 |
| MLP 9 | GDA | 1 | Tansig | 8 | Logsig | 4 | Purelin | 2 |
| MLP10 | OSS | 2 | Logsig | 26 | Tansig | 19 | Purelin | 4 |

## 5    Fuzzy Method

Different approaches can be found in the field of uncertainty to cope with uncertain values based on the analyzed data. According to experts' judgments, fuzzy mathematical programming is a practical approach to this type of uncertainty. In this paper, we use a fuzzy method by Jiménez et al. [22], which is a strong mathematical concept, such as the expected interval and the expected value of fuzzy numbers. Consider the following model in which the parameters are defined as fuzzy triangular numbers. According to Jiménez et al. [22], the equivalent crisp model can be are as follows:

$$x \in N(\tilde{A}, \tilde{b}) = \{x \in R | \tilde{a}_i x \geq \tilde{b}_i, \tilde{a}_i x \leq \tilde{b}_i, i = 1, \ldots, m, x \geq 0\}$$
$$[(1 - \alpha)E_2^{a_i} + \alpha E_1^{a_i}]x \geq \alpha E_2^{b_i} + (1 - \alpha)E_1^{b_i}$$
$$[(1 - \alpha)E_1^{a_i} + \alpha E_2^{a_i}]x \leq \alpha E_1^{b_i} + (1 - \alpha)E_2^{b_i}$$
$$i = 1, \ldots, m; x \geq 0; \alpha \in [0, 1]$$

Based on the above method, Constraints (4) and (5) are converted by:

$$\sum_{s,r,l,d} X_{slrd} \times CL_{lrd} \leq T - \sum_{k=1}^{3} \sum_{s} [(1 - \alpha)E_2^{dur_{ks}} + \alpha E_1^{dur_{ks}}] \times DM_{ks}$$

$$\sum_{r,l,d} X_{slrd} \times CL_{lrd} \leq DE_s \times \sum_{k=1}^{3} \sum_{s} [(1 - \alpha)E_2^{dur_{ks}} + \alpha E_1^{dur_{ks}}] + E_s$$

## 6  Case Study and Results

The results presented in this section are obtained based on the data collected from a private hospital in Tehran. The hospital consists of five specialties, five ORs, two wards, 65 beds. All the ORs are not capable of undergoing any surgery, so some specialties must be executed in a particular operating room. ORs are open eight hours a day, and working days are five in a week from Saturday to Wednesday (Thursday and Friday are holiday in Iran). To perform the surgeries, the department has access to four elective and one emergency ORs. The case hospital has faced some issues in the scheduling MSS table. In this section, we apply our approach to this case. The aim is to provide an MSS that enables the department to handle fluctuating emergency patient demand and at the same time provide a sufficient throughput of elective patients. First, the amount of capacity is reserved for emergency patients. Secondly, the new MSS is introduced, and finally we apply the fuzzy method to obtain a more reliable solution. Table 2 presents the parameters of the model. The model is solved in GAMS software using CPLEX solver. For example, the optimal schedule at the first week of planning horizon is shown in Table 3. It is deduced that the optimum MSS meets all the time blocks assigned to specialties in strategic level.

**Table 2.** Parameters of surgical specialties

| Surgical specialties | $DE_s$ | $dur_{sk}$ |
|---|---|---|
| Orology | (200, 250, 300) | (30, 90, 180) |
| Orthopedic | (90, 130, 170) | (45, 120, 250) |
| General | (280, 340, 400) | (30, 150, 300) |
| Vascular | (350, 400, 450) | (40, 100, 150) |
| Cardiology | (550, 650, 750) | (60, 200, 360) |

**Table 3.** Optimum MSS

| | | OR 1 | OR 2 | OR 3 | OR 4 | OR 5 |
|---|---|---|---|---|---|---|
| Sat | Block 1 | Orthopedic | Orthopedic | General | General | General |
| | Block 2 | Orthopedic | Orthopedic | General | General | General |
| Sun | Block 1 | Orology | Orology | Cardiology | Vascular | Vascular |
| | Block 2 | Orology | Orology | Cardiology | Vascular | Vascular |
| Mon | Block 1 | Cardiology | Cardiology | Orthopedic | General | General |
| | Block 2 | Cardiology | Cardiology | Orthopedic | General | General |
| Tue | Block 1 | Vascular | Vascular | Vascular | Orology | Cardiology |
| | Block 2 | Vascular | Vascular | Vascular | Orology | Cardiology |
| Wed | Block 1 | Orology | Orthopedic | General | Cardiology | Orthopedic |
| | Block 2 | Orology | Orthopedic | General | Cardiology | Orthopedic |

## 7 Conclusion

In this paper, we have developed a mathematical model for the master surgical scheduling (MSS) problem and to provide tactical decision support for managers in a department with both elective and emergency patients. To deal with daily emergency patients, we used neural- network algorithm to predict the demand for emergency patients. Due to current uncertainty in the problem, surgery duration was considered uncertain. Therefore, a fuzzy approach was applied to convert to a crisp model. The proposed model was solved using GAMS software. The results revealed that the model is improved in an uncertain environment. For future studies, it is suggested to consider the cancellation of elective patients, and it might be interesting to investigate the effect of different policies to improve hospital performance.

## References

1. Hamid, M., Hamid, M., Musavi, M., Azadeh, A.: Scheduling elective patients based on sequence-dependent setup times in an open-heart surgical department using an optimization and simulation approach. Simulation **95**(12), 1141–1164 (2019)
2. Hay, J.W.: Hospital cost drivers: an evaluation of 1998–2001 state-level data. Am. J. Manag. Care **9**(spec No 1), SP13–SP24 (2003)

3. Hamid, M., Nasiri, M.M., Werner, F., Sheikhahmadi, F., Zhalechian, M.: Operating room scheduling by considering the decision-making styles of surgical team members: a comprehensive approach. Comput. Oper. Res. **108**, 166–181 (2019)
4. Freeman, N., Zhao, M., Melouk, S.: An iterative approach for case mix planning under uncertainty. Omega **76**, 160–173 (2018)
5. Hans, E.W., van Houdenhoven, M., Hulshof, P.J.H.: A framework for healthcare planning and control. In: Hall, R. (ed.) Handbook of Healthcare System Scheduling. International Series in Operations Research & Management Science, vol. 168, pp. 303–320. Springer, Boston (2012). https://doi.org/10.1007/978-1-4614-1734-7_12
6. Hulshof, P.J., Kortbeek, N., Boucherie, R.J., Hans, E.W., Bakker, P.J.: Taxonomic classification of planning decisions in health care: a structured review of the state of the art in OR/MS. Health Syst. **1**(2), 129–175 (2012)
7. van Essen, J.T., Hans, E.W., Hurink, J.L., Oversberg, A.: Minimizing the waiting time for emergency surgery. Oper. Res. Health Care **1**(2–3), 34–44 (2012)
8. Cardoen, B., Demeulemeester, E., Van der Hoeven, J.: On the use of planning models in the operating theatre: results of a survey in Flanders. Int. J. Health Plan. Manag. **25**(4), 400–414 (2010)
9. Adan, I., Bekkers, J., Dellaert, N., Jeunet, J., Vissers, J.: Improving operational effectiveness of tactical master plans for emergency and elective patients under stochastic demand and capacitated resources. Eur. J. Oper. Res. **213**(1), 290–308 (2011)
10. Testi, A., Tanfani, E., Torre, G.: A three-phase approach for operating theatre schedules. Health Care Manag. Sci. **10**(2), 163–172 (2007)
11. Li, X., Rafaliya, N., Baki, M.F., Chaouch, B.A.: Scheduling elective surgeries: the tradeoff among bed capacity, waiting patients and operating room utilization using goal programming. Health Care Manag. Sci. **20**(1), 33–54 (2015). https://doi.org/10.1007/s10729-015-9334-2
12. Ma, G., Demeulemeester, E.: A multilevel integrative approach to hospital case mix and capacity planning. Comput. Oper. Res. **40**(9), 2198–2207 (2013)
13. van Oostrum, J.M., et al.: A master surgical scheduling approach for cyclic scheduling in operating room departments. OR Spectr. **30**(2), 355–374 (2008)
14. Fügener, A., Hans, E.W., Kolisch, R., Kortbeek, N., Vanberkel, P.T.: Master surgery scheduling with consideration of multiple downstream units. Eur. J. Oper. Res. **239**(1), 227–236 (2014)
15. Batal, H., Tench, J., McMillan, S., Adams, J., Mehler, P.S.: Predicting patient visits to an urgent care clinic using calendar variables. Acad. Emerg. Med. **8**(1), 48–53 (2001)
16. Jones, S.S., Thomas, A., Evans, R.S., Welch, S.J., Haug, P.J., Snow, G.L.: Forecasting daily patient volumes in the emergency department. Acad. Emerg. Med. **15**(2), 159–170 (2008)
17. Boutsioli, Z.: Forecasting the stochastic demand for inpatient care: The case of the Greek national health system. Health Serv. Manag. Res. **23**(3), 116–120 (2010)
18. Ordu, M., Demir, E., Tofallis, C.: A decision support system for demand and capacity modelling of an accident and emergency department. Health Syst. **9**(1), 1–26 (2019)
19. Kam, H.J., Sung, J.O., Park, R.W.: Prediction of daily patient numbers for a regional emergency medical center using time series analysis. Healthcare Inform. Res. **16**(3), 158–165 (2010)

20. Yazdanparast, R., Hamid, M., Azadeh, A., Keramati, A.: An intelligent algorithm for optimization of resource allocation problem by considering human error in an emergency. J. Ind. Syst. Eng. **11**(1), 287–309 (2018)
21. Amalnick, M.S., Habibifar, N., Hamid, M., Bastan, M.: An intelligent algorithm for final product demand forecasting in pharmaceutical units. Int. J. Syst. Assur. Eng. Manag. **11**(2), 481–493 (2019). https://doi.org/10.1007/s13198-019-00879-6
22. Jiménez, M., Arenas, M., Bilbao, A., Rodri, M.V.: Linear programming with fuzzy parameters: an interactive method resolution. Eur. J. Oper. Res. **177**(3), 1599–1609 (2007)

# SKOS Tool: A Tool for Creating Knowledge Graphs to Support Semantic Text Classification

Farhad Ameri(✉), Reid Yoder, and Kimia Zandbiglari

Engineering Informatics Lab, Texas State University, San Marcos, USA
{ameri,rjy15,k_z54}@txstate.edu

**Abstract.** Knowledge graphs are being increasingly adopted in industry in order to add meaning to data and improve the intelligence of data analytics methods. Simple Knowledge Management System (SKOS) is a W3C standard for representation of knowledge graphs in a web-native and machine-understandable format. This paper introduces SKOS Tool; a web-based application developed at the Engineering Informatics Lab at Texas State University. It can be used for creating knowledge graphs and concept schemes based on the SKOS standard. The main feature and functions of SKOS Tool are described in this paper. Beyond creating knowledge graphs, SKOS Tool has additional features that can be used to support semantic document classification based on the Bag of Concepts technique. To demonstrate the utilities of SKOS Tool, a use case related to classifications of manufacturing suppliers with Medical Grade Polymer Tubing capabilities is presented.

**Keywords:** Knowledge graph · Semantic classifier · Natural language processing · Artificial intelligence · SKOS

## 1 Introduction

Semantic Artificial Intelligence (AI) is a branch of AI that uses semantic models for supporting intelligent systems that mimic human-like cognitive functions such as learning, reasoning, and problem solving. Semantic models are intended to represent a model of the reality in a machine-understandable and logical fashion [1]. They can be used to represent the implicit meaning of data and add context to it. There are different types of semantic models ranging form simple controlled vocabularies and taxonomies to more sophisticated formal thesauri and ontologies that vary based on their expressivity and development cost and time. Most formal semantic models can be represented as graphs with nodes (concepts or entities) and edges (relationships). *Knowledge Graph* is a general term that can be applied to the semantic models that are represented as one or more connected graphs [2]. Knowledge graphs can serve as unifying models that can semantically connect and integrate disparate silos of structured and unstructured data. A knowledge graph can provide a strong foundation for various machine learning and cognitive computing projects as it adds a semantic layer on top of metadata and data layers in AI application [3].

© IFIP International Federation for Information Processing 2020
Published by Springer Nature Switzerland AG 2020
B. Lalic et al. (Eds.): APMS 2020, IFIP AICT 592, pp. 263–271, 2020.
https://doi.org/10.1007/978-3-030-57997-5_31

There are multiple standards for representation of knowledge graph. The focus of this paper is on a specific type of knowledge graph that serves as a *concept scheme* or *thesaurus* and is represented using Simple Knowledge Organization System (SKOS) formalism [4]. SKOS is a standard, published by World Wide Web Consortium (W3C), that provides a structured framework for building controlled vocabularies such as thesauri, concept schemes, and taxonomies to be used and understood by both human and machine agents. SKOS models are considered to be lightweight ontologies as they don't have the expressivity of heavyweight, axiomatic ontologies such as OWL models. However, for many applications that require basic semantics in terms of the structural and lexical relationships between various entities, SKOS models can be developed fairly easily without requiring to invest heavily on developing rich, logic-based ontologies.

This paper describes a web-based tool called INFONEER SKOS Tool (or SKOS Tool for short) that is developed for creation and extension of SKOS models. Beyond its core function, SKOS Tool provides some other useful services that can support supervised and unsupervised document classification applications. Although SKOS Tool was originally developed to support a particular application related to classification of manufacturing suppliers based on their website content, it can be used for any type of document classification and semantic similarity measurement applications.

The remainder of this paper is organized as follows. Section 2 provides an overview of the underlying Semantic Model of SKOS. Section 3 describes a use case related to ventilator supply chain. Section 4 presents different functions and features of SKOS Tool. Section 5 describes how SKOS Tool can be used for supporting a supplier classification task related to the ventilator use case.

## 2 SKOS Semantic Model

The building block of a SKOS knowledge graph is called a *Concept*. A SKOS Concept (skos:concept) is any unit of thought such as an idea, an object, or an event. SKOS concepts, as abstract notions in mind, are independent of the terms that are used in natural language to describe them. For example, the English terms *car* and *automobile* point to the same concept, or entity, which is basically an artifact that is used for transporting people. Separation of the concepts form their descriptors (labels) is a core feature of SKOS models. Humans can identify concepts through their labels and machines can identify concepts via their Uniform Resource Identifier (URI) [5].

Each concept in SKOS has exactly one *preferred label* (skos:prefLabel) and can have multiple *alternative labels* (skos:altLabel). Preferred Label is a SKOS element that makes it possible to assign an authorized name to a concept. For example, in the context of metal casting terminology, *Foundry Sand* is the alternative label for *Molding Sand* as it is used frequently for referring to the same concept (Fig. 1). The broader concept of the *Molding Sand* is *Sand*, while *Silica Sand* and *Chromite Sand* are the narrower concepts; meaning that they are more specialized forms of *Molding Sand*. The concept that is semantically *related* to *Molding Sand* is *Mold*. While skos:broader and skos:narrower indicate a *hierarchical* link between two concepts, skos:related represents an *associative* relationships between concepts. Each SKOS concept can also have a definition provided in plain English or any other natural language. One major advantage of the SKOS thesauri is that they can be extended, enriched, and validated incrementally by community crowds and shared as linked open data due to their open and standard syntax and semantics. A SKOS thesaurus forms the nucleus of a knowledge graph that can be continuously enriched to support various data-driven and knowledge-intensive application such as semantic search and reasoning, text mining, data integration and alignment, and data analytic.

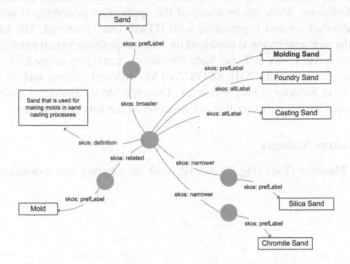

**Fig. 1.** The concept diagram of the Molding Sand based on SKOS terminology.

## 3   Use Case: COVID-19 Response Manufacturing Suppliers

COVID-19 pandemic caused a demand surge for certain medical equipment and supplies such as ventilators and face shields [6]. Supply chains have been slow in responding to this emergency mainly because finding the qualified suppliers with the required set of capability and capacities is a time-consuming process. Using keyword search method for finding suppliers is inefficient because online keyword search doesn't take into account the contextual semantics of the terms. Additionally, the contents of the websites of manufacturers vary significantly in term of quality and depth. Another issue arises from the heavy use of 'tribal knowledge' on the websites of contract manufacturers. The informal terminology that dominates this body of tribal knowledge causes a semantic discontinuity throughout the domain.

In presence of a knowledge graph that captures the important concepts (notions) in medical equipment manufacturing, supplier search can be conducted on a semantic level. For example, the manufacturers' websites can be annotated, or tagged, with the concepts coming from the knowledge graph. Another solution is to use a Semantic Classifier for classifying suppliers, represented by documents extracted from their websites, based on their capabilities.

# 4  INFONEER SKOS Tool

INFONEER SKOS Tool is developed for creating knowledge graphs. It also supports document classification applications by providing means for tokenizing and annotating documents using SKOS concepts. The SKOS Tool runs as a Django web application. Django is a free and open-source web framework that utilizes Python to realize a traditional model-template-view architecture. In addition to Django, various other libraries such as BeautifulSoup4 are bundled in a virtual environment to help carry out the tool's functions. While the back-end of the application is developed with Python, the application's front-end is presented with HTML and JavaScript. The latest stable release of the web application is deployed on a developmental virtual machine running Red Hat Enterprise Linux at Texas State University, providing accessibility for select users through Secure Shell (SSH). SKOS Tool has different gadgets such as Thesaurus Manager, Term Selector, Entity Extractor, Concept Model Builder, Concept Model Manager, and Capability Scorer that are describe in the following sections.

## 4.1  Thesaurus Manager

Thesaurus Manager (TM) (Fig. 2) can be used for creating and extending a SKOS thesaurus.

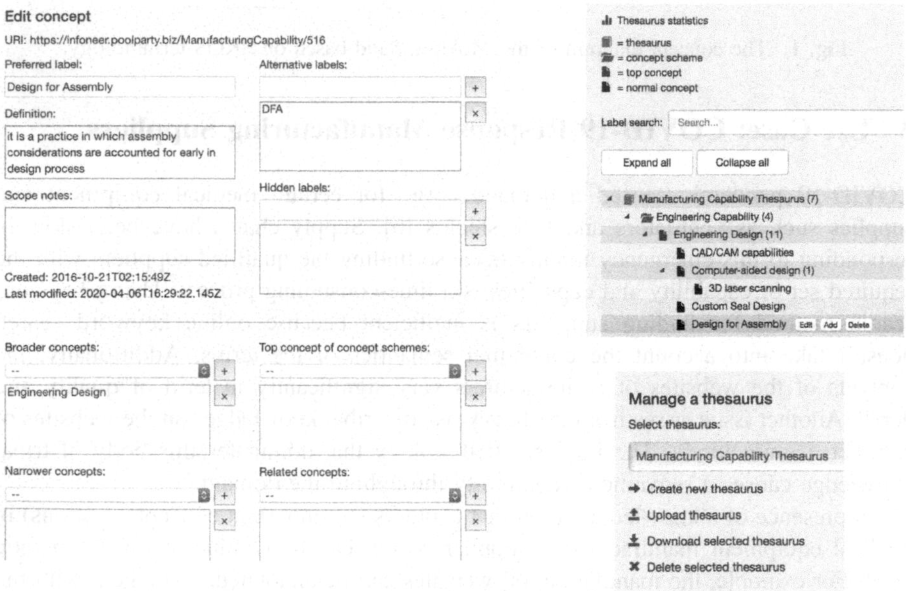

**Fig. 2.** The user interface for Thesaurus Manager and partial view of the Manufacturing Capability Thesaurus

The user can create a thesaurus from scratch by building a taxonomy of concepts, adding the necessary preferred and alternative labels and providing natural language definition for each concept, and relating them to one another. The final model can be exported in RFD/JSON format. For example, in the thesaurus partially shown in Fig. 2, Design for Assembly is a narrower concept for Engineering Design under Engineering Capability concept scheme. Thesaurus imports are also allowed using the same format.

## 4.2 Term Selector

The thesaurus can be extended directly by adding concepts using the TM gadget. An alternative method is to select terms from inserted text and integrate the selected terms with the thesaurus. The Term Selector gadget allows the user to select the relevant terms from a given text (through copy & paste or entering the URL) and add them to the thesaurus directly or export the result as an intermediate CSV file to be integrated with the thesaurus after verification by domain experts.

As shown in Fig. 3, the user needs to specify the parent (skos:broader) concept for each selected term. In the example shown in this figure, "FDA approvable grade" is selected as a new concept to be added to the thesaurus and placed under "Material Capability" is the broader concept.

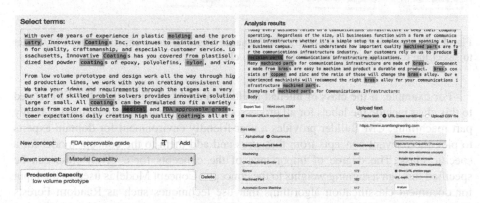

**Fig. 3.** Term Selector (left) user can highlight the terms that should be added to the thesaurus. Entity Extractor (right) identifies the occurrences of the thesaurus concepts in a text (Color figure online)

## 4.3 Entity Extractor

Entity Extractor (Fig. 3-right) is used for tokenizing a text or document. The tokens are the concepts that exist in the treasures and appear in the inserted text through either their preferred labels (highlighted in green) or alternative labels (highlighted in red). The input text can be inserted directly or grabbed from a given URL. The number of occurrences of those concepts is also captured using this gadget. This will result in vectorization of the unstructured text. The resulting concept vector can be exported as a

CSV file. The concept vector for each document can be used for more advanced text analytics processes such as document classification and clustering.

## 4.4  Concept Model (CM) Builder and Manager

A Concept Model (CM) is a subset of the thesaurus that represents a class of interest in a document classification task (Fig. 4-left).

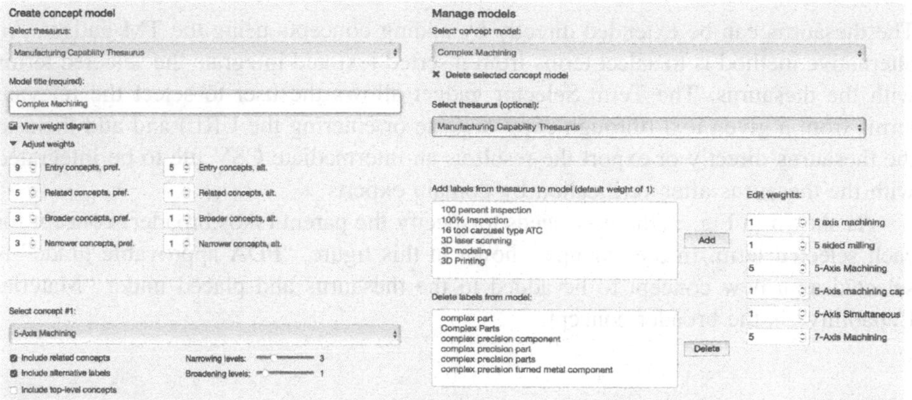

**Fig. 4.** Concept Model Builder (Left), CM Manager (Right) Domain expert can use CM builder to select the representative concepts for a given class of documents

For example, if the class of interest is Heavy Part Machining, then the CM related to this class include the labels for all processes and equipment that can be used in heavy part machining. CM Builder provides a user-friendly environment for domain experts to pick the relevant concepts from thesaurus and add them to the concept model for a specific class. The degree of importance of the concepts for a given class can be specified through assigning weights to the concepts. Concept Model is used as the input for document classification algorithms that use techniques such as Random Forests (RF) and Support Vector Machine (SVM). CM Manger can be used for modifying a concept model through adding or removing concepts and/or changing their weighting.

## 4.5  Capability Scorer

SKOS Tool was originally developed for evaluating the capabilities of manufacturing companies based on the textual description of their services provided on their websites. Capability Scores uses a scoring scheme that assigns a score to a given text based on the normalized frequencies of occurrences of terms that can be mapped to concepts in a given concept model. In the given example in Fig. 5, the company's score with respect to complex machining and heavy machining capabilities is 0.133 and .053, respectively.

**Fig. 5.** A document (company website) scored based on complex machining and heavy machining capabilities

## 5    SKOS Tool for Classification of Manufacturing Suppliers

Going back to the COVID-19 use case discussed earlier, since most ventilators need some sort of silicone and polymer tubing, suppose we want to create a group of suppliers with specialization in "Medical Grade Polymer Tubing". We already have a knowledge graph named Manufacturing Capability Thesaurus (MCT). Through web crawling, all suppliers in North America can be screened and evaluated based on their websites information. If they meet the minimum membership strength threshold, they will be added as a member of this class. Alternatively, using the capability scorer gadget in SKOS Tool, a score can be assigned to each participating supplier. This sore can be used for ranking and initial screening before going through more rigorous capability analysis steps. Using the SKOS Tool, the Manufacturing Capability Thesaurus was extended with the concepts that are related to Medical Grade Polymer Tubing capability. Some of those concepts are shown in Table 1.

To collect these concepts, the websites of about 100 suppliers with medical tubing capability was parsed. This step is equivalent to the training phase of the conventional text classification methods that results in an automatically-generated dictionary of terms (a.k.a Bag of Words) [7]. However, the Bag of Words method often creates a dictionary which is cluttered with irrelevant terms that create a noisy environment for text classification. However, a curated thesaurus ensures that every term included in the Concept Model is terminologically and semantically relevant and meaningful. The collected concepts were then made *skso:related* to one another in order to capture the associative relationships among them. We refer to this semantically enhanced document classification method as Bag of Concepts (BoC) method. Using the Bag of Concepts method, new suppliers can be analyzed to check if they belong to different capability classes of interest. It was demonstrated previously that BoC method significantly improve the precisions of document classifiers [8].

**Table 1.** A subset of concepts related to Medical Grade Tubing concept model

| Materials | Methods | Finishing | Technologies |
|---|---|---|---|
| PTFE Tube | Extrusion | Laser Welding | Tri-TIE |
| Teflon Tube | Tip forming | Laser Machining | Taper-TIE |
| PEEK Tube | Flanging | Tipping | Variable Braid & Coil |
| FEP Tube | flaring | Precision Cutting | Polyimide Shaft Liners |
| TPU Tube | Coextrusion | Precision Machining | Coil & Braid Reinforced |
| PP Tube | Single Lumen | Hole Punching | Sheath Extrusion |
| PEBAX Tube | Multi-Lumen | RF Welding | Proximally Reinforced |
| PE Tube/polyethylene | Tri-Layer Extrusion | Overmolding | Marker Bands |
| Nylon Tube | Intermittent Extrusion | Printing | Super- Tri |
| ABS Tube | Braiding | Plasma Etching | PTFE Coated Mandrels |
| PETG tube | Coiling | Annealing | Multi-Lumen Tubing |

# 6  Conclusion

In this paper, the main feature and functions of SKOS Tool were described and a use case related to supplier classification was discussed. In future, we will extend the medical equipment supplier classification use case by creating multiple capability classes. SKOS Tool will be extended in future to provide more sophisticated functionalities such as creating probabilistic Naïve Bayes networks from unstructured text. SKOS Tool is currently in its alpha test phase and it is being evaluated by a small group of researchers. The beta version will be released to larger group of domain experts for creation of knowledge graphs in various domains.

# References

1. Hagedorn, T., Bone, M., Kruse, B., Grosse, I., Blackburn, M.: Knowledge representation with ontologies and semantic web technologies to promote augmented and artificial intelligence in systems engineering. INSIGHT **23**(1), 15–20 (2020)
2. Wilcke, X., Bloem, P., De Boer, V.: The knowledge graph as the default data model for learning on heterogeneous knowledge. Data Sci. **1**(1–2), 39–57 (2017)
3. Ameri, F., Urbanovsky, C., McArthur, C.: A systematic approach to developing ontologies for manufacturing service modeling. In: Proceedings of the Workshop on Ontology and Semantic Web for Manufacturing, OSEMA 2012, 24 July 2012, pp. 1–14. Sun SITE Central Europe CEUR-WS (2012)
4. Miles, A., Bechhofer, S.: SKOS simple knowledge organization system reference. W3C (2009)

5. Blumauer, A.: PoolParty technical white paper (2017). https://help.poolparty.biz/doc/white-papers-release-notes/poolparty-technical-white-paper
6. Ranney, M.L., Griffeth, V., Jha, A.K.: Critical supply shortages—the need for ventilators and personal protective equipment during the Covid-19 pandemic. New Engl. J. Med. **382**(18), e41 (2020)
7. Korde, V.: Text classification and classifiers: a survey. Int. J. Artif. Intell. Appl. **3**(2), 85–99 (2012)
8. Sabbagh, R., Ameri, F.: A thesaursi-guided text analytics technique for capability based classification of manufacturing suppliers. In: Proceedings of the ASME International Design Engineering Technical Conferences/Computers and Information in Engineering Conference (IDETC/CIE 2017) (2017)

# Data-Driven Services: Characteristics, Trends and Applications

# The Successful Commercialization of a Digital Twin in an Industrial Product Service System

Oliver Stoll[1]([⊠]) [iD], Shaun West[1]([⊠]) [iD], Paolo Gaiardelli[2] [iD],
David Harrison[3] [iD], and Fintan J. Corcoran[4]

[1] Lucerne University of Applied Sciences and Arts, 6048 Horw, Switzerland
{oliver.stoll, shaun.west}@hslu.ch
[2] Università degli studi di Bergamo, 24129 Bergamo, Italy
paolo.gaiardelli@unibg.it
[3] Glasgow Caledonian University, Glasgow G4 0BA, Scotland, UK
D.K.Harrison@gcu.ac.uk
[4] Mebag, Planungs- und Bauträger AG, 6330 Cham, Switzerland
fintan.corcoran@mebag-services.ch

**Abstract.** This paper describes the design, development and commercialization of a digital twin in an industrial product service system (industrial PSS). The twin was one of a number developed as part of a Smart Twin project in Switzerland with multiple industrial partners. The case here follows a commercialization process for digital twin-enabled services and will highlight some of the critical success factors. The service provided with the support of the digital twin was based on the reliable and predictable operation of a server room. Equipment in the room comes from several original equipment manufacturers (OEMs), and a system integrator manages the system. The approach is to apply action research as the methodology on a single case and then to identify and assess the aspects where Service Dominant (S-D) logic supported or hindered the development of the new digital technology-based service that was being co-created between the supplier and the customer. The analysis of the case confirmed that S-D logic supported the development of Smart Service offerings and showed that value co-creation can be developed.

**Keywords:** Smart services · S-D logic · Industrial product service systems

## 1 Introduction

The purpose of this paper is to describe the design, development, and commercialization of a digital twin in an industrial product service system (industrial PSS) based on a real case. The case is a Swiss firm which has developed and commercialized a Digital Twin as a service. The researchers had the opportunity to support and observe the development of these services. Along the way, the firm used experimental methods for design and development. In commercialization traditional methods were used, with which the firm encountered several barriers, therefore adapting the approach. Closer investigation of this use case may allow other firms to develop new digitally enabled services. The barriers to development and commercialization are different for digital

B. Lalic et al. (Eds.): APMS 2020, IFIP AICT 592, pp. 275–282, 2020.
https://doi.org/10.1007/978-3-030-57997-5_32

services, with a greater focus on value co-creation and co-delivery than with traditional services. Therefore, this investigation aims to identify the key success factors (and barriers) which need to be understood to design, develop, and commercialize digital smart services. The motivation was to understand how, where, and why S-D logic assisted or hindered the co-development and delivery of Smart Services.

## 2 Theoretical Background

Industry 4.0 and the internet of things (IoT) are enabling manufacturing firms and system integrators to offer new value propositions to their customers. Anderson [1], stated in 1998 that to build a value proposition for a customer, it was first essential to understand what they valued and how they created value. Firms can use the data from their existing equipment to gain deeper insights that can lead to competitive advantages [2]. One way to seize the opportunities of data insights is the Digital Twin [3]. Digital Twins are, in general, a digital representation of a physical object or a process [4, 5], providing a link between the virtual and the physical [3].

Industrial Product and Service Systems, consisting of many actors across different organizations, machines, and services, includes the design and commercialization of digital services. Industrial PSS has mainly been investigated from the product perspective; very little is written about it in the context of S-D logic [6]. This field now offers the opportunity to investigate the commercialization of digital services in an industrial context, making it possible to examine themes such as ecosystem analysis, actors and their motivation [7], value propositions in an S-D logic context, and value sharing and co-creation [6, 8].

Servitization has been studied for over 30 years [9]. However, today there has been a step-change with digitally enabled servitization [10]. The emerging digital capabilities of original equipment manufacturers (OEMs) increase opportunities to develop smart services using digital technologies such as IoT and advanced data analysis. Kohtamäki [11] identified a range of business models relevant to servitization and highlighted the importance of value creation within the value proposition. West et al., [12] assessed the smartness of services using S-D logic premises by analyzing the service ecosystem, service platform and value co-creation, independent of the type of firm. The use of S-D logic supports the value discovery described by Anderson [1].

## 3 Research Methodology

Although multiple case studies are considered in order to build more robust theory [13] due to their potential for triangulation, single case studies can be more effective to describe complex interactions among several variables characterizing the problem under investigation [14]. Voss et al., [15] suggest single case approaches demonstrate more effective learning on long term cause and effect relationships. The data-driven servitization project by the company highlighted in this case analysis was initiated by a Swiss innovation project between numerous Swiss universities acting as research partners, and multiple other implementation partners. Consequently, throughout all stages of this project continual reviews and constructive discussions took place to verify the direction of the project and assist all implementation partners to overcome any shared complications.

Action research methodology was applied for the reflections on the digital twin roadmap; evidence included identifying the tools used at each stage of the roadmap, and considering their usefulness, as well as the challenges and opportunities identified at that particular point. In this paper, a single case-based approach was used and analyzed on the timeline of the design, development, and commercialization. The main reason for selecting this approach is the scarcity and inconsistency of practical insights on design and commercialization challenges in industrial PSS literature.

Action research is a practically-oriented approach for small projects that aim for fast progress. It incorporates change as a characteristic that allows discoveries on the go, using the framework: plan, act, observe and reflect. The process is cyclic with multiple iterations from researchers and practitioners [16].

## 4   Case Analysis

The starting point for the case is shown in Fig. 1, which presents the digital twin development roadmap developed by the commercial manager for the firm and provides evidence from each of the phases described below. The development was the first digital service for what was a traditional building and facility management firm in Switzerland. This family firm delivers its core values through the execution and

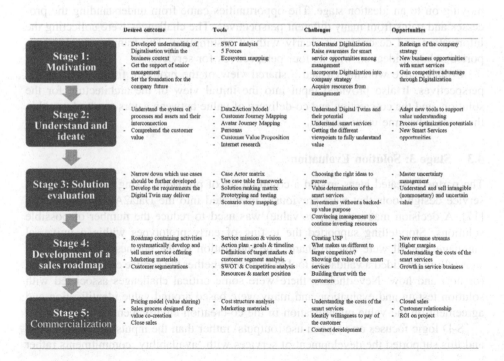

**Fig. 1.** The detailed roadmap developed and provided by the firm

delivery of high-quality services such as, building planning, construction, and long-term management of multiple facilities. Therefore, the idea to pursue a servitized activity came about from a desire to integrate their current services with industry 4.0 and improve the already high quality of their broad range of services.

## 4.1  Stage 1: Motivation

The initial motivation for the project came from the firm's strategy to "do something digital" and to maintain a longer-term relationship with their customers after the handover of a project. The outcome here was to find a solution that supported the daily work routines through the application of smart services. This was intended to create a competitive advantage for the firm by capturing a partner for the longer term. The challenges it created were that both parties needed to understand digitalization, and for the firm there was a need to acquire new resources.

The major dimensions of service platform and value co-creation were considered important when moving from the strategic decision to "do something digital with customers over the longer term". Working with the customer to co-create a service was considered essential for both parties.

## 4.2  Stage 2: Understand and Ideate

Application of the Data2Action framework [17] and additional research identified the processes that cause the most frequent pains for the building occupier. The problems were detailed in collaboration with the actors, and their roles were identified before moving on to an ideation stage. The opportunities came from understanding the processes and pains from many different perspectives. The challenges were collecting the information and describing it clearly without assumption. The framework [18] supported solution ideation with its four perspectives for services.

Collaborative working created a shared view of the problem, from many actors' perspectives. It also provided input into the initial view of the architecture for the solution, and the co-creation and co-delivery of value between actors (multiple) within the system became more evident.

## 4.3  Stage 3: Solution Evaluation

The partners created ideas around a common set of problems, using a set of different service design tools that were previously integrated into the Data2Action framework [17]. A decision matrix (effort vs value) was used to reduce the number of possible solutions. Storytelling supported the testing of early prototypes within a universal language that all were able to share. The integration of the business model into the storytelling provided a validation tool to confirm whether the service could be delivered (or not) and how. Nevertheless, there were some critical challenges associated with solution testing and evaluation, and many were based around value identification and agreement on the value quantification in the co-creation environment.

S-D logic focuses on value in use (outputs) rather than the inputs into the process, and this supported the development of services with 'availability' commitments rather than ones based around basic inputs (e.g., call out times). The value co-creation here was described (often the process was based around three or more actors), it also supported the definition of the rules of exchange and the accommodation of multiple roles as there was a degree of resource integration. The use of the term 'beneficiary' was helpful when assessing the different situations and the perspective of the value that was co-created.

### 4.4 Stage 4: Development of a Sales Roadmap

This phase focused on defining the offer into a form that could be commercialized. The service was clearly defined, and the roles and readabilities clearly described. Customer segmentation and competition analysis were developed, leading to an action plan with a clear aim and timeline. The required resources for the execution of the roadmap were identified in detail and labelled as core/non-core.

The focus on value in use and co-creation of value supported the development of the sales roadmap. Discussions between the parties supported the revenue model and the identity of the firm's core activities and tasks that the customer was best suited to deliver. Revenue models that provided a gain/pain share were preferred to support value co-creation. Roles and responsibilities were clearly defined, also detailed resource integration while keeping an architecture that was designed to be flexible.

### 4.5 Stage 5: Commercialization

The objective was to have a system that was in commercial operation. Based on this, a cost model was built to integrate all of the firm's resources; the design was modular to support different levels of resources. A performance-based agreement was designed that described the obligations of all parties, along with the governance processes to deal with changes flexibly. This flexibility created a challenge, as it resulted in slightly adjusting or moving tasks and obligations to another party within the agreement; this was not appreciated by the legal team. The discussions around revenue models provided opportunities for capturing the value that was co-created.

Legal advisors were unsure of how to apportion roles, responsibilities and obligations – they sought clarity on how to support this based on S-D logic, as they had been trained on Goods-Dominant logic. The framework [12] sustained the co-creation of value, although discussions were needed to understand its practical use and reference to S-D logic. Some of the aspects valued by the customer and used in the revenue model were more akin to Goods-Dominant logic than pricing based on S-D logic principles.

### 4.6 Outcome and Reflection from Commercialization

The two key beneficiaries of the case studied proposed the best approach to pass the digital twin and its services through the procurement process. This approach involved presenting a full package offer, with all service offerings clearly split and, more importantly, detailing the values the customer receives. The structure and pricing for this offer were developed through sampling comparable offers from competitor service providers while also correlating proposed services with current service level agreements. The process of developing a final offer with all functional aspects of the service and the metrics to measure outcomes, sparked discoveries of value and supported the construction and the fees for the customer.

Two departmental directors (service recipients) presented this detailed service proposal to all other relevant head management individuals. The offer was presented directly to the key individuals that make the final purchasing decisions. The process used bypassed the procurement manager and, as such, reduced the opportunities for a rejection or alternative offers. This suggests that procurement may not be well equipped for buying Smart Services and that a new sales channel may be required.

# 5  Discussion

The case here mirrors the findings of Anderson [1], who describes the importance of understanding what customers value. The theme is then to identify, create, and deliver value. The case confirms that the process is complex and requires iteration and further confirmation from the customer. The five-step development road map of the firm with the iterations demonstrated the complexity of the process and the poor understanding of value (initially) from both parties.

Co-creation and testing of the solutions proposed is an example of open innovation [19], which assisted the design of the Smart Service as well as important aspects such as the development and testing of the revenue model. It is unlikely that traditional 'closed' innovation would have led to the proposed solution. It is also in line with Service Design that focuses on development and testing with different stakeholders within the system, in particular the active beneficiaries and providers [7]. The roadmap and the tools used supported the design and commercialization.

The use of S-D logic helped identify the value (and form) that could accrue or be destroyed in the industrial PSS. It also helped understand each actor's motivation, and the consideration of co-creation/co-delivery supported the development of the service processes. Data access and ownership concerns were identified and could be negotiated, based in part on the actor motivations and from the detailed understanding of the resources and operation. Value creation/destruction supported the net value for the beneficiary, helping with both pricing and budgeting.

The customer's procurement actors required more traditional pricing models, so the firm had to translate the value from the S-D perspective to a more traditional product view on pricing. The consequences of this were that many value co-creation propositions were lost. The use of the framework [18] supported ideation by creating four questions. The derivation of the S-D logic axioms [12] made the approach more useable in terms of value discovery. The major difficulties from the 'value in use' model were based around the value discovery in different situations and the equal weighting of all situations.

## 5.1 Theoretical and Practical Contribution

S-D logic is a powerful concept to identify value creation and destruction in a complex industrial PSS. However, it needs both the marketing and the engineering points of view to be understood simultaneously. The value capture process then helped to define the reasonable target cost for the development of the digital twin. Service Design supported pragmatic application of S-D logic so practitioners could apply the approach. The framework [18] aided the development of different customer value propositions and the ultimate route to the commercialized customer value proposition with its revenue model/fee structure.

One of the managerial implications challenges the traditional cost-plus or value-in-exchange approaches, as they do not identify the actual value created. The application of S-D logic supported the identification of the value created, and the identification of relevant KPIs that assess and measure the value of the smart services.

# 6 Conclusions and Recommendations

The concept of S-D logic helped to describe and develop the complex value propositions that unfolded when taking a broader industrial PSS perspective in combination with open innovation and co-development. During the motivation phase, the concept of S-D logic was used by management to create the foundation to understand value co-creation. Building this understanding for individuals who didn't know about S-D logic proved to be complicated. Particularly in the commercialization phase, people without this knowledge couldn't grasp the value of the Smart Service offerings. Traditional value assessment methods of procurement were not able to cope with the S-D logic value propositions, and the firm had to translate the value propositions to meet procurement guidelines, which lost some of the value. This provides additional challenges for detailed service delivery measurements. The major limitation of this work is that it is from a single case. More in-depth research of S-D logic in the context of industrial PSS is needed, along with new methods to operationalize S-D logic.

# References

1. Anderson, J.C., Narus, J.A.: Business marketing: understand what customers value. Harvard Bus. Rev. **76**(6), 53 (1998)
2. Sagiroglu, S., Sinanc, D.: Big data: a review. In: Proceedings of the 2013 International Conference on Collaboration Technologies and Systems, CTS 2013, pp. 42–47 (2013). https://doi.org/10.1109/CTS.2013.6567202
3. Barbieri, C., Rapaccini, M., West, S., Meierhofer, J.: Are practitioners and literature aligned about digital twin? In: Proceeding of the 26th EurOMA Conference, pp. 2781–2790 (2019)
4. Bolton, R.N., et al.: Customer experience challenges: bringing together digital, physical and social realms. J. Serv. Manag. **29**(5), 776–808 (2018). https://doi.org/10.1108/JOSM-04-2018-0113

5. Zhang, H., Ma, L., Sun, J., Lin, H., Thürer, M.: Digital twin in services and industrial product service systems: review and analysis. Procedia CIRP **83**, 57–60 (2019). https://doi.org/10.1016/j.procir.2019.02.131

6. Cedergren, S.I., Elfving, S.W., Eriksson, J., Parida, V.: Analysis of the industrial product-service systems (IPS2) literature: a systematic review. In: 2012 IEEE 6th International Conference on Management of Innovation and Technology, ICMIT 2012, pp. 733–740 (2012). https://doi.org/10.1109/ICMIT.2012.6225897

7. Ekman, P., Raggio, R.D., Thompson, S.M.: Service network value co-creation: Defining the roles of the generic actor. Ind. Mark. Manag. **56**, 51–62 (2016). https://doi.org/10.1016/j.indmarman.2016.03.002

8. Rönnberg Sjödin, D., Parida, V., Wincent, J.: Value co-creation process of integrated product-services: effect of role ambiguities and relational coping strategies. Ind. Mark. Manag. **56**, 108–119 (2016). https://doi.org/10.1016/j.indmarman.2016.03.013

9. Vandermerwe, S., Rada, J.: Servitisation of business: adding value by adding services. Eur. Manag. J. **6**(4), 314–324 (1988)

10. Paschou, T., Rapaccini, M., Adrodegari, F., Saccani, N.: Digital servitization in manufacturing: a systematic literature review and research agenda. Ind. Mark. Manag. 1 (2020). https://doi.org/10.1016/j.indmarman.2020.02.012

11. Kohtamäki, M., Parida, V., Oghazi, P., Gebauer, H., Baines, T.: Digital servitization business models in ecosystems: a theory of the firm. J. Bus. Res. **104**, 380–392 (2019). https://doi.org/10.1016/j.jbusres.2019.06.027

12. West, S., Gaiardelli, P., Rapaccini, M.: Exploring technology-driven service innovation in manufacturing firms through the lens of service dominant logic. IFAC-PapersOnLine. **51**, 1317–1322 (2018). https://doi.org/10.1016/j.ifacol.2018.08.350

13. Yin, R.K.: Case Study Research: Design and Methods, 4th edn. Sage, Thousand Oaks (2009)

14. Dyer Jr., W.G., Wilkins, A.L.: Better stories, not better constructs, to generate better theory: a rejoinder to eisenhardt. Acad. Manag. Rev. **16**(3), 613–619 (1991)

15. Voss, C., Tsikriktsis, N., Frolich, M.: Case research in operations management. Int. J. Oper. Prod. Manag. **22**(2), 195–219 (2002)

16. Denscombe, M.: The Good Research Guide for Small Scale Research Projects. Open University Press (2010). https://doi.org/10.1371/journal.pone.0017540

17. Stoll, O., West, S., Rapaccini, M., Barbieri, C., Bonfanti, A., Gombac, A.: Upgrading the Data2Action framework: results deriving from its application in the printing industry. In: Nóvoa, H., Drăgoicea, M., Kühl, N. (eds.) IESS 2020. LNBIP, vol. 377, pp. 273–286. Springer, Cham (2020). https://doi.org/10.1007/978-3-030-38724-2_20

18. Kowalkowski, C., Ulaga, W.: Service Strategy in Action: A Practical Guide for Growing Your B2B Service and Solution Business. Service Strategy Press, Scottsdale (2017)

19. Chesbrough, H.: The case for open services innovation: the commodity trap. Calif. Manag. Rev. **53**(3), 5–20 (2011). https://doi.org/10.1525/cmr.2011.53.3.5

# Using Service Dominant Logic to Assess the Value Co-creation of Smart Services

Oliver Stoll[1]([⊠]) [iD], Shuan West[1]([⊠]) [iD], and Cosimo Barbieri[2] [iD]

[1] Lucerne University of Applied Sciences and Arts, 6048 Horw, Switzerland
{oliver.stoll,shaun.west}@hslu.ch
[2] Università degli Studi di Firenze, Viale G. Morgagni 40, 50134 Florence, Italy
cosimo.barbieri@unifi.it

**Abstract.** The digital transformation of industrial firms is providing opportunities to improve efficiency, design new value propositions and re-engineer their business models. With the adoption of digital technologies in combination with the use of data, firms can develop new smart services for their internal or external customers, enabling new value co-creation opportunities and, possibly, leading to a competitive advantage. Nevertheless, assessment of the impact of smart services in financial and organizational terms, and the way to reach such a competitive advantage, is problematic for firms. The challenge firms are facing is that the value created through smart services consists of many small improvements which add up rather than a single point of value. This paper introduces the background literature research, then presents and discusses the results from a use-case where the application of enabled smart services was developed. The outcomes show that digitization can support both internal value creation and the development of new customer value propositions based on servitization and allow non-manufacturing firms to develop new value propositions through smart services.

**Keywords:** Smart services · Digital servitization · Smart connected products · S-D logic

## 1 Introduction

Digital technologies (i.e. sensors, cloud computing, machine learning, artificial intelligence, etc.) can create new connections within a business ecosystem and, in combination with big data, enable new value co-creation opportunities and processes [1]. In particular, research shows a growing interest in the digital transformation of industrial firms shifting towards a service business focus (servitization) [2] and existing literature defines this shift from traditional/non-digital offering (goods and services) of manufacturing firms, with the implementation (adoption and use) of digital technologies, as digital servitization [3]. Even if many studies have addressed the role of digital technologies [4], there are many examples of manufacturers that no longer sell products, but rather provide advanced services, smart services, and digitally-enabled product service solutions [2]. The literature agrees that technology-driven innovations can facilitate differentiation of the company's offering, thus bringing a new opportunity for

© IFIP International Federation for Information Processing 2020
Published by Springer Nature Switzerland AG 2020
B. Lalic et al. (Eds.): APMS 2020, IFIP AICT 592, pp. 283–290, 2020.
https://doi.org/10.1007/978-3-030-57997-5_33

capturing value in highly competitive markets [2]. Still, too little attention is given to how the value of Smart Services can be assessed according to the theoretical premises of service science and Service Dominant (S-D) logic. This paper challenges some views of the actual research and sheds further light on this argument. Findings from the analysis of a use case study are discussed in order to answer the research question (RQ):

"How can value co-creation be assessed and captured along the Data2Action smart services development process?".

This research aims to answer this question using an inductive theory building from a case approach. The paper is structured as follows: first, a literature review of the key concepts of Smart Services and value co-creation though the lens of S-D logic; then, the research methodology used to answer the RQ with the results from the use-case; finally, the findings are discussed and conclusions made.

## 2 Literature Review

The context of the paper is industrial Product-Service Systems (industrial PSS), and this limits the scope of the literature review to within this complex B2B environment. The outline of how firms can gain financial benefits from digitally-enabled industrial PSS has recently been described in the literature [5]. The papers identify that organizational shifts are needed for digital servitization to enable the creation and delivery of the collaborative value propositions that can be developed with industry 4.0 technologies. The new value propositions are often predicated on existing industrial PSS augmented with smart services supported through value co-creation and value co-delivery. Such co-creation within the ecosystems experienced in industrial PSS has been further described [6], where three different literature streams were compared to describe the ecosystem and value co-creation processes. As such, the literature review aims to define Smart Services and then define value co-creation according to S-D logic so that the RQ can be answered.

### 2.1 Smart Services

Smart, connected products enable functions and have capabilities referring to monitoring, control, optimization and autonomy [7]. They allow the development of Smart Services, which are pre-emptive product-support services that can be delivered more efficiently and quickly due to hard field intelligence and connectivity [8]. This concept encapsulates more than just technology: it also refers to a more customer-centric view and strategy to transform technology into services with added value from the customer's point of view [9]. In particular, with the concept of servitization [10, 11], it refers to the commercialization of digital services within Industrial PSS.

### 2.2 Value Co-creation According to Service Dominant Logic

S-D logic is a meta-theoretical framework based upon ten foundational premises that define its conceptual domain [12]. It provides a novel perspective that calls for a rethinking and re-evaluation of service innovation [13]. According to the principles of S-D logic [12], value is (co-)created through simultaneous and continuous interactions among a wide set of dynamic operant (active) resources, which form ecosystems of service offerings and exchanges. In this context, technological changes can play a key role. Digital technologies can create new connections and interactions within a service ecosystem, enabling new value co-creation opportunities and processes in different spatial and temporal settings [1].

## 3   Research Methodology

The process of assessing the value of smart services based on S-D logic is complex, so it is essential to use a qualitative approach [14], since that gives the possibility of gaining an understanding of managerial actions and processes in real-life organizational settings [15]. In particular, since research in this domain is in its preliminary stage, we adopted an inductive theory, building from the case approach [16]. In particular, we decided to use a single case study since we found the selected case particularly revelatory [17]. No research protocol was used, the data collection of the use-case has been done through direct observation and open questions (what, why, how). The observation took place during weekly development sessions with the industrial partner. These were both face to face and online meetings, during which the researchers could ask questions.

## 4   Case Description

The case study is a company with a printing-as-a-service business model [18]. In order to guarantee the profitability of contracts, the company has to assure that the right amounts of spare parts and consumables are sent to the customer in time, to fulfil the service level agreement. For this reason, the service department is in charge to validate the orders coming from the customers and manage and optimize the resources in the field. The participants who collaborated were from the service department of the firm, responsible for the delivery of printing-as-a-service. As a team, they wanted to understand how to develop new Smart Services using the data collected from individual printers. Their focus was the order fulfilment system and how they could improve customer experience and at the same time drive out cost (i.e., waste or inventory).

The Data2Action model [18] gave us the structure to understand the problem, ideate solutions, build prototypes and test the prototypes. The model integrates aspects of S-D logic and Service Design approaches, and in this case the focus is on the key tools used to discover and describe value (co-)created for the potential Smart Services that were developed.

The tools used to identify value are shown schematically in Fig. 1 The rating matrix tool was used to rate solutions from the ideation phase in terms of their business value and the feasibility of developing them to a running solution. The rating matrix with its two dimensions - value and feasibility - provided justification and structure for the selection of ideas. The ratings from the team were qualitative and included tangible and intangible value dimensions of the service. Iterations were required to support the convergence of agreement with the positioning of the solutions on the rating matrix. The case/actor matrix was used to identify the context of the problem and the actors involved. This gave the team a tool that allowed them to understand who was involved in a prospective solution, as well as describing the context of the problem. The S-D logic framework was then used as a proxy for the smartness of the solutions according to S-D logic axioms [19]. Some of the data in the table was in effect a copy/paste from the case/actor matrix and supported the five-point scale used when grading the different solutions. For the value assessment three iterations were conducted, as the understanding of the value and the effectiveness grew with every iteration, giving the project team more confidence when selecting the solutions to develop into Smart Services.

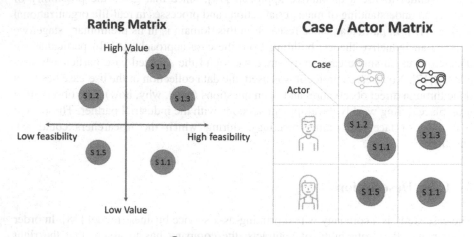

Fig. 1. The three tools used to help identify the value co-creation.

The process for value assessment was iterative and consisted of many tools, all of which provided some information needed for decision making. The value aspect of the matrix (in which the ideas were rated) was the contextual understanding that was developed with customer journey mapping, avatar journey mapping and ecosystem mapping [20]. The value recipient (the actor) was described as a persona, and the actor value was described with the customer value proposition. The relationships between context and actor were summarized in the case actor matrix. With each iteration the context and the actor value propositions became clearer. As the maturity of context and value proposition grew, the confidence for decision making grew. The case actor matrix helped assess the smartness of an idea based on the S-D logic framework, and this supported the value assessment.

Effectiveness is an axis on the matrix that tries to identify how easily an idea could be prototyped or developed. Technical aspects, knowledge, and resource (data) availability can play a role in moving the idea along this axis. The effectiveness can also be related to costs. The technical people in the project team drive the rating for this axis. The Source Target Link matrix from the D2A associated ideas with the data and the analysis methods systematically revealing if the idea was do-able or not.

In early stages the matrix is based on purely qualitative data but, with the increased context development, potential value proxies are identified and translated into KPIs, providing stronger arguments for project decision making.

## 5  Discussion

The discussion is broken up into four sections, the first describes the importance of the input to the process. It then moves on to consider the process of the assessment of the value of the solution based on S-D logic, identifying the challenges as well as the benefits of the approach taken. It closes with discussing the research question and putting it into an industrial implication.

### 5.1  Input Stage

During the development of solutions to the umbrella case of printing-as-a-service, the development group learned that there was not just one value proposition idea but many, depending on the context [21]. The clarity of the ideas for solutions (the output from the ideation phase) was critical for the input to the value estimation of the solutions. Visualizing the solutions gave clearer contextual understanding of the proposed solutions, and this is supported by the literature [22].

### 5.2  Assessment of the Value of the Solution Based on S-D Logic

The rating matrix was a tool for the initial value discussions for a solution. The lack of a formal scale gave the team an opportunity to discover the value and integrate their views of tangible and intangible value creation. The value here was for the beneficiaries identified in the solution idea. The relative scale improved with each iteration, as ideas were modified and improved.

The case/actor matrix allowed the context to be described in a standardized way, and for the actors to be clearly identified. A simple graphic was used – based on the sketch developed in the ideation phase – to communicate the context in a simple and unambiguous way. This is according to value in context [23], because context frames the value creation, according to S-D logic. However, it is often challenging for the development team to initially frame the contextual aspects effectively from multiple perspectives and to clearly identify the beneficiaries. The team in this case were from one general cultural group (i.e., Italian) and so their views may vary from people from other cultural groups [24]. This would mean that there would have to be a re-confirmation of value within other cultural contextual settings.

The smartness rating assessment provides a simple checklist that is based on S-D logic that the development team can use as a check. This in effect operationalizes the S-D logic axioms and foundational premises into a form that can be applied in an industrial setting. The value of doing the assessment after the actor/case matrix is that some of the information can be directly taken over and assessed in more detail using the framework. The five-point Likert-scale (1–5) provides a pragmatic approach to the scoring. In general, the higher the scoring the more likely it is that higher value was co-created with the beneficiary. The value here is captured from both tangible and intangible aspects.

Iterations are important [25] and the return to the rating matrix provides the opportunity to move the solution in both the x and y directions. Each iteration also improves the description of the solution in terms of its value and the effort to develop it, while also supporting convergence.

## 5.3 Assessment of the Research Question

The developers have used a process that has allowed them to identify on a relative basis the value co-created by different actors for a beneficiary within the context of a Smart Service. It does not mean that the value identified will be created and delivered, as this is only in effect a proxy to the value. However, it is closer to the value in use than the traditional value-in-exchange model used by many manufacturers and supports a move to value-based pricing. The model proposed is shown in Fig. 2 and the authors recommend that at least three iterations are required to get convergence on a solution.

## 5.4 Industrial Implications

The industrial implication is that a model that has been tested on one case, could be supported with development of Smart Services, and addresses concerns identified in the literature [25]. This is important, as the application of S-D logic can be difficult for manufacturing firms. The two business axes of efficiency (cost saving) and effectiveness (potentially new value propositions) need to be integrated into the approach.

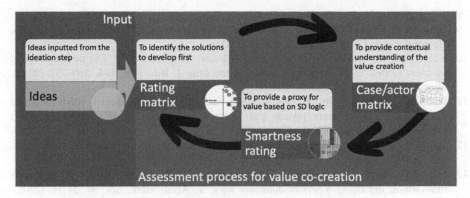

**Fig. 2.** The value discovery and identification process.

## 6 Conclusions and Recommendations

This single case study has shown that with digitally-enabled Smart Services it is possible to use a process to discover and identify value co-creation according to the axioms and foundational premises of S-D logic. A process that assesses the proposed solution in an iterative process is able to provide an approach to identify tangible and intangible value.

This is, however, only a single case study, which thus limits the applicability of the findings. It is therefore recommended that multiple case studies are undertaken to test and further develop the process.

## References

1. Breidbach, C.: Technology-enabled value co-creation: an empirical analysis of actors, resources, and practices. Ind. Mark. Manag. **56**, 73–85 (2016)
2. Baines, T., Lightfoot, H.W.: Servitization of the manufacturing firm: exploring the operations practices and technologies that deliver advanced services. Int. J. Oper. Prod. Manag. **34**, 2–35 (2013). https://doi.org/10.1108/IJOPM-02-2012-0086
3. Vendrell-Herrero, F., Wilson, J.R.: Servitization for territorial competitiveness: taxonomy and research agenda. Compet. Rev. **27**, 2–11 (2017)
4. Ardolino, M., Rapaccini, M., Saccani, N., Gaiardelli, P., Crespi, G., Ruggeri, C.: The role of digital technologies for the service transformation of industrial companies. Int. J. Prod. Res. **56**(6), 2116–2132 (2017). https://doi.org/10.1080/00207543.2017.1324224
5. Kohtamäki, M., Parida, V., Patel, P.C., Gebauer, H.: The relationship between digitalization and servitization: the role of servitization in capturing the financial potential of digitalization. Technol. Forecast. Soc. Change **151**, 119804 (2020). https://doi.org/10.1016/j.techfore.2019.119804
6. Autio, E., Thomas, L.: Value co-creation in ecosystems: insights and research promise from three disciplinary perspectives (2019)
7. Porter, M.E., Heppelmann, J.E.: How smart, connected products are transforming companies (2015)

8. Allmendinger, G., Lombreglia, R.: Four strategies for the age of smart services (2005)
9. Reinartz, W.: Hybrid offerings: research avenues for implementing service growth strategies. elgaronline.com (2014). Research WU-H of SM
10. Kohtamäki, M., Parida, V., Oghazi, P., Gebauer, H., Baines, T.: Digital servitization business models in ecosystems: a theory of the firm. J. Bus. Res. **104**, 380–392 (2019). https://doi.org/10.1016/j.jbusres.2019.06.027
11. Paschou, T., Adrodegari, F., Perona, M., Saccani, N.: The digital servitization of manufacturing: a literature review and research agenda, pp. 1–20, September 2017. https://doi.org/10.13140/rg.2.2.13283.14888
12. Vargo, S.L., Lusch, R.F.: Service-dominant logic: continuing the evolution. J. Acad. Mark. Sci. **36**, 1–10 (2008). https://doi.org/10.1007/s11747-007-0069-6
13. Michel, S., Brown, S.W., Gallan, A.S.: An expanded and strategic view of discontinuous innovations: deploying a service-dominant logic. J. Acad. Mark. Sci. **36**, 54–66 (2008). https://doi.org/10.1007/s11747-007-0066-9
14. Guercini, S.: New qualitative research methodologies in management. Manag. Decis. **52**, 662–674 (2014). https://doi.org/10.1108/MD-11-2013-0592
15. Rynes, S., Gephart, R.P.: Qualitative research and the academy of management journal. Acad. Manag. J. **47**, 454–462 (2004)
16. Eisenhardt, K.M., Graebner, M.E.: Qualitative research and the academy of management journal. Acad. Manag. J. **50**, 25–32 (2007). https://doi.org/10.5465/AMJ.2007.24160888
17. Yin, R.K.: Qualitative Research from Start to Finish, 2nd edn. The Guildford Press, New York (2016)
18. Stoll, O., West, S., Rapaccini, M., Barbieri, C., Bonfanti, A., Gombac, A.: Upgrading the Data2Action framework: results deriving from its application in the printing industry. In: Nóvoa, H., Drăgoicea, M., Kühl, N. (eds.) IESS 2020. LNBIP, vol. 377, pp. 273–286. Springer, Cham (2020). https://doi.org/10.1007/978-3-030-38724-2_20
19. West, S., Gaiardelli, P., Rapaccini, M.: Exploring technology-driven service innovation in manufacturing firms through the lens of Service Dominant logic (2018)
20. Osterwalder, A.: Business Model Canvas. academia.edu (2010). Last YP-S published
21. Barbieri, C., West, S., Rapaccini, M., Meierhofer, J.: Are practitioners and literature aligned about digital twin. In: 26th EurOMA Conference Operations Adding Value to Society (2019)
22. Bitner, M.J., Ostrom, A.L., Morgan, F.N.: Service blueprinting: a practical technique for service innovation. Calif. Manag. Rev. **50**, 66–94 (2008)
23. Chandler, J.D., Vargo, S.L.: Contextualization and value-in-context: how context frames exchange. Mark. Theory **11**, 35–49 (2011). https://doi.org/10.1177/1470593110393713
24. Axtle-Ortiz, M.A.: Perceiving the value of intangible assets in context. J. Bus. Res. **66**, 417–424 (2013). https://doi.org/10.1016/j.jbusres.2012.04.008
25. Blomkvist, J.: Representing future situations of service: prototyping in service design (2014)

# Engineering of Data-Driven Service Systems for Smart Living: Application and Challenges

Henrik Kortum[1], Laura Sophie Gravemeier[1(✉)], Novica Zarvic[1],
Thomas Feld[2], and Oliver Thomas[1,3]

[1] German Research Center for Artificial Intelligence (DFKI) GmbH,
Parkstraße 40, 49080 Osnabrück, Germany
{henrik.kortum, laura_sophie.gravemeier, novica.zarvic,
oliver.thomas}@dfki.de
[2] Strategion GmbH, Albert-Einstein-Straße 1, 49076 Osnabrück, Germany
thomas.feld@strategion.de
[3] Chair of Information Management and Information Systems, Osnabrück
University, Parkstraße 40, 49080 Osnabrück, Germany
oliver.thomas@uni-osnabrueck.de

**Abstract.** Service systems in the smart living domain integrate a multitude of
heterogenous data sources and affect the most private area of human lives.
Therefore, particular challenges for service systems engineering arise in terms of
interoperability of Internet-of-Things (IoT)-devices, privacy concerns and creating truly smart value propositions. By applying a promising approach, this
paper examines smart service systems engineering and reveals the potential for
extensions and adaptations of existing methods. A need for the integration of
data science and software engineering approaches as well as a focus on
acceptance, usability and the business perspective within a holistic smart service
systems engineering method is discussed. This enables smart service systems to
reconcile their human-centered and data-driven qualities.

**Keywords:** Smart service · Smart living · Service engineering · Artificial
Intelligence · Human-centered design

## 1 Introduction

Smart service systems are immanently complex and dynamic since they are comprised
of a variety of data sources, human actors with differing roles and IoT-devices that are
capable of learning and reacting appropriately [1, 2]. While some Service Systems
Engineering (SSE) approaches have been proposed [3], no common standard has been
established. However, for smart service systems and especially the smart living
domain, a more concrete data-driven engineering method could make the complexity
more manageable. Such a method should be closely geared to the domain-specific
needs and provide practical guidance. Therefore, this paper aims at clarifying challenges in smart SSE and the smart living domain in particular. For this purpose, the
recombinant SSE [3] method is applied to a concrete use case: the intelligent gatekeeper, an Artificial Intelligence (AI)-based building access management system.

© IFIP International Federation for Information Processing 2020
Published by Springer Nature Switzerland AG 2020
B. Lalic et al. (Eds.): APMS 2020, IFIP AICT 592, pp. 291–298, 2020.
https://doi.org/10.1007/978-3-030-57997-5_34

Based on this preliminary application, challenges of SSE in the smart living domain are identified and appropriate actions as well as necessary properties of a suitable SSE approach for this domain are discussed.

## 2 Background Information

Past service research has focused on *(1)* the shift from a product-centric exchange of goods towards a service-dominant logic [4, 5], *(2)* the enrichment of product offerings with associated services in the form of product-service systems [6], and an *(3)* integrative service-system-approach emphasizes the interrelationship of people, technologies and other resources with services and products [1, 7]. *Smart Service Systems* extend the concept of digital services [8, 9] by incorporating smart products, which enable the real-time capture, processing and analysis of continuously gathered data. This allows for the alignment and management of the service and its features to be pre-emptive, context-aware and dynamic [8–10]. These characteristics are of special importance in the smart living domain, which is addressed in this paper, and need to be considered for SSE.

### 2.1 Concepts from the Smart Living Domain

The terms smart home and smart living are not yet clearly defined in the literature and often used interchangeably. *Smart Homes* are understood as residences equipped with different smart technologies, which have the purpose of providing their users with tailored services [11]. *Smart Living* broadens the smart home concept beyond the home automatization aspect by including further areas, such as smart energy management and health [12, 13] and extends the view to building complexes and entire cities. Smart living thus combines different, often still completely separate areas, with the aim of improving the quality of life [14]. *Smart Living Services* are smart services that refer to use cases in the smart living domain. These services take into account a large number of dynamic parameters, distributed data sources and behavior variants that need to be processed in near real-time. Developing suitable AI-methods will therefore be a key component of smart living services in order to meet user requirements [15, 16].

### 2.2 Smart Service Systems Engineering

SSE broadens the scope of service engineering [17] by methods for the development of singular value propositions towards "designing integrated conglomerates of products, services, and information technology" [3]. While several methods for the development of classical product-service systems exist with perspectives ranging from general to domain-specific [18–21], there is still a lack of systemic approaches focusing on the orchestration of multiple service and product components with smart capabilities [22]. Based on reviewing different approaches for the engineering of value propositions and service systems, recombinant SSE was introduced [3]. Here, known recombination methods are used for service innovation: through dissociation, existing services can be split into singular elements, which have the potential to form novel services by crafting new combinations in the process of association or become part of an existing service via addition. This is not in pursuit of designing singular value propositions but – aligning with the use case at hand – aimed at the development of integrative smart product-service systems. Following a prototyping approach, certain phases are proposed for the analysis, design and transformation of the envisioned service system [3].

# 3 SSE for the Smart Living Domain

## 3.1 Application of Recombinant SSE in the Smart Living Domain

In the following, the method for recombinant SSE [3] will be applied to a concrete service in the smart living domain (see Fig. 1): *the intelligent gatekeeper.*

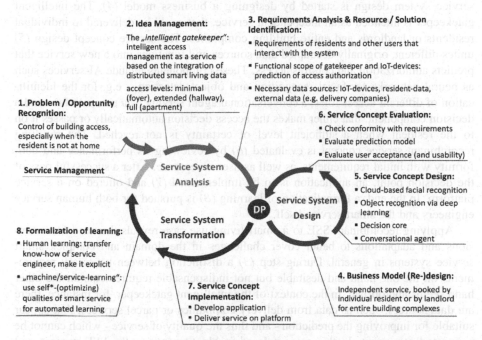

**Fig. 1.** Application of recombinant SSE [3] for the intelligent gatekeeper

When applying the recombinant SSE approach, first an opportunity is identified *(1)*. Given the proliferation of sensors and IoT-devices in smart living contexts, access control of buildings and other assets can be assisted and even automated. On this basis, a more complex idea management *(2)* is initiated. The intelligent gatekeeper is concretized as a smart service concept for access management. A focus group identifies different viable use cases: not only keyless building access for residents, but also emergency access and regular external access for suppliers, parcel carriers and technicians. For example, parcel carriers can be given automatic or regulated access, where the implantation of a user-controlled differentiation of access levels from minimal access to the foyer, extended access to the hallway or full access to the apartment has to be considered. In the following, the use case of regular external building access is further explored. In terms of the requirements analysis and identification of resources and solutions *(3)*, the needs and wants of all involved parties are taken into consideration. This includes residents, landlords and providers of external services like delivery companies. Following this, necessary functions and data sources of the gatekeeper are identified. Besides collecting data from IoT-devices within the building complex, residents should provide data regarding eligible persons for entry and their authorized access levels. On top of that, the integration of data from delivery companies or online retailers is essential to verify the context of a delivery. In addition, modeling current processes of human gatekeepers could prove beneficial for identifying critical steps and possible problem sources. After reaching a satisfying service concept and therefore completing the phase of service system analysis, the process of service system design is started by designing a business model *(4)*. The intelligent gatekeeper is intended as an independent service, that could be delivered to individual residents or landlords and entire building complexes. The service concept design *(5)* unites different, originally decoupled data sources and functions into a new service that predicts authorization and controls access. These components include AI-services such as neural networks for facial recognition and object detection – e.g. for the identification of different access roles, a conversational agent serving as a user interface and a decision component, that either makes the access decision automatically or passes it on to the resident when a sufficient level of certainty is not reached. The resulting recombinant service concept is evaluated *(6)* by reviewing its performance and conformity with initial requirements, as well as user acceptance. After a successful pass of the decision point, an application is to be implemented *(7)* and offered on a service platform. In the end, a formalization of learning *(8)* is pursued for both human service engineers and the smart service itself.

Applying recombinant SSE to a smart living use case reveals the need for extensions and adaptations to better cover challenges in the domain and complex smart service systems in general. During step *(3)* a distinction between necessary requirements on the one hand and desirable but not indispensable requirements on the other hand seems appropriate. In the context of the intelligent gatekeeper, for instance, there are data sources, such as data from delivery companies or parcel services, that appear suitable for improving the prediction - and thus the quality of service - which cannot be connected at present. In this case, it is advisable to continue the SSE process and integrate additional data sources at a later stage. When developing a business model *(4)* an iterative approach has to be emphasized, so that first prototypical design-increments can be implemented without being based on a comprehensive business model. The data-driven design of the service system is mainly handled during step *(5)* of the recombinant SSE approach. However, data analysis and its necessary preceding steps are not considered in detail, even though the parallel use of data science methods, e.g. the CRISP-DM model [23] might be needed. Furthermore, for smart services utilizing machine learning, the formalization of learning *(8)* should include model improvement through continuous evaluation and re-training. On top of that, the recombinant SSE approach defines decision points to assess the present solution. For this assessment, key performance indicators (KPIs) for each decision point would be of practical use. Necessary steps backward whenever decision points are not passed successfully need visual representation in the method. In general, involved products and users in the smart service system should play a more central part in its engineering process.

## 3.2 Challenges for Smart Living Service Systems Engineering

The current smart home landscape is characterized by a multitude of stand-alone solutions [16] only able to handle small tasks, which limits the perceived customer benefit. The goal must therefore be the orchestration of customer-centric services, bundling the functions of individual smart home devices. This combination of previously unrelated resources describes the process of recombinant innovation [24]. A cross-system data exchange, currently hardly possible due to the lack of interoperability [16, 25], is a necessary prerequisite for the implementation of data-driven SSE. This is an even greater obstacle for smart living services, where the boundaries of single smart homes are left behind [26]. Another problem arises from the heterogeneity and multitude of devices and providers: individual service providers usually don't have access to all the data needed to develop meaningful services. The IoT-device manufacturer might only disclose this data to the service providers if they benefit financially. On top of that, the training of machine learning models as a central component of most smart services will be affected by incompatibilities of IoT-devices and heterogeneous user behavior. The recognition of patterns across apartments, e.g. to classify certain activities, will be hindered by variations in data. Thus, the SSE approach should integrate a machine learning perspective. Just as for the intelligent gatekeeper, most smart living use cases are based on personal data [27]. As opposed to industrial contexts, the living space is a private area of human life, where personal behavioral profiles could be gathered that are critical in terms of privacy. Therefore, the circumstances under which residents are willing to share relevant data need to be examined. If consumers are not willing to provide necessary data and thus inhibit the process of value co-creation, the provision of smart living services is hindered. User reservations are expected to be greater where the handling of personal data becomes non-transparent, which is particularly relevant for service providers using cloud applications. Under these circumstances, offering value propositions that are truly beneficial for consumers is crucial. Issues of privacy concerns or negative attitudes might be resolved by taking socio-economic, age-related and personal differences into account. Value-propositions could then be tailored toward customer groups with heterogeneous needs [15] to find a suitable trade-off between service features and privacy requirements. For example, tracking the movement within the apartment might be rejected by most customers, could however be accepted by residents with health impairments in order to ensure emergency care.

## 4 Discussion

Based on the application of recombinant SSE and the consideration of the smart living domain, this chapter discusses implications and opportunities for future SSE methods. A heterogeneous, short-lived infrastructure and the lack of standards are problems not exclusive to smart living but transferable to many domains. This technical complexity asks for compatible solutions and not developing product-specific services. In this light, reusable design patterns could help create sustainable and transferable solutions [28]. While the need for technical interoperability in smart living is already addressed by various platform projects [16], future work has to answer how cooperation between suppliers can be fostered to form unified markets and enable the orchestration of multiple service offerings. In order to react to fast-moving, complex ecosystems, SSE methods should be agile and aimed at fast prototyping. AI models play an important role in realizing characteristics of smart service systems. SSE methods should therefore be combined with data science methods, such as the CRISP-DM model, to create a holistic approach which consistently includes the data-driven idea in all design phases.

In addition to technical complexity, the human factor poses a great challenge for engineering data-driven services. In the smart living domain it is evident that a service can only generate real value by interacting with its users as part of a co-creation process. For this purpose, it is necessary that the user is willing to contribute sensitive, personal data to the service system. SSE should therefore center the user and his requirements throughout the process of service development. The consideration of general conditions such as data security, transparency and explainability appear necessary to increase user acceptance and should be explicitly included in an SSE approach. In addition, smart services should give users agency over the amount and purpose of shared data. This passes on the trade-off between functionality and privacy to the user.

In general, including data science and software engineering methods as well as the business perspective in a consolidated SSE seems to be necessary. Within this integrative approach, user acceptance and usability are crucial to develop truly beneficial value propositions. The use of KPIs for each perspective could support the service systems' continuous improvement. Utilizing indicators of model performance for the data science perspective, profitability and efficiency measures for the business perspective, acceptance and usability scores in relation to the user as well as software engineering performance indicators can quantify progress and give insight during SSE. When developing and enhancing an SSE method for smart services, a simultaneously human-centered and data-driven approach must be pursued. While smart services need to realize the collected data's potential, humans should be in charge of high-level governance.

## 5    Summary and Conclusions

This paper is motivated by challenges in smart living where a complex interplay of IoT-devices, service concepts and stakeholders dominates SSE. In the sense of the system of systems perspective [29], multiple smart products and value propositions supplement each other within the smart service system, which will in turn be connected to other systems. The intelligent gatekeeper exists within the context of a smart home and an even larger scope of smart living, where a heterogenous blend of service systems need to be consolidated. Applying a suitable method for recombinant SSE helps managing a complex process and simultaneously reveals further necessary alterations and perspectives in order to make SSE for smart services data-driven and human-centered.

The focus on these initially conflicting but ultimately symbiotic perspectives during the development of SSE is content of necessary future research on smart service systems.

**Acknowledgements.** This contribution is part of the research project "ForeSight" that aims at advancing the adoption of Smart Living with a consortium of more than 30 partners from science and industry. It was developed in the context of subproject "Smart Service Engineering and Business Models" and is partly funded by the Federal Ministry for Economic Affairs and Energy of the German Government. We would like to thank them for their support.

# References

1. Spohrer, J., Vargo, S.L., Caswell, N., Maglio, P.P.: The service system is the basic abstraction of service science. In: Proceedings of the Annual Hawaii International Conference on System Sciences (2008)
2. Lim, C., Maglio, P.P.: Data-driven understanding of smart service systems through text mining. Serv. Sci. **10**, 154–180 (2018)
3. Beverungen, D., Lüttenberg, H., Wolf, V.: Recombinant service systems engineering. Bus. Inf. Syst. Eng. **60**(5), 377–391 (2018). https://doi.org/10.1007/s12599-018-0526-4
4. Vargo, S.L., Lusch, R.F.: Evolving to a new dominant logic for marketing. J. Mark. **68**, 1–17 (2004)
5. Baines, T.S., et al.: State-of-the-art in product-service systems. Proc. Inst. Mech. Eng. Part B J. Eng. Manuf. **221**, 1543–1552 (2007)
6. Becker, J., Beverungen, D., Knackstedt, R.: Reference models and modeling languages for product-service systems - status-quo and perspectives for further research. In: Proceedings of the Annual Hawaii International Conference on System Sciences (2008)
7. Maglio, P.P., Vargo, S.L., Caswell, N., Spohrer, J.: The service system is the basic abstraction of service science. Inf. Syst. e-Bus. Manag. **7**, 395–406 (2009). https://doi.org/10.1007/s10257-008-0105-1
8. Beverungen, D., Müller, O., Matzner, M., Mendling, J., vom Brocke, J.: Conceptualizing smart service systems. Electron. Mark. **29**(1), 7–18 (2017). https://doi.org/10.1007/s12525-017-0270-5
9. Fischer, M., Heim, D., Hofmann, A., Janiesch, C., Klima, C., Winkelmann, A.: A taxonomy and archetypes of smart services for smart living. Electron Mark. **30**, 131–149 (2020). https://doi.org/10.1007/s12525-019-00384-5
10. Allmendinger, G., Lombreglia, R.: Four strategies for the age of smart services. Harv. Bus. Rev. **83**, 131 (2005)
11. Marikyan, D., Papagiannidis, S., Alamanos, E.: A systematic review of the smart home literature: a user perspective. Technol. Forecast. Soc. Change **138**, 139–154 (2019)
12. Bauer, J., Kettschau, A., Michl, M., Franke, J.: Die intelligente Wohnung als Baustein im Internet der Dinge. In: Erste transdisziplinäre Konferenz zum Thema. Technische Unterstützungssysteme, die die Menschen wirklich wollen, Hamburg (2014)
13. Nikayin, F., De Reuver, M.D.: What motivates small businesses for collective action in smart living industry? J. Small Bus. Enterp. Dev. **22**, 320–336 (2015)
14. Marrone, M., Hammerle, M.: Smart cities: a review and analysis of stakeholders' literature. Bus. Inf. Syst. Eng. **60**(3), 197–213 (2018). https://doi.org/10.1007/s12599-018-0535-3
15. Meyer, S.: Analyse der Mieteranforderungen und Akzeptanz vernetzter Systeme in vermieteten SmartHome-Wohnungen. Sozial und Technikforschung, Berlin im Auftrag von ForeSight, Berlin (2019)

16. Bauer, J., et al.: ForeSight - platform approach for enabling ai-based services for smart living. In: Pagán, J., Mokhtari, M., Aloulou, H., Abdulrazak, B., Cabrera, M.F. (eds.) ICOST 2019. LNCS, vol. 11862, pp. 204–211. Springer, Cham (2019). https://doi.org/10.1007/978-3-030-32785-9_19
17. Leimeister, J.M.: Dienstleistungsengineering und - management. Springer, Heidelberg (2020). https://doi.org/10.1007/978-3-662-59858-0
18. Lindahl, M., Sundin, E., Rönnbäck, A.Ö., Sandström, G.Ö., Östlin, J.: Integrated product and service engineering - the IPSE project. In: Proceedings of the Workshop on Sustainable Consumption Research Exchange (2006)
19. Metzger, D., Niemöller, C., Thomas, O.: Design and demonstration of an engineering method for service support systems. Inf. Syst. e-Bus. Manag. 15(4), 789–823 (2016). https://doi.org/10.1007/s10257-016-0331-x
20. Trevisan, L., Brissaud, D.: Engineering models to support product–service system integrated design. CIRP J. Manuf. Sci. Technol. 15, 3–18 (2016)
21. Andriankaja, H., Boucher, X., Medini, K.: A method to design integrated product-service systems based on the extended functional analysis approach. CIRP J. Manuf. Sci. Technol. 21, 120–139 (2018)
22. Hagen, S., Kammler, F., Thomas, O.: Adapting product-service system methods for the digital era: requirements for smart PSS engineering. In: Hankammer, S., Nielsen, K., Piller, F.T., Schuh, G., Wang, N. (eds.) Customization 4.0. SPBE, pp. 87–99. Springer, Cham (2018). https://doi.org/10.1007/978-3-319-77556-2_6
23. Chapman, P.: The CRISP-DM user guide. In: Brussels SIG Meeting (1999)
24. Cecere, G., Ozman, M.: Innovation, recombination and technological proximity. J. Knowl. Econ. 5(3), 646–667 (2014). https://doi.org/10.1007/s13132-014-0209-4
25. Miori, V., Russo, D., Ferrucci, L.: Interoperability of home automation systems as a critical challenge for IoT. In: 2019 4th International Conference on Computing, Communications and Security, ICCCS 2019. Institute of Electrical and Electronics Engineers Inc. (2019)
26. Bianchini, D., De Antonellis, V., Melchiori, M., Bellagente, P., Rinaldi, S.: Data management challenges for smart living. In: Longo, A., et al. (eds.) IISSC/CN4IoT -2017. LNICST, vol. 189, pp. 131–137. Springer, Cham (2018). https://doi.org/10.1007/978-3-319-67636-4_15
27. Plachkinova, M., Vo, A., Alluhaidan, A.: Emerging trends in smart home security, privacy, and digital forensics. In: AMCIS 2016 Proceedings (2016)
28. Velasco, A.A., McGrory, J., Berry, D.: Patterns within patterns within the smart living experience. In: Conference Papers, p. 288 (2018)
29. Porter, M.E., Heppelmann, J.E.: How smart, connected products are transforming competition. Harv. Bus. Rev. 92, 64–88 (2014)

# The Role of Service Business Models in the Manufacturing of Transition Economies

Slavko Rakic[(✉)] , Nenad Simeunovic , Nenad Medic ,
Marko Pavlovic, and Ugljesa Marjanovic

Faculty of Technical Sciences, University of Novi Sad, Novi Sad, Serbia
slavkorakic@uns.ac.rs

**Abstract.** The use of service in the manufacturing sector is growing in the last decade. Moreover, there are developed and implemented many service business models across the world. Prior studies investigated the role of service business models in the manufacturing sector of developed countries; however, the role of service business models in transition economies (e.g., Serbia) is neglected. This research provides an overview of the use of service business models in the manufacturing sector of the Republic of Serbia from the dataset of 240 manu-facturing firms from the European Manufacturing Survey conducted in 2018. Furthermore, results show a positive impact of service business models on the manufacturing firm's performance.

**Keywords:** Product-service systems · Service business models · Firm performance

## 1 Introduction

Servitization presents a connection between goods, service, and adding value for customers [1]. Throughout history, the idea of Product-Service Systems (PSS) was developed by the servitization process in manufacturing [2, 3]. PSS represents a system of connectedness between products and services, which is developed for increasing customer satisfaction [4]. Moreover, there are many studies, which investigate the service business model in the manufacturing sector of developed countries [5, 6], but this field is neglected in transition economies (e.g., Serbia) [7, 8]. On the other perspective, the Gross Domestic Product (GDP) of the top four economies (i.e., United States of America, China, Japan, Germany) in the world is conducted by services [9]. Also, the manufacturing sector of Serbia had a major share in the GDP creation for 2018, with 14.5% [10]. Unfortunately, the share of service in the GDP of the Republic of Serbia is around 50%, which is 20% under average value in countries from the European Union [9]. Consequently, there is a real need for observation of service business models in the manufacturing sector of Serbia, from both perspectives – theory and practice. The purpose of this paper is to investigate the role of service in the manufacturing sector of developing countries. Moreover, this study provides useful information on which service business models could increase firm performance. With this knowledge, manufacturing firms from developing countries could improve their

Published by Springer Nature Switzerland AG 2020
B. Lalic et al. (Eds.): APMS 2020, IFIP AICT 592, pp. 299–306, 2020.
https://doi.org/10.1007/978-3-030-57997-5_35

position on the market and increase its competitiveness. Research is based on a Serbian dataset from the European Manufacturing Survey (EMS) with a sample of 240 manufacturing firms. Based on the gap in the literature of developing countries, the following research question is proposed:

- RQ: The deployment of service business models will positively affect a firm's performance in the manufacturing sector of the Republic of Serbia?

Figure 1 depicts the proposed research framework based on the theoretical background and research question.

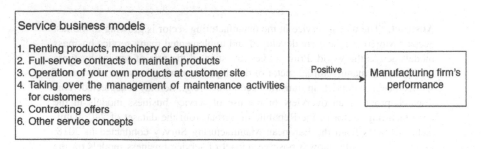

**Fig. 1.** Research framework

## 2 Literature Review

Previous research demonstrated the growing importance of services in the manufacturing sector [2]. Furthermore, studies presented that service business models in manufacturing are developed and mature than in the last decade [3]. PSS business models "refers to the logic of how a firm does business" with the services in the manufacturing sector [11]. A prior study introduced three levels of use of PSS in manufacturing firms: product-oriented, use oriented, and result-oriented [12]. Moreover, these orientations provide an in-depth understanding of their service business models [12]. Customer segmentation and relationships are shown as the key activities in the services business model [13]. Accordingly, authors investigate service business models of *operation of products at customer site/for the customer* and *taking over the management of maintenance activities for the customer to guarantee availability or costs*. Advanced contracts about services offer could increase revenue from service offers [14]. Therefore, the authors introduce the *full-service contracts with a defined scope to maintain products* and *contracting offers (e.g. supply of operating resources such as electricity)*. The service business models which provide *service concepts based on firm performance* are presented as one of the main capabilities for service innovation [15]. Pay per use are service business models that are employed in many firms such as Rolls-Royce Holdings [14]. In order to investigate pay per use services in developing countries authors *introduce renting products, machinery or equipment* as the service business model. Based on the presented literature, EMS consortium [16] considers a list of service business models in manufacturing sectors shown in Fig. 1.

Furthermore, previous research presented that service business models have a different impact on firm performance, according to the use of product innovations [5]. Manufacturing firms with product innovations have a positive long-term effect on firm performance, but without product innovations, they have only short-term positive effects [5]. Additionally, prior research presented that services supporting the clients' actions have a positive and significant relationship with profit growth [17]. Besides, investments in relationships with stakeholders directly contribute to firms' performances and indirectly to firms' value [18]. It could be argued that service business models could construct a positive relationship with customers and long-term positive effects on firm value. On the other hand, the literature presents that service business models do not generate positive effects on firm performance in any case [19]. This occurrence is called the "servitization paradox" [20]. Moreover, Cambridge Service Alliance gives an overview of 75 manufacturing firms from developed countries, which bankrupt with servitization activities [21].

Nevertheless, novel studies show that digital services business models could improve the current situation with the servitization paradox [22]. Moreover, the use of digital services based on Big Data Analysis, Cloud Computing, and Artificial Intelligence are often used in manufacturing firms of developed countries [23]. Unlike from studies from developed countries, previous research from transition economies (e.g., Serbia) measure only the impact of product-related services and digital services on firm performance [8, 24, 25]. However, the role of service-business models in the manufacturing sector of the Republic of Serbia is neglected [25].

# 3 Methodology

Data for this empirical research are collected through European Manufacturing Survey (EMS) with the dataset from the Serbian manufacturing sector (NACE Rev. 2 codes from 10 to 33) from 2018. The EMS is coordinated by the Fraunhofer Institute for Systems and Innovation Research from Germany [16]. The analytical dataset includes 240 observations of manufacturing firms from the Republic of Serbia.

For data visualization and influence between manufacturing sectors, Social Network Analysis (SNA) method is used. SNA is the method of extracting useful information from social structures based on graph theory [26, 27]. Moreover, many studies apply this method in a different type of manufacturing research, such as Industry 4.0 [28], cloud manufacturing [29], logistics [30], collaborative manufacturing [31]. The industry sectors are presented with red circles according to NACE Rev 2.2 classification. While authors labeled service business models with a combination of letters and numbers ranging from BM1 to BM6 according to the research model and they are presented with blue squares in Fig. 2. Furthermore, to analyze the impact of service business models on a manufacturing firm's performance, the authors used linear regression. According to previous research [5, 17], authors employed share of revenue from services as the dependent variable. Moreover, early studies present financial parameters as the measurement for firm performance [17, 32, 33]. Furthermore, Eggert [17] introduce a share of revenue as the ratio for firm performance. Table 1 depicts the sample distribution according to the industry sector.

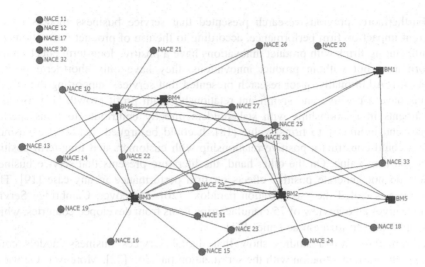

**Fig. 2.** Graph illustrating social network between manufacturing firms and service business models

**Table 1.** Classification of manufacturing sectors according to share on the total sample.

| NACE Rev. 2 | Manufacturing industry | Share on total sample (%) |
| --- | --- | --- |
| 25 | Manufacture of fabricated metal products, except machinery and equipment | 16.7 |
| 10 | Manufacture of food products | 14.4 |
| 22 | Manufacture of rubber and plastic products | 8.6 |
| 28 | Manufacture of machinery and equipment n.e.c. | 8.6 |
| 27 | Manufacture of electrical equipment | 6.9 |
| 14 | Manufacture of wearing apparel | 6.3 |
|  | Other | 38.5 |

## 4 Results and Discussion

Table 2 presents the linear regression model used to test the research question.

In the regression model that tests the research question the overall model was significant, $R^2 = .248$, $F = 3.163$, $p < .001$. Furthermore, results shown that only service business models of *Full-service contracts with a defined scope to maintain products* and *Operation of products at customer site/for the customer* have a positive and significant impact on the share of revenue. As a major finding, our research indicates a significant role in the service business model in the manufacturing sector of the Republic of Serbia.

Additionally, Fig. 2 presents a network between manufacturing sectors according to the use of service business models.

**Table 2.** Results of the impact of service business model on performance

| Service business models | Model parameters |
|---|---|
| Renting products, machinery or equipment | 0.049 |
| Full-service contracts to maintain products | 0.175* |
| Operating of your products at the customer site | 0.279*** |
| Taking over the management of maintenance activities for customer | 0.078 |
| Contracting offers | 0.111 |
| Other service concepts | 0.154 |
| R | 0.461 |
| $R^2$ | 0.213 |
| Sig. | 0.001 |

*Note: ***p < 0,001, *p < 0,05*

Figure 2 shows the results of eigenvector-centrality between manufacturing firms in the two-mode networks. Moreover, eigenvector-centrality shows that:

(1) Manufacture of fabricated metal products, except machinery and equipment,
(2) Manufacture of machinery and equipment n.e.c.,
(3) Manufacture of electrical equipment,
(4) Manufacture of motor vehicles, trailers, and semi-trailers
(5) Manufacture of rubber and plastic products

have the highest relationship between the manufacturing sector of the Republic of Serbia in the use of service business models. Furthermore, the network shows that the *Operation of your own products at customer site/ for the customer (e.g., pay on production)* and *Full-service contracts with a defined scope to maintain your products* are the most used service business models in the manufacturing sector of the Republic of Serbia. The results of the linear regression model are in line with results from SNA analysis. These findings may be useful for production managers. Moreover, this information could provide an in-depth understanding of the role of service business models in manufacturing firms. Thus, production managers can better shape their service business models according to other firms in their industry.

## 5 Conclusion

This research evaluates the use of service business models in the manufacturing sector of the Republic of Serbia. The empirical results indicate a significant and positive impact of service business models on manufacturing firm performance (share of revenue from services). Previous studies showed an overview of servitization in developed countries [34]. Nevertheless, studies presented in the last decade don't study servitization in developing countries [35]. Accordingly, this study provides findings on the example of developing countries. Furthermore, this overview contributes to the existing literature by showing the role of service business models in manufacturing firms in transition economies (e.g., Republic of Serbia). This study confirmed previous findings that presented a revenue model and relationship with the customers as one of the main components in service business models [6]. This study gives a novelty in servitization literature because the authors used a mixed-method approach with SNA and linear regression. Moreover, results show that the most used service business models provide the best effects on firm performance.

This research is limited only to the dataset from one manufacturing industry (i.e., Serbia). There are other transitional economies, which could employ service business models in their manufacturing firms that could be included in future research. Future research should take into consideration different service business models in measuring their impact on manufacturing firm performance. Furthermore, many manufacturing firms are evolving their digital service business models on product offerings so that these business models could be considered in future research.

# References

1. Vandermerwe, S., Rada, J.: Servitization of business: adding value by adding services. Eur. Manag. J. **6**(4) (1988). https://doi.org/10.1016/0263-2373(88)90033-3
2. de Sousa Mendes, G.H., Moro, S.R., Cauchick-Miguel, P.A.: Product-service systems benefits and barriers: an overview of literature review papers. Int. J. Ind. Eng. Manag. **11**(1), 61–70 (2020). https://doi.org/10.24867/IJIEM-2020-1-253
3. Suarez, F.F., Cusumano, M.A., Kahl, S.J.: Services and the business models of product firms: an empirical analysis of the software industry. Manag. Sci. **59**(2), 420–435 (2013)
4. Goedkoop, M.J., van Halen, C.J.G., Te Riele, H.R.M., Rommens, P.J.M.: Product service systems, ecological and economic basics. Report for Dutch ministries environment economic affairs, pp. 1–118 (1999)
5. Visnjic, I., Wiengarten, F., Neely, A.: Only the brave: product innovation, service business model innovation, and their impact on performance. J. Prod. Innov. Manag. **33**(1), 36–52 (2016). https://doi.org/10.1111/jpim.12254
6. Adrodegari, F., Saccani, N.: Business models for the service transformation of industrial firms. Serv. Ind. J. **37**(1), 57–83 (2017). https://doi.org/10.1080/02642069.2017.1289514
7. Lalic, B., Rakic, S., Marjanovic, U.: Use of industry 4.0 and organisational innovation concepts in the Serbian textile and apparel industry. Fibres Text. East. Eur. **27**(3), 10–18 (2019). https://doi.org/10.5604/01.3001.0013.0737
8. Marjanovic, U., Lalic, B., Medic, N., Prester, J., Palcic, I.: Servitization in manufacturing: role of antecedents and firm characteristics. Int. J. Ind. Eng. Manag. **10**(2), 133–144 (2020). https://doi.org/10.24867/IJIEM-2020-2-259
9. World Bank: Services, value added (% of GDP) (2019). https://data.worldbank.org/indicator/NV.SRV.TOTL.ZS
10. Statistical Office of the Republic of Serbia: Gross domestic product (2018). https://www.stat.gov.rs/en-us/vesti/20191001-bruto-domaci-proizvod-2018/
11. Yang, M., Smart, P., Kumar, M., Jolly, M., Evans, S.: Product-service systems business models for circular supply chains. Prod. Plan. Control **29**(6), 498–508 (2018). https://doi.org/10.1080/09537287.2018.1449247
12. Tukker, A.: Eight types of product–service system: eight ways to sustainability? Experiences from SusProNet. Bus. Strategy Environ. **13**(4), 246–260 (2004)
13. Adrodegari, F., Saccani, N.: A maturity model for the servitization of product-centric companies. J. Manuf. Technol. Manag. (2020). https://doi.org/10.1108/jmtm-07-2019-0255

14. Jovanovic, M., Engwall, M., Jerbrant, A.: Matching service offerings and product operations: a key to servitization success: existing conditions, such as product characteristics or market attributes, may determine the success of a move toward servitization. Res.-Technol. Manag. **59**(3), 29–36 (2016). https://doi.org/10.1080/08956308.2016.1161403

15. Kindström, D., Kowalkowski, C.: Service innovation in product-centric firms: a multidimensional business model perspective. J. Bus. Ind. Mark. **29**(2), 96–111 (2014). https://doi.org/10.1108/JBIM-08-2013-0165

16. Jäger, A.: European manufacturing survey. Fraunhofer ISI (2018)

17. Eggert, A., Hogreve, J., Ulaga, W., Muenkhoff, E.: Revenue and profit implications of industrial service strategies. J. Serv. Res. **17**(1), 23–39 (2014). https://doi.org/10.1177/1094670513485823

18. Iazzolino, G., Migliano, G., Dattilo, M.I.: The impact of intellectual capital on firms' characteristics: an empirical analysis on European listed manufacturing companies. Int. J. Ind. Eng. Manag. **10**(3), 219–237 (2019). https://doi.org/10.24867/IJIEM-2019-3-242

19. Lalic, B., Marjanovic, U., Rakic, S., Pavlovic, M., Todorovic, T., Medic, N.: Big data analysis as a digital service: evidence form manufacturing firms. In: Wang, L., Majstorovic, V.D., Mourtzis, D., Carpanzano, E., Moroni, G., Galantucci, L.M. (eds.) Proceedings of 5th International Conference on the Industry 4.0 Model for Advanced Manufacturing. LNME, pp. 263–269. Springer, Cham (2020). https://doi.org/10.1007/978-3-030-46212-3_19

20. Gebauer, H., Fleisch, E., Friedli, T.: Overcoming the service paradox in manufacturing companies. Eur. Manag. J. **23**(1), 14–26 (2005). https://doi.org/10.1016/j.emj.2004.12.006

21. Benedettini, O., Neely, A., Swink, M.: Why do servitized firms fail? A risk-based explanation. Int. J. Oper. Prod. Manag. **35**(6), 946–979 (2015). https://doi.org/10.1108/IJOPM-02-2014-0052

22. Gebauer, H., Fleisch, E., Lamprecht, C., Wortmann, F.: Growth paths for overcoming the digitalization paradox. Bus. Horiz. (2020). https://doi.org/10.1016/j.bushor.2020.01.005

23. Paschou, T., Rapaccini, M., Peters, C., Adrodegari, F., Saccani, N.: Developing a maturity model for digital servitization in manufacturing firms. In: Anisic, Z., Lalic, B., Gracanin, D. (eds.) IJCIEOM 2019. LNMIE, pp. 413–425. Springer, Cham (2020). https://doi.org/10.1007/978-3-030-43616-2_44

24. Medić, N., Anišić, Z., Lalić, B., Marjanović, U., Brezocnik, M.: Hybrid fuzzy multi-attribute decision making model for evaluation of advanced digital technologies in manufacturing: industry 4.0 perspective. Adv. Prod. Eng. Manag. **14**(4), 483–493 (2019). https://doi.org/10.14743/apem2019.4.343

25. Marjanovic, U., Rakic, S., Lalic, B.: Digital servitization: the next "big thing" in manufacturing industries. In: Ameri, F., Stecke, K.E., von Cieminski, G., Kiritsis, D. (eds.) APMS 2019. IAICT, vol. 566, pp. 510–517. Springer, Cham (2019). https://doi.org/10.1007/978-3-030-30000-5_63

26. Sladojevic, S., Anderla, A., Culibrk, D., Stefanovic, D., Lalic, B.: Integer arithmetic approximation of the hog algorithm used for pedestrian detection. Comput. Sci. Inf. Syst. **14**(2), 329–346 (2017). https://doi.org/10.2298/CSIS160229011S

27. Rakic, S., Tasic, N., Marjanovic, U., Softic, S., Lüftenegger, E., Turcin, I.: Student performance on an E-learning platform: mixed method approach. Int. J. Emerg. Technol. Learn. IJET **15**(02), 187–203 (2020). https://doi.org/10.3991/ijet.v15i02.11646

28. Omar, Y.M., Minoufekr, M., Plapper, P.: Lessons from social network analysis to Industry 4.0. Manuf. Lett. **15**, 97–100 (2018). https://doi.org/10.1016/j.mfglet.2017.12.006

29. Škulj, G., Vrabič, R., Butala, P., Sluga, A.: Decentralised network architecture for cloud manufacturing. Int. J. Comput. Integr. Manuf. **30**(4–5), 395–408 (2017). https://doi.org/10.1080/0951192X.2015.1066861

30. Hawe, P., Webster, C., Shiell, A.: A glossary of terms for navigating the field of social network analysis. J. Epidemiol. Community Health **58**(12), 971–975 (2004). https://doi.org/10.1136/jech.2003.014530
31. Leng, J., Jiang, P.: Evaluation across and within collaborative manufacturing networks: a comparison of manufacturers' interactions and attributes. Int. J. Prod. Res. **56**(15), 5131–5146 (2018). https://doi.org/10.1080/00207543.2018.1430903
32. Kastalli, I.V., Van Looy, B.: Servitization: disentangling the impact of service business model innovation on manufacturing firm performance. J. Oper. Manag. **31**(4), 169–180 (2013). https://doi.org/10.1016/j.jom.2013.02.001
33. Kohtamäki, M., Parida, V., Patel, P.C., Gebauer, H.: The relationship between digitalization and servitization: the role of servitization in capturing the financial potential of digitalization. Technol. Forecast. Soc. Change **151**, 119804 (2020). https://doi.org/10.1016/j.techfore.2019.119804
34. Neely, A., Benedetinni, O., Visnjic, I.: The servitization of manufacturing: further evidence. In: 18th European Operations Management Association Conference (2011)
35. Mastrogiacomo, L., Barravecchia, F., Franceschini, F.: A worldwide survey on manufacturing servitization. Int. J. Adv. Manuf. Technol. **103**(9–12), 3927–3942 (2019). https://doi.org/10.1007/s00170-019-03740-z

# System Architecture Analysis with Network Index in MBSE Approach -Application to Smart Interactive Service with Digital Health Modeling-

Toshiya Kaihara, Nobutada Fujii, Daisuke Kokuryo,
and Mizuki Harada(✉)

Graduate School of System Informatics, Kobe University, 1-1 Rokkodai-Cho,
Nada, Kobe, Hyogo 657-8501, Japan
kaihara@kobe-u.ac.jp, nfujii@phoenix.kobe-u.ac.jp,
kokuryo@port.kobe-u.ac.jp,
mizuki@kaede.cs.kobe-u.ac.jp

**Abstract.** In recent years, systems have become large scale and complex due to the development of Internet of Things (IoT). Therefore, it becomes difficult to understand the influence of component specification changes that occur during the system development stage. Thus we focus on Model-Based Systems Engineering (MBSE), which is capable of expressing hierarchical structure and overviewing information. In this paper, we propose a method for analyzing the influence on the smart interactive service with digital health modeling caused by changes in system elements using index of network theory. As a conclusion, we clarified the degree of influence on the whole system caused by changing the specification of each component with using eigenvector centrality, which is one of the network indices.

**Keywords:** Model-Based Systems Engineering (MBSE) · SysML · Network theory · Architecture analysis

## 1 Introduction

In recent years, the realization of Cyber Physical Systems (CPS) accompanying the development of Internet of Things (IoT) technology has increased the number of systems connecting between different fields. As a result, the scale and complexity of the system are even more problematic than before. In the development stage of a system, the specifications of components in the system change due to factors such as changes in the business environment and system environment, mistakes and changes in the definition of requirements. In addition, the specification change influences not only the target component but also the components related to the target. Then, it cause frequent revise processes, which greatly influence the cost and schedule of the whole system

This work was supported by JST-Mirai Program Grant Number JPMJMI17D8, Japan.

development [1]. As a result, it is necessary to analyze the influence by considering the propagation range of the influence due to the change of system specification. In order to consider the range of influence propagation, it is important to clearly understand the relationships and effects in large scale and complex systems. We focused on Model-Based Systems Engineering (MBSE), which has features such as the ability to represent the hierarchical structure of systems and explain multiple causal relationships [2]. MBSE is an approach that focuses on the creation and utilization of models, and achieves the overall optimization of the system, taking into account the diverse values that span multiple disciplines. There is an approach similar to MBSE called Model Driven Architecture (MDA). MDA is an approach to design, development, and implementation in software development using graphical models. And it focuses on the transformation of the model [3]. The common point with MBSE is to use a model. On the other hand, MDA is an approach mainly considered for software, and is not suitable for use at a high abstraction stage including software and hardware. Therefore we use MBSE rather than MDA.

There are related work of change influence analysis. First, there is a scenario-based software architecture modifiability analysis method called Architecture-Level Modifiability Analysis (ALMA) [4]. They define a change scenario for software, rank the impact of the scenario on a five-level scale, and interpret the results to gain strength against changes in the software architecture. Second, there is also an Enterprise Architecture Modifiability Analysis Method (EA-MAM) as a method for scenario-based changeability evaluation for enterprise architectures [5]. This was considered as an adaptation of Software Architecture Analysis Method (SAAM) to enterprise architecture. As for the influence analysis of changes related to model-based systems engineering, change propagation prediction using design structure matrix (DSM) exists [6]. By using DSM, it is possible to identify the relevant component for the case of change. As described above, there are few studies that evaluate the degree of influence of the element change of each element of the system on the system architecture including software and hardware.

In this paper, we propose a method for analyzing the influence on the smart interactive service with digital health modeling caused by changes in system elements using eigenvector centrality, one of the network indices.

## 2  Target System

In this paper, we target the smart interactive service with digital health modeling, one of the projects of JST-Mirai Program [7]. In order to reduce medical and nursing care costs in hyperaging society, it is necessary to provide services to manage health and exercise for each individual. The smart interactive service with digital health modeling aims to realize an innovative multi-side platform type smart interactive service that provides quantification of health degree by modeling health, behavioral change based on disease prediction and individual optimal exercise and lifestyle prescription. Figure 1 shows a conceptual diagram of smart interactive service with digital health modeling.

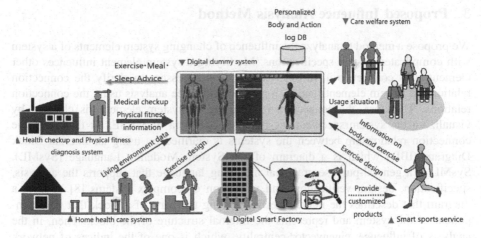

**Fig. 1.** Smart interactive service with digital health modeling

The smart interactive service with digital health modeling consists of the following subsystems.

- **Digital dummy system**
  System that simulates the operation of each system using a digital body model that is completely personalized for each user
- **Home health care system**
  System that maintains and improves user health in households by proposing living fitness designed as exercises with daily activities based on motion simulations of user activities using digital body model
- **Health checkup and Physical fitness diagnosis system**
  System that maintains and improves user health by consulting exercise, meal and sleep based on medical checkup and physical fitness diagnosis informations
- **Care welfare system**
  System that maintains and improves user health by navigating usage settings suitable for user based on simulations of usage situation of nursing care equipment using digital body model
- **Smart sports service system**
  System that maintains and improves user health by advising support suitable for user, such as assisting sports, correcting forms, and training care using digital body model
- **Digital Smart Factory**
  Factory that operates mass customization of various products such as sports products, nursing care equipment, and health-related equipment that are completely customized for each user by using digital body model

In this paper, we target Home health care system, a subsystem of smart interactive service with digital health modeling, for modification influence analysis.

# 3  Proposed Influence Analysis Method

We propose a method to analyze the influence of changing system elements of a system with complicated system specifications. Modifying a system element influences other elements that connect to it. In other words, it is necessary to clarify the connection relations of system elements and then perform influence analysis using the connection relations. Therefore, the connection relationship of system elements is clarified by visualizing the system specifications based on the idea of MBSE. At that time, the connection relationship between the systems is clarified by using an Internal Block Diagram (IBD) which is a diagram of the System Modeling Language (SysML). SysML is a general-purpose graphical modeling language that supports the analysis, specification, design, verification, and validation of complex systems [8]. IBD is a diagram that describes the interconnection among the parts of a block that is a component of the system and represents the internal structure of the block. Then, in the analysis of influence, eigenvector centrality, which is one of the indices of network theory, is used in order to consider an index that can consider the chain of changes such as the change caused by the influences of changes. In order to use the index, the connection relation between the systems shown in IBD is converted into a network. Figure 2 shows a flowchart for influence analysis.

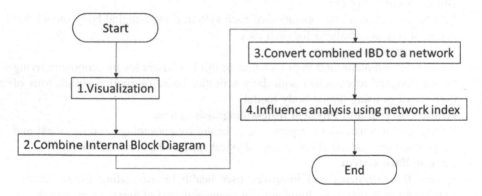

**Fig. 2.** Flowchart for influence analysis

## 3.1  Step1: Visualization

The system specifications of the target system are visualized based on the dual vee model in Systems Engineering using SysML diagrams. Dual vee model is composed of "architecture vee" which represents the decomposition of the target system and "entity vee" which represents the development process of the system elements. It uses Use case diagram, Sequence diagram, Block definition diagram, Internal block diagram and Requirement diagram, which belong to SysML diagrams. As a result, the relationship between the operation scenario of the system and the external system, the required functions, the components that realize the functions, the relationships among the components, and the requirements of the system are clarified.

## 3.2  Step2: Combine Internal Block Diagram

In Sect. 3.1, an IBD is created for each subsystem. In the influence analysis, it is necessary to consider the influence of the change based on the relationship of the whole system. Therefore, the IBD created for each subsystem are combined to create one combined internal block diagram representing the entire target system.

## 3.3  Step3: Convert Combined IBD to a Network

We convert the combined internal block diagram created in Sect. 3.2 to a network structure. The part in the combined internal block diagram is converted into a node in the network, and the connector path is converted into an edge. If there is a connector path to the external system of the target system, the external system is also a node. A part is an element that constitutes a system, and a connecter path is a line that indicates the existence of an interaction between two connected parts. Therefore, the network created in this section represents the relationships between the components of the system.

## 3.4  Step4: Influence Analysis Using Network Index

The network created in Sect. 3.3 is analyzed using network indices. In this paper, we focus on eigenvector centrality among network indices. Since the centrality of eigenvectors takes into account the centrality of adjacent nodes, we believe that it is possible to take into account the chain of changes, such as the secondary changes created by the influence of changes.

**Eigenvector Centrality.** Eigenvector centrality is an index that increases the centrality of nodes connected to nodes of higher degree [9].

$$C_{ev}(i) = \frac{1}{\lambda} \sum_{j=1}^{n} a_{ij} C_{ev}(j) \tag{1}$$

$$C_{ev}^*(i) = \frac{C_{ev}(i)}{\max\{C_{ev}(k)\}, \ (k = 1, 2, \cdots, N)} \tag{2}$$

- $C_{ev}(i)$: Eigenvector centrality of node $i$
- $C_{ev}^*(i)$: Normalized eigenvector centrality of node $i$
- $a_{ij}$: Components of the adjacency matrix $\mathbf{A}$ of the network
- $\lambda$: Maximum eigenvalue of adjacency matrix $\mathbf{A}$
- $n$: Total number of nodes in network $(n = 1, 2, \cdots N)$

## 4   Result of Influence Analysis

According to the flowchart shown in Fig. 2, we analyze the influence of changing the components of the home health care system. In this paper, we show the network obtained in Step3 in Fig. 3 and the result of the influence analysis of Step4 in Table 2.

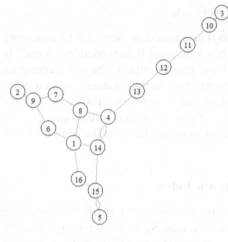

**Fig. 3.**  Network

**Table 1.** Node name

| Label | Name |
|---|---|
| 1 | Terminal |
| 2 | Living environment |
| 3 | User |
| 4 | Database |
| 5 | Digital dummy system |
| 6 | Sensor identification unit |
| 7 | Spatial recognition unit |
| 8 | Furniture detection unit |
| 9 | Near infrared camera |
| 10 | Visible light camera |
| 11 | Skeletal estimation unit |
| 12 | Motion classification unit |
| 13 | Personal identification unit |
| 14 | Calculation exercise unit |
| 15 | Creation exercise unit |
| 16 | Optimisation unit |

Figure 3 is a network obtained by converting the combined internal block diagram of the target system. Table 1 shows the relationship between node labels and names of system components before conversion. Terminal, Living environment, User, Database, Digital dummy system of label 1 to label 5 in Table 1 are external systems of the target system. We calculated the centrality of the eigenvectors of all nodes in the network shown in Fig. 3, and analyzed the influence of changing the components of the system. Table 2 shows the calculation results of eigenvector centrality. The eigenvector centrality is normalized to a maximum value of 1. From Table 2, the node with the highest eigenvector centrality is node 14, which is Calculation exercise unit. The degree of node 14 is 4, which is large in this network. Similarly, the degree of the node connected to node 14 is also 4. From these facts, it was confirmed that the eigenvector centrality became large. Calculation exercise unit (node 14) is a unit that calculates the amount of exercise required to maintain the user's health. If you change the data used to calculate in the Calculation exercise unit, the Database (node 4) which is the data storage must be influenced. Similarly, the Personal identification unit (node 13) and the Motion classification unit (node 12) could be influenced because they are data acquisition units.

A change is also required for the Creation exercise unit (node 15), which uses the calculated amount of exercise. Thus, it is considered that the change of the node having the large eigenvector centrality such as the node 14 has a large influence on other nodes.

**Table 2.** Eigenvector centrality

| Node | 1 | 2 | 3 | 4 | 5 | 6 | 7 | 8 | 9 | 10 | 11 | 12 | 13 | 14 | 15 | 16 |
|---|---|---|---|---|---|---|---|---|---|---|---|---|---|---|---|---|
| Degree | 4 | 2 | 2 | 4 | 2 | 2 | 2 | 3 | 4 | 3 | 2 | 2 | 2 | 4 | 4 | 2 |
| $C_{ev}^*$ | 0.725 | 0.181 | 0.012 | 0.894 | 0.447 | 0.314 | 0.271 | 0.584 | 0.292 | 0.020 | 0.039 | 0.108 | 0.310 | 1.000 | 0.724 | 0.448 |

## 5   Conclusion

In this paper, we analyzed the influence of changing system elements using the network in MBSE for the smart interactive service with digital health modeling. By converting IBD of SysML into a network and using the eigenvector centrality, the degree of influence on the entire system due to component change for each system component could be clarified. As a result, it becomes possible to identify the system elements at an early stage, for which the cost of modification will increase. It can also used to verify the strength of changes to system specifications.

In future work, it is necessary to analyze not only the connection relation of the system but also various factors by using the relation of other diagrams of SysML.

## References

1. Tsumaki, T., Shirogane, J.: Introduction to Requirements Engineering - From Basic Concept to Application of Requirements Engineering. Kindaikagaku Publishing (2009)
2. Suzuki, H.: About the upstream process of systems engineering. SEC J. **12**(4), 26–33 (2017)
3. Object Management Group: Model driven architecture (MDA) MDA guide rev.2.0. OMG document ormsc/2014-06-01 (2014)
4. Bengtsson, P., Lassing, N., Bosch, J., Vliet, H.: Architecture-level modifiability analysis (ALMA). J. Syst. Softw. **69**, 129–147 (2004)
5. Busch, N.R., Zalewski, A.: Enterprise architecture modifiability analysis. In: Kosiuczenko, P., Madeyski, L. (eds.) Towards a Synergistic Combination of Research and Practice in Software Engineering. SCI, vol. 733, pp. 119–134. Springer, Cham (2018). https://doi.org/10.1007/978-3-319-65208-5_9
6. Clarkson, P.J., Simons, C., Eckert, C.: Predicting change propagation in complex design. J. Mech. Des. **126**(5), 788–797 (2004)
7. JST-mirai program smart interactive service with digital health modeling. https://sakamoto21.wixsite.com/mysitehumane. Accessed 27 Mar 2020
8. Sanford, F., Alan, M., Rick, S.: A Practical Guide to SysML. Morgan Kaufmann Publishing, Boston (2009)
9. Masuda, N., Konno, N.: Complex Networks - From Basics to Applications. Kindaika-gaku Publishing (2010)

# The Data-Driven Product-Service Systems Design and Delivery (4DPSS) Methodology

Roberto Sala[1]($\boxtimes$) (iD), Alessandro Bertoni[2] (iD), Fabiana Pirola[1] (iD),
and Giuditta Pezzotta[1] (iD)

[1] Department of Management, Information and Production Engineering,
University of Bergamo, Viale Marconi, 5, 24044 Dalmine, BG, Italy
roberto.sala@unibg.it

[2] Department of Mechanical Engineering, Blekinge Institute of Technology,
37179 Karlskrona, Sweden

**Abstract.** The design of Product-Service Systems (PSS) has been approached from several perspectives like the process, innovation, engineering and operational ones providing, for each one of those, a specific view on the problem. This paper proposes a Data-Driven Product-Service System Design and Delivery (4DPSS) methodology focusing on the collection and exploitation of delivery data to feed the design phase. The logic of the methodology relies on aggregating operational data (collected in the delivery phase) to build a consistent body of knowledge to be exploited in iterative PSS design activities, thanks to better identification of customer needs, and product and service process design issues. This paper presents the 4DPSS methodology at a theoretical level, the implementations of the different methods constituting the methodology are referred to in the text, while its implementation and test as a whole are demanded to future work.

**Keywords:** Product-service system · Data-driven design · Data-driven delivery

## 1 Introduction

Companies approaching the transition towards the offering of Product-Service Systems (PSS) face challenges encompassing the definition of a successful business model, the design of the efficient and sustainable product and service combinations, and the definition of operational procedures supporting the effective PSS delivery. A plethora of methods to support the transition toward PSS has been proposed in the literature. Such methods, despite approaching the challenge from different perspectives, have as a common denominator the capability to correctly capture and fulfil the needs of the customers, and use them to guide the whole PSS design [1] and delivery process [2].

The shift from a traditional product-centric perspective to the PSS perspective has brought researchers and community of practitioners to focus on the multi-disciplinary implications of such a new mindset. The "PSS transition" challenge has been approached from a process perspective, focusing on lean processes and waste reduction in service and maintenance integrating operational data [3, 4], from a PSS innovation perspective, focusing on design space exploration and value and sustainability

© IFIP International Federation for Information Processing 2020
Published by Springer Nature Switzerland AG 2020
B. Lalic et al. (Eds.): APMS 2020, IFIP AICT 592, pp. 314–321, 2020.
https://doi.org/10.1007/978-3-030-57997-5_37

assessment enabled by surrogate modelling [5], and from an engineering practice perspective, focusing on modelling and visualization to address the cognitive limitation of engineers' when making decisions in the presence of multi-disciplinary information [6]. Another factor that should be considered as influencing the transition towards PSS is the digitalization of companies, which can be beneficial in terms of data availability for design and delivery purposes [7]. All of these perspectives have been addressed singularly, without considering their integration. Thus, the paper proposes a methodology that, having roots in methodologies and tools presented in the literature, integrates the different perspectives to improve the PSS design and delivery. In the following sections, the paper introduces the main theoretical foundation of the methodology, explain the research approach, and describe and visualize the details of the proposed methodology.

## 2   Scientific Positioning

### 2.1   Theoretical Foundation

As an answer to need to provide guidance addressing such different dimensions, this paper presents a methodology, named Data-Driven Product-Service Systems Design and Delivery (4DPSS), developed to support the deployment of PSS solutions by creating a virtuous circle of data and information sharing between the PSS design phase and the PSS operations. In particular, the uniqueness of the methodology resides in the adoption of a four-dimensional perspective addressing both the PSS design and the PSS operations during delivery. Figure 1 illustrates such perspectives, that consists in: (1) dealing with the process-oriented view optimizing the design process phases (i.e. the design perspective), (2) assessing the fulfilment of multi-disciplinary and multi-dimensional needs of the different stakeholders, encompassing lifecycle-value and sustainability dimensions (i.e. the value modelling perspective), (3) dealing with the engineering-human dimension of the design activity, introducing the use of boundary objects to nurture discussion and understanding of the multi-disciplinary implications of PSS design decisions (i.e. the PSS visualization perspective), (4) integrating the design process with data from the field, collected during the delivery phase as support for needs identification and effective PSS design (i.e. operational perspective).

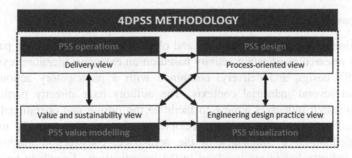

**Fig. 1.**  Four-dimensional perspective of the 4DPSS methodology

Different research contributions address such perspectives one at a time. The proposed methodology builds on some of the main approaches proposed in PSS research, particularly focusing on how the increasing availability of information communication technologies, combined with data science, can enable an effective and efficient PSS deployment. From a process-oriented perspective the PSS Lean Design Methodology (PSSLDM) described in [3], proposes a comprehensive approach to develop PSS along the entire lifecycle, defined by four main phases: the identification of the customer needs, the PSS conceptual design, the PSS design and the monitoring of the PSS performance when on the market. The PSSLDM introduces the adoption of specific KPIs to monitor PSS performances on the market, to facilitate the identification of PSS problems [8].

The iterative use and evolution of value models along the PSS design process have been proposed [5, 6]. Such an iterative process is enabled by the use of surrogate modelling and data mining to explore a wider design space [6]. This triggers design negotiations, forcing the PSS cross-functional team members to "(1) confront each other's perceptions on what the value of a system is, to (2) resolve conflicts where conclusions differ, and to (3) progressively learn what a 'good design' is" [3, p. 18]. To populate such models with reliable information, researchers have investigated how models should be built based on data collected from product operations, historical databases, sensors, and online resources, and how unexpected correlations can be discovered by the use of data mining and machine learning [9]. The effectiveness of using such value models to frontload engineering design activities is strongly related to their effectiveness in enhancing cross-disciplinary and cross-functional collaboration in early design, in other words to their ability to act as effective boundary objects in decision making. This has ultimately led to the proposal of a physical interactive visualization environment and interfaces to enhance the multidisciplinary awareness of decision-making teams when dealing with ill-defined design problems encompassing both a product and service dimensions [6].

From the delivery perspective, the 4DPSS methodology integrates the operational data gatherable during the PSS delivery (e.g. during maintenance services) to improve the recognition of problems at the design or process level. This activity is supported through the implementation of a structured approach, as presented in [4], enhancing the data collection, management and analysis, which are three central aspects for value generation from data [10].

## 2.2 Research Approach

The definition of the research questions and objectives at the basis of the paper is the results of a research clarification activity based on an extensive literature review in the field of PSS design and delivery, combined with a participatory action research approach in several industrial contexts. The authors have directly participated in industrial research initiatives aiming to facilitate the design and operationalization of PSS, as well as contributing to the development of case studies on the topic. Four Swedish medium-large companies in the aerospace, construction machining, and packaging industry have been involved in the investigation of needs in terms of PSS concept design and trade-off, regarding mainly the current PSS design process in terms of phases and data used for decision-making purposes. Similarly, three Italian manufacturing companies, producing bottling and packaging machines, balancing machines and pumps for the Oil&Gas sector, have been engaged to support the definition of the operational characteristics supporting the collection of information to be used later in the design phase. For these interviews, the attention was devoted to the data generated during the maintenance delivery and used for maintenance decision-making (e.g. technician selection and intervention scheduling).

Qualitative data were gathered through semi-structured interviews, workshops and focus groups, initially to compile a comprehensive descriptive analysis of the needs and challenges of PSS design and delivery, and later with the intent to preliminary validate the different steps of the methodology.

# 3   The 4DPSS Methodology

This section deals with the description of the 4DPSS methodology structure. As introduced in Sect. 1, the paper proposed a methodology covering different aspects of the PSS design and delivery, integrating different perspectives and working on different levels, from the process one (definition of the main phases) to the operative one (definition of the sub-phases and the decision-making tools).

The methodology describes how the integration of different perspectives can be concretized by making the best use of the data collection and analysis in the PSS design, implementation and monitoring phases. Figure 1 illustrates visually the four-dimensional perspective adopted by the 4DPSS methodology, encompassing the focus on PSS design, on value modelling for design space exploration and trade-off, visualization for engineering design practice and decision making, and the integration of data from the field.

The integration of the four perspectives described in Fig. 1 results into the Data-Driven Product-Service Systems Design and Delivery (4DPSS) methodology (Fig. 2). Each one of the perspectives contributes in supporting the phases of the 4DPSS by providing different views on the design (e.g. PSS design, PSs value modelling and PSS visualization) and delivery problems (e.g. PSS operations).

The 4DPSS is composed of four consecutive phases: i) Needs identification, ii) Concept generation and design, iii) Implementation and, iv) Monitoring. Each phase can be characterized by one or more sub-phases to carry out specific tasks.

The first phase is characterized by the identification of the needs leading to the conceptualization of the PSS characteristics and components. In particular, needs can stem from three different sources: a) customer, b) product and, c) service. The customers' needs originate from the direct dialogue with the customer and are collected through different means such as interviews, surveys or analysis of customer feedback on social platforms.

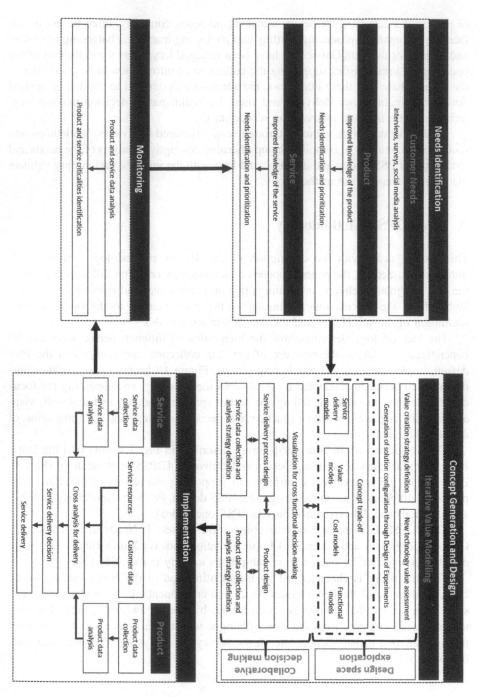

**Fig. 2.** The 4DPSS methodology

Instead, the product and service needs are the results of improved knowledge of the product and service thanks to the data analysis and criticalities identification activities carried out in the Monitoring phase.

The prioritization of the needs is performed according to the criticality of the problem identified, usually associated with the time or cost required to solve the problem.

The second phase, Concept generation and design, uses the information collected in the previous phase as inputs for the creation of PSS concepts. The Value Creation Strategy is updated based on the data collected in the needs identification phase, and it is used to assess the potential value of new technologies. At this stage, a number of potential design modifications of a baseline design are decided and the design space is explored by running simulation models. In case of complex and critical product design, where a set of simulations can take up to days or weeks, such as in aerospace component design, a Design of Experiment setting can be used to generate a large enough set of simulation results to create surrogate models approximating the whole design space (see [6] for more details).

Such information converges in a collaborative decision-making environment, featuring visualization capabilities, where models are used as boundary objects to enhance engineers' awareness decision making. In parallel with the exploration of alternative product design, the PSS design activities are also characterized by the definition of specific data collection and analysis strategies for the service and the product components, as suggested in [4]. The definition of proper data-related strategies is fundamental to enable profitable PSS delivery and to understand what kind of information could be collected and analyzed during the use phase to improve service delivery.

The third phase, Implementation, is focused on the collection of the data from the field supporting the decision-making phase at the operational level. The effectiveness and operational efficiency of this phase are subjected to the decisions made in the previous phase. This phase should support the operational decision making exploiting historical and aggregated data collected during the PSS delivery. Data sources are different and cover both product and service sides, involving also customers as long as their general information is involved. Data collection during PSS use is aimed at creating a comprehensive database supporting the decision-making phase in service delivery [4]. The cross-analysis and the service delivery decision could be supported by tools such as optimization models able to consider product and service information.

The fourth phase, Monitoring, exploits the aggregated data collected in the Implementation phase to extract information concerning the PSS performance to identify problems and criticalities. In particular, analyses are focused both on the product and service-related data. For example, the analysis of maintenance data could be used to identify problems in the product design (e.g. breakdowns and stoppages due to the frequent failure of the same component), or in the way service delivery is designed (e.g. useless activities in the process, wrong tools). Thus, this phase aims to extract information that could be used as input for the following phase, Needs identification. With the proposed approach, needs won't be identified only through the experience of the designer or the direct inputs of the customers, but also through a structured analysis of the data collected from the PSS on the field.

The 4DPSS methodology finds its roots in methodologies and methods discussed in the literature. The innovativeness and the value-added, of the 4DPSS stems from the integration of these methods and methodologies, developed to reduce the wastes along with the PSS design and delivery phases, and improve the effectiveness of the PSS delivery through data-driven design and delivery. Methods and methodologies have been selected due to their synergies concerning the inputs and outputs of each phase in the scope of improving the PSS design and increase the effectiveness of the need identification phase enlarging the pool of sources not only to feedback from customers but considering also the data from the service delivery phase.

## 4   Discussion and Conclusions

The 4DPSS methodology introduces a data-driven decision-making approach exploiting aggregated operational data to identify needs and emerging PSS criticalities from the operational phase and use them in both PSS design and delivery. The 4DPSS methodology shall be seen as a bridge between the literature focusing on PSS development, PSS innovation and design exploration, and PSS visualization for decision-making. The necessity for such a methodology finds its root in the lacks identified through interviews and collaboration with the companies. Specifically, it emerged the incoherence between data collection and exploitation approaches as they are currently carried out in the companies, mainly due to the problems in data management and analysis for design and delivery purposes. For example, some of the interviewed companies had experience with the data-driven design methods part of the "Concept generation and design" phase, but no experience with what is proposed in the "Implementation" phase. Similarly, other companies were experienced with the "Implementation" and "Monitoring" phases but had no experience with the methods proposed in the "Concept generation and design" phase. In this sense, it emerged the interest from companies in introducing digital supports and perspectives able to improve the internal processes related to the design phase and then, improve the ones related to the service delivery [7]. Thus, the research approach allowed identifying the blind spots related to data utilization in the various phases and propose solutions to tackle them through a mix of knowledge taken from literature, company experience and researchers' experience.

The design, implementation, and monitoring of PSS rely on a data-driven approach that works both at the operational and strategic levels and that is aimed at improving, (1) the maintenance delivery through improved operational decisions, (2) the PSS composition through an analysis of the components who fails most frequently and of the service delivery process characteristics, identifying and correcting the most critical activities, (3) the PSS design process by populating value models with a constant flow of information derived from the analysis of the data collected during the PSS operations.

Finally, the proposed methodology should be considered as the results of a prescriptive study and it has not been implemented and validated in its entirety in a real case study. Nevertheless, the methods and approaches proposed in its frame have been singularly validated in the different research initiatives cited in the paper. Future work will focus on the implementation and test of the methodology in a single case study. The validation process of the 4DPSS methodology would require to apply it in its entirety to a single case study to evaluate its effectiveness and the implementation barriers. Given the long time required to collect operational data for new PSS, the identification of needs from operational data will require to identify a company who is already collecting operational data from maintenance in a suitable way, which allows applying the logic part of the 4DPSS.

# References

1. Maussang, N., Zwolinski, P., Brissaud, D.: Product-service system design methodology: from the PSS architecture design to the products specifications. J. Eng. Des. **20**, 349–366 (2009)
2. Tian, G., Zhang, H., Zhou, M., Li, Z.: AHP, gray correlation, and TOPSIS combined approach to green performance evaluation of design alternatives. IEEE Trans. Syst. Man Cybern. Syst. **48**, 1093–1105 (2018)
3. Pezzotta, G., et al.: The product service system lean design methodology (PSSLDM): integrating product and service components along the whole PSS lifecycle. J. Manuf. Technol. Manag. **29**, 1270–1295 (2018)
4. Sala, R., Pirola, F., Dovere, E., Cavalieri, S.: A dual perspective workflow to improve data collection for maintenance delivery: an industrial case study. In: Ameri, F., Stecke, K.E., von Cieminski, G., Kiritsis, D. (eds.) APMS 2019. IAICT, vol. 566, pp. 485–492. Springer, Cham (2019). https://doi.org/10.1007/978-3-030-30000-5_60
5. Bertoni, M., Bertoni, A.: Iterative value models generation in the engineering design process. Des. Sci. 5 (2019)
6. Bertoni, M., Wall, J., Bertoni, A.: Model Driven Decision Arena: an areospace study. In: Proceedings of the International Design Conference, pp. 171–182 (2018)
7. Ardolino, M., Rapaccini, M., Saccani, N., Gaiardelli, P., Crespi, G., Ruggeri, C.: The role of digital technologies for the service transformation of industrial companies. Int. J. Prod. Res. 1–17 (2017)
8. Mourtzis, D., Papatheodorou, A.-M., Fotia, S.: Development of a Key Performance Indicator Assessment Methodology and Software Tool for Product-Service System Evaluation and Decision-Making Support (2018)
9. Bertoni, A., Bertoni, M.: PSS cost engineering: a model-based approach for concept design. CIRP J. Manuf. Sci. Technol. (2018)
10. Zhou, J., Yao, X., Zhang, J.: Big data in wisdom manufacturing for industry 4.0. In: 2017 5th International Conference Enterprise Systems, pp. 107–112 (2017)

# Data-Driven Maintenance Delivery Framework: Test in an Italian Company

Roberto Sala(✉) ⓘ, Fabiana Pirola ⓘ, and Giuditta Pezzotta ⓘ

Department of Management, Information and Production Engineering,
University of Bergamo, Viale Marconi, 5, 24044 Dalmine, BG, Italy
roberto.sala@unibg.it

**Abstract.** Many manufacturing companies are now facing the transition towards the development of a structured service offering in the servitization fashion. Especially in the case of a service like maintenance, the definition of a coherent process, able to collect and exploit in the right way the data from the field for decision-making scopes constitutes the base to run an economically sustainable offering. The authors proposed a structured framework that, considering a dual perspective (asset and service), aims to address this problem and to improve the maintenance decision-making. The paper, using as a case study an Italian manufacturing company willing to accelerate its servitization process, addresses the testing and improvement of the framework. Company A service department's employees were interviewed in the scope of validating the framework and identify improvements for its structure and the related decision-making instruments.

**Keywords:** Maintenance · Decision-making · Product-service systems · Industry 4.0

## 1 Introduction

Manufacturing companies are widening their offering adopting the Product-Service System (PSS) business model, consisting of the joint offering of products and services to satisfy specific customer needs [1]. Researchers [2] expect that the introduction of the Industry 4.0 technologies inside production processes will also improve the service delivery to final customers, creating new revenue streams and solid bonds between users and vendors. Though, expanding the traditional offer with services, e.g. maintenance, does not guarantee additional profits [3], because of a lack of structured processes and tools [4] able to support proper operational decision-making and delivery [5]. Thus, decision-making tools are needed to offer services successfully [6]. Through Industry 4.0, new and unprecedented quantities of data can be exploited for decision-making purposes [7], even if manufacturing companies cannot create value without proper culture or skills [8]. To fill this gap, the authors proposed a framework [9] (Fig. 1) that, considering information from the asset and the field service, can support maintenance delivery as well as the continuous improvement of asset and service design. In this framework, blue rectangles represent phases, while ovals indicate tools and approaches under development (in orange), or already available (in blue) supporting specific steps. The framework is divided into three macro-areas (data collection and analysis, cross-analysis, and improvement) and adopts a dual perspective approach to support decision-makers, considering data from the asset and the maintenance.

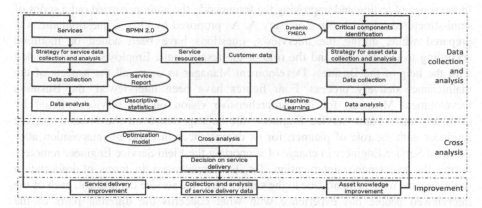

**Fig. 1.** The dual perspective framework for maintenance delivery improvement (Color figure online)

From the service perspective, the framework starts with a deep understanding of the actual service delivery processes that can be achieved by mapping activities, actors and data flows. Based on this, a strategy for the collection and analysis of service-related data should be defined and put in place. The service report [9] is the suggested tool to collect this data in a structured way. Regarding the asset, the first activity is the analysis of the components to identify the critical ones. This activity can be done through dynamic FMECA [10]. Once identified the critical components, the company should define a strategy for asset-related data collection, in terms of which data and how to analyse them. To this purpose, machine learning is suggested to determine the health status of the components. This activity is supported by a framework [11] for the selection of the algorithm based on. The novelty of this framework resides on the cross analysis of service and asset data to support service operations decisions, such as the selection of the maintenance policy and the intervention scheduling. To this purpose, an optimization model has been specifically developed. Once executed, the intervention's data are collected. The analysis of this data along with the asset information would allow the company to identify improvements at both the asset or the service level. The authors are now interested in testing the usefulness of the framework answering to the following research question: *How a data-driven decision-making framework for maintenance delivery should be structured?* This paper reports the results of an interview run in Company A, an Italian manufacturing company producing pumps for the Oil&Gas sector. Traditionally focused on its product-centred portfolio, the company is facing a servitization process, and aims at improving the maintenance service. After a short presentation of the research method (Sect. 2), the paper discusses the interviews (Sect. 3) and the improvements (Sect. 4) before delineating the next steps in the research (Sect. 5).

## 2  Research Method

In the scope of testing and improving the framework, the authors carried out a series of semi-structured interviews in Company A. As proposed by [12], a questionnaire was prepared while, during the interviews, questions have been added or modified according to the situation and the role of the respondents. Employees were selected with the help of the Business Development Manager to cover all the aspects of the maintenance delivery process. Four figures have been interviewed: the Business Development Manager, for its comprehensive vision on the services offered by Company A; a Field Service Engineer, for its experience on the field; a Service Engineer with the role of planner, for its competences in terms of intervention allocation; a Service Engineer in charge of supporting the Field Service Engineer remotely during the maintenance intervention, for its competencies in terms of information retrieving and management. Due to the small size of the service department, each of the interviewed people has experience with what concerns the different parts of the maintenance delivery process even not being specialized in all the tasks. The interviews lasted around 1.5 h each and were divided into two parts. In the first part, the respondents were asked to describe their activities related to the maintenance delivery process as well as the data collected and used to make decisions related to maintenance delivery. This phase of the interview allowed highlighting the current gaps in terms of data usage and sharing, tools and activities in the process. In the second part, based on the problems identified in the first part of the interview, the framework and the related tools were presented, and benefits and barriers related to their implementation were discussed. This phase allowed identifying how the implementation of the framework could improve the current maintenance delivery process in Company A and allowed listing a set of requirements necessary for the correct implementation and exploitation of the framework. All the interviews were recorded and transcribed to favour the following analysis. The authors categorized the information retrieved from the transcripts depending on their relationship with the framework to clarify the list of gaps that emerged during the interviews, identifying commonalities between the ones described by the respondents. In the following section, the authors discuss the results of the interviews.

## 3  Results

### 3.1  Company A

Company A is a manufacturing company headquartered in the northern part of Italy working in the Oil&Gas sector. Originally characterized by a strongly product-oriented portfolio, the company has recently started an internal reorganization introducing a servitization perspective in its business model. Company A has been chosen due to its interest in the development of a proper maintenance offering. The current maintenance delivery process in Company A is structured as follows. The planner receives, via email or phone, a claim from the customers or the vendors on the field. In half of the cases, it is possible to identify the problem immediately and sort it to the right person. In the remaining half, more information from the customer are collected. Once identified the problem, the request is sorted out to a technician on the base of their competencies. First, the owner of the request tries to solve the problem via telephone; otherwise, an intervention is scheduled with the support of the planner. Once the intervention is scheduled, the technician goes to the field and tries to solve the problem. If possible, the problem is solved in a unique session, otherwise, the technician schedules additional sessions. A report, used mainly for the final billing, is written at the end of the intervention. Once the bill is sent to the customer, the report is stored in an internal database.

## 3.2   The Framework

The respondents were asked to discuss how, from their perspective, the framework and the tools could contribute in solving the current gaps considering benefits and barriers connected to its implementation. The interviewees agreed on the structure of the framework and its content. Regarding information sharing among departments, the field service engineer said *"We are trying to restructure the way information is shared between R&D and service department. [...] The framework is aligned with what we are intentioned to create here."* Similarly, the Service Engineer said *"Data sharing would be really useful, even though we need to understand how to handle the situation on the asset side due to the privacy concerns of the customers".* Some suggestions for the improvement were collected from the respondents. Firstly, it is relevant to deepen the asset monitoring aspect since, as the Business Development Manager said, *"The main barrier to the implementation is in the introduction of real-time monitoring technology in the Oil&Gas plants [...]. Moreover, currently, we don't have a historical database to run preventive maintenance".* Also, the Service Engineer stated: *"Something that should be clarified is who is in charge of the infrastructure maintenance. The customer or us? It is something that has to be defined in the contract".* Thus, the framework can be useful to overcome the problem of data collection and exploitation (i.e. for preventive maintenance purposes) and information sharing. In the following, the main areas of the framework are discussed.

**Data Collection and Analysis**
Currently, data collection and analysis in Company A are carried out in an unstructured way. Even when data is collected properly, it is stored in different databases, making more complex the analysis. Information indexing is one of the main problems the company is suffering, resulting in the inability to offer more advanced services, e.g. preventive maintenance. Since service reports are text-intensive and any natural language process algorithms are used, data collected during the interventions are not analysed, preventing the information extraction. The framework proposes the introduction of an approach to data collection and analysis, aimed at favouring the retrieval of useful information when it is needed, e.g. making decisions for maintenance

delivery. As depicted in Fig. 1, first, the company should decide what data and how to collect them. Analyses are performed using techniques able to extract information and determine, for example, the machine health status. Regarding the asset data collection, the Business Development Manager stated *"The problem is that our products are tested for 4 hours internally and then we have no process data. We have no historical database supporting services like preventive maintenance"*. The usefulness of such an approach for data analysis has been confirmed by the Field Service Engineer: *"It would be useful to have unique software to handle data, making it easier the information research"* and by the Planner: *"Service Reports are just stored on an internal database, not analyzed because of the lack of a standard format. The structure that you propose for the data collection and analysis is good. [...] It would be useful to have a historical database of what happened to the machine, it would facilitate the identification of the problem."*

### Cross Analysis

Currently, the Planner is in charge of filtering the requests and assigning each one to the most suitable technician. This work is done only with the calendar, without the support of specific software or a database with information on technicians or past interventions, due to the limited number of service resources available in Company A. When this figure is not available, no one in Company A has the competencies to fully substitute him. To address this issue, the framework proposes an optimization model that integrates the information on service (e.g. list of available interventions, skills required to execute the intervention) and asset (e.g. component health status), the information related to the service department (e.g. resources, schedule, competencies) and to the customer (e.g. location, Service Level Agreement) making it possible to base decisions on historical and field data. The company completely agreed with this. The Planner said: *"It could be very useful to have something like this when I am occupied with other activities. Having data on the usual length of the interventions would facilitate the job for the person who has to substitute me"*.

### Improvement

Currently, due to the lack of a structured approach to data collection and analysis, Company A is not using the data from service reports to identify the main problems in products and services. Information sharing is still limited nowadays, whit only a few meetings organized until now. The framework is built in a continuous improvement fashion. It aims at combining the data from maintenance intervention reports and from the asset (if available) as sources of information to identify improvements both for the service (e.g. service reengineering) and asset sides. This approach to data management is considered beneficial, since, as reported by the Field Service Engineer, *"Recently we had a meeting with the R&D to discuss the problems related to the machine design and the ones related to the incorrect machine usage. [...] The identification of these problems could be one mean to reduce the frequency of these failures and shorten the resolution time"*.

## 3.3   The Framework Tools

The interviews were useful to collect suggestions for the improvement of the tools as described in the following.

**Dynamic FMECA**

Currently, Company A is not keeping track of a structured way of the most problematic components in its machines. This, and the lack of analysis on maintenance interventions, complicates the definition of proper maintenance plans for the machines. The Service Engineer stated: *"I think it is a good idea to update it with new information."* However, he suggested: *"Something that I would improve is the way components Risk Priority Number (RPN) is updated. A component that frequently fails not necessarily fails because it has a problem. The failure could be caused by another component's wrong behavior. So, I would suggest introducing a Root Cause Analysis (RCA) to identify the failure cause of a component and be sure to update the right RPN."*

**Service Report**

Data collection is critical for Company A, especially during maintenance delivery. The proposal of a standard format for service reports was interesting for the respondents, who appreciated its structure and gave suggestions for improvement. For example, the Field Service Engineer said: *"I think it has a good format. Depending on the type of service, a report like this could be really useful. [...] It would be good to have the chance to print only parts of the report depending on the situation and necessity."* Similarly, for the planner *"The logic behind the report structure is good. It would be useful to specify the day of execution for each activity. It would help in understanding their length and impact. It would also be useful to have the length of the single activities, to know what are the simplest ones and the most complex. Sometimes the customer is the cause of a considerable amount of time lost during the intervention because he is not ready. It would be useful to have information like this".* To facilitate the filling phase for the technicians, the structure of the asset identified through the dynamic FMECA (e.g. groups, subgroups, and components) is replicated into the service report.

**Optimization Model**

As emerged from the interviews, there is only one Planner in charge of the scheduling; the other employees do not have enough competencies to substitute him. Thus, the proposal of a tool able to support the task allocation, in conjunction with the idea of creating a competencies database and collect data on the intervention length, was approved by the Planner, who stated: *"The logic behind the model is very similar to the one I use. Sometimes there are contingency factors causing delays to the original schedule. It would be useful to have something that also considers that information."*

# 4   Summary of Improvements

The interviews allowed to validate the structure of the framework and collect information on further improvements. The results are depicted in Fig. 2.

The general structure of the framework received positive feedback and, thus, no modification was necessary. Despite this, suggestions were collected about its implementation barriers (e.g. contractual clauses) and the benefits.

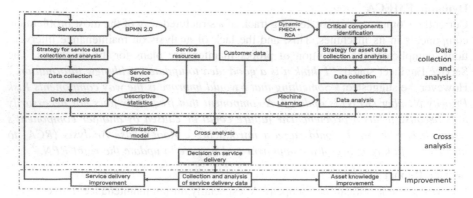

**Fig. 2.** The updated framework

The main suggestions for improvement were focused on the internal structure of the tools rather than on the structure of the framework. For example, the RCA has been integrated into the process of updating the RPN in the dynamic FMECA. Other changes have been integrated into the tools despite being not visible in the framework since related to their internal structure. Specifically, the Service Report has been modified in the structure considering the possibility to specify time losses causes and add more information related to the activities performed.

## 5   Conclusions

The establishment of a structured approach to data collection and analysis is necessary if companies want to offer an efficient maintenance service to their customers. In the scope of validating and improving the framework proposed in [9], this work describes the results of a set of semi-structured interviews run in an Italian manufacturing company operating in the Oil&Gas sector which is currently facing a servitization process. The data collected during the interview demonstrated the possible benefits achievable from the implementation of the framework and of the related instruments. Despite this, also suggestions on improvement actions related to both the framework and the instruments were collected (e.g. joint use of dynamic FMECA and RCA to improve the RPN update). The main contribution of the framework resides in the approach that considers the asset and service perspectives jointly with a focus on operational decision-making. As discussed in [5] and [6] there is a lack of approaches focused to maintenance decision-making at the operational level. The framework wants to cover this gap working at the operative level (e.g. technician selection and scheduling, maintenance typology) and on the strategic and tactical levels through the improvement phase (e.g. redesign of asset or service, re-definition of maintenance policies, spare parts management). Barriers related to the acceptance of the new approach should be discussed to explain the employees its benefits and make them participate in the company improvement journey [8]. Suggestions will be used to improve the whole framework and new interviews will be run to validate the framework and the instruments.

**Acknowledgments.** This research is supported by the French region AURA, via the international project 'Collaboration Franco-italienne pour une industrialisation durable des territoires'. The paper was inspired by the activity of the ASAP SMF, an industry-academia community aimed at developing knowledge and innovation in product-services and service management (www.asapsmf.org).

# References

1. Baines, T., Ziaee, A., Bustinza, O.F., Guang, V., Baldwin, J., Ridgway, K.: Servitization: revisiting the state-of-the-art and research priorities. Int. J. Oper. Prod. Manag. 1–28 (2016)
2. Ardolino, M., Rapaccini, M., Saccani, N., Gaiardelli, P., Crespi, G., Ruggeri, C.: The role of digital technologies for the service transformation of industrial companies. Int. J. Prod. Res. 1–17 (2017)
3. Gebauer, H., Fleisch, E., Friedli, T.: Overcoming the service paradox in manufacturing companies. Eur. Manag. J. **23**, 14–26 (2005)
4. Dahmani, S., Boucher, X., Peillon, S., Besombes, B.: A reliability diagnosis to support servitization decision-making process. J. Manuf. Technol. Manag. **27**, 502–534 (2016)
5. Gopalakrishnan, M., Bokrantz, J., Ylipää, T., Skoogh, A.: Planning of maintenance activities - a current state mapping in industry. Procedia CIRP **30**, 480–485 (2015)
6. Ruiz, P.P., Foguem, B.K., Grabot, B.: Generating knowledge in maintenance from experience feedback. Knowl.-Based Syst. **68**, 4–20 (2014)
7. Qi, Q., Tao, F.: Digital twin and big data towards smart manufacturing and industry 4.0: 360 degree comparison. IEEE Access **6**, 3585–3593 (2018)
8. Vassakis, K., Petrakis, E., Kopanakis, I.: Big data analytics: applications, prospects and challenges. In: Skourletopoulos, G., Mastorakis, G., Mavromoustakis, C.X., Dobre, C., Pallis, E. (eds.) Mobile Big Data. LNDECT, vol. 10, pp. 3–20. Springer, Cham (2018). https://doi.org/10.1007/978-3-319-67925-9_1
9. Sala, R., Pirola, F., Dovere, E., Cavalieri, S.: A dual perspective workflow to improve data collection for maintenance delivery: an industrial case study. In: Ameri, F., Stecke, K.E., von Cieminski, G., Kiritsis, D. (eds.) APMS 2019. IAICT, vol. 566, pp. 485–492. Springer, Cham (2019). https://doi.org/10.1007/978-3-030-30000-5_60
10. Colli, M., Sala, R., Pirola, F., Pinto, R., Cavalieri, S., Wæhrens, B.V.: Implementing a dynamic FMECA in the digital transformation era. IFAC-PapersOnLine **52**, 755–760 (2019)
11. Sala, R., Zambetti, M., Pirola, F., Pinto, R.: How to select a suitable machine learning algorithm: a feature-based, scope-oriented selection framework. In: Proceedings of the Summer School Francesco Turco, pp. 87–93 (2018)
12. Robson, C.: Real World Research: A Resource for Social Scientists and Practitioner-Researchers (2002)

# Towards a Comparative Data Value Assessment Framework for Smart Product Service Systems

Lennard Holst[(⊠)], Volker Stich, Günther Schuh, and Jana Frank

Institute for Industrial Management at RWTH Aachen University,
Campus-Boulevard 55, 52074 Aachen, Germany
lennard.holst@fir.rwth-aachen.de

**Abstract.** This paper contributes to an assessment framework for valuing data as an asset. Particularly industrial manufacturers developing and delivering Smart Product Service Systems (Smart PSS) are comprehensively depended on the business value derived by processing data. However, there is a lack in a framework for capturing and comparing the Smart PSS data value with the purpose of increasing the accountability of data initiatives. Therefore a qualitative data value assessment approach was developed and specified on Smart PSS, based on an industrial case study research.

**Keywords:** Data value · Data value assessment · Smart Product Service Systems · Case study research

## 1 Introduction

The most valuable companies these days regarding their market capitalization are internet and technology companies with almost no physical assets [1]. This determines the high intangible value and the deep economic impact of intangible assets, especially of data in the digital age. Throughout this paper we use the terms "data" and "value" as generic contiguous terms, comprising the assumption that data (symbols and signs) generate a contextual monetary value added within specific use cases. This assumption is conform to the DIKW pyramid, which describes data as the basis for obtaining information, knowledge and wisdom [2]. The access to data and the ability to use it properly are becoming key competitive factors and justify the need for the digital transformation of established business models [3]. For many years manufacturing companies are trying to adapt their established transactional business models being able to offer integrated solutions for their customers [4, 5]. In the early stages manufacturers designed and delivered services accompanying their products, creating so-called Product Service Systems (PSS) [6]. With the rise of digital technologies, falling costs for sensors and their connection via increasingly powerful, internet-capable networks known as the industrial internet of things (IIoT) these PSS are transforming to Smart Product Service Systems (Smart PSS) [7]. In Smart PSS data generation and evaluation are the binding components and the main drivers for engineering smart services and new digital business models around a smart product that delivers constant usage data.

B. Lalic et al. (Eds.): APMS 2020, IFIP AICT 592, pp. 330–337, 2020.
https://doi.org/10.1007/978-3-030-57997-5_39

Whereas in the old transactional business, data was mainly generated within the operational process and stored in intra-divisional silos or historically grown IT system landscapes [3], smart products are delivering an entirely new data-based insight into the usage phase. Thus smart products enable manufacturers to understand their customers' behavior and needs almost in real-time, offering the chance for a comprehensive customer-centric business orientation [3, 8]. However, observing Smart PSS manufacturing firms at every scale, there is an *overarching difficulty deriving, measuring and communicating value from specific digital initiatives* [9]. This leads to a two-sided problem: From an internal perspective, investments in digital product or service initiatives like e.g. the retro-fitting of products in operation with sensor technology are intensively discussed, whether it should be given away for free instead of being sold with a margin [10]. From a market perspective this might lead to the assumption that Smart PSS manufacturing firms are highly underrated. According to the current valuation and balancing standards, physical assets and future cash flow are valued in particular. Realized or potential values from data, that also need to be considered as assets [11], are attributed indirectly, if at all [12]. Although various methods for data valuation have been discussed in research for several years, none has yet established itself as a practicable market standard. Therefore this research focuses on a data value assessment framework for Business-to-Business (B2B) Smart PSS manufacturing firms, as they are already today particularly dependent on the business value added by data generation and usage.

## 2 State of Research

### 2.1 Smart Product Service Systems

The integration of ICT technology in PSS can be described as a digital transformation towards Smart PSS, enabled by embedded micro-devices, software technology and internet-capable interfaces [13]. Smart PSS are defined by (1) a high degree of autonomy and real-time reactivity, (2) a strong customer-centricity, (3) the interchangeability during the operation phase, (4) innovative business models and (5) interconnected components [13, 14]. All of the given attributes either generate or inevitably depend on a constant stream of usage data. An example of the Smart PSS complexity (Fig. 1) and its immanent data value is the offering of printing machines as a subscription. Due to usage and benchmark data, the industrial manufacturer is able to

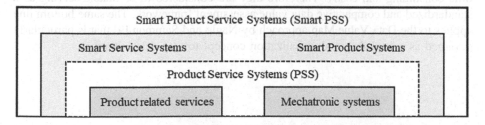

**Fig. 1.** Composition of Smart PSS based on [13, 14]

offer guaranteed performance increases in a pay-per-print model, growing its business along with the customer [8].

- Product related services: *e.g. traditional maintenance services*
- Mechatronic systems: *e.g. car brake systems*
- Product Service Systems: *e.g. installation and implementation of a machine*
- Smart Service Systems: *e.g. machine learning supported spare part orders*
- Smart Product Systems: *e.g. distance control assistants (cyber-physical)*
- Smart Product Service Systems: *e.g. printing machines, sold as a subscription*

## 2.2    Data Valuation Frameworks

In research literature, there are various approaches to the valuation of data, uniformly demanding the consideration of data as an asset with a disclosable business value. The following given research approaches are shortly described and assessed for their practicability in the research context: Already in 1999 Moody and Walsh [11] considered data, respectively information derived from data, as a "valuable but unvalued asset". Based on *7 laws of information* they examined the three major asset paradigms in accounting theory: *Cost* (Or Historical Cost), *Market* (Or Current Cash Equivalent) and *Utility* (or Present Value). Although describing the pros and cons of the paradigms in the context of data valuation and developing general principles and ideas for valuing data, they claim themselves for not providing a complete methodology. Brennan et al. [15] developed and executed a general, survey based approach for a data value assessment. The proposed data value dimensions *Operational Impact, Dataset Replacement Costs, Competitive Advantage, Regulatory Risk* and *Timeliness* served as an important orientation, but are not sufficient for a practicable procedural method solving the issue of deriving and communicating data value on a comprehensive practice-oriented level.

Laney [16] developed an indicator approach for valuing data, proposing three foundational measures *Intrinsic Value, Business Value* and *Performance Value* and three financial measures *Cost Value, Market Value* and *Economic Value*. Formulas are presented that can be used to calculate the respective values. However, the work does not provide any information on how the formulas can be quantified in practice. Within this paper the definition of the "contextual monetary value added by data" is based on the preliminary work of Zechmann and Möller [17] who developed a comprehensive usage based valuation approach, even applied in Smart PSS related case studies. However, already Moody and Walsh [11] stated that usage based valuation methods are time consuming and costly. Therefore they are considered to be unable serving as a standardized and comparative data value assessment framework. The same bottom line applies to the Data Value Map approach by Nagle and Sammon [9] that is particularly designed as a workshop and visualization concept to map data initiatives.

# 3 Research Process

In order to develop a data valuation assessment for Smart PSS manufacturing firms a case-based research method according to Eisenhardt was chosen [18]. The method allows a practice-oriented research process consisting of eight steps, listed in Table 1 [8, 18].

**Table 1.** Case study process and implemented research activities, based on [18]

| Process step | Proposed activities | Implementation during the research process |
|---|---|---|
| I. Getting started | Defining the research question | What are the Smart PSS requirements regarding data valuation and its assessment process? |
| II. Selecting cases | Specifying population | Examination of 7 Smart PSS manufacturers with a diverse product and (digital) service portfolio in the branches printing, milling, laser cutting, medical devices, industrial tools and sensor technology |
| III. Crafting instruments | Combining data collection methods | Telephone and in-person interviews, workshops, internal documents, secondary source documents |
| IV. Entering the field | Overlapping data collection and analysis | Two iterations: 1. Deriving conceptual requirements 2. Transferring results into an assessment framework |
| V. Analyzing data | Within-case analysis | Ranking present data streams to their perceived value (context of use, data quality, monetizing effects) |
| VI. Shaping hypothesis | Iterative tabulation of evidence | Conclusion after 2 iterations: using 6 main requirements and a 6 step assessment approach |
| VII. Enfolding literature | Comparison with conflicting literature | Comparison with existing data valuation approaches and Smart PSS literature presented in Sect. 2.2 |
| VIII. Reaching closure | Theoretical saturation | Observed flattening curve regarding knowledge gain |

# 4 Results

## 4.1 Requirements Derived from the Case Studies

The following Table 2 ranks the requirements towards a data valuation method from the first iteration of the case study research, according to the utility analysis carried out with the Smart PSS manufacturing firms:

**Table 2.** Requirements towards a data valuation method

| Ranked requirements | Description of the specific requirement |
|---|---|
| $R_1$: Data catalogue | A data catalogue with ex-ante formulated valuable data streams |
| $R_2$: Data quality and attributes | Data quality requirements are depended on the use case and should be linked upfront with certain tolerance levels for specific use cases |
| $R_3$: Standardization possibilities | Since individual, usage based valuations are not suitable for standardization, a context/use case catalogue needs to be given ex-ante<br>A neutral third party entity is needed serving as auditor |
| $R_4$: Hybrid valuation method | The data value captured needs to integrate the dimensions *monetization* and *indirect, usage value add* |
| $R_5$: Customer insights* | Customer Insights are considered to have the highest impact on the present and future business value in Smart PSS |
| $R_6$: Qualifying date | When the data value assessment is carried out there needs to be a strong separation between the present and the future data value |

\* Definition of Customer Insights: If customer data from various sources is systematically collected, interpreted and used to derive findings for adapting business processes.

## 4.2    General Framework for a Data Value Assessment

The following Table 3 presents the assessment steps that were developed in the second iteration of the case study analysis. The fundamentals were the requirements derived from the first iteration. The assessment steps are therefore linked to the requirements, depicted in Sect. 4.1 and marked by $R_x$. In addition, the responsibility column differentiates between the responsible authorities, since Smart PSS manufacturing firms are unable to perform a comparative data value assessment on their own. Over and above that there was a demand for a neutral third party serving as a data value auditor (cf. $R_3$).

**Table 3.** General assessment steps for a data valuation framework

| Assessment step | Description of the assessment step | Responsibility |
|---|---|---|
| $S^1$: Setting up the data catalogue ($R_1$, $R_3$, $R_5$) | Initially determining the most valuable data streams for the considered system | Third party/Auditor |
| $S^2$: Setting up the use case catalogue ($R_3$, $R_4$) | Defining a catalogue of relevant use cases for the data streams set up in $S^1$ | Third party/Auditor |
| $S^3$: Establishing data attributes and threshold values ($R_2$) | Setting up data attributes, linking them to use cases Data quality threshold values for the specific use cases | Third party/Auditor |
| $S^4$: Preliminary assessment and software tool support ($R_6$) | Smart PSS manufacturing firms must be guided through a semi-automatic assessment of $S^1$–$S^3$ | Smart PSS manufacturing firms |
| $S^5$: Applying a hybrid data value method ($R_4$, $R_6$) | Combining cost, market and usage based valuation approaches in a standardized data value method | Third party/Auditor |
| $S^6$: Final assessment ($R_3$) | Assessment for examination of the results from $S^{4,5}$ | Third party + Smart PSS |

### 4.3   Smart PSS Specified Framework for a Data Value Assessment

This section specifies the derived assessment steps $S^1$–$S^3$ of Sect. 4.2 on Smart PSS, which was an additional part of the second iteration within the case study research process. The assessment steps $S^4$–$S^6$ are prospect to further development stages and research.

$S^1$ **Setting Up the Data Catalogue:** Within the case study research process Customer Insights were determined to be the most important, data driven value provider to Smart PSS. Therefore a data catalogue for Customer Insights was developed, initially gathering the most valuable data streams with the option of implementing a data stream significance ranking and readjustments in case of further examinations. The data catalogue was structured alongside 4 customer journey phases: (1) *Attention phase* with customer-specific data streams like store visits, website visits, conversations with chatbots, call center activities, social media appearances etc. (2) *Acquisition phase* with data streams like customer master data, sales data from field representatives, sales data from digital distribution channels etc. (3) *Usage phase* with data streams like usage and performance data in real-time or discrete, data from self-service customer portals, data from service tickets, data from remote service diagnostics, complaint data, data from blogs and forums etc. (4) *Loyalty phase* with data streams like the purchase history, internal and external market research data etc.

$S^2$ **Setting Up the Use Case Catalogue:** The data streams from $S^1$ will be individually linked to fixed use cases. This step is the essential part of the data value generation chain to derive a contextual monetary value added. In order to develop a practicable use case catalogue an aggregated level for providing the use cases was chosen. A longlist was set up, including various use cases like *increasing customer satisfaction, deriving marketing measures, submitting individual customer offers, ensuring that customer use offerings correctly and receive a return on investment, quantify the perceived customer value, improve the customer experience, adjust pricing schemes, increase performance of services and products, direct selling of the data asset etc.*

$S^3$ **Establishing Data Attributes and Threshold Values:** For each use case an initial, standardized set of data attributes needs to be classified. Threshold indicators are implemented within the attribute *data quality criteria* and can be checked in the preliminary assessment $S^4$ by the Smart PSS manufacturing firm. The attributes are *Monetization* (direct, indirect, realized in the past vs. in a 3 year forecast with a probability of occurrence), *Data Sourcing* (costs for sourcing and mining the data), *Data Processing and Analysis* (need and ability for analysis, occurred costs), *Data Quality Criteria* (accuracy, quantity, transfer rate, vulnerability, accessibility etc., each criteria with an initial threshold value) *importance for business model and decisions* (criticality, importance for decision makers).

$S^4$ **Preliminary Assessment with Tool Support:** To deliver the assessment steps $S^1$–$S^3$ in a practicable setting a semi-automated tool, including the data catalogue and use cases as well as the possibility to link data attributes is currently being developed.

$S^5$ **Applying a Hybrid Data Valuation:** The hybrid data valuation approach consists of linking the three accountability paradigms (cf. Sect. 2.2) via $S^1$–$S^3$ and is currently being examined with business valuation and auditing experts.

$S^6$ **Final Assessment:** Within the final assessment, the information given by the Smart PSS manufacturing firm in $S^4$ on the current abilities to realize present and future data value need to be audited. To standardize the assessment steps in order to thrive a comparative Smart PSS individual data value a VDI guideline will be set up in the research project *Future Data Assets*.

## 5  Conclusion and Further Research

Based on the derived requirements towards a comparative data value assessment, determined during the practice-oriented case study research process, a new and more standardized data value assessment logic was developed and initially specified on Smart PSS. Therefore existing data valuation methods can serve as fundamentals but are suggested to be put in a more comparative framework by default, respectively fixed data streams, data usage and data attribute dimensions. A third party accompanied data value assessment can help Smart PSS to better evaluate and communicate the benefits of digital initiatives with the various internal and external stakeholders.

Concerning the presented research status further research activities regarding an easy-to-use software tool support and an integrated hybrid data valuation method need to be carried out to complete and standardize a comparative assessment framework. Expanding the perspective, the topic data valuation was found to be relatively uncharted. Thus, forcing researchers and practitioners to work closely together on practicable solutions to communicate the date value internally and externally, since the data economy across all branches is rapidly gaining momentum and business models are becoming increasingly depended on the value derived by data usage.

**Acknowledgement.** The research and development project *Future Data Assets* that forms the basis for this report is funded within the scope of the 'Smart Data Economy' technology program run by the German Federal Ministry for Economic Affairs and Energy (BMWi) and is managed by the DLR project management agency. The authors are responsible for the content of this publication.

## References

1. PwC: Global Top 100 companies by market capitalisation (2019). https://www.pwc.com/gx/en/audit-services/publications/assets/global-top-100-companies-2019.pdf. Accessed 1 Apr 2020
2. Rowley, J.: The wisdom hierarchy: representations of the DIKW hierarchy. J. Inf. Sci. (2007). https://doi.org/10.1177/0165551506070706
3. Porter, M., Heppelmann, J.: How smart, connected products are transforming companies. Harvard Bus. Rev. **93**(10), 97–114 (2015). https://hbr.org/2015/10/how-smart-connected-products-are-transforming-companies

4. Kowalkowski, C., Gebauer, H., Oliva, R.: Service growth in product firms: past, present, and future. Ind. Mark. Manage. (2017). https://doi.org/10.1016/j.indmarman.2016.10.015
5. Oliva, R., Kallenberg, R.: Managing the transition from products to services. Int. J. Serv. Ind. Manag. (2003). https://doi.org/10.1108/09564230310474138
6. van Halen, C., Vezzoli, C., Wimmer, R.: Methodology for product service system innovation. How to develop clean, clever and competitive strategies in companies (2005). ISBN 90 232 4143 6
7. Chowdhury, S., Haftor, D., Pashkevich, N.: Smart product-service systems (Smart PSS) in industrial firms: a literature review. Procedia CIRP **73**, 26–31 (2018)
8. Schuh, G., Frank, J., Jussen, P., Rix, C., Harland, T.: Monetizing Industry 4.0: design principles for subscription business in the manufacturing industry. In: 2019 IEEE International Conference on Engineering, Technology and Innovation (ICE/ITMC), Valbonne Sophia-Antipolis, France, 17–19 June 2019, pp. 1–9. IEEE (2019)
9. Nagle, T., Sammon, D.: The data value map: a framework for developing shared understanding on data initiatives. In: Proceedings of the 25th European Conference on Information Systems (ECIS), pp. 1439–1452 (2017)
10. Möller, D.P.F.: Guide to Computing Fundamentals in Cyber-Physical Systems: Concepts, Design Methods, and Applications. CCN. Springer, Cham (2016). https://doi.org/10.1007/978-3-319-25178-3
11. Moody, D.L., Walsh, P.: Measuring the value of information - an asset valuation approach. In: Proceedings of the Seventh European Conference on Information Systems, ECIS 1999, Copenhagen (1999)
12. Leatherberry, T., Mears, R.: Data as an Asset: Balancing the Data Ecosystem (2010). http://mitiq.mit.edu/IQIS/Documents/CDOIQS_201077/Papers/03_09_4C-1.pdf. Accessed 3 Apr 2020
13. Abramovici, M., Göbel, J.C., Neges, M.: Smart engineering as enabler for the 4th industrial revolution. In: Fathi, M. (ed.) Integrated Systems: Innovations and Applications, pp. 163–170. Springer, Cham (2015). https://doi.org/10.1007/978-3-319-15898-3_10
14. Kuhlenkötter, B., et al.: Coping with the challenges of engineering smart product service systems - demands for research infrastructure. In: DS 87-3 Proceedings of the 21st International Conference on Engineering Design (ICED 2017). Product, Services and Systems Design, Vancouver, Canada, 21–25 August 2017, vol. 3 (2017)
15. Brennan, R., Attard, J., Petkov, P., Nagle, T., Helfert, M.: Exploring data value assessment: a survey method and investigation of the perceived relative importance of data value dimensions. In: 21st International Conference on Information Systems (ICEIS) (2019). https://doi.org/10.5220/0007723402000207
16. Laney, D.B.: Infonomics. Taylor and Francis, London (2017)
17. Zechmann, A., Möller, K.: Finanzielle Bewertung von Daten als Vermögenswerte. CON (2016). https://doi.org/10.15358/0935-0381-2016-10-558
18. Eisenhardt, K.M.: Building theories from case study research. Acad. Manag. Rev. **14**, 532 (1989)

# Impact of Platform Openness on Ecosystems and Value Streams in Platform-Based PSS Exemplified Using RAMI 4.0

Michela Zambetti[1]($\boxtimes$), Till Blüher[2], Giuditta Pezzotta[1],
Konrad Exner[3], Roberto Pinto[1], and Rainer Stark[2,3]

[1] Department of Management, Information and Production Engineering,
University of Bergamo, Dalmine, Italy
{michela.zambetti,giuditta.pezzotta,
roberto.pinto}@unibg.it
[2] Technische Universität Berlin, Pascalstraße 8-9, 10587 Berlin, Germany
{till.blueher,rainer.stark}@tu-berlin.de
[3] Fraunhofer Institute for Production Systems and Design Technology,
Pascalstraße 8-9, 10587 Berlin, Germany
konrad.exner@ipk.fraunhofer.de

**Abstract.** With the digital revolution, the IoT (Internet of Things) platform approach emerges as a supportive way for the implementation of IoT platform-based Product-Service System (PSS) offerings. To exploit the full potential of the platform economy and considering the complexity of the multitude of different actors in all the lifecycle stages, value creation architectures for digital and service platforms are one of the critical points to develop. In this work, the concept of Platform-based PSS is presented, and for representation purposes, an extension of the RAMI 4.0 reference model has been proposed. Specifically, the ecosystem perspective has been added to RAMI 4.0, to approach Platform-based PSS with a multi-actor lens. Moreover, the different contributions and benefits of the main participants in Platform-based PSS are illustrated. Therefore, three different scenarios have been exemplified with the proposed RAMI 4.0 extension relating the actors' possibilities to contribute to Platform-based PSS to the level of openness of a platform.

**Keywords:** Platform-based PSS · Platform openness · RAMI 4.0 · Ecosystem

## 1 Introduction

Digital solutions and communication technologies transform the daily life of people and companies "as fundamental as that caused by the industrial revolution" [1]. However, with the rise of digital platforms and platform economies like e.g. Siemens MindSphere, or the Amazon Market Place, a wide spectrum of challenges regarding the infrastructures and the society have to be addressed reaching from wireless network and computing capabilities, to data ownership and security. While meeting these challenges, the European Commission Data Strategy strives to utilize industrial and commercial data in a common infrastructure to cope with the massive data growth as well as to utilize the

© IFIP International Federation for Information Processing 2020
Published by Springer Nature Switzerland AG 2020
B. Lalic et al. (Eds.): APMS 2020, IFIP AICT 592, pp. 338–346, 2020.
https://doi.org/10.1007/978-3-030-57997-5_40

business potential [2]. One of the key themes for research and development is the value creation for Industry 4.0 and digital servitization that represent two of the most impacted field from platform approach. This includes the understanding of networks with dynamic value creation along the lifecycle as well as value creation models and data valuation. Furthermore, value creation architectures for digital and service platforms [3] are a main development need. Companies show confidence and invest resources to support their servitization approaches with platform-centered architectures with a trend into modularization [4]. Thus, companies use a multitude of technologies and layers (structural tiers of the architecture) to complement their specific infrastructure and business needs [5]. Platform openness is among the decisions that goes to impact the ecosystem configuration and enable different value creation mechanisms, both to the end-users, the platform and to the application developers [6]. Additionally, the design of the architecture for each individual ecosystems have to be determined. Both aspects, the openness and the architecture of the ecosystems are not fully understood in industry and research, and thus, represent the research gap for the paper. Moreover, openness is the only viable approach to achieve the European strategy. Therefore, the main objective of this paper is to analyze the different layers of platforms in correlation with interdependent value creation, providing an exemplification on how an open reference architecture model for Industry 4.0 supports this scope. The paper is structured as follow: Sect. 2 presents Platform-based PSS and platform openness. Industry 4.0 reference models are also presented, since they represent the starting point adopted to describe the Platform-based PSS. Section 3 explains the extension of RAMI 4.0 to address the Platform-based PSS representation while Sect. 4 exemplifies the ecosystem perspective of the architecture with three different scenarios. Section 5 concludes the work.

## 2 Background

### 2.1 Platform-Based PSS and Platform Openess

This paper defines a Platform-based PSS as a Product Service System (PSS) that relies on an IoT Platform Technology stack for their operations. This stack can be represented by three essential elements (Fig. 1): (i) Constrained Devices, (ii) Gateways and (iii) IoT cloud Platform [7]. *Constrained Devices* are the physical end-products of a PSS generating data via sensors or interacting with the environment via actuators. Often these products are limited in their IoT capability, due to, for example, constraints in power supply, computing capacity, etc. The *Gateway* helps overcoming the limitations of constrained devices, e.g. by bridging network latencies or compensate for incompatibilities between different end-devices. Many gateways are able to execute software code and manage an IoT Ecosystem even when a connection to the IoT Cloud platform is lost (edge computing). Finally, the *IoT Cloud platform* is the backend, typically implemented via a cloud infrastructure due to cost and scalability reasons. It executes various digital services, e.g. device and data management, thus enabling smart services. In addition, platform-based PSS differ in the type of data and information that is evaluated in the context of providing offers. Depending on the use case, different types of data are the main asset of individual digital services, such as business data for business forecasts, operational data for predictive maintenance, user data for customization, etc. [8]. Depending on the data, different analysis goals are also pursued and different algorithms are required to achieve these goals. Until now, data management in platform-based PSS and according industrial applications, especially in light of the digital twin, is not yet common practice for many companies [9]. In addition to the value-added by digital services, additional value can be created on platforms through network effects. These synergies arise when several end devices or stakeholders are networked on a platform and create added value, e.g. because more data is exchanged, more services are provided or more devices are networked [10]. In accordance, platform-based PSS derive competitive edge from an intelligent formation of their ecosystem. Therefore, the design of an ecosystem is essential to optimize the value co-creation of different stakeholders in platform-based PSS [11].

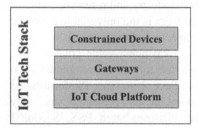

**Fig. 1.** Representation of IoT Technology Stack

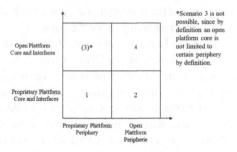

**Fig. 2.** Scenarios of Openness of Platform Core and Periphery (own representation)

The openness of a platform plays an essential role here, as it determines who can participate in a platform and thus what design options an ecosystem has. According to [12], platforms consist of a *platform core, interfaces,* and *periphery* that connects to the platform core through interfaces. While the platform core provides the basic functionality for the ecosystem to operate and is relatively stable over time, the periphery can change and is flexible. The openness of the platform core indicates the extent to which a company has proprietary access to the platform core and thus control over the entire platform and its design [13]. Figure 2 presents scenarios depending on the level of openness of a platform core and it's periphery. Today, many companies are striving to develop a proprietary, that should either extend the benefits of their own products exclusively (*Scenario 1*) or, in addition, integrate products and services from third parties (*Scenario 2*). From an economic point of view, platforms according to Scenario 2 gain considerable market power through hyper-scaling and winner-takes-all situation [14]. However, this situation allows a single company to control large markets, distort competition and possibly exclude third parties from these markets [15]. Open platforms with an open platform core do not focus on capturing profits, but enable broad participation (*Scenario 4*) and are therefore often politically driven.

## 2.2    Industry 4.0 Reference Models

To enable cross-domain interaction, facilitate system interoperability and compatibility and boosting the growth of IoT, different attempts have been made in the definition of a reference model and architecture for IoT systems [16]. Different working groups have proposed reference architectures and the two more discussed are the IIRA and the RAMI 4.0. IIRA model was developed in 2015 by the IIC and it is continually under refinement. It is composed of four viewpoints: business, usage, functional and implementation. It is based on the ISO/IEC/IEEE 42010:2011 standard. In this view, each layer represents a perspective of the stakeholder and decisions from a higher-level viewpoint guide, influence and impose requirements on the viewpoints below. The RAMI 4.0 architecture was developed in Germany in 2015 by BITCOM, VDMA and ZWEI. It takes its roots in the Smart Grid Architecture Model and results as a three-dimensional structure that describes all critical component of Industry 4.0. The three axes are: The Hierarchy Levels, Life Cycle & Value Stream and Layers. The hierarchy level represents the production system, following IEC 62264 and IEC 61512 standards, adding the product and the connected world levels. They represent, respectively, the fact that Industry 4.0. needs smarter and connectable products and the resulting network of enterprises. The lifecycle and Value stream differentiates between the concept of a component and its creation. The vertical axis is composed of six layers, which represent the IT structure of an Industry 4.0 components.

# 3    RAMI 4.0 for the Representation of Platform-Based PSS

The reference models mentioned before are domain-specific for different industries; nevertheless, as presented in some previous research and considering some limitations, the architectures are also suited to represent Platform-based PSS [18, 19]. Indeed, it deploys Industry 4.0 scenarios outside the typical industrial environment [17].

In order to decide which model is the most appropriate for the scope, existing comparisons of reference models have been considered [20, 21] evaluating their views and viewpoints, as summarized in Table 1. Overall, it is possible to state that the RAMI model better fits the Platform-based PSS since it includes specific views, like the Asset and Lifecycle, that are crucial for the description of a general PSS. Additionally, some other works have made successful attempts to describe Platform-based PSS using RAMI 4.0. For example, [17] stated that the underlying design of the ICT platform of such services presents many interesting similarities with RAMI 4.0 and was able to describe a real case within the architecture. Bousdekis et al., designed a predictive maintenance architecture according to RAMI 4.0 and developed a unified predictive maintenance platform that can be exactly seen as one Platform-based PSS [18].

In this work, an evolution of the RAMI4.0 is proposed, considering two changes to include important aspects of Platform-based PSS. The first one is an extension of the "Life Cycle & Value stream" dimension, adding the "Usage" phase. This extension is opportune because the actual service provision and data flow only start from the beginning of the Mid of Life phase. The second change is made on the Hierarchy levels, between "Enterprise" and "Connected world". "Enterprise" level refers to

**Table 1.** IIRA (1) and RAMI 4.0 (2) Viewpoint comparison (adapted from [19, 20])

|     | Business | Usage | Functional | Information | Communication system | System | Asset | Lifecycle/Value chain | Hierarchy |
|-----|----------|-------|------------|-------------|----------------------|--------|-------|----------------------|-----------|
| (1) | X | X | X | | | X | | | |
| (2) | X | | X | X | X | X | X | X | X |

factories where IT systems, like ERP, CRM, SCM, PLM are deployed and monitored on a usual basis. This level directly comes from the IEC 62264 standard, referring to the highest level of the smart factory. The "connected world" level is the representation of the possible integration of information between all different manufactures and IT systems. Authors included the "Ecosystem" between the two hierarchy levels, in order to describe the actors that participate in the value creation process and contribute to the Platform-based PSS. The ecosystem perspective has been recognized as a fundamental of Platform-based PSS, that should be approached with a holistic, multi-actor lens considering the collaboration of interfirm and intrafirm actors [21] (Fig. 3).

## 4   Exemplification of Ecosystem in Platform-Based PSS

Intending to represent the contribution of different actors in Platform-based PSS, we selected three examples, based on [23], that matched the scenarios described in

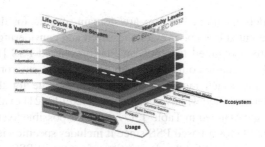

**Fig. 3.** Platform-based PSS RAMI 4.0 architecture (adapted from [22])

Sect. 2.2 and exemplified them with the introduced "RAMI 4.0" architecture. Three main actors have been selected, that are: the product/service provider, the IoT platform provider, and the end-customer. The focus of the exemplification in this paper lies on the usage phase (*Life Cycle & Value Stream*) and *Layers*, so other *Hierarchy Levels* than the Ecosystem level and other life cycle phases other than the proposed Usage phase are excluded for simplification purposes. Figure 4, 5, 6 show the contribution and the benefits of the three actors in the three scenarios on the RAMI 4.0 layers, with grey and white boxes respectively. The three scenarios are the following:

- *Scenario 1*: ThyssenKrupp Max [24]. ThyssenKrupp is a manufacturing company of inter alia elevators. They developed a proprietary platform to deploy predictive maintenance services. The platform core provides data analytics services for failure predictions. Only ThyssenKrupp elevators can connect to the platform core, i.e. it is not open to third parties.

- *Scenario 2:* Siemens MindSphere [25]. The platform core enables data handling and usage of industrial apps that are operated through a scalable MindSphere backend architecture. The platform core is based on open source technology but is modified and controlled by Siemens due to proprietary interfaces. The platform allows connecting any third-party device.
- *Scenario 4:* Gaia-X [26]. Gaia-X is a German initiative designed to provide a safe and sovereign European data infrastructure. The idea of an open platform core is that it is not proprietary. Third parties cannot be excluded from using open platform cores. Consequently, any periphery can also use the platform.

From the representation, it is possible to see how different contributions to value streams are directly impacted by different levels of platform "openness". In Scenario 1, the main value stream is related to the customer data flow that comes from products enabling the provision of more efficient maintenance services and greater elevator uptime for the customer. Those data linked to the provision of analytic capabilities enable also ThyssenKrupp to enhance its asset and reshape business models. Indeed, operational data feed predictive maintenance algorithms and enable service field operators to better schedule required activities and perform them proactively. Other data may also feed the system, e.g. users may directly provide feedbacks during the elevators utilization. This creates a direct link between end-users and the manufacturer and enables the latter to enhance customers' final experience.

| | Ecosystem level – Usage phase | | |
| --- | --- | --- | --- |
| | **P/S - Thyssenkrupp** | **IoT ( Microsoft)** | **End Customer** |
| **Business** | New business models may be deployed Revenues from products, service, platform subscription | Indirect revenue from product sales or PSS contracts | Reduction in down time and improvement in efficiency Risk- sharing |
| **Functional** | Customer data used to enhance functionality and provide proactive services Product and customer visibility | Platform uptime Computing power Back-end functionality | Access new functionality and services |
| **Information** | Different internal unit can access data ( service tec., R&D, Marketing) Know-how help to transform data into information | Algorithms | Access information on one asset typology |
| **Communic.** | Proprietary gateway (Controller Box) | Elevators are connected to the Azure IoT Hub via MQTT | |
| **Integration** | Creation of a large data base to run analytics | Tens of thousands of Thyssenkrupp's elevators are integrated | |
| **Asset** | Customer data used to enhance product and service Elevators | Server infrastructure | Elevator operational data; service data; user feedbacks |

**Fig. 4.** Scenario 1. Ecosystem level on RAMI4.0 for Platform-based PSS (own elaboration)

Ecosystem level – Usage phase

| | P/S providers | IoT (MindShpere) | End Customer |
|---|---|---|---|
| Business | New business models may be deployed Revenues from products, service, platform subscription Use 3rd party services to enlarge portfolio | Royalties from third party P/S providers Network effect | Improvements where services are provided Risk- sharing Network effect |
| Functional | Customer data used to enhance functionality and provide proactive services Product and customer visibility | Selected actors are available to develop functionalities; documentation and developer forums, marketplace Back-end functionality | Access various functionality and services |
| Information | Multiple function can access insight generated by algorithms Know-how help to transform data into information | Several ML and IA analytics tools Platform governance | Access information and insight at system levels |
| Communic. | | Flexibility due to different protocols Mindconnect, proprietary solution uses open communication protocols such as HTTPS, MQTT or PC UA | |
| Integration | Multiple devices can be managed through a single IoT platform; multiple information and system may be integrated | SDKs and APIs for third-party developers | System level vision may be reached |
| Asset | Customer data used to enhance product(s) and service(s) Products | MindSphere can be run on different infrastructure (e.g. AWS, Azure) | Product data |

**Fig. 5.** Scenario 2. Ecosystem level on RAMI4.0 for Platform-based PSS (own elaboration)

In Scenario 2, the functionality of the platform core is handling data and making MindSphere apps available for various applications. The openness to third-party providers also allows for synergy effects as external developers provide apps and other manufacturers connect their devices to the MindSphere platform core, enabling the creation of multiple application at the functional layer both to the end customer and to the P/S provider(s) and network effects at the business layer. MindSphere enables multiple data flows to be integrated together, not only from devices but also for different customer databases and enterprise systems such as ERP, MES and SCADA enabling the possibility to create system-level visions and whole context analysis. In Scenario 3, additional value creation mechanisms are made possible since data are available for all users and a common standard for data and communication interoperability is defined enhancing trust. All users may contribute to the creation of a single database that can be accessed by all participants as well as to the development of new applications and functionalities that contribute to the creation of networks effect, even at the information layer. Even the technical details are still under development, information is accessible to every stakeholder although ownership remains with the data creator. Since the platform core is not proprietary, no profit can be captured so that no data-driven business model for the IoT platform provider is possible.

## 5  Limitations and Outlook

The presented work is a first approach to exemplifying platform-based PSS with an enhanced RAMI 4.0 reference model. The adoption of a three-dimensional model reflected difficulties in the representation of all axis at the same time and even using

| | P/S providers | IoT (Gaia X) | End Customer |
|---|---|---|---|
| | **Ecosystem level – Usage phase** | | |
| Business | New business models may be deployed Revenues from products, service, platform subscription Use 3rd party services to enlarge portfolio Network effect | Network effect | Improvements where services are provided Risk- sharing; Network effect |
| Functional | Customer data used to enhance functionality and provide proactive services Product and customer visibility | Everyone may deploy new platform functionality Back-end functionality | Access various functionality and services Possibility to develop its own application |
| Information | Access insight generated by algorithms Different cloud services may access data Synergies of competences – Network effect Know-how help to transform data into information | Network effect Platform governance | Access information and insight Network effect |
| Communic. | Different cloud services easily interact | Single and shared standard for sharing data | |
| Integration | Multiple devices can be managed through a single IoT platform Customer data used to enhance product(s) and service(s) | Open data infrastructure Structure for data interoperability | End to end visibility may be reached |
| Asset | Products, data | Server infrastructure | Product data |

**Fig. 6.** Scenario 3. Ecosystem level on RAMI4.0 for Platform-based PSS (own elaboration)

only a partial model to exemplify the three scenarios, connecting the layers and describing all relations between them was difficult. Further studies may consider the integration of all the other axis into one single representation, the diversification of different value creations paradigm and formalization of relations between value creation processes of different stakeholders. Furthermore, value creation is closely linked to the development of business models, which are addressed by the layer "Business". However, there is no defined notation for representation of a sophisticated business model logic as, e.g. monetary flows, risk distribution and legal aspects should also be presentable. This limitation should be addressed in the future to take full advantage of RAMI 4.0 for business model development. Finally, in our example, a deeper analysis into the overall structure, starting from the data typology, to the duration of storing, aggregation and analytics to be applied to deploy applications.

# References

1. European Commission: Shaping Europe's digital future (2020)
2. European Commission: The European data strategy (2020)
3. Ngo, L., O'Cass, A.: Value creation architecture and engineering: a business model encompassing the firm-customer dyad. Eur. Bus. Rev. **22**, 496–514 (2010)
4. Frank, A., Dalenogare, L., Ayala, N.: Industry 4.0 technologies: implementation patterns in manufacturing companies. Int. J. Prod. Econ. **210**, 15–26 (2019)
5. Cenamor, J., Rönnberg Sjödin, D., Parida, V.: Adopting a platform approach in servitization: leveraging the value of digitalization. Int. J. Prod. Econ. **192**, 54–65 (2017)
6. Menon, K., Kärkkäinen, H., Wuest, T.: Industrial internet platform provider and end-user perceptions of platform openness impacts. Ind. Innov. **27**, 363–389 (2020)
7. Eclipse Foundation: The Three Software Stacks Required for IoT Architectures (2016)

8. Tomiyama, T., Lutters, E., Stark, R., Abramovici, M.: Development capabilities for smart products. CIRP Ann. **68**, 727–750 (2019)
9. Stark, R., Fresemann, C., Lindow, K.: Development and operation of digital twins for technical systems and services. CIRP Ann. **68**(1), 129–132 (2019)
10. Farrell, J., Klemperer, P.: Coordination and lock-in: competition with switching costs and network effects. In: Handbook of Industrial Organization, vol. 3, pp. 1967–2072 (2017)
11. Eloranta, V., Turunen, T.: Platforms in service-driven manufacturing: leveraging complexity by connecting, sharing, and integrating. Ind. Mark. Manage. **55**, 178–186 (2016)
12. Abdelkafi, N., Raasch, C., Roth, A., Srinivasan, R.: Multi-sided platforms. Electron. Mark. **29**(4), 553–559 (2019). https://doi.org/10.1007/s12525-019-00385-4
13. Parker, G., Van Alstyne, M.: Innovation, openness and platform control. Manage. Sci. **64**(7), 3015–3032 (2017)
14. Eisenmann, T.R.: Managing proprietary and shared platforms. Calif. Manage. Rev. **50**(4), 31–53 (2008)
15. Acatech: Smart Service Welt - Abschlussbericht (2015)
16. Bui, N., Walewski, J.W.: Internet of Things – Architecture Final architectural reference model for the IoT v3 (2013)
17. Corradi, A., et al.: Smart appliances and RAMI 4.0: management and servitization of ice cream machines. IEEE Trans. Ind. Inform. **15**, 1007–1016 (2019)
18. Bousdekis, A., Lepenioti, K., Ntalaperas, D., Vergeti, D., Apostolou, D., Boursinos, V.: A RAMI 4.0 view of predictive maintenance: Software architecture, platform and case study in steel industry. In: Proper, H., Stirna, J. (eds.) Advanced Information Systems Engineering Workshops. CAiSE 2019, vol. 349. Springer, Cham (2019). https://doi.org/10.1007/978-3-030-20948-3_9
19. Weyrich, M., Ebert, C.: Reference architectures for the Internet of Things. IEEE Softw. **33**(1), 112–116 (2016)
20. Exploitation and dissemination of the results: Diversity European Project (2017)
21. Sklyar, A., Kowalkowski, C., Tronvoll, B., Sörhammar, D.: Organizing for digital servitization: a service ecosystem perspective. J. Bus. Res. **104**, 450–460 (2019)
22. Alignment Report for Reference Architectural Model for Industrie 4.0/ Intelligent Manufacturing System Architecture. Sino-German Industrie 4.0/Intelligent Manufacturing Standardisation Sub-Working Group, 23 April 2018
23. Exner, K., Smolka, E., Blüher, T., Stark, R.: A method to design Smart Services based on information categorization of industrial use cases. Procedia CIRP **83**, 77–82 (2019)
24. Thyssenkrupp: Max-The game-changing predictive maintenance service for elevators (2019)
25. Siemens: MindSphere: enabling the world's industries to drive their digital transformations (2018)
26. German Federal Government: Project GAIA-X (2019)

# Industry 4.0 Data-Related Technologies and Servitization: A Systematic Literature Review

Michela Zambetti[✉], Roberto Pinto, and Giuditta Pezzotta

Department of Management, Information and Production Engineering,
University of Bergamo, Dalmine, Italy
{michela.zambetti, roberto.pinto,
giuditta.pezzotta}@unibg.it

**Abstract.** The advancements and adoption of digital technologies enable manufacturers to approach intelligent production and reach a higher level of automation in the wave of Industry 4.0. Even though manufacturing is at the center of this industrial revolution, the impact of digital technologies is more far-reaching: indeed, one of the biggest growth potentials is recognized in the paradigm shift from a traditional product orientation to the provision of bundled solutions. Particularly the possibility to gather and analyze data has been recognized as a key enabler for the advancement of the product-services offering. In this view, the research presented a systematic literature review exploring the state of the art considering on one side the newest technologies related to data and digitalization and on the other side servitization, aiming at understanding the point of contact between them. Four different perspectives have been identified and discussed and possible research directions have been proposed.

**Keywords:** Digital technologies · Servitization · Industry 4.0 · Data-driven

## 1 Introduction

Originated in Germany in 2011, the term "Industry 4.0" refers to a paradigm shift from automated manufacturing toward an intelligent manufacturing concept, enabled by the adoption of digital technologies and associated paradigms, to achieve a higher level of operational efficiency and productivity, as well as a higher level of automation [1]. Even though manufacturing is the main focus, the impact of Industry 4.0's technologies is more far-reaching: indeed, one of the most significant growth potentials is recognized in the paradigm shift from a traditional product orientation to the provision of bundled solutions [2]. The concept that manufacturers need to leverage innovative combinations of services and products to increase the scope of their value creation activities and to face the increasing global competition is not new. There is a rich literature on this trend, which has been mainly discussed under the terms "Servitization" and "Product Service System" (PSS) [3]. Moreover, the advancements in the technologies that allow obtaining real-time data from the environment and act upon this to control, monitor, and interact with the real world are supporting and revolutionizing the "Servitization" trend. In this regard, Information and Communication Technologies (ICT), Internet of things (IoT), cloud computing, data analytics, and the possibility to integrate information along the value chain in real-time, are the most relevant technologies [4]. The adoption of these digital technologies is a key enabler for the provision of many services related to an integrated solution, either i) supporting new functionalities, ii) providing the possibility to offer "Smart Services" or iii) increasing the efficiency of service delivery [2]. For example, connecting products enable manufacturers to provide services such as predictive maintenance and remote control from center for remote-controlled operations. Additionally, the adoption of an intelligent ICT infrastructure enables gathering feedback and data collection from later stages back to the earlier stages of the product lifecycle [5]. It creates the potential to enhance the value co-creation process, which is one of the central premises of the service logic [6]. In this view, this research aims at exploring state of the art in the above-mentioned fields and understand the point of contact between Industry 4.0 and Servitization. To this end, we adopted a broad perspective including both researches that are focused on the "digital servitization" stream, and papers that are focused on the technological and industrial perspective that is not always covered into the servitization domain [7].

The paper is structured as follows: Sect. 2 delineates the methodology followed to perform the systematic literature review, Sects. 3 and 4 report some quantitative analysis of the final sample and the categorized papers considering their content. In the end, Sect. 5 discusses some insights into the analysis proposing possible future research focus and concludes the work.

## 2  Methodology

The systematic literature review has been identified as the best option to pursue research's aims, since it is widely used to explore an emergent topic, investigate the advancement of a specific stream of research as well as to propose recommendations for future studies [8]. A systematic review can be distinguished from different types of publications for its scope and rigorousness. Indeed, a rigorous scientific investigation follows a specific, explicit and, therefore, reproducible methodology and approaches to identify, collect, evaluate and discuss relevant issues on the specific topic [9] limiting bias and random errors [10]. Approaching systematic literature review requires a specific protocol: to this end, we decided to follow the PRISMA statement, which defines a detailed set of steps to be followed during the systematic literature review [11]. In this research, the four main steps, which are (1) identification, (2) screening, (3) eligibility and (4) inclusion have been addressed. All steps followed by authors are described in the following paragraph.

In order to identify a representative corpus of documents for investigation, the first step was the definition of a set of keywords to be included in the research. For each keyword, the specific meaning of the word or concept has been defined as well as a set of synonyms to be included in the query.

The keywords have been chosen separately for the two different topics. For what concerns *"Industry 4.0"*, authors considered only concepts related to the possibility to gather data and enable the data utilization. Particularly, six technologies have been selected, as reported in Table 1. For *"Servitization"*, two main research streams have been found in the literature, that express a similar concept: Servitization and Product Service System.

**Table 1.** Keyword selection – technology domain

| Keyword | Reference |
|---|---|
| Internet of Things | [12] |
| Internet of Services | [13] |
| Digitization | [14] |
| Analytics | [15] |
| Big Data | [16] |
| Cloud Computing | [17] |

After the definition of the keywords, the research was performed using the Scopus database, and the queries have been constructed linking two by two the different concepts: a total of six queries has been used, matching one concept from technologies domain and one from servitization. Screening has been addressed by limiting each query to the English language and year of publication after 2011 since the Industry 4.0 concept emerged in 2011. Moreover, to limit the scope of the research, the subject areas included were: Engineering; Computer Science; Business Management & Accounting and Decision Science. Because of the high number of papers related to those queries, the research was limited to articles published in journals. This choice allows also to have control over the quality of publications [9]. In the end, each query was defined as explained in Table 2, searching the specific keywords in the papers' title and abstract.

The final pool of paper resulted in the aggregation of the results from the six different queries, therefore duplicate removal has been performed. Then, in addition to the filters described in the research query, authors have perused articles in three different rounds, increasing the level of the content incrementally under analysis. First of all, titles have been read, then abstract reading enabled to further restrict the pool and in the end, full texts have been examined. Not all the full-text readings have led to a positive inclusion in the final pool since some works did not meet the eligibility criteria. Thus, a first reading was made to decide the level of coherence and adherence of the content with the scope. Papers have been excluded for two reasons:

(1) The degree of technology innovation cannot be included in the wave of industry 4.0, even if the paper was focused on servitization and technological advancement;

(2) High technological applications and topics were completely disjoint from the service-oriented perspective, and it was not even possible to assume that those solutions would be used as service applications.

**Table 2.** Query definition

| | | |
|---|---|---|
| **Service perspective** | (1) | ((TITLE-ABS-KEY ( pss* ) OR TITLE-ABS-KEY ( "Product-Servi* System*" ) OR TITLE-ABS-KEY ( "Integrated product servi*" ) OR TITLE-ABS-KEY ( "Industrial Product servi* System*" ) OR TITLE-ABS-KEY ( "Integrated Product Servi* Offer*" ) OR TITLE-ABS-KEY ( ipso ) OR TITLE-ABS-KEY ( "Integrated Solutio*" ) OR TITLE-ABS-KEY ( "Product servi*" ) ) ) |
| | (2) | ( ( TITLE-ABS-KEY ( serviti*ation ) OR TITLE-ABS-KEY ( "Smart service" ) OR TITLE-ABS-KEY ( "Servi* Infusion" ) OR TITLE-ABS-KEY ( "Hybrid Value Creation" ) OR TITLE-ABS-KEY ( "Service-oriented Manufacturing" ) OR TITLE-ABS-KEY ( "Customer Solution*" ) OR TITLE-ABS-KEY ( "Product-extension service*" ) OR TITLE-ABS-KEY ( demateriali?ation* ) ) |
| **Technology perspective** | (3) | ((TITLE-ABS-KEY ( "Big Data" ) OR TITLE-ABS-KEY ( "Cloud Computing" ) OR TITLE-ABS-KEY ( digiti?ation ) OR TITLE-ABS-KEY ( analytic* ) ) ) |
| | (4) | ((TITLE-ABS-KEY ( ios ) OR TITLE-ABS-KEY ( "Internet of Serv*" ) ) ) |
| | (5) | ((TITLE-ABS-KEY ("Internet of Thing*") OR TITLE-ABS-KEY ( *iot ) OR TITLE-ABS-KEY ("Internet of Everything") OR TITLE-ABS-KEY ("Industrial internet of thing*") OR TITLE-ABS-KEY ("Industrial internet")) |
| | | **(1)AND(3); (1)AND(4); (1)AND(5); (2)AND(3); (2)AND(4); (2)AND (5)** |
| AND | | (LIMIT-TO (LANGUAGE, "English " ) ) |
| AND | | (LIMIT-TO (SUBJAREA, "ENGI " ) OR LIMIT-TO (SUBJAREA, "COMP " ) OR LIMIT-TO (SUBJAREA, "BUSI " ) OR LIMIT-TO (SUBJAREA, "DECI " ) ) |
| AND | | ( LIMIT-TO (PUBYEAR, 2019 ) OR LIMIT-TO (PUBYEAR, 2018 ) OR LIMIT-TO (PUBYEAR, 2017 ) OR LIMIT-TO (PUBYEAR, 2016 ) OR LIMIT-TO (PUBYEAR, 2015 ) R LIMIT-TO (PUBYEAR,2014) OR LIMIT-TO (PUBYEAR, 2013 ) OR LIMIT-TO (PUBYEAR, 2012 ) OR LIMIT-TO (PUBYEAR, 2011)) |
| AND | | (LIMIT-TO (DOCTYPE , "ar " ) ) |
| AND | | (LIMIT-TO (SRCTYPE , "j " ) |

In Fig. 1 all steps and the corresponding number of papers are reported.

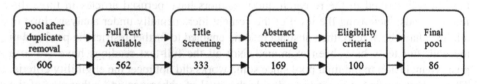

**Fig. 1.** Steps and number of papers along the systematic literature review

## 3   Papers Descriptive Analysis

The first analyses investigated the corpus of the review considering some "demo-graphic" analysis. Specifically, it is possible to notice an interesting increment and constant growth of the number of publications form 2016, as depicted in Fig. 2, proving an ongoing interest in the research field in recent years.

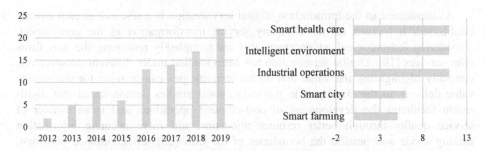

**Fig. 2.** Number of publications over years    **Fig. 3.** Top five applications field (n. of paper)

An analysis has been also performed on the journal source: it revealed that they are widespread from technology, management, service, marketing and other fields and most of them have a technical imprint, as it is possible to see in Fig. 4. The most recurrent journal is the "Journal of ambient intelligent and smart environment" meaning that in the field of Smart Environment the topic is highly debated. Looking at the application field that papers deal with, there is no doubt that the intelligent environment has a core position. It refers to the capacity of sensing of ambient with respect to different factors and the consequent ability of the system to offer services based on necessity, either adapting or calling some "external entities" [18]. Nevertheless, as it is possible to see from Fig. 3, there are not borders in terms of applicability: Smart health care, Industrial operations, Smart city and Smart farming are also at the center of the discussion.

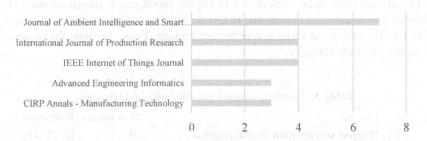

**Fig. 4.** Top 5 journals in the pool (n. of paper)

## 4 Paper Categorization

At the starting point, the final corpus of paper resulted to be heterogeneous since the topic is widespread among different disciplines. Consequently, we decided to categorize papers into homogeneous groups to provide an overall overview of the topic. The categories have been established considering on one side the focuses introduced with the keywords that are related to the service domain and technologies, and on the other side, the most relevant perspectives underlined by the literature.

As mentioned in the introduction, digital servitization is a research stream already established. It focuses on the company service transformation as the core aspect, considering technological advancement that are completely reshaping the way firms offer services [19]. Digital servitization has been studied under different perspectives, generally highlighting the value that digital technologies can provide for the service value delivery to the customer. In particular, some studies demonstrated that digitization facilitates the development of cost-efficient operations and is an enabler of service quality through better resource allocation and more accurate information sharing inside and outside the boundaries of the firm [20]. In accordance with that, attention has been focused by different academics into the integration of servitization and digitalization with other business dimensions, as the manufacturing process and the supply chain. The production perspective emerges, for example, in the work of Coreynen et al. (2017) [21]: they examined how digital technologies can enable different Servitization pathways proposing three different cases, that are Industrial, Commercial and Value Servitization Pathways. Into the Industrial pathway, resources and capabilities are devoted to make the internal manufacturing operations smarter and provide new hybrid services for the customers. For what concern supply chain, for example, Vendrell-Herrero et al., (2017) study how the dematerialization of physical products is transforming the way firms are positioned in the supply chain and their engagement with customers [22].

Starting from these considerations, authors divided the corpus of the paper according to three different focuses, that are the *service*, the *industry* and the *supply chain*. Lastly, a final class has been defined to represent research studies describing from a technological point of view some specific applications based on Industry 4.0 technologies that could potentially be deployed as a service in many circumstances.

The classes have been named: (CL1) Digital servitization transformation; (CL2) Industrial servitization of operations; (CL3) Supply chain and network collaboration; and (CL4) Technological focus in specific applications. Table 3 reports the number and the papers per each category.

**Table 3.** Number of papers per categories and references

| ID | Classes | N of papers | References |
|---|---|---|---|
| CL1 | **"Digital servitization transformation"** | 25 | [7, 21–44] |
| | Papers that deal with digital servitization transformation | | |
| CL2 | **"Industrial servitization of operations"** | 10 | [45–54] |
| | Papers presenting digital technologies, resources and capabilities to make the internal manufacturing operations smarter with adopting concept of servitization | | |
| CL3 | **"Supply chain and network collaboration"** | 10 | [55–64] |
| | Paper dealing with the impact that the adoption of new technologies has on the collaboration practices in the value chain and implications at the network level" | | |
| CL4 | **"Technological focus in specific applications"** | 41 | [65–105] |
| | Papers dealing with the realization of a systems or application towards smart service provision for the technological point of view | | |

CL1 has been created considering papers that deal with digital servitization transformation. This pool represents works studying different aspects of the path of manufacturing companies thought the servitization paradigm leveraging the possibilities that technologies and data gathering are creating. What emerges is that the scope of the services is changing and expanding. Particularly, has been found that products connectivity enables manufacturers to offer new services with new service value proposition [24]. The manufacturer has the possibility to continuously auditing customer operations and expand value creation having the ability to operate within the field of product use including services at customer's operation level [41]. Moreover, if the applications are into business context, the need of a culture of trust with business partners, customer and users emerge more and more, since customers have no intrinsic interest in sharing operational data with machine tool contractor and to hook them up to their data gathering and processing systems [41], because of different privacy and security issues. In this view, value creation and co-creation, which considers the necessity of the customer involvement and engagement into a joint-value creation process [24], are recognized as the basis of the deployment of such solutions. CL2 deals with applications that employ digital technologies, resources and capabilities to make the internal manufacturing operations smarter. Among them, an interesting part considers the cloud manufacturing paradigm as the main impact of service-oriented applications. Indeed, customers can have access to on-demand services, such as engineering design, simulation, production, assembling, testing and management [51]. Some other works deal with the Industrial Product-Service System (IPS2), as an approach to operate in an efficient and effective service-oriented way, enhancing life cycles, delivering solutions that meet customer expectations, providing, for example, a tool to support firms into the decision of an IPSS adoption [52]. CL3 is focused on the positive impact that the adoption of new technologies has on the collaboration practices in the value chain and on the other on the implication at the network level. From the analysis resulted that the adoption of intelligent products and the contribution of ICT enhancement can result in the integration of users together with producers and service providers in closed data and information loops, in a collaborative ecosystem. Inside those works, it is possible to find paper dealing with models supporting a service-oriented enterprise collaboration network [58] or describing the benefits of the Internet of Things (IoT)-based systems into the supply chain context [59]. CL4 is the larger class and the most widespread among different disciplines and fields. Within this class, it is possible to find papers that, for example, describe the realization of a smart service system set up for the maintenance, remote failure diagnosis, quick service response, failure detection and iterative optimization of sugarcane harvesters [95]. Other works describe IoT hybrid monitoring systems for health care environments providing location, status, and tracking of patients and assets [97]. Another proposes a Smart Service Orchestration Architecture to coordinate ubiquitous objects, create interlinked data, and implement versatile smart service in the Smart City context [104]. Within this class, it is possible to find also works that are more focused on the manufacturing side [99] or supply chain and coordination mechanisms [74, 93]. Overall, it is possible to state that with different perspectives and field of applications lot of paper deals with the design and development of complex solutions, which needs the technological competences in the realization of infrastructure, that should be reliable and secure, analytics capabilities and the know-how into the field of applications.

## 5   Discussion, Conclusion and Future Research

This work is concerned with the interconnection between two main emerging phenomena: the Industry 4.0 technologies related to the data domain, and the Servitization. From the analysis of the corpus of the papers, it was possible to draw out first insights, considering that different focuses have emerged, that are: (CL1) Digital servitization transformation; (CL2) Industrial servitization of operations; (CL3) Supply chain and network collaboration; and (CL4) Technological focus in specific applications. Inside those classes, a deeper analysis needs to be performed, as a natural development of the proposed work. Nevertheless, some possible direction emerges from this initial analysis. From this review, it is possible to notice how the two phenomena under investigation maintain separate knowledge and research stream, indeed, as also highlighted by Frank et al., (2019) [7] the connection between Servitization and Industry 4.0 is still emerging. There are some initial attempts of merging but authors maintain most of the time the two concepts disconnected, indeed most of the studies into the CL1 do not consider the manufacturing perspective, while into the other three classes the servitization perspective is weakly addressed. Moreover, even though authors included in the research keywords several concepts related to the possibility to gather data and enable the data utilization, the specific focus on data remains poorly covered in the pool of paper and mostly appears as an underlying enabler. Indeed, studies either focused on the impacts of technologies on service offering (CL1) or on the technical development of solution (CL4), without proposing a holistic view. There is a lack in the overall comprehension of data-related services, both considering their characteristics and development. Additionally, even studies reveal how the information sharing among firms create the potential for collaboration that enables more efficient operations, as emerged both in CL1 and CL3 there are limited works that further investigate value creation mechanisms in a data-enabled ecosystem. Consequently, considering the possibility to further integrate the relation of data technologies and possibilities into the service point of view and vice versa, some interesting direction emerges. Those directions are the result of a cross-analysis of the different classes, not considering what can be done for each of them, but how to move forward to create synergies between them and blurring the boundaries among different pieces of knowledge.

*Research Direction 1:* The creation of a systematic understanding and synthesis of the possibilities that technologies and data availability open in the service field should be addressed, as well as an analysis of value creation practices considering data-related applications. A contribution can be made by means of taxonomies or classification frameworks both regarding service typologies, value proposition and value creation mechanisms that may be achieved from data collection and analysis.

*Research Direction 2:* Structured approaches that enable firms to leverage data to create value, both for customers and for internal applications can be formalized. Those approaches should also be considered to fill the gap that emerges clearly between the technological perspective and the servitization perspective, providing tools and methodologies aiming at synergistically address both domains. Service Engineering methodologies may be proposed, considering including data-driven and industrial lenses.

*Research Direction 3:* New cooperation and collaboration mechanism need to be analyzed and conceptualized to support firms and all actors in this transition. Particularly the ecosystem perspective should be included considering access and sharing of resources, including knowledge, capabilities but also data streams. In particular, the digital ecosystem that characterizes the majority of data-driven services may be analyzed from a platform perspective, that strongly emerges as the tool which supports data collection and analysis as well as application deployment, considering how the design of the technological architecture impact the value creation for different actors.

**Acknowledgement.** This research is supported by the French region AURA, via the international project 'Collaboration Franco-italienne pour une industrialisation durable des territoires'.

# References

1. Kagermann, H., Wahlster, W., Helbig, J.: Securing the future of German manufacturing industry: recommendations for implementing the strategic initiative INDUSTRIE 4.0. Final report of the Industrie 4.0 working group (2013)
2. Kamp, B., Ochoa, A., Diaz, J.: Smart servitization within the context of industrial user–supplier relationships: contingencies according to a machine tool manufacturer. Int. J. Interact. Des. Manuf. (IJIDeM) **11**(3), 651–663 (2016). https://doi.org/10.1007/s12008-016-0345-0
3. Baines, T., et al.: State-of-the-art in product-service systems. Proc. Inst. Mech. Eng. Part B J. Eng. Manuf. **221**(10), 1543–1552 (2007)
4. Ardolino, M., Saccani, N., Gaiardelli, P., Rapaccini, M.: Exploring the key enabling role of digital technologies for PSS offerings. Procedia CIRP **47**, 561–566 (2016)
5. Lee, J., Kao, H.A., Yang, S.: Service innovation and smart analytics for Industry 4.0 and big data environment. Procedia CIRP **16**, 3–8 (2014)
6. Belvedere, V., Grando, A., Bielli, P.: A quantitative investigation of the role of information and communication technologies in the implementation of a product-service system. Int. J. Prod. Res. **51**(2), 410–426 (2013)
7. Frank, A.G., Mendes, G.H.S., Ayala, N.F., Ghezzi, A.: Servitization and Industry 4.0 convergence in the digital transformation of product firms: a business model innovation perspective. Technol. Forecast. Soc. Change **141**, 341–351 (2019)
8. Goodwin, G.M., Geddes, J.R.: Introduction to systematic reviews. J. Psychopharmacol. **18**, 249–250 (2004)
9. Light, R.J., Pillemer, D.B.: Summing Up the Science of Reviewing Research. Harvard Business Press, Boston (1984)
10. Cook, D.J., Mulrow, C.D., Haynes, R.B.: Systematic reviews: synthesis of best evidence for clinical decisions. Ann. Intern. Med. **126**(5), 376–380 (1997)
11. Moher, D., Liberati, A., Tetzlaff, J., Altman, D.: Preferred reporting items for systematic reviews and meta-analyses: the PRISMA statement. PLoS Med. **6**(7), 264–269 (2009)
12. Giusto, D., Iera, A., Morabito, G., Atzori, L.: The Internet of Things. Springer, New York (2010). https://doi.org/10.1007/978-1-4419-1674-7

13. Buxmann, P., Hess, T., Ruggaber, R.: Internet of services. Bus. Inf. Syst. Eng. **1**(5), 341–342 (2009)
14. Kagermann, H.: Change through digitization—value creation in the age of industry 4.0. In: Albach, H., Meffert, H., Pinkwart, A., Reichwald, R. (eds.) Management of Permanent Change, pp. 23–45. Springer, Wiesbaden (2015). https://doi.org/10.1007/978-3-658-05014-6_2
15. Chen, H., Storey, V.C.: Business intelligence and analytics: from big data to big impact. MIS Q. Manag. Inf. Syst. **36**(4), 1165–1188 (2012)
16. Wamba, S.F., Akter, S., Edwards, A., Chopin, G., Gnanzou, D.: How 'big data' can make big impact: findings from a systematic review and a longitudinal case study. Int. J. Prod. Econ. **165**, 234–246 (2015)
17. Demirkan, H., Delen, D.: Leveraging the capabilities of service-oriented decision support systems: putting analytics and big data in cloud. Decis. Support Syst. **55**(1), 412–421 (2013)
18. Nixon, P.A., Wagealla, W., English, C., Terzis, S.: Security, privacy and trust issues in smart environments. In: Cook, D.J., Das, S.K. (eds.) Smart Environments, pp. 249–270. Wiley, Hoboken (2005)
19. Lerch, C., Gotsch, M.: Digitalized product-service systems in manufacturing firms: a case study analysis. Res. Technol. Manag. **58**(5), 45–52 (2015)
20. Kindström, D., Kowalkowski, C.: Service innovation in product-centric firms: a multidimensional business model perspective. J. Bus. Ind. Mark. **29**(2), 96–111 (2014)
21. Coreynen, W., Matthyssens, P., Van Bockhaven, W.: Boosting servitization through digitization: pathways and dynamic resource configurations for manufacturers. Ind. Mark. Manag. **60**, 42–53 (2017)
22. Vendrell-Herrero, F., Bustinza, O.F., Parry, G., Georgantzis, N.: Servitization, digitization and supply chain interdependency. Ind. Mark. Manag. **60**(1), 69–81 (2017)
23. Heinis, T.B., Loy, C.L., Meboldt, M.: Improving usage metrics for pay-per-use pricing with IoT technology and machine learning: IoT technology and machine learning can identify and capture advanced metrics that make pay-per-use servitization models viable for a wider range of applications. Res. Technol. Manag. **61**(5), 32–40 (2018)
24. Sambit, L., Vinit, P., Joakim, W.: Digitalization capabilities as enablers of value co-creation in servitizing firms. Psychol. Mark. **34**(1), 92–100 (2016)
25. Anke, J.: Design-integrated financial assessment of smart services. Electron. Mark. **29**(1), 19–35 (2019)
26. Demirkan, H.: Innovations with smart service systems: analytics, big data, cognitive assistance, and the internet of everything. Commun. Assoc. Inf. Syst. **37**, 35 (2015)
27. Wiegard, R.B., Breitner, M.H.: Smart services in healthcare: a risk-benefit-analysis of pay-as-you-live services from customer perspective in Germany. Electron. Mark. **29**(1), 107–123 (2019)
28. Chouk, I., Mani, Z.: Factors for and against resistance to smart services: role of consumer lifestyle and ecosystem related variables. J. Serv. Mark. **33**(4), 449–462 (2019)
29. De, E., et al.: Business process support for IoT based product-service systems (PSS). Bus. Process Manag. J. **22**(2), 263–270 (2016)
30. Zheng, P., Lin, T.J., Chen, C.H., Xu, X.: A systematic design approach for service innovation of smart product-service systems. J. Clean. Prod. **201**, 657–667 (2018)
31. Mani, Z., Chouk, I.: Consumer resistance to innovation in services: challenges and barriers in the Internet of Things era. J. Prod. Innov. Manag. **35**(5), 780–807 (2018)
32. Boldosova, V.: Telling stories that sell: the role of storytelling and big data analytics in smart service sales. Ind. Mark. Manag. **86**, 122–134 (2020)

33. Opresnik, D., Taisch, M.: The value of big data in servitization. Int. J. Prod. Econ. **165**, 174–184 (2015)
34. Burzlaff, F., Wilken, N., Bartelt, C., Stuckenschmidt, H.: Semantic interoperability methods for smart service systems: a survey. IEEE Trans. Eng. Manag. 1–15 (2019)
35. Shin, H., Jeon, B., Park, J.W.: Method to design and analyze an interactive product based on design elements for creating an IoT-based service. Int. J. Smart Home **10**(10), 229–238 (2016)
36. Helfert, M., Ge, M.: Perspectives of big data quality in smart service ecosystems (quality of design and quality of conformance). J. Inf. Technol. Manag. **10**(4), 72–83 (2019)
37. Ostrom, A.L., Parasuraman, A., Bowen, D.E., Patrício, L., Voss, C.A.: Service research priorities in a rapidly changing context. J. Serv. Res. **18**(2), 127–159 (2015)
38. Maleki, E., et al.: Ontology-based framework enabling smart product-service systems: application of sensing systems for machine health monitoring. IEEE Internet Things J. **5**(6), 4496–4505 (2018)
39. Shao, S., Xu, G., Li, M.: The design of an IoT-based route optimization system: a smart product-service system (SPSS) approach. Adv. Eng. Inform. **42**, 101006 (2019)
40. Verdugo Cedeño, J.M., Papinniemi, J., Hannola, L., Donoghue, I.D.M.: Developing smart services by Internet of Things in manufacturing business. DEStech Trans. Eng. Technol. Res. (icpr) **14**, 59–71 (2018)
41. Kamp, B., Ochoa, A., Diaz, J.: Smart servitization within the context of industrial user–supplier relationships: contingencies according to a machine tool manufacturer. Int. J. Interact. Des. Manuf. **11**(3), 651–663 (2017)
42. Rymaszewska, A., Helo, P., Gunasekaran, A.: IoT powered servitization of manufacturing – an exploratory case study. Int. J. Prod. Econ. **192**, 92–105 (2017)
43. Basirati, M.R., Weking, J., Hermes, S., Böhm, M., Krcmar, H.: Exploring opportunities of IoT for product-service system conceptualization and implementation. Asia Pac. J. Inf. Syst. **29**(3), 524–546 (2019)
44. Zhang, Q., Lu, X., Peng, Z., Ren, M.: Perspective: a review of lifecycle management research on complex products in smart-connected environments. Int. J. Prod. Res. **57**(21), 6758–6779 (2019)
45. Li, Z., Barenji, A.V., Huang, G.Q.: Toward a blockchain cloud manufacturing system as a peer to peer distributed network platform. Robot. Comput. Integr. Manuf. **54**, 133–144 (2018)
46. Liu, B., Zhang, Y., Zhang, G., Zheng, P.: Edge-cloud orchestration driven industrial smart product-service systems solution design based on CPS and IIoT. Adv. Eng. Inform. **42**, 100984 (2019)
47. Rasouli, M.R.: An architecture for IoT-enabled intelligent process-aware cloud production platform: a case study in a networked cloud clinical laboratory. Int. J. Prod. Res **58**(12), 3765–3780 (2019)
48. Yan, J., Ma, Y., Wang, L., Choo, K.K.R., Jie, W.: A cloud-based remote sensing data production system. Future Gener. Comput. Syst. **86**, 1154–1166 (2018)
49. Tao, F., Qi, Q.: New IT driven service-oriented smart manufacturing: framework and characteristics. IEEE Trans. Syst. Man Cybern. Syst. **49**(1), 81–91 (2019)
50. Valilai, O.F., Houshmand, M.: A collaborative and integrated platform to support distributed manufacturing system using a service-oriented approach based on cloud computing paradigm. Robot. Comput. Integr. Manuf. **29**(1), 110–127 (2013)
51. Ren, L., Zhang, L., Tao, F., Zhao, C., Chai, X., Zhao, X.: Cloud manufacturing: from concept to practice. Enterp. Inf. Syst. **9**(2), 186–209 (2015)
52. Wang, X., Durugbo, C.: Analysing network uncertainty for industrial product-service delivery: a hybrid fuzzy approach. Expert Syst. Appl. **40**(11), 4621–4636 (2013)

53. Preuveneers, D., Ilie-Zudor, E.: The intelligent industry of the future: a survey on emerging trends, research challenges and opportunities in Industry 4.0. J. Ambient Intell. Smart Environ. **9**(3), 287–298 (2017)
54. Holler, J., Tsiatsis, V., Mulligan, C.: Toward a machine intelligence layer for diverse industrial IoT use cases. IEEE Intell. Syst. **32**(4), 64–71 (2017)
55. Zhang, Y., Liu, S., Liu, Y., Li, R.: Smart box-enabled product–service system for cloud logistics. Int. J. Prod. Res. **54**(22), 6693–6706 (2016)
56. Nivedha, R.: Service oriented network virtualization. Int. J. Res. Appl. Sci. Eng. Technol. (IJRASET) **4**(XI), 497–501 (2016)
57. Li, Z., Huang, G.Q., Fang, J., Qu, T.: Ontology-based dynamic alliance services (ODAS) in production service system. Int. J. Comput. Integr. Manuf. **27**(2), 148–164 (2014)
58. Zhang, F., Jiang, P., Zhu, Q., Cao, W.: Modeling and analyzing of an enterprise collaboration network supported by service-oriented manufacturing. Proc. Inst. Mech. Eng. Part B J. Eng. Manuf. **226**(9), 1579–1593 (2012)
59. Li, Z., Liu, G., Liu, L., Lai, X., Xu, G.: IoT-based tracking and tracing platform for prepackaged food supply chain. Ind. Manag. Data Syst. **117**(9), 1906–1916 (2017)
60. Rezaei, M., Shirazi, M.A., Karimi, B.: IoT-based framework for performance measurement: a real-time supply chain decision alignment. Ind. Manag. Data Syst. **117**(4), 688–712 (2017)
61. Loukis, E., Kyriakou, N., Pazalos, K., Popa, S.: Inter-organizational innovation and cloud computing. Electron. Commer. Res. **17**(3), 379–401 (2017). https://doi.org/10.1007/s10660-016-9239-2
62. Curtin, J.P., Gaffney, R.L., Riggins, F.J.: Identifying business value using the RFID e-Valuation Framework. Int. J. RF Technol. Res. Appl. **4**(2), 71–91 (2013)
63. Kiritsis, D., Koukias, A., Nadoveza, D.: ICT supported lifecycle thinking and information integration for sustainable manufacturing. Int. J. Sustain. Manuf. **3**(3), 229 (2015)
64. Long, Q.: A framework for data-driven computational experiments of inter-organizational collaborations in supply chain networks. Inf. Sci. (Ny) **399**, 43–63 (2017)
65. Stefan, I., Aldea, C.L., Nechifor, C.S.: Web platform architecture for ambient assisted living. J. Ambient Intell. Smart Environ. **10**(1), 35–47 (2018)
66. Sikeridis, D., Rimal, B.P., Papapanagiotou, I., Devetsikiotis, M.: Unsupervised crowd-assisted learning enabling location-aware facilities. IEEE Internet Things J. **5**(6), 4699–4713 (2018)
67. Hussein, D., Han, S.N., Lee, G.M., Crespi, N., Bertin, E.: Towards a dynamic discovery of smart services in the social internet of things. Comput. Electr. Eng. **58**, 429–443 (2017)
68. Bui, N., Castellani, A.P., Casari, P., Zorzi, M.: The internet of energy: a web-enabled smart grid system. IEEE Netw. **26**, 39–45 (2012)
69. Seungcheon, K.: Smart pet care system using internet of things. Int. J. Smart Home **10**(3), 211–218 (2016)
70. Corradi, A., et al.: Smart appliances and RAMI 4.0: management and servitization of ice cream machines. IEEE Trans. Ind. Inform. **15**(2), 1007–1016 (2019)
71. Ganapathy, K., Vaidehi, V., Poorani, D.: Sensor based efficient decision making framework for remote healthcare. J. Ambient Intell. Smart Environ. **7**(4), 461–481 (2015)
72. Mohammadi, M., Al-Fuqaha, A., Guizani, M., Oh, J.S.: Semisupervised deep reinforcement learning in support of IoT and smart city services. IEEE Internet Things J. **5**(2), 624–635 (2018)
73. Preuveneers, D., Joosen, W.: Security and privacy controls for streaming data in extended intelligent environments. J. Ambient Intell. Smart Environ. **8**(4), 467–483 (2016)
74. Zhou, C., Liu, X., Xue, F., Bo, H., Li, K.: Research on static service BOM transformation for complex products. Adv. Eng. Inform. **36**(2), 146–162 (2018)

75. Zhu, M., Cao, J., Cai, Z., He, Z., Xu, M.: Providing flexible services for heterogeneous vehicles: an NFV-based approach. IEEE Netw. **30**(3), 64–71 (2016)
76. Takenaka, T., Koshiba, H., Motomura, Y., Ueda, K.: Product/service variety strategy considering mixed distribution of human lifestyles. CIRP Ann. - Manuf. Technol. **62**(1), 463–466 (2013)
77. Zhang, X., Guo, X., Guo, F., Lai, K.H.: Nonlinearities in personalization-privacy paradox in mHealth adoption: the mediating role of perceived usefulness and attitude. Technol. Health Care **22**(4), 515–529 (2014)
78. Walsh, L., McLoone, S.: Non-contact under-mattress sleep monitoring. J. Ambient Intell. Smart Environ. **6**(4), 385–401 (2014)
79. Demizu, H., Harano, Y., Hirata, M., Sakaguchi, K.: New approach to product development based on service design process: next-generation event management solution 'EXBOARD'. Fujitsu Sci. Tech. J. **54**(1), 52–57 (2018)
80. Solima, L., Della Peruta, M.R., Maggioni, V.: Managing adaptive orientation systems for museum visitors from an IoT perspective. Bus. Process Manag. J. **22**(2), 285–304 (2016)
81. Georgakopoulos, D., Jayaraman, P.P.: Internet of Things: from internet scale sensing to smart services. Computing **98**(10), 1041–1058 (2016)
82. Ray, P.P.: Internet of things for smart agriculture: technologies, practices and future direction. J. Ambient Intell. Smart Environ. **9**(4), 395–420 (2017)
83. Fragidis, L.L., Chatzoglou, P.D., Aggelidis, V.P.: Integrated nationwide electronic health records system: semi-distributed architecture approach. Technol. Health Care **24**(6), 827–842 (2016)
84. Riel, A., Kreiner, C., Macher, G., Messnarz, R.: Integrated design for tackling safety and security challenges of smart products and digital manufacturing. CIRP Ann. - Manuf. Technol. **66**(1), 177–180 (2017)
85. Abosaq, N.H.: Impact of privacy issues on smart city services in a model smart city. Int. J. Adv. Comput. Sci. Appl. **10**(2), 177–185 (2019)
86. Lee, J.S., Choi, S., Kwon, O.: Identifying multiuser activity with overlapping acoustic data for mobile decision making in smart home environments. Expert Syst. Appl. **81**, 299–308 (2017)
87. Singh, H., Mallaiah, R., Yadav, G., Verma, N., Sawhney, A., Brahmachari, S.K.: iCHRCloud: web & mobile based child health imprints for smart healthcare. J. Med. Syst. **42**(1), 1–12 (2017). https://doi.org/10.1007/s10916-017-0866-5
88. Sung, W.T., Chang, K.Y.: Health parameter monitoring via a novel wireless system. Appl. Soft Comput. J. **22**, 667–680 (2014)
89. Doran, M.A., Daniel, S.: Geomatics and smart city: a transversal contribution to the smart city development. Inf. Polity **19**(1–2), 57–72 (2014)
90. Yan, M., et al.: Field microclimate monitoring system based on wireless sensor network. J. Intell. Fuzzy Syst. **35**(2), 1325–1337 (2018)
91. Newman, K.E., Blei, M.: Evaluation of smart phones for remote control of a standard hospital room. Wirel. Pers. Commun. **75**(2), 1005–1013 (2014). https://doi.org/10.1007/s11277-013-1404-5
92. Takenaka, T., Yamamoto, Y., Fukuda, K., Kimura, A., Ueda, K.: Enhancing products and services using smart appliance networks. CIRP Ann. - Manuf. Technol. **65**(1), 397–400 (2016)
93. Laubis, K., Konstantinov, M., Simko, V., Gröschel, A., Weinhardt, C.: Enabling crowdsensing-based road condition monitoring service by intermediary. Electron. Mark. **29**(1), 125–140 (2019). https://doi.org/10.1007/s12525-018-0292-7

94. Ramachandran, L., Narendra, N.C., Ponnalagu, K.: Dynamic provisioning in multi-tenant service clouds. Serv. Oriented Comput. Appl. **6**(4), 283–302 (2012). https://doi.org/10.1007/s11761-012-0116-0

95. Liu, S., Ju, Y., Wang, J., Yang, F., Ma, S., Wang, S.: Design of a smart after-service system for sugarcane harvesters based on product lifecycle. J. Eur. des Syst. Autom. **51**, 239–257 (2018)

96. Yue, M., Hong, T., Wang, J.: Descriptive analytics-based anomaly detection for cybersecure load forecasting. IEEE Trans. Smart Grid **10**(6), 5964–5974 (2019)

97. Adame, T., Bel, A., Carreras, A., Melià-Seguí, J., Oliver, M., Pous, R.: CUIDATS: an RFID–WSN hybrid monitoring system for smart health care environments. Future Gener. Comput. Syst. **78**, 602–615 (2018)

98. Yoo, M.J., Grozel, C., Kiritsis, D.: Closed-loop lifecycle management of service and product in the internet of things: semantic framework for knowledge integration. Sensors (Switzerland) **16**(7), 1053 (2016)

99. Shibata, T., Kurachi, Y.: Big data analysis solutions for driving innovation in on-site decision making. Fujitsu Sci. Tech. J. **51**(2), 33–41 (2015)

100. Erguido, A., Marquez, A.C., Castellano, E., Parlikad, A.K., Izquierdo, J.: Asset management framework and tools for facing challenges in the adoption of product-service systems. IEEE Trans. Eng. Manag. 1–14 (2019)

101. Doyle, J., et al.: An integrated home-based self-management system to support the wellbeing of older adults. J. Ambient Intell. Smart Environ. **6**(4), 359–383 (2014)

102. Park, W., Na, O., Chang, H.: An exploratory research on advanced smart media security design for sustainable intelligence information system. Multimed. Tools Appl. **75**(11), 6059–6070 (2016)

103. Ojala, A.: Adjusting software revenue and pricing strategies in the era of cloud computing. J. Syst. Softw. **122**, 40–51 (2016)

104. You, L., Tuncer, B., Zhu, R., Xing, H., Yuen, C.: A synergetic orchestration of objects, data, and services to enable smart cities. IEEE Internet Things J. **6**(6), 10496–10507 (2019)

105. Sivamani, S., Bae, N., Cho, Y.: A smart service model based on ubiquitous sensor networks using vertical farm ontology. Int. J. Distrib. Sens. Netw. **9**(12) (2013)

# A Framework to Support Value Co-creation in PSS Development

Martha Orellano[1(✉)], Xavier Boucher[2], Gilles Neubert[3],
and Anne Coulon[4]

[1] Mines Saint-Etienne, Univ Lyon, Univ Jean Moulin, Univ Lumire, Univ Jean
Monnet, ENTPE, INSA Lyon, ENS Lyon, CNRS, UMR 5600 EVS, Institut
Henri Fayol, 42023 Saint-Etienne, France
martha.orellano@emse.fr
[2] Mines Saint-Etienne, Univ Clermont Auvergne, CNRS, UMR 6158 LIMOS,
Institut Henri Fayol, 42023 Saint-Etienne, France
[3] Emlyon Business School, CNRS, UMR 5600 EVS, 42009 Saint-Etienne,
France
[4] Vibratec, 28 chemin du petit bois, 69131 Ecully, France

**Abstract.** The design of innovative offers involves deep collaboration between
the provider and the customer to create higher value than in traditional offers.
Product-Service Systems (PSS) are bundles of products and services and constitute innovative offers designed to fit complex customer needs. The academic
literature on PSS development has a strong focus on the provider perspective,
and only a few works address customer involvement in the process of value co-
creation. This paper proposes a methodological framework composed of a
customer view and a provider view, highlighting the interface between them, in
which value co-creation takes place. The proposed framework aims at supporting the collaboration process between the customer and the provider during
the entire PSS development. The framework has been built within a R&D
project in a French company called Vibratec.

**Keywords:** Value co-creation · PSS development · Customer value · Case
study

## 1 Introduction

The design of innovative offers involves deep collaboration between the provider and
the customer to create and capture higher value than traditional offers [7]. Product-
Service Systems (PSS), which are essentially bundles of products and services, are
considered as innovative offerings designed to fit complex customer needs. Usually, the
literature approaches the process of PSS development from the provider perspective
[10, 11]. Few studies integrate the customer perspective of value creation in PSS
development [2, 4]. In this research, we consider the customer as a key actor on value
co-creation, according to the service-dominant logic (SDL) [6]. This paper proposes a
three-fold conceptual framework composed of a customer view (value expectations); a

© IFIP International Federation for Information Processing 2020
Published by Springer Nature Switzerland AG 2020
B. Lalic et al. (Eds.): APMS 2020, IFIP AICT 592, pp. 361–368, 2020.
https://doi.org/10.1007/978-3-030-57997-5_42

provider view (value proposition), highlighting the interface between both of them; and a general context view.

Customer value is considered here as the point of departure for the process of value co-creation. Indeed, clear visualization of customer value constitutes the key entry for supporting the provider in the development of high value-added offerings [12]. This research aims at exploring the customer and provider perspectives of the value expected from a PSS offer, looking for the alignment of both perspectives. The research question guiding this research can be formulated as follows: *How is the process of value co-creation between the customer and the provider in PSS development?*

Action research is carried out within a small-sized French company called Vibratec. Vibratec is an innovative company in the sector of vibration analysis. The empirical approach adopted is based on a qualitative analysis throughout the deployment of semi-directive interviews with the key actors.

The structure of the paper is as follows. Section 2 presents briefly a literature review on value co-creation and PSS. Section 3 introduces the proposed framework. Section 4 presents the case study, describing the empirical approach and the application of the proposed framework. Finally, conclusions and research perspectives are explained in Sect. 5.

## 2 Value Co-creation and PSS Development

In the literature, there are two main approaches to value co-creation. On the one hand, service-dominant logic (SDL) defines value co-creation as a relational process in which the customer and the provider collaborate to create superior value For the SDL the customer is the beneficiary of the value created and the provider is a facilitator [6]. Indeed, the customer defines what value is according to its needs and experience, which is known as the value in use. On the other hand, the resource-based view (RBV) [1, 3] defines value co-creation as the strategic integration of resources and knowledge coming from several actors (i.e., in a dyadic or a networked relationship) with the aim at developing innovative offerings able to create high value for all the actors.

Focusing on the dyadic customer-provider relationship, the interest for each actor to adopt a co-creation strategy has been analysed. Firstly, the provider is interested in incorporating the customer knowledge and expertise in the offer development from the early stages of idea generation and conceptualization. This allows the provider to respond the closest possible to the customer expectations, reducing the risk of failure during the commercialization phase [9, 12]. Particularly in B2B relationships, a reason to integrate the customer in the offer development corresponds to a strategy of cost and risk-sharing. This case usually takes place in the development of innovative offerings triggered by a specific customer demand [9]. In conclusion, integrating the customer in the offer development process represents an opportunity to be more competitive in a highly dynamic market.

Similarly, according to [9], the customer is interested in co-creating value with its providers for acceding to their missing skills, knowledge, and resources. For instance, in B2B relationships, customers collaborate with providers to increase their capacity, get operational or methodological expertise, obtain market information, or gain in legitimation in their business activities [9]. Moreover, closer collaboration with the providers enables customized solutions, able to fit particular and complex customer needs.

In the context of PSS, the integration of the customer in the process of value creation is a crucial factor to have a successful business model [5]. A few works refer to customer and provider collaboration. For instance, [14] propose an improvement of the BMC by adopting the principles of the service-dominant logic (SDL), which is translated into collaborative practices between customers and providers. Most of the contributions in this category are based on the PSS typology proposed by [13] (i.e., product-oriented, used-oriented, and result-oriented). Besides, [12] highlight the concept of value co-creation as the fact of involving the customer from the early to the later phases of the offer development. For these authors, the value co-creation process aims at achieving a trade-off between the accomplishment of customer's value expectations and the development of feasible value propositions according to the provider capabilities. This research adopts an organisational point of view of PSS development, centred in the collaborative process between customer and provider.

## 3 Methodological Framework to Support Value Co-creation in PSS Development

This methodological framework resumes the global pathway to co-create an innovative offer, and is based on the authors' previous research [8]. It takes into consideration the interactions between the customer and the provider, which is the base of value co-creation. The framework is composed by the two main pillars of value co-creation: the customer view (value expectations), and the provider view (value proposition). Additionally, considering the literature in innovation, a third view concerning the analysis of the general context is added. Figure 1 shows the detailed model.

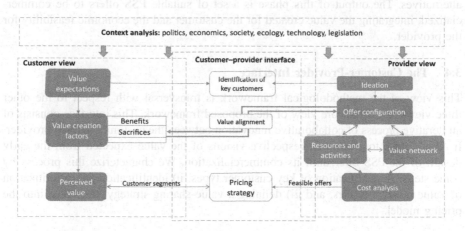

**Fig. 1.** Methodological framework for collaborative PSS development.

### 3.1     General Context Analysis

This step of the methodological framework consists of a deep understanding of the company's internal and external contexts. According to the reviewed literature, several external factors can trigger or block the development of innovative offers development like PSS. External factors coming from competition, politics, economics, society, technology, environmental issues, and legislation, influencing innovative offer development. For this phase, tools for strategic analysis as PESTEL are suitable for having a global view of the context.

### 3.2     Customer View

This view refers to the identification of the potential and current customer segments and their associated factors of value creation. This derives into a deep understanding of the called customer perceived value. From the methodological point of view, an exploratory approach can be adopted during this step. For instance, semi-structured interviews allow getting a qualitative characterization of the customer's expected value. The results of this phase constitute a key entry to ideate PSS opportunities from then provider view.

### 3.3     Provider View

The aim of this view is to identify the provider capabilities to fulfil customer value expectations. Following an iterative process of collaboration with the customer, the provider would be able to entail the PSS offer development process. At this phase, the provider integrates the customer value expectations and confront them with its own capabilities and skills to fulfil them. This phase allows the provider structuring a process of PSS development: i) opportunities ideation, ii) identification of activities and resources needed, iii) value network configuration, and iv) economic analysis of PSS alternatives. The output of this phase is a set of suitable PSS offers to be commercialized, integrating the value created for the customer and the economic feasibility for the provider.

### 3.4     The Customer-Provider Interface

This view of the methodological framework is transversal with respect to the other three views and is the core view of the proposed framework. This interface consists of an iterative process of collaborative innovation between the customer and the provider. It allows them to align their respective visions of the value expected from the early design of the PSS offer until its commercialization. We characterize this process by some steps: i) identification of key customer types, ii) identification and prioritization of value creation factors, and iii) defining a value-sharing strategy, translated into the pricing model.

# 4 The Case of Vibratec: An Action Research Approach

## 4.1 Research Context

The case of a small-sized company in France, called Vibratec, is analysed in this research. Vibratec main activity remains on service provision of specialized analysis of vibrations, applied to different industrial fields (i.e., railway systems, aeronautics, automotive, among others). Recently, in the frame of an R&D project, Vibratec developed a highly-innovative prototype destined to maintenance management in railway systems (i.e., rolling material and infrastructure). The product is in the prototype phase, and the company aims at finishing it to start commercialization. Currently, it is necessary to develop supplementary services around the offer, configuring a bundled offer of products and services to respond to specific customer needs. The company desires to move from a product-based offer towards a PSS offer to be more competitive in a new market.

The action research approach has been implemented to collect the data and be able to analyse the case of Vibratec. The methodology of action research implemented in the company comprehends four steps: i) context analysis; ii) key actors identification; iii) development of interviews; iv) analysis of interviews and conclusions. These steps are concrete support to the proposed framework.

An exploratory approach based on semi-structured interviews was deployed with the key actors identified by Vibratec's commercial department. The main objective of these interviews was to identify the factors of value creation for each customer category throughout the content analysis. 15 interviews have been executed between 2018 and 2020.

## 4.2 Methodological Framework Implementation

The project development is at the second stage of the methodological framework. However, it is possible to draw out some insights for each of the phases.

**Context Analysis.** The railway system in France is a complex ecosystem in which several actors are involved. This complexity corresponds to the relevance of public transport for the development of any society. The PESTEL framework has been implemented to analyse the macro context in this research:

**(P) Politics:** decisions regarding investments on maintenance systems depend on the transport authorities (AOT) at national, regional, and local levels.
**(E) Economics:** the target market of the innovative Vibratec's offer is currently dominated by big-sized and well-positioned companies in the railway sector. Nevertheless, some opportunities for market positioning are possible regarding the company's innovation strengths.
**(S) Society:** the public transport system in France favours the accessibility to any individual, providing multi-modality and high levels of comfort.
**(T) Technology:** current developments correspond to self-driven and hydrogen-based trains. All the political efforts and investments are currently addressed on these directions.

(E) **Ecology:** new policies and technologies address the need for energy-efficient trains.
(L) **Legislation:** a recent law of mobility in France (2019) encourages an augmentation of the use of public transport. It promotes comfort standards related to vibration and acoustics management.

**Customer View: Key Factors for Customer Value Creation.** Firstly, actual and potential customers for the innovative offer of Vibratec are identified.

The targeted customers of Vibratec are AOTs (Transport Authority), transport operators, and technical experts. Firstly, the AOTs are the governmental entities responsible for mobility management in a territory (in this case, regional, or local). They have a financial role in the transport ecosystem. Secondly, the transport operators are contracted by the AOTs and they are responsible for the operations and, then, the maintenance management of the railway system. Finally, the technical experts are private or public companies with expertise on a specific domain of knowledge (e.g., financial, vibrations and acoustics, etc.), which provide services linked to the maintenance activities. Some of the findings of value creation factors are summarized in the following:

**AOT:** this type of customer is placed at a strategic and political level of decision, lacking technical knowledge about maintenance management. For this type of actor, the main factors of value creation correspond to environmental and social issues. For the environmental dimension, the AOTs look for solutions extending the life cycle of the rolling material and the infrastructure. In terms of social value, one of the major interests of the AOTs is to guarantee a tolerable level of noise to the citizens, linked to vibration management.
**Transport operator:** this actor is placed at an intermediate level, dealing with strategic and operational decisions. The main value factor concerns the reduction of maintenance costs in the long-term. Besides, at the technical level, transport operators look for decision-aiding support that allows them to optimize the maintenance activities.
**Technical expert:** this customer type is concerned with specific technical issues. The main factors of value creation identified correspond to the reduction and or the elimination of mechanical failures (e.g., geometry measurements, screeching, short defaults, among others).

**The Provider View: Insights to the Offer Configuration.** After the interviews performed with the targeted customers, Vibratec can elucidate major insights to further develop their PSS offer.

Firstly, it exists an economic barrier considering the customer willingness to pay for the desired offer. This is derived from the general difficulty of the customers to visualize the entire value that the offer can provide them. Giving this fact, some strategies are being studied by Vibratec to guide the offer development, for instance: i) extending the customer target, ii) further development of additional services modules, iii) rethinking the business model associated to the offer, different from product-selling (i.e., pooling, location, among others), and iv) considering the provision of a complete solution for the customer.

The last point appears essential for different customer segments. Indeed, a complete offer means going from the diagnostic of the failure until the maintenance service provision. In this case, Vibratec, whose core business is based on vibration analysis and not in maintenance activities, should considering strategic partnerships with maintenance service providers. It requires the construction of collaborative business models based on win-win value-sharing strategies.

In the continuity of the project, further development of the provider view is considered. Concretely, the deployment of workshops with internal employees of Vibratec is proposed. The aim of the subsequent steps is to generate ideas about the future offer configuration until getting a refined set of PSS alternatives.

**The Customer-Provider Interface: Value Co-creation Process.** This research is currently in the first stages of the value co-creation process, involving key customers identification and value alignment process.

Firstly, concerning the key customer segments, at the beginning of the project, Vibratec delimited the target customers according to their own vision of the offer functionalities and commercialization potential. Nevertheless, as a result of the interviews with the different customers, new key customers were identified and then added to the scope of the study. Then, besides the AOTs and the transport operator (i.e., identified by the commercial engineers at Vibratec before the interviews), the "technique expert" was included (e.g., grinding service provider). They are potential customers, which could integrate Vibratec offer into their own value offer of maintenance.

Concerning the value alignment, new factors of value creation have been elucidated from the customer perspective. For instance, the social value (e.g., preserving employments linked to rudimentary maintenance methods like visual inspection). Further investigation is required to quantify the different value creation factors, establishing the priorities for both customers and the provider.

Finally, the pricing strategy is not yet analysed given the current state of the research. It will be based on the deep analysis of the customer perceived value for each segment, as well as the cost analysis of the final alternatives of the PSS offer and the corresponding business model.

## 5  Conclusions

This methodological framework for PSS design was applied to a French company in the railway transport sector. The framework highlights the importance of defining structured mechanisms to support a strong interaction between the provider and its customers, bringing the two visions within an active value co-creation process. Throughout these structured and managed interactions, the framework aims at enabling a better adaptation and acceptability of the offer, a larger creation of value, as well as a cognitive alignment between both customers' and providers' points of view.

The current case study is still under progress, only the first steps of the framework are described here. Nevertheless some managerial implications can be highlighted based on the insights obtained from the single case study. Firstly, the framework provides to Vibratec a formal and structured base to support their marketing and commercial strategies. Secondly, the framework represents a tool for the commercial department to communicate internally with the technical department (which facilitates the technical development of the PSS offer), and with the decision-makers (guiding financial and organisational decisions).

The perspectives of the paper are to provide a full validation with Vibratec, before any further extension through additional case studies and larger theoretical confrontation.

# References

1. Barney, J.: Firm resources and sustained competitive advantage. J. Manag. **17**(1), 99–120 (1991)
2. Bertoni, A., Bertoni, M., Johansson, C.: Analysing the effects of value drivers and knowledge maturity in preliminary design decision-making. In: Design Information and Knowledge Management. International Conference on Engineering Design. Design Society (2015)
3. Corsaro, D.: The emergent role of value representation in managing business relationships. Ind. Mark. Manage. **43**(6), 985–995 (2014)
4. Edvardsson, B., Kristensson, P., Magnusson, P., Sundstrm, E.: Customer integration within service development—a review of methods and an analysis of insitu and exsitu contributions. Technovation **32**(7), 419–429 (2012)
5. Kindström, D., Kowalkowski, C.: Development of industrial service offerings: a process framework. J. Serv. Manag. **20**(2), 156–172 (2009)
6. Lusch, R.F., Vargo, S.L.: Service-dominant logic: reactions, reflections and refinements. Market. Theory **6**(3), 281–288 (2006)
7. Neubert, G., Lambey-Checchin, C.: The sustainable value proposition of PSSs: the case of ECOBEL "Shower Head". Procedia CIRP **47**, 12–17 (2016)
8. Orellano, M., Medini, K., Lambey-Checchin, C., Neubert, G.: A system modelling approach to collaborative PSS design. Procedia CIRP **83**, 218–223 (2019)
9. Petri, J., Jacob, F.: The customer as enabler of value (co)-creation in the solution business. Ind. Mark. Manage. **56**, 63–72 (2016)
10. Schmidt, D.M., Malaschewski, O., Mrtl, M.: Decision-making process for product planning of product-service systems. Procedia CIRP **30**, 468–473 (2015)
11. Shen, J., Erkoyuncu, J.A., Roy, R., Wu, B.: A framework for cost evaluation in product service system configuration. Int. J. Prod. Res. **55**(20), 6120–6144 (2017)
12. Tran, T., Park, J.Y.: Development of a strategic prototyping framework for product service systems using co-creation approach. Procedia CIRP **30**, 1–6 (2015)
13. Tukker, A.: Eight types of product–service system: eight ways to sustainability? Experiences from SusProNet. Bus. Strategy Environ. **13**(4), 246–260 (2004)
14. Xing, K., Ness, D.: Transition to product-service systems: principles and business model. Procedia CIRP **47**, 525–530 (2016)

# The Future of Lean Thinking
# and Practice

# Utilizing Lean Thinking as a Means to Digital Transformation in Service Organizations

F. P. Santhiapillai[✉] and R. M. Chandima Ratnayake

University of Stavanger (UIS), Department of Mechanical and Structural
Engineering and Material Science, Stavanger, Norway
{felix.santhiapillai,chandima.ratnayake}@uis.no

**Abstract.** Digital transformation (DT) is gaining interest and changing citizens' expectations of service organizations' ability to deliver high-value, real-time digital services. However, from an organizational perspective, DT entails a continuum of transitions that emphasize cultural, organizational, processual and relational changes. Over the past few decades, Lean thinking has been a dominant part of many organizational philosophies and proven to be an important enabler, to cater for the aforementioned changes. With its focus on reducing organizational complexity and increasing value for the end-user, it can support DT through its systematized utilization of methods and tools for improvement. The purpose of this paper is to demonstrate the use of Lean thinking to develop and enhance service processes and its contributing effect to enable DT in service organizations. Accordingly, a conceptual process for Lean digital transformation (LDT) is developed and discussed. In order to test the developed LDT process, action research was conducted in a sales and service organization in Norway, where an after-sales process was selected for current-state analysis. The conducted study resulted in the development and commercialization of a software system, which has been licensed and implemented by approximately 100 users within a year. The findings of this study reveal a great improvement and innovation potential in utilizing Lean thinking to enable and drive DT.

**Keywords:** Lean thinking · Digitization · Digitalization · Lean digital transformation

## 1 Introduction

Digital transformation (DT) is gaining interest and changing citizens' expectations of service organizations' ability to deliver high-value, real-time digital services [1]. As computing capabilities have increased exponentially over recent decades, DT offers enormous value-creating opportunities, in terms of new services, products, processes and skills [2]. It is mostly associated with the effort of using new technologies to create or modify and improve processes and services, following the needs of customers, which goes beyond organizational digitization efforts [3, 4]. According to [4], DT evolves along a continuum of transitions, which is differentiated by digitization, digitalization and digital transformation, where digitization highlights the process of converting information into a digital format or the transition from analog to digital, whereas digitalization is the utilization of digital technologies and digitized data to make changes in processes. Followingly, DT emphasizes the overall cultural, organizational, and relational changes, which constitute a complex field within organizational change management [4].

Over the past few decades, Lean thinking has been a dominant part of many organizational philosophies and proven to be an important enabler to cater for the aforementioned changes [5, 6]. It facilitates a common language and a systematic way of thinking that ensures a centralized focus on customer value and the elimination of waste, variation and/or overburden in an organization [7, 8]. Furthermore, Lean thinking emphasizes principles and tools, such as "pull" system, leveled flow, visual control, standardization, value stream mapping, etc., as enablers of process innovation [9]. For the support and implementation of new technology as a means to improve existing value-creation processes, Lean thinking can complement digitalization, as digitalization can benefit the pursuit of becoming Lean [10, 11]. However, there is a need to further explore the relationship between the two paradigms of Lean and DT and how they can influence or enable each other, from a practical perspective.

Lean thinking, the process of product design and development [12] and design thinking [13] together inspired the development (and modification during and after the project) of a holistic conceptual design for the process of Lean digital transformation (LDT) (Fig. 1). LDT illustrates the application of Lean thinking and tools relative to the transitioning process of DT and product design and development. In order to test and simulate the developed LDT process, an action research project was initiated in a sales and service organization in Norway. The action research strategy included a mixed-method approach of quantitative and qualitative analysis. This paper provides insight into and discusses the results of the presented LDT process.

## 2  Organizational Challenge

The company in this study sells high-end products to a wide range of customer segments. It is a leading franchise, with 25 locations across Norway, whose products are supplied by multiple global suppliers. If its products are delivered with poor quality, or the product is damaged early in its estimated life span, for which the customer is not at fault, the customer has the right to demand a type of compensation under Norwegian law. A central part of the business is to have a customer-satisfying product claim process (PCP), if this occurs after sale. Their current PCP is largely manual and not standardized, which has led to the development of separate and different routines across their 25 locations. From a managerial perspective, there is a lack of total overview and control of all defects and cases that are created. The purpose of this study is to analyze their current state process. Furthermore, the objective is to introduce an improved future state solution for this sales and service organization.

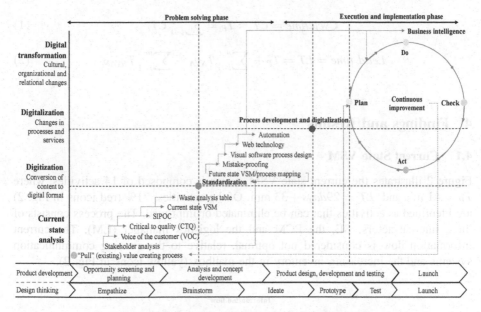

**Fig. 1.** Lean digital transformation process diagram

# 3 Research Methodology

This study intends to generate explicit knowledge that will lead to informed and strategic action for a company. Accordingly, an action research strategy is chosen [14, 15]. The study uses a mixed-method approach, with a combination of qualitative and quantitative analysis [16]. As part of the method, unstructured interviews were conducted in workshops with one of the location's employees. Participants were chosen and categorized based on their position relative to operational, tactical and strategic levels in the organization. Accordingly, one "shop-floor" employee (SE) from the operational level, one product claim manager (PCM) from the tactical level and one location manager from the strategic level participated. However, due to time management and resource capacity, the PCM was the one to actively participate in all workshops. The PCM supplied with necessary input information regarding the PCP based on experience and expertise.

In order to identify the improvement potential, in the form of the digitization and digitalization potential, of the company's PCP, a current state analysis was first initiated. To provide a holistic understanding and snapshot of the PCP "before" and "after", this paper is limited to presenting the following analytical Lean tools: current state value stream mapping (VSM), waste analysis table and future state VSM. Furthermore, the following mathematical formulas for performance measures were applied [17], where cycle time (CT) is the actual time spent completing a task and lead time (LT) is the total time it takes to complete a task, which include CT and time spent on non-value-added activities (NVA) and non-value-added, but necessary activities (NVAN).

$$Cycletime = CT = T_P = \sum_{i=1}^{n} CT_i \tag{1}$$

$$Lead\ time = LT = T_P + \sum_{i=1}^{n} T_{NVA} + \sum_{j=1}^{m} T_{NVAN_i} \tag{2}$$

## 4   Findings and Results

### 4.1   Current State VSM

Figure 2 illustrates the current state VSM, which is composed of 14 activities, where $T_P = 41$ min and $LT = 29 days + 33$ min. Of the activities, 71% (red icons in Fig. 2) are identified as activities that can be eliminated or improved. The process consists of three internal actors: SE, the PCM and the logistics manager (LM). The current information flow is considered not optimal, relative to the existing communication systems and the increasing inventory in the mailbox (yellow icons in Fig. 2).

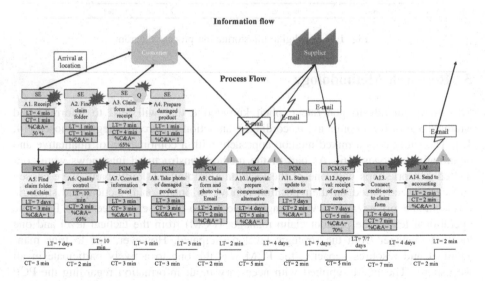

**Fig. 2.**  Current state value stream mapping of claim process (Color figure online)

### 4.2   Waste Identification and Analysis

Based on the current state VSM, constraints, operational waste (OW) and root causes are identified and analyzed. The PCM supplied the necessary information with as much detail as possible to accomplish the aforementioned. Table 1 provides a summarized description of some of the identified OW, NVA and NVAN.

Table 2 illustrates how the activities identified from the current state VSM (Fig. 2) and analyzed in the waste analysis table (Table 1) are evaluated and structured relative to value added (VA), NVA and NVAN. This provides an overview of which activities

**Table 1.** Waste analysis table

| OW | NVA/NVAN | Description |
|---|---|---|
| Over-processing | A1-A3. Manual document handling and excessive paperwork | Finding folder in cabinet and filling out a one-page claim form, one for the PCM and a receipt for the customer. A duplicate is stored in a secondary folder for ongoing cases. When the customer returns to collect his/her product, the SE must find the secondary folder and the correct duplicate matching the given receipt (see Inventory and Transportation). |
| Over-production | A7-A9. Over-production of the same data/information | The same information is processed on three platforms for storage and communication. The original claim form is converted to/in secondary claim form, Excel and email. |
| Defect | A3. Defects in generated claim case, which are first identified when PCM revises claim form after first handover from store employee | There are 40 SEs that can receive and generate a case in the first stage. The PCM observes variation in handling of this stage, due to lack of experience among the SEs, e.g. information is missing, or, as the initial claim form is handwritten, PCM often experiences unintelligible handwriting, which causes rework and information hunting (see Rework). |
| Rework | A6. Rework or correcting as a result of identified defects | Repercussions from Defects, when information is lacking or unintelligible, the PCM must go through the initial information and supply what is missing; this may mean finding the right SE for additional information or extracting the information from their systems. |
| Transportation | A1-A11. Information hunting and excessive processing | Establishing a communication channel with customer based on a physical claim receipt has often led to situations where customer returns to store and has lost the given receipt. This causes information hunting and an additional process for validation. Communication with customer is made through phone first when the supplier has made an evaluation. However, their experience is that customers often make contact via phone to ask for the status on their case; as any one of the 40 SEs may answer, it becomes difficult to provide an adequate answer, as only the PCM knows the status. Internal transmittal of information is not optimal, causing disturbances and poor customer experience. |
| Inventory | A9-A14. Information is converted to three different platforms | Handling an average of 45 claims each month with different suppliers has resulted in a complex and unorganized inventory system in their service mailbox. There are no established systems for providing an overview of collected credit notes from suppliers. Their Excel sheet has also become complex and lost its function. |

to eliminate or improve, according to their value creation, and, further, a foundation for future state VSM.

## 4.3  Future State VSM

The future state PCP is composed of seven activities overall (Fig. 3), meaning, 50% of the activities from the current state VSM are either eliminated or improved. The presented waste in Table 1 is eliminated or reduced, resulting in an estimated

**Table 2.** Waste elimination and improvement table

| Activity | VA | NVAN | NVA | Digital improvement | Eliminate |
|----------|-----|------|-----|--------------------|-----------|
| A1 | ● | | | x | |
| A2 | | | ● | | x |
| A3 | ● | | | x | |
| A4 | ● | | | | |
| A5 | | | ● | | x |
| A6 | | ● | ● | x | x |
| A7 | | | ● | | x |
| A8 | ● | | | x | |
| A9 | ● | | | x | |
| A10 | | ● | | x | |
| A11 | ● | | | x | |
| A12 | | ● | | x | |
| A13 | | | ● | | x |
| A14 | | | ● | | x |
| 100% | 42.9% | 21.4% | 35.7% | | |

$T_P = 15.1$ min and $LT = 11 \ days + 3.1$ min. Furthermore, the new PCP facilitates optimal resource utilization, by releasing LM from the process.

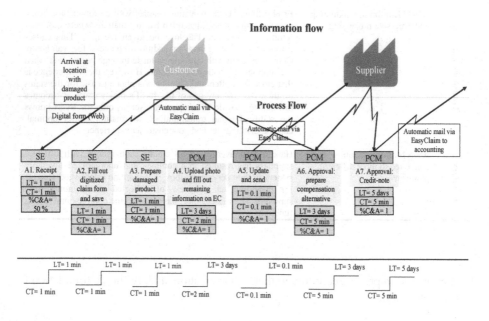

**Fig. 3.** Future state VSM

# 5  Discussion and Conclusion

The testing and implementation of the presented LDT process (Fig. 1) resulted in the development, launching, commercialization and specialization of a lead incident management system within the domain of customer (& supplier) relationship management (CSRM), which goes by the name, Easyclaim [18]. Within a year, this software system has been licensed by two leading service and sales organizations and implemented by approximately 100 locations or users in Norway. Section 4, Findings and Results, provides a snapshot of the entire LDT process and summarizes the current state analysis phase and the improvement that was made for the company. The digitalized PCP is composed of seven activities overall (Fig. 3), meaning, at least 50% of the activities from the current state VSM are either eliminated or improved (Fig. 2). In the digitalized PCP, *LT* is reduced by approximately 62%, where 35.7% of the activities (NVA) are eliminated and 21.4% of the activities (NVAN) are either integrated as part of a VA activity or improved (Table 2).

The findings of this study also reveal and confirm that standardization and conversion of input information at the point of entry enables digitization. This further allowed creative utilization of digital technologies to restructure and digitalize the company`s existing PCP. For instance, as the process was brought into a computerized platform, functionalities, such as mistake-proofing, automation, a notification and prioritization system and visual process management, were integrated, to improve the PCP. Furthermore, from a strategic perspective, the digital transition facilitated the introduction of business intelligence providing business-critical information, such as detailed analysis of the company's products (e.g. defects and variations), economic loss, suppliers, case processing time, etc. – information used for strategic negotiations and decision-making.

DT also entails organizational and relational changes; accordingly, stakeholder analysis and voice of the customer (VOC) were continual in the LDT process. Having a clear overview of the central actors or users with a high level of interest and power of influence in the PCP, and connecting or relating their needs to the different phases or stages of the LDT process (along both axes), facilitated the detailed customization of the user interface and experience. This particularly resulted in effective system- and user-alignment, reduction of resistance to change from employees and ultimately efficient organizational implementation of the digitalized system.

However, challenges and a further need for system and PCP customization were expected and experienced when transitioning to and operating in the testing and implementation phases of the new software system and digitalized PCP. In order to be flexible and adapt to changes, the continuous improvement cycle of PDCA (plan, do, check and act) was integrated as an iterative process for/in these phases. This particularly facilitated the structured re-visiting of previously conducted/implemented phases and/or tools, the modification and/or improvement of the established product and/or process information, and the identification and integration of additional value-creating processes and functions complementing the software system and the digitalized PCP.

Based on the conducted action research (and product design and development project), this study confirms that Lean thinking and tools enable and support DT, which can contribute to improving existing value-creating processes in an organization. From a practical perspective, the results of this study validate the developed and implemented LDT process. However, further research shall explore its theoretical foundation or validity and integrate it with other disciplinary domains or processes, such as software engineering. In order to develop, adapt and modify the presented LDT process, further research shall also test and/or implement it in other service organizations, such as in the public sector, which is less digitally evolved compared to the private sector [19, 20].

# References

1. Kobus, J., et al.: Enabling digitization by implementing lean IT: lessons learned. TQM J. **30**(6), 764–778 (2018)
2. Matzner, M., et al.: Digital transformation in service management. J. Serv. Manag. Res. **2**, 3–21 (2018)
3. Berman, S.J.: Digital transformation: opportunities to create new business models. Strategy Leadersh. **40**(2), 16–24 (2012)
4. Mergel, I., Edelmann, N., Haug, N.: Defining digital transformation: results from expert interviews. Gov. Inf. Q. **36**, 1–15 (2019)
5. Rachman, A., Ratnayake, R.M.: Adoption and implementation potential of the lean concept in the petroleum industry: state-of-the-art. Int. J. Lean Six Sigma **10** (2018)
6. George, M.L.: Lean Six Sigma for Service. The McGraw-Hill Company, New York (2003)
7. Liker, J.K., The Toyota Way: 14 Management Principles from the World`s Greatest Manufacturer. McGraw Hill, New York (2004). 3–289
8. Womack, J.P., Jones, D.T., Roos, D.: The Machine that Changed the World 1990
9. Netland, T.H., Powell, D.J.: The Routledge Companion to Lean Management. Routledge, New York (2016)
10. Lorenz, R., et al.: Lean and digitalization—contradictions or complements? In: IFIP International Conference on Advances in Production Management Systems. pp. 77–84. Springer, Cham (2019)
11. Womack, J.P., Jones, D.T.: Lean Thinking: Banish Waste and Create Wealth in Your Corporation. Rev. and updated edn. ed. (2003). New York Free Press
12. Ulrich, K.T., Eppinger, S.D.: Product Design and Development, 5th edn. McGraw-Hill, New York (2011)
13. Brown, T.: Design thinking. Harvard Bus. Rev. **86**(6), 84–92 (2008)
14. Greenwood, D.J., Levin, M.: Introduction to Action Research. SAGE Publications Inc, Thousand Oaks (1998)
15. Koshy, V.: Action Research for Improving Practices, 1st edn. SAGE Publications, Thousand Oaks (2005)
16. Bryman, A., Bell, E.: Business Research Methods, 3rd edn., p. 675. Oxford University Press Inc., Oxford (2011)
17. Stadnicka, D., Ratnayake, R.M.C.: Enahncing performance in service organizations: a case study based on value stream analysis in the telecommunications industry. Int. J. Prod. Res. **55**(23), 6984–6999 (2017)
18. Moen, I.A.: Easyclaims ystems 2019. https://www.easyclaimsystems.com/
19. Cankar, S.S., Petkovšek, V.: Private and public sector innovation and the importance of cross-sector collaboration. J. Appl. Bus. Res. **29**(6), 1597–1606 (2013)
20. Dröll, P.: Powering European Public Sector Innovation: Towards A New Architecture 2013: Publications Office of the European Union, Luxembourg. p. 57 (2013)

# On the Need of Functional Priority and Failure Risk Assessment to Optimize Human Resource Allocation in Public Service Organizations

F. P. Santhiapillai[(✉)] and R. M. Chandima Ratnayake[(✉)]

University of Stavanger (UIS), Department of Mechanical and Structural
Engineering and Material Science, Stavanger, Norway
{felix.santhiapillai,chandima.ratnayake}@uis.no

**Abstract.** Optimization of resource utilization plays a significant role in the continuous improvement initiatives of an organization providing services. Lean thinking and systematic approaches, such as multicriteria analysis (MCA), are necessary to optimize the utilization (or allocation) of human resources (HR) in a public service organization, especially to assure that functional performance satisfies organizational and public needs and objectives. This manuscript demonstrates the use of functional priority assessment (FPA) and functional failure risk (FFR) assessment to support and optimize human resource allocation (HRA) management in a public sector organization. Action research has been carried out in one Norwegian police district, to investigate the appropriateness of FPA and FFR assessment for HRA. First, functional priorities have been assessed, based on their impact relative to nine central organizational criteria. Further, based on a tailor-made risk matrix composed of six criteria, consequence of failure (CoF) and probability of failure (PoF) have been qualitatively assessed, resulting in a quantitative representation of FFR levels. The suggested Lean and MCA-based methodology provides significant support to strategic management and Lean practitioners who are involved in implementing or locating improvement initiatives in service organizations, especially in optimizing resource utilization.

**Keywords:** Human resource allocation · Lean thinking · Functional failure risk · Functional priority

## 1 Introduction

Lean thinking has become an important business philosophy within the field of organizational governance and improvement [1, 2]. It emphasizes principles such as customer value creation, pull, just-in-time service deliveries, systematic elimination of waste or non-value-added (NVA) activities and employee-driven continuous improvement [2, 3]. Implementation of Lean thinking to support optimal resource utilization can positively impact several aspects of service performance [1, 4]. In the public sector, this is especially relevant, as top level managers are charged with the difficult task of meeting both public service needs and increasing demands for performance, whilst budgets and

© IFIP International Federation for Information Processing 2020
Published by Springer Nature Switzerland AG 2020
B. Lalic et al. (Eds.): APMS 2020, IFIP AICT 592, pp. 379–386, 2020.
https://doi.org/10.1007/978-3-030-57997-5_44

resources are decreasing [5]. Public sector organizations are expected to prioritize and manage their HR and continuously improve their services [6, 7]. However, strategic decisions regarding HRA are usually made based on the experience and intuition of managers [8]. Hence, there is an increasing need for logical approaches and a framework to assist decision makers in prioritizing their limited HR for the execution of functional activities and service enhancement initiatives [9].

In the literature, different approaches have been proposed, aiming to provide improved support to make the task of HRA more efficient. There is an increasing interest in the use of MCA approaches to define directions and guide cultural changes, prioritizing limited resources and improvement opportunities [9–11]. It is proven to be a helpful way to assess current situations and manage major transformational changes in an organization [12, 13]. By utilizing MCA-based approaches, such as FPA and FFR, this study aims to generate knowledge regarding functional priority and failure risk, based on the current performance level in a public service organization, and, furthermore, to support strategic decision makers in optimal HRA management. Action research has been carried out in one Norwegian police district, to investigate the appropriateness of FPA and FFR assessment for HRA and the prioritization of improvement initiatives.

## 2   Organizational Challenge

The Norwegian Police Service is a nationwide government agency in Norway. The police district in this study, which is one of twelve districts, consists of approximately 1250 employees, 12 units, 30 departments and 60 functions with different service areas. It has a hierarchical structure, represented by strategic, tactical and operational management levels. In the existing forecast, the district is expected to enter 2020 with 1200

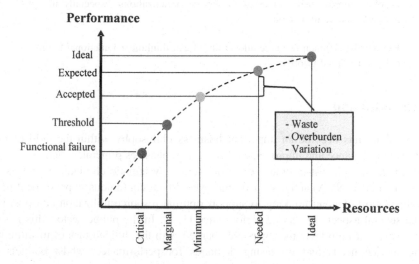

**Fig. 1.** Illustration of the idea for functional failure

employees, without the possibility of new recruitment. Hence, there is a need to monitor, prioritize and adapt the operational environment and its HR utilization and flow. Due to the recruitment freeze, the district may have to adjust the organization, reallocate HR and accelerate systematic improvement initiatives in some functions. This is especially vital in order to avoid functional failure and maintain a satisfying and improving level of service performance in society (Fig. 1).

## 3   Research Methodology

This study has chosen an action research strategy as the objective is to generate new explicit knowledge through participation that will lead to strategic and informed action, [14, 15]. A mixed method approach, with a combination of qualitative and quantitative analysis, is applied. Accordingly, questionnaires and unstructured interviews are used in the implementation phase of this study.

As the district is composed of multiple departments and functions, this manuscript test and present the appropriateness of the developed methodology and MCA models, in order to make adjustments before official implementation in the organization. Accordingly, five functions from different departments, but from the same unit, were chosen to collect data from. As a bottom-up strategy was desired, operational management and employee representatives, responsible for each function, were chosen as participants. Furthermore, the criteria and the developed content were based on close cooperation with disciplinary experts within law enforcement in the district and strategic circulars and documents. Due to sensitive information, content descriptions are not provided in this study.

### 3.1   Functional Priority Assessment

Based on the concept of maturity assessment [13], a questionnaire-based priority matrix was developed, with a total of nine criteria (Table 1). These are described and questioned according to five assessment levels, which are formulated relative to the aspect of impact (or importance).

**Table 1.** Overview of chosen criteria

| Category | Criteria | |
|---|---|---|
| Public impact/importance | 1. | Maintain order and safety in society |
| | 2. | Crime prevention |
| | 3. | Protect public law-abiding activities |
| | 4. | Investigate and prosecute offenses |
| Internal impact/importance | 5. | Requirements for expertise |
| | 6. | Specialized expertise |
| | 7. | Internal cooperation/impact |
| Strategic impact/importance | 8. | Short-term local strategy 0-1 year |
| | 9. | Long-term national strategy 5 years |

## 3.2    Functional Failure Risk Assessment

This study defines functional failure as the termination of the ability of a function to perform its required functional services internally and/or externally [16, 17]. The NORSOK standard, Z-008 Risk-based maintenance and consequence classification, provides the requirements and guidelines for constructing a tailor-made risk matrix, and directions for performing a classification of consequences due to potential failures [16, 18]. Based on the NORSOK standard, a risk matrix (Fig. 2) consisting of six operational consequence criteria was developed (Table 2).

| | Severity | C1 | C2 | C3 | C4 | C5 | C6 | Failure is not expected (1/VL) | Never heard of (2/L) | Has occurred (3/M) | Has been experienced several times (4/H) | Failure will occur (5/VH) |
|---|---|---|---|---|---|---|---|---|---|---|---|---|
| | 5 | | | | | | | M/5 | 10/H | 15/VH | 20/VH | 25/VH |
| | 4 | | | | | | | 4/L | M/8 | 12/H | 16/VH | 20/VH |
| | 3 | | | | | | | 3/VL | 6/L | M/9 | 12/H | 15/VH |
| | 2 | | | | | | | 2/VL | 4/VL | 6/L | M/8 | 10/H |
| | 1 | | | | | | | 1/VL | 2/VL | 3/VL | 4/L | M/5 |

Consequence criteria · Increasing probability · Increasing consequence · Tailor-made content for each combination

Fig. 2. Illustration of risk matrix, adapted from [18]

**Table 2.** Criteria, abbreviations and level of risk categorization

| Criterion | Aspect |
|---|---|
| C1 | Public safety and order |
| C2 | Public trust and reputation |
| C3 | Compliance (with law and guidelines) |
| C4 | Economy |
| C5 | Expertise |
| C6 | HSE |
| *Risk levels* | *Risk categorization* |
| VH | Very high: unacceptable risk – immediate action to be taken |
| H | High: unacceptable risk – action to be taken |
| M | Moderate: acceptable risk – action to reduce risk may be evaluated |
| L | Low: acceptable risk |
| VL | Very low: acceptable risk – insignificant |

# 4 Findings

## 4.1 Functional Priority Assessment (FPA)

Based on the given assessments and leveling for each criterion, an average priority score (P) was calculated for each function. Figure 3 illustrates the distribution of functional priority scores. When comparing the average priority scores, there is variation in impact and/or criticality, relative to the defined criteria. For example, Function B is highly critical or has overall high impact on a majority of criterions compared to Function D.

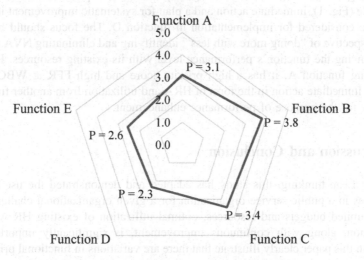

**Fig. 3.** Average functional priority score based on defined criteria

## 4.2 Functional Failure Risk (FFR) Assessment

Based on the developed risk matrix, the participants qualitatively assessed CoF and PoF, resulting in a quantitative representation of the FFR level for each consequence criterion (Fig. 4). Figure 4 illustrates the level of risk category for two assessed scenarios for each function: a worst best case (WBC) and a worst case (WC). These provide two perspectives on the number of HR that can be strategically pulled and reallocated from one function to another before reaching functional failure. For example, WC for Function B is pulling and reallocating nine HR to other functions. This is reflected in the assessed risk levels for each criterion.

| Function | P | WBC | WC | C1 | | C2 | | C3 | | C4 | | C5 | | C6 | |
|---|---|---|---|---|---|---|---|---|---|---|---|---|---|---|---|
| A | 3.1 | 1 | 2 | 12 | 20 | 12 | 20 | 9 | 15 | 1 | 6 | 16 | 25 | 8 | 9 |
| B | 3.8 | 1 | 9 | 1 | 16 | 1 | 20 | 1 | 20 | 6 | 20 | 4 | 16 | 4 | 20 |
| C | 3.4 | 1 | 5 | 6 | 16 | 3 | 16 | 3 | 9 | 3 | 20 | 6 | 16 | 3 | 9 |
| D | 2.3 | 1 | 2 | 20 | 25 | 20 | 25 | 20 | 25 | 20 | 25 | 20 | 25 | 20 | 25 |
| E | 2.6 | 1 | 3 | 8 | 12 | 4 | 12 | 8 | 12 | 8 | 12 | 16 | 20 | 15 | 20 |
| | | | | WBC | WC | WBC | WC | WBC | WC | WBC | WC | WBC | WC | WBC | WC |

**Fig. 4.** Overview of FFR assessment according to WBC and WC

Figure 4 presents a framework that illustrates which functions are in immediate need of HRA or improvement initiatives, according to their priority and FFR. For example, if disciplinary knowledge and expertise is compatible, pulling resources from a highly prioritized function, such as Function B, and reallocating to Function D may not be an optimal solution, as Function B has a very low priority score. However, due to very high FFR at WBC, which arguably indicates a performance level below acceptable (Fig. 1), immediate action and a plan for systematic improvement initiatives should be considered for implementation in function D. The focus should be on the Lean perspective of "doing more with less", identifying and eliminating NVA activities and enhancing the function`s performance level with its existing resources. However, considering function A, it has a high priority score and high FFR at WBC. In this scenario, immediate action in the form of HRA and utilization from another function is necessary for the purpose of performance enhancement.

# 5   Discussion and Conclusion

Based on Lean thinking, this study has adapted and demonstrated the use of MCA approaches in a public service organization for a given organizational challenge. In a time of limited budgets and resources, optimal utilization of existing HR within the organization, along with continuous improvement, is significantly important. The findings in this paper clearly illustrate that there are variations in functional priority and

FFR. It is therefore deemed necessary to utilize MCA approaches, such as FPA and FFR, to systematically generate knowledge regarding the organization and its functions according to current performance level, especially in order to support optimizing HRA and prioritizing the location of improvement initiatives. The suggested FPA and FFR assessment-based methodology and framework is believed to provide support to the strategic management level and practitioners who are involved in implementing Lean thinking in organizations providing services, especially in optimizing the HRA.

However, as the selected criteria in both assessment models are heavily impacted by political, social, economic and technological environments, the presented findings only provide a snapshot of a dynamic environment. Hence, further research related to digital transformation of this methodology, in order to enable continuous planning and data collection, will be carried out. Furthermore, by expanding the implementation of this methodology to all 60 functions in the district, scenarios may arise where several functions are represented equally in relation to average priority score and FFR. In order to distinguish the functions even more, the strategic management level should be able to prioritize or weight the various criteria, to handle scenarios where multiple functions have the same functional priority and failure risk. Further study will therefore investigate the possibility of integrating approaches, such as analytical hierarchy process (AHP), where expert judgments can provide the necessary information for the ranking of various criteria [19].

# References

1. George, M.L.: Lean Six Sigma for Service. The McGraw-Hill Company (2003)
2. Liker, J.K.: The Toyota Way: 14 Management Principles From the World's Greatest Manufacturer, pp. 3–289. McGraw Hill (2004)
3. Womack, J.P., Jones, D.T., Roos, D.: The Machine that Changed the World, p. 352. Free Press (1991)
4. Arias, M., et al.: Human resource allocation in business process management and process mining: a systematic mapping study. Manag. Decis. **56**(2), 376–405 (2018)
5. Callan, T., Nolan, B., Walsh, J.R.: The economic crisis, public sector pay and the income distribution. Res. Labor Econ. **32**(32), 207–225 (2011)
6. Antony, J., Rodgers, B.: Lean six sigma in policing services. Int. J. Prod. Perform. Manag. **67**(5), 935–945 (2018)
7. Bambera, G.J., et al.: Human resource management, lean processes and outcomes for employees: towards a research agenda. Int. J. Hum. Res. Manag. **25**(21), 2881–2891 (2014)
8. Yoshimura, M., et al.: Decision-making support system for human resource allocation in product development projects. Int. J. Prod. Res. **44**(5), 831–848 (2006)
9. Mitton, C., et al.: Allocating limited resources in a time of fiscal constraints: a priority setting case study from Dalhousie University Faculty of Medicine. Acad. Med. **88**(7), 939–945 (2013)
10. Becker, J., et al.: Maturity models in IS Research in European Conference on Information Systems. AISeL (2010)
11. Mitton, C., Donaldson, C.: Twenty-five years of programme budgeting and marginal analysis in the health sector, 1974–1999. J. Health Serv. Res. Policy **6**(4), 239–248 (2001)

12. Ibbs, C.W., Kvak, Y.H.: Assessing project management maturity. Proj. Manag. J. **31**, 32–43 (2000)
13. Becker, J., Knackstedt, R., Peoppelbuss, J.: Developing maturity models for IT management. Bus. Inf. Syst. Eng. **1**(3), 2123–2222 (2009)
14. Greenwood, D.J., Levin, M.: Introduction to Action Research. SAGE Publications, Inc. (1998)
15. Koshy, V.: Action Research for Improving Practices 1ed. SAGE Publications (2005)
16. Ratnayake, R.M.C.: Plant systems and equipment maintenance: use of fuzzy logic for criticality assessment in NORSOK standard Z-008. In: Industrial Engineering and Engineering Management (IEEM) (2013)
17. DNV-OS-F101: Submarine Pipeline Systems in Offshore Standard, Det Norske Veritas AS (2012)
18. Ratnayake, R.M.C.C.: Knowledge based engineering approach for subsea pipeline systems' FFR assessment: a fuzzy expert system. TQM J. **28**(1), 1754–2731 (2016)
19. Samarakoon, S.M.K., Ratnayake, R.M.C.: Strengthening, modification and repair techniques' prioritization for structural integrity control of ageing offshore structures. Reliab. Eng. Syst. Saf. **135**, 15–26 (2015)

# Assessing the Value of Process Improvement Suggestions

Torbjørn H. Netland[1(✉)], Hajime Mizuyama[2], and Rafael Lorenz[1]

[1] D-MTEC, Chair of POM, ETH Zurich, Zurich, Switzerland
tnetland@ethz.ch
[2] Department of Industrial and Systems Engineering, Aoyama Gakuin
University, Tokyo, Japan

**Abstract.** Firms struggle to estimate the expected benefits of improvement suggestions. As a result, pointless or even damaging suggestions are sometimes implemented at the expense of potentially valuable improvement suggestions. This paper reviews, discusses, and advises on the use of available value assessment methods. Thereby, the paper contributes to the production improvement literature and practice with an overview and classification of common value assessment methods.

**Keywords:** Continuous improvement · Manufacturing cost deployment · Kaizen

## 1 Introduction

The ability to continuously identify and implement improvement suggestions is a hallmark of successful organizations. In the lean literature and practice, the term *kaizen*—meaning change for the better in Japanese—is established as the reference method [1, 2]. It involves regular improvement workshops (known as quality circles [3], kaizen blitz, or kaizen bursts), the continual encouragement of improvement suggestions from all employees (sometimes referred to as a continuous improvement culture [4]), and large-scale improvement projects (known as *kaikaku* [1]). While kaizen, by definition, should improve performance, it is often unclear if and how much it does. How the potential gain from a kaizen activity should be measured has been an enduring challenge.

Evaluating production improvement suggestions is a frequent task in manufacturing, but it is usually less rigorous than it should be. Often, managers select improvement projects by taking a leap of faith. In other cases, middle managers battle for the attention and investments of senior management by writing up speculative business cases for their proposed improvement projects. As a result, firms spend a great deal of money on useless improvements, fixing issues that are non-critical or have low or no effect on factory performance. The literature has suggested some structured methods to overcome this challenge, but few are well-known and generally accepted.

It is arguable that a priori value assessment is of less importance because any kaizen is good by definition, and companies should take all the opportunities they can. However, this viewpoint is misguided for four reasons. First, companies operate under

© IFIP International Federation for Information Processing 2020
Published by Springer Nature Switzerland AG 2020
B. Lalic et al. (Eds.): APMS 2020, IFIP AICT 592, pp. 387–395, 2020.
https://doi.org/10.1007/978-3-030-57997-5_45

financial and resource constraints, which creates alternative costs for each investment. Hence, companies should not choose *any* project but the improvements that matter the most for the firm's strategic objectives (e.g., revenue growth; cost reduction; or meeting strategic goals related to sustainability, social responsibility, or other issues). Second, not all intended improvements are effective; sometimes, instead of making things better, changes make things worse (known as *kaiaku*) [5, p. 142]. Besides wasting resources before and after such changes, such results are detrimental to the further motivation of a continuous improvement culture. Third, companies can use quantified improvement data to prescribe the value of new improvement suggestions [6]. Finally, convincing skeptical senior managers to invest money and resources in an improvement project often requires some kind of estimate of its cash flow—even if it is purely based on speculation. Even if one agrees or not with the ubiquitous tendency to measure everything, metrics are part of modern management.

There are plausible reasons why companies do not use rigorous value assessment methods. On the one hand, it is very difficult to correctly assess the cost reduction or revenue growth potential of improvement suggestions. It is also often difficult to assess the cost of implementing the suggestion. On the other hand, for small improvements, a rigorous process may slow down the improvement pace or discourage suggestions from employees. For these reasons, it is not clear when and what form of value assessment methods should be used to support the selection of suggestions for implementation. The challenge is to professionalize the selection method while simultaneously sustaining or growing the improvement culture.

If value assessment is crucial to improvement activities, why does the literature not offer a standard method for it? We assume this is because it is very complicated to take into account all the different requirements and contextual variables needed. Nevertheless, engineers, management researchers, and economists have come up with a range of methods that are used to assess the value of improvements at different stages of pre-implementation. In this paper, we review common value assessment methods from the literature and practice. Additionally, we advise managers on when and how to assess the value of process improvement suggestions.

## 2    Existing Value Assessment Methods

Not surprisingly, companies that use objective prioritization methods report a higher success rate for improvement projects compared to those companies that exclusively use subjective methods [7]. The lack of structured project selection methods leads to lost opportunities, sub-optimization, and inefficient resource allocation. In our review of the literature—and drawing on our insights from working with many manufacturing companies—we found only a few established objective value assessment methods for improvement projects. We discuss these methods in terms of their reliance on different types of qualitative and quantitative data: arbitrary methods (Level 0), qualitative methods (Level 1), operational methods (Level 2), and financial methods (Level 3). Figure 1 illustrates these levels and the typical forms of decision support measurements they involve. These methods are cumulative; financial metrics (in dollars) are derived from operational metrics (changes in time use, quality, etc.) based on some qualitative judgments (e.g., what metrics are recorded), which are influenced by individual judgments.

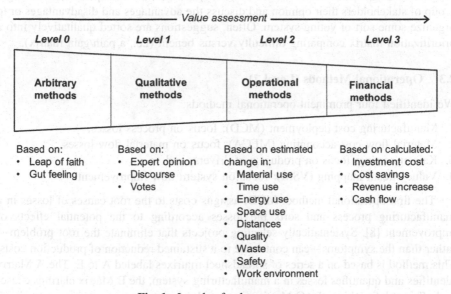

Fig. 1. Levels of value assessment.

We briefly discuss a few common qualitative methods that are used at Levels 0 and 1 before reviewing in more detail objective assessment methods at Levels 2 and 3. At Level 2, companies use operational metrics. For example, suggestion X is expected to reduce material losses by 5% or suggestion Y is expected to decrease energy usage by 3%. While quantitative metrics like these can be convincing, they are incomplete. The financial metrics of Level 3 ultimately provide answers to the question: What will be the return on this investment?

## 2.1   Arbitrary Methods (Level 0)

At Level 0, projects are started purely based on a gut feeling or leap of faith. This complete lack of an objective assessment methods may be justified if the cost of applying the methods would be higher than the expected benefits. Sometimes, the simple rule of thumb is applied to inform the decision to implement or not. For example, 'if an improvement suggestion X makes the workplace more compliant with a certification Y, then it should be implemented.' While this type of value assessment is quick and simple, it risks being incorrect or ineffective.

## 2.2 Qualitative Methods (Level 1)

At Level 1, an elaborate qualitative assessment is conducted that informs the expected effectiveness of suggested improvement ideas. An example is to ask experts if the suggestion has been successful elsewhere in the past. Another example is to ask a larger group of stakeholders their opinion and discuss the advantages and disadvantages or to organize some sort of voting system. Often, suggestions are sorted qualitatively into a prioritization matrix comparing difficulty versus benefit (i.e., a pain/gain matrix).

## 2.3 Operational Methods (Level 2)

We identified four prominent operational methods:

1. Manufacturing cost deployment (MCD): focus on process losses,
2. Material flow cost accounting (MFCA): focus on material flow losses,
3. Kaizen costing: focus on product cost drivers, and
4. Value stream mapping (VSM): focus on system flow improvement.

The first operational method, MCD, assigns costs to the root causes of losses in a manufacturing process and sorts the losses according to the potential effects of improvement [8]. Systematically selecting projects that eliminate the root problem—rather than the symptoms—can contribute to a sustained reduction of production costs. This method is based on a series of spreadsheet matrixes labeled A to E: The A Matrix identifies and quantifies losses in a manufacturing system, the B Matrix clarifies cause-and-effect relationships, the C Matrix connects losses and manufacturing costs, the D Matrix connects causal losses and improvement techniques, and, the E Matrix identifies benefit values and establishes the cost-reduction program. MCD follows a seven-step roadmap [9] from identifying and categorizing losses to selecting improvement projects based on a total cost–benefit analysis. Although the seven steps are straightforward, MCD is an advanced improvement technique, which requires input from both the accounting and production departments. Since it is based on loss calculations, this method is most useful in a technology-intensive environment. MCD is an integrated part of the world class manufacturing program developed by Prof. Hajime Yamashina at Kyoto University and championed by leading automobile companies such as Fiat Chrysler and IVECO.

The second method, MFCA, is an environmental management accounting tool originally proposed in Germany and further refined in Japan, the application procedure for which was standardized as ISO 14051 in 2011 [10]. This six-step method systematically reveals losses and material usage wastes in a manufacturing process and evaluates them in terms of material, energy, system, and waste management costs, thereby supporting improvement projects targeting these losses and wastes. Hence, it focuses only on the physical material flow (and losses) throughout the manufacturing processes. As in the case of MCD, this method needs both operational and accounting data. MFCA has been used to support process improvement in many firms [e.g., 11].

The third method, kaizen costing [12–14], applies to products in the manufacturing phase (as an extension of target costing in the product development phase). When using kaizen costing, firms define a competitive cost for a product and then break the costs of producing it into seven categories: supply chain (including materials); manufacturing; waste; disposal; legal; recruitment; and marketing, sales, and distribution costs. In kaizen costing, cost reduction targets are set regularly (e.g., every month), and teams work to reduce any of the products' seven cost categories. Kaizen costing is a method for involving all employees in the continuous pursuit of cost reduction.

The fourth method is the well-established VSM. The goal of VSM is to visualize the flow of a product from the supplier to the customer through the different processing steps of the plant [15]. VSM draws a map of all the processes and transport for a specific product family. Thereby, it creates transparency about the value adding and non-value adding activities, and the user can derive improvement suggestions, which are visualized as kaizen bursts in the visual map. These improvement suggestions mainly intend to eliminate the non-value adding time and thereby decrease the lead time. However, there is no intention in VSM to combine these suggestions with a cost dimension.

For all these operational methods, the analysis is mainly performed in the operational layer and reveals operators' non-value adding actions, losses of material usage and machine time, and their physical amounts. Improvement suggestions are derived from the potential elimination or reduction of those non-value adding elements. Only by estimating the potential economic effects of eliminating or reducing wastes can these elements be translated into costs with the help of accounting data. Although MCD, MFCA, and kaizen costing calculate cost reduction estimates in monetary terms, these methods are only able to estimate improvements to the *current* production system (kaizen) and not to innovations that are radically new to the system (kaikaku).

## 2.4 Financial Methods (Level 3)

Ultimately, to support an improvement idea, managers want to know how much cash must be invested and how much cash will be received and when. In the field of project finance [16], several approaches are commonly used to evaluate the economic potential of a project. A set of these methods is static, which means that they do not account for the change in values over time. These methods are simple and do not have complex formulas. However, they lack precision in calculating the return. For instance, the break-even point (or payback period) looks at how long it will take for the investment in the improvement to amortize (as a rule of thumb, a payback period longer than 3 years is a hard sell). The return on investment (ROI) can be used to define the invested resources in relation to the expected outcome. It is calculated by dividing the net profit (expected revenue minus expected costs) by the expected costs in order to get a return rate. An alternative to ROI is the internal rate of return (IRR), which is more complicated to calculate but take the time value of money into account.

The second set of methods is dynamic, which means they take into account the potential change in value over time. An example is the net present value (NPV), which compares the monetary inflow with the monetary outflow over time. There are alternatives to this model (e.g., the internal rate of return), all of which are based on the same underlying logic. If there are many projects being proposed, a profitability index calculating the NPV per dollar investment can be used to prioritize and select among them.

In addition, and often based on the method above, numerous sophisticated mathematical optimization models for project prioritization have been suggested in the literature. However, these advanced models find limited use in practice because they are context specific, managers do not understand them, or the model assumptions do not hold.

## 3   Decision Support Model

Improvement suggestions can be very different in scope and impact. They can range from taping the floor to mark the place of a fire extinguisher to changing the layout of a value stream. We posit that the optimal method to evaluate improvement suggestions depends on the type of suggestion. To cluster the improvement suggestions, we differentiate them into two dimensions: impact and scope (see Fig. 2).

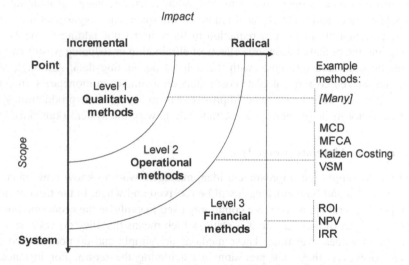

**Fig. 2.** A decision support model for when to prioritize different value assessment methods.

The impact dimension (along the horizontal axis) captures the magnitude of the change. A suggested change can range from incremental (kaizen) to radical (kaikaku). An incremental change would introduce small improvements to an existing system, for instance, changing the location of boxes of screws at an assembly station. A radical suggestion would fundamentally change the process, for example, by automating the screwing process or eliminating the need for screws through a change in the product design.

The scope dimension (along the vertical axis) captures the focus of the improvement. This can range from a point improvement to a system improvement. Point improvements have limited influence beyond the single process or activity improved. System improvements refer to holistic change at the system level, including several processes. For example, consider the redesign of a product where its previously separate parts can be produced in one piece with additive manufacturing. This suggestion would involve many processes in the value stream.

For incremental point improvements on the shop floor, qualitative methods are sufficient. Using a qualitative method helps to motivate and encourage employees to come up with many small improvements. However, if the suggestion becomes more radical or system oriented, operational methods are needed to justify and assure worthwhile investments. Finally, if the suggestions are both radical and system oriented, financial methods need to be used to calculate the hard financial returns of the suggestion.

When using this decision support model, practitioners should consider a range of contextual variables that may affect the choice of using a particular value assessment method. In particular, they should pay attention to existing value assessment practices, managers' affinity for quantitative metrics, data availability, the organization's experience in continuous improvement, resource accessibility (cash, time, and people), and number and quality of improvement suggestions raised. For example, if an organization has no culture for improvement suggestions, using qualitative assessment methods (Level 1) can encourage the kaizen culture to develop. More advanced firms would typically move toward quantitative methods (Levels 2 and 3).

Some mature, lean firms try to assist project selection by moving from traditional accounting to lean accounting. Traditional accounting practices have been criticized for not being able to capture the value of improvement projects besides simple cost-cutting point improvements (e.g., automation of a manual process). As a response, the lean accounting literature has suggested ways to allocate costs to product streams rather than functional cost centers [17]. In the general accounting literature, similar concepts such as activity-based costing (ABC) are well-known but still not widely adopted (a recent survey found that only 18.7% of Irish firms have moved from traditional accounting to ABC [18]). The accurate allocation of overhead to product streams remains one of the main difficulties with ABC. If properly implemented, lean accounting (or ABC) can be used to directly identify improvement potential. ABC can demonstrate how profitable different product streams are to the firm, and the company can use this information to prioritize the improvement of the streams with the highest return. It has been shown that companies that use ABC have a higher improvement rate than companies with traditional accounting systems [19].

# 4  Conclusion

This paper presented a review and discussion of common value assessment methods used in manufacturing improvement activities. We derived four levels of assessment methods (see Fig. 1): no method, qualitative methods, operational methods, and financial methods. Managers can use these assessment methods to assist and increase the effectiveness of decisions related to improvement suggestions. We suggested a simple framework to help practitioners select among the different methods based on two characteristics of the improvement suggestion: its impact and its scope (see Fig. 2).

Managers must be aware of the limitations of the available methods. For example, all quantitative models have problems cost setting soft issues related to human factors and the work environment. Issues related to risk and safety, for example, would usually not be picked up by cost–benefit assessments alone. It is also important to remember that even the most advanced quantitative methods represent simplifications of real-world systems. Moreover, all methods can be manipulated by users who have particular agendas or incentives. It is perhaps pertinent to close with the following quote from W. Edward Deming: "No one knows the cost of a defective product – don't tell me you do. You know the cost of replacing it, but not the cost of a dissatisfied customer" [quoted in 20].

# References

1. Bicheno, J.: Kaizen and kaikaku. In: Taylor, D., Brunt, D. (eds.) Manufacturing Operations and Supply Chain Management: The LEAN Approach, pp. 175–184. Thomson Learning, London (2001)
2. Imai, M.: Kaizen: The Key to Japan's Competitive Success. Random House, New York (1986)
3. Deming, W.E.: Out of the Crisis. Massachusetts Institute of Technology, Boston (1982)
4. Netland, T.H., Powell, D.J.: A lean world. In: Netland, T.H., Powell, D.J. (eds.) The Routledge Companion to Lean Management. Routledge, New York (2016)
5. Ohno, T.: Workplace Management. Productivity Press, Cambridge (1988)
6. Schuh, G., Prote, J.-P., Busam, T., Lorenz, R., Netland, T.H.: Using prescriptive analytics to support the continuous improvement process. In: Ameri, F., Stecke, K.E., von Cieminski, G., Kiritsis, D. (eds.) APMS 2019. IAICT, vol. 566, pp. 46–53. Springer, Cham (2019). https://doi.org/10.1007/978-3-030-30000-5_6
7. Kirkham, L., et al.: Prioritisation of operations improvement projects in the European manufacturing industry. Int. J. Prod. Res. 52(18), 5323–5345 (2014)
8. Yamashina, H., Kubo, T.: Manufacturing cost deployment. Int. J. Prod. Res. 40(16), 4077–4091 (2002)
9. Høeg, P., Knutsen, D.: Roadmap for Manufacturing Cost Deployment. NTNU, Trondheim (2016)
10. Christ, K.L., Burritt, R.L.: Material flow cost accounting: a review and agenda for future research. J. Clean. Prod. 108, 1378–1389 (2015)
11. Schmidt, M., Nakajima, M.: Material flow cost accounting as an approach to improve resource efficiency in manufacturing companies. Resources 2(3), 358–369 (2013)
12. Monden, Y., Hamada, K.: Target costing and kaizen costing in Japanese automobile companies. J. Manag. Acc. Res. 3(1), 16–34 (1991)
13. Kaur, M., Kaur, R.: Kaizen costing technique - a literature reivew. CLEAR Int. J. Res. Commer. Manag. 4(11), 84–87 (2013)
14. Yoshikawa, T., Kouhy, R.: Continuous improvement and Kaizen costing. In: Mitchell, F., Nørreklit, H., Jakobsen, M. (eds.) The Routledge Companion to Cost Management, pp. 108–120. Routledge, New York (2013)
15. Rother, M., Shook, J.: Learning to See: Value Stream Mapping to Create Value and Eliminate Muda. Lean Enterprise Institute, Brookline (2003)
16. Yescombe, E.R.: Principles of Project Finance. Elsevier, San Diego (2002)

17. Maskell, B.H., Kennedy, F.A.: Why do we need lean accounting and how does it work? J. Corp. Acc. Finan. **18**(3), 59–73 (2007)
18. Quinn, M., Elafi, O., Mulgrew, M.: Reasons for not changing to activity-based costing: a survey of Irish firms. PSU Res. Rev. **1**(1), 63–70 (2017)
19. Ittner, C.D., Lanen, W.N., Larcker, D.F.: The association between activity-based costing and manufacturing performance. J. Acc. Res. **40**(3), 711–726 (2002)
20. Lohr, S.: He taught the Japanese. In: The New York Times, p. 6 (1981)

# On the Necessity for Identifying Waste in Knowledge Work Dominated Projects: A Case Study from Oil & Gas-Related Product Development Projects

F. P. Santhiapillai[(✉)] and R. M. Chandima Ratnayake[(✉)]

University of Stavanger (UIS), Department of Mechanical and Structural
Engineering and Material Science, Stavanger, Norway
{felix.santhiapillai, chandima.ratnayake}@uis.no

**Abstract.** Within the field of management, knowledge management (KM) enables the generation, sharing, utilization and management of knowledge and information. In order to optimize the processes of KM, Lean thinking and tools can contribute to identifying and eliminating or reducing waste or activities and/or actions that disrupt or do not add value to the information and knowledge generation that ultimately returns value to the end user. Projects, such as product development projects (PDPs), are in general knowledge work (KW) dominated. This manuscript presents an exploratory case study, conducted at a company providing oil & gas operations' services in Norway. The study examines the initial phases of their PDPs, where KM and KW play a more significant role, as information and knowledge are often limited, and uncertainty is high. It is hypothesized that waste in the early phases causes subsequent underperformance in the overall project. This manuscript first elaborates the notion of waste in knowledge work dominated projects from a theoretical perspective. Furthermore, a mixed-method approach was applied, while a survey and semi-structured interviews were conducted. Finally, the Gioia methodology is utilized to process the findings and present a conceptual framework to support KM as a means to prevent or minimize waste in KW-dominated projects.

**Keywords:** Lean thinking · Lean knowledge work · Product development · Waste management

## 1 Introduction

Lean thinking has become a focal business or organizational philosophy for many companies over the last few decades [1]. It is proven to be a significantly important business philosophy which emphasizes customer value by systematically reducing or eliminating overburden, variation and waste or non-value added activities (NVA) [2]. However, implementing Lean within knowledge work (KW) dominated projects, such as product development projects (PDPs), requires adaptation, due to the nature of the projects [3], which are characterized by several KW-related areas, such as integration management, scope management, time management, cost management, quality management, etc. [4].

© IFIP International Federation for Information Processing 2020
Published by Springer Nature Switzerland AG 2020
B. Lalic et al. (Eds.): APMS 2020, IFIP AICT 592, pp. 396–405, 2020.
https://doi.org/10.1007/978-3-030-57997-5_46

In contrast to a manufacturing environment or an assembly line, which is more repetitive and materialistic, KW is not as repetitive and capable of being defined unambiguously with relative certainty [5]. Hence, understanding the field of KW-related waste is deemed necessary, to potentially enhance performance in the overall project.

The purpose of this study is to identify and understand how waste or NVA and actions in front-end phases or early stages of KW-dominated projects can impact the performance of the overall project. Accordingly, an exploratory case study is conducted at an engineering contractor company providing oil & gas operations' services in Norway. PDPs in one of their design engineering departments is chosen for the purpose of this study. A mixed-method approach is chosen, with a survey in the form of a self-completion questionnaire being developed and conducted, based on a literature review. Furthermore, semi-structured interviews are carried out to further investigate the findings from the survey, which statistically illustrate a low level of operational waste in their PDPs in general. However, findings and analysis from the interviews reveal another dimension of waste which can have a considerable effect on the performance and potentially the outcome of their projects.

## 2 Literature Study

The philosophy of Lean relies heavily on employee-driven and systematic identification and removal of waste; this is believed to be a fundamental and critical aspect to understand, in order to effectively target and apply relevant Lean tools and successfully become Lean [1, 6]. Since its origin in the automobile manufacturing industry, Lean has been widely recognized, studied, adapted and implemented in various industries, in both the private and public sectors [7, 8]. However, applying Lean principles and approaches to KW-dominated projects or environments, has proven remarkably challenging, due to their differences from a manufacturing environment (Table 1) [3, 9]. Compared to an assembly line, which is more materialistic and repetitive, knowledge management and KW involves human expertise and judgement that depend heavily on tacit knowledge and data and information, to generate and utilize knowledge [5].

**Table 1.** Lean principles in manufacturing vs knowledge work, adapted from [9]

| Lean principles | Manufacturing | Knowledge work |
|---|---|---|
| Value | Visible at each step, defined goal | Harder to see/define, emergent goals/deliveries/requirements |
| Value stream | Parts and materials | Data, information and knowledge |
| Flow | Iterations are waste | (Un)planned iterations and/or ad hoc approaches must be efficient |
| Pull | Driven by takt time | Driven by needs of enterprise and/or customer/end-user |
| Perfection | Process repeatable without errors | Process enables enterprise improvement |

From a macroscopic perspective, researchers equate knowledge with professional intellect, which in organizations centres around several contexts or knowledge layers, such as *know-what, know-how, know-why* and *know-with* [10]. Accordingly, the information processing system relative to these layers can be analogously and holistically compared to a value-flow model of a manufacturing system [11]. As mentioned, in manufacturing, physical goods flow through the production system; in KW-dominated projects, this hardware is replaced by information and knowledge in its various forms (Fig. 1).

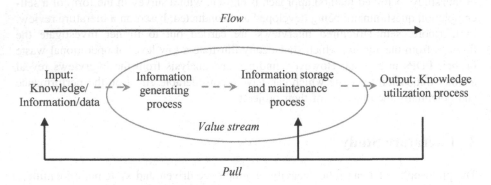

**Fig. 1.** Information processing system, adapted from [11]

Projects, such as PDPs, are in general dynamic, time restricted, multi-disciplinary, goal- and customer-oriented, communication-intensive and KW-dominated, especially in the initial or front-end phases, which to a greater extent are comprised of planning, analysis, creativity, ideation, design processes, etc., often within uncertain conditions with limited information [12, 13]. When describing waste within such environments, the traditional waste categories from manufacturing are also analogously applied when managing Lean in the knowledge-work paradigm. However, due to its complexity, the set of categories cannot be considered all-inclusive [14]. Authors such as [9, 12, 14–19] address this issue by reformulating, adapting and supplementing the traditional operational waste (OW) categories in a PDP environment (Table 2). Due to the complex nature of this environment, interdependency and the formation of a complex causal network between the OW categories must be taken into account (Fig. 2) [14].

**Table 2.** Operational waste categories

| Waste | Description |
|---|---|
| Over-production | Producing and/or distributing unnecessary and superfluous information (e.g. extra features, documents, design etc.,). |
| Over-processing | Unnecessary processing of information/completion of tasks beyond what is required in the process |
| Defect | Defective information which deviates from the standards of its purpose or from the customers expectation; it entails the activities creating and using defective outputs / incomplete or incorrect information for/in the process. |
| Correcting | Correcting relates to the effort involved in re-doing, repairing or reworking information. |
| Transportation | Inefficient or unnecessary transmittal/movement/communication of information, between people, organizations, IT systems, disciplines etc. |
| Motion | In contrast to transportation, motion relates to unnecessary human movement (physically) to acquire needed information. |
| Inventory | Build-up or stockpiling of information (e.g. raw, in-process and/or processed features and material, such as prototypes, that is not being used). |
| Waiting/Delays | Waiting is when the value-creating processes are standing still; as a result, the value stream is considered "non-flowing", this can be due to the lack of necessary inputs, resources, controls, approvals etc., causing delays. |

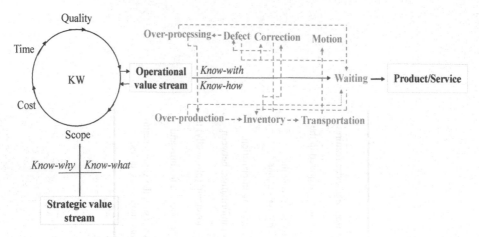

**Fig. 2.** Conceptual illustration of value streams and waste in KW dominated projects, adapted from [14, 16, 17]

## 3   Methodology

As the object is to explore and understand a complicated phenomenon, the philosophical perspective of this study is considered to be an exploratory case study [20]. Case study research is concerned with the complexity and particular nature of the case in question. Such studies typically aim to answer "how" and "why" questions, and in essence explore and investigate contemporary real-life phenomena [21]. The research method is comprised of a survey or self-completion questionnaire and semi-structured interviews.

### 3.1   Lean Maturity Assessment

A survey was developed, in order to assess the department's PDP Lean maturity. The survey was administered to 13 engineers in the department as a self-completion questionnaire. The multicriteria-based matrix consisted of five assessment levels and 37 questions related to commonly identified NVA in PDPs [22].

### 3.2   Gioia Methodology and 5 Whys Analysis

For the 5 whys root-cause analysis, semi-structured interviews were chosen, in order to encourage the interviewees to speak freely. A total of four interviewees participated individually in the analysis. Furthermore, the qualitative structuring and analysis of the findings is based on the adaptation and application of the Gioia methodology, which offers a systematic approach to new concept development and grounded theory articulation [23].

## 4    Case Study Background

The selected case study company supplies mission-critical products and services for the global oil and gas industry. This study investigates a PD design engineering department that provides services in the Nordic region. The department's main role is to support their customers, by developing, upgrading and maintaining the company's installed products and services, as well as providing technical studies and lifetime extension support. Figure 3 provides a broad illustration of their PDP process. As Fig. 3 illustrates, projects experience high uncertainty, complexity and flexibility regarding decision-making in the initial phases, while these decrease as the project develops and information increases. In order to reduce uncertainty, risk and waste in the early stages, the process of KM is seen as an important and central field of their management.

When PDPs reach the implementation phase, they have been executed using the traditional definitions of waste. However, a hypothesis is that the experienced OW or non-value-added activities (NVA) in their implementation phase are results of root causes developed in the early stages of the PDPs. If these activities and root causes are not analysed, the resulting decentralized strategic decisions may continue to produce operational challenges. There is a need to identify and define these in a new conceptual framework, which can be purposed as a tool that contributes to increased value creation and better KM in the early stages.

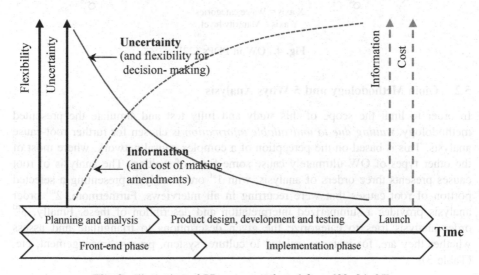

**Fig. 3.** Illustration of PD process, adapted from [22, 24, 25]

# 5    Data Collection and Findings

## 5.1    Lean Maturity Assessment

Considering the average Lean maturity index of 3.8 (dotted line in Fig. 4), the individual maturity scores of Waiting, Transportation, Over-processing, Correction and Defect are below and interpreted as those that should be further investigated. However, statistically, the results illustrate overall low variation between the given categories and high Lean maturity in their projects.

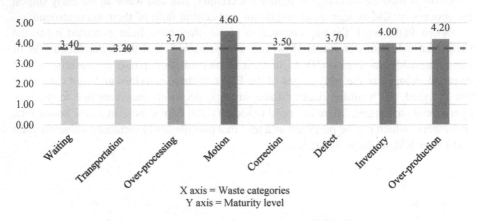

X axis = Waste categories
Y axis = Maturity level

**Fig. 4.** OW in PDPs [22]

## 5.2    Gioia Methodology and 5 Whys Analysis

In order to limit the scope of this study and fully test and simulate the presented methodology, *waiting due to unavailable information* is chosen for further root-cause analysis. This is based on the perception of a complex causal network, where most of the other types of OW ultimately cause some form of waiting. The analysis of root causes presents three orders of analysis, with [1] order analysis presenting a selected portion of root causes that were recurring in all interviews. Furthermore, [2] order analysis provides a summarized interpretation and description of these. Finally, [3] order analysis tries to categorize the given descriptions to triangulate and assess whether they are, for instance, related to culture, system, process, management, etc. (Table 3).

**Table 3.** Analysis of root causes

| 1st order analysis: Root causes from 5 whys analysis | 2nd order analysis | 3rd order analysis |
|---|---|---|
| • Poor capturing of technical requirements/needs, due to lack of expertise/knowledge in initial phases<br>• Details relative to technical changes are not considered when defining the product and project scope<br>• Planning with minimum required resources based on poorly captured requirements<br>• Lack of experience and understanding of tasks and alignment of disciplinary tasks when making decisions<br>• Poor capturing of needed knowledge, leading to coordination and requirement of additional resource capacity and knowledge from disciplines abroad | Managers, customers and/or project participants operating blindly and making strategic decisions without the right information, knowledge, expertise etc., regarding the technical and/or operational aspect of the project and product scope | Lack of operational/technical planning |
| • Poor project/product documentation leading to information hunting<br>• Poor project/product documentation, due to no best-practice guidelines<br>• Poor alignment of entities/disciplines in initial phases causes many targets instead of a common one during the project<br>• Diluted and/or miscommunication of information causing different interpretation of needs or requirements<br>• Multiple people handling the information and not documenting well | Lack of management, handling, documentation, communication, etc., of existing and/or new information/knowledge | Lack of/poor information management |

# 6   Discussion and Conclusion

The findings from the Lean maturity assessment indicate a high level of maturity in the department's PDPs. However, when exploring and analysing Waiting, there are some human activities, actions and/or conditions that are revealed as strategic waste (Fig. 2), which have operational repercussions. From interviews and Table 3, interpreted summarization and categorization for the identified root causes indicate lack of operational and technical knowledge, expertise, information, understanding, etc., among managers and customers, who are more strategically involved and influential regarding decisions in the initial phases of their projects. Arguably, the knowledge layers of "know-why" and "know-what" relative to the project scope are emphasized more than "know-how" and "know-with" relative to the product scope. This causes poor capturing of technical or operational requirements or needs of the design engineers, providing them with a limited product scope that must be developed ad hoc. Another dimension of root cause seems to be a lack of routines, processes or systems for the management, handling, documentation, communication, etc. of shared information in the project. From Fig. 2, these actions, conditions or activities can be considered to be strategic waste (SW).

Accordingly, there is potential for improvement in the early stages that can contribute to improving the management of generating and capturing the necessary knowledge to a greater extent. This study presents a methodological framework to assess Lean maturity and identify waste and root causes in knowledge work dominated projects. A case study was conducted, in order to explore a PDP environment in an oil & gas company, to simulate the implementation of the methodology. However, the study provides a rather isolated and unilateral perspective of waste and its root causes in a highly interrelating and causal network of OW categories. Hence, further study will explore the application of the presented methodology and the notion of SW in other KW-dominated projects or environments, such as in public sector services, law enforcement, criminal cases, strategic management processes, etc. The interrelating causal network of OW and SW will also be further explored.

# References

1. Liker, J.K.: The Toyota Way: 14 Management Principles from the World's Greatest Manufacturer, pp. 3–289. McGraw Hill, New York (2004)
2. Womack, J.P., Jones, D.T., Roos, D.: The Machine that Changed the World, p. 352. Free Press (1991)
3. Rachman, A., Ratnayake, R.M.: Adoption and implementation potential of the lean concept in the petroleum industry: state-of-the-art. Int. J. Lean Six Sigma 10 (2018)
4. PMI: A Guide to the Project Management Body of Knowledge (PMBOK Guide), 5th edn. Project Management Institute (2002)
5. Staats, B., Upton, D.M.: Lean knowledge work. J. Direct Data Digital Mark. Pract. 13(3), 269 (2012)
6. Womack, J.P., Jones, D.T., Roos, D.: The Machine That Changed the World (1990)
7. George, M.L.: Lean Six Sigma for Service. The McGraw-Hill Company (2003)

8. Antony, J., Rodgers, B., Cudney, E.A.: Lean six sigma for public sector organizations: is it a myth or reality. Int. J. Qual. Reliab. Manag. **34**(9), 1402–1411 (2017)
9. McManus, H.L.: Product Development Value Stream Mapping (PDVSM) Manual. Massachusetts Institute of Technology: LAI (2005)
10. Liu, S., et al.: A decision-focused knowledge management framework to support collaborative decision making for lean supply chain management. Int. J. Prod. Res. **51**(7), 2123–2137 (2013)
11. Hicks, B.J.: Lean information management: understanding and eliminating waste. Int. J. Inf. Manag. **27**, 233–249 (2007)
12. Bauch, C.: Lean Product Development: Making waste transparent. Massachusetts Institute of Technology (MIT) (2004)
13. Wysocki, R.K.: Effective Project Management: Traditional, Agile, Extreme, 7th edn. Wiley (2014)
14. Oehmen, J., Rebentisch, E.: Lean Product Development for Practitioners. LAI Paper Series, pp. 2–35 (2010)
15. Pessôa, M.V.P., et al.: Understanding the waste net: a method for waste elimination prioritization in product development. In: Chou, S.Y., Trappey, A., Pokojski, J., Smith, S. (eds.) Global Perspective for Competitive Enterprise, pp. 233–242. Economy and Ecology. Springer, London (2009). https://doi.org/10.1007/978-1-84882-762-2_22
16. Ćatić, A., Vielhaber, M.: Lean product development: hype or sustainable new paradigm. In: International Conference on Engineering Design (2011)
17. Ward, A.C., Sobek, D.K.: Lean product and process development, 2 edn. Lean Enterprise Institute (2014)
18. Freire, J., Alarcon, L.F.: Achieving lean design process: improvement methodology. J. Constr. Eng. Manag. **128**, 248–256 (2002)
19. Poppendieck, M., Poppendieck, T.: Lean Software Development: An Agile Toolkit, p. 240. Addison-Wesley Longman Publishing Co. (2003)
20. Yin, R.K.: Case Study Research: Design and Methods, 4th edn. Sage Publication (2009)
21. Bryman, A., Bell, E.: Business Research Methods, 3th edn, p. 675. Oxford University Press Inc. (2011)
22. Santhiapillai, F.P., Ratnayake, R.M.C.: Identifying and defining knowledge-work waste in product development: a case study on lean maturity assessment. In: IEEE International Conference on Industrial Engineering and Engineering Management (IEEM) (2018)
23. Gioia, D.A., Corley, K.G., Hamilton, A.L.: Seeking qualitative rigor in inductive research: notes on the gioia methodology. Organ. Res. Methods **16**(1), 15–31 (2012)
24. Samset, K., Volden, G.: Front-end definition of projects: Ten paradoxes and some reflections regarding project management and project governance. Int. J. Project Manag. **34**(2), 297–313 (2016)
25. Ulrich, K.T., Eppinger, S.D.: Product Design and Development, 5th edn. McGraw-Hill (2011)

# Lean Thinking: From the Shop Floor to an Organizational Culture

Paulo Amaro (ID), Anabela C. Alves(✉) (ID), and Rui M. Sousa (ID)

Centro ALGORITMI, University of Minho, Campus of Azurém,
4800-058 Guimarães, Portugal
pamaro@efacec.pt, {anabela, rms}@dps.uminho.pt

**Abstract.** In many areas, there is a multitude of terms/designations and definitions for the same concept, leading thus to misunderstanding. This also occurs with the designated Lean Production, which started to be known as a "thing" from the shop floor. However, it was quickly realized that it is much more than that (and should be understood as much more), otherwise the transformation of the operations will not be possible, as each company has its own organizational culture that could enable or inhibit the Lean implementation. Lean Production is underneath Lean Thinking, otherwise designated as philosophy, organizational culture, organizational model, production paradigm and others. This paper intends to present terms/designations and definitions that had been associated with Lean Thinking. The objective is to clarify that Lean Thinking is, in fact, all of that. Companies need to understand this in order to improve their operations, by recognizing value for the customer and eliminate wastes.

**Keywords:** Organizational culture · Philosophy · Lean thinking

## 1 Introduction

Lean Production Systems (LPS) was the designation given by Krafcik [1] to the Toyota Production System (TPS). In this germinal paper, it was recognized how different LPS was, implying a mind-set change from the Fordism, mainly related to work standardization, span control, teamwork, buffers and inventories' interpretation and meaning of repair areas. People should be seen as more than "a pair of hands"; in fact, their "heads" are the most important asset of the company [2]. Buffers and inventories reflect overproduction, considered as the worst waste but common in "just-in-case" scenarios.

Moreover, repair areas should not even exist as they mean production of defects, another waste that implies more consumption of materials, energy and water, as well as more pollutants emission. To accept/make such interpretations, companies need to think and look to their operations from a different viewpoint, but most companies are not used do this. This different thinking was named by Womack and Jones [3] as Lean Thinking but it seems difficult to have these insights and be successful in lean implementation. Inhibitors and enablers have been identified and studied, and organizational culture is pointed out as a context-dependent factor, i.e., could act as both, depending on the context [4]. However, there is a plethora of terminology associated

B. Lalic et al. (Eds.): APMS 2020, IFIP AICT 592, pp. 406–414, 2020.
https://doi.org/10.1007/978-3-030-57997-5_47

with Lean Thinking that is prone to confusion and misunderstanding [5, 6]. With this in mind, this paper characterizes and compares different terminologies used for Lean Thinking, aiming to clarify that Lean Thinking is a philosophy that should be built on a proper organizational culture. In addition, it should work according to an organizational model inside a production paradigm that demands a silo-broken strategy, among other strategies.

This paper is structured in five sections. After this introduction, the second section presents the materials and methods. The third section presents some concepts and definitions. The section four describes the enablers of lean product-oriented systems in a synthetized way. Finally, section five wrap-up some conclusions.

## 2    Materials and Methods

This research was mainly based on a literature review, both classical (e.g. organizational culture origin) and most recent literature. Based also on observations and experience, the authors show the need to view Lean Thinking as an organizational culture transformation of the companies' culture into a lean product-oriented system. In addition, the research used a conceptual methodology to build conceptual constructs and to establish causal relationships about Lean Thinking and their evolution from shop floor operations to the need of an understanding and commitment by the highest levels of the company/organization hierarchy. As referred by Gilson and Goldberg [7], "... *conceptual papers seek to bridge existing theories in interesting ways, link work across disciplines, provide multi-level insights, and broaden the scope of our thinking.*".

## 3    Organizational Culture Background

Schein [8] referred that organizational culture as a concept had a fairly recent origin and that the interest on it comes fundamentally from the emergence of a different management style, the Japanese style [9–11]. Accordingly, other authors, namely, Glynn et al. [12] and Teehankee [13] pointed out the seventies as the decade of the initial interest in this concept. One of first authors that discussed this concept was Pettigrew [14].

According to Schein [15], organizational culture "*is the pattern of basic assumptions that a given group has invented, discovered, or developed in learning to cope with its problems of external adaptation and internal integration - a pattern of assumptions that has worked well enough to be considered valid and, therefore, to be taught to new members as the correct way to perceive, think, and feel in relation to those problems.*". Also he defined, for the first time, three levels of culture: 1) Artifacts - visible organizational structures and processes (hard to decipher); 2) Values – strategies, goals, philosophies (espoused justifications); 3) Underlying assumptions - unconscious, taken for granted belief, habits of perception, thought and feeling (ultimate source of values and action) [16]. In a different paper [9], he defined cultural paradigm as: "*a cultural paradigm as a set of interrelated assumptions that form a coherent pattern.*", related with the human being need for order and consistency. He also stated that not all assumptions are mutually compatible or consistent, and provided some examples of groups' dynamics and behavior, and that organizational culture paradigms are adapted versions of broader cultural paradigms. The underlying cultural paradigm could be in the way the organization, and, particularly, the groups organize the space (open office landscape/individual office and closed doors), informality/formality, among other aspects.

Several authors considered the organizational culture concept as arising from a mixture of organizational psychology, social psychology and social anthropology [12, 14, 17]. Others, namely Teehankee [13], also relate it to organizational and management theory, and to the pioneers of the formal study of organizations, such as Max Weber, Henry Fayol and Frederick Taylor (scientific management techniques). He also linked to the human relations movement in organizational studies of Elton Mayo, Abraham Maslow and Douglas McGregor and systems schools promoted by Daniel Katz and R. L. Kahn. Previously, Roethlisberger and Dickson ([18] and Parsons [19] had made these relations. Finally, Teehankee [13] reinforces that the interest in organizational culture comes from business competition, mainly, Japanese competition. Meanwhile, other contributions were given to the organizational culture definition and understanding [20, 21]. For instance, Gorman [21] defined cultural indicators to assist managers in understanding culture. These are: 1) stories and myths, 2) symbols and their meanings, 3) hero myths, 4) taboos, and 5) rites of passage. He also defined four functions of culture: 1) transmit learning, 2) unite the organization, 3) provide meaning to organization members, and 4) handle strong emotions. Yet, in 1996, Schein [22] considered that the organizational culture concept was not sufficiently discussed, and defined three cultures of management: 1) the "operators" – who make and deliver products; 2) the "engineers" – who design and monitor the technology and what organization does; and 3) the "executives" – who do the financial accountability. These three work and learn individually, thus inhibiting the organization to act as a unit and hindering efficiency and effectiveness. This is related to "what holds the organization together", as Goffee and Jones [23] put it, and it is a continuum [24].

Additionally, Goffee and Jones [23] reinforced the dimensions of sociability and solidarity related to four types of community. High sociability leads to better collaboration, information sharing and openness to new ideas. However, it could also have disadvantages, e.g. the friendship environment created could inhibit discussion. Still, when the organization members felt they are reflected in the organizational culture, the work atmosphere tends to be more pleasurable, which increases morale [24]. Moreover, a growing body of literature supports a connection between an organization's culture and its performance [17, 24–27]. Members of an organization that identifies with the organizational culture, create a positive image and commitment that could outperform others with non-existent culture [24, 28, 29]. From the above, it is recognized that organizational culture is a complex interlinked concept that is not immediately recognized or identified. This means that the change requires a huge effort from the organization and is a long-term project coordinated and led by top management [30]. According to Schein [9], independently of the kind of culture, organizations (more mature or not) that have to manage a culture change, will cross through a painful process and strong resistance. Organizational culture is a deep phenomenon that should be addressed seriously [31]. Hence, knowing the organizational culture can reduce the risk of failure [30] leading thus to the need to diagnose it [24, 32, 33]. In this diagnosis one should be aware that more than one culture, e.g. associated to departments or hierarchy, could co-exist within an organization [33]. This author indicate seven steps to change a culture: 1) conduct a culture audit (diagnosis); 2) cultural assessment and need for change; 3) assess cultural risk; 4) unfreezing the cultural pattern; 5) elicit support from the cultural elite; 6) selecting an intervention strategy; and 7) monitoring and evaluation.

Changing a culture is part of the organization development process. This process implies a structured complex set of trade-offs among structure, systems, people, and culture, allowing the reaching of a particular business strategy [30]. Also, a myriad of other important concepts is also related to organizational culture such as groups, dynamics, strategies, philosophy, leadership, habits, paradigms, sociability, socialization, solidarity, models, traditions, climate, skills, norms, change, behavior, patterns, among others. This shows the richness of an organizational culture and, at the same time, the difficulty to understand, manage and change it. It also explains why so many different designations are used to name "organizational culture", often wrongly used [31].

## 4 Lean Thinking: The Literature Perspective

Lean Production has been implemented in many companies, as reported by [34]. Yet, it is very common to find companies frustrated, trying to implement it without success [35]. Krafcik [1] and Womack et al. [36] described what they found in Japanese companies; particularly, Toyota has reported the differences from Lean production to the mass production and craftsmanship paradigms. Anticipating the difficulties that companies interested in implementing could have, Womack and Jones [3] developed the Lean Thinking principles as a guide to help them. Nevertheless, since it origins, Lean suffered opposition [37], which is common to happen when something new emerges.

Meanwhile, 30 years after Lean designation use, in spite of evidences, a lot of confusion and suspicious environment around Lean Production prevails, keeping people away. Some companies do not even want to hear the word "lean", but accept well a "continuous improvement" program. This reveals that those companies do not know exactly what is Lean, otherwise they will know that continuous improvement, or kaizen, is behind the fifth Lean Thinking principle [3] and is in the centre of TPS [38].

For sure, one of the causes is the misunderstanding of Lean meaning, due to the plethora of terms associated. Among such myriad of terms and concepts, and hided by them, is the organizational culture. This motivates the authors of this paper to initiate this research. It starts with a literature review, of papers (nineties onwards) that present Lean as a different "thinking". In these papers, terms and designations used by the authors for "thinking" were collected but only the most frequent, such as: culture (sometimes appears just this word), organizational culture, model (solely), organization model, paradigm, philosophy and socio-technical system. Lean production/ manufacturing/management, production system, or others similar, were discarded because they are the most common. This review comprehended 75 papers, from 1993 to 2019. Due to the number of analysed papers, it is not possible to present a table with the respective authors; however, the Fig. 1 synthesizes the main findings. The term most used is philosophy (>50%); nevertheless, the combination of culture and organizational culture represents 63%, which means that this aggregation is the most used.

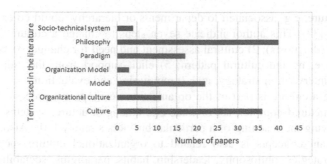

**Fig. 1.** Terms/designations used in the literature by the authors of Lean papers.

As so, some authors have been recognizing Lean as organizational culture. Nevertheless, attending to the extensive literature in Lean [39–41], it is possible to conclude that this is just a small "crumb". Of course, the sample used in this research is also small (75 papers) and biased (just papers related with Lean Thinking as a conceptual term). An important work on highlighting Lean culture ambiguity was the systematic literature review of Dorval et al. (2019). In this research, the authors want to reinforce the need for companies/organizations to recognize Lean Thinking as an organizational culture in the light of the organizational culture definition by the experts, referred in Sect. 3. Also, this strengthens the literature that presents culture as an inhibitor or barrier to Lean implementation, namely, Hodge et al. [42], Salem et al. [43] and Shrimali and Soni [44]. Other barriers, related to terms associated to organizational culture referred in the Sect. 3, could also be pointed out, namely, 1) lack of top management support [44–50], 2) lack of commitment [44, 51–53] and 3) lack of training [44, 52, 54, 55].

Organizational culture is a key factor in successful lean processes implementation [56–58]. This means that before implementing Lean in a company, its culture should be analysed and understood, and the founders/owners/top managers must have sufficient insight into their own culture to make an intelligent transition process possible, as referred by Schein [15]. At the same time, this knowledge will allow them to make a decision if Lean should be implemented or not. Not all companies have to introduce a different culture just because neighbourhood has or is the "flavour" of the moment.

Implementing Lean tools is not synonymous of implementing Lean Thinking. It is possible to implement isolated Lean tools but only with marginal gains. Only with a global approach, it is possible to achieve sustainable results, but this demands an organizational culture change. In either cases, implementing just one tool or changing the organizational culture, demands knowledge about Lean. Even in the first case, it is important to devise what tool could be used without demanding changing the culture. If it is a tool related to changing habits, probably, the hard decision to change the culture must be made. However, changing from a culture that values autonomy is very different of changing from one that values hierarchical authority, as exemplified by Dyer [33], or vice-versa, e.g. a company with roots in Fordism culture, willing to implement Lean.

Consequently, as recommended by Dyer [33] and Schwartz and Davis [30], to change organizational culture, companies needs extensive training, team building, role negotiation, new reward systems and new structures to support the change, namely a good communication system. As referred by Alves et al. [59], Lean promotes thinkers, but it is necessary to provide some conditions, namely the need to become a learning organization. In fact, learning in organizations is vital for the organization success [60] and, according to Revans [61], the rate of learning must be greater than (or at least equal to) the rate of change. Furthermore, Powell and Reke [62] reframe the TPS as a learning system where, rather than on pure process improvement, the focus is on the development of personal competences (both technical and creative), across all levels of the organization (i.e. from shop-floor workers to top managers).

## 5    Conclusions

This paper presents a seminal work about Lean Thinking and the need to recognize it as an organizational culture. The organizational culture concept is relatively recent and emerged because, at that time, a different management style was recognized, the well-succeed Japanese style. This triggered the need to study this phenomenon and understand the reasons of it. While this do not happen, many companies will try to implement Lean without the proper knowledge and mind-set. Nevertheless, they must be aware that changing the organizational culture is a hard endeavor demanding a lot of continuous effort and energy, until it becomes a sustainable and natural Lean culture. The authors recognize some limitations in this research: the sample used is small and biased. Having this in mind, the authors have as objective for future work to develop a systematic literature review about this topic.

**Acknowledgements.** This work has been supported by FCT – Fundação para a Ciência e Tecnologia within the R&D Units Project Scope: UIDB/00319/2020.

## References

1. Krafcik, J.F.: Triumph of the lean production system. Sloan Manag. Rev. **30**(1), 41–52 (1988)
2. Takeuchi, H., Osono, E., Shimizu, N.: The contradictions that drives Toyota's success. Harv. Bus. Rev. (June), 98–104 (2008)
3. Womack, J.P., Jones, D.T.: Lean Thinking: Banish Waste and Create Wealth in your Corporation. Free Press, New York (1996). Press F, editor
4. Amaro, P., Alves, A.C., Sousa, R.M.: Context-dependent factors of lean production implementations: two sides of the same coin. Jordan J. Mech. Ind. Eng. (submitted)
5. Cowger, G.: Half measures gets less than half results. Mech. Eng. Mag. ASME **138**(131), 130–135 (2016)
6. Schonberger, R.J.: The disintegration of lean manufacturing and lean management. Bus. Horiz. **62**(3), 359–371 (2019)
7. Gilson, L.L., Goldberg, C.B.: Editors' comment: so, what is a conceptual paper? Group Organ Manag. **40**(2), 127–130 (2015)
8. Schein, E.H.: Organizational Culture (1988)

9. Schein, E.H.: Coming to a new awareness of organizational culture. Sloan Manag. Rev. **25** (2), 3 (1984)
10. Szostak, C.R.: Success of Japanese management—Lessons for American managers. University of Montana (1984)
11. Culpan, R., Kucukemiroglu, O.: A comparison of U.S. and Japanese management styles and unit effectiveness. Manag. Int. Rev. **33**(1), 27–42 (1993)
12. Glynn, M.A., Giorgi, S., Lockwood, C.: Organizational Culture. Oxford Bibliographies Online (2018)
13. Teehankee, B.: Organizational culture: a critical review. Dialogue Can. Philos. Assoc. **27**(1), 67–92 (1993)
14. Pettigrew, A.M.: On studying organizational cultures. Adm. Sci. Q. **24**(4), 570–581 (1979)
15. Schein, E.H.: The role of the founder in creating organizational culture. Organ. Dyn. Summer **12**(1), 13–28 (1983)
16. Schein, E.H.: Organizational Culture and Leadership. The Jossey. Wiley, Hoboken (2010)
17. Scott, T., Mannion, R., Davies, H., Marshall, M.: The quantitative measurement of organizational culture in health care: a review of the available instruments. Health Serv. Res. **38**(3), 923–945 (2003)
18. Roethlisberger, F., Dickson, W.: Management and the Worker. Harvard University Press, Cambridge (1961)
19. Parsons, T.: The Social System. Routledge (1991)
20. Ott, J.S.: The Organizational Culture Perspective. Brooks/Cole (1989)
21. Gorman, L.: Corporate Culture. Manag. Decis. **27**(1) (1989)
22. Schein, E.H.: Culture: the missing concept in organization studies. Adm. Sci. Q. **41**(2), 229–240 (1996)
23. Goffee, R., Jones, G.: What holds the modern company together? Harv. Bus. Rev. **74**(6), 133–148 (1996)
24. Demir, C., Unnu, N.A., Erturk, E.: Diagnosing the organizational culture of a Turkish pharmaceutical company based on the competing values framework. J. Bus. Econ. Manag. **12**(1), 197–217 (2011)
25. Cheng, Y.C.: Organizational culture: development of a theoretical framework for organization-al research. City Univ. Hong Kong Educ. J. **17**(2), 128–147 (1989)
26. Calori, R., Sarnin, P.: Corporate culture and economic performance: a French study. Organ. Stud. **12**(1), 049–074 (1991)
27. Warrick, D.D.: What leaders need to know about organizational culture. Bus. Horiz. **60**(3), 395–404 (2017)
28. Singh, K.: Predicting organizational commitment through organization culture: a study of automobile industry in India. J. Bus. Econ. Manag. **8**(1), 29–37 (2007)
29. Wilkins, A.L., Ouchi, W.G.: Efficient cultures: exploring the relationship between culture and organizational performance. Adm. Sci. Q. **28**(3), 468 (1983)
30. Schwartz, H., Davis, S.M.: Matching corporate culture and business strategy. Organ. Dyn. **10**(1), 30–48 (1981)
31. Schein, E.H.: What you need to know about organizational culture. Train Dev. J. (Jan), 30–3 (1986)
32. Harrison, R., Stokes, H.: Diagnosing Organizational Culture. Wiley, Hoboken (1992)
33. Dyer, W.G.J.: Organizational culture: analysis and change. Sloan Manag. Rev. (Sept), 1–27 (1983)
34. Amaro, P., Alves, A.C., Sousa, R.M.: Lean thinking: a transversal and global management philosophy to achieve sustainability benefits. In: Alves, A.C., Kahlen, F.-J., Flumerfelt, S., Siriban-Manalang, A.B. (eds.) Lean Engineering for Global Development, pp. 1–31. Springer, Cham (2019). https://doi.org/10.1007/978-3-030-13515-7_1

35. Lean Frontiers: Current State of Lean: Summary of a 2016–2017 Lean Community Delphi Study (2017)
36. Womack, J., Jones, D.T., Roos, D.: The Machine That Changed the World: The Story of Lean Production. Rawson Associates, New York (1990)
37. Berggren, C.: Lean production - the end of history? Work Employ Soc. **7**(2), 163–188 (1993)
38. Liker, J.K., Morgan, J.M.: The Toyota way in services: the case of lean product development. Acad. Manag. Perspect. **20**(2), 5–20 (2006)
39. Ciano, M.P., Pozzi, R., Rossi, T., Strozzi, F.: How IJPR has addressed 'lean': a literature review using bibliometric tools. Int. J. Prod. Res. **57**(15–16), 5284–5317 (2019)
40. Samuel, D., Found, P., Williams, S.J.: How did the publication of the book the machine that changed the world change management thinking? Exploring 25 years of lean literature. Int. J. Oper. Prod. Manag. **35**(10), 1386–1407 (2015)
41. Dorval, M., Jobin, M.H., Benomar, N.: Lean culture: a comprehensive systematic literature review. Int. J. Prod. Perform. Manag. **68**(5), 920–937 (2019)
42. Hodge, G.L., Goforth, K.R., Joines, J.A., Thoney, K.: Adapting lean manufacturing principles to the textile industry. Prod. Plan. Control **22**(3), 237–247 (2011)
43. Salem, R., Musharavati, F., Hamouda, A.M., Al-Khalifa, K.N.: An empirical study on lean awareness and potential for lean implementations in Qatar industries. Int. J. Adv. Manuf. Technol. **82**(9–12), 1607–1625 (2016)
44. Shrimali, A.K., Soni, V.K.: Barriers to lean implementation in small and medium-sized indian enterprises. Int. J. Mech. Eng. Technol. **8**(6), 1–9 (2017)
45. Scherrer-Rathje, M., Boyle, T.A., Deflorin, P.: Lean, take two! Reflections from the second attempt at lean implementation. Bus. Horiz. **52**(1), 79–88 (2009)
46. Antony, J.: Lean implementation in Scottish small and medium sized enterprises (SMEs): an empirical study. In: Proceedings of the 2012 Industrial and Systems Engineering Research Conference, pp. 1–8 (2012)
47. Ravikumar, M.M., Marimuthu, K., Parthiban, P., Abdul Zubar, H.: Critical issues of lean implementation in Indian micro, small and medium enterprises-an analysis. Res. J. Appl. Sci. Eng. Technol. **7**(13), 2680–2686 (2014)
48. Elkhairi, A., Fedouaki, F., Alami, S.El.: Barriers and critical success factors for implementing lean manufacturing in SMEs. IFAC-PapersOnLine **52**(13), 565–570 (2019)
49. Alkhoraif, A., Rashid, H., McLaughlin, P.: Lean implementation in small and medium enterprises: literature review. Oper. Res. Perspect. **6**(1), 100089 (2019)
50. Da Silva, F.W., Alves, A.C., Figueiredo, M.C.B.: Lean production in small and medium sized companies from the free economic zone of Manaus: a reality or just fiction? Gestão e Producão **26**(4) e4237 (2019)
51. Salonitis, K., Tsinopoulos, C.: Drivers and barriers of lean implementation in the Greek manufacturing sector. Procedia CIRP **57**(3), 189–194 (2016)
52. Lodgaard, E., Ingvaldsen, J., Gamme, I., Aschehoug, S.: Barriers to lean implementation: perceptions of top managers, Middle Managers and Workers. Procedia CIRP **57**, 595–600 (2016)
53. AlManei, M., Salonitis, K., Xu, Y.: Lean implementation frameworks: the challenges for SMEs. Procedia CIRP **63**, 750–755 (2017)
54. Simmons, L., Holt, R., Dennis, G., Walden, C.: Lean implementation in a low volume manufacturing environment: a case study. In: IIE Annual Conference and Expo (2010)
55. Leme, J., Tortorella, G., Augusto, B.: Identification of barriers and critical success factors in lean implementation in micro-sized enterprises. Espacios **37**(5), 1–17 (2016)
56. Pakdil, F., Leonard, K.M.: The effect of organizational culture on implementing and sustaining lean processes. J. Manuf. Technol. Manag. **26**(5), 725–743 (2015)

57. Yadav, O.P., Nepal, B.P., Rahaman, M.M., Lal, V.: Lean implementation and organizational transformation: a literature review. Eng. Manag. J. **29**(1), 2–16 (2017)
58. Yadav, V., Jain, R., Mittal, M.L., Panwar, A., Lyons, A.C.: The propagation of lean thinking in SMEs. Prod. Plan. Control **30**(10–12), 854–865 (2019)
59. Alves, A.C., Dinis-Carvalho, J., Sousa, R.M.: Lean production as promoter of thinkers to achieve companies' agility. Learn. Organ. **19**(3), 219–237 (2012)
60. Dean, P.J.: Gower Handbook of Training and Development (1991). Editor John Prior
61. Revans, R.W.: Action Learning: New Techniques for Management. Blond & Briggs (1980)
62. Powell, D., Reke, E.: No lean without learning: rethinking lean production as a learning system. In: Ameri, F., Stecke, K.E., von Cieminski, G., Kiritsis, D. (eds.) APMS 2019. IAICT, vol. 566, pp. 62–68. Springer, Cham (2019). https://doi.org/10.1007/978-3-030-30000-5_8

# Digital Lean Manufacturing and Its Emerging Practices

# A Learning Roadmap for Digital Lean Manufacturing

Anja Bottinga Solheim(✉) and Daryl John Powell

SINTEF Manufacturing AS, Raufoss, Norway
{anja.solheim, daryl.powell}@sintef.no

**Abstract.** Since it was popularized in the 1990s, the adoption of lean production has been a primary driver for continuous improvement efforts worldwide. The next wave of industrial improvement is widely considered to be
driven by industry 4.0 and digitalization. This has more recently led to the
emerging concept of digital lean manufacturing. In this paper, we address a
shortcoming in the extant literature, which presents an abundance of roadmaps
for digitalization but very few addressing this in combination with lean. As such,
we present a learning roadmap for digital lean manufacturing, with a core focus
on cybersecurity. The roadmap has been developed and tested by combining
theory with practical insights at the Norwegian Catapult Lean4zero Lab,
Norway's first and only full-scale digital lean simulator.

**Keywords:** Lean manufacturing · Digitalization · Cybersecurity

## 1 Introduction

Lean manufacturing emerged as an alternative way of organizing and managing
manufacturing enterprises in the 1990s [1]. Since then, lean principles have been
applied in countless organizations across many industries. More recently, the emergence of Industry 4.0 and its associated advanced digital technologies has presented
manufacturers with more novel ways of optimizing production operations [2]. Subsequently, the combination of lean with Industry 4.0 has since resulted in the emergence of Digital Lean Manufacturing (DLM) systems [3]. Given that the manufacturing
industry in general, and small- and medium enterprises (SMEs) in particular are at a
state of low maturity in terms of combining advanced digitalization with existing lean
initiatives, in this paper we present a learning roadmap for realizing the potential
benefits of DLM, which can be used for taking a company from an initial state to an
advanced level of innovation and cooperation. We adopt a particular focus on cybersecurity (an important part of digital transformations which is unfortunately often
overlooked in research and in practice [4]), and build the roadmap based on practical
insights from SINTEF's *Lean4zero Learning Lab* in Raufoss, Norway.

© IFIP International Federation for Information Processing 2020
Published by Springer Nature Switzerland AG 2020
B. Lalic et al. (Eds.): APMS 2020, IFIP AICT 592, pp. 417–424, 2020.
https://doi.org/10.1007/978-3-030-57997-5_48

## 2   Theoretical Background

In this chapter, we present relevant theory in order to shape a theoretical frame for the investigation.

### 2.1   Industry 4.0

There is a general industrial trend towards *Industry 4.0*, which brings new optimization possibilities via the application of advanced digital technologies. [5] presents an overview and classification of Industry 4.0 (I4.0) as nine technologies that are transforming industrial production; Additive Manufacturing, Augmented Reality (AR), Autonomous Robots, Big Data Analytics, The Cloud, Cybersecurity, Horizontal- and Vertical Integration, Industrial Internet of Things (IIoT) and Simulation. [6] attempts to frame these technologies within the context of *smart supply chains, smart manufacturing, smart products and smart working*. The impacts of *Artificial Intelligence* (AI) are discussed, e.g. implying that using AI technology reasonably and effectively can greatly promote valuable creativity and enhance the competitiveness in both humans and machines [7].

In order to start the development towards I4.0, manufacturing companies are expected to apply digital communication platforms and integrate their value chains, sharing data in and between cyber-physical production systems [3]. These developments imply that machines and control systems, so called *Operational Technology* (OT) that are otherwise not originally designed to be exposed on the Internet, are suddenly connected to *Information Technology* (IT) solutions and made available via cloud services, which creates a vulnerability. Companies should therefore count on becoming the target for cyber-attacks and in addition to making preventive measures, become reactive enough to keep the economic loss at a level as low as possible in case of an eventual attack [8].

### 2.2   Lean Production and Digital Lean Manufacturing

Lean production is based on the principles and working processes of the Toyota Production System (TPS) and has been defined as *doing more with less* [9]. In its simplest terms, lean production can be described as the elimination of waste [10]. [11] provided the world with a vision of what lean is about, summarizing lean thinking as five principles: (1) precisely specify value; (2) identify the value stream for each product; (3) make value flow without interruptions; (4) let the customer pull value from the producer; and (5) pursue perfection. More recently, there have been indications that lean thinking and practice is better described as a learning system than a production system [12]. For example, [13] suggests that "*improvement without learning is not lean thinking*".

Digital Lean Manufacturing (DLM), refers to the application of digital technology, such as e-Kanbans, digital problem solving, and kaizen in digital collaborative environments, in order to enhance the lean and learning transformation in manufacturing organizations [14]. Both [15] and [16] present Lean Production in the context of Smart Manufacturing, presenting the main components of a smart production system as *smart products, smart operators, smart machines, smart workstations* and *smart planners*, and subsequently comparing and contrasting these with Just-in-Time (JIT) and Jidoka and JIT, Total Quality Management (TQM), Total Productive Maintenance (TPM) and Human Resource Management (HRM), respectively. In fact, there is a significant emerging extant literature that covers the combination of lean production and digitalization, identifying various levels of lean and digital integration [c.f. 3, 17–21]. Studies of ERP systems from a lean perspective show that contemporary ERP systems can be used to support lean production by offering an array of support functionality for each of the five lean principles [22].

## 2.3 Maturity Models and Roadmaps

Maturity models (MMs) enable users to identify the need for change and to derive the necessary measures to accompany the change process [23]. Several MMs and roadmaps exist for the implementation of both lean and digitalization. For example, [24] presents a MM for assessing I4.0 readiness and maturity of manufacturing enterprises, while [25] presents a capability MM for lean implementation in the context of ERP system integration in SMEs. The overview of Industry 4.0 MMs presented in [23] and based on a literature search comparing 11 different MMs, shows a variety in the number and definition of stages, spanning from 4 to 8 stages, e.g. initial, managed, defined, integrated and operability, and digital-oriented [26], or digitalization awareness, smart networked products, the service-oriented enterprise, thinking in service systems, and the data-driven enterprise [27], with an average of 5,3 and a median of 5 stages. Each of these MMs have more than one dimension, covering e.g. process, monitoring and controlling, technology, and organization; and business, application, information and technical infrastructure.

## 3 Research Approach

This is a conceptual paper based on a literature review in combination with new insights drawn from a single case study, in which the authors were actively involved in the development of the *Lean4zero Learning Lab* – Norway's first and only full-scale training centre for DLM.

### 3.1 Case Description

The *Lean4zero Learning Lab,* hereinafter referred to as "the lab", situated in Raufoss, at one of Norway's first catapult centres, the *Manufacturing Technology Norwegian Catapult* (MTNC), was first opened in August 2009 as a full-scale analogue lean manufacturing simulator. In response to demand from the Norwegian manufacturing industry, efforts began in 2019 to convert the simulator to a DLM learning lab.

The lab today offers courses with a mix of theoretical and action-oriented elements, training course participants in lean principles. The course material is based on lean management and the methodology and tools for efficient pull-based and levelled production with continuous improvement at its core. The courses span from one to three days, including Toyota Kata and learning organization, as well as value stream analysis, aiming at making course participants ready to independently manage lean-focused work when they return to their own organization.

## 3.2  Towards a Learning Roadmap for Digital Lean Manufacturing

As a result of the comparison of the 11 I4.0 MMs mentioned in the previous chapter, we suggest a five stage MM with the following predominant phases as the basis for the development of our Learning Roadmap for DLM:

1) Basic: Actuators and monitoring; 2) Data and system integration: Sensory and information processing; 3) Communication system: Network, interpretation and services; 4) Enhanced performance: Adaption and optimization; 5) Advanced innovation: Innovation and cooperation.

In the Learning Roadmap for DLM, measures for lean, advanced technology and cybersecurity are mapped to these five stages, giving the model a three-dimensional structure, using the environment in the lab as a practical example.

# 4  Discussion

In the next sections we will discuss the five stages identified in the MM above and present structured insights toward a Learning Roadmap for DLM.

## 4.1  Basic

The first stage of the Learning Roadmap for DLM describes an initial stage in a manufacturing environment, illustrated by the initial setup in the lab, from an advanced technology, lean and cybersecurity point of view. The current level of digitization is at a basic *actuators and monitoring* level, in the lab case comprising touch screens at each station for documenting the process and a program that produces statistic graphs, using the data collected via the touch screens, demonstrating the flow balance principles, by visualizing the takt-time and time spent on each station and product.

The Lab is a lean environment; the workplaces with parts and materials are organized based on 5S principles, the operations are standardized and described on standard operation paper sheets, the production is levelled and based on pull principles, and continuous improvement work is manually performed on analogue boards, based on manually gathered data analysed by humans. This environment describes the foundation on which the next I4.0 stage can be built, as digitalizing and automating a system that isn't lean makes only for digital waste [3]. Opening the door to the connected global world should be done after having a risk assessment system in place.

Not having connected any devices to the Internet, the level of technical cybersecurity measures at this stage includes e.g. basic virus protection on the computers, photo documentation control, and checking and limiting physical admission into the building. The organizational cybersecurity and safety management, is as important as the technical aspect, including continuous risk assessment management work being built-in in the continuous improvements work and including test execution of the risk handling plan, e.g. fire and loss of power supply drills, with roles and responsibilities clearly distributed in the organization.

## 4.2  Data and System Integration

In the data and system integration stage of the Learning Roadmap for DLM, the focus is on *sensory and information processing*. At this stage sensors will be introduced in product and process in the Lean Lab, collecting data that will be used in the analysis process of the progress and quality. The parts are here made traceable, providing input to a digitized parts and material flow management, connected to sales and production planning information, through integrating off-line ERP and digital Kanban systems in a digital model of the business. The flow and quality performance data are in this stage being processed digitally and presented on digital continuous improvement boards and *manufacturing planning and control* (MPC) platform pads. At this stage, the *Lean4zero Learning Lab* will introduce cooperative, industrial and transport robots in the production, having them perform simple tasks. In this stage the systems are still not connected to the outer world, but service people installing and upgrading the robotic and digital systems might connect these to the Internet while working. Thus, with robots working in the area it will be important to have these organized in sub-systems, creating a basis for a layered system architecture including a definition of the human place within the system, such as e.g. the Purdue Enterprise Reference Architecture described in [28], having the safety and cybersecurity risk assessment level based on identification of safety issues and business value. There should be worst case scenarios identified and a communication and handling plan for all of these in place.

## 4.3  Communication System

In the communication system stage of the Learning Roadmap for DLM, *network, interpretation and services* are lead words. During this stage the digital flow within the *Lean4zero Learning Lab* becomes a link in a larger digital flow inside the value chain, including suppliers on one side and customers on the other. A communication platform is established, adding information from outside the organization to the internal data, digitally analysing and interpreting the available data, and communicating the results both internally and externally in the value chain. This means that input from customers and suppliers regarding e.g. the quality of the product or delays in the supply chain, will become input to the MPC, be interpreted by the system and trigger continuous improvement actions and changes in the production plan in the ERP system, performed by the human staff. *Virtual Reality* (VR) and *Augmented Reality* (AR) will be introduced as communication tools between the digital and robotic systems and the humans, e.g. instructing the existing or new human staff on new or existing operations. Cybersecurity measures will have to be considered here, e.g. isolation of networks at the different architecture layers of the business, securing that only the highest communication platform level is accessible over the Internet and that the lower levels, including the ERP system level, is guarded by several firewalls. The risk assessment and crisis handling plan should be updated with the cybersecurity risks deriving from connecting the business systems to the Internet. On a technical cybersecurity level, data on normal performance could be gathered, as part of the self-diagnosis of the system, reporting and sending out alarms at identified abnormalities.

## 4.4   Enhanced Performance

In this stage the data processing is lifted to the next level, to some extent letting the system *adapt and optimize*, using a digital twin of the *Lean4zero Learning Lab* with simulation models to test possible scenarios and the possibility to automatically optimize the systems accordingly. Changes in customer needs, supply capacity or internal changes, e.g. machine service or human resource capacity, will hereby be integrated in the dynamic production planning, based on machine learning, and communicated to the human staff. Cybersecurity risk assessment analysis and handling plan will be updated continuously as part of the continuous improvement work, cybersecurity measure will be prioritized based on the outcome of the analysis, and the system will be stress tested.

## 4.5   Advanced Innovation

In this stage of the Learning Roadmap for DLM, the systems and human resources are integrated in *innovation and cooperation* activities. In achieving stage five, lean and cybersecurity measures and countermeasures will become a cohesive part of the system. The robots, digital systems and humans in the lab will perform based on the output from secure data processing in the digital twin, possibly including e.g. diagnosis, prognosis and trial-and-error functions as described in [29], self-organizing in robust human-machine sub-systems, solving their tasks in dynamically optimized ways, e.g. by the deployment of human-in-the-loop hybrid-augmented intelligence systems. Suggesting such a model for safety and security issues, [7] argues that hybrid-augmented intelligence can provide strong technical support and a basic infrastructure framework to meet the increasing challenges in those security areas. It is there recommended to have humans participate in prediction, detection and subsequent disposition, making full use of human intelligence in complex problem judging and of AI in processing massive data.

# 5   Conclusion

In this article, we adopt the stance that manufacturing firms should learn how to systematically combine lean thinking and practice with advanced Industry 4.0 technologies in order to build competitive advantage in the digital era. We present a five-stage Learning Roadmap for DLM distributed across three critical dimensions. These important elements have emerged from a literature review as well as from practical insights in developing a *Lean4zero Learning Lab*.

We suggest that this article has implications for both theory and practice. Firstly, with regard to theory, we present a framework that promises to evolve Lean Production towards an advanced human-machine innovation and cooperation system, through the creation of a flexible, autonomous and self-optimizing system. By adopting the

Learning Roadmap for DLM, practitioners can begin to understand how to identify and take the next step on the DLM journey.

In terms of limitations, though the Learning Roadmap for DLM has been developed based on a literature review, practical experiences are based on a single case study in the *Lean4zero Learning Lab* environment. Future research should therefore further develop and test the model in practice, as well as expand the cybersecurity analysis, specifying its different perspectives across the five levels.

**Acknowledgements.** The authors would like to acknowledge the support of the Research Council of Norway – both through the research project *Lean Digital* and the research program *SFI Manufacturing*.

# References

1. Womack, J.P., Jones, D.T., Roos, D.: The Machine that Changed the World: The Story of Lean Production–Toyota's Secret Weapon in the World Car Wars that is Now Revolutionizing World Industry (2007). https://www.simonandschuster.com/
2. Lasi, H., et al.: Industry 4.0. Bus. Inf. Syst. Eng. **6**(4), 239–242 (2014). https://doi.org/10.1007/s12599-014-0334-4
3. Romero, D., Gaiardelli, P., Powell, D., Wuest, T., Thürer, M.: Digital lean cyber-physical production systems: the emergence of digital lean manufacturing and the significance of digital waste. In: Moon, I., Lee, G.M., Park, J., Kiritsis, D., von Cieminski, G. (eds.) APMS 2018. IAICT, vol. 535, pp. 11–20. Springer, Cham (2018). https://doi.org/10.1007/978-3-319-99704-9_2
4. Gcaza, N., von Solms, R.: Cybersecurity culture: an ill-defined problem. In: Bishop, M., Futcher, L., Miloslavskaya, N., Theocharidou, M. (eds.) WISE 2017. IAICT, vol. 503, pp. 98–109. Springer, Cham (2017). https://doi.org/10.1007/978-3-319-58553-6_9
5. Rüßmann, M., et al.: Industry 4.0: the future of productivity and growth in manufacturing industries. Boston Consult. Group **9**(1), 54–89 (2015)
6. Frank, A.G., Dalenogare, L.S., Ayala, N.F.: Industry 4.0 technologies: implementation patterns in manufacturing companies. Int. J. Prod. Econ. **210**, 15–26 (2019)
7. Zheng, N.-n., et al.: Hybrid-augmented intelligence: collaboration and cognition. Front. Inf. Technol. Electron. Eng. **18**(2), 153–179 (2017). https://doi.org/10.1631/FITEE.1700053
8. Alcaraz, C., Lopez, J., Wolthusen, S.: Policy enforcement system for secure interoperable control in distributed smart grid systems. J. Netw. Comput. Appl. **59**, 301–314 (2016)
9. Womack, J.P., Jones, D.T., Roos, D.: The Machine that Changed the World. Harper Perennial, New York (1990)
10. Liker, J.K.: The Toyota Way: 14 Management Principles From the World's Greatest Manufacturer. McGraw-Hill, New York (2004)
11. Womack, J.P., Jones, D.T.: Lean Thinking: Banish Waste and Create Wealth in Your Corporation. Simon and Schuster, New York (1996)
12. Ballé, M., et al.: The Lean Sensei, Go, See, Challenge. Lean Enterprise Institute, Inc., Boston (2019)
13. Netland, T.H., Powell, D.: A lean world. In: Netland, T.H., Powell, D. (eds.) The Routledge Companion to Lean Management. Routledge, New York (2017)
14. Ashrafian, A., et al.: Sketching the landscape for lean digital transformation. In: Ameri, F., Stecke, K.E., von Cieminski, G., Kiritsis, D. (eds.) APMS 2019. IAICT, vol. 566, pp. 29–36. Springer, Cham (2019). https://doi.org/10.1007/978-3-030-30000-5_4

15. Kolberg, D., Zühlke, D.: Lean automation enabled by industry 40 technologies. IFAC-PapersOnLine **48**(3), 1870–1875 (2015)
16. Mora, E., Gaiardelli, P., Resta, B., Powell, D.: Exploiting lean benefits through smart manufacturing: a comprehensive perspective. In: Lödding, H., Riedel, R., Thoben, K.-D., von Cieminski, G., Kiritsis, D. (eds.) APMS 2017. IAICT, vol. 513, pp. 127–134. Springer, Cham (2017). https://doi.org/10.1007/978-3-319-66923-6_15
17. Romero, D., Gaiardelli, P., Powell, D., Wuest, T., Thürer, M.: Total quality management and quality circles in the digital lean manufacturing world. In: Ameri, F., Stecke, K.E., von Cieminski, G., Kiritsis, D. (eds.) APMS 2019. IAICT, vol. 566, pp. 3–11. Springer, Cham (2019). https://doi.org/10.1007/978-3-030-30000-5_1
18. Romero, D., et al.: Rethinking jidoka systems under automation & learning perspectives in the digital lean manufacturing world. IFAC-PapersOnLine **52**(13), 899–903 (2019)
19. Powell, D., Romero, D., Gaiardelli, P., Cimini, C., Cavalieri, S.: Towards digital lean cyber-physical production systems: Industry 4.0 technologies as enablers of leaner production. In: Moon, I., Lee, G.M., Park, J., Kiritsis, D., von Cieminski, G. (eds.) APMS 2018. IAICT, vol. 536, pp. 353–362. Springer, Cham (2018). https://doi.org/10.1007/978-3-319-99707-0_44
20. Cattaneo, L., Rossi, M., Negri, E., Powell, D., Terzi, S.: Lean thinking in the digital era. In: Ríos, J., Bernard, A., Bouras, A., Foufou, S. (eds.) PLM 2017. IAICT, vol. 517, pp. 371–381. Springer, Cham (2017). https://doi.org/10.1007/978-3-319-72905-3_33
21. Buer, S.-V., Strandhagen, J.O., Chan, F.T.: The link between Industry 4.0 and lean manufacturing: mapping current research and establishing a research agenda. Int. J. Prod. Res. **56**(8), 2924–2940 (2018)
22. Powell, D., Alfnes, E., Strandhagen, J.O., Dreyer, H.: ERP support for lean production. In: Frick, J., Laugen, B.T. (eds.) APMS 2011. IAICT, vol. 384, pp. 115–122. Springer, Heidelberg (2012). https://doi.org/10.1007/978-3-642-33980-6_14
23. Felch, V., Asdecker, B., Sucky, E.: Maturity models in the age of Industry 4.0–Do the available models correspond to the needs of business practice? In: Proceedings of the 52nd Hawaii International Conference on System Sciences (2019)
24. Schumacher, A., Erol, S., Sihn, W.: A maturity model for assessing Industry 4.0 readiness and maturity of manufacturing enterprises. Procedia Cirp **52**(1), 161–166 (2016)
25. Powell, D., Riezebos, J., Strandhagen, J.O.: Lean production and ERP systems in SMEs: ERP support for pull production. Int. J. Prod. Res. **51**(2), 395–409 (2013)
26. De Carolis, A., Macchi, M., Negri, E., Terzi, S.: A maturity model for assessing the digital readiness of manufacturing companies. In: Lödding, H., Riedel, R., Thoben, K.-D., von Cieminski, G., Kiritsis, D. (eds.) APMS 2017. IAICT, vol. 513, pp. 13–20. Springer, Cham (2017). https://doi.org/10.1007/978-3-319-66923-6_2
27. Katsma, C.P., Moonen, H.M., van Hillegersberg, J.: Supply chain systems maturing towards the internet-of-things: a framework. In: Bled eConference (2011)
28. Williams, T.J.: The Purdue enterprise reference architecture. Comput. Ind. **24**(2–3), 141–158 (1994)
29. Vanderhaegen, F.: Autonomy control of human-machine systems. IFAC Proceedings Vol. **43**(13), 398–403 (2010)

# Investigating the Challenges and Opportunities for Production Planning and Control in Digital Lean Manufacturing

Daryl Powell[1,2(✉)], Eirin Lodgaard[1], and Heidi Dreyer[2]

[1] SINTEF Manufacturing, Raufoss, Norway
{daryl.powell,eirin.lodgaard}@sintef.no
[2] Department of Industrial Economics and Technology Management,
Norwegian University of Science and Technology, Trondheim, Norway
Heidi.c.dreyer@ntnu.no

**Abstract.** Digital Lean Manufacturing has emerged as a new approach to Lean Production, combining lean thinking and practice with the new opportunities presented by innovative digital technologies and Industry 4.0 concepts. However, this combined approach also raises certain challenges for the manufacturing industry. In this paper, we explore both the challenges and opportunities presented to manufacturers in light of digitalization *contra* Lean Manufacturing, with a specific focus on Production Planning and Control. Drawing on insights from four diverse explorative industrial cases studies, we identify the challenges and opportunities experienced by manufacturers embarking on a journey towards Digital Lean Manufacturing and highlight important avenues for further research.

**Keywords:** Lean production · Digitalization · Production planning and control

## 1 Introduction

A recent trend in operations management is digitalization and a shift towards Industry 4.0, which is set to dominate the next frontier of operational change and improvement in the manufacturing industry [1]. As such, this has created a so-called lean-digitalization paradox [2] and has even raised the question as to whether digitalization contradicts lean and indeed if digitalization will replace lean [3]. Certainly, in some cases, digitalization may indeed begin to counteract the application of lean, for example when decision-making becomes more centralized in information systems, as opposed to the decentralized and autonomous decision-making principles of lean thinking. However, current research has illustrated that lean thinking and practice is still very much here to stay as a dominant manufacturing concept contributing to efficiency and performance improvements, and that digitalization can behave as an enabler and catalyst for Lean Production [4]. An example is the application of digital algorithms on production planning decisions based on sensor technology and real time ordering and demand data. This is, in fact, in line with previous research that investigated the role of

B. Lalic et al. (Eds.): APMS 2020, IFIP AICT 592, pp. 425–431, 2020.
https://doi.org/10.1007/978-3-030-57997-5_49

information and communication technology (ICT), specifically enterprise resource planning (ERP) systems in lean transformations [5].

The concept of Digital Lean Manufacturing (DLM) has emerged in response to this debate [6]. DLM is realized when traditional lean methods gain a new digitally-enabled edge [7, 8]. However, the integration of digitalization and lean thinking is a two-sided coin. Adopting a limited view of digitalizing lean practices in isolation rather than considering also the change processes and application of lean thinking to digital transformations, risks simply digitalizing unnecessary activities, leading to digital waste [7]. In this paper, we explore the challenges and opportunities that arise during the integration of Lean Production and digitalization with a particular focus on Production Planning and Control (PPC) processes (strategic, tactical and operative).

## 2   Theoretical Background: Beyond the Lean Vs. ICT Paradox – the Emergence of Digital Lean Manufacturing

Production planning and control is a key mechanism in lean manufacturing, since planning puts the organization in a position where future demand can be met with a lean approach to better utilize resources and capacity. Supported by digitalized planning solutions mitigates uncertainty by providing information for better decision-making. Although in some instances considered an enabler for lean production, planning is otherwise strongly challenged by lean principles, since lean makes rigid planning highly sensitive to disturbances [9, 10], in particular variability in supply and demand. For a competitive environment this contradiction is emergent and the role of digitalization in a lean manufacturing setting must be further explored.

Though earlier publications identified Lean- and ICT-based approaches to production planning and control as contradictory [11–13], the more recent scientific literature presents both (therein specifically the integration of) as enablers of competitive advantage since digitalization promises to positively impact on flexibility and capacity utilization [5, 14]. This is an important development in thinking with regards to the contemporary debates around the contradictory or complementary nature of lean and digitalization – and suggests that we must once again revisit the Lean-ICT Paradox [15] in order to exploit potential novel concepts from the paradox [16].

[17] posed the question as to whether lean and ICT were complementary or contradictory in nature. Exploring this challenging issue, [18, 19] explored the support functionality of Manufacturing Execution Systems (MES) and Enterprise Resource Planning (ERP) Systems for Lean Production, respectively. Exploring the concurrent application of lean and ERP through action research, [5] proposed an ERP-based Lean implementation process – suggesting that the ERP implementation acted as a catalyst for the case-company's lean transformation. [20] also explored the support functionality offered by ERP systems for pull production, using multiple case-study research.

Given the complementary nature of contemporary ICT solutions and Lean Production, [6, 7] proceed with presenting both conceptual and practical insights into the complementary nature of Lean and Digitalization – rather than dwelling on the debate as to whether the two paradigms can co-exist or not. As such, [6] discusses Industry 4.0 technologies as enablers of leaner production, while [7] coins the term *Digital Lean*

*Manufacturing,* and subsequently extends the focus beyond production planning and control to also include total quality management (TQM) functions, such as *Jidoka 4.0* [21] and *Quality Management (QM) 4.0* [22].

As a final theoretical discussion, [1] presents and discusses the managerial challenges associated with lean and digitalization, classifying the *Digital Lean Landscape* in terms of a set of paradoxes within organizational design, supply chain planning, decision systems and supplier relationships. As such, these important research themes represent the structure for this investigation.

## 3   Research Design

This paper presents preliminary results from the initial stage of a four-year research project. To fully understand and gain a deep insight into the production planning and control processes of the digital lean manufacturing concepts applied by manufacturing companies, the research design is based on a theory-building case study approach [23]. The unit of analysis is the production planning and control process at strategic and tactical levels, which has been explored by the research question: *What are the challenges and opportunities for Production Planning and Control in Digital Lean Manufacturing?* Aggregated planning is particularly interesting in a DLM context, since the long-term planning horizon absorbs uncertainty and sets more robust direction for lower level planning.

Given the what-type research question [24], we chose to adopt a multiple case study research design and to draw useful insights form the results of semi-structured interviews with representatives from four industrial case companies (for an overview, see Table 1.). In addition, information from two workshops with the four case companies has contributed to contextual insight about the planning and control process. Data from the interviews was compiled in a report and triangulated with other sources, such as company documentation and follow-up discussions. The data has been analyzed according to the constructs *planning challenges* and *digital opportunities* (for planning).

**Table 1.** An overview of the case companies and interviewees.

| Case | Industry | Interviewee |
|------|----------|-------------|
| 1 | Automotive | Project manager – lean responsible |
| 2 | Oil and Gas | Chief Operations Officer (COO) – lean responsible |
| 3 | Construction | Human Resources (HR) manager – lean responsible |
| 4 | Aluminium | Project manager – lean responsible |

## 3.1   Case 1: Automotive

Lean has been the main management model in Case 1 for several years. PPC at Case 1 is largely driven by input from customers and forecasted expectations of sales and market development as well as strategic priorities over a five-year horizon, which then provides the basis for making plans for production, distribution and procurement. In forecasting and planning, various digital planning tools are used, such as ERP and MES. These systems support the planning processes of the various functions at different levels in the organization (strategic, tactical, operational).

Takt-time and capacity are important tactical planning constraints. Planning meetings are conducted in order to consider available resources, equipment, and materials. One challenge in particular is that suppliers have different response times for different requirements which directly affect the inventory and safety stock level. Demands for reduction in inventory and varying response time from the suppliers lead to greater uncertainty in the planning environment and vulnerability in relation to the level of delivery precision. As a countermeasure, the Industrial Internet of Things (IIOT) and supply chain connectivity present an interesting opportunity for Case 1 concerning more advanced analytics about demand and supply, and involvement of suppliers and customers in planning.

## 3.2   Case 2: Oil and Gas

Case 2 processes over 400,000 work orders through its base stations each year, for example for material supplies and maintenance equipment to multiple installations geographically spread. A substantially part of the flow through the base stations are specialized engineer to order material and equipment, delivered on JIT premises. Therefore, the planning and management of supply, operations and demand at base stations presents a grand challenge for Case 2 (the base stations are the central hubs of the value chain that link on-shore and off-shore installations). As such, the PPC task is complex, and the bases are required to coordinate both inbound and outbound material- and information flows from- and to its facilities off-shore, its external suppliers, and its logistics providers. In addition, the base stations serve as (intermediate) consolidation and storage points for equipment and materials. Therefore, effective flow, interaction and coordination in and between base stations presents a key challenge, whereby digitalization can provide a solution in the form of more integrated digital planning.

## 3.3   Case 3: Construction

Case 3 is an engineer-to-order (ETO)/project-based producer, providing systems to the oil and gas industry. As such, the customer's product specifications intervene "deeply" into the company's upstream processes, i.e. in or before engineering and includes the sub-suppliers. This creates a completely different planning environment to the one which is typically found in the traditional commodity manufacturing industry, where demand uncertainty is usually mitigated through the production and storage of standard products. The ETO environment is therefore surrounded by significantly greater uncertainty related to, among other things, lead times, delivery reliability, access to specialized engineering expertise/capacity/resources, etc. This uncertainty also propagates further down the value chain to suppliers. Coordination, integration, planning/management of the processes in these types of organizations and the utilization/role that digitization can have, for example in connection with information capture, the sharing of information between decision steps and levels, product configurators/bill-of-materials/catalogs, organization, integration with suppliers and customers, etc., are critical elements that can greatly affect profitability and competitiveness.

### 3.4    Case 4: Aluminium

Case 4, a producer of aluminum, has developed and implemented an advanced digital model to plan and allocate resources in relation to demand/order requirements. The model is mainly used for the European region and has an accuracy of about 80%, i.e. the inaccuracy of 20% is relatively significant, which in turn has implications for the quality of planning and a need to build capacity (storage, production, transport, etc.) to maintain a high level of delivery precision. The company could benefit further from an analysis of the digital model and its subsequent planning process, as well as the integration of a Big Data analytics module in order to uncover barriers and potential "digital waste" and mitigate uncertainty in Production Planning and Control.

## 4    Discussion

The aim of this paper was to investigate the research question: *What are the challenges and opportunities for Production Planning and Control in Digital Lean Manufacturing?* Results from the multiple case-analysis is summarized in Table 2 and will be discussed below.

**Table 2.** Cross-case analysis.

| Case | Production planning challenges | DLM opportunities |
|---|---|---|
| 1 | Planning uncertainty caused by varying supplier lead times at the same time as reducing stock levels | Supply chain connectivity by Industrial Internet of Things (IIOT) |
| 2 | Complex supply and demand planning for JIT operations | Integrated digital planning |
| 3 | Planning of ETO orders with high uncertainty caused by poor customer specification | Integrated digital production and supply chain planning |
| 4 | Complex production network planning causing low planning accuracy | Exploiting advanced analytics/Big Data technology in network planning |

The research resulted in the identification of challenges and opportunities for PPC in DLM, specifically intra- and inter-organizational integration (with respect to material and information flows). The planning environment in the cases is characterized by uncertainty and complexity, consisting multiple units and their interdependency, and variability in demand and supply which challenges lean management of operations. Critical elements of DLM identified in the cases are the access to and sharing of information for integrated planning and decision support across functions and between customers and suppliers. Next, the results identify the role DLM might have on improving processes and driving change management by the strong emphasis on integrated planning and connectivity in the cases. Further, the cases identify the complexity and systemic component of the planning and control process as critical elements in DLM, but also the potential benefits and novelty coming from investigating the paradox of DLM. We consider this to represent both the fundamental challenge and opportunity for PPC in DLM – traditional lean supply chain practices can certainly be enhanced by novel digital solutions such as IIoT and Big Data analytics.

## 5    Conclusion

By considering the challenges and opportunities for PPC in DLM, it appears that lean paves the way for successful digital transformation and digitalization enriches lean practices. From the results of this investigation, it appears that the combination of lean with digital solutions certainly promises to enable lean thinking to be extended beyond company borders and out into the supply chain. As such, we suggest that further research should investigate *Digital Lean Supply Chains* in more detail.

**Acknowledgements.** The authors acknowledge the support of the Norwegian research project *Lean Digital* and the Norwegian research program *SFI Manufacturing*.

## References

1. Ashrafian, A., et al.: Sketching the landscape for lean digital transformation. In: Ameri, F., Stecke, Kathryn E., von Cieminski, G., Kiritsis, D. (eds.) APMS 2019. IAICT, vol. 566, pp. 29–36. Springer, Cham (2019). https://doi.org/10.1007/978-3-030-30000-5_4
2. Lewis, M.W., Smith, W.K.: Paradox as a metatheoretical perspective: sharpening the focus and widening the scope. J. Appl. Behav. Sci. **50**(2), 127–149 (2014)
3. Lorenz, R., Buess, P., Macuvele, J., Friedli, T., Netland, T.H.: Lean and digitalization—contradictions or complements? In: Ameri, F., Stecke, K.E., von Cieminski, G., Kiritsis, D. (eds.) APMS 2019. IAICT, vol. 566, pp. 77–84. Springer, Cham (2019). https://doi.org/10.1007/978-3-030-30000-5_10
4. Meissner, A., Müller, M., Hermann, A., Metternich, J.: Digitalization as a catalyst for lean production: a learning factory approach for digital shop floor management. Procedia Manuf. **23**, 81–86 (2018)
5. Powell, D., Alfnes, E., Strandhagen, J.O., Dreyer, H.: The concurrent application of lean production and ERP: towards an ERP-based lean implementation process. Comput. Ind. **64**(3), 324–335 (2013)

6. Powell, D., Romero, D., Gaiardelli, P., Cimini, C., Cavalieri, S.: Towards digital lean cyber-physical production systems: industry 4.0 technologies as enablers of leaner production. In: Moon, I., Lee, G.M., Park, J., Kiritsis, D., von Cieminski, G. (eds.) APMS 2018. IAICT, vol. 536, pp. 353–362. Springer, Cham (2018). https://doi.org/10.1007/978-3-319-99707-0_44
7. Romero, D., Gaiardelli, P., Powell, D., Wuest, T., Thürer, M.: Digital lean cyber-physical production systems: the emergence of digital lean manufacturing and the significance of digital waste. In: Moon, I., Lee, G.M., Park, J., Kiritsis, D., von Cieminski, G. (eds.) APMS 2018. IAICT, vol. 535, pp. 11–20. Springer, Cham (2018). https://doi.org/10.1007/978-3-319-99704-9_2
8. Mora, E., Gaiardelli, P., Resta, B., Powell, D.: Exploiting lean benefits through smart manufacturing: a comprehensive perspective. In: Lödding, H., Riedel, R., Thoben, K.-D., von Cieminski, G., Kiritsis, D. (eds.) APMS 2017. IAICT, vol. 513, pp. 127–134. Springer, Cham (2017). https://doi.org/10.1007/978-3-319-66923-6_15
9. Fisher, M.L.: What is the right supply chain for your Product? Harv. Bus. Rev. 75(2), 105–116 (1997)
10. Copra, S., Meidl, P.: Supply Chain Management Strategy, Planning, and Operations. Pearson Education Limited, Essex (2016)
11. Piszczalski, M.: Lean vs information systems. Automot. Manuf. Prod. 2000, 26–28 (2000)
12. Halgari, P., McHaney, R., Pei, Z.J.: ERP systems supporting lean manufacturing in SMEs. In: Cruz-Cunha, M.M. (ed.) Enterprise Information for Systems Business Integration in SMEs: Technological, Organizational, and Social Dimensions, IGI Global, Hershey (2011)
13. Sugimori, Y., Kusunoki, K., Cho, F., Uchikawa, S.: Toyota production system and Kanban system materialization of just-in-time and respect-for-human system. Int. J. Prod. Res. 15(6), 553–564 (1977)
14. Powell, D.: ERP systems in lean production: new insights from a review of lean and ERP literature. Int. J. Oper. Prod. Manag. 33(11–12), 1490–1510 (2013)
15. Powell, D., Strandhagen, J.O.: Lean production Vs. ERP systems: an ICT paradox? Oper. Manag. 37(3), 31–36 (2011)
16. Hargrave, T.J., Van de Ven, A.H.: Integrating dialectical and paradox perspectives on managing contradictions in organizations. Organ. Stud. 38(3–4), 319–339 (2017)
17. Riezebos, J., Klingenberg, W., Hicks, C.: Lean production and information technology: connection or contradiction? Comput. Ind. 60, 237–247 (2009)
18. Powell, D., Binder, A., Arica, E.: MES support for lean production. In: Emmanouilidis, C., Taisch, M., Kiritsis, D. (eds.) APMS 2012. IAICT, vol. 398, pp. 128–135. Springer, Heidelberg (2013). https://doi.org/10.1007/978-3-642-40361-3_17
19. Powell, D., Alfnes, E., Strandhagen, J.O., Dreyer, H.: ERP support for lean production. In: Frick, J., Laugen, B.T. (eds.) APMS 2011. IAICT, vol. 384, pp. 115–122. Springer, Heidelberg (2012). https://doi.org/10.1007/978-3-642-33980-6_14
20. Powell, D., Riezebos, J., Strandhagen, J.O.: Lean production and ERP systems in SMEs: ERP support for pull production. Int. J. Prod. Res. 51(2), 395–409 (2013)
21. Romero, D., Gaiardelli, P., Powell, D., Wuest, T., Thürer, M.: Rethinking jidoka systems under automation & learning perspectives in the digital lean manufacturing world. IFAC-PapersOnLine 52(13), 899–903 (2019)
22. Romero, D., Gaiardelli, P., Powell, D., Wuest, T., Thürer, M.: Total quality management and quality circles in the digital lean manufacturing world. In: Ameri, F., Stecke, K.E., von Cieminski, G., Kiritsis, D. (eds.) APMS 2019. IAICT, vol. 566, pp. 3–11. Springer, Cham (2019). https://doi.org/10.1007/978-3-030-30000-5_1
23. Yin, R.K.: Case Study Research: Design and Methods, 4th edn. Sage Publications, Thousand Oaks (2009)
24. Karlsson, C.: Researching Operations Management. Routledge, New York (2009)

# New Forms of Gemba Walks and Their Digital Tools in the Digital Lean Manufacturing World

David Romero[1]([⊠]), Paolo Gaiardelli[2], Thorsten Wuest[3],
Daryl Powell[4], and Matthias Thürer[5]

[1] Tecnológico de Monterrey, Monterrey, Mexico
david.romero.diaz@gmail.com
[2] University of Bergamo, Bergamo, Italy
paolo.gaiardelli@unibg.it
[3] West Virginia University, Morgantown, USA
thwuest@mail.wvu.edu
[4] SINTEF Manufacturing AS, Vestre Toten, Norway
daryl.powell@sintef.no
[5] Jinan University, Guangzhou, China
matthiasthurer@workloadcontrol.com

**Abstract.** Gemba Walks are an important mean of vertical integration in Lean Manufacturing environments. They ensure that all levels of the company stay connected with the front-line, "the Gemba", where the actual value is created. However, traditionally Gemba Walks have been restricted to one location. This is a shortcoming in production environments characterized by interconnected and often globally dispersed problems where information from several locations is needed simultaneously. In response, this paper explores the emergence of new forms of Gemba Walks enabled by the adoption of new digital technologies. We intend to identify the advantages and disadvantages of using digital technology to support the execution of these new forms of Gemba Walks in more complex, globalized environments and to get a grasp of the extent to which digitalization changes communication characteristics between the parties involved.

**Keywords:** Digital manufacturing · Smart manufacturing · Lean manufacturing · Digital lean manufacturing · Cyber-physical production systems · Industry 4.0 · Augmented reality · Gemba Walks

## 1 Introduction

*Lean managers* agree that it is important for all levels of management to stay connected with the shop-floor, where value is created. An important mean to realize this vertical integration is through *Gemba Walks* [1, 2]. Traditionally, *Gemba Walks* refer to lean managers making an effort to physically "go and see" what is happing on the shop-floor using their human senses to better understand the problems and actual work processes that their employees deal with every day to create value for their customers [1, 2]. However, a managers' physical presence in their organisations' front-lines is not

© IFIP International Federation for Information Processing 2020
Published by Springer Nature Switzerland AG 2020
B. Lalic et al. (Eds.): APMS 2020, IFIP AICT 592, pp. 432–440, 2020.
https://doi.org/10.1007/978-3-030-57997-5_50

helpful unless it enables active problem-solving [3]. The higher the level of management, the higher the control sphere and consequently the more complex the problems to be solved [4]. Contemporary problems are often no longer isolated at the front-line level, where the interconnectedness of problems becomes apparent. To address this properly, several *Gemba Walks* at distant global locations need to be conducted simultaneously.

The emerging *Digital Lean Manufacturing World* builds on "new data acquisition, data integration, data processing and data visualization capabilities to create different descriptive, predictive and prescriptive analytics applications to detect, fix, predict and prevent unstable process parameters and/or avoid quality issues inside defined tolerance ranges that may lead to any type of waste within the cyber- and physical- worlds" [5]. Such capabilities have the promise to support important feedback-loops for continuous improvement cycles [6] as well as managers' double-loop learning cycles, independent of physical location [7]. This provides an important mean to enhance traditional *Gemba Walks*, making them more suitable for complex, globalized production environments.

In this paper, we explore the emergence of new forms of *Gemba Walks* enabled by the adoption of new *digital technologies* at the digital lean factory floor. We aim to achieve this research goal by analysing innovative technology-based *Gemba Walk* solutions available to the industry. Our aim is twofold, firstly, to identify the advantages and disadvantages of using digital technology to support the implementation of this lean technique, and secondly, to grasp the extent to which *digitalization* changes communication characteristics between the parties involved in a *Gemba Walk*.

The research and assessment methods used were an explorative review of scientific and grey literature and empirical observations by the authors as lean consultants.

## 2    Gemba Walks

As a combination of *Gemba* ("the real thing"), *Genchi Genbutsu* ("go and see"), and *Genjitsu* ("real facts"), a *Gemba Walk* is a powerful lean technique to observe, interact, gather information, and understand how work or co-work is performed by humans and/or machines. Specifically, it is an important mean for vertical integration that aims to foster the systematic development of an organisation by developing the human potential to solve problems and identify ideas for improvement.

A *Gemba Walk* is characterised by four distinctive elements: (i) *Location* – observing an operator, a machine, or a team at "the actual location" where the work is being performed; (ii) *Observation* – watching an operator, a machine, or a team perform their work "in person"; (iii) *Teaming* – "interacting" with an operator, a machine, or a team performing work by respectfully asking questions, if appropriate; and (iv) *Reflecting* – after "seeing and listening", on what actions are required to support innovation and continuous improvement [1, 2]. It is specifically this latter part that is important for the success of *Gemba Walks* [2].

*Gemba Walks* are a core *lean management tool* since they provide an up-close, detailed view of behaviours in action and context, thus facilitating "understanding by seeing", and the subsequent identification of process improvement opportunities [2].

Moreover, *Gemba Walks* are an important *lean leadership tool* since they enable lean managers to directly engage with the operators at their actual workplace. By performing regular *Gemba Walks,* lean managers show appreciation for the work of the employees in creating value, boosting morale with their presence, and gaining their trust to share relevant information for continuous improvement [8].

In summary, *Gemba Walks* support organisations' improvement by (i) developing knowledge through the integration and exchange of contextualized information, (ii) supporting managers to make the right decisions that depend on the context in which they are taken, (iii) building *Nemawashi* ("consensus") by getting people through observation and discussion to agree on what the main problem is and how it can be addressed, and (iv) improving the organisations' ability to capture the skills of each human resource through direct interaction with people as they face problems. However, people are often bound to one location, which means they can just observe problems within a given physical perimeter. This limits the usefulness of traditional *Gemba Walks* in ever more complex business environments, where problems are interconnected and often globally dispersed. Therefore, *Gemba Walks* should be enhanced to allow for simultaneous visits of several *Gemba's* or to allow for simple access to information via augmented realities.

## 2.1 New Forms of Gemba Walks

As the adoption of *Digital Technologies* continues to increase rapidly at the factory floor [5], new forms of *Gemba Walks* are emerging. Such new forms identified in this explorative research work are based on the authors' empirical observations and scientific and grey literature reviews. The identified new forms of *Gemba Walks* are:

*Simplified Virtual Gemba Walks* – when lean managers may use of hand-held cameras in a remote location to record or transmit their walk live for others.

*Augmented Gemba Walks* – when lean managers "go to *Gemba*" using wearable technologies [9] such as Augmented Reality (AR) smart glasses. In this new *Gemba Walk* form, lean managers' senses are 'augmented' allowing him/her to 'see and listen' in real-time and in his/her field of view the emerging big data world of digital lean factory floors loaded with relevant and up-to-date information from IIoT-enabled smart, social machines [10] and operators [11] (e.g. real-time performance data). Such an enriched and detailed big data world improves the context- and situational-awareness of *augmented lean managers* as they walk the shop-floor and engage with the operators and machines. This helps to gain a more accurate understanding of the current problems and makes for more effective continuous improvement measures.

*Advanced Virtual Gemba Walks* – when lean managers utilize *digital technologies* to 'remotely interact' with IIoT-enabled smart, social machines and operators through *digital twins,* in Virtual Reality (VR) production environments. In this new form of *Gemba Walk,* lean managers use virtual and digital copies of the production resources [12], and *VR technologies* for creating immersive VR production environments to conduct *Virtual Gemba Walks* [13] without neglecting the essential context- and situational-awareness of being on the actual shop-floor. In these VR environments, *digital twins* can offer a detailed view of a production system, allowing lean managers to simulate and analyse work processes and view them from different perspectives without any disruption of a production resource. Consequently, this contributes to problem-solving and continuous improvement based on advanced simulations and big data analytics [14].

*Automated Guided Gemba Walks* – when lean managers' *Gemba Walks* are 'automated and guided' by data-driven trend predictions provided by IIoT-enabled smart, social machines and operators at digital lean factory floors. This allows them to anticipate deviations from standard operating procedures (SOPs), production system states, or work processes parameters, and take appropriate preventative actions. In this new form of *Gemba Walks*, *Andon systems* [15] could be used, for example, to guide, and augment the walking path of lean managers, showing areas deserving particular attention by highlighting them, for example, with yellow lights.

*Human Cyber-Physical Gemba Walks* – when lean managers and AI-enabled systems (i.e. intelligent personal assistants) become 'joint cognitive systems' [16, 17]. Both are walking the *Gemba* physically and digitally, correspondingly, the path of production with a critical eye for observing and detecting deviations from standard operating procedures or actual work processes abnormalities. In this new form of *Gemba Walks*, humans make use of their (augmented) senses and cognition while the AIs use their network of sensors available in a digital lean factory floor combined with different data analytics tools (e.g. event-driven, real-time data-driven, and trend prediction) for sensemaking (i.e. 5 Whys) of such deviations or abnormalities. Humans and AIs interact in a meaningful way as a joint cognitive system to investigate and understand the root cause of problems.

## 2.2 New Digital Tools for New Forms of Gemba Walks

Supporting lean managers as they "go to *Gemba*", and observe, ask why, take notes, and show respect for people in the *Digital Lean Enterprise,* calls for a new set of digital tools for data collection, sharing, analysis, optimization, and feedback. For *data collection support,* handheld-devices such as tablets and smartphones, equipped with a variety of sensors, will allow the easy-capture of text, images, audio, video, indoor locations, and other measures (e.g. temperature, light, vibrations, etc.). The richness of data in digitally-documented observations will lead to better decision-support and decision-making.

Moreover, for *data sharing support* in information systems, 'tags' as metadata can be utilized to describe a data item and facilitate its categorization, and later search in a database. Tagging and push-information systems can help to guarantee that the right person(s) and/or system(s) will receive the right data for its further processing.

Furthermore, for *data analysis support,* visual analytics tools [18] offer various interactive visualization techniques (i.e. visual data exploration) to support human analytical reasoning for data-driven decision-making. Visual Analytics tools emerge to be indispensable at the big data digital lean factory floors with its ability to generate data at a faster rate than it can be analysed by humans without support.

For *data optimization support,* automatic data analysis tools [19] (e.g. data mining, machine learning) will support the automated filtering, categorization, and analysis of massive and complex datasets that are manually unfeasible in big data digital lean factories. Automatic data analysis tools will help human analysts to generate, evaluate, and refine their data-driven decision models to support their decision-making.

Lastly, for *data feedback support,* virtual *Obeya* rooms [20] can offer person-to-person communication, sharing each other's notes, posting and reading posts, and updating data and events as new things happen. Virtual *Obeya* can help to speed-up feedback cycles for action-taking and continuous improvement by overcoming the boundaries of time and space of traditional *Obeya* rooms.

## 3    Assessing the New Forms of Gemba Walks

Taking into account the critical elements, or dimensions, of the *Gemba Walk* definition, we can characterize the new forms of *Gemba Walks* as reported in Fig. 1.

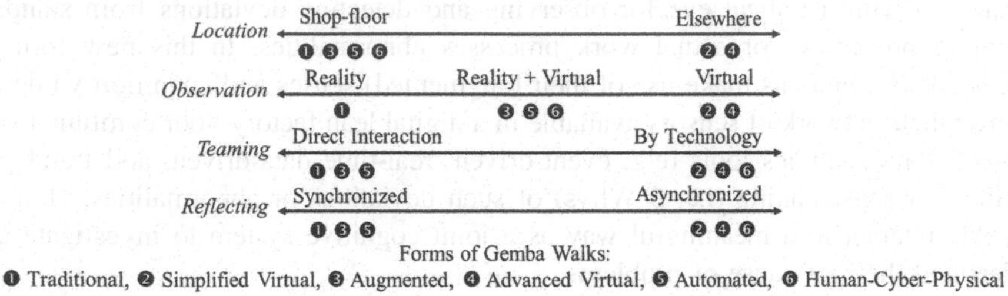

Forms of Gemba Walks:
❶ Traditional, ❷ Simplified Virtual, ❸ Augmented, ❹ Advanced Virtual, ❺ Automated, ❻ Human-Cyber-Physical

**Fig. 1.** Main characteristics of the new forms of Gemba Walks

Concerning *Location,* the introduction of digital technologies may allow the observer to avoid being physically present in the place where the value is generated by intervening remotely. This possibility provides the observer greater accessibility in time and space to the *Gemba,* thus allowing more opportunities for gaining knowledge of the context and the problem of how resources operate by exploiting their skills. The result is a greater opportunity to capture the capabilities of individuals and multiple opportunities to find the right answers and solutions for improvement.

If we refer instead to the way *Observation* takes place, thanks to the use of digital technology it is possible to move from a physical to a virtual perspective, operating in an environment where it is easier to experiment with proposals for improvement even anticipating the behaviour of a productive resource. Where instead there is the possibility of integrating the physical environment with the digital one, with the use of augmented reality, it is possible to obtain more details and information from the field to better understand the context being analysed and therefore make better decisions.

Moreover, the use of technology, with respect to *Teaming,* allows modifying the approach of identifying and sharing information through disintermediation between the supplier and the receiver. If the separation between the parties increases the time available to deal with and solve problems and increases the opportunities to understand the capabilities of each resource, at the same time it reduces the moments of contact making it more complicated for the parties to create an environment of mutual trust.

Finally, as far as *Reflection* is concerned, thanks to the use of new technologies, the logic of analysis of the problem and solutions changes, as technological innovations make possible to study the behaviour of a system or resource, not necessarily at the moment in which it operates. The advantage lies in the possibility of integrating human experience with the speed and flexibility of technology to create better solutions with the risk of relying too much on artificial intelligence, instead of people's knowledge and skills.

The consequent advantages and disadvantages of the new forms of *Gemba Walks* for supporting lean managers double-loop learning cycles are summarised in Table 1.

**Table 1.** New forms of Gemba Walks: advantages and disadvantages

| Forms of Gemba Walks | Advantages | Disadvantages |
|---|---|---|
| Traditional | • Aligning perception with reality<br>• First-hand facts and data<br>• Direct interaction with employees and equipment | • Limit time to ask "why" so to not disrupt the continuous flow<br>• Potential narrow view |
| Simplified virtual | • Seeing and hearing remotely | • Other senses excluded |
| Augmented | • Adding detailed data to remove subjectivity<br>• Better observations mean better decisions | • Putting more attention to data over people thoughts |
| Advanced virtual | • Learning from reality and possible future scenarios | • Indirect interaction with employees and equipment |
| Automated guided | • Being proactive towards detected (negative) trends | • Parts of the processes chains may be skipped |
| Human cyber-physical | • Learning together humans and AI systems, thus accelerating learning | • Relying too much on AI systems, instead of people knowledge and skills |

## 4 Effects on Communication and Feedback

As digital lean factory floors start hosting more cyber-physical productions systems, "going to *Gemba*" will become a "data-driven" continuous improvement effort for the case of *Gemba Kaizen* initiatives (i.e. incremental, exploitative improvement efforts), and will remain more "human-driven" for the case of *Gemba Kaikaku* initiatives (i.e. radical, explorative improvements efforts). Although automation technologies could be seen as more advanced than human-centred ones, there are some complex and special tasks that only humans can accomplish (see [21]).

The effectiveness of the new forms of *Gemba Walks* for enabling continuous improvement and double-loop learning is based on the quality of the feedback loops. Such quality can be measured according to the feedback-loops properties of

(Ci) *Completeness* – as their effectiveness to identify and communicate all "observations" needed to understand the ideas, advice, complaints, and issues detected and collected during a *Gemba Walk;* (Cii) *Conciseness* – as their effectiveness to organise and present the proper amount of information, and avoid information overload (i.e. cognitive *Muri*), in support of agile decision-making; (Ciii) *Consideration* – as their effectiveness to recognize, value, and combine different data-sources coming humans and computer information systems to support an integrated decision-making; (Civ) *Concreteness* – as their effectiveness to call for action based on clear instructions for problem-solving or performance improvement; (Cv) *Courtesy* – as their effectiveness for offering "respect for people" when it comes to negotiating and agreeing to a change or modification in work and/or behaviour; (Cvi) *Clarity* – as their effectiveness to provide clear evidence and justification for the needed change or modification for improvement; and (Cvii) *Correctness* – as their effectiveness to create a positive impact with the change or modification in the processes and people (see Table 2).

**Table 2.** New forms of Gemba Walks: effects on communication & feedback characteristics

| Forms of Gemba Walks | Ci | Cii | Ciii | Civ | Cv | Cvi | Cvii |
|---|---|---|---|---|---|---|---|
| Traditional | REF | REF | REF | REF | REF | REF | REF |
| Simplified virtual | = | = | − | + | − | − | = |
| Augmented | + | + | = | + | = | = | = |
| Advanced virtual | = | + | + | + | − | + | = |
| Automated huided | + | + | + | + | − | + | = |
| Human cyber-physical | + | + | = | + | − | + | = |
| +: Higher impact | =: Same Impact | | | -: Lower Impact | | | |

Regarding the distinctive features of the new forms of *Gemba Walks,* we can state that the *Completeness* is higher where it is possible to integrate both physical and virtual reality making the "observation" more extensive. From this point of view operating in a virtual context remains completely indifferent concerning a real context. Indeed, if the "observation" carried out in a virtual reality environment can be extended in time and space, operating from external place involves the risk of a lower ability to capture the characteristics of the context where the information is generated. Another risk of virtualization is evident regarding *Conciseness*. The excessive use of technology to support data observation and analysis can create conditions of information overload, thus falling into the trap of *Muda* or digital waste [5, 22]. Moreover, if the shift of perspective towards a virtual world favours the possibility of combining information from different sources (i.e. *Consideration*), on the other hand, excessive virtualization leads to disintermediation between subjects, thus losing communicative effectiveness. This principle also applies to *Courtesy*, understood as the ability to create collaboration and mutual trust between people, which inevitably disappears by shifting the focus of the decision-making process from people to machines. The *Concreteness, Clarity,* and *Correctness* of information are potentially higher in a virtual context, as the use of digital information and technologies allows to capture more detailed information and to reprocess it faster to propose better solutions. However, reducing the participation of actors in the process of problem analysis and processing of results risks harming the final effectiveness of the actions undertaken, as the proposed solution is not made by those who have to implement it. Based on these considerations, Table 2 summarizes the relations between the components of the communication and new types of *Gemba Walks*. The evaluation is made with reference (REF) to the traditional *Gemba Walk*.

## 5   Conclusions and Outlook

The success of *Gemba Walks* depends on their capability to enable active problem-solving. Nevertheless, traditionally *Gemba Walks* are bound to one location and current information. This is ill-suited in a production environment where problems are complex, interconnected and often globally dispersed. The new, technology-enhanced forms of *Gemba Walks,* presented in this paper, can bring great benefits for innovation, problem-solving, and continuous improvement of conditions, tools, and procedures at the factory floor in these contexts. They allow to bridge time and space and if used correctly, increase the opportunity to observe operations within our globalized world greatly. However, lean managers must ensure that these new forms do not hinder the main goal of *Gemba Walks* of communicating and collaborating with the operators in their terms, and at their locations. The new technology-enhanced forms of *Gemba Walks* may be perceived as 'policing' (a.k.a. "big brother" is watching you) and thus contradict its original intentions. Lean managers should always show "respect for people" by visiting their operators at their workplace, and keep in mind that their creativity, ingenuity, and innovation, as well as daily standardized work (i.e. standard operating procedures), are the true sources of sustained value-creation, continues improvement, and operational excellence. Outlook – *Genchi-Genbutsu* practice is being revised by Toyota [see 23].

## References

1. Womack, J.: Gemba Walks. Lean Enterprise Institute Inc., Expanded 2nd edn. (2019)
2. Ballé, M. et al.: The Lean Sensei. Lean Enterprise Institute Inc. (2019)
3. Tucker, A.L., Singer, S.J.: The effectiveness of management-by-walking-around: a randomized field study. Prod. Oper. Manage. 24(2), 253–271 (2015)
4. Netland, T., Powell, D. Hines, P.: Demystifying lean leadership. Lean Six Sigma (2019)
5. Romero, D., Gaiardelli, P., Powell, D., Wuest, T., Thürer, M.: Digital lean cyber-physical production systems: the emergence of digital lean manufacturing and the significance of digital waste. In: Moon, I., Lee, G.M., Park, J., Kiritsis, D., von Cieminski, G. (eds.) APMS 2018. IAICT, vol. 535, pp. 11–20. Springer, Cham (2018). https://doi.org/10.1007/978-3-319-99704-9_2
6. Buer, S.-V., et al.: The data-driven process improvement cycle: using digitalization for continuous improvement. IFAC-PapersOnLine 51(11), 1035–1040 (2018)
7. Pearce, A.D., Pons, D.J.: Defining lean change – framing lean implementation in organizational development. Bus. Manage. 12(4), 10–22 (2017)

8. Aij, K.H., Teunissen, M.: Lean leadership attributes: a systematic review of the literature. Health Organ. Manage. **31**(7–8), 713–729 (2017)
9. Perera, C., Liu, C.H., Jayawardena, S.: The emerging internet of things marketplace from an industrial perspective: a survey. IEEE Trans. Emerg. Top. Comput. **3**(4), 585–598 (2015)
10. Li, H., Parlikad, A.K.: Social internet of industrial things for industrial and manufacturing assets. IFAC-PapersOnLine **49**(28), 208–213 (2016)
11. Romero, D., Wuest, T., Stahre, J., Gorecky, D.: Social factory architecture: social networking services and production scenarios through the social internet of things, services and people for the social operator 4.0. In: Lödding, H., Riedel, R., Thoben, K.-D., von Cieminski, G., Kiritsis, D. (eds.) APMS 2017. IAICT, vol. 513, pp. 265–273. Springer, Cham (2017). https://doi.org/10.1007/978-3-319-66923-6_31
12. Negri, E., Fumagalli, L., Macchi, M.: A review of the roles of digital twin in CPS-based production systems. Procedia Manuf. **11**, 939–948 (2017)
13. Kunz, A., Zank, M., Fjeld, M., Nescher, T.: Real walking in virtual environments for factory planning and evaluation. Procedia CIRP **44**, 257–262 (2016)
14. Shao, G., Shin, S.-J., Jain, S.: Data analytics using simulation for smart manufacturing. In: Proceedings of the Winter Simulation Conference (2014)
15. Everett, R.J., Sohal, A.S.: Individual involvement and intervention in quality improvement programmes: using the andon system. Qual. Reliab. Manage. **8**(2), 21–34 (1991)
16. Howard, N.: Intention awareness in human-machine interaction sensemaking in joint-cognitive systems. In: 8th International Conference on Information Science and Digital Content Technology, pp. 293–299. IEEExplorer (2012)
17. Jones, A.T., Romero, D., Wuest, T.: Modeling agents as joint cognitive systems in smart manufacturing systems. Manuf. Lett. **17**, 6–8 (2018)
18. Soban, D., Thornhill, D., Salunkhe, S., Long, A.: Visual analytics as an enabler for manufacturing process decision-making. Procedia CIRP **56**, 209–214 (2016)
19. Hilbrich, M., Weber, M., Tschüter, R.: Automatic analysis of large data sets: a walk-through on methods from different perspectives. In: International Conference on Cloud Computing and Big Data, pp. 373–380. IEEExplorer (2013)
20. Terenghi, F., Cassina, J., Kristensen, K, Terzi, S.: Virtual obeya: a new collaborative web application for running lean management workshops. In: International Conference on Engineering, Technology and Innovation, pp. 1–7. IEEExplorer (2014)
21. Romero, D., Gaiardelli, P., Powell, D., Wuest, T., Thürer, M.: Total quality management and quality circles in the digital lean manufacturing world. In: Ameri, F., Stecke, K.E., von Cieminski, G., Kiritsis, D. (eds.) APMS 2019. IAICT, vol. 566, pp. 3–11. Springer, Cham (2019). https://doi.org/10.1007/978-3-030-30000-5_1
22. Romero, D., Gaiardelli, P., Thürer, M., Powell, D., Wuest, T.: Cyber-physical waste identification and elimination strategies in the digital lean manufacturing world. In: Ameri, F., Stecke, K.E., von Cieminski, G., Kiritsis, D. (eds.) APMS 2019. IAICT, vol. 566, pp. 37–45. Springer, Cham (2019). https://doi.org/10.1007/978-3-030-30000-5_5
23. https://europe.autonews.com/automakers/lockdown-leads-toyota-chief-question-core-tenet

# New Reconfigurable, Flexible or Agile Production Systems in the Era of Industry 4.0

# A Computational Method for Identifying the Optimum Buffer Size in the Era of Zero Defect Manufacturing

Foivos Psarommatis[(✉)], Ali Boujemaoui, and Dimitris Kiritsis

ICT for Sustainable Manufacturing, EPFL SCI-STI-DK, École Polytechnique
Fédérale de Lausanne, Lausanne, Switzerland
foivos.psarommatis@epfl.ch

**Abstract.** Decreasing defects, waste time, meeting customer demand and being adaptable are the goals of a Zero Defect Manufacturing (ZDM) strategy. Scheduling is an important tool to perform that. It should take in account buffer size allocation. In this study, a method to solve the Buffer Sizing Problem (BSP), which is NP-hard problem. The current research work focuses on finding the optimal buffer allocation using Tabu-search (TS) algorithm. The goal is to minimize buffers' sizes while maintaining a certain productivity. The evaluation of the alternative buffer solutions were performed using the following performance indicators; Makespan, Tardiness and the Buffers Cost. In the developed method the following are considered: multitasking machines subjected to non-deterministic failure, non-homogeneous buffer sizing, and non-sequential production line. The propose approach was tested via a real life industrial use case from a leading Swiss company in high precision sensors. The simulation results showed that the proposed methodology can effectively design the buffer strategy for complex production lines.

**Keywords:** Buffer Size Problem · BSP · Zero Defect Manufacturing · ZDM · Optimization · Tabu-search

## 1 Introduction

Modern industry, 4.0, wants to reach new goals. Nowadays, manufacturing includes data to analyze and treat, changing and advancing communication and information technology. Flexible production and batch processes are the path adopted. Furthermore, manufacturers give special attention to the improvement of the quality using one of the latest paradigms, Zero Defect Manufacturing (ZDM) which is achieved by implementing industry 4.0 technologies. ZDM paradigm is relying on a huge data collection about product and processes. In ZDM, not only detection takes place, but also the right reaction must be done [1]. Implementing the ZDM concept can create loses in the performance of the manufacturing system because extra processes are added, such as inspections or part re-work. In addition, to stay competitive, companies should answer properly to customer different customization needs, since the production has changed from mass production to mass customization [2]. The way to do is to move from systematics inspections to a flexible structure, while products are not mass product but

© IFIP International Federation for Information Processing 2020
Published by Springer Nature Switzerland AG 2020
B. Lalic et al. (Eds.): APMS 2020, IFIP AICT 592, pp. 443–450, 2020.
https://doi.org/10.1007/978-3-030-57997-5_51

became in form of batches, augmenting the level of defects probability and occurrence. ZDM is a complex strategy to implement and therefore, new approaches are needed for successful implementation.

The current research work focuses on giving a solution to the Buffer Size Problem (BSP) for unreliable multitask machine in non-sequential production line. Furthermore, the parts waiting time in the buffers are utilized for the ZDM processes. The solution proposed is implemented inside a ZDM oriented scheduling tool [3]. Tabu search is used for both scheduling and Buffer Size optimization. The proposed approach is tested in a real industrial use case from a Swiss leading micro-sensors company. Finally, a comparison is performed between the buffer solution with and without ZDM in order to discover the different needs that ZDM requires.

## 2 State of the Art

Buffer sizing problem (BSP) is a combinatorial problem ranked as a NP-hard [4]. Buffers have a big importance because their presence increases workstations' independence. It eliminates common issues such as starving or blocked machines [5]. However big buffer's size means bigger investment and bigger use costs. The problem can take many forms as shown by many authors. First mathematical formulations are done by Buzacott in 1954 [6]. The most common method for optimizing Buffer Size is metaheuristics algorithms. In general, a solution for the BSP is compound of two parts, an evaluative part that determines performance measures and a generative part based on which the different Buffer size are generated. Evaluation could be done for big cases with simulation, or an approximation is made based on the generalized expansion method like for example [7], the aggregation method in [8] for their serial line using the aggregate model from [9] or the decomposition method used by [10] where they followed the DDX model from [11].

This drives the subject to the generative part of the solution, which is the main part of this paper, that determines the buffer capacity and find the solution. This is typically an optimization problem. Many traditional techniques exist such as Gradient search and degraded ceiling, however their main drawback is that they can trapped into a local optimum. Meta-heuristic are the best solution for medium to large problems because they can avoid local optima by putting some laws to manage the search space [5]. The most widely known meta-heuristic methods are the tabu-search, simulated annealing, genetic algorithm and ant colony. Many authors treated this topic such as Spinellis et al. who used decomposition method with simulated annealing to optimize line's production rate [12], where others have used genetic algorithm to find the optimal buffer sizes [13]. Blumenfeld and Li developed a methodology for solving the BSP for multiple machines but always with identical speeds, number of failures per hour and repair rate [14].

Compared to the current literature, the paper offers new perspectives. The added value of the proposed tabu list is its simplicity and robustness. Indeed, it is simple to tune and quite straightforward for visualizing parameters influence on result. It has proven to be effective on various production network and machine configuration.

In the *current* literature there are no articles discussing the BSP, ZDM and scheduling together. The implementation of ZDM into a manufacturing system can cause great disturbances, because for achieving zero defects numerous of actions are needed to be implemented into the schedule in order to counteract problems or to prevent future problems [1]. ZDM actions might create delays on the production or intensify some bottleneck stations and therefore the correct buffer size is imperative in order to mitigate those effects.

## 3 Methodology and Industrial Case Definition

In this section, the methodology for the buffer size optimization will be analyzed. The difference from existing research works is that the production system under investigation is composed from different machines. In addition, each task can be performed in more than one machine with different processing times. The optimization of the buffer size and the schedule is performed using Tabu-search, because of the good solution quality compared to the computation time. The buffer size optimization is done via tabu-search. Then the scheduling optimization is performed via a different tabu search program. The focus of the current research work is the neighbor creation for the evolution of the initial solution. The neighborhood generation is done in two phases: heterogeneous and homogeneous. Heterogeneous means that neighbors are obtained by adding 1 on each buffer iteration. Homogeneous iteration is used |when a local minimum happens. It forces the generation of buffer profiles that will necessary provide a better objective function. Two approaches to build the neighbor are used. The first is to generate $n$ neighbors from the current buffer distribution, $n$ being the number of buffers. Each neighbor is a vector of size $n \times 1$. They differ from the current buffer distribution by a unity added to one buffer (i.e. to one line in the vector). Neighbors distinguishes themselves by the buffer where the unity is added. This is the heterogeneous distribution. If the current buffer distribution is still better than the neighbor, a new way to generate buffer is adopted. The maximum of the current buffer distribution is put as the size of all other buffers. This is the homogeneous distribution. Each time a new distribution is found, the program goes back by default to the heterogenous distribution. Concerning the objective function computation, it is done inside the associated scheduling tool. Furthermore, if a buffer is full, all the production is stopped and emptying the full buffer becomes the priority. Not emptying a buffer may lead to non-feasible schedule. When this happens, a specifically designed algorithm is dynamically tweaking the schedule in specific points in order to achieve a feasible schedule. Figure 1 illustrates the buffer optimization procedure that is followed in the current research work.

Each buffer solution is fed into a scheduling tool where with the help of Tabu-Search a local optimum solution is produced based on three performance indicators (PIs). The used PIs are the Makespan and the Tardiness, which are described in [15] and the total buffers cost which is a function of the size of the buffer times the cost per square meter times the area that each component needs.

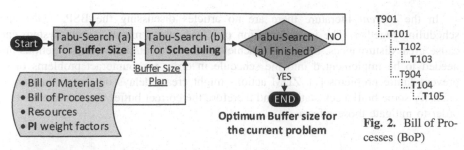

Fig. 1.  Buffer optimization overall framework

Fig. 2.  Bill of Processes (BoP)

Each buffer solution is fed into a scheduling tool where with the help of Tabu-Search a local optimum solution is produced based on three performance indicators (PIs). The used PIs are the Makespan and the Tardiness, which are described in [15] and the total buffers cost which is a function of the size of the buffer times the cost per square meter times the area that each component needs. The comparison of the alternative schedule solutions is performed by aggregating the three PIs into one value.

This is achieved by normalizing each PI value in order to eliminate the units and then perform a weighted sum. The weight factors for each PI is user defined, but the sum of all the weight factors should be 1. The result will be a value in the range [0,1]. The result of the weighted sum is called "Utility Value" and closer to 1 it is the higher the quality of the produced schedule. This procedure is based on Simple Additive Weighting (SAW) method which is explained in details in [16, 17]. In this point should be mentioned that the ZDM is implemented into the scheduling tool via a procedure to re-schedule the production every time that actions are needed in order to mitigate problems and therefore achieve ZDM.

## 3.1   Industrial Case

The propose approach was tested using data coming from a real-life industrial use case from a leading Swiss company in high precision sensors. The case treated in this paper is more realistic but also more complex. Indeed, the literature concentrated on different problems: single production line with two machines or more that are similar, with a sequential organization. Machines in literature also are non-multitask. In the case treated there is no line but a network, in other terms the machines are compound by non-similar workstations The production line/network is not sequential, and machines are multitask, which add more complexity to what is found in literature. Figure 2 shows the bill of process for the product under investigation. In reality the product BoP is more complex but for the current study a simplification was performed and the BoP presented in Fig. 2 illustrates the grouped BoP, composed by seven tasks. Also there are four inspection processes at the following levels of BoP, 904, 102, 101 and 901. If a defected part is detected the part is repaired if it is feasible in order to achieve ZDM. Furthermore, the current industrial case is susceptible to order delays and the financial penalties in case of delays are significant. This is the reason behind the selection of the Makespan and the Tardiness as PI for the current problem. In addition, the buffers cost another aspect that needs to be in balance with the manufacturing times and therefore those three PI are the final choice.

The production line is composed by seven stations, each one has two machines. Each machine in each station has different processing time, failure and repair rates from the other. Furthermore, the buffers are considered to be after each machine. The proposed approach is validated through a real life industrial use case and considers the production of 250 products, which they represent the 30% of the annual sales. In total the investigated product, occupy 0.03 sqm each when fully assembled. For each manufacturing step, the components occupying area were calculated in order to accurately calculate the Buffers cost. In the current study, the cost per sqm is considered 50CHF.

## 4    Experimental Results

The simulations for validating the current method were conducted for a period of three months, which corresponds to 250 parts. In order to demonstrate the evolution of the solution all the alternatives saved in the tabu-list (Tabu-Search (a) Fig. 1) were used for figures Figs. 3, 4, 5 and 6. The tabu-list contains the best alternative solutions revealed during the tabu-search algorithm and therefore worth illustrating their performance. The performance indicators for those solutions are presented in Fig. 3, Fig. 4 and Fig. 5 and corresponds to the Makespan, Tardiness and Buffers cost accordingly. The x-axis of all figures corresponds to the total sum of buffer places for all the workstations. In this point should be mentioned that the buffer size on each machine was considered as separate variable and independent from the rest. For example the solution [3, 5, 6] is treated as different solution than the [1, 3, 10] regardless that the total sum is the same. The total sum of buffers was selected only of demonstrating purposes and for simplifying the graphs.

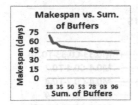

**Fig. 3.** Makespan vs total sum of buffers

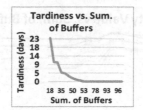

**Fig. 4.** Tardiness vs total sum of buffers

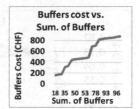

**Fig. 5.** Buffers cost vs total sum of buffers

As someone would expect the Makespan is decreasing as the number of buffer places are increased. Until total buffer places 35 there is a significant drop of the Makespan value were as after that point there Makespan is decreasing with a significant lower rate. Similar trend is observed to the Tardiness, until buffer size 35 the Tardiness is rapidly decreased. After that point, there is a lower decreasing rate until reaches zero, which means that there are not orders due date delays. The Buffers cost is increasing as the number of buffer places is increasing. Having seen the three individual performance indicators is difficult to reach to a conclusion of the best solution. Therefore, the three performance indicators were combined into one value (Utility Value), ranging from [0, 1] with 0 to be the worst and 1 the best possible number [16]. Then the utility value was calculated for different weight factors for each performance indicator and presented in Fig. 6 (M:Makespan, C:Buffers Cost and T:Tardiness).

All the alternatives presented in Fig. 6 show some similarities in their behavior. At the beginning where the absolute number of buffer places is small the solutions are not good and when there is a small increase to a specific workstation the solution becomes significantly better. Interesting is that for total buffer size 35 and 36 all the solutions are very close together with an average standard deviation of 0.0162.

After that point and until total buffer size 54 there is an increase to the quality of the solution for all the cases. From that point three different behaviors are noticed. In the case where the weight for the buffer cost is minimum (0.2) the solution's quality is continuing to getting better slightly. In the case where the weight for the buffer cost is maximum (0.5) the quality of the solution is getting worst as the total buffer size is increased. In all the other cases, the solution can be considered constant. The best solution regardless the PI weight factors was in the neighborhood of 50–54 buffer size with the absolute best solutions to be [9,7,10,7,7,7,7] and [8,7,10,7,6,8,7] for weight factors sets 3,5 and 1,2,4,6,7 respectively. Further to that from the simulation results, it was observed that workstation for T101 is the bottleneck and requires 10 buffer places, whereas the other workstation requires between 6–9. On the other hand, when the same case was simulated without ZDM active then the buffer sizes were [6,3,5,5,12,4] which are significantly different than the results obtained with ZDM active. In this case, the bottleneck is not any more the T101 but the T104 and this is caused because no ZDM actions are required to be implemented to the schedule.

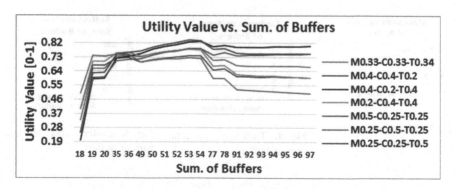

**Fig. 6.** Utility value vs total sum of buffers for different weight factor sets

# 5 Conclusions

The developed method proved to be robust enough to optimize the buffer size problem real complex production line. The results shows that the implementation of ZDM requires a different buffer sizes because of the quality control for every part and the actions that are required for counteracting a problem. The intelligent neighborhood generation method for shifting between heterogeneous and homogeneous buffer distribution proved useful for finding better solutions, because when the Tabu-search is "trapped" to a local maximum, it shifts to a homogeneous buffer distribution. Further to that, the Makespan is not depending on the absolute sum of buffer size, but it is more sensitive to the increase of a certain bottleneck buffer. Decreasing trends for Makespan and Tardiness and the increasing on for cost in function of buffers size is respect the findings in the literature.

**Acknowledgments.** The presented work is supported by the EU H2020 project QU4LITY (No. 825030). The paper reflects the authors' views and the Commission is not responsible for any use that may be made of the information it contains.

# References

1. Psarommatis, F., May, G., Dreyfus, P.-A., Kiritsis, D.: Zero defect manufacturing: state-of-the-art review, shortcomings and future directions in research. Int. J. Prod. Res. **7543**, 1–17 (2019)
2. Mourtzis, D., Doukas, M., Psarommatis, F.: A multi-criteria evaluation of centralized and decentralized production networks in a highly customer-driven environment. CIRP Ann. Manuf. Technol. **61**(1), 427–430 (2012)
3. Psarommatis, F., Kiritsis, D.: A scheduling tool for achieving zero defect manufacturing (ZDM): a conceptual framework. In: Moon, I., Lee, G.M., Park, J., Kiritsis, D., von Cieminski, G. (eds.) APMS 2018. IAICT, vol. 536, pp. 271–278. Springer, Cham (2018). https://doi.org/10.1007/978-3-319-99707-0_34
4. Dolgui, A., Eremeev, A., Kovalyov, M.Y., Sigaev, V.: complexity of buffer capacity allocation problems for production lines with unreliable machines. J. Math. Model. Algorithms **12**(2), 155–165 (2013)
5. Demir, L., Tunali, S., Eliiyi, D.T.: The state of the art on buffer allocation problem: a comprehensive survey. J. Intel. Manuf. **25**(3), 371–392 (2014)
6. Buzacott, J.A., Shanthikumar, J.G.: Stochastic Models of Manufacturing Systems. Prentice Hall, Englewood Cliffs (1993)
7. Cruz, F.R.B., Van Woensel, T., Smith, J.M.G.: Buffer and throughput trade-offs in M/G/1/K queueing networks: a bi-criteria approach. Int. J. Prod. Econ. **125**(2), 224–234 (2010)
8. Abu Qudeiri, J., Yamamoto, H., Ramli, R., Jamali, A.: Genetic algorithm for buffer size and work station capacity in serial-parallel production lines. Artif. Life Robot. **12**(1–2), 102–106 (2008)
9. Li, J.: Overlapping decomposition: a system-theoretic method for modeling and analysis of complex manufacturing systems. IEEE Trans. Autom. Sci. Eng. **2**(1), 40–53 (2005)
10. Shi, L., Men, S.: Optimal buffer allocation in production lines. IIE Trans. (Institute Ind. Eng.) **35**(1), 1–10 (2003)

11. Dallery, Y., David, R., Xie, X.L.: An efficient algorithm for analysis of transfer lines with unreliable machines and finite buffers, IIE Trans. (Inst. Ind. Eng.) **20**(3), 281–283 (1988)
12. Spinellis, D.D., Papadopoulos, C.T.: A simulated annealing approach for buffer allocation in reliable production lines. Ann. Oper. Res. **93**(1–4), 373–384 (2000)
13. Qudeiri, J.A., Mohammed, M.K., Mian, S.H., Khadra, F.A.: A multistage approach for buffer size decision in serial production line. In: SIMULTECH 2015 - 5th International Conference on Simulation Modeling Methodologies, Technologies and Applications, pp. 145–153 (2015)
14. Blumenfeld, D.E., Li, J.: An analytical formula for throughput of a production line with identical stations and random failures (2005)
15. Psarommatis, F., Kiritsis, D.: Identification of the inspection specifications for achieving zero defect manufacturing. In: Ameri, F., Stecke, K.E., von Cieminski, G., Kiritsis, D. (eds.) APMS 2019. IAICT, vol. 566, pp. 267–273. Springer, Cham (2019). https://doi.org/10.1007/978-3-030-30000-5_34
16. Mourtzis, D., Doukas, M., Psarommatis, F.: A toolbox for the design, planning and operation of manufacturing networks in a mass customisation environment. J. Manuf. Syst. **36**, 274–286 (2015)
17. Tzeng, G.-H., Huang, J.-J.: Multiple Attribute Decision Making. Springer-Verlag, Berlin, Heidelberg (2011)

# A Bi-objective Scheduling Model for Additive Manufacturing with Multiple Materials and Sequence-Dependent Setup Time

Reza Tavakkoli-Moghaddam$^{(\boxtimes)}$, Shadi Shirazian,
and Behdin Vahedi-Nouri

School of Industrial Engineering, College of Engineering, University of Tehran,
Tehran, Iran
tavakoli@ut.ac.ir

**Abstract.** Considering the striking achievement of additive manufacturing (AM) as a revolutionary technology, it has increasingly attracted the attention of academia and industrial communities in recent years. Scheduling and production planning in AM play an essential role in the efficient and economical manufacturing of customized products through the saving of time and cost. In this paper, an AM scheduling problem is taken into account with different order specifications, especially the material type and due date on non-identical parallel machines. To formulate the problem, a bi-objective mixed-integer linear programming (MILP) model is proposed to minimize the makespan and the total tardiness penalty. Assuming parts with different material types necessitates the consideration of sequence-dependent setup time that depends on the material type of the current and previous jobs on an AM machine. Finally, an augmented $\varepsilon$–constraint method is applied for the problem to achieve a Pareto-optimal front in an illustrative instance.

**Keywords:** Scheduling · Industry 4.0 · Additive manufacturing ·
Mathematical modeling · Sequence-dependent setup time

## 1 Introduction and Literature Review

Additive manufacturing (AM) or 3D printing as an emerging technology has been developed over the last two decades. Compared to traditional manufacturing, in AM, the process of manufacturing parts is through joining materials layer by layer based on a three-dimensional computer-aided design (CAD) file [1]. AM enjoys significant benefits, such as design freedom, requires fewer materials and resources, and production flexibility [1, 2] that attracts industries (e.g., automotive, aerospace, medical, and defense). Applying AM can lead to the production of small and customized batches economically [3]. AM processes can be classified into three main clusters: powder-based system, liquid-based system, solid or wire extrusion [4]. In this research, a variation of powder-based AM process, namely selective laser melting (SLM), is considered. This variation is capable of the simultaneous production of several parts in one batch for the capacity constraint.

© IFIP International Federation for Information Processing 2020
Published by Springer Nature Switzerland AG 2020
B. Lalic et al. (Eds.): APMS 2020, IFIP AICT 592, pp. 451–459, 2020.
https://doi.org/10.1007/978-3-030-57997-5_52

To start processing a new batch called a job, a series of works are required to set up the associated machine, such as preparing data, filling powder material, adjusting the machine, and filling the protective atmosphere [2]. Then, the layer generation is repeated until all parts inside the building platform of the machine are completed. It means that no part can be removed until the job is finished. Afterward, the machine should be cleaned, and some post-processing (typically manual) might be performed. Accordingly, the production cost and time are dynamically influenced by some factors, such as different combinations of parts in jobs, the maximum height of the parts allocated to a job, the thickness of layers, and build orientation. Also, since the processing and purchasing cost of AM machines is high, optimal assignment of ordered parts into jobs and the scheduling of these jobs on AM machines are of significant importance [1].

Regarding AM, different problems have been explored like sustainability in the AM supply chain [5], part orientation in 3D printers [6] and part placing problem [7]. However, to the best of our knowledge, only a few studies emphasize the production planning and scheduling problems in AM. The AM scheduling problem can be considered as an extension of the batch scheduling problem, in which different part assignments lead to different processing times regarding the volume and height of the parts allocated to a job (batch) [2]. Li et al. [1] presented a mixed-integer linear programming (MILP) model to minimize the average production cost per volume of material on non-identical AM machines. They considered only one type of material and part nesting in the absence of due dates for parts. Also, they proposed two heuristic procedures named 'best-fit' and 'adapted best-fit' to solve this problem. Chergui et al. [8] investigated the problem of scheduling and nesting of parts on parallel identical AM machines to minimize the maximum lateness. They divided the problem into two sub-problems: clustering of parts into a set of batches, and scheduling of batches on parallel machines. Dvorak et al. [9] considered two-dimensional bin packing, nesting, and scheduling of parts on a job shop to minimize the makespan respecting the deadlines of orders. Fera et al. [10] formulated a multi-objective model for a single AM machine scheduling problem that minimizes the time and cost and developed a modified genetic algorithm to solve the problem. Li et al. [11] studied the joint dynamic order acceptance and scheduling problem in AM to maximize the average profit-per-unit-time while minimizing the makespan. Kucukkoc [2] proposed several MILP models to address AM scheduling problems in single, identical parallel and non-identical parallel machine settings that minimize the makespan.

Regarding the literature, researchers have considered only one type of materials in the AM scheduling. However, in the real world, the material type of the received orders might be different, and 3D printers, which are compatible with different metal powders are available on the market. Accordingly, for the first time, this study aims to scrutinize the scheduling problem in AM scheduling, in which the material type of parts are different. In other words, a part is made up of only one material; however, the material type of two parts might be different. In this multi-material AM, setup time between each job on each machine is sequence-dependent, which depends on the material types of parts processed in the associated sequential jobs. The proposed AM problem is assumed in a non-identical parallel machine environment. A bi-objective MILP model is devised to formulate the problem, which minimizes the makespan and the total tardiness cost.

The rest of this paper is organized as follows. Section 2 is devoted to describing the problem, its assumptions, notations, and the proposed bi-objective mathematical model. In Sect. 3, an illustrative problem in a multi-material AM is solved by applying the developed model. Finally, Sect. 4 concludes this study and provides some recommendations for future studies.

## 2   Problem Description

As described above, the presented research concentrate on the scheduling problem in AM. A set of parts $(i \in I)$ with different specification, such as height $(h_i)$, area $(a_i)$, volume $(v_i)$, due date $(d_i)$, tardiness penalty $(p_i)$, and material type $(type_i \in K)$ should be assigned into a set of jobs $(j \in J)$, and scheduled on a set of AM machines $(m \in M)$ that are arranged as non-identical parallel machines. The bi-objective model aims to find Pareto-optimal solutions by minimizing the makespan and the total tardiness cost.

The maximum completion time and accordingly tardiness cost for a part are dynamically impacted by a combination of the parts in its associated job. In other words, the processing time of a job depends on its assigned parts. Since the material type associated with each part could be different and a machine can be filled with only one material at a time, the parts that are grouped in a job must be the same type. As a result, each job is identified with a type $(k, k' \in K)$. After finishing a job, the machines should be cleaned and setup operations are performed. The setup time for jobs is sequence-dependent. For instance, if the material type of the first job differs from the second one, the setup time is longer than a case, in which the material type of sequential jobs is the same. Besides, capacity constraints (i.e., height and area) play a key role in part grouping. Other assumptions of the problem are as follows. The rectangular shape is only considered as the projection of part shapes, and a safety tolerance in the value of $(a_i)$ is regarded between the parts to avoid part damage and simplify the process of removing parts. Build orientation is assumed to be fixed since it has an impact on quality [12]. All parts have the same layer thickness. All parts are ready at time zero. Each AM machine can have specific features (e.g., build speed and laser power). All machines can be reused after finishing a job, and setup times that are sequence-dependent must be performed. Some parts cannot be assigned to some machines due to capacity restrictions. The number of parts is greater or equal to jobs. The other notations of the problem are expressed in Table 1 followed by the proposed bi-objective mathematical model.

**Table 1.** Notations of the developed model

| Parameters | | Variables | |
|---|---|---|---|
| $VT_m^k$ | Time spent for forming per unit volume of material type $k$ on machine $m$ | $x_{mji}$ | 1 if part $i$ is assigned to job $j$ on machine $m$; 0, otherwise |
| $HT_m^k$ | Time spent for powder layering of material type $k$ on machine $m$ | $w_{mj}^k$ | 1 if material type $k$ is utilized for job $j$ on machine $m$; 0, otherwise |
| $STF_m^k$ | Setup time required for the first job with material type $k$ on machine $m$ | $y_{mj}^{k'k}$ | 1 if job $j$ with material type $k$ succeeds job $j-1$ with material type $k'$; 0, otherwise |
| $ST_m^{k'k}$ | Setup time required for a job with material type $k$ on machine m that its previous job is of material type $k'$ | $Tard_i$ | Tardiness of part $i$ |
| | | $C_{mj}$ | Completion time of job $j$ on machine $m$ |
| $MH_m$ | Height capacity of machine $m$ | $PT_{mj}^k$ | Processing time of job $j$ on machine $m$ if its material type is $k$ |
| $\psi_1-\psi_5$ | Large positive numbers | | |
| $MA_m$ | Building platform area capacity of machine $m$ | $PT_{mj}$ | Processing time of job $j$ on machine $m$ |
| | | $C_i$ | Completion time of part $i$ |

$$\text{Min } Z_1 = C_{Max} \tag{1}$$

$$\text{Min } Z_2 = \sum_{i \in I} p_i \times Tard_i \tag{2}$$

s.t.

$$\sum_{m \in M} \sum_{j \in J} x_{mji} = 1; \forall i \in I \tag{3}$$

$$\sum_{i \in I} a_i.x_{mji} \leq MA_m; \forall m \in M, \forall j \in J \tag{4}$$

$$h_i.x_{mji} \leq MH_m; \forall m \in M, \forall j \in J, \forall i \in I \tag{5}$$

$$\sum_{i \in I} x_{m(j+1)i} \leq \psi_1.\sum_{i \in I} x_{mji}; \forall m \in M, \forall j \in J \tag{6}$$

$$\sum_{k \in K} k.w_{mj}^k \leq x_{mji}.type_i + \psi_5(1 - x_{mji}); \forall m \in M, \forall j \in J, \forall i \in I \tag{7}$$

$$\sum_{k \in K} k.w_{mj}^k \geq x_{mji}.type_i - \psi_5(1 - x_{mji}); \forall m \in M, \forall j \in J; \forall i \in I \tag{8}$$

$$\sum_{k \in K} w_{mj}^k \leq 1; \forall m \in, ; \forall j \in J \tag{9}$$

$$w_{mj}^k \leq \sum_i x_{mji}; \forall m \in M, \forall k \in K, \forall j \in J \tag{10}$$

$$y_{mj}^{k'k} + 1 \geq w_{mj}^k + w_{mj-1}^{k'}; \forall m \in M, \forall k \in K, \forall j \in J \text{ and } j \neq 1 \tag{11}$$

$$2y_{mj}^{k'k} \leq w_{mj}^k + w_{mj-1}^{k'}; \forall m \in M, \forall k \in K, \forall j \in J \text{ and } j \neq 1 \tag{12}$$

$$PT_{mj}^k \geq VT_m^k \sum_{i \in I} v_i.x_{mji} + HT_m^k.\max_{i \in I}\{h_i.x_{mji}\} - \psi_2\left(1 - w_{mj}^k\right);$$
$$\forall m \in M, \forall k \in K, \forall j \in J \tag{13}$$

$$PT_{mj} \geq PT_{mj}^k; \forall m \in M, \forall k \in K, \forall j \in J \tag{14}$$

$$C_{mj} \geq C_{mj-1} + PT_{mj} + y_{mj}^{k'k}.ST_m^{k'k}; \forall m \in M, \forall k \in K, \forall j \in J \text{ and } j \neq 1 \tag{15}$$

$$C_{m1} \geq PT_{m1} + STF_m^k - \psi_4(1 - w_{m1}^k); \forall m \in M, \forall k \in K, j = 1 \tag{16}$$

$$C_{Max} \geq C_{mj}; \forall m \in M, \forall j \in J \tag{17}$$

$$C_i \geq C_{mj} - \psi_3(1 - x_{mji}); \forall m \in M, \forall j \in J, \forall i \in I \tag{18}$$

$$C_i \leq C_{mj} + \psi_3(1 - x_{mji}); \forall m \in M, \forall j \in J, \forall i \in I \tag{19}$$

$$Tard_i \geq C_i - d_i; \forall i \in I \tag{20}$$

$$x_{mji}, w_{mj}^k, y_{mj}^{k'k} \in \{0, 1\}; PT_{mj} \geq 0; PT_{mj}^k \geq 0 \tag{21}$$

Equations (1) and (2) represent the two objective functions of the problem, including minimizing the makespan and the total tardiness cost, respectively. Constraint (3) guarantees that each part is allocated to only one job among all machines. Capacity constraints are respected by Constraints (4) and (5). Constraint (6) states that a job on a machine cannot be formed before the formation of its previous job on the machine. Constraints (7) to (10) identify the material type of each job concerning the type of its assigned parts. Constraint (9) guarantees that the material type of a job would not change. Constraint (10) states that if no part is assigned into a job, $w_{mj}^k$ would not take 1. Constraints (11) and (12) state that $y_{mj}^{k'k}$ takes 1 only if job $j$ includes parts with material type $k$ and job $j-1$ includes parts with material type $k'$. Constraints (13) and (14) calculate the processing time for each job of each machine as the function of total volume and maximum height of the parts assigned to. The completion times of jobs are determined by Constraints (15) and (16) according to their setup times and processing times. The makespan, completion times, and tardiness of parts are calculated by Constraints (17) to (20), respectively. Constraint (21) defines the variables of the respected model.

# 3   Computational Experiment

In this section, a simple numerical example with 10 parts, 2 machines, and 2 types of materials is presented to validate the mathematical model. Tables 2 and 3 display the parameters of the problem. Since the proposed model is a bi-objective one, the augmented ε-constraint method is applied to achieve a Pareto-optimal front. This method is a well-known and efficient multi-objective method presented by Mavrotas and Florios [13] and employed in a vast variety of research (i.e., [14, 15]). The original ε-constraint method is based on optimizing one objective and putting others as constraints. To reduce the drawbacks of this method, the augmented ε-constraint method introduced in 2009, in which slack variables are considered to make the equality constraint and the objective function is augmented with the weighted sum of slack variables. Then, the AUGMECON2 was developed as an improvement of the previous method in 2013, which is appropriate for multi-objective integer programming problems [13]. The proposed model was coded in GAMS software using CPLEX solver and executed on an AMD Quad Core A12-9700P CPU 3.4 GHz system with 8 GB RAM. The Gantt charts of single-objective optimal solutions based on the makespan and the total tardiness cost are depicted in Figs. 1 and 2, respectively. For example, in Fig. 1, the parts are assigned into 6 jobs; 2 jobs on machine 1, and 4 jobs on machine 2. The two colors are applied for the jobs to illustrate their material types. For instance, as seen in Fig. 1, the first job of machine 2 includes parts 1 and 8, which both are performed by material type 1. To minimize the makespan, the value of the makespan and the total cost of tardiness are obtained 282.06 and 1023.52, respectively. Then, to optimize the second objective the optimum total cost of tardiness is 51.19 and the makespan is determined 317.06. Also, the Pareto-optimal front of solving this example is shown in Fig. 3. It should be noted that in the AUGMECON2, the makespan is optimized and the second objective is applied as the constraint. Seven non-dominated solutions are generated by adjusting 9 grid points by which the decision-maker can select the most favorable solution among them based on his/her preference.

Table 2.   Parameters related to parts

| $i$ | $h_i$-cm | $a_i$-$cm^2$ | $v_i$-$cm^3$ | $Type_i$ | $d_i$-hr | $p_i$-\$ |
|---|---|---|---|---|---|---|
| 1 | 7.12 | 233.83 | 1718.83 | 1 | 285 | 3 |
| 2 | 26.37 | 184.80 | 2394.82 | 1 | 142 | 3 |
| 3 | 8.21 | 275.27 | 717.19 | 2 | 185 | 6 |
| 4 | 11.63 | 639.58 | 1933.09 | 2 | 285 | 8 |
| 5 | 27.47 | 71.90 | 2240.96 | 2 | 300 | 3 |
| 6 | 18.64 | 383.45 | 920.84 | 1 | 270 | 2 |
| 7 | 15.78 | 741.61 | 380.81 | 1 | 110 | 7 |
| 8 | 15.47 | 439.93 | 1476.41 | 1 | 155 | 7 |
| 9 | 7.15 | 736.59 | 519.70 | 1 | 50 | 5 |
| 10 | 7.12 | 233.83 | 1718.83 | 1 | 285 | 3 |

**Table 3.** Parameters related to machines

|     | $ST_m^{1,1}$ | $ST_m^{1,2}$ | $ST_m^{2,1}$ | $ST_m^{2,2}$ | $STF_m^1$ | $STF_m^2$ | $VT_m^1$ | $VT_m^2$ | $HT_m^1$ | $HT_m^2$ | $MA_m$ | $MH_m$ |
|-----|------|------|------|------|------|------|------|------|------|------|------|------|
| $m1$ | 1.27 | 1.15 | 1.52 | 1.4 | 1.31 | 1.14 | 0.035 | 0.034 | 0.7 | 0.7 | 1000 | 33.4 |
| $m2$ | 1.62 | 1.24 | 1.53 | 1.61 | 1.04 | 1.05 | 0.035 | 0.04 | 0.7 | 0.7 | 900 | 38.7 |

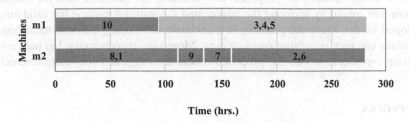

**Fig. 1.** Gantt chart for minimizing the makespan.

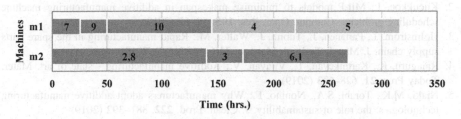

**Fig. 2.** Gantt chart for minimizing the total cost of tardiness

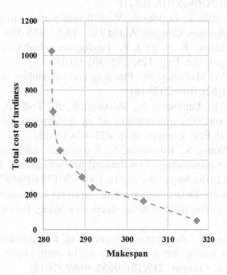

**Fig. 3.** Pareto front of the problem

## 4  Conclusions

This study explored a new scheduling problem in additive manufacturing (AM) with the presence of sequence-dependent setup times. The problem supposed parts with different material types on non-identical AM machines considering a trade-off between two objectives, including minimizing the makespan and the total tardiness cost. A bi-objective MILP model was proposed to formulate the problem, and an illustrative problem was solved by applying the augmented ε-constraint method for validating the developed model. Since the problem is intractable, developing efficient meta-heuristic algorithms can be a promising research area. Moreover, incorporating bin packing and uncertain consideration into the proposed model are suggested for future research.

## References

1. Li, Q., Kucukkoc, I., Zhang, D.Z.: Production planning in additive manufacturing and 3D printing. Comput. Oper. Res. **83**, 157–172 (2017)
2. Kucukkoc, I.: MILP models to minimise makespan in additive manufacturing machine scheduling problems. Comput. Oper. Res. **105**, 58–67 (2019)
3. Holmström, J., Partanen, J., Tuomi, J., Walter, M.: Rapid manufacturing in the spare parts supply chain. J. Manuf. Technol. Manage. **21**(6), 687–697 (2010)
4. Rajaguru, K., Karthikeyan, T., Vijayan, V.: Additive manufacturing - state of art. Mater. Today Proc. **21**, 628–633 (2019)
5. Niaki, M.K., Torabi, S.A., Nonino, F.: Why manufacturers adopt additive manufacturing technologies: the role of sustainability. J. Clean. Prod. **222**, 381–392 (2019)
6. Zhang, Y., Bernard, A., Harik, R., Karunakaran, K.P.: Build orientation optimization for multi-part production in additive manufacturing. J. Intell. Manuf. **28**(6), 1393–1407 (2017). https://doi.org/10.1007/s10845-015-1057-1
7. Canellidis, V., Giannatsis, J., Dedoussis, V.: Efficient parts nesting schemes for improving stereolithography utilization. Comput. Aided Des. **45**(5), 875–886 (2013)
8. Chergui, A., Hadj-Hamou, K., Vignat, F.: Production scheduling and nesting in additive manufacturing. Comput. Ind. Eng. **126**, 292–301 (2018)
9. Dvorak, F., Micali, M., Mathieug, M.: Planning and scheduling in additive manufacturing. Inteligencia Artif. **21**(62), 40–52 (2018)
10. Fera, M., Fruggiero, F., Lambiase, A., Macchiaroli, R., Todisco, V.: A modified genetic algorithm for time and cost optimization of an additive manufacturing single-machine scheduling. Int. J. Ind. Eng. Comput. **9**(4), 423–438 (2018)
11. Li, Q., Zhang, D., Wang, S., Kucukkoc, I.: A dynamic order acceptance and scheduling approach for additive manufacturing on-demand production. Int. J. Adv. Manuf. Technol. **105**(9), 3711–3729 (2019). https://doi.org/10.1007/s00170-019-03796-x
12. Byun, H.-S., Lee, K.H.: Determination of the optimal build direction for different rapid prototyping processes using multi-criterion decision making. Robot. Comput. Integr. Manuf. **22**(1), 69–80 (2006)
13. Mavrotas, G., Florios, K.: An improved version of the augmented ε-constraint method (AUGMECON2) for finding the exact pareto set in multi-objective integer programming problems. Appl. Math. Comput. **219**(18), 9652–9669 (2013)

14. Hamid, M., Tavakkoli-Moghaddam, R., Golpaygani, F., Vahedi-Nouri, B.: A multi-objective model for a nurse scheduling problem by emphasizing human factors. Proc. Inst. Mech. Eng. Part H J. Eng. Med. **234**(2), 179–199 (2020)
15. Vahedi-Nouri, B., Tavakkoli-Moghaddam, R., Rohaninejad, M.: A multi-objective scheduling model for a cloud manufacturing system with pricing, equity, and order rejection. IFAC-PapersOnLine **52**(13), 2177–2182 (2019)

# Dynamic Distributed Job-Shop Scheduling Problem Consisting of Reconfigurable Machine Tools

Mehdi Mahmoodjanloo[1,2(✉)], Reza Tavakkoli-Moghaddam[1],
Armand Baboli[2], and Ali Bozorgi-Amiri[1]

[1] School of Industrial Engineering, College of Engineering,
University of Tehran, Tehran, Iran
mehdi.janloo@ut.ac.ir
[2] LIRIS Laboratory, UMR 5205 CNRS, INSA of Lyon,
69621 Villeurbanne Cedex, France

**Abstract.** Keeping pace with rapidly changing customer requirements forces companies to increase the capability of adaptation of their production systems. To fulfill the market requirements in a reasonable time and cost, distributed manufacturing has been emerged as one of the efficient approaches. Moreover, the ability of reconfigurability makes manufacturing systems and tools to be more adaptable. This research deals with a dynamic production scheduling problem simultaneously in several different shop-floors consisting of reconfigurable machine tools (RMTs) by utilizing the real-time data extracted from a cyber-physical system (CPS). First, a mathematical programming model is presented for the static state. Thereafter, by utilizing the CPS capabilities, a dynamic model is extended to schedule new jobs, in which there have already been some other jobs in each facility. A numerical example is solved to illustrate the validation of the model. Finally, some potential solving approaches are proposed to make the model implementable in real-world applications.

**Keywords:** Distributed manufacturing · Reconfigurable manufacturing systems · Dynamic scheduling · Industry 4.0 · Cyber-physical shop floor

## 1 Introduction

Over the last decades, due to the globalization of the economy and its requirements, enterprises aim to reach higher operational performance at a lower cost. Hence, distributed manufacturing has been emerged as one of the efficient approaches to overcome these requirements. On the other hand, capabilities of new emerging smart factories are enhancing supported by Industry 4.0 technologies, such as a cyber-physical system (CPS), cloud computing, virtual reality, internet of things (IoT) and big data. To gain competitive advantages of these technologies, companies are going to adapt for a more customer-oriented market [1]. Also, new manufacturing systems need to satisfy the main requirements of this market, such as the rapid introduction of new products and high demand fluctuations. A significant approach to cope with these issues is to take advantages of reconfigurability for manufacturing systems and tools.

© IFIP International Federation for Information Processing 2020
Published by Springer Nature Switzerland AG 2020
B. Lalic et al. (Eds.): APMS 2020, IFIP AICT 592, pp. 460–468, 2020.
https://doi.org/10.1007/978-3-030-57997-5_53

Hence, a new class of production machines, called reconfigurable machine tools (RMTs), have been introduced. An RMT machine usually has a modular structure, which makes it be able to obtain different configurations in order to satisfy manufacturing requirements. One of the benefits of developing RMTs is that the use of several different machines that share many costly and common modules while being rarely used at the same time can be prevented [2]. The capacity and functionality of a manufacturing system by relying on abilities of such machines can be adjusted easily. Despite the special capabilities, it seems that the studies in production scheduling in such systems face new challenges considering the high level of dynamism and complexity of needed decisions.

De Giovanni and Pezzella [3] studied a static distributed and flexible job-shop scheduling problem. They developed an improved genetic algorithm (GA) to solve the problem efficiently. However, they did not consider a dynamic environment of the production system. Tian et al. [4] designed a production information management system based on industrial IoT technology to tackle the dynamic flexible job-shop scheduling problem in a rolling horizon. Romero-Silva and Hernández [5] studied in different manufacturing contexts the role of the CPS to provide a company by carrying out a better scheduling task. They found that production systems with uncertain demands and complex production processes could benefit the most from implementing a CPS at a shop-floor level. However, they did not consider the effect of reconfigurability on the studied systems. Recently, Mahmoodjanloo et al. [6] presented a new variant of a job-shop scheduling problem, which contains reconfigurable machine tools. They developed two static models to tackle the scheduling problem in a centralized production system.

In this paper, by utilizing the cyber-physical shop-floor capabilities, a distributed flexible job-shop scheduling problem consisting of reconfigurable machine tools in a dynamic environment is studied.

## 2 Static and Dynamic Model Presentation

### 2.1 Problem Description

There is a set $\mathcal{J}$ of $n$ jobs, where each one should be processed in one of the existing facilities. Job $i$ has a set of $n_i$ operations with a predefined sequence (e.g., $O_{i,1} \rightarrow O_{i,2} \rightarrow \ldots \rightarrow O_{i,n_i}$). The facilities have already been deployed in different geographical areas. In each facility $f \in F$, there is a set of RMTs, in which each RMT $k \in K_f$ has a set of $C_{k,f}$ configurations. It is assumed that operation $O_{ij}$ can be processed at least on one configuration of one of the existing RMTs in each facility. No setup is needed to perform operations in a machine configuration, while to switch to a different configuration on the machine, the RMT needs to a setup that is dependent on two consecutive configurations. The main decisions of the problem include assigning of each job to one facility, allocating of each job operation to an eligible RMT, sequencing of the jobs and determining the appropriate configurations of each machine to perform the allocated operations. The objective is to minimize the total cost.

The scheduling environment can be classified into two main classes; namely, static (offline) and dynamic (online) scheduling. We first present the static model formulation, in which there are several jobs to be processed in the empty facilities. Thereafter, the model will be extended for the dynamic state, in which there are several jobs in each facility that are processing based on a current schedule. By arriving some new jobs, the current schedules should be updated based on a variable-order rescheduling strategy, in which all unprocessed operations can be rescheduled after assigning the new arriving jobs to the facilities.

## 2.2   Static Model Formulation

### Sets and Indices:

$\mathcal{J}$      Set of jobs, where job index $i \in \mathcal{J}$

$N_i$      Set of operations related to job $i$, where operation $j$ of job $i$ is denoted by $O_{ij}$

$F$      Set of facilities, where facility index $f \in F$

$K_f$      Set of machines, where machine index $k \in K_f$

$C_{k,f}$      Set of configurations of machine $k$ in facility $f$, where configuration index $c \in C_{k,f}$

$L_{k,f}$      Set of job positions on machine $k$ of facility $f$, where position index $l \in L_{k,f}$ (i.e.,
$$|L_{k,f}| = \sum_{i \in J} \sum_{j \in N_i} \left( \max_{c \in C_{k,f}} R^f_{ijkc} \right) \text{ and } L = \cup_{f \in F, k \in K_f} L_{k,f}).$$

### Parameters:

$PT^f_{ijkc}$      Processing time of operation $O_{ij}$ on configuration $c$ of machine $k$ in facility $f$

$R^f_{ijkc}$      Binary parameter. If operation $O_{ij}$ can be processed on configuration $c$ of machine $k$ in facility $f$, then $R^f_{ijkc} = 1$; otherwise, $R^f_{ijkc} = 0$.

$PC^f_{ijkc}$      Processing cost of operation $O_{ij}$ on configuration $c$ of machine $k$ in facility $f$

$TT^f_i$      Transportation time of job $i$ from facility $f$

$TC^f_i$      Transportation cost of job $i$ from facility $f$

$ST^f_{c_1,c_2,k}$      Configuration-dependent setup time when configuration is changed from $c_1$ to $c_2$ (i.e., $c_1 \neq c_2$ and $c_1, c_2 \in C_{k,f}$) on machine $k$ in the facility $f$

$SC^f_{c_1,c_2,k}$      Configuration-dependent setup cost when configuration is changed from $c_1$ to $c_2$ (i.e., $c_1 \neq c_2$ and $c_1, c_2 \in C_{k,f}$) on machine $k$ in the facility $f$

$D_i$      Due date of job $i$

$\omega_i$      Tardiness penalty of job $i$ per time unit

### Decision Variables of the Static Model:

$x_{fi}$      1 if job $i$ be assigned to facility $f$; 0, otherwise.

$y^f_{ijklc}$      1 if operation $O_{ij}$ is processed on machine-positions $k$ and $l$ with configuration $c$ of facility $f$; 0, otherwise.

$Z^f_{c_1,c_2,k,l}$     1 if at the beginning of positions $k$ and $l$ of facility $f$, in which the machine's configuration is changed from $c_1$ to $c_2$ (i.e., $c_1 \neq c_2$); 0, otherwise.

$CO_{ij}$     Completion time of operation $O_{ij}$

$CP_{fkl}$     Finishing time of positions $k$ and $l$ in facility $f$

$T_i$     Tardiness of job $i$

**Mathematical Formulation of the Static Problem:**

$$\text{Min } z = \sum_{i \in \mathcal{J}} \sum_{j \in N_i} \sum_{f \in F} \sum_{k \in K_f} \sum_{c \in C_{kf}} \sum_{l \in L_{kf}} PC^f_{ijkc} y^f_{ijklc} + \sum_{i \in \mathcal{J}} \sum_{f \in F} TC^f_i x_{fi} + \sum_{i \in \mathcal{J}} \omega_i T_i$$

$$+ \sum_{f \in F} \sum_{k \in K_f} \sum_{c_1 \in C_{kf}} \sum_{c_2 \in C_{kf}} \sum_{l \in L_{kf}} SC^f_{c_1,c_2,k} Z^f_{c_1,c_2,k,l} \qquad (1)$$

$$c_1 \neq c_1$$

Subject to:

$$\sum_{f \in F} x_{fi} = 1 \qquad \forall i \in \mathcal{J} \qquad (2)$$

$$\sum_{j \in N_i} \sum_{k \in K_f} \sum_{c \in C_{kf}} \sum_{l \in L_{kf}} y^f_{ijklc} \leq n_i \times x_{fi} \qquad \forall f \in F, i \in \mathcal{J} \qquad (3)$$

$$\sum_{f \in F} \sum_{k \in K_f} \sum_{c \in C_{kf}} \sum_{l \in L_{kf}} y^f_{ijklc} = 1 \qquad \forall i \in \mathcal{J}, j \in N_i \qquad (4)$$

$$\sum_{l \in L_{kf}} y^f_{ijklc} \leq R^f_{ijkc} \qquad \forall i \in \mathcal{J}, j \in N_i, f \in F, k \in K_f, c \in C_{kf} \qquad (5)$$

$$\sum_{i \in \mathcal{J}} \sum_{j \in N_i} \sum_{c \in C_{kf}} y^f_{ijklc} \leq 1 \qquad \forall f \in F, k \in K_f, l \in L_{kf} \qquad (6)$$

$$\sum_{i \in \mathcal{J}} \sum_{j \in N_i} \sum_{c \in C_{kf}} y^f_{ijk,l-1,c} \geq \sum_{i \in \mathcal{J}} \sum_{j \in N_i} \sum_{c \in C_{kf}} y^f_{ijklc} \qquad \forall f \in F, k \in K_f, l \in L_{kf}, l \neq 1 \qquad (7)$$

$$\sum_{i \in \mathcal{J}} \sum_{j \in N_i} y^f_{ijk,l-1,c_1} + \sum_{i \in \mathcal{J}} \sum_{j \in N_i} y^f_{ijklc_2} \geq 2 Z^f_{c_1,c_2,k,l} \qquad \begin{array}{l} \forall f \in F, k \in K_f, l \in L_{kf}, \\ c_1, c_2 \in C_{kf}, c_1 \neq c_2 \end{array} \qquad (8)$$

$$\sum_{i \in \mathcal{J}} \sum_{j \in N_i} y^f_{ijk,l-1,c_1} + \sum_{i \in \mathcal{J}} \sum_{j \in N_i} y^f_{ijklc_2} - 1 \leq Z^f_{c_1,c_2,k,l} \qquad \begin{array}{l} \forall f \in F, k \in K_f, l \in L_{kf}, \\ c_1, c_2 \in C_{kf}, c_1 \neq c_2 \end{array} \qquad (9)$$

$$CO_{ij} \geq CO_{i,j-1} + \sum_{f \in F} \sum_{k \in K_f} \sum_{c \in C_{kf}} \sum_{l \in L_{kf}} PT^f_{ijkc} y^f_{ijklc} \qquad \forall i \in \mathcal{J}, j \in N_i \qquad (10)$$

$$CP_{fkl} \geq CP_{fk,l-1} + \sum_{\substack{c_1 \in C_{kf} \\ c_1 \neq c_2}} \sum_{c_2 \in C_{kf}} ST_{c_1,c_2,k}^f Z_{c_1,c_2,k,l}^f + \sum_{i \in \mathcal{J}} \sum_{j \in N_i} \sum_{c \in C_{kf}} PT_{ijkc}^f y_{ijklc}^f$$

$$\forall f \in F, k \in K_f, l \in L_{kf} \tag{11}$$

$$CP_{fkl} \leq CO_{ij} + M \left( 1 - \sum_{c \in C_{kf}} y_{ijklc}^f \right) \quad \forall f \in F, k \in K_f, l \in L_{kf}, i \in \mathcal{J}, j \in N_i \tag{12}$$

$$CP_{fkl} \geq CO_{ij} - M \left( 1 - \sum_{c \in C_{kf}} y_{ijklc}^f \right) \quad \forall f \in F, k \in K_f, l \in L_{kf}, i \in \mathcal{J}, j \in N_i \tag{13}$$

$$CO_{i,n_i} + \sum_{f \in F} TT_i^f x_{fi} - T_i \leq D_i \quad \forall i \in \mathcal{J} \tag{14}$$

$$y_{ijklc}^f, Z_{c_1,c_2,k,l}^f, x_{fi} \in \{0,1\} \quad \forall f \in F, k \in K_f, c \in C_{kf}, l \in L_{kf}, i \in \mathcal{J}, j \in N_i \tag{15}$$

$$C_{ij}, C_{fkl}', T_i \geq 0 \quad \forall f \in F, k \in K_f, l \in L_{kf}, i \in \mathcal{J}, j \in N_i \tag{16}$$

Equation (1) is the objective function, which calculates total system costs. Constraint set (2) ensures that each job should be assigned to one of the facilities. Then, Constraint set (3) guarantees all operations of each assigned job be processed on the machines of the associated facility, where $n_i = |N_i|$, the number of operations which should be done on the job $i$. Constraint set (4) mandates each operation to be assigned to one position of an existing machine configuration of the associated facility. Constraint set (5) prevents the assignment of the operation $O_{ij}$ to any positions of the configuration of machines $k$ and $c$ of facility $f$ if it is not allowed to be performed on the configuration of machine $c$ of machine $k$ ($R_{ijkc}^f = 0$). Constraint set (6) guarantees that in each machine position of a facility, at most one operation can be processed. Constraint set (7) shows that each position can be allocated only when the previous position has already been assigned. For each machine, Constraint sets (8) and (9) guarantee that a proper setup should be done if two consecutive positions be assigned to different configurations. Constraint set (10) shows that each operation $O_{ij}$ can be started only after finishing of the previous operation. Constraint set (11) ensures that the finishing time of each machine position should be greater than the completion time of the previous position plus an associated processing time of the position and a possible setup time. Constraints (12) and (13) guarantee that the completion time of each machine position be set with its associated job operation ($M$ is a big positive number). Constraint set (14) calculates the amount of tardiness for each job. Constraints (15) and (16) define the decision variables.

## 2.3   Dynamic Model Formulation

Herein, we extend the presented model for a dynamic situation, in which some new arriving orders should be scheduled to be produced in the manufacturing system. Utilizing the Industry 4.0 technologies, the required real-time data from the distributed shop-floors (e.g., delayed jobs, current configurations and accessibility of machines) and limitations of the logistics system (i.e., availability of raw materials) can be provided by a cyber-physical shop-floors (CPSF). The provided data can be utilized in the scheduling module to update the current schedules of each shop-floor. The shop-floors under an IoT environment can include three basic levels. The conceptual framework of information flow to provide the autonomous analysis of system status and real-time response to dynamic events is presented in Fig. 1.

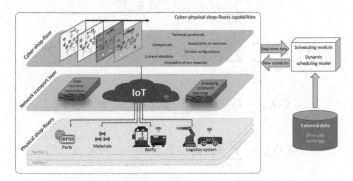

**Fig. 1.** Dynamic scheduling task utilizing CPSF capabilities

### Updated Sets and Indices of the Dynamic Model:

$\mathcal{J}'$    Set of non-delivered jobs, where $\mathcal{J}' \subseteq \mathcal{J}$

$\mathcal{J}''$    Set of new arrived jobs

$N_i'$    Set of all operations of new jobs (for $i \in \mathcal{J}''$) or remained operations of current jobs, where $N_i' \subseteq N_i$ for $i \in \mathcal{J}'$

$c_{k,f}'$    Index of current configuration of $k$ th machine in facility $f$, where $c_{k,f}' \in C_{k,f}$

$L_{k,f}'$    Set of unoccupied machine-positions

$l_{k,f}'$    Index of the first unoccupied position of $k$ th machine in facility $f$ after arriving new jobs, where $L_{k,f}' = \left\{ l_{k,f}', l_{k,f}' + 1, \ldots, l_{k,f}' + \left| L_{k,f}' \right| - 1 \right\}$

Considering the optimal value of the variables $x_{fi}^* \forall i \in \mathcal{J}$ and $CP_{f,k,l_{k,f}-1}^*$ as the initial conditions of the dynamic model and substituting the sets $\mathcal{J}' \cup \mathcal{J}''$, $N_i'$ and $L_{k,f}'$ respectively instead of the previous sets $\mathcal{J}$, $N_i$ and $L_{k,f}$, the dynamic model can be defined as follows.

**Mathematical Formulation of the Dynamic Problem:**

$$\text{Min } z = \sum_{i \in \mathcal{J}' \cup \mathcal{J}''} \sum_{j \in N_i'} \sum_{f \in F} \sum_{k \in K_f} \sum_{c \in C_{kf}} \sum_{l \in L_{kf}'} PC_{ijkc}^f y_{ijklc}^f + \sum_{i \in \mathcal{J}''} \sum_{f \in F} TC_i^f x_{fi} +$$

$$\sum_{i \in \mathcal{J}' \cup \mathcal{J}''} \omega_i T_i + \sum_{f \in F} \sum_{k \in K_f} \sum_{c_1 \in C_{kf}} \sum_{c_2 \in C_{kf}} \sum_{l \in L_{kf}'} SC_{c_1,c_2,k}^f Z_{c_1,c_2,k,l}^f \qquad (17)$$

$$c_1 \neq c_1$$

Constraints (4)–(13), (15) and (16) should be considered replacing updated the sets $\mathcal{J}' \cup \mathcal{J}''$, $N_i'$ and $L_{kf}'$ respectively instead of the previous sets $\mathcal{J}$, $N_i$ and $L_{kf}$.

$$\sum_{f \in F} x_{fi} = 1 \qquad \forall i \in \mathcal{J}'' \qquad (18)$$

$$\sum_{j \in N_i'} \sum_{k \in K_f} \sum_{c \in C_{kf}} \sum_{l \in L_{kf}'} y_{ijklc}^f \leq n_i \times x_{fi} \qquad \forall f \in F, i \in \mathcal{J}'' \qquad (19)$$

$$CO_{i,n_i} - T_i \leq D_i - \sum_{f \in F} TT_i^f x_{fi}^* \qquad \forall i \in \mathcal{J}' \qquad (20)$$

$$CO_{i,n_i} + \sum_{f \in F} TT_i^f x_{fi} - T_i \leq D_i \qquad \forall i \in \mathcal{J}'' \qquad (21)$$

## 3   Computational Results and Discussions

In this section, a small-sized example is illustrated to validate the proposed models. The main data of the example are presented in Table 1. At first, jobs 1 to 4 are considered to be scheduled by the static model. The optimum schedule is presented in Fig. 2. Thereafter, it is supposed that job 5 is arrived at $t = 85$. Moreover, based on the obtained real-time data from the CPSF, it is estimated that the needed time for providing the manufacturing system in facility 1 and 2 are 90 and 45 time units, respectively. In the optimum solution of the dynamic model, the new arriving job is assigned to the facility 1. As can be seen in Fig. 3, the unprocessed operations until $t = 175$ containing $O_{1,3}, O_{1,4}, O_{3,3}$ and all operations of job 5 are rescheduled.

A sensitive analysis on $\Delta t$ shows that the total cost is strongly affected by this parameter. Hence, the performance of the manufacturing system directly is related to the response time. To make the method applicable in real-world problems, the system must be equipped with some major "hard" and "soft" technological requirements. A significant issue to improve the performance is to enhance the agility of the logistics system. Developing an appropriate smart logistics system can be helpful to make the manufacturing system much more flexible. Also, the decision-making approach and the related computational time should be considered. For example, the proposed models is coded in GAMS 24.1.3 software and solved by CPLEX solver. The written codes are performed on a computer with a 2/5 GHz Intel Core(TM) i7-4710HQ CPU and 8 GB RAM. The static and dynamic models use 496 and 273 s of CPU time to be solved, respectively. Hence, developing an efficient algorithm to solve the problem in a reasonable time can be interesting.

**Table 1.** Data for the illustrated example

| $f,k,c$ | Job 1 | | | | Job2 | | | | | Job3 | | | Jo4 | | | | Job5 | | |
|---|---|---|---|---|---|---|---|---|---|---|---|---|---|---|---|---|---|---|---|
| | 1 | 2 | 3 | 4 | 1 | 2 | 3 | 4 | 5 | 1 | 2 | 3 | 1 | 2 | 3 | 4 | 1 | 2 | 3 |
| 1,1,1 | | | | | 75 | | | 51 | | 87 | 91 | | | 52 | 57 | 72 | | 65 | 74 |
| 1,1,2 | | 72 | | 86 | 54 | | | | | 96 | | | | | | | 53 | | |
| 1,2,1 | | 65 | 55 | 61 | | 62 | 81 | | 86 | | | 59 | 86 | | 76 | 54 | | | |
| 1,2,2 | 93 | 97 | 63 | | | | | 90 | | 67 | 96 | 62 | | | | | 76 | 50 | 62 |
| 2,1,1 | 81 | | 71 | | 70 | 55 | | | | 83 | 85 | | 95 | | | | 83 | 71 | |
| 2,1,2 | | | | 80 | | 97 | 77 | | | 63 | 75 | 60 | | | | | | | 55 |
| 2,1,3 | 60 | 58 | | | | | | 99 | | | | | | 84 | | | | 82 | |
| 2,2,1 | | | | | 75 | | | 51 | | 87 | 91 | | | 52 | 57 | 72 | | | |
| 2,2,2 | | 72 | | 86 | 54 | | | | | 96 | | | | | | | 53 | | |
| $D_i,w_i$ | 430,100 | | | | 650,150 | | | | | 400,65 | | | 400,50 | | | | 650,70 | | |

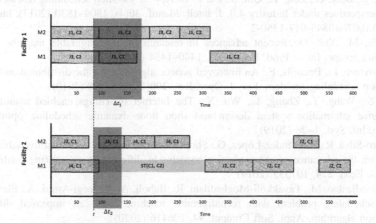

**Fig. 2.** Optimal schedule of the illustrated example with $z^* = 153500$

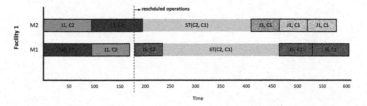

**Fig. 3.** Rescheduled operations of the illustrated example $z_{new}^* = 210110$

# 4 Conclusions

Because of current globalization trend, many manufacturing systems have shifted to a distributed production network instead of a single factory production. Moreover, information technology has been utilized to make producers more competitive in today's rapidly changing market requirements. These evolutions can affect many areas of decision making, including scheduling. In this paper, a mathematical model has been presented for a distributed flexible job-shop scheduling in a dynamic environment by utilizing cyber-physical shop-floor capabilities. The full adoption of the framework presented will help companies enhance their global competitiveness, improve the flexibility of their domestic manufacturing systems, and obtain new market opportunities.

Due to the different aspects of the decision environment, the high complexity of the problem, and a requirement for real-time decision making, a multi-agent approach can be effective to solve it. Moreover, because of high volume data generated in the shop-floor agents, machine learning approaches by doing a general analysis of data can be utilized to facilitate solving some of specific tasks.

# References

1. Zhang, J., Ding, G., Zou, Y., Qin, S., Fu, J.: Review of job shop scheduling research and its new perspectives under Industry 4.0. J. Intell. Manuf. 30(4), 1809–1830 (2017). https://doi.org/10.1007/s10845-017-1350-2
2. Gadalla, M., Xue, D.: Recent advances in research on reconfigurable machine tools: a literature review. Int. J. Prod. Res. 55(5), 1440–1454 (2017)
3. De Giovanni, L., Pezzella, F.: An improved genetic algorithm for the distributed and flexible job-shop scheduling problem. Eur. J. Oper. Res. 200(2), 395–408 (2010)
4. Tian, S., Wang, T., Zhang, L., Wu, X.: The Internet of Things enabled manufacturing enterprise information system design and shop floor dynamic scheduling optimisation. Enterp. Inf. Syst. 1–26 (2019)
5. Romero-Silva, R., Hernández-López, G.: Shop-floor scheduling as a competitive advantage: a study on the relevance of cyber-physical systems in different manufacturing contexts. Int. J. Prod. Econ. 224, 107555 (2019)
6. Mahmoodjanloo, M., Tavakkoli-Moghaddam, R., Baboli, A., Bozorgi-Amiri, A.: Flexible job shop scheduling problem with reconfigurable machine tools: an improved differential evolution algorithm. Appl. Soft Comput. 94, 106416 (2020)

# Towards a Non-disruptive System for Dynamic Orchestration of the Shop Floor

Milan Pisarić[1]([⊠]) [iD], Vladimir Dimitrieski[2] [iD], Marko Vještica[2] [iD],
and Goran Krajoski[1] [iD]

[1] KEBA AG, Industrial Automation, Linz, Austria
{pisa,krgo}@keba.com
[2] University of Novi Sad, Faculty of Technical Sciences, Novi Sad, Serbia
{dimitrieski,marko.vjestica}@uns.ac.rs

**Abstract.** One of the main challenges of Industry 4.0 is the adaptation of existing production lines. Robots are substituting human workers in modern smart factories, as they are much more suitable for repetitive tasks. In contrast to that, Industry 4.0 predicts a high rise in product customization. The total disruption of the current factories, although the easiest solution, is not welcomed by the traditional industry stakeholders. To offer adaptation rather than disruption, and to promote man-machine collaboration rather than complete substitution of the human workforce, we present a Digital Factory solution capable of orchestrating different types of resources —humans, machines, robots— according to their capabilities. The core component of the solution is a real-time Orchestrator that orchestrates factory resources in order to produce the desired product. Orchestrator is a complex, modular, highly scalable, and pluggable software, responsible for dynamical matching, scheduling, and executing of production steps, allowing high customization and lot-size-one production.

**Keywords:** Orchestration · Digital factory · Smart manufacturing · Flexible manufacturing systems · Production planning · Industry 4.0

## 1 Introduction

The industrial world is evolving. Although some researchers suggest a revolution or a total disruption of the current industrial automation setting, existing industry stakeholders are rather hoping for stabile transition and adaptation to the wave of Industry 4.0 proposals. Highly frequent repetitive tasks are a common playground for robots in production, but a trend in Industry 4.0 is extensive product customization rather than a huge number in lot-size of products [1]. The substitution of the human workforce with robots is not always motivated by the cost or the efficiency of the production itself, but rather a social trend —as new generations seem less willing to work as low-skilled operators [2]. Industry stakeholders also face the problem of preservation of current knowledge and skills of experienced workers who have nobody to transfer it to [3]. In contrast to that, in the current, rigid production environment, robots are still not fit to do some of the high complexity tasks that mid- and high-skilled human workers do, nor they are fit for high customization of the products because of the lengthy time required

© IFIP International Federation for Information Processing 2020
Published by Springer Nature Switzerland AG 2020
B. Lalic et al. (Eds.): APMS 2020, IFIP AICT 592, pp. 469–476, 2020.
https://doi.org/10.1007/978-3-030-57997-5_54

for conversion to other product. Robots are not going to completely replace human workers soon, but a proportion of collaboration between a man and a machine will increase in the near future [2].

Our approach, in opposition to a total disruption, is to enable the integration of the existing participants in the production into a flexible manufacturing system of the next generation. Legacy equipment and information systems will be adapted by using a specific hardware-software component in order to create a corresponding proxy, able to coexist, and cooperate with the proposed system. In this paper, we present a Digital Factory solution with an intelligent, real-time Orchestrator as its core component. The Orchestrator is a complex system that orchestrates a safe collaboration of all factory resources —humans, machines, robots— with the goal of producing a requested product. Formally described production processes are fed to the Orchestrator which in turn is responsible for the orchestration —matching, scheduling, and enriching the process— and for the execution on final production steps in a smart factory Digital Twin (DT). Execution commands are propagated from the DT to its corresponding smart device where they are realized at a shop floor level while allowing for lot-size-one production.

## 2  Related Work

Digitalization of the complete production process is a crucial step in reaching any of the Industry 4.0 goals —including automated shop floor reconfiguration and service or task-oriented programming of machines. Therefore, not only products but also processes and resources need to have digital descriptions [4]. Based on these descriptions, modern industrial software systems orchestrate delegation of instructions and their assignment to smart resources [5]. Based on the desired product and by matching required resources with available smart resources and their offered capabilities, these systems can act as self-organizing systems and execute the complete production process [6, 7]. This matching is enabled by the introduction of semantic knowledge of the manufacturing environment, which formalizes the rules and the relationships between the participating objects [8].

Production flexibility is achieved not only on the execution level but also in the production process modeling phase. Domain-specific modeling language can be designed for this purpose —not only to enable process customization but also to enable visualization of the process monitoring and graphical simulation of the production process model [9]. Even though modern, flexible manufacturing relies on computer systems, many production lines still lack the possibility of simulating the production process itself. The development of simulators, as generic as possible, that can mimic any give shop floor of the production process is still a promising approach within the industry [10]. Simulation is to act as a digital twin of the production system, that is able to simulate individual process steps or complete production. Production process simulation has been addressed in several solutions with a focus on assembling —to validate the result of assembly planning, to detect the errors of the product design, and to make appropriate modifications to the generated execution plan [5, 7]. Simulation in our solution is practically a digital twin of the product being produced. It can be used as a visualization of the executed production while collecting adequate data for in- or post-production analysis. Otherwise, it can be alienated from the production process as a pure simulation. By simulating the complete process, potential production failures are reduced, resource consumption is optimized and the safety of participating human workers is enhanced. Various forms of cooperation between machine and a human have already been addressed in the area of modern production systems [11]. Vernim et al. have already proposed the integration of human workers as a special type of a factory resource in a capability-based production planning [12]. In addition to this work, we address the orchestration of a human worker, by sending generic instructions for the final execution. A human operator is basically used as Human as a service, with a focus still being on collaboration with machines in this adaptation of existing shop floors.

## 3 Architecture

In the presented solution (Fig. 1), **Orchestrator** denotes software that can be used to orchestrate factory resources with a goal of producing a requested product. On one hand, it can be run as a self-contained black box (e.g. on an industrial PC). On the other hand, several core elements and external parts of the Orchestrator are pluggable and offer the possibility of adapting the solution to the factory or use-case specific requirements e.g. Dashboard or Analytics. Pluggable elements are denoted with a plus symbol in Fig. 1. The red line depicts the orchestration flow starting from the user interface and ending with the execution of production. The overall architecture is modular and is implemented as a basic **Container and Agent infrastructure**. With the actors as the software components packaged within the containers, it is possible to realize smart, modular, and pluggable software infrastructure. An actor is an individual entity with some intelligence attached to the software components. Software containers also enable high scalability and running on cross-platform with minimum time to setup. This is achieved by introducing de-coupled containers that start, stop, and run independently and can be seen as complete and isolated services. These containers can be run on-demand, based on a multitude of factors such are the number of requests or the load on the existing container instances.

**Customer interface** (1) offers flexible and intelligent ways to interact with the production facility. In a generic pluggable fashion, customers can express individual products in various formats which are later parsed or transformed into a generic product model or digital product description (such as Computer-Aided Design —CAD, or Computer-Aided Manufacturing —CAM diagrams). A user-defined product description is an input for the orchestrator. **Orchestration Agent** (2) is an essential component that operates the complete orchestration process. It is a state machine that runs each user's product order through various states —matching to execution —in order to create the desired product. **Process Reasoner** (3) uses the digital product description as an input, to reason upon required capabilities, steps, and order of the sequences and generates the digital process description as an output. The process description is a technological description without any resource allocation in it. It also holds the information about the bill of materials, quantities, timing constraints, acceptance, and

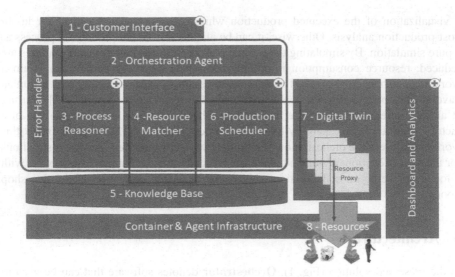

**Fig. 1.** Orchestrator architecture

completion criteria. Process Reasoner is also implemented in a pluggable fashion to answer to use-case specific requirements. Once the production process specification is inferred, it can be adapted by using the provided process modeler. This tool allows not only altering the existing production processes, to fine-tune them for production, but also creating them from scratch and thus enriching or substituting the customer interface. This creation of process specifications is of utmost importance as some product specifications are not provided in a machine-readable form.

**Resource Matcher** (4) takes up the responsibility to match all the required capabilities, constraints, acceptance and completion criteria on the input, with the available resources, based on their offered capabilities stored in **Knowledge Base** (5), to the processes and the required capabilities. The result of the matching process is a set of possible production processes with allocated **Resources** (8). This is represented as a set of directed graphs where each graph represents a single process —practically a variety of production process description. The next step is the enrichment of generated processes. It is done gradually in a sequence of customizable enrichers. The result is production process variations improved in resource level enrichment —which includes the preparation steps for a product order, and in logistic enrichment —which describes the material flow during the production process. The result of this phase is another set of directed graphs, where each graph represents an enriched variation of a process description.

**Knowledge Base (KB)** is a storage facility for the semantic data models of resources, capabilities, constraints, factory logistics, collaboration models, and interface contracts. It also stores semantics of products and processes and plays a key role in the orchestration of production. Any new version of the process, even when a previous version exists, is stored in the KB. KB offers production knowledge in a machine-readable form and is based on well-defined and formal meta-models. It also holds information on physical and logical connections between devices and required physical connections in the system. A topology inside KB contains information on which device can interact with which other devices to create an appropriate flow of operations based on the inputted processes. It also includes all the spare resources on the shop floor (e.g. machines that are currently being maintained). The Discovery mechanism enables additional resources to enter the shop floor dynamically when they are inserted in the KB in a plug-and-produce fashion. KB also supports inference and query mechanism that can dynamically find connections between all resources. This enables Orchestrator to search for semantic connections and orchestrate the production.

**Production Scheduler** (6) receives a graph of all possible process descriptions with resources and offered capabilities, process steps, and material allocations. It then performs a scheduling algorithm with the variants of cost functions. It is done in a multilayered sequence of matching-scheduling graders that lean on information stored in KB. Different optimization functions act like graders for the scheduler and enable an optimization via a specific combination of criteria, such as reduced times and energy consumption or optimized material consumption and preferred technological steps used. According to the pluggable architecture, these criteria are organized in factory-specific graders and every graph is then ranked according to the desired set of graders. The result of this phase is an enriched and scheduled list of production process steps ready to be executed.

**Digital Twin (DT)** (7) is the component of the Digital Factory that takes an executor role and oversees the final execution of commands. DT is a faithful representation of the factory shop floor where each digital element represents an actual resource that it can communicate with. This enables the usage of DT representation as a Simulation only, as well as a simultaneous execution and visual representation of the production process. For each process step, DT sends the appropriate command to a targeted element, which then propagates the execution command to its resource via a resource Proxy. Proxies generate machine-specific commands and are the functional and behavioral interface between DT and the physical assets of the Digital Factory. The hardware platform is still open, and although the structure of execution commands may be common among all the types of resources, the proxies are factory specific in the end. A **resource** is an asset involved in the production process. In the proposed architecture, humans, robots, and production machines are considered as resources that are differentiated by their capabilities, interaction, and interface description. A **human worker** is modeled with its capabilities (i.e. inspection, pick-n-place, turning...) that are not necessarily different from robot capabilities (i.e. pick-n-place, milling, drilling...) but are differentiated by their constraints. Robots can operate with heavier loads or with less fatigue, while human workers will still be of greater trust in some type of jobs (e.g. inspection) for some time in the future. Also, there are still some competences and man-machine interactions that are hardly going to be replaced by a machine until a production completely based on Artificial Intelligence (AI). Although the executor sends generic commands to any resource, a human worker interacts via a human-machine interface (HMI) while machines communicate via a standardized interface. Interaction with non-standard resources, especially legacy non-smart machines, is to be enriched by their appropriate and use-case specific interfaces.

All system components communicate with each other through an internal communication layer based on a highly-scalable communication backbone (in Zero Messaging Queue). An intra-module communication is established through a broker implementation. Every component provides logging and tracing data to the logging-bus module. It is a rudiment for the rule-based **Error handling** which is triggered according to the information provided in logs and provides event-based error mechanisms for all the components including matching and scheduling. Additional pluggable components, that also lean heavily on the communication layer are **Dashboard and Analytics** modules of various kinds. The proposed infrastructure and architecture are foundations for high-scalability and a large flow of information. System components are modular, independent, and scalable, which enables both horizontal and vertical scalability. The current proposal is also technology agnostic with the possibility to run on a single PC, distributed on several industrial PCs or in a cloud.

## 4   Use Case (Proof of Concept)

Several use-cases were used while analyzing and testing the architecture flow presented on Fig. 1. One assembly use-case was used to set up a laboratory conditions testbed, alongside a corresponding simulation. Test arena comprises of several elements — smart shelves and material area, smart assembly tables, an autonomously guided vehicle (AGV) with an industrial robot mounted on it, 3D printer, LEGO bricks of various sizes and colors and additional industrial robot fixed on the assembly table. Simulation encompasses real-world device simulation models and a graphical preview of the simulated system and the Digital Twin (7). The simulation is created using ROS environment because of the ease of usage and understanding to the non-robotics community, in a way to resemble the desired test arena as much as possible. The human operator is also a part of the testbed, depending on the use-case variation.

There are two mobile applications available for human participants —one is used as a communicator to the human operator, and the second is a starting point of interaction with the Digital Factory. This interface (1) allows the upload of a digital description of the product. In the particular case, there is a GUI set up on a tablet device, that enables a user to design a custom flag. The desired flag is to be assembled out of LEGO bricks, using the resources existing in the Knowledge Base (5) and without any additional coding. All the participants of the testbed - smart areas, inventory, bricks, and assembly table —are regarded as resources (8). After the user designs a flag, the Orchestration Agent (2) initiates the orchestration mechanisms and the flag is then being processed. The Process Reasoner (3) generates the production process specification from the inputted digital description of the product, and stores it in the KB (5). In this use-case, the raster, shape, dimensions, and number of bricks to be used are extracted from the input, and a digital specification of the production process is generated as an output of this element. All the production steps are deduced according to the factory-specific topology and use-case. It is then possible to make changes or additions to the generated process in the dedicated Process Tool, with the optimization being the main goal. Additionally, the execution process can be reviewed in the tool, thus acting as a secondary DT. The digital description is a recipe that is used for further orchestration of all the resources towards the product being delivered. The Resource Matcher (4) uses the semantic information stored in KB to match the existing resources (8), their capabilities and constraints, and offers an optimal match for every production step described in the generated production process. In this use-case, the available resources capable of assembling are limited to two robots and a human. Matcher first produces a production process variation in which it assigns these resources to their dedicated production steps (e.g. AGV is to pick a targeted brick, the robot is to assemble a targeted brick on the targeted table; human is to prepare a targeted brick, etc.). This production variation is later enriched in several layers of enrichment. This re-matching or deeper matching refinement is done according to the availability of the resources in the testbed, current topology of the machines, physical limitations of the collaboration between resources, etc. In this use-case, there is a safety limitation of human being too close to the industrial robots, and this information is therefore additionally calculated in the matching process.

The Production Scheduler (6) is scheduling the execution order of all the matched production steps to find an optimal schedule. Time was the only optimization grader used in this use-case, intending to assemble the LEGO flag as quickly as possible. This led to bricks being transferred from a material area to the assembly table in higher volume and not brick by brick. After the matching and scheduling phases are done, the participating resources receive the commands via dedicated Resource Proxies. These proxies are elements of Digital Twin (7) which is practically acting as an executor. Generic commands (e.g. Pick blue brick of size 2 × 2 from location A) received as a result of previous phases are transformed in a set of factory-specific instructions and are then propagated to the designated resources. In the described use-case, commands are sent via ROS bridge for robots, and a tablet or smartwatch for human workers, who receive instructions and send feedback when their activity is finished. The human worker provides additional bricks that are out of stock or delivers a brick created additionally in the 3D printer. If a brick is to be created or to be delivered by a human worker, the AGV reaches the targeted material area where the human operator and the 3D Printer are, and where the collaboration is safe. In the end, the fixed robot assembles the flag vertically by placing LEGO bricks one by one on the assembly table.

## 5 Conclusions and Future Work

We have presented the concept of a Digital Factory as a pluggable software system, that automatically extracts instructions from the given input, sets up the factory shop floor accordingly, and executes the production itself. Both the simulation and the real-time testbed set in a laboratory are used as a proof of concept. Not only are the machines orchestrated but a human worker in collaboration with robots as well.

We are continuing the work on the presented solution. Several areas of investigation are still open, including the introduction of AI-based scheduling graders that determine main properties of delivering the optimized execution graphs; decentralization of the orchestrator process to the participating assets; automatic extraction of the production process steps out of the existing CAD/CAM diagrams or recipes; deducing the missing information on process descriptions based on AI previous knowledge, etc.

**Acknowledgment.** The research in this paper is supported by KEBA AG Linz.

# References

1. Lu, Y.: Industry 4.0: a survey on technologies, applications and open research issues. J. Ind. Inf. Integr. **6**: 1–10 (2017). https://doi.org/10.1016/j.jii.2017.04.005
2. The risk of automation for jobs in OECD Countries: a comparative analysis (2016). https://doi.org/10.1787/5jlz9h56dvq7-en
3. Müller, J.M., Voigt, K.-I.: Sustainable industrial value creation in SMEs: a comparison between industry 4.0 and made in China 2025. Int. J. Precis. Eng. Manuf. Green Technol. **5** (5), 659–670 (2018). https://doi.org/10.1007/s40684-018-0056-z
4. Backhaus, J., Reinhart, G.: Digital description of products, processes and resources for task-oriented programming of assembly systems. J. Intell. Manuf. **28**(8), 1787–1800 (2015). https://doi.org/10.1007/s10845-015-1063-3
5. Keddis, N.: Capability-based system-aware planning and scheduling of workflows for adaptable manufacturing systems (2016)
6. Michniewicz, J., Reinhart, G.: Cyber-physical-robotics – modelling of modular robot cells for automated planning and execution of assembly tasks. Mechatronics **34**, 170–180 (2016). https://doi.org/10.1016/j.mechatronics.2015.04.012
7. Zhang, Y., Qian, C., Lv, J., Liu, Y.: Agent and cyber-physical system based self-organizing and self-adaptive intelligent shopfloor. IEEE Trans. Ind. Inf. **13**, 737–747 (2017). https://doi.org/10.1109/TII.2016.2618892
8. Alsafi, Y., Vyatkin, V.: Ontology-based reconfiguration agent for intelligent mechatronic systems in flexible manufacturing. Robot. Comput. Integr. Manuf. **26**, 381–391 (2010). https://doi.org/10.1016/j.rcim.2009.12.001
9. Vještica, M., Dimitrieski, V., Pisarić, M., Kordić, S., Ristić, S., Luković, I.: Towards a formal description and automatic execution of production processes. In: Proceedings of 15th IEEE International Scientific Conference on Informatics (Informatics 2019), pp. 450–455. IEEE, Poprad, Slovakia (2019)
10. Boschert, S., Rosen, R.: Digital twin—the simulation aspect. In: Hehenberger, P., Bradley, D. (eds.) Mechatronic Futures, pp. 59–74. Springer, Cham (2016). https://doi.org/10.1007/978-3-319-32156-1_5
11. Romero, D., et al.: Towards an operator 4.0 typology: a human-centric perspective on the fourth industrial revolution technologies. In: Proceedings of International Conference on Computers & Industrial Engineering, pp. 1–11, Tianjin, China (2016)
12. Vernim, S., Walzel, H., Knoll, A., Reinhart, G.: Towards capability-based worker modelling in a smart factory. In: 2017 IEEE International Conference on Industrial Engineering and Engineering Management (IEEM), pp. 1576–1580. IEEE, Singapore (2017). https://doi.org/10.1109/IEEM.2017.8290158

# Assembly Process Design: Performance Evaluation Under Ergonomics Consideration Using Several Robot Collaboration Modes

Anthony Quenehen[✉], Stephane Thiery, Nathalie Klement,
Lionel Roucoules, and Olivier Gibaru

Arts et Métiers Institute of Technology, LISPEN, HESAM Université,
59000 Lille, France
anthony.quenehen@ensam.eu

**Abstract.** This paper aims at studying the combination of different collaboration modes between operator and collaborative robot in order to optimize an assembly process for both economic and ergonomic objectives. Based on a real case study, and using a energy expenditure ergonomic model, the authors have determined by experiment the different ergonomic and economic variables under each possible collaboration mode. They propose a set of indicators to evaluate the quality of assignment solutions, as well as a multi-objective cost function to determine optimal trade-offs between the different collaboration modes. An initial set of trials has indicated that combining several modes of collaboration may deliver benefits for both economic and ergonomic performance.

**Keywords:** Collaborative robotics · Process design · Ergonomics performance · Collaboration modes · Optimization

## 1 Introduction

Collaborative robotics has opened new ways for introduction of automation into manual processes. Indeed, the opportunity for human and collaborative robot (cobot) of sharing the same environment without physical safety device (under certain circumstances) has made their interaction potentially smoother. This may lead to design a collaborative (human and cobot) process using work balancing approach. Besides their inherent limitations in handling complex assembly tasks, most cobots have limited payload and speed compared to industrial robots. This guarantees safe interaction with operators, but hinders cobots economic competitiveness. Nevertheless, their ability to execute or assist human tasks delivers solutions for process ergonomics improvement, thus representing a competitive asset when it comes to balance both economic and ergonomic performance, opening way for repetitive stress injuries reduction and/or management of disabled workforce within the production environment.

© IFIP International Federation for Information Processing 2020
Published by Springer Nature Switzerland AG 2020
B. Lalic et al. (Eds.): APMS 2020, IFIP AICT 592, pp. 477–484, 2020.
https://doi.org/10.1007/978-3-030-57997-5_55

## 2   Related Works

**Several Types of Safe Interaction** can be foreseen in the context of assembly operations, ranging from physical separation between operator and cobot to simultaneous action on the same work piece. Thiemermann [9] proposes a classification based on spatial and temporal separation, highlighting four interaction categories, see Fig. 1. In the process of designing a collaborative assembly process, we propose to focus on the 'synchronisation' and 'cooperation' categories, which are specific to cobot. Synchronisation enables to handle the task allocation as a balancing problem under constraints. Usual constraints may be precedence of tasks, resource availability, along with potential for automation of task based on technical feasibility factors [4, 5, 10]. As a result of this decision process, task may be allocated to either operator or cobot. Cooperation category follows a similar decision process, offering an additional allocation option towards 'operator and cobot', hence using both resources for the concerned task [1]. In both cases, proposed solutions are evaluated against performance metrics, as Cycle Time (CT) or makespan [7] for instance.

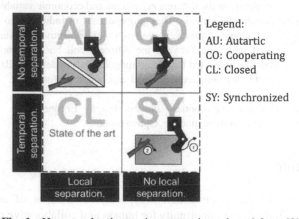

**Fig. 1.**  Human robot interaction categories, adapted from [9]

**Ergonomic improvement,** also representing a potential benefit of cobot usage, has already received attention from researchers. The subsequent trade offs between economical performance and ergonomic improvements have been studied in the form of multi objective optimization, based on applicable ergonomic models [7, 11]. Nevertheless, this has been done under the assumption of task allocation towards either operator or cobot.

**Several ergonomic models,** such as RULA (Rapid Upper Limb Assessment) [6], are available to assess and quantify the strain generated by posture, efforts and movements throughout the execution of process tasks. Additional approaches based on energy expenditure propose more quantitative evaluation and results [3]. They also express the ergonomic load as a necessary relaxation time (RT), required when the energy spent during the task exceeds a given threshold value [2]. Based on formulas related to each type of movement, they can offer quick calculation of the energy expenditure for each work element. More interestingly, they express the ergonomic cost (relaxation time) in the same dimension as the economic cost (cycle time), providing more realistic view of the trade off between the two objectives. For these reasons we will select the PMES (Predetermined Motion Energy System) model proposed by [2], and give further details in following section.

Building on existing work, we propose to design a process considering a three way trade off between operator, cobot, or joint action of operator and cobot for each task (cooperative mode). Indeed, allocating task to cobot whose motion speed is slow will improve ergonomic performance at the expense of an increased task time (TT), as using cooperation mode will deliver less ergonomic improvement, but without impacting TT. Nevertheless, both resources will be required for a single task in that case. Our motivation is to enlarge the field of possible solutions, since each option dominates the other two (see Table 1) on one of the criteria of the problem (economic performance, ergonomic, resource mobilisation). Additionally, we propose to ground our work on an experimental case study, as we deem important to test the relevancy and applicability of the proposed solutions, specially when the supporting model complexity has been increased.

**Table 1.** A qualitative comparison of collaboration modes under performance criteria

|                        | Operator | Cobot | Cooperation  |
|------------------------|----------|-------|--------------|
| Eco. performance       | High     | Low   | High         |
| Ergo. performance      | Low      | High  | Intermediate |
| Parallelisation of tasks | High   | High  | Low          |

## 3  Proposed Problem Modelisation

**Assignment Notations.** We note $t = 0$ the starting time of the process cycle, and represent an assignment solution $S$ by $[[t_1, A_1], [t_2, A_2], \ldots [t_N, A_N]]$, where $N$ notes the number of tasks, $ti$ the starting time of task $i$, and $A_i \in \{'10','01','11'\}$ its allocation (respectively '10' to an operator, '01' to cobot, and '11' to both in cooperation mode). An assignment solution $S$ provides operator's and cobot's respective cycles times $CT_o(S)$ and $CT_c(S)$ (defined as "the time when the operator, resp the cobot, finishes his last task"), and the required relaxation time $R_{tot}(S)$ for the operator.

**Cost Function.** We define an economic cost $C_{eco}(S)$ as equal to the process cycle time. Assuming that in case of idle time between two tasks, operator will rather slow down his pace to fill this gap with continuous work than stopping and relaxing, we consider that relaxation can only happen after operator's cycle is completed. Thus, we define an ergonomic cost $C_{ergo}(S)$ as the remaining amount of relaxation time after cycle completion (in case of the operator finishes first i.e. $CT_c(S) - CT_o(S) > 0$, he can start relaxing while the cobot finishes the process cycle, otherwise this cost is $R_{tot}(S)$). This leads to the following cost expressions:

$$\begin{cases} C_{eco}(S) = \max\{CT_o(S), CT_c(S)\} \\ C_{ergo}(S) = \max\{0, R_{tot}(S) - C_{eco}(S) - CT_o\} \end{cases} \tag{1}$$

Economic cost and ergonomic cost being expressed in the same unit (time in second), we can easily design a cost function. As part of an upcoming work, we aim at finding assignment solutions $S$ minimizing the following cost function:

$$J_\alpha(S) = (1 - \alpha) \cdot C_{eco}(S) + \alpha \cdot C_{ergo}(S) \tag{2}$$

where $\alpha \in [0, 1[$ stands for a given trade-off between ergonomic and economic cost. The apparent complexity to solve this problem by a solver, as an optimization problem under constraints (precedence and resources availability), points towards an evolutionary algorithm based solutions. We plan to use genetic algorithm or reinforcement learning.

**Key Performance Indicators.** To assess the performances of an assignment solution $S$, we output the followings economic and ergonomic indicators:

$$I_{eco}(S) = \frac{C_{ref}}{C_{eco}(S)} \text{ and } I_{ergo}(S) = \min\left\{\frac{C_{eco}(S)}{CT_o(S) + R_{tot}(S)}, 1\right\} \tag{3}$$

with $C_{ref}$ representing the cycle time of a full manual process. The higher $I_{eco}$, the better the economic performance. Compared to a full manual process, cooperative mode assignment would enable to significantly reduce the ergonomic cost, but also to marginally reduce the cycle time. Therefore, achieving $I_{eco} > 1$ is possible. Note that an upper bound exists, corresponding to perfect parallelisation of tasks between operator and cobot, assuming compliance to all precedence and feasibility constraints are achieved. For example, if the cobot is $k$ times slower than operator, this bound is $I_{eco} = 1 + 1/k$. Further work will determine applicable maximum values for $I_{eco}$ (setting $\alpha = 0$ in Eq. 2). Concerning $I_{ergo}$, the closest to 1, the best the ergonomic performance is. Indeed $I_{ergo}$ inferior to 1 means a remaining relaxation time is still required after completion of the process. If $C_{eco}(S)/(CT_o(S) + R_{tot}(S)) > 1$, operator finishes to relax before end of process cycle. From ergonomic point of view, this situation does not represent any additional benefit (only inefficiency of resource usage). Therefore, as per Eq. 3, $I_{ergo}$ maximum value has been set to 1.

Also, as a sub KPI, we compute the resource usage ratio as percentage of the cycle time, where $Idle_o$ and $Idle_c$ are the respective idle times of the operator and the cobot during the cycle:

$$\begin{cases} U_o(S) = \dfrac{C_{eco}(S) - Idle_o(S) + \min\{C_{eco}(S) - CT_o(S), R_{tot}\}}{C_{eco}(S)} \times 100 \\ U_c(S) = \dfrac{C_{eco}(S) - Idle_c(S)}{C_{eco}(S)} \times 100 \end{cases} \tag{4}$$

Indeed, when the cobot finishes last, idle time at the end of operator's cycle can be used for relaxation.

# 4  Application: Problem Setting

In order to support this approach, the assembly process of a pneumatic cylinder has been selected as a case study. Offering different types of operations (picking, setting, inserting, screwing), with various levels of complexity, it may give relevance to the potential for automation. The simple geometric nature of most sub components may also permit relatively simple handling operation from the cobot with standard effectors.

This assembly process is divided in fourteen tasks, with a limited number of precedence constraints (see Fig. 2). Thus, it should offer a large number of possibilities for parallelisation of tasks, and open sufficient areas for solutions to understand the potential and limitations of the proposed model.

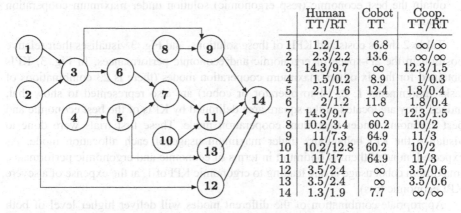

| | Human TT/RT | Cobot TT | Coop. TT/RT |
|---|---|---|---|
| 1 | 1.2/1 | 6.8 | $\infty/\infty$ |
| 2 | 2.3/2.2 | 13.6 | $\infty/\infty$ |
| 3 | 14.3/9.7 | $\infty$ | 12.3/1.5 |
| 4 | 1.5/0.2 | 8.9 | 1/0.3 |
| 5 | 2.1/1.6 | 12.4 | 1.8/0.4 |
| 6 | 2/1.2 | 11.8 | 1.8/0.4 |
| 7 | 14.3/9.7 | $\infty$ | 12.3/1.5 |
| 8 | 10.2/3.4 | 60.2 | 10/2 |
| 9 | 11/7.3 | 64.9 | 11/3 |
| 10 | 10.2/12.8 | 60.2 | 10/2 |
| 11 | 11/17 | 64.9 | 11/3 |
| 12 | 3.5/2.4 | $\infty$ | 3.5/0.6 |
| 13 | 3.5/2.4 | $\infty$ | 3.5/0.6 |
| 14 | 1.3/1.9 | 7.7 | $\infty/\infty$ |

**Fig. 2.** Precedence graph of our problem, with Task Time (TT) and Relaxation Time (RT) in seconds for each type of task assignment.

The description of the manual assembly process can be seen on the following URL: bit.ly/2w8Iwf0. Based on the video analysis of several cycles of the assembly process, repeatable time values have been determined for each work element of every task, in order to populate the model. Likewise, each work element has been assessed through PMES to calculate its relative energy expenditure, using the formulas proposed in [3], and determine related relaxation time if applicable. In order to populate each possible task execution mode (operator, cobot, or cooperative), two versions of the process have been run and analyzed: fully manual version (100% of tasks done by operator), and a version where cooperation mode has been maximized to re-calculate TT and RT. Cobot related TT have been determined by applying a coefficient of $k = 5.9$ on the operator TT, based on previous work in the cobot usage for similar case study [8]. When task could not be allocated to cobot due to its complexity (i.e. bolt tightening), or cooperation mode is irrelevant (i.e. task consists in moving a single piece), related TT and/or RT have been set to the $\infty$ value, to exclude them from potential selection based on a cost function. Overall results are presented in Fig. 2.

## 5 Identification of Solution Areas

Initial trials were done by maximizing utilisation of each specific collaboration mode (operator, cobot, cooperation), in compliance with precedence constraints, but without investigating potential benefit of altering assembly sequence at this stage. Thus, we considered the following four specific assignment solutions:

- $S_{manual}$: full manual process. Each task is allocated to the operator.
- $S_{cobot}$: process with allocation to the cobot, except for tasks 3, 7, 12, 13 done in parallel by the operator the earliest possible (no usage of cooperation mode).
- $S_{coop-eco}$ (resp $S_{coop-ergo}$): process with highest usage of cooperation mode. Tasks 1, 2, 14, not eligible for cooperation, are assigned to the operator (resp the cobot) to obtain the best economic (resp ergonomic) solution under maximum cooperation mode.

Table 2 shows costs and KPIs of these solutions, and Fig. 3 visualises their relative position in the 2D-space of ergonomic and economic performances. In Fig. 3, KPIs obtained for the six others maximum cooperation modes (there is 23 combinations of tasks assignments 1, 2, 14 to operator or cobot) are also represented to show that, indeed, they are located in the square area delimited by KPIs of the best economic and best ergonomic under maximum cooperation mode. These first trials were done to visualize the KPI behaviours under maximum usage of each allocation mode. As expected, none of them is optimum in terms of economic and ergonomic performance (maximum cobot usage is one leading to ergonomic KPI of 1, at the expense of a severe KPI economic loss).

Appropriate combination of the different modes will deliver higher level of both economic and ergonomic performance. The upcoming algorithm development will aim at characterising such KPI solution areas, and their borders for a same fixed trade-off $\alpha$. Resolution will be done respectively with and without the cooperation mode. By comparing respective solutions, we will be in a position to assess the additional benefits of the cooperative mode.

**Table 2.** Costs and KPIs of initial trials

| Solution | $CT_o$ | $R_{tot}$ | $CT_c$ | Costs (Eq. 1) $C_{eco}$ | $C_{ergo}$ | KPI (Eq. 3) $I_{eco}$ | $I_{ergo}$ | Usage (Eq. 4) $U_o$ | $U_c$ |
|---|---|---|---|---|---|---|---|---|---|
| $S_{manual}$ | 88.4 | 72.8 | 0 | 88.4 | 72.8 | 1 | 0.548 | 100% | 0% |
| $S_{cobot}$ | 67.8 | 24.2 | 311.4 | 311.4 | 0 | 0.284 | 1 | 19.2% | 100% |
| $S_{coop-eco}$ | 83 | 20.4 | 81.7 | 83 | 20.4 | 1.065 | 0.803 | 100% | 94.22% |
| $S_{coop-ergo}$ | 98.6 | 15.3 | 106.3 | 106.3 | 7.6 | 0.832 | 0.933 | 80.81% | 100% |

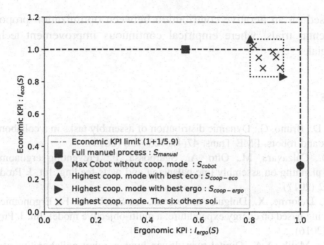

**Fig. 3.** Relative KPI's position of the different initial trials.

In order to assess the validity of the proposed model and results the solutions $S_{coop\text{-}eco}$ and $S_{coop\text{-}ergo}$ have been actually implemented (see video footage). Despite minor discrepancies in task times when recombining them into new processes, it appeared that a significant factor is the possible mismatch between the end condition of a task and start condition of the next depending on their respective collaboration mode. This leads to adjust the content of the concerned tasks, impacting their TT. Modeling and populating such phenomenon would increase significantly problem complexity, for potential limited benefit in prediction accuracy. Besides, as per regular automation approach, continuous improvement loops may be applied to several tasks involving cobot (trajectory optimization), improving further the economic performance. Furthermore, as it can be seen on the process video footage, the cyclic nature of the production enables to parallelise the last tasks of an instance and the first tasks of the next. This factor is not reflected in the current problem setting and will require updating $C_{eco}$ and $C_{ergo}$ expressions.

## 6  Conclusion and Further Work

In this article, we have proposed an analysis of both economic and ergonomic KPIs through the combination of several collaboration modes between operator and cobot. A part of upcoming work will be the resolution of our optimization problem based on the designed cost function, using genetic algorithm or reinforcement learning. This will support a more accurate definition of solutions areas, and offer more quantitative evaluations of additional benefits brought by the combination of the different collaboration modes. Additionally, experimental phase has highlighted valuable elements that may benefit to the initial model, and open way to study a comprehensive process design approach, based on an iterative contribution between optimization proposed solution and experimental trials, where empirical continuous improvement techniques may prove beneficial.

# References

1. Antonelli, D., Bruno, G.: Dynamic distribution of assembly tasks in a collaborative workcell of humans and robots. FME Trans. **47**(4), 723–730 (2019)
2. Battini, D., Calzavara, M., Otto, A., Sgarbossa, F.: Preventing ergonomic risks with integrated planning on assembly line balancing and parts feeding. Int. J. Prod. Res. **55**(24), 7452–7472 (2017)
3. Battini, D., Delorme, X., Dolgui, A., Persona, A., Sgarbossa, F.: Ergonomics in assembly line balancing based on energy expenditure: a multi-objective model. Int. J. Prod. Res. **54**(3), 824–845 (2016)
4. Bilberg, A., Malik, A.A.: Digital twin driven human–robot collaborative assembly. CIRP Ann. **68**(1), 499–502 (2019)
5. Malik, A.A., Bilberg, A.: Collaborative robots in assembly: a practical approach for tasks distribution. In: 52nd CIRP Conference on Manufacturing Systems, vol. 81, pp. 665–670 (2019)
6. McAtamney, L., Corlett, E.N.: Rula: a survey method for the investigation of work-related upper limb disorders. Appl. Ergon. **24**(2), 91–99 (1993)
7. Pearce, M., Mutlu, B., Shah, J., Radwin, R.: Optimizing makespan and ergonomics in integrating collaborative robots into manufacturing processes. IEEE Trans. Autom. Sci. Eng. **15**(4), 1772–1784 (2018)
8. Quenehen, A., Pocachard, J., Klement, N.: Process optimisation using collaborative robots-comparative case study. IFAC-PapersOnLine **52**(13), 60–65 (2019)
9. Hiemermann, S.: Direkte Mensch-Roboter-Kooperation in der Kleinteilemontage mit einem SCARA-Roboter (2005)
10. Tsarouchi, P., Matthaiakis, A.S., Makris, S., Chryssolouris, G.: On a human-robot collaboration in an assembly cell. Int. J. Comput. Integr. Manuf. **30**(6), 580–589 (2017)
11. Weckenborg, C., Spengler, T.S.: Assembly line balancing with collaborative robots under consideration of ergonomics: a cost-oriented approach. IFAC-PapersOnLine **52**(13), 1860–1865 (2019)

# A Method of Distributed Production Management for Highly-Distributed Flexible Job Shops

Daiki Yasuda[1], Eiji Morinaga[2(✉)], and Hidefumi Wakamatsu[1]

[1] Graduate School of Engineering, Osaka University, Osaka, Japan
{daiki.yasuda,wakamatu}@mapse.eng.osaka-u.ac.jp
[2] Graduate School of Humanities and Sustainable System Sciences,
Osaka Prefecture University, Osaka, Japan
morinaga@kis.osakafu-u.ac.jp

**Abstract.** Recent developments of computer technology and information and communication technology are realizing highly-distributed manufacturing systems (HDMSs) in which each machine is computerized and can communicate with other machines. For this type of manufacturing system, a distributed method of discrete event simulation and a distributed method of job shop production scheduling were proposed, respectively. Because these methods use a common distributed sequencing algorithm for HDMSs, they can be integrated and an integrated method of distributed simulation and scheduling was also proposed for job shops. This paper describes an extension of the method to flexible job shops, in which an operation is processed by one of multiple machines. A distributed algorithm for selecting the machine which processes the next operation of an intermediate job based on a given dispatching rule was proposed. By incorporating this algorithm, the conventional method can be applied to flexible job shops. In addition, a method of optimizing the machine selection by adjusting the ratio of each of multiple dispatching rules was proposed. The feasibility of the proposed method was shown by computer experiments.

**Keywords:** Distributed production management · Highly-distributed manufacturing systems · Flexible job shop · Dispatching rules · Simulated annealing · Internet of things

## 1 Introduction

Diversified customers' needs have caused the transition from low-mix high-volume production to high-mix low-volume production and agile manufacturing in this half century. In these styles of production, it is important to flexibly respond to fluctuations in production conditions, and it is required to develop a method for real-time production management. To achieve this flexible manufacturing, it is necessary to immediately generate, evaluate, modify and determine an operation plan which is suitable for the new condition. As for the immediate generation of an operation plan, there have been proposed many methods for reactive scheduling that utilize meta-

B. Lalic et al. (Eds.): APMS 2020, IFIP AICT 592, pp. 485–492, 2020.
https://doi.org/10.1007/978-3-030-57997-5_56

heuristics [1], knowledge-based systems [2], neural networks [3], multi-agent systems [4–6] and so on. As for the evaluation of an operation plan, manufacturing simulation has been discussed and many commercial simulators have been developed. However, those simulators are not used for the purpose of immediate evaluation because of the heavy load of model construction [7].

Recent developments of computer technology and information and communication technology are realizing highly-distributed manufacturing systems (HDMSs) in which each machine is computerized and can communicate with other machines. With this type of manufacturing systems, distributed discrete event simulation can be performed by providing each machine with a function to simulate its behavior by constructing a simulation sub-model on its own computational resource and with a function to exchange information about itself for executing events in chronological order in the entire system. Based on this concept, highly-distributed manufacturing system simulation has been discussed [8, 9].

Along with such a distributed method for evaluating an operation plan, it is desirable to also develop a distributed method for generating an operation plan. As for distributed production scheduling, methods using combinatorial auction [10], mediator architecture [11] and active database [12] have been proposed. However, from the point of view of performing production scheduling together with the immediate evaluation of the generated schedule by the highly-distributed manufacturing system simulation, it is desirable to develop another distributed scheduling method which is based on the same architecture that the simulation method has. For this reason, highly distributed scheduling methods utilizing the time management mechanism of the highly-distributed manufacturing system simulation have been proposed [13–16].

These distributed methods of scheduling and simulation for HDMSs can be integrated because they are based on the same time management mechanism. The integration makes it possible to generate better operational plans efficiently. It is also possible to obtain good plans by incorporating an optimization method in the integrated method. For this aim, a method to integrate them and perform optimization was given for job shops [17]. In actual production, it is common that there are multiple machines which can process a certain operation [18, 19]. This paper describes an extension of the integrated method to flexible job shops.

## 2   Highly-Distributed Manufacturing Management System for Job Shops [17]

This paper considers a manufacturing system composed of an automated storage/retrieval system (AS/RS) and machining centers (MCs). Each job (product) is initially stored in the AS/RS, transported to MCs which process its required operations, and finally returned to the AS/RS. Each MC has a buffer of finite capacity for storing pending jobs and processed jobs, and processes the pending jobs stored in it one by one. The processed job is passed to the MC which is responsible for the next operation by automated guided vehicles (AGVs). Each job is temporarily returned to the AS/RS when the buffer of the recipient MC is full. Production ends when the final operation of all jobs is completed and the AS/RS receives all finished products.

Each of the AS/RS and MCs, which is a component of this production system, has a calculation function and a communication function, and can perform autonomous decision-making about itself and exchange information by communication with other components. In transport using AGVs, it is important to avoid collision between AGVs. In production sites, a practical method for avoiding the collision is adopted. In the method, the transport path is divided into plural sections (called *zones* in this paper) with a switch for controlling an incoming AGV based on the presence or absence of an AGV in the section. In this paper, the zones are dealt with components of the production system. Each zone is assumed to have a calculation function and a communication function also as well as the AS/RS and MCs. The role of a zone is to simulate transport of intermediate products and finished products between machines by passing information about an AGV between zones by communication. There is a constraint that an AGV cannot enter a zone with another AGV until the preceding AGV goes out from the zone. To deal with uncertainty caused by this constraint, it is necessary to perform simulation.

The highly-distributed manufacturing system simulation [8, 9] executes a discrete event simulation in the highly distributed environment described above. Events that cause a change in the system status occur at discrete points in time. The execution of the simulation is realized by repeating the following steps. Step 1: Advance the simulation time (simulation clock) to the next discrete time point; Step 2: Extract all events that can occur at the new time; Step 3: The process associated with the occurrence of each event is executed to change the state of the system. In order to execute this in a distributed environment, it is necessary to generate events that occur one after another in various places in the system, while maintaining temporal consistency. For this purpose, the machine is ordered based on the earliest event occurrence time of each machine, and the right to execute simulation is given to the machine with the earliest time.

There are four types of events to be executed on the machine which has acquired the right for simulation: job reception, starting processing, finishing processing, and a transport. Each process is as follows: In the case of an event of job reception, the events of starting processing and finishing processing for the next process of the received job are generated. If the machine is idle, the occurrence time of the generated event of starting processing is determined to the time when the job is received. If the machine is processing another job, the occurrence time of the generated event is determined to the time at which the current process is finished.

In the case of an event of starting processing, first, the event list is checked whether there are plural earliest events of starting processing of stored jobs having the same occurrence time. If there are such events, one of the jobs is selected using pregiven dispatching rules (SPT, LWKR, etc.), the weights of which are optimized using similar technique as that for flexible job shops described in Sect. 3.2. The event of starting processing for the selected job is executed, and then the occurrence time of the event of finishing processing of the job is determined. The occurrence time of the events of starting processing of the unselected jobs are changed to the time at which the processing of the selected job finishes. If there are not plural earliest events of starting processing with the same occurrence time, the earliest event of starting processing is executed, and the occurrence time of the event of finishing processing is determined.

In the case of an event of finishing processing, a request to transport the job to the machine that processes the next operation of the job is assigned to an AGV.

In the case of an event of transport, information of the zone having the right for simulation is passed to the zone in the direction of travel of the AGV and vice versa, and the information about the AGV and the object being transported is transmitted to the recipient zone. The zone receiving the AGV generates an event of transport within itself.

In this system, sequencing is performed using two types of algorithms. One is that called *initial sorting algorithm*, which is mainly used in the initial stage of simulation. This sorting algorithm orders the priorities of all machines by having each machine inform all other machines of its time and adjust its priority based on received information. The other is that called *re-sorting algorithm*, which is mainly used for performing sequencing in intermediate stages of simulation. This algorithm reorders the priority of all machines by having the machine the time of which has changed inform all other machines of the change and the related machines adjust their priorities based on received information.

# 3    Highly-Distributed Manufacturing Management System for Flexible Job Shops

## 3.1    Processing Machine Selection and Prioritization

In job shops, an operation of a job is processed by a pre-specified machine. But, in flexible job shops, there are a plurality of machines that can process the operation. In job shop scheduling, the MC responsible for each operation of each job is determined in advance, so the transfer of jobs between operations can be simple processing. However, in flexible job shop scheduling, before processing a job for delivery, it is necessary to select an MC to be in charge of the next operation of the job. A common dispatching rule for performing this selection is PT rule that gives priority to a high-performance MC, and a highly distributed scheduling method using this rule has been proposed [16]. In this approach, before assigning a job, each machine autonomously determines the initial value of the priority of the machine in accordance with the PT rule that prioritizes high-performance MC. This process is called *initial sorting*. Each machine broadcasts the required processing time $PT_i$ and the ID number $ID_i$ to other machines. Thereafter, each machine receives a message from another machine ($ID_j$) and analyzes the magnitude relationship with the required time $PT_j$ of the sender machine. If the required time $PT_i$ is larger, the value of $S_i$ (initial value is 1), which represents the own priority of the machine for each product, is incremented by one to lower the priority. If they are equal, the one with the smaller ID number has priority. By performing this set of processes, the correct priority sequence of all machine is obtained.

An example of processing is shown below. First, AS/RS assigns each job to one of the MCs that can take charge of processing its first operation. At this time, the priorities of the MCs based on the PT rule is calculated and the job is assigned to the MC with the highest priority. A transportation event and a job reception event are then generated by job allocation. Next, by the initial sorting algorithm, a machine (AS/RS, MC or zone) with the earliest event is determined, and the machine executes its earliest event. After that, the priorities of the generated events are ordered by the re-sorting algorithm, so that a machine with the earliest event is determined, and the machine executes its earliest event. When the job arrives at the MC, the MC executes the event of starting processing for the job. After that, when the event of finishing processing for the job is executed, the MC responsible for the next operation of the job is determined by performing the machine selection based on the PT rule. If the selected MC has multiple jobs in its buffer when it reaches the idle time, the priorities of those jobs is calculated and the event of starting processing for the job with the highest priority is executed.

## 3.2 Machine Selection Optimization

If only the PT rules is used, jobs may be excessively concentrated on high-performance machine, resulting in a poor schedule. Thus, if only one dispatching rule is adopted, the shortcomings of the rule will have a significant effect on the schedule. Therefore, it can be expected that the shortcomings of each rule can be compensated by using some dispatching rules together. There are various rules for machine selection other than the PT rule. In this study, the excessive concentration of jobs to a machine is suppressed by using the NINQ rule, which can be expected to reduce the machines that become idle, together with the PT rule. The NINQ rule is a rule that, when assigning jobs, assigns to the MC that has the least number of jobs in the buffer among the assignable MCs. The evaluation value of the PT rule is time, and the evaluation value of the NINQ rule is the number of jobs. Therefore, when these are used together, it is necessary to perform normalization to make the value range uniform. The following shows how to normalize the PT rule and the NINQ rule respectively.

$$V_{PT} = \frac{PT - PT_m}{PT_M - PT_m} \tag{1}$$

$PT$: Processing time (If the MC is unavailable, a large value is set to this variable.)
$PT_m$: Minimum processing time for one operation in all machine
$PT_M$: Maximum processing time for one operation in all machine

$$V_{NINQ} = \frac{Number\ of\ Jobs}{Buffer\ Size} \tag{2}$$

*NumberofJobs*: Number of jobs in the buffer
*BufferSize*: Buffer capacity of each MC
The evaluation value $V_i$ is calculated for each rule and multiplied by the rule weight $W_i$. The sum of them is regarded as the priority $P_{MC}$ of each job as follows.

$$P_{MC} = W_{PT} * V_{PT} + W_{NINQ} * V_{NINQ} \tag{3}$$

Since each $V_i$ is defined by the rule that a small value is good, the MC with the smallest $P_{MC}$ value is preferentially selected. Using the weight $W_i$ of each rule in this equation as a solution, the weight is optimized by simulated annealing (SA). Since $W_i$ is a continuous variable, it generates a neighborhood solution using normal random numbers. Normal random numbers are generated by the Box-Muller method. If the random variables $X$ and $Y$ are independent of each other and both follow a uniform distribution on [0, 1], then, $z_{i1}$ defined by the following formula becomes independent random variables according to the standard normal distribution $N(0, 1)$ with mean 0 and variance 1.

$$z_{i1} = \sqrt{-2 \log X} * \cos 2\pi Y \tag{4}$$

The random variable $x$ following the normal distribution $N(\mu, \sigma)$ is expressed as follows.

$$x = \mu + \sigma z_{i1} \tag{5}$$

Since the neighborhood solution $\tilde{W}_i$ of the solution $W_i$ is a normal random number according to $N(W_i, \sigma)$, the neighborhood solution is obtained by the following equation.

$$\tilde{W}_i = W_i + \sigma z_{i1} \tag{6}$$

Weight adjustment is performed by the above method.

## 4  Numerical Example

Processing flows based on the proposed algorithms and concept were coded in the C language and the proposed method was implemented on a generic workstation in semblance by interprocess communication with sockets due to machine constraints. The method was applied to an example of flexible job shops of 10 jobs which require 10 operations using 3 machining centers (MCs), 1 automated storage/retrieval system (AS/RS) and 2 AGVs shown in Fig. 1.

As a result of optimizing the makespan with the number of iterations in SA set to 200, a schedule with a makespan of 281 was obtained. Table 1 shows the numbers of

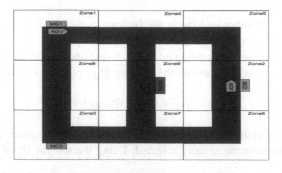

**Fig. 1.** Example used for case study.

message exchange which occurred in the simulation. Assuming that the number of machines is $n$, $n(n - 1)$ times of communication are required for the initial sorting algorithm, and $2(n - 1)$ times of communication are required for the re-sorting algorithm. When the number of jobs is $o$, the number of operations is $p$ and the maximum transport distance is $q$ zone, the maximum number of events from the start to the end of production is $op(q + 3)$. By these characteristics of the communication algorithms, the number of message exchange tends to be large. Assuming that a message is sent based on TCP and its size is 80 byte, the total size is about 792 MB. If the communication is performed using a standard of wireless LAN (IEEE 802.11n), it can be completed in about 9.9 s. This result shows a potential of the proposed method for practical use.

Table 1. Number of message exchange which occurred in the simulation.

| Machine type | Number of message exchange |
| --- | --- |
| AS/RS | 547837 |
| MC1 | 1086559 |
| MC2 | 1071049 |
| MC3 | 865399 |
| Zone1 | 639457 |
| Zone2 | 589978 |
| Zone3 | 944737 |
| Zone4 | 829597 |
| Zone5 | 592567 |

## 5  Conclusions

This paper described an extension of a highly-distributed manufacturing management system to flexible job shops. A method for handling multiple dispatching rules and performing optimization has been applied to a set of processing flows of the management system for flexible job shops. Numerical experiments implied that the proposed method can generate an optimal operation plan with a practical number of message exchanges.

**Acknowledgement.** This work was supported by JSPS KAKENHI Grant Number JP18K03872.

## References

1. Zheng, L., Gao, L.: A hybrid genetic algorithm and tabu search for a multi-objective dynamic job shop scheduling problem. Int. J. Prod. Res. 51(12), 3516–3531 (2013)
2. Szelke, E., Kerr, R.M.: Knowledge-based reactive scheduling. Prod. Plann. Control 5(2), 124–145 (1994)

3. Garetti, M., Taisch, M.: Using neural networks for reactive scheduling. In: Kerr, R., Szelke, E. (eds.) Artificial Intelligence in Reactive Scheduling. IAICT, pp. 146–155. Springer, Boston, MA (1995). https://doi.org/10.1007/978-0-387-34928-2_11
4. Archimede, B., Coudert, T.: Reactive scheduling using a multi-agent model: the SCEP framework. Eng. Appl. Artif. Intell. **14**(5), 667–683 (2001)
5. Lou, P., Liu, Q., Zhou, Z., Wang, H.: Multi-agent-based proactive–reactive scheduling for a job shop. Int. J. Adv. Manuf. Technol. **59**(1–4), 311–324 (2012)
6. Sabuncuoglu, I., Kizilisik, O.B.: Reactive scheduling in a dynamic and stochastic FMS environment. Int. J. Prod. Res. **41**(17), 4211–4231 (2003)
7. Fujii, S., Hibino, H., Iwamura, K., Tsumaya, A., Sashio, K.: Simulation of manufacturing system under ubiquitous environment. J. Jap. Soc. Precis. Eng. **74**, 1016–1019 (2008). (In Japanese)
8. Fujii, S., et al.: A basic study on a highly distributed simulation of manufacturing systems under the ubiquitous environment. In: Proceedings of the ASME/ISCIE 2012 International Symposium on Flexible Automation, ISFA2012-7208, pp. 321–324 (2012)
9. Morinaga, E., et al.: A study on highly-distributed manufacturing system simulation. Procedia Manuf. **39**, 50–57 (2019)
10. Kaihara, T., Fujii, N., Toide, S., Ishibashi, H., Nakano, T.: Optimization method using combinatorial auction for production scheduling with batch processing. J. Adv. Mech. Des. Syst. Manuf. **4**(3), 588–596 (2010)
11. Matsumoto, T., Kato, Y., Nagafune, S., Wakamatsu, H., Shirase, K., Arai, E.: Advanced autonomous distributed manufacturing system using active database. Trans. Jap. Soc. Mech. Eng. **65**(630), 837–843 (1999). (In Japanese)
12. Tönshoff, H-K., Seilonen, I., Teunis, G., Leitão, P.: A mediator-based approach for decentralized production planning, scheduling, and monitoring. In: Proceedings of the CIRP International Seminar on Intelligent Computation in Manufacturing Engineering, pp. 113–118 (2000)
13. Morinaga, E., Takagi, A., Sakaguchi, Y., Wakamatsu, H., Arai, E.: Basic study on production scheduling method for highly-distributed manufacturing systems. J. Adv. Mech. Des. Syst. Manuf. **8**(5), JAMDSM0072 (2014)
14. Morinaga, E., Sakaguchi, Y., Wakamatsu, H., Arai, E.: A distributed production scheduling method for highly-distributed manufacturing systems. In: Grabot, B., Vallespir, B., Gomes, S., Bouras, A., Kiritsis, D. (eds.) APMS 2014. IAICT, vol. 438, pp. 531–538. Springer, Heidelberg (2014). https://doi.org/10.1007/978-3-662-44739-0_65
15. Morinaga, E., Nakamura, T., Wakamatsu, H., Arai, E.: A method for highly-distributed manufacturing systems. In: Proceedings of the 23rd International Conference on Production Research, ICPR23, Manila, Philippines, 31 July 2015–6 August 2015, p. 1100 (2015)
16. Morinaga, E., Nakamura, T., Wakamatsu, H., Arai, E.: Flexible job-shop scheduling method for highly-distributed manufacturing systems. J. Smart Process. **6**(5), 181–187 (2017)
17. Yasuda, D., Morinaga, E., Wakamatsu, H.: Integrated production scheduling and simulation for highly-distributed manufacturing systems. In: Proceedings of 2020 JSPE Spring Conference, pp. 345–346 (2020). (In Japanese)
18. Kopp, S., Dauzère-Pérès, S., Yugma, C.: Flexible job-shop scheduling with extended route flexibility for semiconductor manufacturing. In: Proceedings of the 2014 Winter Simulation Conference, pp. 2478–2489 (2014)
19. Alvarez-Valdes, R., Fuertes, A., Tamarit, J.M., Giménez, G., Ramos, R.: A heuristic to schedule flexible job-shop in a glass factory. Eur. J. Oper. Res. **165**, 525–534 (2005)

# A Digital Twin Modular Framework
# for Reconfigurable Manufacturing Systems

Hichem Haddou Benderbal[1]([⊠]) [iD],
Abdelkrim R. Yelles-Chaouche[1,2] [iD], and Alexandre Dolgui[1] [iD]

[1] IMT Atlantique, LS2N-CNRS, Nantes, France
{hichem.haddou-ben-derbal, abdelkrim-ramzi.yelles-
chaouche, alexandre.dolgui}@imt-atlantique.fr
[2] IRT Jules Verne, Bouguenais, France

**Abstract.** The emergence of Industry 4.0 and its related technologies transformed modern manufacturing environment by making them more intelligent.
This is associated with the fast evolution of data acquisition technologies and the
enormous amount of generated data. Among these modern manufacturing
environment, Reconfigurable Manufacturing System (RMS) is a concept able to
cope with the current market conditions, characterized by an increasingly personalized and volatile demand. At the same time, Digital Twin (DT) emerged as
a new concept. DT represents a new data-driven vision that combines real time
data analytics, optimization and simulation. When managing modern and
complex manufacturing systems, DT provides new insights and potentials in
decision-making process support. In this context, this paper is an attempt to
present an integrated RMS digital twin (RMS-DT) modular framework. RMS-
DT is a model that can represent the system state at any moment in time while
allowing a holistic system visibility to improve its performances and enable
flexible decision-making. The paper is concluded with a discussion, future
challenges and perspectives in order to enhance the proposed RMS digital twin
framework.

**Keywords:** Digital twin · Reconfigurable manufacturing system · Modular
framework · RMS digital twin

## 1 Introduction

The current markets are characterized by an increasingly personalized and volatile
demand. As a result, companies are seeking for responsiveness and customization.
Thus, many research attempt to provide new solutions in order to achieve the aforementioned challenges. In this regard, Reconfigurable Manufacturing System (RMS) is
considered as one of the most suitable solution. Such system was proposed by Koren
et al. [13]. The differences of this system from all other concepts of manufacturing
systems are presented in [6]. RMS is characterized by reconfigurability *i.e.* the ability to
quickly change and reorient components (hardware and/or software) easily to adjust
production (in terms of functionality and capacity) in response to abrupt changes. This
is possible thanks to reconfigurable machine tools (RMT) that are a major components

of RMS. Such machines have a modular structure allowing to be reconfigured in order to fulfill different functionalities and capacities.

RMS is a part of the industry 4.0 [3]. The latter is driven by the rapid evolution of information, data acquisition and communication technologies, which are the main foundation of the so-called smart factory. This is achievable due to digitalization, where all components of an industry are linked and can communicate in real time. In this context, Digital Twin (DT) appeared as a concept that benefits from these technologies to achieve intelligent manufacturing [22]. Indeed, it provides a high-fidelity virtual representation of a physical system. DT comprises two main parts (physical and virtual) with real data transmission between them. DT will process, analyze and evaluate the enormous amount of collected data (Real-time/offline), allowing a better system transparency. As a result, a wide range of information can be collected and used for many applications, such as tracking the state of the system, making predictions, diagnosis, simulation and optimization of the system (e.g. planning, scheduling, configuration/reconfiguration selection, etc.).

In a reconfigurable environment, where unpredictable changes in demand and flexibility are challenging, a DT may prove to be very useful in a decision-making process at all levels. In fact, designing and selecting an RMS configuration is shown to be complex [14], since the number of configurations grow significantly with the number of RMTs. Thus, a DT can help to achieve a flexible decision-making process (*e.g.* choosing an appropriate configuration based on real time, predicted and historical data). The DT applications are various and have proven to be very useful in a manufacturing context. However, few research works consider both RMS and DT [22]. Moreover, to the best of our knowledge, the software reconfiguration part of the RMS reconfigurability characteristic is rarely treated by researchers. In this regard, this paper is an attempt to present a generic and modular framework that integrates both RMS and DT concepts. This latter includes the software reconfiguration part through a "plug & play" type of software as module components. Furthermore, the idea is to shed light on the considerable gap in this matter and rise attentions to the importance of research around it.

## 2    Related Works

RMS literature covers various areas like system design, process planning, scheduling and reconfigurable control as demonstrated by several state of the arts reviews in recent years [2–4]. Moreover, Industry 4.0 covers a lot of new emerging concepts and technologies [16]. However, this section will only focus on a small portion of these fields that includes respectively: RMS design, digitalization (digital twin) and how it is integrated in RMS.

One of the major issues found through the RMS literature is RMS design. The objective is to use their core characteristic (i.e. reconfigurability) to design responsive systems. RMS design problems are more complex, this is due to the fact that these systems are characterized by dynamic capacities to change and to integrate change. Besides, RMS properties, including reconfigurability, emerge after the deployment of the manufacturing system [1, 9]. RMS focuses on scalability and responsiveness, supported by adding or removing functionalities. This allows these systems to be easily scalable to maintain the life cycle of the manufacturing system itself. Thus, to meet these requirements with these properties, reconfigurability must be incorporated into system design from the outset in order to have the best responsiveness when facing changes [14]. Hence, all system components as well as its different levels must be considered and prepared for change. This kind of perspective of the system (on the production and on the design problem) is favored by reconfigurability [8].

Reconfigurability represents a non-functional requirement of the system, linked to its long-term behavior [1]. This implies that classical approaches, which consider only the immediate requirements of the system will not necessarily lead to dynamically changeable systems. Besides, instead of achieving the objectives of reconfigurability, they cause the designed system to quickly become obsolete when facing market variations. Furthermore, for a system to be easily reconfigurable, certain characteristics must be fulfilled such as modularity, integrability, convertibility, diagnosability, customization and scalability [7, 13], as well as automatibility [19, 20]. Based on the previous statements, we see that there is a need to adapt existing approaches and/or develop new design methodologies to design systems with dynamic capacity for change by including the essential parameters of reconfigurability. These methodologies must consider reconfigurability as a dynamic property of the manufacturing system. Thus, a key characteristic towards industry 4.0 is the development of changeable and reconfigurable manufacturing systems.

Industry 4.0 affects the different performance dimensions of a production system, thus it must be considered as factor when designing RMS. The latter needs to be responsive to adapt quickly to changing conditions. This becomes possible in the context of industry 4.0 thanks to digital twin emergence [10]. Xu et al. [21] stressed that the realisation of industry 4.0 is hindered by the lack of powerful tools especially formal methods and systems methods. Authors continue to show the unpreparedness to support digital transformation by current infrastructures and the need of new ones. To tackle that, they argued that there is a need to develop digital twin with added-value decision-making services. The concept of DT has been expanded from product to manufacturing system [5, 17, 18]. In this context, [22] conducted a systematic study on the related research and application of DT. Authors underlined that most DT research lacks referable application cases and are considered in theoretical stage. They also argued that there is a lack of clearness of the proposed application methods and application framework. Based on that, authors proposed an application framework of DT for product lifecycle management. In a reconfigurable environment, [15] proposed a rapid reconfiguration of automated manufacturing system using a novel digital twin-driven approach. The authors attempted to find an optimal reconfiguration solution through a bi-level programming model of upper-level productivity rebalancing and lower-level reconfiguration cost.

RMS reconfiguration complexity increases remarkably when considering both machine-level and system-level (in both hardware and software) [12]. Thus, the number of configurations grow significantly with the number of RMTs. This makes the process of designing then selecting a RMS configuration very complex [14]. Developing comprehensive approaches seems to be very difficult due to the huge variety of possible manufacturing tasks. As a result, integrating digital twin within RMS could be more efficient. This is due to the fact that DT can be oriented to focus on specific problems like diagnosability, predictive maintenance, training, reconfiguration selection or scheduling, etc. Moreover, DT can optimize all activities within the system due to its comprehensive and real-time control of information flow. However, to the best of our knowledge, research work are focusing more on specific parts of DT applications and little research work considered the benefits of a global framework integrating digital twin within RMS while considering its core characteristics as well as software reconfiguration. In this context, our paper presents a first attempt to fill this gap. The goal is to profit from the digital twin concept and propose a modular framework that can be used to ensure an easy reconfiguration of the software part of the RMS by adding new software blocks (e.g. simulation, control …) as needed when needed in "plug & play" manner, which will eventually help in a better selection and gives a better insight and a flexible decision-making process (e.g. hardware reconfiguration).

## 3   RMS-DT Modular Framework

In this section, we present the proposed RMS-DT modular framework for a digital twin within RMS (Fig. 1), explain its various blocks/modules as well as the information flow. The proposed framework, which focuses on the virtual space, is based on broad interpretation of the DT concept. Thus, we did not focus on all the possible technologies related to/can be used within industry 4.0. DT core components are physical space, virtual space, and the data/information flow between them. Nevertheless, this paper focuses only on the virtual space. Our RMS-DT framework is modular and describes the process of the virtual modeling and the construction idea for application subsystems of DT. It is introduced to solve amongst other, complex reconfiguration problems. As the number of machine (RMTs) increases, RMS configurations number increases faster than a natural exponential function [14]. In this regard, RMS-DT represent an attempt to tackle the complexity of reconfiguration problems in a reconfigurable environment.

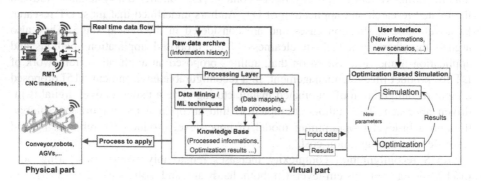

**Fig. 1.** RMS-DT framework

Using the RMS-DT framework, this problem can be solved following two step process. The first step considers executing reconfiguration experiments on high-fidelity virtual space of the RMS-DT. Moreover, the Real-time data flow between the two spaces (physical and virtual) is seamless. This creates and favors high-fidelity conditions that helps to explore all the possible reconfigurations, optimize, simulate and evaluate them on the virtual space. In a second step, the feedback from the virtual space (e.g. optimized production, best reconfiguration, maintenance …) can be used to apply efficiently on the physical space.

The objective of the RMS-DT modular structure is to ensure an easy reconfiguration of the software (adding, modifying and/or removing blocks/modules) in a "plug & play" manner. This makes the framework extensible and adaptable to different needs by integrating new technologies or adapting/developing new behaviours/tasks. For example the "Optimization based simulation" module can be replaced by a solver intended for other tasks like finding the best maintenance strategy instead of finding "the best reconfiguration".

To ensure high-fidelity conditions for solving the problem, the data collected from the physical part—using data acquisition technologies like sensors for example—is transmitted in real-time to the virtual part (green arrow in Fig. 1). Data is collected from different sources (manufacturing systems, machines, AGVs, PLCs, etc.). The real-time raw information collected will then be redirected to two modules (i) *"Raw data archive"* and (ii) *"Processing layer"*.

The **"Raw data archive"** module will simply store the data as it is collected from the physical space. This raw data archive can be used later as historical data, which can be an input for the *"Data Mining/Machine Learning (ML) techniques"* module that will be detailed hereafter.

The **"Processing layer"** module connects information flow between physical space and virtual space through information mapping, processing and storing. The data interaction within this module allows the interoperation of both spaces(physical and virtual). This module comprises three main function modules that are respectively:

- **The "Processing bloc" module:** This module is responsible for processing, mapping and analysing real-time data from the physical space. First, the raw data is processed through cleaning (*e.g.* rule based), structuring and clustering. The clean data is mapped to match and extract the needs of the decision-maker patterns, decision variables, and information. The resulted data is then analyzed and compared with data stored in the *"Knowledge base"* module. After the comparison we are left with two scenarios:

  1. The processed information does not exist in the knowledge base. In this case, the data is stored in the Knowledge base and then redirected to the *"Optimization based simulation"* module to find a new solution corresponding to the new data.
  2. The knowledge base already has this data. In this case, the corresponding solution to apply is fetched and redirected to the physical space.

- **The "Knowledge base" module:** Stores data from both spaces (physical and virtual). All data stored is considered as processed data. That means the data is coming from the *"processing bloc"* module or it represent new data from the *"Data mining/Machine Learning (ML)"*. The physical space data comprises (but not limited to) equipment data (capacity, functionality, re-configurations, tools, …), workshop environment data, production data, etc. For virtual space data we can find (also not limited to) decision data, simulation/optimization evaluation results, and prediction data and new inferred models or patterns, etc.

- **The "Data Mining/Machine Learning (ML)" module:** Its role is to infer/find new patterns and correlations between various collected information collected/stored within both the *"Knowledge base"* module and the *"Raw data archive"* module

Once the real-time data flow treated by the *"processing layer* and redirected to the **"Optimization based simulation"** module (Fig. 2), the latter will try to find the best solution. This Module follow a looped two step process. First, the optimization of an objective function subject to constraints—as defined by the decision-maker or a team of experts—is conducted. Then, a stochastic simulation is used to evaluate the optimization results as well as the objective(s) function(s) and its respective constraints. The process is then repeated until fulfilling a stop criteria (e.g. a time limit, stable solutions, …).

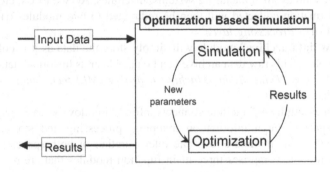

**Fig. 2.** Optimization based Simulation module

The *"Optimization based simulation"* module can also be used directly in asynchronous mode to the physical space through the **"User interface"**. This latter offer to the user (e.g. decision-maker) the possibility to test and evaluate new scenarios or introduce new parameters of the production process/system. The goal is to get insights about them and to predict, control, and optimize the system in exploitation in its environment.

## 4 Conclusion and Perspectives

In this paper, a framework, which describes the use of the digital twin (DT) in an RMS is provided. The framework shows how a DT can be used to achieve the needed RMS flexibility and responsiveness during its operating phase by providing a flexible decision-making process. This is done by continuously collecting real time data from the RMS components. Subsequently, these are stored, processed and analyzed by using information analytic, simulation and optimization module blocs. Based on this, DT can quickly provide critical decisions such as the appropriate RMS configuration to efficiently cope with sudden changes. Due to space limitations, we do not provide in details how the data are collected and exchanged between the RMS and the DT. Instead, we only focus on the virtual part.

For future research perspectives, a comprehensive framework, which includes not only the virtual part, but also a detailed descriptions of the physical part and the connection protocols between them will be provided. More, we are looking forward to develop an online optimization based simulation approach for RMS configuration selection based on what have been done in [11]. This will constitute a first step towards achieving the proposed framework. Accordingly, a DT can be used in an RMS context to achieve diagnosability, which is a core characteristic of such systems and is defined as the ability of an RMS to be easily diagnosed. To the best of our knowledge, few papers study this feature. Since DT offers system transparency and real time feedback, this can be used to detect and prevent root causes of machine and system failures. Finally, an interesting work direction is to study how other RMS characteristics can be integrated using this RMS-DT as well as its general use towards Industry 4.0.

**Acknowledgment.** This work was financially supported by the IRT PERFORM program, managed by IRT Jules Verne (French Institute in Research and Technology in Advanced Manufacturing) as well as by the Region Pays de la Loire.

# References

1. Andersen, A.L.: Development of changeable and Reconfigurable Manufacturing Systems: supporting context-specific design of changeability. Ph.D. thesis, Aalborg University (2017)
2. Benyoucef, L. (ed.): Reconfigurable Manufacturing Systems: From Design to Implementation. SSAM. Springer, Cham (2020). https://doi.org/10.1007/978-3-030-28782-5
3. Bortolini, M., Galizia, F.G., Mora, C.: Reconfigurable manufacturing systems: literature review and research trend. J. Manuf. Syst. **49**, 93–106 (2018)
4. Brahimi, N., Dolgui, A., Gurevsky, E., Yelles-Chaouche, A.R.: A literature review of optimization problems for reconfigurable manufacturing systems. IFAC- PapersOnLine **52** (13), 433–438 (2019)
5. Ding, K., Chan, F.T., Zhang, X., Zhou, G., Zhang, F.: Defining a digital twin-based cyber-physical production system for autonomous manufacturing in smart shop floors. Int. J. Prod. Res. **57**(20), 6315–6334 (2019)
6. Dolgui, A., Proth, J.M.: Useful Methods and Techniques. Springer, London (2010). https://doi.org/10.1007/978-1-84996-017-5
7. ElMaraghy, H.A.: Flexible and reconfigurable manufacturing systems paradigms. Int. J. Flex. Manuf. Syst. **17**(4), 261–276 (2005)
8. ElMaraghy, H.A., Wiendahl, H.P.: Changeability - an introduction. In: ElMaraghy, H. (ed.) Changeable and Reconfigurable Manufacturing Systems. Springer Series in Advanced Manufacturing, pp. 3–24. Springer, London (2009). https://doi.org/10.1007/978-1-84882-067-8_1

9. Farid, A.M.: An engineering systems introduction to axiomatic design. In: Farid, A.M., Suh, N.P. (eds.) Axiomatic Design in Large Systems, pp. 3–47. Springer, Cham (2016). https://doi.org/10.1007/978-3-319-32388-6_1

10. Grieves, M., Vickers, J.: Digital twin: mitigating unpredictable, undesirable emergent behavior in complex systems. In: Kahlen, F.-J., Flumerfelt, S., Alves, A. (eds.) Transdisciplinary Perspectives on Complex Systems, pp. 85–113. Springer, Cham (2017). https://doi.org/10.1007/978-3-319-38756-7_4

11. Haddou-Benderbal, H., Dahane, M., Benyoucef, L.: Hybrid heuristic to minimize machine's unavailability impact on reconfigurable manufacturing system using reconfigurable process plan. IFAC-PapersOnLine 49(12), 1626–1631 (2016)

12. Huang, S., Wang, G., Shang, X., Yan, Y.: Reconfiguration point decision method based on dynamic complexity for reconfigurable manufacturing system (RMS). J. Intell. Manuf. 29 (5), 1031–1043 (2017). https://doi.org/10.1007/s10845-017-1318-2

13. Koren, Y., et al.: Reconfigurable Manufacturing Systems. In: Dashchenko, A.I. (ed.) Manufacturing Technologies for Machines of the Future, pp. 627–665. Springer, Heidelberg (2003). https://doi.org/10.1007/978-3-642-55776-7_19

14. Koren, Y., Gu, X., Guo, W.: Reconfigurable manufacturing systems: principles, design, and future trends. Front. Mech. Eng. 13(2), 121–136 (2017). https://doi.org/10.1007/s11465-018-0483-0

15. Leng, J., et al.: Digital twin-driven rapid reconfiguration of the automated manufacturing system via an open architecture model. Robot. Comput. Integr. Manuf. 63, 101895 (2020)

16. Oztemel, E., Gursev, S.: A taxonomy of industry 4.0 and related technologies. In: Industry 4.0-Current Status and Future Trends. IntechOpen (2020)

17. Tao, F., Zhang, H., Liu, A., Nee, A.Y.: Digital twin in industry: state-of-the-art. IEEE Trans. Ind. Inf. 15(4), 2405–2415 (2018)

18. Tuegel, E.J., Ingraffea, A.R., Eason, T.G., Spottswood, S.M.: Reengineering aircraft structural life prediction using a digital twin. Int. J. Aerosp. Eng. 2011, 14 (2011)

19. Wiendahl, H.P., et al.: Changeable manufacturing-classification, design and operation. CIRP Ann. 56(2), 783–809 (2007)

20. Wiendahl, H.P., Heger, C.: Justifying changeability. A methodical approach to achieving cost effectiveness. J. Manuf. Sci. Prod. 6(1–2), 33–40 (2004)

21. Xu, L.D., Xu, E.L., Li, L.: Industry 4.0: state of the art and future trends. Int. J. Prod. Res. 56 (8), 2941–2962 (2018)

22. Zheng, Yu., Yang, S., Cheng, H.: An application framework of digital twin and its case study. J. Ambient Intell. Humaniz. Comput. 10(3), 1141–1153 (2018). https://doi.org/10.1007/s12652-018-0911-3

# Reconfigurable Digitalized and Servitized Production Systems: Requirements and Challenges

Magdalena Paul[1(✉)], Audrey Cerqueus[2], Daniel Schneider[1],
Hichem Haddou Benderbal[3], Xavier Boucher[2], Damien Lamy[4],
and Gunther Reinhart[1]

[1] Institute for Machine Tools and Industrial Management, Technical University
of Munich, 85748 Garching, Germany
magdalena.paul@iwb.tum.de
[2] Mines Saint-Etienne, University of Clermont Auvergne, CNRS, UMR 6158
LIMOS, Institut Henri Fayol, 42023 Saint-Etienne, France
[3] IMT Atlantique, LS2N-CNRS, Nantes, France
[4] Mines Saint-Etienne, Institut Henri Fayol, 42023 Saint-Etienne, France

**Abstract.** Reconfigurable manufacturing systems (RMS) emerged in literature during the last two decades with the aim to respond to the rapid increase in product demand and variations. The implementation of such solutions in the industry is very recent and remains difficult. In this article, an analysis of the industrial requirements and challenges involving four key aspects of RDSS (reconfigurability, digitalization, servitization and sustainability) is based on semi-structured interviews conducted with representatives from the industry. Further, the identified requirements and challenges are compared to those extracted from an extensive literature review. The findings of the comparison are divided into technology and organization oriented issues and show a strong interconnection of the four key aspects: Digitalization offers possibilities for the implementation of sustainable systems, servitization creates the possibility for companies to achieve more flexibility through reconfigurable systems and the further development of RMS offers more possibilities for digitalization and thus a better adaptation to current requirements.

**Keywords:** Reconfigurability · Digitalization · Servitization · Sustainability

## 1 Introduction

Today's challenges in the manufacturing industry include the constantly changing requirements, a more volatile demand, increasingly varied products and new expectations in the field of sustainability. To meet these challenges, companies must deploy flexible and reconfigurable systems and operate them digitally within a network. Additionally, new business models and services can be applied. In [1] a framework was developed that shows the connection of digitalization, servitization and sustainability in the field of RMS. To apply the framework in the industry, it is important to understand the challenges and requirements that arise for companies when using reconfigurable,

B. Lalic et al. (Eds.): APMS 2020, IFIP AICT 592, pp. 501–508, 2020.
https://doi.org/10.1007/978-3-030-57997-5_58

digitized, servitized and sustainable (RDSS) systems. For that purpose, semi-structured interviews were conducted and their results were evaluated on the basis of an extensive literature analysis. This paper provides an overview of the technologically and organizationally oriented issues of using RDDS and explores whether the literature and interviews agree or disagree. The authors also provide an outlook on the future research needed in the field of RDSS.

## 2 Related Works

An RMS is defined as a system with several components that can be rearranged, moved and replaced quickly and reliably to adapt production in response to changes in market demand or technology [2]. This paper focuses on the requirements and challenges of digitalization, servitization and sustainability in RMS.

**Reconfigurable Manufacturing Systems.** RMS literature covers various areas, such as system design, process planning, scheduling and reconfigurable control [3]. One of the major issues found in the relevant literature is RMS design. The objective is to leverage their core characteristic (i.e. reconfigurability) to design responsive systems. For a system to be easily reconfigurable, certain characteristics such as modularity, integrability, convertibility, diagnosability, customization and scalability must be met [2], as well as automatability [4]. RMS design problems are more complex than those of conventional systems. This is due to (i) the system's dynamic capacities to change and to integrate change; and (ii) its properties, including reconfigurability, that emerge after the deployment of the manufacturing system [5]. The scalability of RMS is supported by adding or removing functionalities to maintain the lifecycle of the manufacturing system itself. To have the best responsiveness to change, system design must take into account reconfigurability from the outset [2]. The system perspective on production and design problems is favored for reconfigurability [4]. This implies that classical approaches will not necessarily lead to dynamically changeable systems. Besides, the designed system becomes quickly obsolete, when facing market variations, rather than achieving reconfigurability. Therefore, existing approaches and methodologies need to be adapted for designing systems with dynamic capacity by including the essential parameters for reconfigurability developed.

**Digitalization of Reconfigurable Production Systems.** Based on the recent advancements in technologies in Industry 4.0 and digitalization, the development of RMS and modern manufacturing systems is entering a new era [6]. New technologies enable RMS to adapt quickly to changing conditions. Zangiacomi et al. derive from a case study on the implementation of Industry 4.0 strategies and methods in the manufacturing industry that the definition of company-specific strategies is needed to avoid standalone implementations of new technologies [7]. Koren et al. show that techniques for big data and cyber physical manufacturing systems can improve the design of RMS [6]. Based on advanced monitoring and analysis capabilities, intelligent real-time maintenance and production planning decisions can be made more effectively and intelligently. Nevertheless, current infrastructures are often not fully prepared to support digital transformation [8]. Based on new infrastructures, two current research-oriented approaches could yield operational results: (i) the exploitation of data science and analysis and their scalability in digitized production environments; (ii) the development of digital twin with value-added decision-making services [9]. Furthermore, manufacturers' security concerns, especially vulnerability to interference and cyber-attacks, increase with prevalence of increasingly digitized environments [10].

**Servitization of Reconfigurable Production Systems.** Until now, scientific literature has developed the fields of manufacturing servitization and RMS as two distinct fields. Yet, a strong convergence can be highlighted. Brad and Murar underline that Product Service Systems and RMS share 'patterns towards similar goals', with RMS focusing specifically on manufacturing environments [11]. The convergence can be emphasized on three levels: The first level of RMS servitization considers the business model (BM) supporting the deployment of RMS. Determining and modeling key strategical aspects of the BM configuration is crucial for the design of reconfigurable systems. The second level is the system level, i.e. reconfigurability management at the level of a production segment, line or station. At this level, servitization of RMS leads first to taking into account that the overall functionality of any production system component involves both tangible technological components and intangible value-added of associated services and secondly, that the implemented services could ensure an optimum interoperability and reconfigurability of all the subsystems. Key challenges are associated with (i) digital interoperability of these subsystems [11], (ii) organizational management and planning of both manufacturing and service operations [12], (iii) modularity of both service and products, but also (iv) the need of decision-making solutions for managing the organizational performance of the changing configurations in an existing RMS. At a third level, RMS servitization has to be addressed at the operational level of manufacturing resource reconfigurability. This issue is more usual in literature [13], but key questions remain with regard to the adaptability of such solutions to small and medium enterprises and the integration of new artificial intelligence solutions, to increase the added value of manufacturing life cycle traceability.

**Sustainability in Reconfigurable Production Systems.** In recent years, new objectives emerged for the design of production systems such as sustainability and reducing waste [14]. Faulkner et al. propose a methodology for improving the sustainability performance of a manufacturing line, which covers the three pillars of sustainability, namely economic, environmental and societal aspects [15]. More recently, [16] argues that RMS level of sustainability is an important aspect requiring investigation. Liu et al. study and model the energy consumption of a system as a multi-objective problem for sustainable RMS design [17]. The performance of the RMS is evaluated using criteria for energy-related costs, throughput and storage costs. Zhang et al. introduce the concept of energy-efficient RMS (REMS) and design a discrete event simulation model to evaluate the system's energy efficiency [18]. Meanwhile, the recent survey provided in [19] shows that if many possibilities can be addressed by RMS, as demonstrated in the literature, only a few research projects actually consider reconfiguration as an instrument for energy efficiency and sustainability in production.

# 3  Methodology

In order to better understand the industry's requirements and challenges regarding RMS, the authors conducted interviews with representatives from different industries in Germany and France. The structure of these interviews was derived from an analysis of the industrial needs and framework presented in [1]. The goal is to identify more precisely the needs of the industry for tools to help with the implementation and operation of reconfigurable systems. The survey focused primarily on four topics: reconfigurability, digitalization, sustainability, and servitization. Industry experts from 10 different companies were interviewed. The criteria of the quantitative research developed by [20] were followed to ensure valid, easy-to-generate, reliable, and objective results. The interviews were carried out in a semi-structured way, individually drawing out increasingly specific evidence regarding the interviewee's assets. 6 out of 10 companies are active in the mechanical engineering sector, 2 in the automotive sector and 2 in the aerospace sector. The interviewees fill different positions in the companies, ranging from management to technical development as well as production planners and managers. 5 of the companies can be classified as providers of production systems, all being part of the mechanical engineering sector and 5 companies are users of production systems.

# 4  Results

**Reconfigurability.** The interviews showed that reconfigurability as a concept is known to most of the companies. All interviewees express the need for a flexible or reconfigurable production system in order to adapt to the quick changes in demand. However, the perception and level of maturity regarding reconfigurability varies significantly between the companies and mainly depends on the size of the company. While large companies are either pursuing extensive research in this field or are already using RMS production systems, mid-sized companies view reconfiguration more as the process of retrofitting, which is still often done manually. One interviewee, a provider of customized production systems, deals with machines very differently. As development costs cannot be shared among various customers or products, it would be too expensive to design each of these machines as reconfigurable ones. Other companies are trying to tackle this problem by modularizing certain functional parts of their machines to make reconfiguration possible. Other providers of production solutions, however, expect increasingly reconfigurable production systems in the future and adapt their services and products accordingly.

**Digitalization.** Regardless of their size, companies see potential in collecting and using production data. Such data are collected in order to optimize the production system, to forecast demand or to implement predictive maintenance. However, unreliable and unexploited data, low levels of digitalization and redundancy of the software used lead, especially for SMEs, to a considerable lack of holistic integration and to interface problems. The interviewees cite digital consistency as a main prerequisite for flexible production systems, whose degree of abstraction must be considered when dealing with RMS. In addition, data security is a major challenge that still needs to be overcome, since the fear of excessive transparency in the transfer of sensitive data to third parties deters medium-sized companies from implementing digitization solutions. These problems make it difficult for large companies to further improve the level of digitalization among their customers. However, they also see economic potential for themselves, since many customers have a considerable need for further support in the transformation phase towards more digitized or even reconfigurable production. Model-based approaches are helpful, in which virtual models or digital twins are used to facilitate and support digitization efforts.

**Sustainability.** The conducted interviews also concerned the effects of RMS on the sustainability of production systems. The interest in sustainability aspects varies and depends on whether the companies are providing or using reconfigurable production systems. For users of reconfigurable systems, possible financial improvements resulting from the implementation of RMS on an operational level and the possibility of avoiding fines after regulatory changes are most important. Furthermore, being able to control the system's energy consumption and to schedule production in periods of low-cost energy are adding to both the economic and ecological potential. Additionally, RMS enable the socially appropriate alignment of employees' skills with the new tools of the production systems and externalization of highly specific skills by experts. On the other hand, providers increasingly emphasize the substantial impact RMS have on the sustainability of production systems, considering the whole lifecycle of production systems and the ecological impact of re-using production machines, in addition to economical and human viewpoints. It was thus observed that flexible/reconfigurable production systems are currently the most efficient way for large companies to fulfill the production program. Furthermore, the interviews highlighted the importance of developing metrics for measuring the sustainability of RMS. A return on investment indicator considering the possibilities posed by reconfigurability, a measure of costs and benefits from an ecological standpoint and a metric for reconfigurability potential could help decision-makers to adopt RMS.

**Servitization.** Many of the interviewed companies were familiar with the concept of servitization. However, most of the interviewed companies raised the concern of knowledge loss, which might arise in conjunction with servitizing certain parts of their production, as significant technological know-how might be exposed. If introduced, the companies would, therefore, start implementing servitized production processes in the field of secondary rather than primary processes. Furthermore, the technical prerequisites would have to be clearly defined. The companies did express a strong interest and would further consider it, especially if profitable use cases were presented. Other than that, two providers of production systems showed an interest in production management as a service. The first one seeks a closer relationship with its client by developing tools based on production data. The second one considers digital twins to be an opportunity to offer certain production management tasks as a service. Holistic approaches seem to be very difficult to develop because of the huge variety of possible tasks. However, digital twin solutions, which focus only on specific problems like bottleneck analysis, predictive maintenance or scheduling, could be more feasible due to the corresponding high complexity. For a smaller specialized provider, servitization is not attractive, as financial effort to keep their customers' production systems up to date would have to be underpinned by the company itself. The company currently benefits greatly from this circumstance by frequently selling new machines. The belief that manufacturing as a service leads to considerable cannibalization effects does prevail.

## 5  Discussion

Taking into account the results of the literature research and the interviews, a comparison between academic and industrial challenges is presented. The gap between these two visions is shown in Table 1, emphasizing that despite the shared vision of industry and academics on the importance of the four key issues, considerable work remains to be done to enable their consistent integration into business practice.

**Table 1.** Key factors relating to the gap between industrial and academic visions

| Technology oriented issues | |
| --- | --- |
| **RMS.** All industrial companies are very concerned about flexibility and are aware of the challenges of reconfigurability, but RMS often seem not to be adapted to their proper context yet. The literature is mainly concerned with an elaborate complex design of RMS, but understandable and cost-effective systems are a key factor, especially for small companies. For some companies, flexibility through modularization is more feasible than reconfigurability | **Digitalization.** Appears to be the topic most frequently addressed by the industry and the one with the least differences between literature and industry practice. There is a significant gap between the technical possibilities of future or current data-related technologies and the current basis for possible use. The interviews also showed a need for the development of new tools that enable software interoperability, especially for the integration of machines into old systems |
| **Organization oriented issues** | |
| **Servitization.** Many companies integrate servitization in their market offer. Integrating it at the level of the inner industrial model with 'manufacturing as a service' is still at a very early stage of development. Especially large companies worry about the loss of know-how and are opposed to service models for primary activities. There is a lack of new relevant business model ideas here | **Sustainability.** Shared agreement on the importance of research in sustainability, with two key industrial focal points (energy, competence). Sustainability is still considered as a secondary factor with no specific urgency. There is a lot of research on energy efficiency, but implementation is still poor. The potential of RMS to enhance sustainability remains unexploited in industry |

Other general conclusions can be highlighted. Firstly, digitalization appears to be a key factor for industrial/academic convergence and thus for further research into a new generation of RMS. Secondly, the four key concepts seem to be strongly linked. In addition, linking the aspects together may lead to the possibility of a further dimension.

Digitalization offers possibilities for the implementation of sustainable systems, while servitization offers companies the possibility to create more flexibility through reconfigurable systems and further development of the technology RMS can create more possibilities for their digitalization and thus a better adaptation to current requirements.

# 6 Conclusion

This paper highlights the needs and challenges of the industrial application regarding reconfigurability, RMS digitalization, RMS servitization and RMS sustainability, comparing them to the ones referred to in the literature. The strong interconnection of these four topics and their complementarity makes it a strong value added for further research steps. With acceptability and adopting practices being two of the main concerns for companies, it is a significant requirement for research and will necessitate to demonstrate increases in performance over the entire lifecycles through suitable indicator systems and specific demonstrators. An in-depth analysis of both the literature and the industrial interviews will be used to update the framework previously presented in [1], in particular by focusing on the requirements of decision support tools with the aim to be used as a research roadmap.

**Acknowledgment.** The research is developed with the support of the Franco-German Alliance for Factory Supported by the Federal Ministry of Education and Research (BMBF) and the Free State of Bavaria under the Excellence Strategy of the Federal Government and the Länder, and the French alliance for the industry of the future, in the context of the German-French Academy for the Industry of the Future of Institut Mines-Télécom (IMT) and Technical University of Munich (TUM).

# References

1. Boucher, X., et al.: Towards reconfigurable digitalized and servitized manufacturing systems: conceptual framework. In: Ameri, F., Stecke, K.E., von Cieminski, G., Kiritsis, D. (eds.) APMS 2019. IAICT, vol. 566, pp. 214–222. Springer, Cham (2019). https://doi.org/10.1007/978-3-030-30000-5_28
2. Koren, Y., Heisel, U., Jovanc, F., et al.: Reconfigurable manufacturing systems. CIRP Ann. **48**(2), 527–540 (1999). https://doi.org/10.1016/S0007-8506(07)63232-6
3. Bortolini, M., Galizia, F.G., Mora, C.: Reconfigurable manufacturing systems: literature review and research trend. J. Manuf. Syst. **49**, 93–106 (2018). https://doi.org/10.1016/j.jmsy.2018.09.005
4. ElMaraghy, H.A., Wiendahl, H.-P.: Changeability – an introduction. In: ElMaraghy, H.A. (ed.) Changeable and Reconfigurable Manufacturing Systems, vol. 55, pp. 3–24. Springer, London (2009)
5. Andersen, A.-L.: Development of Changeable and Reconfigurable Manufacturing Systems. Aalborg University Press (2017)
6. Koren, Y., Gu, X., Guo, W.: Reconfigurable manufacturing systems: Principles, design, and future trends. Front. Mech. Eng. **13**(2), 121–136 (2017). https://doi.org/10.1007/s11465-018-0483-0

7. Zangiacomi, A., Pessot, E., Fornasiero, R., et al.: Moving towards digitalization: a multiple case study in manufacturing. Prod. Plan. Control **31**(2–3), 143–157 (2020). https://doi.org/10.1080/09537287.2019.1631468

8. Xu, L.D., Xu, E.L., Li, L.: Industry 4.0: state of the art and future trends. Int. J. Prod. Res. **56** (8), 2941–2962 (2018). https://doi.org/10.1080/00207543.2018.1444806

9. Zhang, C., Zhou, G., He, J., et al.: A data- and knowledge-driven framework for digital twin manufacturing cell. Procedia CIRP **83**, 345–350 (2019). https://doi.org/10.1016/j.procir.2019.04.084

10. Fatorachian H, Kazemi H (2018) A critical investigation of Industry 4.0 in manufacturing: theoretical operationalisation framework. Production Planning & Control 29(8): 633–644. https://doi.org/10.1080/09537287.2018.1424960

11. Brad, S., Murar, M.: Employing smart units and servitization towards reconfigurability of manufacturing processes. Procedia CIRP **30**, 498–503 (2015). https://doi.org/10.1016/j.procir.2015.02.154

12. Delaram, J., Valilai, O.F.: A novel solution for manufacturing interoperability fulfillment using interoperability service providers. Procedia CIRP **63**, 774–779 (2017). https://doi.org/10.1016/j.procir.2017.03.141

13. Pourabdollahian, G., Copani, G.: Toward development of pss-oriented business models for micro-manufacturing. Procedia CIRP **47**, 507–512 (2016). https://doi.org/10.1016/j.procir.2016.03.220

14. Jawahir, I.S., Badurdeen, F., Rouch, K.E.: Innovation in sustainable manufacturing education. Technische Universität Berlin (2013)

15. Faulkner, W., Templeton, W., Gullett, D., Badurdeen, F.: Visualizing sustainability performance of manufacturing systems using sustainable value stream mapping: In: 2012 International Conference on Industrial Engineering and Operations Management (2012)

16. Huang, A., Badurdeen, F., Jawahir, I.S.: Towards developing sustainable reconfigurable manufacturing systems. Procedia Manuf. **17**, 1136–1143 (2018). https://doi.org/10.1016/j.promfg.2018.10.024

17. Liu, M., An, L., Zhang, J., et al.: Energy-oriented bi-objective optimisation for a multi-module reconfigurable manufacturing system. Int. J. Prod. Res. **57**(19), 5974–5995 (2019). https://doi.org/10.1080/00207543.2018.1556413

18. Zhang, J., Li, Z., Frey, G.: Simulation and analysis of reconfigurable assembly systems based on R-TNCES. J. Chin. Inst. Eng. **41**(6), 494–502 (2018). https://doi.org/10.1080/02533839.2018.1504694

19. Battaïa, O., Benyoucef, L., Delorme, X., Dolgui, A., Thevenin, S.: Sustainable and energy efficient reconfigurable manufacturing systems. In: Benyoucef, L. (ed.) Reconfigurable Manufacturing Systems: From Design to Implementation. SSAM, pp. 179–191. Springer, Cham (2020). https://doi.org/10.1007/978-3-030-28782-5_9

20. Denzin, N.K., Lincoln, Y.S. (eds.): The SAGE Handbook of Qualitative Research, 5th edn. SAGE, Los Angeles (2018)

# The Impact of Dynamic Tasks Assignment in Paced Mixed-Model Assembly Line with Moving Workers

S. Ehsan Hashemi-Petroodi[1]([✉]), Simon Thevenin[1], Sergey Kovalev[2], and Alexandre Dolgui[1]

[1] IMT Atlantique, LS2N, CNRS, La Chantrerie, 4, rue Alfred Kastler, B.P. 20722, 44307 Nantes Cedex 3, France
{seyyed-ehsan.hashemi-petroodi,simon.thevenin, alexandre.dolgui}@imt-atlantique.fr
[2] INSEEC Business School, 25 rue de l'Université, 69007 Lyon, France
skovalev@inseec.com

**Abstract.** With the rise of mass customization, manufacturing companies are increasingly adopting mixed-model assembly lines. These lines can produce multiple products instead of a single one in a dedicated manufacturing system. Consequently, mixed-model assembly lines can benefit from reconfigurations of the workforce and equipment to adjust the line to the production requirements. This study investigates the impact of dynamic task assignment on the design of a mixed-model assembly line with walking workers. In the dynamic task assignment strategy, the assignment of tasks to stations changes depending on the item sequence. In this work, we propose a scenario-based integer linear program to design such an assembly line. The numerical results show that the dynamic task assignment strategy significantly reduces the number of required workers when compared to the fixed task assignment strategy, but it slightly increases the total equipment costs.

**Keywords:** Mixed-model assembly line · Reconfigurability · Workforce assignment · Dynamic task assignment

## 1 Introduction

With the rise of mass customization, various manufacturing companies have transformed their dedicated manufacturing systems into mixed-model assembly lines (MMAL) [14]. Such lines can assemble different items in any sequence, and the manufactured items can be significantly different from one another. Lines with moving workers are superior in such circumstances since the workers can move from a station to another to adjust the station's capacity to the set of items on the line [2]. As a result, mixed-model assembly lines with moving workers are common in practice, for instance in the automotive industry [1].

© IFIP International Federation for Information Processing 2020
Published by Springer Nature Switzerland AG 2020
B. Lalic et al. (Eds.): APMS 2020, IFIP AICT 592, pp. 509–517, 2020.
https://doi.org/10.1007/978-3-030-57997-5_59

In this work, we investigate the impact of dynamic task reassignment on the design of the MMAL with moving workers. In the dynamic task assignment strategy, the assignment of tasks to stations changes depending on the item sequence. In practice, this dynamic task assignment requires the flexible assembly equipment [3], and the equipment selection is a complex decision since the most flexible pieces of equipment are often the most expensive. In other words, the objective is to select the equipment with the right level of flexibility (flexible enough to reassign the tasks for each predefined item sequence, but not too flexible to reduce the costs).

Task reassignments along with worker movements adjust the line to the production requirements. Consequently, these strategies increase the reconfigurability of the assembly line. Note that we use the term reconfigurability rather than flexibility since worker movements modify the line's characteristics by a physical change of the system [8]. This definition is in line with the literature on Reconfigurable Manufacturing System [13], where a system is said reconfigurable if its components can be added, removed, or moved. The reconfiguration takes place to create the capacity and functionality that is needed, when it is needed.

The present paper proposes a scenario-based integer linear program (ILP) for the design of a MMAL with moving workers and task reassignments. Such a problem integrates operational decisions in the design of the MMAL. The design stage assigns the equipment to the work stations. At the operational level, the production sequence is revealed, and the tasks and workers are assigned to the stations. The objective is to design a line that respects the takt time for all given item sequences, and that minimizes the cost related to the workers and equipment. We conduct a numerical comparison between the fixed and dynamic task assignment strategies. Our results suggest that the dynamic task reassignment allows to significantly reduce the number of required workers when the equipment cost is low.

The paper is organized as follows. A short literature review is given in Sect. 2. Section 3 gives the problem description, a simple example, and an integer linear program. Section 4 presents some numerical experiments. Finally, the paper ends with the conclusion and some future research directions in Sect. 5.

## 2   Literature Review

In the literature on MMAL balancing, each task is usually assigned to a single station [10]. A few works exist on the dynamic task assignment in MMAL balancing for different production environments, such as parallel two-sided MMAL with fixed workers (working at both sides) [e.g., 14], or MMAL with fixed workers [e.g., 4]. For instance, in [14], the assignment of tasks to the stations depends on the production cycle, where a production cycle corresponds to different combinations of models. However, to the best of our knowledge, there exists no work on the design of the MMAL with moving workers and task reassignment. In the literature on the MMAL balancing with moving workers, the tasks assigned to the stations are either fixed or given [e.g., 1,6,9,12]. The present work aims to fill this gap in the literature. Indeed, the decisions on task and workforce assignment must be made simultaneously, since any change in task assignment may imply changes in workforce assignment [5].

# 3    Problem Description

To describe the problem, the general characteristics of the MMAL is presented below, before stating the assumptions related to the equipment and workers.

We consider a MMAL with a set $S = \{1 \ldots S\}$ of stations. The line produces a set $I = \{1 \ldots I\}$ of models, which flow in any order through the line. These models flow from one station to the next at regular time intervals $C$, called takt time. Each model $i$ requires a set $O_i$ of tasks. We denote $O$ the set of all tasks. Moreover, we consider the precedence relationship between the tasks, and $(o, o')$ is in the set of precedence $A$ if task $o$ must be performed before task $o'$.

To process a task, the required equipment must be available at the station. More precisely, each task $o$ requires exactly one equipment that must be fixed to the station, and the set of equipment is denoted $\mathcal{E}$. The parameters $R_{oe}$ equals 1 if equipment $e$ is able to perform task $o$, and each equipment $e$ has a cost $c_{se}$ at each station $s$. In this study, the workers can move from a station to another at any takt time, and the processing time $p_{io}^l$ of each task $o$ of model $i$ depends on the number $l$ of workers on the station. Workers are assumed fully skilled and identical, and their movement time between stations is negligible.

**Table 1.** Compatibility between tasks and equipment, and the cost of equipment in each station.

|  | Task 1 | Task 2 | Task 3 | Task 4 | Task 5 | Station 1 | Station 2 |
|---|---|---|---|---|---|---|---|
| Equipment 1 | ✓ |  |  |  |  | 100 | 110 |
| Equipment 2 |  | ✓ | ✓ | ✓ |  | 130 | 150 |
| Equipment 3 | ✓ |  | ✓ | ✓ | ✓ | 170 | 200 |
| Equipment 4 | ✓ | ✓ | ✓ | ✓ | ✓ | 220 | 250 |

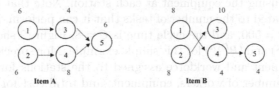

**Fig. 1.** The precedence graph of the simple example.

At the design stage, the problem (denoted $P^{Dyn}$) is to decide the number $Y$ of workers and the positions of the equipment (the variable $w_{se}$ equals 1 if equipment $e$ is at station $s$, and 0 otherwise). At the operational stage, the sequence $\omega$ of items is known at the beginning of the day, and $P^{Dyn}$ is to assign the tasks and workers to the stations. To evaluate the impact of the dynamic task assignment, we also consider the problem with fixed task assignments (denoted $P^{Fix}$). More precisely, $P^{Fix}$ is similar to $P^{Dyn}$, but the tasks are assigned to the stations at the design stage, and their assignment is the same for all sequences at the operational stage.

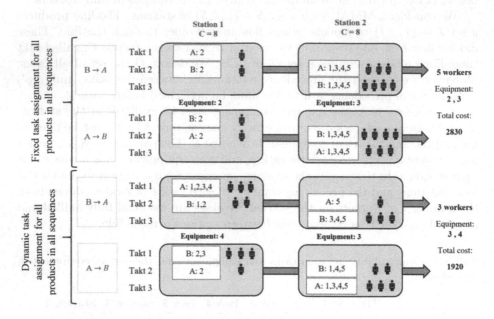

**Fig. 2.** The optimal solution of $P^{Fix}$ and $P^{Dyn}$ in the simple example.

To clarify the problem, we provide a simple example with two stations, two models A and B, and the two possible sequences (A; B) and (B; A). Figure 1 gives the precedence graphs and processing times for each item with a common set of 5 tasks. Table 1 presents the compatibility between equipment and tasks, and the cost of using the equipment at each station. Note that the cost of each equipment is related to the number of tasks that it can perform. Finally, the cost of a worker is $\alpha = 500$, and the cycle time is $C = 8$. Figure 2 shows the optimal solution of ($P^{Fix}$) and ($P^{Dyn}$) for this simple example. More precisely, Fig. 2 gives the task, equipment and workforce assigned to the stations for each sequence, as well as the number of workers, equipment, and total cost for the worst takt. The optimal solution of ($P^{Fix}$) requires 5 workers and a total equipment and workforce cost of 2830, whereas ($P^{Dyn}$) leads to a solution with 3 workers and a total equipment and workforce cost of 1920.

The mathematical formulation of $P^{Dyn}$ (1)–(11) relies on the set $\Omega$ of all possible item sequences. Given a sequence $\omega$, we can infer the station $s_{it}^{\omega}$ where item $i$ is at each takt. Similarly, $i_s^{t\omega}$ denotes the item at station $s$ at takt $t$ for sequence $\omega$. The operational decisions (affectation of workers and tasks) depend on the sequence, and they require to define three decision variables.

- $b_{sl}^{\omega t}$ equals 1 if there are $l$ workers at station $s$ in period $t$ for sequence $\omega$ (with $l \in \mathcal{L} = \{1 \ldots l_{max}\}$), and 0 otherwise.
- $b_{oil}^{\omega t}$ equals 1 if $l$ workers perform task $o$ of item $i$ in period $t$ for sequence $\omega$, and 0 otherwise.
- $x_{soi}^{\omega}$ equals 1 if task $o$ of item $i$ is performed on station $s$ for sequence $\omega$, and 0 otherwise.

$$\min \quad \alpha\, Y + \sum_{s \in S} \sum_{e \in \mathcal{E}} w_{se} c_{se} \tag{1}$$

s.t.

$$\sum_{s \in S} \sum_{l=1}^{l_{max}} l\, b_{sl}^{\omega t} \leqslant Y \qquad \omega \in \Omega,\ t \in \mathcal{T} \tag{2}$$

$$\sum_{l=1}^{l_{max}} b_{sl}^{\omega t} = 1 \qquad s \in S,\ \omega \in \Omega,\ t \in \mathcal{T} \tag{3}$$

$$\sum_{s \in S} x_{soi}^{\omega} = 1 \qquad \omega \in \Omega,\ o \in O,\ i \in I \tag{4}$$

$$b_{oil}^{\omega t} \leqslant x_{soi}^{\omega} \qquad l \in \mathcal{L},\ \omega \in \Omega,\ o \in O,\ i \in I,\ t \in \mathcal{T},\ s = s_{it}^{\omega} \tag{5}$$

$$b_{oil}^{\omega t} \leqslant b_{sl}^{\omega t} \qquad l \in \mathcal{L},\ \omega \in \Omega,\ o \in O,\ i \in I,\ t \in \mathcal{T},\ s = s_{it}^{\omega} \tag{6}$$

$$b_{oil}^{\omega t} \geqslant b_{sl}^{\omega t} + x_{soi}^{\omega} - 1 \qquad l \in \mathcal{L},\ \omega \in \Omega,\ o \in O,\ i \in I,\ t \in \mathcal{T},\ s = s_{it}^{\omega} \tag{7}$$

$$\sum_{o \in N_i} \sum_{l=1}^{l_{max}} p_{io}^{l}\, b_{oil}^{\omega t} \leqslant C \qquad \omega \in \Omega,\ t \in \mathcal{T},\ s \in S,\ i = i_s^{t\omega} \tag{8}$$

$$x_{soi}^{\omega} \leqslant \sum_{e \in E} R_{oe} w_{se} \qquad s \in S,\ o \in O,\ i \in I,\ \omega \in \Omega \tag{9}$$

$$\sum_{s \in S} s\, x_{soi}^{\omega} \leqslant \sum_{s' \in S} s'\, x_{s'o'i}^{\omega} \qquad (o, o') \in A_i,\ i \in I,\ \omega \in \Omega \tag{10}$$

$$x_{soi}^{\omega},\ b_{sl}^{\omega t},\ w_{se} \in \{0, 1\} \qquad \text{and} \qquad Y \geqslant 0 \qquad \text{and} \qquad b_{oil}^{\omega t} \leqslant 1 \tag{11}$$

The objective function (1) is to minimize the costs associated with the workers and equipment amortization, where $\alpha$ represents the salary of a worker. Constraints (2) prevent to affect more workers to the stations than the total number of workers. Constraints (3) state that a single number of worker must be chosen for each station in each takt and sequence. Constraints (4) state that each task must be affected to a single station for each sequence. The constraints (5), (6), and (7) compute the value of $b_{oil}^{\omega t}$ based on the values of $b_{sl}^{\omega t}$ and $x_{soi}^{\omega}$. Finally, constraints (8), (9) (10) give the classical takt time, equipment, and precedence constraints, respectively.

The mathematical formulation of $P^{Fix}$ is similar to (1)–(11), but the assignment of tasks to stations is a design decision. Therefore, they do not depend on the sequence and constraint (12) is added to (1)–(11).

$$x_{soi}^{\omega} = x_{soi'}^{\omega'} \quad \omega, \ \omega' \in \Omega, \quad t \in \mathcal{T}, \quad o \in O, \quad i, i' \in \mathcal{I}, \quad s = s_{it}^{\omega} \qquad (12)$$

## 4   Numerical Experiments

The numerical experiments are performed with instances generated by extending the well known simple assembly line balancing instances from [15]. To generate an instance with $I$ items and $|O|$ tasks, the precedence graph and processing times of each item $i$ correspond to different instances from [15] with $|O|$ tasks. These instances have been generated with different order strength values (in the range [0, 1]), where a high order strength value refers to a dense precedence graph. More precisely, each of our instances merges $I$ consecutive (sorted by ascending order of instance's numbers) instances of [15] with a specific order strength range. In this work, we consider the instances with 3 items, 3 stations, and 5 takts ($I = 3, S = 3, T = 5$). $\Omega$ includes all possible sequences with a single unit of each item ($|\Omega| = 3! = 6$). The cycle time is set to 1000. The equipment costs at each station are generated randomly in the range [100, 300]. Two different values for workers salary are considered ($\alpha = \{500, 50\}$). Finally, the matrix of compatibility between tasks and equipment is generated manually such that an expensive equipment is able to perform a wide range of tasks. The resulting matrix is given in Table 2.

**Table 2.** Compatibility matrix of equipment and tasks (T1–T20).

| | T1 | T2 | T3 | T4 | T5 | T6 | T7 | T8 | T9 | T10 | T11 | T12 | T13 | T14 | T15 | T16 | T17 | T18 | T19 | T20 |
|---|---|---|---|---|---|---|---|---|---|---|---|---|---|---|---|---|---|---|---|---|
| Equipment 1 | 1 | 0 | 0 | 0 | 0 | 1 | 0 | 0 | 0 | 1 | 0 | 0 | 0 | 1 | 0 | 0 | 0 | 0 | 0 | 0 |
| Equipment 2 | 0 | 1 | 0 | 0 | 0 | 0 | 1 | 0 | 0 | 1 | 0 | 1 | 0 | 0 | 0 | 0 | 1 | 0 | 1 | 1 |
| Equipment 3 | 0 | 0 | 1 | 1 | 1 | 0 | 0 | 0 | 1 | 0 | 0 | 1 | 1 | 1 | 0 | 1 | 0 | 1 | 0 | 0 |
| Equipment 4 | 0 | 1 | 0 | 0 | 1 | 1 | 0 | 1 | 0 | 1 | 1 | 0 | 1 | 0 | 1 | 1 | 0 | 0 | 0 | 1 |
| Equipment 5 | 1 | 0 | 1 | 1 | 0 | 0 | 1 | 1 | 1 | 1 | 1 | 0 | 0 | 0 | 1 | 0 | 1 | 1 | 1 | 0 |

The mathematical model is solved with CPLEX 12.9, and the numerical experiments are run on a processor Intel(R) Core(TM) i7-8650U CPU @ 1.90 GHz 2.11 GHz with a time limit of one hour. As our goal is to investigate the benefit of dynamic task assignment, we provide the results for the instances which were solved optimally within one hour.

Table 3 gives for each order strength the average total cost, number of workers, number of equipment duplications (Nr. Dup.), and execution time in second for $P^{Fix}$ and $P^{Dyn}$, as well as the percentage gap between the total costs in $P^{Fix}$ and $P^{Dyn}$ (see Eq. (13)). Note that the instances of [15] do not cover all the order strength ranges, for instance, there is no instance with order strength in $[0.4, 0.5)$. The dynamic task affectation in $P^{Dyn}$ leads to a lower number of workers (4 and 7 workers in average when $\alpha$ is equal to 500 and 50, respectively) than the fixed task assignment in $P^{Fix}$ (6.1 and 7.5 workers in average when $\alpha$ is equal to 500 and 50, respectively), but slightly larger equipment cost (1168.6 versus 1012.2 in average when $\alpha = 500$, and 712.2 versus 710.4 in average when $\alpha = 50$) and smaller total cost. In addition, $P^{Dyn}$ is harder to solve with an average execution time of 483 s versus 56.7 s for $P^{Fix}$. When the workers salary decreases ($\alpha = 50$), both problems are solved faster, but $P^{Dyn}$ is still harder to solve (102.2 s versus 28.9 s in average). Besides, a large order strength increases the average number of workers and total cost for both $P^{Fix}$ and $P^{Dyn}$. Finally, the dynamic task assignment is preferable in both cases when $\alpha = \{500, 50\}$, but manufacturers should use the dynamic task assignment when the amortization cost of equipment is lower than the cost of workers (e.g. steering column assembly in the automotive industry [11]).

$$Gap = \frac{Cost(P^{Fix}) - Cost(P^{Dyn})}{Cost(P^{Fix})} * 100 \tag{13}$$

**Table 3.** Number of workers and equipment cost in the optimal solutions of $P^{Dyn}$ and $P^{Fix}$.

| Order strength | Nr. instances | $\alpha$ | Fixed task assignment | | | | | Dynamic task assignment | | | | | Gap (%) |
|---|---|---|---|---|---|---|---|---|---|---|---|---|---|
| | | | Cost | Eq. cost | Y | Nr. Dup | CPU | Cost | Eq. cost | Y | Nr. Dup | CPU | |
| [0.1, 0.2) | 53 | 500 | 3566.4 | 936.9 | 5.2 | 1.15 | 73 | 2811.1 | 1086.8 | 3.5 | 1.56 | 342 | 21.1 |
| | | 50 | 986.2 | 646.6 | 6.8 | 0.03 | 48 | 979.8 | 648.6 | 6.6 | 0.03 | 165 | 0.7 |
| [0.2, 0.3) | 41 | 500 | 3707.8 | 976.1 | 5.4 | 1.14 | 96 | 2925.6 | 1084.1 | 3.7 | 1.63 | 648 | 21 |
| | | 50 | 1035.1 | 685.1 | 7 | 0.14 | 32 | 1009.7 | 679.2 | 6.6 | 0.12 | 121 | 2.4 |
| [0.3, 0.4) | 9 | 500 | 3883.3 | 1105.5 | 5.5 | 1.8 | 68 | 3105.5 | 1161.1 | 4 | 2.1 | 397 | 20 |
| | | 50 | 1107.7 | 746.6 | 7.2 | 0.33 | 45 | 1063.3 | 746.6 | 6.3 | 0.33 | 96 | 4 |
| [0.8, 0.9) | 73 | 500 | 4659.7 | 1056.9 | 7.2 | 1.8 | 20 | 3627.2 | 1305.3 | 4.6 | 2.24 | 503 | 22.1 |
| | | 50 | 1185 | 766.5 | 8.3 | 0.65 | 10 | 1161.6 | 772.6 | 7.7 | 0.61 | 46 | 2 |
| Average | All | 500 | 4069 | 1012.2 | 6.1 | 1.46 | 56.7 | 3191.3 | 1168.6 | 4 | 1.89 | 483 | 21.5 |
| | | 50 | 1086.3 | 710.4 | 7.5 | 0.33 | 28.9 | 1066.4 | 712.2 | 7 | 0.31 | 102.2 | 1.8 |

## 5   Conclusion

In this paper, we propose a scenario-based integer linear problem to design a mixed-model assembly line with dynamic task assignment and moving workers. Our computational experiments suggest that dynamic task assignment leads to significant cost savings when it is compared to the fixed task assignment strategy. However, the resulting optimization problem is difficult to solve. Consequently, the future works concern the design of efficient exact methods or (meta-)heuristics to solve the large scale instances. Besides, future works include the evaluation of the ergonomic impact of such dynamic assembly lines on the well being of the workers. On the one hand, this dynamic context may have some side effects in terms of ergonomics (e.g., workers get stress or over-loaded). On the other hand, job rotation is often used to reduce the exposure to ergonomics risks [7,16]. Finally, the considered problem can be extended to the context of hybrid human-robot collaboration systems, where dynamic task assignments is common. This extension requires to account for non-identical resources (e.g., different speed), resources skills, movable equipment, etc.

**Acknowledgement.** The authors of this paper would like to thank the Region Pays de la Loire, France (www.paysdelaloire.fr).

# References

1. Battaïa, O., et al.: Workforce minimization for a mixed-model assembly line in the automotive industry. Int. J. Prod. Econ. **170**, 489–500 (2015)
2. Biele, A., Mönch, L.: Hybrid approaches to optimize mixed-model assembly lines in low-volume manufacturing. J. Heuristics **24**(1), 49–81 (2017). https://doi.org/10.1007/s10732-017-9357-6
3. Bukchin, J., Tzur, M.: Design of flexible assembly line to minimize equipment cost. IIE Trans. **32**(7), 585–598 (2000). https://doi.org/10.1023/A:1007646714909
4. Choi, G.: A goal programming mixed-model line balancing for processing time and physical workload. Comput. Ind. Eng. **57**(1), 395–400 (2009)
5. Cortez, P.M., Costa, A.M.: Sequencing mixed-model assembly lines operating with a heterogeneous workforce. Int. J. Prod. Res. **53**(11), 3419–3432 (2015)
6. Delorme, X., Dolgui, A., Kovalev, S., Kovalyov, M.Y.: Minimizing the number of workers in a paced mixed-model assembly line. Eur. J. Oper. Res. **272**(1), 188–194 (2019)
7. Diego-Mas, J.A.: Designing cyclic job rotations to reduce the exposure to ergonomics risk factors. Int. J. Environ. Res. Public Health **17**(3), 1073 (2020)
8. Dolgui, A., Hashemi-Petroodi, S.E., Kovalev, S., Kovalyov, M.Y., Thevenin, S.: Workforce planning and assignment in mixed-model assembly lines as a factor of line reconfigurability: state of the art. IFAC-PapersOnLine **52**(13), 2746–2751 (2019)
9. Dolgui, A., Kovalev, S., Kovalyov, M.Y., Malyutin, S., Soukhal, A.: Optimal workforce assignment to operations of a paced assembly line. Eur. J. Oper. Res. **264**(1), 200–211 (2018)
10. Dolgui, A., Proth, J.M.: Supply Chain Engineering: Useful Methods and Techniques. Springer, London (2010). https://doi.org/10.1007/978-1-84996-017-5
11. Graves, S.C., Redfield, C.H.: Equipment selection and task assignment for multiproduct assembly system design. Int. J. Flex. Manuf. Syst. **1**(1), 31–50 (1988). https://doi.org/10.1007/BF00713158
12. Hwang, R., Katayama, H.: Integrated procedure of balancing and sequencing for mixed-model assembly lines: a multi-objective evolutionary approach. Int. J. Prod. Res. **48**(21), 6417–6441 (2010)
13. Koren, Y., et al.: Reconfigurable manufacturing systems. Ann. CIRP **48**(2), 527–540 (1999)
14. Kucukkoc, I., Zhang, D.Z.: Simultaneous balancing and sequencing of mixed-model parallel two-sided assembly lines. Int. J. Prod. Res. **52**(12), 3665–3687 (2014)

15. Otto, A., Otto, C., Scholl, A.: Systematic data generation and test design for solution algorithms on the example of SALBPGen for assembly line balancing. Eur. J. Oper. Res. **228**(1), 33–45 (2013)
16. Padula, R.S., Comper, M.L.C., Sparer, E.H., Dennerlein, J.T.: Job rotation designed to prevent musculoskeletal disorders and control risk in manufacturing industries: a systematic review. Appl. Ergon. **58**, 386–397 (2017)

# Balancing and Configuration Planning of RMS to Minimize Energy Cost

Audrey Cerqueus, Paolo Gianessi, Damien Lamy, and Xavier Delorme[✉]

Mines Saint-Etienne, Univ Clermont Auvergne, CNRS, UMR 6158 LIMOS,
Institut Henri Fayol, 42023 Saint-Etienne, France
{audrey.cerqueus,paolo.gianessi,damien.lamy,
xavier.delorme}@mines-stetienne.fr

**Abstract.** In this paper, we investigate the use of the scalability property of RMS to reduce the energy cost during the production. The corresponding optimization problem is a new Bilevel Optimization problem which combines a line balancing problem with a planning problem. A heuristic based on a simulated annealing algorithm and a linear program is proposed. An illustrative example is presented to highlight the potential of this new approach compared to the cost obtained with a classic production line.

**Keywords:** Energy · Scalability · Reconfigurable manufacturing systems

## 1 Introduction

The industry is responsible for more than 50% of the energy consumption worldwide, and its electricity use is expected to grow as a result of an increase in product demand [17]. Moreover, the societal environmental concern urges companies towards energy-efficient and sustainable production systems. Thus, energy consumption has to be considered from a strategic level to an operational level [8]. The design and management of energy-efficient manufacturing systems (MS) requires to increasingly consider renewable energy sources, whose use alongside classical ones is expected to grow in the next decades [1]. When considering energy consumptions of production systems, three energy measures are usually referred to: (1) total energy consumption; (2) time-of-use pricing (TOU); (3) peak power limit.

Production systems are subject to volatility of the market and need to quickly adapt their throughput to the demand. The notion of Reconfigurable MS (RMS), introduced by [10], aims to achieve such reactivity by reconfiguring the production system. Typical RMS are composed of several workstations organized in serial manner with multiple parallel identical machines used in each workstation, as shown in Fig. 1. Parts are moved from a workstation to the next by a conveyor and a gantry. The machines on each workstation are generally computer numerical control machines, reconfigurable machine tools, but can also consist

© IFIP International Federation for Information Processing 2020
Published by Springer Nature Switzerland AG 2020
B. Lalic et al. (Eds.): APMS 2020, IFIP AICT 592, pp. 518–526, 2020.
https://doi.org/10.1007/978-3-030-57997-5_60

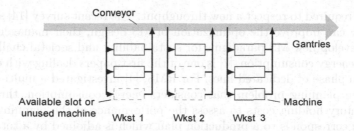

**Fig. 1.** RMS layout as seen by [9]

in other types of resources (e.g., workers with cobot). RMS can be an interesting lever to deal with variable energy availability or pricings as it is the case with TOU, which require to modulate the energy consumption. In costlier periods, a less consuming configuration, even with lower productivity, can be used, before switching to a higher-throughput higher-consumption configuration in periods with lower energy prices so as to satisfy a given demand.

In this paper, a Bilevel Optimization problem is addressed, optimizing the energy cost while satisfying a given demand. The upper-level problem is a balancing problem to determine the design of the RMS and thus the set of configurations which can be used. The lower-level problem consists in finding an optimal planning, i.e. an assignment of configurations to energy cost periods that minimizes the total energy cost while meeting the desired demand. A specific iterative heuristic approach to solve the problem is also investigated.

The remainder of the paper is organized as follows: Sect. 2 introduces the related works. Section 3 formulates the considered problem and its assumptions. Section 4 presents the developed method and Sect. 5 gives a numerical illustration. Conclusions and perspectives are given in Sect. 6.

## 2 Related Works

RMS have been introduced in [10]. They aim to reach as high throughput as dedicated lines and as much flexibility as flexible MS. This is enabled by their capacity to integrate new machines and/or change modules on workstations.

The literature on RMS deals with system design, process planning, scheduling and reconfigurable control [2]. RMS rely on specific characteristics such as modularity, integrability, convertibility, diagnosability, customization and scalability [11]. The scalability of RMS is obtained by adding or removing functionalities in order to have a production system that fits the market demand. According to [11], it might be the most important characteristic of RMS. [6] investigated a model for assessing the scalability capacity of a make-to-order RMS considering different demand scenarios and w.r.t. different performance measures. In [18], a scalability planning methodology for reconfigurable manufacturing is explored. Starting with an existing system, the approach consists in changing its capacity by successive reconfigurations. The objective is to minimize the number of machines required to respect a new throughput. The recent survey [14] state that scalability can improve the optimization of MS design, their management and help to develop new MS paradigms for sustainability and societal challenges.

As to energy consumption, [7] is one of the first papers dealing with energy at the design phase of dedicated lines. For RMS, [4] investigated a multi-objective production planning problem that considers energy consumption, throughput, and inventory holding costs to assess the performance of the planning. A configuration corresponds to a production plan which is adjoined by a total energy consumption. [19] introduced the concept of energy-efficient RMS and investigated a discrete event simulation model to evaluate the system's energy efficiency. In [13], a multi-objective RMS consisting of a rotary table and a set of machines and modules is studied. The approach consists in two stages: the system's design and its control, with the goal to minimize the cycle time and the overall costs that include energy costs. The recent survey [1] showed that few research projects consider reconfigurations to improve energy efficiency and sustainability in production and that RMS have great potential in this respect.

To conclude, as far as we are aware of, no study has considered both scalability and energy consumption in the context of RMS.

## 3  Problem Definition

In this study, we consider a paced production line, dedicated to a single product. The production process is known, i.e. the precedence constraints between the $n$ operations composing it are known and their processing times $t_j$ and their energy consumption $e_j$ are deterministic. The assignment of operations to $K_{\max}$ workstations, i.e. the Assembly Line Balancing Problem (ALBP) defined in [16], is the core strategic decision problem of the production line.

Given a balancing of the line, i.e. such an assignment, a set of parallel machines can be associated with each workstation, so that different configurations can be obtained by turning on/off some of them. We suppose to deal with a RMS with such a feature, i.e. in which all the configurations descend from one balancing and are thus defined by the number $r_k$ of machines turned on for each workstation $k$. In such a setting, it is reasonable to consider as negligible the time required to reconfigure the system.

A configuration is characterized by two measures: takt time and energy consumption. The takt time is based on the processing time of the operations. The sum of the processing time of the operations assigned to a workstation $k$ is its workload $W_k$. The cycle time $c_k$ of a workstation $k$ is its workload divided by the number of its parallel machines, i.e. $c_k = W_k/r_k$. It is the average time required to process one piece. The takt time $c$ of a configuration is the maximum cycle time of the workstations. The idle time of the workstation $k$ is $I_k = c - W_k/n_k$.

The energy $E$ consumed during a takt time is the sum of the energy consumed by each workstation. The energy consumption $E_k$ of workstation $k$ is the sum of the energy consumption of operations assigned to it $(\eta_k)$ and of a residual consumption during idle time that depends by a coefficient $\alpha$ on the number $r_k$

of machines, the idle time $I_k$ and the average consumption per time unit $\eta_k/W_k$:

$$E_k = \eta_k + \alpha I_k r_k \frac{\eta_k}{W_k} \tag{1}$$

In this article, we consider the energy consumption by unit of time $Q = \frac{E}{c}$.

Let us now suppose to deal with a TOU pricing scheme with $P$ time periods $p \in \{1 \ldots P\}$, each defined by an energy cost $U_p$ and a duration $D_p$ over a time horizon $T$, i.e. such that $\sum_p D_p = T$. We want to solve the planning problem of finding the configurations used in each period $p$ that minimize the total energy cost while fulfilling a given overall demand $\Delta$ within the timespan $T$.

Considering the cost of energy since the design stage of the production system gives rise to a *Bilevel Optimization Problem* in which the design (balancing) of the production system is the *upper-level* decision problem, while the planning problem represents the *lower-level* decision-making. The decision variables are:

- upper-level assignment variables $x_{jk} \in \{0, 1\}, \forall j \in \{1 \ldots n\}, k \in \{1 \ldots K_{\max}\}$
- lower-level planning variables $0 \le y_{ip} \le 1, \forall i \in \mathcal{C}(x), p \in \{1 \ldots P\}$

where $\mathcal{C}(x)$ is the set of configurations that descend from the balancing $x$.

The Bilevel nature of the problem mainly resides in the intertwinement of the two levels, as the suitability of a balancing cannot be evaluated without solving the planning problem, which in turn cannot be solved without knowing the balancing. We refer the reader to [5] for an introduction to Bilevel Optimization.

The Bilevel optimization model is the following:

$$\min_x \mathcal{T}(x, y^\star); \ \max_x \mathcal{R}(x) \tag{2}$$
$$\text{s.t. } \mathcal{B}(x) \le 0 \tag{3}$$
$$y^\star = \operatorname{argmin}_y \mathcal{E}(x, y) \tag{4}$$
$$\text{s.t. } \mathcal{P}(y) \le 0 \tag{5}$$

where $\mathcal{T}$, $\mathcal{R}$ and $\mathcal{E}$ are, respectively, an overall cost function (which may include cost terms other than energy, related e.g. to workstations and tools), a reconfigurability measure of $x$, and the energy cost of planning $y$ based on the configurations of $\mathcal{C}(x)$. $\mathcal{B}(x)$ and $\mathcal{P}(y)$ are the balancing and planning constraints.

## 4 Proposed Method

In the following, we propose a sequential, two-phases decomposition heuristic to the Bilevel Optimization problem proposed in Sect. 3. Phase 1 addresses the design problem to obtain a candidate balancing $x$ and a set $\mathcal{C}(x)$ of configurations from it. These are used in the Phase 2 to find a planning that fulfils a demand $\Delta$ over a timespan $T$ at a minimum energy cost w.r.t. a given TOU pricing scheme. Since the number of workstation is bounded, we will not consider it in the cost function and $\mathcal{T}$ will be reduced to the energy cost.

## 4.1    Phase 1: Generation of a Set of Configurations

This phase assigns operations to workstations so as to define the type of machines needed for each workstations. The configurations derived from a balancing offer different levels of productivity with different energy consumption. To increase the productivity of the system, an additional machine have to be turned on for the bottleneck workstation, which has the highest cycle time $c_k$. This property defines a method to derive configurations from a balancing: allocate one machine to each workstation to define the first configuration, then iteratively add a machine in the bottleneck workstation.

Further restrictions are needed to avoid unrealistic situations (all operations assigned to the same workstation, an infinity of machines on a workstation ...) and conform to industrial constraints:

- There is at least one machine per workstation.
- There is no more than $r_{\max} = 3$ machines per workstation.
- The maximum number of machines in a configuration, $R_{\max}$, is $n/2$.
- The maximum number of operations per workstation is $n_{\max} = 40\% n$.

The definition of configurations is the same as in [3], in which the authors studied the scalability of different derived configurations. They showed that the scalability is not correlated with the classical line balancing indicators (takt time, smoothness ratio...). They proposed to evaluate the scalability by a bi-objective analysis (takt time, number of machines) of the balancing and by computing a hypervolume metric $\mathcal{H}$. We adopt this approach here and compute such a metric on takt time and per-time-unit energy consumption of the configurations. Note that by doing so the metric $\mathcal{H}$ actually aggregates a reconfigurability measure ($\mathcal{R}$) with an energy consumption measure ($\mathcal{T}$).

Let $c^i$ and $Q^i$ be the takt time and energy consumption per time unit of the $|\mathcal{C}(x)|$ configurations derived from a same balancing and sorted by decreasing takt time. The hypervolume measures the area above the points $(c^i, Q^i)$:

$$\mathcal{H} = (p_c - c^1)(p_Q - Q^1) + \sum_{i=2}^{|\mathcal{C}(x)|} (c^{i-1} - c^i)(p_Q - Q^i) \qquad (6)$$

A reference point $(p_c, p_Q)$ is used as an upper bound on the values of takt time and energy consumption, with $p_c = \sum_j t_j + 1$ and $p_Q = R_{\max} \max_j \frac{e_j}{t_j} + 1$. We refer the reader to [3] for further explanations of the hypervolume.

In order to find the line balancing maximizing the hypervolume computed on its derived configurations, we implemented a simulated annealing [12]. The generation of an initial balancing is random, taking into account the precedence constraints, $n_{\max}$, and limiting the number of workstations to $R_{\max}$. Two balancings are neighbors if all operations are assigned to the same workstation, except one. The neighborhood search randomly selects one neighbor of the current balancing. At the end of the simulated annealing execution, the configurations derived from the best balancing are given to Phase 2.

**Table 1.** Features of the eight configurations from the instance Heskia

| $i$ | 1 | 2 | 3 | 4 | 5 | 6 | 7 | 8 |
|---|---|---|---|---|---|---|---|---|
| $c^i(s)$ | 309 | 284 | 180 | 154.5 | 142 | 135 | 116 | 103 |
| $Q^i(\times 10^3)$ | 80.88 | 89.51 | 135.64 | 157.76 | 172.51 | 182.79 | 209.72 | 236.21 |
| $E^i$ | | 24.992 | 25.419 | 24.414 | 24.374 | 24.495 | 24.676 | 24.327 | 24.329 |

## 4.2   Phase 2: Assignment of Configurations

We set up a Linear Program (LP) in order to decide how to deploy the configurations, returned by the Phase 1, over a given time horizon $T$. The objective is to fulfill a given demand $\Delta$ while minimizing the overall economic cost of the associated energy consumption. The associated decisions can be represented by nonnegative real variables $y_{ip} \geq 0$, equal to the percentage of the period $p \in \{1 \dots P\}$ allocated to configuration $i \in \mathcal{C}(\boldsymbol{x})$. The proposed LP model is:

$$\min \sum_{i \in \mathcal{C}(\boldsymbol{x}), p \in \{1 \dots P\}} D_p \cdot U_p \cdot Q^i \cdot y_{ip} \tag{7}$$

$$\text{s.t.} \sum_{i \in \mathcal{C}(\boldsymbol{x}), p \in \{1 \dots P\}} \frac{D_p}{c^i} \cdot y_{ip} \geq \Delta \tag{8}$$

$$\sum_{i \in \mathcal{C}(\boldsymbol{x})} y_{ip} \leq 1 \qquad \forall p \in \{1 \dots P\} \tag{9}$$

Term (7) represents the economic cost to minimize. Inequality (8) is the demand fulfillment constraint, and relations (9) enforce the fact that the use of some configurations over an energy cost period must not exceed its duration.

## 5   Numerical Example

To illustrate our approach, in this section we present the result obtained for the instance Heskia [15], which features 28 tasks, for which we generated energy consumption values. LP Model of Phase 2 is solved using IBM ILOG CPLEX.

A balancing of operations of five workstations (named $S_1$ to $S_5$), with a takt time of 309 s, is output by simulated annealing in Phase 1. Eight configurations are derived from this balancing: Table 1 shows their takt time and energy consumptions. Figure 2 depicts configuration $i = 2$ and gives the values of $W_k$, $I_k$ and $\eta_k$ for each workstation $k$ (which are common to all configurations). For this configuration, the takt time is 284 s. From (1), and using $\alpha = 0.1$, the energy consumption of $S_1$ is $4.382 + 0.1 \times 104 \times 1 \times \frac{4.382}{180} = 4.635$. Similarly we get 8.392 for $S_2$, 6.929 for $S_3$, 4.153 for $S_4$ and 1.310 for $S_5$. Thus the total energy consumption of configuration $i = 2$ is $E^2 = 25.419$, and $Q^2 = 89.51 \times 10^{-3}$.

As to Phase 2, we defined $P = 6$ periods over a 24 h time horizon, the duration and the cost of energy of which are shown in Fig. 3, along with the planning returned by Phase 2 for a demand $\Delta = 601$. Grayed areas represent production

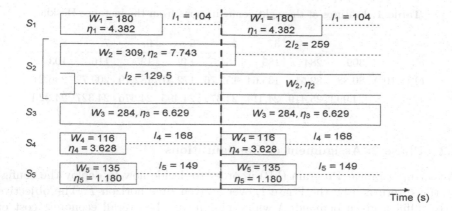

**Fig. 2.** The second configuration for the instance Heskia

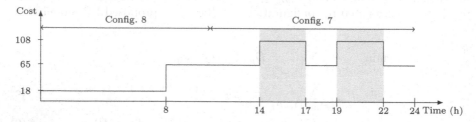

**Fig. 3.** Pricing scheme over the 24 h time horizon and planning output by Phase 2.

interruptions. The optimal energy cost is 175.186. Only two configurations are used. Configuration 8 (with the lowest takt time) is used in the first period and 47% of the second, allowing to stop production during the costliest periods. Configuration 7, with the lowest $E^i$ value, is used to produce the remaining demand. In this example, periods are either used fully or not at all: this is not a constraint of the LP, and not all instances show this behaviour.

A dedicated line with one machine per workstation would require 8 workstations and have a takt time of 143 s. If such a line was used during the 24 h to satisfy the demand, the energy cost would amount to 242.573. Our method enables an almost 30% energy cost reduction by using a RMS instead.

## 6  Conclusion and Perspectives

In this article, we studied the Bilevel optimization problem of balancing and configuration planning of a RMS to satisfy a given demand with minimum energy cost w.r.t. a TOU energy pricing scheme. The main motivation of this work is to show how RMS can be beneficial when dealing with questions arising from more variable energy sources, an issue nowadays more and more sensitive.

To solve this problem, we defined a two-phases method. We developed a simulated annealing for Phase 1 that evaluates the different configurations derived from a same balancing, taking simultaneously into account their takt time and energy consumption. A linear programming model is used in Phase 2 to plan the use of the configurations over a time horizon. The numerical example showed that increasing the production on low-cost periods and not producing on high-cost periods can lead to a significant reduction of the overall energy cost.

Further tests on a wider instance set would allow to better assess the potential savings that could be achieved using this approach. Moreover, it would be interesting to consider some industrial constraints, such as a power peak limit.

# References

1. Battaïa, O., Benyoucef, L., Delorme, X., Dolgui, A., Thevenin, S.: Sustainable and energy efficient reconfigurable manufacturing systems. In: Benyoucef, L. (ed.) Reconfigurable Manufacturing Systems: From Design to Implementation. SSAM, pp. 179–191. Springer, Cham (2020). https://doi.org/10.1007/978-3-030-28782-5_9
2. Bortolini, M., Galizia, F.G., Mora, C.: Reconfigurable manufacturing systems: literature review and research trend. J. Manuf. Syst. **49**, 93–106 (2018)
3. Cerqueus, A., Delorme, X., Dolgui, A.: Analysis of the scalability for different configurations of lines. In: Benyoucef, L. (ed.) Reconfigurable Manufacturing Systems: From Design to Implementation. SSAM, pp. 139–160. Springer, Cham (2020). https://doi.org/10.1007/978-3-030-28782-5_7
4. Choi, Y.C., Xirouchakis, P.: A holistic production planning approach in a reconfigurable manufacturing system with energy consumption and environmental effects. Int. J. Comp. Integ. Manuf. **28**(4), 379–394 (2015)
5. Colson, B., Marcotte, P., Savard, G.: Bilevel programming: a survey. 4OR **3**(2), 87–107 (2005)
6. Deif, A.M., ElMaraghy, H.A.: Assessing capacity scalability policies in RMS using system dynamics. Int. J. Flex. Manuf. Syst. **19**(3), 128–150 (2007)
7. Gianessi, P., Delorme, X., Masmoudi, O.: Simple assembly line balancing problem with power peak minimization. In: Ameri, F., Stecke, K.E., von Cieminski, G., Kiritsis, D. (eds.) APMS 2019. IAICT, vol. 566, pp. 239–247. Springer, Cham (2019). https://doi.org/10.1007/978-3-030-30000-5_31
8. Giret, A., Trentesaux, D., Prabhu, V.: Sustainability in manufacturing operations scheduling: a state of the art review. J. Manuf. Syst. **37**, 126–140 (2015)
9. Koren, Y., Gu, X., Guo, W.: Reconfigurable manufacturing systems: principles, design, and future trends. Front. Mech. Eng. **13**(2), 121–136 (2018). https://doi.org/10.1007/s11465-018-0483-0
10. Koren, Y., et al.: Reconfigurable manufacturing systems. CIRP Ann. **48**, 2 (1999)
11. Koren, Y., Wang, W., Gu, X.: Value creation through design for scalability of reconfigurable manufacturing systems. Int. J. Prod. Res. **55**(5), 1227–1242 (2017)
12. Laarhoven, P.J.M., Aarts, E.H.L.: Simulated Annealing: Theory and Applications. Kluwer Academic Publishers, USA (1987)
13. Liu, M., An, L., Zhang, J., Chu, F., Chu, C.: Energy-oriented bi-objective optimisation for a multi-module reconfigurable manufacturing system. Int. J. Prod. Res. **57**(19), 5974–5995 (2019)
14. Putnik, G.: Scalability in manufacturing systems design and operation: state-of-the-art and future developments roadmap. CIRP Ann. **62**(2), 751–774 (2013)
15. Scholl, A.: Data of assembly line balancing problems. Technical report, Darmstadt Technical University, Institute for Business Studies (BWL) (1995)

16. Scholl, A.: Balancing and Sequencing of Assembly Lines. Springer, Heidelberg (1999)
17. U.S. Energy Information Administration: International Energy Outlook 2019. https://www.eia.gov/outlooks/ieo/pdf/ieo2019.pdf
18. Wang, W., Koren, Y.: Scalability planning for reconfigurable manufacturing systems. J. Manuf. Syst. **31**(2), 83–91 (2012)
19. Zhang, J., et al.: Modeling and verification of reconfigurable and energy-efficient manufacturing systems. Discrete Dyn. Nat. Soc. **2015**(1), 1–14 (2015)

# Operations Management
# in Engineer-to-Order Manufacturing

# Factors Affecting Shipyard Operations and Logistics: A Framework and Comparison of Shipbuilding Approaches

Jo Wessel Strandhagen[1](✉) ⓘ, Yongkuk Jeong[2] ⓘ,
Jong Hun Woo[3] ⓘ, Marco Semini[1], Magnus Wiktorsson[2] ⓘ,
Jan Ola Strandhagen[1] ⓘ, and Erlend Alfnes[1] ⓘ

[1] NTNU – Norwegian University of Science and Technology,
Trondheim, Norway
jo.w.strandhagen@ntnu.no
[2] KTH Royal Institute of Technology, Södertälje, Sweden
[3] Seoul National University, Seoul, Korea

**Abstract.** Shipyards around the world have several differences that affect the logistics processes at each yard. The purpose of this paper is to develop a framework for mapping the key factors affecting shipyard logistics. We test and validate the framework by applying it to three case shipyards—one Norwegian and two South Korean. To develop the framework, we first identify key factors affecting shipyard logistics, based on a review of the existing literature. The framework is then applied using data from the three cases. Through a comparative analysis of the collected data, we identify and outline the main logistics differences and the key factors' main implications for the shipyards. The findings from the analysis indicate that there are important differences between the shipyards, and these have implications for their scope of planning and execution of shipyard activities, their primary focus of coordination, and their primary flows, among others. Through the framework development and comparative analysis, the paper contributes to an enhanced understanding of shipyard logistics, as well as how it is affected by internal and external yard characteristics.

**Keywords:** Shipbuilding · Shipyard · Logistics · Engineer-to-order manufacturing

## 1 Introduction

The shipbuilding industry is currently under strong economic pressure, and the drastic reduction in the oil price, from around 2015, caused significant changes in the global shipbuilding market. Fierce global competition has driven the margins of shipbuilding companies down, making cost-efficient operations more important than ever before. Efficient shipyard logistics—defined here as the coordination of shipyard operations related to the flow of materials through a yard up to the completion of a ship—is, therefore, increasingly significant. However, research on the topic remains scarce. Shipyards also operate under differing conditions, which affect the logistics processes

© IFIP International Federation for Information Processing 2020
Published by Springer Nature Switzerland AG 2020
B. Lalic et al. (Eds.): APMS 2020, IFIP AICT 592, pp. 529–537, 2020.
https://doi.org/10.1007/978-3-030-57997-5_61

at yards. Increased knowledge of the factors that affect a shipyard's logistics activities can increase the understanding of how to achieve efficient yard logistics. Norway and South Korea are examples of two strong, but different, shipbuilding nations. Norway, with its long coastline, has strong traditions in the shipbuilding industry, which remains an important industry for the country [1]. Due to Norway's high labor costs, competing on price is difficult. Norwegian shipbuilding has focused on the low volume production of high-quality, highly customized vessels, with innovative features, for the offshore industry. South Korea, on the other hand, with lower wages and strategic government support, has become a leading shipbuilding nation through the higher volume production of large tankers and cargo carriers [2]. Accordingly, contextual factors affect how shipbuilders should approach their shipyard logistics.

The existing literature includes various studies comparing different aspects within shipbuilding. Eich-Born and Hassink [3] conducted a comparative analysis of shipbuilding regions in Germany and South Korea, focusing on how local, regional, and national factors affect global competition. Bai et al. [4] compared the information technology, production technology, and local characteristics of Chinese, Korean, and Japanese shipyards, albeit without a structured framework. Pires Jr. et al. [5] presented a methodology for shipbuilding performance assessment, based on yard characteristics, production patterns, and industrial surroundings. Colin and Pinto [6] analyzed the asset turnover of several shipbuilding companies, while Semini et al. [7] compared different offshoring strategies in ship production. Despite the range of shipbuilding studies, there is a lack of studies aimed at shipyard logistics.

This paper addresses the need for an increased knowledge of the factors that affect a shipyard's internal logistics. The purpose of this paper is to develop a framework for mapping the key factors affecting shipyard logistics. Such a framework may enable comparative analyses of shipyards and provide useful descriptions of the characteristics and challenges related to shipyard logistics. We test the framework by applying it to a Norwegian shipyard and two South Korean shipyards.

## 2   Research Approach and Framework Development

Figure 1 shows the overall research approach taken in this study. The first step in developing the framework was to identify the relevant factors affecting shipyard logistics, based on a literature review. Following the factor identification, and inspired by Jonsson and Mattsson's [8] original planning environment framework, we developed the framework by establishing the factors and their respective items and content. The framework was then applied to map three different shipyards: Ulstein Verft AS (UVE), Hyundai Heavy Industries Ulsan (HHI Ulsan), and STX Offshore and Shipbuilding Jinhae (STX Jinhae). The first is a Norwegian newbuilding shipyard, and the next two are large and medium-sized shipyards in South Korea. The authors' strong relationship with the case shipyards allowed access to data through interviews and site observations, and various yard documentation and records were made available to the authors. The data collection also provided new insights that were used to revise and improve the framework. Therefore, the framework development became an iterative process with new revisions, as data from the cases were collected and analyzed. The final step was to conduct a cross-case comparative analysis, based on the mapping of the shipyards, and discuss the findings of the analysis.

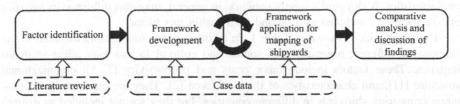

**Fig. 1.** The paper's research approach.

From an operations management perspective, shipyards are different from traditional manufacturing systems, due to the distinct characteristics of their production environment. Following Buer et al.'s [9] definition of production environment, we define a shipyard logistics environment as the sum of internal and external factors that affect shipyard logistics processes. Based on the literature, we include four factors: yard characteristics, product and market characteristics, process characteristics, and supply chain characteristics. Each factor consists of several items.

As shipyards are different from traditional manufacturing systems, we treat yard characteristics as a separate factor. First, a yard's facilities and available equipment influence both the activities that can be carried out and how they can be carried out. Second, shipbuilding is the production of large-scale products that require a certain amount of physical space and number of workers. Although shipbuilding is typically characterized as production in a fixed-position layout, several options exist within that main layout type, eventually affecting how material flows through a shipyard. Finally, a yard's logistics is affected by its levels of process automation and information technology (IT) in terms of IT systems to support logistics processes.

A production environment's product and market characteristics typically include the placement of the customer order decoupling point, product volume and variety, level of customization, and product complexity. However, the description of a shipyard requires items that are adapted to the shipbuilding context. Shipyards can vary based on the types of vessels they produce, as different types may require different material handling equipment or different organization of the activities at a shipyard. The vessel type can also indicate the complexity associated with building it. The number of vessels produced per year and whether a shipyard typically produces one-offs or a series of several ships per order are additional aspects that affect shipyard logistics.

A yard's process characteristics include the main shipbuilding processes it performs, as processes may be outsourced to other yards. There are also different possible building practices for outfitting operations in shipbuilding, i.e., the installation of a ship's equipment in its hull. As the hull is typically constructed by joining hull blocks together, outfitting may be done on single blocks before they are joined to erect a ship. Outfitting after ship erection reduces accessibility to the point of installation, as the hull is then a closed structure. The final item within this factor is the throughput time, i.e., the total time from production start to ship completion.

Shipyards may differ greatly in how their supply chains are organized. The degree of vertical integration has been found to have a particularly significant impact on shipbuilding productivity [10]. Thus, it is included as an item within supply chain characteristics. A shipyard's supply network, in general, may also influence its logistics and is, therefore, included as a second item within this factor.

The framework is shown in Table 1. In addition to the four factors included in the framework, different organizational, social, and cultural factors may affect shipyard logistics. These factors include labor costs and productivity [2, 5], organizational structure [11], and characteristics of the workforce [2]. They are particularly relevant when comparing shipyards in different countries, but they are not included as distinct factors in the mapping framework. Similarly, economic factors, such as the shipbuilding company's financial performance and eventual government support [2, 5], while relevant factors, are not included in the framework at the current stage.

**Table 1.** Framework for mapping factors affecting shipyard logistics.

| Factors | Items | Content | Ref. |
|---|---|---|---|
| Yard characteristics | Yard facilities | Main production facilities, docks, and quays | [6] |
| | Yard equipment | Main yard equipment for material handling | [5] |
| | Yard size | Total number of shipyard workers, total yard area | [10] |
| | Yard layout | Shape and direction of material flow through the yard | [2] |
| | Automation level | Level of automation of shipbuilding processes | [6] |
| | IT level | Level of IT systems infrastructure and integration | [5] |
| Product and market characteristics | Vessel types produced | Tankers, bulk carriers, cargo/passenger ships, fishing vessels, and offshore vessels | [12] |
| | Customization | Degree of customization | [13] |
| | Total production volume | Average number of vessels produced per year | [9] |
| | Order size | Average number of similar ships per customer order | [9] |
| | Type and size of market | Type and size of the market the shipyard competes in | [2] |
| Process characteristics | Throughput time | Average throughput time of a customer order | [9] |
| | Main shipbuilding processes | Main shipbuilding processes performed at own shipyard | [7] |
| | Building practices | Degree of advanced outfitting | [12] |
| Supply chain characteristics | Supply network | Characteristics of the supply network | [5] |
| | Vertical integration | Shipyard's integration with hull yard, ship designer, main equipment suppliers, and shipowner | [10] |

# 3 Framework Application: A Comparison of Shipyards in Norway and South Korea

Norway's high cost levels affect performance, especially in labor-intensive production, by driving up product costs through higher direct and indirect labor costs [14]. A consequence of this is the offshoring of most steel-related tasks to countries with lower cost levels [7]. Therefore, Norwegian yards primarily perform the more advanced outfitting tasks, such as the installation of machinery and deck equipment, electrical systems, and accommodation, while the steel structure is built in lower-cost countries [7]. With these high cost levels, there is also a need to focus on high value-added and knowledge-based products, making access to competence and innovation vital. Norway's maritime industry is supported by a network of maritime clusters, and proximity to customers, suppliers, competitors, and research institutions provides benefits that compensate for the high labor costs [14]. Organizational, social, and cultural factors also have implications for the Norwegian shipbuilding industry. Examples include the flat and informal organizational structures, autonomous employees, a skilled workforce, and the small local communities [14]. These locational characteristics provide Norway with a competitive advantage in the production of highly customized products of high quality and with innovative features. This has enabled Norwegian shipbuilders to be global leaders in the market for highly specialized offshore vessels. The performance of Norwegian shipyards has been affected by fluctuations in the oil and gas market, which has forced them to pursue, and adapt to, alternative markets [15].

After entering the shipbuilding industry in the 1970s, South Korea has strengthened its position as a leading shipbuilding nation through lower wages and a national strategic focus [2]. The country's shipbuilding industry has benefited from the large domestic production of steel and a strong marine equipment industry [16], and their large shipyards have dominated for the past decade [2]. South Korean shipyards produce a variety of different ship types, with the main types being larger vessels, such as container ships and various tankers [16]. South Korea's dominance in the shipbuilding industry is a result of advanced technological developments, innovation, and governmental research and development support, in addition to the potential to compete on price. However, the fierce global shipbuilding environment also challenges South Korea, and with many shipyard's struggling to stay in business, the national industry is currently seeing significant restructuring, through several mergers between shipbuilding companies.

Table 2 shows the mapping of the three case shipyards after the application of the framework. The main differences and their implications for logistics are discussed in Sect. 4.

**Table 2.** Framework application on the three case shipyards.

| Items | UVE | HHI Ulsan | STX Jinhae |
|---|---|---|---|
| Yard facilities | Pipe fabrication, outfitting, painting; quay (208 m), 1 graving dock | Steel and pipe fabrication, assembly, outfitting, painting, pre-erection, erection; quay (7.4 km), 10 graving docks | Steel and pipe fabrication, assembly, outfitting, painting; pre-erection, erection; quay (1.8 km), 2 graving docks |
| Yard equipment | 2 main traveling cranes (250 tonnes), 4 dockside and quayside cranes | 9 goliath cranes (max 1,600 tonnes), 33 transporters | 4 goliath cranes, 6 transporters |
| Yard size | Around 75,000 m$^2$ and 300 shipyard workers | Around 6,320,000 m$^2$ and 15,000 shipyard workers | Around 1,000,000 m$^2$ and 1,000 shipyard workers |
| Yard layout | L-shaped, with material flow directed towards hull in dock or at quay | U-shaped from steel entry through fabrication, assembly, and erection to docks and quaysides | |
| Level of automation | Mostly manual operations, with some automation of fabrication | High automation of steelwork and block assembly. Mostly manual operation on painting, outfitting, and ship erection | High automation of steelwork and medium automation of block assembly. Mostly manual operation on painting, outfitting, and ship erection |
| IT level | IT systems used for all business processes but with a low level of integration between systems | IT systems used for all main business processes. High level of integration in the design phase. Low integration at the production site | |
| Vessel types produced | Offshore support vessels (PSV, OCV, SOV) and passenger ships (ROPAX, cruise) | Large size commercial carriers, offshore platform systems, and support vessels | Tankers, gas carriers, cargo carrying vessels (container ships, bulk), and LNG bunkering |
| Customization | Very high | Very high | Very high |
| Total production volume | 2 vessels per year | 70 vessels per year | 10 vessels per year |
| Order size | Few—between 1 and 2 | Several—up to 20 | Several—up to 10 |
| Type and size of market | Mainly offshore, cruise, and passenger markets | Maritime transport market and offshore market | Maritime transport market |

*(continued)*

**Table 2.** (*continued*)

| Items | UVE | HHI Ulsan | STX Jinhae |
|---|---|---|---|
| Throughput time | 20 months | 10 months | 12 months |
| Main shipbuilding processes | Outfits complete hull structures in dry dock and at quayside | Performs all main processes at own shipyard (integrated yard) | Performs all main processes at own shipyard (integrated yard) |
| Building practices | All outfitting work performed on closed hull | Pre-outfitting of hull blocks | Pre-outfitting of hull blocks |
| Supply network | Hull production at a yard in Poland. Mostly local equipment suppliers | Domestic and foreign suppliers of steel. Partly outsourced hull block construction. Two engine suppliers. Several domestic suppliers of other equipment | |
| Vertical integration | Medium. Vertical integration with ship designer. Partnership with hull yard in Poland | Very high. In-house ship design. Vertical integration with main equipment suppliers | Low. Some in-house design-activity |

# 4 Discussion

One of the main differences between the three yards studied concerns the shipbuilding processes performed at each yard. UVE mainly performs outfitting operations, with the other main shipbuilding processes performed at a partner yard. From a logistics perspective, UVE can keep its focus on the outfitting operations. However, as ships spend only a part of the total construction time at UVE's yard, it must operate with a tighter schedule, as there is less room for flexibility in the planning and execution of the outfitting activities performed at their yard. HHI Ulsan and STX Jinhae, on the other hand, are fully integrated yards, and must coordinate the whole range of shipbuilding processes and handle the logistics activities related to these processes.

Another main difference is the large variation in production volumes between the yards. While they all build customized vessels, UVE is more focused on building highly specialized vessels, in a market with lower global demand, than the South Korean yards. While UVE mostly produces one-offs, the South Korean yards build series of several ships. One implication for logistics is the total number of ships being built at the respective yard at any given time. Having up to 20 ships at the yard at a time requires significant interproject coordination, i.e., coordination between projects. UVE mainly has to focus on intraproject coordination, i.e., coordination within each shipbuilding project, as each project makes up a higher share of the total sales value.

The yards' production volumes are naturally linked with their capacity in terms of the number of docks, number and lifting capacity of cranes, and the yards' sizes. Producing tens of ships per year requires the facilities and space of a different magnitude compared to the production of only a handful of ships. As HHI Ulsan and STX Jinhae, both integrated shipyards, perform all the main shipbuilding processes, they need equipment and transporters that can handle and move hull blocks. For instance, yards of the size of HHI Ulsan typically have around 500 hull blocks located at different areas of their yard, and every day more than 100 blocks are transported. UVE, on the other hand, only performs outfitting operations on complete hulls. It does not need heavy-duty material handling equipment, as there is no transportation of hull blocks. The heaviest material handling process at UVE is the lifting of equipment by tower cranes for installation on ships in the dock or at the quay. Accordingly, UVE's main concern regarding layout-related issues is how to improve productivity in their outfitting operations. The primary flow that UVE has to plan and control to perform outfitting operations is the flow of workers to and from the dock or quay and on and off the ship being built. The South Korean yards are, to a larger extent, concerned with planning and controlling the flow of blocks and larger ship structures around their yards.

## 5  Conclusions, Limitations, and Further Research

This paper has proposed a framework for mapping the key factors affecting shipyard logistics. Yard characteristics, product and market characteristics, process characteristics, and supply chain characteristics have implications for a shipyard's logistics, and this has been illustrated through mapping three shipyards by applying the framework. The factors' key implications for shipyard logistics include the scope of planning and execution of shipyard activities, the primary focus of coordination (intraproject versus interproject), and the yards' primary flows.

The low number of cases is one of the paper's limitations. A larger number of cases would enhance the generalizability of the results. Moreover, the presented framework is focused on the shipbuilding industry and the shipyard environment and is currently a first version that needs additional work to be developed further. Future work should consider comparing shipyards with the production environments in other industries.

Nevertheless, the paper contributes to an enhancement of the understanding of shipyard logistics, as there is a lack of related research in the shipyard logistics area, and addresses how logistics challenges are affected by internal and external yard characteristics. The results of this paper can help shipbuilders understand the internal logistics environment and support them in selecting and designing appropriate logistics planning and management systems. The paper offers a guide to further research, which should aim to investigate the main logistics challenges in different shipyard contexts, with the specific objective of developing a typology of shipbuilding logistics. The future work on shipyard logistics should also address how the need for digitalization and the use of Industry 4.0 technologies differs, based on shipyard logistics differences.

# References

1. OECD: Peer review of the Norwegian shipbuilding industry (2017)
2. ECORYS: Study on competitiveness of the European shipbuilding industry (2009)
3. Eich-Born, M., Hassink, R.: On the battle between shipbuilding regions in Germany and South Korea. Environ. Plan. A **37**(4), 635–656 (2005)
4. Bai, X., Nie, W., Liu, C.: A comparison of Chinese, Japanese, and Korean shipyard production technology. J. Mar. Sci. Appl. **6**(2), 25–29 (2007)
5. Pires Jr., F., Lamb, T., Souza, C.: Shipbuilding performance benchmarking. Int. J. Bus. Perform. Manage. **11**(3), 216–235 (2009)
6. Colin, E.C., Pinto, M.M.O.: Benchmarking shipbuilders' turnover of main assets. J. Ship Prod. **25**(4), 175–181 (2009)
7. Semini, M., Brett, P.O., Hagen, A., Kolsvik, J., Alfnes, E., Strandhagen, J.O.: Offshoring strategies in Norwegian ship production. J. Ship Prod. Des. **34**(1), 59–71 (2018)
8. Jonsson, P., Mattsson, S.-A.: The implications of fit between planning environments and manufacturing planning and control methods. Int. J. Oper. Prod. Manage. **23**(8), 872–900 (2003)
9. Buer, S.-V., Strandhagen, J.W., Strandhagen, J.O., Alfnes, E.: Strategic fit of planning environments: towards an integrated framework. In: Temponi, C., Vandaele, N. (eds.) ILS 2016. LNBIP, vol. 262, pp. 77–92. Springer, Cham (2018). https://doi.org/10.1007/978-3-319-73758-4_6
10. Lamb, T., Hellesoy, A.: A shipbuilding productivity predictor. J. Ship Prod. **18**(2), 79–85 (2002)
11. Hellgren, S., Hänninen, M., Valdez Banda, O.A., Kujala, P.: Modelling of a cruise shipbuilding process for analyzing the effect of organization on production efficiency. J. Ship Prod. Des. **33**(2), 101–121 (2017)
12. Eyres, D.J., Bruce, G.J.: Ship Construction, 7th edn. Butterworth-Heinemann, Oxford (2012)
13. Semini, M., Haartveit, D.E.G., Alfnes, E., Arica, E., Brett, P.O., Strandhagen, J.O.: Strategies for customized shipbuilding with different customer order decoupling points. Proc. Inst. Mech. Eng. Part M J. Eng. Marit. Environ. **228**(4), 362–372 (2014)
14. Semini, M., Brekken, H., Swahn, N., Alfnes, E., Strandhagen, J.O.: Global manufacturing and how location in Norway may give factories a competitive advantage. In: Paper presented at the 23rd EurOMA Conference, Trondheim, Norway (2016)
15. Menon Economics: GCE Blue Maritime Cluster – Global Performance Benchmark 2019 (2019)
16. OECD: Peer review of the Korean shipbuilding industry and related government policies (2014)

# Using the Smartphone as an Augmented Reality Device in ETO Industry

Niklas Jahn$^{(\boxtimes)}$ ⓘ, Axel Friedewald, and Hermann Lödding

Hamburg University of Technology, Hamburg, Germany
{niklas.jahn, friedewald, loedding}@tuhh.de

**Abstract.** Industrial Augmented Reality (IAR) has proven its potential in ETO industry by improving productivity and acting as a key technology for consistent digital information flows. In order to leverage these potentials on a significant scale, broad distribution of IAR inside a company should be aimed for. However, most applications have not yet overcome a prototype state and failed to make the step into production. Primary limiting factors are inadequate device availability and acceptance of current IAR solutions, which focus on smart glasses and tablet devices. The aim of this paper is to examine whether smartphones have the potential to serve as a platform for IAR in ETO industry. First the user interface of an existing tablet IAR prototype is adapted to a smartphone in order to later evaluate user experience. Hence a survey to assess worker preferences between tablet and smartphone devices for common IAR supported tasks is developed. The survey design is tested on a group of workers from ETO industry.

**Keywords:** Industrial Augmented Reality (IAR) · Mobile devices · Engineer-to-order (ETO) · User experience

## 1 Introduction and Motivation

Digitalization initiatives in ETO industry transform the future way workers access information by focusing on consistent digital information flows between product design and shop floor and digitalized operator support [1]. Industrial Augmented Reality (IAR) is a special form of digitalized operator support, which visualizes information as virtual content superimposed with reality. It is broadly researched in manufacturing [2] and in particular in the ETO industry for maritime products [3, 4]. In this field mobile devices are the most common type of hardware due to native capabilities that foster the implementation of IAR, such as sensors, display technologies and software frameworks [4]. IAR can reduce the necessary amount of 2D drawings with their high creation costs by allowing for simple access to the underlying 3D CAD data and derived information, e.g. measurements [5].

For leveraging the potentials, it is implied that the predominant device and software need to be widely accepted in a company in terms of *user friendliness*, *reliability* and *scalability* [6]. These fundamental requirements are still not sufficiently fulfilled by head-mounted devices or wearable technology [7].

© IFIP International Federation for Information Processing 2020
Published by Springer Nature Switzerland AG 2020
B. Lalic et al. (Eds.): APMS 2020, IFIP AICT 592, pp. 538–546, 2020.
https://doi.org/10.1007/978-3-030-57997-5_62

In contrast, smartphones and tablets are routinely used in private and business areas. Smartphones, in particular, are carried around by almost everyone due to their compactness, which makes them a highly available information carrier. While broad research on tablet-based IAR in ETO industry exists, smartphones still lack examination.

This paper identifies the challenges for smartphone-based IAR and introduces a prototypical smartphone adaption of an existing UI for a tablet-based IAR information system for workers in ETO industry, like e.g. on a shipyard. Subsequently a study design for determining user preferences in comparison with the tablet solution is proposed. The results of a preliminary test of the study design are finally presented.

# 2 Industrial Augmented Reality in ETO Industry

The basic principle of Augmented Reality is to overlay real environments with virtual content while maintaining a constant positional reference between those two and allowing the user to interact with the virtual content in real-time [8]. Industrial Augmented Reality is a subset of AR and aims at industrial fields of application and their distinct requirements. E.g. most environments in ETO industry do not offer consistent connectivity. Therefore, IAR applications must be designed to focus on daily updates of the most relevant data instead of live streaming it. The main reason for use of IAR, especially in ETO industry, is its positive impact on productivity and product quality.

## 2.1 Productivity Impact

In previous research, Halata, Friedewald et al. [5, 9] extensively studied the use of AR in one-of-a-kind production for products, which are produced in a prepared environment, like cruise ships in a yard and assessed the individual potentials of different IAR devices. They concluded that handheld devices bear the biggest potential to improve key activities found in productivity analysis for assembly processes in ETO industry, which requires more flexible work planning than in BTO or MTO industries. Although focusing on tablets for prototyping and evaluation, they anticipate similar potentials for smartphones. Studies with workers from ETO industry in a test environment revealed a significant labor productivity increase of up to 19% with a tablet-based prototype [9].

The productivity increase results from the impact of an IAR system on those activities which are summarized as information gathering. An example is gathering information about the final state of a work package in order to plan the task execution ad-hoc and to check for engineering changes, which occur more often than in other industries due to the ETO approach. A target-actual comparison after a work package is finished, reveals deviations from target state. AR is not only a more intuitive way of completeness check in comparison to the use of drawings, evaluations have also shown an increased error detection rate and improved product quality, which reduces rework [9].

## 2.2   Standard User Interface for Tablet-Based IAR

In the research project SUPER [10] an IAR prototype based on the fundamental concept of Halata et al. [5, 9] has been developed, which offers additional features like displaying a product structure and advanced filtering. Its UI is shown in Fig. 1 and consists of three main areas. There are two collapsible *2D content areas* on each side of the screen (1), which can hold different groups of information and associated functionalities, called modules. A module is for example the searchable product structure on the left side of the screen, which a worker uses to find and inspect relevant parts for a work package. A *3D content area* is using nearly the entire screen space when 2D content areas are collapsed (2). It either displays an entirely virtual environment (CAD mode) or an augmented reality visualization (AR mode). Two constantly visible *control bars* at the top and bottom of the screen (3) contain buttons to control these visualization modes as well as the activation state of modules in the 2D content areas. Further buttons allow for user interactions affecting the 3D content area in terms of navigation, e.g. automatic movement of the camera towards a selected part in CAD mode.

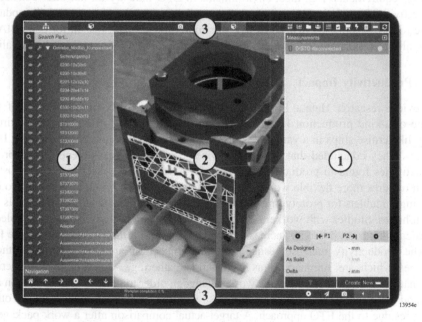

**Fig. 1.** User interface of a tablet-based IAR prototype

# 3   Adapting the User Interface to the Smartphone Screen

Since the hardware performance is comparable between smartphones and tablets, the smaller screen size of smartphones in particular makes the difference. In the following the focus therefore is on solving the resulting challenge of maintaining user experience despite the smaller screen size, when IAR is brought to smartphones.

In order to develop an adapted UI design and to implement it in a prototypical application, requirements are formulated, that aim for good user experience.

## 3.1   Fundamental Requirements

A satisfying user experience is tightly coupled with user friendliness and reliability of an application. In order to incorporate these aspects in a UI design, requirements have been compiled, which are of special importance for a smartphone UI:

- **Device Orientation.** Unlike tablets, which are primarily used in landscape orientation, for smartphones portrait orientation is the more common one [11]. This is especially due to its allowance for one hand operation. Also there is higher relevance of device orientation due to the larger aspect ratio of the screen, resulting in a bigger difference in field of view when viewing a 3D scene. A smartphone UI therefore has to adapt to frequent changes in device orientation, since users tend to change it depending on the displayed content and situations requiring one-hand operation.
- **Restricted Screen Zones.** Smartphones include a variety of sensors, like cameras and brightness sensors, which are necessarily placed at the front of the device facing the user, e.g. to perform video calls. Many devices have display notches that integrate the sensors but make parts of the screen resolution invisible. On top of that the native operation systems of smartphones reserve other restricted areas to place controls such as a virtual home menu buttons. A smartphone UI therefore has to take into account both of these restricted screen zones.
- **Information Access.** The UI should allow easy and fast access to any information and functionality and therefore require the least possible amount of interactions. This can be challenging. A multi-level dropdown menu is an example for a common UI element, which requires little screen space, but tends to obstruct the information it is linked to, because it requires multiple inputs for information at a deeper menu level.
- **Predictability.** The UI should give the user the feeling of being in control by having a predictable, i.e. reproducible behavior. Automatic UI reactions should be kept at a minimum and should be simple enough for the user to understand. A menu that automatically sorts itself based on the elements a user often uses, might appear helpful in the first place, but it is not very predictable since the user will find himself in situations where buttons changed positions, resulting in a feeling of uncertainty.
- **Intuitive Interactions and Layout.** Smartphone operating systems have basic design guidelines for their target device which foster intuitive use, e.g. size of interaction items like buttons should be suitable to be reliably clicked without misses. Another aspect of these guidelines requires, that the UI layout should be organized in a fixed grid, so the user can easily internalize it.

- **User Focus.** The limited screen size of smartphones can lead to unavoidable conflicts about which areas of the UI should be in focus and therefore use more screen space. The UI should support the user in establishing focus by allowing him to maximize certain areas of interest and minimize others. Where possible the UI can taking control over this automatically under consideration of aforementioned *predictability*.

## 3.2  Design of the User Interface

These fundamental requirements have been taken into account to create a prototype optimized for smartphones. The underlying design activities and decisions can be consolidated into three main activities.

**Streamlining the UI.** Many common smartphones have space-limiting notches at the top of the screen. However, the two 3D mode control buttons fit in this area (1) as shown in Fig. 2 a), where they are quickly accessible, but hardly pressed accidentally. The majority of buttons for controlling module visibility can be combined in a single menu strip large enough to view a reasonable number of buttons in parallel (2). It allows to access further menu items by horizontal scrolling.

Additionally both 2D content areas of the tablet UI can be combined into a single one to substantially reduce the need for screen space (3). Since most modules are designed to be used independently, the 2D content area can be restricted to only contain one module at a time. Lastly the bottom control bar is resized to fit larger buttons, which demand for less typing precision (4).

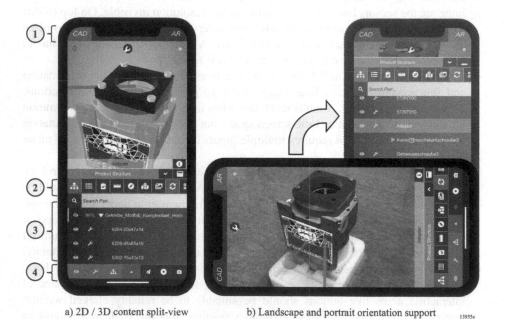

a) 2D / 3D content split-view          b) Landscape and portrait orientation support

**Fig. 2.** UI of the smartphone-based IAR prototype

**Adding User Control over the Layout.** Reduction of the UI to two content areas already increases clarity, but can be further improved by allowing the user to decide which area to primarily work with. It leads to a reduction of the split-attention effect [12], that the user experiences when using the 2D and 3D area simultaneously as shown in Fig. 2 a). Therefore the UI is extended with controls to expand and minimize the 2D area, hiding or expanding the 3D visualization area as a result (see Fig. 2 b).

If the smartphone's orientation changes from vertical to horizontal, the user interface automatically reacts by minimizing the 2D area and maximizing the 3D area to give the user a greater field of view for AR and CAD mode.

**Improving Interaction with Lists.** Lists will automatically react to changing selection in the 3D area by expanding items and scrolling to the relevant list entry (auto-scroll) as shown in Fig. 3. When using the search bar on top of a list (1), the 2D area is automatically expanded to full screen (1*). Selecting a search result (2) also leads to the aforementioned auto-scroll behavior (2*).

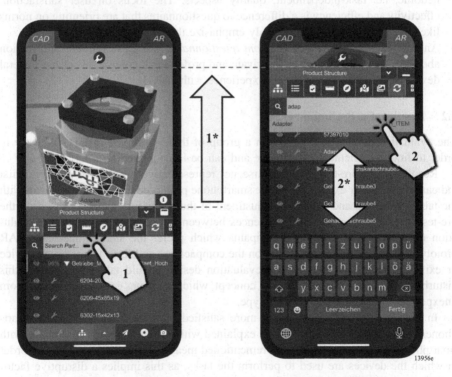

**Fig. 3.** Optimized user interactions with lists (1, 2) by automatic UI reactions (1*, 2*)

The UI design has been implemented in a prototypical IAR application. In the following, the goal is to examine the resulting user experience in comparison with the tablet-based prototype, which has been introduced in Sect. 2.2.

# 4   Comparative Study on User Experience

## 4.1   Methodology

To cover both task-related and task-independent aspects concerning the user experience, the proposed evaluation method combines three questionnaires. Participants perform different IAR related tasks with each device and then answer the questionnaires.

- The *NASA Task Load Index (TLX)* quantifies the overall workload of a person for performing a task based on six individual factors measured on a 20-step scale [13]. It serves as a standardized questionnaire to evaluate whether the device type effects the effort to achieve certain tasks performed with a designated software prototype.
- The *User Experience Questionnaire (UEQ)* captures the overall impression of a user interacting with a software [14]. This is represented by six different scales, which are assigned to two categories of either pragmatic, i.e. task-related, or hedonic, i.e. task-independent, quality aspects. The focus on user satisfaction, effectivity and efficiency is a difference to questionnaires that are orienting on norms like ISO 9241/110-S, which mainly emphasize the latter two aspects.
- An additional self-developed *custom questionnaire* is used to retrieve information about the user's device usage in private and professional context, his or her general device preferences and previous experience with IAR.

## 4.2   Results of a Preliminary Test

The evaluation method was tested on a group of three workmen in ETO industry in order to find out whether it is suitable and can be later applied on a larger group.

Results of the pre-test are of course not representative but deliver a helpful first indication about user experience of the smartphone prototype in direct comparison with the tablet prototype and needs for adjustment of the evaluation method. Based on the pre-test, the following relevant differences between the devices that affect the evaluation design can been found. Participants which prefer the smartphone-based IAR prototype often reason their decision on the compactness and form factor of the device or existing practice and habit. The evaluation design should take into account this disturbance factor by using a blocking concept, which separates experienced users from unexperienced ones for each device type.

In this pre-test participants were more satisfied with their task results on smartphones than on tablets. This might be explained with a higher amount of practice with smartphones and emphasizes the aforementioned measure. It also depends on the order in which the devices are used to perform the tasks, as this implies a disruptive factor due to a training effect on the task execution when the other type of device is used to repeat the task. In order to reduce this interference, the starting device type must also be taken into account when blocking.

## 5  Outlook

The presented IAR prototype presented in this paper is the foundation for process-related research on the use of smartphones as an IAR device for ETO industry. The pre-tested study allows to compare devices in terms of the user experience and is intended to be used on a larger scale in future research. The measurement of user experience aims at determining the device that mostly satisfies workers' needs.

However, an additional productivity analysis of both devices in a laboratory environment would enable to also take into account the economic impact to a company.

**Acknowledgments.** The authors would like to express their gratitude to the Research Council of Norway (MAROFF-2) for funding this research in the project "SmartYard" (No. 282365). We are also grateful for the dedicated contribution of the participants who took part in the pre-test.

## References

1. Strandhagen, J.W., Buer, S.-V., Semini, M., Alfnes, E.: Digitalized manufacturing logistics in engineer-to-order operations. In: Ameri, F., Stecke, K.E., von Cieminski, G., Kiritsis, D. (eds.) APMS 2019. IAICT, vol. 566, pp. 579–587. Springer, Cham (2019). https://doi.org/10.1007/978-3-030-30000-5_71
2. Bottani, E., Vignali, G.: Augmented reality technology in the manufacturing industry: a review of the last decade. IISE Trans. **51**(3), 284–310 (2019). https://doi.org/10.1080/24725854.2018.1493244
3. Helle, S., Korhonen, S., Euranto, A., Kaustinen, M., Lahdenoja, O., Lehtonen, T.: Benefits achieved by applying augmented reality technology in marine industry. In: Bertram, V. (ed.) COMPIT 2014, pp. 86–97. Verlag Schriftenreihe Schiffbau, Hamburg (2014)
4. Fraga-Lamas, P., Fernandez-Carames, T.M., Blanco-Novoa, O., Vilar-Montesinos, M.A.: A review on industrial augmented reality systems for the industry 4.0 shipyard. IEEE Access **6**, 13358–13375 (2018). https://doi.org/10.1109/ACCESS.2018.2808326
5. Halata, P.S., Friedewald, A., Lödding, H.: Augmented reality supported information gathering in one-of-a-kind production. In: Bertram, V. (ed.) COMPIT 2014, pp. 489–503. Verlag Schriftenreihe Schiffbau, Hamburg (2014)
6. Navab, N.A.: Developing killer apps for industrial augmented reality. IEEE Comput. Graph. Appl. **24**(3), 16–20 (2004). https://doi.org/10.1109/mcg.2004.1297006
7. Merhar, L., Berger, C., Braunreuther, S., Reinhart, G.: Digitization of manufacturing companies: employee acceptance towards mobile and wearable devices. In: Ahram, T.Z. (ed.) AHFE 2018. AISC, vol. 795, pp. 187–197. Springer, Cham (2019). https://doi.org/10.1007/978-3-319-94619-1_18
8. Azuma, R.T.: A survey of augmented reality. Presence Teleoperators Virtual Environ. **6**(4), 355–385 (1997). https://doi.org/10.1162/pres.1997.6.4.355
9. Friedewald, A., Halata, P.S., Meluzov, N., Lödding, H.: Die Produktivitätswirkung von Augmented Reality in der Unikatfertigung. In: Schlick, C.M. (ed.): Megatrend Digital-isierung - Potenziale der Arbeits- und Betriebsorganisation, pp. 141–162. GITO, Berlin (2016)
10. Wanner, M.-C., Lödding, H., et al.: Schiffbauliche Unikatproduktion mit Erweiterter Realität (SUPER). Final Report, Center of Maritime Technologies e.V. (CMT), Hamburg (2019)

11. Smartphone and tablet portrait orientation usage 2017 Q3. https://www.scientiamobile.com/smartphone-tablet-portrait-orientation-usage-2017-q3. Accessed 2 Apr 2020
12. Chandler, P., Sweller, J.: The split-attention effect as a factor in the design of instruction. British J. Educ. Psychol. **62**(2), 233–246 (1992). https://doi.org/10.1111/j.2044-8279.1992.tb01017.x
13. Hart, S.G., Staveland, L.E.: Development of NASA-TLX (Task Load Index): results of empirical and theoretical research. In: Hancock, P.A., Meshkati, N. (eds.) Human Mental Workload, Advances in Psychology, vol. 52, pp. 139–183. Elsevier, Amsterdam (1988). https://doi.org/10.1016/S0166-4115(08)62386-9
14. Rauschenberger, M., Schrepp, M., Perez-Cota, M., Olschner, S., Thomaschewski, J.: Efficient measurement of the user experience of interactive products. How to use the user experience questionnaire (UEQ). Example: Spanish language version. IJIMAI **2**(1), 39–45 (2013). https://doi.org/10.9781/ijimai.2013.215

# Exploring the Path Towards Construction 4.0: Collaborative Networks and Enterprise Architecture Views

Ovidiu Noran[1,3(✉)], David Romero[2], and Sorin Burchiu[3]

[1] Griffith University, Brisbane, Australia
O.Noran@griffith.edu.au
[2] Tecnológico de Monterrey, Monterrey, Mexico
david.romero.diaz@gmail.com
[3] University of Constructions Bucharest, Bucharest, Romania
sburchiu@gmail.com

**Abstract.** Construction 4.0 is an engineering and construction paradigm derived from Industry 4.0 that describes the fourth industrial revolution. Construction 4.0 promises to revolutionize the way buildings are constructed and managed; however, there are several major hurdles to be overcome, such as the human skilling and degree of automation, the information systems aspect, and especially the heterogeneous nature of the projects and the supply chains involved. This paper elaborates on these challenges in achieving the Construction 4.0 paradigm and describes possible solutions using various concepts based on Collaborative Networks and Enterprise Architecture disciplines to enable the full potential of the Construction 4.0 paradigm.

**Keywords:** Construction 4.0 · Collaborative networks · Enterprise Architecture

## 1 Introduction

*Construction 4.0* is an engineering and construction paradigm derived from Industry 4.0, covering "the industrial use of new construction systems and digital technologies on projects and in structures delivered" [1]. Furthermore, it calls for new professions and skills in the construction sector as a result of the adoption of new digital technologies. These technologies encompass (a) *industrial production systems* such as prefabrication, 3D-printing and assembly, and offsite manufacture; (b) *cyber-physical systems* incl. sensors, drones, autonomous vehicles, and robots; and (c) *digital technologies* like BIM (building information modelling), laser scanning, AI and cloud computing, big data and data analytics, blockchain, and augmented reality) [2].

The *Construction 4.0 paradigm* promises to revolutionize the way buildings are constructed and construction sites are managed. While the awareness and readiness of construction professionals steadily improve [3], there are still major challenges ahead to be overcome by this traditional heavy industry. Some of these challenges have been identified by Oesterreich and Teuteberg [4]: (a) the complexity of construction projects, (b) the uncertainty over tangible and intangible constraints within the individual projects, (c) a highly fragmented supply chain, (d) short-term thinking as a result of the temporary nature of construction projects, and (e) rigid culture, resistant to changes.

This paper elaborates in the following opportunity areas for the construction sector: (a) technology-enhanced construction management *functions* towards more fluid, faster projects with fewer errors, (b) interoperable *information* management systems for effective communication and coordination, (c) improved human *resources* digital skills towards the construction worker of the future, and (d) better approaches for the dynamic *organisation* and management of the construction supply chains, guided by the disciplines of *Collaborative Networks* [5] and *Enterprise Architecture* [6].

## 2  Technology-Enhanced Construction Management Functions

*Digital Transformation* of the construction sector, as one of the oldest industries [7], represents a significant set of opportunities for the effective management of construction projects, and the improvement of their productivity and supply chains [7–9]. According to [8], the *Construction 4.0 design principles* can be summarized in (a) *interconnection and interoperability* – aimed at supporting effective communication and coordination among stakeholders; (b) *information transparency* – enabled by virtual and augmented realities; (c) *decentralized decision-making* – using cloud-based building information systems for collaboration throughout a building lifecycle, and (d) *technical assistance* – by robots and drones usage for hazardous and unsafe works for humans as well as new human-machine collaborations for higher levels of productivity than neither can achieve in their own. Furthermore, the *Operational and Informational Technologies* (OT/IT) in the construction sector can be categorized into three big groups according to [9]: (a) *workflow automation technologies* – focused on improving structured data manipulation and handling such as CAD, ERP, CRM, and more recently BIM (Building Information Modelling[1]) systems; (b) *communication and collaboration technologies* – focused on enhancing the handling of unstructured data (like text, voice, images, and videos) by using (i) big data analytics for better understanding customers' expectations, (ii) augmented reality for very informative and

---

[1] BIM is a digital representation of the physical and functional characteristics of a facility, and a shared, reliable knowledge resource for decision-making about a faculty during its lifecycle [10].

interactive e-brochures, (iii) virtual reality for mock-ups walk-throughs, and (iv) wearable devices for anywhere, anytime communication, coordination and collaboration among stakeholders; and (c) *operational technologies* – spanning from (i) smart sensors for real-time data acquisition, (ii) fast building systems based on prefabrication, preassembly, modularization and 3D-printing approaches, and (iii) robotics and automation for performing repetitive and/or dangerous processes for humans, and artificial intelligence for aiding construction workers with smart equipment and tools to do better their jobs.

Moreover, Hossain and Nadeem [8] propose a *strategic framework* to implement the *Construction 4.0 paradigm* at supply chain level among construction companies by following a step-by-step procedure that (a) maps out the construction supply chain and its digital maturity; (b) selects construction partners for a pilot project; (c) builds digital capabilities by incorporating new construction technologies to the supply chain partners' bag of assets; and (d) starts performing data analytics towards a data-driven decision-making culture; finally (e) transforms and (f) sustains a new digital way of operating using appropriate digital tools and standards for higher productivity levels.

## 3   Interoperable Information Management Systems

BIM [10] is becoming the core of information management in the construction industry to allow all stakeholders to exchange and manage information throughout the lifecycle of a building. Unfortunately, however, the BIM adoption rate in the construction sector has been much slower than anticipated [11], even though BIM offers the capability of *digitising* building projects information based on established information technologies within the various professional areas involved in the building lifecycle phases. Thus, BIM is an essential component of new *Cyber-Physical Building Management Systems (CP-BMSs)* proposed by Noran et al. [12], which constitute a major stepping stone towards the *Construction 4.0 paradigm* attainment. Hence, a *CP-BMS* can be defined as "a building management system that leverages the advances brought by intelligent cyber-physical systems for real-time information management of a building state during its lifecycle" [12].

Importantly, the full benefits brought by CP-BMSs and BIM can only be achieved if *digital technologies* facilitate the prompt and free flow and ubiquity of information among construction stakeholders under cloud-based interoperable information systems [13], whereby the appropriate *cloudification* and *interoperability standards* have to be achieved in terms of structure [14] and extent [15] (see Fig. 1). Also, the use of large amounts of information gathered by smart sensors towards data-driven decision-making poses the challenge of proper interpretation to achieve self- and situational-awareness as described in [12] and [16], possibly using situation and domain level theories through channel logic [17] as further detailed in [18].

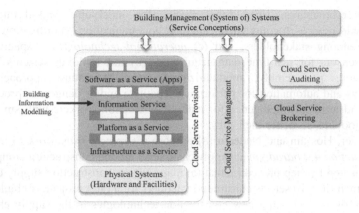

Fig. 1. CP-BMS and BIM cloudification (based on the model described in [12])

# 4   Human Resources Digital Skills Development

Although more *digital skills* are gradually starting to be demand in the construction sector, there is still a high degree of resistance to change in this traditional industry [3]. In this sense, the *Operator 4.0* concept defined by Romero et al. [19] can be specialised to define several stages in the development of a construction worker skillset towards the *Construction Worker 4.0,* as follows: (stage 1) construction workers continue to conduct manual and dextrous work with support from mechanical tools and manually operated machines; (stage 2) construction workers make use of computer-aided tools such as CAD systems, possibly integrated into other enterprise information systems like ERPs, and motor-powered construction machinery; (stage 3) construction workers get involved in cooperative work with robots, drones, and other machines and computer tools in human-robot collaborations; and (stage 4) construction workers evolve to the usage of wearable devices enhancing their physical, sensorial, and cognitive capabilities.

In this fourth stage, the construction worker evolution is represented by a *smart* and *skilled* operator who performs work aided by machines *if* and *as needed.* Automation here is seen as a further enhancement of the human's physical, sensorial, and cognitive capabilities through the usage of *Human Cyber-Physical Systems (H-CPSs)* [19, 20]. The implementation of the *Construction Worker 4.0* concept would evolve the current state of human-machine interaction in the construction sector, and thus, become an essential enabler for the *Construction 4.0 paradigm.* Moreover, the application of the *Human-in-the-Loop (HITL)* feedback control systems in construction projects can lead to systems that require human interaction [20] by (a) letting the operator directly control the operation under supervisory control, (b) letting automation monitor the operator and take appropriate actions, or (c) a hybrid of 'a' and 'b', where automation monitors the operator, and takes human input for the control and acts appropriately. HITL control models, although being challenging due to the complex physiological, sensorial, and cognitive nature of human beings, are an important enabler for the achievement of the *balanced human-automation symbiosis,* especially in the construction sector, usually featuring hesitation and delays in adopting robotics and automation technologies.

## 5 Dynamic Supply Chain Organization and Management

The construction sector has traditionally been known for custom-built projects for one-off designs; unfortunately, this tradition constitutes an important challenge in achieving the *Construction 4.0 paradigm* as, for example, *new industrial production systems* like "fast building systems" based on prefabrication, preassembly, modularization and 3D-printing, and *advanced operational technologies* like construction automation [21] and robotics systems would benefit from more standardization and usage for higher levels of productivity and construction quality.

The construction industry is one of the major raw materials consumers; moreover, its products (i.e. buildings) account for 30% of global greenhouse emissions [22]. In the current climate change situation and efforts to control it, (a) waste minimization during construction and (b) the creation of sustainable and energy-efficient buildings is paramount [23]. The *Circular Economy* concept, populated with interconnected sensing enterprises, intelligent assets, and CPSs [24] can help meet these goals. Unfortunately, however, a significant barrier in achieving the necessary circularity and efficiency is the heterogeneity of the suppliers involved in the construction effort, resulting in quality control, time, and budget issues. Concepts such as *Logistics 4.0* attempt to address the issue [25], however, they are mainly snapshot-based and focused on technology rather than taking a holistic, lifecycle-based approach, and also including other important aspects such as "human aspects" with automation boundary or distinction between management and production activities [26].

## 6 Collaborative Networks and Enterprise Architecture Views

### 6.1 Collaborative Networks Models in the Construction 4.0 Context

This paper proposes to engage the concept of *Collaborative Networks (CNs)* [5], which has been proven in various areas and now is reaching the Industry 4.0 paradigm as communities or ecosystems of smart entities [27]. CNs have been traditionally used to allow collaborative enterprises to bid for one-of-a-kind projects requiring competencies beyond those of a single organisation [28]. Many construction projects such as large buildings (or clusters thereof) or infrastructure (i.e., roads, bridges, tunnels) fit this image. In addition, the management of the completed buildings can also benefit from the CNs virtual enterprise models in the form of potential *Service Virtual Enterprises (SVEs)* [28] usable towards providing mgmt. and maintenance services (see Fig. 2).

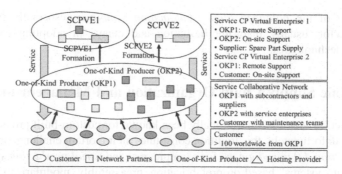

**Fig. 2.** Collaborative service model (based on [28])

The heterogeneous feature of construction projects has endured to this day. The advent of advanced ICTs, such as the Internet of Things, Services, and People (IoTSP), has prompted efforts to use it towards a new *Collaborative Networks 4.0* paradigm; however, as shown above, this is currently limited to a snapshot approach focused on the current technology. The proposed CNs approach, based on *Virtual Enterprises* [5, 28], has been proven in the industry in the past; moreover, when coupled with lifecycle reference frameworks it has been shown to also be able to support in a *holistic* and *integrated* manner the upcoming Industry 4.0 paradigm [27]. As such, it is highly likely to also be useful for the Construction 4.0 endeavours.

In the Industry 4.0 context, the CNs 4.0 can enable a group of smart enterprises to be selected from a pool of certified participants to promptly come together to form a *Virtual Cyber-Physical Enterprise (VCPE)* as shown in Fig. 2. This VCPE will employ agreed-upon standardized protocols and processes that can be digitalised and (partially or fully) executed by other CPSs. The VCPE can thus support an evolved CNs 4.0 paradigm addressing the heterogeneity problem of the Construction 4.0 paradigm.

The CNs concept makes the most sense when applied in a lifecycle context as one can understand how the various participants can interact depending on their current and future lifecycle phases. While there can be many ways one can model lifecycles of entities, intuitively the best way would be to choose a framework that integrates aspects deemed of importance to the project at hand in the context of participants' lifecycles. The *extent of digital maturity* appears to be the basis of the classification for any Industry, it, therefore, follows that a framework that integrates this aspect in a lifecycle context would be best suited.

Another important aspect is the distinction between management/control and the mission accomplishment (a product or service) of an entity. This allows to clearly define essential aspects such as organisational culture and *agility*, i.e. the capacity of an entity to adapt in response to changes in its environment to cope with them.

## 6.2    Enterprise Architecture Modelling in the Construction 4.0 Context

This paper will make use of the *GERA modelling framework* [6], depicted like a three-dimensional structure integrating several dimensions incl. those defined as important for the *Construction 4.0 paradigm*. For this paper, the authors shall use only a 'slice' (extract) of the modelling framework at the model level; moreover, the third dimension featuring aspects such as Function, Information, Resources, and Organization (FIRO), previously used in the paper will be flattened for the sake of clarity. The result is a modelling construct such as shown in Fig. 3. Of course, once the basic concept is agreed upon by the stakeholders, richer (and implicitly more complex) models can be created reintroducing additional aspects while preserving the lifecycle context, and the mgmt. vs. production viewpoint.

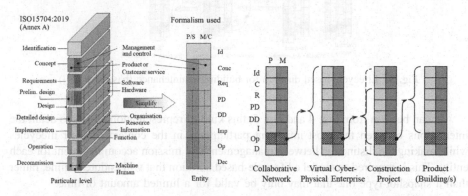

**Fig. 3.** GERA MF based construct (based on [6])

**Fig. 4.** Creation of the VCPE (based on [29])

Using the above-defined construct, one can model how the CNs concept can help the *Construction 4.0* endeavour. The modelling principle is shown in Fig. 4, whereby a CN composed of certified (qualified) suppliers creates a VCPE which then, in turn, creates (and typically also operates) a project whose purpose is to construct one or more buildings. The modelling construct allows depicting the creation and operation of Service VCPE for the maintenance of buildings, in the context of the lifecycles of all involved entities. Thus, Fig. 5 shows how several potential partners can agree (possibly at the initiative of the largest or most influential partner, the leading partners in the figure) to form a CN to be able to bid for and accomplish projects beyond their individual competencies.

Thus, the Service Collaborative Network will be able, based on pre-agreed processes and protocols, to quickly form an entity having all the necessary competencies to bid for and accomplish a service (e.g., building maintenance) project. At the same time, potential suppliers and contractors will go through a certification process to achieve readiness to support an SVCPE as required.

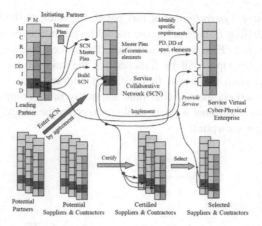

**Fig. 5.** Lifecycle-based diagram for building maintenance (based on [29])

As can be seen from Fig. 4 and Fig. 5, this kind of representation allows to detail the interactions between the most important participants in the context of their lifecycles while making the distinction between management and mission accomplishment for each entity. This is required to model a lifecycle-based solution that will endure in time, rather than a snapshot-type one that may only be valid for a limited amount of time.

# 7   Conclusions and Further Work

Achieving the *Construction 4.0* paradigm must overcome several hurdles specific to this domain; this paper has detailed some of them and proposed also some solutions. In the human area, the "Construction Worker 4.0" will be assisted by automation when and where required only. In the "Information Systems" area, adequate cloudification and interoperability standards have to be achieved. Lastly, the heterogeneity of construction stakeholders present in a construction project setup and management has to be addressed. The paper has proposed the use of the proven *Collaborative Networks* paradigm applied within a construction lifecycle project to assist in the proper implementation of the Industry 4.0 paradigm based features in the construction industry. Further work will concentrate on the development of "enterprise reference models" for the *Construction 4.0* paradigm.

# References

1. BIM World. https://bim-w.com/en/construction-4-0
2. Sawhney, A., Riley, M., Irizarry, J.: Construction 4.0 for the Build Environment. Routledge, London (2020)
3. Osunsanmi, T., et al.: Appraisal of stakeholders' willingness to adopt construction 4.0 technologies for construction projects. Built Environ. Proj. Asset Manage. (2020)

4. Oesterreich, T.D., Teuteberg, F.: Understanding the implications of digitisation and automation in the context of industry 4.0. Comput. Ind. **83**, 121–139 (2016)
5. Camarinha-Matos, L., et al.: Collaborative networked organizations: concepts and practice in manufacturing enterprises. Comput. Ind. Eng. **57**(1), 46–60 (2009)
6. ISO/IEC, Annex A: GERAM, in ISO15704-2019. https://www.iso.org/standard/71890.html
7. Klinc, R., Turk, Ž.: Construction 4.0 – digital transformation of one of the oldest industries. Econ. Bus. Rev. **21**(3), 393–410 (2019)
8. Aslam Hossain, M.D., Nadeem, A.: Towards digitizing the construction industry: state of the art of construction 4.0. In: Structural Engineering and Construction Management, pp. 1–6 (2019)
9. Rastogi, S.: Construction 4.0. In: Indian Lean Construction Conference, pp. 1–11 (2017)
10. National BIM Standard – United States. https://www.nationalbimstandard.org/faqs
11. Walasek, D., Barszcz, A.: Analysis of the adoption rate of building information modeling and its return on investment. Procedia Eng. **172**, 1227–1234 (2017)
12. Noran, O., Sota, I., Bernus, P.: Towards next generation building management systems. In: E3S Web Conferences, Les Ulis: EDP Sciences, vol. 111, pp. 1–9 (2019)
13. Fernandes, P.: Advantages and Disadvantages of BIM Platforms on Construction Site. University of Porto, Portugal, Master's thesis in Civil Engineering (2013)
14. Liu, F., et al.: NIST Cloud Computing Reference Architecture. NIST-SP500-292, US (2011)
15. Noran, O., Bernus, P.: Business cloudification: an enterprise architecture perspective. In: 19th International Conference on Enterprise Information Systems, pp. 353–360. ScitePress (2017)
16. Bernus, P., Noran, O.: Data rich – but information poor. In: Camarinha-Matos, L.M., Afsarmanesh, H., Fornasiero, R. (eds.) PRO-VE 2017. IAICT, vol. 506, pp. 206–214. Springer, Cham (2017). https://doi.org/10.1007/978-3-319-65151-4_20
17. Barwise, J., Seligman, J.: Information Flow: The Logic of Distributed Systems. Cambridge Tracts in Theoretical Computer Science. Cambridge University Press, Cambridge (2008)
18. Noran, O., Bernus, P.: Improving digital decision making through situational awareness. In: Information Systems Development: Designing Digitalization Proceedings, pp. 1–12 (2018)
19. Romero, D., Bernus, P., Noran, O., Stahre, J., Fast-Berglund, Å.: The Operator 4.0: human cyber-physical systems & adaptive automation towards human-automation symbiosis work systems. In: Nääs, I., Vendrametto, O., Reis, J.M., Gonçalves, R.F., Silva, M.T., von Cieminski, G., Kiritsis, D. (eds.) APMS 2016. IAICT, vol. 488, pp. 677–686. Springer, Cham (2016). https://doi.org/10.1007/978-3-319-51133-7_80
20. Munir, S., et al.: Cyber-physical system challenges for human-in-the-loop control. In: Feedback Computing, pp. 1–4 (2013)
21. Ozevin, D., et al.: Construction automation: research areas, industry concerns and suggestions for advancement. Autom. Constr. **94**, 22–38 (2018)
22. WEF: Shaping the Future of Construction: A Breakthrough in Mindset and Technology (2016)
23. Karlessi, T., et al.: The concept of smart and NZEB buildings and the integrated design approach. Procedia Eng. **180**, 1316–1325 (2017)
24. Romero, D., Noran, O.: Towards green sensing virtual enterprises: interconnected sensing enterprises, intelligent assets and smart products in the cyber-physical circular economy. IFAC Papers Online **50**(1), 11719–11724 (2017)
25. Winkelhaus, S., Grosse, E.H.: Logistics 4.0: a systematic review towards a new logistics system. Prod. Res. **58**(1), 18–43 (2020)
26. Naoum, S.: People and Organizational Management in Construction. Thomas Telford, London (2001)

27. Camarinha-Matos, L.M., Fornasiero, R., Afsarmanesh, H.: Collaborative networks as a core enabler of industry 4.0. In: Camarinha-Matos, L.M., Afsarmanesh, H., Fornasiero, R. (eds.) PRO-VE 2017. IAICT, vol. 506, pp. 3–17. Springer, Cham (2017). https://doi.org/10.1007/978-3-319-65151-4_1
28. Hartel, I., Billinger, S., Burger, G., Kamio, Y.: Virtual organization of after-sales service in the one-of-a-kind industry. In: Camarinha-Matos, L.M. (ed.) PRO-VE 2002. ITIFIP, vol. 85, pp. 405–420. Springer, Boston, MA (2002). https://doi.org/10.1007/978-0-387-35585-6_44
29. Bernus, P., et al.: Using the globemen reference model for virtual enterprise design in after sales service. In: Global Engineering and Manufacturing in Enterprise Networks, pp. 71–90 (2002)

# The Potential for Purchasing Function to Enhance Circular Economy Business Models for ETO Production

Deodat Mwesiumo[1(✉)], Nina Pereira Kvadsheim[1,2], and Bella Belerivana Nujen[2,3]

[1] Faculty of Logistics, Molde University College, Britvegen 2, Molde, Norway
{Deodat.E.Mwesiumo,Nina.P.Kvadsheim}@himolde.no
[2] Møreforsking Molde, Britvegen 4, Molde, Norway
[3] Faculty of International Business, Norwegian University of Science and Technology, Ålesund, Norway
bella.nujen@ntnu.no

**Abstract.** Inclusion of 'circular principles' in the activities of the purchasing process from the initial stages to the end of product life can help all actors in the value chain to deliver sustainability goals through an active, cost-effective and accountable approach. Yet, research on this linkage has been virtually nonexistent. This study extends perspectives and theories on purchasing and circular economy business models (CEBMs) for engineer-to-order (ETO) production. Based on a case study, a framework that identifies critical purchasing activities relevant for enhancing the implementation of CEBMs is developed. The framework advocates that engaging in the proposed activities can compel the purchasing function to increase its strategic focus by being proactive and relentless in embracing circularity in its agenda. In addition to accentuating the relevance of purchasing function in ETO production, the framework shows how harnessing it can benefit circular strategies.

**Keywords:** Circular economy business models · Strategic purchasing · ETO production

## 1 Introduction

The potential for the purchasing function to unleash strategic benefits is well documented. Nonetheless, a gap still exists between the potential strategic role of purchasing and the operational role it continues to exhibit. As such, purchasing must abandon the status quo by focusing on issues beyond cost cash savings and start building long-term capabilities for making broader contribution to the organization's value creation [1]. Since value creation processes of a firm are embodied by its business model (BM), creating strategic value will require purchasing to play an active role in enhancing the implementation of organizations' BMs. Currently, there is a wide consensus that adopting circular economy (CE) is critical for realizing sustainability ambitions and for the promotion of economic growth [2]. However, achieving these ambitions will only be possible if businesses start to embrace CE strategically and

B. Lalic et al. (Eds.): APMS 2020, IFIP AICT 592, pp. 557–564, 2020.
https://doi.org/10.1007/978-3-030-57997-5_64

operationally along with the enactment of appropriate and consistent regulations [3]. Thus, businesses must implement circular economy business models (CEBMs) [4], which can be defined as "the rationale of how an organization creates, delivers, and captures value with and within closed material loops" [5].

Despite being critical for economic growth and a sustainable future, the adoption rates of CEBMs have been fairly low [2]. Among other things, the required changes in product design, production, and logistics systems pose a challenge in the implementation of CEBMs [6]. Conceivably, ways for enhancing the adoption of CEBMs warrant attention. The present paper explores the potential role of the purchasing function in enhancing the CEBMs for ETO production. The ETO context is selected for two reasons. First, CEBMs for ETO production has so far received limited attention despite its importance [7]. Second, purchasing plays a vital role in accomplishing ETO projects [8]. Therefore, insights provided by the present study are relevant to purchasing practitioners working in an ETO environment as well as scholars who investigate ETO related matters.

## 2   Strategic Purchasing in the ETO Production Environment

Strategic purchasing can be defined as "the process of planning, implementing, evaluating, and controlling strategies and operating purchasing decisions for directing all activities of the purchasing function toward opportunities consistent with the firm's capabilities to achieve its long-term goals" [9, p. 201]. Stated differently, strategic purchasing is exemplified by its focus, involvement, and visibility in the creation of firms' competitive advantage [10]. Thus, to be strategic, a purchasing function must be aware of the firm's strategic plans, proactive in its operations, willing to take risks, and relentless in pursuing strategic objectives. More so, purchasing must participate in the strategic processes of the firm [11]. This will allow alignment of the purchasing strategy with the firm's business strategy, which according to [12], is important for contributing to the competitive advantage.

Broadly, ETO refers to a production strategy whereby a product is designed, engineered, and produced according to the specifications provided by a specific customer [13]. This way, ETO products tend to be highly customized and produced in low volumes (often one-of-a-kind). Since the design of ETO products starts when a customer places an order, it is challenging to accurately forecast demand, identify all the required materials and produce the products in advance [14]. Like other products, the value of ETO products can be distinguished into customer's perceived value versus supplier's perceived value [15]. As ETO products are customized according to the customer's specifications, their business viability is only possible when the customer's perceived value surpasses the ETO vendor's perceived value [16]. Taken together, the features of ETO production have implications on the purchasing strategy of the firm. For instance, the sequence that engineers decide how the product should be assembled may not necessarily be the optimal sequence for purchasing the required inputs. Following [12] and [17], this indicates that for a purchasing function to deliver strategic benefits in an ETO environment, it must participate in the strategic processes of the firm and calibrate its activities accordingly. In some cases, it may also need to be proactive in initiating strategic initiatives.

## 3 Potential CEBMs for ETO Production

In the emerging field of CEBMs, Kvadsheim et al. [7] examine ETO products and propose their relevant CEBMs, which are briefly described in this section: 1) *Circular supplies* that involve replacing traditional production inputs with renewable, bio-based or recovered materials that can influence the conceptualization of ETO product design and manufacturing process; 2) *Product life extension* aims to extend the life of products (e.g. through reuse, remanufacturing). This is desirable from a CE perspective, as it implies ETO products and materials embedded in them would remain in the system for a long time, thereby reducing extraction of new resources; 3) *Product as a service* offers product access and retain ownership to internalize benefits of circular resource productivity. With this model, ETO firms have an advantage in selling services and recapturing residual value at end-of-life and 4) *Resource recovery* involves production of secondary raw materials from waste streams. This model is a good fit for most ETO firms, especially where waste material from products can be reclaimed through take-back management and reprocessed cost effectively.

Building on the work of [18] and [19] in distinguishing CEBMs from linear models, [20] categorize CEBMs according to the mechanisms by which resources flow through a system. *Slowing loops* is about designing long-life products and extending the life of products to slow down the flow of resources. *Closing loops* is about recycling to close the loop between post-use and production, and *narrowing loops* aims at using fewer resources per product (e.g. through efficient manufacturing processes and lightweight product design). What is more, while slowing and closing resource loops clearly characterize CE, the narrowing loops strategy also fits in the current linear economy [21]. From these aforementioned CEBMs, it can be concluded that *product life extension* and *product-as-a-service* models seek to retain product value by slowing resource loops. Furthermore, that the *resource recovery* model contributes to closing resource loops by retaining the material value, and the *circular supplies* model seeks to narrow resource loops by retaining material value as well. Combining these key strategies with their respective CEBMs allows developing a framework for guiding the role of the purchasing function in enhancing the CEBM implementation.

## 4 Research Methodology

The present study deploys case study method. According to [22], case study method is useful in studying issues related to purchasing and supply management particularly when investigating contextual issues such as understanding purchasing in particular settings. Since the present study focuses on the potential role of purchasing in one particular context– ETO production, case study method is deemed appropriate. Specifically, a single case study is preferable considering the exploratory nature of the study.

The selected company, hereafter pseudomized as Promaker, is an ETO company that manufactures and supplies custom-made propulsion, positioning and maneuvering systems to domestic and international shipyards and ship owners. The production of the propulsion systems is done on-site and organized as projects that involve engineering design, procurement and production functions. All these functions are kept in-house to ensure quality of the end product. In order to meet or exceed customers' perceived value, Promaker ensures clear understanding of customer requirements, which forms the basis for determining components and subsystems needed to create the end product. Over the past few years, Promaker mostly applied single sourcing strategy and maintained close relations with its suppliers. However, in order to reduce costs and increase quality, the company is in the process of introducing a multiple sourcing strategy.

Data collection was conducted as follows. Firstly, data were collected through semi-structured interviews with individual managers of key functional areas (i.e. product development/engineering, purchasing, production, logistics, and aftersales) to enhance the understanding of processes and issues pertaining to their operations and their viewpoints on the implications of adopting CEBMs. Interviewing all these informants ensured an adequate understanding of Promaker's current BM. Secondly, the information provided by the key informants was triangulated with direct, non-participant observation and document review. In terms of analysis, the study deploys identification and delineation approaches [23], which allowed us to develop a framework that envisions ways through which the purchasing function can enhance the implementation of CEBMs in ETO production. Finally, we performed a quasi-validation of the framework through an expert interview. Similar to [24], the selected expert has deep knowledge and extensive experience in leading various functions in ETO companies and is currently a CEO of an ETO company different from Promaker.

## 5  Analysis and Discussion

The identification and delineation of the purchasing activities that are relevant for enhancing CEBMs in the context of ETO production were achieved through a synthesis and categorization of the collected data. To begin with, CEBMs for ETO production were identified and categorized according to key strategies for moving towards CE, that is, slowing loops, closing loops and narrowing loops. Subsequently, activities involved in a purchasing process were distinguished into three main categories: pre-selection, selection and contracting, and post-award activities. Finally, based on the understanding of the ETO production developed through the case study, relevant purchasing activities were identified for the ETO CEBMs. The activities were then refined through an expert interview. Figure 1 presents the resulting framework that identifies purchasing activities relevant for enhancing the implementation of CEBMs for ETO products.

As shown in Fig. 1, the purchasing function can contribute to the enhancement of such CEBMs right from the pre-selection phase of the purchasing process. This phase consists of activities such as needs identification and analysis, material specifications, discussion with sales people, and supply market analysis. Purchasing function can

| CE strategies | ETO CEBMs | Purchasing activities | | |
|---|---|---|---|---|
| | | Pre-selection activities | Selection and contracting activities | Post award activities |
| Slowing loops | Product life extension / Product as a service | • Emphasize circularity in the discussions with internal clients and suppliers<br>• Market research to explore possibilities for obtaining product as a service and used/repaired products/components<br>• Explore possibilities for designing products in a way that increases durability/maintainability<br>• Discussion on needs analysis and ideas for improved products with other stakeholders (e.g. customers, experts) | • Assess potential to improve products based on circularity and technical specifications (technical dialogue with suppliers)<br>• Acquire product as a service<br>• Consider used/repaired products/components<br>• Consider product longevity<br>• Consider product maintenance services and product warranties<br>• Consider upgrading services<br>• Consider refurbishment/remanufacturing of components<br>• Consider direct reuse of products/components<br>• Consider supplier take-back agreements<br>• The contract regime must be flexible enough to allow CEBM | • Coordination for effective product maintenance<br>• Close collaboration with suppliers, customers and third-party operators |
| Closing loops | Resource recovery | • Emphasize circularity in the discussions with internal clients and suppliers<br>• Explore possibilities for industrial symbiosis<br>• Explore potentials for exploiting the residual value of resources (upcycling and/or downcycling)<br>• Explore the performance characteristics of recovered materials | • Consider geographically proximate partners (i.e. with comparably low logistics costs)<br>• Coordinate verification of the partner suitability<br>• Consider valorization of the materials contained in waste streams (i.e. ensure that their unit cost is lower relative to market price of finished materials)<br>• Consider recovered materials with high certainty of performing as required<br>• The contract regime must be flexible enough to allow CEBM | • Coordination for effective product flow<br>• Crafting and developing synergistic partnerships |
| Narrowing loops | Circular supplies | • Emphasize circularity in the discussions with internal clients and suppliers<br>• Explore potentials for exploiting the residual value of resources (upcycling and/or downcycling)<br>• Explore the performance characteristics of recovered materials | • Emphasize long lasting components<br>• Consider replacing traditional production inputs with renewable or recovered materials<br>• Consider integrating locally derived secondary materials into the supply chains<br>• Emphasize recovered materials to be good substitutes for the traditional materials they replace, as well as sufficiently available and affordable<br>• Consider purchasing finished fully machined parts<br>• Improve resource efficiency (i.e. reducing scrap when machining/cutting parts)<br>• The contract regime must be flexible enough to allow CEBM | • Coordination for effective product maintenance and upgrading services<br>• Close collaboration with suppliers and customers |

**Fig. 1.** Framework to guide the purchasing function in enhancing the implementation of CEBMs in ETO production

enhance ETO CEBMs during this phase by considering and embedding relevant CE principles, depending on the specific CEBM a firm chooses to implement. In addition to potential bidders, a dialogue between purchasers and other stakeholders (e.g. customers, experts) can provide valuable information that would help specify purchasers' needs. For example, in the case of product as a service BM, undertaking an extensive market research in order to get information on customers' willingness to pay for product use without owning the product themselves. Such information may be meaningful in order to keep the final contract within a certain budget frame. Likewise, CE principles can be considered and embedded during the selection and contracting phase. This phase consists of activities such as analysis of supplier proposals, negotiation and selection of suppliers. During this phase, not only CE principles should be included in the evaluation process, but it is an opportunity for the purchasing function to discuss with potential suppliers on their role in supporting the implementation of CEBM fit for their firm. Among the activities suggested in this phase, flexible contracting emerged as an important element for all CEBMs. This coincides with [25] who argues that contracting is a strategically critical capability in forming and shaping relationships across supply chains. Particularly, we argue that flexible contracting must take center stage in the implementation process to ensure that upstream activities are aligned with the selected CEBMs. After signing the contract with the preferred supplier, relevant post-award activities must engage to support the agreed terms related to the selected CEBMs. These can include activities such as nurturing a strategic alliance as well as coordination for effective product maintenance and effective product flow. For instance, effective take-back arrangements and upgrading services will require continued relationship with suppliers.

Although the proposed framework focuses on ETO production, most of the proposed activities can also be relevant for other production strategies such as Make-to-order, Assemble-to-order, and Make-to-stock. While an activity such as collaborating with internal and external clients during the needs analysis phase is specifically relevant for ETO production, other activities such as exploration of possibilities for industrial symbiosis, flexible contract regimes, and close collaboration with suppliers can be useful in the implementation of CEBMs even in other contexts than ETO production. However, important to mention is that large volumes and wide range of products involved in other production strategies may hamper the implementation of some of the proposed activities in the developed framework. In such cases, creating and maintaining strategic relationships with a large number of suppliers in order to enhance CEBMs may become challenging.

## 6 Closing Remarks

The underlying premise of this paper is that the purchasing function can play a key role in enhancing CEBMs. Since the suitability of CEBMs is context dependent, the paper focuses its analysis on the ETO context and proposes relevant purchasing activities for enhancing ETO-CEBMs. Like any other new practice in an organization, enhancing the implementation of CEBMs will require major changes in the purchasing function. Overall, the implementation of the proposed activities can compel the purchasing function to increase its strategic focus by being proactive and relentless in embracing circular principles in its agenda. In addition to looking for opportunities to introduce circular principles with the current product lines, the purchasing function must seek possibilities to innovate with suppliers on new circular products. This will require building a strong business case through quantification of the gains to be achieved. Notably, the purchasing business case must be aligned with the firm's vision and business strategy. Following [26] line of reasoning, we argue that innovating with existing and potential suppliers for supporting CEBMs will require that the purchasing function: (1) explores unmet needs and anticipates future needs by working closely with other functions and clients (2) explores external opportunities for enhancing CE beyond first-tier suppliers (3) involves suppliers in CE projects.

Although the present study provides useful insights, it is important to outline some limitations as they provide opportunities for further research. Firstly, the study has developed a framework based on a single case study, hence future studies may further explore the subject based on multiple ETO cases. Secondly, given the increasing recognition to embrace CEBMs across different industries, future studies may consider investigating the potential role of the purchasing function in enhancing CEBMs in settings other than ETO production.

# References

1. Knoppen, D., Sáenz, M.J.: Purchasing: Can we bridge the gap between strategy and daily reality? Bus. Horiz. **58**(1), 123–133 (2015)
2. Fehrer, J.A., Wieland, H.: A systemic logic for circular business models. J. Bus. Res. (2020). https://doi.org/10.1016/j.jbusres.2020.02.010
3. Guglielmo, C., Nitesh, M.: Circular Business Models for the Built Environment (2017)
4. Kirchherr, J., Reike, D., Hekkert, M.: Conceptualizing the circular economy: an analysis of 114 definitions. Res. Conserv. Recycl. **127**, 221–232 (2017)
5. Mentink, B.: Circular Business Model Innovation: a process framework and a tool for business model innovation in a circular economy (2014)
6. Ünal, E., Shao, J.: A taxonomy of circular economy implementation strategies for manufacturing firms: analysis of 391 cradle-to-cradle products. J. Clean. Prod. **212**, 754–765 (2019)
7. Kvadsheim, N.P., Mwesiumo, D., Emblemsvåg, J.: Examining circular economy business models for engineer-to-order products. In: Ameri, F., Stecke, K.E., von Cieminski, G., Kiritsis, D. (eds.) APMS 2019. IAICT, vol. 566, pp. 570–578. Springer, Cham (2019). https://doi.org/10.1007/978-3-030-30000-5_70
8. Shah, S., Hasan, S.: Procurement Practices in project based manufacturing environments. MATEC Web of Conferences **76**, 02007 (2016)
9. Carr, A.S., Smeltzer, L.R.: An empirically based operational definition of strategic purchasing. Eur. J. Purch. Supply Manage. **3**(4), 199–207 (1997)
10. Paulraj, A., Chen, I.J., Flynn, J.: Levels of strategic purchasing: Impact on supply integration and performance. J. Purch. Supply Manage. **12**(3), 107–122 (2006)
11. Nair, A., Jayaram, J., Das, A.: Strategic purchasing participation, supplier selection, supplier evaluation and purchasing performance. Int. J. Prod. Res. **53**(20), 6263–6278 (2015)

12. Martínez, S., Mediavilla, M., Bäckstrand, J., Bernardos, C.: Alignment of the purchasing strategy to the business strategy: an empirical study on a harbour cranes company. In: Grabot, B., Vallespir, B., Gomes, S., Bouras, A., Kiritsis, D. (eds.) APMS 2014. IAICT, vol. 440, pp. 51–58. Springer, Heidelberg (2014). https://doi.org/10.1007/978-3-662-44733-8_7
13. Gosling, J., Naim, M.M.: Engineer-to-order supply chain management: a literature review and research agenda. Int. J. Prod. Econ. **122**(2), 741–754 (2009)
14. Bertrand, J.W.M., Muntslag, D.R.: Production control in engineer-to-order firms. Int. J. Prod. Econ. **30–31**(C), 3–22 (1993)
15. Lefaix-Durand, A., Kozak, R.: Comparing customer and supplier perceptions of value offerings: an exploratory assessment. J. Bus. Mark. Manage. **4**(3), 129–150 (2010)
16. Mol, P.: Purchasing in an engineer-to-order environment - Part I | Genius ERP. GeniusERP. https://www.geniuserp.com/blog/purchasing-in-an-engineer-to-order-environment. Accessed 6 Mar 2020
17. Formentini, M., Ellram, L.M., Boem, M., Da Re, G.: Finding true north: design and implementation of a strategic sourcing framework. Ind. Mark. Manage. **77**, 182–197 (2019)
18. McDonough, W., Braungart, M.: Cradle to Cradle: Remaking the Way We Make Things. North Point Press, New York, NY (2002)
19. Stahel, W.R.: The Performance Economy (2010)
20. Bocken, N.M.P., de Pauw, I., Bakker, C., van der Grinten, B.: Product design and business model strategies for a circular economy. J. Ind. Prod. Eng. **33**(5), 308–320 (2016)
21. Ludeke-Freund, F., Gold, S., Bocken, N.M.: A review and typology of circular economy business model patterns. J. Ind. Ecol. **23**(1), 1–26 (2018)
22. Dubois, A., Salmi, A.: A call for broadening the range of approaches to case studies in purchasing and supply management. J. Purch. Supply Manage. **22**(4), 247–249 (2016)
23. MacInnis, D.J.: A framework for conceptual contributions in marketing. J. Mark. **75**(4), 136–154 (2011)
24. Tunn, V.S.C., Bocken, N.M.P., van den Hende, E.A., Schoormans, J.P.L.: Business models for sustainable consumption in the circular economy: an expert study. J. Clean. Prod. **212**, 324–333 (2019)
25. Cummins, T.: Strategic contracting as a source of organizational success. J. Strateg. Contract. Negot. **1**(1), 7–14 (2015)
26. Legenvre, H., Gualandris, J.: Innovation sourcing excellence: three purchasing capabilities for success. Bus. Horiz. **61**(1), 95–106 (2018)

# Planning Procurement Activities in ETO Projects

Kristina Kjersem[1(✉)] and Marte Giskeødegård[2]

[1] Møreforsking Molde AS, Britvegen 4, 6410 Molde, Norway
Kristina.kjersem@himolde.no
[2] NTNU, Ålesund, Norway
Marte.giskeodegard@ntnu.no

**Abstract.** The complexity of ETO projects reflects also in the challenges of planning and controlling them. Most ETO companies apply planning procedures based on elements from the traditional project management literature with a linear approach that cannot deal with the challenges of such an environment. Moreover, most of these procedures focus on planning the production activities with little focus on planning the design-, engineering-, and procurement activities. This research looks into how ETO characteristics affect the planning of procurement activities since their outcome have a significant effect on the total cost of the project. The studied literature reveals a need for more knowledge on how to actually plan procurement activities since delayed materials and components contribute to major costs overruns and delays in ETO projects.

**Keywords:** ETO projects · Procurement · Planning

## 1 Introduction

Most Engineer-To-Order (ETO) products are highly customized, unique, and are delivered through a project based approach where the customer is involved in all phases from design to testing and delivery [1]. Usually, this production strategy involves a large number of specialized suppliers that contribute with products, materials, and services at different stages of the project. For example, 60–80% of the value added in shipbuilding projects is procured from external suppliers that must be coordinated by the entity responsible for delivering the final product. Hence, shipbuilding companies had to develop a core competence in integrating such a large number of project participants, an approach that requires considerable coordination and collaboration [2]. Nevertheless, dealing with all these suppliers becomes a challenge especially when several teams perform the procurement activities at different project phases. For example, a specialized procurement team (SPT) together with the design team negotiate delivery terms for the key-components, then the procurement team (at the main yard) negotiate the rest of the components and equipment, while the hull yard negotiate the equipment and materials within their scope of work. There are also other big work packages that are outsourced to specialized suppliers, e.g., electro, accommodation, piping. These suppliers are often in charge of negotiating the procurement of the materials and equipment within their scope of work and within the frame of the project.

© IFIP International Federation for Information Processing 2020
Published by Springer Nature Switzerland AG 2020
B. Lalic et al. (Eds.): APMS 2020, IFIP AICT 592, pp. 565–572, 2020.
https://doi.org/10.1007/978-3-030-57997-5_65

This is a phase-based project management approach where different entities deliver specific parts of the project through well-defined contractual agreements [3].

In a recent research performed together with a Norwegian shipbuilding company, the research team discovered that delayed procurement activities increased significantly the total cost of the project. Since one of the main activities in that research is to analyze the project planning as performed by the case company, we decided to look at how the procurement activities are in fact planned and controlled. One of the preliminary findings shows that even though some procurement activities are included in the project plan, none of the purchasers managed to report the real status of their activities. In fact, the number of issues to be solved together with the customer, design-, engineering-, and production teams while dealing with each specific supplier, overwhelmed the procurement team. They were on a constant firefighting and they had to prioritize placing purchasing orders (POs) based on what items were most delayed. Even though they were working overtime daily, they were never á jour with placing POs within the recommended time frame. The result of delayed POs was higher costs for a significant number of purchased items since suppliers had to deliver them as express orders. Following the plan created at the beginning of the project was an appealing topic, but the negotiating process as well as delayed information from customer, engineering team and suppliers, took too much of their daily work. A closer look at the identified challenges, reveal that many of them were related to the ETO characteristics, e.g., customer involvement, unclear specification, as well as outsourcing and customization. Hence, the main research question for this article is: How do ETO characteristics challenge the planning of procurement activities?

## 2   Theoretical Background

ETO is a production strategy where design-, engineering- and production activities commence only after a customer order is confirmed [4]. This is also applicable to the procurement phase since it cannot be started without information from the customer, the engineering- and the production teams. The ETO environment is characterized by the following elements: products that are customer specific, produced in low volumes and highly customized. To achieve such deliveries, ETO companies apply non-repetitive processes that are labor intensive and demand highly skilled labor [5]. Moreover, several phases and parts of an ETO project are outsourced to specialized suppliers [6, 7] increasing the number of organizations participating in each project [8]. These ETO characteristics have a strong influence on the total planning process [9], that includes the planning of procurement activities.

Hicks, et al., [10] found that most ETO companies use a reactive approach to procurement where functions are departmentalized and predominantly clerical in nature. That is endorsed by [11] who discuss the negative influence and the waste created by the contracting practices that tend to limit procurement performances through focus on contractual specification. Most research regarding procurement in ETO projects refers to the strategies needed to identify the right tactics in choosing and managing their large network of suppliers [12]. Among others, [13, 14], discuss suppliers integration in customer-driven environments, proposing different approaches to categorize and treat the relationships between the participating entities. These studies contribute to a better understanding on the necessity to integrate both customers and suppliers in the decision process. Yet, based on the studied literature, there is a knowledge gap on how to actually plan procurement activities in ETO project given the particularities of this strategy.

Since most ETO products are delivered through a project-based approach [15], the management methods applied by these ETO companies are inspired from the traditional project management literature. Such an approach emphasizes the focus on e.g. contractual agreements, risk management issues, setting the scheduled dates, and communication with the suppliers. These elements are included in a procurement management plan [16] without in fact focusing on planning these activities. That is because planning procurement activities is not seen as part of planning of both engineering and production activities. Yet, since engineering, procurement, and production phases are often performed concurrently, most ETO companies are dependent on an effective collaboration and a dynamic planning process [9] as well project participants that are committed to the planning process [17]. To the best of our knowledge, there is no well-defined planning process for procurement activities in ETO projects.

Moreover, the traditional approach to planning ETO projects, do not take into consideration the iterative nature of most engineering activities, the concurrency among project phases [8], or the uncertainty within ETO product specifications. A consequence of such working models is that procurement activities are at times chaotic and fall behind the schedule resulting in delayed project deliveries and cost overruns.

## 3    Research Method

This research adopts an explorative approach to the topic of the role of planning purchasing activities in ETO projects. The data analyzed in this article stem from a thematically broader research project, on integrated planning in the shipbuilding sector. Within this project, we have conducted 28-semi-structured interviews with the entire project organization at the yard, internal, and external. In addition, the researchers have observed seven project planning meetings. The purpose of this data gathering process was to get a better understanding of key issues in the project management process, and more specifically, the role of planning in this respect. Other sources of data include document analysis of project plans, reports and so forth, and three master thesis written within the project. The collected data was then structured in NVIVO by topics (e.g. planning, digitization), phases and levels of planning for each department.

Planning purchasing activities emerged as a central topic in the analysis and seemed to be an issue permeating in all levels of the project. As the challenges of planning purchasing activities became central, the project team initiated a comparative project at another yard targeting specifically planning of purchasing activities in ETO projects. The yard chosen as the second empirical case is relevant due to its role as a key player in the industry. The study was designed by outlining a topic for a master thesis, supervised by the project leader. In this master thesis, five interviews were conducted, specifically targeting planning of purchasing activities from several different perspectives.

At this yards, two project planners, two purchasers and one production manager were interviewed. Thus, the methodological strategy in this article is explorative, following up on emerging topics identified through systematic analysis of the preliminary findings. One of the most relevant challenge in both companies is that they do not have a follow-up system that can in fact visualize the effects of delayed procurement activities. While the current article recognizes this as a key issue, we identify a need for a more extensive study on planning purchasing activities in ETO projects. Because our research project is still going, the results presented here are preliminary.

## 4    Case Company – Challenging Issues

The main case company uses an ETO approach to deliver highly customized vessels to several markets like offshore, cruise, fishing and shipping. They use advanced planning software to create a project plan after the contract is signed and this plan includes a certain number of procurement activities. Nevertheless, these activities are usually the ones falling behind the schedule as soon as the project has started and many of the reasons are connected to the ETO characteristics as discussed later.

Like other similar companies, the main case company divides the procurement responsibilities between several entities: SPT and basic design (BD), procurement department (PD) located at the main yard, procurement team at the hull yard and procurement performed by other participating organizations (e.g., piping, electro, etc.). Based on information from customer and BD, the SPT negotiates conditions for most of the key-components in the beginning of the project. The negotiation process contains several phases: a) choose the suppliers that are relevant for each specific item; b) customer approves the selected suppliers; c) start negotiation based on preliminary product specifications; d) agree on delivery dates for the preliminary documentation that is needed by the design and engineering departments; e) agree on delivery dates for the physical product; f) agree the destination to be delivered (e.g., hull yard or main yard). Each of these phases might contain several iterations until agreements with each supplier and the customer can be reached.

The PD takes over the procurement process after the customer has signed the contract for the new vessel. They further negotiate equipment and materials while considering customer requirements and engineering recommendations. Since the case company applies some levels of concurrency between engineering, procurement and production phases, this issue adds several iterations during the procurement process. Some of the iterations are included in the project plan, still, most of them appear as a result of customer involvement in defining the product features after the project has started.

After rating the best alternatives, the PD negotiates with one or more suppliers the delivery terms and the necessary documentation. If customers and/or suppliers propose changes to the materials or equipment, a new discussions with the customer, engineers, production and class are necessary. When all parts agree on all the terms of the delivery and the customer approves the drawings/models, the production can start. Sometimes, due to pressure on project delivery, production activities have already been started based on the preliminary drawings and incomplete information.

Typically, the contract with the customer is based on the specifications document (Spec) that defines all the features and components on the final product. The level of detail in the Spec varies from project to project and quite often it contains items that are described in uncertain terms. According to some purchasers, that is because "*a more detailed description would give suppliers a lot more negotiating power and eventually, higher prices for the respective items. We have written such a general Spec that no one knows what we actually want*" (I1). Therefore, each key component and equipment gets more details while the iterative negotiating process with suppliers and customers is ongoing. Since each project deals with a large number of specialized suppliers, negotiating with each of them is often a demanding task that results in a lack of prioritization and POs that are placed so late that suppliers have to deliver more or less on express rates. Hence, the estimated price that was based on normal lead time is then changed to higher rates. An example in one of the interviews was an item that costs about 250 thousand euros at the beginning of the project, but due to a delayed PO, the price increased to 350 thousand euros. Or as a purchaser put it "*it costs so much more, that you get dizzy when you look at the total price we pay for an express deliveries*" (I2).

Another challenging issue for planning procurement activities is that each project purchaser has to deal with over 400 suppliers that can deliver several hundred items to each project. In average, one purchaser at the main case company works with about 25–30 suppliers per day the whole project duration. Planning all these activities becomes a challenging task. Yet, the interviewed purchasers stated that they were interested in a better planning process for their activities because "*If we would have had time to plan these activities, the total cost of the procurement, and implicitly the project, would have been reduces a lot*" (I1). The same purchasers referred to challenges originating in the volatile market that leads to ups and downs on the order level, which in turn challenges shipbuilding companies to adapt to less known environments.

In a similar line of thoughts, one project planner at the second company argues for better planning and control on the procurement activities by stating: "*The main challenge is that the phases are concurrent. We start with the plan for the hull and in the same time, we are planning the engineering and procurement phases. Then we try matching these plans, but it never matches. There are always collisions in dates and time, so our main challenge is to find ways to do planning in a better way*" (I2).

Based on the arguments presented above, the planning practice for procurement activities is in need for improvements that can support a better control over deliveries of the required documents, materials and components in ETO projects.

## 5   Discussion

The aim of this article is to identify and analyze how ETO characteristics influence the planning of procurement activities. As indicated in Sect. 2, the existing literature on ETO reveals following characteristics: highly customized products, extensive outsourcing, project-based procurement approach, iterations, concurrency, and project-based type of management. These characteristics have a strong influence on the total planning process [9] including the procurement activities that usually are planned only partially. Table 1, summarizes the ETO characteristics described in Sect. 2, and how they challenge the planning of the procurement activities.

**Table 1.** ETO characteristics and their influence on planning procurement activities

| ETO characteristics | Procurement challenges |
| --- | --- |
| Customization | Customers select and approve the components, equipment and materials to be mounted on the vessel. Approving process can affect the procurement plan by delaying negotiations with suppliers |
| Outsourcing to specialized supplier | Large network of suppliers to be handled and included in the project plan. Each supplier demands a signed contract before they start delivering documents and information. Delays with one supplier can affect negotiations with other suppliers. The contracting practices between shipyards and suppliers are often limiting a proper integration through the planning process due to information sensitivity or other specific issues |
| Project-based approach | Materials, components and equipment are specifically purchased for each project and cannot be ordered before the contract is signed. Key-items, especially the customized ones, may need long lead times and placing POs late leads to unplanned extra costs |
| Iterations | Engineering department is dependent on the information from the procurement and vice versa. Meanwhile, the procurement team must collect information (from one or more suppliers) discuss it with engineering- and production teams while negotiating further. Not all iterations can be planned and that leads to extra working hours on solving unplanned issues |
| Concurrency | Engineering, procurement and production teams are dependent on a dynamic information flow among them. Delays from one team affect the progress and the results for the others |
| Incomplete specifications | Customers delay the decision process as long as possible and that reduces negotiating possibilities for the procurement team. Identifying proper solutions is dependent on iterative and demanding negotiation process with customers, suppliers and class societies. The result is an increased number of negotiations periods and iterations. As a way to guard themselves against high process, the shipyards reveal pieces of information about the needed product while the negotiating process has started. Such approach extends the procurement process since everyone has to clarify the specifications within own company before continuing the negotiating process |
| Phase-based project management | Procurement is divided between several entities: SPT, design, engineering, production, hull yard, and suppliers. Each entity creates own project plans that are difficult to match with each other. This approach leads to lack of control on the status of procurement activities at the project level |

The type and nature of the challenges presented in Table 1, show a complex picture about the difficulties in planning procurement activities in ETO projects. Such challenges cannot be solved only by using existing planning software that are quite rigid and unable to integrate a large number of project participants. There is a need for a better planning process for the procurement activities in order to facilitate coordination and collaboration among all entities involved in each project. However, the existing planning approaches applied to ETO projects are based on a sequential type of thinking that do not consider the challenges originating in ETO characteristics. That is because the traditional project planning methods applied by most ETO companies are based on a linear strategy that implies dependent, sequential phases executed according to a plan established at the beginning of the project [18]. A proper planning process implies all activities of collecting and delivering right information at the right time to the right people so that procurement activities can be performed as planned.

Based on the presented data, shipbuilding companies, a representative ETO environment in Norway, are in need for a better system that can in fact visualize the effects of delayed procurement. Most of the interviewed people are aware of such cost overruns, however, no one could provide a clear number about the degree to which these are due to POs that are placed later than planned. Continuous firefighting demands attention to solving each issue within the current frames at the moment these issues must be solved. Often, it implies express rates for a large amount of the POs, and according to most purchasers, these rates could be avoided through better planning and control of the procurement activities. A future research step would be to collect data from other types of ETO companies to see if their planning of the procurement activities is as challenging as in the observed shipbuilding companies. While these are typical ETO shipbuilding projects, broader studies on cost overruns due to lack of planning are necessary to be able to claim such challenges critical for ETO projects in general.

As also observed by e.g., [13, 14], customer involvement in the procurement process requires different approaches to categorization and integration strategies applied to the large network of suppliers. This line of thinking should also be applied to the planning of procurement activities in ETO since customer involvement in the process of approving the supplies, the drawings and the product affect the results of the planning process in its entirety. Yet, most literature on ETO project planning addresses planning of production activities with little focus on design- and engineering activities [19], and even less focus on procurement activities. In other words, planning procurement activities in ETO project must be improved as part of the whole project planning process.

**Acknowledgements.** We want to thank master students Kristian Granberg and Vetle Terland for the data collected at the second shipbuilding company.

# References

1. Haartveit, D.E.G., Semini, M., Alfnes, E.: Integration alternatives for ship designers and shipyards. In: Frick, J., Laugen, B.T. (eds.) APMS 2011. IAICT, vol. 384, pp. 309–316. Springer, Heidelberg (2012). https://doi.org/10.1007/978-3-642-33980-6_35
2. Held, T.: Supplier integration as an improvement driver: An analysis of some recent approaches in the shipbuilding industry. In: Engelhardt-Nowitzki, C., Nowitzki, O., Zsifkovits, H. (eds) Supply Chain Network Analysis, pp. 369–384 (2010)
3. Ciobanu, I.C., Neupane, G.P.: Phase-Based Project Management at Aker Yards: A Lean Shipbuilding Perspective in Logistics. Molde University College, Norway (2008)
4. Rudberg, M., Wikner, J.: Mass customization in terms of the customer order decoupling point. Prod. Plann. Control 15(4), 445–458 (2004)
5. Powell, D., et al.: A New Set of Principles for Pursuing the Lean Ideal in Engineering-to-Order Manufacturers in CIRP Conference on Manufacturing Systems, Windsor, Ontario, Canada (2014)
6. Kjersem, K., Jünge, G.H.: Categorizing engineer-to-order companies through their project execution strategy. In: Nääs, I., Vendrametto, O., Reis, J.M., Gonçalves, R.F., Silva, M.T., von Cieminski, G., Kiritsis, D. (eds.) APMS 2016. IAICT, vol. 488, pp. 919–926. Springer, Cham (2016). https://doi.org/10.1007/978-3-319-51133-7_108
7. Semini, M., et al.: Offshoring Strategies in Norwegian Ship Production. J. Ship Prod. Design 34(1), 59–71 (2018)
8. Kjersem, K., Emblemsvåg, J.: Literature review on planning design and engineering activities in shipbuilding. In: 22nd Annual Conference of the International Group for Lean Construction IGLC 22, pp. 677–688. Springer, Oslo (2014)
9. Kjersem, K., Jünge, Gabriele H., Emblemsvåg, J.: Project execution strategy and planning challenges. In: Lödding, H., Riedel, R., Thoben, K.-D., von Cieminski, G., Kiritsis, D. (eds.) APMS 2017. IAICT, vol. 514, pp. 243–250. Springer, Cham (2017). https://doi.org/10.1007/978-3-319-66926-7_28
10. Hicks, C., McGovern, T., Earl, C.F.: Supply chain management: A strategic issue en engineer to order manufacturing. Int. J. Prod. Econ. 65(2), 179–190 (2000)
11. Sarhan, S., et al.: Institutional waste within the uk construction procurement context: a conceptual framework. Eng. Proj. Organ. J. 8, 36–64 (2018)
12. Shlopak, M., Rød, E., Jünge, G.H.: Purchasing strategies, tactics, and activities in engineer-to-order manufacturing. In: Ameri, F., Stecke, K.E., von Cieminski, G., Kiritsis, D. (eds.) APMS 2019. IAICT, vol. 566, pp. 562–569. Springer, Cham (2019). https://doi.org/10.1007/978-3-030-30000-5_69
13. Bäkstrand, J.: A method for customer-driven purchasing - aligning supplier interaction and customer-driven manufacturing. Department of Industrial Engineering and Management 2012, School of Engineering, Jönköping University, Sweden
14. Wikner, J., Bäkstrand, J.: Triadic perspective on customization and supplier interaction in customer-driven manufacturing Prod. Manuf. Res. 6(1), 3–25 (2017)
15. Mello, M.H., Strandhagen, O.J.: Supply chain management in the shipbuilding industry: challenges and perspectives. J. Eng. Maritime Environ. 225(3), 261–270 (2011)
16. PMBOK®: A guide to the Project Management Body of Knowledge (PMBOK guide), 5th edn. P.M. Institute. 2013a: Project Management Institute (2013)
17. Zidane, Y.J.-T., et al.: Barriers and challenges in employing of concurrent engineering within the Norwegian construction projects. Procedia Econ. Finance 21, 494–501 (2015)
18. Fernandez, D.J., Fernandez, J.D.: Agile project management - agilism versus traditional approaches. J. Comput. Inf. Syst. 49(2), 10–17 (2009)
19. Little, D., et al.: Integrated planning and scheduling in the engineer-to-order sector. Int. J. Comput. Integr. Manuf. 13(6), 545–554 (2000)

# Maturity Model for Successful Cost Transformation in ETO Companies

Johann Gregori and Ralph Riedel(✉) (iD)

Chemnitz University of Technology, 09107 Chemnitz, Germany
ralph.riedel@mb.tu-chemnitz.de

**Abstract.** Companies are more and more required nowadays to monitor and to improve their cost structure. Hereby, ETO enterprises experience particular difficulties, due to the high complexity and dynamics as well as less opportunities for standardization which are an intrinsic part of their products and processes. Therefore, a systematic and holistic approach for cost management is needed, considering hard factors as well as soft factors, like organizational and behavioral aspects. In this paper, we introduce a product cost maturity model, which integrates a multitude of success factors for cost transformation from different categories in an ETO environment. Hereby companies will be enabled to determine and evaluate their current state as well as a future state to derive a roadmap for necessary actions. The maturity model is based on a thorough literature research and on practical experiences in ETO companies. It is complemented with a systematic procedure for cost transformation projects. We describe the maturity model and its application as far as possible in detail, hereby also justifying every design decision we made.

**Keywords:** Cost transformation · Maturity model · Engineer to Order

## 1 Introduction

The importance of Engineer-to-Order (ETO) companies has been and is still increasing due to a higher demand for customized products [19]. The ETO industry is characterized by individualized products, low volumes, low standardization, high complexity, dynamism, long lead times and a project based approach for order processing [3, 6, 19].

Traditionally, the main competitive advantage of ETO industry has been to fulfill individual customer requirements and to master the resulting complexity and dynamism; costs resp. the price was not that important [6]. Since global competition has increased together with low-cost countries' ability to manage complexity and to produce ETO products at low costs, improving the cost efficiency of ETO processes has become vital for high-cost countries [3].

Due to their particularities, the conditions for cost reduction programs in ETO companies are not the best: it is difficult to standardize products, the heterogeneity of processes is rather high and learning curves are rather flat. Compared to serial production ETO companies usually have only one chance to design and to manufacture a cost efficient product for a specific customer, which in turn has a considerable impact on their competitiveness already in the quotation phase and also later on when a

© IFIP International Federation for Information Processing 2020
Published by Springer Nature Switzerland AG 2020
B. Lalic et al. (Eds.): APMS 2020, IFIP AICT 592, pp. 573–580, 2020.
https://doi.org/10.1007/978-3-030-57997-5_66

reasonable price-cost-ratio is necessary. Therefore, thinking and acting in a cost-efficient manner affects all processes.

Following recent studies, the success rate of cost reduction initiatives is rather bad, i.e. only around fifty percent [14]. The challenge therefore is, to transform an ETO company to an entity, which is able to continuously review and decrease its costs. For such a transformation process a precise determination of the current position (where to start from) as well as the determination of a future state (where to strive for) and development path, which systematically leads from the current to the future state, are essential. Maturity models are a common approach to support this [18]. Following the argumentation above, a product cost maturity model (PCMM) is needed especially for ETO companies, which should not be focused on a single product's cost structure, but rather on the company's ability for (cost) transformation and resulting cost efficient processes.

In this article we describe the concept of a product cost maturity model and its application in ETO industry. The work is based on the design science research approach [16, 21] and includes the derivation of success factors from research as well as empirical insights from many cost reduction projects in industrial practice, namely from a big ETO company in south Germany, which produces equipment for the beverages industry. In the remainder of the article we briefly address some scientific basics of maturity models, explain then the development process for the PCMM as well as its results, and give some hints for the application of the model. At the end, we give some conclusions and an outlook on further work.

## 2   Maturity Models in an ETO Environment

Maturity models support the evaluation of the quality of a company's processes, often against some specific target state. The purpose of a maturity model is to identify gaps which can subsequently be closed by improvement measures [2, 21]. Famous maturity models are the capability maturity model (CMM) and its successor, the capability maturity model integrated (CMMI). Although CMMI has its origins and application in software industry, Alfnes [2] demonstrated its applicability in an ETO environment for materials management under engineering change situation. Another substantial argumentation, that practices of the CMMI can also be applied in ETO companies, can be found for instance in [24].

Maturity models usually consist of maturity levels, maturity dimensions and indicators, optionally weighted, and a maturity level - parameter-matrix [1]. Frameworks or procedures for designing maturity models are for instance provided by [4, 13]. The development process of maturity models should be closely intertwined with their later application process [21].

In our development process we chose the design science research approach [16], which was specified for maturity models [21], as a general framework. In the rigor cycle we identified a suitable methodology for the PCMM design and we derived categories, criteria, characteristics of success factors for cost transformation, in general as well as especially in an ETO environment. In the relevance cycle we considered the state of the art, especially insights from ETO practice. Hereby, the design-build and evaluation phases are passed-through several times, continuously improving the model. The design process itself followed the procedure proposed by [13].

# 3 Development of a Product Cost Maturity Model

The possible and selected design alternatives for the PCMM are shown in Fig. 1.

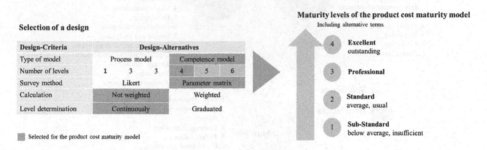

**Selection of a design**

| Design-Criteria | Design-Alternatives | | | | | |
|---|---|---|---|---|---|---|
| Type of model | Process model | | Competence model | | | |
| Number of levels | 1 | 3 | 3 | 4 | 5 | 6 |
| Survey method | | Likert | | Parameter matrix | | |
| Calculation | | Not weighted | | Weighted | | |
| Level determination | | Continuously | | Graduated | | |

■ Selected for the product cost maturity model

**Maturity levels of the product cost maturity model**
Including alternative terms

4 **Excellent** outstanding

3 **Professional**

2 **Standard** average, usual

1 **Sub-Standard** below average, insufficient

**Fig. 1.** Design approach for the PCMM

For our purpose we chose the approach of a competence model [12] instead of a process model [2], because we consider competencies of management and employees to have a decisive role for a successful transformation. The other design specifications are explained in the following sections.

## 3.1 Success Factors and Key Areas

The *indicators* of the PCMM are defined by success factors [7] for cost transformation. (Critical) success factors are actions and processes that can be controlled by management to achieve an organization's goals [9]. The success factors are subsumed in key areas which form the *dimensions* of the PCMM.

Product cost reduction in combination with the necessary transformation is a complex field. Following our methodology explained in Sect. 2, a thorough literature research focusing on cost management, cost reduction, cost transformation in conjunctions with success factors, change management, project management has led to an initial list of possible success factors which are grouped in five key areas (exemplarily [5, 8, 11, 17, 20, 22, 25, 26], categories from [23] and others); those are shown in Fig. 2.

"Hard factors" are ETO-specific processes, which all need to pursue the goal of cost-efficiency and cost-improvement, as well as projects, i.e. the transformation of the processes together with the whole company. The framework for both is provided by the involved people (employees), leadership and culture – the "soft factors". It could be shown that behavioral and organizational factors have a substantial role in transformations endeavors [17]. In turn, those factors are – and need to be – affected by the transformation.

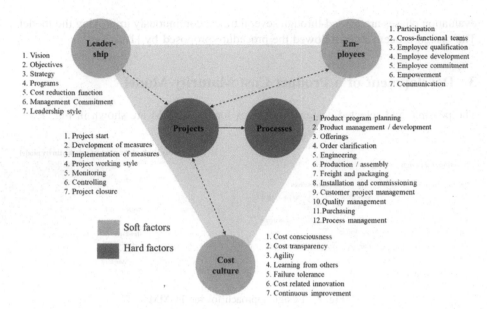

1. Vision
2. Objectives
3. Strategy
4. Programs
5. Cost reduction function
6. Management Commitment
7. Leadership style

**Leader-ship**

**Em-ployees**

1. Participation
2. Cross-functional teams
3. Employee qualification
4. Employee development
5. Employee commitment
6. Empowerment
7. Communication

1. Project start
2. Development of measures
3. Implementation of measures
4. Project working style
5. Monitoring
6. Controlling
7. Project closure

**Projects**

**Processes**

1. Product program planning
2. Product management / development
3. Offerings
4. Order clarification
5. Engineering
6. Production / assembly
7. Freight and packaging
8. Installation and commissioning
9. Customer project management
10. Quality management
11. Purchasing
12. Process management

Soft factors

Hard factors

**Cost culture**

1. Cost consciousness
2. Cost transparency
3. Agility
4. Learning from others
5. Failure tolerance
6. Cost related innovation
7. Continuous improvement

**Fig. 2.** Key areas (categories, dimensions) and success factors (sub-categories, indicators)

## 3.2   Maturity Levels

The maturity will be determined by a scoring procedure. There are two alternatives to choose from: statements, combined with a Likert-scale, or open questions and the assignment of answers to a parameter matrix. In the latter, the manifestations of the different maturity levels are described by objective, quantifiable or observable criteria [1]. As statements on a Likert scale do not provide instructions how to move from one level to another, we decided to define open questions and detailed descriptions of each maturity level. Based on this, indications are available how to develop from on level to the next one.

Typically, maturity models consist of three to six levels. The higher the number of levels, the more complex a differentiation will be. In order to limit this kind of complexity, parameter matrix based maturity models are usually limited to four or even three levels [15]. For our PCMM we defined four maturity levels, with designations in accordance with common management language: sub-standard, standard, professional, excellent.

For the scoring itself, a continuous or a staggered evaluation can be used [15]. With a continuous evaluation a total value is aggregated from all indicators and dimensions, independent from their particular maturity levels. In a staggered evaluation the maturity level of a dimension can only be as high as the lowest maturity level of its indicators. Likewise, the overall maturity level can only be as high as the lowest maturity level of its dimensions. For our PCMM, we chose the continuous evaluation method, because this provides a more transparent picture; the maturity levels of particular success factors should be the starting point for improvement. Furthermore, we did not include weighs for indicators or dimensions in order to produce an unfiltered view.

In the PCMM the overall maturity level M is calculated as the arithmetic mean of the maturity levels $d_i$ of its dimensions i. The maturity level $d_i$ of a dimension i is calculated as the arithmetic mean of the maturity levels $i_{ij}$ of its assigned indicators j. The maturity level of a particular indicator ij is calculated as the arithmetic mean of all evaluations of the assigned questions $q_{ijk}$ in the parameter matrix.

### 3.3 Parameter Matrix

The core element of the product cost maturity model is the evaluation tableau or parameter matrix. Its structure is illustrated with an example in Fig. 3.

| Vision | Sub-Standard | Standard | Professional | Excellent |
|---|---|---|---|---|
| **To what extend orders are clarified before starting value adding activities?** | No order clarification | Order clarification exists as a process, but orders are also processed without | Capacity and time is provided for clarification; sales people are enabled; orders are completely clarified | Key questions are formalized as checklists |
| **To what extend a design freeze is consequently performed ?** | No design freeze | Design freeze is discussed, but not performed consistently | Design freeze is part of contracts; open issues are clarified in time | Design freeze is used proactively to avoid change costs; vendor and customer intend to utilize the design freeze to reduce complexity |
| **To what extend an optimum is achieved between customer benefit and low costs?** | Copying of similar solutions without questioning | Utilization of proven technical concepts; usage of experiences with certain customers | Utilization of proven modules; intensive dialogue with contributing partners | No perfectionism; effort-benefit ratio is stressed |

**Fig. 3.** Parameter matrix for the success factor "order clarification"

For each success factor up to four open questions are formulated. The manifestations for the four maturity levels are described for each question. Hereby, the manifestations of lower levels are also valid for higher levels.

Usually only the optimal manifestation for a success factor can be derived from literature or from best practice. A gradation, which is necessary for the parameter matrix, needs to be defined based on practical experience. This input is gained from structured interviews with experts/practitioners.

## 4   Application of the PCMM in Transformation Projects

The application of the product maturity model should happen in four steps, which follow an initiating phase, see Fig. 4.

The PCMM is suitable to be applied by an auditor or as a self-assessment tool [13]. For the auditor approach, often an external expert is engaged, who evaluates the maturity level and provides recommendations. Hereby, management and employees take a rather passive role. However, there is a risk, that the evaluation remains rather

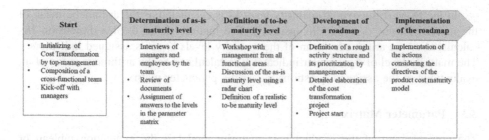

Fig. 4. Application of the PCMM for transformation

abstract, identification with the result is rather low and recommended measures are not implemented. A self-assessment can be done by one person or by a cross-functional team with and without the support of experts [15]. If a person does the assessment on its own, it might happen that the as-is analysis is biased. Studies show, that with a cross-functional team, different perspectives can be considered, and that after an intensive discussion the team reaches a consensus which in turn leads to a high level of commitment so that the process is kept going [10].

The as-is maturity level is determined with the help of a series of interviews. It is important to involve all affected persons. Hereby, diverse perspectives are generated, which form in the end a holistic view on the situation. For some questions it is also recommendable to consult existing artefacts, for instance documents, to verify the right answer.

A to-be maturity level (target state) shall be defined in a management workshop with managers from all functional areas. The as-is maturity level serves as a basis for discussion. The target state does not need to be necessarily the highest maturity level, but depends on the current state. Targets need to be challenging but also realistic and to be considered as achievable. So moving step-b-step from one level to the next might be an appropriate strategy. Also, not every success factor needs to be at the same level.

In order to manage the transition from the current to the target state, a roadmap is necessary, which should provide a rough structure, defined by management. This serves as the framework for a change project which should be detailed and consequently realized by executives and employees.

## 5   Conclusion and Further Work

In this paper, we argued that especially ETO companies face the challenge of cost reduction, but that the particularities of this type of business makes it even more difficult to succeed. Cost reduction needs to be considered from a strategic perspective as a continuous and anticipating activity [17]. Being cost-efficient and continuously striving for cost reduction is a capability, that a company needs to develop and to sustain. This, in turn, will be significantly supported by a systematic approach, involving different success factors, which should serve as an anchor for evaluating the actual state of a company and as a landmark for future development. In our research we used such success factors to compose a maturity model for product cost reduction (PCMM), following an established procedure [13].

The first version of the PCMM is currently based on an extensive literature review, which revealed a lot of success factors for cost reduction and cost transformation projects in ETO environments but also in industrial enterprises in general. Those factors are matched with the author's empirical experiences from a multitude of cost reduction projects in an ETO environment.

In a next iteration, following the design science approach, this first version is validated and adapted, based on experts' opinions gathered in structured interviews and workshops. Adaptations comprise the list of success factors which form the indicators of the PCMM and the description of their manifestation for different maturity levels in the parameter matrix. We only selected experts with a high level of experience in ETO industry. Experts will be invited to comment on the formulations and gradations as well as to add examples of best practices and also not so good practices.

The model and the systematic procedure it is embedded in will then be applied in case studies in the involved ETO company. The insights gained from this might lead to another improvement cycle.

# References

1. Akkasoglu, G.: Methodik zur Konzeption und Anwendung anwendungsspezifischer Reifegradmodelle unter Berücksichtigung der Informationsunsicherheit. Shaker, Aachen (2014)
2. Alfnes, E.: Capability maturity model for engineering change management in ETO environment. In: Nääs, I. (ed.): Proceedings of the Production Management Initiatives for a sustainable world. IFIP WG 5.7 International Conference, APMS 2016, Iguassu Falls. Advances in Production Management Systems (2016)
3. Arica, E., Magerøy, K., Lall, M.T.M.: Barriers and success factors for continuous improvement efforts in complex ETO firms. In: Moon, I., Lee, Gyu M., Park, J., Kiritsis, D., von Cieminski, G. (eds.) APMS 2018. IAICT, vol. 535, pp. 124–130. Springer, Cham (2018). https://doi.org/10.1007/978-3-319-99704-9_16
4. Becker, J., Knackstedt, R., Pöppelbuß, J.: Developing maturity models for IT management. Bus. Inf. Syst. Eng. 1(3), 213–222 (2009)
5. Berk, J.: Cost Reduction and Optimization for Manufacturing and Industrial Companies. Wiley (2010)
6. Birkie, S.E., Trucco, P.: Understanding dynamism and complexity factors in engineer-to-order and their influence on lean implementation strategy. Prod. Plann. Control 27(5), 345–359 (2016)
7. Boynton, A., Zmud, R.: An assessment of critical success factors. Sloan Mngmt. Rev. 25(4), 17–27 (1984)
8. Bragg, S.M.: Cost Reduction Analysis: Tools and Strategies. Wiley (2010)
9. Brotherton, B., Shaw, J.: Towards an identification and classification of critical success factors in UK hotels. Int. J. Hospitality Manag. 15(2), 113–135 (1996)
10. Chiesa, V.P., Voss, C.: Development of a technical innovation audit. J. Product Innov. Manag. 13(2), 105–136 (1996)
11. Couto, V., Plansky, J., Caglar, D.: Fit for Growth: a Guide to Strategic Cost Cutting, Restructuring, and Renewal. Wiley (2017)

12. Crawford, K.: The project management maturity model. Inf. Syst. Manag. 23(4), 50–58 (2006)
13. de Bruin, T., Rosemann, M., Freeze, R., Kulkami, U.: Understanding the main phases of developing a maturity assessment model. In: 16th Australasian Conference on Information Systems, Sydney. Australasian Association for Information Systems (2005)
14. Deloitte: Thriving in uncertainty. Deloitte's fourth biennial cost survey: Cost improvement practices and trends in the Fortune 1000 (2016)
15. Fraser, P., Moultrie, J., Gregory, M.: The use of maturity models/grids as a tool in assessing product development capability. In: Proceedings of the IEEE International Engineering Management Conference, Cambridge UK, vol. 1, pp. 244–249 (2002)
16. Hevner, A.R.: A three cycle view of design science research. Scand. J. Inf. Syst. 19(2), 87–92 (2007)
17. Himme, A.: Critical success factors of strategic cost reduction. J. Manag. Control 23(3), 183–210 (2012)
18. Jording, T.: Entwicklung und Konzeption eines Reifegradmodells des Supply Chain Managements: Der Supply Chain Management Maturity Cube (SCMMC). In: Logistik und Supply Chain Management 18. University of Bamberg Press (2018)
19. Kjersem, K., Giskeødegård, M.F.: Changing markets: implications for the planning process in ETO companies. In: Ameri, F., Stecke, K.E., von Cieminski, G., Kiritsis, D. (eds.) APMS 2019. IAICT, vol. 566, pp. 554–561. Springer, Cham (2019). https://doi.org/10.1007/978-3-030-30000-5_68
20. Kotter, J.: Accelerate! Havard Business Review, November 2012
21. Mettler, T.: Maturity assessment models: a design science research approach. Int. J. Soc. Syst. Sci. 3(1/2), 81–98 (2011)
22. Schein, E.H., Schein, P.: Organisational Culture and Leadership, 5th edn. Wiley (2017)
23. Sharma, C.: Business Process Transformation. The Process Tangram Framework. Springer, New Delhi (2015). https://doi.org/10.1007/978-81-322-2349-8
24. Veldman, J., Klingenberg, W.: Applicability of the capability maturity model for engineer-to-order firms. Intern. J. Technol. Mngmt 29(7), 539–545 (2009)
25. Westerveld, E.: The Project Excellence Model®: linking success criteria and critical success factors. Int. J. Project Mngmt. 21(6), 411–418 (2003)
26. Zhang, S., Bartol, K.: Linking empowering leadershipand employee creatitity: the influence of psychological empowerment, intrinsic motivation, and creative process engagement. Acad. Manag. J. 53(1), 107–128 (2010)

# Backlog Oriented Bottleneck Management – Practical Guide for Production Managers

Roman Ungern-Sternberg$^{(\boxtimes)}$ , Christian Fries ,
and Hans-Hermann Wiendahl

Fraunhofer Institute for Manufacturing Engineering and Automation IPA,
70569 Stuttgart, Germany
roman.ungern-sternberg@ipa.fraunhofer.de

**Abstract.** Today's productions systems become more and more complex, comprising a multitude of different resources interacting with each other. The Theory of Constraints (TOC) describes the dilemma that the overall output of such a system is constrained by one or more resources called "bottlenecks". Identifying those bottlenecks has been subject of many research papers. Classical approaches focus typically solely on the bottleneck utilization and neglect accumulated deviations against the planned utilization. This so-called backlog is critical as it has a direct effect on the on-time-delivery. This paper therefore provides a practical approach that can be used by the operative management in order to identify, prioritize and manage bottlenecks in a backlog situation efficiently and effectively.

**Keywords:** Bottleneck · Management guide · Production logistics

## 1 Introduction

A bottleneck is a resource whose capacity requirement exceeds the available capacity in a period [2, 3]. If all production orders have to pass through the bottleneck, the maximum production output corresponds to that of the bottleneck [6: p. 115], resulting to the fact that an hour lost at a bottleneck is an hour lost for the overall system [3]. Classical approaches focus solely on the bottleneck utilization and do rarely provide guidelines for their management. Furthermore, accumulated deviations, which are represented in backlog, are typically neglected. Backlog however, is critical as it has a direct effect on the on-time-delivery. This paper therefore develops a practical two-step approach for analyzing and improving operations. The intended users are productions managers in need of a systematic but practical approach to select critical bottlenecks in manufacturing to improve on-time-delivery.

## 2 Literature Review

This section gives an overview of existing identification methods and defines the terms bottleneck and backlog.

© IFIP International Federation for Information Processing 2020
Published by Springer Nature Switzerland AG 2020
B. Lalic et al. (Eds.): APMS 2020, IFIP AICT 592, pp. 581–589, 2020.
https://doi.org/10.1007/978-3-030-57997-5_67

## 2.1  Bottlenecks

**Definition.** Within this paper, the capacity bottleneck is defined as the resource with the highest load factor (load divided by maximum capacity) during a defined period. A selection of methods for detecting and managing bottlenecks is summarized in the following section.

**Management.** Adams uses a graph based iteration process to detect bottlenecks based on throughput time and lateness. The Shifting Bottleneck method (SB) solves bottlenecks from iteration to iteration for all machines. In each iteration step, the machine with the largest maximum delay is selected. Then the bottleneck is solved on this machine and an optimal processing sequence of the orders is determined [1].

Based on the duration a machine is active without interruption Roser develops the Active Period Method [8]. Bottlenecks are detected based on the idea that the longer a machine is working without interruption, the more likely it is constraining the overall systems performance [9].

H.-P. Wiendahl describes the Bottleneck Oriented Logistic Analysis (BOLA) as a method for identifying capacitive bottlenecks in the material flow [16, 17]. This method allows to derive problem specific measures based upon analyzing the logistics behavior using the concept of the logistics operating curves [6]. The BOLA is thereby a permanent control's task and thus a continuous process for improving logistics [5: p. 170].

The existing approaches consider backlog only indirect by observing lateness as a relevant parameter. As backlog is a critical parameter in production control, it will be directly considered in the presented method.

## 2.2  Backlog in Order Based Production Systems

**Definition.** The backlog corresponds to the amount of work that a resource should have completed by a certain date but has not yet completed. Thus, the backlog is calculated as the difference between the planned and actual output [7: p. 65f, 14: p. 148, 18: p. 80].

The backlog range is the time needed to reduce the backlog to zero (assuming that no new orders are planned) and calculated as the backlog divided by the planned capacity per period of the relevant resource [14: p. 149]. Figure 1 shows an overall backlog situation with more late orders (too late done) than advanced orders (too early done) for one resource.

**Management.** Unmanaged backlog generally leads to longer throughput-times, which in turn leads to sequence deviations; both typically cause low on-time-delivery rates. For backlog management there are three general approaches sorted by effectiveness:

1. Allocation of **additional capacity** (e.g. overtime, extra shifts) to reduce backlog; given that sufficient work-in-progress is available at the backlog resource [4: p. 551].
2. Planning of **less work content** in future periods to use the free capacity for backlog reduction, e.g. by external processing or declining orders in the respective periods.

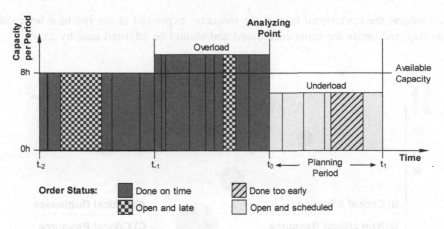

**Fig. 1.** Resource order schedule (assigned by due date, showing a backlog situation)

3. **Rescheduling/postponement** of existing production orders to reduce the calculated backlog is generally not solving the problem but shifting it. If directly linked customer orders cannot be postponed (e.g. as customers refuse later delivery dates) this leads to low on-time-delivery rates.

## 3 Proposed Heuristic Approach

This paper develops a two-step approach for the operative bottleneck management: (1) Critical bottlenecks are prioritized based on their backlog situation and general management guidelines are derived. (2) The contributions of different causes to the overall backlog are described, quantified and countermeasures are suggested.

### 3.1 Prioritization/Resource Selection and General Management Guidelines

Real world production systems have many resources. Therefore, a practical prioritization approach is required in order to wisely use the limited management capacity.

**Prioritization/Analysis.** The task of factory planning is to evaluate and design static, long-term bottlenecks. For a first structured and qualitative identification of requirements for the PPC design and operation, the turbulence profile can be used [12]. For the evaluation and prioritization of actions, short-term bottlenecks with already fixed production orders (and due dates) additionally the backlog situation should be considered for taking appropriate actions while keeping high on-time-delivery rates. To facilitate the analysis the so-called Backlog-Load-Portfolio is introduced (see Fig. 2): On the y-axis the current resource situation is expressed by backlog range. For benchmarks or heterogeneous backlog tolerances, a relative backlog range is recommended [15]. On the x-axis the potential to reduce backlog by capacity increase expressed by the load factor (or alternatively the utilization) is depicted. The bubble size reflects the operational cost of the resource, expressed in the machine-hour rate. The depicted limits are experience based and should be adjusted case-by-case.

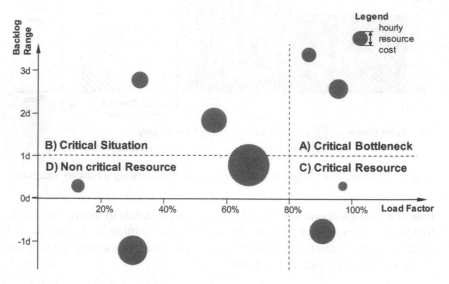

**Fig. 2.** Backlog-Load-Portfolio, based on [13: p. 208f]

**General Management Sequence and Approaches.** Based on the relative backlog and demand situation four general strategies are recommended in the following sequence:

a. **Critical bottleneck:** The resource has high backlog and capacity demand. Alternative modes of flexibility (e.g. alternative or external resources) and/or the re-negotiation of due dates with customers should be considered.
b. **Critical situation:** The resource has high backlog but low demand. The high short-term capacity flexibility allows capacity adjustments for reducing the backlog.
c. **Critical resource:** The resource has low backlog but high demand. The resource should be monitored closely in order to avoid an additional backlog situation, e.g. by avoiding starvation or breakdowns.
d. **Non-critical resource:** The resource has low backlog and demand. Because of its high short-term capacity flexibility any potential backlog situation can be counteracted. The resource should be planned efficiently, yet flexible if capacity is required.

## 3.2   Quantification and Countermeasures of Backlog for Selected Resources

Generally, backlog is caused by due-date deviation, throughput-time deviation or start-date deviation. Figure 3 depicts a more detailed hierarchy of backlog causes. This section describes definitions of the respective causes, approaches for quantification and potential countermeasures.

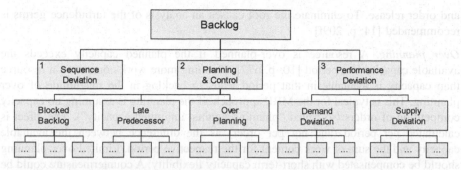

**Fig. 3.** Reasons for Backlog, based on cause-effect relationships of [4]

**Sequence Deviation.** Sequence deviation is the deviation of the planned and the actual rank of an order [4: p. 85]. Within this paper the sequence deviation is measured roughly, i.e. all orders within one planning period have the same rank, so sequence deviations within a planning period do not affect the backlog situation.

Sequence deviations lead to symmetrical backlog and advance situations. Thus, their effect on the overall backlog is the minimum of too late and too early orders. E.g. a resource processed 8 h of work too early and is late for 20 h, thus 8 h of the backlog is caused by sequence deviation (the overall backlog equals 12 h).

Countermeasures are disciplinary measures or technical restrictions such as blocking of sequence deviations by IT or physical setup on the shop-floor e.g. by FiFo-rail.

**Planning and Control.** These backlog causes can be split into three groups.

*Blocked Backlog.* Orders that are too late and available at the resource, but not processable cause blocked backlog. An order is not processable if it cannot be started, independently from the capacity situation at the resource [5: p. 218].

The backlog effect of blocked orders (or blocked WIP) is the sum of orders in backlog which are not (yet) processable. Delayed processability regularly leads to sequence deviations [4: p. 103].

For effective countermeasures, further analysis is required. Main reasons for not processable orders are missing closures due to technical quality defects, materials (in assembly processes) or manufacturing tools [5: p. 218]. Depending on the order release strategy, limiting the work-in-progress by postponement of order release is helpful to keep stable throughput times [4: p. 102].

*Late Predecessor.* Orders that already late, but didn't yet (physically) arrive at the resource for processing cause backlog due to late predecessor, e.g. by order creation with past due dates or late order processing, both leading to start deviation for the resource.

The backlog effect of late preceding processes is the sum of all orders in backlog at a resource, but are not yet available.

The problem should be analyzed and solved going upstream starting at the last resource, including the planning activities such as production and sales order creation and order release. To eliminate the root causes an analysis of the turbulence germs is recommended [14: p. 209f].

*Over planning.* A resource is over-planned if the planned capacity exceeds the available capacity in a period [10: p. 677]. Planning more work content on a resource than capacity is available in that period leads to backlog in the magnitude of over planning. This is typical for the MRP approach, if the planning is assuming no capacity competition of orders (so called "planning against unlimited capacity"). The effect is calculated per period (and not per order) as the difference between the available capacity and the sum of work content for the respective period. Limited over-planning should be compensated with short-term capacity flexibility. A countermeasure could be the use of APS (advanced planning and scheduling) with limited capacity planning approaches.

**Performance Deviation.** This difference between planned and actual performance within a period can be caused by supply and/or demand deviations.

Underperformance (because of lower capacity than promised or higher demand, i.e. standard times, then planned) leads to backlog in the magnitude of the deviation between planned and actual performance. Two cases of performance deviation can be separated within an analysis period:

1. Cases with a reduced performance compared to the planned performance within an analytical period. Here the causes are ambiguous and cannot be assigned clearly to supply or demand deviations. Thus, the guideline is to increase the sampling frequency of the time series data to reach the second case (see Fig. 4).
2. Cases with non-performance within an analytical period. These cases generally can be classified unambiguously as supply deviations with planned (e.g. maintenance) and unplanned non-performance (e.g. breakdowns) periods, where the latter contributes to the backlog.

The higher sampling frequency required for the second case are commonly achieved by data recording at resource level as production feedback data usually do not have such a high resolution. Thus a first action is tracking the resource status with high sampling frequency, e.g. by machine data acquisition or cyber-physical-systems. Remaining periods with less than expected performance (but not non-performance) can be caused by supply or demand deviations and need further analysis.

Countermeasures for backlog due to supply deviation (e.g. lower than planned resource performance) are generally programs for higher performance, such as preventive maintenance. Countermeasures for demand deviations (e.g. wrong standard times) are adapted demand data, e.g. by advanced calculation methods for standard times.

The distinction between supply and demand deviations in complex systems such as semi-automated assemblies with changing operator performance (supply deviations) but also learning curve effects (demand deviation) is ambiguous. The definition of distinctive criteria between the two categories as well as the required statistical analysis of these multi-causal issues is beyond the scope of this article.

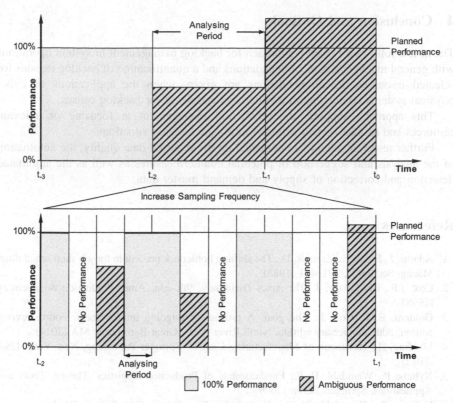

**Fig. 4.** Increase of sampling frequency to identify performance deviations unambiguously.

### 3.3 Limitations

The article's approach is on backlog management of single resources. However backlog can be inherited from other resources, e.g. due to wrong transition times or late finalization of preceding operations. As shown in above not all effects can be exactly quantified or even assigned to one exact cause. The analysis focuses on the current situation and does not cover past backlog dynamics over time or the proactive detection of bottlenecks by prediction. Sufficient data quality is a prerequisite for precise and trustable analytics [11, 12: p. 8ff, 222ff].

The order creation and calculation of the due dates is not part of the approach, e.g. the scheduling procedure applied or the handling of customer requests with shorter than standard lead times (so called express orders). In addition, an effective application of the presented results requires profound logistical competence of the managers.

## 4 Conclusion and Outlook

The article follows a two-step approach for backlog management in system operations with general management recommendations and a quantification of backlog reasons for selected resources. Recommendations are given, when the applications of cyber physical systems could support a better understanding for backlog causes.

This approach supports the production management in focusing on relevant resources and to take correct actions to mitigate backlog situations.

Further research should be conducted on the required data quality, the automation of the analysis and suggestion of potential countermeasures as well as the automated detection and correction of supply and demand master data.

## References

1. Adams, J., Balas, E., Zawack, D.: The shifting bottleneck procedure for job shop scheduling. Manag. Sci. **34**(3), 391–401 (1988)
2. Cox, J.F., Blackstone, J., H.: Apics Dictionary, 9th edn. Amer Production & Inventory (1998)
3. Goldratt, E.M.; Cox, J.: The goal. A process of ongoing improvement. Fourth revised edition, 30th anniversary edition. North River Press, Great Barrington, MA (2014)
4. Lödding, H.: Handbook of Manufacturing Control. Springer Publishing, New York, USA (2012)
5. Nyhuis, P., Wiendahl, H.-P.: Fundamentals of Production Logistics. Theory, Tools and Applications. Springer, Berlin (2009)
6. Nyhuis, P.; Wiendahl, H.-P.: Logistische Kennlinien. Grundlagen, Werkzeuge und Anwendungen. 3. Aufl. Springer Vieweg (VDI-Buch), Berlin (2012)
7. Petermann, D.: Modellbasierte Produktionsregelung. Diss. Universität Hannover 1995, published in: Fortschr.-Berichte VDI, Reihe 20, Nr. 193, VDI Verlag, Düsseldorf (1996)
8. Roser, C., Nakano, M., Tanaka, M.: A practical bottleneck detection method. In: Winter Simulation Conference Proceedings, vol. 2, pp. 949–953 (2001)
9. Roser, C., Nakano, M., Tanaka, M.: Detecting Shifting Bottlenecks. In: International Symposium on Scheduling. Hamamatsu, Japan, pp. 59–62 (2002)
10. Schönsleben, P.: Integrales Logistikmanagement. Springer, Heidelberg (2016). https://doi.org/10.1007/978-3-662-48334-3_1
11. Wang, R.Y., Strong, D.M.: Beyond accuracy: what data quality means to data consumers. J. Manag. Inf. Syst. **12**(4), 5–33 (1996)
12. Wiendahl, H.-H.: Turbulence germs and their impact on planning and control – root causes and solutions for PPC design. CIRP Ann. **56**(1), 443–446 (2007)
13. Wiendahl, H.-H.: Situative Konfiguration des Auftragsmanagements im turbulenten Umfeld. Heimsheim: Jost-Jetter, 2002. (IPA-IAO – Forschung und Praxis, Nr. 358). Zugl. Stuttgart, Univ., Diss. (2002)
14. Wiendahl, H.-H.: Auftragsmanagement der industriellen Produktion. Grundlagen, Konfiguration, Einführung. Springer (VDI-Buch), Berlin, Heidelberg (2011)
15. Wiendahl, H.-H., Steinberg, F.: Montageversorgungsanalyse in der Einzelfertigung. Ist-Situation, Potentiale und Ursachen. WT Werkstattstechnik **105**(9), 597–603 (2016)
16. Wiendahl, H.-P.: Load-Oriented Manufacturing Control. Springer, Heidelberg (1995)

17. Wiendahl, H.-P., Nyhuis, P.: Engpassorientierte Logistikanalyse. Methoden zur kurzfristigen Leistungssteigerung in Produktionsprozessen. TCW-Verl., München (1998)
18. Yu, K.-W.: Terminkennlinie. Eine Beschreibungsmethodik für die Terminabweichung im Produktionsbereich. Diss. Universität Hannover 2001, published in: Fortschritt-Berichte VDI, Reihe 2, Nr. 576, VDI-Verlag, Düsseldorf (2001)

# Cross-Functional Coordination Before and After the CODP: An Empirical Study in the Machinery Industry

Margherita Pero[1(✉)] and Violetta G. Cannas[2]

[1] Politecnico di Milano, Department of Management, Economics and Industrial Engineering, Via Lambruschini 4B, 20156 Milan, Italy
margherita.pero@polimi.it
[2] Carlo Cattaneo University - LIUC, Corso G. Matteotti, 22, 21052 Castellanza, VA, Italy
vcannas@liuc.it

**Abstract.** Cross-functional coordination among engineering, sales and production departments is known to be beneficial for improving order fulfillment processes. In Engineer-to-Order (ETO) companies, sales, design and production activities are strongly interrelated and sometimes they overlap, thus requiring cross-functional coordination. In these companies, design and production activities can be both partially performed before the customer order arrival. ETO companies pursue different objectives and implement different managerial approaches before and after the customer order decoupling point (CODP). However, despite its relevance for company performance, how ETO companies manage cross-functional coordination and how departments are coordinated before and after the CODP is still understudied. This paper sheds light on this topic by investigating 12 case studies in the Italian machinery industry. Results suggest that the coordination mechanisms used before and after CODP are different, and vary depending on the CODP configuration chosen.

**Keywords:** ETO · Cross-functional coordination · Machinery industry · CODP

## 1 Introduction

The Customer Order Decoupling Point (CODP) is defined as the point in the value chain where a product becomes linked to a specific customer order [1]: before the CODP, activities are forecast-driven, while, after the CODP, activities are planned and controlled based on actual customer orders. CODP positioning is a strategic choice for the company [2], and it has implications on the ability of the company either to provide customers with a high degree of choice (i.e. flexibility) or to maintain high internal efficiency [3].

In Engineer-to-Order (ETO) companies, engineering and production activities have been traditionally considered by the literature as performed after the customer order arrival [4]. However, recently, ETO companies are simultaneously facing the challenges of maintaining high flexibility while reducing costs and lead-times [5]. To face

B. Lalic et al. (Eds.): APMS 2020, IFIP AICT 592, pp. 590–597, 2020.
https://doi.org/10.1007/978-3-030-57997-5_68

this challenge, changes to company's and supply chain processes are advisable [6]. To addres these challenges, ETO companies started to perform some engineering and production activities to forecast, moving their CODP closer to the customer [7, 8]. This change poses new challenges for ETO companies: among the others, how to guarantee the coordination among engineering, production and sales [9–11]. In particular, Cannas et al. [12], highlighted that, in ETO companies, before and after the CODP the objectives and the managerial practices to be applied to pursue these objectives change, with a consequent need for different coordination mechanisms.

However, to the best of our knowledge, there is little research on how ETO companies are coordinating engineering, production and sales activities before and after the CODP. Thus, the purpose of this research is to explore cross-functional coordination mechanisms between engineering, sales and production functions adopted in ETO companies. In doing so, we aim to answer the following research question (RQ):

RQ: How do ETO companies manage engineering, production and sales processes, before and after the CODP?

The study answers to the RQ by empirically observing and analyzing a specific ETO sector, i.e., the machinery industry, by means of multiple case studies.

## 2  Background

Coordinating engineering, production and sales processes requires to manage three sets of coordination mechanisms related to, respectively, engineering and production, engineering and sales, and sales and production. As far as engineering and production is concerned, Adler [13] distinguishes among "Standard", "Schedule and Plan", "Mutual adjustment" or "Team". The same interface has been studied when engineering and production activities are performed by different companies Twigg [14]. As far as engineering and sales coordination is concerned, Griffin and Hauser [15] proposed six general approached to integrate the efforts of engineering and sales: relocation and physical facilities design, personnel movement (multi-functional training), informal social systems, matrix organizations and project teams, incentives and rewards, and formal integrative management processes such as phase review process, stage-gate process, product and cycle time excellence (PACE) and quality function deployment (QFD). Finally, Lamberti and Pero [16] discusses marketing, supply chain and product development interfaces in an electromechanical company. Whereas, Tang [17] presented a framework for the sales-production interface models in which he proposed: integrated decision models (mathematical models), balanced scorecards to avoid sub-optimization, cross-functional teams for developing coordinated plans, iterative negotiation and joint planning to move towards a more collaborative relationship among marketing and operations. Some of the mechanisms proposed for these two interfaces, engineering-sales and production-sales, are in common with the one proposed for engineering-production by [13].

In the ETO cross-functional coordination literature, Mello et al. [9] promoted the application of the coordination mechanisms developed by [13] in ETO companies. Mello et al. [10] included the integration of engineering and production activities in the list of principles to improve coordination in ETO supply chains; more precisely, they proposed the following mechanisms to integrate engineering and production: "Co-located teams", "Integrated IT systems", "Establishment of common goals", "Direct communication among the two functions", "Similar organizational culture".

Cannas et al. [12] demonstrated that in ETO companies the coordination needs of engineering and production processes change upstream and downstream of the CODP. Upstream of the CODP engineering and production coordination reduces unexpected design updates, reworks and late defects as much as possible, as they cause delays and additional costs. While, downstream of the CODP, engineering and production coordination reduces the risk of exceeding the stock holding costs due to obsolescence, excessive space occupation, etc. or facing stock-outs. Despite this contribution, little studies addressed how ETO companies can manage cross-functional coordination and how engineering, sales and production departments are coordinated before and after the CODP. For this reason, this study empirically analyzes ETO companies operating in the machinery industry, aiming to extend and refine the existing frameworks in the literature and adapt them to the complex ETO context.

## 3  Methodology

This research was conducted using multiple case studies, taking as the unit of analysis the company's core product families (the ones that have the major impact on the company's turnover). This research counts twelve case studies in nine companies operating in the Italian machinery industry. To ensure replication and variations within the sample, the criterion for selecting companies to be included in the sample was including companies operating in different sectors (e.g. machine tools, plastic and rubber, automotive and food) and producing different products (e.g. cutting machines, automated assembly lines, packaging lines and machine tools). In the data collection phase, the main sources of information were: semi-structured face-to-face interviews, official documents and internal documents. Semi-structured interviews (that lasted about 2 h each), collected information on the core product family of the company interviewed, focusing on how the company coordinates engineering, production and sales activities, before and after CODP. The informants have been chosen on the basis of their involvement in the key processes subject of the analysis (e.g. Operations Manager, Engineering Manager, Sales Manager, Plant Manager, etc.). Each interview was recorded with the informants' consensus and then transcribed to deeply analyze all the information collected.

## 4  Findings

The results shown that there is a difference in the coordination mechanisms employed by the companies based on the CODP positioning. In particular, in the sectors analysed, this difference depends on the number of engineering and production activities, performed before and after the order. Accordingly, the units of analysis have been mapped into the two-dimensional (2D) CODP framework proposed by Cannas et al. [11], which is the most recent taxonomy for classifying CODP positioning strategies in ETO companies (for details on this framework, please refer to this reference). What emerges from these results is that almost all the product families of the interviewed companies fall into the four main decoupling configurations identified by [11], namely: Special Machines (C, H), Customized Machines (E, G), Standard-customized machines (A, D, F) and Modular machines (B, I). Table 1 summarizes the coordination mechanisms adopted by the companies in the sample before and after the CODP depending on the configuration.

**Table 1.** Summary of coordination mechanisms used before and after the CODP

| | Configuration | Before-CODP | After-CODP |
|---|---|---|---|
| Engineering-Production | Special Machines | Standards | Teams and Mutual adjustment |
| | Customized Machines | | Mutual adjustment |
| | Standard-customized machines | | |
| | Modular machines | | |
| Engineering-Sales | Special Machines | Teams and Mutual adjustment | |
| | Customized Machines | Teams | |
| | Standard-customized machines | Standards | |
| | Modular machines | | |
| Sales-Production | Special Machines | No coordination | |
| | Customized Machines | | |
| | Standard-customized machines | | |
| | Modular machines | | |

## 4.1 Engineering-Production Coordination

The outcomes of the case study analysis show that, in all the cases, the mechanisms adopted to coordinate engineering and production activities, before and after the order arrival, are different. *Before the CODP*, when all the production-related activities are performed internally (cases A, C, E, D), companies adopt coordination mechanisms belonging to the standard coordination mode category, such as: (i) compatible CAD/CAM software through which companies exchange information; (ii) stage-gate process, i.e., a determined set of tasks is performed by a function and reviewed by another function which decide to go/not to go on; and (iii), visual work instructions software, which is a coordination mechanism not considered in the previous literature, representing a software tool providing work instructions to employees of the assembly department. *After the CODP*, companies providing customers with special machines (C, H) chose mechanisms falling into Team and Mutual adjustment (both meetings and coordination roles). Whereas, companies providing customers with customized machines (E, G), adopt only mutual adjustment mechanisms (both meetings and coordination roles). Finally, companies that provide customers with standard-customized machines (A, D, F) and modular machines (B, I), chose mutual adjustment mechanisms falling only into meetings. Among team mechanisms there are the transition teams, i.e., design engineers are temporarily transferred into the production department to be available in case design reviews are required. Among mutual adjustment mechanisms, the mostly applied are: (i) meetings, such as kick-off, i.e., a first meeting after the order is received in which interest parties gather to analyze order details and plan future activities, and weekly project review to monitor the state of progress of a current order; (ii) coordinating roles such as the line managers, which are responsible for inter-functional communication, and the project engineers, which are technical project managers in charge of coordinating the effort of engineering and production resources of a specific project.

## 4.2 Engineering-Sales Coordination

For what concerns coordination among engineering and sales, coordination mechanisms adopted before and after the order are different and this is true for all the CODP configurations. *Before the CODP*, companies providing customers with special machines (C, H) favor coordination mechanisms based on team, i.e., cross functional teams, and mutual adjustment, i.e., the coordinating role of sales engineers, people with a strong technical background belonging to the sales department supporting sales managers during the negotiation phase, acting as a reference point of the engineering department. This underlines a high coordination effort needed. While, *after the CODP* these companies mainly rely on one-time meetings (i.e. Kick-off), thus indicating a lower coordination effort needed among engineering and sales once the order has been acquired. For companies that anticipate some activities before the order, the coordination effort seems more balanced before and after CODP, but for sure is high *before the CODP*, since they adopt coordination mechanisms based on team, i.e. cross-functional teams and coordinating groups (E and G). *After the CODP*, they rely on meetings because they do not include people with strong technical competences (e.g. sales engineers) into the sales department. Finally, companies that provide customers with standard-customized machines (A, D, F) and modular machines (B, I), *before the CODP*, rely on the use of standard coordination mechanisms such as: (i) design rules, which can be used by product engineers in the design phase to assure the producibility of their designs; (ii) design configurator, i.e., software used by sales managers allowing the automation of the tendering and design phase leveraging on CAD and PLM platforms to generate ready-made bill of materials and product descriptions; and (iii), standard procedures, i.e., commercial offers created using pre-defined standard forms. While, *after the CODP*, they mainly adopt meetings (i.e. kick off and project review meetings). Interestingly, since face-to-face coordination underlines a higher coordination effort, with respect to standard coordination modes, the coordination effort in this case seems to be higher once the order is received.

### 4.3 Sales-Production Coordination

The mechanisms used to coordinate the effort of sales department and internal production vary upstream and downstream of the CODP. Company A, which is totally vertical integrated, employ cross-functional teams *before the CODP* and mutual adjustment, through line managers, *after the CODP*. While, it has emerged that, for all the other cases, which outsource part or most of the production, *before the CODP* there is no coordination among sales and production related activities performed internally. *After the CODP*, the great majority of these cases, adopt meetings (kick-off or project review). Therefore, it is reasonable to assume that the choice of coordination mechanisms, in this case does not depend on the CODP configuration the company adopts. Finally, concerning coordination among sales department and external suppliers, the companies analyzed do not adopt any coordination mechanisms, since the department in charge of managing the interface with external suppliers is the Purchasing department for all the cases.

## 5 Discussion and Conclusions

This paper investigates through a case study research whether and how cross-functional coordination mechanisms vary before and after the CODP. Results show that, *before the order (pre CODP)*, the companies interviewed recognize a high coordination effort needed for engineering-sales interfaces. Thus, they rely on mechanisms belonging to team and mutual adjustment, when customization levels are high; while, moving towards more standard product configurations, cross-functional coordination is achieved through standardization of procedures, sales' experience from previous project, the use of IT tools, which of course correspond to a lower coordination effort to be sustained. Differently, *after the order (post CODP)*, our findings revealed that coordination regards mainly engineering and production activities (both internally and externally performed) and the choice of coordination mechanisms is influenced by the type of products. In particular, also in this case, the higher the customization level of the product, the higher the intensity of coordination. When products are highly customized, after the CODP it is necessary to employ different modes of mutual adjustment (e.g. project engineers, kick-off meetings) and teams. Finally, findings concerning sales-production interface show that coordination happens after the order and only with the internal production. Moreover, for this interface, the mechanisms adopted are the same for each type of product.

The novelty of this study consists of (i) introducing a new temporal dimension when studying cross-functional coordination mechanisms (i.e. pre and post CODP), (ii) studying cross-functional coordination in the machinery industry, and (iii) considering in the same research more interfaces (i.e. engineering-sales, engineering-production and sales-production). The results underline the importance for studies focusing on ETO cross-functional coordination of considering all the possible interfaces, including also the sales department and differentiating between the activities performed before and after the customer order. This can be considered an interesting research direction for future studies. Surely, this study presents also limitations.

Although the research was designed considering all the relevant aspects for ensuring the reliability of the results, the focus on one specific industry, as well as the size of the sample, could limit the generalizability of the results. Thus, further research addressing different ETO sectors and/or adopting methodologies that study larger samples, such as survey-based research, are recommended to extend and validate the results of this research.

# References

1. Hoekstra, S., Romme, J.: Integral Logistic Structures: Developing Customer-oriented Goods Flow (1992)
2. Amaro, G., Hendry, L., Kingsman, B.: Competitive advantage, customisation and a new taxonomy for non make-to-stock companies (1999). https://doi.org/10.1108/01443579910254213
3. Barlow, J., Childerhouse, P., Gann, D., Hong-Minh, S., Naim, M., Ozaki, R.: Choice and delivery in housebuilding: lessons from Japan for UK housebuilders. Build. Res. Inf. **31**, 134–145 (2003). https://doi.org/10.1080/09613210302003
4. Wortmann, J.C.: Production management systems for one-of-a-kind products. Comput. Ind. (1992). https://doi.org/10.1016/0166-3615(92)90008-B
5. Birkie, S.E., Trucco, P.: Understanding dynamism and complexity factors in engineer-to-order and their influence on lean implementation strategy. Prod. Plan. Control **27**, 345–359 (2016). https://doi.org/10.1080/09537287.2015.1127446
6. Patrucco, A., Ciccullo, F., Pero, M.: Industry 4.0 and supply chain process re-engineering. Bus. Process Manage. J. (2020). https://doi.org/10.1108/BPMJ-04-2019-0147. ahead-of-print
7. Willner, O., Powell, D., Gerschberger, M., Schönsleben, P.: Exploring the archetypes of engineer-to-order: an empirical analysis. Int. J. Oper. Prod. Manag. **36**, 242–264 (2016). https://doi.org/10.1108/IJOPM-07-2014-0339
8. Cannas, V.G., Gosling, J., Pero, M., Rossi, T.: Determinants for order-fulfilment strategies in engineer-to-order companies: Insights from the machinery industry. Int. J. Prod. Econ., 107743 (2020) https://doi.org/10.1016/j.ijpe.2020.107743
9. Mello, M.H., Strandhagen, J.O., Alfnes, E.: The role of coordination in avoiding project delays in an engineer-to-order supply chain. J. Manuf. Technol. Manag. (2015). https://doi.org/10.1108/JMTM-03-2013-0021
10. Mello, M.H., Gosling, J., Naim, M.M., Strandhagen, J.O., Brett, P.O.: Improving coordination in an engineer-to-order supply chain using a soft systems approach. Prod. Plan. Control (2017). https://doi.org/10.1080/09537287.2016.1233471
11. Mello, M.H., Strandhagen, J.O., Alfnes, E.: Analyzing the factors affecting coordination in engineer-to-order supply chain. Int. J. Oper. Prod. Manag. (2015). https://doi.org/10.1108/IJOPM-12-2013-0545
12. Cannas, V.G., Gosling, J., Pero, M., Rossi, T.: Engineering and production decoupling configurations: An empirical study in the machinery industry. Int. J. Prod. Econ. **216**, 173–189 (2019)
13. Adler, P.S.: Interdepartmental Interdependence and coordination: the case of the design/manufacturing interface. Organ. Sci. **6**, 147–167 (1995). https://doi.org/10.1287/orsc.6.2.147
14. Twigg, D.: Managing the design/manufacturing interface across firms. Integr. Manuf., Syst (2002)

15. Griffin, A., Hauser, J.R.: Integrating R&D and marketing: a review and analysis of the literature. J. Prod. Innov. Manag. Int. Publ. Prod. Dev. Manag. Assoc. **13**, 191–215 (1996)
16. Pero, M., Lamberti, L.: The supply chain management-marketing interface in product development: an exploratory study. Bus. Process Manage. J. **19**(2), 217–244 (2013). https://doi.org/10.1108/14637151311308295
17. Tang, C.S.: A review of marketing-operations interface models: from co-existence to coordination and collaboration. Int. J. Prod. Econ. **125**, 22–40 (2010). https://doi.org/10.1016/j.ijpe.2010.01.014

# Production Management in Food Supply Chains

# Short Agri-Food Supply Chains: A Proposal in a Food Bank

Aguinaldo Eduardo de Souza[1,2]([✉]) [iD], João Gilberto Mendes dos Reis[1,3] [iD],
Antonio Carlos Estender[1] [iD], Jorge Luiz Dias Agia[1] [iD],
Oduvaldo Vendrametto[1] [iD], Luciana Melo Costa[4] [iD],
and Paula Ferreira da Cruz Correia[1] [iD]

[1] Paulista University - UNIP, PPGEP, São Paulo, Brazil
souza.eduaguinaldo@gmail.com
[2] UNIBR, São Vicente, Brazil
[3] Federal University of Grande Dourados - UFGD, PPGA, Dourados, Brazil
[4] Federal University of São Paulo - UNIFESP, Santos, Brazil

**Abstract.** Many communities are interested in acquiring healthy food without pesticides and chemical preservatives. At the same time, they want to protect local production and cultural characteristics. In this sense, the academy starts to discuss a change in food supply chains and called of Short Agri-Food Chains. These networks have proven to be a reliable substitute for conventional supply chains creating empowerment from family farmers. The present study investigated the role of food banks' on the structural basis of short food supply chains. The results pointed out that food banks may be an important instrument for consolidating these supply chains contributing to the development of Family Farm and Small producer.

**Keywords:** Agri-Food chains · Family farm · Food bank · Logistics

## 1 Introduction

Food supply chains suffer from a high number of wastes and losses between farm to fork. Around 30% of the food produced in the world is wasted or lost mainly due to the logistics process [1, 2]. Therefore, the efficiency alongside supply chain management is fundamental as a source of social well-being, reduction of the use of natural resources, and to increase food access [3].

Contrary to the common belief the agri-food networks are lead by Family Farms [4–8] that are negatively affected by the global supply chains [2, 4, 9–13]. These supply chains usually raise the product price to consumers due to intermediaries' agents but reduce profitability to small producers.

On the other hand, studies point out a new paradigm of global consumption, where consumers have preferred healthy foods, produced locally, with their own cultural characteristics and guaranteeing social justice [2, 4, 9–13].

Currently, one alternative to this scenery is the Alternative Food Networks - AFN which is an option to the traditional agri-food system. The AFNs have as characteristics

© IFIP International Federation for Information Processing 2020
Published by Springer Nature Switzerland AG 2020
B. Lalic et al. (Eds.): APMS 2020, IFIP AICT 592, pp. 601–608, 2020.
https://doi.org/10.1007/978-3-030-57997-5_69

the development of local initiatives, use of local input, and low production scale with a focus on quality, to the detriment of high productivity [14].

It is in this context that emerges the Short Food Supply Chain - SFSC concept. A model substitute for conventional supply chain where foods reflect the characteristics of "local", "natural", "healthy" and "reliable" [15].

According to [16] Short Agri-Food Chains, they are specific chains of agricultural products intended for human consumption. The authors reveal that these chains excel in proximity between producers and consumers. Far beyond the spatial aspect, but a connection that allows interactivity so that both know each other's purposes and needs

The aim of this study is to demonstrate the role of Food Bank as a catalyst for the model of Short Agri-Food Chains. To this end, we chose to conduct field research through a case study with the Itanhaém Food Banks, located on the southern coast of the state of São Paulo.

## 2    Background

### 2.1    Food Bank

Food Banks are intended to combat hunger and food insecurity [17]. They have physical structures that aim to capture, select and distribute free foodstuff that would be wasted throughout the production chain [18]. These entities may be public or private, under the management of civil society organizations of social interest, non-profit organizations [19].

The Food Bank originated in 1967 in the United States in Phoenix city, through the initiative of volunteers who requested donations of foodstuffs, which would be discarded by supermarkets and industry. Initially, the donations were intended to prepare meals for those in need. However, the volume of donations was exceeding the capacity to prepare meals, starting to be stored and distributed to philanthropic organizations [20].

In Brazil, the National System of Food and Nutrition Security aims to guarantee the Human Right to Adequate Food. For this purpose, the government articulates public policy at the three levels of government: federal, state, municipality, through different sectors and civil society, with a view to promoting Food and Nutrition Security and combating hunger. These actions are operationalized through public food and nutrition security equipment. Public Equipment is structures aimed at serving and supporting citizens in nutritional vulnerability [19].

The first movements of Food Bank in Brazil emerged from the initiative of the Social Trade Service - SESC, with the urban harvesting program in 1997. Later in 2000, the first Food Bank was inaugurated in the city of Rio de Janeiro [20].

Therefore, Food Banks are important arrangements for promoting food security in Brazilian municipalities, aiming to eradicate hunger.

## 2.2 Short Agri-Food Chains

Sustainable agri-food systems play a key role in combating malnutrition [21]. However, the Short Supply Chains have proved to be an option for traditional supply chains as well as an alternative to AF's sustainability. They can nullify two problems faced by farmers: the increase of the production cost; and the new global trend of consumption, with a strong call for healthy eating, based on sustainable production, aiming at food security [16].

Moreover, Short Supply Chains propose a direct relationship between the producer and consumer, reducing the number of intermediaries and the distance between the producer and the final consumer [14].

The small farmers are the main benefit of short supply chains, the obtaining of fairer recipes. The relationship between producer and consumer is the main characteristic of the SFSC, and, therefore, contribute to the economic development of the locations where they are inserted, besides providing the autonomy of producers [15].

## 2.3 Family Farm in Brazil

The legal definition of Family Agriculture is contained in Decree No. 9,064 [22]. In order to be framed as a family farmer, the producer must develop his practices in rural areas. What characterizes the family agriculture of the non-family is the fact that is management is shared between family members and agricultural production activities are the main source of income of the family [23].

Regarding the profile of Family Agriculture in Brazil, data from the Brazilian Institute of Geography and Statistics - IBGE [24] indicate that of the 5.07 million rural establishments located in 351.2 million hectares, The Family Farm accounts for 3.9 million establishments (77%), which together occupy a total area of 80.9 million hectares, i.e. 23% of the country's agricultural area.

## 3  Methods

To meet the objectives of this work, we opted for an exploratory and descriptive methodological approach. The study was developed in the municipality of Itanhaém (SP) through field research with the Association of Rural Producers of the Rio Branco Hydrographic Watershed, Artisanal Fishermen, Aquaculture and Indigenous Peoples of Itanhaém and Region - AMIBRA, composed of 52 family farmers and the Itanhaém Food Bank.

For data collection, a semi-structured questionnaire was applied in order to quantify the volume of food purchase, food type, main suppliers (farmers), logistics flow (receipt and distribution), recipients, related to the operations of 2018. The study population comprises family farmers from the AMIBRA farmers association and Itanhaém Food Bank. The collected data was compiled into an electronic database of the Microsoft Excel program®. From there it was possible to structure and understand a model of Short Agri-Food Chains.

# 4 Result and Discussion

The Itanhaém Food Bank is responsible for operationalizing Food and Nutrition Security - SAN programs in the municipality through the Food Acquisition Program - PAA. Created in 2007, the Itanhaém Food Bank is the result of the agreement between the Municipality of Itanhaém and the Federal Government.

In 2019, BRL 300,000.00 from the Ministry of Social Development was contributed, which ensured the socioeconomic inclusion of family farmers in the municipality, registered as suppliers of the Food Acquisition Program. Together the farmers provided more than 90 tonnes of food to the municipality's program, which were transferred to ten entities registered with the Municipal Social Assistance Council - CMAS (Fig. 1) including about 2,500 families.

| PRODUCT | Social Assistance Entities | | | | | | | | | | TOTAL (kg) |
|---|---|---|---|---|---|---|---|---|---|---|---|
| | 1 | 2 | 3 | 4 | 5 | 6 | 7 | 8 | 9 | 10 | |
| Zucchini Girl/organic | 150.00 | 141.70 | 160.00 | 150.00 | 750.00 | 141.70 | 141.70 | 141.70 | 150.00 | 299.92 | 2,226.72 |
| Hydroponic Lettuce | 500.00 | 480.00 | 550.00 | 500.00 | 2,400.00 | 500.00 | 600.00 | 600.00 | 480.00 | 793.84 | 7,403.84 |
| Banana Silver | 2,800.00 | 2,600.00 | 2,800.00 | 2,600.00 | 15,852.09 | 2,600.00 | 3,000.00 | 2,800.00 | 2,600.00 | 3,000.00 | 40,652.09 |
| Sweet Potato | 173.54 | 190.00 | 200.00 | 175.00 | 900.00 | 230.00 | 234.92 | 173.54 | 150.00 | 300.00 | 2,727.00 |
| Zucchini | 270.00 | 260.00 | 300.00 | 300.00 | 1,350.00 | 350.00 | 413.98 | 258.52 | 260.00 | 300.00 | 4,062.50 |
| Cabbage | 180.00 | 180.00 | 200.00 | 160.00 | 800.00 | 220.00 | 230.91 | 159.09 | 170.00 | 200.00 | 2,500.00 |
| Organic Cabbage | 400.00 | 360.00 | 450.00 | 360.00 | 1,800.00 | 450.00 | 500.00 | 450.00 | 360.00 | 478.96 | 5,608.96 |
| Cassava Vacuum s/bark | 580.00 | 600.00 | 600.00 | 600.00 | 3,330.89 | 650.00 | 700.00 | 650.00 | 580.00 | 800.00 | 9,090.89 |
| Passion Fruit Azedo | 310.00 | 350.00 | 320.00 | 310.00 | 1,650.00 | 450.00 | 458.60 | 309.81 | 310.00 | 400.00 | 4,868.41 |
| Palmito Pupunha Peeled | 200.00 | 200.00 | 200.00 | 200.00 | 1,000.00 | 250.00 | 401.10 | 194.44 | 200.00 | 210.00 | 3,055.54 |
| Palmito Pupunha/organic | 169.97 | 169.97 | 169.97 | 169.97 | 1,175.91 | 169.97 | 225.26 | 169.97 | 169.97 | 169.97 | 2,760.93 |
| Fish | 225.25 | 225.28 | 225.97 | 225.26 | 1,983.49 | 225.26 | 225.26 | 225.26 | 225.26 | 225.26 | 4,011.53 |
| Tahitian Lemon | 150.00 | 131.66 | 150.00 | 150.00 | 700.00 | 131.66 | 131.66 | 131.65 | 140.00 | 252.34 | 2,068.97 |
| | 6,108.76 | 5,888.59 | 6,325.94 | 5,900.23 | 33,692.38 | 6,368.59 | 7,263.39 | 6,263.98 | 5,795.23 | 7,430.29 | 91,037.38 |

**Fig. 1.** Entities benefited from the PAA in 2019. Source: Adapted Itanhaém Food Bank

As shown in Fig. 1, about 95% of the food purchased was hortifrúti, especially banana (40 t), the most produced item due to the characteristics of the region. The remaining 5% was intended for the purchase of fish, offered by fishermen from Itanhaém city.

The income of the 52 farmers was around BRL 5,679.00 (1,750 kg/month) where the lowest income was BRL 2,000.00 (454 kg/month) and the highest, BRL 6,500.00 (2.600 kg/month).

Another source of acquisition is food from "urban collection". Products without commercial value, but that retain their nutritional characteristics, which are donated by local retailers to Itanhaém Food Bank. About two tons per month of hortifrúti food are received, selected, packaged, stored and subsequently destined for the "Capillarity Project" (Fig. 2).

The "Capillarity Project" serves people in a state of social and nutritional vulnerability, who are informally referred to Itanhaém Food Bank through the Social Care Reference Center - CRAS, Health Secretary (sick with diabetes, cancer, HIV) and other entities that are not registered by CMAS. Once routed, these families are registered in the project and become benefited from food baskets.

Before                    During                    After

**Fig. 2.** Capillarity Project. Source: Authors

Given its logistical functional ability (reception, selection, storage, and distribution), the Food Bank can be presented as an important instrument for consolidating the Short Agri-Food Chains, contributing to the development of Family Farm and social rise of the small producer [9, 15, 16].

In the specific case of Itanhaém Food Bank, its logistics structure ensures the development of a model of Short Chains, as can be observed in Fig. 3.

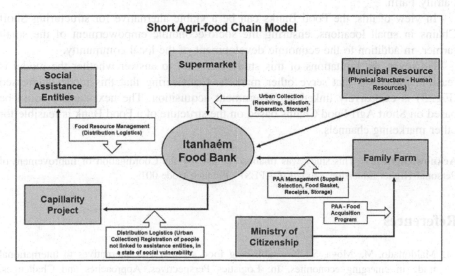

**Fig. 3.** Structure of a Short Agri-Food Chain. Source: Authors

The Short Chain model elaborated in Fig. 3 presents Itanhaém Food Bank as the main articulator of the logistics activities of this chain. However, three activities gain greater prominence, supplier management, food acquisition, storage, and distribution.

In addition, it accounts for dimensions of economic, environmental and social sustainability [25].

Two operations are performed in this model presented. In the management of the PAA, o Itanhaém Food Bank is responsible for defining food purchase items, considering the specificities of local agricultural culture, as well as the productive potential of farmers, in addition to the receipt, storage and shipment of food acquired for registered entities.

In the Operation Capillarity Project, Itanhaém Food Bank is responsible for maintaining the agreement with donor companies. In addition, it manages the logistics functions of the project such as receiving donated foods, selection, and separation of products, the composition of baskets, storage and distribution for registered families that are withdrawn from the bank itself.

## 5  Final Considerations

In order to present the Food Bank as a proposal of Short Agri-Food Chains, it can be concluded that the Itanhaém Food Bank in its attributions, develops the main activities that make up the premises of Short Agri-Food Chains.

In this model Itanhaém, the Bank is the only intermediate agent, allowing a direct connection between the field and the table, and therefore, fairer revenues for farmers. Moreover, institutional sale to the PAA is an opportunity for market diversification for Family Farm.

In view of this, the Food Banks can be a viable alternative for structuring Short Chains in small locations, ensuring the socio-economic empowerment of the small farmer, in addition to the economic development of the local community.

However, the limitations of this study were not to answer whether the model is feasible for chains that serve other markets. Considering that this model addressed (Fig. 3) is exclusively linked to government acquisition. The next studies could be based on Short Agri-Food Chains based on the structure of a Food Bank is feasible for other marketing channels.

**Acknowledgments.** This study was financed in part by the Coordination of Improvement of Personal Higher Education - Brazil (CAPES) - Finance Code 001

## References

1. Maldonado, M., Moya, S.: In establishing food security and alternatives to international trade in emerging economies. In: Logistics Perspectives, Approaches and Challenges, pp. 1–34. Nova Science Publishers Inc
2. Todorovic, V., Maslaric, M., Bojic, S., Jokic, M., Mircetic, D., Nikolicic, S.: Solutions for more sustainable distribution in the short food supply chains. Sustainability **10**(10), 3481 (2018). http://www.mdpi.com/2071-1050/10/10/3481

3. Gonzalez-Feliu, J., Osorio-Ramirez, C., Palacios-Arguello, L.: Local production-based dietary supplement distribution in emerging countries: Bienestarina distribution in colombia. In: Establishing Food Security and Alternatives to International Trade in Emerging Economies, pp. 297–315. IGI Global (2018)

4. Hill, B.: The 'myth' of the family farm: defining the family farm and assessing its importance in the European community. J. Rural Stud. 9(4), 359–370 (1993). https://linkinghub.elsevier.com/retrieve/pii/074301679390048O

5. Toader, M., Roman, G.V.: Family farming – examples for rural communities development. Agric. Agric. Sci. Procedia 6, 89–94 (2015). https://linkinghub.elsevier.com/retrieve/pii/S221078431500176X

6. Graeub, B.E., Chappell, M.J., Wittman, H., Ledermann, S., Kerr, R.B., Gemmill- Herren, B.: The state of family farms in the world. World Dev. 87, 1–15 (2016). https://linkinghub.elsevier.com/retrieve/pii/S0305750X15001217

7. Godoy-Durán, N., Galdeano-Gómez, E., Pérez-Mesa, J.C., Piedra-Muñoz, L.: Assessing eco-efficiency and the determinants of horticultural family-farming in Southeast Spain. J. Environ. Mange. 204, 594–604 (2017). https://linkinghub.elsevier.com/retrieve/pii/S030147971730899X

8. USDA, D.d.A.d.E.U.: Family farms|national institute of food and agriculture. https://nifa.usda.gov/family-farms

9. Goodman, D.: The quality 'turn' and alternative food practices: reflections and agenda. J. Rural Stud. 19(1), 1–7 (2003). https://linkinghub.elsevier.com/retrieve/pii/S0743016702000438

10. Bloom, J.D., Hinrichs, C.C.: Moving local food through conventional food system infrastructure: value chain framework comparisons and insights. Renewable Agric. Food Syst. 26(1), 13–23 (2011). https://www.cambridge.org/core/product/identifier/S1742170510000384/type/journal_article

11. King, R.P., Hand, M.S., DiGiacomo, G., Clancy, K., Gómez, M.I., Hardesty, S.D., Lev, L., McLaughlin, E.W.: Comparing the Structure, Size, and Performance of Local and Mainstream Food Supply Chains, pp. 187–189 (2010). https://foodsystemsjournal.org/index.php/fsj/article/view/33

12. Chiffoleau, Y., Millet-Amrani, S., Rossi, A., Rivera-Ferre, M.G., Merino, P.L.: The participatory construction of new economic models in short food supply chains. J. Rural Stud. 68, 182–190 (2019). https://linkinghub.elsevier.com/retrieve/pii/S0743016718304157

13. Mancini, M., Menozzi, D., Donati, M., Biasini, B., Veneziani, M., Arfini, F.: Producers' and consumers' perception of the sustainability of short food supply chains: the case of parmigiano reggiano PDO. Sustainability 11(3), 721 (2019). http://www.mdpi.com/2071-1050/11/3/721

14. Pivoto, D., Mores, G.d.V., Silva, R.F.d., Finocchio, C.P.S.: Cadeias curtas de suprimentos de alimentos: Uma oportunidade para os produtores rurais? 54. https://www.researchgate.net/publication/304893058_Cadeias_curtas_de_suprimentos_de_alimentos_uma_oportunidade_para_os_produtores_rurais

15. Aguiar, L.d.C., DelGrossi, M.E., Thomé, K.M.: Short food supply chain: characteristics of a family farm. Ciência Rural 48(5) (2018). http://www.scielo.br/scielo.php?script=sci_arttext&pid=S0103-84782018000500800&lng=en&tlng=en

16. Scarabelot, M., Schneider, S.: As cadeias agroalimentares curtas e desenvolvimento local – um estudo de caso no município de nova veneza/SC 14(19), 101. http://e-revista.unioeste.br/index.php/fazciencia/article/view/8028

17. Knoblock-Hahn, A., Brown, K., Medrow, L., Murphy, A.: How community food banks support school breakfast: strategies used and lessons learned. J. Acad. Nutr. Diet. 116(7), 1187–1192 (2016). https://linkinghub.elsevier.com/retrieve/pii/S2212267216001003

18. Davis, L.B., Sengul, I., Ivy, J.S., Brock, L.G., Miles, L.: Scheduling food bank collections and deliveries to ensure food safety and improve access. Socio-Econ. Plann. Sci. **48**(3), 175–188 (2014). https://linkinghub.elsevier.com/retrieve/pii/S0038012114000172
19. CIDADANIA, M.D.: SISAN - sistema nacional de se- gurança alimentar e nutricional. http://mds.gov.br/assuntos/seguranca-alimentar/direito-a-alimentacao/sistema-nacional-de-seguranca-alimentar-e-nutricional-sisan/sisan
20. Belik, W.B., Cunha, A.R.A.d.A., Costa, L.A.: Crise dos alimentos e estratégias para a redução do desperdício no contexto de uma política de segurança alimen- tar e nutricional no brasil 0(38). http://www.ipea.gov.br/ppp/index.php/PPP/article/view/277
21. Gillespie, S., van den Bold, M., Hodge, J.: Nutrition and the governance of agri- food systems in south asia: a systematic review. Food Policy **82**, 13–27 (2019). https://linkinghub.elsevier.com/retrieve/pii/S0306919218308376
22. Government, F.: Decree no. 9,064. http://www.planalto.gov.br/ccivil_03/_Ato2015-2018/2017/Decreto/D9064.htm
23. Medina, G., Almeida, C., Novaes, E., Godar, J., Pokorny, B.: Development conditions for family farming: lessons from Brazil. World Dev. **74**, 386–396 (2015). https://linkinghub.elsevier.com/retrieve/pii/S0305750X15001412
24. IBGE, B.I.o.G.a.S.: Agricultural census (2017). https://sidra.ibge.gov.br/pesquisa/censo-agropecuario/censo-agropecuario-2017
25. Martins, C., Melo, M., Pato, M.: Redesigning a food bank supply chain network in a triple bottom line context. Int. J. Prod. Econ. **214**, 234–247 (2019). https://linkinghub.elsevier.com/retrieve/pii/S092552731830450X

# Analysis of the New Frontier of Soybean Production in Brazil

José Alberto de Alencar Luz[1,2]($\boxtimes$) (iD), João Gilberto Mendes dos Reis[1,3]($\boxtimes$) (iD),
and Alexandre Formigoni[1,4] (iD)

[1] RESUP/PPGEP - Universidade Paulista, São Paulo, Brazil
josealberto@socimol.com.br, betomendesreis@msn.com
[2] Production Engineering UNIP/UNIFSA, Teresina, Brazil
[3] Agribusiness, Universidade Federal da Grande Dourados, Dourados, Brazil
[4] Gestão Tecnologia em Sistemas Produtivos, Centro Paula Souza, São Paulo, Brazil

**Abstract.** Brazil is one of the main country growers in soybean production. With the purpose to maintain this position, the production is going to the new areas in the country seeking the low cost of land. In this sense, the Piaui state appears as a new frontier of growth. However, it causes a direct impact on infrastructure in the corridor of exportation. The study intends to analyze the production of soybean in Piauí state, Brazil, and the main logistics barriers. The work was carried out through qualitative research that allowed to characterize the producers regarding the size, productivity, costs, the origin of the input, transport, and issues in logistics infrastructure. The results showed the competitive advantages of soybean production in Piaui, as well as the main challenges pointed out by producers.

**Keywords:** Food supply chains · Production management · Soybean · Logistics

## 1 Introduction

The agricultural sector is essential to the Brazilian economy. In 2017, the agribusiness supply chains are responsible for 23% of country GDP [1]. Among the several products commercialized, the country is the world second soybean grower facing the US for the first place. Moreover is the largest soybean exporter [2]. However, soybean market are controlled by large multinational corporations that operate all stages of the production chain, offering seeds, pesticides, machinery, fertilizers, transport, and storage. Therefore, they have direct influence over the costs and competitiveness of commodities in all the countries.

Soybean production in Brazil is controlled by Archer Daniels Midland, Bunge, Cargill, Louis Dreyfus, CofCo, Glencore. Moreover in Brazil we have Amaggi, Caramuru, and Algar [3]. The soybean complex comprises a production chain that involves grain production and export, and the processing of the product using a industrial processes called crushing where soybean is transformed in oil

© IFIP International Federation for Information Processing 2020
Published by Springer Nature Switzerland AG 2020
B. Lalic et al. (Eds.): APMS 2020, IFIP AICT 592, pp. 609–615, 2020.
https://doi.org/10.1007/978-3-030-57997-5_70

and soybean meal [4,5]. Of the crushed grain, approximately 80% is converted to soybean meal and the rest to oil [6].

Among the factors that contribute to the increase the world consumption of soybean is mainly the growing purchasing power of the population in developing countries, which has been causing a change in eating habits. Thus, the exchange of cereals for beef, pork, and chicken is increasingly observed. All of this results in a greater demand for soybean as an ingredient that makes up 70% of the feed for these animals [4]. Soybean meal is the fundamental input for animal production, being used in the feeding of poultry and pigs to produce meat and eggs. The intensification of soybean crushing has caused an increasing link among industry, agriculture and livestock.

All this demand is pressing soybean supply chains to find out new areas of production. In this sense, Piaui emerges due to favorable aspects such as productivity and landing low cost. One of the main areas of production in the south of the state where Uruçui has an important role in the production [7].

This research investigated the soybean production in Piaui to identify productivity, costs, logistics and reason to production to be implemented in that area. To do so, we conducted a survey in 20 farms of the state in the municipalities of Bom Jesus, Ribeiro Goncalves and Uruçuí.

## 2   Methodology

The present study consists of a survey of soybean growers in Piaui state, Brazil. The investigation was based on the dialectical method [8] which seeks to understand the causes of a process in a way to argue, analyze, and promote a synthesis, whose technical procedures were based on bibliographic, documentary and survey research.

The survey took place through interviews with a structured questionnaire. Table 1 presents a summary of the subjects covered in the survey, which accounts for a total of 18 questions.

**Table 1.** Content of survey

| Questions by subject | Quantity |
|---|---|
| Characterization | 4 |
| Agricultural inputs | 2 |
| Suppliers | 2 |
| Storage and transport | 2 |
| Advantages of Soybean production | 3 |
| The role of Companhia Nacional de Abastecimento | 1 |
| Soybean price | 1 |
| Logistics | 2 |
| Profitability | 1 |

The questionnaire was applied between January and February 2020 with the 20 soybean producers in Piaui. Among them, 18 farms are located in the municipality of Uruçuí, 1 in Ribeiro Gonçalves and 1 in Bom Jesus, Fig. 2. The locations were established based on the availiability of growers to meet the researches. The Uruçuí was the main place due to assistance of local cooperative (Fig. 1).

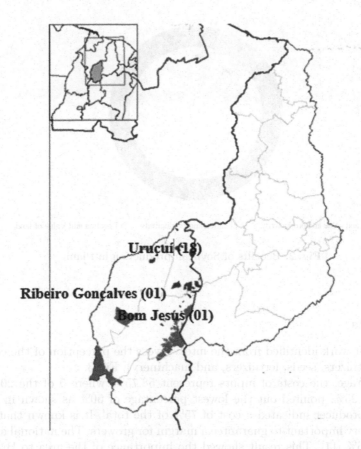

**Fig. 1.** Municipalities where the survey was conducted

# 3   Results and Discussion

## 3.1   Productivity and Reasons to Produce in Piaui

The productivity data in the 2017/2018 crop year in Piaui was 3, 4 metric tons per hectare [9] while among 20 producers was slightly less, around 3,3 metric tons per hectare. The source of the productivity results is according to the Brazilian organization responsible for providing statistical indicators on agricultural production.

Most parts of the growers are migrants from the south of the country that bring the culture and knowledge of soybean production. The main reason to produce in Piaui according to the survey is the cost of land acquisition and productivity (86%), Fig. 3. This result confirm the advance of agriculture production in the state [10].

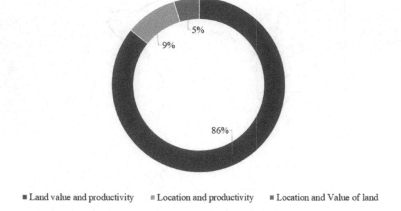

■ Land value and productivity    ■ Location and productivity    ■ Location and Value of land

**Fig. 2.** Benefits of Soybean production in Piaui

## 3.2   Costs

The present work identified from the interviewees the perception of the costs of inputs (fertilizers, seeds, fertilizers, and machinery), Fig. 3.

On average, the costs of inputs represent 58.75%, where 5 of the 20 interviewed, or 25%, pointed out the lowest percentage of 50% as shown in Fig. 3. Only one producer indicated a cost of 75% of the total. It is known that these costs are very important to guarantee a margin for growers. The national average cost is 61.6% [11]. This result showed the importance of the area to Brazilian agriculture production.

## 3.3   Logistics

The studied scenario considers a flow of soybeans through road transport, as it is the only mode of transport used in the operation to the sea port. Located in the North of the region, covering approximately 700 km.

One of the aspects that draw attention in the research is the assessment of road conditions in the savanna of Piaui states. This aspect was highlighted by all interviewees as the point of greatest logistical difficulty for the grower in the region. Around 75% of the growers evaluated the conditions of the soybean roads in Piaui as poor and very bad. Moreover, the other 25% classify the roads as

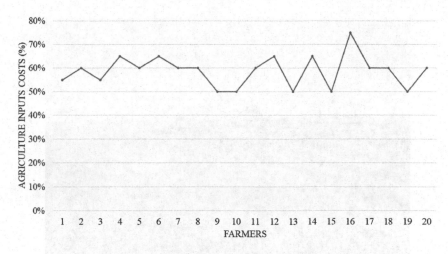

**Fig. 3.** Percentage of agricultural input costs

regular. This is a relevant factor in the research because of the logistical costs and waste increase with the compromise of the conditions of the roads, in addition to lagging the service level of the production chain, as the lead time becomes longer.

It is known that there are many unpaved stretches of both state and federal highways, such as BR's 135/324 and PI's 392/397 with an extension of more than 250 km. Figure 4 depicts the reality of one of the main highways in the Piaui region, Transcerrados.

The survey found that supplier logistics involves only national suppliers, including seeds, manure, machinery, and fertilizers. Part of the transport logistics is carried out with its own eet, about 15% of the Producers. This configuration influences the cost of production calculated at work. Logistical difficulties may be associated with increases in production costs, 75% of the survey a rmed that entry costs are up to 60%, considered high for the segment under analysis. Another point that is highlighted is the susceptibility of inputs to changes in exchange, as they are commodities, subject to changes in the dollar exchange. The literature states an average cost that represents approximately 50%, slightly below what the interviewed producers indicated.

## 4   Final Remarks

According to a study carried out by Paiva et al. [12], it is noted that the growth in soy production is mainly due to the expansion of the planted area. Productivity data collected in our study are in line with the national average. In addition, incentives such as the acquisition value of properties in Piaui states being less costly compared to land prices in other regions of savannahs in the country affects this soybean movement.

**Fig. 4.** Piaui roadways

The relevance of the research will be given by the size of the area corresponding to the Research Producers equivalent to 150,400 hectares. However, the conclusions of this research cannot be universalized, taking into account that the other locations in the region and in the country they are influenced by other variables that modify the production scenario. Rain is considered the main climatic factor that can limit the production of the grain crop according to its frequency and quantity since the vast majority of soybean crops for grain production are grown in large areas and under rainfed conditions.

It is possible to verify the high size of the enterprises in the region covered in the research, considering that 95% of the properties have more than 6,500 planted hectares. The majority, that is, 75% of the producers work with soy stock on the farm, inducing a policy of storage and the presence of silos to store the grain. The growers mention that they prefer the cultivation of soybean over other crops, due to the greater ease of commercialization, pointed out by 80% of the interviewees. Other justifications are the knowledge of the soybean production process and the productivity achieved in the region.

Finally, the challenges permeate the structural conditions, mainly in the roadway logistics, as the roads do not have asphalt pavement and the access conditions are poor. The factor that only increases distribution costs and stores grain. It can generate a tradeoff, low production cost, and high distribution cost.

# References

1. Confederation of Agriculture and Livestock of Brazi. www.cnabrasil.org.br/central-comunicacao/boletins

2. USDA: Oilseeds: world markets and trade (2017). https://apps.fas.usda.gov/psdonline/circulars/oilseeds.pdf

3. Pereira, P.: Novos e velhos atores na soja no centro-oeste e no norte do Brasil. Ph.D. thesis, Federal Fluminense, Rio de Janeiro (2016)

4. Freitas, M.: The soybean crop in Brazil: the increase of the Brazilian production and the emergence of a new agricultural frontier. Enciclopédia Biosfera **7**(12) (2011)

5. dos Reis, J.G.M., Amorim, P., Cabral, J.A.S.: Effects of price and transportation costs in Soybean trade. In: Nääs, I., et al. (eds.) APMS 2016. IAICT, vol. 488, pp. 563–570. Springer, Cham (2016). https://doi.org/10.1007/978-3-319-51133-7_67

6. Lourega, L.D.O.: Análise da participação do complexo soja nas exportações do Brasil no período de 2004 a 2014, p. 17 (2015). http://bibliodigital.unijui.edu.br:8080/xmlui/bitstream/handle/123456789/3174/La%C3%ADs%20de%20Oliveira%20Lourega.pdf?sequence=1

7. Silva, A.J.D., Monteiro, M.D.S.L., Barbosa, E.L.: Territorialização da agricultura empresarial em Uruçuí/PI: de "espaço vazio" aos imperativos do agronegócio. Caderno de Geografia **27**(1), 138–158 (2017). http://periodicos.pucminas.br/index.php/geografia/article/view/p.2318-2962.2017v27nesp1p138

8. Sposito, E.S., Oliveira, A.U.D.: Geografia e filosofia: contribuição para o ensino do pensamento geográfico. Ed. UNESP, São Paulo (2004). oCLC: 57522797

9. Companhia Nacional de Abastecimento: portaldeinformacoes.conab.gov.br/index.php/safra-serie-historica-dashboard

10. Flexor, G., Leite, S.P.: Land market and land grabbing in brazil during the commodity boom of the 2000s. Contexto Internacional **39**, 393–420 (2017). http://www.scielo.br/scielo.php?script=sci_arttext&pid=S0102-85292017000200393&nrm=iso

11. Meade, B.: Corn and Soybean production costs and export competitiveness in Argentina, Brazil, and the United States. Econ. Inf. Bull. **154**, 52 (2016)

12. Paiva, M.D.S., Nagano, M.S., Hongyu, K.: Análise da Expansão da Soja: Uma Aplicação de Análise Multivariada e Redes Neurais Artificiais. Sigmae **8**(2), 554–563 (2019). http://publicacoes.unifal-mg.edu.br/revistas/index.php/sigmae/article/view/1035, number: 2

# Prediction of Cold Chain Transport Conditions Using Data Mining

Clayton Gerber Mangini⬤, Nilsa Duarte da Silva Lima⬤,
and Irenilza de Alencar Nääs$^{(\boxtimes)}$⬤

Graduate Studies in Production Engineering, Paulista University,
São Paulo, SP 04026-002, Brazil
clayton.mangini@gmail.com, irenilza@gmail.com,
nilsa.lima@stricto.unip.br

**Abstract.** Ensuring the delivery of temperature-controlled products in transportation is an increasing challenge, especially in countries with continental extension and tropical climate such as Brazil. Products with this type of specificity generally have a higher added value and involve specialized equipment and labor. Thus, route mapping is necessary for the logistics of the cold chain. The study aimed to predict the transport conditions in the cold chain. The data set analyzed includes the temperature of the loads and the route information (Southeast to Northeast and South of Brazil). The classification of temperature excursions considered data below 15 °C or above 30 °C. The Naïve Bayes and Multilayer Perceptron algorithms are used to predict the optimal temperature excursion model. The Multilayer Perceptron algorithm proved to be the most suitable for a thermal route mapping model. With this identified standard, logistics decision making can be improved to reducer o waste and ensure product integrity with less recourse.

**Keywords:** Classifiers · Naïve Bayes · Multilayer Perceptron

## 1 Introduction

The cold chain begins in the production phase. The raw materials needed to produce a specific product are processed, followed by the transport of the product at low temperatures under strict conditions, refrigerated storage and its subsequent distribution by land, sea or air, finally, is acquired by the patient [1, 2]. The cold chain is part of the supply chain, where temperature monitoring plays a vital role in the system. At the same time, automatic data collection is an essential aspect of cold chain management [2–7].

Cold chain logistics refers to a systematic operation where perishable products require a low-temperature environment. They are collected in an environment with specific temperature ranges in each process before reaching the final consumer. It is necessary temperature management in the production, transportation, storage, distribution, and marketing of these drugs, which not only guarantee a high-quality product but reduce waste in transportation and reduce cost [1, 2, 5, 7]. Therefore, the manufacturer must balance the two situations and choose the best product distribution

© IFIP International Federation for Information Processing 2020
Published by Springer Nature Switzerland AG 2020
B. Lalic et al. (Eds.): APMS 2020, IFIP AICT 592, pp. 616–623, 2020.
https://doi.org/10.1007/978-3-030-57997-5_71

strategy to avoid degradation and maintain product quality [4, 5, 8]; and increased public health [9–11].

In this way, continuous temperature monitoring and the availability of reliable reports for these products are essential [12, 13]. Thus, the relevance of this theme is justified because, despite technological advances, temperature monitoring in the cold chain of pharmaceutical products is still a challenge for the value chain of pharmaceutical products. This study aimed to classify the transport conditions of pharmaceutical products using data mining techniques.

## 2   Materials and Methods

The study included temperature excursion trials in two Brazilian regions during the summer and winter of 2019.

### 2.1   Parameters Tested During Transport Tests

The drugs were conditioned in thermal packaging under adequate environmental conditions and transported land ways by truck to the Northeast and South regions of Brazil, the parameters included in the tests to determine the optimal temperature excursion are presented in Table 1.

**Table 1.** Temperature excursion parameters set by manufacturers.

| Excursions | Optimal temperature excursion conditions |
|---|---|
| 15 a 30 °C | Yes |
| <15 a >30 °C | No |

Source: [14].

### 2.2   Prediction of Optimal Temperature Excursion Conditions

The study data were collected at a pharmaceutical distribution company in São Paulo and contain anonymous records regarding transportation and temperature excursion. Data mining applies to this study, through techniques (algorithms), to support the transportation planning of pharmaceutical products in search of strategic information that allows the extraction of implicit information existing in the databases, contributing to the process identify and classify new standards [15–17]. The steps of the data mining process are selection, pre-processing, data mining, and post-processing for knowledge discovery [16, 17]. The results obtained with data mining can be used in information management, information request processing, decision making, and process control. The data contained in the databases are used to learn a particular target concept [15–18]. Tasks performed by data mining techniques (such as classification) allow the building of models that can be applied to unclassified data. Such a procedure categorizes them into classes, to relate the meta attribute (whose value will be predicted) and a set of prediction attributes [15–18].

Data pre-processing of the data was performed in Microsoft Excel® spreadsheets for further processing in Weka® data mining software version 3.8 [19–22]. The attributes used for the construction of the predictive model in data mining by the classification technique (*modeling classification*) were: "seasons," "period," "forecasted-routes," "temperature," and "optimal-temperature-excursion." A pre-processing stage was performed in the data to obtain the best result in the classification. In that stage, we performed a discretization of the attributes "period" (late, night, dawn and morning) and "optimal-temperature-excursion" (yes and no, Table 1). Discretization reduces and simplifies data, making learning faster, and results in denser [15].

The algorithms Naïve Bayes (weka.classifiers.bayes.NaiveBayes) and Multilayer Perceptron (weka.classifiers.functions.MultilayerPerceptron) were applied to the construction of a model of rules for the prediction of the temperature excursion depending on the route (northeast, south), the period (dawn, morning, afternoon, night) and the season (summer, winter). The validation of the model was parameterized using *cross-validation*. The validation was applied both for the training set with 75% (5,308 instances) of the total data. The testing was done using 25% (1,770 instances) of the total data (7,078 instances).

The classification process was performed in two stages. In the first step, a training model (training set) was constructed that describes a predetermined set of data classes. In the second step, the model is used for sorting. The validation method is a simple technique that uses a labeled class test set. The test samples are randomly selected and are independent of the training samples. The filter was used *Stratified Remove Folds* to stratifying the data set, to separate the training set and the test set. All classification algorithms used in this study used the cross-validation test option (*cross-validation*).

## 2.3    Evaluation of the Prediction Model

The last step is to evaluate the prediction; this analysis was made based on the performance values obtained through the prediction model test [23]. The performance evaluation measures of prediction models used were confusion matrix, accuracy, precision, sensitivity (recall), and Matthews correlation coefficient (MCC). The Kappa statistic measures the learning capacity of the algorithm. The confusion matrix is a matrix with results obtained during the model test step, widely used in models that use classification algorithms. It is also called the confusion matrix of a hypothesis, this hypothesis offers a valid measure of the classification model, by showing the number of correct classifications versus the predicted classifications for each class, over a set of examples. The number of hits, for each class, is on the main matrix diagonal, and the other elements represent errors in the classification (Table 2). The confusion matrix of an ideal classifier has all these elements equal to zero since it does not make mistakes.

**Table 2.**  Confusion matrix

| Prediction | Observed true | Observed false |
|---|---|---|
| Expected true | TP | FP |
| Expected false | FN | TN |

TP = true positive; FN = false positive;
FP = false negative; TN = true negative.
Source: [23].

# 3 Results and Discussion

The mean metrics for unbalanced classes of the Naïve Bayes algorithm presented the following results: the correctly classified instances were equal to 86.61%, instances classified incorrectly equal to 13. 39%, with Kappa statistics equal to 0.64. Considering the average accuracy detailed by class, the true positive rate was equal to 0.87, the false positive rate 0.21, accuracy 0.87, sensitivity 0.87 (recall), and the MCC was equal to 0.64. For the Multilayer Perceptron, the average metrics for unbalanced classes were 93.73% for correctly classified instances, 6.27% for incorrectly sorted instances, 0.82 for Kappa statistics. For the average accuracy detailed by class, the results were equal to 0.94 for true positive rate, 0.16 for false-positive rate, 0.94 for accuracy, 0.94 for sensitivity (recall), and 0.82 to MCC. The results of the comparison of Naïve Bayes and Multilayer Perceptron algorithms comparing unbalanced and balanced classes are presented below in Table 3.

**Table 3.** Classifier performance for unbalanced class prediction models

| Class imbalanced | Classifier model - stratified cross-validation | | | | | |
|---|---|---|---|---|---|---|
| Metrics | Naïve Bayes | | | Multilayer Perceptron | | |
| Correctly classified instances | 86.61% | | | 93.73% | | |
| Incorrectly classified instances | 13.39% | | | 6.27% | | |
| Kappa statistic | 0.64 | | | 0.82 | | |
| Detailed accuracy by class | Class | | | Class | | |
| | Yes | No | WA* | Yes | No | WA* |
| TP rate | 0.90 | 0.75 | 0.87 | 0.98 | 0.79 | 0.94 |
| FP rate | 0.24 | 0.10 | 0.21 | 0.21 | 0.02 | 0.16 |
| Precision | 0.92 | 0.71 | 0.87 | 0.94 | 0.94 | 0.94 |
| Recall | 0.90 | 0.75 | 0.87 | 0.98 | 0.79 | 0.94 |
| MCC | 0.64 | 0.64 | 0.64 | 0.82 | 0.82 | 0.82 |

*WA = Weighted average.

The performance of the Multilayer Perceptron, within the unbalanced classes, was higher than the Naïve Bayes. That includes the lower false-positive rate, the higher percentage of correctly classified instances, lower percentage of ranked instances incorrectly and the Kappa statistic close to 1 (0.82) indicating the proper performance of the algorithm to classify the temperature excursion to the northeast and southern regions of Brazil (Table 3).

The metrics for balanced classes of the Naïve Bayes algorithm presented mean values of 73.48% for correctly classified instances, 26.52% for instances classified incorrectly, with Kappa statistics equal to 0.47. The average accuracies detailed by class presented values equal to 0.73 for the true positive rate, 0.26 for the false-positive rate, 0.75 for accuracy, 0.74 for sensitivity (recall), and 0.48 for the MCC.

The Multilayer Perceptron presented average performance metrics for balanced classes, higher than the Naïve Bayes with 96.07% of correctly classified instances, 3.93% of instances sorted incorrectly, including 0.92 for Kappa statistics. The results were equal to 0.96 for true positive rate considering the average accuracy detailed per class; 0.04 for false-positive rate, 0.96 for accuracy, 0.96 for sensitivity (recall), and 0.92 to MCC. The results of the comparison of algorithms comparing unbalanced and balanced classes for the Naïve Bayes and Multilayer Perceptron algorithms are presented below in Table 4.

**Table 4.** Classifier performance for balanced class prediction models

| Class balanced | Classifier model - Stratified cross-validation | | | | | |
|---|---|---|---|---|---|---|
| Metrics | Naïve Bayes | | | Multilayer Perceptron | | |
| Correctly classified instances | 73.48% | | | 96.07% | | |
| Incorrectly classified instances | 26.52% | | | 3.93% | | |
| Kappa statistic | 0.47 | | | 0.92 | | |
| Detailed accuracy by class | Class | | . | Class | | |
| | Yes | No | WA* | Yes | No | WA* |
| TP rate | 0.62 | 0.85 | 0.73 | 0.98 | 0.94 | 0.96 |
| FP rate | 0.85 | 0.38 | 0.26 | 0.06 | 0.02 | 0.04 |
| Precision | 0.80 | 0.69 | 0.75 | 0.94 | 0.98 | 0.96 |
| Recall | 0.62 | 0.85 | 0.74 | 0.98 | 0.94 | 0.96 |
| MCC | 0.48 | 0.48 | 0.48 | 0.92 | 0.92 | 0.92 |

*WA = Weighted average.

In class balancing, Multilayer Perceptron performance outperformed Naïve Bayes, including lower false-positive rate, the higher percentage of correctly classified instances, lower percentage of instances misclassified and Kappa statistics. These class performance metrics presented values close to 1 (TP Rate, Precision, Recall, MCC) that indicates the proper performance of the algorithm to classify the temperature excursion condition for the northeast and southern regions of Brazil (Table 4).

The Naïve Bayes algorithm correctly classified the "yes" class for optimal temperature excursion (true positive = TP), with an average rate of 87% for unbalanced classes and 73% for balanced classes. The class "no," for an excursion outside the temperature parameters presented a rate of 75.47% for unbalanced classes and 84.81% for balanced classes (true negative = TN) indicating a proper performance of the algorithm in the classification task (Table 5).

However, the Multilayer Perceptron algorithm correctly classified the "yes" class for optimal temperature excursion (true positive = TP). With an average rate of 94% for unbalanced classes and 96% for balanced classes, and the "no" class for an excursion outside the temperature parameters had a rate of 79.21% for unbalanced classes and 94.16% for balanced classes (true negative = TN) indicating better

**Table 5.** Naïve Bayes classification confusion matrix

| Class imbalanced - Naïve Bayes | | | |
|---|---|---|---|
| a | b | Total | Classified as |
| 1.210 | 132 | 1,342 | a = yes |
| 105 | 323 | 428 | b = no |
| 1,315 | 455 | 1,770 | |
| Class balanced - Naïve Bayes | | | Classified as |
| 549.99 | 335.01 | 885 | a = yes |
| 134.40 | 750.0 | 885 | b = no |
| 684.39 | 1085.61 | 1,770 | |

**Table 6.** Multilayer Perceptron classification confusion matrix

| Class imbalanced - Multilayer Perceptron | | | |
|---|---|---|---|
| a | b | Total | Classified as |
| 1,320 | 22 | 1,342 | a = yes |
| 89 | 339 | 428 | b = no |
| 1,409 | 361 | 1,770 | |
| Class balanced - Multilayer Perceptron | | | Classified as |
| 867.19 | 17.81 | 885 | a = yes |
| 51.69 | 833.31 | 885 | b = no |
| 918.88 | 851.12 | 1,770 | |

performance than Naïve Bayes in the classification task (Table 6). The results obtained confirm the possibility of predicting the optimal temperature specifications in the transport of pharmaceutical products.

When connecting the results of the present study with the advantages of real-time cargo tracking, we can build rules for reducing logistics operations costs. We might also manage expenses, minimize product value loss, and maximizing the total value of items. Other advantages ate to contribute to decision-making related to distribution and storage planning, finding possible quality failures, and identifying risks for real-time action to mitigate such risks [3, 6, 24].

The cold chain refers to the transportation of perishable products, which are temperature sensitive throughout a supply chain through thermal and refrigerated packaging methods, and planning logistics to protect the integrity of shipments [1, 2, 25, 26]. The products can be damaged in the complex transport operations; the strategic use of environmental sensors in transportation and storage is essential. Damage can be mainly by shock or temperature variations. Perishable products maintain chemical reactions whose rate can be attenuated by low temperatures. However, delays and poor planning can have negative consequences or reduce the efficiency of the shipping shipment [27, 28].

## 4 Conclusions

The Multilayer Perceptron algorithm integrated with performance metrics determined better results with superior stability to solve problems and predict temperature excursion within the optimal standard of transport specification regardless of the use of class balancing filter.

**Acknowledgment.** The first author wishes to thank the Coordination of Superior Studies (Capes) for the scholarship.

## References

1. Campos, Y., Villa, J.L.: Technologies applied in the monitoring and control of the temperature in the cold chain. In: 2nd IEEE Colombian Conference on Robotics and Automation (CCRA), pp. 1–6. IEEE Press, New York (2018). https://doi.org/10.1109/ccra.2018.8588118
2. Rodrigue, J.P.: The Cold Chain and Its Logistics. The Geography of Transport Systems. Routledge/Taylor & Francis, New York (2016)
3. Bogataj, M., Bogataj, L., Vodopivec, R.: Stability of perishable goods in cold logistic chains. Int. J. Prod. Econ. **93**, 345–356 (2005)
4. Ammann, C.: Stability studies needed to define the handling and transport conditions of sensitive pharmaceutical or biotechnological products. AAPS PharmSciTech **12**, 1264–1275 (2011)
5. Chen, K.Y., Shaw, Y.C.: Applying backpropagation network to cold chain temperature monitoring. Adv. Eng. Inform. **25**, 11–22 (2011)
6. Lee, H., Jo, S.K., Lee, N., Lee, H.W.: A method for co-existing heterogeneous IoT environments based on compressive sensing. In: 18th International Conference on Advanced Communication Technology (ICACT), pp. 206–209. IEEE Press, New York (2016). https://doi.org/10.1109/icact.2016.7423330
7. Kim, K., Kim, H., Kim, S.K., Jung, J.Y.: I-RM: an intelligent risk management framework for context-aware ubiquitous cold chain logistics. Expert Syst. Appl. **46**, 463–473 (2016). https://doi.org/10.1016/j.eswa.2015.11.005
8. Sharma, S., Pai, S.: Analysis of operating effectiveness of a cold chain model using bayesian Netw. Bus. Process. Manag. J. **21**, 722–742 (2015). https://doi.org/10.1108/bpmj-10-2014-0105
9. Ou, C.M., Tu, J.F.: The WSN and 3G/NFC embedded into IoV (Internet-of-Vehicle) fulfill cold chain logistics. Microsyst. Technol. **24**, 3977–3983 (2018). https://doi.org/10.1007/s00542-017-3594-3
10. Öcal, M., Kaya, İ.A.: Food safety and GIS applications. In: 4th International Conference on Agro-Geoinformatics, pp. 85–90 (2015)

11. Li, C.M., Nien, C.C., Liao, J.L., Tseng, Y.C.: Development of wireless sensor module and network for temperature monitoring in cold chain logistics. In: 2012 IEEE International Conference on Wireless Information Technology and Systems (ICWITS), pp. 1–4. IEEE (2012)
12. Lippi, G., et al.: Suitability of a transport box for blood sample shipment over a long period. Clin. Biochem. **44**(12), 1028–1029 (2011)
13. Kulkarni, N.S., Niranjan, S.: Multi-echelon network optimization of pharmaceutical cold chains: a simulation study. In: Proceedings of the 2013 Winter Simulation Conference: Simulation: Making Decisions in a Complex World, pp. 3486–3498. IEEE Press (2013)
14. The US Pharmacopeia. Packaging and storage requirements, Rockville 6801 (2018)
15. Larose, D.T., Larose, C.D.: Wiley Series on Methods and Applications in Data Mining. Data Mining and Predictive Analytics. Wiley, Hoboken (2015)
16. Frank, E., et al.: Weka-a machine learning workbench for data mining. In: Maimon, O., Rokach, L. (eds.) Data Mining and Knowledge Discovery Handbook, pp. 1269–1277. Springer, Boston (2009). https://doi.org/10.1007/978-0-387-09823-4_66
17. Ngai, E.W.T., Xiu, L., Chau, D.C.K.: Application of data mining techniques in customer relationship management: a literature review and classification. Expert Syst. Appl. **36**(2), 2592–2602 (2009)
18. Naik, A., Samant, L.: Correlation review of classification algorithm using data mining tool: weka, rapidminer, tanagra, orange and knime. Procedia Comput. Sci. **85**, 662–668 (2016)
19. Holmes, G., Donkin, A., Witten, I.H.: Weka: a machine learning workbench (1994)
20. Witten, I.H., Frank, E., Trigg, L.E., Hall, M.A., Holmes, G., Cunningham, S.J.: Weka: practical machine learning tools and techniques with Java implementations (1999). http://www.springer.com/lncs. Accessed 21 Nov 2016
21. Markov, Z., Russell, I.: An introduction to the weka data mining system. ACM SIGCSE Bull. **38**(3), 367–368 (2006)
22. Hall, M., Frank, E., Holmes, G., Pfahringer, B., Reutemann, P., Witten, I.H.: The WEKA data mining software: an update. ACM SIGKDD Explor. Newslett. **11**(1), 10–18 (2009)
23. Bowes, D., Hall, T., Gray, D.: Comparing the performance of fault prediction models which report multiple performance measures: recomputing the confusion matrix. In: Proceedings of the 8th International Conference on Predictive Models in Software Engineering, pp. 109–118 (2012)
24. Gessner, G.H., Volonino, L., Fish, L.A.: One-up, one-back ERM in the food supply chain. Inf. Syst. Manag. **24**(3), 213–222 (2007). https://doi.org/10.1080/10580530701404561
25. Uthayakumkar, R., Priyan, S.: Pharmaceutical supply chain and inventory management strategies: optimization for a pharmaceutical company and a hospital. Oper. Res. Health Care **2**(3), 52–64 (2013)
26. Raab, V., Petersen, B., Kreyenschmidt, J.: Temperature monitoring in meat supply chains. Br. Food J. **113**(10), 1267–1289 (2011)
27. Kumar, N., Jha, A.: Temperature excursion management: a novel approach of quality system in pharmaceutical industry. Saudi Pharm. J. **25**(2), 176–183 (2017)
28. Montanari, R.: Cold chain tracking: a managerial perspective. Trends Food Sci. Technol. **19**(8), 425–431 (2008)

# Environmental Impact Classification of Perishable Cargo Transport Using Data Mining

Manoel Eulálio Neto[1,2] (ID), Irenilza de Alencar Nääs[1(✉)] (ID),
and Nilsa Duarte da Silva Lima[1] (ID)

[1] Graduate Studies in Production Engineering, Paulista University, São Paulo,
SP 04026-002, Brazil
{manoeleulalio,irenilza}@gmail.com, nilsa.
lima@stricto.unip.br
[2] Centro Universitário Santo Agostinho, Teresina, PI 64.019-625, Brazil

**Abstract.** The study presents a model for classifying the environmental impact caused by the transport of vegetables from the production centers of several Brazilian states to a distribution center in Teresina, Brazil, using data mining. The distances from production regions to the distribution center were calculated. $CO_2$-eq emissions and Global Warming Potential (GWP) were estimated. The GWP indicates the potential for the environmental impact that gas causes in each period (usually 100 years). We applied the data mining approach using the Rapid Miner Studio® software to build up the models. The target was the environmental impact indexed as "low", "average", and "high". Results indicated that considering the on-road modal transport presented in the trees, the "product," "distance," and "quantity" classification for high environmental impact depends on the amount of product transported as well as the distance traveled. The found trees classify the impact and can be used as guidance for the decision-maker, as it can be used when planning and purchasing fruit and vegetables for public consumption.

**Keywords:** Classifiers · Random forest · Transportation of vegetables · Food supply chain

## 1 Introduction

The Global Warming Potential (GWP) compares the amount of heat retained by a certain mass of $CO_2$ gas to the amount of heat captured by a similar mass of carbon dioxide along a period, usually 100 years. The GWP of an anisotropic gas indicates the potential for the environmental impact that gas causes in each given period. The report by the Intergovernmental Panel on Climate Change [1] estimates that greenhouse gas (GHG) emissions should be reduced by 40 to 70% by 2050 compared to 2010 levels, to avoid an increase of more than 2 °C at the global average temperature. Such an objective can avoid the more severe climate and, eventually, reduce the impacts.

B. Lalic et al. (Eds.): APMS 2020, IFIP AICT 592, pp. 624–630, 2020.
https://doi.org/10.1007/978-3-030-57997-5_72

However, without a clear research policy, initiatives to overcome the problems of large emerging economies and large territorial countries (for example, China, India, and Brazil) that depend on road transport is a significant challenge [2, 3].

The transport of fruit and vegetables in Brazil takes place from the producing region to regional distribution centers (Ceasa). Consumer centers are located close to large urban centers, usually in the capitals of Brazilian states. Transport is the logistical activity that plays a vital role within the supply chain. It enables sectors of the economy and the use of trucks to transport cargo can provide, in several situations, greater flexibility in the operations of distributing products and inputs, in a more agile way, because it can cover almost all regions of the country.

With the development of computers and automation, the storage and recovery of large volumes of data have been increased. As a result, machine learning techniques, including data mining, have become a useful tool for identifying and exploring patterns and relationships between many variables [4, 5]. Data mining applications offer classification models in some research areas, including health diagnosis and prognosis [6] and identifying gaps in education data [7].

The present study aimed to develop environmental impact estimation models using the data mining approach. The subject was the on-road cargo transportation, from part of the logistics chain for the distribution of fruit and vegetables (tomatoes, lettuce, bell peppers, cucumbers, and cabbage) from the production centers in several Brazilian states to the 'Nova Ceasa' distribution center in Teresina, Piauí State, Northeast Brazil.

## 2   Materials and Methods

The products transported (tomatoes, lettuce, bell peppers, cabbage, and cucumbers) are produced in different regions of the country and distributed in Teresina by 'Nova Ceasa,' which is the fresh food distribution center. These products are transported in 'road modes' using cargo trucks from the farms in production centers to the distribution center from January to October 2019. The production distances were calculated, assuming that the transport trucks consume an average of 10 L/km of fuel (diesel). $CO_2$-eq emissions and GWP were calculated in an online spreadsheet [8]. The values found for GWP were discretized into three conditions "low," "average," and "high." The data obtained were inserted and organized in an Excel® spreadsheet and further used in data processing using the data mining approach.

The Random forest approach in the data mining scenario was selected to describe the environmental impact of on-road transportation of fresh food perishable products. The Random forest classifier used for this study consists of using randomly selected features or a combination of features at each node to grow a classifying tree.

The complete dataset (containing the distances, km; amount transported, t; and the discretized values of GWP) was used to build a decision tree using Rapidminer® Studio, a software-based on Java version 9.2 (RapidMiner, Inc. Boston, Mass., USA). The alternative classification was found while processing the dataset, considering the final focus (target) as the environmental impact of cargo transport (GWP).

The operators used were 'retrieve data,' 'split data,' and 'Random forest' as a classifying algorithm. In the present study, we used 70% of the data to train the algorithm and 30% to develop the model as input values for the 'split' operator. The subsequent set of characteristics in the data training set is recognized by the attributes that discriminate several samples more precisely [9]. Amongst the trees found within the Random forest applied algorithm, three trees were selected, the first focusing on the transported product, the second on the transport distance, and the third focusing on the quantity of product transported.

The percentage of correctly classified samples compared to the number of all examples is named accuracy (Eq. 1).

$$\text{Accuracy} = TP + TN/TP + FP + FN + TN \tag{1}$$

where TP = true positive, TN = true negative, FP = false positive, and FN = false negative.

Figure 1 shows the data processing scheme of the present study.

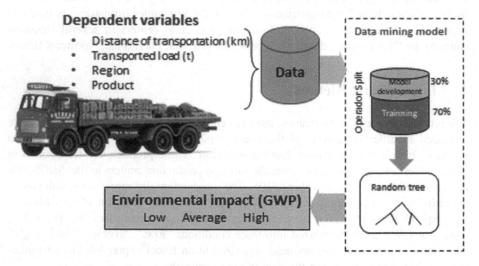

**Fig. 1.** Schematic of data processing used in the present study.

## 3 Results and Discussion

The trees found were selected for the model accuracy (75%), containing the classification of environmental impact (high, average, and low). The trees were selected whose processing classified the 'product,' 'distance,' and 'quantity' transported. Fig. 2, 3, and 4 show the selected trees that were obtained from the processing results of the Random forest.

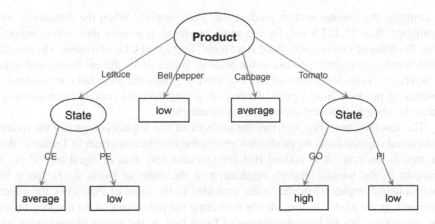

**Fig. 2.** Random tree with a focus on the environmental impact mainly due to the product transported.

The classifying tree shown in Fig. 2 indicates the level of impact on $CO_2$ emissions, considering the concepts, arbitrated, pre-established in this work (A = high, M = medium, and B = low). When analyzing the origin of the products by the state (or region) of production, it appears that for the tomato production from the State of Goiás (GO), it has a high environmental impact compared to the GWP of the other states that supply tomato products. It is highlighted the transport from Pernambuco (PE) with low impact.

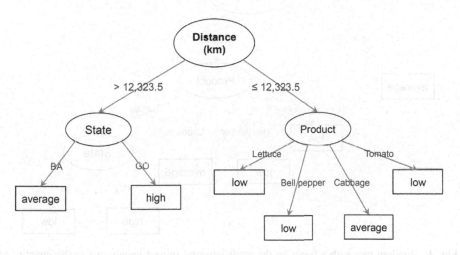

**Fig. 3.** Random tree with a focus on the environmental impact, mainly due to the distance the products were transported.

The analysis of the tree concerning the distance between the producers and the distribution center resulted that for a distance less than or equal to 12,323.5 km, the lettuce, bell pepper, and cabbage products have a "low" environmental impact (GWP).

In contrast, the tomato product produces a "low" impact. When the distance is more significant than 12,323.5 km, for the same products, it is seen that, when importing from the State of Goiás (GO), there is a "high" impact on $CO_2$ emissions. On the other hand, when acquired the product in the State of Bahia (BA), the environmental impact is "average." Thus, the presented tree objectively guides the analyzed consequences of purchasing products from a particular region, giving decision-makers the possibility to make the choices that best protect the environment

The resulting tree (Fig. 4) focus the analysis of the impact concerning the quantity transported on-road from the production area to the distribution center in Teresina. When the tree is analyzed, it is noticed that for amounts less than or equal to 862 (t), the transport of the tomato product, originating in the State of Goiás (GO), has a high environmental impact. However, when provided in the State of Piauí (PI), the effect is classified, in the model, as low, clearly indicating the influence that the distance traveled has, since there is a higher consumption of fossil fuel, in the modal transportation used, with direct reflection in the GWP. It is seen that for quantities less than or equal to 862 (t) for lettuce and bell peppers, the impact is low. On the other hand, when the amount exceeds 862 (t), the GWP presents a medium environmental impact, and the decision-maker might, given these indicators, make a choice that best protects the environment, not disregarding other variables considered by the consumers.

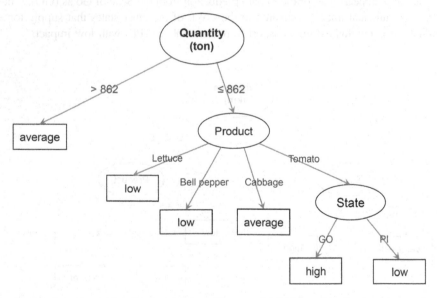

**Fig. 4.** Random tree with a focus on the environmental impact mainly due to the quantity of products transported.

The claims of 'local food' chains propose improvements in the relations between the urban and rural areas [10]. Within the 'local food' debate, environmental impacts are not restricted to GHG emissions. However, carbon reduction policies may provide potential trade-offs in the overall ecological sustainability issue until other impacts are measured [11].

Policy contexts need to address how environmental impact will be assessed and managed as governments attempt to meet the schedule of emissions cuts [12]. In a similar study, [13] provides a scenario of food on-road transportation in Brazil, stating that such an array of food distribution without impacting the environment is a difficult task in continental countries.

## 4  Conclusions

The objective of the present study was the development of an environmental impact estimation model (GWP) using data mining to transport loads in the road mode. This is part of the logistics chain for the distribution of fruit and vegetables from production centers in several Brazilian states to the 'Nova Ceasa' fresh food distribution center in Teresina, State of Piauí, Northeast of Brazil.

The models obtained as Random forest are useful to support tool for decision making since they can present graphical information to guide managers in their decisions. From the found trees, it was possible to verify that the vegetables from the Goiás state produce high environmental impact. The trees might guide the decision-maker, as they can be used when purchasing fruit and vegetables considering the environmental impact. It is reasonable to believe that the choice of the production center should favor the one that least contributes to the emission of polluting gases.

## References

1. IPCC- Intergovernmental Panel on Climate Change. Fifth assessment report, p. AR5 (2014)
2. Muratori, M., Smith, S.J., Kyle, P., Link, R., Mignone, B.K., Kheshgi, H.S.: Role of the freight sector in future climate change mitigation scenarios. Environ. Sci. Technol. **51**, 3526–3533 (2017)
3. Dente, S.M.R., Tavasszy, L.: Policy-oriented emission factors for road freight transport. Trans. Res. D **61**, 33–41 (2018)
4. Díez, J., et al.: Using machine learning procedures to ascertain the influence of beef carcass profiles on carcass conformation scores. Meat Sci. **73**, 09–115 (2006)
5. Pereira, D.F., Miyamoto, B.C.B., Maia, G.D.N., Sales, T., Magalhães, M.M., Gates, R.S.: Machine vision to identify broiler breeder behavior. Comput. Electron. Agr. **99**, 194–199 (2013)
6. Zhuang, X., Bi, M., Guo, J., Wu, S., Zhang, T.: Development of an early warning algorithm to detect sick broilers. Comput. Electron. Agr. **144**, 102–113 (2018)
7. Baker, R.S.J., Isotani, S., Carvalho, A.M.J.B.: Mineração de dados educacionais: oportunidades para o brasil. Rev. Bras. Informática Educação **19**(2), 3 (2011)
8. CFC-Carbon Footprint Calculator Vehicle $CO_2$ emissions footprint calculator (2018). https://www.commercialfleet.org/tools/van/carbon-footprint-calculator
9. Lavrac, N.: Selected techniques for data mining in medicine. Artif. Intell. Med. **16**, 3–23 (1999)

10. DuPuis, M., Goodman, D.: Should we go 'home' to eat? Towards a reflexive politics in localism. J. Rural Stud. **21**(3), 359–371 (2005)
11. Hall, G., et al.: Potential environmental and population health impacts of local urban food systems under climate change: a life cycle analysis case study of lettuce and chicken. Agr. Food Secur. **3**, 6 (2014)
12. Rothwell, A., Ridoutt, B., Page, G., Bellotti, W.: Environmental performance of local food: trade-offs and implications for climate resilience in a developed city. J. Clean. Prod. **114**, 420–430 (2016)
13. Duarte, G.T., Nääs, I.A., Innocencio, C.M., Cordeiro, A.F.S., Silva, R.B.T.R.: Environmental impact of the on-road transportation distance and product volume from farm to a fresh food distribution center: a case study in Brazil. Environ. Sci. Pollut. Res. **26**(32), 33694–33701 (2019)

# Economic and Environmental Perfomance in Coffee Supply Chains: A Brazilian Case Study

Paula Ferreira da Cruz Correia[1,2(✉)] ⓘ,
João Gilberto Mendes dos Reis[1,2,3] ⓘ, Rodrigo Carlo Toloi[2,4] ⓘ,
Fernanda Alves de Araújo[1,2] ⓘ, Silvia Helena Bonilla[1] ⓘ,
Jonatas Santos de Souza[1,2] ⓘ, Alexandre Formigoni[5] ⓘ,
and Aguinaldo Eduardo de Souza[1,2,6] ⓘ

[1] Postgraduate Program in Production Engineering, Universidade Paulista, São Paulo, Brazil
paulafecruz@gmail.com
[2] RESUP - Supply Chain Research Group, Production Engineering, Paulista University, São Paulo, Brazil
[3] Federal University of Grande Dourados - UFGD, PPGA, Dourados, Brazil
[4] Federal Institute of Mato Grosso Campus Rondonópolis, Rondonópolis, Mato Grosso, Brazil
[5] Logistics and Operations, Gestão de Tecnologia em Sistemas Produtivos, CPS, São Paulo, Brazil
[6] UNIBR São Vicente, São Vicente, Brazil

**Abstract.** The concern to meet food needs of the world population and preserve the environment is frequent today. In this context, Brazil has a significant participation in world agriculture. For instance, the country is the largest producer and exporter of green coffee grain. Coffee, besides being part of cultural habits in many countries, still corresponds significantly in the Brazilian trade balance, in the generation of jobs and income in the food industry chain worldwide, having its consumption associated with meetings and socialization and also as food base of children in a situation of economic and social vulnerability. The aim of this work is to discuss the economic and environmental performance, through the analysis of different combinations of cargo vehicles in different paving and non-paving conditions for the flow of coffee grain production from Guaxupé/MG to the Port of Santos/SP. It was observed that the best combination for load is "rodotrem" because it presents the best economic performance due to lower costs with diesel per ton of coffee grain transported and the best environmental performance which is maintained in all load combinations. It is clear that the Brazilian road network needs investments related to paving, technologies to improve fuel use and tire performance.

**Keywords:** Cargo vehicle combinations · Economic performance · Environmental performance · Coffee

© IFIP International Federation for Information Processing 2020
Published by Springer Nature Switzerland AG 2020
B. Lalic et al. (Eds.): APMS 2020, IFIP AICT 592, pp. 631–639, 2020.
https://doi.org/10.1007/978-3-030-57997-5_73

632    P. F. da Cruz Correia et al.

# 1 Introduction

The projection of the world population for 2030 is 8.5 billion [1] and there is a concern to meet their needs, especially related to food production and environment. Thereby, Brazil plays a strategic role in global agribusiness, leading world grain production [2]. The country is favored by its edaphoclimatic [3, 4], is the largest coffee producer and exporter [5, 6], generates, by along the production chain, more than 400 thousand jobs [7], and in addition, it is the second-largest consumer of the beverage [5, 6].

For many of children in the world, who are in vulnerable situation, the combination of coffee with flour or milk is the only source of food [8], and due to its stimulating and exotic properties, it has become, for decades, a very complex beverage and it is appreciated in almost all countries of the world [9].

The international market is a major consumer of Brazilian coffee and the blends prepared in the country are appreciated around the world [10].

Thus, it is possible to affirm that coffee is part of the cultural habits in many countries. Its consumption is associated with meetings and socializations [11, 12].

Minas Gerais state, located in the southeast region of the country, is the main producer and exporter, with 82% of what is exported by the country [13]. The main port of exportation is Santos, located about 382 km far and the transportation is made by road [14].

One of the major barriers to the flow of coffee production is the availability of transport modes to efficiently meet production. Logistical inefficiency results in the raise of the costs and impacts negatively in the environment.

As transport activities are responsible for 14% of global anthropogenic emissions [15], the effects of environmental transport problems become critical, especially for food production chains in underdeveloped countries [16].

Regarding to the environment, there is a movement towards a change of habits and sustainable conditions are inserted in logistics processes for exports. The green seal is something which adds value to the grain. With these ideas in mind, this work seeks to answer questions related to the flow of coffee grain production and economic and environmental aspects inherent to the process.

The aim of this work is to discuss economic and environmental issues of different types of combinations of cargo vehicles related to the conditions of the roads for traffic, inherent to the process of flow of coffee grain production from Guaxupé, Minas Gerais, through highways to the Port of Santos, São Paulo.

# 2 Methodology

In order to discuss the economic and environmental issues of the processes of coffee production flow in Minas Gerais, an exploratory, bibliographic and descriptive research was carried out to contextualize the scenario [17].

When discussing these questions, some concepts were inserted to facilitate understanding and, to achieve the proposed methodology, it was organized in two stages:

## 2.1 Economic Analysis

To pull the different types of semitrailer, it was used a tractor truck 420HP 6X4. The values for Fuel Consumption in Scale (km/L), Life of new tires (Km) and service life of retreaded tires (Km) were acquired by research with professional drivers (variable values for each type of driving). Diesel oil prices were defined based on the average price practiced in the State of Minas Gerais [18]. And values of cost of new tires and cost of retreaded tires were delimited by dividing the average tire value by the average kilometers driven in each proposed situation.

## 2.2 Environmental Analysis

For calculations of greenhouse gas emissions, only one factor was taken into account, namely the emission factor related to combustion of diesel used [19].

$$Emission\ of\ Diesel\colon E_jk = (FE_i * Qdiesel/Km * D_jk) \tag{1}$$

Where: Ejk corresponds to the total emission of $CO_2$ by municipality of origin j and port of destination k; The FE corresponds to the $CO_2$ emission factor of diesel, Q is diesel consumed per kilometer, and D is the distance traveled from origin j and destination port k in km.

A route was specified between the city of Guaxupé/MG and the Port of Santos/SP, an average distance of 382 km. As a functional unit in the environmental aspect, 1 kg of coffee grain was stipulated allowing comparisons with other studies (such as work-related to soybeans by [20]), since there is a scarcity in this type of study in the coffee area.

The data were compiled in a table to enable their discussion. The variables analyzed were extracted from the literature consulted [20–29] and pointed out in the research.

# 3   Results and Discussion

Three distinct situations were evaluated (highway with good and poor quality pavement and unpaved road) regarding the economic and environmental performance of vehicle combinations, data compiled in Table 1.

For better understanding, some information is relevant in the context of the proposed situation. Cargo transport in Brazil is predominantly carried out through the road modal [30, 31], corresponding to 61.1% of the amount carried out with about 485 million tons per useful kilometer [27].

In this perspective, coffee is transported by road modal to the Port of Santos. Among the combinations of vehicles for transport, the usual is the use of a tractor truck and a semitrailer, which can vary from 5 to 9 axles, and its maximum transport capacity varies between 41.5 and 74 tons [28]. These different combinations have different fuel and tire consumption, being directly linked to economic and environmental issues [22, 23]. With a focus on the environmental issue, transport modes are required to have lower consumption of fossil fuels with consequent lower $CO_2$ emissions and longer life

**Table 1.** Behavior of combinations of cargo vehicles in pavement modalities.

| Grain body type (pulled by 420 hp tractor with 6×4) | Good quality paved highway | | | | Low quality paved highway | | | | Unpaved highway | | | |
|---|---|---|---|---|---|---|---|---|---|---|---|---|
| | Rodotrem 9 axes 25 m | Bitrem articulate 7 axes (up to 30 m) | Truck | Stump | Rodotrem 9 axes 25 m | Bitrem articulate 7 axes (up to 30 m) | Truck | Stump | Rodotrem 9 axes 25 m | Bitrem articulate 7 axes (up to 30 m) | Truck | Stump |
| Total gross cargo weight (PBTC) (tons) | 74 | 57 | 48.5 | 41.5 | 74 | 57 | 48.5 | 41.5 | 74 | 57 | 48.5 | 41.5 |
| Net weight (tons) | 50 | 38 | 30 | 25 | 50 | 38 | 30 | 25 | 50 | 38 | 30 | 25 |
| Fuel consumption with scale load (Km/L) | 1.7 | 1.9 | 2.5 | 2.8 | 1.45 | 1.62 | 1.92 | 2.21 | 1.23 | 1.38 | 1.67 | 1.88 |
| Diesel oil cost (BRL/km) | 2.22 | 1.99 | 1.51 | 1.35 | 2.61 | 2.33 | 1.97 | 1.71 | 3.07 | 2.74 | 2.26 | 2.01 |
| Tire quantity | 34 | 26 | 22 | 18 | 34 | 26 | 22 | 18 | 34 | 26 | 22 | 18 |
| New tire life (Km) | 250 000 | 280 000 | 290 000 | 290 000 | 212 500 | 238 000 | 246 500 | 246 500 | 180 625 | 202 300 | 209 525 | 209 525 |
| Cost with new tires (BRL/km) | BRL 0.20 | BRL 0.14 | BRL 0.11 | BRL 0.09 | BRL 0.24 | BRL 0.16 | BRL 0.13 | BRL 0.11 | BRL 0.28 | BRL 0.19 | BRL 0.16 | BRL 0.13 |
| Unit cost of new tire (BRL/ton of coffee grain) | BRL 1.56 | BRL 1.40 | BRL 1.45 | BRL 1.42 | BRL 1.83 | BRL 1.65 | BRL 1.70 | BRL 1.67 | BRL 2.16 | BRL 1.94 | BRL 2.01 | BRL 1.97 |
| Retreaded tire life (Km) | 140000 | 150000 | 150000 | 160000 | 119000 | 127500 | 127500 | 136000 | 101150 | 108375 | 108375 | 115600 |
| Cost of retreaded tires (BRL/km) | R$0,15 | R$0,10 | R$0,09 | R$0,07 | R$0,17 | R$0,12 | R$0,10 | R$0,08 | R$0,20 | R$0,14 | R$0,12 | R$0,09 |
| Unit cost of retreaded tire (BRL/ton of coffee grain) | BRL 1.11 | BRL 1.05 | BRL 1.12 | BRL 1.03 | BRL 1.31 | BRL 1.23 | BRL 1.32 | BRL 1.21 | BRL 1.54 | BRL 1.45 | BRL 1.55 | BRL 1.43 |
| Consumption in liters of diesel to cover | 224.71 | 201.05 | 152.80 | 136.43 | 263.45 | 235.80 | 198.96 | 172.85 | 310.57 | 276.81 | 228.74 | 203.19 |

(continued)

**Table 1.** (continued)

| Grain body type (pulled by 420 hp tractor with 6×4) | Good quality paved highway | | | | Low quality paved highway | | | | Unpaved highway | | | |
|---|---|---|---|---|---|---|---|---|---|---|---|---|
| | Rodotrem 9 axes 25 m | Bitrem articulate 7 axes (up to 30 m) | Truck | Stump | Rodotrem 9 axes 25 m | Bitrem articulate 7 axes (up to 30 m) | Truck | Stump | Rodotrem 9 axes 25 m | Bitrem articulate 7 axes (up to 30 m) | Truck | Stump |
| average distance from Guaxupé/MG to the Port of Santos (382 km) | | | | | | | | | | | | |
| Unit cost of diesel (BRL/ton of coffee grain) | BRL 16.99 | BRL 20.00 | BRL 19.25 | BRL 20.63 | BRL 19.92 | BRL 23.46 | BRL 25.07 | BRL 26.14 | BRL 23.48 | BRL 27.54 | BRL 28.82 | BRL 30.72 |
| CO2 emission | 602.22 | 538.81 | 409.51 | 365.63 | 706.05 | 631.95 | 533.21 | 463.24 | 832.33 | 741.85 | 613.03 | 544.55 |
| CO2 emission per kg of coffee grain | 0.012 | 0.014 | 0.014 | 0.015 | 0.014 | 0.017 | 0.018 | 0.019 | 0.017 | 0.019 | 0.020 | 0.022 |

of tires (which are manufactured from rubber) [23]. On the other hand, Brazil has 1,720,756 km of highways, has poor quality infrastructure with about 12.3% of the paved highways and of this total 58.2% are poorly maintained [22, 32].

The use of the road modal is deeply linked to anthropogenic $CO_2$ emissions. There is a projection indicating that in 2020 emissions will be 270 million tons of $CO_2$, about 60% higher than in 2009 [21, 33].

After a brief contextualization of the Brazilian scenario in relation to the most used transport modal and the concern about it being the largest $CO_2$ emitter, an analysis will be presented regarding the different types of combinations of cargo vehicles in relation to paving conditions of the roads.

## 3.1    Economic and Environmental Efficiency Analysis

It is observed that, in general, from an economic point of view, the use of retreaded tires for any type of vehicle is better. The expenses (BRL/ton of coffee grains) on retreaded tires are on average 26% lower than with new tires. The average for new tires is BRL 1.46 and for retreads are BRL 1.08 per ton of coffee grains transported.

Regarding the expenses on diesel (BRL/ton of coffee grains) it is observed that in decreasing order of economic efficiency there is: rodotrem (BRL 16.99), truck (BRL 19.25), bitrem (BRL 20.00) and stump (BRL 20.63).

Thus, considering the total expenses sum of diesel and tires, per ton of coffee grains transported from Guaxupé to the port of Santos, the most economical is that of the rodotrem with retreaded tires (BRL 18.10), and the least economical is the stump with new tires (BRL 22.05), which means a difference of 18%.

From this point of view of economic efficiency, the same is observed in relation to the highway with low quality paving and unpaved road. That is, whatever the quality of the highway, the rodotrem with retreaded tires is shown to be the best option and the stump with new tires, the worst.

It was expected that the consumption of tires and diesel will be higher on highways with low quality paving and even higher on unpaved roads. On average, compared with the respective values observed on highways with good quality paving, the expenses with tires are 17.3% higher on highways with low quality paving and 38.6% higher on unpaved roads; diesel spending is 23% higher on a highway with low quality paving and 43.8% higher on unpaved roads.

This observation reflects the impact on economic costs of the lack of road investments through improvement, maintenance, and rehabilitation of pavements, as highlighted in the work [34, 35].

In addition to the quality of the roads, another determining factor in the increase in economic costs is related to the competence of the driver, as they can generate a difference in fuel consumption of 10% to 12% when comparing the best and worst drivers [36].

From an environmental point of view, [37] emphasize that $CO_2$ emissions are directly proportional to the amount of fuel consumed by a vehicle.

In this sense, $CO_2$ emissions on a highway with low-quality paving and on unpaved roads are higher than on highways with good-quality pavement, because the increase in emissions is enhanced by deficiencies in the infrastructure of the highways, as it affects the inertia, rolling resistance, air resistance and slope of the road and prevents speed from being constant [37].

## 4  Final Remarks and Outlooks

In order to discuss economic and environmental issues, with different combinations of cargo vehicles and different road conditions (good paving, poor paving and no paving) the present work presented data reporting the conjuncture by which the production of coffee grain in Guaxupé is exposed when transported to the Port of Santos.

That said, the use of the tractor truck 420HP 6X4 for all the proposed situations standardized the evaluations, ensuring that the differences to be evaluated would be in the use of semitrailers.

It was observed that, in general, it is more economical to use retreaded tires instead of new tires. This fact can be considered as beneficial to the environment, as it is possible to retread a "new" tire twice before it is discarded as scrap. Another fact associated with the cost of tires is that for the different combinations of vehicles the difference in cost with tires per ton of coffee grain transported is not relevant.

In economic terms, the factor that has the greatest relevance is the cost of diesel per ton of coffee grain transported and the "rodotrem" is the best combination for cargo, because it has the lowest consumption of diesel per ton of coffee grain transported.

In the environmental aspect, the "rodotrem" is the combination of load with the best performance in all of the paving conditions which have been evaluated.

As a result of the above, it is evident that the quality of road paving is a primary factor for better economic and environmental performance for the transport of coffee grains. By comparing the total distances covered by paved and unpaved roads, it is possible to identify that Brazil's transportation matrix needs investments, technologies to improve fuel consumption and tire performance.

Finally, it is important to highlight that this study contributes to national efforts to mitigate anthropogenic GHG emissions in Brazilian food production chains, however the reduction of GHG emissions will depend on the development of the model of transport matrix that the government intends to follow.

This study was financed in part by the Coordenação de Aperfeiçoamento de Pessoal de Nível Superior Brasil (CAPES) Finance Code 001.

## References

1. Organização das Nações Unidas, D.d.A.E.e.S.: Probabilistic population projections based on the world population prospects: the 2017 revision. Technical report, United Nations, New York (2017). http://esa.un.org/unpd/wpp/index.htm
2. de Abastecimento CONAB, C.N.: Conab - srie histrica das safras (2020). http://www.conab.gov.br/info-agro/safras/serie-historica-das-safras
3. Läderach, P., et al.: Systematic agronomic farm management for improved coffee quality. Field Crops Res. **120**(3), 321–329 (2011)

4. WIPO: World intellectual property report 2017: intangible capital in global value chains. World Intellectual Property Report, Place of publication not identified (2017). https://www.wipo.int/publications/en/details.jsp?id=4225

5. Ministry of agriculture, livestock, and food supply (2019). http://www.agricultura.gov.br/assuntos/politica-agricola/cafe/cafeicultura-brasileira

6. CECAFÉ fatia do brasil nas exportaes globais de café deve aumentar (2019). https://www.cecafe.com.br/publicacoes/fatia-do-brasil-nas-exportacoes-globais-de-cafe-deve-aumentar-20190116/

7. Ferro, R.G., De Muner, L.H., Fonseca, A.F.A.d., Ferro, M.A.G.: Caf Conilon. In- caper, Vitria/ES (2016)

8. Encarnação, R.d.O., Lima, D.R.: O café e a saúde humana. Technical report, Embrapa Café, Braslia (2003). http://ainfo.cnptia.embrapa.br/digital/bitstream/item/32759/1/Cafe-e-saude-humana.pdf

9. Boaventura, P.S.M., Abdalla, C.C., Arajo, C.L., Arakelian, J.S.: Value co-creation in the specialty coffee value chain: the third-wave coffee movement. Rev. Adm. Empres. 58(3), 254–266 (2018)

10. Sindicato da Indústrias de Café de Minas Gerais: Café no Mundo. Technical report, SindiCafe-MG, Belo Horizonte (2004). http://sindicafe-mg.com.br/cafe-no-mundo

11. Rodrigues, H.L., Dias, F.D., Teixeira, N.d.C.: A origem do café no brasil: a semente que veio para ficar. Revista Pensar Gastronomia 1(2) (2015)

12. ICO, I.C.O.: A história do café. Technical report, International Coffee Organization, London (2020). http://www.ico.org/pt/coffee_storyp.asp

13. da Cruz Correia, P.F., dos Reis, J.G.M., de Souza, A.E., Cardoso, A.P.: Brazilian coffee export network: an analysis using SNA. In: Ameri, F., Stecke, Kathryn E., von Cieminski, G., Kiritsis, D. (eds.) APMS 2019. IAICT, vol. 566, pp. 142–147. Springer, Cham (2019). https://doi.org/10.1007/978-3-030-30000-5_19

14. Campos, A., Souza, R., Portual Jr, P., Oliveira, G., Souza, G.: Desafios logísticos para o escoamento da produção de café no sul de minas gerais. In: 12th Simpósio de Excelência em Gestão e Tecnologia - SEGeT. p. 12. Associação Educacional Dom Bosco (2015)

15. Bunsen, Till e Cazzola, P.e.G.M.e.P.L.e.S.S.e.S.R.e.T.J.e.T.J.: Global ev outlook: Rumo eletrificao cross-modal (2018)

16. Pathways, C.R.: Adaptation, mitigation, and sustainable development. In: Field, C.B., Barros, V.R., Dokken, D.J., Mach, K.J., Mastrandrea, M.D. (eds.) Climate Change 2014 Impacts, Adaptation, and Vulnerability, pp. 1101–1131. Cambridge University Press, Cambridge (2014)

17. Lima, T.C.S., Mioto, R.C.T.: Procedimentos metodológicos na construção do conhecimento científico: a pesquisa bibliográfica. Revista Katálysis 10(SPE), 37–45 (2007)

18. ANP, A.N.d.P.: Sistema de levantamento de preços. Technical report, Braslia (2020)

19. Pachauri, R.K., Mayer, L., Change, I.P.C.C. (eds.): IPCC: Climate change 2014: synthesis report. Intergovernmental Panel on Climate Change, Geneva, Switzerland (2015)

20. Toloi, R.C., et al.: Cargo vehicle combinations: an economic and environmental approach to soybean supply chain in mato grosso, brazil. In: 8th International Conference on Information Systems, Logistics and Supply Chain. Texas State University, Austin

21. Agency, I.E.: $CO_2$ Emissions from fuel combustion highlights 2015. Technical report, Frana (2015)

22. Guimarães, P.: Consumo de combustível em duas combinações veiculares de carga no transporte rodoviário florestal. Ph.D. thesis (2014)

23. Klvac, R., Kolařík, J., Volná, M., Drápela, K.: Fuel consumption in timber haulage. Croatian J. For. Eng. J. Theor. Appl. For. Eng. 34(2), 229–240 (2013)

24. Moreira, L., Santos, S., Oliveira Neto, R., Silva Junior, L.: Revisão bibliográfica sobre o modal de transporte rodoviário no Brasil. Res. Soc. Dev. **8**(3), 38 (2019)
25. CNT, C.a.N.d.T.: Transporte rodoviário - desempenho do setor, Infraestrutura e Investimentos (2017)
26. Soliani, R.D., Argoud, A.R.T.T., Lopes, L.J.: A sustentabilidade no transporte rodoviário de cargas no brasil. In: XXVII SIMPEP (2017)
27. Torres, O., Fagundes, M., Figueiredo, A., Tredezini, C.: Impacto da Implantação do Custo do Pedágio na BR-163 em Relação ao Transporte de Soja do Estado de Mato Grosso. Rev. Economia Sociologia Rural **55**(3), 533–550 (2017)
28. DNIT, Departamento Nacional *de* Infraestrutura *de* Transportes: Quadro de fabricantes de veículos. departamento nacional de infra-estrutura de transportes. Technical report, Braslia (2012)
29. Toloi, M.N.V., Toloi, R.C., Silva, H.R.O., dos Reis, J.G.M., Bonilla, S.H.: $CO_2$ Gas emissions of soybean production and transportation in the different macro-regions of Mato Grosso State - Brazil. In: Ameri, F., Stecke, Kathryn E., von Cieminski, G., Kiritsis, D. (eds.) APMS 2019. IAICT, vol. 566, pp. 187–194. Springer, Cham (2019). https://doi.org/10.1007/978-3-030-30000-5_25
30. Gonçalves, D.N.S., Goes, G.V., D'Agosto, M., Bandeira, R.: Energy use and emissions scenarios for transport to gauge progress toward national commitments. Energy Policy **135**, 110997 (2019)
31. Marchetti, D., Wanke, P.: Brazil's rail freight transport: efficiency analysis using two-stage DEA and cluster-driven public policies. Socio.-Econ. Plann. Sci. **59**, 26–42 (2017)
32. Ministério de Minas e Energia: Empresa de pesquisa energética: plano decenal de expansão de energia 2026 (2017). http://www.epe.gov.br/sites-pt/publicacoes-dados-abertos/publicacoes/PublicacoesArquivos/publicacao-40/PDE2026.pdf
33. Danao, M.G.C., Zandonadi, R.S., Gates, R.S.: Development of a grain monitoring probe to measure temperature, relative humidity, carbon dioxide levels and logistical information during handling and transportation of soybeans. Comput. Electron. Agric. **119**, 74–82 (2015)
34. Bryce, J., Brodie, S., Parry, T., Presti, D.L.: A systematic assessment of road pavement sustainability through a review of rating tools. Resour. Conserv. Recycl. **120**, 108–118 (2017)
35. Dente, S.M.R., Tavasszy, L.: Policy oriented emission factors for road freight transport. Transp. Res. Part D Transp. Environ. **61**, 33–41 (2018)
36. CAT: caterpillar performance handbook. Technical report Edition 44, Caterpillar, Illinois (2014). http://www.puckettmachinery.com/images/CatPerformanceHandbook.pdf
37. Demir, E., Bekta, T., Laporte, G.: A review of recent research on green road freight transportation. Eur. J. Oper. Res. **237**(3), 775–793 (2014)

# Managing Perishable Multi-product Inventory with Supplier Fill-Rate, Price Reduction and Substitution

Flemming Max Møller Christensen[✉], Kenn Steger-Jensen, and Iskra Dukovska-Popovska

Centre for Logistics (CELOG), Materials and Production,
Aalborg University, Aalborg, Denmark
fmmc@mp.aau.dk

**Abstract.** Order-sizing in replenishment planning and control for perishable products is studied in grocery retail context. There is a need for age-based policies that consider multiple products, the impact from price reduction (due to close-to-expiration), and product substitution in order to reduce waste, increase availability and improve freshness. This study develops a theoretical extension to known EWA-models considering positive and/or negative interdependence in substitution between products, impact from price reduction and expired products, as well as the inventory impact from other products safety stocks.

**Keywords:** Inventory control · Shelf-life · Perishable · Substitution

## 1 Introduction

The grocery market faces ever-growing requirements to product availability and freshness [1]. Majority of consumers often feel disappointed with fresh food products' (FFP) availability and freshness when grocery shopping [2]. The FFPs have down to few days shelf-life with high waste-levels when comparing with other product types [3]. Increasing remaining shelf-life one day causes improved freshness, availability and waste [4].

Grocery demand is stochastic and non-stationary over the week with high sales in weekends [5]. This, as well as the increased focus on food waste and use of automated replenishment systems across product assortments [6], put high requirements on the FFP replenishment planning and control at wholesaler and retail store. Different heuristics have been suggested to manage perishables in automated replenishment systems when considering the product's remaining shelf-life [5, 7–9]. However, they do not reflect certain real-life situations. Grocery wholesaler/retailer faces different product characteristics that influence the order-size decision-making of FFPs:

1. Price-reduction: if "FFP A" is close to expiration, its price is reduced (in rounds) to minimize waste. The demand for the price-reduced "FFP A" depends on the reduction i.e. price elasticity, which influences the available inventory in different degrees.

B. Lalic et al. (Eds.): APMS 2020, IFIP AICT 592, pp. 640–648, 2020.
https://doi.org/10.1007/978-3-030-57997-5_74

2. Order fill-rate: FFPs to be delivered in the future, not yet in transit, may be influenced by (suddenly) reduced fill-rate due to factors such as, e.g. sudden raw-material unavailability. This influences the safety stock, hence the ability to withstand variation in demand level, thus order-sizing of FFPs.
3. Substitution demand: if "FFP A" is out-of-stock it may be substituted with "FFP B", causing extraordinary substitution demand on "FFP B" – and vice versa, depending on the products' positive and/or negative interdependence [10].
4. Substitution inventory: FFPs have asymmetrical financial losses[1] with increased food waste focus. Therefore, instead of buying too many "FFP B" (due to e.g. minimum order quantities) which causes excess inventory, hence increased risk of waste from expiration, the available inventory from substituting "FFP A" may satisfy "FFP B"'s demand, thereby mitigate risk.

By investigating current heuristics for perishable (automated) replenishment planning and control, it is possible to see how substitution, price reduction and reduced fill-rate in future orders may be included in the decision-making. The following presents the background, the developed multi-product $EWA_{3SL}$, and ends with the conclusion.

## 1.1 Inventory Control for Perishable Products

Numerous inventory control systems have been introduced for perishable products with fixed or random shelf-life and fixed or continuous review period, modelling deterministic or stochastic demand [11–15]. Fixed shelf-life is a known and deterministic time period where a product deteriorates (e.g. fresh meat, dairy and chilled food products), while random shelf-life is a probabilistic time period where a product deteriorates (e.g. fruits and vegetables). Recent studies primarily concern single items assuming deterministic demand, mainly focusing on pricing and lot-sizing or multi-echelon – and shortages are considered through back-ordering [14]. For products with particular short shelf-life, i.e. one day, the newsboy problem is considered appropriate [15]. Extended versions covering two periods with stochastic demand are suggested by e.g. [16].

For products with up to few weeks shelf-life such as fresh meat and dairy products the OIR policy [8], age-and-stock-based (CASB) policy [9] and the EWA policy [5] are considered. The old inventory ratio (OIR) policy is a two-step policy minimizing the expected number of outdated products given a predetermined allowance for out-of-stock. The inventory position is raised to order-up-to level, and then, if the ratio between old (i.e. outdated) and total inventory position on hand is larger than a specified threshold, an additional order quantity corresponding to the number of outdated products is ordered. Simulation results for blood products show significant reduction in outdated products (19,6% to 1,04%) while keeping sufficiently high fill-rate [8]. A variation of the OIR is the CASB policy with a continuous review [9]. An order quantity is suggested either when total inventory position drops to a specified number of products (re-order point) or when the oldest batch has aged $t$ units of time;

---

[1] Too few products mean lost sales i.e. profit – too many means lost purchase and handling costs.

whichever comes first [9]. Since the review is continuous, the required safety stock is lower [15].

The EWA policy considers the estimated number of products to outdate within the review period. Based on [15] the EWA batches store orders according to case sizes with positive lead-times and weekly time-varying demand, as known in the grocery industry [5]. They obtain 17,7% increase in inventory availability and 3,4% waste reduction for products with 4–7 days shelf-life when comparing to stock-based policy. [7] extends the EWA to $EWA_{SS}$ considering the size of safety stock relative to the expected number of products outdated within the review period. They simulate grocery products with short shelf-life and compare with a stock-based policy and obtain improved results on waste reduction compared to [5]: 10,3% increase in inventory availability and 10,7% waste reduction. The latest $EWA_{SS}$ suggested by [7] is in Eq. (1)–(2):

If,

$$I_t - \sum_{i=t+1}^{t+R+L-1} \widehat{O}_i < \sum_{i=t+1}^{t+R+L} E[D] + SS \tag{1}$$

then,

$$Q_t = \begin{cases} \max\left(\dfrac{\sum_{i=t+1}^{t+R+L} E[D] + \sum_{i=t+1}^{t+R+L-1} \widehat{O}_i - I_t}{B}, 0\right) & \text{if}, SS < \sum_{i=t+1}^{t+R+L-1} \widehat{O}_i \\[4mm] \max\left(\dfrac{\sum_{i=t+1}^{t+R+L} E[D] + SS - I_t}{B}, 0\right) & \text{if}, SS \geq \sum_{i=t+1}^{t+R+L-1} \widehat{O}_i \end{cases} \tag{2}$$

$E[D]$ = expected product demand within review time
$I_t$ = inventory position of product at time $t$
$\widehat{O}_i$ = estimated number of products to expire within review time
$SS$ = safety stock for product

Although $EWA_{SS}$ includes the size of safety stock relative to the estimated number of products that will outdate, it is for a single product as with EWA, OIR and CASB. Since including only one product, they do not consider the additional demand created from other products sold out and out-of-stock (i.e. substitutions demand). Further, they do not include the impact of when selling product close to expiration at a reduced price.

## 1.2    Product Characteristics

Different planning environment characteristics influence FFPs [17]. In this study, the focus is on the impact of price reduction when FFPs are close to expiration, the supplier order fill-rate for future orders and impact from substitution on demand and inventory.

Due to FFPs short shelf-life, any excess inventory will be prone to the risk of expiration and thus subject to a price reduction. Depending on how excessive the inventory level is, a price reduction can be used as a tool to increase the demand in due time [13]. This decreases the inventory level with the desired speed and timing. Price-elasticity can support the order sizing of FFPs by estimating how much the inventory position will decrease each time products are reduced in the price, and is also suggested by [18].

The FFPs are processed down to every day with immediate shipment from the supplier, for fresh meat products see e.g. [17]. The raw materials for FFPs are scarce and can usually not be stored for any longer time, as well as they are often influenced from factors such as, e.g. available only in certain season(s) and nature (storm, rain etc.). Sudden scarcity may, therefore, influence future orders, not yet in transit, within the review period. By including a supplier order fill-rate, this order sizing of FFPs may encounter this and increase order size as needed.

The last two product characteristics concern substitutions and the impact on demand and inventory availability [10, 19]. Focusing on "FFP A", we consider substitution demand for "FFP A" when "FFP B" has too low inventory, and substitution inventory from "FFP B" when "FFP A" has too low inventory. [10] describes how the well-used exogenous substitution factors may be used for creating a substitution probability matrix. We represent the two by available substitution inventory of other FFPs and substitution demand from other FFPs.

## 2  A Multi-product EWA with Supplier Fill-Rate, Price Reduction and Substitution

To control inventories in a way which reflects the consumer requirements (availability and freshness) and impact from substitution as well as mitigates the risk of causing quality reduction and food waste, it is necessary to use a multi-product approach. To ensure the size of safety stock relative to outdating products, we build on the $EWA_{SS}$. As with both current EWA policies [5, 7], we use a fixed review period. This fits with the grocery industry and wholesaler/retail stores placing orders at specified time points regardless of demand type (normal or campaign demand). Having a safety stock for perishable items means a chance for reducing the sales price of the product to adjust the inventory position, so waste is avoided. Based on the four FFP characteristics, $EWA_{3SL}$ is suggested. The 3SL in $EWA_{3SL}$ relates to the supplier (S), shelf-life (SL) and substitution (S). It follows the logic as depicted in Fig. 1, where one of three different order-sizing decisions applies.

To ensure simplicity in presentation, we first define the available inventory as in Eq. (3). For product $p_1$ at time $t$ we consider current inventory level (on hand and in transit), plus all quantities ordered but not yet received/in transit multiplied by the fill-rate ($\beta$) for each supplier ($l$), minus already reserved quantities[2], within the review- and lead-time ($i$) [15]. Then, the estimated outdated (i.e. expired) quantities and estimated quantities sold at a reduced price (due to close to expiration) up until the immediate prior time period are subtracted. For quantities sold at a reduced price, please notice

---

[2] Customer orders placed long time in advance, e.g. pre-orders for campaigns.

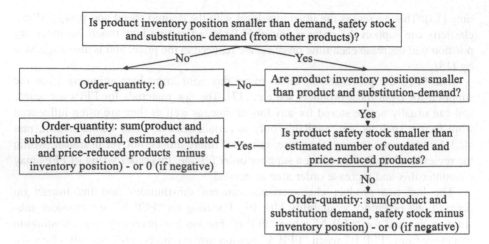

**Fig. 1.** Decision diagram for EWA$_{3SL}$

that there may be products with different expiration dates, i.e. different price-reduced quantities each day as identified by $\varepsilon$.

$$I_{p_1,t}^{available} = I_{p_1,t} + \sum_{i=t+1}^{R_{p_1}+L_{p_1}} \sum_{l=1}^{S_1 \to S_x} Q_{p_1,i,l}^{ordered} \beta_{p1,i,l} - \sum_{i=t+1}^{R_{p_1}+L_{p_1}} Q_{p_1,i}^{reserved}$$
$$- \sum_{i=t+1}^{R_{p_1}+L_{p_1}-1} \widehat{Q}_{p_1,i}^{outdate} - \sum_{i=t+1}^{R_{p_1}+L_{p_1}-1} \sum_{k=1}^{\varepsilon_{p_1}} \widehat{Q}_{p_1,i,k}^{reduced}$$

(3)

$I_{p_1,t}$ = starting inventory position, after expired products are subtracted

$Q_{p_1,i,l}^{ordered}$ = number of product $p_1$ already ordered but arriving later, within review time

$\beta_{p1,i,l}$ = fill-rate on ordered quantities of product $p_1$ from supplier $l$ ($S_1 \to S_x$)

$Q_{p_1,i}^{reserved}$ = number of product $p_1$ reserved from inventory due to, e.g. campaign or customer

$\widehat{Q}_{p_1,i}^{outdate}$ = estimated number of product $p_1$ to expire within review time

$\widehat{Q}_{p_1,i,l}^{reduced}$ = estimated number of product $p_1$ sold a reduced price within review time

In addition to the classical demand plus safety stock as order-up-to point, the EWA$_{3SL}$ considers the substitution effect, when evaluating relative to available inventory. Also, that the substitution for "FFP A" and "FFP B" may not necessarily be one-to-one, i.e. equal interdependence. As an example, while a substitute for ground beef 8–12% may be ground beef 4–7%, the substitute for 4–7% may be a completely different product, i.e. thus not necessarily symmetrical demand-effect.

In step 1 (Eq. 4, below) in the $EWA_{3SL}$, if the available inventory of product $p_1$ at time $t$ is less than the sum of expected demand within the review- and lead-time, the safety stock and the expected substitution-demand from other products (not having sufficient inventory) (product $2$ to $x$, $p_2 \rightarrow p_x$), then continue to step 2. $E\left[D_{j,i}^{sub}\right]$ is expected substitution demand for all products $p_j$, when product $p_1$ has excess inventory and $p_j$ has too low inventory to satisfy demand and thus substitute with product $p_1$. This is influenced by the substitution probability factor $\mu_{p_1|j}$ for all $j$ products [10]. Similarly, when the substituting products $p_j$ have excess inventory, allowing substituting demand from product $p_1$. In the formula we account for an FFP may have several other substituting FFPs as the case of, e.g. multiple brands (brand#1, brand#2 and private label). For expected demand, this may be particularly relevant when a certain product may not be available from the supplier for a (longer) period. This is depicted in Eq. (4).

In step 2 (Eq. 5), the substituting inventory available from the product $p_2 \rightarrow p_x$ is included when evaluating against product $p_1$ demand and product $p_2 \rightarrow p_x$ substitution demand. If the total available inventory is less than the total expected demand, proceed to step 2a. Here the evaluation of safety stock and outdated/price-reduced products determines the order-size as described by [7]. In the $EWA_{3SL}$, we additionally add the number of products price-reduced due to close to expiration as well as the substituting demand from other products if safety stock is smaller than the two. This is depicted in Eqs. (5-9).

In step 3, if the available inventory is larger or equal to the expected product and substitution demand, no order should be placed. This may be of particular relevance if experiencing too high inventory levels of substituting products that need to be reduced. Depending on the substitutability, different products inventories may be included in the calculation. Thus, $EWA_{3SL}$ includes risk mitigation by evaluating with substitution inventory that could otherwise end up as potential waste if inventory levels are high. This is depicted in Eq. (10).

1) **If:**

$$I_{p_1,t}^{available} < \sum_{i=t+1}^{R_{p_1}+L_{p_1}} E\left[D_{p_1,i}\right] + SS_{p_1} + \sum_{j=1}^{p_2 \rightarrow p_x} \sum_{i=t+1}^{R_{p_1}+L_{p_1}} E\left[D_{j,i}^{sub}\right]\mu_{p_1|j} \tag{4}$$

where:

$$D_{j,i}^{sub} = 0 \quad if \quad I_{j,i}^{available} \geq D_{j,i} \text{ and } D_{j,i}^{sub} > 0 \quad if \quad I_{j,i}^{available} < D_{j,i}$$

$$\mu_{p_x|j} = \begin{pmatrix} 0 & \mu_{p_1 2} & \cdots & \mu_{p_1 j} & \cdots \\ \mu_{p_2 1} & 0 & \cdots & \mu_{p_2 j} & \cdots \\ \vdots & \vdots & \ddots & \vdots & \cdots \\ \mu_{p_x 1} & \mu_{p_x 2} & \cdots & 0 & \cdots \\ \vdots & \vdots & \vdots & \vdots & \ddots \end{pmatrix}$$

then,

for all $I_{p_x,t}^{available} < E[D_{p_x,i}]$,

2) if,

$$I_{p_1,t}^{available} + \sum_{j=1}^{p_2 \to p_x} \sum_{i=t+1}^{R_{p_1}+L_{p_1}} I_{j,i}^{sub.avail.} < \sum_{i=t+1}^{R_{p_1}+L_{p_1}} E[D_{p_1}] + \sum_{j=1}^{p_2 \to p_x} \sum_{i=t+1}^{R_{p_1}+L_{p_1}} E[D_{j,i}^{sub}] \mu_{p_1|j} \quad (5)$$

then,

2a) if,

$$SS_{p_1} < \sum_{i=t+1}^{R_{p_1}+L_{p_1}-1} \widehat{Q}_{p_1,i}^{outdate} + \sum_{i=t+1}^{R_{p_1}+L_{p_1}-1} \sum_{l=1}^{\varepsilon_{p_1}} \widehat{Q}_{p_1,i,l}^{reduced} \quad (6)$$

then,

$$Q_{p_1,t} = \max \left( \left( \begin{array}{c} \sum\limits_{i=t+1}^{R_{p_1}+L_{p_1}} E[D_{p_1}] + \sum\limits_{i=t+1}^{R_{p_1}+L_{p_1}-1} \widehat{Q}_{p_1,i}^{outdate} + \sum\limits_{i=t+1}^{R_{p_1}+L_{p_1}-1} \sum\limits_{l=1}^{\varepsilon_{p_1}} \widehat{Q}_{p_1,i,l}^{reduced} \\ + \sum\limits_{j=1}^{p_2 \to p_x} \sum\limits_{i=t+1}^{R_{p_1}+L_{p1}} E[D_{j,i}^{sub}] \mu_{p_1|j} - I_{p_1,t}^{available} \end{array} \right), 0 \right)$$

$$(7)$$

2b) if,

$$SS_{p_1} \geq \sum_{i=t+1}^{R_{p_1}+L_{p_1}-1} \widehat{Q}_{p_1,i}^{outdate} + \sum_{i=t+1}^{R_{p_1}+L_{p_1}-1} \sum_{l=1}^{\varepsilon_{p_1}} \widehat{Q}_{p_1,i,l}^{reduced} \quad (8)$$

then,

$$Q_{p_1,t} = \max \left( \left( \sum_{i=t+1}^{R_{p_1}+L_{p_1}} E[D_{p_1,i}] + \sum_{j=1}^{p_2 \to p_x} \sum_{i=t+1}^{R_{p1}+L_{p1}} E[D_{j,i}^{sub}] \mu_{p_1|j} + SS_{p_1} - I_{p_1,t}^{available} \right), 0 \right) \quad (9)$$

for all $I_{p_x,t}^{available} \geq E[D_{p_x,i}]$,

3) if,

$$I_{p_1,t}^{available} + \sum_{j=1}^{p_2 \to p_x} \sum_{i=t+1}^{R_{p_1}+L_{p_1}} I_{j,i}^{sub.avail.} \geq \sum_{i=t+1}^{R_{p_1}+L_{p_1}} E[D_{p_1}] + \sum_{j=1}^{p_2 \to p_x} \sum_{i=t+1}^{R_{p_1}+L_{p_1}} E[D_{j,i}^{sub}] \mu_{p_1|j} \quad (10)$$

then,

$$Q_{p_1,t} = 0$$

$I_{p_1,t}^{available}$ = inventory position (on hand plus in transit) at time t for product $p_1$

$I_{j,i}^{sub.avail.}$ = beginning inventory at time i for substituting product $j$ ($p_2 \rightarrow p_x$)

$\hat{Q}_{p_1,i}^{outdate}$ = estimated number of product $p_1$ to expire within review time

$\hat{Q}_{p_1,i,l}^{reduced}$ = estimated number of product $p_1$ sold a reduced price within review time

$E\left[D_{j,i}^{sub}\right]$ = expected substitution demand from product $j$ ($p_2 \rightarrow p_x$)

$E\left[D_{p_1,i}\right]$ = expected demand from product $p_1$

$SS_{p_1}$ = safety stock for product $p_1$

$Q_{p_1,t}$ = order quantity for product $p_1$

$\mu_{p_1|j}$ = substitution matrix for product $j$ ($p_2 \rightarrow p_x$) substituting with product $p_1$ when $I_{j,i}^{available} < D_{j,i}$

$\varepsilon_{p_1}$ = price elasticity of product $p_1$ for price reduction when $p_1$ gets close to expiration

## 3  Conclusion

This study extends the inventory control for stochastic demand and fixed review time to a multi-product model, by suggesting a new heuristics considering four product characteristics. The model includes substitution factors across all products as well as includes potential noise in supply-signal through estimated fill-rate during future orders to receive. It is based on previous studies on EWA. By allowing asymmetrical evaluation according to the product characteristics, the EWA$_{3SL}$ reflects the real-life situations, even more, causing effective decision-making when order-sizing. This means that, e.g. the impact from different rounds of price-reduction on the product demand is considered. The EWA$_{3SL}$ is expected to bring even lower waste and improved availability than previous results by supporting the mitigation of risks across products. For practical implications, determining the substitution factor may be challenging and rather subjective given the limited literature on the subject matter and the influence from the geographical area, culture etc. [10, 19]. A solution may be to then apply a binary system: 0 if not substitutable and 1 if substitutable. Further, the model is yet to be tested, and further research governs checking how robust the heuristic is, the impact on inventory levels, fill-rate and waste.

# References

1. Hübner, A.H., Kuhn, H., Sternbeck, M.G.: Demand and supply chain planning in grocery retail: an operations planning framework. Int. J. Retail. Distrib. Manag. **41**, 512–530 (2013). https://doi.org/10.1108/IJRDM-05-2013-0104
2. BlueYonder: customer experience in grocery retail: the fresh opportunity customers in fresh - a global survey of 4,000 consumers shine light on customer experience in fresh and product availability (2017)
3. Mena, C., Terry, L.A., Williams, A., Ellram, L.M.: Causes of waste across multi-tier supply networks: cases in the UK food sector. Int. J. Prod. Econ. **152**, 144–158 (2014). https://doi.org/10.1016/j.ijpe.2014.03.012
4. Broekmeulen, R.A.C.M., van Donselaar, K.H.: Quantifying the potential to improve on food waste, freshness and sales for perishables in supermarkets. Int. J. Prod. Econ., 1–9 (2017). https://doi.org/10.1016/j.ijpe.2017.10.003
5. Broekmeulen, R.A.C.M., van Donselaar, K.H.: A heuristic to manage perishable inventory with batch ordering, positive lead-times, and time-varying demand. Comput. Oper. Res. **36**, 3013–3018 (2009). https://doi.org/10.1016/j.cor.2009.01.017
6. RELEX: Planning for every future in grocery retail, survey-based research study (2020)
7. Kiil, K., Hvolby, H.H., Fraser, K., Dreyer, H., Strandhagen, J.O.: Automatic replenishment of perishables in grocery retailing: the value of utilizing remaining shelf life information. Br. Food J. **120**, 2033–2046 (2018). https://doi.org/10.1108/BFJ-10-2017-0547
8. Duan, Q., Liao, T.W.: A new age-based replenishment policy for supply chain inventory optimization of highly perishable products. Int. J. Prod. Econ. **145**, 658–671 (2013). https://doi.org/10.1016/j.ijpe.2013.05.020
9. Lowalekar, H., Ravichandran, N.: A combined age-and-stock based policy for ordering blood units in hospital blood banks. Int. Trans. Oper. Res. **24**, 1561–1586 (2017). https://doi.org/10.1111/itor.12189
10. Hübner, A.H.: Retail Category Management Decision Support Systems. LNE. Springer, Heidelberg (2011). https://doi.org/10.1007/978-3-642-22477-5
11. Nahmias, Steven: Perishable inventory theory: a review. Oper. Res. **30**, 680–708 (1982)
12. Raafat, F.: Survey of literature on continuously deteriorating inventory models. J. Oper. Res. Soc. **42**, 27–37 (1991). https://doi.org/10.1057/jors.1991.4
13. Goyal, S.K., Giri, B.C.: Recent trends in modeling of deteriorating inventory. Eur. J. Oper. Res. **134**, 1–16 (2001). https://doi.org/10.1016/S0377-2217(00)00248-4
14. Bakker, M., Riezebos, J., Teunter, R.H.: Review of inventory systems with deterioration since 2001. Eur. J. Oper. Res. **221**, 275–284 (2012). https://doi.org/10.1016/j.ejor.2012.03.004
15. Silver, E.A., Pyke, D.F., Peterson, R.: Inventory Management and Production Planning and Scheduling. Wiley, Hoboken (1998)
16. Nahmias, S., Pierskalla, W.P.: Optimal ordering policies for a product that perishes in two periods subject to stochastic demand. Nav. Res. Logist. Q. **20**, 207–229 (1973). https://doi.org/10.1002/nav.3800200202
17. Christensen, F.M.M., Jonsson, P., Dukovska-Popovska, I., Steger-Jensen, K.: Differentiated Demand Information Sharing in Perishable Product Supply Chains: A Supplier Planning Environment Contingency on environmental munificence. Prod. Plan. Control (2020, under rev.)
18. van Donselaar, K., van Woensel, T., Broekmeulen, R., Fransoo, J.: Inventory control of perishables in supermarkets. Int. J. Prod. Econ. **104**, 462–472 (2006). https://doi.org/10.1016/j.ijpe.2004.10.019
19. Gruen, T.W., Corsten, D.S., Bharadwaj, S.: Retail Out-of-Stocks: A Worldwide Examination of Extent, Causes and Consumer Responses. Grocery Manufacturers of America, Washington (2002)

# Digital Technology Enablers for Resilient and Customer Driven Food Value Chains

Christos Emmanouilidis[1](✉) and Serafim Bakalis[2]

[1] Cranfield University, Cranfield MK43 0AL, UK
christosem@cranfield.ac.uk
[2] University of Nottingham, Nottingham NG7 2RD, UK

**Abstract.** Food production chains have to respond to disrupted global markets and dynamic customer demands. They are coming under pressure to move from a supply to a demand-driven business model. The inherent difficulties in the lifecycle management of food products, their perishable nature, the volatility in global and regional supplier and customer markets, and the mix of objective and subjective drivers of customer demand and satisfaction, compose a challenging food production landscape. Businesses need to navigate through dynamically evolving operational risks and ensure targeted performance in terms of supply chain resilience and agility, as well as transparency and product assurance. While the industrial transition to digitalised and automated food production chains is seen as a response to such challenges, the contribution of industry 4.0 technology enablers towards this aim is not sufficiently well understood. This paper outlines the key features of high performing food production chains and performs a mapping between them and enabling technologies. As digitalisation initiatives gain priority, such mapping can help with the prioritisation of technology enablers on delivering key aspects of high performing food production chains.

**Keywords:** Food production · Customer–driven models · Industry 4.0

## 1 Introduction

Food value chains involve wide range and versatile processes with a very diverse range of stakeholders situated all the way from primary and manufacturing producers to the end customer. At the low value end lie commodity products, characterised by high production and supply volumes but with tight profitability margins. At the high value end it is increasingly common to identify prime products and services associated with them targeting niche markets or individual customers [1]. A wide range of products and services populate the space between the two ends. Supply chain agility and resilience [2–4], customer orientation [5, 6], as well as traceability [7, 8] and transparency [9] are among the most important considerations when managing production and in particular food value chains. Extensive research and several surveys dealing with the digital transformation of supply chains have been published [9–13]. Such transformation is associated with dynamic and evolving business models [14, 15] but the extent to which different technology enablers of digital transformation contribute to innovative and in

© IFIP International Federation for Information Processing 2020
Published by Springer Nature Switzerland AG 2020
B. Lalic et al. (Eds.): APMS 2020, IFIP AICT 592, pp. 649–657, 2020.
https://doi.org/10.1007/978-3-030-57997-5_75

particular to consumer – driven food value chains is less well explored. This paper contributes to filling this gap by (a) outlining the key challenges of consumer – driven food value chains; (b) discussing the main characteristics of demand-driven food chains; (c) mapping the extent to which different enabling technologies for digitalized food production chains contribute to addressing the challenges and to the desired characteristics of demand-driven food value chains.

## 2 Visual Analytics on Relevant Literature

A literature search for journal articles has been performed in both the Web of Science (WoS) core collection and Scopus on "food production" and "supply chain" aimed at identifying the key concepts that have been targeted in the last 3 years in these areas. The intention was not to perform a detailed literature analysis but to inform a higher-level meta-analysis on the interrelationship between key challenges, requirements, and potential solution enablers. To this end, the obtained results were analysed through the graph network bibliometric visualisation tool VOSviewer (VOSviewer.com). The tool was employed to build network graphs of terms employed in article titles and abstracts. The key visualization features are determined by scores and weights and are visualised with bubbles and connectors. High scores correspond to more frequently used terms and are depicted with larger bubbles. Thicker connectors correspond to more frequent co-occurrence of terms. Trimming out weak connections and infrequent terms while not allowing significant cluster fragmentation, WoS produced two main clusters, one "red cluster" contained terms relevant to the overall "food ecosystem" (Fig. 1).

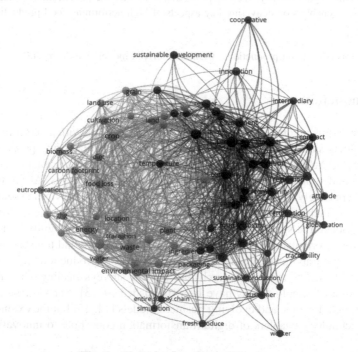

**Fig. 1.** WoS visual analysis of literature

The green cluster was mostly relevant to resources and sustainability. There was very limited evidence of Industry 4.0 technology enablers in the terms. The Scopus picture has similarities with WoS and displays three main clusters (Fig. 2). The green one is largely about resources and sustainability. Instead of a single food ecosystem cluster two clusters are formed: one relevant to the stakeholders of the production ecosystem and associated processes and characteristics; and one relevant to biological aspects, including health, risk, and ingredients.

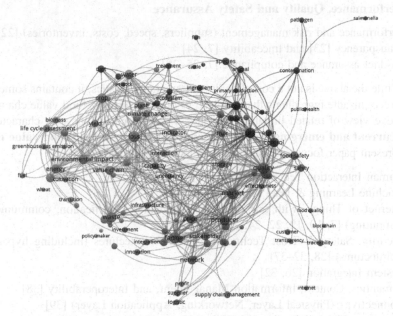

**Fig. 2.** Scopus visual analysis of food production and supply chain literature (Color figure online)

This reflects the somewhat different disciplines covered by the two databases, with Scopus covering more engineering and technology, compared to WoS. However, this is less significant compared to the observation that in none of the two cases can one identify any strong presence of digital enabling technologies. Both cases avoided explicitly including digitalisation terms in the search so as to explore whether such terms are already prevalent in the literature, rather than directing the search towards them. This indicates that relevant research still has to catch up with employing such technologies.

## 3 Characteristics of Resilient Customer Driven Food Chains

Successful and sustainable food value chains with strong customer orientation are expected to exhibit some key characteristics, which are largely considered to fall under the broad categories of (i) food ecosystem; and (ii) performance, encompassing:

### Food Ecosystem and Market Agility and Resilience

- Food ecosystem stakeholders integration [16, 17]
- Business models and innovation [5, 14–16, 18, 19]
- Sustainability [5, 20]
- Resilience/agility (logistics routing, suppliers, returns, last mile, local chain) [2, 3, 5, 19]
- Personalised customer experience, prosumers, and behavioural changes [21]

### Performance, Quality and Safety Assurance

- Performance and risk management (suppliers, speed, costs, inventories) [22]
- Transparency [23] and traceability [7, 24]
- Product assurance and compliance [7, 25–28]

While the above is not a complete list of key characteristics, it contains some of the most recognizable ingredients that can lead to high-performing food value chains. The birds-eye view of related literature indicates a clear need to link such characteristics with **current and emerging technology enablers for digitalized food value chains.** The present paper focuses on several such technology enablers:

- Human Interaction Technologies [6, 10, 13]
- Machine Learning & Data Analytics [7, 29]
- Internet of Things (with one or more of sensing, identification, communication, computing) [7, 10, 12, 22, 24, 28, 30–32]
- Security, Safety & Trust Technologies and Architectures (including hyperledger architectures) [28, 32–37]
- System Integration [26, 32]
- Semantics, Context, Information Management, and Interoperability [38]
- Connectivity (Physical Layer, Networking, Application Layer) [39]
- Augmented/Virtual Reality (AR/VR) [13]
- Simulation [40, 41]
- Cloud – based platforms [42]
- Automation and Robotics [10]
- Advanced/smart materials and packaging (includes embedded/printed electronics) [13, 27, 43, 44]

All the above are typically associated with Industry 4.0. The last one can be considered as part of automation and robotics, but is listed separately to indicate the critical role it has within internal and external logistics, and retailing. Table 1 maps the extent to which the above technologies contribute to delivering the key characteristics. Food ecosystem integration heavily depends on overall system integration, interoperability and cross-layer connectivity and requires cloud-based platforms. Security and trust technologies are of paramount importance, while automation and robotics are key operational technologies that enable production and logistics workflows. Ensuring customer engagement is complex and relies to a significant extent on involving nearly all listed technology enablers, starting from human interaction ones. Performance and risk management, as well as resilience and agility requires the inclusion of higher added value enablers, such as AI, IoT, simulation, and advanced packaging, on top of others.

**Table 1.** Mapping between technology enablers and food chain characteristics

| | Ecosystem/stakeholders integration | Personalised customer experience & engagement | Performance and risk management (suppliers, speed, costs, inventories) | Business models | Sustainability | Resilience and agility: logistics, routing, suppliers, returns, last mile | Transparency and traceability | Product assurance and compliance |
|---|---|---|---|---|---|---|---|---|
| Human interaction technologies | X | XXX | | | X | X | XX | |
| Machine learning-AI analytics | | XXX | XXX | X | X | XX | XX | X |
| Internet of Things (With one or more of sensing, identification, communication, computing) | XX | XXX | XXX | XX | XXX | XXX | XXX | XXX |
| Security &trust technologies and architectures | XXX | XXX | XX | XXX | X | XX | XXX | XXX |
| System integration | XXX | XX | XXX | XXX | XXX | XXX | XX | x |
| Connectivity | | | | | | | | |
| Physical layer | XX | XX | XX | X | XX | XXX | XXX | XXX |
| Networking | XXX | XXX | XXX | XX | XXX | XXX | XXX | XXX |
| Application layer | XXX | XXX | XX | XXX | XX | XXX | XX | XX |
| Interoperability, including semantics and context information management | XXX | XXX | X | X | XX | X | X | XX |
| AR/VR | X | XXX | X | X | XX | X | X | XX |
| Simulation | XXX | XX | XXX | XX | XXX | XXX | XXX | XX |
| Cloud-based platforms | XXX | XXX | XXX | XXX | X | XXX | XXX | x |
| Automation and robotics | | XX | XXX | XXX | X | XXX | XXX | x |
| Advanced/smart materials and packaging (includes embedded/printed electronics) | X | XX | XXX | XXX | XXX | XXX | XXX | XXX |

Business models are enabled by application layer connectivity, integration, cloud platforms for stakeholders integration, as well by automation technologies and smart packaging. Simulation is key for sustainability regarding the design perspective, while operational delivery requires integration, connectivity, and advanced packing to inform consumer behaviour. IoT is key for transparency, traceability, and product assurance, together with security & trust, connectivity, and cloud platforms, integrating also automation technologies and smart packaging for transparent and efficient workflows. Nonetheless, the mapping, currently based on literature and own judgement, requires a more systematic analysis and this needs to include also consumer behavioural studies.

## 4  Conclusion

Food value chains are increasingly driven by changing individual customer demands and are required to respond to highly disruptive market changes. Facing such challenges, food production ecosystems are undergoing digital transformation. Although relevant literature is rich with respect to the emerging characteristics of future resilient food value chains, as well as regarding the use of digitalisation enablers, the contribution of such enablers towards consumer oriented or driven food value chains and their agile and resilient characteristics is less well established. Customer – driven products specifically depend on more complex food value chains, compared to conventional supply models and their dependence on efficient end-to-end digitization is evident. This paper analysed current literature in this area and proposed a mapping between relevant technology enablers that support such digital transformation. While the mapping takes into account current literature together with own judgement to produce a rated mapping of technology enablers contribution, more systematic research, which includes empirical findings is needed to establish its validity and indeed apply appropriate adjustments and extensions. Such a mapping is a valuable tool towards devising a model for prioritising digitization interventions for food value supply chains.

## References

1. Dreyer, H.C., Strandhagen, J.O., Hvolby, H.H., Romsdal, A., Alfnes, E.: Supply chain strategies for speciality foods: a Norwegian case study. Prod. Plan. Control. **27**, 878–893 (2016). https://doi.org/10.1080/09537287.2016.1156779
2. Stone, J., Rahimifard, S.: Resilience in agri-food supply chains: a critical analysis of the literature and synthesis of a novel framework. Supply Chain Manag. **23**, 207–238 (2018). https://doi.org/10.1108/SCM-06-2017-0201
3. Ali, I., Nagalingam, S., Gurd, B.: A resilience model for cold chain logistics of perishable products. Int. J. Logist. Manag. **29**, 922–941 (2018). https://doi.org/10.1108/IJLM-06-2017-0147
4. Rotz, S., Fraser, E.D.G.: Resilience and the industrial food system: analyzing the impacts of agricultural industrialization on food system vulnerability. J. Environ. Stud. Sci. **5**(3), 459–473 (2015). https://doi.org/10.1007/s13412-015-0277-1

5. Todorovic, V., Maslaric, M., Bojic, S., Jokic, M., Mircetic, D., Nikolicic, S.: Solutions for more sustainable distribution in the short food supply chains. Sustainability **10**(10), 3481 (2018). https://doi.org/10.3390/su10103481
6. Giannikas, V., McFarlane, D., Strachan, J.: Towards the deployment of customer orientation: a case study in third-party logistics. Comput. Ind. **104**, 75–87 (2019). https://doi.org/10.1016/j.compind.2018.10.005
7. Alfian, G., et al.: Improving efficiency of RFID-based traceability system for perishable food by utilizing IoT sensors and machine learning model. Food Control **110**, 107016 (2019). https://doi.org/10.1016/j.foodcont.2019.107016
8. Badia-Melis, R., Mishra, P., Ruiz-García, L.: Food traceability: new trends and recent advances. Rev. Food Control. **57**, 393–401 (2015). https://doi.org/10.1016/j.foodcont.2015.05.005
9. Astill, J., et al.: Transparency in food supply chains: a review of enabling technology solutions. Trends Food Sci. Technol. **91**, 240–247 (2019). https://doi.org/10.1016/j.tifs.2019.07.024
10. Miranda, J., Ponce, P., Molina, A., Wright, P.: Sensing, smart and sustainable technologies for agri-food 4.0. Comput. Ind. **108**, 21–36 (2019). https://doi.org/10.1016/j.compind.2019.02.002
11. Büyüközkan, G., Göçer, F.: Digital supply chain: literature review and a proposed framework for future research. Comput. Ind. **97**, 157–177 (2018). https://doi.org/10.1016/j.compind.2018.02.010
12. Lezoche, M., et al.: Agri-food 4.0: a survey of the supply chains and technologies for the future agriculture. Comput. Ind. **117**, 103187 (2020). https://doi.org/10.1016/j.compind.2020.103187
13. Vanderroost, M., Ragaert, P., Verwaeren, J., De Meulenaer, B., De Baets, B., Devlieghere, F.: The digitization of a food package's life cycle: existing and emerging computer systems in the logistics and post-logistics phase. Comput. Ind. **87**, 15–30 (2017). https://doi.org/10.1016/j.compind.2017.01.004
14. Spendrup, S., Fernqvist, F.: Innovation in agri-food systems – a systematic mapping of the literature. Int. J. Food Syst. Dyn. **10**, 402–427 (2019). https://doi.org/10.18461/ijfsd.v10i5.28
15. Nosratabadi, S., Mosavi, A., Lakner, Z.: Food supply chain and business model innovation. Foods **9**(2), 132 (2020)
16. Stancová, K.C., Cavicchi, A.: Smart specialisation and the agri-food system: a European perspective (2018). https://doi.org/10.1007/978-3-319-91500-5
17. Zondag, M.M., Mueller, E.F., Ferrin, B.G.: The application of value nets in food supply chains: a multiple case study. Scand. J. Manag. **33**, 199–212 (2017). https://doi.org/10.1016/j.scaman.2017.10.002
18. Utami, H.N., Alamanos, E., Kuznesof, S.: Co-creation benefits by re-configuring the value network in creative agri-food transformation through the SMEs e-commerce channel: a business market perspective, vol. 98, pp. 63–68 (2019). https://doi.org/10.2991/icot-19.2019.14
19. Nakandala, D., Lau, H.C.W.: Innovative adoption of hybrid supply chain strategies in urban local fresh food supply chain. Supply Chain Manag. **24**, 241–255 (2019). https://doi.org/10.1108/SCM-09-2017-0287
20. Herrmann, C., Schmidt, C., Kurle, D., Blume, S., Thiede, S.: Sustainability in manufacturing and factories of the future. Int. J. Precis. Eng. Manufact.-Green Technol. **1**(4), 283–292 (2014). https://doi.org/10.1007/s40684-014-0034-z

21. Kumar, A., Singh, R.K., Modgil, S.: Exploring the relationship between ICT, SCM practices and organizational performance in agri-food supply chain. Benchmarking **27**, 1003–1041 (2020). https://doi.org/10.1108/BIJ-11-2019-0500

22. Tsang, Y.P., Choy, K.L., Wu, C.H., Ho, G.T.S., Lam, C.H.Y., Koo, P.S.: An internet of things (IoT)-based risk monitoring system for managing cold supply chain risks. Ind. Manag. Data Syst. **118**, 1432–1462 (2018). https://doi.org/10.1108/IMDS-09-2017-0384

23. Hsiao, H.I., Huang, K.L.: Time-temperature transparency in the cold chain. Food Control **64**, 181–188 (2016). https://doi.org/10.1016/j.foodcont.2015.12.020

24. Liu, K.: Research on the food safety supply chain traceability management system base on the internet of things. Int. J. Hybrid Inf. Technol. **8**(6), 25–34 (2015). https://doi.org/10.14257/ijhit.2015.8.6.03

25. Aung, M.M., Chang, Y.S.: Traceability in a food supply chain: Safety and quality perspectives. Food Control **39**, 172–184 (2014). https://doi.org/10.1016/j.foodcont.2013.11.007

26. Shih, C.W., Wang, C.H.: Integrating wireless sensor networks with statistical quality control to develop a cold chain system in food industries. Comput. Stand. Interfaces **45**, 62–78 (2016). https://doi.org/10.1016/j.csi.2015.12.004

27. Fang, Z., Zhao, Y., Warner, R.D., Johnson, S.K.: Active and intelligent packaging in meat industry. Trends Food Sci. Technol. **61**, 60–71 (2017). https://doi.org/10.1016/j.tifs.2017.01.002

28. Bouzembrak, Y., Klüche, M., Gavai, A., Marvin, H.J.P.: Internet of things in food safety: literature review and a bibliometric analysis. Trends Food Sci. Technol. **94**, 54–64 (2019). https://doi.org/10.1016/j.tifs.2019.11.002

29. Elijah, O., Rahman, T.A., Orikumhi, I., Leow, C.Y., Hindia, M.N.: An overview of internet of things (IoT) and data analytics in agriculture: benefits and challenges. IEEE Internet Things J. **5**, 3758–3773 (2018). https://doi.org/10.1109/JIOT.2018.2844296

30. Gialelis, J., Theodorou, G., Paparizos, C.: A low-cost internet of things (IoT) node to support traceability: logistics use case. In: ACM International Conference Proceeding Series, pp. 72–77 (2019). https://doi.org/10.1145/3342428.3342661

31. O'Sullivan, M.G.: A Handbook for Sensory and Consumer-Driven New Product Development: Innovative Technologies for the Food and Beverage Industry. Woodhead Publishing (2017)

32. Verdouw, C.N., Robbemond, R.M., Verwaart, T., Wolfert, J., Beulens, A.J.M.: A reference architecture for IoT-based logistic information systems in agri-food supply chains. Enterp. Inf. Syst. **12**, 755–779 (2018). https://doi.org/10.1080/17517575.2015.1072643

33. Mc Carthy, U., Uysal, I., Badia-Melis, R., Mercier, S., O'Donnell, C., Ktenioudaki, A.: Global food security – issues, challenges and technological solutions. Trends Food Sci. Technol. **77**, 11–20 (2018). https://doi.org/10.1016/j.tifs.2018.05.002

34. Doinea, M., Boja, C., Batagan, L., Toma, C., Popa, M.: Internet of things based systems for food safety management. Inform. Econ. **19**(1), 87–97 (2015). https://doi.org/10.12948/issn14531305/19.1.2015.08

35. Mondal, S., Wijewardena, K.P., Karuppuswami, S., Kriti, N., Kumar, D., Chahal, P.: Blockchain inspired RFID-based information architecture for food supply chain. IEEE Internet Things J. **6**, 5803–5813 (2019). https://doi.org/10.1109/JIOT.2019.2907658

36. Leng, K., Bi, Y., Jing, L., Fu, H.C., Van Nieuwenhuyse, I.: Research on agricultural supply chain system with double chain architecture based on blockchain technology. Futur. Gener. Comput. Syst. **86**, 641–649 (2018). https://doi.org/10.1016/j.future.2018.04.061

37. Caro, M.P., Ali, M.S., Vecchio, M., Giaffreda, R.: Blockchain-based traceability in agri-food supply chain management: a practical implementation. In: 2018 IoT Vert. Top. Summit Agric. - Tuscany, IOT Tuscany 2018, pp. 1–4 (2018). https://doi.org/10.1109/IOT-TUSCANY.2018.8373021
38. Geerts, G.L., O'Leary, D.E.: A supply chain of things: the EAGLET ontology for highly visible supply chains. Decis. Support Syst. **63**, 3–22 (2014). https://doi.org/10.1016/j.dss.2013.09.007
39. Villa-Henriksen, A., Edwards, G.T.C., Pesonen, L.A., Green, O., Sørensen, C.A.G.: Internet of things in arable farming: implementation, applications, challenges and potential. Biosyst. Eng. **191**, 60–84 (2020). https://doi.org/10.1016/j.biosystemseng.2019.12.013
40. Raba, D., Juan, A.A., Panadero, J., Bayliss, C., Estrada-Moreno, A.: Combining the internet of things with simulation-based optimization to enhance logistics in an agri-food supply chain. In: Proceedings of the Winter Simulation Conference 2019-Decem, pp. 1894–1905 (2019). https://doi.org/10.1109/WSC40007.2019.9004952
41. Verboven, P., Defraeye, T., Datta, A.K., Nicolai, B.: Digital twins of food process operations: the next step for food process models? Curr. Opin. Food Sci. (2020). https://doi.org/10.1016/j.cofs.2020.03.002
42. Verdouw, C.N., Wolfert, J., Beulens, A.J.M., Rialland, A.: Virtualization of food supply chains with the internet of things. J. Food Eng. **176**, 128–136 (2016). https://doi.org/10.1016/j.jfoodeng.2015.11.009
43. Ghaani, M., Cozzolino, C.A., Castelli, G., Farris, S.: An overview of the intelligent packaging technologies in the food sector. Trends Food Sci. Technol. **51**, 1–11 (2016). https://doi.org/10.1016/j.tifs.2016.02.008
44. Majid, I., Ahmad Nayik, G., Mohammad Dar, S., Nanda, V.: Novel food packaging technologies: innovations and future prospective. J. Saudi Soc. Agric. Sci. **17**, 454–462 (2018). https://doi.org/10.1016/j.jssas.2016.11.003

# Gastronomic Service System Design

# Human–Robot Hybrid Service System Introduction for Enhancing Labor and Robot Productivity

Takeshi Shimmura[1,2(✉)], Ryosuke Ichikari[2], and Takashi Okuma[2]

[1] College of Gastronomic Management, Ritsumeikan University,
1-1-1, Noji-Higashi, Kusatsu, Shiga, Japan
t-shinmura@gankofood.co.jp
[2] National Institute of Advanced Industrial Science and Technology, Kashiwa
II Campus, University of Tokyo, 6-2-3, Kashiwanoha, Kashiwa, Chiba, Japan

**Abstract.** This study introduces service robots to improve restaurant industry labor productivity because restaurant productivity is the lowest among service industries. Furthermore, this study represents an attempt to improve robot productivity because low robot productivity is the main hindrance to robot introduction into service industries. Service robot systems developed based on AGV robot systems were incorporated into operations of an actual restaurant. Staff operations changed. The AGV replaced conveyance operations to reduce staff work loads. Moreover, the AGV systems are refined to increase AGV work loads: the number of AGV battery chargers was increased to avoid electric battery power shortages, AGV boards were changed from fixed type to removable type. Moving patterns increased from 1 to 4 to adopt AGV operation for restaurant operation situation changes. Results indicate that the system redesign improves labor productivity. It reduces working time and increases service quality. Furthermore, the AGV system refinement enhances robot productivity: in fact, the total AGV daily moving distance was doubled.

**Keywords:** Productivity · Restaurant · Service engineering · Service robot

## 1 Introduction

Generally speaking, service industry productivity is low, even though service industries represent key industries, accounting for around 75% of Japanese GDP. "The growth of service economy" trend is not only true for Japan, but also for all industrialized countries such as the US, the UK, France, and Germany. Enhancing service industry productivity is an important strategy for these countries and service companies worldwide. Moreover, restaurant industry productivity is the lowest among service industries. The cause of low productivity is so-called "labor intensive" production systems. The industry must evolve a human-based production system to achieve a productivity breakthrough.

In the 1950s, the US restaurant industry introduced chain store operation systems to enhance industry productivity [1]. Chain store operation systems have adopted central kitchens, similar to food factories, to reduce the total number of cooking staff at

© IFIP International Federation for Information Processing 2020
Published by Springer Nature Switzerland AG 2020
B. Lalic et al. (Eds.): APMS 2020, IFIP AICT 592, pp. 661–669, 2020.
https://doi.org/10.1007/978-3-030-57997-5_76

restaurants. Furthermore, systems have introduced multi-restaurant strategies to realize volume economies. The restaurant industry has even reduced ingredient costs through bulk buying. The system simplifies menu and service operations to reduce staff skill dependence. A simplification strategy is intended to reduce average labor costs. In the 1970s, the Japanese restaurant industry introduced operation systems. Consequently, the industry has become a key industry in Japan.

In the 1980s, the restaurant industry introduced point of sales (POS) systems to improve restaurant operations [2]. Before POS introduction, restaurants recorded order information using paper checks: when a service staff member receives an order, the staff member writes it down on the order sheet, walks from dining room to the kitchen, and hands it to the cooking staff. Several minutes are necessary for order information transmission. Furthermore, a paper is sometimes lost. In such cases, service staff members must stroll around the restaurant to find the customer who ordered a certain dish. By contrast, POS systems automatically transmit order information via a wireless communication network. For that reason, service staff need not enter the kitchen. Also, POS systems record the order information in a POS terminal. A sheet can be reprinted if a service staff member loses it [3].

In the 1990s, the restaurant industry introduced new cooking equipment to realize cooking automation. For instance, the industry introduced convection ovens for automated steaming, baking, and boiling [4]. Also, the industry combines plural cooking equipment and machines to realize automation-based kitchen systems. A typical example is so-called "Kaiten sushi" (conveyer sushi). The purpose of machine introduction and kitchen systems is maximization of production capacity and reduction of the total number of cooking staff [5]. In addition, the industry has launched some studies for kitchen operation system enhancement. For instance, the cooking capacity of individual cooking machines is measured and compared with the volume of customer orders of individual cooking machines to find a bottleneck. Based on that comparison, the number of cooking machines or menu varieties might be redesigned to optimize supply (cooking capacity) and demand (customer order) [6]. In addition, a new cooking system, a line and cell production combination system, is introduced into an actual restaurant to improve productivity. The results of the study indicate it as useful for productivity enhancement [7].

Early in this century, AI and simulation technologies were developed for use in industry. For instance, kitchen simulation systems were developed based on a factory simulation system, and were introduced for actual restaurant redesign [8]. In addition, simulation systems for central kitchens were introduced into restaurants [9].

Although conventional studies continuously resolve low-productivity problems, some difficulties remain. The first difficulty is how to overcome "service product characteristics [10]. Actually services have special characteristics. By and large they are intangible, indicating their fundamental Intangibility. Therefore, services can not be stocked. They are therefore known for their Perishability. Consequently, service products should be produced simultaneously with a customer order. Services therefore have Simultaneity. For instance, service staff should take order at the same time a customer order it, and they should serve dishes at the same time chef finish the order cooking. If conveyance operation are replaced from human to robot, productivity of service staff will be enhanced. A second problem is that production systems evolve.

Conventional studies and methods mainly address individual production modes such as humans, machines, or IoT. For instance, convection oven machine is stand-alone system for simmered food; it is not much more than tool for cooking staff. Point-of-sales system is order information and account control system for restaurant; staff and the system do not make cooperation. Restaurant service systems should combined all three factors synergistically, as human, machine, and IoT hybrid systems. As society 5.0 proposes, service industries should mix these technologies and combine them with human-based service systems [11]. A third problem is robot productivity itself. At present, service robot productivity is markedly low, compared to that of factory robots. The reason is simple: actual service sites are not accommodative of robots. For instance, service staff members have only insufficient experience operating robots, controlling robots. Service staff stop using robot and work themselves if restaurant become busy, because it is quicker and robot operation is messy. In addition, service robot operation speed is kept low to avoid accidental contact between humans and robots. Different from factory robots, service robots, and staff work together. Therefore, robot speed should be controlled slow. To enhance service productivity, robot productivity must be enhanced along with labor productivity.

This study developed a human–robot hybrid service system for restaurants and introduced it into an actual Japanese cuisine restaurant store to enhance labor productivity and robot productivity.

## 2  Human–Robot Hybrid Service System for Restaurant

### 2.1  System Structure

Traditionally, traditional restaurants are operated by skillful staff because human-based service systems provide core value for customers. Kitchen staff cook dishes, the catering staff check food quality, add garnish, and top sauces. Subsequently, the conveyance staff move the dishes from the kitchen to a dining room before service staff members serve it to customers. Catering staff support the conveyance staff in resolving delays because long waiting times lead to customer dissatisfaction if a dish can not be moved from the kitchen to a dining room because of high workloads.

Restaurant value for customers is fundamentally created by kitchen staff members because the purpose of dining out is to be entertained with fine foods. Furthermore, customers are entertained by in-floor service because customers enjoy interaction with service staff members, as well as eating foods. However, conveyance operations are also important for restaurant operations because they are indispensable processes with cooking and service. Nevertheless, the process does not create value for customers. Consequently, conveyance processes can replace humans with robots.

Figure 1 presents the hybrid service system structure for the restaurant industry. Cooking and service processes are done by humans. Conveyance processes are operated by service robots. The service robot system comprises four automated guided vehicles (AGV), 1 AGV control server, an AGV operation program, 50 RFID devices for operation control transmissions, 9 tablets for AGV operation by staff members, 1 non-contact battery charger, 2 contact battery chargers, and a magnet guide line.

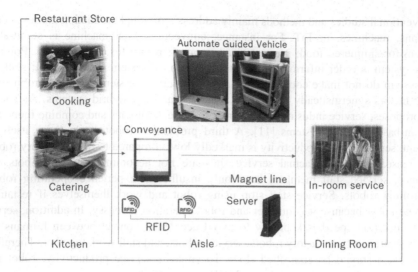

**Fig. 1.** System structures.

## 2.2    System Introduction

The robot system was introduced for use in a Japanese traditional cuisine restaurant (1,648.2 m², 441 sheets, and 1 kitchen). Before system introduction, robot operation training was conducted for restaurant staff. Thereafter, staff members had some discussions about "how to change the restaurant operation." The restaurant then undertook service robot system introduction. Service operations were changed based on the system hypothesis. The cooking staff cooks dishes. Then the dishes are loaded on AGV by catering staff. The staff destination of the AGV is designated by referring to the order information. The AGV automatically moves from the kitchen to the dining site. A service staff picks up the delivery and takes it to the customer.

Service staff members sometimes discuss operation improvements intended for enhancing labor productivity. Each staff member changes work scheduling. A conveyance staff shifts from conveyance operations to in-room service operations so that service staff can concentrate on dish serving and conversations with customers. In addition, catering staff members shift from conveyance to cooking for enhancing dish quality and reducing lead times. Based on operation changes, the store manager changes the shift roster to reduce the restaurant store working times.

Sales per work hour are measured as a KIP for enhancing labor productivity. Daily sales are calculated by the POS system. Actually, the system records individual orders. From them, it calculates daily sales by summing up unit prices. Daily work hours are measured by an attendant management system. When a staff member starts working, the staff member inputs the employee ID and pushes a "start working" button. Then the system records the clock time. When the staff member finishes working, the system records the clock time when the "finish working" button is pushed. Sales per work hour are calculated as the sales revenues divided by work hours. The measurement is conducted for 9 weeks from 2 months after AGV system introduction because the operation efficiency worsens immediately after the system introduction. Typically, staff members are not accustomed to using system operations. Sales per work hour are compared to those of the same week the prior year because sales differ from season to season.

At two months after the system introduction, the store manager, head chef, service manager, system designer, and store designer hold meetings to improve AGV productivity. Based on their discussions, the system was actually redesigned several times. First, the AGV base board was redesigned from a fixed type to a retractable type because dishes put on an AGV and stopped in an area lead to AGV immobility. It can not be moved because the dishes should be served to the nearby customer. Staff members need only retract the board to operate an AGV if an AGV base board is retractable. Second, contactless battery chargers were increased from 1 to 2. Also, the contact chargers were increased from 2 to 4 to avoid shortcomings caused by weak batteries. Different from factory robots, service robots are operated without a power supply cable. Therefore, they sometimes stop if a battery is low. Battery charge methods and timing are important factors for AGV operation. Furthermore, basic operation patterns were changed from 1 to 4 because operation situations differ from time to time: open preparation times, rush times (lunch/dinner), setup times (idle time), and closure operations.

One year after AGV introduction, the average AGV running distance per day per customer was compared as a KPI for robot productivity, because if AGV convey many foods, its moving distance gets long. The daily individual AGV running distance was recorded by an AGV server. The average running distance was calculated as the daily total running distance divided into the working AGV number. In addition, the total numbers of customers the respective days were recorded by the POS system and were downloaded from the POS server. The average AGV running distance was compared with the same week during the prior year because sales differ from season to season.

## 3  Results and Discussion

### 3.1  Results

Average daily sales of conventional service ecosystem (prior year) were 2,237,302 yen (SD = 559,053). Daily service staff work hours were 292.2 h (SD = 32.4 h). Average sales per work hour were 8,000 yen. The coefficient of correlation was 0.74. Average daily sales of the redesigned service ecosystem (prior year) was 2,416,935 yen (SD = 682,249). Daily service staff work hours were 270.6 h (SD = 33.7 h). Therefore, the average sales per work hour were 8,932 yen. The coefficient of correlation was 0.87. Figure 2 (left) presents work hours and sales point diagrams for the prior year. Figure 2 (right) shows those of the present year. Assuming equal variance with one-sample $t$ tests, we found a significant difference in the means ($t(63) = 5.382, p < 0.05$)

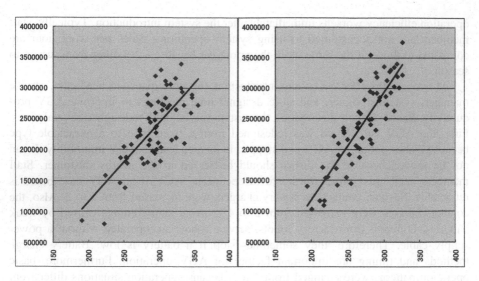

**Fig. 2.** Work hours and daily sales point diagram: horizontal axis, work hour (hour); vertical line, daily sales (1,000 Yen).

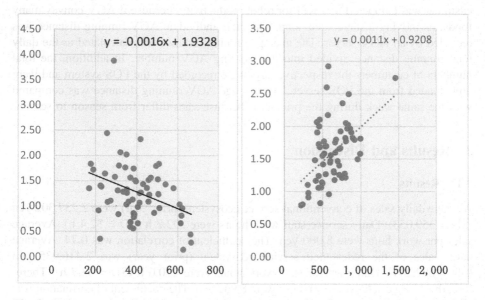

**Fig. 3.** Robot moving distance and a number customer point diagram: horizontal axis, daily customers (person); vertical line, AGV moving distance per customer (meter).

The average moving distance per customer of the first year was 1.27 m (SD = 0.58 m). The average total distance of 1 AGV was 511 m. The coefficient of correlation was 0.12. Also, the average moving distance per customer of the second year was 1.60 m (SD = 0.47 m). The average total distance of an AGV was 1,012 m. The coefficient of correlation was 0.24. Assuming equal variance with one-sample $t$ tests, we found a significant difference in the means ($t(124) = 3.434$, $p < 0.01$).

## 3.2  Discussion

First, labor productivity improvement can be discussed based on sales per work hour. The main purpose of AGV system introduction was to replace conveyance operations conducted by humans with work done by AGV robots. Mainly, AGV systems take over the tasks of conveyance staff members. Thereby, conveyance staff members reduce their workload. In addition, catering staff reduce the frequency for conveyance because they need only to put dishes on the AGV. Therefore, they need not convey them by themselves. Based on the operation changes, the store manager reduces the total daily working time. Results show that work hours of the restaurant are reduced compared to those before AGV introduction. Results demonstrated that AGV introduction did not reduce service quality because daily sales were not reduced by AGV introduction. Instead, daily sales increased from 2,237 K to 2,416 K yen. Therefore, the system might enhance service quality. As explained earlier, the conveyance staff shifted their tasks from conveyance to in-room service support. Therefore, service staff can concentrate on customer service. Also, service staff need not pick up dishes at the kitchen because the AGV automatically convey them. Service staff get good feedback about service quality from customer. Catering staff shifted their tasks from conveyance to cooking. Therefore, dish quality improved because the total work hours at the kitchen were increased. Cooking staff evaluate food layout is improved by catering staff rework. Productivity comprises two factors: reduced labor input and increased added value. The restaurant system redesign realized both.

Secondly, robot productivity improvement is discussed based on results data. As results indicate, the AGV moving distance per customer increased 126.0% (1.27 m → 1.60 m); the daily total AGV moving distance increased 198.0% (511 m → 1,012 m). Results show that AGVs saved some time. That time is represented by increased AGV moving distance. Also, staff abilities for AGV operation improved because they became accustomed with AGV operations. Their efforts increased the AGV workload. They used AGVs because they have sufficient leeway for AGV operations if the restaurant is idle. However, if the restaurant is busy, they have insufficient leeway. Then they conveyed dishes by themselves because they became accustomed to it. As Fig. 3 (left) shows, the AGV moving distance increased when the restaurant was idle, but it decreased as the restaurant become busy (approximate line have a negative slope in proportion as sales increase). However, proficiency for AGV operations changes the situation. They use AGVs continuously for conveyance if the restaurant is idle. They use AGV systems for conveyance because they have sufficient leeway for AGV operation if the restaurant becomes busy. As a result, the average AGV moving distance for one customer increases if the restaurant becomes busy (Fig. 3 (right)).

## 4  Conclusions

For this study, service robot system is introduced in an actual Japanese cuisine restaurant to enhance productivity. Staff members changed their operations. Conveyance staff replaced human operations with those of AGV robots. Catering staff also replace the operation to reduce workloads. In addition, the conveyance staff supports the in-room service staff to improve service quality. Catering staff support cooking staff to enhance food quality. Based on operation changes, the store manager reduced the total working time. In addition, the AGV system was refined. The number of AGV battery chargers was increased to avoid electric battery power shortages. Also, the AGV board was changed from a fixed type to a removable type. The moving patterns were increased from 1 to 4 to adapt AGV operations to changes in the restaurant operation situation. Results indicate that the system redesign improved labor productivity: it reduced working time and also increased service quality. The AGV system refinement definitely enhanced robot productivity: the total AGV daily moving distance was doubled.

**Acknowledgments.** This work was supported by JST-OPERA Program Grant Number JPMJOP1612.

## References

1. Chase, R.B., Apte, U.M.: A history of research in service operations: what's the big idea? J. Oper. Manag. **25**(2), 375–386 (2007)
2. Stein, K.: Point-of-sales systems for foodservice. J. Am. Diet. Assoc. **105**(12), 1861–1863 (2005)
3. Shimmura, T., Takenaka, T., Akamatsu, M.: Improvement of restaurant operation by sharing order and customer information. Int. J. Organ. Collecting Intell. **1**(3), 54–70 (2010)
4. Danowsca-Oziewicz, M., Karpinsca-Tymoszczyk, M., Borowski, J.: The effect of cooking in a steam-convection oven on the quality of selected dishes. J. Food Serv. **18**(5), 187–197 (2007)
5. Ngai, E.W.T., Suk, F.F.C., Lo, S.Y.Y.: Development of an RFID-based sushi management system: the case of a conveyorbelt sushi restaurant. Int. J. Prod. Econ. **112**(2), 630–645 (2008)
6. Sill, B.: Operations engineering: improving multiunit operations. Cornell Hoteland Restaurant Adm. Q. **35**(3), 64–71 (1994)
7. Shimmura, T., Takenaka, T., Ohura, S.: Improving productivity and labor elasticity at multiproduct Japanese cuisine restaurant introducing cell production system. In: Proceeding of International Conference Advances in Production Management Systems, pp. 11–17, Pennsylvania, September 2013
8. Shimamura, T., et al.: Using a cooking operation simulator to improve cooking speed in a multiproduct Japanese cuisine restaurant. In: Grabot, B., Vallespir, B., Gomes, S., Bouras, A., Kiritsis, D. (eds.) APMS 2014. IAICT, vol. 439, pp. 556–563. Springer, Heidelberg (2014). https://doi.org/10.1007/978-3-662-44736-9_67

9. Fujii, N., Kaihara, T., Uemura, M., Nonaka, T., Shimmura, T.: Facility layout planning of central kitchen in food service industry: application to the real-scale problem. In: Prabhu, V., Taisch, M., Kiritsis, D. (eds.) APMS 2013. IAICT, vol. 415, pp. 33–40. Springer, Heidelberg (2013). https://doi.org/10.1007/978-3-642-41263-9_5
10. Wölfl, A.: Productivity growth in service industries assessment of recent patterns and the role of measurement. OECD Science, Technology and Industry Working Papers (2003)
11. What is society 5.0. https://www8.cao.go.jp/cstp/english/society5_0/index.html

# Forecasting Customers Visiting Using Machine Learning and Characteristics Analysis with Low Forecasting Accuracy Days

Takashi Tanizaki[1]([✉]), Yuta Hanayama[1], and Takeshi Shimmura[2]

[1] Graduate School of Systems Engineering, Kindai University,
1 Takaya-Umenobe, Higashi-Hiroshima 739-2116, Japan
tanizaki@hiro.kindai.ac.jp
[2] Ritsumeikan University, 1-1-1 Nogi-Higashi, Kusatsu 525-8577, Japan

**Abstract.** In this paper, the number of customers visiting restaurants is forecasted using machine learning and statistical analysis. There are some researches on forecasting the number of customers visiting restaurants using past data on the number of visitors. In this research, in addition to the above data, external data such as weather data and events existing in ubiquitous was used for forecasting. Bayesian Linear Regression, Boosted Decision Tree Regression, Decision Forest Regression and Random Forest Regression are used for machine learning, Stepwise is used for statistical analysis. Among above five methods, the forecasting accuracy using Bayesian Linear Regression was the highest. The forecasting accuracy did not tend to improve even if the training data period was extended. Based on these forecasting results, the characteristics of days with low forecasting accuracy are analyzed. It was found that the human psychology around the payday and the reservation customers affected the number of visitors. On the other hand, the weather data such as temperature, precipitation and wind speed did not affect the accuracy.

**Keywords:** Forecasting customers visiting · Machine learning · Statistical analysis

## 1 Introduction

The service industry is an important industry that accounts for about 70% of Japan's GDP. It has a very high impact on the Japanese economy. However, its productivity is low compared to the manufacturing industry. In many countries, the productivity growth of the service industry is lower than that of the manufacturing industry. Among them, Japan has a big difference in productivity growth, and improving the productivity of the service industry is an important issue for the country. In order to solve such problems, it is important to change the method of business improvement in the service industry from "experience and intuition" to "engineering method". From the above background, we are researching the improvement of the productivity of the restaurant using the engineering method. The goal of our research is ways to improve store management by improving employee job arrangements and cocking material orders based on accurate forecasts of restaurant customer numbers. As the first step, we research a method for forecasting the number of customers visiting restaurants.

There are some research papers on forecasting the number of Customer Visiting using machine learning. In [1], a comprehensive literature review and classification of restaurant sales and consumer demand techniques are presented. In addition, the data used for the forecasting in the surveyed literature are also summarized. Multiple Regression, Autoregressive Integrated Moving Average, Artificial Neural Networks, Bayesian Network Model and other methods are used as the forecasting method. The paper reports that it is difficult for forecasters to choose the right technique for their unique situations. Data such as the past number of customers and sales, seasons, and days of the week are used for forecasting. In [2], it is proposed an approach to forecasting how many future visitors would go to a restaurant using big data and supervised learning. It is used for big data involving restaurant information, historical visits, and historical reservations in this method. In the past research, internal data, such as the past number of customers and reservations were used for forecasting, but external data were not used.

From the above, we are researching forecasting methods using internal data such as Point-of-Sales and external data in the ubiquitous environment such as weather, events, etc. in order to improve the accuracy of forecasting. In this paper, we analyze the relation between training data and forecasted results by machine learning and statistical analysis and discuss the characteristics with low forecasting accuracy days.

## 2 Forecasting Method

In this research, the number of customers visiting is forecasted using machine learning and statistical analysis with internal data and external data in the ubiquitous environment. Bayesian Linear Regression, Boosted Decision Tree Regression, Decision Forest Regression and Random Forest Regression are used for machine learning, Stepwise is used for statistical analysis. We used Azure Machine Learning and Python as a machine learning tool and SPSS as a statistical analysis tool.

(1) Bayesian Linear Regression

Bayesian Linear Regression (Bayesian) is a method of applying Bayesian network to machine learning. Bayesian network is a probabilistic model in which conditional dependencies among a plurality of random variables are represented by a graph structure and dependency relationships between the random variables are represented by conditional probabilities [3]. By using the Bayesian network, we can obtain probability distribution about unobserved variables when observing some variables, and treat the value with the highest probability value as the predicted value of that variable.

(2) Boosted Decision Tree Regression

Boosted Decision Tree Regression (Boosted) is a method machine learning using boosting. Boosting refers to a general and provably effective method of producing a very accurate forecasting rule by combining rough and moderately inaccurate rules of thumb [4]. In this method, as a result of learning using N learning machines, learning is focused on the case by increasing the weight of the incorrectly forecasted.

(3) Decision Forest Regression

Decision Forest Regression (Decision) is a method of machine learning using Random Forest [5]. Random Forest is an ensemble learning method that constructs a forest using multiple decision trees and performs majority decision on the result of learning for each decision tree. In order to prevent extreme bias in learning of each decision tree, learning data used in each decision tree is extracted with randomness. As a result, overfitting is prevented and high generalization performance is obtained.

(4) Random Forest Regression

There are two types of methods in the random forest: "classification" and "regression" [6]. The difference between the two methods is that "classification" is used if data can be divided into classes, and "regression" is used to forecast continuous data such as time series. In this research, we use Random Forest Regression (Random) because we forecast time series data.

(5) Stepwise

Stepwise is a method of constructing a regression model by searching for a combination of objective variables that can most explain the explanatory variable by sequentially increasing or decreasing the objective variable [7]. When adding highly objective variables to regression formulas, there are variables that have already been added, which become useless due to their relevance to objective variables added later. Therefore, each time an objective variable is added, the variable that becomes insignificant for the explanatory variable is deleted from the regression formula.

## 3    Forecasting the Number of Customers Visiting

Using the customers visiting data of four stores from restaurant chain A of the joint research, the number of customers visiting was forecasted. The number of customers visiting from '18/5/1 to '19/4/30 was forecasted using the customer visiting result from '14/5/1 to '18/4/30. The weather data used was the data from the Japan Meteorological Agency's observation station closest to the location of each restaurant.

We compared the forecasted results with customer visiting results during the same period. Table 1 shows explanatory variables used for forecasting. The forecasting ratio $\alpha$, that is ratio of the number of forecasted customers to that of actual customers, is calculated using the Eqs. (1) and (2).

$p_{i}$:    Actual number of customers visiting on $i$−th day
$e_{i}$:    Forecasted number of customers visiting on $i$−th day
$N$:    Forecasting period
$\alpha_{i}$:    Forecasting ratio on $i$−th day

**Table 1.** Explanatory variable

| Category | Explanatory variable | Definition | Category | Explanatory variable | Definition |
|---|---|---|---|---|---|
| Month | January | Jan/1-Jan/31 | Event | January 1st | January 1st |
| | February | Feb/1-Feb/28 | | January 2nd | January 2nd |
| | March | Mar/1-Mar/31 | | January 3rd | January 3rd |
| | April | Apr/1-Apr/30 | | Year-end | Dec/29-Dec/31 |
| | May | May/1-May/31 | | End of year party | Weekday of December |
| | June | Jun/1-Jun/30 | | Christmas eve | December 24 |
| | July | Jul/1-Jul/31 | | Coming-of-age day | Second Monday in January |
| | August | Aug/1-Aug/31 | | Setsubun | February 2nd |
| | September | Sep/1-Sep/30 | | Obon | Aug/13-Aug/15 |
| | October | Oct/1-Oct/31 | | New year's party | Weekday till the coming-of-age day except Jan/1-Jan/3 |
| | November | Nov/1-Nov/30 | | Farewell party | Weekday in March |
| | December | Dec/1-Dec/31 | | Welcome party | Weekday in April |
| The day of the week | Monday | Weekday and the next day is weekday | Weather | Average wind speed | Average wind speed per day (m/s) |
| | Tuesday | Weekday and the next day is weekday | | Maximum wind speed | Maximum wind speed per day (m/s) |
| | Wednesday | Weekday and the next day is weekday | | Highest temperature | Highest temperature in a day (℃) |
| | Thuesday | Weekday and the next day is weekday | | Lowest temperature | Lowest temperature in a day (℃) |
| | Fryday | Weekday and the next day is weekday | | Amount of precipitation | Amount of precipitation in a day (mm) |
| | Saturday | Even if the target day is a holiday it is Saturday. | | Maximum precipitation | Maximum amount of precipitation in ten minutes (mm) |
| | Sunday | Sunday and the next day is weekday | | Maximum instantaneous wind speed | Maximum instantaneous wind speed in a day (m/s) |
| | | Even if the target day is a holiday it is Sunday. | | | |
| | Sunday during holidays | Sunday and the next day is holiday | | | |
| | | Even if the target day is a holiday it is Sunday. | | | |
| | Holiday | Holiday and the nextday is weekday | | | |
| | Holiday during holidays | Holiday and the nextday is holiday | | | |
| | Before holiday | Weekday and the next day is holiday | | | |
| | Lastday during holidays | The last day of three or more consecutive holidays | | | |

$$\alpha_i = \sum_{i=1}^{N} \frac{p_i - |p_i - e_i|}{p_i} \tag{1}$$

$$\alpha = \frac{\sum_{i=1}^{N} \alpha_i}{N} \tag{2}$$

Table 2 shows the forecast results for four restaurants in Restaurant Chain A. The highest forecasting ratio for each restaurant and the training data period is marked in yellow. Bayesian had a high forecasting ratio for all four restaurants. Figure 1 shows a graph of actual numbers and forecasted numbers of customers visiting by Bayesian using learning data for two years at Restaurant Z, which has the highest forecasting ratio. There is a difference between the forecasted number and the actual number during the Bon holiday period in August and the welcome and farewell party period from the end of March to the beginning of April. Based on these forecasting results, we analyzed the characteristics of days with low forecasting accuracy.

**Table 2.** Forecast results

| Restaurant | Data period | Bayesian | Boosted | Decision | Random | Stepwise |
|---|---|---|---|---|---|---|
| W | Four years | 82.7 | 78.3 | 75.2 | 81.1 | 82.4 |
| | Three tears | 83.1 | 79.1 | 79.8 | 81.4 | 82.4 |
| | Two Years | 82.7 | 75.1 | 79.0 | 81.3 | 82.2 |
| | One Year | 81.8 | 73.4 | 79.6 | 77.5 | 81.4 |
| X | Four years | 77.0 | 72.4 | 73.6 | 70.6 | 77.6 |
| | Three tears | 75.9 | 74.7 | 74.1 | 72.4 | 76.0 |
| | Two Years | 76.8 | 70.2 | 71.7 | 75.0 | 76.6 |
| | One Year | 77.0 | 64.6 | 72.8 | 74.6 | 76.2 |
| Y | Four years | 77.2 | 77.4 | 74.8 | 73.8 | 73.2 |
| | Three tears | 73.5 | 73.7 | 75.9 | 72.2 | 71.1 |
| | Two Years | 76.3 | 73.3 | 75.0 | 72.2 | 75.4 |
| | One Year | 78.4 | 72.4 | 75.3 | 76.3 | 76.9 |
| Z | Four years | 81.7 | 81.6 | 82.2 | 82.8 | 81.4 |
| | Three tears | 82.9 | 81.6 | 82.5 | 83.1 | 82.9 |
| | Two Years | 83.8 | 80.0 | 82.8 | 82.6 | 83.8 |
| | One Year | 73.0 | 77.5 | 81.5 | 82.4 | 82.4 |

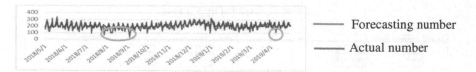

**Fig. 1.** Actual and forecasted numbers of customers visiting at Z (Bayesian, two years)

# 4    Analysis of Characteristics with Low Forecasting Accuracy Days

The characteristics with low forecasting accuracy days were analyzed by focusing on the difference between the actual and forecasted numbers of customers visiting, explanatory variables such as days of the week, weather, events, and the number of reservation customers. The method and the training data period that had the highest forecasting accuracy for each restaurant were selected and analyzed. We analyzed the forecasting results of Bayesian with three years training data for restaurant W, the forecasting results of Stepwise with for years training data for X, the forecasting results of Bayesian with one-year training data for Y, and the forecasting results of Bayesian with two years training data for Z.

## 4.1    Characteristics Analysis for Week and Day of Week

We analyzed week and day of week characteristics for the days when the forecasted numbers exceeded the error range calculated by Eqs. (3) to (6).

$q_{ij}$:    Forecasted number of customers visiting on $i$ − th day using method $j$. $J$ is the combination of method and training data period ($j = 1, 2, ..., 20$)

$y_j$:    The annual sum of the absolute value of the difference between forecasted number using method j and actual number

min($y_j$): Minimum value of $y_j$

$Y$:    Annual average of $min(y_j)$

$\bar{p}$ :    Annual average of actual values

$\beta$ :    Error ratio

$k_i$:    Error range on $i$-th day

$$y_j = \sum_{i=1}^{365} |p_i - q_{ij}| \tag{3}$$

$$Y = \frac{\min(y_j)}{365} \tag{4}$$

$$\beta_j = \frac{Y}{\bar{p}} \tag{5}$$

$$k_i = x_i \pm \beta\bar{p} \tag{6}$$

Table 3 shows the results. The cases that exceed more than half of the applicable annual days are marked in yellow. In restaurants W and X, there were many days outside the error range in the fourth and fifth weeks. In Japan, there are paydays in the fourth or fifth weeks. Therefore, it is considered that human psychology after salary income may affect the use of restaurants. However, in restaurants Y and Z, there is no tendency to be low for the forecasting accuracy of the fourth and fifth weeks. Therefore, the effect of human psychology after salary income is considered to be limited.

**Table 3.** Results of characteristics analysis for week and day of week

| Restaurant | Week | Mon | Tue | Wed | Thu | Fri | Sat | Sun | Total |
|---|---|---|---|---|---|---|---|---|---|
| W | 1st | 4(33%) | 7(58%) | 5(42%) | 5(42%) | 5(42%) | 5(42%) | 5(42%) | 36 |
| | 2nd | 5(42%) | 2(17%) | 4(33%) | 4(33%) | 5(42%) | 4(33%) | 2(17%) | 26 |
| | 3rd | 1(8%) | 8(67%) | 4(33%) | 6(50%) | 5(42%) | 6(50%) | 6(50%) | 36 |
| | 4th & 5th | 8(50%) | 10(63%) | 10(50%) | 7(44%) | 9(56%) | 8(50%) | 6(38%) | 58 |
| | Total | 18 | 27 | 23 | 22 | 24 | 23 | 19 | 156 |
| X | 1st | 4(33%) | 5(42%) | 9(75%) | 6(50%) | 6(50%) | 4(33%) | 6(50%) | 40 |
| | 2nd | 7(58%) | 5(42%) | 6(50%) | 4(33%) | 5(42%) | 5(42%) | 4(33%) | 36 |
| | 3rd | 3(25%) | 7(58%) | 2(17%) | 2(17%) | 3(25%) | 5(42%) | 2(17%) | 24 |
| | 4th & 5th | 5(31%) | 5(31%) | 9(56%) | 9(56%) | 8(50%) | 6(38%) | 8(50%) | 50 |
| | Total | 19 | 22 | 26 | 21 | 22 | 20 | 20 | 150 |
| Y | 1st | 2(17%) | 3(25%) | 8(67%) | 8(67%) | 1(8%) | 4(33%) | 5(42%) | 31 |
| | 2nd | 4(33%) | 4(33%) | 3(25%) | 6(50%) | 6(50%) | 5(42%) | 5(42%) | 33 |
| | 3rd | 2(17%) | 7(58%) | 6(50%) | 5(42%) | 5(42%) | 4(33%) | 5(42%) | 34 |
| | 4th & 5th | 7(44%) | 7(41%) | 5(31%) | 6(38%) | 7(44%) | 10(63%) | 6(38%) | 48 |
| | Total | 15 | 21 | 22 | 25 | 19 | 23 | 21 | 146 |
| Z | 1st | 6(50%) | 6(50%) | 4(33%) | 7(58%) | 8(67%) | 6(50%) | 8(67%) | 45 |
| | 2nd | 4(33%) | 7(58%) | 5(42%) | 3(25%) | 3(25%) | 6(50%) | 5(42%) | 33 |
| | 3rd | 6(50%) | 3(25%) | 5(42%) | 4(33%) | 6(50%) | 4(33%) | 4(33%) | 32 |
| | 4th & 5th | 9(56%) | 5(29%) | 5(31%) | 8(50%) | 7(44%) | 5(31%) | 7(44%) | 46 |
| | Total | 25 | 21 | 19 | 22 | 24 | 21 | 24 | 156 |

## 4.2    Characteristics Analysis for Weather

We analyzed the weather data that could be a factor that changes human behavior. In this research, we focused on three factors: temperature, precipitation, and wind speed. Based on the definition of forecast terms by the Japan Meteorological Agency, criteria for "temperature", "precipitation" and "wind speed" were set.

(1) Temperature

If the temperature difference is extremely large compared to the normal temperature of the season, If the temperature difference is extremely large compared to the normal temperature in the season, the human's behavior may be different. If the temperature is higher than normal in summer or lower than normal in winter, you may hesitate to go out. On the other hand, if the temperature is lower than normal in summer or higher than normal in winter, you may go out positively. From this, in this research, the criterion with a large difference in temperature was ±5 °C of the monthly average maximum temperature and the monthly minimum temperature.

(2) Precipitation

If the precipitation is strong, you may hesitate to go out. The Japan Meteorological Agency defines strong precipitation as having an hourly precipitation of 20 mm or more [8]. From this, in this study, the criteria with strong rainfall are that both of the following conditions are satisfied.

- 10 min precipitation is 3.5 mm or more
- Total precipitation per day is 20 mm or more

(3) Wind speed

There is a possibility that hesitating to go out in case of strong wind. The Japan Meteorological Agency defines strong wind as the average wind speed of 20 m/s or more [8]. From this, in this study, the criterion of a strong wind is that the average wind speed, the maximum wind speed, or the maximum instantaneous wind speed is 20 m/s or more.

A statistical test was performed to determine whether the weather deviated from any of the above three criteria influenced forecasting the number of customers visiting. For this purpose, we performed a $x^2$ test for the following null hypothesis using a cross-tabulation table.

Null hypothesis: There is no relation between the weather outside the criteria and the forecasted number of customers visiting.

Alternative hypothesis: There is some relation between the weather outside the criteria and the forecasted number of customers visiting.

Table 4 shows $x^2$ value for the number of weather data that deviated from each criteria value. According to Table 4, the null hypothesis cannot be rejected because the $x^2$ value does not exceed the one-sided 5% point of 3.84 at all four restaurants. Therefore, weather data does not affect the forecasted number of customers visiting.

**Table 4.** $x^2$ value for weather data

| Restaurant | W | X | Y | Z |
|---|---|---|---|---|
| Temperature | 0.06 | 0.05 | 0.38 | 3.16 |
| Precipitation | 0.18 | 0.26 | 0.15 | 0.15 |
| Wind speed | 1.30 | 0.05 | 1.34 | 0.32 |

## 4.3   Characteristics Analysis for Reservation Customers

There are reservation customers who make reservations in advance and come to the restaurant. Since reservation customers rarely cancel reservations, it is thought that if there are many reservation customers, this may cause a difference between the actual number and the forecasted number. Therefore, we analyzed whether there was a difference in the ratio of the number of reservation customers to that of actual customers between the group where the forecasted number of visiting customers coming was within the error range and the group where that was outside the error range. For this purpose, we performed the Mann-Whitney U test for the following null hypothesis.

Null hypothesis: The average ratio of the number of reservation customers to that of actual customers is equal for groups with forecasted customers within and outside the error range.

Alternative hypothesis: The average ratio of the number of reservation customers to that of actual customers is different for groups with forecasted customers within and outside the error range.

$R_i$:    The number of reservation customers on $i$-th day
$\gamma_i$ :    The ratio of the number of reservation customers to that of actual customers on $i$-th day
$R_A$:    Sum of ranks within the error range
$R_B$:    Sum of ranks outside the error range
$m$:    Number of days within error range
$n$:    Number of days outside error range
$U$:    Either $U_A$ or $U_B$

$$\gamma_i = \frac{R_i}{p_i} \tag{7}$$

$$U_A = R_A - \frac{n(n+1)}{2} \tag{8}$$

$$U_B = R_B - \frac{m(m+1)}{2} \tag{9}$$

$$Z = \frac{U - \frac{nm}{2}}{\sqrt{\frac{nm(n+m+1)}{12}}} \tag{10}$$

Table 5 shows the statistics Z calculated by Eqs. (7) to (10) for each restaurant. The statistic Z has the property of following the standard normal distribution under the null hypothesis. The statistics Z is out of $\pm 1.96$ which is the 5% point on both sides of the standard normal distribution in all restaurants. Therefore, the null hypothesis is rejected and the alternative hypothesis is adopted. Since the average ratio of the number of reservation customers to that of actual customers is different for groups with forecasted customers within and outside the error range, the number of reserved customers affects the forecasting the number of customers visiting.

**Table 5.** Statistics Z for each restaurant

| W | X | Y | Z |
|---|---|---|---|
| 2.26 | -3.10 | -2.25 | -2.93 |

## 5   Conclusion

In this paper, we analyze the relation between training data and forecasted results calculated by machine learning and statistical analysis and discuss the characteristics on days with low forecasting accuracy. The following results were obtained.

(1)  Forecasting results of customers visiting
Among the five methods, the forecasting accuracy using Bayesian was the highest. The forecasting accuracy did not tend to improve even if the training data period was extended.

(2)  Analysis of characteristics with low forecasting accuracy days
It was found that the human psychology around the payday and the reservation customers affected the number of visitors. On the other hand, the weather data such as temperature, precipitation and wind speed did not affect the accuracy.

In future research, we improve the forecasting ratio by conducting data analysis considering human behavior patterns and restaurant locations and developing new methods and forecasting models using new machine learning or deep learning with additional explanatory variables. After further improving the forecasting ratio, we plan to study how to improve store management.

# References

1. Lasek, A., Cercone, N., Saunders, J.: Restaurant sales and customer demand forecasting: literature survey and categorization of methods. In: Leon-Garcia, A., et al. (eds.) SmartCity 360 2015-2016. LNICST, vol. 166, pp. 479–491. Springer, Cham (2016). https://doi.org/10.1007/978-3-319-33681-7_40
2. Xu, M., Yanshan, T., Chu, L., Yuehui, Z.: Predicting future visitors od restaurants using big data. In: Proceedings of 2018 International Conference on Machine Learning and Cybernetics, vol. 1, pp. 269–274 (2018)
3. Motomura, Y., Kurata, T., Yamamoto, Y.: Community-based participatory service engineering: case studies and technologies. In: Kwan, Stephen K., Spohrer, James C., Sawatani, Y. (eds.) Global Perspectives on Service Science: Japan. SSRISE, pp. 63–78. Springer, New York (2016). https://doi.org/10.1007/978-1-4939-3594-9_5
4. Bernard, S., Fabio, R., Flavio, R., Fabricio, F., Jonice, O.: Scholar performance prediction using boosted regression trees techniques. In: European Symposium on Artificial Neural Networks 2017 Proceedings, pp. 329–334 (2017)
5. Antonio, C., Jamie, A., Ender, K.: Decision forests: a unified framework for classification, regression, density estimation, manifold learning and semi-supervised learning. Found. Trends Comput. Graph. Vis. 7(2-3), 81–227 (2012)
6. Sebastian, R.: Python Machine Learning (Japanese Edition), pp. 86–87. Impress Corp (2016)
7. Boich, B.W., Huang, C.J.: Applied Statistics analysis (Japanese Edition), pp. 27–28, pp. 167–172. Morikita Publishing Co. Ltd. (1968)
8. Japan Meteorological Agency: Rain and wind. https://www.jma.go.jp/jma/kishou/books/amekaze/amekaze.pdf. Accessed 3 Mar 2020. (in Japanese)

# A Study on Menu Planning Method
# for Managed Meal -Consideration
# of the Cost of Ordering Ingredients-

Kyohei Irie(✉), Nobutada Fujii, Daisuke Kokuryo, and Toshiya Kaihara

Graduate School of System Informatics, Kobe University,
1-1 Rokkodai-cho, Nada, Kobe 657-8501, Japan
irie@kaede.cs.kobe-u.ac.jp, nfujii@phoenix.kobe-u.ac.jp,
kokuryo@port.kobe-u.ac.jp, kaihara@kobe-u.ac.jp

**Abstract.** Japan's aging is rapidly progressing, and it is important to extend healthy life expectancy considering the increase in social security costs such as medical expenses and long-term care benefits and the decline of local cities. Nutritional management is considered to play a major role in extending healthy life expectancy. This study focuses on the menu plan for managed meals provided by hospitals or nursing homes. This study has proposed a menu planning method using Genetic Algorithm for 30 days (90 meals) in consideration of the order of provision so as not to get tired of a meal. This paper proposes a menu planning method that takes into account not only the variety of meals but also the cost of ordering ingredients.

**Keywords:** Genetic algorithm · Menu planning · Managed meal

## 1 Introduction

In Japan, the aging is rapidly progressing, and the average life expectancy is expected to further increase. By 2025, households with only elderly people aged 65 and over are expected to account for more than a quarter of all households. Considering the increase in social security costs such as medical and nursing care benefits and the decline of local cities, it is important to extend healthy life expectancy. Improving the quality of nutrition assessment and management of the people leads to maintenance and promotion of health, prevention and severity of lifestyle-related diseases, and prolongs healthy life expectancy. In this research, the menu of meals provided in hospitals and nursing homes (hereinafter called managed meal) has been focused on. The requirements for menus of managed meal are following [2].

- Three meals a day, long-term (4 or 6 weeks) menu planning
- To take into account changes and duplication of foods so that the meal can be enjoyed

B. Lalic et al. (Eds.): APMS 2020, IFIP AICT 592, pp. 679–685, 2020.
https://doi.org/10.1007/978-3-030-57997-5_78

- To adjust the nutrient amount based on the dietary intake standards [3] and the nutrient amount depending on the disease state
- To take into account food costs

Dietitians have prepared menus that take the above into account, but it is difficult to consider all of them by using only their experience and intuition. Therefore, the purpose of this research is to automate planning menus for managed meal.. This study extended the method of the previous study [4] and has proposed a menu planning method that considers three points of "long-term menu," "change and duplication of food," and "nutrition management," and has verified its effectiveness. This paper proposes a menu planning method that takes into account not only above three points but also the cost of ordering ingredients. The less the types of ingredients used, the lower the cost of ingredients, while it is difficult to have variations in the menu. Therefore, this paper confirms that there is actually a trade-off relationship by conducting experiments while changing the severity of restrictions on food costs. Nutrition management is intended for low-salt food, taking into account salt and calories. The upper limit of the salt amount is the amount recommended by the Japanese Society for Hypertension [5]. The target amount of energy shall be the value specified in the dietary intake standard [3].

## 2 Menu Planning Using Genetic Algorithm

### 2.1 Database of Dishes

The database of dishes is created from the recipe site "Delicious Health: Delicious Daily Food and Health Management" [6], and the number of dishes registered in the database is 300. The information of each dish data is as follows.

- Index numbers assigned to the dish (1–5: staple for breakfast, 6–10: staple for lunch/dinner, 11–50: staple for breakfast, 51–160: staple for lunch/dinner, 161–1200: breakfast side dishes, 201–300: lunch and dinner side dishes)
- Name of the dish
- The amount of salt and energy contained in the dish
- Numbers that represent the characteristics of the dish

In consideration of variations in the characteristics of the dishes, the characteristics of the main and side dishes are quantified as follows. Staple foods are not considered in this study because they have few features.
The characteristics of the main dish are quantified as shown below.

**Characteristic 1 (genre of dishes)**
    1: Japanese 2: Western 3: Chinese
**Characteristic 2 (foodstuff)**
    1: Pork/Beef 2: Chicken 3: Fish 4: Other
**Characteristic 3 (cooking method)**
    1: Grilling 2: Stewing 3: Frying 4: Stir frying 5: Other

The characteristics of the side dish are quantified as shown below.

**Characteristic 1 (genre of dishes)**
1: Japanese 2: Western 3: Chinese
**Characteristic 2 (vegetable genre)**
1: Fruit vegetables 2: Leaf vegetables 3: Root vegetables 4: Other
**Characteristic 3 (cooking method)**
1: Raw 2: Dressing/Pickling 3: Frying 4: Poaching/Stir frying

## 2.2 Genetic Algorithm

The flow of the genetic algorithm (GA) in this study is shown below.

**Step1** Generate individuals randomly. If there is a constraint violation, the individual is discarded, and the individual is regenerated until the predetermined number of individuals is obtained.
**Step2** Calculate the evaluation value of the individual.
**Step3** If the number of generations has not been reached, go to step 4. If it has, end.
**Step4** Individuals to leave for the next generation are selected according to the evaluation value of each individual. At that time, the best individual in that generation remains in the next generation.
**Step5** Two individuals are selected at random, and uniform crossover is performed with a certain probability. If a constraint is violated, the individual is discarded and crossover is performed until a predetermined number of individuals are obtained.
**Step6** Mutation is performed for each individual with a certain probability. If there is a constraint violation, the mutation is repeated until the individual has no constraint violation. Return to step 2.

Regarding gene coding, genes are arranged in the order of staple food for breakfast, main dishes for breakfast, side dishes for breakfast, staple food for lunch, main dishes for lunch, side dishes for lunch, staple food for dinner, main dishes for dinner and side dishes for dinner. The genes in each of these nine categories are ordered in the order of dishes served on day 1, day 2, day 3, ..., day 30, respectively. Each gene has a corresponding index numbers assigned to the dish.

## 2.3 Evaluation Value Calculation

Based on the evaluation calculation method in the previous study [4], the entropy of the moving section that measures the variation in the order of appearance of each feature of the main and side dishes is calculated. The sum of these values and the ratio of the genres (Japanese, Western and Chinese) of the main dish and side dish in one meal is used as the evaluation function, and the calculated value is used as the evaluation value of the genetic selection. The calculation of the entropy of each feature is the number of items of the feature. The following shows the formulas and the meaning of the characters in the formulas.

$$H = \sum_{m=1}^{M} \sum_{i=1}^{I} \frac{H_{m,i}}{H_{m,i}^*} + G \tag{1}$$

$$H_{m,i} = -\frac{1}{T_{m,i} - J|_{m,i} + 1} \sum_{t=1}^{T_{m,i} - J|_{m,i} + 1} \sum_{j|_{m,i}=1}^{J|_{m,i}} P_{j|_{m,i}}(t) \log P_{j|_{m,i}}(t) \tag{2}$$

$$P_{j|_{m,i}}(t) = \frac{1}{J|_{m,i}} \sum_{p=0}^{J|_{m,i}-1} \alpha_{j|_{m,i}}(t+p) \tag{3}$$

$$T_{m,i} = D + 2(J|_{m,i} - 1) \tag{4}$$

$$G = \frac{\sum_{d=1}^{D} \beta_t}{D} \tag{5}$$

- $m = 1, 2$: Type of dish (1: main dish, 2: side dish)
- $i = 1, 2, ..., I$: Characteristic of dish
- $j|_{m,i} = 1, 2, ..., J|_{m,i}$: Items of characteristic $i$ where the type of dish is A
- $t = 1, 2, ..., T_{m,i}$: Gene ordinal numbers rearranged at the time of calculating the evaluation values for dish type $m$ and characteristic $i$
- $P_{j|_{m,i}}$: Serving frequency ratio in one section from $t$ for dishes with characteristic $j|_i$ of type $m$
- $\alpha_{j|_{m,i}}(t)$: 1/0 binary variable indicating the provision/non-supply of a dish with a feature $j|i$ of a dish type $m$ in $t$
- $\beta_t$: 1/0 binary variable indicating the genre of main and side dishes in $t$ is the same/not the same
- $H_{m,i}$: Average of entropy of characteristic $i$ of all sections of dish type $m$
- $H_{m,i}^*$: Maximum value of $H_{m,i}$
- $H$: Sum of $H_{m,i}$ divided by $H_{m,i}^*$
- $d = 1, 2, ..., D$: Ordinal number of meal in menu planning
- $G$: Rate of total meals that have the same genre of main and side dishes (Japanese, Western and Chinese)

In the entropy calculation of Eq. (1), because the evaluation value of the main dish and the side dish are calculated separately, they are rearranged in the order of appearance separately. In addition, in order to consider the boundary conditions, the entropy calculation is performed by adding, at the beginning and the end, dishes that are one less than the number of feature items; additional dishes are not included in the menu.

## 2.4    Constrains

Equation (6) shows a constraint equation regarding the amount of salt. Equation (7) shows a constraint equation regarding the amount of energy. Equation (8) shows the constraint equation relating to the cost of ordering ingredients.

The ordering cycle shall be 5 days, and the ingredients shall be ordered at the beginning of each period in 1 to 6 periods.

$$\sum_{l=1}^{L} s_l < S \tag{6}$$

$$\frac{|E - \sum_{l=1}^{L} e_l|}{E} \leq \delta \tag{7}$$

$$\frac{1}{N} \sum_{k=1}^{K} \sum_{f \in F_k} n_{k,f} P_f \leq C \tag{8}$$

$$n_{k,f} = \underset{n \in \mathbb{N}, nR_f > w_{k,f} - s_{k,f}}{\arg\min} \quad nR_f - (w_{k,f} - s_{k,f})$$

$l$ is the locus, $s_l$ is the amount of salt contained in the dish with the dish number of the locus $l$, $e_l$ is the amount of energy contained in the dish with the dish number of the locus $l$, and $S$ is the upper limit of salt intake in 30 days, $E$ is the target value of energy intake, and $\delta$ is the difference between the target value of energy intake and energy intake. $N$ is the number of meals served, $k$ is the ordering period, $F_k$ is the set of ingredients required for menu in the $k$ period, $w_{k,f}$ is the weight required for the $k$ period of the ingredients $f$, $s_{f,k}$ is the weight of ingredient $f$ in stock during $k$ period, $R_f$ is the minimum lot of ingredients f, $P_f$ is a lot ordered in the $k$ period of ingredients $f$, $P_f$ is the purchase price of the minimum lot of ingredients $f$, and $C$ is the upper limit of the quantity of ingredients ordered per person. Ingredient purchase price data (minimum lot and its price) is created with reference to "M-Mart Co., Ltd. [7]".

## 3   Computer Experiments

### 3.1   Experimental Conditions

In the experiment, the cooking data described in Sect 2.2 is used. To meet the salt requirement of less than 6 grams per day recommended by the Japanese Society for Hypertension [5], the salt intake in 30 days is less than 180 grams ($S = 180$). The target amount of energy is 66000 kcal ($E = 66000$), which is defined as the estimated energy requirement for men aged 70 and over based on dietary intake standards [3]. Restrictions are set so that the error between the energy intake and the target value is within 5% ($\delta = 0.05$). Three cases are performed in the experiments; in the case where there is no restriction on food costs, the case where the value of $C$ (upper limit of the order quantity of food per person) is set to 18000 and the case where it is set to 20000. The experiments were performed 10 times. Regarding the parameters in GA, the population is set to 300, the number of generations is 10000, the selection method is tournament selection, the crossover method is uniform crossover, the crossover rate is 0.9, and the mutation rate is 0.1.

## 3.2  Experimental Results

Table 1 summarizes the average evaluation values $H$ and the value of the food cost per person in 10 trials when there is no restriction on the food ordering cost, $C$ is 20000, and $C$ is 18000. A menu is obtained in which the cost of ordering

**Table 1.** Experiment result

| $C$ | $H$ | Cost per person |
|---|---|---|
| No constraint | 4.86 | 21221.48 |
| 20000 | 4.50 | 19208.00 |
| 18000 | 4.22 | 17768.09 |

ingredients is within the set upper limit. In addition, the constraints on salt content and energy content were satisfied in all cases, and high evaluation values were obtained. In other words, a menu satisfying the points that "similar dishes do not last" and "the amount of nutrition required" was obtained. However, the more restrictive, the lower the evaluation value, confirming that the variety of menu dishes is lost. In order to reduce the cost of ordering ingredients, it is effective to reduce the types of ingredients used, so that the variety of dishes is lost.

## 4  Conclusion

This paper proposed a 30-day menu planning method for managed meals provided at hospitals and nursing homes, taking into account the order of serving so as not to get tired of meal, nutrition, and food ordering costs. As results of a computer experiments, a menu was obtained in which the cost of ordering food was kept within the set upper limits. However, it was confirmed that the entropy, which is the evaluation value, became lower as the constraints became stricter. As a future task, it is necessary to create a menu that keeps the variety of dishes and reduces the cost of ingredients. Since there is a trade-off between food ordering cost and variety of dishes, it is considered effective to define the food ordering cost as an objective function and solve it as a multi-objective optimization problem.

## References

1. Ministry of Health, Labor and Welfare: Report on the Study Group on Nutrition Management in the Food Distribution Business that Promotes Health Support for Elderly People in the Community (Japanese). https://www.mhlw.go.jp/stf/seisakunitsuite/bunya/0000158814.html

2. Tosa, S., Sasaki, A.: Principles of menu planning and meals at hospitals. In: Nutrition Care, vol. 4, no. 4. Medica Publishing
3. Ministry of Health, Labor and Welfare: Report on the Committee on Formulating Japanese Dietary Intake Standards (2015). (Japanese). https://www.mhlw.go.jp/stf/shingi/0000041824.html
4. Kashima, T., Orito, Y., Someya, H.: Consecutive meals planning on meals support system: verification of solutions obtained by permutation GA. In: Technical Meeting on "Information Systems", IEE Japan (2017). (Japanese)
5. Salt Reduction Committee, Japanese Society of Hypertension (Japanese). https://www.jpnsh.jp/com_salt.html
6. Delicious health: Daily delicious food and health management (Japanese). https://oishi-kenko.com
7. Commercial wholesale market—M-Mart Co., Ltd. (Japanese). https://www.m-mart.co.jp/

# Service System Design Considering Employee Satisfaction Through Introducing Service Robots

Tomomi Nonaka[1](✉), Takeshi Shimmura[1], and Nobutada Fujii[2]

[1] College of Gastronomy Management, Ritsumeikan University,
1-1-1 Noji-Higashi, Kusatsu, Shiga 525-8577, Japan
nonaka@fc.ritsumei.ac.jp
[2] Graduate School of System Informatics, Kobe University, Kobe, Japan

**Abstract.** In this paper, we perform a basic analysis on employee satisfaction and production planning by introducing a service robot which delivers dishes in restaurant service. As an example of a service robot introduced in a Japanese restaurant, we focus on the pantry staff, kitchen staff, and customer service staff, as well as production planning that individual employees implicitly plan and update in their heads. The service robots are used to deliver the dishes prepared at the kitchen to the customer service floor, where the worker specifies the destination and transports the dishes while patroling the restaurant. By analyzing the productivity and employee satisfaction before and after the introduction of the service robots into the categories of serving, cooking area, and customer service, how employees can identify and coordinate work between humans and machines and change process design. From December 2019 to January 2020, an analysis was conducted based on the results of employee questionnaires and interviews conducted at a restaurant.

**Keywords:** Service system design · Employee satisfaction · Productivity · Restaurant service

## 1 Introduction

The use of robots in the service industry is progressing in order to improve labor productivity and shortage of labor in the service industry. Part-time employment is very severe in the food service industry, especially in the restaurant industry, and the decrease in the working population is an urgent issue. Many of the food service sites are labor-intensive, and research and development to improve productivity in the service industry is underway by industry, government, and academia. Single-function robots have already been introduced into service areas such as inns, hotels, and restaurants [1], and their productivity has been improved.

Economic activity in the service industry is increasing, creating important jobs not only in developed countries but also in developing countries. The service industry accounts for about 70% of Japan's GDP and two-thirds of the country's employment. In the food service industry, which is classified as a food service industry, production is carried out by an intensive labor force. Staff working on the service floor of a restaurant

© IFIP International Federation for Information Processing 2020
Published by Springer Nature Switzerland AG 2020
B. Lalic et al. (Eds.): APMS 2020, IFIP AICT 592, pp. 686–692, 2020.
https://doi.org/10.1007/978-3-030-57997-5_79

provide face-to-face service to customers. In the kitchen, there are still many hand-crafted processes in service operations that create value [2, 3]. Therefore, the working conditions of the staff may affect the delivery of the service. The importance of employee satisfaction in providing good service has been pointed out [4–6]. A previous study [4] showed that there is a substantial relationship between individual job satisfaction and individual performance. If employee performance improves, the quality of service is expected to improve. In terms of service satisfaction [7], the relationship between service quality and customer satisfaction has been shown to be independent but closely related [8]. The importance of the linkage effect is mentioned in order to improve overall satisfaction, including customer satisfaction, employee satisfaction, and management satisfaction [7, 9].

In order to improve both employee satisfaction and service quality, it is necessary to examine employee satisfaction and clarify its structure. In the previous study [10], the authors analyzed employee satisfaction by looking at the results of a questionnaire distributed to restaurant staff. First, we build a structural model of employee satisfaction. The questions were categorized into seven questions: "Work environment," "Work efficiency and quality of service", "Relationship with supervisor," "Rules", "Education system", "Attitude and willingness to work" and "Interest in multi-skill development". The results of the questionnaire examined the relationship between employee satisfaction and the seven categories from multiple perspectives. As a result, differences between employee satisfaction structures and attributes such as job title, employment status, age group, and duration of continuous employment were analyzed from multiple perspectives. The results were analyzed using two approaches: correlation analysis and covariance structure analysis.

This paper presents a basic analysis of employee satisfaction and production planning with the introduction of robot serving in a restaurant service. Using a serving robot introduced in a Japanese restaurant as a case study, we focus on the operations of the serving staff, kitchen staff, and customer service staff, as well as the production planning that each employee implicitly plans and updates in his or her head. This delivery robot carries the food prepared in the kitchen to the customer's floor, where the operator specifies the destination and carries the food while patrolling the restaurant. They are also responsible for carrying the dishes from the lower table to the washing area. We analyze the results of employee questionnaires and interviews conducted from December 2019 to January 2020 at a store where robots were introduced.

## 2 Employee Satisfaction and Productivity in Restaurant Services

### 2.1 Job Categories in a Restaurant Service

The employees working in a restaurant can be divided into three categories: kitchen staff in charge of cooking, floor staff in charge of serving customers and serving food to customers, and cashiers, and serving and washing staff. In this paper, we define the difference between these tasks as occupations. The role of serving is to arrange the dishes that are prepared individually for each customer between the kitchen and the floor, and to assemble a set menu, etc. Focusing on these three occupations, the authors propose a model of employee satisfaction that takes into account the customer contact and customer orientation in different occupations and the customer contact and customer orientation in different occupations. A questionnaire survey was conducted in restaurants, and the structure of the relationship between improved customer service and employee satisfaction awareness was modelled through structural analysis of covariance [11]. The restaurant locations where the service delivery robots were installed in this paper are the same restaurant chain with similar menus and service forms, but on a larger scale. In addition to the traditional customer service staff, there are auxiliary staff who assist in serving food and support the overall service of the store in cooperation with the serving staff and the customer service staff. In this paper, we analyze kitchen staff, catering staff, customer service staff, and assisting customer service staff.

## 2.2    Employee Satisfaction and Productivity

In the field of service research, in addition to customer satisfaction (CS), the importance of employee satisfaction (ES) has been pointed out, and the cycle of success model [13] and the "service profit chain" [12], which describes the relationship between employees and customers as a satisfaction mirror, influence each other. Especially in interpersonal service situations where employees and customers face each other directly, the state of employees and their feelings have a significant impact on service quality.

Labor productivity is calculated by dividing value added by labor input, and increasing labor productivity is a combination of increasing the value added in the numerator and reducing the labor input in the denominator. In restaurant services, there are difficulties with both numerator and denominator approaches due to the heterogeneity of services and the labor-intensive nature of the work.

# 3    Questionnaire and Interview Surveys for Employees

## 3.1    Targets

Employee questionnaires and interviews were conducted between December and January 2019 for employees working in four occupations: hospitality staff, hospitality auxiliary staff, culinary staff, and catering staff. Types of employment include both formal and informal employment. Interviews were conducted with executives, leaders, regular staff, and long and short years of service, respectively. The employee questionnaire received valid responses from 18 employees. Employee interviews were conducted with 12 employees in semi-structured interviews lasting approximately 25 min on December 20, 23, and 24.

## 3.2 Questionnaire Design

The questionnaire consists of questions on employee satisfaction and productivity, in addition to the attribute survey and job satisfaction, by recalling two time points immediately after the introduction of the service robot and after the passage of time. A six-point Likert scale ranging from "very much agree" to "don't agree at all" was used as a choice questionnaire and an open-ended questionnaire. In detail, the questions (Q1) and (Q2) are questions that assume the awareness/motivation and quality of provision of work, and (Q2) and (Q3) are questions that assume two time points immediately after and after the introduction of the serving robot, respectively. Questions related to work efficiency, service delivery quality, teamwork, and the operability and awareness of using the robot were set up. The questions on perceived quality took into account the characteristics of the target restaurant and the business and restaurant in question, such as the quality of the food served, the speed at which it was served, and the response and satisfaction of the customers.

Employee interviews examine efficiency and operational changes, customer satisfaction and employee satisfaction in the implementation of service robots. The objective is to find out how service robots are used in the work that employees are responsible for and what changes in operation will lead to quality, efficiency, and customer and employee satisfaction.

As a measure of employee satisfaction, Gazzoli et al. categorized the questionnaire questions into three categories: empowerment, job satisfaction and perceived service quality [14]. Empowerment includes questions such as "Is my job important to me" and "I have discretion on how I do proceed my job". In addition, it has been shown that a single indicator of job satisfaction is correlated with the use of the overall job satisfaction scale [15]. As for perceived service quality, conventional studies have been proposed that question items are required to be tailored to the characteristics of the target service, such as restaurant [14] and bank [16].

The questionnaire survey used in this paper is based on a questionnaire survey on employee satisfaction [11] conducted by the authors at the same restaurant chain and was developed by adding questions about service robots. Questions included in empowerment include, "Is work important to me?" and "Do I have freedom in how I proceed with my work? In the questionnaire survey used in this paper, questions related to empowerment, job satisfaction and perceived quality were set, respectively. In the question on perceived quality, the questions were set in consideration of the characteristics of the restaurant. This questionnaire consists of questions on perceived quality to directly ascertain the effects and influences of the introduction of service robots and questions to indirectly ascertain the effects of the introduction of service robots on employees in terms of their feelings and job satisfaction. In addition to the questions on empowerment, job satisfaction, and perceived quality, the questions on perceived quality included questions on the quality of food delivery, speed of food delivery, and customer response and satisfaction, taking into account the characteristics of the restaurant location [11]. In the (Q2) and (Q3), two scenes were set up for the question items, one immediately after the introduction of the service robot and the other at the present time. The same question items are set up to be answered for each of the two periods. Respondents are asked to describe their feelings and conditions both when the service robot was introduced and their current feelings and conditions. Some questions are about work efficiency, provision quality, teamwork, and operation using the robots by introducing the robots. Regarding questions related to perceived quality, the following questions are set considering the characteristics of restaurants including quality of serving food, food serving speed, and customer response and satisfaction.

During employee interviews, we examine changes in efficiency and operations, customer satisfaction, and employee satisfaction when introducing the service robots. The purpose is to examine how the service robots are used in work for which the employee is responsible, and to assess what changes in the operations result in improved quality, efficiency, and customer and employee satisfaction.

## 4   Discussions

First, the results of the employee questionnaire are presented. We compared the mean values of the current Likert scale immediately after the introduction and after the passage of time with respect to the effect of introducing the service robot in question categories (Q2) and (Q3).'The skills to operate the service delivery robot have been acquired so that we are able to provide high quality service. The positive results for the introduction of robots were obtained (Q41). In this question, a significant difference (the average of gap is 0.45) was found as a result of the difference test of the mean value of the t-test (one-tailed test, P-value: 0.03). However, although we were able to confirm a certain number of positive changes in the number of subjects for the other question items, we were not able to confirm any significant differences between the current and immediate introduction. Since this questionnaire analysis was conducted on a single store, quantitative verification by increasing the number of stores and the number of survey targets is a future issue.

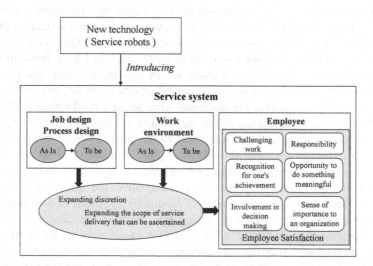

**Fig. 1.** The outline of the impact of technology implementation on service systems and employee satisfaction

According to the results of the employee interviews, it was mentioned that the serving staff was able to stay in the serving area and work because the distance travelled from the serving area to the table in question on the hospitality floor was significantly reduced. This suggests that people are reducing the non-value-added tasks of movement and avoiding more time for other tasks or original tasks that can contribute to value-added and service quality improvement. In addition, the ability to strategically instruct the robot on the timing, location, and movement of food to be placed on the serving robot increased productivity by allowing the robot to perform other tasks, such as serving food, in its free time within its own work time. As a secondary effect of the introduction of the robot, we heard the opinion that the introduction of the tablet to check the position of the service robot in the store and its status made it possible to grasp the entire store. In [11], many of the serving staff had the perception that they work independently between the cooking and customer service staff. On the other hand, the staff in question also felt that the motivating factors increased employee satisfaction, while they felt that their work was more rewarding and that they had acquired new skills (Fig. 1). On the other hand, it was observed that the service assistant staff actively promoted the use of the service delivery robot and helped the service staff to focus on more value-added tasks close to the customers. Although some subjects in the interview survey mentioned certain improvements in quality and efficiency, the questionnarire survey did not reveal any significant differences, except for (Q41). For example, "As a result of the improvement and efficiency of our operations, we are now able to satisfy our customers (Q42), I feel my work efficiency has improved and my physical load has been reduced (Q44), and I feel that I have a high level of value-added work I am now able to devote more time to work that I couldn't do before (Q46), and to work with customers. It is now possible to devote more time to direct customer service (Q50). Further analysis is needed to take into account the differences in occupations and intention to use the robot.

## 5 Conclusions

This paper discusses the impact of the introduction of service delivery robots on employee satisfaction and productivity. The next challenge is to increase the scope of the survey and propose a more quantitative evaluation and employee satisfaction model.

**Acknowledgements.** This work was supported in part by JSPS KAKENHI Grant Number 7H01827.

## References

1. Qing-xiao, Y., Can, Y., Zhuang, F., Yan-zheng, Z.: Research of the localization of restaurant service robot. Int. J. Adv. Robot. Syst. **7**(3), 227–238 (2010)

2. Shimamura, T., Takenaka, T., Ohura, S.: Improving labor productivity and labor elasticity at multiproduct Japanese cuisine restaurant introducing cell-production system. In: Prabhu, V., Taisch, M., Kiritsis, D. (eds.) APMS 2013. IAICT, vol. 415, pp. 11–17. Springer, Heidelberg (2013). https://doi.org/10.1007/978-3-642-41263-9_2

3. Takenaka, T., Shimmura, T., Ishigaki, T., Motomura, Y., Ohura, S.: Process management in restaurant service - a case study of a Japanese restaurant chain. In: Proceeding of International Symposium of Scheduling 2011 (ISS2011), Osaka, Japan, 2–4 July, pp. 191–194 (2011)

4. Judge, T.A., Thoresen, C.J., Bono, J.E., Patton, G.K.: The job satisfaction-job performance relationship: a qualitative and quantitative review. Psychol. Bull. **127**, 379–407 (2001)

5. Iaffaldano, M.T., Muchinsky, P.M.: Job satisfaction and job performance: a meta-analysis. Psychol. Bull. **97**, 251–273 (1985)

6. Harter, J.K., Schmidt, F.L., Hayes, T.L.: Business-unit-level relationship between employee satisfaction, employee engagement, and business outcomes: a meta-analysis. J. Appl. Psychol. **87**(2), 268–279 (2002)

7. Fujii, N., Toshiya, K., Nonaka, T., Oda, J., Shimmura, T.: A study on staff shift scheduling improving service satisfaction in restaurant business - proposal of planning method considering difference in employee abilities. In: 23rd Conference on the Japan Society of Mechanical Engineers, Design and Systems Division (in Japanese) (USB), p. 2314 (2013)

8. Sureshchandar, G.S., Rajendran, C., Anantharaman, R.N.: The relationship between service quality and customer satisfaction - a factor specific approach. J. Serv. Mark. **16**(4), 363–379 (2002)

9. Fujii, N., Kaihara, T., Uemura, M., Nonaka, T., Shimmura, T.: Facility layout planning of central kitchen in food service industry: application to the real-scale problem. In: Prabhu, V., Taisch, M., Kiritsis, D. (eds.) APMS 2013. IAICT, vol. 415, pp. 33–40. Springer, Heidelberg (2013). https://doi.org/10.1007/978-3-642-41263-9_5

10. Nonaka, T., et al.: Employee satisfaction analysis in food service industry – resultant of questionnaire to the restaurant staff. In: Maeno, T., Sawatani, Y., Hara, T. (eds.) ICServ 2014, pp. 23–36. Springer, Tokyo (2016). https://doi.org/10.1007/978-4-431-55861-3_2

11. Nonaka, T., Fujii, N., Shimmura, T., Takahashi, T., Kaihara, T.: An employee satisfaction model considering customer satisfaction -difference analysis of staff work positions in restaurant services. J. Jpn. Ind. Manag. Assoc. **67**(1), 59–69 (2016)

12. Heskett, J.L., Jones, T.O., Loveman, G.W., Sasser Jr., W.E., Schlesinger, L.A.: Putting the service-profit chain to work. Harv. Bus. Rev. **72**, 164–174 (1994)

13. Schlesinger, L.A., Heskett, J.L.: Breaking the cycle of failure in services. Sloan Manag. Rev. **32**(3), 17–28 (1991)

14. Gazzoli, G., Hancer, M., Park, Y.: The role and effect of job satisfaction and empowerment on customers' perception of service quality a study in the restaurant. Ind. J. Hosp. Tour. Res. **34**(1), 56–77 (2010)

15. Wanous, J.P., Richers, A.E., Hudy, M.J.: Overall job satisfaction: how good are single-item measures? J. Appl. Psychol. **82**(2), 247–252 (1997)

16. Schneider, B., Bowen, D.E.: Employee and customer perceptions of service in banks: replication and extension. J. Appl. Psychol. **70**(3), 423–433 (1985)

# Product and Asset Life Cycle
# Management in the Circular Economy

# Exploring Synergies Between Circular Economy and Asset Management

Federica Acerbi$^{(\boxtimes)}$ ⓘ, Adalberto Polenghi ⓘ, Irene Roda ⓘ,
Marco Macchi ⓘ, and Marco Taisch ⓘ

Department of Management, Economics and Industrial Engineering, Politecnico
di Milano, Piazza Leonardo da Vinci 32, 20133 Milan, Italy
{federica.acerbi,adalberto.polenghi,irene.roda,
marco.macchi,marco.taisch}@polimi.it

**Abstract.** Circular economy (CE) has been recently considered one of the most promising sustainable strategies for industrial companies, aiming at reducing resources consumption, extending resources life cycle and making recirculate resources within the life cycle stages. The transition from a linear economy towards a circular one requires the internal reorganization of companies without limiting the focus on product life cycle management, also considering how to appropriately manage internal assets, both physical, e.g. machines, and social, e.g. workforce. Indeed, the objective of the present work is to investigate the adoption of CE in industrial asset management (AM), thus focusing on the physical assets. A systematic literature review has been performed with a two-fold goal: firstly, to envisage the synergies between CE and AM and, secondly, to identify existing research gaps. Through this review, it was possible to notice the shared life cycle orientation of the two theories but the still embryonic adoption of it in the AM for a circular aim. Indeed, the major focus in the AM theory, from a CE perspective, is on the role of maintenance activities to extend asset life cycle during its Middle of Life stage while CE adoption at the Beginning of Life of industrial assets is still lagging. This limits a life cycle orientation which would boost industrial companies' sustainability. In order to encounter policymakers' expectations these two theories should be furtherly integrated.

**Keywords:** Circular economy · Asset management · Literature review

## 1 Introduction

Nowadays, due to the scarcity of resources registered in the last decades, forecasted to further increase together with the augment of pollution generation [1], the entire society looks towards sustainable development. Out of all the sectors, industrial companies are considered one of the major responsible of materials and energy usage, while undeniably leading also towards the augment of emission generations [2]. Indeed, the attention on industrial companies has been increased and the adoption of a new industrial economy, called circular economy (CE), has been widely supported by policymakers too [3]. CE is defined as an *"industrial economy that is regenerative and*

B. Lalic et al. (Eds.): APMS 2020, IFIP AICT 592, pp. 695–702, 2020.
https://doi.org/10.1007/978-3-030-57997-5_80

*restorative by intention and design"* [4]. This definition is reflected into the adoption by industrial companies of strategies willing to modify the entire organization structure in order to address the CE values of slowing (extending), narrowing (reducing) and closing (recirculating) resources loops [5]. As stated by Stahel (2007) *"the shift from a linear manufacturing economy to a circular or service economy means a change in economic thinking, from flow (throughput) management to stock (asset) management"* [6]. Thus, according to this vision, this transition requires to adequately manage not only products flows, but also all the internal assets, both physical, like machineries, and social, like workforce, necessary to enable the circularity of resources flows.

Asset Management (AM) is a novel approach focusing on the management of physical assets (such as machineries, industrial equipment and plants) in an integrated and holistic way along their life cycle [7]. The corresponding body of international standards about AM [8] pushes towards the adoption of sustainable strategies to support AM. Nevertheless, it does not provide any practical way to correlate them.

For these reasons, it is interesting to study how CE can contribute for sustainable AM practices. In this paper, the extant scientific literature is analyzed addressing the following research question: "What are the synergies and gaps on the adoption of CE strategies in AM?".

To this end, the paper is structured as follows. Section 2 is the basement of the research and both CE and AM are briefly introduced. Section 3 provides the research methodology adopted explaining the motivations behind it. Section 4 presents the major results out of the state-of-the-art (SOTA) of the scientific literature. In Sect. 5 the discussion about the SOTA of the extant scientific literature is proposed. Section 6 presents the conclusions and the main limitations of the present work.

## 2 Theoretical Background

This section creates the grounding of the present research by reporting the theoretical background of the two areas of investigation, separately, that are CE and AM.

### 2.1 Circular Economy

CE is defined as an *"industrial economy that is regenerative and restorative by intention and design"* [4]. CE is driven by three main CE values of slowing, narrowing, and closing resources loops, which aim to limit resources consumption, extend resources life cycle and enable the reintroduction of resources in new life cycles, respectively [5]. Over the years, relying on these CE values, different strategies have been adopted by companies to undertake the transition towards CE. Among them, some strategies are more AM-related such as reuse (e.g. [9]), remanufacturing (e.g. [10]), recycling (e.g. [11]), disassembly (e.g. [12]) and circular design (e.g. [13]). CE strategies aim to cover all the CE values and, they all foster a life cycle orientation by going beyond the single interested life cycle stage, in order to understand the related consequences in the next stages.

## 2.2 Asset Management

AM, defined as *"the coordinated activities of an organization to realize value from assets"* [8], is a quite recent theory that finds its roots in maintenance management (MM), considering both Total Productive Maintenance (TPM) and Reliability Centered Maintenance (RCM) approaches [7, 14]. MM is considered one of the main function within AM [15] and it promotes sustainable manufacturing since it enables asset reliability and availability during its usage [2, 16]. Nevertheless, AM goes beyond the traditional MM goals – mainly related to the operational phase of the assets – looking for an integrated methodology to govern the assets over the entire life cycle – thus covering the whole life from Beginning of Life (BoL), through Middle of Life (MoL) up to the End of Life (EoL) stages. Moreover, AM is not only characterized by a life cycle orientation. Other principles, besides life cycle orientation, are at its background: system orientation, risk orientation and asset centric orientation. Based on such principles, AM takes place at the three main control levels within organizations [7]:

- strategic control level refers to long-term strategy definition, guiding the tactical level towards business objectives;
- tactical control level involves the medium-term planning, planning tasks and reporting performance to support higher strategic level;
- operational control level refers to shop-floor activities driven by tactical-dictated tasks and report current performance.

## 3  Literature Review Methodology

A systematic literature review has been performed in order to envisage, in a structured and systematic way, the current scientific advances in the adoption of CE strategies in AM. Scopus was chosen as search engine for this review, being it widely used for industrial engineering researches. The first set of keywords considered appropriate to query the search engine were: "Circular Economy" AND "Asset Management", nevertheless these led to only six documents. Indeed, considering the theoretical background above reported about AM, the final string selected is: "Circular Economy" AND ("Asset Management" OR "Maintenance"). This enabled to identify 85 documents, out of which, after a screening process, 37 were selected to perform the review. Indeed, the documents discarded consider the "asset" as a "product" and, thus, their focus is on the "traditional" CE perspective on product life cycle management, starting from the products newly developed and then managed throughout their life cycle, and not on asset life cycle management with a circular aim, considering the assets as portfolio/systems of assets and individual assets to be managed throughout the life cycle within industrial facilities [8]. Last, the sample of the selected papers was analyzed through a theoretical framework, as discussed in Sect. 4. Indeed, the framework was used to develop a reasoning around the SOTA to envisage the synergies already exploited, and to deductively propose envisioned gaps. In particular, each CE strategy is analyzed through the AM lenses, which are control levels and asset life cycle stages.

# 4 Theoretical Framework and Results

Figure 1 represents the theoretical framework developed by relying on the SOTA of the extant scientific literature. The CE strategies in each paper have been analysed and framed according to the suitable asset control level and asset life cycle stage considered. In some cases, the same paper covers more than one life cycle stage or more than one CE strategy and, thus, it is reported more than one time in the framework.

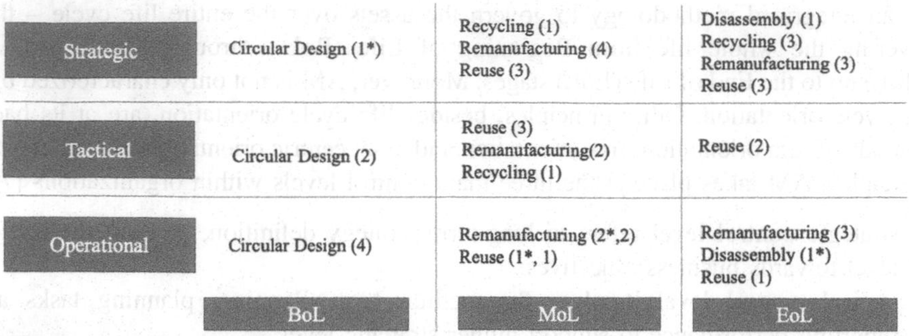

| Strategic | Circular Design (1*) | Recycling (1) Remanufacturing (4) Reuse (3) | Disassembly (1) Recycling (3) Remanufacturing (3) Reuse (3) |
|---|---|---|---|
| Tactical | Circular Design (2) | Reuse (3) Remanufacturing(2) Recycling (1) | Reuse (2) |
| Operational | Circular Design (4) | Remanufacturing (2*,2) Reuse (1*, 1) | Remanufacturing (3) Disassembly (1*) Reuse (1) |
| | BoL | MoL | EoL |

**Fig. 1.** CE and AM: theoretical framework. (The numbers next to the CE strategies represent the amount of papers focused on a certain control level and a certain life cycle stage; * represents those papers focused on AM, while the others, without *, are focused on MM within AM.)

The analysis and mapping of the CE strategies, reported below, allowed to draw first results regarding the goal of this research work.

Concerning the synergies between the two theories, as visible in Fig. 1, a prominent position is gained by remanufacturing, reuse and recycling. These CE strategies are investigated homogeneously at different control levels and, in most of the cases these strategies are adopted both during asset MoL and EoL. Referring to the asset and its components, these strategies take over maintenance as a mean towards asset regeneration with a long term orientation to enable the extension of the life cycle [17, 18]. Disassembly too has been adopted in AM as a CE strategy. Indeed, AM also understands the need to pay attention on asset disassembly performances, such as time, to ease maintenance activities [19]. Nevertheless, disassembly under this perspective has been considered in few papers and only one paper claims a strategic vision of its adoption [17].

Concerning the missing synergies, the life cycle orientation with a circular vision is still not comprehensive of all the asset life cycle stages. It is especially lagging under the concept of industrial AM in BoL. Indeed, circular design has been proposed only by few researches and the most diffused ones are in non-manufacturing industry. For instance, reporting some works, major appliances have been designed to ease their maintenance and their components replacement [20], and buildings have been designed to ensure their robustness, durability [21] and adaptability [22]. In industrial AM, the most CE oriented work with a long term orientation is the one developed in [23], in which environmental oriented appraisal is conducted during asset acquisition at BoL.

This latter work has a higher circular long-term vision of the asset life cycle, but it is still not exhaustive, being it only partially focused on CE values. Indeed, the appraisal is limited on environmental issues, close to the narrowing value, and does not include the other CE values that have been covered in other industries through for instance design for adaptability and durability [21, 22].

In addition to the above mentioned strategies, others emerged from the extant review to have potentialities in supporting AM sustainability. Among them, servitization, cleaner production, material efficiency and waste management gain momentum in the scientific literature even though less asset-related strategies and more enterprise and operating business models oriented ones.

Servitization is implemented to provide to the asset user all the maintenance services required to optimize the asset utilization and extend its life cycle [24]. Indeed, service maintenance activities are in fact performed by the asset producers to optimize assets utilization through preventive or predictive maintenance [25] during the MoL of the asset, i.e. with a limited life cycle orientation and a more operational vision. Nevertheless, it is also underlined the usefulness of servitization in order to support maintenance activities to enable more responsible production and consumption from a strategic viewpoint [26]. As final remark, servitization is proposed, taking a long term orientation, only within the construction industry, with the goal to provide a maintenance service of assets already designed with a circular aim [27].

As opposed to servitization, which involves the asset provider, maintenance activities might be undertaken also by the asset users themselves [2]. In this latter case, the maintenance activities are no more considered under the service perspective and are performed in order to increase machines reliability by optimizing production processes to reduce inefficiencies and scraps. The CE strategy adopted in these cases are cleaner production and resources efficiency since the goal is to enable the assets to be more reliable during its MoL by limiting avoidable resources consumption due to inefficiencies [28] or by monitoring asset material corrosion [29].

## 5 Discussion

From the SOTA of the scientific literature emerged that the synergic point between CE and AM is majorly found in the "maintenance" scope. Maintenance has been already considered a way to support industrial companies' sustainability [2], and, with a CE orientation, maintenance activities are performed through different CE strategies. On the other hand, the gaps envisioned through this review are mainly of four categories: (i) General gap, (ii) CE-related gap, (iii) CE-AM related gap, (iv) AM-related gap.

(i) General gap. There is a shortage of scientific researches dealing with the synergic vision of CE and AM, that is expressed by the limited number of papers identified during the research process. AM is still a relatively recent theory, not deeply investigated yet. Instead, in CE adoption, there is limited attention on physical assets as machineries, being CE more focused on the management of products.

(ii) <u>CE-related gap</u>. Although CE strategies are driven by the three main CE values, used as further lenses for the analysis, the wide number of papers are focused on only two out of the three values – "slowing" and "narrowing" – to manage the physical assets; these are the most coherent ones with the traditional sustainable vision. Indeed, through maintenance activities it is supported the extension of asset life cycle and asset components' life cycle (i.e. slowing), and the improvement of industrial efficiency through the reduction of resources consumption, thus also pollution generation (i.e. narrowing) [30]. The "closing" value is still lagging, and it is addressed only in those works aiming to make recirculate obsolete resources.

(iii) <u>CE-AM related gap</u>. Looking at Fig. 1, it is evident that not all the CE strategies were resulting in the AM research; for instance, closed-loop supply chain is not considered (which might also support the life cycle orientation), this is still missing as reported below in the AM-related gaps.

(iv) <u>AM-related gap</u>. The asset life cycle orientation vision integrated with CE values is still embryonic. The majority of the papers focus the attention on the asset MoL and EoL, and very few on BoL (see Fig. 1), while, from a CE perspective, BoL would facilitate CE adoption along asset life cycle. Indeed, although the great impact on companies productivity is caused by machines inefficiencies [31], which inevitably impacts also on the increase of resources consumption, there is still not a long term vision anticipated in the asset BoL. Maintenance activities are then performed during the MoL, or in the worst cases, when components or machines need to be replaced in the EoL, whereas sustainability might be improved by including CE values during the asset BoL. Therefore, CE may gain momentum by giving value to CE-related decisions and information in the asset selection and acquisition: all this would boost a life cycle orientation, aiming at including CE values appraisal during asset acquisition or leasing.

# 6   Conclusion

AM has an inherent life cycle orientation which is coherent with the CE one. Nevertheless, in the extant scientific literature has not yet emerged the exploitation of this synergy as the majority of the researches remains still mainly focused on asset MoL, searching solutions to act during the asset usage to extend its useful life. Therefore, further researches should be developed to include a CE long term orientation and, thus, CE values, starting from the BoL of the asset. Indeed, including at BoL considerations on asset MoL and EoL, which will inevitably arise in the future, would foster industrial companies' sustainability. Considering the valuable role of physical assets in an industrial company, and considering the current need to embrace CE to improve industrial companies' sustainability, further researches should be developed to integrate CE values in AM. To this end, it could be useful to investigate CE strategies adopted for products to transfer and adapt those concepts to physical assets, whenever possible.

   The gaps identified within this paper can be used for paving the way for future researches. They would be particularly relevant to develop empirical investigations and, at the same time, important to attract the attention of policymakers to meet their expectations too on new areas, such as AM and MM, where to implement CE.

It is worth remarking that the present literature review might be biased by the choice of the keywords, especially "Maintenance", which narrows the eligible papers in the MoL and EoL.

# References

1. OECD: Global material resources outlook to 2060. OECD (2019)
2. Franciosi, C., Lambiase, A., Miranda, S.: Sustainable maintenance: a periodic preventive maintenance model with sustainable spare parts management. IFAC-PapersOnLine 50(1), 13692–13697 (2017)
3. European Commission: Circular Economy Action Plan (2020)
4. The Ellen MacArthur Foundation: Towards a Circular Economy: Business Rationale for an Accelerated Transition (2015)
5. Bocken, N., Miller, K., Evans, S.: Assessing the environmental impact of new circular business models. In: New Business Models - Exploring a changing view on organizing value creation – Toulouse, France, pp. 16–17, June 2016
6. Stahel, W.R.: Sustainable development and strategic thinking, 2857 (2007)
7. Roda, I., Macchi, M.: A framework to embed asset management in production companies. J. Risk Reliab. 232(4), 368–378 (2018)
8. ISO 55000:2014(E): Asset management—overview, principles and terminology. BSI Stand. Publ, vol. 2014 (2014)
9. Liu, B., et al.: The effect of remanufacturing and direct reuse on resource productivity of China's automotive production. J. Clean. Prod. 194, 309–317 (2018)
10. Sitcharangsie, S., Ijomah, W., Wong, T.C.: Decision makings in key remanufacturing activities to optimise remanufacturing outcomes: a review. J. Clean. Prod. 232, 1465–1481 (2019)
11. Zhong, S., Pearce, J.M.: Tightening the loop on the circular economy: coupled distributed recycling and manufacturing with recyclebot and RepRap 3-D printing. Resour. Conserv. Recycl. 128, 48–58 (2018)
12. Marconi, M., Germani, M., Mandolini, M., Favi, C.: Applying data mining technique to disassembly sequence planning: a method to assess effective disassembly time of industrial products. Int. J. Prod. Res. 57(2), 599–623 (2019)
13. den Hollander, M.C., Bakker, C.A., Hultink, E.J.: Product design in a circular economy: development of a typology of key concepts and terms. J. Ind. Ecol. 21(3), 517–525 (2017)
14. Pintelon, L., Parodi-Herz, A.: Maintenance: an evolutionary perspective. In: Pintelon, L., Parodi-Herz, A. (eds.) Complex System Maintenance Handbook, pp. 21–48. Springer, Heidelberg (2008). https://doi.org/10.1007/978-1-84800-011-7_2
15. BS EN 16646:2014: Maintenance—maintenance within physical asset management. BSI Stand. Publ. (2014)
16. Franciosi, C., Voisin, A., Miranda, S., Riemma, S., Iung, B.: Measuring maintenance impacts on sustainability of manufacturing industries: from a systematic literature review to a framework proposal. J. Clean. Prod. 260, 121065 (2020)
17. Diez, L., Marangé, P., Levrat, É.: Maintenance best way for meeting best of the challenge of the regenaration. IFAC-PapersOnLine 49(28), 49–54 (2016)
18. Diener, D.L., Kushnir, D., Tillman, A.: Scrap happens: a case of industrial end-users, maintenance and component remanufacturing outcome. J. Clean. Prod. 213, 863–871 (2019)

19. Belhadj, I., Khemili, I., Trigui, M., Aifaoui, N.: Time computing technique for wear parts dismantling. Int. J. Adv. Manuf. Technol. **103**(9–12), 3513–3527 (2019). https://doi.org/10.1007/s00170-019-03692-4
20. Fiore, E., Tamborrini, P., Norese, M.F.: Designing major appliances: a decision support model. In: 2016 Electronics Goes Green (2016)
21. Farrar, S.J.: Towards a code of practice for the use of bio-based materials in construction (2019)
22. Farrar, S.J.: The 'Eco - Shed': an example of a domestic scale building constructed using the principals of the circular economy (2019)
23. Korse, M., Ruitenburg, R.J., Toxopeus, M.E., Braaksma, A.J.J.: Embedding the circular economy in investment decision-making for capital assets - a business case framework. Procedia CIRP **48**, 425–430 (2016)
24. Iung, B., Levrat, E.: Advanced maintenance services for promoting sustainability advanced maintenance services for promoting sustainability. Procedia CIRP **22**, 15–22 (2014)
25. Bressanelli, G., Adrodegari, F., Perona, M., Saccani, N.: Exploring how usage-focused business models enable circular economy through digital technologies. Sustainability **10**, 639 (2018)
26. Pialot, O., Millet, D., Bisiaux, J.: 'Upgradable PSS': clarifying a new concept of sustainable consumption/production based on upgradablility. J. Clean. Prod. **141**, 538–550 (2017)
27. Azcárate-Aguerre, T., Den Heijer, J.F., Klein, A.: Integrated fades as a product-service system -business process innovation to accelerate integral product implementation. J. Facade Des. Eng. **6**(1), 41–56 (2018)
28. Guo, J., Cai, L.: Study on the theory and application of ecological industry. In: World Automation Congress Proceedings (2012)
29. Taylor, C., Sours, A.N.S.: Materials stewardship: a framework for managing and preserving materials in the circular economy. In: NACE - International Corrosion Conference Series (2018)
30. Olivier, S., Pires, S.P., Loures, E.R.F., Santos, E.A.P., Cestari, J.M.P.A.: Knowledge management for sustainable performance in industrial maintenance. In: IIE Annual Conference Expo, June 2015
31. Wakiru, J., Pintelon, L., Muchiri, P.N., Chemweno, P.: Maintenance optimization: application of remanufacturing and repair strategies. Procedia CIRP **69**(May), 899–904 (2018)

# Information Flows Supporting Circular Economy Adoption in the Manufacturing Sector

Federica Acerbi and Marco Taisch

Department of Management, Economics and Industrial Engineering, Politecnico di Milan, Piazza Leonardo da Vinci 32, 20133 Milan, Italy
{federica.acerbi,marco.taisch}@polimi.it

**Abstract.** Circular economy (CE) is considered one of the drivers pushing towards sustainable development. Indeed, this economy is defined as an "industrial economy that is regenerative and restorative by intention and design" and thus, it boosts responsible consumption and production which is one the sustainable goals promoted by policymakers. In particular, from the extant literature emerged that to pursue the transition towards CE, manufacturers adopt different CE strategies. Their implementation implies to have a clear vision about stakeholders involved along product life cycle and about the implications that are encountered during the decision process of the producer thus, by its companies' functions. Indeed, all the actors involved should operate concurrently for a single and common direction. For this reason, the objective of the present work is to investigate the vertical information flow within a manufacturing company at strategic, tactical and operational levels while adopting CE strategies to appropriately manage product lifecycle. The paper objective is pursued through a literature review on Scopus together with practitioners' interviews. The outcome is the development of a conceptual framework to support the decision process. The framework structures the information flow for adopting CE across the three levels above mentioned. Indeed, the main finding of this research is the key role of information as a facilitator for the adoption of CE strategies in manufacturing.

**Keywords:** Circular economy · Manufacturing · Information flow

## 1 Introduction

Nowadays, the limited resource availability of our planet is one of the main criticalities that our society is facing [1]. For this reason, sustainable objectives have been proposed to be fulfilled by people in their daily activities and by companies while running their industrial activities, among which production and transportation. These are commonly called "*sustainable development goals*" and, they promote sustainable development in respect of planet resources generation such as "responsible consumption and production" [2]. In order to achieve these goals, structured guidelines should be promoted, and specific sustainable strategies should be designed. A first attempt has been done by The Ellen MacArthur Foundation, which promoted the adoption of circular economy (CE).

© IFIP International Federation for Information Processing 2020
Published by Springer Nature Switzerland AG 2020
B. Lalic et al. (Eds.): APMS 2020, IFIP AICT 592, pp. 703–710, 2020.
https://doi.org/10.1007/978-3-030-57997-5_81

This economy is defined as *"an industrial economy that is restorative and regenerative by intention and design"* [3] and it might be used as mean towards sustainable development by the society as a whole, but especially by manufacturers. Indeed, considering the prominent position of manufacturers in consuming resources generated by natural systems, in the extant literature more than one CE strategy has been studied as a possible application boosting the sustainable development of this sector. More in detail, different research streams have been identified and what they all have in common is the need to define a structured decision process supporting the adoption of CE [4]. Indeed, manufacturers usually are forced by internal rigidity, and this limits them to efficiently undertake the transition from a linear economy towards a circular one.

Indeed, the objective of this paper is to develop a conceptual framework aiming to facilitate this transition by structuring the vertical information flows of the company's functions, (i.e. the one occurring among the strategic, tactical and operational hierarchical levels), that emerged to be the most affected during the transition, by allocating to each level the corresponding decisions and related information required to manage the product along its life cycle with a circular vision. This has been partially proposed in the extant literature to design the right reverse logistics network [5]. Nevertheless, the perspective of the focal firm has been neglected in the extant literature, and whenever present, it has been tackled only from the strategical perspective. Therefore, this paper aims to cover this lack, by including in the analysis the strategic, tactical and operational perspectives through the producer's lenses to facilitate the adoption of CE.

The structure of the present work is the following: (2) "Methodology" to explain how the research has been conducted, (3) "Theoretical background" to elucidate both the CE concept and the traditional decision process of manufacturers, in order to put the basis of this research, (4) "Practitioners' interviews" to add value and validate the literature findings by observing the industrial field, (5) The section "Information flow for circular economy adoption" in which results and discussions are reported relying on both scientific literature and practitioners' interviews. In this section, it is presented the conceptual framework to structure the vertical information flow of the different company' functions involved in the transition, (6) "Conclusions" to elucidate and discuss the main findings and limitations of the work.

## 2 Methodology

To create the ground for this research, a first overview of CE strategies adoption in the manufacturing sector has been provided, together with an overview of manufacturers' organization structure and internal decision process. Then, a literature review has been performed to envisage the main information required to take adequate decisions to manage the product along its life cycle under CE. The main findings from the review have been benchmarked and validated through practitioners' interviews. Indeed, leveraging on both scientific literature and practitioners' interview, a conceptual framework has been developed. This aims to clear-out the main information flows required, in a structured manufacturing company, to facilitate the transition from a linear economy towards CE of the company itself enabling to appropriately manage the product along its life cycle. In particular, the vertical information flow regards the three main hierarchical levels related to the company's functions mainly involved in the transition towards CE.

The literature review has been developed by using Scopus as search engine that was queried with the following keywords: (i) (("circular economy" AND "manufacturing") OR "circular manufacturing") AND ("decision*" OR "data" OR "information"); (ii) ("decision process" AND "Strategic*" AND "tactic*" AND "operat*"). These two strings of keywords were first used separately in parallel and then together. The literature review developed, together with the experts' interviews, enabled to classify the main issues faced by the manufacturer during the transition, and the information required according to the level of responsibility, in order to establish the right information flow through the strategic, tactical and operational levels while adopting CE strategies.

## 3 Theoretical Background

### 3.1 Circular Economy

CE aims to ensure resource regeneration and restoration and it is characterized by three main pillars: (i) preserve and enhance natural capital, (ii) optimize resource yields, (iii) foster system effectiveness [3]. These pillars have been adopted by manufacturers and created the ground for the development of several CE strategies [6]. Among the possible CE strategies there are: circular design practices [7], remanufacturing, recycling, reuse [8], closed-loop supply chain [9] and others. Moreover, the transition from a linear economy towards CE modifies the internal structure of companies since new stakeholders are involved and different activities are undertaken [10]. According to the extant scientific literature, the companies' functions most involved while adopting these CE strategies are procurement (e.g. [11]), product design (e.g. [7]), production (e.g. [12]), logistics (e.g. [13]) and customer care (e.g. [14]) and they all require specific sets of information. Actually, the most challenging barrier in adopting CE strategies is information management and sharing [15]. It emerged the need to have a structured decision-making process relying on an adequate information management [4]. Therefore, to embrace CE, it is required to manage information about the entire product life cycle [16], which exits companies' boundaries and requires the firm to gather and manage information not only referred to internal processes, but also referred to other actors' behaviours, both internal and external to the supply chain, which are involved along circular product life cycle [13].

### 3.2 Decision Process Within a Manufacturing Company

According to the extant literature, the main barrier to adopt CE in manufacturing companies is information management, which becomes a challenge for the decision process. Indeed, the structure of manufacturing companies usually leads towards a high level of rigidity especially whenever the dimensions in terms of human resources and plants are huge. Therefore, companies require to coordinate their internal activities both among functions, thus horizontally, but also vertically among different levels of responsibility. Actually, managers, in this context, hold a relevant position to guide their companies in moving towards CE adoption [17]. To streamline the vertical information flow and to facilitate the decision process to efficiently manage enterprises, the distinction among strategic, tactical and operational levels, that are the three major hierarchical levels, has been proposed for years [18]. Information granularity is different according to the levels, which are characterized by specific responsibilities. These are reflected in determined decisions to be taken and required information whose aggregation level increases in line with the augment of the responsibility. In particular, the strategic level requires aggregated information to make decisions covering the longest time horizon thus, these are the most difficult to be changed and impact the entire organization's main direction. The tactical one must be highly integrated and aligned with the strategic level to pursue a common and shared direction. The time horizon characterizing this level is shorter and its role is to guide the operational level, in charge of making daily decisions covering a limited time horizon, towards the concrete adoption of the general guidelines proposed at the strategic level [5]. The major barrier stands into gathering the right information according to the level, to appropriately take decisions by streamlining the vertical flow of information, and push the entire company in embracing CE pillars.

## 4 Practitioners' Interviews

Practitioners' interviews were conducted with Italian manufacturing companies characterized by one of the two following issues: (i) they have the intention to undertake the transition, (ii) they have already put in place specific actions towards CE. The interviews were developed to understand in practical terms the main issues regarding the decision process encountered in adopting CE strategies. The main barriers, highlighted by most of them, are reported below and they all agreed that the enabler would be the adequate information sharing and management. The decisions to be made and the required information are reported in Subsect. 5.1 together with literature findings.

The first obstacle is to educate final users to prevent the product from becoming waste and to enable its restoration. This is possible only if the product itself is designed to allow its disassembly and reusability or the recyclability of its components and materials. Therefore, to educate end-users, once the product has been designed with circular characteristics, adequate information should be given to them to avoid the final landfill. Once the product becomes "waste" its juridical status changes and it cannot be anymore restored as a resource. Thus, in this latter case, all the circular end-of-life practices cannot be adopted and, the disposal becomes the only action to be undertaken.

Second, they observed difficulties in managing products end-of-life whenever they do not own all the information related to product components and materials. This becomes a problem especially when the producer is not the same actor managing product end-of-life, thus it should be promoted the tracking of the product information.

Third, they observed the need to structure the information flow across the organization value chain since they consider essential to provide a common direction. Indeed, being already many the trade-offs to be balanced, even without the introduction of CE adoption, it would be difficult to efficiently move the entire organization towards CE. For this reason, the integration must be done not only horizontally but also vertically starting from the strategic level.

# 5 Information Flow in Circular Economy Adoption

According to the findings in the scientific literature regarding the CE adoption in the manufacturing sector, there is still not an overall framework enabling the structured vertical information management flow within the company, even though the transition towards CE impacts the entire company and all its internal activities. This is the reason why the unique direction must be given first by the highest level of responsibility, in order to ensure awareness in the entire company about the transition [17]. Moreover, this direction must be translated into guidelines and more operative tasks to be assigned at lower levels in the company hierarchy. Nevertheless, in the extant literature, the CE concept has been usually tackled from a strategic point of view. Since, both from the scientific literature and also from practitioners emerged the need to integrate the entire vertical structure of manufacturing companies with the CE pillars to efficiently undertake the transition, the two concepts and the results from the field and from the literature have been merged into a unique framework. The explanation is reported in Sect. 5.1.

## 5.1 Strategic, Tactical and Operational Decisions Towards CE Adoption in a Manufacturing Company

The decision process supporting the transition towards CE is quite complex being it impacted by heterogeneous stakeholders affecting the product life cycle, and for this reason, some functions' decisions are highly impacted during this transition by external actors and need to coordinate themselves. Moreover, all the decisions are governed by CE principles, sustainable government regulations, and sustainable-related standards, and are characterised by three levels as reported in the framework in Fig. 1.

The strategic level is the one that guides the entire company by taking decisions that cover a longer time horizon and it requires a low level of information granularity [5]. This level owns the responsibility to clearly state in the mission of the company the willingness to adopt CE principles, thus the information to be managed are at firm level with a general overview of the external context in which the company operates. In this way, the company can both show to the external stakeholders its "circular values", while simultaneously make aware of these values the company's internal stakeholders. This concerns also the definition of new strategies and overall principles to be followed for the single company's area. Moreover, at this level should be defined as the capital allocated for the investments in technologies and software that enable to efficiently support the transition [19]. The technology type is defined at the tactical level since the needs are different according to the area. The functionalities are defined at the operational one where the requirements necessary to conduct daily activities are well known.

To manage more concretely the transition, the tactical level must be involved. At the tactical level, managers must concurrently operate to build systems in line with the

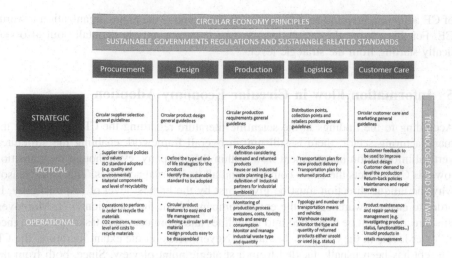

**Fig. 1.** Information flow framework for circular economy adoption in manufacturing

overall mission. They need to put in place the general guidelines proposed by the strategic level. Concerning the selection of suppliers, their benchmark should be done by investigating the standards adopted, the internal policies with the related values and the materials supplied. In particular, there should be information about the material components and the possibility to recycle them [20]. Moreover, designers should consider the circular end-of-life management practices the product should be able to perform and the sustainable standard to be used, both affecting product features. The production plan should be defined according to market demand and sustainable standards. Moreover, during the production process, industrial waste might be generated and, the tactical level should define either the policies to reuse that scrap or industrial partner to sell the waste. According to the demand, returned products, distribution points, and retailers' localization, the definition of transportation plan should be defined for the logistic [21]. For customer care, they should manage their feedbacks to improve product design and monitor the demand to align the production. Moreover, they should define returned-back policies and maintenance and repair service [22]. Therefore, at tactical level, the information required is focused on the firm's functions, and on the basis of internal general information such as on product characteristics and processes ones, the information to be gathered need to be extended also over external actors belonging to the supply chain. This requires to better understand customers' behaviours and suppliers' characteristics and thus to be able to gather this type of information.

Last, at the operational level, all these decisions must be translated into concrete information and data. Considering the procurement of materials and components, at this level must be gathered information about the operations to be done in order to recycle the materials and the relative costs and $CO_2$ emissions. For the design area, the information required is related to the definition of a circular bill of material. This is reflected in the definition of circular product features that must facilitate the circular product life cycle, among which the possibility to easily disassemble the product.

Indeed, it is required to ensure easy product maintenance, reparability, reuse, remanufacturing and recycling. Regarding the production, the information gathered should enable the monitoring of production process costs, $CO_2$ emissions, toxicity level, and energy consumption, but also information regarding the type and quantity of industrial waste created during the production process [12]. The logistic should have the information required to monitor the type and quantities of returned products (both used and unsold products), to manage the warehouse capacity and the transportation in terms of localization and quantity. Customer care should be devoted to understand the main issues regarding unsold products in the retailers and to manage the product maintenance and repair service by investigating for each product the status and functionalities. At this level, product-related information must be gathered and managed to take right operational decisions.

## 6  Conclusion

To efficiently undertake the transition towards CE and thus, to appropriately manage the entire product life cycle, different companies' functions should be involved at all the hierarchical levels. In particular, those highly affected are procurement, design, production, logistics and customer care. These need to be guided starting from the top management, thus the strategic level, to then translate the overall strategy into more operational tasks, passing through the tactical level. Indeed, the company must be cohesive both horizontally and vertically to face this challenging transition.

The framework proposed in the present work aims to cover the lack identified in the extant literature regarding the need to study the adoption of CE, through the lenses of the focal firm, not only with a strategical perspective, but by digging deeper also in the other levels to operationalize the transition. In future researches, this framework should be applied to a case study and it should be extended by studying in detail all the information and data required. Data management is the core aspect of this context. Indeed, to make the right decisions, the information must be gathered carefully and should rely on adequate data, whose collection might be done either though software or other technologies. Indeed, data management systems should be adopted, and their functionalities and characteristics should be defined in future researches. A conceptual data model could be developed in order to define the required classes of data and their relationships.

## References

1. OECD: Global Material Resources Outlook to 2060. OECD (2019)
2. United Nations: Sustainable development goals (2019). https://sustainabledevelopment.un.org/?menu=1300
3. The Ellen MacArthur Foundation. Towards a Circular Economy: Business Rationale for an Accelerated Transition (2015)
4. Acerbi, F., Sassanelli, C., Terzi, S., Taisch, M.: Towards a data-based circular economy: exploring opportunities from digital knowledge management. In: Rossi, M., Rossini, M., Terzi, S. (eds.) ELEC 2019. LNNS, vol. 122, pp. 331–339. Springer, Cham (2020). https://doi.org/10.1007/978-3-030-41429-0_33

5. Misni, F., Lee, L.S.: A review on strategic, tactical and operational decision planning in reverse logistics of green supply chain network design. J. Comput. Commun. **05**(08), 83–104 (2017)
6. Lieder, M., Rashid, A.: Towards circular economy implementation: a comprehensive review in context of manufacturing industry. J. Clean. Prod. **115**, 36–51 (2016)
7. den Hollander, M.C., Bakker, C.A., Hultink, E.J.: Product design in a circular economy: development of a typology of key concepts and terms. J. Ind. Ecol. **21**(3), 517–525 (2017)
8. Zhou, Z., Zhao, W., Chen, X., Zeng, H.: MFCA extension from a circular economy perspective: model modifications and case study. J. Clean. Prod. **149**, 110–125 (2017)
9. Lapko, Y., Trianni, A., Nuur, C., Masi, D.: In pursuit of closed-loop supply chains for critical materials: an exploratory study in the green energy sector. J. Ind. Ecol. **23**(1), 182–196 (2019)
10. Parida, V., Burström, T., Visnjic, I., Wincent, J.: Orchestrating industrial ecosystem in circular economy: a two-stage transformation model for large manufacturing companies. J. Bus. Res. **101**, 715–725 (2019)
11. Rogers, Z.S., Carter, C.R., Kwan, V.: Making tough choices: a policy capturing approach to evaluating the tradeoffs in sustainable supplier development initiatives. J. Purch. Supp. Manag. **25**(5), 100574 (2019)
12. Ren, S., Zhang, Y., Liu, Y., Sakao, T., Huisingh, D., Almeida, C.M.V.B.: A comprehensive review of big data analytics throughout product lifecycle to support sustainable smart manufacturing: a framework, challenges and future research directions. J. Clean. Prod. **210** (10), 1343–1365 (2019)
13. Accorsi, R., Manzini, R., Pini, C., Penazzi, S.: On the design of closed-loop networks for product life cycle management: economic, environmental and geography considerations. J. Transp. Geogr. **48**, 121–134 (2015)
14. Wastling, T., Charnley, F., Moreno, M., Wastling, T., Charnley, F., Moreno, M.: Design for circular behaviour: considering users in a circular economy. Sustainability **10**(6), 1743 (2018)
15. Masi, D., Day, S., Godsell, J.: Supply chain configurations in the circular economy: a systematic literature review. Sustainability (Switzerland) **9**(9), 1602 (2017)
16. Dunque Ciceri, N., Garetti, M., Terzi, S.: Product lifecycle management approach for sustainability. In: Proceedings of the 19th CIRP Design Conference – Competitive Design (2009)
17. Ünal, E., Urbinati, A., Chiaroni, D.: Managerial practices for designing circular economy business models: the case of an Italian SME in the office supply industry. J. Manuf. Technol. Manag. **30**(3), 561–589 (2019)
18. Doumeingts, G., Ducq, Y.: Enterprise modelling techniques to improve efficiency of enterprises. Prod. Plan. Control **12**(2), 146–163 (2001)
19. Neligan, A.: Digitalisation as enabler towards a sustainable circular economy in Germany. Intereconomics **53**(2), 101–106 (2018). https://doi.org/10.1007/s10272-018-0729-4
20. Liou, J.J.H., Tamošaitiene, J., Zavadskas, E.K., Tzeng, G.H.: New hybrid COPRAS-G MADM model for improving and selecting suppliers in green supply chain management. Int. J. Prod. Res. **54**(1), 114–134 (2016)
21. Chileshe, N., Jayasinghe, R.S., Rameezdeen, R.: Information flow-centric approach for reverse logistics supply chains. Autom. Constr. **106**, 102858 (2019)
22. Zhang, Z., Liu, G., Jiang, Z., Chen, Y.: A cloud-based framework for lean maintenance, repair, and overhaul of complex equipment. J. Manuf. Sci. Eng. Trans. ASME **137**(4), 1–16 (2015)

# A Conceptual Model of the IT Ecosystem for Asset Management in the Global Manufacturing Context

Adalberto Polenghi(✉) , Irene Roda , Marco Macchi ,
and Alessandro Pozzetti

Department of Management, Economics and Industrial Engineering,
Politecnico di Milano, Piazza Leonardo da Vinci 32, 20133 Milan, Italy
{adalberto.polenghi,irene.roda,marco.macchi,
alessandro.pozzetti}@polimi.it

**Abstract.** This research proposes a new conceptual model of the IT ecosystem required in the scope of global asset management. To accomplish this aim, the functionalities required by maintenance management are integrated with those required by Asset Management needs, thus extending the current scope of work of extant IT systems to a lifecycle management perspective. The allocation of the functionalities to three asset control levels (operational, tactical, strategic) is propaedeutic to derive the IT ecosystem structure based on three main software families. The model has been built along a collaborative project with a world leading company in the food sector. Lessons learnt on the proposed IT ecosystem for a centralized AM over geographically dispersed production plants are reported.

**Keywords:** Asset Management · Maintenance management · Software · IT ecosystem

## 1 Introduction

Industry 4.0 is the well-known paradigm characterizing the last decade of manufacturing transformation built upon digitization. Amongst the fundamentals of Industry 4.0, Cyber-Physical Systems (CPS) are the building blocks to develop future smart factories [1], bringing to the emergence of many characteristics such as the connectivity and the networking capabilities, the high degree of autonomy leading to self-capabilities (e.g., self-awareness, self-diagnosis, self-healing), the use of sensors and actuators to collect information about the physical operations in real-time. All in all, it is leading to a basis to build advanced systems to monitor and control the industrial assets along with their degradation. This capability leads to provide a detailed insight on a production system and its assets, which finally promotes maintenance as a key function to achieve operational excellence based on digital capabilities. Therefore, the manufacturing companies are becoming sensitive to this new role; indeed, the current evolution is now determining a perception of maintenance as a data-driven decision making process [2].

© IFIP International Federation for Information Processing 2020
Published by Springer Nature Switzerland AG 2020
B. Lalic et al. (Eds.): APMS 2020, IFIP AICT 592, pp. 711–719, 2020.
https://doi.org/10.1007/978-3-030-57997-5_82

This perspective is not yet systematically integrating the evolution of the management discipline towards the inclusion of a lifecycle perspective as promoted by the Asset Management approach. Looking at maintenance in this extended scope, requires to embrace a wider digitalization to support the Asset Management (AM) system [3]. This should consider that the set of decisions is larger than the ones maintenance is used to, and theory is correspondingly extended [4]. Henceforth, it is worth pointing out that the ever-growing number of data sources is not reflected consistently in advancements of maintenance support systems: nowadays as in past years, most of the effort appears to be put on enhancing and improving computerized maintenance management systems (CMMS), see some recent studies such as [5–7]. Nevertheless, the adoption of AM by global players has further exacerbated the already existing criticalities related to information and data management solely bounded to the maintenance scope [8, 9]. This motivates the need to reflect upon the IT ecosystem of industrial software tools, as the CMMS appears to be not enough for meeting the challenges brought by AM in a global manufacturing context.

Indeed, we believe that there is a need to review the IT ecosystem on which maintenance is relying, by extending its functionalities and scope of work towards a more AM-oriented ecosystem, to finally comply with future evolutions integrating the lifecycle management of complex industrial facilities. This is particularly escalated for those companies owning multisite production systems since it involves both local and global management of the operations. To this end, this research aims at proposing a conceptual structure of the IT ecosystem, with the purpose to extend the "traditional" CMMS functionalities with the new ones claimed by AM needs.

For what concern the methodology to accomplish the objective of the research, two steps enable building the conceptual model: firstly, a systematic review of the scientific literature aims at summarizing the functionalities related to CMMS as consolidated basis; secondly, a review of the literature, including also selected references from grey literature, enables to integrate AM-oriented functionalities. Findings bring to locate the CMMS functionalities and to integrate the AM-oriented ones within a structure of three asset control levels (operational, tactical, strategic); it finally leads to establish a hierarchical structure of software families with their own uses.

Furthermore, the conceptual model has been developed along a collaboration with a world leading company of the food sector, challenged by the need to coordinate the management across geographically dispersed production plants. This collaboration allowed to collect feedbacks and insights relevant for future improvements.

The paper is so structured. Section 2 deals with the literature on the CMMS functionalities. Section 3 describes the proposed model of the IT ecosystem for global AM. Section 4 discusses the lessons learnt from the project, valid for large enterprise acting at global level. Finally, Sect. 5 draws conclusions and envisions future researches.

## 2   Literature Review on CMMS Functionalities

The CMMS functionalities are identified through a systematic literature review (SLR) on WoS (Web of Science) database. The research protocol is so defined: keywords (*maintenance* AND *CMMS*), only English-written documents and restrictions only to the field of Industrial Engineering. The searching process results in a set of 52 papers. A further screening process is performed, looking at those CMMS functionalities useful to manage the assets; the screening does not consider user-related characteristics like "ease of use", important for selecting software [10] but out of scope of this research.

Figure 1 reports the agglomerated results, showing the main functionalities of the CMMS as retrieved in the analyzed documents with relative frequency of citations. The identified functionalities could be grouped in modules since some of them are parts of the same process, e.g. issue work order and record work order are functionalities grouped under the Work orders management module. The derived functional modules are Report management, Information and data management, Work orders management, Maintenance planning/scheduling, Spare parts management, Budget/Cost analysis, Supplier management. The relative citations of the modules are summarized in the top right-hand part of Fig. 1 as collected from the selected papers.

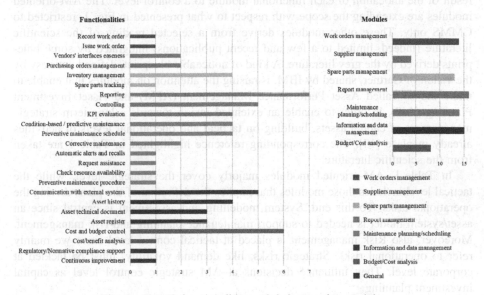

**Fig. 1.** CMMS functionalities and their grouping modules.

The identified modules are the consolidated basis to support maintenance management; the IT ecosystem for global AM will be completed by AM-oriented modules.

## 3  Model of the IT Ecosystem for Asset Management in Global Manufacturing Context

It is widely recognised in maintenance and AM literature the existence of three control levels in order to better manage the assets: operational, tactical and strategic (see [11] for maintenance management, and [4] for AM). Therefore, the whole set of modules could be framed in a three-level structure in accordance with the asset control levels. The discriminant to assign a module to a specific control level is its scope of work [12]:

- Operational control level involves day-by-day activities aiming at work task controlling at tactical level, and measurement and reporting of technical performance always in compliance with what required at the tactical level;
- Tactical control level is devoted to the coordination and planning of tasks at operational level, and to the control and reporting of KPIs (Key Performance Indicators) to orient decisions towards the strategic level;
- Strategic control level includes analysis and evaluation of feedbacks from tactical level and provide long-term guidance for the tactical level.

It is worth noting the central role of tactical level that works as an important junction to align business objectives with day-by-day activities. Table 1 shows the result of the allocation of each functional module to a control level. The AM-oriented modules are extending the scope with respect to what presented in Fig. 1, restricted to CMMS only. These other modules derive from a selected reading of the scientific literature (indeed, limited to a few and recent publications) integrated by some blueprints derived by the grey literature. A kind of noticeable blueprint, defined courtesy by the vision of Gartner, shared by IBM, is raising the attention on modules that enable to make the so called Asset Performance Management (APM) and Asset Investment Planning (AIP), in order to enable an extended vision towards a long-term strategic management of capital assets, building on tactical and operational levels of activities already in place [13]. The corresponding reference highlighted in Table 1 are taken from the scientific literature.

In Table 1, AM-oriented modules majorly cover the strategic level, while the tactical level includes those modules that implies the definition of the plans driving the operational tasks. To this end, System modelling and assessment is central since an asset/system model is needed to support maintenance planning and risk management. Moreover, also Risk management is placed at tactical control level since we mainly refer to operational risks. Strategic risks, like demand volatility, must be tackled at corporate level. They influence decisions at AM strategic control level as capital investment planning.

The three-level structure of the IT ecosystem for global AM can then be correspondingly related to software families proposed on the market [13]. Therefore, it is possible to associate to each control level a precise software family:

1. *Operational control level*: Enterprise Asset Management (EAM) software that aims at governing shop-floor activities and reporting performance indicators to support better planning. Historically the CMMS and the EAM were not clearly differentiated, as described in [19]; indeed, the difference was blurred in past discussions;

**Table 1.** Conceptual model of IT ecosystem: allocation of functionalities to control levels.

| Asset control level | Functional modules |
|---|---|
| Strategic | Business objectives alignment [14] |
| | Capital investment planning [15] |
| | Asset portfolio/fleet management [16] |
| Tactical | Budget/Cost analysis |
| | Risk management [17] |
| | System modelling and assessment [18] |
| | Supplier management |
| | Information and data management |
| | Maintenance planning |
| | Spare parts management |
| Operational | Report management |
| | Maintenance scheduling |
| | Work orders management |

anyhow, [20] notices that the difference may reside in the fact that the EAM is enterprise-wide, while the CMMS is local.

2. *Tactical control level*: Asset Performance Management (APM) software, which aims at transferring the long-term business objectives to medium-/short- term decision, in relation to maintenance plans, suppliers and risk management, by developing component/system models determining performance.
3. *Strategic control* level: Asset Investment Planning (AIP) software; it is devoted to govern the entire asset portfolio/fleet, by establishing proper capital investment decisions to respond to business needs.

The hierarchical structure of the IT ecosystem for global AM is represented in Fig. 2. The three-level structure allows to join the business objective/needs with current asset functioning/condition, thus creating a virtuous loop that makes strategic decisions aligned with operational tasks and vice versa.

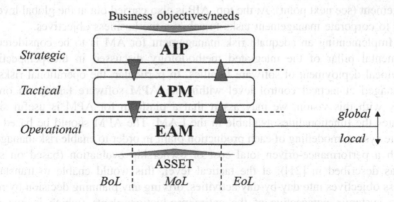

**Fig. 2.** Proposed IT ecosystem for global AM.

Figure 2 proposes also an integrated view with the lifecycle stages of the assets. Moreover, it offers a first insights a lesson learnt on global/local deployment of the EAM to enhance centralized AM for global operations, as better described in Sect. 4.

# 4   Lessons Learnt on the Proposed Model of the IT Ecosystem

This section summarizes lessons learnt from the implementation of the proposed IT ecosystem during a collaborative project with a world leader food company. The proposed model helps in better framing the existing software tools and platforms the company already owns to boost centralized AM over geographically dispersed plants:

1. Integration of activities along the asset lifecycle stages;
2. Support to local/global deployment of EAM, APM and AIP software families;
3. Implementation of risk management in APM, enabled by system modelling;
4. Management of data ownership through role-based module access;
5. Support to technology planning of the IT ecosystem evolution.

**1.** The three software families allow an integration of the activities done on the assets over all their lifecycle (BoL – Beginning of Life, MoL – Middle of Life, and EoL – End of Life). To this concern, an important challenge may typically regard the interface between the BoL and the MoL: a mismatch between what designed for the assets and what performed on the assets, tends to exist as a consequence of the lack of complete information and the partial data exchange between software systems.

**2.** The IT ecosystem allows to discern between software systems to be used at local level and at global level for centralized control in a global manufacturing scope (see the *global/local* perspective raised in Fig. 2). On one hand, the EAM is envisioned to have primarily a local usage, being integrated in an enterprise-wide perspective; on the other hand, the EAM has also a global use since it may enable an auditing system to control the correct implementation of decisions taken at tactical level, e.g. maintenance plans. To complete this viewpoint, APM has also a global perspective as it helps to translate the business objectives to the local production plants. As recommended within our conceptual model, this can be accomplished by means of the relevant lever of risk management (see next point). At the top, AIP is also carried out at the global level as it relates to corporate management tasks to achieve the business objectives.

**3.** Implementing an adequate risk management for AM is to be considered as a fundamental pillar of the integrated methodology discussed in the perspective of global/local deployment of software families. In particular, the operational risks must be managed at tactical control level within the APM software family. In order to comply with this vision, we may assert that a platform for APM is useful since it integrates the functionalities available in the EAM. The APM should be based on an accurate system modelling of each production plant in order to enable risk management through a performance-driven total cost of ownership evaluation (based on similar steps as described in [21]); at the tactical level, this would enable to translate the business objectives into day-by-day activities, driving any planning decision by relying upon a systemic perspective of the entire production plants (which is one of the principle of AM [4]).

**4.** The proposed three-level structure helps in defining a proper data ownership strategy. By separating the three asset control levels with as many software families, the access to information could be better managed and shaped according to the key users and their roles. When a global AM organizational department is present, composed by local maintenance managers, global maintenance managers and a global asset manager, this would lead to restrict the access to EAM to maintenance managers only, both local and global, while a more tactical and strategic level would be prerogative of the global asset manager and the asset management team.

**5.** The proposed model of IT ecosystem for global AM may support both a medium-term and a long-term planning of the IT development. In the medium-term, it is possible to establish a plan aimed to integrate or substitute functionalities/modules at each control level, to enhance a better centralized control, and between lifecycle stages, to share design and operational data. In the case of a more long-term perspective, a more cumbersome and demanding activity of re-structuring the entire IT ecosystem may be considered, to renew an extant ecosystem to better support a central control for global AM.

## 5 Conclusions

This research aims at proposing a conceptual model of the IT ecosystem for global AM. The IT ecosystem is built on the CMMS as basic software used for maintenance; therefore, a systematic literature review is used to collect the functionalities already implemented in the CMMS; as literature findings, a synthesis of these functionalities in modules is performed (see Fig. 1). The functionalities are also integrated with AM-oriented modules identified from additional scientific literature and even from grey literature, in order to look at the IT vendor perspective to consider the relative novelty of such kind of systems. All the functionalities are allocated to the three asset control levels defined in the AM theory (see Table 1), leading to the final contribution of this paper.

The proposed model of the IT ecosystem relates to different problems currently experienced in the scope of AM such as the missed information and data exchange between asset lifecycle stages and asset control levels, or the data ownership in complex management context with different organizational roles involved. Indeed, the collaborative project with a world leading company with production plants in numerous countries confirms the envisioned potential uses to manage such problems in IT management for AM. The so structured IT ecosystem is thus especially thought for those companies willing to implement a global AM from different starting points: i) companies with an already established IT ecosystem can check whether all the AM-related functionalities are present, or the ultimate goals are being pursued (Sect. 4); ii) companies looking after such an ecosystem can understand the needed functionalities and organize them against control levels and allocate them according to a local or global view.

If applied in company with a single plant, the potential uses blur and implementation effort could be not repaid in our current understanding; thus, our model should be downsized; this could regard future practical work. Besides, further work should concentrate on the strategic control level of AM. The developed IT ecosystem is built starting from maintenance, so partially limiting the entire set of decisions within the AM scope. Especially, capital investment decisions need to be further explored to include, within the IT ecosystem, appropriate modules to support their deployment.

# References

1. Napoleone, A., Macchi, M., Pozzetti, A.: A review on the characteristics of cyber-physical systems for the future smart factories. J. Manuf. Syst. **54**, 305–335 (2020)
2. Bokrantz, J., Skoogh, A., Berlin, C., Wuest, T., Stahre, J.: Smart maintenance: an empirically grounded conceptualization. Int. J. Prod. Econ. **223**, 107534 (2019)
3. Amadi-Echendu, J.E.: Managing physical assets is a paradigm shift from maintenance. In: 2004 IEEE International Engineering Management Conference (IEEE Cat. No.04CH37574), vol. 3, pp. 1156–1160. IEEE (2004)
4. Roda, I., Macchi, M.: A framework to embed asset management in production companies. Proc. Inst. Mech. Eng. Part O J. Risk. Reliab. **232**(4), 368–378 (2018)
5. Lopez-Campos, M.A., Marquez, A.C., Fernandez, J.F.G.: Modelling using UML and BPMN the integration of open reliability, maintenance and condition monitoring management systems: an application in an electric transformer system. Comput. Ind. **64**(5), 524–542 (2013)
6. Lopes, I., et al.: Requirements specification of a computerized maintenance management system - a case study. Procedia CIRP **52**, 268–273 (2016)
7. Munyensanga, P., Widyanto, S.A., Aziz, M.N.A., Rusnaldy, Paryanto: Information management to improve the effectiveness of preventive maintenance activities with computerized maintenance management system at the intake system of circulating water pump. Procedia CIRP **78**, 289–294 (2018)
8. Tsang, A.H.C., Yeung, W.K., Jardine, A.K.S., Leung, B.P.K.: Data management for CBM optimization. J. Qual. Maint. Eng. **12**(1), 37–51 (2006)
9. Borek, A., Parlikad, A.K., Woodall, P., Tomasella, M.: A risk based model for quantifying the impact of information quality. Comput. Ind. **65**(2), 354–366 (2014)
10. Fumagalli, L., Polenghi, A., Negri, E., Roda, I.: Framework for simulation software selection. J. Simul. **13**(4), 286–303 (2019)
11. Marquez, A.C., Gupta, J.N.D.: Contemporary maintenance management: process, framework and supporting pillars. Omega **34**(3), 313–326 (2006)
12. Haider, A., Koronios, A., Quirchmayr, G.: You cannot manage what you cannot measure: an information systems based asset management perspective. In: Mathew, J., Kennedy, J., Ma, L., Tan, A., Anderson, D. (eds.) Engineering Asset Management, pp. 288–300. Springer, Heidelberg (2006). https://doi.org/10.1007/978-1-84628-814-2_32
13. Gartner: Market guide for asset performance management (2018)
14. El-Akruti, K.O., Dwight, R.: A framework for the engineering asset management system. J. Qual. Maint. Eng. **19**(4), 398–412 (2013)
15. El-Akruti, K.O., Dwight, R., Zhang, T.: The strategic role of engineering asset management. Int. J. Prod. Econ. **146**(1), 227–239 (2013)
16. Petchrompo, S., Parlikad, A.K.: A review of asset management literature on multi-asset systems. Reliab. Eng. Syst. Saf. **181**, 181–201 (2019)

17. Polenghi, A., Roda, I., Macchi, M., Trucco, P.: Risk sources affecting the asset management decision-making process in manufacturing: a systematic review of the literature. In: Ameri, F., Stecke, K.E., von Cieminski, G., Kiritsis, D. (eds.) APMS 2019. IAICT, vol. 566, pp. 274–282. Springer, Cham (2019). https://doi.org/10.1007/978-3-030-30000-5_35
18. Roda, I., Macchi, M., Parmigiani, C., Arata, A.A.: System-oriented reliability-based methodology for optimal joint maintenance and production planning. In: Lödding, H., Riedel, R., Thoben, K.D., von Cieminski, G., Kiritsis, D. (eds.) APMS 2017. IAICT, vol. 513, pp. 92–100. Springer, Cham (2017). https://doi.org/10.1007/978-3-319-66923-6_11
19. Bradshaw, L.: Improved CMMS and asset management systems. Maint. J. **17**(2), 7–14 (2004)
20. Gartner: Magic quadrant for enterprise asset management software (2018)
21. Roda, I., Macchi, M., Albanese, S.: Building a total cost of ownership model to support manufacturing asset lifecycle management. Prod. Plan. Control. **31**(1), 19–37 (2019)

# Production Ramp-Up Strategies for Product

# Part Selection for Freeform Injection Molding: Framework for Development of a Unique Methodology

Elham Sharifi[1(✉)], Atanu Chaudhuri[1], Brian Vejrum Wæhrens[1],
Lasse G. Staal[2], and Saeed D. Farahani[3]

[1] Department of Materials and Production, Aalborg University,
Fibigerstræde 16, 9220 Aalborg, Denmark
elham@m-tech.aau.dk
[2] AddiFab ApS, Møllehaven 12A, 4040 Jyllinge, Denmark
[3] Maersk Mc-Kinney Moller Institute, Southern Denmark University,
Campusvej 55, 5230 Odense, Denmark

**Abstract.** The purpose of this study is to provide an overview of a methodology, which will enable industrial end-users to identify potential components to be manufactured by Freeform Injection Molding (FIM). The difference between the technical and economic criteria needed for part selection for Additive Manufacturing (AM) and FIM will be discussed, which will lead us towards proposing a new methodology for part selection for FIM. Our proposed approach starts by identifying the most similar components (from end-user part libraries) to some reference parts, which can be produced by FIM. Identification will be followed by cluster analysis based on important factors for FIM part selection. As there are some interdependency between the factors involved in the clusters, some decision rules using Fuzzy Interference System (FIS) will be applied to rank the parts within each cluster using user-defined technical and economic criteria. Once the first set of potential FIMable parts have been identified, Design of Experiment (DOE) will be conducted to investigate which factors are most important and how they interact with each other to generate the desirable quality of the FIM parts. The DOE results will be validated in order to finetune the ranges of the parameters, which gives the best results. Finally, a predictive model will be developed based on the optimum feasible range of FIM parameters. This will help the end-users to analytically find the new FIMable parts without repeating the algorithm for the new parts.

**Keywords:** Freeform injection molding · Additive manufacturing · Part identification · Technical and economic factors

## 1 Introduction

Injection molding is a widely used production technology, which is very cost effective for higher volumes of parts. For low-volume production, the lead time and costs of injection mold tooling are often a challenge, and molding investments may be difficult to recover. Moreover, the design freedom of plastic parts for traditionally made steel

B. Lalic et al. (Eds.): APMS 2020, IFIP AICT 592, pp. 723–730, 2020.
https://doi.org/10.1007/978-3-030-57997-5_83

tools are limited due to the necessity for "ejecting" the molded part from a rigid tool. For low volume production e.g. spare parts, Additive Manufacturing (AM) may be a more viable option [1]. But AM has multiple limitations, including slow process speed, poor dimensional accuracy compared to some conventional processes, rough surface finish [2], problems with process predictability and repeatability [3], restricted choice of materials [4], insufficient material properties, difficulties with material removal, high process costs and high energy intensity [5]. In particular, manufacturers find it difficult to justify AM as a direct alternative for injection molded parts, where performance requirements are often impossible to meet. Therefore, other advanced manufacturing technologies such as indirect 3D-printing [6] should be investigated.

## 2 What Is Freeform Injection Molding (FIM)?

There are two main indirect 3D-printing technologies: 3D Printed Injection Molds (3DPIM), which is also known as "soft tooling" and FIM. 3DPIM (Fig. 1a) can address the prolonged lead-time and high costs associated to the design and manufacturing of mold tools. It has been shown that 3DPIM allows 80–90% production costs reduction as compared with a conventionally machined tool. Furthermore, the production lead-time will be reduced in the range of 60–70% compared to the time needed to machine mold tools [6]. 3DPIM are mostly produced by Polyjet 3D printing or Stereolitography (SLA) due to the high level of accuracy and good surface finish. 3DPIM tools are designed as split tools (the same as traditional mold tools) and, therefore, do not benefit from AM design freedom. The lifetime of the 3DPIM tools are limited due to the thermal shocks which will result in propagation of micro-cracks and failure [7]. Another limiting factor regarding 3DPIM is that printing materials are not temperature and pressure resistant and therefore, engineering materials cannot be processed. This is especially true where materials are brittle (e.g. in the case of metal or ceramic feed-stocks) or where materials have a tendency to stick to the mold surfaces. The above-mentioned drawbacks with 3DPIM can be addressed by FIM, a patent pending concept, introduced by Danish company AddiFab. FIM uses single-use sacrificial closed-cavity mold inserts that are made with a soluble polymer.

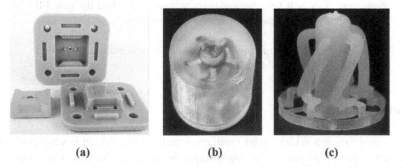

(a)                    (b)                    (c)

**Fig. 1.** **a**: 3D printed injection molds with Polyjet machine (image courtesy of Promolding), **b**: FIM mold with internal cavity, **c**: Injection molded part with FIM.

The FIM mold inserts are printed by a DLP machine in a patent-pending resin (IM 2.0 GP). The composition of IM 2.0 GP cannot be revealed due to confidentiality. The FIM mold (Fig. 1b) basically consists of a block of solidified resin with an internal cavity of the desired part (Fig. 1c). FIM can alleviate the shortcomings of both AM and injection molding by additively manufacturing low cost mold inserts of any complexity, which can then be used for producing low volume injection molded parts. FIM combines the short lead-times, low start-up costs and design freedom of AM with the versatility and scalability of injection molding. The key FIM objectives are to allow manufacturers to bring products to the market faster, cheaper and with lower risk, and to maintain the relevance of these products through easy customization and adaptations once they have been launched. The overview of the FIM value-chain can be seen in Fig. 2.

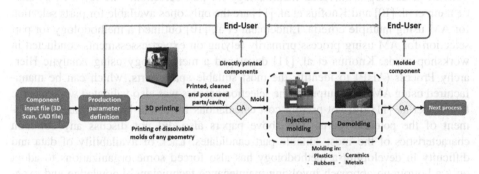

**Fig. 2.** High-level view of FIM process chain

## 3 Why Is Part Selection Important?

One key barrier for companies to adopt new technologies like AM or FIM is lack of understanding related to which parts can be produced using the technologies and difficulty in creating strong business cases for these parts [8]. Therefore, a number of methodologies and tools have been developed to support identification of parts suitable for manufacturing by AM [9]. Without such tools, it is very difficult and, in some cases, impossible for companies with large numbers of components to develop "short lists" of parts from their existing portfolio, which can be produced using AM technologies. Not only the part manufacturing companies have benefitted from the development of part identification tools for AM, the whole AM community has benefitted. More components identified or (re) designed for AM has meant increased AM volume, to the benefit of hardware (HW) vendors, materials vendors, service bureaus and other AM related services including software (SW). To the best of our knowledge, no standardized methodology has been developed to identify the most suitable components to be manufactured by FIM, which combines AM with IM. This makes it difficult for manufacturing companies with large numbers of components to build "short lists" of components from their existing portfolio that may be successfully manufactured using FIM. Therefore, development of a novel methodology to successfully screen and assess part candidates for FIM is needed. Industrial manufacturers have large numbers of legacy products/spare parts would strongly benefit from part identification tool for FIM to quickly filter out those parts and components, which may be produced using FIM.

## 4   Part Selection for AM

Selecting the suitable parts, which can be manufactured by AM pose significant challenges for manufacturers [8]. Company specific part characteristics, availability of data across multiple databases and in multiple forms, the need to consider multiple factors and the relationships of those factors with company specific objectives make it difficult to develop a universal methodology for part selection. The research by Lindemann et al. [10] and Knofius et al. [11] are the only ones available for parts selection for AM using multiple criteria. Lindemann et al. [10] outlined a methodology for part selection for AM using process primarily relying on expert assessments conducted in workshop mode. Knofius et al. [11] developed a methodology using Analytic Hierarchy Process (AHP) to identify the most suitable spare parts, which can be manufactured using AM. The output of the selection process was also validated with experts. Knofius et al. [11] did not present cost calculations for actual business case development of the potential parts. The above papers also did not discuss any common characteristics of the most suitable part candidates. Lack of availability of data and difficulty in developing a methodology has also forced some organizations to adopt only a bottom-up approach involving maintenance technicians' knowledge and experience to identify spare parts for AM. This empirical approach is the basis for commercially available tools developed for part selection for AM (e.g., Exalead, Cadenas and etc.). In these tools, the selection process starts with some manufacturable parts by AM as reference geometries. Accordingly, the most similar parts (from part library) to those reference geometries, will be identified and clustered based on user-defined criteria. Such an approach may not be suitable for an individual manufacturer, which is trying to identify parts, which are suitable for AM, for the first time without access to reference parts.

### 4.1   Factors Considered for Part Selection for AM

Some of the factors used for part selection for AM [9–11] have been summarized in Fig. 3. As it can be seen, these factors can be classified into two categories: technical factors and economic/supply chain parameters. In the study done by Knofius et al. [11] and Frandsen et al. [9], the focus has been on supply chain criteria for spare part selection for AM. In the work done by Lindemann et al. [10], the focus has been more on technical parameters needed for part selection for AM.

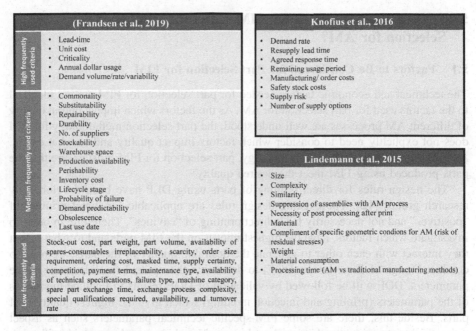

**Fig. 3.** Factors for selection of parts to be manufactured by AM

## 4.2 Methodologies Used for Part Selection for AM

Figure 4 summarizes some of the methodologies used for part selection for AM [9–11]. The methodologies used for part selection for AM can be categorized into two classes: bottom-up and top-down approaches. In the bottom-up approach [10] the selection process relies on the inputs from AM expert assessments conducted in workshop mode. Some attempts have been done by Knofius et al. [11] to develop a top-bottom approach for part selection, but this approach is still in its infancy and further research will be needed.

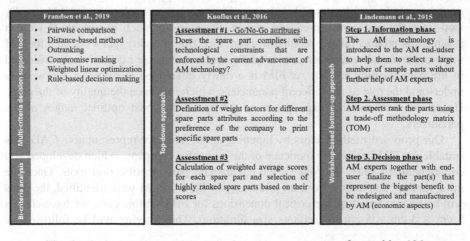

**Fig. 4.** Methodologies used for selection of parts to be manufactured by AM

# 5 Why Is Part Selection for FIM Different from Part Selection for AM?

## 5.1 Factors to Be Considered for Part Selection for FIM

The technical and economic factors needed for part selection for FIM are not identical to the factors used for part selection for AM. As the factors which impact output quality of different AM processes are well-understood, the part selection methodology for AM does not explicitly need to consider which factors impact quality and to what extent. As FIM is a recently developed technology, part selection for FIM must ensure that the parts produced using FIM meet the desired quality.

The design rules for direct printing of parts using DLP have been developed by research groups [12]. The existing design rules are applicable for direct printing of "positives" and not necessarily for indirect printing of "cavities". Therefore, in order to investigate which factors, have the highest impact on the FIM parts and to what extent they interact with each other to generate the desirable quality of the parts, we need to conduct Design of Experiment (DOE) to determine the optimal feasible range of the parameters. DOE will be followed by validation of DOE results to finetune the ranges of the parameters (printing and injection molding) which give the highest quality FIM parts. Beside this, there are some FIM-specific technical parameters such as aspect ratio, thickness ratio etc. that need to be considered during the part identification process for FIM. In addition to the technical differences between FIM and AM, the economic parameters for part selection for FIM is not identical to part selection for AM.

## 5.2 Proposed Methodology for Part Selection for FIM

Due to the difference between the factors for part selection for AM and FIM and the uniqueness of the FIM process, there is a need for developing a new methodology for part selection for FIM. In this study, we propose a hybrid approach, which combines the empirical methods with experimentation (Fig. 5). It should be noticed that the sequence of the screening and filtering steps in our approach differ from those suggested in academic literature [9–11]. Prior literature on part selection for AM usually stop once the parts are scored and ranked. Such an approach is suitable if we can assume that product quality requirements are met. But in reality, parts selected for AM may not meet quality requirements as quality requirements are explicitly not considered in the part selection model. As FIM is a newly developed technology, we want to understand the role of the different parameters, which influence the quality of the parts. Hence, we will conduct experiments to determine the most optimal ranges of the parameters.

Our proposed method starts by inputting some reference/representative CAD files suitable for FIM based on experience of the innovator company, which developed and commercialized FIM, into one of the commercial part identification tools. Once the most similar components from the end-user part library/PLM were identified, the parts will be filtered based on the critical dimensions for FIM (in this case, we have chosen 5 cm × 5 cm × 5 cm to facilitate size filtration). This filtering will be followed by cluster analysis to group the identified parts based on important factors for FIM part selection such as aspect and thickness ratio. As the clusters can be quite different and the factors involved are interdependent, we need to apply some decision rules using Fuzzy Interference System (FIS) to rank the parts within each cluster using user-defined technical and economic criteria. At this stage, we should have a set of parts potentially manufacturable by FIM. If substantial number of parts are identified at this stage of the process, a preliminary screening based on lifecycle cost will be conducted. Lifecycle cost is the cost of raw materials, production (man hours, machine hours, energy etc.), inventory and transportation costs over the lifecycle of the usage of the part.

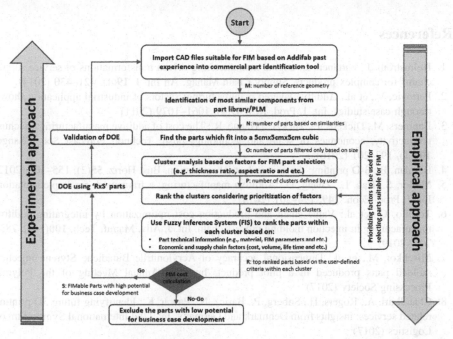

**Fig. 5.** Proposed hybrid methodology for part selection for FIM

After the above-mentioned process steps are conducted, we will be ready to start the experimentation part of our approach, in which we will produce and evaluate a number of the components identified. The reason behind the experimentation is that we lack knowledge about which factors are most important and how they interact with each other to generate the desirable quality of the FIM parts. To address this lack of knowledge, we need to conduct a Design of Experiment (DOE) followed by validation of the DOE results to finetune the ranges of the parameters which gives the best results. Finally, the optimum feasible range of FIM parameters will be used to develop a predictive model to analytically find the new FIMable parts without repeating the algorithm for the new parts.

# 6  Conclusion and Discussion

The existing literature on part selection for AM cannot be used to evaluate indirect FIM printing where the objective is to print a mold insert with an inner cavity. Therefore, development of a part screening tool for FIM is perceived as essential. This research bridges the gap and provides a framework for part selection for FIM. The proposed generic framework will be suitable for any new hybrid manufacturing technology which combines AM with conventional manufacturing as for such technologies, the critical factors and the relationships between them will be identified while selecting parts which can be produced with desired quality by those technologies.

# References

1. Holmström, J., Partanen, J.: Digital manufacturing-driven transformations of service supply chains for complex products. Supply Chain Manag. An Int. J. **19**(4), 421–430 (2014)
2. Petrovic, V., et al.: Additive layered manufacturing: sectors of industrial application shown through case studies. Int. J. Prod. Res. **49**(4), 1061–1079 (2011)
3. Baumers, M., Dickens, P., Tuck, C., Hague, R.: The cost of additive manufacturing: machine productivity, economies of scale and technology-push. Technol. Forecast Soc. Change. **102**(1), 193–201 (2016)
4. Berman, B.: 3-D printing: the new industrial revolution. Bus. Horiz. **55**(2), 155–162 (2012)
5. Mellor, S., Hao, L., Zhang, D.: Additive manufacturing: a framework for implementation. Int. J. Prod. Econ. **149**, 194–201 (2014)
6. Tosello, G., et al.: Value chain and production cost optimization by integrating additive manufacturing in injection molding process chain. Int. J. Adv. Manuf. Tech. **100**(1–4), 783–795 (2019)
7. Mischkot, M., et al.: Dimensional accuracy of Acrylonitrile Butadiene Styrene injection molded parts produced in a pilot product. In: 33rd Annual Meeting of the Polymer Processing Society (2017)
8. Chaudhuri, A., Rogers, H., Søberg, P., Baricz, N., Pawar, K.: Identifying future 3D printing related services: insights from Denmark and Germany. In: 22nd International Symposium on Logistics (2017)
9. Frandsen, C.S., Nielsen, M.M., Chaudhuri, A., Jayaram, J., Govindan, K.: In search for classification and selection of spare parts suitable for additive manufacturing: a literature review. Int. J. Prod. Res. **58**(4), 970–996 (2020)
10. Lindemann, C., Reiher, T., Jahnke, U., Koch, R.: Towards a sustainable and economic selection of part candidates for additive manufacturing. Rapid. Prototyp. J. **21**(2), 216–227 (2015)
11. Knofius, N., Van der Heijden, M.C., Zijm, W.H.: Selecting parts for additive manufacturing in service logistics. J. Manuf. Technol. Manag. **27**(7), 915–931 (2016)
12. Redwood, B., Schffer, F., Garret, B.: The 3D printing handbook: technologies, design and applications. 3D Hubs, Amsterdam, Netherlands (2017)

# A Model for Cost-Benefit Analysis
# of Production Ramp-up Strategies

Khaled Medini[1]([✉]), Antoine Pierné[2], John Ahmet Erkoyuncu[3],
and Christian Cornet[4]

[1] Mines Saint-Etienne, Univ Clermont Auvergne, CNRS, UMR 6158 LIMOS,
Henri Fayol Institute, 42023 Saint-Etienne, France
khaled.medini@emse.fr
[2] Mines Saint-Etienne, 42023 Saint-Etienne, France
[3] Through-Life Engineering Services Centre, School of Aerospace,
Transport and Manufacturing, Cranfield University, Cranfield MK43 0AL, UK
[4] Centre Technique des Industries Mécaniques, 42000 Saint-Etienne, France

**Abstract.** Production ramp-up is a critical step in product life cycle as it could
lead to either success or failure of product introduction into the market. The
criticality of this step is owed to several factors including the uncertainty
underlying this step regarding both expected costs and benefits, and thus to the
complexity of decision-making. In order to enlighten decision makers particularly in multi-variant production contexts, this paper elaborates on an analytical
model supporting cost-benefit analysis of production ramp-up strategies. The
model takes into account capacity planning decisions and learning curves in
determining cost-benefit estimates. The model is illustrated and discussed
through a keyrings manufacturing process.

**Keywords:** Ramp-up · Cost-Benefit · Costing · Analytical model · Variety

## 1 Introduction

Manufacturing and service industries are challenged more than ever by market
volatility and shortened product life cycles. As a result, frequent production and service
introduction into the market and increasingly varied offerings has become key features
of nowadays industry. However, successfully introducing products into markets is not
an easy task particularly in high variety production [1, 2]. More specifically, the shift
from prototype development to stable production is a critical phase entailing high
uncertainty and lack of relevant information to take proper decisions [3, 4]. This is
heightened by high offering variety aiming to offer customers a wider spectrum of
choice [5]. High variety production ramp-up is a critical step in product life cycle as it
could lead to either success or failure of product introduction into the market [2, 6]. The
criticality of this step is owed to several factors including the challenging costing and
cost-benefit analysis tasks of unstable production [7]. Accordingly, this paper addresses
the following questions: *What are the challenges of ramp-up management particularly
with regards to cost modelling and cost-benefit estimate? Do existing ramp-up models
cover the cost perspective of multi-variant production ramp-up? And, how to adapt*

© IFIP International Federation for Information Processing 2020
Published by Springer Nature Switzerland AG 2020
B. Lalic et al. (Eds.): APMS 2020, IFIP AICT 592, pp. 731–739, 2020.
https://doi.org/10.1007/978-3-030-57997-5_84

*traditional models to production ramp-up*? To address these questions, the remainder of the paper is organized as follows: Sect. 2 reviews ramp-up challenges and identifies the main gaps in the literature. Section 3 derives a model supporting cost-benefit analysis of ramp-up management strategies. The model results from a joint research effort of researchers and practitioners. Section 4 illustrates the model using a simple use case. The paper ends with discussion and concluding remarks in Sect. 5.

## 2  Ramp-up Management Overview and Challenges

In their effort to consistently deliver customized products and services, companies are faced with a continuous multi-product development and ramp-up [1]. While ramp-up is very determinant phase in product life cycle, it received less attention than both design and stable production phases in particular considering high variety production environments [2, 6, 7]. While there are several definitions of ramp-up, it is commonly accepted that ramp-up is the connecting phase between product development and series production [8]. Ramp-up phase plays a major role in successful new and innovative products introduction into the market. Production ramp-up is however challenged by increasing product variety resulting in high operations complexity [4, 9] (see Fig. 1). This challenge is partly owed to evolving customer requirements and new interoperability issues underlying Industry 4.0 concept [8, 10]. As such, the complexity spans over both product and processes, thus adding to the criticality of decisions on production volume. This figure is prevailing in multi-variant and small-lot size production [11]. Therefore, adequate approaches and operational frameworks are needed to holistically address ramp-up management of multi-variant production. Depending on product and process complexities, different ramp-up strategies can be distinguished focusing on achieving volume production of standard products (i.e. high-volume-low-mix) or ramping up the production of a set of products variants at low volumes (i.e. low-volume-high-mix) [2].

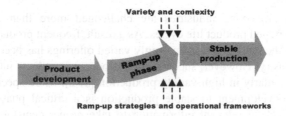

**Fig. 1.** Ramp-up management in product life cycle

As a matter of fact, ramp-up management decisions particularly impact on and are impacted by capacity planning, learning effects and operations cost, which have in turn mutual influences [7, 12, 13]. Capacity is usually limited at the beginning of and during the ramp-up phase, which requires increasing it incrementally in particular in high complexity production [13]. Such increase involves however investment decisions which should be supported by a cost-benefit analysis. Furthermore, there is high uncertainty underlying operations before reaching production steady state which decreases progressively with the increase of experience-based learning acquired by the personnel [14]. Both of these factors greatly impact on operations' cost during the ramp-up phase. In this sense, authors such as [7, 12] highlighted the lack of attention to holistically addressing several ramp-up management perspectives such as cost, capacity and learning.

Ball et al. [7] proposed an analytical model to fill such gap, through modelling the impact of changes within the ramp-up phase. The model was however not explicitly described. Furthermore, product-mix and variety in general are not considered. Most of cost models which apply to ramp-up consider learning and learning curves [10]. Arguably, learning is progressively improved during ramp-up therefore cost effectiveness is also improved. Subsequently, it could be reasonably inferred that speeding up the ramp-up phase is at stake for manufacturing and service companies as a means to reduce costs and to ensure a timely introduction into the market [4, 9]. In this sense, learning can be introduced as a factor in cost modelling during ramp-up and different scenarios can be distinguished in order to enlighten decision makers. The idea of holistically addressing ramp-up was partly addressed in a more recent study from [13]. While the proposed planning model is relatively comprehensive, it was focused upon operational performance with no explicit representation of the cost dimension.

Costing during the ramp-up phase is only partially dealt with, firstly because of the lack of holistic frameworks allowing to consider the joint effect of different factors. In this sense, more tailored costing models are needed, which can be derived from the most common approaches such as bottom-up, analogous, and parametric costing [15]. In fact, while sound models have been developed consistently with these basic approaches, most of them do not consider the ramp-up learning and capacity effects. In a nutshell, an adequate costing model should reflect learning effects, capacity and production features. Further on, to effectively support informed decisions on a given alternative ramp-up strategy both investment and operations costs (outflow) and operations income (inflow) should be holistically depicted and analyzed. In this sense existing cost models should be complemented with inflow models. Next section elaborates a model for addressing these issues in the context of ramp-up management.

## 3   Cost-Benefit Analysis of Ramp-up Management Strategies

This section elaborates on a model aimed at enabling support decision-making on ramp-up management strategies in discrete manufacturing. It applies to the life cycle phase starting right after finishing realizing product development. Indices and sets, and indicators for assessing ramp-up strategies are detailed in the following.

| $H$ | Set of time-box periods covering the ramp-up phase |
| --- | --- |
| $\mathcal{A} = \{a_1, \ldots, a_A\}$ | Set of products included in company's portfolio |
| $d_a^t$ | Demand volume of article $a$ at period $t$ |

*(continued)*

(continued)

| | |
|---|---|
| $H$ | Set of time-box periods covering the ramp-up phase |
| $v_a$ | Selling price of product $a$ |
| $\mathcal{M} = \{m_1, \ldots, m_M\}$ | Set of potential equipment to be invested in |
| $c_m$ | Purchasing cost of equipment $m$ |
| $l_m^t$ | Maintenance cost of equipment $m$ at period $t$ |
| $k_m^t$ | Maximum capacity of equipment $m$ at period $t$ |
| $\delta_m$ | Binary variable such that $\delta_m = 0$ if $m$ is automated |
| $L_m : H \rightarrow [0, 1]$ | Learning function, such that $L_m^t = L_m(t)$ is the learning level about equipment $m$ at period $t$. The closer is $L_m(t)$ to 1 the higher is the learning effectiveness. |
| $T_m^x$ | Wage (per period) of operating equipment $m$ |
| $\mathcal{B}$ | Set of raw material and components |
| $q_b^a$ | Bill of material coefficient referring to quantity of raw material or component $b$ required to produce one unit of product $a \in \mathcal{A}$ |
| $n_a^t$ | Production volume of product $a$ during period $t$ |
| $s_m$ | Salvage value of equipment $m$ |
| $T_m$ | Useful life time of equipment $m$ |
| $f_b$ | Unit cost function of raw material or component $b \in \mathcal{B}$ |
| $\phi(m, a, t)$ | Binary function such that $\phi(m, a, t) = 1$ if equipment $m$ is used to produced product $a$ at period $t$ |

The learning process is assumed to follow a specific function which generally increases with experience. It is assumed that equipment is used continuously and extensively thus limiting forgetting risk, subsequently forgetting effects are not considered. Furthermore, it is assumed that demand is known for the periods belonging to the ramp-up phase, automated equipment does not require human resources. The model suggests to evaluate a given ramp-up strategy through a cost-benefit computing function. To this end, sales turnover (benefit) is calculated based on demand volumes and on planned production volumes. Besides, variable and fixed costs are calculated (cost) based on planned production volumes and on the chosen investment strategy in capacity and considering learning function. Following a straight-line depreciation, depreciation $D$ can be written as follows, we assume that $\forall m, T_m \geq H$:

$$D = \sum_{m \in \mathcal{M}} \sum_{t \in H} \frac{c_m - s_m}{T_m} \times \max_{t_0 \leq t} \left( \left\lceil \frac{\sum_{a \in \mathcal{A}} n_a^{t_0} \phi(m, a, t_0)}{k_m^{t_0} L_m^{t_0}} \right\rceil \right) \qquad (1)$$

Assuming that demand of given period is satisfied exclusively by the production of the same period, operations cost can be calculated as follows:

$$C = \sum_{t \in H} \sum_{m \in \mathcal{M}} (l_m^t + T_m^x \delta_m) \left\lceil \frac{\sum_{a \in \mathcal{A}} n_a^t \phi(m, a, t)}{k_m^t L_m^t} \right\rceil + \sum_{t \in H} \sum_{a \in \mathcal{A}} \sum_{b \in \mathcal{B}} n_a^t q_b^a f_b (n_a^t q_b^a) \qquad (2)$$

Sales turnover can be written as follows, such that $n_a^t \leq d_a^t$:

$$S = \sum_{t \in H} \sum_{a \in A} v_a \times n_a^t \qquad (3)$$

Since the main objective of the model is to enlighten decision maker through cost-benefit analysis of a given strategy, decision variables involve selected equipment $m$ (capacity and number) as well as planned production volumes $n_a^t$. These variables depend on a variety of factors which are not exhaustively addressed by the model. In fact, the scope of the current model is limited to show the impact of a given ramp-up strategy rather than providing an optimal solution. In fact, current model is intended for supporting a cost-benefit analysis through integrating both investment and operations' costs (cost) and sales (inflow). This scope is quite consistent with the commonly used Profitability Index (*PI*) which is derived from the Net Present Value (NPV) concepts. NPV supports the evaluation and comparison of several alternative investment options. *PI* represents the rate of present value of cash inflow to required investments. In the current model, *PI* can be written as follows:

$$PI = \frac{S}{D+C} \qquad (4)$$

## 4   Illustrative Use Case – Keyrings Manufacturing

The illustrative use case involves a small SME providing accessories and concerned with ramp-up the production of keyrings $A = \{a_1, a_2, a_3, a_4, a_5\}$. The horizon of the ramp-up amounts to 24 months. For each of the articles $a \in A$, two profiles are considered for the demand $d_a$ (Fig. 2). A seasonality is introduced in demand forecast of three of the five articles in the second profile (D2). Selling prices $v_a$ are as follows 10 €, 10 €, 14 €, 8 € and 12 €, respectively.

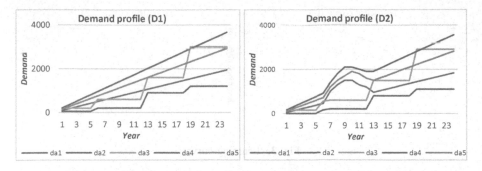

**Fig. 2.** Demand profiles throughout ramp-up phase

All five products have one-level bill of material, raw materials unit costs and consumptions are shown in Table 1.

**Table 1.** Material consumption

| Material | Designation | Cost function | Quantities | | | | |
|---|---|---|---|---|---|---|---|
| | | | $a_1$ | $a_2$ | $a_3$ | $a_4$ | $a_5$ |
| $w_1$ | Grey paste | $f_1(q) = 8$ | $0,01$ | $0,01$ | $0,01$ | | |
| $w_2$ | Purple paste | $f_2(q) = 8$ | $0,01$ | | $0,01$ | | |
| $w_3$ | Blue paste | $f_3(q) = 10$ | $0,01$ | $0,01$ | | | |
| $w_4$ | Plastic | $f_4(q) = 7$ | | | | $0,012$ | $0,012$ |
| $w_5$ | Ring | $f_5(q) = 0,5$ | $1$ | $1$ | | | |
| $w_6$ | Ring-luxury | $f_6(q) = 1,5$ | | | $1$ | $1$ | $1$ |
| $w_7$ | Water | $f_7(q) = 0,01$ | $0,001$ | $0,001$ | $0,001$ | | |

In order to meet market demand, the company needs to plan its capacity based on a set of available equipment. Characteristics of the possible equipment to produce the keyrings are detailed in Table 2. For each equipment (Equip.) we assume salvage value $(s_m)$ represents 20% of purchasing cost $(c_m)$ and $T_m = 36$ months. Two learning functions are considered as shown in Fig. 3. Monthly operator wage is $T_x = 2000$ €.

**Table 2.** Equipment characteristics

| Equip. | Operation | Products | Purchasing cost | Maintenance cost | Maximum capacity |
|---|---|---|---|---|---|
| $m_1$ | Preparation | $a_1, a_2, a_3$ | 5 000 € | 50 €/month | 9 600 unit/month |
| $m_2$ | Cutting | $a_1, a_2, a_3$ | 7 500 € | 100 €/month | 3 200 unit/month |
| $m_3$ | Cutting | $a_4, a_5$ | 10 000 € | 100 €/month | 4 800 unit/month |
| $m_4$ | Assembly | $\forall a \in \mathcal{A}$ | 7 500 € | 200 €/month | 3 200 unit/month |
| $m_5$ | Decoration | $\forall a \in \mathcal{A}$ | 10 000 € | 200 €/month | 1 600 unit/month |
| $m_6$ | Cooking | $a_1, a_2, a_3$ | 12 500 € | 100 €/month | 3 200 unit/month |
| $m_7$ | Finishing | $\forall a \in \mathcal{A}$ | 5 000 € | 50 €/month | 3 200 unit/month |

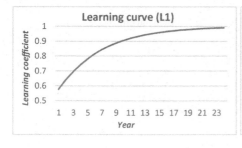 

**Fig. 3.** Learning curves

In order to illustrate the model, a parallel ramp-up policy was adopted which consists of simultaneously ramping-up the production of all products. The ramp-up process is ruled by a capacity matches-demand planning strategy, aiming to align equipment investments with demand forecast. In total, four scenarios were evaluated considering two demand profiles and two learning curves. The model was implemented in Excel for illustration purposes. Results were double checked for consistency. A summary of the scenarios, main model inputs, demand profile, learning function (in addition to above data) and outputs, *PI* are provided in Table 3.

**Table 3.** Ramp-up strategies evaluation results

| Scenarios | Demand profile | Learning function | PI |
|-----------|----------------|-------------------|------|
| D1-L1 | $D_1$ | $L_1$ | 1.55 |
| D1-L2 | $D_1$ | $L_2$ | 1.37 |
| D2-L1 | $D_2$ | $L_1$ | 1.50 |
| D2-L2 | $D_2$ | $L_2$ | 1.40 |

It can be seen from Table 3 that Profitability Index is sensible to both the learning and demand profile. However the impact of learning curves was higher with almost 10% variation in *PI* value compared to less than 1% variation induced by introducing seasonality in demand profile. As shown in Fig. 4, all four scenarios uncover an initial period with total costs exceeding sales profit. This period, ranging from 3 to 6 months, is higher when the learning process follows the second learning curve (L2) (top right hand side in Fig. 4). The impact of seasonality is reflected basically in the new trends of sales and cost curves (bottom graphics in Fig. 4). Both demand and learning can be assumed to be exogenous variables to the decision making process on production ramp-up. The case study shows however how these variables can impact the ramp-up phase from a cost-benefit perspective.

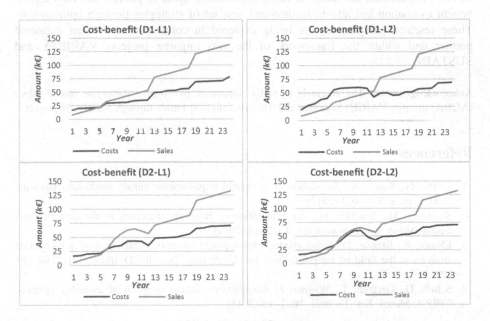

**Fig. 4.** Cost-benefit results

## 5 Discussion and Concluding Remarks

Increasingly evolving business environment and technological advances uncovered promising opportunities to reinforce customer-oriented operations. Conversely, this poses new challenges to both manufacturing and service sectors, which is to frequently develop and introduce new customized products. This adds to the complexity of ramp-up management as scaling up high-mix production is much more challenging than low-mix production.

The current model supports the decision making process during production ramp-up while considering both product mix and ramp-up phase peculiarities, i.e. learning and capacity planning decisions. The model relies on cost-benefit analysis to evaluate ramp-up strategies. While there is a well-established body of literature on cost modelling and estimation, it is argued that peculiarities of ramp-up phase requires both adaptation of these approaches and enrichment to integrate the benefit perspective. Through integrating a bottom up cost modelling and profitability assessment, current model complements existing literature by integrating cost modelling and benefit assessment of ramp-up strategies. Furthermore, the model contributes to addressing the lack of operational frameworks for ramp-up management through its ease of use and relatively limited amount of required data.

In a nutshell, the paper sheds more light on the economic perspective of ramp-up phase while integrating factors such learning and demand profile. While the case study was selected for illustration purposes, it uncovered very promising research opportunities that are being explored and addressed in ongoing research and projects. This includes the analysis of different ramp-up strategies of multi-variant production in order to build a set of contextualized recommendations to some specific business environments. Furthermore, the model is being improved in order to provide not only a cost-benefit evaluation but also to recommend best set of strategies through optimization. These research perspectives are being explored in collaboration with an industrial partner and within the framework of the two ongoing projects VARIETY and SUSTAIN.

**Acknowledgements.** The research is partly supported by *Région Auvergne Rhône Alpes* (AURA) through VARIETY project and Thomas Jefferson Funds through SUSTAIN project.

## References

1. Lanza, G., Sauer, A.: Simulation of personnel requirements during production ramp-up. Prod. Eng. **6**, 395–402 (2012)
2. Slamanig, M., Winkler, H.: An exploration of ramp-up strategies in the area of mass customisation. Int. J. Mass Cust. **4**, 22–43 (2011)
3. Elstner, S., Krause, D.: From product development to market introduction: a co-citation analysis in the field of ramp-up. Proc. Int. Conf. Eng. Des. ICED 1(DS75-01), 289–298 (2013)
4. Schuh, G., Gartzen, T., Wagner, J.: Complexity-oriented ramp-up of assembly systems. CIRP J. Manuf. Sci. Technol. **10**, 1–15 (2015)

5. ElMaraghy, H., et al.: Product variety management. CIRP Ann. Manuf. Technol. **62**, 629–652 (2013)
6. Christensen, I.: New product fumbles – organizing for the ramp-up process. Copenhagen Business School (2018)
7. Ball, P.D., Roberts, S., Natalicchio, A., Scorzafave, C.: Modelling production ramp-up of engineering products. Proc. Inst. Mech. Eng. Part B J. Eng. Manuf. **225**, 959–971 (2011)
8. Schmitt, R., et al.: On the future of ramp-up management. CIRP J. Manuf. Sci. Technol. **23**, 217–225 (2018)
9. Von Cube, J.P., Schmitt, R.: Execution of ramp-up projects in day-to-day operations through a quantitative risk management approach. Procedia CIRP **20**, 26–31 (2014)
10. Doltsinis, S., Ferreira, P., Mabkhot, M.M., Lohse, N.: A decision support system for rapid ramp-up of industry 4.0 enabled production systems. Comput. Ind. **116**, 103190 (2020)
11. Brecher, C., Storms, S., Ecker, C., Obdenbusch, M.: An approach to reduce commissioning and ramp-up time for multi-variant production in automated production facilities. Procedia CIRP **51**, 128–133 (2016)
12. Terwiesch, C., Bohn, R.E.: Learning and process improvement during production ramp-up. Int. J. Prod. Econ. **70**, 1–19 (2001)
13. Wochner, S., Grunow, M., Staeblein, T., Stolletz, R.: Planning for ramp-ups and new product introductions in the automotive industry: extending sales and operations planning. Int. J. Prod. Econ. **182**, 372–383 (2016)
14. Glock, C.H., Grosse, E.H.: Decision support models for production ramp-up: a systematic literature review. Int. J. Prod. Res. **53**, 6637–6651 (2015)
15. Datta, P.P., Roy, R.: Cost modelling techniques for availability type service support contracts: a literature review and empirical study. CIRP J. Manuf. Sci. Technol. **3**, 142–157 (2010)

# Key Factors on Utilizing the Production System Design Phase for Increasing Operational Performance

Md Hasibul Islam$^{(\boxtimes)}$ (ID), Zuhara Chavez, Seyoum Eshetu Birkie (ID), and Monica Bellgran (ID)

KTH Royal Institute of Technology, 151 81 Södertälje, Sweden
mhisla@kth.se

**Abstract.** Production system lifecycle includes phases ranging from concept pre-study to ramp-up and operations. Manufacturing companies often face challenges to reach operational performance targets during ramp-up time and operation phase. The design phase is considered crucial as major decisions related to the future production system are taken during this phase. There is an opportunity to utilize the production system design phase to improve the operational performance during both the ramp-up and operation phase. This research aims to identify the critical factors of the design process that affect the performance in the ramp-up and operational phase. A case study was conducted in a pharmaceutical company where a completed project of launching a new production line for a new product was followed in retrospect. Data were collected by conducting interviews with different members involved in the project and the production team on the shop floor. By qualitative data analysis, critical factors affecting the project's operational performance were identified; such as level of internal technical competency; involvement level of future line manager, operator and project sponsor within the project team; project team's competency; pre-study of the business case; time pressure to complete the project; expertise of product and process; organization's continuous improvement culture; and relationship with the supplier.

**Keywords:** Sustainable production · Production system design · Ramp-up · Factors · Production system design process

## 1 Introduction

Production systems design is one of the critical competencies for companies to achieve desired operational results [1]. For the last couple of decades, a lot of attention has been given by researchers and practitioners to improve the operational performance on the shop-floor to achieve the desired efficiency and output. Apart from disturbances during the operation phase, many manufacturing companies face economic losses due to low productivity concentrated in the ramp-up phase [2]. Introducing a new product in the market, integrating new manufacturing technologies for new products or existing products, often lead to different challenges associated with the ramp-up phase, such as low productivity, new technical problems, quality-related deviations [18]. Therefore, it

© IFIP International Federation for Information Processing 2020
Published by Springer Nature Switzerland AG 2020
B. Lalic et al. (Eds.): APMS 2020, IFIP AICT 592, pp. 740–748, 2020.
https://doi.org/10.1007/978-3-030-57997-5_85

is crucial to put attention to the design phase of a new production system/line or to the upgrading of an existing system, to comply with the challenges both during ramp-up and operation phase [3].

Manufacturing companies launch a new production system or upgrade the existing production system, such as assembly lines, to improve the capacity and/or operational performance [1]. In addition, there are many activities associated with the design process of a new production system, such as identify requirements, design the equipment, design layout and logistics flow and select equipment suppliers, that take years of time [1, 4]. Though production system design teams usually face the pressure to reduce the time-to-volume period and deal with a lot of uncertainty, designing a robust production system is crucial in order to reduce disturbances during operation and ramp-up time [3, 5]. Hence, utilizing the design phase of the complete production system life cycle offers the opportunity to achieve performance objectives during the later stages of the life cycle.

In practice, usually within a large manufacturing organization, activities of the designing production system process are handled by a separate team or department and are considered as a project [3]. Therefore, the team adopts project management concepts to carry out their functions, requiring the involvement of experts from various company departments like production, quality, health & safety, maintenance, finance, etc., in some cases also adding equipment and raw material suppliers [3]. The design team needs to solve several challenges, such as specifying the requirements of the production equipment to align with practices like Lean and Green [6, 7], choosing the right equipment supplier, finishing the project within a short period of time and limited budget and supporting the learning process during ramp-up after installation of equipment [1]. Solving these tasks requires a standard procedure to perform the related activities and be able to deliver information effectively with strong collaboration among team members of different departments and equipment suppliers [3]. However, utilizing the potential of the design phase of the production system by considering challenges in later stages is often ignored. Therefore, this research aims at exploring how the design phase of the production system lifecycle could be utilized to increase the operational performance in the ramp-up and operation phase. In compliance with this aim, this paper will address the following research question:

RQ: What are the critical factors of the design process that affects the operational performance in the ramp-up and operational phase?

## 2 Literature Review

To search for existing literature within this specific research context, different terms- *"Production Equipment Acquisition"*, *"Production system design"*, *Factors* AND *"Production system design"*, *Factors* AND *"Production Equipment Acquisition"*- were used to search within articles title, abstract and keywords in scientific database- Scopus and Web of Science. Based on the found articles brief theoretical background relevant to this research are presented as follows.

## 2.1 Production System Design Process

The production system design phase is a part of the lifecycle of the production system. A model of lifecycle of production system proposed by Wiktorsson [8] includes several phases- planning, design, realization or construction, start-up, operation, operation refinement, and finally termination or re-use. The activities in design stage has been elaborated in production system development framework presented by Bellgran [1] where the design phase is categorized in two stages; preparatory design and detailed design. In the preparatory design stage; by doing background study and pre-study the requirement specification is generated which act as input for the detailed design stage. In the detailed design stage, conceptual production system alternatives based on the requirement specification are generated, evaluated and finally, a detailed design is carried out of the chosen production system.

## 2.2 Challenges and Factors of the Production System Design Phase

There are several challenges associated with the production system design process mentioned in previous research. For instance, difficulties in coordinating the whole design process [9], lack of a systematic working structure [3], managing the project team with members from different specialized function [10], lack of well-defined objectives of the production system at the beginning [11], uncertainties in information flow between different stakeholders, and difficulties to align with business and manufacturing strategies [3].

Earlier research suggested remedies to the possible challenges in the design phase. For instance, strong collaboration with suppliers to design production equipment [4], proper information flow to manage uncertainty and equivocality with suppliers [12], assigning a contact with sufficient technical knowledge with suppliers [13], well-established design process with proper documentation, standardization and review system [13]. These remedies suggested by earlier researchers could be considered as factors that affects the performance during ramp-up and operation phase. However, based on the literature study, it has been observed that there is a lack of empirical studies on how to conduct the design process that targets the operational performance objectives already during the design phase. To the best of our knowledge, this subjected research question has not been specifically addressed in previous research. Therefore, considering this as a research gap, the research presented in this paper tries to identify factors during production system design phase that affect the ramp-up and operational phase and sets out to contribute to the theory building.

## 3 Research Methodology

This research has adopted an exploratory type case study method [14]. A case study approach allows to get rich and detail data that provides an in-depth understanding of a situation [14, 15]. The case study was done in a pharmaceutical production company, located in Sweden, where a completed project (referred in this paper as Project-Y) of launching a new production line for a new product was followed in retrospect.

The data was collected by reviewing project-related documents like- machine specifications, project charter, and conducting in total 7 h of interviews of six different professionals worked in the project. The interviewees were three project managers working in the project-Y consecutively, the process engineer, the line manager, and the current line manager. Interviews were recorded and later transcribed to text for further analysis. To validate the information collected from each interviewee, crucial information was cross-checked by other interviewees. The interview data was analyzed based on progressive coding techniques: Open Coding, Axial Coding and Selective Coding [16]. At first, based on the context, initial codes were generated during the open coding phase. The generated codes were categorized and used in axial coding phase to generate more meaningful information.

### 3.1 Case Description of Project-Y

In this company, production system design activities are carried out by a separate department. The company launched an internal program, referred in this paper as Program-X, to reduce its ramp-up time and to solve the challenges related to their production system design model. A finished Project-Y, was selected by the manager of Program-X to investigate and collect data that will assist them to set strategies to fulfil the objectives of Program-X.

The aim of the project-Y was to build a production line to supply an existing (not new) product to market at a specific time. The company used to supply the product for the market while being manufactured by a supplier. However, it was decided to shift to production in-house. The project started in the middle of 2015 and had a strict deadline to supply the commercial batches by mid-2017. It was a new product with a new production process from the production perspective, and the production department did not have the necessary expertise for some of the production processes. A team was formed to carry out the project comprising experts from different departments, such as investment, logistics, production, process, quality, health & safety, etc.

## 4  Result and Analysis

Based on the analysis of the interview data, factors in the design process that affected the operation performance of the case project-Y is presented in following Table 1.

**Table 1.** Factors impacting the performance in ramp-up and operation phase

| Factors | Elaboration of factors | Reason/Impact during design, ramp-up and operations phase in project-Y |
|---|---|---|
| Internal technical competency | Strong Internal technical competency to solve deviations | Suppliers competency was not adequate to solve the machine-related deviations |
| | | Synchronize different equipment supplied by different suppliers |
| | | Eliminated false alarm in machines |
| Relationship with supplier | Strong relation with key equipment suppliers | Facilitated redesigning of the equipment |
| Members involved within Project team | Future line manager involved since beginning of project | Focused on increasing automation to minimize operators number |
| | | Developed machine specification considering different lean principles |
| | | Tried to design layout and establish SOP (standard operating procedure) to minimize operator number |
| | Project sponsor actively involved | Showed direction quickly during project considering financial issues |
| | Operator involvement at beginning of project | Skilled operators were recruited |
| | | Operators used Mock practice with machines as training exercise |
| | | Operators were involved in developing SOP from scratch |
| | | Operators were responsible to teach each other operators |
| | | Strategy was to make operators skilled enough to do small maintenance and remove technician |
| Project team's competency | Team members with relevant knowledge and expertise | Acted proactively to reduce possible uncertainties |
| | | First line manager had knowledge on process, equipment, maintenance, and operators' selection process |
| Proper pre-study of business case | Poor business case | No Pre-study was done about the project |
| | | Lack of proper information sharing to project team |
| | | One machine was not regulated with ISO standard |
| | | Had to redesign some equipment |
| | | Forced to work with particular suppliers |
| | | Poor relation with a particular supplier |
| Time pressure | Strict deadline to supply market | Mock test performed during redesign |
| | | Test run before process validation was cancelled due to time pressure |
| | | Lack of confidence on solving technical issues related to machines |

(*continued*)

Table 1. (continued)

| Factors | Elaboration of factors | Reason/Impact during design, ramp-up and operations phase in project-Y |
|---|---|---|
| Product/process expertise | New product- never produced before | Lack of reliability on information regarding quality deviation parameters |
| | | Lack of information on quality deviation parameter |
| | New equipment- never worked with before | Poor performance of machine after installation |
| | | No previous knowledge about handling the machines |
| Organization's continuous improvement culture | Mindset to continuous improvement of existing system | Project team developed new way of communication within project |
| | | Project team developed new way of reviewing documents |
| | | All relevant units were involved in the project |

## 5  Discussion

Based on the factors (presented in Table 1), one of the factors was strong internal technical competency to solve technical issues associated with production equipment. Detecting and fixing technical issues with equipment is one of the major concern in ramp-up phase and company requires strong technical competency to solve them [17]. When designing a production system, it is very common to purchase different equipment from different suppliers, and fitting them together in an assembly line was one of the challenges mentioned during interviews. Therefore, strong internal technical competency was important not only to assist in solving technical issues during the ramp-up period, but also to assist the production system design team to select the desired equipment.

Another factor identified was the strong relationship with the equipment supplier that have been highlighted by previous researchers [4, 12]. For the case project-Y, the company had strong relation with some suppliers which facilitated the reengineering process of some of the equipment where the design was modified jointly by supplier and production team. In contrary, the company had weak relationship with a particular equipment supplier which clearly affected the design process negatively. Therefore, this situation indicates that, lack of strong relationship with one equipment supplier could affect the whole design process, no matter how strong the relationship with other equipment suppliers.

How the design team was formed in terms of competency could be considered a crucial factor. As mentioned in the literature review, managing the production system design team from different functions/disciplines is a challenge, and deciding about the project team is hence an important question [1]. In this case project-Y, the future line manager, project sponsor and operators participated actively from the beginning of the project and their high expertise proved to be advantageous during the whole project. Therefore, high involvement level of production team, especially at early stage in production system design process, allows them to design the production system considering future operational perspective that usually impacts on the operational performance.

Apart from this, level of expertise on product and manufacturing process affects the design process. For the studied case project-Y, the product and related manufacturing process was new and the company had not produced the specific product line before. Therefore, due to lack of internal competency and knowledge about the production process for the product, it took some time to reach the quality level internally set as acceptable, to develop standard operating procedure and to learn about the different technical issues related to equipment. As product and process maturity level has already been highlighted as major issue during ramp-up [17, 18], it affect the design process as well.

For case project-Y, the project team had a strict deadline to finish the project and to comply with that test run of machines after the installation was shortened. This affected the training time and quality for the operators and technicians. As a consequence, in the operation phase production team had less confidence to fix technical errors with the machines and it affected the quality and technical availability of the products. Lack of training has been pointed as one of the challenges during the ramp-up period [17]. Therefore, time pressure to design a production system can have an impact on the performance during ramp-up and operation phase as it affects the training time and quality.

The organization's culture on continuous improvement is also found to be an important factor. In the case of project-Y, the team adopted several innovative approaches that could speed up the process, such as a new way of reviewing documents by the team members, new way of conducting a meeting to remain more attentive, involving other departments actively and providing freedom to the first line manager. It indicates their mindset to improve existing system which could be related to organizations culture on continuous improvement.

Finally, the proper pre-study of a business case for initiating a new production system affects the design process. For the case project-Y, several interviewees stated that the business case was poorly designed which affected some critical activities in the design process, such as selecting equipment supplier, defining machine specification, etc. Proper pre-study and business case development has been pointed out as crucial step for production system design process due to its impact during the operation phase [1].

# 6  Conclusion, Practical Implication and Future Research

The presented research contributes to existing knowledge on the management of production system design process by mainly addressing the important factors that need to be considered during the design phase of the production system so that the operational performance in the ramp-up and operation phase increases. The case study identified some of the factors based on investigation of a completed project in a pharmaceutical company. These factors are: strong internal technical competency; involvement level of future line manager, operator and project sponsor within the project team; project team´s competency; proper pre-study of business case; time pressure to complete the project; expertise of product and manufacturing process; organization's continuous improvement culture; and relationship with equipment supplier.

As for practical implication, findings from this research could be utilized by practitioners by addressing the factors into their existing management system of the production system design process to upgrade it, and to develop their strategy for ramp-up as well. For instance, companies can chose to modify the involvement level of production team, to develop the internal technical competency rather relying on suppliers´ expertise. Also this factors could be utilized as guideline for practitioners who wish to review or to develop their production system management process from scratch, especially for new companies.

For future research, as the factors presented here is based on a single case study, it is relevant to execute multiple case studies at the case company as well as at other companies to validate or modify the factors to establish general theory. In addition, different numerical or quantitative analysis method could be used to prioritize the factors which is missing in the current research. Furthermore, a framework of the management of production system design process could be developed to support the practical implications mentioned here.

# References

1. Bellgran, M., Säfsten, E.K.: Production Development: Design and Operation of Production Systems. Springer, London (2010). https://doi.org/10.1007/978-1-84882-495-9
2. Viles, E., Bultó, R., Mateo, R., Jurburg, D.: Production ramp up in European automotive production systems: a performance analysis. Prod. Plann. Control 1–18 (2020)
3. Bruch, J.: Management of design information in the production system design process. Doctoral dissertation, Mälardalen University (2012)
4. Rönnberg-Sjödin, D.: A lifecycle perspective on buyer-supplier collaboration in process development projects. J. Manuf. Technol. Manag. 24(2), 235–256 (2013)
5. Barton, J.A., Love, D.M., Taylor, G.D.: Design determines 70% of cost? A review of implications for design evaluation. J. Eng. Des. 12(1), 47–58 (2001)
6. Smith, L., Ball, P.: Steps towards sustainable manufacturing through modelling material, energy and waste flows. Int. J. Prod. Econ. 140(1), 227–238 (2012)
7. Yusup, M.Z., Wan Mahmood, W.H., Salleh, M.R., Mohd Yusof, S.A.: The adoption of lean and cleaner production–a preliminary study for malaysia manufacturing industry. Appl. Mech. Mater. 660, 949–953 (2014)
8. Wiktorsson, M.: Performance assessment of assembly systems: linking strategy to analysis in early stage design of large assembly systems (2002)
9. Cochran, D.S., Arinez, J.F., Duda, J.W., Linck, J.: A decomposition approach for manufacturing system design. J. Manuf. Syst. 20(6), 371–389 (2001)
10. Love, D.: The design of manufacturing systems. Int. Encycl. Bus. Manage. 4, 3154–3174 (1996)
11. Chryssolouris, G.: Manufacturing Systems: Theory and Practice. Springer, Heidelberg (2013)
12. Sjödin, D.R., Frishammar, J., Eriksson, P.E.: Managing uncertainty and equivocality in joint process development projects. J. Eng. Technol. Manag. 39, 13–25 (2016)

13. Bruch, J., Bellgran, M.: Design information for efficient equipment supplier/buyer integration. J. Manuf. Technol. Manag. **23**(4), 484–502 (2012)
14. Yin, R.K.: Case Study Research and Applications: Design and Methods. Sage Publications, Thousand Oaks (2017)
15. Eisenhardt, K.M.: Building theories from case study research. Acad. Manag. Rev. **14**(4), 532–550 (1989)
16. Strauss, A., Corbin, J.: Basics of Qualitative Research Techniques. Sage Publications, Thousand Oaks (1998)
17. Surbier, L., Alpan, G., Blanco, E.: A comparative study on production ramp-up: state-of-the-art and new challenges. Prod. Plan. Control **25**(15), 1264–1286 (2014)
18. Almgren, H.: Pilot production and manufacturing start-up: the case of Volvo S80. Int. J. Prod. Res. **38**(17), 4577–4588 (2000)

# Business Model Development for a Dynamic Production Network Platform

Stefan Wiesner[1](✉) ⓘ, Larissa Behrens[2],
and Jannicke Baalsrud Hauge[1,3] ⓘ

[1] BIBA - Bremer Institut für Produktion und Logistik GmbH at the University
of Bremen, Hochschulring 20, 28359 Bremen, Germany
{wie,baa}@biba.uni-bremen.de
[2] Karlsruher Institut Für Technologie (KIT), Institut für Fördertechnik
und Logistiksysteme, Gotthard-Franz-Str. 8, 76131 Karlsruhe, Germany
larissa.behrens@kit.edu
[3] KTH – Royal Institute of Technology, Kvarnbergagatan 12, Södertälje,
Sweden

**Abstract.** Fully dynamic cross-company production networks that adapt to
individual customer orders are a core vision in Industry 4.0. For different reasons, like failure of machines of a supplier or a sudden increase of demand,
additional production capacities might be required at short notice. However,
there are barriers to finding and integrating suppliers with free capacities into
existing ordering and logistics processes. A Dynamic Production Network
Broker (DPNB), which is an online marketplace that actively connects suppliers
and consumers of production resources to dynamic, cross-company production
networks, might bridge this gap. New generic service-based business models are
required for operation and usage of the DPNB platform. In this paper, such a
business model is drafted.

**Keywords:** Production network · Business model · Platform economy ·
Industry 4.0

## 1 Introduction and Problem

Fully dynamic cross-company production networks that adapt to individual customer
orders are a core vision in Industry 4.0 [1]. Due to failures in own or suppliers
machines, other delivery failures or increased demand, production capacities are regularly required at very short notice, e.g. in the area of drawing and special parts. The
European Tool & Die making industry is a highly fragmented market. In Germany, the
share of SMEs in the manufacturing sector is around 98% [2]. This results in a high
effort for a buyer to find a manufacturer being able to deliver on time with acceptable
quality and price, and to integrate this supplier into existing ordering and logistics
processes.

The existing business model of contract manufacturing implies that all costs are
covered by the cash flow of the customers [3]. With such a business model, the
machines cannot be utilized to capacity, and the idle times of the machines must be

© IFIP International Federation for Information Processing 2020
Published by Springer Nature Switzerland AG 2020
B. Lalic et al. (Eds.): APMS 2020, IFIP AICT 592, pp. 749–757, 2020.
https://doi.org/10.1007/978-3-030-57997-5_86

included in the price of production [4]. Therefore, much effort has been put on developing concepts and tools that allow to share resources for matching of demands and supply [5], i.e. by offering underutilized capacity on platforms, also providing access to new customer groups [6]. A higher utilization of the machines through data analysis to identify suitable productions demands leads to cost benefits for producers and customers [7].

Accordingly, the aim is to develop business models and analyse market and customer segments for the platform, identifying suitable compensation models as well as promise a good value proposition for the participants [8]. In this paper, a concept for a service-based business model of a production platform based on the use case of a "Dynamic Production Network Broker" (DPNB) is presented. The intention is to support the dynamic formation of production networks by means of a modular service system. This includes (i) the matching of supply and demand for short-term availability of production capacities while at the same time ensuring the necessary transport capacities, (ii) the short-term onboarding of suppliers, and (iii) the possibility of making complex assembly activities compatible for outsourcing. The crucial use cases for designing an appropriate business model are elaborated and on this basis, a generic business model is developed in the Business Model Canvas [9].

The paper is structured as follows: The next section explains the research approach and methodology, followed by an overview of the state-of-the art in the field of production platforms. Section 4 presents the DPNB platform, whereas Sect. 5 illustrates the resulting canvas for the identified business model for the platform. Finally, in Sect. 6 next steps and future work are discussed.

## 2  Methodology

A mixed method approach has been applied for research: a literature review on platforms in the manufacturing sector, in combination with a use case analysis for a dynamic production network platform, based on which a business model has been drafted for the DPNB platform. In order to formalize the required functionalities and to shed some light on suitable business models, three use cases for such a platform have been modeled according to the method described by Jacobson et al. [10]. Furthermore, the actual business model was developed using a user centric and participatory approach in a workshop, based on the St. Gallen Business Model Navigator by Gassmann [11] and the Business Model Canvas [12]. Participants from the manufacturing industry, transport service industry and research institutes have been involved to combine different requirements and perspectives. This approach supports the analysis of the value proposition, value creation and revenue model, in order to get an overview of all relevant aspects of the platform business model.

# 3    State-of-the-Art

In order to make it easier to find and integrate a reliable business partner, certain conditions have to be established. It must be possible to have an overview of the offers on the market and the participants must commit themselves to the rules of the market and execute the contracts properly. Today, many business-2-consumer (B2C) markets have adopted a form of Internet-based platforms (e.g. Amazon or eBay). These platforms provide benefits by creating a link between customers and suppliers [6].

In order to establish a link between customers and the highly fragmented market of production companies in the manufacturing sector in Europe, a platform would ideally allow a customer to find a supplier, who can provide capacities according to the demand (e.g. dimensions, quantity and material). If the platform allows the selection between the offers of different suppliers, it also allows competition on quality, costs and delivery times, making product transactions more efficient [13]. Such business-2-business (B2B) marketplaces and eCommerce order portals for production capacities are currently being developed, mainly driven by start-ups. Their business models are based on offering brokering services and collaboration support [14].

Production platforms like KREATIZE [15], established 2015 and Shift from 2017 provide basic marketplace services for manufacturers and customers, however they do not offer instant pricing and require manual entry and acceptance of orders through a web portal. Instant pricing is offered by other platforms for production capacities, like Xometry [16], fictive [17] and 3D Hubs [18], all of which have been established in 2013, as well as Laserhub [19] founded in 2017. Xometry for example offers a large number of available technologies, a large production network capacity (over 2,500 producers) and quality guarantee. All of them still require manual entry and acceptance of orders through a web portal.

One of the more advanced production capacity platforms today is fabrikado [20], established in 2016. It is an example of a supplier-independent portal that anonymously matches production orders with contract manufacturers and itself appears as a "contract manufacturer without a machine". Fabrikado offers a wide range of production technologies, such as 3D printing, cutting and machining. The special value of fabrikado is the possibility to install an information management system that reports free production capacities to the platform, which makes it the only permanent interface between customer and contract manufacturer. The fabrikado platform also offers instant price calculation, from which a 10–15% commission is charged for successful order placement. The quality assurance is based on a certification by fabrikado.

In addition to this concept, further models are being developed like V–INDUS-TRY [21] that started 2018 and provides UMTS retrofits to connect machine tools directly to the platform and also offers instant pricing. All these platforms can be differentiated by whether the suppliers appear anonymously or publicly and whether they are portals (marketplaces) open to suppliers or webshops of a supplier. The billing models also differ.

Although these platforms are good enablers for sharing production capacities, they are not yet sufficiently equipped to provide automatically capacities in highly dynamic environments. The existing platforms are not able to commission supplier networks, if no single supplier can satisfy a demand on its own. This could improve resilience and make better use of the prevailing SME capacities in the manufacturing sector. For this purpose, the necessary ad-hoc transport relationships have to be included by logistics service providers. In addition, services are required that go beyond the placement of orders and the exchange of production-relevant data to allow rapid onboarding of production and logistics processes. For this, large amounts of background knowledge (e.g. production plans, assembly instructions) would have to be linked with real-time data, e.g. from machines.

## 4  Dynamic Production Network Broker Platform

The use case analysis is centered on a production platform developed in the DPNB project with the objective of closing the gap mentioned in the previous section [22]. It is established as a two-sided market, in which the platform automatically matches the demand of customers to the capacity of suppliers, as depicted in Fig. 1:

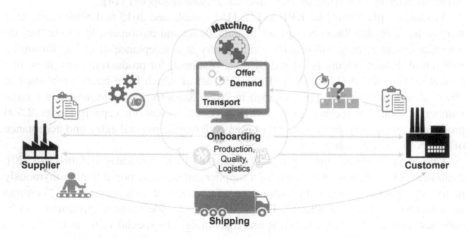

**Fig. 1.**  DPNB platform process overview, according to [22]

A centralized architecture that allows providers of production resources to participate in the market without their own revenue management system is implemented. Customers can directly access the providers' resources without having to rely on services from third parties. Thus, the platform targets a larger potential user group than established systems, as the barriers to entry are relatively low for both suppliers and customers.

The overall vision of the DPNB platform has been divided into three use cases that have been further detailed: The onboarding of participants, order planning and the execution of production orders. The different use cases are described below.

Figure 2 illustrates the initial use case for DPNB, describing the onboarding of participants to the platform. Suppliers and customers are able to register themselves through a web frontend. Once the legacy data, like name and address, is provided, their basic suitability for DPNB is assessed, i.e. by checking the credit rating. When approved, suppliers are able to specify their manufacturing qualifications (e.g. ISO certifications) and competencies, which are validated by the platform. After that, they describe their facilities and machine capabilities and optionally send a physical sample to the platform operator for verification. An initial participant rating is automatically generated from all the information provided, which can be continuously updated by the participant. It is optional for the suppliers to install a host system, which provides a direct interface between the platform and the enterprise information systems, such as ERP.

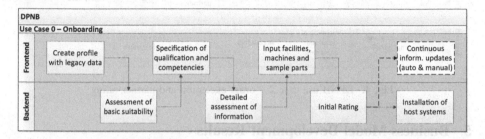

**Fig. 2.** DPNB use case 0 – supplier and customer onboarding

Once participants have registered, manufacturing orders can be placed, as shown in Fig. 3. The customer is able to enter the required product through the frontend and further specify the order. This is processed against the production capacities reported by the suppliers and a functional specification containing possible manufacturing steps is created by the platform. Suitable production capacities are tentatively blocked for planning. A matching algorithm combines supplier and order information to prepare different tender options, which can be filtered and selected in the frontend. The selected tender is used to block the required production capacities finally and will be executed.

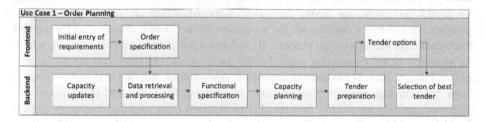

**Fig. 3.** DPNB use case 1 – order planning and tender selection

For execution, as presented in Fig. 4, matching orders are bundled to achieve an optimal capacity usage through the platform. The order is the processed on the reserved capacities, while the customer is able to track the progress in the web frontend. Accounting takes care of invoicing the customer and tracking the payment of the order. Once the manufactured parts are delivered, customer and supplier can rate each other in several aspects. This input is used to update the participant rating on the platform, which is displayed in the legacy data.

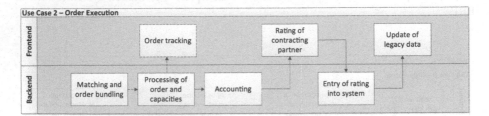

**Fig. 4.** DPNB use case 2 – order execution and partner rating

## 5  Business Model Development Results

The DPNB business model was developed during a one-day workshop with participants from two research institutes, two manufacturing companies and one transport service provider. The main goal was to create a Business Model Canvas for the platform, utilizing the use cases for DPNB as an input. After introducing different business model frameworks, the participants reviewed their own organizations' business models through the lens of the St. Gallen Business Model Navigator [11]. The different perspectives and background of the partners proved to be valuable to gain a holistic understanding of the business model. Next, the DPNB Business Model Canvas was modeled, taking into account the instructions by Osterwalder [9]. The result is illustrated in Fig. 5.

Below, the findings of the workshop will be explained in more detail. The main **value** of the platform is to create a dynamic and more or less automated marketplace for production capacities among the participants. Matching algorithms provide suggestions for optimal value chains for a certain product, while quality can be tracked throughout the manufacturing process. It contains a *full-package* service option, where the platform is the contracting party for the participants and takes care of all organizational issues, such as payment or insurance. Anonymous ordering and multi-sourcing from different suppliers are also possible. In contrast, for *individual transactions* the platform can only be used to find suitable production capacities and exchange legacy data between the participants. Organization of order processing and payment has to be arranged directly between customer and supplier.

Main **customer segments** for the platform from the supplier side include job shoppers (mainly but not exclusively SMEs), transport and assembly service providers. From the customer side, the *full package* is intended for a fast provision of missing

| Key partnerships | Key activities | Value offer | Customer relationships | Customer segment |
|---|---|---|---|---|
| • Machine manufacturer<br>• IT integrator for ERP / MES / TMS<br>• Assembly partners<br>• Transport exchange<br>• Payment and insurance providers | • Connection to platform<br>• Matching between supplier and customer<br>• Big data analysis<br>• Manage order processing | • Access to market participants on the platform<br>• Match between supplier & customer<br>• Quality tracking | • Assisted order procurement<br>• Acquisition of production capacities<br>• Intermediary<br>• Partner rating<br>• Online support | • Job shopper (SME)<br>• Transport service provider<br>• Assembly service provider |
| | **Key resources** | **Full-Package**<br>• Fast provision of capacities<br>• Liability for payments<br>• Integration to company systems<br>• Anonymization<br>• Multi-sourcing | | **Full-Package**<br>• Companies with bottlenecks<br>• Small series production<br>• Prototype production<br>• Private customers |
| | • Platform architecture<br>• Matching algorithm<br>• Participants' production capacities<br>• Participants' profiles<br>• Trustee | | **Channels** | |
| | | | • Digital platform<br>• Web portal<br>• Hosts serve as interfaces to company systems | |
| | | **Individual transaction**<br>• Fast access to capacities<br>• Support of information exchange<br>• Establish business relationships | | **Individual transaction**<br>• Companies with series production |

| Cost structure | Sources of income | |
|---|---|---|
| • Maintenance and development of the platform and services<br>• Participant support<br>• Acquisition costs | • Membership fees          • Brokerage fees | |
| | **Full-Package**<br>• Margin on value added | **Individual transaction**<br>• Matching and add. services fee |

**Fig. 5.** DPNB business model canvas

capacities to companies with a bottleneck, or for small series and prototypes, potentially also for private customers. The *individual transaction* is rather intended to support establishing long-term business relationships for series production.

Sources of **income** for the platform also differ between the two options. While different fees for membership and brokerage are discussed in general, the *full package* will retain a margin of the value added, while for the *individual transaction* matching and all additional services will have to be paid separately. Associated platform **costs** include the maintenance and further development of DPNB, support of existing participants and acquisition of new participants.

In order to set up the platform and enable the derived business model, several **key partners** are needed. First, it is crucial to involve major manufacturers of production equipment, in order to automate capability and capacity reporting as much as possible. The same applies to IT companies, providing the interfaces between the platform and the enterprise information systems. Assembly and transport exchanges take care of the finalization and delivery of the products, while payment and insurance providers support the financial aspects.

## 6  Conclusions and Future Work

The research objective of this paper to draft a business model for sharing production capacities in dynamic environments has been achieved by developing a Business Model Canvas for the DPNB platform. The value offer includes services closing the gap identified in the existing production platforms, i.e. the ad-hoc onboarding and implementation of production networks with manufacturing SMEs, logistics and assembly providers. Suitable compensation models that can generate sufficient revenue for the operators as well as promise a good value proposition for the participants have been identified.

Because the DPNB platform is still in development, the business model has not yet been implemented in a real case. Therefore, validation of its practicability is still to be carried out. A number of research issues are thus still to be analyzed more closely, such as the value of different data types or suitable pricing models, which will be accepted by the market. Possible competitive advantages and key resources for "order-driven production" have to be investigated in more detail to refine "Industry as a Service" business models. Furthermore, the service building blocks in the business model will be further expanded. The business models developed for the DPNB project could provide the basis for further expansion of the platform economy in production. Furthermore, aspects like matching algorithms are applicable for multi-sided B2B platforms in other sectors. The necessary alignments form an additional field of research.

**Acknowledgements.** This research has been funded by the German Federal Ministry of Education and Research (BMBF) under the programme "Innovationen für die Produktion, Dienstleistung und Arbeit von morgen" and is supervised by Projektträger Karlsruhe (PTKA). The authors wish to acknowledge the funding agency and all the DPNB project partners for their contribution.

# References

1. Bundesministerium für Wirtschaft und Energie (BMWi): Fortschreibung der Anwendungsszenarien der Plattform Industrie 4.0 (2016). https://www.plattform-i40.de/PI40/Redaktion/DE/Downloads/Publikation/fortschreibung-anwendungsszenarien.pdf?__blob=publicationFile&v=8
2. Statistisches Bundesamt: wirtschaft und Statistik (2011)
3. Wiesner, S., Padrock, P., Thoben, K.-D.: Extended product business model development in four manufacturing case studies. Procedia CIRP **16**, 110–115 (2014). https://doi.org/10.1016/j.procir.2014.01.014
4. Vogel-Heuser, B., Bauernhansl, T., Ten Hompel, M.: Handbuch Industrie 4.0 Bd. 1. Produktion. Springer, Heidelberg (2017). https://doi.org/10.1007/978-3-662-45279-0
5. Baalsrud Hauge, J., Kalverkamp, M., Forcolin, M., Westerheim, H., Franke, M., Thoben, K.-D.: Collaborative serious games for awareness on shared resources in supply chain management. In: Grabot, B., Vallespir, B., Gomes, S., Bouras, A., Kiritsis, D. (eds.) APMS 2014. IAICT, vol. 439, pp. 491–499. Springer, Heidelberg (2014). https://doi.org/10.1007/978-3-662-44736-9_60
6. Blaurock, U., Schmidt-Kessel, M., Erler, K. (eds.): Plattformen: geschäftsmodell und verträge, 1st edn. Schriften der Ernst-von-Caemmerer-Stiftung, Band 10. Nomos, Baden-Baden (2018)
7. Kaufmann, T.: Geschäftsmodelle in Industrie 4.0 und dem Internet der Dinge. Springer, Wiesbaden (2015). https://doi.org/10.1007/978-3-658-10272-2
8. Nagl, A., Bozem, K.: Geschäftsmodelle 4.0. Springer, Wiesbaden (2018). https://doi.org/10.1007/978-3-658-18842-9
9. Osterwalder, A., Pigneur, Y.: Business Model Generation. Game Changers, and Challengers. Wiley, Hoboken, A Handbook for Visionaries (2013)

10. Jacobson, I., Spence, I., Kerr, B.: Use-case 2.0. Commun. ACM. **59**(5), 61–69 (2016). https://doi.org/10.1145/2890778
11. Gassmann, O., Frankenberger, K., Csik, M.: The Business Model Navigator: 55 Models That Will Revolutionise Your Business. Pearson, Harlow (2014)
12. Grote, S., Goyk, R. (eds.): Führungsinstrumente aus dem Silicon Valley: Konzepte und Kompetenzen. Springer, Berlin (2018). https://doi.org/10.1007/978-3-662-54885-1
13. Täuscher, K., Laudien, S.M.: Understanding platform business models: a mixed methods study of marketplaces. Eur. Manag. J. **36**(3), 319–329 (2018). https://doi.org/10.1016/j.emj.2017.06.005
14. Wirtz, B.W.: B2B digital business models. In: Wirtz, B.W. (ed.) Digital Business Models. PI, pp. 161–173. Springer, Cham (2019). https://doi.org/10.1007/978-3-030-13005-3_9
15. KREATIZE (2020). https://kreatize.com/
16. Xometry: CNC machining, 3D printing, sheet metal & injection molding services (2020). https://www.xometry.com/
17. Fictiv: On-demand manufacturing (2020). https://www.fictiv.com/
18. D Hubs: On-demand manufacturing: quotes in seconds, parts in days (2020). https://www.3dhubs.com/
19. Laserhub - Ihr digitaler Komplettanbieter für Blechteile (2020). https://laserhub.com/#
20. fabrikado GmbH (2020). https://fabrikado.com/en
21. V-INDUSTRY – Kollaborative Industrie 4.0 Plattform (2020). https://v-industry.com/
22. DPNB - Broker für dynamische Produktionsnetzwerke (2020). https://www.dpnb.de/

# Changeable Closed-Loop Manufacturing Systems: A Case Study of Challenges in Product Take-Back

Markus Thomas Bockholt[1], Ann-Louise Andersen[1(✉)],
Thomas Ditlev Brunoe[1], Jesper Hemdrup Kristensen[1], Michele Colli[1],
Peter Meulengracht Jensen[2], and Brian Vejrum Wæhrens[1]

[1] Department of Materials and Production, Aalborg University,
Aalborg, Denmark
ala@mp.aau.dk
[2] Group Environment CoE, Group EHS, GRUNDFOS Holding A/S,
Bjerringbro, Denmark

**Abstract.** Product take-back programs are becoming increasingly popular and widespread driven by continuous focus on sustainability and circular economy. As a result, manufacturing systems need to be designed to handle not only disassembly, but also reprocessing of materials, re-assembly, and remanufacturing in a cost-efficient way. Compared to traditional manufacturing, this involves higher need for changeability due to higher uncertainty e.g. in terms of timing, quantity, and quality of received items to handle, and in particular due to significant variety in returned items. Therefore, the aim of this paper is to provide empirical insight on how changeability and reconfigurability can be applied to meet challenges in development of closed-loop manufacturing systems for product take-back.

**Keywords:** Remanufacturing · Closed-loop manufacturing · Changeability · Reconfigurability · Product take-back

## 1 Introduction

Product take-back programs are becoming increasingly relevant for manufacturing companies, which is driven by a growing demand for more sustainable and environmentally friendly business models [1–3]. In this regard, a truly closed-loop supply chain can be defined as a supply chain with zero waste that reuses, recycles, or composts all materials [4]. Thus, a closed-loop supply chain involves both forward flow of materials and reverse flow of materials that are processed by the closed-loop manufacturing system, involving activities such as inspection, cleaning, testing, sorting, disassembly, repair, remanufacturing, re-distribution, and disposal [5]. Therefore, the closed-loop manufacturing systems should be designed not only for new processes such as cleaning, sorting, and disassembly, but also with high robustness against fluctuations and high levels of changeability in processing, handling, and routing of a large variety of products, parts, components, and materials [5]. As a consequence,

© IFIP International Federation for Information Processing 2020
Published by Springer Nature Switzerland AG 2020
B. Lalic et al. (Eds.): APMS 2020, IFIP AICT 592, pp. 758–766, 2020.
https://doi.org/10.1007/978-3-030-57997-5_87

business cases of such closed-loop systems are highly likely to become unattractive due to e.g. high changeover times, difficulty in automation, and high labor cost [1, 6], which makes it difficult for manufacturers to efficiently meet increasing demands for zero-waste and eventually make attractive business cases. Various approaches and solutions towards these closed-loop manufacturing challenges have been addressed in research, e.g. product design for remanufacturing, utilization of additive or industry 4.0 smart technologies, or forecasting, planning, and control models for remanufacturing [3, 7, 8]. However, while changeable and reconfigurable manufacturing concepts have been widely recognized and exploited for traditional manufacturing systems involving small batch sizes, high need for variety and product customization, short product life-cycle, and high variability/uncertainty in demand [9, 10], these principles have been less addressed specifically in the context of remanufacturing and design of closed-loop manufacturing systems. For instance, it has been widely covered in both research and practice how reconfigurability in terms of modular software and hardware with standard interfaces can be utilized in design of manufacturing systems to achieve both cost-efficiency and rapid reconfiguration [9, 11–13]. However, potential use of reconfigurability principles for activities in later stages of product lifecycles have received less attention, but appears relevant as well [14–16]. Therefore, the aim of this paper is to provide empirical insight on how changeability and reconfigurability as manufacturing system paradigms can be applied to meet challenges in development of closed-loop manufacturing systems. The remainder of the paper is structured as follows: Sect. 2 describes related research and Sect. 3 outlines the applied case research method. Section 4 presents the case study findings, and Sect. 5 concludes the paper and describes future research directions.

## 2 Related Research

The focus of this paper lies in the intersection between the following domains and search terms: 1) "Manufacturing system" or "production system", 2) "Changeable manufacturing", "changeability", "reconfigurable manufacturing", or "reconfigurability", and 3) "Remanufacturing", "closed loop manufacturing", "circular economy", "circular supply chain", "sustainability", or "product take-back". By combining the search terms in each domain, a literature search was conducted in Scopus searching specifically in title, abstract and keywords. As a result, 31 documents were retrieved and screened for relevance. 19 papers were considered relevant and excluded papers covered mainly machine tool design or planning and control of traditional manufacturing with sustainability included as a general term. Further, a snowball approach revealed additional relevant papers to include. In the following, the findings of the review are summarized.

Initially, the concept of the Reconfigurable Manufacturing System (RMS) was introduced by Koren in the mid 1990's with the aim of providing capacity and functionality on demand [17, 18]. However, competitive factors going beyond rapid responsiveness and lower cost increase the relevance of reconfigurability. Bi [11] addressed different manufacturing system paradigms and their abilities to support sustainability. Additional conceptual evaluations of RMS in the context of sustainable manufacturing have been proposed by e.g. Koren et al. [19] stating that e.g. modular machine tools and systems can increase sustainability and allow manufacturing systems to support easier redesign, conversion to produce from virgin and recycled materials. Brunoe et al. [16] investigated how circular supply chains can be supported by different changeability classes including reconfigurability for different end-of-life product strategies. Garbie [20, 21] considered not only the reconfigurable manufacturing system in a sustainability context, but the entire manufacturing enterprise. Going beyond reconfigurable manufacturing as a paradigm that can increase sustainability of manufacturing, some research particularly addressed traditional reconfigurability characteristics in this context. For instance, Barwood et al. [22] explored the adoption of RMS principles for electronic waste recycling systems and proposed a concept of reconfigurable recycling system (RRS) with the ability to rearrange and modify processes in order to match characteristics of the waste stream. Further, Huang et al. [23] explored RMS characteristics in connection to sustainable manufacturing performance defined in terms of emission, waste, water use, and efficiency, as well as different types of cost. Particularly in relation to product development, Mesa et al. [24] addressed the application of modular product development principles as a basis for RMS and for increased sustainability. In relation to this, research on cascading use methodology provides insights on identifying new EoL solutions for products and materials [25]. Research in relation to reconfigurability and sustainability can also be identified on both hardware and software levels. On a machine level, Fan et al. [26] propose a reconfigurable multi-process combined machining method to solve the challenge of limited flexibility of machining equipment, low efficiency, and high cost of remanufacturing. Likewise, Bi et al. [27] considered how existing machines can be reconfigured to achieve higher sustainability of manufacturing systems, while Peukert et al. [28] proposed an approach for modular and reconfigurable machine tool frames to make a sustainable footprint [28]. In regard to planning, Touzout and Benyoucef [29] addressed process plan generation in a reconfigurable manufacturing environment considering emission criterion as an environmental factor. Several other works also address production and process planning in a reconfigurable manufacturing system aiming at improving different sustainability criteria [29–31]. To summarize, research on reconfigurability as support for closed-loop manufacturing covers: 1) reconfigurability on a system/paradigm concept level for closed-loop manufacturing, 2) exploration of RMS characteristics in connection with sustainability of manufacturing, 3) reconfigurable hardware design for closed-loop manufacturing, and 4) production and process planning in reconfigurable system considering sustainability factors. Furthermore, the review shows that reconfigurability is a means for closed-loop manufacturing, however, insights are primarily driven by conceptual explorations or mathematical representations rather than investigations in industry.

## 3   Case Research Methodology

In this paper, the strengths of case research is its ability to support a relatively full understanding of product take-back in a real-life manufacturing context, in order to identify and explore related challenges and the potential of changeability as means for meeting some of these challenges. The case company is a large enterprise with headquarters located in Denmark and numerous global manufacturing plants and sales offices. With an annual output of more than sixteen million products, the company is the market leader within its product domain. Due to the diverse condition of incoming products e.g. product age, type, wear and tear, the disassembly process is entirely manual (manual pressing tools) and the company has not yet identified or developed a more automated manufacturing system with sufficient degree of changeability. The unit of analysis in this paper is the take-back program of a small discrete manufacturing product, where returns are from both internal and external sources, e.g. End-of-Life, warranty cases, insurance cases e.g. pallet slip, etc. In the case company, the product take-back project has been running for several years, and longitudinal data is available to support this study. In this regard, each returned product type and its value recovery process was investigated to achieve comparability and to allow for extraction of prominent characteristics. All identified challenges have been extracted, compared, and discussed in four phases. The first two phases mainly focused on challenges and the last two on potential changes in the manufacturing system considering RMS principles. In the first phase, the researchers conducted semi-structured interviews with the lead project manager overseeing the circular economy initiatives, aiming at gaining an overview of the take-back project, the returned products, the reverse supply chain, and the recycling/remanufacturing process. The current system was mapped and assessed as well. Based on this, a workshop was conducted in the second phase with the regional sales representative, distribution center manager, production supervisors, and external waste handlers. The workshop was used to discuss the overview created during the first phase, as well as to identify challenges that affected design and operation of the system. In the third phase, data was collected to analyze identified disassembly processes in order to measure takt and cycle time as performance indicators. Here, various stakeholders within production provided data. The fourth phase consisted of analyzing the results and presenting the findings to the lead project manager in order to ensure validity.

## 4  Case Study Findings

### 4.1  Challenges in Closed-Loop Manufacturing for Product Take-Back

For presentation of the results, all identified challenges have been assigned to different superordinate categories using an Ishikawa diagram as a semantic tool (see Fig. 1).

The first identified category is the disassembly process. An inefficient disassembly process is one of the main symptoms leading to the poor performance of the closed loop manufacturing system. On closer examination we found that three distinct challenges are responsible for this. First, the current process is purely manual, which has a significant impact on the economic performance. The root cause of the manual process design is the high demands on flexibility to heterogenous products and product conditions. The second challenge is the unbalanced disassembly steps. Root causes for this are the general layout of the line, which is not optimized for operation efficiency and the heterogenic condition of incoming goods, which leads to a fluctuation of takt times

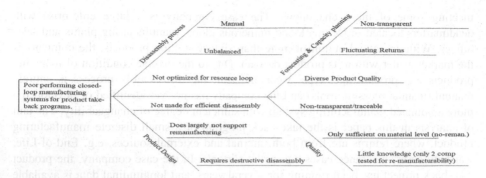

**Fig. 1.** Categorized challenges identified in the case study.

that creates or worsens existing bottle-necks. A third challenge which is responsible for the inefficient disassembly process is that the process is not optimized to the individual resource loops in which parts and materials circulate. Recycling only recovers raw material value, which allows for efficient, destructive separation of raw materials, albeit the case company disassembles products manually. However, as a general rule, disassembly only makes sense financially when functional value is recovered.

The second identified category is forecasting and capacity planning. The case company is not applying any forecasting methods, which hinders the ability to optimize the capacity planning of the disassembly line. Root causes for this is mainly non-transparent return flows. The external market acts as a "black-box" to the case company, which does not give any indication on potentially upcoming returns. Another root cause which leads to poor supply forecasting and capacity planning are fluctuating returns. Longitudinal case data allowed us to observe up to 42% fluctuation of incoming EoL products from the same system within a time frame of 5 years. A third identified root cause is the diverse quality of returned products. The return volume consist of a mix of 3 product types, where the share of each individual product type fluctuates from batch to batch. This in turn disrupts the workflow, as each type requires different steps/tools.

The third category playing a major role in the performance of the closed-loop manufacturing system is the product design. We observed three different root causes in this category. First, the product design process did not consider EoL handling, disassembly or any other value recovery strategies. This results in a complex and partly destructive disassembly process. Second, product design only allows remanufacturing on a component level, whereas the number of remanufacturable components is limited to two.

The fourth category of challenges is quality. Adapting the output quality of closed-loop manufacturing systems to the quality level of the case company's conventional manufacturing process is a major challenge. One root cause is the low level of transparency in returned products. Currently, the case company struggles to identify remanufacturable components, as numerous incremental design changes have been conducted throughout a product's lifespan. Also, in a majority of cases, value only remains in raw materials, since long and intense use phases wear down the product and demolish the functional value. Another challenge identified is the limited knowledge about technical and financial feasibility of remanufacturing. Only two components across the three different product types have been tested. Thus, arguably a lot of remanufacturing potential is currently lost due to lack of knowledge.

## 4.2    Reconfigurable System Scenarios for Closed-Loop Manufacturing

In order to meet the challenges reported in the previous section, redesign initiatives for the closed-loop manufacturing system were initiated in the case company. The aim was to develop a system capable of changing configurations to fulfill different functions in present and future applications. Evidently, not all challenges in terms of poor performance of the closed-loop manufacturing system can be met by designing a reconfigurable system. However, a reconfigurable line can in particular support challenges in the two first categories. The redesign largely followed the three steps of 1) requirement analysis, 2) concept design considering RMS principles, and 3) concept evaluation.

In the requirement analysis and specification, products or product families to include in the design process were determined, as well as their required processing tasks. Three distinct product groups were identified having significant impact on the disassembly process. These three processes varied between 9 and 12 processing steps and had current cycle times between 100 to 160 s. However, due to the heterogeneous condition of the products (e.g. corroded press connections or screws) deviations of up to 50% in cycle times could be determined in individual cases. The current line facilitates the three different products in parallel to each other, which results in significant movement of product and operators. A workflow analysis showed that 21% of the throughput time was non-value adding. Thus, increased convertibility of the layout was required in the new setup, which was solved by a modular approach to workstations and their integration. Moreover, in order to develop requirements, a scenario approach considering uncertainties in existing and future product commonality, product volume, product variety, and needed process changes was applied. The outcome of this was three distinct scenarios that system configurations should be designed to meet, covering not only the immediate requirements in output unit/hour and product mix, but also future more long-term changes. The three scenarios clearly showed a need for high scalability and convertibility of the system, i.e. being able to reconfigure the capacity and functionality of the system on both short term basis in terms of mix changes, and on long term-basis in terms of more significant volume changes. The first scenario considered only 25,000 units/year, while the third scenario considered 1,000,000 units/year. Thus, a modular system architecture was considered in the concept design phase in order to enable different alternative system configurations. By exploiting a potential modular system design, different levels of automation, different configurations of layouts, and different capacity levels could be reached by changing, adding, or removing system modules. Thus, considerations of alternating between modular system configurations in response to changes in demand were made, i.e. increasing capacity in a step-wise manner by adding more parallel workstations or automating some process steps e.g. inspection or some disassembly steps. Moreover, considerations of moving from pure recycling to recovery of functional value through remanufacturing was also included. In the final evaluation of concepts, the degree to which remanufacturing could be introduced significantly impacted the attractiveness of the scenarios and configurations of the closed-loop manufacturing system. As a remaining task not covered in this paper, the reconfigurable concept should be designed in detail and the performance evaluated.

## 5 Conclusions and Future Research

This paper contributes with insights from a case study on challenges in closed-loop manufacturing systems for product take-back programs and considerations on how reconfigurability can support and meet these challenges. The findings of the paper shows significant challenges in developing well-performing closed-loop systems, e.g. high degree of manual work, difficulty in balancing flows, limited ability to recover functional value rather than recycling, low transparency in incoming products, fluctuating quantity and quality of returns, and products not designed for EoL and disassembly. This paper considers how reconfigurability principles can be applied to aid at some of the challenges. In particular the low transparency, high uncertainty, and significant fluctuation in incoming products. Limitations to this study are first of all that solving these challenges requires efforts beyond manufacturing system design, involving various stakeholders in the company. Also, the challenges need to be validated in further industrial settings beyond the case company. Future research should also explore the performance of reconfigurable systems to support disassembly and remanufacturing.

## References

1. Seitz, M.A., Peattie, K.: Meeting the closed-loop challenge: the case of remanufacturing. Calif. Manag. Rev. **46**(2), 74–89 (2004)
2. Subramoniam, R., Huisingh, D., Chinnam, R.B.: Remanufacturing for the automotive aftermarket-strategic factors: literature review and future research needs. J. Clean. Prod. **17** (13), 1163–1174 (2009)
3. Tolio, T., Bernard, A., Colledani, M., et al.: Design, management and control of demanufacturing and remanufacturing systems. CIRP Ann. **66**(2), 585–609 (2017)
4. Golinska, P., Fertsch, M., Gómez, J.M., Oleskow, J.: The concept of closed-loop supply chain integration through agents-based system. In: Gómez, J.M., Sonnenschein, M., Müller, M., Welsch, H., Rautenstrauch, C. (eds.) Information Technologies in Environmental Engineering. Environmental Science and Engineering (Environmental Engineering), pp. 189–202. Springer, Heidelberg (2007). https://doi.org/10.1007/978-3-540-71335-7_20
5. Kondoh, S., Nishikiori, Y., Umeda, Y.: A closed-loop manufacturing system focusing on reuse of components, pp. 453–457. IEEE (2005)
6. Bockholt, M.T., Kristensen, J.H., Wæhrens, B.V., et al.: Learning from the nature: enabling the transition towards circular economy through biomimicry, pp. 870–875. IEEE (2019)
7. Matsumoto, M., Yang, S., Martinsen, K., et al.: Trends and research challenges in remanufacturing. Int. J. Precis. Eng. Manuf.-Green Technol. **1**(3), 129–142 (2016)
8. Dittrich, M., Schleich, B., Clausmeyer, T., et al.: Shifting value stream patterns along the product lifecycle with digital twins. Procedia CIRP **86**, 3–11 (2019)

9. Koren, Y.: The rapid responsiveness of RMS. Int. J. Prod. Res. **51**(23–24), 6817–6827 (2013)
10. ElMaraghy, H., AlGeddawy, T., Azab, A., ElMaraghy, W.: Change in manufacturing – research and industrial challenges. In: ElMaraghy, H. (ed.) Enabling Manufacturing Competitiveness and Economic Sustainability, pp. 2–9. Springer, Heidelberg (2012). https://doi.org/10.1007/978-3-642-23860-4_1
11. Bi, Z.: Revisiting system paradigms from the viewpoint of manufacturing sustainability. Sustainability **3**(9), 1323–1340 (2011)
12. Andersen, A., Brunoe, T.D., Nielsen, K., et al.: Towards a generic design method for reconfigurable manufacturing systems - analysis and synthesis of current design methods and evaluation of supportive tools. J. Manuf. Syst. **42**, 179–195 (2017)
13. Andersen, A.-L., Brunoe, T.D., Nielsen, K.: Reconfigurable manufacturing on multiple levels: literature review and research directions. In: Umeda, S., Nakano, M., Mizuyama, H., Hibino, H., Kiritsis, D., von Cieminski, G. (eds.) APMS 2015. IAICT, vol. 459, pp. 266–273. Springer, Cham (2015). https://doi.org/10.1007/978-3-319-22756-6_33
14. Koren, Y., Gu, X., Badurdeen, F., et al.: Sustainable living factories for next generation manufacturing. Procedia Manuf. **21**, 26–36 (2018)
15. Singh, A., Gupta, S., Asjad, M., et al.: Reconfigurable manufacturing systems: journey and the road ahead. Int. J. Syst. Assur. Eng. Mgt. **8**(2), 1849–1857 (2017)
16. Brunø, T.D., Andersen, A., Nielsen, K.: Changeable manufacturing systems supporting circular supply chains, pp. 1423–1428 (2019)
17. Koren, Y.: General RMS characteristics. Comparison with dedicated and flexible systems. In: Dashchenko, A.I. (ed.) Reconfigurable Manufacturing Systems and Transformable Factories, pp. 27–45. Springer, Heidelberg (2006). https://doi.org/10.1007/3-540-29397-3_3
18. Koren, Y., Heisel, U., Jovane, F., et al.: Reconfigurable manufacturing systems. CIRP Ann.-Manuf. Technol. **48**(2), 527–540 (1999)
19. Koren, Y., Gu, X., Badurdeen, F., et al.: Sustainable living factories for next generation manufacturing. Procedia Manuf. **21**, 26 (2018)
20. Garbie, I.H.: DFMER: design for manufacturing enterprise reconfiguration considering globalisation issues. Int. J. Ind. Syst. Eng. **14**(4), 484–516 (2013)
21. Garbie, I.H.: DFSME: design for sustainable manufacturing enterprises (an economic viewpoint). Int. J. Prod. Res. **51**(2), 479–503 (2013)
22. Barwood, M., Li, J., Pringle, T., et al.: Utilisation of reconfigurable recycling systems for improved material recovery from E-waste. Procedia CIRP **29**, 746–751 (2015)
23. Huang, A., Badurdeen, F., Jawahir, I.S.: Towards developing sustainable reconfigurable manufacturing systems. Procedia Manuf. **17**, 1136–1143 (2018)
24. Mesa, J.A., Esparragoza, I., Maury, H.: Modular architecture principles MAPs: a key factor in the development of sustainable open architecture products. Int. J. Sustain. Eng. **13**(2), 1–15 (2019)
25. Khan, M.A., Kalverkamp, M., Wuest, T.: Cascade utilization during the end-of-life of product service systems: synergies and challenges. In: Pehlken, A., Kalverkamp, M., Wittstock, R. (eds.) Cascade Use in Technologies 2018, pp. 1–7. Springer, Heidelberg (2019). https://doi.org/10.1007/978-3-662-57886-5_1
26. Fan, X., Zhang, Z., Jin, X., et al.: Technology of reconfigurable multi-process combined machining for remanufacturing, pp. 1–4. IEEE (2010)
27. Bi, Z., Pomalaza-Ráez, C., Singh, Z., et al.: Reconfiguring machines to achieve system adaptability and sustainability: a practical case study. Proc. Inst. Mech. Eng. Pt. B: J. Eng. Manuf. **228**(12), 1676–1688 (2014)

28. Peukert, B., Benecke, S., Clavell, J., et al.: Addressing sustainability and flexibility in manufacturing via smart modular machine tool frames to support sustainable value creation. Procedia CIRP **29**, 514–519 (2015)
29. Touzout, F.A., Benyoucef, L.: Sustainable multi-unit process plan generation in a reconfigurable manufacturing environment: a comparative study of three hybrid-meta-heuristics, pp. 661–668. IEEE (2018)
30. Ghanei, S., AlGeddawy, T.: A new model for sustainable changeability and production planning. Procedia CIRP **100**(57), 522–526 (2016)
31. Khezri, A., Benderbal, H.H., Benyoucef, L.: A sustainable reconfigurable manufacturing system designing with focus on environmental hazardous wastes, pp. 317–324. IEEE (2019)

# Author Index

Printed in the United States
by Baker & Taylor Publisher Services

Printed in the United States
by Baker & Taylor Publisher Services